PETER MARSHALL

Demanding the Impossible

A History of Anarchism

Be Realistic: Demand the Impossible!

PM

For Dylan and Emily

Demanding The Impossible: A History Of Anarchism
Peter Marshall

ISBN: 978-1-60486-064-1
Library Of Congress Control Number: 2009901374

PM Press
PO Box 23912
Oakland, CA 94623
www.pmpress.org

Cover design by John Yates/Stealworks

Printed in the USA on recycled paper.

PETER MARSHALL is a philosopher, historian, biographer and travel writer. He has written fifteen highly acclaimed books which are being translated into fourteen different languages. They include *William Godwin*, *Nature's Web*, *Riding the Wind*, *The Philosopher's Stone* and *Europe's Lost Civilization*. His circumnavigation of Africa was made into a TV series. His website is www.petermarshall.net

From the reviews of *Demanding the Impossible*:

'Large, labyrinthine, tentative: for me these are all adjectives of praise when applied to works of history, and *Demanding the Impossible* meets all of them.'
GEORGE WOODCOCK, *Independent*

'I trust that Marshall's survey of the whole heart-warming, head-challenging subject will have a large circulation ... It is a handbook of real history, which should make it more valuable in the long run than all the mighty textbooks on market economics and such-like ephemeral topics.'
MICHAEL FOOT, *Evening Standard*

'Infectious in its enthusiasm, attractive to read ... There is more information about anarchism in this than in any other single volume.'
NICOLAS WALTER, *London Review of Books*

'Immense in its scope and meticulous in its detail . . . It covers every conceivable strand in the libertarian little black book.'
ARTHUR NESLEN, *City Limits*

'A wide-ranging and warm-hearted survey of anarchist ideas and movements . . . that avoids the touchy sectarianism that often weakens the anarchist position.'
JAMES JOLL, *Times Literary Supplement*

'There's no mistaking the fact that *Demanding the Impossible* is timely . . . a gigantic mural in which every celebrated figure who has ever felt hemmed in by law and government finds a place.'
KENNETH MINOGUE, *Sunday Telegraph*

'Peter Marshall, clearly a convinced impossibilist, has set himself a sisyphean task. His book is a kind of model of what it talks about – a sphere of near-structureless co-existence, a commune or "phalanstery" for all the friends of libertarianism from Wat Tyler to Walt Whitman to Tristan Tzara.'
LORNA SAGE, *Independent on Sunday*

BY THE SAME AUTHOR

William Godwin
Journey through Tanzania
Into Cuba
Cuba Libre: Breaking the Chains?
William Blake: Visionary Anarchist
Journey through Maldives
Nature's Web: An Exploration of Ecological Thinking
Around Africa: From the Pillars of Hercules to the Strait of Gibraltar
Celtic Gold: A Voyage around Ireland
Riding the Wind: A New Philosophy for a New Era
The Philosopher's Stone: A Quest for the Secrets of Alchemy
World Astrology: The Astrologer's Quest to Understand the Human Character
Europe's Lost Civilization: Uncovering the Mysteries of the Megaliths
The Theatre of the World: Alchemy, Astrology and Magic in Renaissance Prague

CONTENTS

ACKNOWLEDGEMENTS

I would like to thank Heiner Becker, John Clark, John Crump, Caroline Cahm, David Goodway, Carl Levy, Geoffrey Ostergaard, Hans Ramaer, and Vernon Richards for commenting on different chapters of this work. Tom Cahill and Graham Kelsey kindly provided me with materials. I am indebted to John Burrow for encouraging, many years ago, my interest in the history of anarchist ideas. I much appreciate the pioneering work in the history of anarchism undertaken by Paul Avrich, Daniel Guérin, James Joll, Jean Maitron, Max Nettlau and George Woodcock, although I do not always share their emphases or interpretations. In preparing the book for publication, the editorial advice of Philip Gwyn Jones has proved unfailingly perceptive and relevant.

My thanks are due to the staff of both the National Library of Wales and the British Library, and to the librarians of Coleg Harlech, the University College of North Wales, and the University of London for facilitating my research.

My children Dylan and Emily have been bemused by my work on something impossibly called 'anarchism', but have been an inspiring example of constructive anarchy in action. I am grateful to my mother Vera for first awakening in me a sense of justice and equality. My brother Michael has given his warm support at all times. Above all, I must thank Jenny Zobel for her constant help and encouragement during the composition of this long study; only she knows the depth of my indebtedness. My friends Richard Feesey, Jeremy Gane, Graham Hancock, David Lea, and John Schlapobersky have in their different ways all inspired me to complete my task.

For this new edition, I have added an epilogue bringing anarchism up to date in the twenty-first century and given my own suggestions on the way forward.

I would like to thank John Clark in particular for his very perceptive and detailed comments. Ruth Kinna helped me with some materials. Elizabeth Ashton Hill kindly read the epilogue. My thanks also to Rosalind Porter and Essie Cousins at Harper Perennial and Ramsey Kanaan at PM Press who have brought out this new edition.

I welcome any readers' comments on my website:

www.petermarshall.net

PETER MARSHALL, Little Oaks, July 2007

INTRODUCTION

ANARCHY IS TERROR, the creed of bomb-throwing desperadoes wishing to pull down civilization. Anarchy is chaos, when law and order collapse and the destructive passions of man run riot. Anarchy is nihilism, the abandonment of all moral values and the twilight of reason. This is the spectre of anarchy that haunts the judge's bench and the government cabinet. In the popular imagination, in our everyday language, anarchy is associated with destruction and disobedience but also with relaxation and freedom. The anarchist finds good company, it seems, with the vandal, iconoclast, savage, brute, ruffian, hornet, viper, ogre, ghoul, wild beast, fiend, harpy and siren.[1] He has been immortalized for posterity in Joseph Conrad's novel *The Secret Agent* (1907) as a fanatic intent on bringing down governments and civilized society.

Not surprisingly, anarchism has had a bad press. It is usual to dismiss its ideal of pure liberty at best as utopian, at worst, as a dangerous chimera. Anarchists are dismissed as subversive madmen, inflexible extremists, dangerous terrorists on the one hand, or as naive dreamers and gentle saints on the other. President Theodore Roosevelt declared at the end of the nineteenth century: 'Anarchism is a crime against the whole human race and all mankind should band against anarchists.'[2]

In fact, only a tiny minority of anarchists have practised terror as a revolutionary strategy, and then chiefly in the 1890s when there was a spate of spectacular bombings and political assassinations during a period of complete despair. Although often associated with violence, historically anarchism has been far less violent than other political creeds, and appears as a feeble youth pushed out of the way by the marching hordes of fascists and authoritarian communists. It has no monopoly on violence, and compared to nationalists, populists, and monarchists has been comparatively peaceful. Moreover, a tradition which encompasses such thoughtful and peaceable men as Godwin, Proudhon, Kropotkin, and Tolstoy can hardly be dismissed as inherently terroristic and nihilistic. Of the classic anarchist thinkers, only Bakunin celebrated the poetry of destruction in his early work, and that because like many thinkers and artists he felt it was first necessary to destroy the old in order to create the new.

The dominant language and culture in a society tend to reflect the values and ideas of those in power. Anarchists more than most have been victims of the tyranny of fixed meanings, and have been caught up in what Thomas Paine called the 'Bastille of the word'. But it is easy to see why rulers should fear anarchy and wish to label anarchists as destructive fanatics for they question the very foundations of their rule. The word 'anarchy' comes from the ancient Greek αναρχια meaning the condition of being 'without a leader' but usually translated and interpreted as 'without a ruler'. From the beginning, it made sense for rulers to tell their subjects that without their rule there would be tumult and mayhem; as Yeats wrote: 'Things fall apart; the centre cannot hold;/Mere anarchy is loosed upon the world.'³ In the same way, upholders of law argued that a state of 'lawlessness' would mean turmoil, licence and violence. Governments with known laws are therefore necessary to maintain order and calm.

But it became increasingly clear to bold and independent reasoners that while States and governments were theoretically intended to prevent injustice, they had in fact only perpetuated oppression and inequality. The State with its coercive apparatus of law, courts, prisons and army came to be seen not as the remedy for but rather the principal cause of social disorder. Such unorthodox thinkers went still further to make the outlandish suggestion that a society without rulers would not fall into a condition of chaotic unruliness, but might produce the most desirable form of ordered human existence.

The 'state of nature', or society without government, need not after all be Hobbes' nightmare of permanent war of all against all, but rather a condition of peaceful and productive living. Indeed, it would seem closer to Locke's state of nature in which people live together in a state of 'perfect freedom to order their actions', within the bounds of the law of nature, and live 'according to reason, without a common superior on earth, with authority to judge between them'.⁴ Anarchists merely reject Locke's suggestion that in such a condition the enjoyment of life and property would be necessarily uncertain or inconvenient.

For this reason, Pierre-Joseph Proudhon, the first self-styled anarchist, writing in the nineteenth century, launched the apparent paradox: 'Anarchy is Order.' Its revolutionary import has echoed ever since, filling rulers with fear, since they might be made obsolete, and inspiring the dispossessed and the thoughtful with hope, since they can imagine a time when they might be free to govern themselves.

The historic anarchist movement reached its highest point to date in two of the major revolutions of the twentieth century – the Russian and the Spanish. In the Russian Revolution, anarchists tried to give real meaning to the slogan 'All Power to the Soviets', and in many parts, particularly in the Ukraine, they established free communes. But as the Bolsheviks concentrated their power, the anarchists began to lose ground. Trotsky, as head of the Red Army, crushed the anarchist movement led by Nestor Makhno in the Ukraine, and then put down the last great libertarian uprising of sailors and workers known as the Kronstadt Mutiny in 1921.

By far the greatest anarchist experiment took place in Spain in the 1930s. At the beginning of the Spanish Civil War, peasants, especially in Andalucía, Aragón and Valencia, set up with fervour a network of collectives in thousands of villages. In Catalunya, the most highly developed industrial part of Spain, anarchists managed the industries through workers' collectives based on the principles of self-management. George Orwell has left a remarkable account of the revolutionary atmosphere in his *Homage to Catalonia* (1938). But the intervention of fascist Italy and Germany on the side of Franco and his rebels, and the policy of the Soviet Union to funnel its limited supply of arms through the Communists, meant that the experiment was doomed. Communists and anarchists fought each other in Barcelona in 1937, and Franco triumphed soon after. Millions of Spanish anarchists went underground or lost their way.

The Second World War which followed shattered the international anarchist movement, and the most dedicated were reduced to running small magazines and recording past glories. Only Gandhi's strategy of civil disobedience used to oust the British from India and his vision of a decentralized society based on autonomous villages seemed to show a libertarian glimmer. When George Woodcock wrote his history of anarchism at the beginning of the 1960s, he sadly concluded that the anarchist movement was a lost cause and that the anarchist ideal could principally help us 'to judge our condition and see our aims'.[5] The historian James Joll also struck an elegiac note soon after and announced the failure of anarchism as 'a serious political and social force', while the sociologist Irving Horowitz argued that it was 'foredoomed to failure'.[6]

Events soon proved them wrong. Anarchism as a volcano of values and ideas was dormant, not extinct. The sixties saw a remarkable revival, although in an unprecedented and more diffuse form. Many of the themes of the New Left – decentralization, workers' control, participatory democracy – were central anarchist concerns. Thoughtful Marxists like E. P. Thompson began to call themselves 'libertarian' socialists in order to distance themselves from the authoritarian tactics of vanguard parties. The growth of the counter-culture, based on individuality, community, and joy, expressed a profound anarchist sensibility, if not a self-conscious knowledge. Once again, it became realistic to demand the impossible.

Tired of the impersonality of monolithic institutions, the hollow trickery of careerist politics, and the grey monotony of work, disaffected middle-class youth raised the black flag of anarchy in London, Paris, Amsterdam,

Berlin, Chicago, Mexico City, Buenos Aires, and Tokyo. In 1968 the student rebellions were of libertarian inspiration. In Paris street posters declared paradoxically 'Be realistic: Demand the impossible', 'It is forbidden to forbid' and 'Imagination is seizing power'. The Situationists called for a thorough transformation of everyday life. The Provos and then the Kabouters in Holland carried on the tradition of creative confrontation. The spontaneous uprisings and confrontations at this time showed how vulnerable modern centralized States could be.

The historians took note. Daniel Guérin's lively *L'Anarchisme: de la doctrine à l'action* (1965) both reflected and helped develop the growing libertarian sensibility of the 1960s: it became a best-seller and was translated into many languages. Guérin concluded that it might well be State communism, and not anarchism, which was out of step with the needs of the contemporary world, and felt his prediction fully vindicated by the events of 1968 in Prague and Paris.[7] Joll was obliged to acknowledge that anarchism was still a living tradition and not merely of psychological or historical interest.[8] Woodcock too confessed that he had been too hasty in pronouncing anarchism to be moribund. Indeed, far from being in its death throes, it had become 'a phoenix in an awakening desert'.[9]

The hoped-for transformation of everyday life did not occur in the seventies, but the anarchist influence continued to reveal itself in the many experiments in communal living in Europe and North America which attempted to create free zones within the Corporate State. The movement for workers' control and self-management echoed the principles of early anarcho-syndicalism. The peace and women's movements have all been impressed by the anarchist critique of domination and hierarchy, and have adopted to different degrees the anarchist emphasis on direct action and participatory democracy. The Green movement is anarchist in its desire to decentralize the economy and to dissolve personal and political power. Anarchists are influential in the fields of education, trade unions, community planning and culture. The recent trend towards more militarized, centralized and secretive governments has created a counter-movement of people who challenge authority and insist on thinking for themselves.

In the remaining authoritarian socialist regimes, there is a widespread demand for more self-determination and fundamental freedoms. In the independent republics of the former Soviet Union, the role of the State is once again back on the agenda, and young radicals are reading Bakunin and Kropotkin for the first time. Before the tanks rolled in, the student-inspired demonstrations in China in May 1989 showed the creative possibilities of non-violent direct action and led to calls for autonomous unions and self-management on anarchist lines.

In the West, many on the Right have also turned to anarchist thinkers for inspiration. A new movement in favour of 'anarcho-capitalism' has emerged which would like to deregulate the economy and eradicate governmental interference. Although in practice they did the opposite, Prime Minister Margaret Thatcher in Britain tried 'to roll back the frontiers of the State', while in the USA President Ronald Reagan wanted to be remembered principally for getting 'government off people's backs'. The Libertarian Party, which pushes these ideas further, became the third largest party in the United States in the 1980s.

It is the express aim of this book to show that there is a profound anarchist tradition which offers many ideas and values that are relevant to contemporary problems and issues. It is not intended, like many studies of anarchism, to be a disguised form of propaganda, attacking Marxist and liberal critics alike, in order simply to establish the historical importance and relevance of anarchism. Nor does it offer, as David Miller's recent work does, an account of anarchism as an ideology, that is to say, as a comprehensive doctrine expressing the interests of a social group.[10]

Demanding the Impossible is primarily a critical history of anarchist ideas and movements, tracing their origins and development from ancient civilizations to the present day. It looks at specific thinkers but it does not consider their works merely as self-contained texts. It tries to place the thinkers and their works in their specific historical and personal context as well as in their broader traditions.

Where one begins and who one includes in such a study is of course debatable. It could be argued that a study of anarchism should begin with Pierre-Joseph Proudhon, the first self-styled anarchist, and be confined only to those subsequent thinkers who called themselves anarchists. Such a study would presumably exclude Godwin, who is usually considered the first great anarchist thinker, as well as Tolstoy, who was reluctant to call himself an anarchist because of the word's violent associations in his day. It would also restrict itself to certain periods of the lives of key individual thinkers: Proudhon, for instance, lapsed from anarchism towards the end of his life, and Bakunin and Kropotkin only took up the anarchist banner in their maturity.

In general, I define an anarchist as one who rejects all forms of external government and the State and believes that society and individuals would function well without them. A libertarian on the other hand is one who takes liberty to be a supreme value and would like to limit the powers of government to a minimum compatible with security. The line between anarchist and libertarian is thin, and in the past the terms have often been used interchangeably. But while all anarchists are libertarians, not all libertarians are anarchists. Even so, they are members of the same clan, share the same ancestors and bear resemblances. They also sometimes form creative unions.

I have followed in this study the example of Kropotkin who, in his famous article on anarchism for the *Encyclopaedia Britannica* (1910), traced the anarchist 'tendency' as far back as Lao Tzu in the ancient world.[11] I am keen to establish the legitimate claims of an anarchist tradition since anarchism did not suddenly appear in the nineteenth century only when someone decided to call himself an anarchist. I would also like to uncover what Murray Bookchin has called a 'legacy of freedom' and to reconstruct a strand of libertarian thinking which has been covered or disguised by the dominant authoritarian culture in the past.[12] I have primarily restricted myself to thinkers; poets like Shelley and novelists like Franz Kafka, B. Traven and Ursula K. LeGuin who express a profound anarchist sensibility have been reluctantly left out; and the rich vein of anarchist art is only touched upon.[13] I have been chiefly motivated in my choice to show the range and depth of anarchist philosophy and to dispel the popular prejudice that the anarchist tradition has not produced any thinkers of the first order.

Demanding the Impossible is therefore intended as a history of anarchist thought and action. While it attempts to place thinkers and ideas in their historical and social context, the emphasis will be on the development of anarchism as a rich, profound and original body of ideas and values. It should therefore be of both historical and philosophical interest. It is not written with any propagandist intentions, but my own sympathies will no doubt shine through.

A study of anarchism will show that the drive for freedom is not only a central part of our collective experience but responds to a deeply felt human need. Freedom is necessary for original thought and creativity. It is also a natural desire for we can see that no animal likes to be caged and all conscious beings enjoy the free satisfaction of their desires. Anarchism further seeks in social life what appears to operate in nature: the call for self-management in society mirrors the self-regulation and self-organization of nature itself.

Anarchism has been dismissed by its opponents as puerile and absurd. Authoritarian Marxists echo Lenin and dismiss it with other forms of 'left-wing' communism as an 'infantile disorder'.[14] In this respect, they find company with orthodox Freudians who believe that civilization can only exist on the basis of severe repression of instinctual drives. Anarchists, it is suggested, project on to the State all the hatred they felt for parental authority. A serious moral and social philosophy is thus reduced to a badly resolved parricide wish or dismissed as a form of therapy for an infantile neurosis. It is further claimed that anarchism lacks philosophical rigour and that its appeal is fundamentally emotional.

If these criticisms were accurate, it would be difficult to explain why some of the best minds of the twentieth century, such as Bertrand Russell and Noam Chomsky, have taken anarchist philosophy so seriously, even if they have not unreservedly endorsed its conclusions. It would also prove hard to account for the widespread influence of anarchism as a social movement in the past, especially in Spain, if it did not offer a rational and meaningful response to specific historical conditions. Far from being utopian or atavistic, anarchism grapples directly with the problems faced by individuals and communities in advanced industrial societies as well as in predominantly agricultural ones.

The continued appeal of anarchism can probably be attributed to its enduring affinity with both the rational and emotional impulses lying deep within us. It is an attitude, a way of life as well as a social philosophy. It presents a telling analysis of existing institutions and practices, and at the same time offers the prospect of a radically transformed society. Above all, it holds up the bewitching ideal of personal and social freedom, both in the negative sense of being free from all external restraint and imposed authority, and in the positive sense of being free to celebrate the full harmony of being. Whatever its future success as a historical movement, anarchism will remain a fundamental part of human experience, for the drive for freedom is one of our deepest needs and the vision of a free society is one of our oldest dreams. Neither can ever be fully repressed; both will outlive all rulers and their States.

PART ONE

Anarchism in Theory

To be governed is to be watched over, inspected, spied on, directed, legislated, regimented, closed in, indoctrinated, preached at, controlled, assessed, evaluated, censored, commanded; all by creatures that have neither the right, nor wisdom, nor virtue . . . To be governed means that at every move, operation, or transaction one is noted, registered, entered in a census, taxed, stamped, priced, assessed, patented, licensed, authorized, recommended, admonished, prevented, reformed, set right, corrected. Government means to be subjected to tribute, trained, ransomed, exploited, monopolized, extorted, pressured, mystified, robbed; all in the name of public utility and the general good. Then, at the first sign of resistance or word of complaint, one is repressed, fined, despised, vexed, pursued, hustled, beaten up, garroted, imprisoned, shot, machine-gunned, judged, sentenced, deported, sacrificed, sold, betrayed, and to cap it all, ridiculed, mocked, outraged, and dishonoured. *That* is government, *that* is its justice and its morality!
                                PIERRE-JOSEPH PROUDHON

Man is truly free only among equally free men.
                MICHAEL BAKUNIN

Every State is a *despotism*, be the despot one or many.
                MAX STIRNER

I

The River of Anarchy

ANARCHY IS USUALLY DEFINED as a society without government, and anarchism as the social philosophy which aims at its realization. The word 'anarchy' comes from the ancient Greek word αναρχια in which αν meant 'without' and αρχια meant first a military 'leader' then 'ruler'. In medieval Latin, the word became *anarchia*. During the early Middle Ages this was used to describe God as being 'without a beginning'; only later did it recapture its earlier Greek political definition. Today it has come to describe the condition of a people living without any constituted authority or government. From the beginning, anarchy has denoted both the negative sense of unruliness which leads to disorder and chaos, and the positive sense of a free society in which rule is no longer necessary.

It would be misleading to offer a neat definition of anarchism, since by its very nature it is anti-dogmatic. It does not offer a fixed body of doctrine based on one particular world-view. It is a complex and subtle philosophy, embracing many different currents of thought and strategy. Indeed, anarchism is like a river with many currents and eddies, constantly changing and being refreshed by new surges but always moving towards the wide ocean of freedom.

While there are many different currents in anarchism, anarchists do share certain basic assumptions and central themes. If you dive into an anarchist philosophy, you generally find a particular view of human nature, a critique of the existing order, a vision of a free society, and a way to achieve it. All anarchists reject the legitimacy of external government and of the State, and condemn imposed political authority, hierarchy and domination. They seek to establish the condition of anarchy, that is to say, a decentralized and self-regulating society consisting of a federation of voluntary associations of free and equal individuals. The ultimate goal of anarchism is to create a free society which allows all human beings to realize their full potential.

Anarchism was born of a moral protest against oppression and injustice. The very first human societies saw a constant struggle between those who wanted to rule and those who refused to be ruled or to rule in turn. The first anarchist was the first person who felt the oppression of another and rebelled against it. He or she not only asserted the right to think independently but challenged authority, whatsoever form it took.

As a recognizable trend in human history, the thread of anarchism, in thought and deed, may be traced back several thousands of years. Kropotkin once observed that 'throughout the history of our civilization, two traditions, two opposing tendencies have confronted each other: the Roman and the Popular; the imperial and the federalist; the authoritarian and the libertarian.'[1] Anarchism is part of the latter tradition. It is a tradition opposed to domination, a tradition which sees the self-governing community as the norm and the drive to create authoritarian and hierarchical institutions as an aberration.

Anarchism began to take shape wherever people demanded to govern themselves in the face of power-seeking minorities – whether magicians, priests, conquerors, soldiers, chiefs or rulers. Throughout recorded history, the anarchist spirit can be seen emerging in the clan, tribe, village community, independent city, guild and union.

The anarchist sensibility made its first appearance amongst the Taoists of ancient China, and has been with us ever since. It is clearly present in classical Greek thought. During the Christian era, its message found direct political expression in the great peasants' revolts of the Middle Ages. The factions of the extreme Left which flourished during the English Revolution, especially the Diggers and the Ranters, were deeply imbued with its spirit. Equally, it was to infuse the lively town meetings in the New England of the seventeenth century.

Nevertheless, these manifestations are, strictly speaking, part of the prehistory of anarchism. It required the collapse of feudalism in order for anarchism to develop as a coherent ideology, an ideology which combined the Renaissance's growing sense of individualism with the Enlightenment's belief in social progress. It emerged at the end of the eighteenth century in its modern form as a response partly to the rise of centralized States and nationalism, and partly to industrialization and capitalism. Anarchism thus took up the dual challenge of overthrowing both Capital and the State. But it soon had to struggle on two fronts, against the existing order of State and Church as well as against authoritarian tendencies within the emerging socialist movement.

It was of course the French Revolution which set the parameters for many of the arguments and struggles which preoccupied the Left during the nineteenth century. Anarchist sentiments and organization can be seen in the districts and municipalities during the Revolution. But the term 'anarchist' was still used as a term of abuse by the Jacobins and the Girondins when attacking the extreme *sans culottes* and the *enragés* who advocated federalism and the abolition of government. The real father of anarchism is to be found on the other side of the Channel. It was William Godwin who gave the first clear statement of anarchist principles, looking forward eagerly to the dissolution of that 'brute engine' of political government.[2]

The nineteenth century witnessed a great flood of anarchist theory and the development of an anarchist movement. The German philosopher Max Stirner elaborated an uncompromising form of individualism, firmly rejecting both government and the State. The first person deliberately to call himself an anarchist was the Frenchman Pierre-Joseph Proudhon; he insisted that only a society without artificial government could restore natural order: 'Just as man seeks justice in equality, society seeks order in anarchy.'[3] He launched the great slogans 'Anarchy is Order' and 'Property is Theft'.

The Russian revolutionary Michael Bakunin described anarchism as 'Proudhonism broadly developed and pushed to its extreme consequences'.[4] He popularized the term 'anarchy', exploiting the two associations of the word: with the widespread discord of revolutionary upheaval, and with the stable social order of freedom and solidarity which would follow. Providing a charismatic example of anarchy in action, Bakunin also helped forge the identity of the modern anarchist movement.

His aristocratic compatriot Peter Kropotkin tried, in the latter half of the century, to make anarchism more convincing by developing it into a systematic social philosophy based on scientific principles. He further refined Bakunin's collectivism – which had looked to distribute wealth according to work accomplished – by giving it a more communistic gloss. Reacting against Kropotkin's mechanistic approach, the Italian Errico Malatesta brought about a major shift by emphasizing the importance of the will in social struggle. During this period Benjamin R. Tucker in America also took up Proudhon's economic theories but adopted an extreme individualist stance.

Although Tolstoy did not publicly call himself an anarchist because of that title's associations with violence, he developed an anarchist critique of the State and property based on the teachings of Christ. As a result, he helped develop an influential pacifist tradition within the anarchist movement.

In the twentieth century, Emma Goldman added an important feminist dimension, while more recently Murray Bookchin has linked anarchism with social ecology in a striking way. More recent anarchist thinkers have, however, been primarily concerned with the application of anarchist ideas and values. The Russian Revolution and the Spanish Republic both proved great testing-grounds for anarchism before the Second World War. After it, the flood of anarchy subsided, but it did not disappear; the demographic complexion of the movement merely became more middle-class, and, since the sixties, the New Left, the counter-culture, the peace, feminist and

Green movements have all taken up many central anarchist themes.

But while anarchism is a broad river, it is possible to discern a number of distinctive currents. What principally divides the family of anarchists is their different views of human nature, strategy and future organization. The mainstream is occupied by the social anarchists, but the individualists form an important part of the flow. Amongst the social anarchists, there are mutualists, collectivists, communists, and syndicalists who differ mainly on the issue of economic organization. Some may be grouped according to their ideas, like the spiritual and philosophical anarchists; others according to their strategies, like the pacifist anarchists.

The social anarchists and individualists often work together but bear differing emphases. The individualists see the danger of obligatory co-operation and are worried that a collectivist society will lead to the tyranny of the group. On the other hand, the social anarchists are concerned that a society of individualists might become atomistic and that the spirit of competition could destroy mutual aid and general solidarity. Such differences do not prevent both wings coming together in the notion of communal individuality, which attempts to achieve a maximum degree of personal freedom without destroying the community.

The boundaries between the different currents of anarchism are not clear-cut; indeed they often flow into each other. Mutualism, collectivism, communism, and syndicalism might well exist side by side within the same society, as different associations and districts experiment with what best meets their specific wants and demands. No anarchist would be comfortable laying down an incontrovertible blueprint for future generations.

Spiritual anarchists see humans as primarily spiritual beings capable of managing themselves without the curb of external government. Most of them reject man-made laws in favour of a prior obligation to natural law or the law of God; some go even further to insist that in a state of grace no law, whether human or divine, is applicable. They generally assume that human impulses are fundamentally good and beneficent. Spiritual anarchism is not linked to any particular creed or sect, but its adherents all reject organized religion and the hierarchical church.

Like Tolstoy and Gandhi, many spiritual anarchists subscribe to pacifist beliefs. Pacifist anarchists refuse to use physical violence even to repel violence. They see the State and government as the ultimate expressions of organized violence, agreeing, with Randolph Bourne, that 'War is the Health of the State'. In their vocabulary, the State stands for legalized aggression, war mass murder, conscription slavery, and the soldier a hired assassin. They argue that it is impossible to bring about a peaceful and free society by the use of violence since means inevitably influence the nature of ends. It therefore follows, as Bart de Ligt argued, 'the greater the

violence, the less revolution'.⁵ The preferred tactics of the pacifist anarchists are non-violent direct action, passive resistance and civil disobedience;
they engage in strikes, boycotts, demonstrations and occupations.

Philosophical anarchism has often been despised by militants, although
clearly any action executed without thought is just an arbitrary jerk. All
anarchists are philosophical in a general sense, but it is usual to call those
thinkers philosophical anarchists who have reached anarchist conclusions
in their search for universal principles without engaging in any practical
activity. While the philosophical anarchists like Godwin have tended to stay
aloof from direct action, the great anarchist thinkers of the nineteenth
century – Proudhon, Bakunin and Kropotkin – were actively involved in
promoting the application of their distinctive strain of anarchism.

Proudhonism was the first current in anarchism to emerge (in Europe
from the 1840s on) as an identifiable social movement, with federalism as
the means of organization, mutualism as the economic principle and anarchy
as the goal. The indispensable premiss of mutualism was that society should
be organized, without the intervention of a State, by individuals who are
able to make free contracts with each other. To replace the existing State
and Capital, mutualists proposed, and tried to create, a co-operative society,
comprising individuals who exchange the necessities of life on the basis of
labour value and obtain free credit through a people's bank. Individuals and
small groups would still possess their instruments of labour, and receive
the produce thereof. Associations based on *mutualité* (reciprocity) would
ensure that exchange took place in the proper fashion by employing a system
of labour notes valued according to the average working time it took to
make a product.

On a larger scale, mutualists suggested that local communities link up
in a federalist system. Society would thus become a vast federation of
workers' associations and communes co-ordinated by councils at the local,
regional, national and international level. Unlike parliaments, the members
of the councils would be delegates, not representatives, without any executive authority and subject to instant recall. The councils themselves would
have no central authority, and consist of co-ordinating bodies with a minimal
secretariat.

Mutualism was not only taken up by members of the first International
Working Men's Association (IWMA); many revolutionaries in the Paris
Commune of 1871 called themselves mutualists. Since it made no direct
attack on the class system, mutualism tended to appeal to craftsmen and
artisans, shopkeepers and small farmers, who valued their independence
rather more than did the industrial working class .

It was not long before delegates within the federalist wing of the IWMA
developed Proudhon's mutualist economic doctrine towards collectivism.

Bakunin used the term for the first time at the Second Congress of the League of Peace and Liberty at Bern in 1868. Collectivists believed that the State should be dismantled and the economy organized on the basis of common ownership and control by associations of producers. They wished to restrict private property only to the product of individual labour, but argued that there should be common ownership of the land and all other means of production.

Collectivists in general look to a free federation of associations of producers and consumers to organize production and distribution. They uphold the socialist principle: 'From each according to his ability, to each according to work done.' This form of anarchist collectivism appealed to peasants as well as workers in the labour movement who wanted to create a free society without any transitional revolutionary government or dictatorship. For a long time after Bakunin, nearly all the Spanish anarchists were collectivists.

After the demise of the First International in the 1870s the European anarchist movement took a communist direction. At first the distinction between communism and collectivism was not always readily apparent; 'collective socialism' was even used as a synonym for 'non-authoritarian communism'. Nevertheless, anarchist communists came to believe, like Kropotkin, that the products of labour as well as the instruments of production should be held in common. Since the work of each is entwined with the work of all, it is virtually impossible to calculate the exact value of any person's labour. Anarchist communists therefore conclude that the whole society should manage the economy while the price and wage system should be done away with.

Where collectivists see the workers' collective as the basic unit of society, communists look to the commune composed of the whole population – consumers as well as producers – as the fundamental association. They adopt as their definition of economic justice the principle: 'From each according to their ability, to each according to their need.' In a free communist society, they are confident that drudgery could be transformed into meaningful work and that there could be relative abundance for all. Economic relations would at last express the natural human sympathies of solidarity and mutual aid and release spontaneous altruism.

Anarchist communists hold a different view of human nature from the individualists, stressing that man is a social being who can only realize his full potential in society. Where the individualists talk about the sovereignty of the individual and personal autonomy, the communists stress the need for solidarity and co-operation. The proper relationship between people, they argue, is not one of self-interest, however enlightened, but of sympathy.

Anarcho-syndicalism shares their concern with mutual aid. Its roots may be traced to the First International which insisted that the emancipation of the workers must be the task of the workers themselves. But it developed, as a recognizable trend, out of the revolutionary trade union movement at the end of the last century, especially in France, where workers reacted against the methods of authoritarian socialism and adopted the anarchist rejection of parliamentary politics and the State. Syndicalism in general redirected the impulses of the advocates of 'propaganda by the deed' and took over many of the most positive ideas of anarchism about a free and equal society without government and the State.

The advocates of anarcho-syndicalism take the view that trade unions or labour syndicates should not only be concerned with improving the conditions and wages of their members, although this is an important part of their activity. They should take on a more positive role and have an educational as well as social function; they should become the 'most fruitful germs of a future society, the elementary school of Socialism in general'.[6] By developing within the shell of the old society, the syndicates should therefore establish institutions of self-management so that when the revolution comes through a general strike the workers will be prepared to undertake the necessary social transformation. The syndicates should in this way be considered the means of revolution as well as a model of the future society.

The most constructive phase of syndicalism was from 1894 to 1914, especially in France and Italy; anarcho-syndicalists also played a significant part in the Russian Revolution. After the First World War, however, anarcho-syndicalism began to lose its way, except in Spain and to a lesser extent in Latin America. It tended to flourish in countries where the labour movement was not well-organized and the class struggle was sharp and bitter. The international movement however regrouped at a Congress in Berlin, Germany, in 1922. It called itself the International Working Men's Association and in its declaration of principles asserted:

> Revolutionary Syndicalism is the confirmed enemy of every form of economic and social monopoly, and aims at its abolition by means of economic communes and administrative organs of field and factory workers on the basis of a free system of councils, entirely liberated from subordination to any government or political party. Against the politics of the State and parties it erects the economic organization of labour; against the government of men, it sets up the management of things. Consequently, it has for its object, not the conquest of political power, but the abolition of every State function in social life.

Its aims were to be put to the test in the last remaining bastion of anarcho-syndicalism in Spain during the Spanish Revolution, when the syndicates took over the industries in Catalunya and demonstrated that they were capable of running them on efficient and productive lines.

Despite its historical importance, many anarchists have argued that anarcho-syndicalism with its emphasis on class struggle has too narrow a vision of a free society. On the one hand, it concentrates on problems of work and can easily become entangled in day-to-day struggles for better wages and conditions like any other union. On the other hand, it places a utopian confidence in the general strike as inaugurating the social revolution. Above all, it is principally concerned with the liberation of producers and not the whole of society.

Individualist anarchism is the most self-regarding form of anarchism. Socially, the individualists conceive society not as an organic whole but as a collection of separate and sovereign individuals. Morally, they celebrate individuality as the supreme value, and are fearful of the individual submerging himself or herself in the community. Economically, they want each person to have the free disposal of the products of his or her labour.

Individualist anarchism comes closest to classical liberalism, sharing its concepts of private property and economic exchange, as well as its definitions of freedom as the absence of restraint, and justice as the reward of merit. Indeed, the individualist develops the liberal concept of the sovereignty of the individual to such an extent that it becomes incompatible with any form of government or State. Each person is considered to have an inviolable sphere which embraces both his body and his property. Any interference with this private sphere is deemed an invasion: the State with its coercive apparatus of taxation, conscription, and law is the supreme invader. Individuals may thus be said to encounter each other as sovereign on their own territory, regulating their affairs through voluntary contracts.

Anarcho-capitalism is a recent current which has developed out of individualist anarchism. It wishes to dismantle government while retaining private property and to allow complete *laissez-faire* in the economy. Its adherents stress the sovereignty of the individual and reject all governmental interference in everyday life. They propose that government services be turned over to private entrepreneurs. Even the symbolic spaces of the public realm like town halls, streets and parks would be made into private property. Radical libertarianism has recently had a considerable vogue in the USA, where the Libertarian Party has taken up many of its ideas, and in Great Britain where the right wing of the Conservative Party talk its language.

While all anarchists are individualist to some degree in that they do not want to be ruled by others, collectivists and communists maintain that social problems cannot be solved on an individual basis or by the invisible hand of the market. In order to change existing society and establish an equitable replacement, it is necessary, they argue, to combine with others and work together.

In recent times, the various currents of anarchism have flown closer together. There are genuine differences between those who are strict pacifists and those who would allow a minimal use of violence to achieve their common goal. Militants are often critical of the more philosophically inclined, and communists keep reminding the individualists of the importance of solidarity. But the different currents have not split off into different streams or hardened into sects. The concept of 'anarchism without adjectives' is being discussed again in the context of creating a broad front to face the challenges of the third millennium.

Except for a few diehard fanatics, most anarchists would see the various currents as expressing a different emphasis rather than an unbridgeable chasm. Indeed, some would find it quite acceptable to call themselves individualists in everyday life, syndicalists in wanting self-management at work, and communists in looking forward to a society in which goods are shared in common. For all the different philosophical assumptions, strategies and social recommendations, anarchists are united in their search for a free society without the State and government. They all flow in the broad river of anarchy towards the great sea of freedom.

2

Society and the State

ANARCHISTS MAKE A CLEAR distinction between society and the State. While they value society as a sum of voluntary associations, they reject the State as a particular body intended to maintain a compulsory scheme of legal order.[1] Most anarchists have depicted the State as an extraneous burden placed on society which can be thrown off, although more recently some, like Gustav Landauer, have stressed that the State is a certain relationship between human beings and overlaps society.

Society

Society for anarchists is, as Thomas Paine wrote, invariably 'a blessing', the repository of all what is good in humanity: co-operation, mutual aid, sympathy, solidarity, initiative, and spontaneity.[2] It is therefore quite misleading, as Daniel Guérin has done, to suggest that the anarchist 'rejects society as a whole'.[3] Only the extreme individualist Stirner attacks society as well as the State, and even he calls for an association or 'union of egoists' so that people can achieve their ends together. Godwin may have considered society only as an 'aggregate of individuals', but he speaks on behalf of most anarchists when he asserts that 'The most desirable condition of the human species, is a state of society.'[4]

Anarchists argue that the State is a recent development in human social and political organization, and that for most of history human beings have organized themselves in society without government and law in a peaceful and productive way. Indeed, in many societies social order exists in inverse proportion to the development of the State.

Pure anarchy in the sense of a society with no concentration of force and no social controls has probably never existed. Stateless societies and peasant societies employ sanctions of approval and disapproval, the offer of reciprocity and the threat of its withdrawal, as instruments of social control. But modern anthropology confirms that in organic or 'primitive' societies there is a limited concentration of force. If authority exists, it is delegated and rarely imposed, and in many societies no relation of command and obedience is in force.

Ever since man emerged as *homo sapiens*, he has been living in stateless communities which fall roughly into three groups: acephalous societies, in which there is scarcely any political specialization and no formal leadership (though some individuals have prestige); chiefdoms, in which the chief has no control of concentrated force and whose hereditary prestige is largely dependent on generosity; and big-man systems, in which the charismatic big man collects his dues for the benefit of society. Anthropologists have described many different types of indigenous anarchies. They vary from gardeners to pastoralists, small groups like pygmies and Inuits in marginal areas to vast tribes like the Tiv in Nigeria or the Santals in East India.[5] But while human beings have been living in such communities for forty or fifty thousand years, they have nearly all been absorbed or destroyed by states in the last couple of centuries.

Many of these organic societies are quite libertarian but some are characterized by ageism and sexism. They often have strong collective moral and religious systems which make people conform. Powerful moral and social pressures as well as supernatural sanctions are brought to bear on any anti-social behaviour. Yet for all their limitations, they show that the Hobbesian nightmare of universal war in a 'state of nature' is a myth. A society without hierarchy in the form of rulers and leaders is not a utopian dream but an integral part of collective human experience. Anarchists wish to combine the ancient patterns of co-operation and mutual aid of these organic societies with a modern sense of individuality and personal autonomy.

Apart from extreme individualists, anarchists thus see society as the natural condition of human beings which brings out the best in them. They consider society to be a self-regulating order which develops best when least interfered with. When asked what would replace government, numerous anarchists have answered 'What do you replace cancer with?' Proudhon was more specific and replied 'Nothing':

> Society is eternal motion; it does not have to be wound up; and it is not necessary to beat time for it. It carries its own pendulum and its ever-wound-up spring within it. An organized society needs laws as little as legislators. Laws are to society what cobwebs are to a bechive; they only serve to catch the bees.[6]

Anarchists thus believe that existing religious and political institutions are for the most part irrational and unnatural and prevent an orderly social life. Left to its own devices, society will find its own beneficial and creative course. Social order can prevail in the fundamental sense of providing security of persons and property.

This fundamental distinction between society and the State is held by liberal as well as anarchist thinkers. Locke depicted men in a state of nature as free and equal and regulated by the law of nature from which natural rights are derived. His notion of natural order existing independently of the State provides the theoretical grounds for the classic liberal defence of *laissez-faire*. He only differed from the anarchists in thinking that life in a state of nature could be uncertain and inconvenient without known laws and a limited government to protect the natural rights to life, liberty and property. Anarchists agree with Locke that humanity has always lived in society but argue that government simply exasperates potential social conflict rather than offering a cure for it.

Anarchists therefore believe that people can live together in peace and freedom and trust. The social anarchists look towards natural solidarity to encourage voluntary co-operation, while the individualists consider it possible to regulate affairs through voluntary contracts based on rational self-interest. Even those few anarchists like Sébastien Faure who see a struggle for survival in the state of nature believe that without laws, masters and repression, the 'horrible struggle for life' can be replaced by 'fertile agreement'.[7] There is therefore simply no need for the nightwatchman State of the liberal, let alone for the roaring Leviathan of authoritarian communists and fascists. Natural order can spontaneously prevail.

Natural Order

A fundamental assumption of anarchism is that nature flourishes best if left to itself. A Taoist allegory goes:

> Horses live on dry land, eat grass and drink. When pleased, they rub their necks together. When angry, they turn round and kick up their heels at each other. Thus far only do their natural dispositions carry them. But bridled and bitted, with a plate of metal on their foreheads, they learn to cast vicious looks, to turn the head to bite, to resist, to get the bit out of the mouth, or the bridle into it. And thus their natures become depraved.[8]

The same might be said of human beings. It is interfering, dominating rulers who upset the natural harmony and balance of things. It is only when they try to work against the grain, to block the natural flow of energy, that trouble emerges in society. The anarchist confidence in the advantages of freedom, of letting alone, is thus grounded in a kind of cosmic optimism. Without the interference of human beings, natural laws will ensure that spontaneous order will emerge.

In their concept of nature, anarchists tend to see the natural ground of society not in a historical sense of 'things as they now are or have become', *natura naturata*, but in a philosophical sense of 'things as they may become', *natura naturans*. Like Heraclitus, they do not regard nature as a fixed state but more as a dynamic process: you never put your foot in the same river twice. Where conservative thinkers believe that nature is best expressed in 'things as they are', that is, what history has produced so far, progressive thinkers look to nature to fulfil its potential. Most anarchists believe that the best way to bring about improvement is to let nature pursue its own beneficent course.

This confidence in the beneficence of nature first emerges amongst the Taoists in ancient China. The early Greeks, especially the Stoics, also felt that if human beings lived in conformity with nature, all would be well. By the time of the Middle Ages, nature came to be perceived in terms of a Great Chain of Being, composed of an infinite number of continuous links ranging in hierarchical order from the lowest form of being to the highest form – the Absolute Being or God. Woodcock has suggested that in their view of man's place in the world, anarchists believed in a modified version of the Great Chain of Being.[9] In fact, the conception of the universe as a Chain of Being, and the principles which underline this conception – plenitude, continuity, and gradation – were deeply conservative. Moreover, the hierarchical cosmogony of the Chain of Being, with its gradations from beast to angels with man in the middle, reflected the social hierarchy of the period. In the eighteenth century, it led to the belief that there could be no improvement in the organization of society and to Pope's conclusion that 'whatever is, is right'.[10]

Indeed, it was only towards the end of the eighteenth century when the static notion of a Chain of Being was temporalized and replaced by a more evolutionary view of nature that progressive thinkers began to appeal to nature as a touchstone to illustrate the shortcomings of modern civilization. The primitivist Rousseau reacted against the artificiality of European civilization by suggesting that we should develop a more natural way of living. The natural goodness of man had been depraved by government and political institutions; it was therefore necessarily to create them anew in order to let the natural man flourish.

There is undoubtedly a strong strand of primitivism in anarchist thought. It takes both a chronological form, in the belief that the best period of history was before the foundation of the State, and a cultural form, in the idea that the acquisitions of modern civilization are evil. These beliefs can combine in a celebration of the simplicity and gentleness of what is imagined to be the primitive life. Most anarchists however do not look back to some alleged lost golden age, but forward to a new era of self-conscious freedom. They are therefore both primitivist and progressive, drawing inspiration from a happier way of life in the past and anticipating a new and better one in the future.

This comes clearly through in the work of Godwin, the first to give a clear statement of anarchist principles at the end of the eighteenth century. He saw nature in terms of *natura naturans*, things as they may become. He never lost his confidence in the possibility of moral and social progress. Even when an atheist, he believed that truth is omnipotent and universal. In his old age, he began to talk of some mysterious and beneficent power which sustains and gives harmony to the whole universe. Proudhon also believed in universal natural law and felt that there was an immanent sense of justice deep within man: 'he carries within himself the principles of a moral code that goes beyond the individual . . . They constitute his essence and the essence of society itself. They are the characteristic mould of the human soul, daily refined and perfected through social relations.'[11]

Bakunin looked at nature and society in a more dialectical way and saw change occurring through the reconciliation of opposites: 'the harmony of natural forces appears only as the result of a continual struggle, which is the real condition of life and of movement. In nature, as in society as well, order without struggle is death.' Nature itself only acts in an unconscious way according to natural laws. Nevertheless, universal order exists in nature and society. Even man with his powers of reasoning is 'the material product of the union and action of natural forces'.[12]

Kropotkin not only felt, like Proudhon, that the moral sense is innate but that nature evolves principally through mutual aid to higher and more complex forms. Malatesta questioned Kropotkin's excessive optimism and suggested that anarchy is 'the struggle, in human society, against the disharmonies of Nature'. But even though he felt that 'natural man is in a continuous state of conflict with his fellows', he believed social solidarity and harmony were possible.[13] Modern theorists like Murray Bookchin and John Clark follow Kropotkin's lead in trying to link anarchism with ecology, and to show that the ecological principles of unity in diversity and of harmony through complexity apply to a free society.

All anarchists thus believe that without the artificial restrictions of the State and government, without the coercion of imposed authority, a harmony of interests amongst human beings will emerge. Even the most ardent of individualists are confident that if people follow their own interests in a clear-sighted way they would be able to form unions to minimize conflict. Anarchists, whatever their persuasion, believe in spontaneous order. Given common needs, they are confident that human beings can organize themselves and create a social order which will prove far more effective and beneficial than any imposed by authority.[14] Liberty, as Proudhon observed, is the mother, not the daughter of order.

But while all anarchists call for the dissolution of the State and believe that social order will eventually prevail, they base their confidence on different premises and models.[15] Individualists like Stirner and Tucker developed Adam Smith's economic vision in which a hidden hand will translate private interest into general good and promote a coincidence of interests. Since economic activity involves countless decisions and operations it cannot be successfully regulated or directed by one individual or a group of individuals. It should therefore be left to itself and a system of self-regulating economic harmony would result. In Saint-Simon's celebrated phrase, the 'administration of things' would eventually replace 'the government of men'.

Godwin based his model of a harmonious free society on the reign of reason in accordance with universal moral laws. Through education and enlightenment, people would become more rational and recognize universal truth and their common interests and act accordingly. All would listen to the voice of truth. Proudhon felt that people were necessarily dependent on each other and would gain from co-ordinating voluntarily their economic interests. Bakunin believed that conscience and reason were sufficient to govern humanity, although he was enough of a Hegelian to depict human consciousness and society developing through history in a dialectical way. Only popular spontaneous organizations could meet the growing diversity of needs and interests.

Both Kropotkin and Tolstoy based their vision of social harmony on their observations of tribal organizations and peasant villages. They were impressed by the way in which such communities arranged their lives without law and government according to custom and voluntary agreement. At the same time, Kropotkin tried to ground anarchism in the scientific study of society and natural history and to demonstrate that it was a rational philosophy which sought to live in accordance with natural and social laws. Human beings, he argued, had evolved natural instincts of sympathy and co-operation which were repressed or distorted in authoritarian and capitalist States. In the spontaneous order of a free society, they would re-emerge and be strengthened.

State and Government

The State did not appear until about 5500 years ago in Egypt. While great empires like those of the Chinese and Romans ebbed and flowed, with no clear boundaries on their outer limits, most of the world's population continued to live in clans or tribes. Their conduct was regulated by customs and taboos; they had no laws, political administration, courts, or police to maintain order and cohesion.

The State emerged with economic inequality. It was only when a society was able to produce a surplus which could be appropriated by a few that private property and class relations developed. When the rich called on the support of the shaman and the warrior, the State as an association claiming supreme authority in a given area began to emerge. Laws were made to protect private property and enforced by a special group of armed men. The State was thus founded on social conflict, not, as Locke imagined, by rational men of goodwill who made a social contract in order to set up a government to make life more certain and convenient.

Kropotkin in his study of the origins of the State argues that the Roman Empire was a State, but that the Greek cities and the medieval city republics were not. In European nations, he argues, the State barely dates from the sixteenth century when it took over the free towns and their federations. It resulted from a 'Triple-Alliance' of lords, lawyers and priests who dominated society.[16] They were later joined by the capitalists who continued to strengthen and centralize the State and crush free initiative. The people in the mean time were persuaded to co-operate with the process and grew accustomed to voluntary servitude.

Most anarchists would accept this version of history in general terms. While society is invariably a blessing, they accept that the State is an artificial superstructure separate from society. It is an instrument of oppression, and one of the principal causes of social evil. They therefore reject the idealist view put forward by Rousseau that the State can express the General Will of the people. They will have none of the Hegelian mysticism which tries to see the State as the expression of the spirit of a nation. They do not believe that it forms a moral being or a body politic which is somehow greater than the sum of its parts. They look through its mystifying ceremony and ritual which veil its naked power. They question its appeals to patriotism and democracy to justify the rule of the ruling minority. They do not even accept the liberal contention that the State can be considered a centre of sympathy and co-operation in certain areas.

On the other hand, anarchists have no trouble in accepting Max Weber's definition of the State as a body which claims the monopoly of legitimate use of physical force within a given territory. It uses its monopoly of force, through the army and police, to defend itself against foreign invasion and internal dissension. As the supreme authority within a given territory, it claims the sole legitimate right to command its citizens and to be obeyed.

Anarchists also agree with socialists that the State is invariably controlled by the rich and powerful and that its legislation is inevitably made in the interests of the dominant elite. Godwin saw, like Marx, that the rich are always 'directly or indirectly the legislators of the state' and that government perpetuated the economic inequality in society. Kropotkin argued that the State has always been both in ancient and modern history

'the instrument for establishing monopolies in favour of ruling minorities'.[17]
With the abolition of the State, anarchists assume that greater equality will
eventually be achieved but they propose widely different economic systems,
ranging from *laissez-faire* based on private property to voluntary communism.

There is of course a difference between the State and government.
Within a given territory, the State remains while governments come and
go. The government is that body within the State which claims legitimate
authority to make laws; it also directs and controls the State apparatus.
It follows certain procedures for obtaining and using power, based in a
constitution or on custom. Tucker defined the State as a 'monopoly of
government' in a particular area, and government as an 'invasion of the
individual's private sphere'.[18]

Most anarchists however use the terms State and government loosely
as if they were synonymous for the repository of political authority in society.
While all anarchists are opposed to the State, a few are ready to allow
government in an attenuated form in a transitional period. Godwin, at a
time when Nation-States in Europe were beginning to take on their modern
form, wrote mainly about the evils of government. He argued that men
associated at first for the sake of mutual assistance, but the 'errors and the
perverseness of the few' led to the need for restraint in the form of government. But while government was intended to suppress injustice, its effect
had been to perpetuate it by concentrating the force of the community
and aggravating the inequality of property. Once established, governments
impede the dynamic creativity and spontaneity of the people:

> They 'lay their hand on the spring there is in society, and put a stop
> to its motion'. Their tendency is to perpetuate abuse. Whatever was
> once thought right and useful they undertake to entail to the latest
> posterity. They reverse the general propensities of man, and instead
> of suffering us to proceed, teach us to look backward for perfection.
> They prompt us to seek the public welfare, not in alteration and
> improvement, but in a timid reverence for the decisions of our ances-
> tors, as if it were the nature of the human mind always to degenerate,
> and never to advance.[19]

The individualist Stirner, on the other hand, focused on the State as the
cause of evil. 'Every State is a *despotism*, be the despot one or many.'[20] Its
one purpose is to limit, control and subordinate the individual.

Not all anarchists are as consistent as Godwin and Stirner. Proudhon
asserted that the government of man by man is servitude, but he paradoxically defined anarchy as the absence of a ruler or a sovereign as a 'form of
government'. In a late work on federalism, he even saw a positive role for

the State 'as a prime mover and overall director' in society.[21] Nevertheless, he acknowledged that 'anarchical government' is a contradiction in terms and left one of the most damning descriptions of government and bureaucracy ever made:

> To be governed is to be watched over, inspected, spied on, directed, legislated, regimented, closed in, indoctrinated, preached at, controlled, assessed, evaluated, censored, commanded; all by creatures that have neither the right, nor wisdom, nor virtue ... To be governed means that at every move, operation, or transaction one is noted, registered, entered in a census, taxed, stamped, priced, assessed, patented, licensed, authorized, recommended, admonished, prevented, reformed, set right, corrected. Government means to be subjected to tribute, trained, ransomed, exploited, monopolized, extorted, pressured, mystified, robbed; all in the name of public utility and the general good. Then, at the first sign of resistance or word of complaint, one is repressed, fined, despised, vexed, pursued, hustled, beaten up, garroted, imprisoned, shot, machine-gunned, judged, sentenced, deported, sacrificed, sold, betrayed, and to cap it all, ridiculed, mocked, outraged, and dishonoured. *That* is government, *that* is its justice and its morality![22]

Bakunin reserved some his finest rhetoric for his condemnation of the State for crushing the spontaneous life of society. But he too was not always consistent. In the First International, Bakunin and his supporters allowed the terms 'regenerate State', 'new and revolutionary State', or even 'socialist State' to stand as synonyms for 'social collective'. But aware of the ambiguity which could be exploited by the authoritarian socialists and Marxists, they went on to propose *fédération* or *solidarisation* of communes as a more accurate description of what they wanted to see to replace the existing State. In his speech at the Basel Congress of 1869, Bakunin thus made clear that he was voting for the collectivization of social wealth by which he meant 'the expropriation of all who are now proprietors, by the abolition of the juridical and political State which is the sanction and sole guarantor of property as it now is'. As to the subsequent form of organization, he favoured the *solidarisation* of communes because such *solidarisation* entails the 'organization of society from the bottom up'.[23]

The practice amongst some anarchists to confuse the government and the State appears most clearly in Malatesta. In his pamphlet *Anarchy* (1891), he defined the State as

> the sum total of political, legislative, judiciary, military and financial institutions through which the management of their affairs, the control over their personal behaviour, the responsibility for their personal

safety, are taken away from the people and entrusted to others who, by usurpation or delegation, are vested with the powers to make the laws for everything and everybody, and to oblige the people to observe them, if need be, by the use of collective force.

But he added that in this sense the word *State* means *government*, or to put it another way, it is 'the impersonal, abstract expression of that state of affairs personified by government'. Since the word State is often used to describe a particular human collectivity gathered in a particular territory, and to mean the supreme administration of a country, he preferred to replace the expression 'abolition of the State' with the 'clearer and more concrete term *abolition of government*'.[24]

Kropotkin was concerned about abolishing both the government and the State. He defined anarchism as the 'No government system of socialism' and as 'a principle or theory of life and conduct under which society is conceived without government'.[25] In his work on the origins of *The State* (1897), Kropotkin distinguished between the State and government. He does not consider all governments to be equally bad for he praises the medieval cities and their governmental institutions, with their assemblies, elected judges, and military force subordinate to the civil authority. But when the State emerged it not only included the existence of a power situated above society like the government but also a '*territorial concentration and a concentration of many or even all functions of society in the hands of a few*'. It implies some new relationships between members of society which did not exist before the formation of the State. It had been the historical mission of the State 'to prevent the direct association among men, to shackle the development of local and individual initiative, to crush existing liberties, to prevent their new blossoming – all this in order to subject the masses to the will of minorities'.[26]

This century the anarchist critique of the State has become more sophisticated. Gustav Landauer has suggested that 'the State is a condition, a certain relationship between human beings, a mode of behaviour; we destroy it by contracting other relationships, by behaving differently'. Only when people make the existing connection between them a bond in an organic community can the legal order of the State be made obsolete.[27]

More recently, Murray Bookchin has argued persuasively that the State is not merely a constellation of bureaucratic and coercive institutions but also a state of mind, 'an instilled mentality for ordering reality'. In liberal democracies this century, its capacity for brute force has been limited, but it continues to have a powerful psychological influence by creating a sense of awe and powerlessness in its subjects. Indeed, it has become increasingly difficult to fix its boundaries and the line between the State and society has become so blurred that now 'the State is a hybridization of political with social institutions, of coercive with distributive functions, of highly punitive with regulatory procedures, and finally of class with administrative needs'.[28]

Liberal Democracy

It is on the issue of the State that anarchists part company with their liberal and socialist allies. Liberals maintain that a State as a compulsory legal order is necessary to protect civil liberties and rights, to deal with disputes and conflicts in society with an unfettered economy. As the liberal thinker L. T. Hobhouse wrote:

> The function of State coercion is to override individual coercion, and, of course, coercion exercised by any association of individuals within the State. It is by this means that it maintains liberty of expression, security of person and property, genuine freedom of contract, the rights of public meeting and association, and finally its own power to carry out common objects undefeated by the recalcitrance of individual members.[29]

Anarchists argue, on the other hand, that even the most minimal 'nightwatchman' State advocated by modern libertarians would be controlled by the rich and powerful and be used to defend their interests and privileges. However much it claims to protect individual rights, the government will always become 'an instrument in the hands of the ruling classes to maintain power over the people'.[30] Rather than providing healthy stability, it prevents positive change; instead of imposing order, it creates conflict; where it tries to foster enterprise, it destroys initiative. It claims to bring about security, but it only increases anxiety.

Although anarchists feel that representative democracy is preferable to monarchy, aristocracy or despotism, they still consider it to be essentially oppressive. They rebut the twin pillars of the democratic theory of the State – representation and majority rule. In the first place, no one can truly represent anyone else and it is impossible to delegate one's authority. Secondly, the majority has no more right to dictate to the minority, even a minority of one, than the minority to the majority. To decide upon truth by the casting up of votes, Godwin wrote, is a 'flagrant insult to all reason and justice'.[31] The idea that the government can control the individual and his property simply because it reflects the will of the majority is therefore plainly unjust.

Anarchists also reject the liberal theory of a social contract beloved by Hobbes, Locke and Rousseau. No government, in their view, can have power over any individual who refuses his consent and it is absurd to expect someone to give his consent individually to all the laws. The American individualist Lysander Spooner exploded the contractual theory of the State by analysing the US Constitution. He could find no evidence of anyone ever making a contract to set up a government, and argued that it was absurd to look to the practice of voting or paying taxes as evidence of tacit consent. 'It is plain', he concluded, 'that on the general principles of law and reason . . . the Constitution is no contract; that it binds nobody, and never did anybody; and that all those who pretend to act by its authority . . . are mere usurpers, and that every body not only has the right, but is morally bound, to treat them as such.'[32]

Not all anarchists share the same view of contracts amongst individuals. Godwin rejected all forms of contract since they usually result in past folly governing future wisdom. If an action is right, it should be performed; if not, avoided. There is no need for the additional obligation of a contract. On the other hand, both Proudhon and Kropotkin looked to contracts in the form of voluntary agreements to regulate affairs between people in an anarchist society without the State. But since such contracts are not legally enforceable and carry no sanctions, they are more like declarations of intent than binding contracts in the conventional sense. The only reason why people would keep them is the pragmatic one that if an individual habitually broke his contracts, he would soon find few people to enter into agreement with him.

Anarchists have few illusions about the nature of liberal democracy and representative government. When Proudhon entered briefly the National Assembly during the 1848 Revolution, it confirmed what he had long suspected: 'As soon as I set foot in the parliamentary Sinai, I ceased to be in touch with the masses. Fear of the people is the sickness of all those who belong to authority; the people, for those in power, are the enemy.'[33] Henceforth he declared 'Universal Suffrage is the Counter-Revolution' and insisted that the struggle should take place in the economic and not the political arena. Bakunin never entered a parliament as a representative or joined a political party. From the beginning he was well aware that 'Whoever talks of political power, talks of domination' and insisted that 'All political organization is destined to end in the negation of freedom.'[34] Although during the Spanish Civil War anarchists did participate for a short while in the republican government in order to fight Franco's rebels, the historic anarchist movement has consistently preached abstention from conventional politics. Hence the popular slogans: 'Whoever you vote for, the government always gets in', or better still, 'If voting changed anything, they'd make it illegal'.

As a result of the social struggles of the last two centuries, the modern liberal State has of course been obliged to provide welfare and education for its citizens. Some anarchists like Nicolas Walter have suggested that not all State institutions are wholly bad since they can have a useful function when they challenge the use of authority by other institutions and when they promote certain desirable social activities: 'Thus we have the liberatory state and the welfare state, the state working for freedom and the state working for equality.'[35]

Nevertheless, the principal role of the State has always been to limit freedom and maintain inequality. Although it may have a benevolent face, the Welfare State can be restrictive by intensifying its grip on the lives of its subjects through registration, regulation and supervision. It creates a surly and overblown bureaucracy. It can, as George Woodcock has argued, become 'just as ingenious a means of repression and regimentation as any more overtly totalitarian system'.[36] It singularly fails to make people happy, and by offering a spurious security it undermines the practice of mutual aid. It tends to be wasteful by not directing resources to those most in need. Instead of paying taxes to the State which then decides who is in need, anarchists prefer to help directly the disadvantaged by voluntary acts of giving or by participating in community organizations.

The same arguments against the liberal State apply to the socialist State, only more so. Anarchists reject the claim made by democratic socialists that the State is the best means of redistributing wealth and providing welfare. In practice, the socialist State tends to spawn a vast bureaucracy which stifles the life of the community. It creates a new elite of bureaucrats who often administer in their own interest rather than in the interest of those they are meant to serve. It encourages dependency and conformity by threatening to withdraw its aid or by rewarding those its favours. By undermining voluntary associations and the practice of mutual aid, it eventually turns society into a lonely crowd buttressed by the social worker and policeman. Only if social democrats adopt a libertarian and decentralized form of socialism can anarchists join them in their endeavours and encourage them to adopt the principles of voluntary federation and association.

The Marxist State

At first sight, anarchists and Marxists would seem to have much in common. Both criticize existing States as protecting the interests of the privileged and wealthy. Both share a common vision of a free and equal society as the ultimate ideal. But it is with Marxist-Leninists that anarchists have encountered the greatest disagreement over the role of the State in society. The issue led to the great dispute between Marx and Bakunin in the nineteenth century which eventually led to the demise of the First International Working Men's Association.

In *The Origin of the Family, Private Property and the State* (1884), Engels argued like Kropotkin that the State had emerged recently in human history as an apparatus of rule separate from society: 'The state, then, has not existed from all eternity. There have been societies that did without it, that had no idea of the state and state power.'It had developed only with the division of society into classes and became a coercive machine for maintaining the rule of one class over another. The capitalist State provided liberty only for those who owned property and subjection for the rest – workers and peasants. Engels however was confident that his generation was approaching a stage in the development of production when classes and the State would inevitably fall. When that time comes

> Society, which will reorganise production on the basis of a free and equal association of the producers, will put the whole machinery of the state where it will then belong: into the museum of antiquities, by the side of the spinning-wheel and the bronze axe.[37]

Although Marx and Engels felt it was necessary for the proletariat to take over the State to hold down their adversaries and to reorganize production, they both looked forward to a time when the proletariat would abolish its supremacy as a class and society would become 'an association in which the free development of each is the condition for the free development of all'.[38] It was Engels's contention in his *Anti-Dühring* that the interference of the State becomes superfluous in one sphere after another so that the government of persons is replaced by the administration of things. In the process, 'The state is not "abolished", *it withers away.*'[39]

Engels however still insisted on the need for a State in a transitional period of socialism before communist society could be established. While Bakunin and the anarchists claimed the direct democracy of the Paris Commune provided a model of a free society, Engels argued that

> The anarchists put the thing upside down. They declare that the proletarian revolution must *begin* by doing away with the political organization of the state . . . But to destroy it at such a moment would be to destroy the only organism by means of which the victorious proletariat can assert its newly conquered power, hold down its capitalist adversaries, and carry out that economic revolution of society . . .[40]

Lenin developed Marx's and Engels's view of the State. As a general principle, he declared that 'we Marxists are opposed to all and every kind of State'.[41] In his pamphlet *The State and Revolution*, written in August 1917 on the eve of the Bolshevik seizure of power, Lenin gave 'the most idyllic, semi-anarchist account' of the proletarian revolution, describing how the State could begin to wither away immediately after its victory.[42] Indeed,

Lenin considered the issue of the State to be of the utmost importance in the coming revolution. In his commentary on Plekhanov's pamphlet *Anarchism and Socialism* (1894), he criticizes Plekhanov for contriving completely to ignore 'the most urgent, burning, and politically most essential issue in the struggle against anarchism, viz., the relation of the revolution to the state, and the question of the state in general!'[43] He further differed from Engels who believed that a factory is necessarily authoritarian in its organization, by maintaining that it would be possible under communism to operate modern industrialized society without the need for compulsion or narrow specialization.

But Marxists and anarchists disagree profoundly over the means of realizing this desirable state of affairs. Marx suggested the need for the 'dictatorship of the proletariat' in a transitional socialist period and it has since become a central part of Marxist-Leninist orthodoxy. Yet the difference between anarchists and Marxists is more than simply a question of tactics. It also involves substantial theoretical differences. Marx's dispute with Bakunin did have an important historical dimension, but it was fired by theoretical considerations as well. He attacked Stirner in *The German Ideology* and Proudhon in *The Poverty of Philosophy* for their failure to appreciate dialectical materialism. Where Marx tried to reverse Hegel's position and give primacy to the capitalist economy over the bourgeois State, many anarchists persisted in seeing the State as a determining influence over the economy. Rather than recognizing the need to wait for economic conditions to develop before abolishing the State, some placed their confidence in the creative power of revolutionary will. Marx also opposed the anarchists' rejection of imposed authority; he was keen to alter the form of authority in a communist society but did not seek to abolish the principle of authority altogether. He thought it was not only necessary to seize State power in order to defend the revolution but also to develop new kinds of social control of the productive forces.

The anarchists failed in Marx's eyes to develop a coherent class analysis, either by taking an individualist position like Stirner, by adopting a 'petty-bourgeois' approach like Proudhon in his defence of the peasantry, or by having an 'opportunist' and 'voluntarist' faith like Bakunin in the creative energies of the undefined 'people' and the 'lumpenproletariat'. There is of course some substance to this criticism. Unlike Marxists, anarchists do not have a specific class base. They recognize the differences in power and wealth between the rich and poor, and align themselves with the 'people', and stress the role of different classes at different times. Proudhon started his career mainly concerned with the peasantry only to finish up considering favourably the political capacity of the working class. Bakunin sometimes used the rhetoric of the 'working class' and the 'proletariat' but when he specified who the revolutionary workers were, they turned out to be the less-educated urban proletarians and the peasants. Although he felt, like Marx, that the proletarians would lead the revolution, he went out of his way to stress the revolutionary potential of the peasantry. In addition, he looked to the dispossessed and disinherited to rise up since they had nothing to lose but their chains.

Above all, Marx criticized the anarchists for struggling on the economic and cultural level only and failing to grasp the need for the working class to conquer political power. Politics even in its parliamentary form could be progressive for Marx; he even entertained the view that it was possible to use political means in order to go beyond conventional politics. In his 'Instructions' to the Geneva Congress of the International, he argued against the Proudhonists that the working class could win reforms through 'general laws, enforced by the power of the state' and 'in enforcing such laws, the working class do not fortify government power. On the contrary, they transform that power, now used against them, into their own agency'.[44] Referring to Bakunin, he declared contemptuously : 'this ass cannot even understand that any class movement, as such, is necessarily and always has been, a political movement'.[45] In particular, he condemned Bakunin for believing that 'The will, and not economic conditions, is the foundation of social revolution.'[46]

In his dealings with Stirner, Proudhon and Bakunin, Marx certainly emerges 'at his least appealing and at his most hectoring and heavy-handed'.[47] He not only revealed the authoritarian tendency of his own social and political thought, but also the authoritarian nature of his own personality. Moreover, his anti-anarchist manoeuvres which led to the demise of the First International ensured that future Internationals in the control of Marxists would become rigid and monolithic and that Marxism itself would harden into a dogmatic creed which brooked no dissent.

Lenin more than any one else helped contribute to this process. He took issue with the anarchists primarily on the role of the State in the revolution. He argued that they went wrong not in wanting to abolish the State, but in wanting to abolish it overnight. Lenin felt it was essential to 'smash' the inherited bureaucratic military State machine. But this did not mean doing away with State power altogether since it was necessary for the proletariat to use it during its dictatorship in a transitional period. Like Marx, Lenin believed in 'democratic centralism'; it was therefore necessary to strengthen and centralize the State power in order to oppose counter-revolutionary forces and 'to crush the resistance of the bourgeoisie'.[48]

Lenin has been accused of hypocrisy in his call for the withering away of the State immediately before his seizure of power in Russia.[49] Certainly after the Bolshevik seizure of power in October 1917, he proceeded to undermine the power of the Soviets and establish a hierarchical and centralized structure of command by the 'vanguard' Communist Party. In his work *'Left-Wing' Communism, An Infantile Disorder* (1920), he proceeded to castigate anarchists and socialist revolutionaries for their immature 'opportunism' in wanting to abolish the State immediately on the morrow o the revolution. He narrated how Bolshevism became 'steeled' in its struggle against *'petty-bourgeois revolutionism* which smacks of, or borrows something from, anarchism' and which easily goes to revolutionary extremes but is 'incapable of perseverance, organization, discipline and steadfastness'. Indeed, he declared that anarchism was 'not infrequently a sort of punishment for the opportunist sins of the working-class movement'. He found to his dismay that certain sections of the Industrial Workers of the World and anarcho-syndicalist trends in Russia continued to uphold the 'errors of Left-Wing Communism' for all their admiration of the Soviet system.[50]

Yet despite his centralizing and strengthening of the State and his liquidation of the anarchist opposition, Lenin still firmly believed that the withering away of the State was the final goal of communism. In a lecture on the State, he insisted that while it was necessary to place the machine (or 'bludgeon') of the State in the hands of the class that is to overthrow the power of capital, he looked to a time when they 'shall consign this machine to the scrap heap. Then there will be no state and no exploitation'.[51]

Whatever Lenin's ultimate ideal, his reliance on a vanguard Communist Party to steer the 'Dictatorship of the Proletariat' led eventually not only to the dictatorship of the Party but also to the dictatorship of one man – Stalin – in the Soviet Union. Moreover, in the other major Marxist-Leninist revolutions this century, in China, North Korea, Vietnam and Cuba, 'democratic centralism' has resulted in practice in highly hierarchical and authoritarian States controlled by an elitist party. The dire warnings of Bakunin that a 'Workers' State' would lead to a new 'red bourgeoisie' have been tragically confirmed. The Communist States that have emerged this century amply demonstrate the anarchists' fear that a 'People's State' or 'Revolutionary Government' would not only perpetuate but extend tyranny.

Law

The anarchists like liberals see the State as primarily a legal association and law as its mode of action.[52] It is designed to maintain a compulsory degree of legal order. Its principal bodies – the legislature, judiciary, and executive – are responsible for making, interpreting and enforcing the law. Strictly speaking, a law is a rule of conduct made by government and enforced by the State.

Tolstoy describes laws vividly as 'rules, made by people who govern by means of organized violence, for non-compliance with which the non-compliant is subjected to blows, to loss of liberty, or even to being murdered'.[53] Laws restrict our liberty by making us act or refrain from acting regardless of our wishes; they stand like high hedges, keeping us on the straight and narrow. The methods used by the State to enforce its laws are those of compulsion: the ultimate power of the law is the coercive power of the State. As Hobbes recognized, the authority of Leviathan is ultimately based on the sword – or its modern equivalent, the policeman's cosh or the soldier's gun. Indeed, as Tolstoy observed, the characteristic feature of government is that 'it claims a moral right to inflict physical penalties, and by its decree to make murder a good action'.[54] Since they reject the State, it is therefore inevitable that anarchists reject its most coercive expression in the law; in the words of Jean Grave, 'anarchy demonstrates that there cannot be any good laws, nor good governments, nor faithful applications of the law . . . all human law is arbitrary.'[55]

Of all anarchists, Godwin was the earliest and most trenchant critic of law. In the first place, he argued that man-made law is unnecessary since 'immutable reason is the true legislator'. Men can do no more than declare and interpret the rules of universal justice as perceived by reason. Secondly, the principal weakness of law is its status as a general rule. No two actions are the same and yet the law absurdly tries to reduce the myriad of human actions to one common measure, and as such operates like Procrustes' bed in the Greek legend which cuts or stretches whoever lays on it. Thirdly, law is inevitably made in the interest of the lawmakers and as such is a 'venal compact by which superior tyrants have purchased the countenance and alliance of the inferior'.[56] Above all, like government it fixes the human mind in a stagnant condition and prevents that unceasing progress which is its natural tendency.

Godwin was certain that the punishment – the voluntary infliction of evil on a vicious being – threatened or imposed by law is not an appropriate way to reform human conduct. Since men are products of their environment, they cannot strictly speaking be held responsible for what they do: an assassin is no more guilty of the crime he commits than the dagger he holds. Since they are in the grip of circumstances, they do not have free will. There can therefore be no moral justification in punishment, whether it be for retribution, example or reform. All punishment is 'a tacit confession of imbecility'; indeed, it is worse than the original crime since it uses force where rational persuasion is enough. Coercion cannot convince or create respect; it can only sour the mind and alienate the person against whom it is used.

Godwin was convinced that law, like government, is not only harmful but unnecessary. His remedy for anti-social acts was to reduce the occasion for crime by eradicating its causes in government and accumulated property and by encouraging people through education to think in terms of the general good rather than private interest. Since vice is principally error, enlightenment will be enough to make people virtuous.

Godwin is realistic enough to recognize that even in a free society it may be necessary to restrain violent people on a temporary basis, but they should always be treated kindly and kept within the community as far as possible. Instead of resorting to courts and professional lawyers, disputes could be solved by popular juries who consider the specific circumstances of each case: 'There is no maxim more clear than this, "Every case is a rule to itself".'[57] The aim should always be to resolve conflict rather than apportion blame. Eventually, Godwin believed, it would only be necessary to recommend rather than enforce the decisions of juries. In place of law, the power of public opinion would suffice to check anti-social acts. And once the 'rules of justice' were properly understood by the community, then laws would become unnecessary.

After Godwin, Kropotkin offered the most cogent anarchist criticism of the law. All legislation within the State, he asserted, has always been made with regard to the interests of the privileged classes. He traced the origins of law first to primitive superstitions, and then to the decrees of conquerors. Originally human relations were regulated by customs and usages, but the dominant minority used law to make immutable those customs which were to their advantage. Law thus made its appearance 'under the sanction of the priest, and the warrior's club was placed at its service'.[58]

Kropotkin divided the millions of laws which exist to regulate humanity into three main categories: the protection of property, the protection of governments, the protection of persons. The first is intended to appropriate the product of the worker's labour or to deal with quarrels between monopolists; as such they have no other object than to protect the unjust appropriation of human labour. The second category, constitutional law, is intended to maintain the administrative machine which almost entirely serves to protect the interests of the possessing classes. The third category, the protection of persons, is the most important since such laws are considered indispensable to the maintenance of security in European societies. These laws developed from the nucleus of customs which were useful to human communities, but since they have been adopted by rulers to sanctify their domination they have become as useless and injurious as the other categories of law.

Kropotkin argued that the main supports for crime are idleness, law and authority. But since about two-thirds of existing crimes are crimes against property, 'they will disappear, or be limited to a quite trifling amount, when property which is now the privilege of a few, shall return to its real source – the community'.[59] For those people who will still be anti-social and violent, Kropotkin insists that punishment is not appropriate since the severity of punishment does not diminish the amount of crime. Talking from his own experience of Russian and French prisons, he condemned prisons for killing physical energy, destroying the individual will, and encouraging society to treat the liberated prisoner as 'something plague-stricken'.[60]

It is not possible to improve prisons. The more prisons are reformed, the more detestable they become: modern penitentiaries are far worse than the dungeons of the Middle Ages. The best cure for anti-social tendencies is to be found in human sympathy. Kropotkin concludes:

> Peoples without political organization, and therefore less depraved than ourselves, have perfectly understood that the man who is called 'criminal' is simply unfortunate; that the remedy is not to flog him, to chain him up, or to kill him on the scaffold or in prison, but to help him by the most brotherly care, by treatment based on equality, but the usages of life amongst honest men.[61]

Anarchists assume that there would be a greater harmony of interests amongst individuals living in a society without government, law and unequal property. But they do not think that everyone would immediately behave in a responsible fashion and there would be no more disputes or conflicts. In place of the force of law, Godwin and Kropotkin recommended the influence of public opinion and mutual censure to reform conduct. There is of course a possibility that the tyranny of public opinion could replace the oppression of law. But while Godwin and Kropotkin allow censure as a form of social control, they insist that people should decide for themselves how they should behave.

Again, in a society where anti-social individuals are considered to be sick and in need of a cure, psychological manipulation can be more coercive and tyrannical than imprisonment. The use of psychiatry to reform dissidents has become notorious in authoritarian societies. Stirner put the problem succinctly: '*Curative means* or *healing* is only the reverse side of *punishment*, the *theory of cure* runs parallel to the *theory of punishment*; if the latter sees in an action a sin against right, the former takes it for a sin of the man *against himself*, as a decadence from his health.'[62]

With their concern for personal autonomy and individual freedom, anarchists more than any other socialists are aware of the inhumanity of both physical punishment and manipulative cure for anti-social members of the community. They look to reasoned argument and friendly treatment to deal with criminals and wish to respect their humanity and individuality.

The Nation-State

The Nation-State has become the norm of modern political organization and the main object of citizens' loyalties. The State is considered the guardian of a nation's identity, and colonized peoples who win their independence invariably strive to set up their own Nation-State. Yet many nations exist without their own States, and many States consist of several different nations. The Nation and the State are not therefore synonymous. Nor are they necessarily desirable. From the beginning, the anarchists have questioned the legitimacy of Nation-States and strongly resisted their formation.[63] They have not however ignored the strong emotional pull of nationalism and patriotism, and some, notably, Proudhon and Bakunin, have succumbed to it.

Like the ancient Stoics, the anarchists have always been cosmopolitan and internationalist in outlook, and considered themselves 'citizens of the world'. In general, they have supported national liberation struggles as part of a wider struggle for freedom, but they have opposed the statist aspirations and exclusive loyalties of the nationalists. They are particularly critical of patriotism which makes the ruled identify with their rulers and become their obedient cannon-fodder. They also recognize that rivalry between Nation-States is one of the principal causes of war.

Godwin was highly critical of Rousseau and others who exhorted people to love their country and to 'sink the personal existence of individuals in the existence of the community' as if it were an abstract being. The love of our country is 'one of those specious illusions which are employed by impostors for the purpose of rendering the multitude the blind instruments of their crooked designs'. It makes us consider whatever is gained for country as so much gained to 'our darling selves'. Patriotism moreover leads to 'a spirit of hatred and all uncharitableness towards the countries around us'. In place of a narrow patriotism, Godwin taught universal benevolence: we should help the most needy and worthy, regardless of our personal connections. We should act as impartial spectators and not be swayed by the ties of family, tribe, country, or race. And since ideas of great empire and of legislative unity are plainly 'the barbarous remains of the days of military heroism', Godwin looked to a decentralized society of federated parishes to replace the Nation-State.[64]

Tolstoy like Godwin also rigorously condemned patriotism. He saw it inextricably linked with government. By supporting government and fostering war, he declared patriotism to be a 'rude, harmful, disgraceful, and bad feeling, and above all, immoral' since it influences man to see himself the 'son of his fatherland and the slave of his Government, and commit actions contrary to his reason and his conscience'.[65] He felt that if people could understand that they are not the sons of some fatherland or other, nor of Governments, but the sons of God, they would be neither slaves nor enemies to each other.

Not all anarchists however have condemned patriotism so roundly as Godwin and Tolstoy. Proudhon was undoubtedly a French nationalist. As he grew older, he not only celebrated the French revolutionary tradition but also the French people and their heritage. He was markedly anti-Semitic. Nevertheless, he argued that federalism is the only answer to end the rivalry between nations and to dissolve empires. Like Rousseau, he felt that the larger a nation in territory or population, the greater the danger of tyranny. He therefore urged a process of decolonization, as the United States and Canada had from England, and looked to a time when Algeria would constitute itself an 'African France'.[66]

Bakunin was a nationalist before becoming an anarchist. He tended to harbour nationalist prejudices, celebrating the freedom-loving and spontaneous Slavs and condemning the militaristic Germans. He thought Marx was a thorough-going authoritarian partly because he was a German and a Jew. However, Bakunin's early support for Polish nationalism and Panslavism was motivated by a desire to break up the Russian empire and to set its colonized peoples free. He expressed 'strong sympathy for any national uprising against any form of oppression' and declared that every people has 'the right to be itself and no one is entitled to impose its costume, its customs, its language, its opinions, or its laws'.[67]

While Bakunin believed that nationalism was a 'natural fact' and that each nation had an incontestable right to free development, he did not think nationalism acceptable as a legitimate political principle because it has an exclusive tendency and lacks 'the power of universality'.[68] In a subtle analysis of patriotism, he distinguished three types. The first is 'natural', an 'instinctive, mechanical, uncritical attachment to the socially accepted hereditary or traditional pattern of life'. But while it is an expression of social solidarity, it exists in an inverse ratio to the evolution of humanity. The second is 'bourgeois', the object of which is to maintain the power of the Nation-State, that is 'the mainstay of all privileges of the exploiters throughout the nation'. The third is 'proletarian', the only truly acceptable form of patriotism, which ignores national differences and State boundaries and embraces the world.[69]

Bakunin therefore looked to a 'large, fraternal union of mankind' and extended the principle of federalism to the world as a whole. As a transition to a federation of all nations, he called for a United States of Europe as the only way of making a civil war between the different peoples in the 'European family' impossible. The 'United States' he had in mind however would not be a centralized, bureaucratic and military federation, but organized from the bottom up with member nations having the right to secession. True internationalism, he insisted, rests on self-determination: 'each individual, each association, commune, or province, each region and nation, has the absolute right to determine its own fate, to associate with others or not, to ally itself with whomever it will, or break any alliance, without regard to so-called historical claims or the convenience of its neighbour'.[70] Only in this way would nations cease to be the products of conquest and historical and geographical distortion. In the long run, however, Bakunin believed that the national question is secondary to the social revolution and the social revolution should become a world revolution.

Rudolf Rocker has provided the most incisive condemnation of the Nation-State in his vast study *Nationalism and Culture* (1937). For Rocker, the nation is not the origin but the product of the State: *'It is the state which creates the nation, and not the nation the state'*. The nation cannot therefore exist without the State. But he does not deny local feelings of attachment to a culture and land. He distinguishes between a people, which the 'natural result of social union, a mutual association' brought about by a common language and particular conditions of living, and the nation, which is the 'artificial struggle for political power'.[71] A people always consists of a community with narrow boundaries, while a nation often encapsulates a whole array of different peoples who have by more or less violent means been pressed into the frame of a common state. He therefore condemned nationalism for trying to create artificial barriers and disturbing the organic unity of the community.

Gustav Landauer, who was strongly influenced by Proudhon, made an interesting attempt to combine nationalism and anarchism. He contrasted like Rocker the 'Community' against the 'State'; the people in a statist society do not find themselves together in the organism of true community. Community however exists alongside and outside the State, but it has not yet been fully realized. A free community is therefore not the founding of something new, but 'the actualization and reconstitution of something that has always been present, which exists alongside the state, albeit buried and laid waste'.[72] It is necessary to develop this community made from the union of persons and families into various communities, and communities into associations.

The 'nationhood' of a people, according to Landauer, remains once 'Statehood' has been superseded. Nationhood consists of the closeness of people together in their way of life, language, tradition, and memories of a common fate and works to create real communal living. It follows that 'nothing but the rebirth of all peoples out of the spirit of regional community can bring salvation'.[73] But while Landauer wanted to revive old communal traditions and dissolve the State, his vision was not parochial. It would seem that the essential features of Rocker's concept of a 'people' are to be found in Landauer's concept of the 'nation'. The nation for Landauer is not an artificial whole but a community of communities. The individual moreover should not identify only with his nation, but see it as one ring in the widening circle of humanity.

The anarchists have thus mounted the most consistent and rigorous critique of the State, whether in its liberal, social democratic, or Marxist form. While the State may have been intended to suppress injustice and oppression, they argue that it has only aggravated them. It fosters war and national rivalries; it crushes creativity and independence. Governments, and the laws through which they impose their will, are equally unnecessary and harmful. At the same time, their confidence in natural order leads anarchists to believe that society will flourish without imposed authority and external coercion. People thrive best when least interfered with; without the State, they will be able to develop initiative, form voluntary agreements and practise mutual aid. They will be able to become fully realized individuals, combining ancient patterns of co-operation with a modern sense of individuality. The anarchist critique of the State not only questions many of the fundamental assumptions of political philosophy but challenges the authoritarian premisses of Western civilization.

Freedom and Equality

ANARCHISM IS A PHILOSOPHY in its own right. Although as a social movement it has developed a wide variety of strands from extreme individualism to communism, all anarchists share certain common concerns. They offer a critique of the existing order, a vision of a free society, and a way of moving from one to another. Above all, they reject all coercive forms of external authority in order to achieve the greatest degree of freedom and equality. In the process they illuminate many of the fundamental principles of moral and political philosophy. While they may not always be consistent, they cannot be accused of having a naive or simplistic view of the great ideals of liberty and equality launched by the French Revolution.

It is usual to see absolute freedom as the anarchists' supreme ideal and their central commitment. Sébastien Faure wrote in the twenties: 'The anarchist doctrine may be resumed in one word: liberty'.[1] For Herbert Read freedom is 'the value of all values'.[2] Anarchists certainly see freedom as a permanent and necessary factor in the life and progress of humanity, as an intrinsic good without which it is impossible for human beings to reach their full stature. The American individualist Josiah Warren speaks for most anarchists when he writes: 'Man seeks freedom as the magnet seeks the pole or water its level, and society can have no peace until every member is really free.'[3]

As philosophers are only too well aware, the notion of freedom can be a conceptual labyrinth and it is important to consider its different meanings. Anarchists wish to expand human freedom in the negative sense of being free from restraint. Most anarchists also see freedom in the positive sense of being free to do what one likes and to realize one's full potential.[4] But freedom is always a triadic relation and involves not only freedom *from* something in order *to* do something, but also the freedom *of* certain agents.[5] In the anarchists' case, they are not concerned with the freedom of a particular class or elite, but the freedom of all human beings. They recognize that the freedom of all is the necessary condition for the freedom of each; as Bakunin declared, 'Man is truly free only among equally free men.'[6]

Herbert Read distinguishes between 'liberty' as a political ideal, which is expressed in social organization, and 'freedom' in which man achieves spontaneity and creativity.[7] While this verbal distinction is peculiar to

English, most anarchists reject the Roman sense of *libertas* as popular government embodied in a republican constitution. Their principal concern is with freedom from external political authority. They do not accept like Locke that the State is necessary to protect individual liberty. They equally reject Rousseau's notion of civil liberty in which one can be legitimately forced to obey the laws one makes for oneself. They have no truck with Hegel's idealist definition of liberty as 'necessity transfigured' so that the individual somehow realizes his 'higher self' in obeying the law of the State.

On the contrary, anarchists believe that genuine freedom can only be achieved in a society without the State. They therefore embrace the traditional socialist freedoms such as freedom from want and insecurity as well as the liberal freedoms of expression, thought, assembly and movement. When they talk about economic freedom, they mean both the liberal sense of freedom from the economic controls of the State and the socialist sense of freedom from economic hardship. The alleged 'freedom' of the few on the other hand to exploit and to command is not a desirable form of freedom since it leads to oppression. They are thus the most coherent and consistent advocates of freedom.

Some anarchists have taken up Rabelais' motto 'Do what you will!' Faure insists that 'the man who does not do what he wants, only what pleases him and which suits him, is not free.'[8] But few anarchists believe that one should do what one wants whatever the consequences. Elisée Reclus sees in anarchism the 'right to act according to one's own agreement, to do "what one wants"', but adds immediately 'while associating one's will to those of other men in all collective works'.[9] Similarly, Godwin makes a distinction between freedom and licence. He rejects the positive right to do as we please on the grounds that we have a permanent duty to contribute to general happiness. Freedom from constraint (except that of reasons presented to the understanding) is of the utmost importance, but 'moral independence' is always injurious.[10] We should therefore be free from political constraints, not moral constraints. Godwin's position resembles Spinoza's description of a free man as one who lives according to the dictates of reason alone. Bakunin went even further to argue that the idea of absolute independence from natural law is a 'wild absurdity', the brainchild of metaphysicians: 'absolutely self-sufficient freedom is to condemn oneself to nonexistence'.[11] As with Marx and Engels, freedom for Bakunin involves control over ourselves and over external nature which is founded on a knowledge of natural law.

Anarchists are not therefore immoralists asserting absolute freedom for themselves alone. They do not, like Dostoevsky's Underground Man, believe that it is right to assert one's independence whatever it may cost and wherever it may lead, or maintain that the greatest good is 'one's own free and unfettered volition, one's own caprice, however wild, one's own fancy, inflamed sometimes to the point of madness . . ."[12] To see freedom entirely in personal terms in this way would seem to justify the kind of self-assertion which leads to the oppression or exploitation of others.

Malatesta argued for instance that the simple desire to be free to do as one pleases is not enough to make an anarchist: 'That aspiration towards unlimited freedom, if not tempered by a love for mankind and by the desire that all should enjoy equal freedom, may well create rebels who, if they are strong enough, soon become exploiters and tyrants, but never anarchists.'[13] Malatesta believed that men are not naturally harmonious, and that living together in society involves a limitation on freedom since we must sacrifice desires which are irreconcilable with those of others. He called for freedom as the power to do as one wishes with the important proviso that it must be 'freedom for everybody and in everything, with the only limit of the equal freedom for others'. [14]

Even the most extreme individualist anarchist Max Stirner does not entirely reject morality and believes voluntary co-operation with other rational egoists desirable. While refusing to accept binding moral rules imposed from without, anarchists look to some form of morality to replace political authority. Kropotkin looked to our innate moral sense as a compass in a free society, and argued that moral principles should replace man-made laws as a guide to human conduct. Even the arch-individualist Benjamin Tucker insisted on a moral code, even if he did reduce the only moral law to 'Mind your own business'.[15]

To adopt moral rules for oneself is not therefore inconsistent with anarchism. Government, with its laws, restricts our freedom by the threat of force, but if a person imposes rules on himself he is not being compelled but acting voluntarily. Freedom in the sense of government by reason is quite acceptable. As Tucker wrote: 'If the individual has a right to govern himself, all external government is tyranny'.[16] The idea of ruling oneself rather than being ruled by others is implicit in the anarchists' advocacy of self-government and self-management. The whole thrust of the anarchist argument for social freedom is that the absence of laws would not lead to a state of moral chaos or disorder since people are capable of governing themselves.

Nevertheless, they do not accept that rational freedom in the sense of governing oneself through constraints imposed from within is enforceable in any way. It is not for the community to compel one to obey the general will; anarchists will have no truck with Rousseau's pernicious paradox that it is possible to 'be forced to be free'.[17] On the other hand, they would accept Kant's view of autonomy as self-imposed rules which have been freely chosen for oneself.

The anarchist stress on personal morality does not of course mean a commitment to past values. Kropotkin sees the value of age-old patterns of co-operation and mutual aid, but would like to combine them with a modern sense of individuality. Most anarchists call, like Nietzsche and Emma Goldman, for a transvaluation of values, a going beyond existing definitions of good and evil, to forge a new morality for a free society.[18]

While rejecting man-made laws, all the classic anarchist thinkers except Stirner recognize the force of natural law as a way of achieving social cohesion in the absence of government and man-made laws. Godwin believed that the universe was governed by universal laws and believed that truth is always victorious over error. He was convinced that morality is independent of positive institutions; that it is 'immutably true' that whatever tends to procure a balance of happiness and pleasure is to be desired.[19] Proudhon too based his whole case for anarchy on the existence in nature and human nature of immanent justice which was revealed through his moral sense.

Bakunin presented himself as a 'scientific' anarchist and argued that natural law is the foundation of our liberty. He celebrated the liberty which consists in the full development of our potential,'the liberty which recognizes no other restrictions than those which are traced for us by the laws of our own nature'. But according to Bakunin these are no real restrictions since 'these laws are not imposed on us by some outside legislator, beside us or above us; they are immanent in us, inherent, constituting the very basis of our being, material as well as intellectual and moral; instead, therefore, of finding them a limit, we must consider them as the real conditions and effective reason for our liberty.'[20]

Kropotkin, too, argued that anarchism should be based on the method of modern science. He believed the same laws governed nature and society, especially the law of sociability, which gave rise to a social instinct in animals and humanity and enabled them to survive in the struggle for existence and develop a moral sense. Although Malatesta criticizes the attempt to make anarchism 'scientific', since this would deny free will, he still recognized 'the great law of solidarity, which predominates in society as in nature'.[21]

It should now be clear that anarchists do not take absolute freedom as their ideal. Given the physical and social limits we all experience, the very idea of absolute freedom is strictly speaking absurd. Without recognizable limits, a definition of freedom is empty and meaningless. Such 'freedom' if it could exist would be like the senseless and hopeless 'inviolability' which K experiences in Kafka's *The Castle* when people have broken off relationships with him and left him alone.[22]

It has even been questioned whether freedom is the supreme ideal of anarchists. As Malatesta wrote, since living in society necessarily involves curbing some of our desires '*freedom*, in its absolute sense, could not solve the question of a happy and voluntary co-existence'.[23] In addition, for those who principally define freedom negatively as freedom from restraint it is difficult to see how it can be a supreme value. Even as a necessary condition of self-development it is valued as a means, not an end. Godwin, for instance, argued that civil liberty is chiefly desirable as a means to encourage a certain type of personality: 'To be free is a circumstance of little value, if we could suppose men in a state of external freedom, without the magnanimity, energy and firmness that constitute almost all that is valuable in a state of freedom.'[24]

  Again, the anarchists' readiness to use public opinion, censure and social pressure to reform conduct in place of law and punishment might suggest that they do not value freedom above everything else. Censure, even in the form of reasoned argument, curtails the freedom of some in an anarchist society to enable the maximum amount of freedom for all. By wishing to combine the greatest individual development with the greatest communal unity, Alan Ritter has argued that their overriding goal is 'communal individuality' and that they therefore cannot strictly speaking be called 'libertarians'; their libertarianism is 'not of direct intention, but of oblique effect'.[25] Freedom is thus valued more as a means than an end.

  This view, while pointing to an important element in the anarchist conception of freedom, is not comprehensive enough. Stirner, Tucker and other individualist anarchists, for instance, do not see community as supporting individuality. But it does remind us that anarchists accept that liberty has physical and social limits and recognize that personal freedom is inevitably curtailed in some way by the freedom of others. For the strict individualist other people must inevitably stand as a constant threat to his or her freedom.

  Afraid of those who would invade his 'sphere of discretion' and reduce him to clockwork uniformity, Godwin felt compelled to conclude that 'everything that is usually understood by the term co-operation is, in some degree, an evil.'[26] But the more collectivist anarchist thinkers like Proudhon, Bakunin and Kropotkin believed that since we are social beings we can only be free to realize ourselves in the company of others. Individuality, in their case, is based on reciprocal awareness. As Proudhon put it, the individual 'recognizes his own self in that of others'.[27] People need not therefore be a threat but a help.

  Anarchists experience freedom as potentially joyous. Malatesta became an anarchist precisely because of his aspirations towards a society which reconciles 'the liberty of everyone with co-operation and love among men'. For him freedom is not an abstract right but the possibility of acting. It is the isolated individual who is powerless; it is 'by co-operation with his fellows that man finds a means to express his activity and his power of initiative'.[28]

While celebrating personal and social freedom as a central if not supreme ideal, anarchists are strongly aware that it cannot easily be achieved. They are aware of the strong social, cultural and psychological obstacles which block the way to a free society. Randolph Bourne not only noted that war is the health of the State but that a herd instinct drives the individual into obedience and conformity since 'You feel powerful by conforming, and you feel forlorn and helpless if you are out of the crowd'. The State – 'the organization of the entire herd' – is founded on these impulses and makes careful use of them.[29] Anarchists are also aware, as Erich Fromm pointed out, that many people fear freedom because of the responsibility it entails and in times of economic insecurity and social unrest look to strong leaders to tell them what to think and do. Isolated and rootless individuals in modern society readily resort to devotion and submission to authoritarian organizations or the State. Like Adam after his expulsion from the Garden of Eden for rebelling against the authority of God, newly won freedom can appear to modern man as a curse; 'he is free *from* the sweet bondage of paradise, but he is not free *to* govern himself, to realize his individuality.'[30]

Again, anarchists appreciate the insights of Wilhelm Reich who has shown how the subject person only too easily becomes an active participant in his own subjection. The utter powerlessness of the modern citizen can often lead to the primary masochism of internalized submissiveness so that he begins to identify with the agent who has thwarted his vital energy. He becomes, as Etienne de la Boétie pointed out, a voluntary slave. Moreover, modern man's experience of our ancient patriarchal and authoritarian society and culture encourages '*an armouring against nature within himself and against social misery outside himself*' leading to 'helplessness, craving for authority, fear of responsibility, mystical longing, sexual misery'.[31]

Yet for all their appreciation of the psychology of obedience and dependence and the powerful influence of the State and culture in shaping conforming citizens, anarchists still believe that all human beings are ultimately capable of breaking out of the Crystal Palace, of releasing themselves from their physical manacles and mental chains of illusion. They call for freedom for all from all forms of imposed authority as well as the freedom to achieve the active realization of the individual self.

Clearly anarchists do not have a naive or crude view of freedom. Moreover, their aspiration to create a free society need no longer appear a utopian dream as it has done in the past. Malatesta at the turn of the century argued that 'All specifically human life is a struggle against outside nature, and every forward step is adaptation, is the overcoming of a natural law'.[32] In our post-scarcity society of relative abundance, the objective conditions are there (in the West at least) to enable us to pass from the historic realm of economic necessity to the realm of freedom. For the first time in human history, we are now free to choose our needs. Desire no longer may be seen as a form of bondage to be controlled by reason since the free satisfaction of desire is possible to a large degree. Indeed, Bookchin has even argued that human beings while freeing themselves are now in a position to create a '*free* nature' by helping it to realize its evolutionary trend towards consciousness and subjectivity.[33]

Of all political doctrines, anarchism responds most to the deeply felt human need for freedom which is essential for creativity and fulfilment. It holds up the ideal of personal freedom as a form of autonomy which does not restrict the freedom of others. It proposes a free society without government in which people make their own free structures. It looks to a time when human beings are not only free from each other, but are able to help each other and all life-forms to realize their full potential.

Authority

Another way of saying that anarchism takes freedom as its ultimate goal is to claim that it opposes authority. 'All anarchists', George Woodcock insists, 'deny authority'.[34] Certainly many anarchists have argued this to be the case. Bakunin, who called himself an 'anti-authoritarian', advocated the '*absolute rejection of every authority*' while Kropotkin maintained that anarchism works 'to destroy authority in all its aspects'.[35] Malatesta also defined anarchy as '*society organized without authority*', meaning by authority 'the power to *impose* one's will'.[36] More recently, Colin Ward has called an anarchist society 'a society which organizes itself without authority'.[37]

This definition of anarchism as an opposition to authority comes from the common definition of the State as the supreme authority within a given territory, and since all anarchists are opposed to the State, it is inferred that they are opposed to authority. Authority however is more fundamental and exists prior to the foundation of the State. In addition, it might be misleading to define anarchy as an absence of authority for strictly speaking it would appear that a society without some form of authority is virtually inconceivable.[38]

Nevertheless, it is true to say that all anarchists are opposed to political authority in the sense that they deny anyone the legitimate right to issue commands and have them obeyed. As Robert Paul Wolff has argued, since 'the state is authority, the right to rule', anarchism which rejects the State is the only political doctrine consistent with autonomy in which the individual alone is the judge of his moral constraints.[39] Anarchists also reject legal authority as defined by Max Weber as 'a belief in the "legality" of enacted rules and the right of those elevated to authority under such rules to issue commands'.[40] Communist anarchists further reject what they call 'economic authority'; as Faure pointed out, 'Authority dresses itself in two principal forms: the political form, that is the State; and the economic form, that is private property'.[41]

Anarchists however are less clear-cut about traditional authority resting on a belief in ancient traditions and the legitimacy of the holders of the tradition. Kropotkin, for instance, stressed repeatedly that customs precede man-made laws to regulate human affairs, and thought they could replace them again in the future. Proudhon even accepted the need for patriarchal authority within the family while opposing it in wider society. Anarchists are also prone to being influenced by charismatic authority, that is by the exemplary character of an exceptional person. Godwin appeared to Shelley as a wise mentor and did not reject the role. Bakunin undoubtedly possessed enormous charisma and exploited it to influence his comrades. Many were also affected by Kropotkin's saintly aura and were prepared to be his followers. Apart from Bakunin, they all saw the dangers of unthinking obedience to or slavish imitation of a leader.

It has been argued that anarchism does not preclude the legitimacy of every type of authority and that anarchists are really opposed only to 'imposed authority, or authoritarianism'.[42] Again, it has been asserted that libertarians reject 'command-authority' in coercive institutions, but are willing to accept 'belief-authority' in which a person voluntarily legitimizes the influence any other person may have upon them.[43]

There is some evidence to support this view. Some anarchists have accepted certain attenuated forms of authority. Bakunin, while rejecting the government of science, accepts the authority of superior or technical knowledge. However, while recognizing the authority of technical competence, he insists that the advice of an expert should only be accepted on the basis of voluntary consent: if I am to accept the authority of the cobbler in the matter of shoes, my decision to act on his advice is mine and not his. Malatesta also believes that it is inevitable that a person who has greater understanding and ability to carry out a given task will succeed more easily in having his opinion accepted, and that it is all right for him to act as guide in his area of competence for those less able than himself.

It is also the case that many anarchists look to some kind of censure in the shape of public opinion or social pressure as a means of influencing the behaviour of others in the absence of positive laws. Such censure can be extremely authoritarian by making people comply with threats. Indeed, in a society without public authority, Godwin wrote that 'general inspection' could provide a force 'not less irresistible than whips and chains' to reform conduct.[44] Bakunin also argued that the 'only great and all powerful authority . . . we can respect is the collective and public spirit'.[45]

More recently, Giovanni Baldelli has followed Bakunin in arguing that the 'rule of authority' is acceptable if it is based on competence as well as consent.[46] David Wieck has gone even further to defend delegated authority if it does not entail power over persons.[47] Alan Ritter has also tried to elaborate an anarchist justification of authority by claiming that it is legitimate if it is shared by all and if it is 'intimate, particular and internal and cannot issue directives of a legal sort'.[48] And Miller argues that anarcho-communists accept a form of authority, although it is 'non-compulsory, non-coercive, functionally specific, and exercised collectively in a particular locality or shares a particular interest'.[49]

But it would be wrong to infer from this that despite their alleged claims to the contrary, anarchists in fact all accept some form of authority. Bakunin's defence of the authority of superior knowledge, for instance, would be anathema to Godwin as an infringement of the right of private judgement. Any reliance on someone with superior knowledge is for him the most pernicious form of authority since it prevents independent thought and encourages a spirit of dependence. Again, while accepting that the influence of public opinion is preferable to the tyranny of the law, Godwin rightly insists that 'coercion cannot convince, cannot conciliate, but on the contrary alienates the mind of him against whom it is employed'.[50] People may advise and admonish an individual, but he should act by his own deliberation and not theirs.

In general, anarchists reject the use of physical force or even manipulation by unconsciously changing beliefs and actions. They deny anyone the right to issue orders and have them obeyed. They are highly critical of political and bureaucratic authority and do not wish to become dominating leaders, even within small, informal groups. Instead, they prefer to influence others through persuasion, offering rational arguments for their anarchist beliefs and practices. Some may accept a temporary form of leadership based on competence, but most believe in leaderless groups and have no time for bosses or masters. Even if in practice anarchists have voluntarily followed charismatic leaders, they are aware of the dangers of such a form of leadership.

Michael Taylor argues that if we get a person to do something he would not otherwise have done by using convincing reasons, we are still exercising authority.[51] But this would seem to confuse persuasion with authority. What distinguishes authority from persuasion and influence is its claim to legitimacy, a claim which all anarchists deny. Authority is also invariably exercised in a clearly defined hierarchy in which superiors assert the right to issue commands and subordinates are obliged to obey. Of the classic anarchist thinkers, only Bakunin was ready to resort to manipulation through his 'invisible dictatorship' and his secret societies.

If they do not reject all forms of authority outright, all anarchists are suspicious of authority, especially that imposed from above, and seek to minimize its influence in society. They certainly do not want to erect an 'anarchist authority', even if all participate in it.[52] What distinguishes anarchists from other socialists is the precise fact that they are 'anti-authoritarian'. Unlike Engels, they believe it is quite possible to organize production and distribution without authority. For anarchists, organization without compulsion, based on free agreement and voluntary co-operation, is the only cure for authority. To this end, anarchists call for the decentralization of authority and finally for its maximum dissolution.

Power

Authority is clearly a manifestation of power, but they are not identical. Power may best be defined as the ability to impose one's will. Power is different from authority for where the latter asserts the right to command and the right to be obeyed, the former is the ability to compel compliance, either through the use or threat of force. A society without political authority can still have coercive power relationships.

In general, anarchists believe not only that power corrupts, and absolute power corrupts absolutely, but that power destroys both the executioner and victim of power. Their awareness of the corrupting nature of power is the basis of their criticism of concentrated power and their reluctance to relinquish any power to leaders and rulers. The State consists of nothing more than a small elite who have more power than the rest of society. Anarchists therefore call for the decentralization of political power in the short term and would like to see it dissolved as much as possible in the long term.

But power is not only political. Bertrand Russell defines power as 'the production of intended effects'.[53] Power in this sense in existing society is ubiquitous, diffuse and often concealed. Power over human beings may usefully be classified by the manner of influencing individuals or by the type of organization involved. An individual may be influenced by direct physical power over his body, (army and police); by rewards and punishments which act as inducements (economic organizations); by the sway of opinion or propaganda (schools, churches, political parties). Indeed, the distinctions between the organizations are not always so clear cut as they often use different forms of power at the same time.

Within society, there is also traditional power (an ancient form based on custom); newly acquired power (such as law based on coercive power of the State or 'naked' military power); and revolutionary power (of party or group). Anarchists would condemn all three, though some like Kropotkin would accept the first as the least pernicious, and others like Bakunin would accept the last in the form of a mass uprising. All however would oppose any centralization of power, which, as Alex Comfort has argued, leads to psychopathic leadership: 'The greater the degree of power, and the wider the gap between governors and the governed, the stronger the appeal of office to those who are likely to abuse it, and the less the response which can be expected from the individual'.[54] Even 'anarcho-capitalists' like Murray Rothbard assume individuals would have equal bargaining power in a market-based society.

At the same time, while opposing power over others, anarchists are not necessarily averse to power over oneself in the form of self-discipline, self-management, or self-determination. Given the unequal distribution of power between the rulers and the ruled, Bookchin has borrowed the language of liberation movements and made out a case for 'empowering' the weaker members of society.[55] And they are not merely concerned with political power in the form of the State and government, but with economic power in society and patriarchal power in the family.

Anarchists are opposed to all power which is coercive and non-reciprocal, especially in the sense of domination which involves force and conflict between two parties. But they sometimes wield a form of power in trying to influence others by making things unpleasant. Indeed, in the place of law, Godwin and Kropotkin both look to public censure to reform wrongdoers. Tucker might well reduce ethics to the sole moral law of 'Mind your own business', but he is ready to exert 'the influence of reason; the influence of persuasion; the influence of example; the influence of public opinion; the influence of social ostracism; the influence of unhampered economic forces; the influence of better prospects . . .'[56] The two principles would seem to be contradictory, and the latter form of influence undoubtedly involves a form of coercive power.

The desire to have power over oneself is quite compatible with the anarchist position. But as Paul Goodman has pointed out, people live quite happily without 'power' that manages or coerces from outside. Most human activities moreover do not need external motivations in the form of reward or punishment.[57]

Anarchists are well aware that an authoritarian upbringing and education produce people who are either submissive or imperious types. As Alfred Adler observed, 'the servile individual lives by the rules of others, and this type seeks out a servile position almost compulsively'.[58] At the same time, they recognize with Hobbes and Adler that the will to power over others is a common tendency amongst human beings. They are aware that, given the opportunity, not only do ex-slaves often try to become masters, but oppressed men try to find weaker beings to lord it over. But anarchists do not see that this tendency is intrinsic in human nature, but rather a product of our authoritarian and hierarchical society. They reject the view that the only possible human relationship is that in which one issues orders and the other obeys, one asserts himself and the other cringes. Such an unequal distribution of power enslaves both the ruler and the ruled. Anarchists look to a time when there will no longer be masters and servants, leaders and followers, rulers and ruled.

Anarchists have therefore principally been concerned with the way in which organizations and individuals have acquired power over people's lives. In the past, anarchists rejected power over each other, but still thought it was necessary to increase power and control over nature. Kropotkin not only entitled one his books *The Conquest of Bread* but argued like Marx that industrial progress required 'conquest over nature'.[59] Despite this, Malatesta still criticized Kropotkin for his view of natural harmony, and insisted that men must combine to harness the 'hostile forces of Nature'. He even went so far as to define anarchy as 'the struggle, in human society, against the disharmonies of Nature'.[60]

More recently however anarchists have been increasingly concerned not only with the unequal distribution of power between human beings, but man's power over nature. Indeed, Murray Bookchin has traced the origin of man's destructive domination of nature to man's domination over man and woman and calls for the dissolution of hierarchy.[61] Breaking with the historical Western anarchist tradition, he has developed an organicist view which see man as an integral part of nature. Working within a similar framework of social ecology, John Clark has also argued that a thorough-going anarchist critique is 'a critique of all forms of domination' that block the attainment of the goal of 'universal self-realization'.[62]

Anarchism as a philosophy wishes to dissolve all forms of authority and power, and if possible, seeks their complete abolition. All anarchists reject political authority in the form of the State and government, and most reject the moral authority of exceptional individuals. Where some allow the authority of competence, they stress that it must be based on accountability and consent. The ideal still remains for all people to judge and act for themselves and not to rely on experts.

Given the present unequal distribution of power, they would prefer it to be spread more evenly. They recognize the right of the individual to have power over his or her own person, but ultimately they prefer a situation where no one has the possibility or desire to impose his or her will on others. More recently, anarchists have gone beyond traditional humanism and called for an end to power over nature itself. In a condition of anarchy, there would be no State and thus no concentration of force or political specialization.[63] Human beings would be equal partners in a non-hierarchical world without domination. And while it may be impossible to realize in practice, the ultimate goal would be to achieve the complete absence of imposed authority and coercive power.

Equality

What distinguishes the democratic ideal from other political ideals is its attempt to combine liberty and equality. Anarchists are democratic in a broad sense. They would agree with Plato that the ends of democracy are liberty, equality and variety, and most would add like the French revolution-aries, fraternity. But it is a commonplace of liberal political theory that liberty and equality are incompatible. Anarchists are as aware as De Tocqueville and J. S. Mill of the potential dangers of the tyranny of the majority and the triumph of mediocrity. They do not want to submerge the individual in the community or level all society to one common standard of grey uniformity. They reject all rulers, whether one man, a few, or the 'people'. Government, even in Abraham Lincoln's definition as 'government of the people by the people for the people', is inadmissible. Nevertheless, unlike socialists and liberals, they seek a genuine resolution of liberty and equality, and believe that everyone has an equal claim to be free.

Anarchists go beyond the liberal concept of equality as equality before the law. Equality before the law, they point out, does not mean the end of injustice, for all people could be treated with equal unfairness under unjust laws. Moreover, if structural inequalities exist in society, the application of the law is likely to be unequal: one law for the rich, and another for the poor. Since they reject man-made law as an interference with personal freedom, clearly any legal concept of equality is inadequate.

As for the doctrine of equal opportunity to develop one's talents, anarchists do not deny that everyone should have an equal claim to self-development. But they recognize that the principle of equal opportunity is fundamentally conservative since existing society with its hierarchy of values only supports the opportunity to develop those talents and abilities which it considers worth developing. The application of the principle will also increase inequalities by creating a society ruled by a meritocracy. Above all, it is founded on an antagonistic, competitive model of society in which there are more losers than winners in the race for goods and status.

In general, then, anarchists go beyond the liberal concept of equality as equality before the law or equality of opportunity. Like the socialists, they have a commitment to economic and social equality. But different anarchist thinkers try to combine equality with liberty in very different ways.

Godwin, for instance, believed that humanity had a common nature and advocated sexual and racial equality, but did not think all people should be treated equally. By defining justice as utility and linking it with the principle of impartiality, he maintained that we should give preferential treatment to those most likely to increase human happiness: in a fire where I could only save one person, I should save a benevolent philosopher who might contribute to the happiness of thousands before his vicious maid, even if she happened to be my mother.

Proudhon, on the other hand, accepted that men and women had equal rights and duties, but he believed that 'if one compares sex with sex, women are inferior'.[64] His notion of justice involved the idea of equality of respect, but his insistence on exchange of equal shares based on labour time meant that he tolerated economic inequality. One of his principal criticisms of authoritarian communism is that it would produce an equality of slaves. The individualist Tucker was even more willing to countenance economic inequalities which might result from the superiority of muscle or brain. As for the 'beautiful world' in which absolute equality had been achieved, 'who would live in it?', he asks. 'Certainly no freeman'.[65]

Bakunin had an entirely different approach. He asserted that all humanity was physically and socially equal, and insisted that since man is truly free only among equally free men, the '*freedom* of each is therefore realizable only in the equality of all. The realization of freedom through equality, in principle and in fact, is *justice.*'[66] Yet by retaining a collectivist system of distribution according to work done he endorsed like Proudhon economic inequality.

Kropotkin went one step further than Bakunin. He shared his belief in human equality but adopted a communist definition of justice: from each according to ability, to each according to need. Clearly this is also an unequal principle, since under a system of voluntary communism the distribution of burdens and rewards will depend on different abilities and needs. In practice, the communist idea of just distribution according to need is more concerned with fair shares than equal shares.

Malatesta was a communist like Kropotkin, but he tried to bring equality and freedom together in his definition of social freedom as 'equal freedom for all, an equality of conditions such as to allow everybody to do as they wish, with the only limitation, imposed by inevitable natural necessities and the equal freedom of others'.[67] More recently, Bookchin has been inspired by the concept of the 'irreducible minimum' practised by organic societies in which everyone has their basic needs satisfied. He also calls for an 'equality of unequals' which recognizes differences between human beings within an overall framework of social equality and economic communism.

In general, anarchists see no contradiction between freedom and equality, but believe that one reinforces the other. Over the last two centuries, they have extended the principle of equality to embrace all humanity. At the same time, their concern with individuality has prevented them from calling for absolute economic equality. While advocating the impartial consideration of everyone's worth and need, they do not insist on equal treatment and equal shares. They would accept John Rawls' principle in his definition of justice as fairness that each person has 'an equal right to the most extensive liberty compatible with a like liberty for all', although they would add the proviso that any inequalities in a free society would ideally be the result of voluntary agreement.[68] But they go beyond Rawls who believes that citizens of a country do not object to there being different offices of government. Because they adopt a principle of justice that *everyone* has an *equal* claim to a maximum of freedom they reject all political authority as an illegitimate interference with freedom. As Tucker put it, they seek the 'greatest amount of liberty compatible with equality of liberty'.[69]

PART TWO

Forerunners of Anarchism

Love, and do what you will.
ST AUGUSTINE

All men have stood for freedom ... For freedom is the man
that will turn the world upside down.
GERRARD WINSTANLEY

In vain you tell me that Artificial Government is good, but
that I fall out with the Abuse. The Thing! The Thing itself
is the Abuse!
EDMUND BURKE

Society is produced by our wants, and government by our
wickedness; the former promotes our happiness *positively* by
uniting our affections, the latter *negatively* by restraining our
vices. The one encourages intercourse, the other creates distinctions. The first is patron, the last a punisher.

Society in every state is a blessing, but government even in
its best state is but a necessary evil; in its worse state an
intolerable one.
THOMAS PAINE

Taoism and Buddhism

Taoism

ANARCHISM IS USUALLY CONSIDERED a recent, Western phenomenon, but its roots reach deep in the ancient civilizations of the East.
The first clear expression of an anarchist sensibility may be traced back
to the Taoists in ancient China from about the sixth century BC.
Indeed, the principal Taoist work, the *Tao te ching*, may be considered
one of the greatest anarchist classics.[1]

The Taoists at the time were living in a feudal society in which law was
becoming codified and government increasingly centralized and bureaucratic. Confucius was the chief spokesman of the legalistic school supporting
these developments, and called for a social hierarchy in which every citizen
knew his place. The Taoists for their part rejected government and believed
that all could live in natural and spontaneous harmony. The conflict between
those who wish to interfere and those who believe that things flourish best
when left alone has continued ever since.

The Taoists and the Confucians were both embedded in ancient
Chinese culture. They shared a similar view of nature, but differed strongly
in their moral and political views. They both had an attitude of respectful
trust to human nature; the Christian notion of original sin is entirely absent
from their thought. Both believed that human beings have an innate predis-
position to goodness which is revealed in the instinctive reaction of anyone
who sees a child falling into a well. Both claimed to defend the Tao or the
way of the ancients and sought to establish voluntary order.

But whereas the Taoists were principally interested in nature and identified with it, the Confucians were more worldly-minded and concerned
with reforming society. The Confucians celebrated traditionally 'male' virtues like duty, discipline and obedience, while the Taoists promoted the
'female' values of receptivity and passivity.

Although it has helped shape Chinese culture as much as Buddhism
and Confucianism, Taoism by its very nature never became an official cult.
It has remained a permanent strain in Chinese thought. Its roots lay in the

popular culture at the dawn of Chinese civilization but it emerged in the sixth century BC as a remarkable combination of philosophy, religion, proto-science and magic.

The principal exponent of Taoism is taken to be Lao Tzu, meaning 'Old Philosopher'. His year of birth was some time between 600 and 300 BC. He was probably of a noble family in Honan province. He rejected his hereditary position as a noble and became a curator of the royal library at Loh. All his life he followed the path of silence – 'The Tao that can be told is not the eternal Tao', he taught.[2] According to legend, when he was riding off into the desert to die, he was persuaded by a gatekeeper in north-western China to write down his teaching for posterity.

It seems likely that the *Tao te ching* (The Way and its Power) which is attributed to Lao Tzu, was written in the third century BC. It has been called by the Chinese scholar Joseph Needham 'without exception the most profound and beautiful work in the Chinese language'.[3] The text consists of eighty-one short chapters in poetic form. Although often very obscure and paradoxical, it offers not only the earliest but also the most eloquent exposition of anarchist principles.

It is impossible to appreciate the ethics and politics of Taoism without an understanding of its philosophy of nature. The *Tao te ching* celebrates the *Tao*, or way, of nature and describes how the wise person should follow it. The Taoist conception of nature is based on the ancient Chinese principles of *yin* and *yang*, two opposite but complementary forces in the cosmos which constitute *ch'i* (matter-energy) of which all beings and phenomena are formed. *Yin* is the supreme feminine power, characterized by darkness, cold, and receptivity and associated with the moon; *yang* is the masculine counterpart of brightness, warmth, and activity, and is identified with the sun. Both forces are at work within men and women as well as in all things.

The *Tao* itself however cannot be defined; it is nameless and formless. Lao Tzu, trying vainly to describe what is ineffable, likens it to an empty vessel, a river flowing home to the sea, and an uncarved block. The Tao, he asserts, follows what is natural. It is the way in which the universe works, the order of nature which gives all things their being and sustains them.

> The great Tao flows everywhere, both to the left and the right.
> The ten thousand things depend on it; it holds nothing back.
> It fulfils its purpose silently and makes no claim.(34)

Needham describes it not so much as a force, but as a 'kind of natural curvature in time and space'.[4]

Like most later anarchists, the Taoists see the universe as being in a continuous state of flux. Reality is in a state of process; everything changes, nothing is constant. They also have a dialectical concept of change as a dynamic interplay as opposing forces. Energy flows continually between the poles of *yin* and *yang*. At the same time, they stress the unity and harmony of nature. Nature is self-sufficient and uncreated; there is no need to postulate a conscious creator. It is a view which not only recalls that of the Greek philosopher Heraclitus but coincides with the description of the universe presented by modern physics. Modern social ecology, which stresses unity in diversity, organic growth and natural order, further reflects the Taoist world-view.

The approach to nature recommended by Lao Tzu and the Taoists is one of receptivity. Where the Confucian wants to conquer and exploit nature, the Taoist tries to contemplate and understand it. The Taoists' traditionally 'feminine' approach to nature suggests that their way of thinking may well have first evolved in a matriarchal society. While at first sight it might seem a religious attitude, in fact it encouraged a scientific and democratic outlook amongst Taoists. By not imposing their own preconceptions, they were able to observe and understand nature and therefore learn to channel its energy beneficially.

The Taoists were primarily interested in nature but their conception of the universe had important corollaries for society. A definite system of ethics and politics emerges. There are no absolute Taoist values; for good and bad, like *yin* and *yang*, are related. Their interplay is necessary for growth, and in order to achieve something it is often best to start with its opposite. Nevertheless, an ideal of the wise person emerges in Taoist teaching who is unpretentious, sincere, spontaneous, generous and detached. For the Taoists, the art of living is to be found in simplicity, non-assertion and creative play.

Central to Taoist teaching is the concept of *wu-wei*. It is often translated as merely non-action. In fact there are striking philological similarities between 'anarchism' and '*wu-wei*'. Just as αναρχια in Greek means absence of a ruler, *wu-wei* means lack of *wei*, where *wei* refers to 'artificial, contrived activity that interferes with natural and spontaneous development'.[5] From a political point of view, *wei* refers to the imposition of authority. To do something in accordance with *wu-wei* is therefore considered natural; it leads to natural and spontaneous order. It has nothing to do with all forms of imposed authority.

The *Tao te ching* is quite clear about the nature of force. If we use force, whether physical or moral, to improve ourselves or the world, we simply waste energy and weaken ourselves: 'force is followed by loss of strength'(30). It follows that those who wage war will suffer as a result: 'a violent man will die a violent death'(42). By contrast, giving way is often the best way to overcome: 'Under heaven nothing is more soft and yielding than water. Yet for attacking the solid and strong, nothing is better; it has no equal. The weak can overcome the strong; the supple can overcome the stiff.'(78) The gentle peacefulness recommended by the Taoists is not a form of defeatist submission but a call for the creative and effective use of energy.

'Practise non-action. Work without doing'(63), Lao Tzu recommends. In their concept of *wu-wei*, the Taoists are not urging non-action in the sense of inertia, but rather condemning activity contrary to nature. It is not idleness that they praise, but work without effort, anxiety and complication, work which goes with and not against the grain of things. If people practised *wu-wei* in the right spirit, work would lose its coercive aspect. It would be undertaken not for its useful results but for its intrinsic value. Instead of being avoided like the plague, work would be transformed into spontaneous and meaningful play: 'When actions are performed/Without unnecessary speech,/People say, "We did it!"'(17).

If people followed their advice, the Taoists suggest, they would live a long life and achieve physical and mental health. One of their fundamental beliefs was that 'Whatever is contrary to Tao will not last long'(55), while he who is filled with virtue is like a new-born child. In order to prolong their lives the Taoists resorted to yoga-like techniques and even alchemy.

The most important principle at the centre of their teaching however was a belief that 'The world is ruled by letting things take their course. It cannot be ruled by interfering.'(48) The deepest roots of the Taoist view of *wu-wei* probably lies in early matriarchal society in ancient China. The Taoist ideal was a form of agrarian collectivism which sought to recapture the instinctive unity with nature which human beings had lost in developing an artificial and hierarchical culture. Peasants are naturally wise in many ways. By hard experience, they refrain from activity contrary to nature and realize that in order to grow plants they must understand and co-operate with the natural processes. And just as plants grow best when allowed to follow their natures, so human beings thrive when least interfered with.[6] It was this insight which led the Taoists to reject all forms of imposed authority, government and the State. It also made them into precursors of modern anarchism and social ecology.

It has been argued that Taoism does not reject the State as an artificial structure, but rather sees it as a natural institution, analogous perhaps to the family.[7] While the *Tao te ching* undoubtedly rejects authoritarian rule, it does read at times as if it is giving advice to rulers to become better at ruling:

> If the sage would guide the people, he must serve with humility.
> If he would lead them, he must follow behind.
> In this way when the sage rules, the people will not feel

oppressed(66)

Bookchin goes so far as to claim that Taoism was used by an elite to foster passivity amongst the peasantry by denying them choice and hope.[8]

Certainly Lao Tzu addresses the problem of leadership and calls for the true sage to act with the people and not above them. The best ruler leaves his people alone to follow their peaceful and productive activities. He must trust their good faith for 'He who does not trust enough will not be trusted.'(17) If a ruler interferes with his people rather than letting them follow their own devices, then disorder will follow: 'When the country is confused and in chaos, Loyal ministers appear.'(18) In a well-ordered society,

> Man follows the earth.
> Earth follows heaven.
> Heaven follows the Tao.
> Tao follows what is natural.(25)

However a closer reading shows that the *Tao te ching* is not concerned with offering Machiavellian advice to rulers or even with the 'art of governing'. The person who genuinely understands the *Tao* and applies it to government reaches the inevitable conclusion that the best government does not govern at all.[9] Lao Tzu sees nothing but evil coming from government. Indeed, he offers what might be described as the first anarchist manifesto:

> The more laws and restrictions there are,
> The poorer people become.
> The sharper men's weapons,
> The more trouble in the land.
> The more ingenious and clever men are,
> The more strange things happen.
> The more rules and regulations,
> The more thieves and robbers.

> Therefore the sage says:
> I take no action and people are reformed.
> I enjoy peace and people become honest.
> I do nothing and the people become rich.
> I have no desires and people return to the good and simple life.(57)

Contained within the marvellous poetry of the *Tao te ching*, there is some very real social criticism. It is sharply critical of the bureaucratic, warlike, and commercial nature of the feudal order. Lao Tzu specifically sees property as a form of robbery: 'When the court is arrayed in splendour, The fields are full of weeds,/And the granaries are bare.'(53) He traces the causes of war to unequal distribution : 'Claim wealth and titles, and disaster will follow.'(9) Having attacked feudalism with its classes and private property, he offers the social ideal of a classless society without government and patriarchy in which people live simple and sincere lives in harmony with nature. It would be a decentralized society in which goods are produced and shared in common with the help of appropriate technology. The people would be strong but with no need to show their strength; wise, but with no pretence of learning; productive, but engaged in no unnecessary toil. They would even prefer to reckon by knotting rope rather than by writing ledgers:

> A small country has fewer people.
> Though there are machines that can work ten to a hundred times faster than man, they are not needed.
> The people take death seriously and do not travel far.
> Though they have boats and carriages, no one uses them.
> Though they have armour and weapons, no one displays them.
> Men return to the knotting of rope in place of writing.
> Their food is plain and good, their clothes fine but simple, their homes secure;
> They are happy in their ways.
> Though they live within sight of their neighbours,
> And crowing cocks and barking dogs are heard across the way,
> Yet they leave each other in peace while they grow old and die.(80)

The anarchistic tendency of the Taoists comes through even stronger in the writings of the philosopher Chuang Tzu, who lived about 369–286 BC. His work consists of arguments interspersed with anecdotes and parables which explore the nature of the Tao, the great organic process of which man is a part. It is not addressed to any particular ruler. Like the *Tao te ching*, it rejects all forms of government and celebrates the free existence of the self-determining individual. The overriding tone of the work is to be found in a little parable about horses:

> Horses live on dry land, eat grass and drink water. When pleased, they rub their necks together. When angry, they turn round and kick up their heels at each other. Thus far only do their natural dispositions carry them. But bridled and bitted, with a plate of metal on their foreheads, they learn to cast vicious looks, to turn the head to bite, to resist, to get the bit out of the mouth or the bridle into it. And thus their natures become depraved.[10]

As with horses, so it is with human beings. Left to themselves they live in natural harmony and spontaneous order. But when they are coerced and ruled, their natures become vicious. It follows that princes and rulers should not coerce their people into obeying artificial laws, but should leave them to follow their natural dispositions. To attempt to govern people with man-made laws and regulations is absurd and impossible: 'as well try to wade through the sea, to hew a passage through a river, or make a mosquito fly away with a mountain!'.[11] In reality, the natural conditions of our existence require no artificial aids. People left to themselves will follow peaceful and productive activities and live in harmony with each other and nature.

In an essay 'On Letting Alone', Chuang Tzu asserted three hundred years before Christ the fundamental proposition of anarchist thought which has reverberated through history ever since:

> There has been such a thing as letting mankind alone; there has never been such a thing as governing mankind.
>
> Letting alone springs from fear lest men's natural dispositions be perverted and their virtue left aside. But if their natural dispositions be not perverted nor their virtue laid aside, what room is there left for government?[12]

The Taoists therefore advocated a free society without government in which individuals would be left to themselves. But while pursuing their own interests, they would not forget the interests of others. It is not a sullen selfishness which is recommended. The pursuit of personal good involves a concern for the general well-being: the more a person does for others, the more he has; the more he gives to others, the greater his abundance. As the Taoist text *Huai Nan Tzu* put its, 'Possessing the empire' means 'self-realization. If I realize myself then the empire also realizes me. If the empire and I realize each other, then we will always possess each other.'[13]

Human beings are ultimately individuals but they are also social beings, part of the whole. Anticipating the findings of modern ecology, the Taoists believed that the more individuality and diversity there is, the greater the overall harmony. The spontaneous order of society does not exclude conflict but involves a dynamic interplay of opposite forces. Thus society is described by Chuang Tzu as

> an agreement of a certain number of families and individuals to abide by certain customs. Discordant elements unite to form a harmonious whole. Take away this unity and each has a separate individuality . . . A mountain is high because of its individual particles. A river is large because of its individual drops. And he is a just man who regards all parts from the point of view of the whole.[14]

Taoism thus offered the first and one of the most persuasive expressions of anarchist thinking. Its moral and political ideas were firmly grounded in a scientific view of the world. Although Taoist philosophy (*Tao chia*) contains spiritual and mystical elements, the early Taoists' receptive approach to nature encouraged a scientific attitude and democratic feelings. They recognized the unity in the diversity in nature and the universality of transformation. In their ethics, they encouraged spontaneous behaviour and self-development in the larger context of nature: production with possession, action without self-assertion and development without domination. In their politics, they not only urged rulers to leave their subjects alone and opposed the bureaucratic and legalistic teaching of the Confucians, but advocated as an ideal a free and co-operative society without government in harmony with nature.

Taoism was not aimed by an elite at peasants to make them more docile and obedient. The Taoists' social background tended to be from the small middle class, between the feudal lords and the mass of peasant farmers. Nor were they merely offering advice on how to survive in troubled times by yielding to the strong, keeping a low profile, and by minding their own business. On the contrary, Taoism was the philosophy of those who had understood the real nature of temporal power, wealth and status, sufficiently well to find them radically wanting. Far from being a philosophy of failure or quietude, Taoism offers profound and practical wisdom for those who wish to develop the full harmony of their being.

Buddhism

While the Taoists have long been recognized as forerunners of anarchism, the libertarian tendency within Buddhism is not immediately so obvious. It is difficult to reconcile the teachings of the Buddha, for instance, with the triumphant State in modern Sri Lanka, where Sinhalese nationalism is supported most vehemently by the Buddhist clergy. But as with contemporary Taoism (*Tao chiao*) and organized Christianity, the distortions of institutionalized religion do not invalidate the original message. The poet Gary Snyder has not been the only one to find in 'Buddhist anarchism' a positive force 'with nation-shaking' implications.[15]

Buddhism was originally an Indian religion, founded in the fifth century BC by Siddhartha Gautama, known as the Buddha (the enlightened one). Buddha found the cause of evil in this world to be ignorance which encourages a person to try and satisfy his or her desires. Craving, whether for possessions, wealth, power or status, inevitably brings suffering and pain. But there is a way out. The four 'Noble Truths' which Buddha taught may be summed up as: '(a) the omnipresence of suffering; (b) its cause, wrongly directed desire; (c) its cure, the removal of the cause; and (d) the Noble Eightfold path of self-development which leads to the end of suffering.'[16]

To avoid suffering it is therefore necessary to overcome one's ego and eradicate all desire. To escape the painful cycle of rebirth in this world of illusion or *maya*, the individual must also try and become enlightened and realize that he or she ultimately has no self. Only by recognizing that *sansara*, the wheel of life, is *nirvana*, nothingness, will a person achieve complete liberation.

In the beginning Buddhism was principally restricted to ethics and meditation exercises. It began to spread in India five hundred years prior to Christ and separated from Hinduism by rejecting the scriptures, rituals and social system. It eventually split into two separate branches, one becoming more rationalistic, formalized and scholastic (Theravada) and the other more mystical (Mahayana). By 1200 Buddhism had practically disappeared in India, but became well established in Sri Lanka, Tibet and Thailand.

While institutional Buddhism has been ready to support inequalities and tyrannies, the disaffiliation, voluntary poverty and traditional harmlessness of practising Buddhists express a strong libertarian sensibility. Snyder has found in the practical systems of meditation developed by Mahayana Buddhism a powerful means of liberating individuals from their 'psychological hang-ups and cultural conditionings'. He also believes that Buddhist Tantrism, or Vajrayana, offers probably the finest and most modern statement of the ancient view that 'man's life and destiny is growth and enlightenment in self-disciplined freedom'.[17] But it was in its Zen form however that Buddhism developed its libertarian potential to the fullest.[18]

Zen Buddhism developed in China after it was brought from India in the sixth century. During the following five hundred years, the Chinese called the school Ch'an. It reached Japan in the twelfth century where it came to be known as Zen. Here two main sects developed, the first Rinzai, which carried on the 'sudden' technique of the founder, and the second Soto, the more gentle way.

Zen has rightly been called the 'apotheosis of Buddhism'.[19] It is uniquely iconoclastic, attempting to reach truth and enlightenment by ultimately transcending the use of concepts, scriptures, and ritual. Where Theravada Buddhism became neatly arranged and systematized, with its twelve-fold chain of Causation, Zen adepts see in the Buddha the first rebel: 'The Buddha was not the mere discoverer of the Twelvefold Chain of Causation,' Suzuki informs us, 'he took the chain in his hands and broke it into pieces, so that it would never again bind him to slavery.'[20] The familiar props of religion are thrown away. The four central statements of Zen are:

> A special transmission outside the Scriptures;
> No dependence upon words or letters;
> Direct pointing to the soul of man;
> Seeing into one's nature and the attainment of Buddhahood.[21]

Traditionally Zen aspirants have learned from a teacher. He is usually called master, but more in the sense of schoolmaster than lord. His task is to help them break out of their everyday perceptions and intellectual habits. Buddhist monks are therefore exemplars, not intermediaries between the individual and God like Christian priests. They may carry sticks and not be averse to using them, but the blows are ways of shaking people out of their habitual way of seeing. In the Rinzai school, where the treatment is particularly vigorous, the discipline is used primarily to develop the pupil's character from within and to increase his or her moral strength.

Zen thus offers a fiery baptism. However rough or gentle, it is intended to bring the student back to his original state of freedom which he has lost through ignorance. It is aimed at creating self-disciplined freedom, not dependence on masters. The successful Zen practitioner controls sound, colour and form and lives out the truth as he sees it. He leaves behind the rules of social and monastic life which helped him on his way. Even the robes which the monks wear and the bells which call them to their meditation are ladders to be finally discarded.

While a teacher may point the way, the individual must ultimately make his own choices and walk alone on his journey. Awakening cannot be achieved by another's power. The Buddha said: 'Work out your own salvation with diligence.'[22] Buddhism thus knows no authority for truth save the mindfulness of the individual, and that is authority for himself alone. It is very egalitarian: everyone can become enlightened on their own through learning by direct and immediate experience. When Daiju visited the teacher Baso in China, and told him he was seeking enlightenment, Baso said: 'You have your own treasure house. Why do you search outside?'[23]

In China, the Ch'an Zen masters did not follow the Buddha but aspired to be his friends and to place themselves in the same responsive relationship with the universe. Zen is an experience and has never become the doctrine of a sect. There are no set rules or regulations; the end at all times dominates the choice of means. As the greatest exponent in China Wei Lang (also known as Hui-neng) declared: 'If I tell you that I have a system of Law to transmit to others I am cheating you. What I do to my disciples is to liberate them from their own bondage with such devices as the case may need.'[24]

The aim is to achieve a state of enlightenment in which one sees directly into one's own nature and realizes that it is not separate from Nature, but part of an organic whole. Opposites are transcended. One feels clear, calm, whole. One becomes uncircumscribed and free. One is beyond conventional definitions of good and evil, moral codes and laws. If you have Zen, you have no fear, doubt or craving. You live a simple life, serene and complete:

> Imperturbable and serene the ideal man practises no virtue;
> Self-possessed and dispassionate he commits no sin;
> Calm and silent he gives up seeing and hearing;
> Even and upright his mind abides nowhere.[25]

It is an ideal shared by many anarchists who seek simplicity and peace.

In the natural world, there are no grounds for hierarchy or domination and we are all born free and equal. This equality for Buddhism is both spiritual and social. People are spiritually equal in the sense that all are equally capable of achieving enlightenment. In their social life, Zen monks live and work communally. Even amongst teachers and pupils, there should be equal obligation and equal treatment; as some Zen parables put it, 'no work, no food', and all should share 'sour miso'.[26] In wider society, Buddha rejected the caste system and Zen Buddhism in particular is no respecter of persons. One story has it that the Governor of Kyoto came to visit a Zen master and sent in his visiting card with his title on it. It was returned. Only when he sent it in again with his title crossed out, was he received.[27]

The Zen Buddhist concept of freedom is also spiritual and social. In a spiritual sense, we are born free. Our fetters and manacles are not the true condition of our existence but forged by our ignorance. Such chains of ignorance, wrought by sensuous infatuation and misused reason, cling to us like wet clothes. But it is the aim of the Zen teachers to help us return to our original state of freedom. Zen tries to break the logjam of our mind, and to free us from the finite world of power, wealth and status. But it attempts this in no fixed pattern. According to Ummon, the great Chinese master, 'in Zen there is absolute freedom; sometimes it negates and at other times it affirms; it does either way at pleasure.'[28]

The most anti-authoritarian statement in the Zen tradition is probably I-Hsuan's. Speaking metaphorically, he declared:

> Kill anything that you happen on. Kill the Buddha if you happen to meet him. Kill a patriarch or an arhat [saint] if you happen to meet him. Kill your parents or relatives if you happen to meet them. Only then can you be free, not bound by material things, and absolutely free and at ease . . .

I-Hsuan added, 'I have no trick to give people. I merely cure disease and set people free . . .'[29]

We are also free to seek our own salvation. Zen finds no contradiction between free will and determinism. It accepts that there is universal determinism, and that all effects have causes. A man's character is the sum total of his previous thoughts and acts. Our lives and all existence are ruled by *karma*, that is to say every action has a reaction. But while the present is determined by the past, the future remains free. Every action we make depends on what we have come to be at the time, but what we are coming to be at any time depends on our will. Every person is thus free within the limitations of his self-created *karma*. By right thought and action, I can change myself and shape my destiny.

While Buddhism seeks personal enlightenment, it does not turn its back on this world. The seeker in the famous story of the Bull, who eventually tames and releases himself from his worldly self, returns to the marketplace with dusty clothes to find the trees living. Again, while the emphasis in Zen is placed on personal autonomy, others are not neglected. Like the Taoists, the Japanese Zen Master Mumon Ekai commented:

> Do not fight with another's bow and arrow.
> Do not ride another's horse.
> Do not discuss another's faults.
> Do not interfere with another's work.[30]

While only the individual can work out his own salvation, he should still think of others. For all its spiritual interests, Zen Buddhism is not an otherworldly mysticism but is concerned with all beings here and now. As the teacher Gasan told his pupils:

> Those who speak against killing and who desire to spare the lives of all conscious beings are right. It is good to protect even animals and insects. But what about those persons who kill time, what about those who are destroying wealth, and those who destroy political economy? We should not overlook them.[31]

While Zen goes beyond conventional definitions of good and evil, and has no commandments enforced by threat of punishment, certain moral values do emerge in the koans and stories. Evil itself is not considered part of nature but man-made: 'Nature has no demons; they are human creations.'[32] The fundamental principle which Buddha taught was compassion for all sentient beings. Since life is one and indivisible, whoever breaks the harmony of life will suffer accordingly and delay his or her own development. If I hurt some other being, I therefore hurt myself.

Zen Buddhism also rejects private property and sees the craving for possessions as just another chain preventing spiritual development. In giving and taking, the receiver should not feel gratitude; if anything, the giver, not the receiver, should be thankful for having the opportunity to give. Many Zen Buddhists would like to see an economy based on the gift relationship, not exchange or barter. The most valuable thing however is natural beauty which no one can take or steal.

Buddhism, particularly in its Zen form, thus has, like Taoism, a strong libertarian spirit. Both reject hierarchy and domination. Both seek growth in self-disciplined freedom and assert that all are capable of enlightenment. Both are concerned with personal autonomy and social well-being. They recognize that each person is not only part of society, but of organic nature itself, as many modern anarchists in the West recognize. The voluntary poverty, compassionate harmlessness, and love of life and beauty of the greatest practitioners of Taoism and Buddhism offer a sound moral base for a free society. Above all, the vision of social freedom makes them a major source of the anarchist sensibility, which if properly understood, must pose as a profound threat to any existing State and Church.

The Greeks

THE WORD ANARCHY NOT only came from the Greeks, but it had from the beginning both a negative and a positive sense of living without rulers, in a condition of spontaneous order or of unruly chaos. The mainstream of Greek political philosophy however was rooted in the idea that the search for justice and the civilized life could only be achieved within the confines of the State. Thus for Plato democracy was a form of unjust government which was always 'anarchical'. His pupil Aristotle referred to those outside the State as 'lawless dangerous beasts' and felt that the fundamental problem of democracy was precisely how to prevent it from slipping into 'anarchy'. But while Plato and Aristotle both felt the need for a hierarchical State with strong laws to maintain social order, not all Greek thinkers were so authoritarian.

Many Greeks drew a distinction between man-made and divine or natural laws. Sophocles depicted the conflict between the two in his great drama of rebellion *Antigone* (*c.*441 BC) When Creon ascends to the throne of Thebes and forbids the burial of the traitor Polynices, his niece Antigone defies his order and gives her brother a token burial. She appeals above Creon's head to the laws of nature:

> For it was not Zeus that had published me that edict; not such are the laws set among men by the Justice who dwells with the gods below; nor deemed I that thy decrees were of such form, that a mortal could override the unwritten and unfailing statutes of heaven. For their life is not of to-day or yesterday, but from all time, and no man knows when they were first put forth.[1]

Heraclitus from Ephesus, who lived around 500 BC expressed views remarkably similar to those of the Taoists in China. Known as the 'riddler' for the mystical obscurity of his thought, he was the most important of the pre-Socratic thinkers. From the fragments of his work *On Nature* which remain, it seems he argued that reason should look beyond common sense and realize that the appearance of stability and permanence presented to our senses is false. All things are in a constant flux, even the 'unchanging' hills. Everything flows. His follower Cratylus popularized his teaching: 'You cannot step twice in the same river.'

Like the Taoists, Heraclitus saw change as a dynamic interplay of opposites: 'cold things warm themselves, warm cools'. He concluded that since all opposites are polar they are united: 'The up and the down is one and the same.'² Change takes place dialectically through the dynamic unity of opposites. But while everything changes, there is also a natural order. He pictured the world as 'an everliving fire, kindling in measures and going in measures'.³ It is the 'reason' or 'destiny' which keeps everything in order and ensures the orderly succession of events. Although Heraclitus had a pessimistic view of the human condition, which earned him the title of 'weeping philosopher', he is the first philosopher in the Western tradition to anticipate the anarchist belief that constant change takes place within a natural order. But he was no democrat and was very scornful of his contemporaries. Only force could make them act for their own good: 'Every beast is driven to the pasture with blows.' He believed strife is justice, and celebrated war. 'War is the father of all and the king of all; and some he has made gods and some men, some bond and some free.'⁴

The case for Socrates as a libertarian is founded on his insistence that one should question authority and think for oneself. He offers the earliest defence of liberty of thought, insisting on the indefeasible right of conscience of the individual and the social importance of criticism and discussion. Although Socrates was an elitist – he opposed the democracy which triumphed in Athens in 403 BC – he bravely opposed his private judgement against the Athenian State. In 399 BC he was persecuted and put to death for being an atheist and a corrupter of youth. His 'crime' was to have argued that we should approach everything with an open mind and examine popular beliefs in the light of reason, undeterred by the dictates of authority or the opinions of the majority. When Socrates said that it was necessary to live by the law and die by the law, he was not simply asserting the need for law for its own sake. In keeping with his characteristic irony, he wished to clarify the accusation made against him by the Athenian State and to bring out its true nature.

As Plato makes clear in his *Apology*, Socrates insisted on the supremacy of individual conscience so that no one should allow themselves to be compelled by any human authority to do what they think is wrong. He also emphasized the public value of free discussion since truth best emerges through the clash of opposing opinions. Socrates not only chose free discussion as his method of teaching but insisted that 'Daily discussion of the matters about which you hear me conversing is the highest good for man. Life that is not tested by such discussion is not worth living.'⁵

Plato, Socrates' most brilliant pupil, failed to heed his teacher's advice. While the communism of goods and women in *The Republic* inspired some later socialists, Plato's ideal State has a rigid social hierarchy ruled by a small elite of guardians and soldiers. It is moreover a completely totalitarian State with no freedom of thought or action: religion is chosen on utilitarian grounds and must be obeyed on fear of punishment or death. If Socrates appears as one of the great libertarians, Plato stands at the fountainhead of the great authoritarian river which subsequently swamped Western thought.

After the death of Socrates, the comparative freedom of discussion which prevailed enabled many schools of philosophy to flourish. The most significant were the Epicureans, the Cynics and the Stoics who all aimed at securing peace for the individual soul in a period of social turmoil. The Epicureans, Cynics and Stoics were extreme individualists for whom the State counted little; they celebrated the natural authority of the individual over that of the State. They looked to a world of universals in nature beyond civil society. Where the theories of Plato and Aristotle were for the improvement of a few, they extended their teaching to all men and recognized them as brothers.

Aristippus, active in the fourth century (born *c*.430 BC), was the founder of the Cyrenaic or Epicurean (also known as Hedonistic) school of philosophy which took pleasure to be the highest good. He was the first of Socrates' pupils to take money for his teaching, but told Socrates that he did not wish to belong to either the governing or the governed class. He taught philosophy at Athens and Aegina, and spent much of his life in the court of Dionysus the tyrant in Syracuse, where he earned a reputation as a voluptuary. It was this experience which no doubt led him to teach that the wise should not give up their liberty to the State. His daughter Arete adopted his doctrines and passed them on to her son Aristippus the Younger.

The Cynics of the third century came even closer to anarchism. They did not develop into a school like the Epicureans and the Stoics, but they interpreted the two fundamental Greek concepts of *Physis* and *Nomos* in a radical way. Usually translated as Nature and Custom respectively, *Physis* can refer to the natural form of an object, a person's nature, or the natural order of things; *Physis* can refer to usage, convention or law. Most Greek thinkers sought to reconcile these two concepts – Aristotle for instance wished to impose law on the natural occurrence of things. The Cynics alone however rejected *Nomos* in favour of *Physis*; they wished to live purely 'according to Nature'. Since the Greek *polis* was based on the rule of custom or convention, by rejecting *Nomos*, the Cynics denied the right of established authority to prescribe the limits of their actions.[6] Since laws are made by men and could have been otherwise, and customs vary from country to country, they held that they had no validity. They denied the competence of courts to judge actions and argued that all social laws, hierarchies and standards are without moral foundation.

The real founder of the Cynics was Antisthenes (*c*.444–370 BC). He was the son of an Athenian father and Thracian mother. He fought at Tanagra in 426 BC, and died in Athens. A friend of Socrates, he turned his back on his former aristocratic circle in order to pursue simple goodness amongst working people. In his desire to 'return to nature', he preached at open-air meetings that there should be no government, no private property, no marriage and no established religion. He despised the artificial pleasures of the senses, declaring 'I had rather be mad than delighted'.[7]

His pupil Diogenes of Sinope became even more famous for his doctrines and his eccentric way of living. Like the Taoists, Diogenes condemned the artificial encumbrances of civilization. He decided to live like a 'dog', and therefore was called a 'cynic' which means 'canine'. Rejecting all conventions, reducing his needs to a minimum, he is said to have lived in a barrel or 'tub', (probably a large pitcher used for burials). When Alexander the Great visited him and tried to corrupt him by offering anything he wished, he asked him 'only to stand out of my light'. The simple beggar was no respecter of persons. He not only rejected the institution of slavery but declared his brotherhood with all beings, including animals. He considered himself to be a 'citizen of the world'.

Diogenes was not therefore 'cynical' in the modern sense, for he pursued moral freedom in liberation from desire and fear, and was deeply anxious about the nature of virtue. As he saw it, only by being indifferent to fame or fortune can a person become truly free. But his teaching was not only aimed at the individual, requiring him to lead a simple and contented life; it had important social implications. One of his most famous paradoxes was his call to 'deface the currency'. The son of a money-changer, he wished to transform his father's activity on a universal scale. The Greek for 'currency' was *nomisma*, derived from the word *Nomos* (custom). Since Diogenes felt that the standard of society was wrong, his call to deface the currency represented an attack on all prevailing customs, rules and laws. It was also coupled with a demand for complete freedom of speech and action. In his own life, he rejected the conventions of religion, manners, dress and even food. As a result, he may be considered one of the great forerunners of anarchism.

The Stoics took up the doctrine of the Cynics but they did not reject the benefits of civilization. Socrates had shown that laws may be unjust and public opinion may be wrong, but he offered no alternative guiding principle except that of reason. The Stoics however found in the law of nature a guide which is prior and superior to all human customs and written laws. They looked beyond civil society to the world of universals in nature. In so doing, they reached anarchist conclusions, developing the ideals of individualism, rationalism, equality, internationalism and cosmopolitanism.[8]

Stoicism found adherents in the outlying parts of the Greek world, especially in Asia Minor, where Greeks and Orientals mingled. It made a strong appeal to educated Romans of the second century and influenced Roman jurisprudence, particularly in ideas of universal law and citizenship.

Kropotkin called the founder of Stoicism, Zeno of Citium (336–264 BC), the 'best exponent of Anarchist philosophy in ancient Greece'.[9] Zeno was a Phoenician born at Citium in Cyprus, and educated in Athens. Attracted to the Cynics, Zeno became principally interested in virtue, and adopted a materialist philosophy of common sense. He went on to proclaim the supremacy of natural law over man-made law. Zeno further opposed Plato's State communism by offering his own ideal of a free community without government.

The starting-point and end for Zeno is nature. He identifies God with Nature which is the most excellent of all things. Virtue results when the will of the individual is in harmony with nature. The wise person, like the Taoist, sees how things happens and conforms his will accordingly. Zeno recommends a life in agreement with nature, which is also a life according to reason. He taught:

> The end may be defined as life in accordance with nature, or, in other words, in accordance with our own human nature as well as that of the universe, a life in which we refrain from every action forbidden by the law common to all things, that is to say, the right reason which pervades all things, and is identical with Zeus, lord and ruler of all that is.[10]

Natural man is an individual and social being. Although the Stoic doctrine tended towards self-sufficiency, they believed that man is 'naturally made for society and action'.[11] Zeno believed that together with the instinct of self-preservation which leads to egoism, there is also a social instinct which makes us join others and co-operate for the common good. While pleasure or freedom from pain might be an advantage it is not a good, for Zeno asserted the official Stoic doctrine that virtue is the only desirable good.

If human beings followed their natural instincts and were guided by reason, they would be able to live in peace and harmony without the need for coercive institutions. In Zeno's *Republic*, according to the fragments preserved for us by Diogenes Laertius, there are no lawcourts, police, armies, temples, schools, money or even marriage. People live as a single 'herd' without family and property, with no distinctions of race or rank, and without the need for money or courts of law. Above all, there is no longer any need for compulsion. People fulfil their natures living in a stateless society of complete equality and freedom which spreads across the whole globe.

It is their attitude to the State which was the most original contribution of the Stoics to political philosophy and which marks them out as anarchist forerunners. The wise man, they taught, 'will take part in politics, if nothing hinders him'.[12] But it is the nature of the State to hinder. A statesman must inevitably either displease the gods or displease the people. All States are therefore equally bad. It follows that since man is endowed with reason and has social instincts, the State in any form is an unnecessary evil. The Stoics extended this reasoning beyond the Greek *polis* with its slaves to embrace not only the 'barbarians' but the whole of humanity. Where Plato wanted to exclude the foreigner from his State, the Stoics considered themselves citizens of the world.

It was not only Greek philosophy which inspired later anarchists like Godwin and Kropotkin. Greek society produced one of the most remarkable examples of democracy which the world has ever known. Prior to the conquests of Philip of Macedon, the Greeks were city dwellers, relating to each other as members of the *polis*. While the *polis* has often been called a 'city-state', it was not a State in the modern sense and may best be described as 'political society'. It formed a social entity, politically autonomous and economically self-sufficient.

In Athens, Greek democracy reached its apogee in the fifth century. Its great lawgiver Solon had claimed that the best-policed city is 'the city where all citizens, whether they have suffered injury or not, equally pursue and punish injustice'. Under the guidance of Pericles, it developed into a remarkable form of direct democracy. At the height of Athens's splendour at the end of the first year of the Peloponnesian War, Pericles declared in his Funeral Oration:

> Our constitution is called a democracy because power is in the hands not of a minority but of the whole people. When it is a question of settling private disputes, everyone is equal before the law; when it is a question of putting one person before another in positions of public responsibility, what counts is not membership of a particular class, but the actual ability which the man possesses. No one, so long as he has it in him to be of service to the state, is kept in political obscurity because of poverty. And just as our political life is free and open, so is our day-to-day life in relations with each other . . . I declare that in my opinion each single one of our citizens, in all the manifold aspects of life, is able to show himself the rightful lord and owner of his own person, and to do this, moreover, with exceptional grace and exceptional vitality.[13]

Thucydides observed that because of his intelligence and integrity, Pericles could respect the liberty of the people and at the same time hold them in check: 'It was he who led them, rather than they who led him.' Nevertheless, he was continuously accountable to the members of the assembly (*ecclesia*) and absolutely dependent on their approval. He had to persuade the people to vote for every measure that he wished to pass. On a good day it has been estimated that in the last quarter of the fifth century six thousand might attend the assembly out of a citizen population of about thirty thousand. Athenian policy was thus determined by mass meetings of the citizenry on the 'advice of anyone who could win the people's ear'.[14] The system, with its regular assemblies, its rotating Council of Five Hundred, and its elected juries, was deliberately organized to prevent the creation of a permanent bureaucracy and to encourage active participation of the citizens. In practice, this process of direct democracy affirmed citizenship as a form of direct action.[15]

Athenian democracy was based on the Greek concept of *autarkia*, of individual self-sufficiency, but it managed to foster a sense of community and civic duty. In his Funeral Oration, Pericles maintained that in the ordinary life of Athenians

> far from exercising a jealous surveillance over each other, we do not feel called upon to be angry with our neighbour for doing what he likes, or even indulge in those injurious looks which cannot fail to be offensive, although they inflict no positive penalty. But all this ease in our private relations does not make us lawless as citizens.[16]

There were of course limits to Athenian democracy. It did not embrace women, slaves, and resident aliens who made up the majority of the population. But it is misleading to say that it was 'based' on slavery and therefore somehow invalid. The great majority of citizens earned their living by working with their hands and only about a third owned slaves.[17] Nevertheless, even this degree of slavery shows that Athens did not fully understand democracy. Another sign was its readiness to go to war; its imperial ambitions led to the Peloponnesian War which finally brought about its downfall towards the end of the third century.

For all its shortcomings, the libertarian legacy of Greek philosophy and Athenian democracy remains impressive and should not be overshadowed by the dominating presence of Plato and Aristotle. The right to private judgement and the freedom of thought and action were first defended by the Greeks. They not only made the fundamental distinction between nature and convention which runs like a silver thread through all anarchist thinking, but developed a strong sense of the common destiny of all humanity to live a life of virtue. They recognized that justice was a universal principle. They loved laughter and friendship and all that is human. Above all, they saw in education the means to awaken the understanding which alone can bring humanity to personal and social freedom.

6

Christianity

AT FIRST SIGHT, IT may seem strange to link Christianity with anarchism. Many of the classic thinkers, imbued with the scientific spirit of the nineteenth century, were atheists or agnostics. Like the *philosophes* of the Enlightenment, they tended to dismiss organized Christianity as part of the superstition and ignorance of the Middle Ages. They saw the Church aligned with the State, and the priest anointing the warrior and the king. For the most part, they thought Christianity taught a slavish morality with its stress on humility, piety, submission. The traditional image of God as an authoritarian father-figure was anathema to them, and they felt no need for a supernatural authority to bolster temporal authority.

There is of course some basis for these views in the theory and practice of Christianity. Genesis asserts that man is created from the dust of the earth and given special authority over the rest of creation: 'Let us make man in our image, after our likeness: and let them have dominion over the fish of the sea, and the fowl of the air, and over the cattle, and over all the earth . . . Be fruitful, and multiply, and replenish the earth, and subdue it.' (Genesis 1: 26–8)

In the Garden of Eden, there was no mine or thine; all things were enjoyed in common. But disobedience, according to Genesis, was man's first sin. Having rebelled against the authority of God and eaten of the tree of knowledge of good and evil, humanity was banished from the Garden and condemned to a life of pain, toil and mortality. The whole of nature became corrupted.

Since man was a fallen and depraved creature it followed for many that he needed powerful rulers to curb his wayward behaviour. The Fall thus made law necessary for deceitful and weak Man required the restraint of positive law. 'Wherefore then serveth the law?' St Paul asked rhetorically. 'It was added because of transgression.'(Galatians 3: 19) As Christianity developed, there was a growing stress amongst certain theologians on the nothingness of sinful man and the omnipotence of God, a trend which culminated in Calvin who argued that the worst tyrant was better than the absence of civil power or anarchy.

Most European anarchists have followed Proudhon, Stirner and Bakunin in their rejection of Christianity. They are opposed to all forms of imposed authority, religious as well as political, and have been profoundly perturbed by the close historical link between Church and State. But this does not mean that they have all been atheists. Anarchism is not necessarily atheistic any more than socialism is. Indeed, the relationship between anarchism and religion is intricate and in many ways the appeal of anarchism lies precisely in the way it manages to combine religious fervour with philosophical rigour.

The legacy of Christianity is not moreover merely repressive. On the one hand, there is a conservative, quietist and authoritarian tendency originating in the Pauline Church in Rome; on the other, a radical, communal and libertarian one which emerged from the Jamesian church in Jerusalem.[1] Many anarchists have belonged to the latter trend. Tolstoy is the most famous, but not the only one to base his anarchism on a radical interpretation of Christianity. Indeed, Jacques Ellul has recently argued that 'biblical thought leads directly to anarchism, and that this is the only "political anti-political" position in accord with Christian thinking'.[2]

The teaching of the Old Testament about political power is that its use is invariably harmful. The Chronicles' account of the kings in Israel and Judaea shows that their rule was systematically bad. Daniel, for instance, who refused to bow to the king, was thrown into the lion's pit. There would seem to be little validation for political power in the Old Testament.

In the New Testament, we find Paul's dictum: 'there is no authority except God.'(Romans 13: 1) While from Constantine onwards this has been appealed to by the Church to justify the theology of the State, the Gospels and Revelation are consistently opposed to authority. Jesus's attitude is radically negative. He counsels his disciples not to imitate the kings of nations: 'kings and governors have dominion over men; let there be none like that among you.' In fact, Jesus consistently held political authority up to derision. When, for instance, he said 'Render unto Caesar', he did not necessarily mean, as it is usually understand, that subjects should obey their governors. The advice was made in relationship to taxes. Since Caesar, having created money, is its master, Jesus was in all probability implying that a Christian cannot serve Mammon and God at the same time.

Alongside the libertarian trend in Christianity has been a communal one. Jesus' voluntary poverty, his attack on riches (it is more difficult for a rich man to go to heaven than to pass through 'the eye of a needle'), and his sharing of goods (particularly bread and fishes) all inspired many early Christians to practise a form of communism. The communal life of the early Christian Church endured throughout the ministry of Paul.[3]

These early Christian communists probably had connections with the Essenes, a Jewish sect who practised the community of goods and brotherly love. Wishing to release the soul from the prison-house of the flesh, they were ascetic but did not withdraw from the world. They despised marriage and the 'lasciviousness' of women but looked after the children of others. They cannot however be considered forerunners of anarchism for they kept strict religious observances and regarded themselves as a moral elite.[4]

There are solid grounds for believing that the first Christian believers practised a form of communism and usufruct. The account in Acts is explicit: 'And all that believed were together, and had all things common; And sold their possession and goods, and parted them to all *men*, as every man had need.'(Acts 2: 44–5) Again Acts records: 'And the multitude of them that believed were of one heart and of one soul: neither said any *of them* that ought of the things which he possessed was his own; but they had all things common.'(Acts 4: 32) The early Christian fathers were clear on the matter too. Ambrose in the fourth century asserted in no uncertain terms: 'Nature has poured forth all things for all men for common use . . . Nature therefore has produced a common right for all, but greed has made it a right for a few.' He anticipated Kropotkin by concluding 'in accordance with the will of God and the union of nature, we ought to be of mutual help one to the other'.[5]

In the thirteenth century Thomas Aquinas summed up the principal teaching of the Christian fathers, attempting to combine the Christian and Greek traditions of thought in a new way. He recognized the right to property for personal 'use', but believed that any superfluity should be distributed to others who are in need. The right to property is therefore strictly speaking a right of administration or stewardship. The possessor of wealth is an administrator who should distribute it according to his judgement for the good of humanity. Possessions are not merely private property for personal enjoyment: 'Quantum ad hoc non debet homo habere res exteriores ut propias, sed ut communes.' The holder of wealth therefore has a continual duty to practise almsgiving according to his individual conscience. Wealth is held in trust for the public good. Property is not an indefeasible right: where death threatens or there is no other source of sustenance, it is permissible to take what is necessary for others. Such an act cannot be considered robbery or theft. It is a view that was to be later adopted by the father of anarchism, William Godwin.

In general, the position of the early Christian Church was not so much an endorsement of communism but a condemnation of the abuse of wealth. But the communistic tradition in early Christianity acted like the power of myth and had a considerable influence on the later development of anarchism and socialism.

Developing the anti-political trend in Christ's teaching, the Church fathers of the late Roman world continued to separate Christianity from the

State. But increasingly Christianity came to be interpreted in social and political terms. In the fifth century, Augustine in his *City of God* (413–26) offered the first Christian-inspired political utopia in history. Although he stressed the corruption of human nature through the fall of man, Augustine presented redemption as a historical event in the future, not as a memory of some 'golden age' in the past. Since all political power is a form of coercion, he denounced politics as evil, and saw that only with the coming of the kingdom of God would coercion cease.[6] His most subversive teaching was 'Love, and do what you will.'

The influence of Augustine led some to withdraw entirely from politics into monasticism; for others, it fired their millenarian hopes. The Apocalypse and the Second Coming were no longer considered as spiritual metaphors but imminent events in history. For an increasing number, particularly amongst the downtrodden and impoverished, the millennium of God's kingdom of earth was about to be realized.

An influential figure in this development was Joachim of Fiore (*c.*1145–1202), a Cistercian abbot and hermit from Calabria. After many years spent meditating on the scriptures, he developed a widely influential prophetic system. He was convinced that he had found a key to the understanding of the course of history. In a series of commentaries on the apocalyptic books of the Bible, he divided the history of humanity into three ages, corresponding to the three branches of the Holy Trinity. The first was the age of the Father, under the Jewish Laws of the Old Testament, laws based on fear and servitude; the second, of the Son, under the Gospel, the age of faith and filial obedience. In the coming third age of the Holy Spirit, he taught that all law would pass away since all people would act according to the will of God. All masters, both spiritual and temporal, would disappear and the Everlasting Gospel – a new understanding of the meaning of the Bible – would prevail. It would be the age of love and spiritual liberty for the Children of God, an age of joy and ecstasy. This state would prevail until the Last Judgement. This vision of the coming age of liberty was taken up by the Ranters during the English Revolution. The abolition of the monarchy was only the first act in a thorough-going change which would entirely transform society. At the time of the French Revolution, in Britain William Blake was preaching a similar message.

At the beginning of the thirteenth century, the attempt of Francis of Assisi to return to the life of the historical Jesus also had revolutionary implications. As is well known he preached a sermon to the birds, wrote a hymn to the sun, and called the donkey his brother. He has become a symbol of Christian pacifism. Although no vegetarian, his love for animals reflects a mystical awareness of the unity of being which is generally alien to the main Judaeo-Christian tradition. His contemporaries described him as taking 'an inward and outward delight in almost every creature, and when he handled or looked at them his spirit seemed to be in heaven rather than on earth'.[7] He felt the same delight in water, rocks, flowers and trees, and by all accounts lived a life of ecstatic joy. For Francis, God is immanent in the world, and the Trinity through Christ has become the comrade of man.

With a small band of companions (a brotherhood of eleven), Francis tried to live like Christ in voluntary poverty. He repudiated all notion of property, including those things retained for personal use. His original affinity group was united in perfect communion, but once his followers were accepted into the Catholic Church, the Franciscans developed into a hierarchical monastic order like the rest, founded on poverty, chastity and obedience. Nevertheless, Francis' message of mystical poverty had a profoundly subversive influence: it showed up the Church and State to be lost in ostentation and opulence, and presented the poor as the only community capable of redemption. Those who wanted to follow Francis' personal example were called Spirituals and were eventually dismissed as heretics. By the end of the thirteenth century, they were also propagating Joachim's prophecies of the coming age of spiritual liberty.

The Spirituals were only one thread in a growing millenarian movement in the Middle Ages alongside the Brethren of the Free Spirit, the Taborites and Hussites, and the Anabaptists of the Reformation. It emerged in the radical wing of the republican movement in the English Revolution, especially amongst the Diggers and Ranters. These groups found inspiration from texts like Augustine's 'Love, and do what you will' and Paul's 'Where the spirit of the Lord is, there is liberty'.(II Corinthians 2: 17) They rejected the Church and State and all temporal law because they felt they were in a state of God's grace and could commit no sin. They denied all earthly government, believing that God-given reason was sufficient to guide their actions. They looked to the Second Coming of Christ and the immediate realization of heaven on earth in which people would live in perfect freedom and complete equality.

This underground libertarian tradition within Christianity surfaced again at the end of the eighteenth century in the writings of William Blake. He too expressed his social aspirations in Biblical language, wishing to replace the Babylon of existing Church and State with the Jerusalem of a free society in which all people would live according to the Everlasting Gospel of forgiveness and love. Like Lao Tzu, he saw reality as a dynamic interplay of opposites. 'Without contraries is no progression.' But he hoped to realize a higher synthesis, a Marriage of Heaven and Hell which would bring about a reconciliation between mind and body, imagination and reason, conscience and desire, rich and poor, humanity and nature.

Blake did not separate religion from politics: indeed, he asked, 'Are not Religion & Politics the Same Thing?'; and insisted 'Brotherhood is Religion'. He drew inspiration from the mythical social paradise, the Garden of Eden, where man and woman lived in a condition of innocence and wholeness, without private property, class distinctions, or human authority. After the Fall, humanity was condemned to toil and suffering, weighed down by Church and State, oppressed by Lord and King. They were obliged to inhabit a world riddled with contradiction: between Nature and Man, State and Society, Capital and Labour, Church and Christianity. Optimistically, Blake looked to a world revolution which would usher in a new millennium in which such contradictions would be no more.

Like later anarchists, Blake regarded authority as the principle source of injustice: 'A Tyrant is the Worst disease & the Cause of all others.' It is the oppressive structures of the State which impede the divine potential within humanity. Blake felt not only that 'Every Body hates a King', but wrote also: 'Houses of Commons and Houses of Lords seem to me fools; they seem to me to be something Else besides Human Life.' The State had no right to make laws, especially as no law could be sufficiently extensive so as adequately to cover every case: 'One Law for the Lion & Ox is Oppression.' Moreover, law encourages crime and transgression, just as the State creates disorder in society: 'Prisons are built with stones of Law, Brothels with bricks of Religion.' Indeed, since it is law which alone defines a crime, incites people to commit it, and promises dire punishment, Blake insisted: 'All Penal Laws court Transgression & therefore are cruelty & Murder'. As a great libertarian, he concluded: 'When the Reverence of Government is lost, it is better than when it is found.'[8]

When it comes to the Church, Blake is no less iconoclastic. The modern Church, he thought, 'Crucifies Christ with the Head Downwards'. He rejected all political and religious authority since human beings are made in the Divine Image and can govern themselves. He identified with the rebel Jesus against the tyrannical Jehovah God of the Old Testament: 'Jesus was all virtue, and acted from impulse, not from rules.' Since man is innocent and natural desires are beneficial, it followed for Blake that any hindrance is harmful and unnecessary. Indeed, at the heart of his visionary anarchism is the belief that 'The Gospel is Forgiveness of Sins & Has No Moral Precepts'. He looked forward to a time when every individual would be 'King & Priest in his own House' in a society of complete forbearance, for 'What is Liberty without Universal Toleration?'.[9]

At the same time, Christianity influenced Blake's contemporary William Godwin in an indirect way and helped him become the father of anarchism. Godwin was an extreme Calvinist in his youth and was trained to become a Dissenting minister. As a young man, he concluded that the God of the Old Testament acted like a 'political legislator' in a theocratic State and yet had 'not a right to be a tyrant'.[10] When he wrote his *Enquiry concerning Political Justice* (1793), he had under the influence of the French *philosophes* become an atheist, but his moral and economic beliefs had been largely shaped by his early Calvinism.[11] He developed Aquinas' notion of steward-ship of the good things of the earth in a communist direction: the individual should distribute any surplus wealth he possessed to the most needy. Godwin's anarchism moreover resulted from a strict application of the Dissenters' right of private judgement from the religious to the political realm.

The great nineteenth-century anarchist thinkers Proudhon, Stirner and Bakunin were all imbued with the scientific spirit of the Enlightenment and identified Christianity with the existing authoritarian Church. Proudhon wanted to show that Catholicism was the counterpart of a hierarchical system of secular government. Since the Catholic God is considered the authority on which all other authorities rest, governments can be nothing less than 'God's scourges set up to *discipline* the world'. Even from a moral point of view, Proudhon was convinced that 'God is tyranny and poverty; God is evil'. It is therefore the first duty of the thinking free man to banish the idea of God from his mind. Since we acquire knowledge and social life in spite of God, 'Each step in our progress represents one more victory in which we annihilate the Deity'.[12] But although Proudhon was militantly anti-Catholic, he still interpreted the Christian doctrine of original sin as a symbol of man's ineradicable inclination towards evil and he sought to create a social order which would restrain his evil tendencies. Moreover, he talked of the idea of Justice inherent in nature as if it were a divine principle. In the form of natural law, it provided an ultimate reference point for his morality and operated as a kind of disguised Providence.

Stirner, on the other hand, thought God, along with the State and Morality, was just another spook to delude humanity. He argued forcibly that the State had come to be considered sacred like the Church, and laws were presented as if they were God's commandments:

> If the Church had *deadly sins*, the State has *capital crimes*; if the one had *heretics*, the other has *traitors*; the one *ecclesiastical penalties*, the other *criminal penalties*; the one *inquisitorial* processes, the other *fiscal*; in short, there sins, here crimes, there inquisition and here – inqui-sition. Will the sanctity of the State not fall like the Church's?[13]

Bakunin for his part was haunted by the problem of God's existence in his youth. But he eventually became a militant atheist, adopting the slogan 'Neither God nor Master'. For him, the Christian God, who judged every action and threatened eternal punishment, was the ultimate symbol of authority. Like Stirner, he argued that God does not exist but is an abstraction which men project into heaven to worship.

Bakunin believed that Christianity taught:

> God being everything, the real world and man are nothing. God being truth, justice, good, beauty, power, and life, man is falsehood, iniquity, evil, ugliness, impotence, and death. God being master, man is the slave . . .[14]

Christianity had understood this better than all other religions. As a result, it was the absolute religion, and the Roman Church the only consistent and logical one.

Like Nietzsche, Bakunin declared the death of God and argued that we must transcend Christian values and create our own. The destruction of religion is a prerequisite of a free society since '*The idea of God implies the abdication of reason and of justice; it is the most decisive negation of human liberty, and necessarily ends in the enslavement of mankind, both in theory and practice.*' Bakunin was at his most passionate in his denunciation of Christianity, but he made his case for the death of God in the form of a syllogism: 'If God exists, man is a slave; now, man can and must be free; then, God does not exist. I defy anyone whomsoever to avoid this circle.' Loving human freedom and considering it to be the absolute condition for all he respected in humanity, Bakunin reverses the phrase of Voltaire to affirm: '*if God really existed, it would be necessary to abolish him*'.[15] For this reason, he praised Satan for being the first rebel and the 'emancipator of worlds'.

According to Bakunin, the Church represents the interests of the clergy, as the State represents those of the bourgeoisie. 'Does She', he asked rhetorically, 'not turn what is living into a corpse, cast aside freedom, preach the eternal slavery of the masses for the benefit of tyrants and exploiters? Is it not this implacable Church that tends to perpetuate the reign of shadows, of ignorance, of poverty and of crime?' He therefore affirmed that the abolition of the Church and the State must be 'the first and indispensable condition of the true liberation of society'.[16] These sentiments, particularly in Latin countries where the Catholic Church was so dominant, had a widespread influence. Bakunin was no doubt partly responsible for the militant atheism of the Spanish anarchists which led to many cases of church-burning during the opening period of the Spanish Revolution.

Not all nineteenth-century anarchists were atheists; others inferred their philosophy directly from their Christian beliefs. The American Adin Ballou reached anarchist conclusions in his *Practical Christian Socialism* (1854) from a more rational route. Since man has only an obligation to obey God and his divine government, he has no obligation to obey the law of the land or human government. Human government is the will of man exercising 'absolute authority over man, by means of cunning and physical force'. God on the other hand divides his authority with no creature; he is the absolute sovereign. The will of man has therefore no intrinsic authority, 'no rightful claim to the allegiance of man'. Ballou therefore asks rhetorically about government: 'Is it not a mere cypher?'

Although he did not call himself an anarchist, Ballou preached against voting, office-holding, legislating, or punishing since 'Majorities often decree folly and inequity. *Power* oftener corrupts its possessor, than benefits the powerless.' Instead, he argued that the true Christian should resist war and develop his moral power. And if 'non-resistants' should ever become the great majority of any community, he thought they could manage public affairs through voluntary assemblies in which the 'law of love and the counsels of wisdom will prevail without strife'.[17]

Tolstoy of course is the most well-known Christian anarchist, and it was a radical interpretation of the Gospels which led him to anarchist conclusions. He believed that they taught that one should live at peace with all men and not promise an oath nor resist evil. It followed for Tolstoy that all governments, laws, armies, and all protection of life or property are immoral: 'I cannot take part in any Government activity that has for its aim the defence of people and their property by violence; I cannot be a judge or take part in trials; nor can I help others to take part in law-courts and Government offices,' he declared.[18] Since *The Kingdom of God Is Within You* and you can be guided by the divine light of reason, governments are both unnecessary and harmful.

If people could but understand that they are 'sons of God', Tolstoy wrote, 'and can therefore be neither slaves nor enemies to one another – those insane, unnecessary, worn-out, pernicious organizations called Governments, and all the sufferings, violations, humiliations, and crimes they occasion, would cease.'[19] Tolstoy inspired a long tradition of anarchist pacifists, while his greatest disciple Gandhi developed his doctrine of civil disobedience into a highly effective form of non-violent direct action.

While Tolstoy rejected both Church and State, and was excommunicated from the Russian Orthodox Church for his views, Ammon Hennacy and Dorothy Day in this century have found it possible to be Catholic anarchists. Dorothy Day, who founded the *Catholic Worker* in 1933, became one of the staunchest advocates of Christian pacifism and anarchism. She felt that the authority of God only made her a better rebel. It gave her courage to oppose those who sought wrongly to carry over the concept of authority from the supernatural field to the social one where it did not belong. She did not think that it was contradictory or unethical to choose to obey the authority of God and reject the authority of the State since 'we were *born into* a state and could not help it, but accepted God of our own free will'.[20]

Influenced by Tolstoy and Proudhon, she sought with the anarchist Peter Maurin and the Catholic Worker Group to decentralize society and establish a community of families, with a combination of private and communal property. While most people associated the *Catholic Worker* with voluntary poverty and community, she stressed above all the need for love: 'We have all known the long loneliness and we have learned that the only solution is love and that love comes with community.'[21]

Hennacy, for his part, was inspired by the 'true rebel Jesus' and his idea of God 'was not an authority whom I obeyed like a monarch but a principle of good as laid down by Jesus in the Sermon on the Mount'.[22] If the forces of the State conflicted with his ideals, he would follow his ideals and disobey the State. Hennacy preached 'the one-man revolution within the heart' based on voluntary poverty and pacifism. Drawing out his legacy, he wrote: 'The way of Jesus, of St Francis, of Tolstoy, and of Gandhi teaches us to love our enemy, to establish justice, to abolish exploitation, and to rely upon God rather than on politicians and governments.'[23]

In the preface to his autobiography, Hennacy gave the clearest and most eloquent statement of his principles and their source in Christianity:

> Christian-anarchism is based upon the answer of Jesus to the Pharisees when He said that he without sin was to cast the first stone; and upon the Sermon on the Mount which advises the return of good for evil and the turning of the other cheek. Therefore, when we take any part in government by voting for legislative, judicial and executive officials, we make these men our arm by which we cast a stone and deny the Sermon on the Mount.
>
> The dictionary definition of Christian is: one who follows Christ, kind, kindly, Christ-like. Anarchism is voluntary co-operation for good, with the right of secession. A Christian-anarchist is, therefore, one who turns the other cheek, overturns the tables of the money-lenders, and who does not need a cop to tell him how to behave. A Christian-anarchist does not depend on bullets or ballots to achieve his ideal; he achieves that ideal daily by the One Man Revolution with which he faces a decadent, confused and dying world.[24]

Where Day and Hennacy were primarily activists, the Russian philosopher Nicholas Berdyaev developed like Tolstoy a form of revolutionary Christianity which was non-institutional and liberating. Both saw the Kingdom of God as an existential condition rather than a social regime but for Berdyaev it took the form of creative autonomy rather than non-resisting love.

Berdyaev defined freedom as 'the duty of man to be a personality, to display the strength of the character of personality'. The free man is a self-governing being who transcends both State and society since 'The self-government of society, and of a people is still the government of slaves.' But for Berdyaev the concept of the free personality can only be understood in a religious context: Christ was the freest man bound only by love and 'God is the guarantee of the freedom of personality from the enslaving power of nature and society, of the Kingdom of Caesar and of the object world.'[25]

The anarchism of Berdyaev is based on the incompatibility of the Gospel and the State, between what he calls *The Realm of the Spirit and the Realm of Caesar* (1946). The ethics of the Gospel, he insists, are invariably opposed to the ethics imposed by the State. The prosperity of the State does not represent the community and always involves the death of innocents. 'The law of the State is that in order to save the State even the innocent must be sacrificed', Berdyaev writes, and yet 'the death of a single man is an event more important and more tragic than the death of a State or an Empire.' Moreover, the Church has become such an intimate partner of the State that it has turned the State into another Church. By recognizing the State, the Church has accepted the incumbent power, whatever it may be, so that 'Sovereignty and the divine character of power exist in equality!'[26] The remedy for this state of affairs is to deny the sovereignty of the State and anyone who claims political authority.

Like the non-resistant anarchists Tolstoy and Ballou, Berdyaev develops the Christian concepts of the Second Coming and the Divinity of Christ in a revolutionary direction. He does not look to any particular class as the agents of change: master and slave, ruler and ruled are victims of the same spiritual affliction. It is the unique individual who concerns him. He introduces into his philosophical framework the spiritual concept of the human 'personality' as our essential feature: man is a person, whose conduct is to be explained in terms of intentions and beliefs, not by his external behaviour or forces. For Berdyaev therefore it is creative autonomy, rather than non-resisting love, which constitutes the existential centre, the true inner kingdom: 'Personality in man is the triumph over the determination of the social group . . . emancipation from dependence upon nature, from dependence upon society and the state.'[27]

Slavery in man is his sin, his Fall. Man seeks slavery as well as freedom. But the free man goes beyond the correlatives of master and slave 'to exist in himself', to become like Christ, the freest of the sons of men who was only bound by love. The truly free man is freed from psychological and physical violence, from the State and social pressures, to be entirely self-governing. As a complete person, he is creative in the 'ecstasy of the moment' which is outside time. It is only 'the gathering together of freedom, truth and love which realizes personality, free and creative personality'.[28]

Berdyaev finally envisages the end of history, which for him is marked by the victory of 'existential time' over historical time, as the complete liberation of humanity.

It should be clear that despite the opposition of many of the classic anarchist thinkers to Christianity in the nineteenth century, and the close historical link between the Church and the State, anarchism is by no means intrinsically anti-religious or anti-Christian. Indeed, its forerunners were inspired by the minor libertarian and communal trend within Christianity, especially in the Middle Ages and during the Reformation. Tolstoy was the outstanding Christian anarchist thinker in the past, but this century has witnessed a remarkable flourishing of Christian anarchism from different traditions.

In fact it could be argued that Christian anarchism is not an attempt to synthesize two systems of thought but rather an attempt to realize the message of the Gospels. Like the mystical anarchists of the Middle Ages, Ciaron O'Reilly has recently claimed that the free society already exists in embryo: 'To the Christian the revolution has already come in the form of the resurrection. It is merely a matter of living out that promise, not living by the standards of the fallen world. The Kingdom of God exists within the social organism, it is our role to make it universally manifest.'[29]

To deny the authority of the State and Church does not necessarily mean a denial of the authority of God. The law of God, like natural law, can offer a standard by which to live and to oppose man-made law. We are coerced into accepting the latter, while we can accept or reject the former according to voluntary choice. Jesus undoubtedly provides an enduring libertarian example by refusing to collaborate with the Roman rulers, by rejecting the financial benefits of the Sadducees, and by encouraging people to liberate themselves and to form communities based on voluntary association and common property. Jesus dealt with wrongdoers by confronting them and then forgiving them. By suggesting that we should do unto to others as we have done unto ourselves, he offered a universal moral principle which does not require the sanction of law. By not resisting evil, by turning the other cheek, he taught that we should not participate in violence to others. Since government is organized violence *par excellence*, a genuine reading of the Sermon on the Mount must logically lead to the rejection of all earthly government. As with the other major world religions, Christianity has left a mixed legacy, but it has been a source of great inspiration to anarchism as well as to socialism, and no doubt will continue to be so in the future.

The Middle Ages

Mystical and Millenarian Anarchists

TAOISM, BUDDHISM AND CHRISTIANITY were not the only religious movements to produce libertarian thinkers and tendencies. In the Middle East, just before the birth of Muhammad, a prophet called Mazdak appeared around AD 487 in Persia.

Retaining Zoroaster's concepts of light and darkness, Mazdak preached a dualistic religion, but with socialist principles. He believed that all men are born equal but suffer from the unequal distribution of wealth and women, and since most fighting is caused by them, he proscribed private property and marriage. People should share their goods and women like water, fire and grazing. They should also maintain respect for animals, thereby putting an end to slaughter. Mazdak's ideal was a stoical and simple life, and he urged contentment and austerity.

Mazdak's followers took from the rich and gave what they did not need to the poor. They even called for the overthrow of the king. Amongst themselves, they had no private property and their children did not know their fathers.[1] Thousands joined the movement, but in AD 523 King Qobbath arranged a massacre. Mazdak was arrested and executed in AD 528 or 529. His followers were virtually wiped out, although Babik tried unsuccessfully to revive the movement in the ninth century. Some of Mazdak's teachings later found expression in the Ismaeliya Movement in general, and in particular in the influential cultural organization known as Ikhwan al-Safa (the Brothers of Purity). They also may have influenced Al-Quramitta who established the first Islamic socialist society in southern Iraq and Bahrain. In the Middle East today 'Mazdak' is still used to describe someone who is rebellious and intractable.

In the Europe of the Middle Ages, as the established Church began to share power with temporal rulers and impose its own dogma, an underground movement developed within Christianity which often took on a revolutionary form in times of unrest and scarcity. It challenged the power of the both State and Church and tried to establish a society based on the community of the apostles. The most radical heresy came to be known as the Heresy of the Free Spirit. Although less known than the Catharist or Albigensian heresies, it was probably more important in the social history of Western Europe.[2]

The Heresy of the Free Spirit was one of many Christian millenarian groups in the Middle Ages which, inspired by Revelation 20: 4–6, looked forward to the Second Coming of Christ who would establish a messianic kingdom on earth and reign for a thousand years before the Last Judgement. While the original teaching held that only the Christian martyrs would be resurrected before the general resurrection of the dead at the Last Judgement, it came to be interpreted to mean that the suffering faithful would be resurrected in their own lifetime. This millenarian doctrine, spread by holy beggars, had considerable appeal for the rootless poor of Western Europe who came to believe in the imminent possibility of terrestrial, collective and total salvation. Unmarried women and widows, who had no clear social role, were particularly attracted to the movement.

The Heresy of the Free Spirit as an identifiable heresy emerged at the close of the twelfth century amongst a mystical brotherhood of Sufis in Islamic Spain, particularly in Sevilla. After a period of initiation in which they had to give blind obedience to a master, the members of the sect would enjoy total freedom in which every impulse was seen as a divine command. The heresy spread rapidly towards the end of the thirteenth century throughout Christian Europe and emerged in full view in the fourteenth century.

In the process, the heresy developed within a Neoplatonic metaphysical framework three principal doctrines. In the first place, its adherents believed that 'God is all that is' and that 'Every created thing is divine'. At the end of time, all will be reabsorbed into God like a drop of wine in the sea. Secondly, they thought that there is no afterlife of reward or punishment, but heaven and hell are merely states of the soul in this world. Thirdly, and this had most important moral and political consequences, they held that once a person has knowledge of God, he or she is in heaven and is incapable of sin: 'Every creature is in its nature blessed'. United with God, the individual rises above all laws, churches and rites and can do whatever he or she wishes. This view became linked amongst some groups to an Adam cult which saw its members (known as Adamites) restored to the state of innocence before the Fall.

In the fourteenth century Heinrich Suso, a disciple of the German mystic Meister Eckhart and an ex-flagellant, emerged from the miasmic underground to record his encounter with an apparition of the Free Spirit in Köln around 1330:

Whence have you come?, Suso asked. 'I come from nowhere.' Tell me, what are you? 'I am not.' What do you wish? 'I do not wish.' This is a miracle! Tell me, what is your name? 'I am called Nameless Wildness.' Where does your insight lead into? 'Into untrammelled freedom.' Tell me, what do you call untrammelled freedom? 'When a man lives according to all his caprices without distinguishing between God and himself, and without looking before or after.'³

This deviant form of medieval mysticism (also found amongst contemporary Sufis) was spread by holy beggars who formed a restless intelligentsia. Their followers have been called mystical anarchists. Indeed, the adepts of the Free Spirit were distinguished from all other medieval sects by their total amoralism: 'The free man is quite right to do whatever gives him pleasure', they taught. Another insisted: 'I belong to the Liberty of Nature, and all that my nature's desires I satisfy.'⁴ It even became a proof of salvation to experience no conscience or remorse. As antinomians, they felt no longer bound by religious commandments, moral rules or civil laws. They rejected private property and shared their wealth. They were sexually promiscuous and rejected the marriage tie.

But for all their stress on self-deification and individual liberty, it is difficult to see them as anarchists in the modern sense for they formed an elite and exploited and oppressed people outside the sect. If anything, they are closer to those followers of Nietzsche who asserted themselves at the expense of others and lived beyond conventional definitions of good and evil. A female adept is reported to have argued in the fourteenth century that God created all things to serve a person who is 'one with God', adding 'A man whom all heaven serves, all people and creatures are indeed obliged to serve and to obey.'⁵ Another female initiate was taught 'You shall order all created beings to serve you according to your will, for the glory of God.' They were thus convinced of their infinite superiority and believed that all things and beings were made to serve their purposes. In practice, they thought cheating, theft, and robbery with violence were all justified: 'Whatever the eyes sees and covets, let the hand grasp it.'⁶

Marguérite Porete, who was tried and burned in Paris in 1311, has left us *Mirouer des simples âmes*, the only complete work by a medieval adept to survive. She taught that at the seventh stage of illumination the soul becomes united with God and by his grace is liberated from sin. It needs no Church, no priesthood and no sacraments. She makes clear that those souls who are at one with God should 'do nothing but what pleases them; or if they do, they deprive themselves of peace, freedom and nobility. For the soul is not perfected until it does what it pleases, and is not reproached for taking its pleasure.' Again, this doctrine of amoral self-assertion is taught at the expense of others: 'Such souls use all things that are made and created, and which nature requires, with such peace of mind as they use the earth they walk on.'[7] It is such teaching which could easily be used to justify immoralism or foster the kind of unrest which broke out in the medieval peasant revolts.

The Heresy of the Free Spirit formed a clandestine tradition which not only emerged in the great peasant rebellions of the Middle Ages and on the extreme left in the English Revolution, but welled up in the writings of William Blake. A modern version of the cult of the Free Spirit, with its stress on the total emancipation of the individual and call for universal peace and love, can be even recognized in the counter-culture of the nineteen sixties.

Clearly such libertarian beliefs had revolutionary implications for medieval society. By the middle of the fourteenth century, the profound economic and social changes were creating serious tensions. Unrest among peasants broke out not so much where they had been prosperous and relatively free, but where a multitude of petty civil and ecclesiastical lords were attempting to extend and formalize their jurisdiction at their expense.[8] Amongst the dispossessed and the rootless poor there was also a great yearning to return to the natural justice of the Garden of Eden. But the great mass insurrections which occurred – notably the English Peasants' Revolt in 1381, the Hussite Revolution in Bohemia at Tabor in 1419–21, the German Peasants' Revolt led by Thomas Münzer in 1525, and the Münster Commune of 1534 – were often contradictory. It is not always easy to uncover anarchist roots in them. While they certainly fostered millenarian and libertarian hopes, they usually had realistic and limited social aims. Their call for freedom was undoubtedly libertarian, but it often ended in authoritarian rule.

The Peasants' Revolt in England in 1381 began as a mass protest of yeomen in Essex and Kent against increasingly heavy taxes – especially the Poll Tax that had been recently introduced. They feared that the nobles were trying to destroy the feudal status of the yeoman and reduce him to a serf. The obscure clergyman John Ball expressed their belief in a former era of equality and freedom in his famous distich:

> When Adam delved and Eve span,
> Who was then a gentleman?

Before the insurrection, John Ball delivered a revolutionary sermon, recorded by the French chronicler Jean Froissart:

Things cannot go well in England, nor ever shall, till everything be made common, and there are neither villeins nor gentlemen, but we shall be all united together, and the lords shall be no greater masters than ourselves. What have we deserved that we should be kept thus enslaved? We are all descended from one father and mother, Adam and Eve. What reasons can they give to show that they are greater lords than we, save by making us toil and labour, so that they can spend? [9]

Although he attacks private property and inequality, John Ball does not specifically attack government. He even argues that the people should appeal to the King and complain about their slavery, although he suggests pointedly: 'tell him we shall have it otherwise, or else we will provide a remedy ourselves.'

The rebels in Kent elected Wat Tyler of Maidstone as their captain and appointed Jack Straw as his chief lieutenant. As they marched to London, 100,000 strong, they captured towns and castles in Essex and Kent and then entered the capital. When they arrived there, the people of London prevented the gates from being shut against the rebels, and joined forces with them. The men of Essex agreed to turn back when the king, Richard II, promised, at Mile End, that he would free the villeins and turn personal service into cash rent. But the men of Kent went on to destroy the Savoy Palace (then home of the chief royal advisor John of Gaunt), to burn Temple Bar, open the prisons (including John Ball's), and to kill the Archbishop of Canterbury and occupy his palace.

Their demands were not great, merely calling for wage labour, a reduction in taxes, free buying and selling, and an ending of feudal dues and obligations. Young King Richard met Tyler and Straw twice and granted most of their demands. At their second meeting at Smithfield, Tyler told the king that 'there should be no more villeins in England, and no serfdom or villeinage, but that all men should be free and of one condition.'[10] Behind the limited demands placed before Richard was a millenarian vision of the sudden restoration of a golden age of liberty and equality. This transpires in the burning of the Savoy Palace without it being sacked, and in Jack Straw's alleged declaration that in the end the rich and clergy (except the begging orders) would have to be killed off.

The hopes of the rebels were never to be realized. At the meeting at Smithfield, during the negotiations, William Walworth, the Mayor of London, wounded Tyler. Discovering that he had been taken to St Bartholomew's Hospital, the mayor had Tyler dragged out and beheaded. The king's promises were then revoked, John Ball and Jack Straw were executed with many others, and the rebellion crushed.

But it was not the end of it. John Ball's message was not forgotten:

> In the beginning all human beings were created free and equal. Evil men by an unjust oppression first introduced serfdom against the will of God. Now it is the time given by God when the common people could, if they would, cast off the yoke they have borne so long and win the freedom they have always yearned for. Therefore they should be of good heart and conduct themselves like the wise husbandman in the scriptures who gathered the wheat into his barn, and uprooted and burnt the tares which had almost choked the good grain; for the harvest time was come. The tares were the great lords, the judges and the lawyers. They must all be exterminated, and so must everyone else who might be dangerous to the community of the future. Then, once the great ones had been cut off, men would all enjoy equal freedom, rank, and power, and share all things in common.[11]

William Morris was to revive *A Dream of John Ball* (1888) five hundred years later. The English Peasants' Revolt was based on the myth of a Golden Age, but in due course the Revolt itself took on the power of myth. Some of the anarchist participants in the anti-Poll Tax riots in London in 1990, for instance, were conscious of this earlier revolt against unjust taxation.

Despite Richard II's rearguard action, kings throughout Europe were unable to prevent feudalism from collapsing any more than the Church could stem the rising tide of the Reformation. After the Peasants' Revolt in England, the most anarchic insurrection took place in Bohemia in the following century in 1419. It was part of a rebellion initially provoked by the execution of Jan Hus, a moderate reformer who had attacked the abuses of the church. He had also defended the British Protestant John Wycliffe who had argued that the Church would be better served without a pope and prelates. Wycliffe had declared in resounding Latin:

> Firstly, that all good things of God ought to be common. The proof of this is as follows. Every man ought to be in a state of grace; if he is in a state of grace he is lord of the world and all it contains; therefore every man ought to be the lord of the whole world. But because of the multitudes of men, this will not happen unless they all hold all things in common: therefore all things ought to be in common.

During the unrest which followed in Bohemia, the insurgents called themselves Taborites after having given the biblical name Tabor to a town on a hill near Prague. They tried to establish an anarcho-communist order in which there was to be no private property or taxes and no human authority of any sort. They took the Bible as the sole authority for their faith and practice. They insisted that 'All shall live together as brothers, none shall be subject to another.' While calling for popular democracy, they still accepted the ultimate authority of God: 'The Lord shall reign, and the Kingdom shall be handed over to the people of the earth.'[12] They were extreme millenarians, believing that the Second Coming of Christ (disguised as a brigand) was imminent. All laws would then be abolished, the elect would never die, and women would bear children painlessly. Some even began acting as if the millennium had already arrived, wandering through the woods naked, singing and dancing; they claimed that they were in state of innocence like Adam and Eve before the Fall.

The Taborites set up communal chests and shared their wealth equally amongst themselves. Although their economic system has been called a communism of consumption, there is some evidence that they socialized production.[13] But they were unable to organize production on a large scale, or to exchange goods efficiently between the city and peasant communes. When their wealth ran out, they began to take from the neighbouring people. The experiment collapsed after a couple of years. Nevertheless, it has been called the first attempt to found a society on the principle that liberty is the mother and not the daughter of order.[14]

The Taborites were ready to fight. They called for a warrior Christ to make war on the Antichrist in Babylon, and declared: 'All lords, nobles and knights shall be cut down and exterminated in the forests like outlaws.'[15] Some however objected to such violence and withdrew under the guidance of Peter Chelšický to rural Bohemia to found a community of pacifists. He lamented how so-called servants of God carried the sword and committed 'all sorts of injustice, violence, robbery, oppression of the labouring poor ... Thereby all brotherly love is infiltrated with bloodlust and such tension created as easily leads to contest, and murder results.' Satan had seduced them into thinking that they were angels who must purify Christ's world of all scandals and judge the world; the result was that they 'committed many killings and impoverished many people'.[16]

In his principal work, *The Net of Faith* (c.1450), Peter Chelčický opposed the 'two whales' of the Church and State. He believed that the State and political power were the result of original sin, and were necessary evils to keep order in an unregenerate world. But in any true community of Christians they were superfluous; love and peace would suffice. The community Chelčický founded had no outward organization, and was held together only by love and by following the example of Christ and his apostles. The sect eventually became the Moravian Brothers. Rudolf Rocker later recognized Chelčický as a forerunner of Tolstoy, and Kropotkin acknowledged him as a precursor of anarchism.[17]

The Reformation, set in motion by the great reformers Luther, Zwingli and Calvin, unleashed forces which were difficult for the Church and State to control. It coincided with the breakup of the hierarchical feudal order with its network of rights and obligations, and freed the economy to competition and usury. The reformers' appeal to the Bible and their insistence of salvation by faith and predestination had enormous consequences. In the three score years following Luther's three great Reformation tracts of 1520, a tremendous movement at the core of Christendom got underway which has been called the radical Reformation. It marked a 'radical break from existing institutions and theologies in the interrelated drives to restore Christian Christianity, to reconstruct and to sublimate'.[18] It consisted of a loose movement of Anabaptists (who believed in adult baptism), Spiritualists (who stressed the divine immediacy), and Evangelical Rationalists. They believed on principle in the separation of the Church from the State, sought to spread their version of the Christian life through missions, martyrdom and philanthropy, and rejected all forms of coercion except the ban. They had an antinomian streak which in its mildest form meant a stress on grace over law, but in a more pronounced form led to the repudiation of all organization and ordinances in church life.

The Anabaptists in the sixteenth century were in many ways successors to the Brotherhood of the Free Spirit, cultivating brotherly love and sharing their goods. They regarded the State with suspicion, considering it irrelevant to true Christians like themselves. They refused to hold official positions in the State or to take up arms on its behalf. Although they were millenarians in that they looked forward to the coming of the Kingdom of God, they were prepared to wait for its arrival. They were mostly pacifists.

This was not the case of Thomas Münzer who opposed Luther in Germany at the time of the Peasants' Revolt. The peasants were looking forward to a society of independent yeoman farmers and free labourers as well as a return to their common rights in land. Luther, who indirectly helped to provoke the unrest, came to defend the rulers who were introducing the new serfdom. 'The only way to make Mr Everyman do what he ought', he declared, 'is to constrain him by law and the sword to a semblance of piety, as one holds wild beasts by chains and cages.'[19]

In 1523, Thomas Münzer began organizing in secret a revolutionary army called the League of the Elect. Basing his vision on the apocalyptic Book of Daniel, he announced the immediate coming of the war between the forces of the Devil and the League of the Elect which would usher in the millennium. Taking the town of Mühlhausen in Thuringia, he made it his base and attracted support from the peasants. Because of Engels' praise of Münzer in *The Peasants' War in Germany* (1850), he has become a Marxist revolutionary saint, but in fact he only called for a community of goods in the last days at Mühlhausen and he ran away from the final battle in 1525 at Frakenhausen in which the peasant army was defeated.

After the debacle, itinerant preachers spread the gospel of violent millenarianism in the Low Countries and South Germany. The bookseller and printer Hans Hut, who had escaped from the battle of Mühlhausen, called for a social revolution, echoing both the views of John Ball and the Taborites: 'Christ will give the sword and revenge to them, the Anabaptists, to punish all sins, stamp out all governments; communize all property and slay those who do not permit themselves to be rebaptized.'[20] Hut was arrested and executed, but his message spread rapidly in South Germany. Millenarian groups sprang up, many of them rejecting all rites and sacraments, living according to the Inner Light, and holding their possessions in common.

It was however in Münster, a small ecclesiastical city-state in north-west Germany, that the radical Anabaptists tried under the inspiration of Jan Bockelson (John of Leyden) to establish a New Jerusalem in 1534. They called on their brothers and sisters to live in a community without sin and held together by love. They pooled their goods, including food, and gave up money. But the authoritarian tendencies in their teaching came to dominate: they burnt all books save the Bible. Although Münster had been governed by an elected council, Bockelson set up a new government of twelve elders. In their name, he introduced a new legal code which made practically every crime or misdemeanour a capital offence, from treason to answering back one's parents. Although an abundance of women led them to accept polygamy (based on the text in Genesis: 'be fruitful and multiply' [1: 22]), he imposed a strict morality with the death penalty for adultery.

In the end, Bockelson, the self-proclaimed Messiah of the Last Days, crowned himself King of the People of God and Ruler of the New Zion. A master of manipulating the people through pageants and feasts, his programmes met with little resistance and life seems to have been a round of constant exultation. Unlike the Taborites, he managed to introduce a communism of production as well as consumption, and guild members worked without wages. The sense of community was all-important in its success. But weakened by a prolonged siege and famine, Münster eventually fell in 1535.

The experience led the Anabaptists to become rigorous pacifists. They continued to set up communities, especially in Eastern Europe. Jacob Hutter, an extreme millenarian, communitarian and pacifist had a widespread influence in Moravia which led to his martyrdom. The *Hutterite Chronicles* record how his group moved to a village near Austerlitz in 1528 and 'spread out a cloak before the people, and every man did lay his substance down upon it, with a willing heart and without constraint, for the sustenance of those of necessity, according to the doctrine of the prophets and apostles (Isaiah 23, 18; Acts 2, 4–5)'.[21] Although the local prince said he would defend their refuge against Vienna, the leaders replied: 'Since you promise to resort to the sword, even to protect us, we cannot stay.' The Hutterite colonies were highly successful and although they believed in decent poverty the efficiency of their communist economy made them wealthy. The members of the colonies practised godly watchfulness on each other, and the marriages were arranged with the help of the elders. The Moravian nobles were forced by the Church and Empire to expel them from their estates in 1622. They scattered, eventually to find their way to the United States and Canada.

The peasant revolts of the Middle Ages cannot all be said to be entirely libertarian. They called for a freeing of feudal ties and rejected the new serfdom being imposed on them by the nobility in the form of heavy taxes. They appealed to their traditional rights under 'common law', but also wanted to become free labourers. The millenarian sects which emerged often channelled their discontent and aspirations, looking to divine law to replace man-made law. They rejected the claims of the upholders of political power as well as the ordinances of the moribund Church. The more extreme sects, like the Brethren of the Free Spirit, believed that once united with God, no law, divine or temporal, applied, and the individual could do what he or she would. While this celebration of freedom anticipates anarchism, in practice many of the Spiritualists were libertines who despised and exploited those who were not in 'a state of grace' like them.

The same ambivalence is to be found in the various millenarian attempts to realize heaven on earth. The Taborites came nearest to establishing an anarcho-communist order, but their communism did not go far beyond consumption and they were reduced to taking from their neighbours. The Anabaptists in Münster went farther in their communism, but ended up establishing a regime of terror. And while subsequent Anabaptists became pacifist, their communities were in many ways intolerant. Like Christianity itself, the legacy of the revolutionary millenarians and mystical anarchists of the Middle Ages is mixed.

The English Revolution

WHILE THE GREAT MEDIEVAL rebellions clearly had libertarian and egalitarian aspirations, they took place within a world view which gave little importance to the individual. Every person had his or her allotted place in a hierarchical society which existed within a great Chain of Being which descended from God. The king was seen as God's representative on earth, and ruled by divine right. The community of peasants was based on mutual aid and shaped by custom, but they allowed little room for nonconformity or autonomy. Even the medieval cities with their guilds celebrated by Kropotkin had strict rules and codes of conduct. It was only with the Reformation and Renaissance in Europe that the individual was considered to be an autonomous person with a right of private judgement.

In the Civil War and Revolution in England in the seventeenth century, this new sense of the rights of the individual was added to the old demands for economic security and freedom from tyranny. For the first time, a recognizably anarchist sensibility can be discerned.

Just as in the periods of social unrest in the Middle Ages, millenarian sects came to the fore during the turmoil of the English Revolution. There was even a hectic if short-lived revival of the 'Free Spirit' amongst groups known as the Diggers and the Ranters who formed the extreme left wing of the republican movement. Unlike the constitutionalist Levellers who accepted the sanctity of private property and retained a faith in Parliament, they claimed they were True Levellers and demanded economic as well as political equality.[1] There had been communist theories before, but the Digger spokesman Gerrard Winstanley was the first to assert clearly that 'there cannot be a universal liberty till this universal community is established'.[2] They understand the crucial point that State power is intimately linked to the system of property.

The English Revolution was a time when it seemed possible to turn the world upside down, not only overthrow the existing State and Church but to end the Protestant ethic with its stress on work, asceticism and discipline. Winstanley and the Diggers were convinced that 'the present state of the old world is running up like parchment in the fire, and wearing away'.[3] There was a new mobility and freedom: 'masterless men', a hitherto unthinkable concept, stalked the land calling for the abolition of all masters;

even some husbandless women were claiming the right to choose whom to kiss. They happily combined the myth of an equal society in the Garden of Eden before the Fall with the myth of Anglo-Saxon freedom before the Norman Yoke. As Christopher Hill has pointed out, there was a remarkable liberation of energy during the English Revolution: 'Men felt free: free from hell, free from priests, free from fear of worldly authorities, free from the blind forces of nature, free from magic.'[4]

Beneath the surface stability of rural England at the time, there was a seething underground of forest squatters and itinerant labourers and vagabonds. Many travellers went from city to city and congregated in London. These masterless men and women prized independence more than security, freedom more than comfort. They were like the beggars romanticized in Richard Brome's *A Joviall Crew* (1641) who have an authentic anarchist ring about them:

> The only freemen of a common-wealth;
> Free above scot-free; that observe no law,
> Obey no governor, use no religion,
> But what they draw from their own ancient custom
> Or constitute themselves.[5]

It was from their ranks that the supporters of the Diggers and Ranters emerged.

The Diggers, inspired by Gerrard Winstanley, tried to set up a colony on wasteland on St George's Hill near Walton-on-Thames in Surrey in April 1649. They declared in their manifesto *The True Levellers' Standard Advanced*: 'We may work in righteousness and lay the foundation of making the earth a common treasury for all.'[6] There were initially about forty people. They came in peace, dug up and manured the wasteland and planted beans, wheat, rye, parsnips and carrots. Winstanley prophesized that their numbers would soon swell to thousands.

Despite their peaceful and productive husbandry, not only the local clergy, landlords, and magistrates harassed them but also the neighbouring freeholders. Their seedlings were trampled on, their tools were taken away, their crude huts pulled down. Yet they persevered for almost exactly a year. They were summoned before General Fairfax to explain themselves and a band of troops was sent to intimidate them. In a sense, Cromwell was right to see their experiment as profoundly subversive for the motley band of Diggers threatened the very foundations of his totalitarian rule. Winstanley after all had warned in *A Watch-Word to the City of London* (1649) that 'All men have stood for freedom ... For freedom is the man that will turn the world upside down, therefore no wonder he hath enemies.'[7]

It was exhaustion from continued harassment which finally ground the

Diggers down on St George's Hill (or rather George's Hill, as they called it, for the radical Protestant tradition rejected saints). It seems likely however that they were only the tip of the iceberg of True Levellerism. But while there were many more experiments throughout the Home Counties, none survived much later than 1650.[8]

Winstanley more than any other gave theoretical form to the Diggers' aspirations, and the Diggers in turn spoke 'for and in the behalf of all the poor oppressed people of England and the whole world'.[9] The son of a Wigan mercer, Winstanley had failed in the cloth trade in London. He was then obliged to become a hired labourer. He first began writing mystical religious pamphlets but rapidly moved from mysticism to a system of progressive and democratic rationalism. Like other radicals of his day, he expressed his social aspirations in religious terms and in a vigorous vernacular prose. Christ for him was a symbol of liberty: 'True freedom', he wrote, 'lies in the community in spirit and community in the earthly treasury, and this is Christ the true man-child spread abroad in the creation, restoring all things into himself.'[10]

Like the adepts of the Free Spirit before him, and like Tolstoy after him, Winstanley believed that God is not a personal deity or Supreme Being but a 'spirit that dwells in all mankind'. He identified God with Reason and Reason with the law of the universe: it is 'Reason that governs the whole Creation' and 'the spirit that will purge mankind is pure reason'.[11] Every person subject to Reason becomes the Son of God. They are no longer ruled from without but from within, by their conscience, love or reason. As Winstanley wrote in the *True Levellers' Standard*, 'the flesh of man being subject to reason, his maker, hath him to be his teacher and ruler within himself, therefore needs not run abroad after any teacher and ruler without him'.[12] It is the 'ruling and teaching power without [that] doth dam up the spirit of peace and liberty, first within the heart, by filling it with slavish fears of others; secondly without, by giving the bodies of one to be imprisoned, pounished and oppressed by the outward power of another'.[13] This is the key to Winstanley's anarchism: external government is no longer necessary if people govern themselves according to their God-given reason.

Impressed by the interdependence of all human beings, Winstanley concluded that reason operates in society as a principle of order for the common preservation of humanity and that the government of rational beings is therefore superfluous. It is private property, not unruly human nature, which is the principal source of social conflict. From these premisses Winstanley in his early pamphlets attacked the social and political order and advocated an anarchist form of communist society, without the State, army and law.[14]

In his *The New Law of Righteousness* (1649), issued two months before the setting up of the colony on George's Hill, Winstanley recognized the close link between property and government: 'buying and selling earth from one particular hand to another saying this is mine, upholding this propriety by a law of government of his own making thereby restraining other fellow creatures from seeking nourishment from their mother earth'.[15] He also realized that once men gain power, they intensify exploitation and oppression:

> everyone that gets an authority into his hands tyrannizes over others; as many husbands, parents, masters, magistrates, that live after the flesh do carry themselves like oppressing lords over such as are under them, not knowing that their wives, children, servants, subjects are their fellow creatures, and hath an equal privilege to share them in the blessing of liberty.[16]

Once established, the owners of property maintain their domination by government and law:

> Let all men say what they will, so long as such are Rulers as call the Land theirs, upholding this particular propriety of *Mine* and *Thine*, the common-people shall never have their liberty, nor the Land ever [be] freed from troubles, oppressions and complainings; by reason whereof the Creator of all things is continually provoked.[17]

It was clear to Winstanley that the State and its legal institutions existed in order to hold the lower classes in place. Winstanley at this stage suggested that the only solution would be to abolish private property and then government and church would become superfluous. Magistrates and lawyers would no longer be necessary where there was no buying and selling. There would be no need for a professional clergy if everyone was allowed to preach. The State, with its coercive apparatus of laws and prisons, would simply wither away: 'What need have we of imprisonment, whipping or hanging laws to bring one another into bondage?'[18] It is only covetousness, he argued, which made theft a sin. And he completely rejected capital punishment: since only God may give and take life, execution for murder would be murder. He looked forward to a time when 'the whole earth would be a common treasury', when people would help each other and find pleasure in making necessary things, and 'There shall be none lords over others, but everyone shall be a lord of himself, subject to the law of righteousness, reason and equity, which shall dwell and rule in him, which is the Lord.'[19]

Winstanley did not call for mass insurrection or the seizure of the lands of the rich. He was always opposed to violence, although he was not an absolute pacifist and advocated an extreme form of direct action. He estimated that between half and two-thirds of the country were wastelands which the poor could work together. He was prepared to eat his bread with the sweat of his brow and helped organize the mass squat on George's Hill. Out of the experience he wrote his famous *The Law of Freedom in a Platform, or True Magistracy Restored* (1652) which offered a plan to reorganize English society on the basis of a system of common ownership.

The work has been called by Christopher Hill 'a draft constitution for a communist commonwealth' but it appears more like a blueprint for a communist State.[20] In fact there are two clear phases to Winstanley's thought. In his early work, he depicted an anarchist society, but after the experience of the Diggers' colony at George's Hill he began to revise his views about the immediate possibility of a free society.[21]

In *The Law of Freedom in a Platform*, he thus offered a new and authoritarian version of communist society. His fundamental premisses were the same. He held firm to his belief in God as the principle of motion and interdependence in nature, and in the efficacy of love, reason and justice in human affairs. He continued to assert with his doctrine of inner light that human beings act rationally and in accordance with natural law. He saw the natural state of humanity to be a co-operative and united society held together by common preservation. Above all, he still celebrated freedom as the free development of every individual and saw it only possible where there was economic security: 'True freedom lies where a man receives his nourishment and preservation, and that is in the use of the earth'.[22]

But the experience of the Diggers' colony on George's Hill, especially of the Ranters within and the hostile freeholders without, made him have second thoughts about human nature. Man might be sociable and reasonable by nature, but in existing society he often appeared unruly and confused. Digger covetousness suggested to Winstanley the need for some form of external social control. Thus because 'transgression doth and may arise from ignorance and rude fancy in man', he now felt that law and government would be necessary in a commonwealth to regulate society.[23]

During the struggle to keep the colony on George's Hill together, Winstanley had already begun to argue that the Diggers were opposed to the government which locks up 'the treasures of the earth from the poor' and not against 'righteous government' as such.[24] Now he went so far as to assert 'Government is a wise and free ordering of the earth and the manners of mankind by observation of particular laws and rules, so that all the inhabitants may live peacefully in plenty and freedom in the land where they are born and bred.'[25] He further defended the need for law as 'a rule whereby man and other creatures are governed in their actions, for the preservation of the common peace'. An army, in the form of a popular militia would be needed to enforce the laws, to protect the community against the 'rudeness of the people' and 'to resist and destroy all who endeavour to keep up or bring in kingly bondage again'.[26]

Winstanley now proposed an annual parliament as the supreme governing body in the land and drew up a rigidly artificial code of laws. The subtitle of *The Law of Freedom* was 'True Magistrary Restored' and was dedicated to the arch-statist and general Oliver Cromwell because 'the power of the land [is] in your hand'.[27] He suggested that magistrates should be elected annually. All citizens had to work by law and only those who contributed to the common stock could benefit from it. The laws were based on the principle of revenge – 'an eye for eye' – although they were intended to be corrective rather than punitive. Sanctions would include whipping, forced labour and loss of civil rights. The death penalty was rehabilitated for murder, buying and selling, rape or following the trade of lawyer or parson. He upheld the authority of the father in the family and advocated 'overseers'(planners) to direct the economy and enforce the laws, and 'taskmasters' to reform criminals. While allowing complete freedom of religious belief and opinion, he called for compulsory and general education. Winstanley had come to believe that the people were not ready to be free and a long process of education and preparation was first necessary before they were capable of governing themselves.

At his lowest ebb, he now defines freedom in the narrow economic sense of a 'freeman' enjoying the fruits of his labours, being capable of choosing or being a representative, and having young men or maids to be his servants in his family. Liberty was no longer universal. Clearly, Winstanley's libertarian genius had left him after his exhausting experience of practical communism. If *The New Law of Righteousness* is one of the first great anarchist texts, *The Law of Freedom* for all its rugged language reads like a proto-Marxist tract. Hill has suggested that it was a 'possibilist' document dedicated to Cromwell in the hope that he would implement its suggestions, but it seems unlikely that Winstanley could seriously believe that Cromwell would be converted to the cause of the true Levellers.[28]

Winstanley wrote nothing more after his communist utopia disintegrated, and he disappeared into obscurity; he seems to have become a prosperous farmer and possibly a Quaker. The Ranter Lawrence Clarkson accused him later of misusing his Reason to hold sway over others and to win personal fame: 'There was self-love and vainglory in his heart.' Clarkson also lamented Winstanley's 'most shameful retreat from George's-hill with a spirit of pretended universality, to become a mere tithe-gatherer of prosperity'.[29]

The libertarian communism of Winstanley and the Diggers was lost on the early anarchist and socialist movement. William Godwin, whose rationalist scheme of philosophical anarchism so closely resembles Winstanley's, dismissed the doctrines of Winstanley and the Diggers as 'scarcely indeed worthy to be recorded' in his mammoth *History of the Commonwealth of England* (1824–8).[30] It was only towards the end of the nineteenth century that socialists rediscovered him, and only this century that the Diggers have been acknowledged as 'the earliest recognizably anarchistic movement'.[31]

It was the Ranters, whom Winstanley despised, who proved the most consistent libertarians and the true heirs of the Heresy of the Free Spirit. They are the most anarchistic individuals to emerge in the English Revolution. As antinomians, they sought total emancipation from all laws and rules, and advocated free love. They attacked private property and called for its abolition, and rejected all forms of government, whether ecclesiastical or civil. They hoped humanity would be returned to its original state where there would be no private property, class distinctions or human authority.

Because of their persecution from all sides, many Ranters adopted a private language and carried on a clandestine propaganda. They formed part of the 'lunatic fringe' in the English Revolution, and were quite happy to play out their radical madness in the darkness of Cromwellian sanity. They emerged after the defeat of the Levellers at Burford in 1649 which put an end to the most serious threat to Cromwell's rule from the Left. The most famous amongst the Ranters were Abiezer Coppe and Lawrence Clarkson, although Joseph Salmon and Jacob Bauthumely or Bottomley also left some writings.

The Ranters were often confused with the Quakers, and many may have crossed over from one group to the other. Both discarded outward forms of worship and believed that true religion was to be found in the 'indwelling spirit' or 'inner light' in the individual soul, and that the power of love would be enough to bring about a new era of peace and freedom. A contemporary, Thomas Collier, asserted that the doctrines of the Ranters and the Quakers were identical: 'no Christ but within; no Scripture to be a rule; no ordinances, no law but their lusts, not heven nor glory but here, no sin but what men fancied to be so.'[32]

Like the adepts of the Free Spirit, the Ranters adopted a kind of materialistic pantheism: God is essentially in every creature; all created things are united; there is neither heaven nor hell except in the human breast. A person with God could therefore commit no evil. Joseph Salmon, a former army officer, records how in a brief period of exaltation:

> I saw heaven opened unto me and the new Jerusalem (in its divine brightness and corruscent beauty) greeting my Soule by its humble and gentle discensions . . . I appeared to my selfe as one confounded

into the abyss of eternitie, nonentitized into the being of beings; my
Soule split, and emptied into the fountaine and ocean of divine fulness:
expired into the aspires of pure life.[33]

Most Quakers and Diggers, however, thought they were far too extreme
and turbulent. It was probably his experience of Ranters in the George's
Hill colony that led Winstanley to believe that some laws and rules were
necessary in his ideal commonwealth to deal with the idle and the 'self-
ended spirits'.[34] After meeting some of them in prison, the Quaker leader
George Fox complained that they claimed they were God and would 'rant,
and vapour, and blaspheme'. At one of his meetings, he found that they
were 'very rude, and sung, and whistled, and danced'.[35] William Penn
further asserted that the Ranter wing among the Quakers 'would have had
every man independent, that as he had the principle in himself, he should
only stand and fall to that, and nobody else'.[36] If the mainstream Quakers
were shocked then it is no wonder that the upright Dissenting divine
Richard Baxter should condemn their 'Cursed Doctrine of *Libertinism*'
which led them to assert that 'to the Pure all things are Pure, (even things
forbidden)'.[37]

It was their total amoralism which most shocked their contemporaries.
Lawrence Clarkson in his Ranter period believed that since all acts are
from God, there can be no sinful act before God. He affirmed 'there was
no sin, but as man esteemed it sin, and therefore none can be free from
sin till in purity it be acted as no sin, for I judged that pure to me, which
to a dark understanding was impure, for to the pure all things, yea all acts,
are pure.'[38] He recalled how he believed that 'God had made all things
good, so nothing evil but as man judged it; for I apprehended there was no
such thing as theft, cheat, or a lie, but as made it so: for if the creature had
brought this world into no propriety, as *Mine* and *Thine*, there had been no
such title as theft, cheat or a lie, for the prevention thereof *Everard* and
Gerrard Winstanley did dig up the Common.'[39] He argued moreover that
there was no evil in swearing, drunkenness, adultery and theft: 'sin hath
its conception only in the imagination'.[40] He advocated absolute self-
exaltation:

> Behold, the King of glory is come
> T' reduce God, and Devil to their Doom;
> For both of them are servants unto Me
> That lives, and rules in perfect Majesty . . .[41]

Clarkson joined a Ranter group called '*My one flesh*' who were the most
uncompromisingly antinomian sect, practising free love and revelling in
bouts of drinking and feasting.

The same anarcho-communistic attitudes found in the Free Spirit continue amongst the Ranters. They felt the earth was a treasury for all to enjoy and that they should have one purse. Abiezer Coppe declared: 'All things which God created are common!'[42] This extended not only to property but also to women. In Samuel Sheppard's *The Joviall Crew, or, The Devill turn'd Ranter* (1651), his intended satire has an authentic ring when he describes their communism:

> ... our women are all in common.
> We drink quite drunk together, share our Oaths,
> If one man's cloak be rent, all tear their Cloaths.

and their rebellious spirit:

> No hell we dread when we are dead
> No Gorgon nor no Fury:
> And while we live, wee'l drink and ****
> In spight of judge and jury.[43]

The Ranters in fact went beyond the Puritan sexual revolution which sought to replace property marriage by a monogamous partnership. Coppe declared 'give over thy stinking family duties', argued that fornication and adultery were no sin, and advocated a community of women.[44] The Ranters asserted the right of the natural man to behave naturally.

Without birth control, this call for freedom tended to be for men only. Nevertheless, many women, who had formed an important part of the Heresy of the Free Spirit, were quick to accept the arguments of the radicals who maintained that the soul knows no difference of sex. The Quaker George Fox asked: 'May not the spirit of Christ speak in the female as well as in the male?'[45] Winstanley had insisted that 'Every man and woman shall have the free liberty to marry whom they love.'[46] The Ranters however advocated and practised free love and refused to be possessive; they were notorious for their celebration of wine, women and song. Coppe felt that sex had a divine power: 'by wanton kisses, kissing hath been confounded; and externall kisses, have been made the fiery chariots, to mount me swiftly into the bosom of him whom the soul loves, [his excellent Majesty, the King of glory].' [47]

The Ranters offered a unique opportunity for women to become independent and voluntary beings with a right to sensual pleasure. Not surprisingly, the Ranter teaching which seemed to offer such a lively and joyful affirmation of life and freedom attracted many women. A description of a female Ranter in the hostile tract *The Routing of the Ranters* (1650) conjures up wonderfully their Dionysian exuberance:

she speaks highly in commendation of those husbands that give liberty
to their wives, and will freely give consent that she should associate
her self with any other of her fellow creatures, which she shall make
choice of; she commends the Organ, Viol, Symbal and Tonges in
Charterhouse-Lane to be heavenly musick[;] she tosseth her glasses
freely, and concludeth there is no heaven but the pleasures she injoyeth
on earth, she is very familiar at the first sight, and danceth the Canaries
at the sound of a hornpipe.[48]

The most celebrated Ranter was Abiezer Coppe who was born in
Warwick in 1619. He left university at the outbreak of the Civil War and
became an Anabaptist preacher in the Warwick area. He felt he was at one
with humanity, especially the wretched and the poor. He recounts how he
once met a strange, deformed man on the road, and his conscience – the
'wel-favoured harlot' – tempted him to give this man all he had, take off his
hat and bow seven times to the beggar. Coppe was no elitist, and felt the
greatest privilege was to be able to give and to share.

His first important work *Some Sweet Sips of Some Spirituall Wine* (1649)
was extremely critical of formal Christianity. But it was *A Fiery Flying Roll*
(bound together with *A Second Fiery Flying Roule*), dated 1649 but published
in 1650, within a year of the execution of the king, which brought him
notoriety. Subtitled 'A Word from the Lord to all the Great Ones of the
Earth', in it Coppe not only attacked organized religion but presented a
vision of a purged society in which property was to be held in common.
Where the Levellers had excluded servants and others from their notion of
equality, Coppe extended it to embrace all men and women. Like the
Diggers, he also advocated a form of voluntary communism which echoes
the early Apostolic Church and the visions of John Ball: 'give, give, give,
give up your houses, horses, goods, gold, Lands, give up, account nothing
your own, have ALL THINGS common'.[49]

Like most Ranters, Coppe was a pacifist, rejecting 'sword levelling, or
digging-levelling'.[50] He insists that he never drew a sword or shed one drop
of blood: 'we (holily) scorne to fight for any thing; we had as live be dead
drunk every day of the weeke, and lye with whores i'th market place, and
account these as good actions as taking the poor abused, enslived plough-
mans money from him.'[51] Nevertheless, he warned the wealthy and
powerful: 'Kings, Princes, Lords, great ones, must bow to the poorest
Peasants; rich men must stoop to poor rogues, or else they'l rue for it.'[52]
He was adamant that it was necessary to chop at one blow 'the neck of
horrid pride, murder, malice and tyranny, &c.' so that 'parity, equality,
community' might bring about on earth 'universall love, universall peace,
and perfect freedome'.[53] Coppe joined a group of Ranters who believed
that all humanity was one and that we should recognize our brotherhood

and sisterhood. He joyously declared the death of sin and called for a life beyond good and evil: 'Be no longer so horridly, hellishly, impudently, arrogantly wicked, as to judge what is sinne, what not . . . sinne and trangression is finisht, its a meere riddle.'[54]

Coppe was not content to preach merely but turned himself into a surrealistic work of art. He became a master of happenings. In London, he would charge at carriages of the great, gnashing his teeth and proclaiming the day of the Lord had come. He wanted to make his listeners' ears 'tingle'. But it was always with a subversive aim: ' I am confounding, plaguing, tormenting nice, demure, barren *Mical* with *Davids* unseemly carriage, by skipping, leaping, dancing like one of the fools; vile, base fellowes, shamelessely, basely, and uncovered too, before handmaids.'[55] His supreme confidence was based on his conviction that his message came from 'My most Excellent Majesty [in me] who is universall love, and whose service is perfect freedome'.[56]

It was all too much for the government and the Protestant Establishment. It was not enough merely to dismiss Coppe as mad; he and his fellow Ranters posed a real threat to Cromwell's rule. The publication of the *Fiery Flying Rolls* prompted the government to pass an Act of Parliament against 'Atheistical, Blasphemous and Execrable Opinions'. They were condemned by Parliament to be publicly burned. Coppe was arrested and imprisoned in Newgate prison. When brought before the Committees of Examination, he apparently feigned madness, talking to himself, and 'throwing nut-shells and other things about the room'.[57] Obliged to recant he issued in 1651 *A Remonstrance of the sincere and zealous Protestation* and *Copps Return to the wayes of Truth*. Written in his best ranting manner, Coppe replied to his accusations, although he remained true to his social message.[58] The Wings of the Fiery Flying Roll were not entirely clipped. While denying the belief that there is no sin, he declares that all men are equally sinful in the eyes of God. Again, he reasserts that he will call nothing he has his own: 'As for community, I own none but that Apostolical, saint-like Community, spoken of in the Scriptures . . . I own none other, long for none other, but the glorious (Rom. 8) liberty of the Sons of God. Which God will hasten in its time.'[59]

For all their enthusiasm and originality, the Ranters never developed into a coherent or organized movement. They mainly formed loose associations or affinity groups, probably with a dozen or score of people. They drew support mainly from the lower strata of the urban poor who shared the aspirations of John Ball. The Ranters became quite numerous for a time, especially in London, and at their height there was no part of England which did not feel their influence. But their leaders were picked off in 1650 and 1651; five years later they were in serious decline. But their influence lingered on and was still strong enough in 1676 for the respectable Quaker Robert Barclay to publish an attack on *The Anarchy of the Ranters and other Libertines*. Fox also reported that Ranters were at work in New England in 1668.

The exact nature and influence of the Ranters is still open to dispute. The term 'Ranter' like anarchist today was often used in a pejorative way to describe anyone with extreme or dangerous opinions; Ranterism came to represent 'any anti-social manifestations of the light within'.[60] To a large extent, the image of the Ranter as an immoral rascal was developed by sensationalist pamphleteers working on behalf of established Protestantism who wanted to suppress its 'lunatic fringe'. In a similar vein, the Marxist historian A. L. Morton called them 'confused mystical anarchists' who drew support from 'the defeated and declassed' groups after Cromwell had crushed the Levellers.[61] But men like Coppe and Clarkson were far from despairing and for a time after the execution of the king it seemed possible in England that true levelling could lead to a genuine commonwealth of free and equal individuals. In the event, as in so many later revolutions, the military dictator Cromwell crushed the extreme left which had helped to bring him to power.

For all their mystical language, the Ranters expressed a wonderful sense of exuberant irreverence and earthy nonconformity. They are not only a link in the chain that runs between Joachim of Fiore and William Blake, but from peasant communism to modern anarcho-communism. They looked back to the Brotherhood of the Free Spirit of the Middle Ages and anticipated the counter-culture of this century.

The French Renaissance and Enlightenment

ONE OF THE CONSEQUENCES of the Renaissance, with its interest in antiquity, and the Reformation, with its stress on the right to private judgement, was a revival of anti-authoritarian tendencies in secular matters. Of all the countries in Europe in the second half of the sixteenth century, it was France that produced the most powerful libertarian thinkers. This was doubtless a response to the centralizing tendencies of the French monarchy and the growth of a strong Nation-State.

François Rabelais

The most colourful and rumbustious French libertarian was the incomparable François Rabelais. An ex-Franciscan and Benedictine monk who practised and taught medicine, Rabelais came to hate monks and scholasticism. In his masterpiece *Gargantua and Pantagruel* (1532–64) he delighted in satirizing the religious, political, legal and social institutions and practices of sixteenth-century France. The work contains a wonderful mixture of bawdy humour, sharp satire and zest for life.

At the same time, there is a serious side to Rabelais. He adopted a form of naturalistic optimism which led him to anarchist conclusions. He believed that human nature is fundamentally good and only corrupted by our education and environment. He therefore called for the full development of our faculties 'because free people, well-born and well-educated, keeping good company, have by nature an instinct and incentive which always encourage them to virtuous acts, and hold them back from vice.'[1] It follows that if people are left to themselves their 'honour' or moral sense is sufficient to govern their behaviour without the need for any external rules or laws.

Rabelais gave flesh and blood to these abstract principles in Book I of *Gargantua and Pantagruel* (1534) where he describes the founding of the abbey of Thélème. Gargantua gives the abbey to Friar John (Frère Jean des Entommeures: Friar John of the Hearty Eaters) for his help in the war against the power-mad despot Picrochole, who has a 'bitter bile' (the meaning of his name in Greek). Friar John has all the faults of monks but none of their vices. He is ignorant, dirty and gluttonous, but also brave, frank and lusty. His abbey is built like a magnificent and luxurious country house without walls, the very opposite of a convent or monastery. Its name Thélème in Greek means 'will' or 'pleasure'. The gifted and well-bred members are free to leave whenever they choose. There is no chastity, poverty and obedience: they can marry, be rich, and live in perfect freedom. They have no need for laws and lawyers, politics, kings and princes, religion, preachers and monks, money and usurers. All their life is spent 'not in laws, statutes or rules, but according to their own free will and pleasure'. The only rule is 'fais ce que voudras!' (Do what you will!).

Rabelais's ideal commonwealth anticipates the exuberant licence of Fourier's phalansteries in which the satisfaction of all desire is considered positive and healthy. But it is primarily a utopia for the new aristocrats of the Renaissance like Rabelais himself who looked to a society based on intelligence and knowledge rather than on power and wealth. His rebellion remains an individual and imaginative one and does not translate itself into action against the structure of society. While he opposed tyranny in all its forms, in the real world Rabelais hoped for nothing more than a peaceful and benevolent monarchy. He might have called for the freedom of noble men and women in his chivalric utopia, but it was not until the eighteenth century that *philosophes* asserted the natural nobility of all free men and women. Nevertheless, Rabelais, for his exuberant and joyful celebration of freedom, deserves an honourable mention in any history of libertarian thought.

Etienne de la Boétie

Unknown to Rabelais, there was another writer in France at the same time asking why free-born people should so readily accept their servitude. His name was Etienne de la Boétie, and he was born in 1530, the son of a judge with powerful connections in Church and State. He went on to study law and became a counsellor in the Bordeaux *parliament* (assembly of lawyers) where he called for religious toleration for the persecuted Protestant Huguenots. A poet and classical scholar, he also was a friend of the great humanist Montaigne. In his short life, la Boétie appeared a devout member of the Catholic Church and a loyal subject to the king but as young man he wrote sometime between 1552 and 1553 a *Discours de la servitude volontaire*, one of the great libertarian classics. He undoubtedly admired all his life those classical writers who had defended liberty in ancient Greece and Rome. After his death in 1563, Montaigne, who was his literary executor, was too prudent and timid to publish the manuscript, although he admitted it was written 'in honour of liberty against tyrants'. He dismissed it as a youthful folly, a mere literary exercise, yet he admitted that la Boétie had believed in every word of it and would have preferred to be born in the liberty of Venice than in France.

The first full version of the essay appeared in Holland in 1576 and was used as propaganda by the Huguenots against the Catholic regime. It went largely unnoticed until the eighteenth century when it was read by Rousseau and reprinted at the beginning of the French Revolution. Since then it has been recognized as a minor classic of political theory for asking the fundamental question of political obligation: why should people submit to political authority or government?

La Boétie's answer contains not only a powerful defence of freedom but his bold reasoning led him to conclude that there is no need for government at all. It is only necessary for humanity to wish that government would disappear in order for them to find themselves free and happy once again. People however choose to be voluntary slaves: 'liberty alone men do not want, not for any other reason, it seems, except that if they wanted it, they would have it. It is as if they refuse to have this fine acquisition, only because it is too easy to obtain.'[2]

Although the style is rhetorical and repetitive, it is possible to discern three stages in la Boétie's argument. In the first part he argues that government exists because people let themselves be governed, and dissolves when obedience ends. In the next part he asserts that liberty is a natural instinct and a goal, and slavery is not a law of nature but merely a force of habit. Finally, it is shown that government is maintained by those who have an interest in its rule.

La Boétie bases his case on natural right theory. He believes that 'if we lived with the rights that nature has given us and with the lessons it teaches us, we would naturally obey our parents, be subjects to reason, and serfs of nobody'.[3] There is simply no point discussing whether liberty is natural since it is self-evident; one cannot keep anyone in servitude without harming them. This is even true of animals, whether they be elephants or horses.

Although he does not accept the social contract theory of government, he suggests that people do behave as if there were a 'contract' to obey their rulers. But since their obedience is voluntary, they are equally able to act as if there were no contract, and thus disobey their rulers. The crucial point is that the people are the source of all political power, and they should choose to allocate this power to rulers or to remove it as they see fit. As such, la Boétie clarifies the nature of political obligation and develops the notion of popular sovereignty.

In his essay, he celebrates that 'liberty which is always such a pleasant and great good, that once lost, all evils follow, and even the goods which remain after it, lose entirely their taste and savour, corrupted by servitude'.[4] He then condemns tyrants and bad princes in swelling rhetoric full of classical allusions. In his view there are three types of tyrant: those who possess a kingdom through the choice of the people; those by force of arms; and those by hereditary succession. Although he thinks the first kind of tyrant is the most bearable, he nevertheless believes that all three types have the same effect: they swallow people up and hold them in servitude. And once enslaved, people forget their freedom so quickly and profoundly that 'it seems impossible that they will awake and have it back, serving so freely and gladly that one would say, to see them, that they have not lost their liberty, but won their servitude'.[5]

The principal reason for this voluntary servitude according to la Boétie is custom: 'the first reason why men serve voluntarily is because they are born serfs and are brought up as such.'[6] The support and foundation of tyranny moreover is not the force of arms but rather the self-interest of a group of people who find domination profitable: 'they want to serve in order to have goods'.[7] The result is that 'these wretches see the treasures of the tyrant shine and look in amazement at the rays of his boldness; and, attracted by this light, they draw near, and do not see that they put themselves in the flame which can only burn them.'[8] But there is a way out. Just as people give power to their rulers, they can take it back. Although he does not say as much, the whole drift of la Boétie's essay is to imply the need for political disobedience.[9]

Not long after the publication of Machiavelli's handbook for unscrupulous statecraft *The Prince* (1532), la Boétie brilliantly demonstrated the economic and psychological grounds for voluntary servitude. Human beings are born free and yet put chains on themselves and their children. They could cast them off if they so wished, but they do not. As a result, voluntary slaves make more tyrants in the world than tyrants make slaves. Montaigne rightly recognized the subversive message of la Boétie's essay – and wrongly tried to suppress it.

This highly original work does not easily fit into any one tradition of political thought. Its analysis of political power lay the groundwork for the concept of civil disobedience, and as such it can take an honoured place within the pacifist tradition. Emerson knew of it and wrote a poem to its author. Tolstoy was the first important anarchist to recognize the importance of the essay and translated it into Russian. Max Nettlau is correct to include la Boétie in his list of early thinkers who envisaged a society without laws and government.[10] Since then the anarchists Gustav Landauer, Rudolf Rocker, Bart de Ligt, and Nicolas Walter have all recognized its honourable place within any history of anarchist thought. More recently, it has also appealed to libertarians of the Right like Murray N. Rothbard who appreciate its emphasis on personal initiative and improvement.[11] There can be no doubt that the *Discours de la servitude volontaire* reveals a profound anarchist sensibility and orientation.

Gabriel de Foigny

In France in the seventeenth century, the process of creating a nation out of the many regional communities gathered momentum. Louis XIV in particular struggled to unite the country in a strongly centralized State symbolized in the person of the monarch. He proudly announced: '*L'État, c'est moi*'. But not all were impressed by his passion for luxury and war which led to the neglect of agriculture and the misery and ignorance of the peasants.

Since it was too dangerous to express radical views directly, libertarian thinkers used the device of an imaginary voyage to a utopia to criticize existing society and suggest alternative institutions and practices. Gabriel de Foigny for one knew only too well how difficult it was to entertain radical ideas and to act independently. Born in Ardennes in 1630, he entered a monastery of the Order of the Cordeliers (Franciscans) and became a Catholic preacher. His unruly behaviour however led him to be unfrocked. He changed his religion and moved to Calvinist Geneva, but again he soon fell into difficulties with the authorities because of his penchant for girls and wine. On one occasion, he is said to have vomited in front of the altar while taking the service in a Temple. With little chance of becoming a solid French or Swiss citizen, he published anonymously in 1676 *Les Aventures de Jacques Sadeur dans la découverte de la Terre Australe*, translated in a truncated version in 1693 as *A New Discovery of Terra Incognita Australis*. The work landed him in jail, although he was eventually released on indefinite bail.

It is easy to see why the authorities of Geneva should be disturbed. In his utopia set in Australia, Foigny attacks all the foundations of religion. Although the inhabitants believe in God, they never mention him and spend their time in meditation rather than prayer. They are born free, reasonable and good and have as little need for religion as they do for government. They have no written laws and no rulers. Private property does not exist. Even sex amongst the 'hermaphrodite' Australians is no longer necessary and the family has no role. The imaginary traveller Jacques Sadeur, a hermaphrodite himself, never found out how they reproduced but reports:

> I have only observed, that they loved one another with a cordial love, and that they never loved any one more than another. I can affirm I neither saw quarrel nor animosity amongst them. They know not how to distinguish between mine and thine and there is more perfect sin-

cerity and disinterestment amongst them than exist between men and women in Europe.[12]

Education takes place in communal houses like monasteries from the age of two to thirty-five. They spend the first part of each day at school or in scientific research, the second part gardening, and the third part in public exercise. Since they only eat fruit, they have no need for agriculture beyond gardening, and since they wear no clothes and have little furniture there is no need for industry. The society is entirely egalitarian. As an Old Man explains to Jacques Sadeur: 'we make a profession of being all alike, our glory consists in being all alike, and to be dignified with the same care, and in the same manner.'[13]

But the most interesting thing about Foigny is that he is the first utopian to conceive of a society without government. The Old Man expounds what might be called a philosophy of anarchism:

> It was the Nature of Man to be born, and live free, and that therefore he could not be subjected without being despoiled of his nature . . . The subjection of one man in another was a subjection of the human Nature, and making a man a sort of slave to himself, which slavery implied such a contradiction and violence as was impossible to conceive. He added that the essence of man consisting in liberty, it would not be taken away without destroying him . . . This does not signify that he does not often do what others desire, but he does not do so because others compel or command him. The word of commandment is odious to him, he does what his reason dictates him to do; his reason is his law, his rule, his unique guide.[14]

These freedom-loving people have no central government and all the decisions about their lives are taken at the local assemblies of each district or neighbourhood. Each morning food is brought by the members of each district to the common storehouse when they meet for their morning conference. They are a peaceful people and never fight amongst each other, but they are ready to defend their country against foreign invasions. But even in war, they have no leaders or commanders and they take up positions without previous discussions. The order and harmony prevailing in their society results primarily from the 'Natural Light' of their reason: 'this adherence to strict reason, which unites them amongst themselves, carries them to what is good and just.'[15]

Foigny's Australians, with their commitment to reason, universal benevolence and perfect sincerity, anticipate Swift's Houyhnhnms in the fourth part of *Gulliver's Travels*; indeed, they are so close one wonders whether the Tory Dean was inspired by Jacques Sadeur's imaginary voyage. There is even a comparison at the end of Foigny's book between the virtue and reason of the Australians and our own Yahoo knowledge 'by the assistance of which we only live like beasts'.[16] Godwin too, if had discovered the work, would have been impressed by the Australians' practice of political justice in their society without government.

Fénelon

Another priest in France, though considerably more illustrious, used the device of the imaginary voyage to express his moral and political views. He was the Archbishop François de Salignac de La Mothe Fénelon (1651– 1715). He wrote the didactic novel *Télémaque* (1699) for his pupil, the duc de Bourgogne, grandson of Louis XIV, and the future king. Ostensibly relating to the adventures of Telemachus, the son of Ulysses, it uses an imaginative narrative full of classical mythology as an excuse to discuss politics, morals, education and religion.

There are two utopias embedded in the work, the first in the country of La Bétique, and the second in the city of Salente. In the idyllic country of La Bétique the sun always shines, and there is a natural abundance, but the citizens hold their goods in common and lead simple lives. It is puritanical compared to Rabelais' Abbey of Thélème; the natives are against vain riches and deceitful pleasures. At the same time, they live in a state of libertarian and pacifist communism and do not want to extend their dominion. They show no signs of pride, haughtiness or bad faith.

In the city of Salente, Telemachus's friend Mentor is asked to mend the administration. He does this by establishing a reign of frugal austerity: gold, foreign merchandise, even effeminate music, are banished. The puritanical tendency in Fénelon also comes to the fore and he argues that well-being is to be achieved by the restriction not the satisfaction of desires: 'Deceptive riches had impoverished them, and they became effectively rich in proportion as they had the courage to do without them.'[17]

No wonder Louis XIV was not amused; Fénelon lost favour at court and was exiled to his diocese. But *Télémaque* proved the model of many a religious and political dissertation disguised as a novel written by the *philosophes* in the following century. In addition, it profoundly influenced the young Godwin who argued in his *Enquiry concerning Political Justice* (1793) that it is preferable to save a benevolent philosopher like Fénelon in a fire rather than his maid, even if she were one's own mother, because of his superior ability to contribute to human happiness.

The Enlightenment

In the work of Foigny and Fénelon we can see the kind of audacious thinking which was to inspire the French Enlightenment of the eighteenth century. After Descartes had established his method of systematic doubt and rational enquiry, the *philosophes* went out of their way to challenge received ideas and prejudices and to analyse society in the light of reason. They took nature as their yardstick and reason as their guide.

Central to the world-view of the Enlightenment was a belief in the perfectibility of man. Man is not irretrievably fallen in a state of sin, the *philosophes* argued, but largely the product of his circumstances. If you change his circumstances, than you can change his conduct. And the best way to achieve that is through enlightenment and education. Man is therefore perfectible, or at least susceptible to continual improvement. History moreover shows that progress has taken place in the past, and there is no good reason to think that it should not so continue in the future.

But while all the *philosophes* believed in the progressive nature of man, they did not all reach anarchist conclusions. Voltaire introduced the liberal ideas of Locke into France in the eighteenth century and like him thought government necessary to protect life and property. He did not go beyond criticizing individual abuses and monarchical despotism. In public Diderot advocated with Voltaire a constitutional monarchy as long as the king made a social contract with the people, and only in private contemplated a society without government and law. While Rousseau was a product of the Enlightenment, he came to question the prevailing confidence in reason and science to bring about social and moral progress. People, he thought, are naturally good and have become depraved by existing institutions. But he did not call like later anarchists for the abolition of all such institutions but their replacement by a new social contract. Only less well-known thinkers like Jean Meslier and Morelly carried the *philosophes*' criticism of the existing regime to the borders of anarchism. Their works however were known only to a few and they did not exert much influence in their day.

Jean Meslier

Little is known of Jean Meslier except that he was a country priest of Étre-pigny in Champagne. He did not dare publish his atheistic and revolutionary beliefs in his own lifetime but wrote them down in a *Testament* in the 1720s for the edification of his parishioners after his death in 1729. Although some manuscript versions circulated in Paris in the middle of the century, Voltaire and Holbach were the first to publish a truncated version which only included his anti-clerical sentiments. The full text did not appear until 1864.

Written in an angry, unpolished and convoluted style, the argument of Meslier's *Testament* are set out in a series of 'proofs'. The title however gives the essence of his message: 'Memoirs of the thoughts and sentiments of Jean Meslier concerning part of the errors and false conduct and government of mankind, in which can be seen clear and evident demonstrations of the vanity and falseness of all divinities and religions . . .'

The village *curé* in fact reached the shattering conclusion that all religions are not only false but their practices and institutions are positively harmful to the well-being of humanity. In the name of reason and nature, he rejected the claims of Christianity and theism. God simply does not exist and no soul lives on after death. According to Meslier, the idea of the Fall of Man bringing about all the afflictions of this life simply because of a mild act of disobedience in eating some apple is quite incomprehensible.

Meslier has been called 'more of an anarchist than an atheist'.[18] He certainly thought that man is naturally drawn to appreciate 'peace, kindness, equity, truth and justice' and to abhor 'troubles and dissension, the malice of deceit, injustice, imposture and tyranny'.[19] But why, he asked, had the desire for happiness common to every human heart been frustrated? It was simply because some people were ambitious to command and others to earn a reputation for sanctity. As a result, two forces had come into being, one political and the other religious. When they made a pact between themselves the fate of the common people was sealed. The source of existing ills was not therefore to be found in the Fall of Man, but rather in the 'detestable political doctrine' of Church and State:

> for some wishing unjustly to dominate their fellows, and others wishing to acquire some empty reputation of holiness and sometimes even of divinity; both parties have cleverly made use, not only of force and violence, but also of all sorts of tricks and artifices to lead the peoples astray, in order to achieve their ends more easily . . . and by these means, one party has made itself honoured and respected or even adored as divinities . . . and the members of the other party have made themselves rich, powerful and formidable in the world, and both parties being, by these kinds of artifices, rendered rich enough, powerful enough, respected or formidable enough to make themselves feared or obeyed, they have openly and tyrannically subjected their fellows to their laws.[20]

To end this state of affairs, Meslier calls on the poor and oppressed to exclude both ecclesiastical and political parties from society so that they can live in peace and virtue once again. He insists that the salvation of the common people lies in their own hands. Only a violent social revolution could eradicate evil from the face of the earth: 'Let all the great ones of the earth and all the nobles hang and strangle themselves with the priests' guts, the great men and nobles who trample on the poor people and torment them and make them miserable.'[21]

Morelly

Meslier was not the only one to entertain such visionary thoughts. One Morelly, whose exact identity is still not known, wrote an allegorical poem called the *Basiliade* in 1753 which depicted an ideal society organized by Adam and Eve who are prudent enough not to commit any errors before founding a family. Morelly's *Code de la nature*, which appeared anonymously in 1755, elaborates the social theory implicit in the first work in an uneven and turgid style. The first three sections attack the existing moral and political system, with its unequal property relations and class divisions, and the fourth section presents Morelly's own ideal pattern of laws.

Morelly's starting-point is nature which is a constant moral order governed by eternal laws. Unfortunately, men are not content to follow the dictates of nature; hence, 'you will see quite clearly the simplest and most excellent lessons of Nature continually contradicted by everyday morals and politics.'[22] In particular, the system of private property has aggravated the unnatural 'desire to possess' which is the basis and vehicle of all the other vices.

But it need not always be like this. Man is not born vicious and wicked. He is naturally social and benevolent, but corrupted by the institutions surrounding him. God or rather Supreme Wisdom (Morelly is a deist, not an atheist like Meslier) has created in man a sense of self-interest (*amour propre*) in order to preserve his existence, but existing institutions transform it into vicious selfishness. However, man is also capable of *attraction morale*; since he cannot always satisfy his needs alone, he feels benevolent affection towards those who help him. The desire to be happy is fundamental and if 'you want to be happy, be benevolent'.[23]

It follows for Morelly that if people would only obey the laws of nature and return to their original integrity and values, then no artificial laws would be necessary. And if they replaced the existing system of private property with communal ownership, there would be little cause for vicious conduct since 'Where no property existed, none of its pernicious consequences could occur'.[24]

Nothing, he concluded in his proposed code of laws, should belong to anyone individually as his sole property except such things as he puts to his personal use, whether for his needs, his pleasure or his daily work. He expected every citizen to contribute his share to the commonweal according to his abilities and be maintained at the public expense. Like later anarchists,

Morelly felt that human beings are not lazy by nature, but are made so by social institutions.

By seeing private property rather than government as the main cause of evil, Morelly was a forerunner of communism. Moreover, he attempted to lay down in the fourth part of his *Code de la nature* a 'Model of Legislation conforming to the intentions of Nature', that is to say, laws of society which would correspond to natural laws. His proposed communist society was austere and authoritarian with strict education and compulsory labour and marriage. The family would be the base of a social hierarchy composed of tribes organized in cities and provinces. The administration of the economy would be merely a matter of accounting, with a minimal government period-ically rotated. There would be a strict overall plan and the only philosophy taught would support the laws. The result would be a 'very fine order'. Those who oppose that order would be punished, the worst offenders being isolated in caverns which eventually would become their tombs. He thought a transitional society of 'some severity' may be necessary to achieve com-munism.

Morelly inspired the egalitarian and communist wing of the French Revolution. Gracchius Babeuf, who led the 'Conspiracy of Equals' claimed that the author of the *Code de la nature* was the true leader of the conspiracy; both certainly confused authority with security. At the same time, Morelly's insistence that institutions must conform to the intentions of nature has an authentic libertarian ring about it. His interest in creating circumstances to encourage benevolence and to bring about happiness anticipates Charles Fourier. It was not without reason that Proudhon should praise his 'negation of government'.[25] Later anarcho-communists like Kropotkin drew more libertarian conclusions because they simply interpreted the lessons of nature in a different way.

Denis Diderot

The case of Denis Diderot is also somewhat curious. As co-editor of the *Encyclopédie ou dictionnaire raisonné des sciences, des arts et des métiers*, he shared the *philosophes'* confidence in gradual progress through the diffusion of practical and theoretical knowledge. By presenting knowledge as a coherent whole, the *Encyclopédie* became a fountain of radical and subversive thought.

In his practical politics, Diderot accepted the monarchy, but in a more enlightened form. In his essay *Autorité politique* (1751) he argued that the king should have a contract with the people, consult them continually, and govern in their interest. In his memoir for Catherine II, Empress of Russia, he further recommended nationalizing church property, providing free uni-versal education, and ensuring complete religious toleration. As a utilitarian, he argued that happiness is the only basis of all good legislation. Adopting Rousseau's notion of the general will, he maintained that the individual should bend to the interest of humanity as a whole.

Diderot was also an ambivalent thinker and could not always make up his mind on central philosophical issues. As a result, he felt most at ease in the dialectical genre of the dialogue which enabled him to destroy dogmatic opinion and encourage open discussion. He was strictly speaking a determinist and materialist but in his dialogue *Jacques le fataliste* (1796) found it difficult to accept the corollary of moral determinism with its rejection of responsibility. Jacques believes in fate but acts as if he were free. Again, Diderot sometimes felt that the animal instincts in man should be curbed, but more often than not he believed that the passions 'always inspire us rightly' and it is the mind which leads us astray.[26]

This theme runs through the story of *Le Neveu de Rameau* (written in 1762 but not published until 1823), a dialectical satire on contemporary society and conventional morality. Rameau's nephew is a musician and an amoral individualist who claims that happiness is living according to one's nature. He principally enjoys sensual pleasures and is insensitive to the 'charms of virtue'. He declares 'long live the wisdom of Solomon – drink good wine, blow yourself out with luscious food, have a tumble with lovely women, lie on soft beds. Apart from that the rest is vanity.'[27]

While drawn to such hedonism, Diderot still feels virtue brings its own reward. Like Morelly, he also hoped that man-made laws would mirror the laws of nature. The best legislation, he argued, conformed most closely to nature, and this is to be achieved not by 'opposing the passions of men, but on the contrary by encouraging and applying them to both public and private interest'.[28]

This was Diderot's public stance; in private, he entertained much more radical ideas. It was his belief that 'Nature gave no man the right to rule over others.' When he was offered, albeit as a party-joke, the opportunity to become a monarch and legislator, he refused. It so happened that for three years he found the bean in the traditional cake on Twelfth Night which according to French custom obliged him to present a code of laws. His initial response was to assert in a poem his wish to unite people, not divide them. He further expressed his love of liberty and called on others to feel the same:

> Divide and rule, the maxim is ancient,
> It's not mine; it was made by a tyrant.
> I love freedom, to unite you is my will
> And if I have one wish
> It's that everyone make their own.[29]

On winning the bean for the third successive year, Diderot decided to abdicate the kingly role once and for all. He renounced even the right to decree like Rabelais' wayward monk 'each should do what he wills'. With impeccable anarchist sentiments, he declared that he did not want to obey any law or make them for others:

> Never for the public's sake
> Has man been willing to surrender his rights!
> Nature has made neither servant nor master;
> I neither want to give nor receive laws![30]

In a short story called 'Conversation of a Father with His Children', Diderot makes the patriarch declare that 'no one is permitted to break the laws'. His son, the narrator, insists however that 'nature has made good laws for all eternity' and argues that one should follow the law of nature rather than man-made laws. He appeals to 'natural equity' as his guide in difficult moral problems. In the discussion that follows, the children rebel against paternal authority, and when the father breaks up the gathering his son asserts that 'there are no laws at all for the wise'.[31] Diderot, while seeing both sides of the argument, clearly sympathizes with the son. Moreover, he is prepared to extend moral and social freedom beyond the intellectual elite of his own circle.

In a more considered statement, Diderot, like Foigny and Swift, criticized existing European civilization by contrasting it with an imaginary society in the tropics. After Louis-Antoine de Bougainville had published in 1771 a description of his travels around the world, Diderot wrote a fictitious account of Bougainville's visit to Tahiti which he called *Supplément au voyage de Bougainville*. His bold reasoning led him to entertain anarchist ideas but his prudence held him back from publishing them. Just as Voltaire did not want to discuss the existence of God in front of the servants, so Diderot did not want his daughter to live out his daring moral speculations. His *Supplément* did not see the light of day until after the French Revolution in 1796.

Diderot not only used the 'primitive' paradise in the Pacific to attack Western civilization with its repressive religion and warring States but presented an anarchist society without government and law. His Tahitians, though noble, are not savages; they effectively condemn by contrast the hypocrisy and meanness of Christian civilization. They follow the 'pure instincts of nature', have no distinction between 'mine' and 'thine', and have no private property in land or women. They enjoy free love and have no words for fornication, incest and adultery. They have no idea of crime or sin or jealousy. Having few wants and living in a fertile land, they have reduced the sum of their labours to the minimum, because nothing seems more preferable to them than repose. The entire island seems like one large family with each hut like an apartment in a great house.

Although the Tahitians' wants are simple, it is not a simplicity imposed by necessity but a rational code of conduct. The Tahitian Orou in a talk with the visiting chaplain appeals to nature and reason and argues that the only moral rule is the 'general good' and 'particular utility'.[32] A love of liberty is their deepest feeling. But it does not extend to sexual licence; there is a strict taboo on intercourse before maturity to avoid unwanted babies.

In a dialogue between Bougainville and a Tahitian elder, the Old Man laments how the newly arrived Europeans have spoiled their happiness, created dissension and shame amongst the women, introduced disease, guilt, 'artificial needs' and 'imaginary virtues'.[33] His indignation is fired by Western greed and bellicosity, but above all by their repressive sexual code. In a discussion of the island society that follows, Diderot suggests that 'by basing morality on the eternal relations which subsist between men, religious law perhaps becomes superfluous, and civil law must only be the enunciation of the law of nature', adding that 'the Tahitian who scrupulously holds to the law of nature, [is] closer to good legislation than any civilized people'.[34] The whole dialogue is a celebration of the natural law and natural order as preferable to man-made law and civilized disorder. To the question whether it is necessary to civilize man or abandon him to his instinct, Diderot's spokesman replies:

> I appeal to all political, civil and religious institutions: examine them thoroughly, and if I am not mistaken you will find the human species bent from century to century under the yoke which a handful of knaves have sworn to impose on it. Beware of the person who comes to put things in order. To order things is always to make oneself master of others by disturbing them: and the people of Calabria are almost the only ones who have not yet had the flattery of legislators imposed on them.[35]

And asked whether the 'anarchy of Calabria' is agreeable, he is ready to wager that 'their barbarism is less vicious than our urbanity'.

Jean-Jacques Rousseau

If Diderot was cautious about publicizing his most radical views, Rousseau had no such qualms. He was, to boot, one of the most paradoxical writers of the eighteenth century. A product of the Enlightenment and a member of its party of *philosophes*, he remained an isolated figure and attacked some of its most fundamental premisses. While he used his own reason to magnificent effect, he declared 'the man who meditates is a depraved animal' and encouraged the cult of sensibility associated with Romanticism. He celebrated individuality and asserted his personal independence and yet hankered after authority. He appears as a great libertarian in his early writings only to call for a corporate State based on a totalitarian democracy in his later ones.

But this was not all. Although he was a righteous moralist who believed that conscience is a 'divine instinct', he gave his children away to the public orphanage. A lyrical advocate of natural religion, he changed his religious creed twice for political convenience. A great imaginative writer and powerful thinker, he was also the voice of Voltaire's *canaille* or mob.

Rousseau first came to prominence by winning the prize at the academy of Dijon in 1750 with *A Discourse on the Moral Effects of the Arts and Science*. It proved to be a thorough-going and hard-hitting critique of contemporary culture. But it is not an attack on all arts and sciences; if anything, it is a defence of virtue against useless knowledge. Rousseau criticizes the way the arts and sciences are misused by those in power to corrupt morals and taste, to encourage hypocrisy and to mislead people:

> so long as power alone is on one side, and knowledge and understanding alone on the other, the learned will seldom make great objects their study, princes will still more rarely do great actions, and the people will continue to be, as they are, mean, corrupt, and miserable.[36]

Nourished by luxury, idleness and ambition, intellectuals will inevitably corrupt the populace.

In his next work for the Dijon academy, *A Discourse on the Origin of Inequality* (1754), Rousseau developed his central theme of man's tragic departure from his essential nature. He sets out with the intention 'to distinguish properly between what is original and what is artificial in the actual nature of man' but made clear that he was offering only 'hypothetical reasonings' and 'conjectures', not historical facts.[37] Like Meslier and Morelly, he argues that man is naturally good but depraved by existing institutions. According to Rousseau, in his natural state man lived a solitary, independent and self-sufficient life. He was by nature gentle and compassionate, a purely instinctive creature devoid of intellectual and moral attributes. But man has two principles prior to reason, one which leads to self-preservation, and the other which makes him feel repugnance at the sight of another sensible being's suffering. It is this innate sense of compassion which supplies the place of 'laws, morals and virtues' in a state of nature.[38]

Above all, man is a free agent and perfectible, that is to say, he has the faculty of self-improvement. It is the latter which takes him out of his natural state. It produces in him his vices as well as his virtues and makes him at length 'a tyrant both over himself and over nature'. As human beings began to associate with each other to satisfy their wants, their natures further changed since the 'bonds of servitude are formed merely by the mutual dependence of men on one another'.[39] Co-operation sows the seed of man's downfall. The desire for self-preservation became transformed into *amour-propre*, a factitious feeling which leads each individual to make more of himself than of any other and fosters pride, ambition and competition. Thinking moreover only makes matters worse, for 'it is reason that engenders *amour-propre*, and reflection that confirms it'.[40]

According to Rousseau, the most important incident in human history and the chief cause of social inequality is the foundation of private property. The second part of his *Discourse* opens with the resounding statement:

> The first man who, having enclosed a piece of ground, bethought himself of saying 'This is mine,' and found people simple enough to believe him, was the real founder of civil society. From how many crimes, wars, and murders, from how many horrors and misfortunes might not any one have saved mankind, by pulling up the stakes, or filling up the ditch, and crying to his fellows: 'Beware of listening to this impostor; you are undone if you once forget that the fruits of the earth belong to us all, and the earth itself to nobody.'[41]

As people became more industrious, their simple wants multiplied into new needs. Agriculture and industry further depressed mankind: 'it was iron and corn which first civilized men, and ruined humanity.' Property, once recognized, gave rise to growing inequality and the first rules of justice. It also had disastrous psychological effects in encouraging dissimulation: 'it now became the interest of men to appear what they really were not.' Eventually the rich, in order to enjoy their property in peace, suggested the need for government as a supreme power to govern with laws. The people were duped into agreeing: 'All ran headlong to their chains, in hopes of securing their liberty; for they had just wit enough to perceive the advantages of political institutions, without experience enough to enable to foresee the dangers.'[42] Such was the origin of government and law which bound new fetters on the poor and gave new powers to the rich. Nations then entered into a state of nature with each other.

Rousseau considered liberty as the 'noblest faculty of man'; it is 'a gift which they hold from nature as being men'.[43] He rejected outright those apologists of slavery who argue that man has a natural propensity to servitude. With all the eloquence of sincere anger, Rousseau exclaims:

> when I see free-born animals dash their brains out against the bars of their cage, from an innate impatience of captivity; when I behold

numbers of naked savages, that despise European pleasures, braving hunger, fire, the sword, and death, to preserve nothing but their independence, I feel that it is not for slaves to argue about liberty.[44]

Rousseau therefore argued that government is an artificial institution set up by free men in the hope of making life easier. But while government did not begin with arbitrary power, it eventually brought about 'just the law of the strongest, which it was originally designed to remedy'.[45] Rousseau further asserted that the different forms of government owe their origin to the differing degrees of inequality which existed between individuals when they were set up. The establishment of laws and the rights of property was the first stage, the institution of magistracy the second, and the conversion of legitimate into arbitrary power the third and last.

Rousseau's analysis of the origins of social inequality and government is brilliant, and most anarchists have followed him in seeing a close link between property and government. Indeed, he recognized in his *Confessions* that 'everything depended radically on politics' and 'no people would ever be anything but what the nature of its government made it'.[46] But despite his celebration of the natural state of man, and his favourable contrast between the 'savage' and the 'civilized', particularly since the former knows how to live within himself and the latter only knows how to live 'in the opinion of others', Rousseau did not call for a return to a primitive state of nature as is commonly supposed.[47] In his second *Discourse*, he suggested that the ideal state of humanity, the happiest and most stable of epochs, must have been in the youth of society when the expansion of the human faculties kept 'a just mean between the indolence of the primitive state and the petulant activity of our *amour-propre*'.[48]

Godwin recognized the importance of Rousseau's insights and praised him for seeing that 'government, however formed, was little capable of affording solid benefit to mankind'. By a 'very slight mistake', he had unfortunately substituted 'as the topic of his eulogium, that period that preceded government and laws, instead of the period that may possibly follow upon their abolition'.[49] Far from calling for the abolition of government, Rousseau insisted on the need for a new social contract to set up a government which would express the general will and safeguard popular sovereignty. He tried to sketch the outlines of a legitimate State and give grounds why the citizen should obey it. He wanted to create a new moral man for a new moral society.

Rousseau undoubtedly gave priority to freedom as a basis of social life and celebrated individuality in many works.[50] He opened his treatise on education, *Emile* (1762), with the resounding statement: 'Everything is good as it comes from the hands of the author of nature, everything degenerates in the hands of man.'⁵¹ To remedy this state of affairs, he called for a system of 'well-regulated freedom' to bring up a child in isolation from corrupting society. The aim of education, he insisted, must be to excite curiosity and to form the judgment, and the best way to encourage learning is by doing. It was a message which impressed Godwin and Kropotkin.

But despite his libertarian aims in education and his desire to create the autonomous individual, Rousseau falls back on authoritarian means. His ideal tutor is an all powerful puppet-master who manipulates the child without him knowing it, and tries to impose a certain cast of mind. In the end, Emile is psychologically bound to his master and cannot escape him. Although his tutor abdicates his authority and hands his charge over to his new wife – 'your guardian from now on' – the docile young couple ask him to continue to 'advise' and 'govern' them.⁵²

Rousseau saw a close link between morals and politics and believed that we must study society through individuals, and individuals through society. In his *Social Contract*, published in the same year as *Emile*, he tried to find a way in which people could enjoy the advantages of common association without being subjected to each other's will, 'and in which each, while uniting himself with all, may still obey himself alone, and remain free as before'.⁵³ He found the solution to this paradox in a new social contract based on a constitution to ensure political legitimacy.

The democratic aspect to Rousseau's thought comes through in his defence of popular sovereignty. The people are the first and last voice; the legislative power remains with them. It is also apparent in his insistence that people must formulate and decide upon their own policies:

> Sovereignty, for the same reason as makes it inalienable, cannot be represented; it lies essentially in the general will, and will does not admit to representation: it is either the same, or other; there is no intermediate possibility. The deputies of the people, therefore, are not and cannot be its representatives: they are merely its stewards, and can carry through no definitive acts. Every law the people has not ratified in person is null and void – is, in fact, not a law. The people of England regards itself as free; but it is grossly mistaken; it is free only during the election of members of parliament. As soon as they are elected, slavery overtakes it, and it is nothing. The use it makes of the short moments of liberty it enjoys shows indeed that it deserves to lose them.⁵⁴

By making a social contract, the individual is obliged to alienate all his rights to the whole community and to put himself in common under the supreme direction of the 'general will' which will express their common interest and realize the general good. The exact nature of the general will remains ambiguous; it is more than the will of all or the sum of private interests, and emerges when people consider the common interest. With this notion, Rousseau believed he had discovered the way to ensure that popular sovereignty prevails. But the act of association according to Rousseau created a corporate and collective body, a 'public person' and a 'moral person' no less. In practice, it would mean the complete immersion of the individual in the community: every citizen would be obliged to give up all his natural rights (including his life and property) to 'society'.

Rousseau defines government as executive and revocable 'solely a commission . . . an intermediary body set up between the subjects and the Sovereign' charged with the execution of the laws. He was not doctrinaire about calling for a particular type of government and suggested that different forms are appropriate for different countries. In practice, he preferred small States and proposed for Poland a federal State with an elected monarchy.

It soon becomes clear however that Rousseau's State would be all-encompassing. It is to be founded by the 'legislator', an exceptional man or group of men, who interprets the general will and manipulates like Emile's tutor the people for their own good. In addition, Rousseau argues that 'the larger the State, the less the liberty' since the government must be tightened. Censorship would be used to preserve morality and the death penalty would be imposed for anyone who shows by their actions that they do not believe the articles of the State's civic religion. His Eurocentricity comes out when he declares: 'despotism is suitable to hot climates, barbarism to cold countries, and good polity to temperate regions.'[55]

For all his concern with equality and popular sovereignty, Rousseau's proposed social contract hardly adds up to a 'society of free men'.[56] On the contrary, it is clearly a recipe to create an absolute and omnipotent State. He will allow no partial society in the corporate State and there would be no safeguards for minorities. He expects complete unanimity in which the individual who differs from the majority is expected to blame himself and feel guilty for not conforming. Moreover, the man who boldly declared 'Man is born free; and everywhere he is in chains' and 'To renounce liberty is to renounce being a man' goes on to provide an excuse for generations of tyrants by arguing that in order to make a refractory citizen realize his better self and to obey the general will 'he will be forced to be free'.[57] In Rousseau's hands, the general will becomes an all-consuming moral imperative, 'the voice of all for the good of all' – whether one likes it or not. It would be a society fit for Emiles, but not for free men and women.

As Godwin observed, 'the superiority of his genius' deserted Rousseau in his *Contrat social* (1762) and his *Considérations sur le gouvernement de Pologne* (1771).[58] The great libertarian individualist ended up as an apologist for authoritarian and totalitarian democracy; in Bakunin's words, 'the true creator of modern reaction'.[59] Rousseau's notion of the general will is an abstraction which is impossible to discover and demands a terrifying unanimity. He not only advocates political imposture to maintain the rule of the State but also his writings abound with hymns to the rule of law.[60]

Rousseau insisted over and over again that freedom was more valuable to him than anything else. But what he meant by freedom is not always clear. He speaks of at least three kinds of liberty – natural, civil, and moral liberty – which prevail in different types of society.[61] In the natural state, men have natural liberty, that is to say, they are not dependent on one another. But they are not yet moral beings and can have no real conception of liberty. In civil society, Rousseau hoped to discover the form of association in which a person might unite with others while remaining free, and believed that he had found the solution in the case of a man obeying laws that he has made for himself. Civil liberty thus becomes the right to do what the laws do not forbid. Moral liberty which exists in moral society is on the other hand obedience to self-imposed laws – 'obedience to a law which we prescribe to ourselves'.[62]

But while Rousseau's treatment of freedom is undoubtedly subtle, it makes way for authoritarian sophists to masquerade as freedom-loving liberals. Rousseau failed to realize that being free and being subject at the same time is logical nonsense and practically impossible. Ultimately, he parts company with anarchists because for him law does not enslave but liberates. Some might accept a definition of freedom as a form of self-discipline, in the sense of being free from passions and instincts or being master of oneself, but none would accept it as obedience to a higher law enforced by the State.

It is possible to understand the paradox of Rousseau's love of freedom and his hankering after authority in the context of his personal revolt against his society. The son of a Swiss watchmaker, he experienced in his wandering life as a valet, secretary, and writer the modern anxiety of being an isolated individual born in a world which appears out of joint. He was always keen to assert his personal independence, yet longed for a supervising father-figure. Alienated and ostracized from his society, he sought the wholeness of true community. In his strengths and weaknesses, he speaks directly to our age.

Yet this does not excuse the authoritarian streak in his personality and thinking. It is clear in his view and treatment of women, for instance, that he had a strong patriarchal and chauvinist tendency. He not only resented the dominance of his mistress-patrons, but treated his servant-mistress abominably – sending her children by him to the public orphanage. He always considered women as the 'sex which ought to obey'.[63] Four of the five books of his treatise on education are devoted to the education of Emile, while only one deals with the upbringing of the girl who is to become his pliant handmaiden. Rousseau asserts that it is a law of nature that 'woman is made to please and to be subjugated' and 'must make herself agreeable to man'.[64] Where men are active and strong, women are weak and feeble.

While Godwin turned away from the later Rousseau, it is not surprising that the dictator Robespierre in the bloodiest stage of the French Revolution should canonize him. Nevertheless, Rousseau deserves a prominent place in the anarchist tradition for his stress on the close link between property and government, his attack on social inequality, his criticism of elitist culture, his concern with popular democracy and sovereignty, his belief in the natural goodness of humanity, and his praise for the simple life close to nature. He was fully aware of the psychological disorders fostered by Western civilization, especially the ways in which it made people anxious, restless, competitive and hypocritical. He showed how history is a depressing record of humanity's failure to realize its full potential and how modern man is alienated from his true self and society. In his writings and his life, Rousseau demonstrated that by nature men are free, but they readily enslave each other. More than any other writer of the Enlightenment, he thus revealed the tensions between a libertarian and an authoritarian approach to democracy which eventually led to the split between the anarchist and statist wings of the socialist movement in the nineteenth century.

10

The British Enlightenment

AFTER THE COLLAPSE OF the English Revolution and the restoration of the monarchy in 1660, there was little social or intellectual room in Britain for the further development of libertarian theory. After the 'Glorious Revolution' of 1688 which checked the power of the king, parliamentary democracy was established in Britain and has held sway ever since. John Locke, the philosopher of common sense and moderation, justified the event and gave the ultimate liberal defence of government.

The 'state of nature' according to Locke, is a state of 'perfect freedom' but competition between roughly equal human beings would make life uncertain and property relations unstable. Hence the need for government and law to enable them to protect life, liberty and property. The latter was most important since for Locke life and liberty could be considered as a form of personal property. He therefore recommended that a social contract be made between people to set up a government to make common laws which would ensure the secure enjoyment of property: 'Political power, then, I take to be a right of making laws, with penalties of death, and consequently of all less penalties for the regulating and preserving of property, and employing the force of the community in the execution of such laws.'[1] While recognizing that it is only labour that creates wealth, he added that it is legitimate for owners to expropriate the wealth created by the labour of their servants and their slaves.

It was an advance on the theory of the divine right of kings, but Locke summed up the ideology of the emerging middle class who wished to wrest power from the landed aristocracy. As such it was a theory of 'possessive individualism', which saw the ownership of private property as sacrosanct.[2] The ideology was to find its ultimate expression in the American Constitution of 1776 which recognized that human beings (or rather male Europeans) are born free and equal and have a right to 'life, liberty and the pursuit of happiness'.

Jonathan Swift

While Locke developed the classic liberal defence of government by close reasoning, Jonathan Swift at the beginning of the eighteenth century entertained anarchist ideas in his imaginative writings. It might at first seem odd to consider the Anglo-Irish Tory Dean Swift as a libertarian thinker. By 'liberty', Swift principally meant a condition of the citizens in a parliamentary monarchy.[3] He shared this view with Locke but he wanted to restrict suffrage even further to only large landowners. Moreover, in his writings Swift often appears as a cynical misanthrope; he called, for instance, the bulk of the English nation 'the most pernicious Race of little odious vermin that Nature ever suffered to crawl upon the Surface of the Earth'.[4] But although Swift had a low estimate of humanity and used savage satire to lambaste their foibles and vices, he undoubtedly wrote for their betterment and enlightenment. He hated tyranny and consistently opposed British imperialism, especially in Ireland.

Inspired by the new accounts of foreign lands by European travellers, Swift, in his *Gulliver's Travels* (1726), used the popular genre of the imaginary voyage to create a work of fantasy in which he violently attacked the values of his own society and age. Middleton Murry described *Gulliver's Travels* as 'the most savage onslaught on humanity ever written'.[5] Gulliver is a frustrated aristocrat who comes back to England from his voyages defeated, railing against the dominant values of his day.

Swift uses a series of utopias and anti-utopias to criticize the vices and follies of his own country. In Lilliput, for instance, there is a rigid division of society and absurd political pretensions. In Brobdingnag, the inhabitants are hard-working and live a life of few wants and simple virtue. No law is allowed to exceed the number of letters in the alphabet. The flying island of Laputa is a direct satire of the state of England and Ireland.

The most interesting voyage however is Gulliver's visit to the country of the Houyhnhnms in Book IV which mounts a direct attack on the European States with their law, government, commerce and war. The work has often been considered unremittingly anti-utopian, and Swift is as ironical and ambiguous as can be, but Godwin, for one, was profoundly influenced by this anarchist arcadia and maintained that Swift had 'a more profound insight into the true principles of political justice, than any preceding or contemporary author'.[6]

Swift of course satirizes the depraved and bestial nature of some human beings in his portrayal of the Yahoos. These hairy creatures in human form are avaricious, perverse, restive, cunning, and passionate. They fight over food and shining stones and move around in packs waging war on each other. They live in a state of 'anarchy' in the negative sense of violent disorder and mayhem. They would be more at home in Hobbes' 'state of nature' than Locke's.

By contrast Swift presents the Houyhnhnms as dignified horses who believe that reason is enough to govern rational creatures: 'Nature and

Reason were sufficient Guides for a reasonable Animal, as we pretended to be, in shewing us what we ought to do, and what to avoid.'[7] Their reason however is not so much a tool of analysis, or a power of drawing logical inferences from observed facts, but more like an organ of cool common sense. They live in a society practising universal benevolence and perfect sincerity. They also live in a golden age of primitive communism: they have no metal or clothes and few wants. Their fundamental maxim is that nature is very easily satisfied. Population is controlled by moral restraint and abstinence. Males and females receive the same education which encourages temperance, industry, exercise and cleanliness.

Since the Houyhnhnms can govern themselves they have no need for political authority, law and coercion. Government is reduced to a periodic representative council of the whole nation which meets for five or six days every fourth year to co-ordinate distribution and regulate the population growth. They try to reach unanimity in all decisions. The council does not make laws but only issues exhortations, for they have 'no Conception how a rational Creature can be *compelled*, but only advised, or *exhorted*; because no Person can disobey Reason, without giving up his Claim to be a rational Creature'.[8] The society is therefore not governed by law but by the dictates of 'reason' which everyone voluntarily accepts. In this anarchist society, Gulliver exalts in the fact that

> I had no Occasion of bribing, flattering or pimping, to procure the Favour of any great Man, or his Minion. I wanted no Fence against Fraud or Oppression: Here was neither Physician to destroy my Body, nor Lawyer to ruin my Fortune: No Informer to watch my Words and Actions, or forge Accusations against me for Hire: Here were no Gibers, Censurers, Backbiters, Pickpockets, Highwaymen, House-breakers, Attorneys, Bawds, Buffoons, Gamesters, Politicians, Wits, Spleneticks, tedious Talkers, Controvertists, Ravishers, Murderers, Robbers, Virtuoso's; no Leaders or Followers of Party and Faction; no Encouragers to Vice, by Seducement or Examples: No Dungeon, Axes, Gibbets, Whipping-posts, or Pillories.[9]

At the same time, there are some strongly negative aspects to this anarchist utopia. The unit of society is a strongly patriarchal family and the economy is based on the labour of the Yahoos. The rational Houyhnhnms have no human warmth or passion and are strongly ascetic. They have no love in the sexual sense, or partiality for their own children. The economy is that of the stone age. No apparent interest exists in science and technology: there are no wheels or metals in the land. It would even seem that yet again Swift was being slyly ironic in presenting the Houyhnhnms as supposedly ideal beings. But it remains the case that when Gulliver returns home to

England he comes to prefer the smell and company of his horse to his family, and tries to apply the 'excellent lessons of virtue' he had learnt among the Houyhnhnms.

George Orwell claims that Swift was intermittently 'a kind of anarchist' and that Book IV of *Gulliver's Travels* is a picture of an anarchistic society. But for him it also illustrates the totalitarian tendency which he claims is explicit in the anarchist or pacifist vision of society. The only arbiter of behaviour is public opinion which can be less tolerant than any system of law: 'When human beings are governed by "thou shalt not", the individual can practise a certain amount of eccentricity: when they are supposedly governed by "love" or "reason", he is under continuous pressure to make himself behave and think in exactly the same way as everyone else.'

It certainly is the case that the Houyhnhnms are unanimous on almost all subjects, have no word for 'opinion' in their language, and express no difference of sentiments in their conversations. But Orwell goes too far in suggesting that this is 'the highest stage of totalitarian organization'.[10] He uses the example of the Houyhnhnm society to attack anarchism and pacifism in general. Yet the Houyhnhnms do not persecute dissidents or force people to conform in thought or action.

Orwell's point about the potential tyranny of reason is more telling. In the rational society of the Houyhnhnms there would be no room for personal idiosyncrasies or bizarre tastes; no one would be able to stick out their tongue or tell their neighbours to go to hell. But Orwell overlooks the point that unlike Yahoo humanity, the Houyhnhnms are genuinely governed by reason. For them, there is no conflict between reason and passion, conscience and desire. Since truth for them is universal and self-evident it inevitably happens that as purely rational beings they recognize it and act accordingly. Godwin was to make a similar point at the end of the century.

Swift's position is undoubtedly ambivalent and paradoxical. He is a Tory Dean who appears at times as a rational anarchist. The son of English settlers in Ireland, he called for Irish economic independence. He despised the human race and yet was at great pains to improve it. Orwell catches the ambivalence of his position when he calls him 'a Tory anarchist, despising authority while disbelieving in liberty, and preserving the aristocratic outlook while seeing clearly that the aristocracy is degenerate and contemptible'.[11] Nevertheless, Swift's picture of the country of the Houyhnhnms is genuinely libertarian, however flawed. Its view of the 'state of nature' in which spontaneous order prevails without government may well be more accurate than Hobbes' romantic myth of universal war. It is for this reason that the first great anarchist thinker William Godwin described the Voyage to the Houyhnhnms as 'one of the most virtuous, liberal and enlightened examples of human genius'.[12]

Edmund Burke

Since most literary historians cannot understand the feasibility of anarchism, they invariably suggest that works by great authors advocating a free society must be ironic. This is the case with Swift, and Edmund Burke. Burke has been best remembered for his attack on all innovation in his *Reflections on the Revolution in France* (1790), but it is often forgotten that as a young man he was a liberal Whig who supported American Independence and advocated economic reform. In addition, he wrote *A Vindication of Natural Society* (1756) which offers one of the most powerful arguments for anarchist society made in the eighteenth century. His starting-point, which he shares with the Taoists and the French *philosophes*, is a confidence in nature which 'if left to itself were the best and surest Guide'.[13]

Human beings in a state of nature originally lived 'with their Brethren of the other Kinds in much equality' and were wholly vegetarian. In the 'natural' society in which they lived, they followed their 'natural Appetites and Instincts, and not in any positive institution'. Governed by reason, they had no need for external government: 'We begin to think and to act from Reason and Nature alone.'[14] Unfortunately, human beings invented artificial rules to guide nature. They created a political society held together by laws which became a violation of nature and a constraint on the mind. Since religion and government are closely connected, once government is considered to be necessary, it draws in an artificial religion and 'Ecclesiastical Tyranny under the Name of Church Government'.[15]

Political regulations, Burke further suggests, create social conflict, and political society is responsible for war since in the state of nature it is impossible to form armies; thus 'All Empires have been cemented in Blood.' The artificial division of mankind into separate groups further produces hatred and dissension. And while in the state of nature man acquires wealth in proportion to his labours, in the state of artificial society with government it is an invariable law that 'those who labour most, enjoy the fewest things; and that those who labour not at all, have the Greatest Number of Enjoyments.'[16]

Burke examines the different forms of government – despotism, aristocracy, and democracy – but finds them all wanting. Although democracy is preferable, he argues that all governments must frequently infringe justice to support themselves. He therefore draws the anarchist conclusion: 'In vain you tell me that Artificial Government is good, but that I fall out only with the Abuse. The Thing! The Thing itself is the Abuse!' Rejecting all artificial laws and the alliance of Church and State, Burke declares at the end of his eloquent and penetrating work: 'We should renounce their

"Dreams of Society", together with their Visions of Religion, and vindicate ourselves into perfect liberty."[17]

When Burke became a Tory after the French Revolution and thundered against all improvement, he disowned his *Vindication of Natural Society* as a youthful folly. Most commentators have followed suit, suggesting that he was trying to parody the manner of Bolingbroke. But Godwin, while recognizing Burke's ironic intention, took him seriously. He acknowledged that most of his own arguments against political society in *An Enquiry concerning Political Justice* (1793) may be found in Burke's work – 'a treatise, in which the evils of the existing political institutions are displayed with incomparable force of reasoning and lustre of eloquence'.[18] In the following century, the radical secularist George Holyoake reprinted Burke's work under the title *The Inherent Evils of all State Governments Demonstrated* (1858). The editor declared enthusiastically that it was 'one of the soberest productions ever-written' and referred in an appendix to the anarchists Pierre-Joseph Proudhon and Josiah Warren for further clarification of Burke's 'great truth that State governments will never give real freedom to their subjects'.[19]

Thomas Paine

The outbreak of the French Revolution in 1789 sparked off one of the greatest political debates in British history. Burke's *Reflections on the Revolution in France* (1790) fell as a bombshell amongst radicals like Thomas Paine, Thomas Holcroft, William Godwin, Mary Wollstonecraft and William Blake. Wollstonecraft made one of the first replies to Burke, in her *Vindication of the Rights of Men* (1790), and then went on to write *A Vindication of the Rights of Woman* (1792), which established her reputation as the first great feminist. She made a powerful plea that mind has no gender and that women should become independent and educated beings. But although she attacked hereditary distinctions and economic inequality, she still looked to a reformed government to protect natural rights.

Paine also used the language of natural rights in his celebrated *Rights of Man* (1791–2), but his libertarian sensibility took him to the borders of anarchism. The son of a Quaker staymaker of Thetford, Norfolk, he had tried his trade in London before becoming an excise-man in Lewes, Sussex. His Quaker background undoubtedly encouraged his plain style and egalitarian sentiments, as well as his confidence in the 'inner light' of reason and conscience to lead him to truth and virtue. He liked to boast that 'I neither read books, nor studied other people's opinions. I thought for myself.'[20] He believed that man was fundamentally good, and saw the world as a garden for enjoyment rather than as a valley of tears. Above all, he valued personal liberty: 'Independence is my happiness,' he wrote in his maturity, 'and I view things as they are, without regard to place or person; my country is the world, and my religion is to do good.'[21]

Paine was a man of his industrial age. He adopted Newton's view of the world as a machine governed by universal laws. Applying the same analytical method to society and nature, he felt that both could be refashioned according to reason. Just as he spent many years designing an iron bridge, so he tried to redesign society on the same simple and rational principles. He was a mechanical and social engineer: 'What Archimedes said of the mechanical powers', he wrote, 'may be applied to Reason and Liberty: "*Had we*", he said, "*a place to stand upon, we might raise the world.*"'[22]

Dismissed from service in Lewes, Paine decided to try his luck in the American colonies. On his arrival, he rapidly threw himself into the social and political struggles of the day. He wrote articles in a direct and robust style which advocated female emancipation and condemned African slavery and cruelty to animals. In 1775, he called eloquently for an end to the legal and social discrimination against women:

> Even in countries where they may be esteemed the most happy [women are] constrained in their desires in the disposal of their goods; robbed of freedom and will by the laws; slaves of opinion which rules them with absolute sway and construes the slightest appearances into guilt; surrounded on all sides by judges who are at once tyrants and their seducers ... for even with changes in attitudes and laws, deeply engrained and oppressing social prejudices remain which confront women minute by minute, day by day.[23]

It was however only in the following year that Paine came to prominence with his pamphlet *Common Sense* (1776), the first work to argue for the complete independence of the thirteen colonies from England. He advocated a people's war to throw off the English yoke and hoped America would become a land of freedom, thereby offering an inspiration to the peoples living under European tyrannies. His internationalism and love of freedom come across in his rousing call:

> O ye that love mankind! Ye that dare oppose, not only the tyrrany, but the tyrant, stand forth! Every spot of the old world is over-run with oppression. Freedom hath been hunted round the globe. Asia, and Africa, have long expelled her. – Europe regards her like a stranger, and England hath given her warning to depart. O! receive the fugitive, and prepare in time an asylum for mankind.[24]

The experience of the American Revolution had a marked effect on Paine. He was deeply impressed by the orderly nature and decorum of American society after the dissolution of the colonial government before the establishment of a new constitution. In his famous opening to *Common Sense*, Paine like later anarchists distinguished between society and government. He felt that they are not only different, but have different origins:

> Society is produced by our wants, and government by our wickedness; the former promotes our happiness *positively* by uniting our affections, the latter *negatively* by restraining our vices. The one encourages intercourse, the other creates distinctions. The first is patron, the last a punisher.
>
> Society in every state is a blessing, but government even in its best state is but a necessary evil; in its worse state an intolerable one; for when we suffer, or are exposed to the same miseries *by a government*, which we might expect in a country *without a government*, our calamities is heightened by reflecting that we furnish the means by which we suffer. Government, like dress, is the badge of lost innocence; the palaces of kings are built on the ruins of the bowers of paradise. For were the impulses of conscience clear, uniform, and irresistibly obeyed, man would need no other lawgiver.[25]

But despite the example of the American colonists organizing their own affairs peacefully without government, Paine believed that it was necessary for the people to make a social contract in order to set up a minimal government on the secure basis of a constitution which would guarantee the rights of life, liberty, and the pursuit of happiness.

After the successful outcome of the American War of Independence, Paine returned to England with hopes of building his iron bridge. The outbreak of the French Revolution in 1789 renewed his revolutionary fervour and Burke's apostasy led him to write his *Rights of Man*. It was, he recognized, 'an age of Revolutions, in which everything may be looked for'.[26]

Burke, in his *Reflections on the Revolution in France*, had maintained that government and society are complex, fragile and organic entities based on the wisdom of ancestors and could only be interfered with at great peril. He dismissed the 'clumsy subtlety' of *a priori* political theorizing (which he had indulged in boldly in his *Vindication*) and suggested that if scholars no longer enjoyed the patronage of the nobility and clergy, learning would be 'trodden down under the hoofs of the swinish multitude'.[27]

Paine spoke on behalf of and to the 'swinish multitude', rejecting Burke's apology for 'the authority of the dead over the rights and freedom of the living'.[28] He was not a particularly original thinker and adopted the liberal commonplaces of eighteenth-century political theory developed from Locke. But he developed them in a more libertarian and democratic direction. If what he said was not particularly new, how he said it undoubtedly was. Where the accepted language of political discourse was elegant and refined, Paine chose to write in a direct, robust, and simple style which all educated working people could understand. He refused to be 'immured in the Bastille of a word' and threatened the dominant culture by his style as well as the ruling powers by his arguments.[29]

The First Part of the *Rights of Man* principally consists of a history of the French Revolution and of a comparison between the French and British constitutions. Paine is mainly concerned here to assert the rights of man against arbitrary and hereditary power. He bases his doctrine of natural rights on the alleged original equality and unity of humanity and argues that they include 'intellectual rights' and 'all those rights of acting as an individual for his own comfort and happiness'.[30] But Paine suggests like Locke that in the state of nature the individual does not have the power to enjoy these rights in security. He therefore recommends that individuals deposit their natural rights in the 'common stock' of civil society and set up a government which will protect them. The government itself has no rights as such and must be considered only as a delegated 'trust' which the citizens can always dissolve or resume for themselves. The only authority on which a government has a right to exist is on the authority of the people. The end of government is to ensure 'the good of all' or '*general* happiness'.[31] As for engendering the Church with the State, as Burke recommended, Paine dismisses such a connection as 'a sort of mule-animal, capable only of destroying and not of breeding up'.[32]

While these arguments were part of the common eighteenth-century liberal defence of government, in Part II of the *Rights of Man* Paine broke new theoretical ground which brought him to the verge of anarchism. At the end of Part I he acknowledged: 'Man is not the enemy of Man, but through the medium of a false system of government.'[33] He now returns to his distinction between society and government made at the opening of *Common Sense* and insists that:

> Great part of that order which reigns among mankind is not the effect of government. It has its origin in the principles of society and the natural constitution of man. It existed prior to government, and would exist if the formality of government was abolished. The mutual dependence and reciprocal interest which man has upon man, and all the parts of a civilized community upon each other, create that great chain of connexion which holds it together ... Common interest regulates their concerns, and forms their law; and the laws which common usage ordains, have a greater influence than the laws of government. In fine, society performs for itself almost everything which is ascribed to government.[34]

In a Rousseauist vein, Paine further maintains that man is naturally good but depraved by governments: 'man, were he not corrupted by governments, is naturally the friend of man.' Human nature therefore is not itself vicious.

Not only is a great part of what is called government 'mere imposition', but everything that governments can usefully do has been performed by the common consent of society without government. Indeed, 'The instant formal government is abolished, society begins to act. A general association takes place, and common interest produces common security.'[35] Looking back on the riots and tumult in English history, Paine argued, like modern anarchists, that they had not proceeded from 'the want of government, but that government was itself the generating cause; instead of consolidating society it divided it . . . and engendered discontents which otherwise would not have existed.'[36] But Paine does not look backward to some mythical golden age of social harmony, rather forward to a more civilized society. He suggests as a general principle that 'the more perfect civilization is, the less occasion has it for government, because the more does it regulate its own affairs, and govern itself.'[37] Since all the great laws of society are laws of nature, it follows for Paine that civilized life requires few laws.

But unlike his contemporary William Godwin, Paine did not carry his bold reasoning to the anarchist conclusion that government is always an unnecessary evil. He felt as long as the natural wants of man were greater than his individual powers government would be necessary to ensure freedom and security. He therefore proposed a minimal government – no more than a 'national association' – with a few general laws to protect the natural rights of man. Its end is limited and simple, to secure 'the good of all, as well individually as collectively'. Paine had a definite preference for republican and representative government based on majority rule, and he wished to anchor it firmly in a constitution. He even praised the American Constitution as 'the political bible of the state'.[38]

By calling on the British people to follow the American and French to form a new social contract and set up a limited government based on a constitution, Paine ultimately departs from the anarchist tradition. At the end of the *Rights of Man*, he even gives a distributive role to government by proposing that it helps to educate the young and support the old through a progressive inheritance tax.

While Paine has been called the father of English socialism, he was in fact a staunch advocate of business enterprise: universal and free commerce would extirpate war. He never advocated economic equality and thought private property would always remain unequal. His capitalist way of thinking led him to defend representative government in terms of a limited company with citizen shareholders: 'Every man is a proprietor in government, and considers it a necessary part of his business to understand. It concerns his interest, because it affects his property.'[39] In his last major work, *Agrarian Justice* (1797), he did not call, like his contemporary Thomas Spence, for the nationalization and common ownership of land but for a society of small landowners to be achieved through a land tax of ten per cent. Paine's final vision was of a representative and republican democracy of independent property owners in which every citizen has an equal opportunity to develop his talents.

Paine developed liberal theory to the threshold of anarchism but he did not cross over. In fact, he was the greatest spokesman for bourgeois radicalism, exhorting the rising middle class to take over the State from the monarchy and aristocracy. But, inspired by the American and French Revolutions, he recognized the ability of people to govern themselves and thereby contributed to the pool of ideas and values out of which anarchism and socialism were to spring.

PART THREE

Great Libertarians

Government is begotten of aggression, by aggression.
HERBERT SPENCER

I call it the State where everyone, good or bad, is a poison-drinker: the State where universal slow suicide is called – life.
FRIEDRICH NIETZSCHE

That government is best which governs not at all.
HENRY THOREAU

Disobedience, in the eyes of anyone who has read history, is man's original virtue. It is through disobedience that progress has been made, through disobedience and through rebellion.
OSCAR WILDE

French Libertarians

IN FRANCE THE DIFFERENCE between libertarian and anarchist was not clearly defined and the terms were often used interchangeably. De Sade and Fourier were both libertarian in the sense that they wished to expand human freedom, but they were not always anarchist in wanting to abolish the State completely. De Sade for a time during the French Revolution entertained the idea of a society without law, although in the end called for a minimal State. Fourier was one of the most original utopian thinkers of the nineteenth century and his vision of a free society inspired many later anarchists and anticipated social ecology.

Marquis de Sade

The spirit of free enquiry sparked off by the Enlightenment led to increasingly bold questioning of existing social and moral laws in the latter half of the eighteenth century. The boldest thinker of them all was the Marquis de Sade. Donatien Alphonse François de Sade of course is remembered for his perversity, and sadism is associated with an abnormal pleasure in cruelty. In fact, the picture of de Sade as a monster is largely the work of prudish and puritanical moralists who have never read his books. The imaginary portraits of de Sade as a dashing Casanova are as inaccurate as his reputation: he was a plump little man with fair hair, blue eyes and a tiny mouth.

De Sade's writings were denied official publication by the French courts as late as 1957 and are still not widely available. This is unfortunate, for de Sade was not only an arch-rebel but a highly original thinker. His contribution to an understanding of sexual psychopathology is well-known; less recognized is his importance as a social philosopher. Poets have most appreciated his libertarian genius: Swinburne called him 'That illustrious and ill-requited benefactor of humanity', while Apollinaire declared that he was 'the freest spirit that has yet existed'.[1]

De Sade knew of the tyranny of men at first hand, both from within himself and from others. After completing a Jesuit education, which endowed him with a lifelong hatred of religion, he acquired various military ranks and served in the Seven Years' War. The experience made him a staunch opponent to offensive war. After his marriage at twenty-three in the presence of the King and Queen and most of the higher members of the Court, his sexual escapades landed him in prison in 1778.

Although de Sade conscientiously explored all imaginable extensions of sexual pleasure, his known behaviour (which includes only the beating of a housemaid and an orgy with several prostitutes) departs greatly from the clinical picture of active sadism.[2] From 1778, with no legal charge brought against him, de Sade spent all but ten of the remaining thirty-seven years of his life in close confinement. In prison, he drew on his experiences to write in earnest, partly in self-justification, partly in wish-fulfilment. Throughout this time, his wife supported him with courage and devotion.

At the outbreak of the French Revolution, de Sade had been held for five years in the notorious 'Tour de la Liberté' of the Bastille. One of seven prisoners left, he was removed eleven days before the people of Paris stormed it. The Constituent Assembly released him on Good Friday in 1790. The relative freedom of the press at the time enabled him to publish the following year *Justine, ou les malheurs de la vertu* which had been written in 1788.

De Sade actively supported the republicans, and served in the revolutionary 'Section des Piques' and was elected president of his group. In 1792, he wrote a pamphlet entitled *Idée sur la mode de la sanction des loix* which proposed that all laws brought forward by the representatives should be directly voted on by the populace at large. His proposal was based on his awareness of the ability of power to corrupt: 'I have studied men and I know them; I know the difficulties that they make in giving up any power that is granted to them, and that nothing is more difficult than to establish limits to delegate power.'[3]

In 1791, de Sade wrote *An Address of a Citizen of Paris to the King of France*, calling on Louis XVI to respect the powers entrusted to him by men who are 'free and equal according to the laws of Nature'. Ironically, the republican de Sade was arrested again for his alleged royalist sympathies. He was released after the fall of Robespierre in 1794. During the following seven years of freedom, he published in 1797 the ten volumes of his bombshell *La Nouvelle Justine, ou les malheurs de la vertu suivie de l'histoire de Juliette sa soeur*. He was rearrested in 1801 and Napoleon's ministers had all the copies that could be found destroyed. No authoritarian government could allow the exposures of the mechanisms of despotism contained in them and de Sade was confined to an asylum for the rest of his life. A quarter of his entire output, ranging from plays to short stories were burnt during Napoleon's rule.

Although de Sade has been remembered for his erotica, he appears in his writings more preoccupied with religion than sex. Indeed, far from being an amoralist, he was not only obsessed by moral issues but had a powerful conscience. He called honour 'man's guiding rein'. He had a profound and continuous awareness of the difference between good and evil, had no delusions about the 'roses and raptures of vice'.[4] Like Blake and Nietzsche, he wanted to go beyond existing definitions of good and evil and to forge his own ethical code. And like the *philosophes*, he tried to follow nature, arguing that the experience of pleasure is a sign that we are acting in accordance with our own nature and nature as a whole: 'All acts which give pleasure ... must be natural and right.'[5] He who abandons himself most to the promptings of nature will also be the happiest. In this sense, de Sade was a consistent hedonist.

In his metaphysics, de Sade was a militant atheist and philosophical materialist, completely opposed to the tyranny of the Church and the repressive nature of Christian doctrine. The Christian God, with his threat of divine retribution, is for de Sade too immoral and base to be acceptable. In place of God, he puts Nature as the prime mover of the universe.

The attributes of nature are not entirely clear in de Sade's writing. At first nature appears as a beneficent force: the law of nature is interpreted as 'Make others as happy as you wish to be yourself.' But gradually in his work, nature begins to turn into a sort of malevolent goddess – a 'cruel stepmother' – so that the law of nature degenerates into: 'Please yourself, no matter at whose expense.'[6] De Sade eventually came to believe that nature is fundamentally destructive (its sole object in creation is to have the pleasure of destruction) and proceeds by corruption. It follows that by satisfying his destructive instincts man is following nature. This is the metaphysical and moral foundation of sadism: if making others feel pain gives pleasure, it is natural and right. To be moral in the conventional sense is to oppose nature; existing virtue is therefore unnatural and the result of a false education.

In his politics, de Sade challenged the fundamental premisses of European civilization. He had a very low opinion of politics; it is a 'science born of falsehood and ambition' which teaches 'men to deceive their equals without being deceived themselves'.[7] In every book, he stresses that society is divided into two antagonistic classes founded on property. Anticipating Proudhon, he defines property as 'a crime committed by the rich against the poor'. The origin of the right of property is in usurpation: 'the right is in origin itself a theft, so that the law punishes theft because it attacks theft'.[8] Speaking from direct experience, de Sade knew that the lawcourts only dispense justice in favour of the wealthy: 'The laws of a people are never anything but the mass and the result of the interests of the legislators.'[9] As for war between nations, it is simply authorized murder in which hired men slaughter one another in the interests of tyrants: 'The sword is the weapon of him who is in the wrong, the commonest resource of ignorance and stupidity.'[10]

In place of the existing class-ridden and unjust society, de Sade proposed several alternatives at different stages in his life. Before the outbreak of the French Revolution, in the second volume of *Aline et Valcour*, written in 1788 and published in 1795, he depicted a utopia in the city of Tamoe in the South Seas. The king Zamé had as a young man visited Europe and found that the greatest causes of misery were private property, class distinctions, religion and family life. He therefore chooses to avoid these ills by making the State control manufacture and employ all the people. All have equal commodities and comforts, and there is no prison or death penalty.

After witnessing the rise to power of Robespierre, the strengthening of the French State, and the Terror which followed, de Sade had second thoughts about the beneficial role of the State in society. In *Juliette*, written in 1794 and published in 1797, he tackled the question of government and law head on and concluded that anarchy is best. In a conversation between two Italians, one interlocutor rejects the social contract à la Rousseau since it serves only the general will but not particular interests. He goes on to reject the restraint of law:

> Let us convince ourselves once and for all that laws are merely useless and dangerous; their only object is to multiply crimes or to allow them to be committed with impunity on account of the secrecy they necessitate. Without laws and religions it is impossible to imagine the degree of glory and grandeur human knowledge would have attained by now; the way these base restraints have retarded progress is unbelievable; and that is the sole service they have rendered to man.[11]

The passions, he maintains, have done more good to mankind than laws. Indeed, individuals who are not animated by strong passions are merely mediocre beings: 'Compare the centuries of anarchy with those of the strongest legalism in any country you like and you will see that it is only when the laws are silent that the greatest actions appear.' We should therefore do away with laws: if man returns to a state of nature, he would be far happier than is possible under the 'ridiculous yoke' of the law. There is absolutely no need for laws to obtain justice, for nature has given man the instinct and necessary force to get justice for himself. The universal law which nature imprints in every heart is 'to satisfy ourselves to refuse our passions nothing, whatever the cost to others'. If this means oppressing another, the oppressed would have the right to revenge himself, and could check the oppressor. As a result, 'I have far less reason to fear my neighbour's passion than the law's injustice.' Anarchy therefore has nothing to do with despotism and is best:

> Tyrants are never born in anarchy, you only see them raise themselves up in the shadow of the laws or get authority from them. The reign of laws is therefore vicious and inferior to anarchy; the strongest proof of my proposition is the necessity a government finds itself in to plunge itself into anarchy when it wishes to remake its constitution.[12]

In the last volume of *Juliette*, the theme is taken up again at length and another Italian declares: 'Give man back to Nature; she will lead him far better than your laws.'[13] It is the conclusion towards which the most daring thinkers of the Enlightenment were groping.

De Sade did not however leave it at that. Conscious of the immediate practical task of remaking French society, and concerned at the authoritarian direction the French Revolution was taking, he include in his *Philosophie dans le boudoir* (1795) a long address entitled *Frenchmen, a further effort if you wish to be Republicans*! It offers a political programme for a 'free State'; a State which he would like to keep to a minimum. As such it is a synthesis of his two earlier positions.

The address continues to reject religion completely. De Sade calls on his fellow countrymen to replace the 'theistic follies' introduced by the 'infamous Robespierre' with social precepts to be taught by a system of national education. Although he would give the State this task to perform it still would have little power as a legal order. A new society would develop new morals and in a State based on liberty and equality there would be practically no crimes to be punished. The laws which might remain should be 'so clement and so few that all men whatever their character can comply with them'.[14] At a time when the French government had just pronounced the respect of private property, de Sade maintained that there should only be a law which punishes not the robber but the man who is careless enough to let himself be robbed.

De Sade always insisted that crimes are committed out of want or passion, and the best way to avoid them is to eradicate the interest in breaking the law. As for those who commit crime because it is a crime, one should try and win them by kindness and honour. Above all, the death penalty should be abolished forever. Although murder is a horror, de Sade recognized that some killing may be necessary to defend a country and as such should be tolerated in a republic. As a crime of passion, however, it should not be revenged by another judicial murder.

As for those crimes motivated by lust (including rape, sodomy and incest), de Sade suggests that the 'it is less a question of repressing this passion in ourselves than in regulating the means by which it can be satisfied in peace.'[15] He therefore recommends public brothels where people can satisfy their wishes to command and be obeyed. To avoid public disorder, de Sade advocates unbridled promiscuity: 'give free play to these tyrannous desires, which despite himself torment him [man] ceaselessly'.[16] The satisfaction of physical love as a natural passion should not be bound by marriage bonds, false modesty or even that love – called the 'madness of the soul' – which is selfish and exclusive.[17] And consistent with his doctrine of complete equality, de Sade insists that women should have the equal opportunity and the same licence as men to satisfy their own desires:

> no act of possession can ever be exercised on a free person; it is as unjust to possess a woman exclusively as it is to possess slaves; all humans are born free and with equal rights; let us never forget that; consequently no sex can have a legitimate right to the exclusive possession of another, and no sex or class can possess the other exclusively.[18]

De Sade's attitude to sex has often been misunderstood. He was the first to recognize the overwhelming importance of sex: 'Lust is to the other passions what the nervous fluid is to life; it supports them all, it lends strength to them all.'[19] But sadism is not merely a branch of sex. It has been defined more broadly as 'the pleasure felt from the observed modifications on the external world produced by the will of the observer'.[20] The crucial point is that the action is willed and that any act which produces visible and audible changes in another has a component of sexual pleasure. It so happens that for de Sade pleasure tends to be pain diminished, and pain is the absolute. It is easier to affect people by pain than pleasure, by destruction than creation, but this does not mean that constructive sadistic pleasure is not possible. And while he shows that the object of power is pleasure (which consists in applying sanctions to those in one's control), de Sade's egalitarian morality made him see all those who seek or acquire such power as evil.

Having witnessed the excesses of the nobles before the French Revolution and the Terror of the revolutionaries, he was fully aware of the desire for domination in human beings and wanted it to be channelled into sexual activity rather than cause social havoc. It is extremely difficult to follow de Sade in his fantasies of torture, murder and arson but at least he had the courage and frankness to recognize the existence of such desires and tried to sublimate them. Both the feminist Simone de Beauvoir and the novelist Alain Robbe-Grillet have acknowledged positively the cathartic function of the sexual cruelty described by de Sade.[21]

De Sade was also a revolutionary thinker in attacking the right to property. He saw the real struggle as lying between the people and the ruling class – made up of the crown, aristocracy, and clergy, as well as the bourgeoisie. For this he has been called the 'first reasoned socialist'.[22] He undoubtedly anticipated Fourier in his project of a harmonious society based on the free play of passions.[23] Like Wilhelm Reich, he also realized that repressed sexuality can lead to tyrannical behaviour on a large scale and that a real democracy must be sexually liberated.

This knowledge forms the basis of de Sade's libertarian philosophy: aware that men in positions of unrestrained power over others, whether in governments or prisons, will dominate and torture, he argued that they should not be given such power and their desires are best satisfied in play. His abiding passion was freedom from oppression. Indeed, no writer at the turn of the nineteenth century expressed more lucidly the incompatibility of traditional religion and conventional morality with the idea of freedom.[24]

Charles Fourier

Charles Fourier was also one of France's greatest libertarian thinkers. He not only influenced the young Proudhon (they both came from Besançon), but Kropotkin later acknowledged Fourier to be a 'forerunner of Anarchy'.[25] Murray Bookchin has recently described him as 'the most libertarian, the most original, and certainly the most relevant utopian thinker of his day, if not of the entire tradition'.[26] Fourier not only influenced the surrealists but his teachings found a direct echo in the counter-culture of the sixties and seventies.

Fourier was born in Besançon in 1772, and he studied at the local academy. He abandoned his studies to become a commercial traveller, covering Holland, France and Germany. During the revolutionary Terror, he was imprisoned and nearly guillotined, but emerged to do two years' military service. He then pursued his desultory commercial career and developed a grandiose scheme to replace the corrupt civilization of his day which he knew so well.

Bookchin observes that Fourier was in many ways the earliest social ecologist to surface in radical thought. Certainly Fourier conceived of the universe as a vast living organism. In order to complete Newton's work, he proposed his own 'law of passionate attraction' in which even stars have sexual proclivities. In his 'theory of universal analogy', he presents man as a microcosm of the universe: the universe is a unified system, a web of hidden correspondences, and man is at its centre. Man is not therefore separate from nature, but an integral part of it. Moreover, behind the apparent chaos of the world, there is an underlying harmony and natural order governed by universal law. If the universal law is understood it would 'conduct the human race to opulence, sensual pleasures and global unity'.[27]

Fourier went far beyond the ideas of liberty, equality and fraternity put forward by the lawyers of the French Revolution. He recognized that social liberty without a degree of economic equality is meaningless. The *philosophes* of the eighteenth century were right to vaunt liberty – 'it is the foremost desire of all creatures' – but they forgot that in civilized societies liberty is illusory if the common people lack wealth: 'When the wage-earning classes are poor, their independence is as fragile as a house without foundations.'[28] While accepting the inequality of talents and remuneration according to work done, Fourier's utopia undoubtedly presupposes the gradual levelling of the privileges of the wealthy and the end of class antagonism.

Like de Sade, Fourier applied the notion of rights to women as well as men. It was Fourier and not Marx who first asserted as a general proposition that 'Social progress and changes of period are brought about by virtue of the progress of women towards liberty' and that the extension of the privileges of women is the fundamental cause of all social progress. Rejecting the degradation and bondage of women and conjugal slavery in modern civilization, he observes: 'A slave is never more contemptible than when his blind submission convinces the oppressor that his victim is born for slavery.' Fourier's egalitarian and libertarian vision even embraces animals. He does not recommend vegetarianism but it is a rule in his ideal society that 'a man who mistreats them is himself more of an animal than the defenceless beasts he persecutes.'[29]

The method Fourier adopted in his social analysis involved 'absolute doubt' and 'absolute deviation'.[30] The uncompromising application of this method led him to mount a devastating indictment of Western civilization and capitalism. His critique of its dehumanized market relations warped by deceit and falsehood, its punishing and repulsive work, and its psychic and sexual frustration are trenchant indeed. He rejected the whole economic system based on free competition and the work ethic itself. Freedom for Fourier not only meant free choice, but freedom from the psychological compulsion to work. In place of the existing order, he proposed a hedonistic utopia called 'Harmony' in which there would be agreeable and voluntary labour, non-repressive sexuality, communal education and communal living. Passion, pleasure, abundance, and love would all find their place in his new moral world.

Each community of Harmony would be a Phalanx housed in a palace or 'phalanstery'. Each Phalanx would consist of a self-managing and self-sustaining association of co-operative workers. The members would work in voluntary groups of friends or a series of groups who have gathered together spontaneously and who are stimulated by active rivalries. Work would be made as attractive as possible, and the division of labour would be carried to the supreme degree in order to allot suitable tasks to different individuals. While work would be co-operative and property enjoyed in common, members would receive dividends proportional to their contributions in capital, work and talent. Everyone would have a right to work and as a key principle Fourier insists on a 'social minimum', a guaranteed annual income. Every effort would be made to combine personal with social freedom and promote diversity in unity. The equality of unequals would prevail.

When it came to desire, Fourier was even more revolutionary. Although a rationalist, he rejected the mechanical rationalization of contemporary society which repressed the passions; they are natural and meant to be expressed. He stands as a forerunner of psychoanalysis in his understanding of the dynamics of repression: 'Every passion that is suffocated produces its counter passion, which is as malignant as the natural passion would have been salutary. This is true of all manias.'[31]

Rather than being disruptive in society, the gratification of individual desire and passion serve the general good: 'the man who devotes himself most ardently to pleasure becomes eminently useful for the happiness of all.'[32] In his notebooks collectively entitled *The New Amorous World*, Fourier called for the satisfaction of material and psychological needs, a 'sexual minimum' as well as a 'social minimum'. He was convinced that complete sexual gratification would foster social harmony and economic well-being. The only kind of sexual activity he condemned as vicious was where a person was abused, injured, or used as an object against his or her will. Only in Harmony could such 'amorous anarchy' prevail.[33]

Fourier's imaginary world is undoubtedly libertarian in many respects, but as it appears in his most succinct formulation in *Le Nouveau monde industriel et sociétaire* (1829) it contains many contradictions. Women are to be liberated from patriarchal constraints, but they are still expected to serve the men domestically and sexually. Again, Fourier's elegant tableaux of sexual and gastronomic delights reflect an aristocratic taste. His 'amorous code' manipulated by an elaborate hierarchy of officials in the 'Court of Love' is not for everyone. His description of sex appears somewhat mechanical and utilitarian. His child psychology is also naive and dogmatic. He not only denies infantile sexuality but asserts dogmatically that since 'Two thirds of all boys have a penchant for filth' they should be organized into 'little hordes' to do the disgusting and loathsome work.[34] Little girls of course like finery.

Finally, the arrangements of everyday life in 'Harmony' are described so minutely that its members are left little room for manoeuvre or renovation. Those who like privacy would not feel at home. While Fourier tried to foster individual autonomy and self-realization in allocating attractive work to suit particular tastes, the life he proposes is undoubtedly regimented. Communal life is so well-organized that to some it might appear more like a prison than a paradise. The whole is orchestrated by the puppet strings of the master.

Fourier distributed his works to the rich and powerful, but to little avail. By 1830, nonetheless, he had managed to attract a small band of followers in the area around Besançon. With the help of the young Victor Considérant, he then managed to turn the small Fourierist group into a movement, winning over some disenchanted followers of Saint-Simon in 1832. In the following year the first community was set up, only to collapse soon afterwards. Only after his death in 1837 did Fourierist movements spring up in most of the European countries and in the United States. In France, Considérant helped to turn Fourierism into a movement for 'peaceful democracy'; and it became a real political force in the last years of the July Monarchy and in the early phase of the 1848 French Revolution. In America, it spawned three dozen short-lived communities, including Brook Farm. Fourier's ideas even influenced Alexander Herzen and the Petrashevsky Circle in Tsarist Russia. But while communities failed, and his revolutionary message got watered down, he did have an influence on the developing co-operative movement, especially in Britain. Most authoritarian socialists, however, went on to dismiss Fourier's utopian visions, as Marx and Engels did, as a 'fantastic blueprint', despite its 'vein of true poetry' and satirical depiction of bourgeois society.[35]

Nevertheless, despite all the regimented and static aspects of his utopia, Fourier was the most libertarian of the nineteenth-century French utopians. His wish to transform repulsive work into meaningful play, his call for the free satisfaction of sexuality, his stress on the social and sexual minimum, and his organic cosmology continue to inspire anarchists and ecologists alike.

12

German Libertarians

THERE HAVE BEEN TWO remarkable libertarians in Germany who scotch the myth that the German character is intrinsically authoritarian and given to State worship. While Hegel was denying the distinction between society and the State and arguing that citizens could only realize themselves through the State, his near contemporary Wilhelm von Humboldt narrowly drew the limits of legitimate State action. In the latter half of the nineteenth century, Friedrich Nietzsche too reacted against growing German nationalism and Bismarck's attempt to create a strong centralized State. He developed one of the most eloquent defences of individualism ever made, and deserves a central place in any history of libertarian thought.

Wilhelm von Humboldt

Humboldt's reputation as a libertarian thinker rests on one book. But while *The Limits of State Action* (1792) came close to anarchism, Humboldt ultimately remained in the liberal camp.[1] The work was not published in English until 1854 as *The Sphere and Duties of Government*; it considerably influenced John Stuart Mill in his essay *On Liberty* (1859). However, the anarchist historian Max Nettlau has called Humboldt's work 'a curious mixture of essentially anarchist ideas and authoritarian prejudice'.[2] More recently, Noam Chomsky has been inspired by Humboldt and through him his ideas have reached a new generation of libertarians and anarchists.[3]

Humboldt absorbed the radical message of the Enlightenment, particularly Leibniz's theory of human perfectibility, Rousseau's belief that moral self-determination is the essence of human dignity, and Kant's stress on the need to treat each individual as an end and never simply as a means. To this, he added an idealized version of the ancient Greek model of the fully rounded and harmonious human personality.

Humboldt's starting-point is the creative individual and his ultimate aim is to achieve the greatest individuality with the widest freedom possible in a variety of situations. It is his belief that only the spontaneous and creative energies of the individual constitute the vitality of a society. Self-education is thus the key concept of his political theory.[4]

Humboldt wrote:

The true end of Man or that which is prescribed by the eternal and immutable dictates of reason and not suggested by vague and transient desires, is the highest and most harmonious development of his powers to a complete and consistent whole. Freedom is the first and indispensable condition which the possibility of such a development presupposes.[5]

The most desirable condition is therefore the one in which each individual 'enjoys the most absolute freedom of developing himself by his own energies, in his perfect individuality'.[6] This principle must be the basis of every political system.

While Humboldt saw the individual and society in organic and aesthetic terms – as flowering plants and works of art – he insisted that the State is nothing more than a piece of machinery. Like later anarchists, he distinguishes between the State and society, or what he calls the State constitution and the national community: 'And it is strictly speaking the latter – the free cooperation of the members of the nation – which secures all those benefits for which men longed when they formed themselves into society.' He further recommends small associations, since in a large one a person easily becomes merely an instrument: 'The more a man acts on his own, the more he develops himself.'[7]

The basis of Humboldt's criticism of government is that it restricts personal autonomy and initiative:

Whatever does not spring from a man's free choice, or is only the result of instruction and guidance, does not enter into his very being, but still remains alien to his true nature; he does not perform it with truly human energies, but merely with mechanical exactness.[8]

Freedom, he argued, 'is but the possibility of a various and indefinite activity'; Humboldt was therefore concerned with 'greater freedom for human energies, and a richer diversity of circumstances and situations'.[9]

The paternalist State which seeks the positive welfare of the citizen is therefore harmful. By treating its subjects as children, it prevents them from learning from their own experience, it lessens the quality of their experience by imposing its own uniform character, and it weakens their initiative and independence. By trying to do good, it saps energy and weakens sympathy and mutual assistance. It can never improve the morals of its citizens since 'all moral culture springs solely and immediately from the inner life of the soul' and 'The greater a man's freedom, the more self-reliant and well-disposed towards others he becomes.'[10]

Rejecting unnecessary political regulations, Humboldt contemplates the possibility of an anarchist society:

If we imagine a community of enlightened men – fully instructed in their truest instances, and therefore mutually well-disposed and closely bound together – we can easily imagine how voluntary contracts with a view to their security, would be entered into among them . . . Agreements of this kind are infinitely to be preferred to any State arrangements.[11]

Humboldt's ideal society based on fellowship in which each individual is independent and yet part of society has something akin to libertarian socialism. It was precisely his aim to outline the kind of political organization which would allow 'the most diverse individuality and the most original independence' to coexist equally with 'the most diverse and profound associations of human beings with each other – a problem which nothing but the most absolute liberty can ever help to solve'.[12] Nevertheless, Humboldt retains the need for the nightwatchman State to stand guard over its citizens. Its principal role is negative: to maintain security, against both the external attacks of foreign enemies and internal dissension. Like Thomas Paine, he sees that State is a necessary means; 'and since it is always attended with restrictions of freedom, a necessary evil'.[13] The only justification for State interference is to prevent harm to others. Thus, while he came to the borders of anarchism, Humboldt ultimately remained in the liberal camp. This cannot be said of his compatriot Friedrich Nietzsche who came to anarchist conclusions quite independently.

Friedrich Nietzsche

Despite his erroneous reputation as the inventor of fascism, Nietzsche may be counted amongst the great libertarians for his attack on the State, his rejection of systems, his transvaluation of values, and his impassioned celebration of personal freedom and individuality. His libertarian views formed only part of his revolutionary attempt to reorientate totally European thought and sensibility. As a result, his influence was far-reaching and complex.

At the turn of the century, Nietzsche's form of individualism won many converts in bohemian and artistic circles throughout Europe – much to Kropotkin's dismay as he considered it too epicurean and egoistic.[14] Amongst anarchist thinkers, Emma Goldman also welcomed him into the family and admired his 'giant mind' and vision of the free individual.[15] Rudolf Rocker admired his analysis of political power and culture.[16] Herbert Read acknowledged that he was the first to make people conscious of the importance of the individual in evolution.[17] But his influence was not only restricted to anarchist intellectuals – Salvador Segui, the Catalan syndicalist who helped found the Spanish Confederación Nacional del Trabajo, was also deeply impressed by his message.

Nietzsche did not call himself an anarchist. He claimed that the anarchist of his day was, like the Christian, a decadent, 'the mouthpiece of a declining strata of society' because his complaints about others and society came from weakness and a narrow spirit of revenge.[18] Clearly this is true of some anarchists as well as some socialists. When the resentful anarchist demands with righteous indignation that his rights be respected he fails to see that his real suffering lies in his failure to create a new life for himself. At the same time, Nietzsche admired those anarchists who asserted their rights: many fail to assert rights to which they are perfectly entitled because 'a right is a kind of *power* but they are too lazy or too cowardly to exercise it'.[19]

With considerable psychological acumen, Nietzsche argued that anarchists of his day demonstrated that

> The desire for *destruction*, change, and becoming can be an expression of overfull, future-pregnant strength (my term for this, as one knows, is the word 'Dionysian'); but it can also be the hatred of the misdeveloped, needy, underprivileged who destroys, who must destroy, because the existing, and even all existence, all being, outrages and provokes him.[20]

Nietzsche was probably thinking of Bakunin here, whom his friend Richard Wagner knew. Those followers of Bakunin and the terrorists who destroy and maim in the name of freedom and justice are clearly motivated by hatred. Most anarchist thinkers, however, especially Godwin, Proudhon, Kropotkin and Tolstoy, were motivated by a sense of the overflowing richness and vitality of life in their wish to overthrow existing values and institutions.

Nietzsche thought that literary decadence sets in when instead of a work of art forming a whole, there is 'an anarchy of atoms'.[21] As a child of his age, he too recognized that he was a decadent but he tried to resist it. His work does not form a coherent whole, indeed he deliberately rejected system-making as a distortion of the truth. The will to construct a system shows a lack of integrity, and, moreover, ineradicable convictions are prisons.

Nietzsche's method is therefore experimental; he approaches his subjects tangentially. His style is aphoristic, rhapsodic and ironic. Engulfed in iconoclastic fervour, he is deliberately paradoxical. He wanted to soak his thoughts in blood, to show that knowledge has to be lived to be understood. It is not surprising that Nietzsche should often have been misinterpreted.

The most serious accusation against him is that he was a forerunner of

Nazism. This accusation was made possible by the work of his sister, who selectively edited his works when he became mad towards the end of his life, and by Nazi ideologues who took certain of his phrases and redeployed them completely out of their context. It is only by radically distorting his message that Nietzsche can be seen as an anti-Semite, a racist, or a German nationalist.[22] He despised and detested German culture, was utterly opposed to German nationalism, and thought the State the poison of the people. One of the main reasons why he broke with Wagner was because of the composer's anti-Semitism. Nietzsche's metaphor of the 'blond beast' became a model for the elevation of the Aryan German, but he was no racist, and even recommended racial mixing. Certainly he celebrated war, but like Blake he was thinking of intellectual not physical strife; he was well aware that 'blood is the worst witness of truth'.[23]

Nietzsche's atrocious views on women however cannot be explained away. 'In woman,' he wrote in *Thus Spoke Zaruthustra*, 'a slave and a tyrant have all too long been concealed. For that reason, woman is not capable of friendship: she knows only love.' A woman should be trained 'for the recreation of the warrior: all else is folly'. In the same work, Nietzsche ironically makes an old woman say 'Are you visiting women? Do not forget your whip!'[24]

Like Proudhon's and Tolstoy's, Nietzsche's attitude to women is lamentable. But his rehearsals of traditional misogyny can at least be better understood when we remember that his childhood was dominated by his mother, sister, grandmother and two aunts; his life as a lonely bachelor visiting European spas was full of frivolous women; and his relationship with the only love of his life, Lou Salomé, ended in failure. His complex relationship with women was aggravated by the fact that he became infected with syphilis from prostitutes as a young man. The disease eventually made him mad in the last ten years of his life and finally killed him. Ironically, the great philosophical misogynist was once photographed pulling a cart with Lou Salomé holding a whip in her hand! Nonetheless, all his antics did not prevent Emma Goldman from admiring his libertarian insights.

The most important premiss of Nietzsche's philosophy is his uncompromising atheism. Kropotkin acknowledged that next to Fourier, Nietzsche was unequalled in undermining Christianity.[25] He not only popularized the slogan 'God is Dead' but joked that there was only one Christian and he died on the cross. Like Bakunin, Nietzsche believed that traditional Christianity is a form of slave morality, with its stress on humility, pity and piety. Above all, it was decadent because it tried to extirpate the passions.

Unlike Bakunin, however, Nietzsche did not believe that law or morality could be derived from nature. Nature is entirely arbitrary and contingent: Lord Chance rules. Indeed, Nature is so disordered that given infinite time, finite space and constant energy in the world, Nietzsche argued, everything is likely to recur eternally. In this scheme of things man appears as a 'thoughtless accident', standing on a rope stretched over an abyss. His mind and body are two aspects of one being. The will, not reason, is paramount and determines both his thought and action. In Nietzsche's view of history there is no rational pattern or moral purpose to be discovered.

The problem for Nietzsche was to find meaning in a godless and arbitrary world based on chance and eternal recurrence. But he did not give into nihilistic despair. In our own lives, we are free to decide whether we want to be sickened or exhilarated by the journey, whether we want to follow the herd and act out inherited beliefs or to create our own life and values. Coming from nowhere, and going nowhere, we can nevertheless create ourselves and shape the world around us.

As in nature so in art: out of chaos human beings can create order. At first Nietzsche called the emotional element in life and art 'Dionysus', and its antithesis 'Apollo'. He saw Greek tragedy as the upshot of Apollo's harnessing of Dionysus, that is to say the creative force overcoming the 'animal' in the individual. Dionysus came to epitomize the sublimated will to power, and was therefore synonymous in Nietzschean vocabulary with *übermensch*, the man in whom the will to power is sublimated into creativity.[26]

What most characterizes Nietzsche's work is his libertarian insistence that the individual can throw off inherited values and beliefs and create his own. Like Stirner, he recognized that values are not given by God or nature but are human creations: every people has its own language of good and evil. While all moral codes are relative, their common element is the will to power.

Nietzsche perceptively saw that vengeance or resentment is at the core of most moral codes, which reveal themselves in their stress on punishment. He also recognized that public opinion, which many anarchists rely on to replace law, inevitably checks the individual from realizing himself: the 'You' of the crowd is older than the 'I'. In these circumstances, the love of one's neighbour is often a vicious form of selfishness, the result of bad love of oneself. In modern mass society, 'One man runs to his neighbours because he is looking for himself, and another because he wants to lose himself.'[27]

In higher and mixed cultures Nietzsche maintains that master and slave moralities have developed, and are often juxtaposed within one person. The rulers determine the master morality which exalts those states of being which determine the order of rank, such as severity and power. The ruled create a slave morality stressing pity, humility and patience to help them endure the burden of existence. Master and slave have contrary definitions of morality: according to the master, the 'good' man inspires fear; according to the slave, the 'evil' man inspires fear while the good man is harmless.[28] But Nietzsche would have us transcend these types of morality; the emancipated person goes beyond existing definitions of good and evil and creates his own anew. In his own moral revaluation, Nietzsche himself valued honesty, courage, self-discipline, strength, and generosity.

Nietzsche argued that our fundamental drive is the will to power. Even the pursuit of truth is often a disguised will to power. Nietzsche's concept of the will to power is one of his most misunderstood doctrines. He celebrates not power over nature or over others but over oneself. He considered the will to power over others to be the will of the weak: the really strong person seeks power only over himself in order to forge his own destiny. The only person one should obey is oneself, and great power reveals itself in self-mastery and is measured by joy. The will to power is therefore an 'instinct to freedom', to transcend and perfect oneself.

Nietzsche calls the developed person *übermensch*. It is usually translated as 'superman' but a more accurate translation is 'overman'. The 'overman' overcomes himself and sublimates his will to power into creativity. His greatest creation is himself. He is able to face the arbitrary nature of the world without pity, nausea and fear, and affirm life with all its suffering. Where for Hobbes power is essentially a means of security, for Nietzsche it is 'the state of being that man desires for its own sake as his own ultimate end'.[29]

Nietzsche's ideal of transformed humanity is that of the individual who overcomes his feelings of pity and terror and makes a work of art out of himself. His call 'You must come who you are' is a call for every individual to reach his or her full stature, to realize their complete potential as an act of creative will: '*to become them who we are* – the new, the unique, the incomparable, those who give themselves their own laws, those who create themselves'.[30] The emancipated human being is an egoist concerned with developing himself, but he helps the unfortunate not out of pity but because he overflows with generosity and strength. He values freedom, creativity, joy, and laughter. He lives dangerously and makes a Dionysian affirmation of life. His ultimate ideal is to realize in himself the 'eternal joy of becoming'.[31]

Freedom for Nietzsche is 'the will to self-responsibility'. He thought the struggle to achieve freedom more important than its attainment since it brings out the best in people. It can be measured in individuals and nations by 'the resistance which has to be overcome, by the effort it costs to stay *aloft*'.[32] Freedom is something one has and does not have, something one wants and achieves. To expand human freedom is a never-ending process of struggle in which one seeks mastery over desire for mere happiness or well-being. In politics and art, Nietzsche observed that the claim to independence, to free development, to *laissez aller* is advanced most heatedly by precisely those for whom 'no curb *could be too strong*'. Nietzsche thus understood progress in the sense of a return to nature but it is not a going back but a '*going-up*' into a high, free even frightful nature and naturalness, such as plays with great tasks, is *permitted* to play with them.'[33] The ideal for Nietzsche is complete self-creation and self-determination, to become a 'self-propelling wheel' who transforms chance into conscious intention.[34] The symbols of Zarathustra are the eagle and the serpent, creatures of power and knowledge who fly the highest and creep the lowest; a tree on a mountainside, the roots of which plunge deeper into the earth as the branches reach for the sky; and a laughing lion, a combination of strength, control and joy.

With these assumptions, it is no surprise that Nietzsche despised his contemporaries. His critique of European culture and politics is unparalleled in its spiteful vehemence:

> Just look at these superfluous people! They steal for themselves the works of inventors and the treasures of the wise: they call their theft culture – and they turn everything to sickness and calamity.
>
> Just look at these superfluous people! They are always ill, they vomit their bile and call it a newspaper. They devour one another and cannot even digest themselves.
>
> Just look at these superfluous people! They acquire wealth and make themselves poorer with it. They desire power and especially the lever of power, plenty of money – these impotent people!
>
> See them clamber, these nimble apes! They clamber over one another and so scuffle into the mud and the abyss.
>
> They all strive towards the throne: it is madness they have – as if happiness sat upon the throne! Often filth sits upon the throne – and often the throne upon filth, too.[35]

Nietzsche makes clear that the new idol of his contemporaries was the State. There were still peoples and herds in the world, but in Europe there were only States. He defined the State in terms which no anarchist could deny:

> The state? What is that? Well then! Now open your ears, for now I shall speak to you of the death of the peoples.
>
> The state is the coldest of all cold monsters. Coldly it lies, too; and this lie creeps from its mouth: 'I, the state, am the people.'
>
> It is a lie! It was creators who created peoples and hung a faith and a love over them: thus they served life.

It is destroyers who set snares for many and call it the state: they hand a sword and a hundred desires over them.

Where a people still exists, there the people do not understand the state and hate it as the evil eye and sin against custom and law.[36]

Nietzsche goes on to say that the State was invented for the superfluous. 'I call it the State where everyone, good and bad, is a poison-drinker: the State where everyone, good and bad, loses himself: the State where universal slow suicide is called – life.' It beckons the 'preachers of death'. It claims that there is nothing greater on earth and that it is 'the regulating finger of God'. It is nothing less than a 'cunning device of Hell . . . a horse of death jingling with the trappings of divine honours'. The church moreover is a kind of State and the State is a 'hypocrite dog' because it wants absolutely to be the most important beast on earth.[37]

Nietzsche did not restrict his criticism only to the Prussian State, for he attacked the whole conception of politics and political parties. Once they have been attained, he argued that liberal institutions immediately cease to be liberal and subsequently nothing is more harmful to freedom. Liberalism comes to mean the '*reduction to the herd animal*'.[38]

As for the relationship between culture and the State, Nietzsche insisted that the two are antagonists. Those who gain political power pay heavily for 'power *makes stupid*'. Culture and the State live off each other, one thrives at the expense of the other: 'All great cultural epochs are epochs of political decline: that which is great in the cultural sense has been unpolitical, even *anti-political*.'[39]

Certainly Nietzsche was no egalitarian. He despised the 'rabble' and saw his contemporaries as superfluous in their pursuit of wealth and status. They were utterly corrupted by *decadence* and *ressentiment* in their ethics of material comfort and envy. In thinking that there had been only a few truly developed human beings in the past, Nietzsche however was an elitist rather than an aristocrat. Ability is not related to blood. Even the slave can show nobility by rebelling. Humanity is not condemned forever: the earth still remains free for great souls who can lead free lives. In the final analysis, Nietzsche's philosophy is a song of freedom and creativity for the individual to make himself or herself anew. The individual and the moment have infinite value: 'so live that you must wish to live again.'

It cannot be denied that Nietzsche's extreme individualism leaves little room for community. His own experience of community was that it crushed individuality; he felt that a free life in his own time could only be possible for solitaries or couples. It is not unreasonable however to infer that his ideal of transformed humanity could exist like Stirner's union of egoists, a voluntary association of individualists who meet to fulfil their particular desires. Human beings for Nietzsche may not be equal in the sense of being uniform, but this does not mean they are not equally capable, regardless of race and sex, of creating themselves and society anew. He would have man fit for intellectual war and woman fit for bearing children, 'but both fit for dancing with head and heels'.[40] The dance for Nietzsche epitomized the union of creative energy with form, a joyful affirmation against all those who would renounce living in gloomy abstractions under moribund rules and regulations.

Emma Goldman, who was strongly influenced by Nietzsche, rightly insisted that he should not be decried as a hater of the weak because he believed in the *übermensch*: 'It does not occur to the shallow interpreters of the giant mind that his vision of the *übermensch* also called for a state of society which will not give birth to a race of weaklings and slaves.'[41] His 'aristocracy', she pointed out, was neither of birth nor of wealth but of the spirit: 'In that respect Nietzsche was an anarchist, and all true anarchists were aristocrats.'[42] Because of this, Nietzsche still speaks directly and eloquently to all those who wish to develop their full individuality, overthrow accepted values and received ideas, and to transform everyday life. He remains an inspiration, offering the hardest task of all, to create a free work of art out of oneself.

13

British Libertarians

WITH ITS STRONG LIBERAL tradition, Britain has produced many great libertarian thinkers. With their Protestant background, they are suspicious of authority and wish to defend the right of private judgement. They celebrate individuality and are fearful of the individual being lost in the community or overwhelmed by the oppressive State. They follow John Locke in seeing a negative role for government in guaranteeing the rights to life, liberty and property. With Adam Smith, they believe that if all people are allowed to pursue their own interests in the long run it will result in the general good.

Amongst the great nineteenth-century libertarians, only William Godwin extended liberalism to anarchism. Nevertheless, the philosophers John Stuart Mill and Herbert Spencer both persuasively defended the individual against the State while retaining a faith in limited government. Towards the end of the century, the writers William Morris, Edward Carpenter and Oscar Wilde all condemned private property and envisaged a world without government. Although they remained on the fringes of the organized anarchist movement, their libertarian vision, combining a love of beauty with a concern for personal freedom, remains one of the most inspiring and far-sighted.

John Stuart Mill

John Stuart Mill in his essay *On Liberty* (1859) insisted that individuality is one of the essential elements of human well-being. To this end, he quoted the German libertarian Wilhelm von Humboldt that 'the end of man ... is the highest and most harmonious development of his powers to a complete and consistent whole' and that the two requisites for individuality are 'freedom, and variety of situations'.[1] He further acknowledged his debt to the 'remarkable American' individualist anarchist Josiah Warren for the use of the phrase 'the sovereignty of the individual'.[2]

But while being a great libertarian and individualist, Mill was no democrat. He dreaded the ignorance of the masses and was fearful of the tyranny of the majority which socialism might involve. He seems to have mistaken Bakunin for the whole of the First International, and associated its socialism with general revolutionary destruction. Of the socialists, he was most impressed by Saint-Simon and Charles Fourier who retained a degree of inequality in their systems.[3]

Nevertheless, Mill was not a complete believer in *laissez-faire* and he wanted a fairer distribution of wealth. He came very close moreover to the anarchist goal of communal individuality in his famous formula:

> The social problem of the future we considered to be, how to unite the greatest individual liberty of action with a common ownership in the raw material of the globe, and equal participation of all in the benefits of combined labour.[4]

Mill has played an important part in the philosophical and the practical defence of individual and social freedom. He defended liberty on the grounds of utility, truth and individuality. He opposed the tyranny of government, of the majority, and of opinion. In his essay *On Liberty*, one of the great classics of libertarian thought, he insisted on an unbridled freedom of speech and thought. He did not, like Godwin, think that truth always triumphs over error, but he argued that free enquiry is best in pursuing truth. No one is infallible and can be sure that the opinion they are suppressing is true. Truth is most likely to emerge in the clash of opposing opinions. And only by defending and explaining our views can we have 'a living apprehension of a truth'.[5] Mill stands beside all those anarchists who believe that people should question authority and think for themselves.

Mill insists that 'The only freedom which deserves the name is that of pursuing our own good in our own way, so long as we do not attempt to deprive others of theirs, or impede their efforts to obtain it.'[6] It was on these grounds that he defended the liberty of conscience, of thought and feeling, of tastes and pursuits, of expression, and of association. In personal terms, he defined freedom in a negative way as doing what one desires – 'all restraint, *qua* restraint, is an evil.'[7] He even went further than most anarchists in pointing out the dangers of public opinion and social pressure in trying to make people conform, a tyranny which could be more oppressive than political authority. He celebrated individuality and diversity as good in themselves, and encouraged eccentricity and different 'experiments of living'.[8]

Making a distinction between self- and other-regarding actions, Mill argues that 'self-protection', either individual or collective, is the only legitimate reason for coercing anyone into doing something he or she does not want to do. People should only be interfered with when they intend definite harm or suffering to others; their own good does not offer sufficient grounds. We all have a right to be left alone: 'Over himself, over his own body and mind, the individual is sovereign.'[9]

Mill presents human beings as self-reliant and capable of responding to rational argument. On these grounds, he opposed 'a State which dwarfs its men, in order that they may be more docile instruments in its hands even for beneficial purposes – will find that with small men no great thing can really be accomplished.'[10] All this is admirably libertarian.

Although Mill often appears almost anarchistic, ultimately he remains, like Humboldt, in the liberal camp. He advocated women's suffrage and argued for proportional representation for minority voices. He was opposed to excessive regulation and centralization. He wanted to restrict government to the regulation of contracts and provision of public works. Yet in arguing his case for representative government, he called for plural voting in which the educated would have more votes than the ignorant. Above all, he followed Rousseau in arguing that 'Despotism is a legitimate mode of government in dealing with barbarians,' thereby justifying colonial rule.[11]

It is Mill's belief in the guiding role of an intellectual elite which prevents him from being regarded as an anarchist. He may have been a great libertarian in his defence of the freedoms of thought, expression and individuality, but he frequently stresses the need for intellectual authority rather than 'intellectual anarchy'.[12] He often pictured the happy society as one in which the people are voluntarily led by an elite of wise guardians. In the long run, the elitist in Mill gets the better of the democrat and the libertarian.

Herbert Spencer

Herbert Spencer, a father of modern sociology, developed a very different organic and evolutionary philosophy from Mill's, but he shared the same concern for individual freedom and fear of excessive government. In two classics of Victorian political thought, *Social Statics* (1851) and *The Man versus The State* (1884), he took up the defence of individuality and severely restricted the legitimate limits of the State. They were sufficiently libertarian to impress Kropotkin, who suggested that he had arrived at the same conclusions as Proudhon and Bakunin; and Emma Goldman, who thought that Spencer's formulation of liberty was the most important on the subject.[13]

Spencer tried like his contemporary Social Darwinists to ground his moral and political beliefs in a philosophy of nature. He was one of the first to apply Darwin's theory of natural evolution to social life and coined the phrase 'the survival of the fittest'. In his view, just as in nature the 'fittest' survive in the struggle for existence, so in society competition enables the best to emerge. But where Darwin defined the 'fittest' to be those most adapted to their environment, Spencer saw fitness in terms of the most successful individuals. The fittest societies are those of the fittest individuals.

At the same time, Spencer argued that societies operate like living organisms, growing more complex as their parts become more mutually dependent. Since they are inherently self-equilibrating, they need the struggles of their members for their further evolution. But where struggle took a military form in feudal society, Spencer would like to see the combination of competition and co-operation prevalent in industrial society take its place. In addition, he was confident that evolution operated as a kind of 'invisible hand' transforming private interest into the general good.[14] The long term direction of evolution was from egotism to altruism. In the process, social life would achieve the greatest development of individuality together with the greatest degree of sociability.

Drawing on contemporary anthropology, Spencer argued like Kropotkin that societies originally regulated their affairs by custom. On the other hand, 'Government is begotten of aggression and by aggression.'[15] A state of war established the authority of a chief who eventually developed into a king. Subsequent history was the record of aggressive war between States, and of class war within States. While all progress has depended on the efforts of individuals to achieve their private ends, governments have always thwarted the growth of society and never been able to enhance it. Rather than establishing rights, as Bentham argued, governments have merely recognized existing claims, especially the claim to property. Spencer concludes from all this that the future function of true liberalism will be that of 'putting a limit to the power of Parliaments'.[16] Like Mill, but from his own evolutionary perspective, he prophesized 'that form of society towards which we are progressing' is 'one in which *government* will be reduced to the smallest amount possible, and *freedom* increased to the greatest amount possible.'[17]

Spencer was equally critical of the socialism and liberalism of his day. He was hostile to representative government which he considered inferior to monarchical government because it results in the tyranny of the majority, the triumph of mediocrity, and inefficiency of administration. It is best only for securing justice, and worst for all other purposes.[18] The power of parliaments should therefore be restricted: 'The great political superstition of the present is the divine right of parliaments.'[19]

As for socialism, which he knew in its Marxist form via H. M. Hyndman, Spencer declared that 'all socialism involves slavery'. The essence of slavery is to make everything a possession; under socialism the citizen becomes owned by the State:

Judge what must under such conditions become the despotism of a graduated and centralized officialism, holding in its hands the resources of the community, and having behind it whatever amount of force it finds requisite to carry out its decrees and maintain what it calls order. Well may Prince Bismarck display leanings towards State-socialism.[20]

Spencer considered existing societies to be of 'the semi-militant semi-industrial type', whereas genuine freedom could only exist in an industrial society based on voluntary co-operation and competition. The socialists however wanted to recreate a military society based on compulsory co-operation. If they got their way, the ultimate result would be like the rigid and tyrannical society of ancient Peru.[21]

Spencer's criticisms of existing liberalism and socialism were made, like Mill's, from the point of view of individual freedom. In his political theory, he consistently opposed what he called 'Over-Legislation'(1853), so much so that T. H. Huxley accused him of 'Administrative Nihilism'.[22] In reply, Spencer claimed that the term might apply to Humboldt, whom he had never read, but certainly not to him.[23] Nevertheless, Spencer looked to a society in which *laissez-faire*, economic competition, voluntary co-operation, and the division of labour would ensure autonomy and general well-being.

But although Spencer pitches the individual against the State, he does not call for its abolition. As Kropotkin observed, he does not endorse all the conclusions about government which ought to be drawn from his system of philosophy.[24] Spencer's individualism was formulated in *The Proper Sphere of Government* (1842) where he argued like Humboldt and Mill that the duty of the State only lies in the protection of its citizens against each other. It may direct its citizens for security – both against external hostility and internal aggression – and for the enforcement of contract. But it should confer nothing beyond the opportunity to compete freely. Its function is 'simply to defend the natural rights of men – to protect person and property, to prevent the aggression of the powerful on the weak; in a word, to administer Justice'.[25]

Spencer wanted to make the State more efficient as a 'negatively regulative' body in preventing aggression and administering justice. Unlike Proudhon (whom he mentions), Spencer held that

within its proper limits governmental action is not simply legitimate but all-important . . . Not only do I contend that the restraining power of the State over individuals, and bodies or classes of individuals, is requisite, but I have contended that it should be exercised much more effectually, and carried out much further, than at present.[26]

Later in his life, Spencer gave the State a more positive role in promoting the moral law, that is the 'law of equal freedom' in which 'every man has freedom to do all that he wills, provided he infringes not the equal rights of every other man.'[27]

Spencer was as far removed from socialism as he was from genuine anarchism. He may have been a bold critic of the excessive power of the State, but he remained true to his background of middle-class provincial radicalism.[28] He feared the demands of the working class which he felt would lead to 'degeneracy', and what is even worse, to 'communism and anarchism'. Any attempt to bring about equal return for labour, he argued, leads to communism – then would come 'anarchism and a return to the unrestrained struggle for life, as among brutes'.[29]

Spencer undoubtedly anticipates modern anarcho-capitalists in his individualism, his economic *laissez-faire*, and his distrust of the powers of the State. Possessive individualism is the final premiss of his political thought.[30] For all his fine libertarian expressions, Spencer ultimately remains a spokesman for early industrial capitalism rather than modern anarchism. But while it may be a small irony of history that his tomb opposite Karl Marx's resplendent bust in Highgate Cemetery, London, is neglected and overgrown, his libertarian vision still lives on.

Edward Carpenter

Towards the end of the nineteenth century in Britain, anarchism exerted a considerable influence amongst radical literary circles. British intellectuals and artists were undoubtedly influenced by the liberal tradition of individualism found in the work of John Stuart Mill and Spencer, but their response to the triumph of capital and empire led them to a deeper analysis of exploitation and a more radical remedy. The clamour of the growing anarchist movement on the Continent also crossed the English Channel, and some of the more distinguished exponents like Prince Kropotkin took political refuge in the comparatively tolerant atmosphere of Britain.

Although the poet Edward Carpenter did not call himself an anarchist, his highly personal form of libertarian socialism comes very close to it. Kropotkin was the leading anarchist spokesman in Britain at the time, and Carpenter contributed to his journal *Freedom*, but the poet perceived in him a 'charming naïveté which summed up all evil in one word "government"'. Nevertheless, Henry W. Nevinson, to whom this remark was made, wrote about Carpenter: 'By temperament, if not by conviction, he was a complete anarchist, detesting all commandments, authority and forms of government.' He believed moreover that 'external law' must always be false and only acknowledged the internal law of self-expression.[31]

The key to Carpenter's libertarian socialism is to be found in his attitude to personal affections: he wanted a society in which men and women could be lovers and friends. He wanted to release what he called 'The Ocean of Sex' within each person. To this end, he urged the creation of 'The Intermediate Sex', a new type of being combining the male and the female, which would appear in *Love's Coming of Age* (1897) – dismissed predictably by Bernard Shaw as 'sex-nonsense'. Like many anarchists at that time, Carpenter turned to anthropology to back up his call for a new kind of humanity and he wrote a study of social evolution entitled *Intermediate Types among Primitive Folk* (1914). While he was far more radical than Spencer, he shared his evolutionary outlook and belief in social progress.

In his analysis of the causes of modern civilization, Carpenter followed Rousseau and Shelley in thinking that it corrupted and disintegrated natural man. The institution of private property in particular broke up the unity of his nature and drew him away from his true self and made him prey to every form of disease. Civilization founded on property had introduced: 'slavery, serfdom, wage-labour, which are various forms of the domination of one class over another; and to rivet these authorities it created the State and the policeman'.[32] Having destroyed the organic structures of earlier society, the institution of property had thus given rise to strong central government which was 'the evidence in social life that man has lost his inner and central control, and therefore must result to an outer one'.[33] Crime moreover is a symptom of social illness, poverty, inequality and restriction.[34]

But all is not lost and there is a cure for civilization. If every person were linked organically to the general body of his fellows, then no serious disharmony would occur. Carpenter thought it possible for a free and communist society to exist without external government and law which are only 'the travesties and transitory substitutes of Inward Government and Order'. Anarchy could therefore exist with no outward rule as 'an inward and invisible spirit of life'.[35]

Carpenter returned to this theme in his *Non-Governmental Society* (1911), a work which deeply impressed Gandhi and Herbert Read. Like Kropotkin, Carpenter was convinced that human societies can maintain themselves in good order and vitality without written law and its institutions. Indeed, he felt that custom, which takes a gentler form and is adaptable to the general movement of society when exerting pressure on individuals, is far superior to law. A study of 'native races' showed that the competition and anxiety of modern society need not exist if people were left to themselves. A 'free non-governmental society' could them emerge which would be practicable because it was vital and organic:

a spontaneous and free production of goods would spring up, followed
of course by a spontaneous free exchange – a self-supporting society,
based not on individual dread and anxiety, but on the common fulness
of life and energy.[36]

Work would be based on voluntary choice according to taste and skill
and there would be common property. A non-governmental society would
therefore be a free and communal society.

But while Carpenter put forward his case in reasoned arguments with
careful evidence in his pamphlets, he was primarily a poet. As a young man,
Shelley's libertarian world had been his ideal. When he came across Walt
Whitman at twenty-five, he felt a great surge of joy. To these influences
was added a deep reading of the *Bhagavadgita*. Carpenter went on to express
his own vision of a free world in his extraordinary rhapsody *Towards Democracy* (1883) which embraced the sexual revolution, direct democracy, vegetarianism and pacifism. Whatever his contemporaries thought of him, he
refused to still his song:

> O Freedom, beautiful beyond compare, thy kingdom is established!
> Thou with the thy feet on earth, thy brow among the stars, for ages
>   us thy children
> I, thy child, singing daylong nightlong, sing of joy in thee.[37]

In place of existing civilization, which pressed on people and left them
'cabin'd, cribb'd, confin'd', Carpenter called for a simple life in a decentralized society of fields and workshops in which every person would have a
cottage and sufficient land. Freedom emerges once the people love the
land:

> Government and laws and police then fall into their places
> – the earth gives her own laws; Democracy just begins to open
> her eyes and peep! and the rabble of unfaithful bishops, priests,
> generals, landlords, capitalists,lawyers, kings, queens, patronisers
> and polite idlers goes scuttling down into general oblivion.[38]

The individual would then live in harmony with himself, his fellows, and
his natural environment. Carpenter hoped moreover that he would develop
a higher form of consciousness in which the personal self is experienced as
part of the universal Self in 'The Everlasting Now'. But the Self can only
find expression in Democracy – equality or freedom – for they come to the
same thing.

Carpenter was no idle poet or mystic. He inherited a small independent
income after being a teacher, but he tried to realize his ideal by building
his own house, living off the land, and making sandals. It is for trying to
practise what he preached that Carpenter has rightly been called the 'Eng-

lish Tolstoi'.[39] And while he remained on the fringes of the anarchist movement, and felt private property was more important than government in bringing about the downfall of humanity, his decentralized vision of free society without law is entirely anarchistic.

William Morris

The poet and artist William Morris was a friend of Carpenter; he admired the simplicity of his lifestyle, while Carpenter respected his love of work and humanity. They were both involved for a time with the Democratic Federation and Socialist League in the 1880s and 1890s. But while Morris drew conclusions similar to those of Carpenter, he was more directly involved in the socialist movement and its political struggles. At the same time, he developed an original form of libertarian socialism which stemmed from a hatred of modern civilization with its physical ugliness and emotional constraint. His aim was not only to create beautiful things but also a beautiful society. The 'idle singer of an empty day', as he appeared in his early epic poem *The Earthly Paradise* (1868–70), moved from idealizing the Middle Ages and elaborating Celtic and Norse mythology to an anarchist vision of a free society.

Morris claimed that as a middle-class Englishman he had to cross a 'river of fire' before becoming a socialist.[40] But his socialism began with an intense desire for 'complete equality of condition', and he became a communist, before he knew anything about the history of socialism.[41] Ruskin had taught him that art is primarily the expression of a person's pleasure in work; he became convinced that it would only be just if all humanity could find such joy in work. Since this was impossible under capitalism, Morris the cultivated pagan became a practical socialist and joined the aforementioned Democratic Federation and then the more left-wing Socialist League.

There is a strong libertarian temper to Morris's writings and he was well aware of the anarchist case against government and political authority. G. K. Chesterton wrote him off as 'a sort of Dickensian anarchist'. There is no doubt that he hated the centralized State. He had, as he noted in 1887, 'an English-man's wholesome horror of government interference & centralization which some of our friends who are built on the German pattern are not quite enough afraid of'.[42]

It is not therefore surprising that many of his political essays have inspired anarchists. In 'Useful Work versus Useless Toil', he made a classic indictment of the capitalist division of labour which separated mental and manual work and reduced the worker to a mere machine operative. In clear and eloquent prose, he rejects capitalism, the 'society of contract', for its classes, its crude utilitarianism, its mass production, its machine domination and its compulsory labour. In its place, he advocates agreeable and voluntary work, with appropriate technology minimizing the time spent in unattractive labour.

In another essay, 'The Society of the Future', Morris sketched his libertarian ideal more boldly. His ultimate aim is 'the freedom and cultivation of the individual will'.[43] In place of existing political society, he calls like Kropotkin for a federation of self-governing communes. Life then would become unconstrained, simple and natural. It would be

> a society which does not know the meaning of the words rich and poor, or the rights of property, or law or legality, or nationality: a society which has no consciousness of being governed; in which equality of condition is a matter of course, and in which no man is rewarded for having served the community by having the power given to injure it.
>
> It is conscious of a wish to keep life simple, to forgo some of the power over nature won by past ages in order to be more human and less mechanical, and willing to sacrifice something to this end.[44]

In his utopian novel *News from Nowhere*, written in 1889 for successive issues of *Commonweal*, Morris offered one of the most persuasive glimpses of what a free society might be like. The revolution in England, we are told, has passed through two stages, not without bitter civil war, but a free and classless society has eventually emerged. Although for a time 'State socialism' doled out bread to the proletariat such a 'slough' was brought to an end.[45] In addition, the Committee of Public Safety set up to oppose the existing government at the beginning of the struggle was eventually dissolved.

There is nothing of the over-organized life and none of the centralized institutions obligatory in authoritarian utopias. For Morris, it is common sense, as clear as daylight, that government is unnecessary: 'a man no more needs an elaborate system of government, with its army, navy, and police, to force him to give way to the will of the majority of his *equals*, than he wants a similar machinery to make him understand that his head and a stone wall cannot occupy the same space at the same moment.'[46] The site of the Houses of Parliament has become a dung market, for there is no longer any need to house parliament ('a kind of watch-committee sitting to see that the interests of the Upper Classes took no hurt') since 'the whole people is our parliament'. Government, that 'machinery of tyranny' which protects the rich from the poor, has become obsolete in an equal society.[47]

In Morris's 'utopian romance', there is no government, private property, law, crime, marriage, money or exchange. Society consists of a federation of communes (based on the old wards and parishes). Affairs are managed by general custom reached by general assent. If differences of opinion arise, the Mote or assembly of neighbours meets and discusses the matter until there is general agreement which is measured by a show of hands; the majority will never impose its will on the minority, however small. If agreement cannot be reached, which is rare, the majority must accept the *status quo*.

It is a world in which Morris's ideal commonwealth has become a reality, in which human beings live in equality of condition, fully aware that harm to one would mean harm to all. They enjoy an abundance of life, and there is space and elbow-room for all. Factories have been replaced by workshops and people find joy in their work. Nothing is made except for genuine use and all work which is irksome to do by hand is done by improved machines. The only reward of labour is the reward of life and creation. Their happiness is thus achieved 'by the absence of artificial coercion, and the freedom for every man to do what he can do best, joined to the knowledge of what productions of labour we really wanted'.[48] They live simple yet beautiful lives in harmony with nature. The salmon leap in the river Thames which is only spanned by stone bridges. The picture Morris depicts is very reminiscent of Godwin's free society except that in place of lawcourts there is 'no code of public opinion which takes the place of such courts, and which might be as tyrannical and unreasonable as they were . . . no unvarying conventional set of rules by which people are judged; no bed of Procrustes to stretch or cramp their minds and lives'.[49]

While all this is entirely anarchistic, Morris has been called a Marxist dreamer.[50] He knew Engels and read Marx and certainly accepted the need for class struggle. He saw communism as completing socialism in which the resources of nature would be owned by 'the whole community for the benefit of the whole'.[51] However, his communist sympathies did not come from reading *Capital* – although he thoroughly enjoyed the historical part, its economic theories made him suffer 'agonies of confusion of the brain'.[52] They came from the study of history and it was the love and practice of art that made him hate capitalist civilization. He turned to Marx and aligned himself for a time with the authoritarian socialists Belfort Bax, H. M. Hyndman and Andreas Scheu because he wanted a 'practical' form of socialism which contrasted with his previous utopian dreams. He was, if anything, an original socialist thinker whose criticism of capitalism was merely reinforced by, if not 'complementary' to, Marxism.[53]

Morris liked Kropotkin, and his decentralized society is very similar to the one envisaged in Kropotkin's *Fields, Factories and Workshops*. He was also inspired by Carpenter's attempt to live a simple, communal and self-sufficient life in the country. Morris was always amiable in print towards those he called 'my Anarchist friends'. But just as he learned from Mill –

against *his* intention – that socialism was necessary, so he joked that he learned from the anarchists, quite against their intention, that anarchism was impossible.[54] His disagreement with the anarchists came to a head in the Socialist League when the anarchist group (led by Joseph Lane, Frank Kitz and Charles Mowbray) secured a majority after the Haymarket Massacre in Chicago in 1888 and began to advocate acts of violence. Repelled by the terrorist outrages throughout Europe in the early 1890s, Morris asked his anarchist friend James Tochatti, who edited *Liberty*, to repudiate the recent anarchist murders, adding: 'For I cannot for the life of me see how such principles [of anarchy], which propose the abolition of compulsion, can admit of promiscuous slaughter as a means of converting people.'[55]

Morris's principal theoretical objection to anarchism was over the question of authority. In a letter to the Socialist League's journal *Commonweal* of 5 May 1889, he reiterated his belief in communism, but argued that even in a communist society some form of authority would be necessary. If freedom from authority, Morris maintained, means the possibility of an individual doing what he pleases always and under all circumstances, this is 'an absolute negation of society'. If this right to do as you please is qualified by adding 'as long as you don't interfere with other people's rights to do the same', the exercise of some kind of authority becomes necessary. He concluded: 'If individuals are not to coerce others, there must somewhere be an authority which is prepared to coerce them not to coerce; and that authority must clearly be collective.' Furthermore, in an equal society some desires could not be satisfied without clashing with 'collective society' and in some instances 'collective authority will weigh down individual opposition'.[56] He did not want people to do exactly as they please; he wanted them to consider and act for the good of the commonweal.

It is of course Mill's and Spencer's argument that some restriction of freedom in the form of political authority are necessary to protect freedom. But, unlike Mill and Spencer, Morris had faith in the ability of people to arrange their affairs through mutual agreement. In reality, the differences between Morris and the anarchists are very slight. When he attacks anarchism, he is clearly thinking of a Stirnerite or Nietzschean type of anarchist individualism. In an interview with *Justice* on 27 January, 1894, after a French member of the Autonomie Club blew himself up while allegedly on his way to destroy the Royal Observatory at Greenwich, Morris made it clear that he had come to oppose the anarchists not only because of their inexpedient insurrectionary methods, but because anarchism 'negatives society, and puts man outside it'.

But many anarchist communists, including Kropotkin, would also repudiate such a view. While sharing Morris' concern with the problem of the anti-social individualist, they believe that persuasion rather than coercion is the best means of dealing with such people in the long run. In addition, many anarchists would not disagree with Morris's view that there should be a 'common rule of conduct' or 'common bond' in any group, that is 'the conscience of the association voluntarily accepted in the first instance', although they would not call it 'authority' as Morris did.[57] Morris insisted that by authority he was not pleading for something arbitrary or unreasonable but 'for a *public conscience* as a rule of action: and by all means let us have the least possible exercise of authority'.[58]

While Morris accepted reluctantly the need for a transitional socialist period of 'collective authority' before moving towards communism he wrote to Georgie Burne-Jones in 1888 that in itself it was a 'pretty dull goal'. Moreover, his daughter May Morris emphasized that 'he would no more accept the tyranny of a Collectivism that would crush individuality than he would accept the tyranny of Capitalism.' He was fully aware in a post-revolutionary society of 'the danger of the community falling into bureaucracy, the multiplication of boards and offices, and all the paraphernalia of official authority'.[59] Morris may have appreciated Marx's view of history, and wanted to give a practical expression to his utopian dreams, but in the final analysis Morris belongs more to the extended anarchist family rather than to authoritarian socialism.

Oscar Wilde

Wilde admired Morris as a poet and as a book designer, and they shared a common friend in the Russian revolutionary Stepniak. Their concern with freedom was mainly inspired by their concern for art and their desire to create a beautiful life. They both came to realize that art for art's sake is an insufficient standard; it is not enough merely to call for the beautification of life, for there must be a political and social context to aestheticism. Wilde concluded that only in a free society without government would an artist be able to express himself fully.

From his early childhood, he had a strong utopian sensibility which led him to conjure up imaginary islands. He remained convinced that

> a map of the world that does not include Utopia is not worth glancing at, for it leaves out the one country at which Humanity is always landing. And when Humanity lands there, it looks out, and, seeing a better country, sets sail. Progress is the realization of Utopias.[60]

Wilde's love of liberty was encouraged by his mother who saw herself as 'a priestess at the altar of freedom'.[61] Unlike her, however, he saw nothing noble in suffering and sought to create a beautiful life without ugliness and

pain and compulsion. As a student at Oxford, he came to the conclusion
not only that '*La beauté est parfaite*' but that 'Progress in thought is the
assertion of individualism against authority.'[62]

After leaving Oxford, Wilde wrote in his twenties a play called *Vera; or,
The Nihilist* (1880). He was already calling himself a socialist, but it is clear
from the play that he considered socialism to be not a levelling down but
the flowering of personality. Prince Paul declares: 'in good democracy, every
man should be an aristocrat.'[63] The nihilists detest torture and martial law
and demand the abolition of marriage and the right to labour. To make
them as authentic as possible, Wilde even borrowed an oath from Nechaev's
Catechism of a Revolutionary which Bakunin may have helped edit.

He later described agitators as

> a set of interfering, meddling people, who come down to some perfectly
> contented class of the community, and sow the seeds of discontent
> amongst them. That is the reason why agitators are so absolutely
> necessary.[64]

Even though he hated violence, he admired sincere revolutionaries – 'these
Christs who die upon the barricades'. Moreover, he saw a beneficial tendency in all rebellion:

> Disobedience, in the eyes of any one who has read history, is man's
> original virtue. It is through disobedience that progress has been made,
> through disobedience and through rebellion.[65]

But Wilde's anarchistic sentiments were not just limited to vague calls for
liberty and disobedience. More than once he quoted Chuang Tzu to the
effect that 'there is such a thing as leaving mankind alone; and there has
never been such a thing as governing mankind.' Giving his own gloss to
this ancient Chinese wisdom, Wilde wrote:

> All modes of government are wrong. They are unscientific, because
> they seek to alter the natural environment of man; they are immoral
> because, by interfering with the individual, they produce the most
> aggressive forms of egotism; they are ignorant, because they try to
> spread education; they are self-destructive, because they engender
> anarchy.[66]

He was also convinced that the accumulation of wealth is the origin of evil
by making the strong violent and the weak dishonest: 'The order of nature
is rest, repetition and peace. Weariness and war are the results of an artificial
society based on capital; and the richer this society gets, the more thoroughly
bankrupt it really is.'[67]

Wilde not only had his genius to declare; he told an interviewer in
France in the spring of 1894: 'I think I am rather more than a Socialist. I

am something of an Anarchist, I believe, but, of course, the dynamite policy is very absurd indeed.'[68] He knew what he was talking about. He met Kropotkin and considered his life to be one of the two most perfect lives he had ever come across; indeed, Kropotkin was 'a man with a soul of that beautiful white Christ which seems [to be] coming out of Russia'.[69]

Wilde gave his own considered version of anarchism in his brilliant essay *The Soul of Man under Socialism* (1891), a work which was translated into many languages and proved particularly influential in Tsarist Russia.

Wilde had long been drawn to socialism and had expressed his sympathies publicly early in 1889 in a review of a book edited by Carpenter, *Chants of Labour: a Song-Book of the People*. He found in socialism a new motif for art and hoped art could help in the construction of an 'eternal city'. Yet he was clearly already concerned to make socialism humanitarian and libertarian, 'for to make socialists is nothing, but to make socialism human is a great thing'. He took up the theme, two years later, in his great essay. It was initially inspired by a meeting on socialism which he attended in Westminster where the chief speaker was Bernard Shaw. But Wilde's socialism could not be more different from Shaw's for it is as pure an anarchism as you can get: 'there is no necessity to separate the monarch from the mob; all authority is equally bad', he declares.[70]

With the air of a paradox, Wilde argues that socialism is of value simply because it will lead to individualism. But this can be achieved only if socialism is libertarian. With prophetic acumen, he warns: 'If the Socialism is Authoritarian; if there are Governments armed with economic power as they are now with political power; if, in a word, we are to have Industrial Tyrannies, then the last state of man will be worse than the first.'[71] Such authoritarian socialism would mean the enslavement of the entire community instead of only a part.

According to Wilde, all modes of government are failures and social democracy means simply 'the bludgeoning of the people by the people for the people'. Equally all authority is quite degrading: 'It degrades those who exercise it, and degrades those over whom it is exercised.' By bribing people to conform, authority produces 'a very gross kind of overfed barbarism'.[72] He therefore agrees with Chuang Tzu that there is 'such a thing as leaving mankind alone' and concludes with Thoreau that 'The form of government that is most suitable to the artist is no government at all.'[73]

Instead of governing, the State should become merely a 'voluntary association' that will organize labour and be responsible for the manufacture and distribution of necessary commodities. Wilde insists that all associations must be quite voluntary. Man should be free not to conform. In all this Wilde agrees with Godwin, but he takes leave of him when he declares categorically that public opinion – 'that monstrous and ignorant thing' – is of no value whatsoever to reform human conduct.[74] People are good only when they are left alone.

Wilde argues like Nietzsche that it is wrong for the rich to pity the poor and give charity, and that there is no point to the poor feeling gratitude: 'it is finer to take than to beg.'[75] But unlike most individualists he does not see that private property is a guarantee of personal independence; indeed, for Wilde, it crushes true individualism. It should therefore be converted into public wealth by 'Socialism, Communism, or whatever one chooses to call it' and co-operation substituted for competition to ensure the material well-being of each member of the community.[76] With the abolition of private property, there will no longer be any marriage; love will then be more beautiful and wonderful. In the long run, it is not material things that are important; what is really valuable is within.

There are other great advantages to follow from the dissolution of political authority. Punishment will pass away – a great gain since a community is infinitely more brutalized by the habitual employment of punishment than it is by the occasional occurrence of crime. What crime will remain after the eradication of its principal cause in property will be cured by care and kindness. No compulsion should be exercised over anyone and every person should be free to choose his or her work.

According to Wilde, it is nonsense to talk about the dignity of manual labour: 'Man is made for something better than disturbing dirt.'[77] Most of it is degrading and should be done by machines, the helots of the future, so that all can enjoy cultivated leisure. Useful things can thus be made by machines, beautiful ones by the individual. The value of art is immense for

> Art is Individualism, and Individualism is a disturbing and disintegrating force. Therein lies its immense value. For what it seeks to disturb is monotony of type, slavery of custom, tyranny of habit, and the reduction of man to the level of the machine.[78]

For Wilde socialism is a means to an end; the goal is the full development of the personality. He insists that the artist would only be able to flourish in a society without government, but it is not only political authority that he is concerned with. He suggests that there are three kinds of despotism: 'There is the despot who tyrannizes over the body. There is the despot who tyrannizes over the soul. There is the despot who tyrannizes over the body and soul alike. The first is called the Prince. The second is called the Pope. The third is called the People.'[79] All three should be done away with.

Wilde admires Christ since he urged man to 'Be thyself.' But he made no attempt to reconstruct society and preached that man could realize a form of individualism only through pain or in solitude. Wilde insists that man is naturally social and the aim of life and art is joy. He therefore calls his new individualism a 'new Hellenism' which combines the best of Greek and Christian culture. It looks to socialism and science as its methods and aims at an intense, full and perfect life. If successful it will bring pleasure for 'When man is happy, he is in harmony with himself and his environment.'[80]

Wilde faces the stock objections to his ideal of anarchy that it is impractical and goes against human nature. Firstly, the only thing that one really knows about human nature is that it changes, and once existing conditions are changed human nature will change. Evolution is a law of life and the tendency of evolution is towards individualism. Secondly, Wilde claims that his form of individualism will not be selfish or affected. Man is naturally social. Selfishness is not living as one wishes to live, it is asking others to live as one wishes to live. It aims at creating an absolute uniformity of type. Unselfishness, on the other hand, is 'letting other people's lives alone, not interfering with them'.[81] When man has realized true individualism, he will also realize sympathy and exercise it freely and spontaneously. In a society without poverty and disease, man will have joy in the contemplation of the joyous life of others.

Daring to oppose conventional morality, Wilde was imprisoned for homosexuality. It broke his health, but not his spirit. The experience only confirmed his analysis of the judicial system and government. He wrote afterwards to a friend that he wished to talk over 'the many prisons of life – prisons of stone, prisons of passions, prisons of intellect, prisons of morality and the rest. All limitations, external or internal, are prisons.'[82]

Furthermore, the experience inspired one of the most moving poems in the English language, *The Ballad of Reading Gaol* (1896), the simple form of which expresses the deepest of emotions. The poem concerns a soldier who is about to be hanged for murdering his lover; the theme implied is that such cruelty is widespread ('each man kills the thing he loves'), but Wilde insists that the murderer's punishment by a guilty society is the greater cruelty. He directly sympathizes with the condemned man, drawing the inevitable conclusion:

> But this I know, that every Law
>   That men have made for Man,
> Since first Man took his brother's life,
>   And the sad world began,
> But straws the wheat and saves the chaff
>   With a most evil fan.

> The vilest deeds likes poison weeds
>   Bloom well in prison-air;
> It is only what is good in Man
>   That wastes and withers there:
> Pale Anguish keeps the heavy gate,
>   And the Warder is Despair.[83]

Wilde is the greatest of all libertarians. He recognized that art by its nature is subversive and the artist must rebel against existing moral norms and political institutions, but saw that only communal property can allow individuality to flourish. He argued that every person should seek to make themselves perfect by following their own inner impulses. This could be made possible only by the break-up of habit and prejudice, a thorough transformation of everyday life. He placed art and thought at the centre of life, and realized that true individualism leads to spontaneous sympathy for others. He had a wonderful sense of play and wit, and was blessed with overflowing creative energy. As a result, Wilde's libertarian socialism is the most attractive of all the varieties of anarchism and socialism. Bernard Shaw observed that contemporary Fabian and Marxian socialists laughed at his moral and social beliefs, but Wilde as usual got the last laugh. He will be long remembered after they have been forgotten.

14

American Libertarians

THERE IS A LONG TRADITION in North America of hostility to the State and defence of personal autonomy; the United States is after all the oldest liberal democracy in the world. The Protestant right of private judgement or conscience became a central part of American political culture, and formed the basis of the defence of freedom of thought and speech. It also accounts for the deeply ingrained sense of individualism in American society.

After the American War of Independence, the founding fathers of the new republic felt compelled to introduce government to protect private property and individual rights to life, liberty and the pursuit of happiness. But they were keen to keep government interference to a minimum and adopted the principle of federation to spread political authority throughout the regions. Immediately after the Revolution, the Articles of Confederation established minimal government, libertarian and decentralized, although its powers were inexorably strengthened in the following decades.

The self-reliant settlers were well aware without reading Tom Paine's *Common Sense* (1776) that 'Society in every state is a blessing, but government even in its best state is but a necessary evil; in its worst state an intolerable one'. They shared for the most part the maxim attributed to Thomas Jefferson: 'That government is best which governs least.' The principle has become a rallying-cry for libertarians ever since, although anarchists have added that the best government is that which governs not at all.

In the nineteenth century, American anarchism developed mainly in an individualist direction in the hands of Josiah Warren, Stephen Pearl Andrews, Lysander Spooner and Benjamin Tucker. While they came close to anarchism, the writers Emerson, Whitman and Thoreau expressed most keenly the libertarian ideal. Their independent stance directly inspired later anarchists and their combination of 'Transcendental Individualism' with a search for a creative life close to nature finds echoes in the counter-culture and Green movements of the late-twentieth century.

Ralph Waldo Emerson

Ralph Waldo Emerson was the elder guru of the Transcendentalists of New England. After Harvard University, he entered the ministry, only to abandon it and sail to Europe, where he became a friend of Carlyle. He returned to Massachusetts and was soon installed as 'the Sage of Concord', attracting a literary-philosophical coterie. At Concord, he developed his philosophy – relying on intuition as the only access to reality – in prose of uncommon lyricism. Believing in the 'divine sufficiency of the individual', he refused to accept the inevitability or objective existence of evil. Emerson based his libertarian vision on a belief that 'reason is potentially perfect' in everyone and that 'a man contains all that is needful to his government within himself'.[1] Conscience moreover is sacrosanct and capable of leading us to moral truth. 'Judge for yourself . . . reverence yourself', he taught. An inevitable inference of his doctrine was that each man should be a State in himself; we should develop our individual character as rational and moral beings rather than set up oppressive and superfluous State institutions. Indeed, in his essay on 'Politics' (1845), Emerson declared as a radical Jeffersonian:

> the less government we have the better – the fewer laws and the less confided power. The antidote to this abuse of formal government is the influence of private character, the growth of the Individual . . . To educate the wise man the State exists, and with the appearance of the wise man the State expires. The appearance of character makes the State unnecessary. The wise man is the State.[2]

He went on to advise Americans to 'give up the government, without too solicitously inquiring whether roads can still be built, letters carried, and title deeds secured when the government of force is at an end'.[3] When in 1850 a fugitive slave bill was passed by Congress and supported by the President, he characteristically declared: 'I will not obey it, by God!' He once wrote the lines which the anarchist Benjamin Tucker was fond of quoting:

> When the Church is social worth,
> When the State-house the hearth,
> Then the perfect state has come, –
> The republican at home.

In place of government by force, Emerson proposed the popular assembly of a town meeting as the forum for decision-making. It had served well in seventeenth-century new England, and could serve well again. But there were limits to Emerson's libertarianism. Having freely accepted to be bound by the rules of a society, he believed that one had an obligation to obey them or else try and change them from within or withdraw. On these grounds, Emerson upheld the Harvard regulation for compulsory chapel.

Emerson's social views were only a minor part of his Transcendental philosophy which stressed the unity of all things. Everything in this world is a microcosm of the universe and 'the world globes itself in a drop of dew'. The universe is also ordered by a Supreme Mind or Over-Soul. Since man's soul is identical with the Over-Soul, and human nature is divine, it follows that there is no need of external authority and tradition. Because there is a higher law in the universe, man does not need human law. The individual can therefore rely on his direct experience for guidance; hence Emerson's motto 'Trust thyself.'

Walt Whitman

Walt Whitman was not a member of Emerson's literary circle in Concord, but the Sage recognized him immediately as a kindred spirit. When the first edition of his rhapsodic book of poems *Leaves of Grass* (1855) appeared, he greeted Whitman 'at the beginning of a great career', and wished him 'joy of your free and brave thought'.[4] After their meeting, Emerson went on to praise Whitman's lawless nature.

Whitman had a completely different background from Emerson. He left school at eleven and held several odd jobs, but gradually began earning a living through printing and journalism. He became the editor of the Brooklyn Democrat paper *Eagle*, but was sacked for supporting the Freedom movement. He then founded his own paper the *Freeman* but it folded within a year. Little of his early writing anticipated the remarkable originality of his first volume of twelve untitled poems which became expanded in *Leaves of Grass*. Whitman intended his poetry, with its remarkable mixture of the earthy and the mystical, to be read by the working man and woman of America. Yet, apart from Emerson's approval, it was not well received.

A strong democratic and egalitarian impetus and sensibility fire all Whitman's work. He felt that the New World needed poems of 'the democratic average and basic equality'.[5] In 'A Thought by the Roadside', he wrote:

> Of Equality – as if it harm'd me, giving others the same chances
> and rights as myself – as if it were not indispensable to my
> own rights that others possess the same.[6]

At the same time, Whitman like Emerson was a great individualist. He sang a song of himself and offered an exposé of his own personality in his poems of freedom. But while he celebrated the sacredness of the self, he also

praised the love of comrades. He therefore combined his love of comradeship with a strong sense of individuality; he wanted his poems to stress
American individuality and assist it – 'not only because that is a great lesson
in Nature, amid all her generalizing laws, but as a counterpoise to the
leveling tendencies of Democracy'. It was the ambitious thought of his song
to form 'myriads of fully develop'd and enclosing individuals'.[7]

As a journalist, Whitman knew at first hand the corrupting nature of
everyday politics. He also directly suffered at the hands of the State. He
served as a nurse in the military hospitals of Washington during the Civil
War and revealed his sympathy for the common soldier and his hatred of
war in *Drum-Taps* (1865). Afterwards, he became a clerk in the Department
of the Interior until the Secretary discovered he was there and dismissed
him as the author of a 'vulgar' book.

Whitman therefore had good reason to consider politicians and judges
as 'scum floating atop of the waters' of society – 'as bats and night-dogs
askant in the capitol'.[8] He also advised the working men and women of
America thus:

> To the States or any one of them, or any city of the States,
> *Resist much, obey little,*
> Once unquestioning obedience, once fully enslaved,
> Once fully enslaved, no nation, no state, city of this earth, ever
> afterwards resumes its liberty.[9]

Whitman spoke on behalf of most anarchists when he asked 'What do you
suppose will satisfy the soul, except to walk free and own no superior?' But
although a radically democratic conception of society emerges from his
poetry, he did not offer any clear or definite vision of a free society.

Henry David Thoreau

This cannot be said of Henry David Thoreau, whom Whitman admired
deeply. 'One thing about Thoreau keeps him very close to me', he remarked.
'I refer to his lawlessness – his dissent – his going his absolute own road
hell blaze all it chooses.'[10]

Although Thoreau came under Emerson's direct influence, he combined mysticism with a Whitmanesque earthiness, and he took Transcen-
dentalism in a more naturalistic direction. He also was not content merely
to preach, but strove to act out his beliefs.

Thoreau was born at Concord, and while he spent most of his youth
there, he eventually followed Emerson and became a student at Harvard
University. After his studies he became a teacher, but he soon returned to
Concord. The experience had not entirely been in harmony with his nature:

he rapidly tired of modern civilization and sought a new way of life. For a while he lived under Emerson's roof as a general handyman and pupil, but still he was not satisfied. He therefore decided in 1845 to undertake what was to be his famous experiment in simple living: he built himself a shack on Emerson's land on the shores of Walden Pond. He lived and meditated there for two years, two months and two days. But the State would still not leave him alone and he was arrested and imprisoned for one night in 1845 for refusing to pay his poll tax. The experience led him to write a lecture on 'The Rights and Duties of the Individual in relation to Government'. Printed in a revised form, it became first the essay 'Resistance to Civil Government' and then finally *On the Duty of Civil Disobedience* (1849). It proved to be Thoreau's greatest contribution to libertarian thought.

Thoreau's refusal to pay a poll tax was a symbolic protest against America's imperialistic war in Mexico. He could not bring himself to recognize a government as his own which was also a slave's government. He accepted his imprisonment on the moral principle that 'Under a government which imprisons any unjustly, the true place for a just man is also in prison.'[11]

Emerson rightly called Thoreau a 'born Protestant'. He combined the Dissenters' belief in the right of private judgement with Locke's right to resist tyranny. He added to them and developed a highly personal and influential form of individualism which was to influence many anarchists and libertarians, including Gandhi and Martin Luther King. Thoreau's key principle is the absolute right to exercise his own judgement or moral sense: 'The only obligation which I have a right to assume is to do at any time what I think is right.'[12]

Like Godwin, he opposed this individual right against man-made laws. If a person considers that a law is wrong, he has no obligation to obey it; indeed, he has a duty to disobey it. Morality and man-made law therefore have little to do with each other: 'Law never made men a whit more just; and, by means of their respect for it, even the well-disposed are daily made the agents of injustice.'[13]

It was his belief that a person need only follow a higher law discerned by his conscience which led Thoreau to renounce external authority and government. He therefore went beyond the Jeffersonian formula 'That government is best which governs least' to the anarchist conclusion 'That government is best which governs not at all.'[14] Thoreau felt that the same objection against governments may be brought against standing armies: both oblige men to serve the State with their bodies as if they were mindless machines.

Beyond the close argument about moral and political obligation, what emerges most prominently from Thoreau's essay on civil disobedience is his passion for freedom: 'I was not born to be forced', he declares. 'I will breathe after my own fashion.' After leaving prison his first impulse was to walk in a nearby huckleberry field on the highest hill where 'the State was nowhere to be seen'.[15]

It was the same impulse which made him celebrate the wilderness as 'absolute freedom', an oasis in the desert of modern urban civilization.[16] Thoreau believed that the preservation of the world is to be found in the wilderness; his social ecology was so radical that he went beyond politics: 'Most revolutions in society have not power to interest, still less to alarm us; but tell me that our rivers are drying up, or the genus pine is dying out in the country, and I might attend.'[17]

Thoreau asked his compatriots:

> Do you call this the land of the free? What is it to be free from King George and continue to be slaves of King Prejudice? What is it to be born free and not to live free? What is the value of political freedom, but as a means to moral freedom? Is it a freedom to be slaves or a freedom to be free, of which we boast? We are a nation of politicians, concerned about the outmost defences of freedom. It is our children's children who may perchance be really free.[18]

In *Walden; or, Life in the Woods* (1854), he described the 'quiet desperation' or alienation of urban industrialized man, alienated from nature, himself and his fellows as a producer and a consumer. In the process of searching for profit and power, modern man had lost his way. Servitude not only took the form of Negro slavery, but many subtle masters enslaved society as a whole. Worst of all, people made slave-drivers of themselves. It was to overcome this state of affairs that Thoreau chose to live as self-sufficiently as possible by the pond at Walden. He went into the woods to confront only the essential facts of life, wanting to live in simplicity, independence, magnanimity and trust.

Thoreau had a singular yearning towards all wildness. He had a passion for the primitive. He delighted in the sensuous vitality of his body (while being unable to appreciate women) and was awed by the teeming life in nature. A chaste and literate loner, he was one of the first imaginary Indians. Yet he did not want to return to a primitive way of life and turn his back on all the gains of Western civilization. Although fascinated by the culture of American Indians, he was repelled on occasion by their 'coarse and imperfect use of nature'. Following an unhappy moose-hunt in Maine, he recalled: 'I, already, and for weeks afterwards, felt my nature coarser for this part of my woodland experience, and was reminded that our life should be lived as tenderly and daintily as one would pluck a flower.'[19]

Thoreau did not therefore reject all the achievements of so-called civilization. He not only condemned in *Walden* a 'Life without Principle' but called for a life according to 'Higher Laws' (the second name chosen for the same chapter). In the section on 'Reading' he recommended a study of the oldest and best books, whose authors are 'a natural and irresistible aristocracy in every society, and, more than kings or emperors, exert an influence on mankind'.[20] Thoreau was for the simple life, but not for a life without learning and manners.

He stood half-way between heaven and earth, the civilized and the wild, the railroad and the pond, a Transcendental savage who gloried in the primitivism of the lost race of American Indians and who sought the 'Higher Laws' of oriental mysticism. He was well aware of the dualism in his character and he found 'an instinct toward a higher, or, as it is named, spiritual life, as do most men, and another toward a primitive rank and savage one, and I reverence them both. I love the wild not less than the good.'[21] But he went beyond the alternative of 'civilization' and 'barbarism' to make a creative synthesis of the two. He wanted the best in nature and culture for himself and his fellow citizens.

While Thoreau was a great rebel, he saw rebellion largely in personal terms. But his individualism was not the rugged or narrow individualism of capitalism, but one which wished to preserve individuality in the face of the coercive institutions and conformist behaviour of modern civilization. Neither did he reject society nor the companionship of his fellows. In *Civil Disobedience*, he insists that he is 'as desirous of being a good neighbour as I am of being a bad subject'.[22] He served American society by trying to reveal its true nature to its citizens.

In place of the hectic and anxious life of commerce and the interfering force of the State, Thoreau recommended a decentralized society of villages. If people lived simple lives as good neighbours they would develop informal patterns of voluntary co-operation. There would then be no need for the police or army since robbery would be unknown. Such a society moreover need not be parochial. Like Kropotkin after him, Thoreau called for the leisure to develop our full intellectual and social potential: 'It is time that villages were universities . . . To act collectively is according to the spirit of our institutions . . . Instead of noblemen, let us have noble villages of men.'[23]

Apart from a brief foray into the campaign against slavery, Thoreau made no attempt to become involved in any organized political movement. He was exceptionally jealous of his personal freedom and felt that his connection with and obligation to society were 'very slight and transient'. He considered what is normally called politics so superficial and inhuman that 'practically I have never fairly recognized that it concerns me at all'.[24] He derided politics and politicians for making light of morality and considered voting merely 'a sort of gaming, like checkers or backgammon, with a slight moral tinge to it, a playing with right and wrong, with moral questions'.[25]

But while practising the 'one-man revolution', Thoreau did not deny his wider bonds with humanity. He called for acts of rebellion, of resistance and non-cooperation: 'let your life be a counter-friction to stop the machine' – the machine of government, of war and of industrialization.[26] Despite his influence on Gandhi and Martin Luther King, he was not an absolute pacifist and defended direct action in *A Plea for Captain John Brown* (1860), after the famous abolitionist had seized Harpers Ferry in 1859 as a protest against Negro slavery.

Thoreau was fully aware of the coercive nature of the State. He met his government, he said, once a year in the person of the tax-gatherer, and if he denied the authority of the State when it presented him its tax bill, he knew it would harass him without end. But he did not try to overthrow it by force. He simply refused allegiance to the State, withdrew and stood aloof from it if it performed acts he did not agree with.

In fact, Thoreau was a gradualist and 'unlike those who call themselves no-government men, I ask for, not at once no government, but *at once* a better government.' He might not like the government and the State, but this did not mean that he would have nothing to do with it: 'I quietly declare war with the State, after my fashion, though I will still make what use and get what advantage of her I can.'[27] While he refused to pay tax to finance war, he was willing to pay tax for roads and schools. Like the Greek Stoics whom he admired, he considered himself beyond politics, and however the State dealt with his body, his mind would always be free: 'If a man is thought-free, fancy-free, imagination-free . . . unwise rulers or reformers cannot fatally interrupt him.'[28]

Although Thoreau shares the ultimate anarchist goal of a society without a State, he is willing to make use of it in the present and believed that a long period of preparation would be necessary before it eventually withered away. Nevertheless, he anticipates modern anarchism by envisaging a world of free and self-governing individuals who follow their own consciences in a decentralized society. He is also a forerunner of social ecology in recognizing that by preserving the wilderness of nature, we preserve ourselves.

PART FOUR

Classic Anarchist Thinkers

Our destiny is to arrive at that state of ideal perfection where
nations no longer have any need to be under the tutelage
of a government or any other nation. It is the absence of
government; it is anarchy, the highest expression of order.
ELISÉE RECLUS

Once annihilate the quackery of government, and the most
homebred understanding might be strong enough to detect
the artifices of the state juggler that would mislead him.
WILLIAM GODWIN

Freedom without Socialism is privilege and injustice . . .
Socialism without freedom is slavery and brutality.
MICHAEL BAKUNIN

All governments are in equal measure good and evil. The best
ideal is anarchy.
LEO TOLSTOY

Mind your own business.
BENJAMIN TUCKER

15

William Godwin

The Lover of Order

WILLIAM GODWIN WAS THE first to give a clear statement of anarchist principles. In his own day, his principal work *An Enquiry concerning Political Justice* (1793) had an enormous impact. 'He blazed', his fellow radical William Hazlitt wrote,

> ·as a sun in the firmament of reputation; no one was more talked of, more looked up to, more sought after, and wherever liberty, truth, and justice was the theme, his name was not far off . . . No work in our time gave such a blow to the philosophical mind of the country as the celebrated *Enquiry concerning Political Justice*.[1]

The Prime Minister William Pitt considered prosecuting the author, but decided against it on the grounds that 'a three guinea book could never do much harm among those who had not three shillings to spare.' In fact, the *Political Justice* was sold for half the price, and many workers banded together to buy it by subscription. Pirated editions appeared in Ireland and Scotland. There was sufficient demand for Godwin to revise the work in 1796 and 1798 in cheaper editions. It not only influenced leaders of the emerging labour movement like John Thelwall and Francis Place, but obscure young poets like Wordsworth, Southey and Coleridge.[2]

The very success of Godwin's work, despite its philosophical weight and elegant style, shows how near the Britain of the 1790s was to revolution. The war declared by Pitt on revolutionary France however soon raised the spectre of British patriotism. His systematic persecution of the radical leaders and the introduction of Gagging Acts in 1794 eventually silenced and then broke the reform movement for a generation. Godwin came boldly to the defence of civil liberties and of his radical friends in a series of eloquent pamphlets, but by the turn of the century he too had fallen into one common grave with the cause of liberty. Thrown up by the vortex of the French Revolution, he sunk when it subsided. Most people in polite society, De Quincey wrote, felt of Godwin with 'the same alienation and horror as of a ghoul, or a bloodless vampyre'.[3]

But not all was lost. It was with 'inconceivable emotions' that the young Percy Bysshe Shelley found in 1812 that Godwin was still alive and he went on not only to elope with his daughter but to become the greatest anarchist poet by effectively putting Godwin's philosophy to verse.[4] Robert Owen, sometimes called the father of British socialism, became friendly soon after and acknowledged Godwin as his philosophical master. In the 1830s and 1840s, at the height of their agitation, the Owenites and Chartists reprinted many extracts from Godwin's works in their journals, and brought out a new edition of *Political Justice* in 1842. Through the early British socialist thinkers, especially William Thompson and Thomas Hodgskin, Godwin's vision of the ultimate withering away of the State and of a free and equal society began to haunt the Marxist imagination.

Godwin at first sight appears an unlikely candidate for the title of first and greatest philosopher of anarchism. He was born in 1756 in Wisbech (the capital of North Cambridgeshire), the seventh of thirteen children. His father was an obscure independent minister who moved to the tiny village of Guestwick in northern Norfolk soon after William's birth. But a strong tradition of rebellion existed in the area. There had not only been a peasants' revolt against the land enclosures in 1549, but during the English Revolution East Anglians had formed the backbone of the Independent movement. Godwin's father would sit in his meeting-house in 'Cromwell's chair', so named because it was said to have been a gift from the leader of the English Revolution.

Godwin moreover was born into a family of Dissenters who rejected the Church of England and its articles of faith. They defended at all costs the right of private judgement. Although officially tolerated since 1689, the Dissenters were unable to have their births registered, to enter the national universities, or to hold public office. The result was that they formed a separate and distinct cultural group and made up a permanent opposition to the State of England. Godwin was steeped in this tradition: his grandfather had been a leading Dissenting minister, his father was a minister, and he aspired from an early age to follow in their footsteps.

As a boy Godwin was deeply religious and intellectually precocious. It was decided to send him at the age of eleven to become the sole pupil of a Reverend Samuel Newton in the great city of Norwich. It was to prove the most formative period of Godwin's life. Newton's harsh treatment of Godwin left him with a hatred of punishment and tyranny. But Newton was also an extreme Calvinist, a follower of the teachings of Robert Sandeman, and the pious Godwin soon adopted his new tutor's creed.

Sandeman lay great stress on reason: grace was to be achieved not by good works or faith, but by the rational perception of the truth, the right or wrong judgement of the understanding. The Sandemanians interpreted the teachings of the New Testament literally: they sought to practise brotherly love and share their wealth with each other. They were also democratic and egalitarian, both rejecting majority rule in favour of consensus and annihilating the distinctions of civil life within the sect. All men and women, they affirmed, are equally fit to be saved or damned.

Godwin went on to pull the Calvinist God down from the heavens and to assert the innocence and perfectibility of man, but he retained much of the social and economic teaching of the Sandemanians. He not only traced his excessive stoicism and condemnation of the private affections to his early Calvinism, but specifically held Sandemanianism responsible for his belief that rational judgement is the source of human actions.

On leaving Newton's intellectual and emotional hothouse, at the age of seventeen Godwin entered the Dissenting Academy at Hoxton – one of the best centres of higher education in eighteenth-century England. Here he received a thorough grounding in Locke's psychology, which presented the mind as a blank sheet; in Newtonian science, which pictured the world as a machine governed by natural laws; and in Hutcheson's ethics, which upheld benevolence and utility as the cornerstones of virtue. At the same time, Godwin formed a belief in 'necessity', that is to say, that all actions are determined by previous causes, and in 'immaterialism', that is, that the external world is created by the mind. These twin pillars of his thought underwent little subsequent change.

Although the tutors were extremely liberal in religion and politics and encouraged free enquiry, Godwin left Hoxton as he entered: a Sandemanian and a Tory. He tried to become a minister, but three times he was rejected by rural congregations in south England. It proved a period of reassessment and self-examination. His intellectual development was rapid. The political debate raging over the American War of Independence at the time soon led him to support the Whig opposition to the war, and a reading of the Latin historians and Jonathan Swift made him a republican overnight.

The most important influence was to come from a reading of the French *philosophes*. In Rousseau, he read that man is naturally good but corrupted by institutions, that private property was the downfall of mankind, and that man was born free, but everywhere was in chains. From Helvétius and d'Holbach, he learned that all men are equal and society should be formed for human happiness. When he closed the covers of their books, his whole world-view had changed. They immediately undermined his Calvinist view of man, although for the time being he became a follower of Socinus (who denied the divinity of Christ and original sin) rather than an atheist. Realizing that he was not cut out to be a minister, Godwin decided to go to London and try to earn his living by teaching and writing.

In quick succession, Godwin wrote a life of William Pitt, two pamphlets supporting the Whig cause, a collection of literary imitations, and three shorts novels. Eager to get rid of his sermons, he published a selections as *Sketches of History* (1784), but not without the observation that God in the Bible acts like a 'political legislator' in a 'theocratic state', despite the fact that he has 'not a right to be a tyrant'. Godwin in this respect was deeply impressed by Milton's depiction of the Devil in *Paradise Lost* – 'a being of considerable virtue', as he later wrote, who rebelled against his maker because he saw no sufficient reason for the extreme inequality of rank and power which had been created. He continued to rebel after his fall because 'a sense of reason and justice was stronger in his mind than a sense of brute force'.[5]

The most important political work of this period was undoubtedly *An Account of the Seminary* (1783) which Godwin intended to open in Epsom for the instruction of twelve pupils in the Greek, Latin, French and English languages. Although no pupils turned up, the prospectus remains one of the most incisive and eloquent accounts of libertarian and progressive education. It shows Godwin believing that children are not only born innocent and benevolent, but that the tutor should foster their particular talents and treat them gently and kindly. The ex-Tory student and Calvinist minister had come to recognize that:

> The state of society is incontestably artificial; the power of one man over another must be always derived from convention or from conquest; by nature we are equal. The necessary consequence is, that government must always depend upon the opinion of the governed. Let the most oppressed people under heaven once change their mode of thinking and they are free.
>
> Government is very limited in its power of making men either virtuous or happy; it is only in the infancy of society that it can do anything considerable; in its maturity it can only direct a few of our outward actions. But our moral dispositions and character depend very much, perhaps entirely, upon education.[6]

Five years before the French Revolution, Godwin had already worked out the main outlines of *Political Justice*. His friendship with the radical playwright Thomas Holcroft further persuaded him to become an atheist and confirmed the evils of marriage and government.

Since none of his early works brought him much money, Godwin was obliged to work in Grub Street for the Whig journals to earn a living. He wrote about the oppression carried out by Pitt's government in Ireland and

India. In a history of the revolution in Holland, he prophesized in 1787 that the 'flame of liberty' first sparked off by the American Revolution had spread and that 'a new republic of the purest kind is about to spring up in Europe'.[7]

When the French Revolution broke out in 1789, it was not entirely unexpected. Godwin was thirty-three, and, no less than William Blake's and William Wordsworth's, his 'heart beat high with great swelling sentiments of Liberty'.[8] He did not remain idle. When Tom Paine's publisher faltered, Godwin helped bring out the first part of *Rights of Man* (1791). He also wrote a letter at this time to the Whig politician Sheridan declaring that 'Liberty leaves nothing to be admired but talents & virtue . . . Give to a state but liberty enough, and it is impossible that vice should exist in it.'[9] As his daughter Mary later observed, Godwin's belief that 'no vice could exist with perfect freedom' was 'the very basis of his system, the very keystone of the arch of justice, by which he desired to knit together the whole human family.'[10]

Burke's *Reflections on the Revolution in France* (1790) had triggered off a pamphlet war, but Godwin decided to rise above the controversies of the day and write a work which would place the principles of politics on an immovable basis. As a philosopher, he wanted to consider universal principles, not practical details. He therefore tried to condense and develop whatever was best and most liberal in political theory. He carefully marshalled his arguments and wrote in a clear and precise style. The result was *An Enquiry concerning Political Justice, and its Influence on General Virtue and Happiness* (1793).

As Godwin observed in his preface, the work took on a life of its own, and as his enquiries advanced his ideas became more 'perspicuous and digested'. He developed a theory of justice which took the production of the greatest sum of happiness as its goal and went on to reject domestic affections, gratitude, promises, patriotism, positive rights and accumulated property. His changing view of government further gave rise to an occasional inaccuracy of language. He did not enter the work, he acknowledged, 'without being aware that government by its very nature counteracts the improvement of individual mind; but . . . he understood the proposition more completely as he proceeded, and saw more distinctly into the nature of the remedy.'[11] The experience of the French Revolution had already persuaded him of the desirableness of a government of the simplest construction but his bold reasoning led him to realize that humanity could be enlightened and free only with government's utter annihilation. Godwin thus set out very close to the English Jacobins like Paine, only to finish a convinced and outspoken anarchist – the first great exponent of society without government.

Political Justice was not the only work to bring Godwin instant fame. In 1794, he published his novel *Things as They Are; or, The Adventures of Caleb Williams*, a gripping story of flight and pursuit intended to show how 'the spirit and character of the government intrudes itself into every rank of society.'[12] It too was to be hailed as a great masterpiece. It is not only a work of brilliant social observation, but may be considered the first thriller and the first psychological novel which anticipates the anxieties of modern existentialism.

Godwin's *Political Justice* was published a fortnight after Britain declared war on revolutionary France – at a time when the public was 'panic struck' with 'all the prejudices of the human mind . . . in arms against it'.[13] Pitt's government tried to crush the growing reform movement by arresting its leaders Holcroft, Horne Tooke, Thelwall and others for High Treason. Godwin sprang to their defence in some well-argued *Cursory Strictures* (1794). Partly due to the influence of Godwin's pamphlet, a jury threw out the charge. Again, when the government introduced its notorious Gagging Acts to limit the freedom of speech, assembly and the press, Godwin responded with some incisive *Considerations* (1795) signed by 'A Lover of Order'. The pamphlet was mainly a denunciation of Pitt's policy of repression but it also criticized the methods of the new political associations, particularly the London Corresponding Society, for simmering the 'cauldron of civil contention' through its lectures and mass demonstrations.[14] While Godwin was as vigorous and uncompromising as ever in defending hard-won liberties, he believed that genuine reform was best achieved through education and enlightenment in small independent circles. Such circles anticipated the 'affinity groups' of later anarchists. His criticisms of the inflammatory methods of his contemporaries, however, meant that he was bitterly attacked by Jacobin agitators like Thelwall.

In the mean time, Godwin had become intimate with Mary Wollstonecraft, the first major feminist writer who had asserted in her celebrated *Vindication of the Rights of Woman* (1792) that mind has no sex and that women should become rational and independent beings rather than passive and indolent mistresses. Although Godwin was diffident and occasionally pedantic, Wollstonecraft recognized in him an independent spirit who was capable of deep emotion as well as high thinking. They soon became lovers, but aware of the dangers of cohabitation, decided to live apart.

Wollstonecraft had an illegitimate daughter by a previous relationship and had experienced the full force of prejudice in the rigid society of late eighteenth-century England. She had already tried to commit suicide twice. When she became pregnant again with Godwin's child, she felt unable to face further ostracism and asked Godwin to marry her. Although Godwin had condemned the European institution of marriage as the 'most odious of all monopolies', he agreed. His enemies were delighted by this apparent turnabout, and the accusation that he had a hot head and cold feet has reverberated ever since. Godwin however as a good anarchist believed that there are no moral rules which should not give way to the urgency of particular circumstances. In this case, he submitted to an institution which he still wished to see abolished out of regard for the happiness of an individual. After the marriage ceremony, he held himself bound no more than he was before.

Although Governmental Terror was the order of the day, Godwin still believed that truth would eventually triumph over error and prejudice. He therefore revised carefully *Political Justice*, a new edition of which appeared in 1796. Wollstonecraft had helped him recognize the importance of the feelings as a source of human action and the central place of pleasure in ethics. Godwin also made his arguments more consistent by showing from the beginning of the work the evils of government and by clarifying the section on property. Kropotkin was therefore wrong to follow De Quincey in thinking that Godwin had retracted many of his beliefs in the Second Edition.[15] It not only retained the great outlines of the first but offered a more substantial and convincing exposition of his anarchism. In the Third Edition of 1798, he further removed a few of the 'crude and juvenile remarks' and added a 'Summary of Principles'.

While revising the second edition of *Political Justice*, Godwin also wrote some original reflections on education, manners and literature which were published as a collection of essays called *The Enquirer* (1797). The work contains some of the most remarkable and advanced ideas on education ever written. Godwin not only argues that the aim of education should be to generate happiness and to develop a critical and independent mind, but suggests that the whole scheme of authoritarian teaching could be done away with to allow children to learn through desire at their own pace and in their own way.

Godwin's thoughts on economics in *The Enquirer* are no less challenging. Indeed, the essay 'Of Avarice and Profusion' offered such a trenchant account of exploitation based on the labour theory of value that it inspired Malthus to write his tirade against all improvement, the *Essay on the Principle of Population* (1798). Godwin's devastating survey 'Of Trades and Professions' in a capitalist society also led the Chartists to reprint it in 1842 at the height of their agitation.

The period spent with Wollstonecraft was the happiest in Godwin's life: it was a union of two great radical minds. Through them the struggles for men's freedom and women's freedom were united at the source. But it was to be tragically short-lived: Wollstonecraft died in giving birth to their daughter Mary. Godwin consoled himself by editing her papers and by

writing a moving and frank memoir of her life which was predictably dismissed by the Anti-Jacobins as a 'convenient Manual of speculative
debauchery'.[16] Godwin never got over the loss of his first and greatest love.
All he could do was to recreate her in his next novel *St Leon* (1799) which
showed the dangers of leading an isolated life and celebrated the domestic
affections.

Godwin did his best to stem the tide of reaction in some calm and
eloquent *Thoughts. Occasioned by the Perusal of Dr Parr's Spital Sermon* (1801),
the apostasy of a former friend. He took the opportunity to clarify his notion
of justice by recognizing the claim of the domestic affections. He also
refuted his chief opponent Malthus by arguing that moral restraint made
vice and misery unnecessary as checks to population. But it was to no avail.
Godwin was pilloried, laughed at and then quietly forgotten. Never again
in his lifetime was he able to capture the public imagination.

The rest of Godwin's life is a sad tale of increasing penury and obscurity. He married a neighbour called Mary Jane Clairmont who already had
two illegitimate children and bore him a son, thereby increasing the family
to seven. But there was no great passion or intellectual inspiration between
the two, and she alienated his close friends like Coleridge and Charles
Lamb. To earn a living, they set up a Juvenile Library which produced an
excellent series of children's books but involved Godwin in endless worry
and debt. A government spy correctly noted that he wished to make his
library the resort of preparatory schools so that in time 'the principles of
democracy and Theophilanthropy may take place universally'.[17]

Godwin continued writing in earnest with so many mouths to feed,
producing disastrous plays as well as a fine life of Chaucer. He wrote
some more powerful novels, especially *Fleetwood* (1805) which showed the
shortcomings of the 'New Man of Feeling' and revealed a critical awareness
of the new factory system, and *Mandeville* (1817), set in the seventeenth
century but containing an astonishing account of madness. He returned in
Of Population (1820) to attack his principal opponent Malthus, with a powerful critique of his philosophical principles and his ratios of population
growth and food supply.

Although Godwin lived a quiet and retired life, younger spirits took up
his message. A poet called Percy Bysshe Shelley, who had been expelled
from Oxford for writing a pamphlet on atheism and spurned by his wealthy
baronet father, burst into Godwin's life in 1812, with *Political Justice* in his
pocket and fiery visions of freedom and justice in his imagination. Godwin
was at first delighted with his new disciple, although he tried to check his
ardour in fomenting rebellion in Ireland. His sympathy however changed
to indignation when Shelley proceeded to elope with his sixteen-year-old
daughter Mary (a 'true Wollstonecraft') in keeping with his own best

theories of free love. His stepdaughter Mary Jane (also known as Claire) joined them and ended up having a child called Allegra with Byron. Mary went on to write *Frankenstein* (1818) and other impressive novels.

For his part Shelley raised vast loans for Godwin on his expected inheritance, in keeping with their view that property is a trust to be distributed to the most needy. On the other hand, Shelley's intellectual debt to Godwin was immense. What the Bible was to Milton, Godwin was to Shelley. The creed of *Political Justice* was transmuted into the magnificent and resounding verse of the greatest revolutionary narrative poems in the English language. Indeed, in *Queen Mab* (1812), *The Revolt of Islam* (1818), *Prometheus Unbound* (1819) and *Hellas* (1822), Shelley openly professed an anarchist creed and systematically celebrated the Godwinian principles of liberty, equality and universal benevolence.

In his *Philosophical Review of Reform* (1820), he further warned against the 'mighty calamity of government', proposed in its place a 'just combination of the elements of social life', and declared like Godwin that poets and philosophers are the 'unacknowledged legislators of the world'.[18] Although Shelley was never an uncritical disciple and was increasingly drawn to Platonism, he remained to the end faithful to the radiant vision of *Political Justice*. If Godwin is the greatest philosopher of anarchism, Shelley is its poet.

The most impressive work of Godwin's old age was *The History of the Commonwealth* (1824–8) in four volumes which treated his favourite period. Although he only makes the briefest mention of Winstanley and the Diggers, whose thought resembled his own so closely, he asserts that the five years from the abolition of the monarchy to Cromwell's *coup d'état* challenge in its glory any equal period of English history. He defended moreover the execution of Charles I on the grounds that natural justice means that it is sometimes right 'to reinvest the community in the entire rights they possessed before particular laws were established'. There comes a point when 'resistance is a virtue'.[19]

Godwin wrote a collection of philosophical essays in *Thoughts on Man* (1831) which show that at the end of his life he still held firm to the fundamental principles of *Political Justice*. In his metaphysics, he recognizes that our feelings and sensations lead us to believe in free will and the existence of matter, but he remains strictly speaking a 'necessarian', upholding determinism, and an 'immaterialist', claiming that mind is all-pervasive in the world. In his politics, he points out to the reformers who were calling for the secret ballot that it is a symbol of slavery rather than liberty. He is still ready to imagine that 'men might subsist very well in clusters and congregated bodies without the coercion of law.'[20]

Indeed, *Thoughts on Man* is a sustained celebration of the achievements and possibilities of the godlike being which makes up our species. After a long and difficult life, Godwin's faith in the perfectibility of humanity remained unshaken, and he ends the book in the confident belief that 'human understanding and human virtue will hereafter accomplish such things as the heart of man has never yet been daring enough to conceive.'[21]

Godwin found it increasingly difficult to squeeze out a living from his writing; so when the new Whig Prime Minister Grey offered him a pension at the age of seventy-seven, he reluctantly accepted. His official title was Office Keeper and Yeoman Usher, and he was given lodgings in the New Palace Yard next to the Houses of Parliament. It was the supreme irony of Godwin's complicated life that he should end his days looking after an obsolete institution which he wished to see abolished. But his story was not without a final twist. In October 1834, a great fire destroyed the old Palace of Westminster. Godwin was responsible for the fire-fighting equipment, but he had quietly absconded to the theatre at the time. No one thought afterwards to accuse him of succeeding where Guy Fawkes had failed!

Godwin eked out his last days with a small pension, his aged wife, his curious library, and his rich memories, principally cheered by visits from his daughter. He died peacefully in his bed on 7 April 1836. He had just turned eighty. Only a handful of friends attended his funeral and he left no organized movement of followers. His final request was to be buried next to his greatest love Mary Wollstonecraft: in death as in life, the union of the first great anarchist and the first great feminist symbolized the common struggle for the complete emancipation of men and women.

Philosophy

Godwin's principal aim was to examine the philosophical principles on which politics depended and to place the subject on an immovable basis. His approach was strictly deductive, proceeding by argument and demonstration, and he tried to express himself as clearly and precisely as possible. While he addressed the calm friend of truth, this did not prevent him from the occasional burst of fervent rhetoric.

As the full title of his principal work *An Enquiry concerning Political Justice, and its influence on General Virtue and Happiness* implies, Godwin was principally concerned with the relationship between politics and ethics. He further based his ethical principles on a particular view of the universe and human nature. Of all the anarchist thinkers, Godwin was the most consistent in trying to show the philosophical assumptions on which he based his libertarian conclusions.

Godwin's starting-point is a belief in universal determinism or 'necessity' as he called it: nature is governed by necessary laws. In history as in the lives of individuals, nothing could have happened otherwise. The regular succession of causes and effects has the advantage of enabling us to make predictions and to model our judgements and actions accordingly. At the same time, Godwin admits that we cannot know the exact nature of causality and that any prediction is based only on high probability.

It was Godwin's meditations on this doctrine of 'necessity' that led him to become an atheist whilst writing *Political Justice*. 'Religion', he concluded, is merely 'an accommodation to the prejudices and weaknesses of mankind'.[22] Nevertheless, Godwin's early religious beliefs clearly affected his moral and political beliefs. His anarchism was largely the application of the Protestant right of private judgement from the religious to the moral and political sphere. His early exposure to the Sandemanian version of Calvinism encouraged his rationality and stoicism as well as his democratic and egalitarian sympathies.

Godwin only remained an atheist for a few years, and like most anarchists believed in a kind of cosmic optimism. Just as nature when left to itself flourishes best, so society thrives when least interfered with. Under the influence of Coleridge, Godwin adopted later in life a kind of vague theism, and came to talk of some 'mysterious power' which sustains and gives harmony to the whole of the universe.[23]

Human Nature

Human nature no less than external nature is governed by laws of necessity. Godwin rejects the theory of innate ideas and instincts and asserts, as one of his chapter titles puts it, that the 'Characters of Men Originate in their External Circumstances'. We are born neither virtuous nor vicious but are made so according to our upbringing and education. Since we are almost entirely the products of our environment, there are also no biological grounds for class distinctions or slavery. It follows for Godwin that we have a common nature and substantial equality. From this physical equality Godwin deduces moral equality: we should treat each other with equal consideration and recognize that what is desirable for one is desirable for all.

But while Godwin argues that human nature is malleable, it does have certain characteristics. In the first place, we are social beings and society brings out our best abilities and sympathies. At the same time, we are unique individuals and cannot be truly happy if we lose ourselves in the mass. Secondly, we are rational beings, capable of recognizing truth and acting accordingly. In the great chain of cause and effect, our consciousness is a real cause and indispensable link. Thirdly, because we have conscious minds, we are voluntary beings, that is to say, we can choose our actions with foresight of their consequences. As Godwin puts it in another chapter title: 'The Voluntary Actions of Men Originate in their Opinions'. The most desirable condition in his view is to widen as far as possible the scope of voluntary action.

It is through reason that Godwin reconciles his philosophy of necessity and human choice. While every action is determined by a motive, reason enables us to choose what motive to act upon. Rather than making moral choices impossible, Godwin believed that the doctrine of necessity enabled us to be confident that real causes produce real effects, and that new opinions can change people's behaviour.

The fourth characteristic of our species is that we are progressive beings. Godwin based his faith in the 'perfectibility of man' on the assumptions that our voluntary actions originate in our opinions and that it is in the nature of truth to triumph over error. He made out his case in the form of a syllogism:

> Sound reasoning and truth, when adequately communicated, must always be victorious over error: Sound reasoning and truth are capable of being so communicated: Truth is omnipotent: The vices and moral weaknesses of man are not invincible: Man is perfectible, or in other words susceptible of perpetual improvement.[24]

Since vice is nothing more than ignorance, education and enlightenment will make us wise, virtuous and free. Thus we may be the products of our environment, but we can also change it. We are, to a considerable degree, the makers of our destiny.

Several objections have been raised to Godwin's view of the perfectibility of man, but they usually overlook his own clarifications. In the first place, by perfectibility, he did not mean that human beings are capable of reaching perfection but rather that they can improve themselves indefinitely. Indeed, he was well aware of the power of evil, the disrupting force of passion, and the weight of existing institutions. Progress, he stressed, will be gradual, often interrupted, and may even have to pass through certain necessary stages.

Next, it is sometimes claimed that there is no immutable and universal truth and that truth does not always triumph over error. Although Godwin talked of immutable truths in a Platonic way, he made it clear that he did not mean absolute truth but 'greater or less probability'. He was moreover fully informed of the fragility of truth and the strength of prejudice and habit. Nevertheless, Godwin assumed like John Stuart Mill that truth can fight its own battles, and put error to rout. On this reasonable assumption, he based his eloquent defence of the freedom of thought and expression.

Finally, Godwin has been accused of being too rational. Certainly, in the first edition of *Political Justice*, he argued that an action can flow from the rational perception of truth and described the will as the last act of the understanding. But he also stressed that passion is inseparable from reason and that virtue cannot be 'very strenuously espoused' until it is 'ardently loved'. In subsequent editions, he gave even more room to feelings, and suggested that reason is not an independent principle but from a practical view merely 'a comparison and balancing of different feelings'.[25] Although reason cannot excite us to action, it regulates our conduct and it is to reason that we must look for the improvement of our social condition. It is a subtle argument which cannot easily be dismissed.

Ethics

From these substantial assumptions about human nature, Godwin developed his system of ethics. He considered it the most important of subjects; indeed, there was no choice in life, not even sitting on the left or the right hand side of the fire, that was not moral in some degree. Ethics moreover was the foundation of politics.

Godwin is a thoroughgoing and consistent utilitarian, defining morality as that 'system of conduct which is determined by a consideration of the greatest general good'.[26] He is an act-utilitarian rather than a rule-utilitarian. While he recognizes that general moral rules are sometimes psychologically and practically necessary, he warns against too rigid an application of them. Since no actions are the same, there can be no clearer maxim than 'Every case is a rule to itself.'[27] It is therefore the duty of a just man to contemplate all the circumstances of the individual case in the light of the sole criterion of utility. Such reasoning led Godwin to become an anarchist for he rejected all rules and laws except the dictates of the understanding.

In his definition of good, Godwin is a hedonist: 'Pleasure and pain, happiness and misery constitute the whole ultimate subject of moral enquiry.'[28] Even liberty, knowledge and virtue are not for Godwin ends in themselves but means in order to achieve happiness. But while he equates happiness with pleasure, some pleasures are preferable to others. Intellectual and moral pleasures are superior to the physical; indeed, Godwin dismisses sexual pleasure as a very trivial object. The highest form of pleasure is enjoyed by the man of benevolence who rejoices in the good of the whole. But Godwin does not think that the higher pleasures should exclude the lower, and he makes clear that the most desirable state is that in which we have access to all these sources of pleasure and are 'in possession of a happiness the most varied and uninterrupted'.[29]

As a utilitarian, Godwin defines justice as 'coincident with utility' and infers that 'I am bound to employ my talents, my understanding, my strength and my time for the production of the greatest quantity of general good.'[30] Combined with the principle of impartiality, which arises from the fundamental equality of human beings and is the regulator of virtue, Godwin's view of utility led him to some novel conclusions.

While all human beings are entitled to equal consideration, it does not follow that they should be treated the same. When it comes to distributing justice I should put myself in the place of an impartial spectator and discriminate in favour of the most worthy, that is, those who have the greatest capacity to contribute to the general good. Thus in a fire, if I am faced with the inescapable choice of saving either a philosopher or a servant, I should choose the philosopher. Even if the servant happened to my brother, my father, my sister, my mother or my benefactor, the case would be the same. 'What magic', Godwin asks, 'is there in the pronoun "my" that should justify us in overturning the decisions of impartial truth?'[31]

Godwin concluded that sentiments like gratitude, friendship, domestic and private affections which might interfere with our duty as impartial spectators have no place in justice. It might be more practical for me to prefer my friends and relatives, but it does not make them more worthy of my attention. Godwin came to recognize the importance of the private and domestic affections in developing sympathetic feelings and apprehended them to be 'inseparable from the nature of man, and from what might be styled the culture of the heart'.[32] But while charity might begin at home, he always insisted that it should not end there and that we should always be guided by considerations of the general good.

Godwin's strict application of the principle of utility led him to an original treatment of duty and rights. 'Duty' he defined as 'the treatment I am bound to bestow upon others'; it is that mode of action on the part of the individual which constitutes 'the best possible application of his capacity to the general benefit'.[33] In order for an action to be truly virtuous, however, it must proceed from benevolent intentions and have long-term beneficial consequences. This duty to practise virtue has serious implications for rights.

While the American and French Revolutions had enshrined lists of rights and Tom Paine was vindicating the *Rights of Man* and Mary Wollstonecraft the *Rights of Woman*, Godwin on utilitarian grounds argued that we have no inalienable rights. Our property, our life and our liberty are trusts which we hold on behalf of humanity, and in certain circumstances justice may require us to forfeit them for the greater good. But while Godwin held that any active or positive right to do as we please is untenable, he did allow two rights in a negative and passive sense. The most important is the right to private judgement, that is a certain 'sphere of discretion' which I have a right to expect shall not be infringed by my neighbour.[34] Godwin also acknowledged the right each person possesses to the assistance of his neighbour. Thus while I am entitled to the produce of my labour on the basis of the right of private judgement, my neighbour has a right to my assistance if he is in need and I have a duty to help him. These rights however are always passive and derive their force not from any notion of natural right but from the principle of utility: they may be superseded whenever more good results from their infringement than from their observance.

Godwin's defence of the right of private judgement is central to his scheme of rational progress and leads him to reject all forms of coercion. As people become more rational and enlightened, they will be more capable of governing themselves, thereby making external institutions increasingly obsolete. But this can only happen if they freely recognize truth and act upon it. Coercion must therefore always be wrong: it cannot convince and only alienates the mind. Indeed, it is always a 'tacit confession of imbecility'.[35] The person who uses coercion pretends to punish his opponent because his argument is strong, but in reality it can only be because it is weak and inadequate. Truth alone carries its own persuasive force. This belief forms the cornerstone of Godwin's criticism of government and law.

On similar grounds, Godwin objects to the view that promises form the foundation of morality. Promises in themselves do not carry any moral weight for they are based on a prior obligation to do justice: I should do something right not because I have promised so to do, but because it is right to do it. In all cases, I ought to be guided by the intrinsic merit of the case and not by any external considerations. A promise in the sense of a declaration of intent is relatively harmless; a promise may even in some circumstances be a necessary evil; but we should make as few of them as possible. 'It is impossible to imagine', Godwin declares, 'a principle of more vicious tendency, than that which shall teach me to disarm future wisdom by past folly.'[36] It follows that all binding oaths and contracts are immoral.

Given Godwin's concern with the independent progress of the mind and rejection of promises, it comes as no surprise that he should condemn the European institution of marriage. In the first place, the cohabitation it involves subjects its participants to some inevitable portion of thwarting, bickering and unhappiness. Secondly, the marriage contract leads to an eternal vow of attachment after encounters in circumstances full of delusion. As a law, marriage is therefore the worst of laws; as an affair of property, the worst of all properties. Above all, 'so long as I seek to engross one woman to myself, and to prohibit my neighbour from proving his superior desert and reaping the fruits of it, I am guilty of the most odious of all monopolies.'[37] The abolition of marriage, Godwin believed, would be attended with no evils although in an enlightened society he suggested that relationships might be in some degree permanent rather than promiscuous.

Politics

Politics for Godwin is an extension of ethics and must be firmly based on its principles. Since these principles are universal, he felt it was possible to deduce from them the 'one best mode of social existence'.[38] Hence the enquiry into 'political justice'. The term however is somewhat misleading since Godwin does not believe that justice is political in the traditional sense but social: his idea of a just society does not include government. His overriding aim was to create a society which was free and yet ordered. His bold reasoning led him to conclude that ultimately order could only be achieved in anarchy.

Like all anarchists, Godwin distinguishes carefully between society and government. With Kropotkin, he argues that human beings associated at first for the sake of 'mutual assistance'. With Paine, he believes that society is in every state a blessing. Man by nature is a social being; without society, he cannot reach his full stature. But society does not create a corporate identity, or even a general will, but remains nothing more than an 'aggregation of individuals'.

It was the 'errors and perverseness of the few' who interfered with the peaceful and productive activities of people which made the restraint of government apparently necessary. But while government was intended to suppress injustice, its effect has been to embody and perpetuate it. By concentrating the force of the community, it gives occasion to 'wild projects of calamity, to oppression, despotism, war and conquest'. With the further division of society into rich and poor, the rich have become the 'legislators of the state' and are perpetually reducing oppression to a system.[39]

Government moreover by its very nature checks the improvement of the mind and makes permanent our errors. Indeed, government and society are mutually opposed principles: the one is in perpetual stasis while the other is in constant flux. Since government even in its best state is an evil, it follows that we should have as little of it as the general peace of society will allow. In the long run, however, Godwin suggests:

> With what delight must every well informed friend of mankind look forward to the auspicious period, the dissolution of political government, of that brute engine which has been the only perennial cause of the vices of mankind, and which ... has mischiefs of various sorts incorporated with its substance, and not otherwise removable than by its utter annihilation![40]

Not surprisingly, Godwin rejects the idea that the justification for government can be found in some original social contract. Even if there had been a
contract, it could not be binding on subsequent generations and in changed
conditions. Equally, the idea of tacit consent would make any existing
government however tyrannical legitimate. As for direct consent, it is no
less absurd since it would mean that government can have no authority over
any individual who withholds his or her approval. Constitutions are open
to similar objections: they not only mean that people are to be governed by
the '*dicta* of their remotest ancestors' but prevent the progress of political
knowledge.[41]

In fact, Godwin asserts that all government is founded in opinion. It is
only supported by the confidence placed in its value by the weak and the
ignorant. But in proportion as they become wiser, so the basis of government
will decay. At present it is the mysterious and complicated nature of the
social system which has made the mass of humanity the 'dupe of Knaves'
but 'once annihilate the quackery of government, and the most homebred
understanding might be strong enough to detect the artifices of the state
juggler that would mislead him'. Godwin therefore looked forward to the
'true euthanasia' of government and the 'unforced concurrence of all in
promoting the general welfare' which would necessarily follow.[42]

Laws no less than governments are inconsistent with the nature of the
human mind and the progress of truth. Human beings can do no more
than declare the natural law which eternal justice has already established.
Legislation in the sense of framing man-made laws in society is therefore
neither necessary nor desirable: 'Immutable reason is the true legislator . . .
The functions of society extend, not to the making, but the interpreting of
law.'[43] Moreover, if the rules of justice were properly understood, there
would be no need for artificial laws in society.

Godwin's criticism of law is one of the most trenchant put forward by
an anarchist. Where liberals and socialists maintain that law is necessary to
protect freedom, Godwin sees them as mutually incompatible principles.
All man-made laws are by their very nature arbitrary and oppressive. They
represent not, as their advocates claim, the wisdom of ancestors but rather
the 'venal compact' of 'superior tyrants', primarily enacted to defend economic inequality and unjust political power.[44] There is no maxim clearer
than this, 'Every case is a rule to itself,' and yet, like the bed of Procrustes,
laws try to reduce the multiple actions of people to one universal standard.
Once begun laws inevitably multiply; they become increasingly confusing
and ambiguous and encourage their practitioners to be perpetually dishonest and tyrannical. 'Turn me a prey to the wild beasts of the desert',
Godwin's hero in his novel *Caleb Williams* exclaims, 'so I be never again
the victim of a man dressed in the gore-dripping robes of authority!'[45]

Punishment, which is the inevitable sanction used to enforce the law, is both immoral and ineffective. In the first place, under the system of necessity, there can be no personal responsibility for actions which the law assumes: 'the assassin cannot help the murder he commits, any more than the dagger.' Secondly, coercion alienates the mind and is superfluous if an argument is true. Punishment or 'the voluntary infliction of evil', is therefore barbaric if used for retribution, and useless if used for reformation or example.[46] Godwin concludes that wrongdoers should be restrained only as a temporary expedient and treated with as much kindness and gentleness as possible.

With his rejection of government and laws, Godwin condemns any form of obedience to authority other than 'the dictate of the understanding'.[47] The worst form of obedience for Godwin occurs however not when we obey out of consideration of a penalty (as for instance when we are threatened by a wild animal) but when we place too much confidence in the superior knowledge of others (even in building a house). Bakunin recognized the latter as the only legitimate form of authority, but Godwin sees it as the most pernicious since it can easily make us dependent, weaken our understanding, and encourage us to revere experts.

Godwin's defence of freedom of thought and expression is one of the most convincing in the English language. All political superintendence of opinion is harmful, because it prevents intellectual progress, and unnecessary, because truth and virtue are competent to fight their own battles. If I accept a truth on the basis of authority it will appear lifeless, lose its meaning and force, and be irresolutely embraced. If on the other hand a principle is open to attack and is found superior to every objection, it becomes securely established. While no authority is infallible, truth emerges stronger than ever when it survives the clash of opposing opinions. Godwin adds however that true toleration not only requires that there should be no laws restraining opinion, but that we should treat each other with forbearance and liberality.

Having established his own political principles. Godwin offered a resounding criticism of existing political practices. In the first place, he completely rejects Rousseau's idea that society as a whole somehow makes up a moral 'individual' in whose overriding interest certain policies must be pursued. The glory and prosperity of society as a whole, he declares, are 'unintelligible chimeras'. Indeed, patriotism or the love of our country has been used by impostors to render the multitude 'the blind instruments of their crooked designs'.[48]

Of all political systems, monarchy is the worst. By his upbringing and his power, 'every king is a despot in his heart', and an enemy of the human race.[49] Monarchy makes wealth the standard of honour and measures people not according to their merit but their title. As such, it is an absolute imposture which overthrows the natural equality of man. Aristocracy, the outcome of feudalism, is also based on false hereditary distinctions and the unjust distribution of wealth. It converts the vast majority of the people into beasts of burden. Democracy on the other hand is the least pernicious system of government since it treats every person as an equal and encourages reasoning and choice.

Godwin's defence of republican and representative democracy is however essentially negative. Republicanism alone, he argues, is not a remedy that strikes at the root of evil if it leaves government and property untouched. Again, representation may call on the most enlightened part of the nation, but it necessarily means that the majority are unable to participate in decision-making. The practice of voting involved in representation further creates an unnatural uniformity of opinion by limiting debate and reducing complicated disputes to simple formulae which demand assent or dissent. It encourages rhetoric and demagoguery rather than careful thought and the cool pursuit of truth. The whole debate moreover is wound up by a 'flagrant insult upon all reason and justice', since the counting of hands cannot decide on a truth.[50]

In Godwin's day, the secret ballot was for many reformers one of the principal means of achieving political liberty. Yet Godwin as an anarchist could scarcely conceive of a political institution which is a 'more direct and explicit patronage of vice'. Its secrecy fosters hypocrisy and deceit about our intentions whereas we should be prepared to give reasons for our actions and face the censure of others. The vote by secret ballot is therefore not a symbol of liberty but of slavery. Communication is the essence of liberty; ballot is the 'fruitful parent of ambiguities, equivocations and lies without number'.[51]

A further weakness of representative assemblies is that they create a fictitious unanimity. Nothing, Godwin argues, can more directly contribute to the depravation of the human understanding and character than for a minority to be made to execute the decisions of a majority. A majority for Godwin has no more right to coerce a minority, even a minority of one, than a despot has to coerce a majority. A national assembly further encourages every man to connect himself with some sect or party, while the institution of two houses of assembly merely divides a nation against itself. Real unanimity can only result in a free society without government.

Godwin is quite clear that political associations and parties are not suitable means to reach that society. While the artisans were organizing themselves into associations in order to put pressure on parliament for reform, Godwin spelled out the dangers. Members soon learn the shibboleth of party and stop thinking independently. Without any pretence of delegation from the community at large, associations seize power for themselves. The arguments against government are equally pertinent and hostile to such associations. Truth cannot be acquired in crowded halls amidst noisy debates but is revealed in quiet contemplation.

Economics

Godwin argued that it is not enough to leave property relations as they are. In this, he departs from the liberal tradition and aligns himself with socialism. Indeed, he considers the subject of property to be the 'key-stone' that completes the fabric of political justice.

Godwin's economics, like his politics, are an extension of his ethics. The first offence, he argues with Rousseau, was committed by the man who took advantage of the weakness of his neighbours to secure a monopoly of wealth. Since then there has been a close link between property and government for the rich are the 'indirect or direct legislators of the state'. The resulting moral and psychological effects of unequal distribution have been disastrous for both rich and poor alike. Accumulated property creates a 'servile and truckling spirit', makes the acquisition and display of wealth the universal passion, and hinders intellectual development and enjoyment.[52] By encouraging competition, it reduces the whole structure of society to a system of the narrowest selfishness. Property no longer becomes desired for its own sake, but for the distinction and status it confers.

To be born to poverty, Godwin suggests, is to be born a slave; the poor man is 'strangely pent and fettered in his exertions' and becomes the 'bond slave of a thousand vices'. The factory system, with its anxious and monotonous occupations, turns workers into machines and produces a kind of 'stupid and hopeless vacancy' in every face, especially amongst the children.[53] Painfully aware of the consequences of the Industrial Revolution, Godwin laments that in the new manufacturing towns if workers managed to live to forty, 'they could not earn bread to their salt'. The great inequalities in European countries can only lead to class war and incite the poor to reduce everything to 'universal chaos'.[54]

In place of existing property relations, Godwin proposes a form of voluntary communism. His starting-point is that since human beings are partakers of a common nature, it follows on the principle of impartial justice that the 'good things of the world are a common stock, upon which one man has as valid a title as another to draw for what he wants'.[55] Justice further obliges every man to regard his property as a trust and to consider in what way it might be best employed for the increase of liberty, knowledge and virtue.

Godwin recognizes that money is only the means of exchange to real commodities and no real commodity itself. What is misnamed wealth is merely 'a power invested in certain individuals by the institutions of society, to compel others to labour for their benefit'.[56] Godwin could therefore see no justice in the situation in which one man works, and another man is idle and lives off the fruits of his labour. It would be fairer if all able-bodied people worked. Since a small quantity of labour is sufficient to provide the means of subsistence, this would inevitably increase the amount of leisure and allow everyone to cultivate his or her understanding and to experience new sources of enjoyment.

Godwin deepens his analysis by distinguishing between four classes of things: the means of subsistence, the means of intellectual and moral improvement, inexpensive pleasures, and luxuries. It is the last class that is the chief obstacle to a just distribution of the previous three. From this classification, Godwin deduces three degrees of property rights. The first is 'my permanent right in those things the use of which being attributed to me, a greater sum of benefit or pleasure will result than could have arisen from their being otherwise appropriated'. This includes the first three classes of things. The second degree of property is the empire every person is entitled to over the produce of his or her own industry. This is only a negative right and in a sense a sort of usurpation since justice obliges me to distribute any produce in excess of my entitlement according to the first degree of property. The third degree, which corresponds to the fourth class of things, is the 'faculty of disposing of the produce of another man's industry'.[57] It is entirely devoid of right since all value is created by labour and it directly contradicts the second degree.

Godwin thus condemns capitalist accumulation. On the positive side, he argues that all members of society should have their basic needs satisfied. But just as I have a right to the assistance of my neighbour, he has a right of private judgement. It is his duty to help me satisfy my needs, but it is equally my duty not to violate his sphere of discretion. In this sense, property is founded in the 'sacred and indefeasible right of private judgement'. At the same time, Godwin accepts on utilitarian grounds that in exceptional circumstances it might be necessary to take goods by force from my neighbour in order to save myself or others from calamity.[58]

Godwin's original and profound treatment of property had a great influence on the early socialist thinkers. He was the first to write systematically about the different claims of human need, production and capital. Marx and Engels acknowledged his contribution to the development of the theory of exploitation and even considered translating *Political Justice*.[59] In the anarchist tradition, he anticipates Proudhon by making a distinction between property and possession. In his scheme of voluntary communism, however, he comes closest to Kropotkin.

Godwin saw no threat from the growth of population to upset his communist society. Like most anarchists, he rested his hopes on a natural order or harmony: 'There is a principle in the nature of human society by means of which everything seems to tend to its level, and to proceed in the most auspicious way, when least interfered with by the mode of regulation.'[60] In addition, there is no evidence for natural scarcity; much land is still uncultivated and what is cultivated could be improved. Even if population did threaten to get out of hand there are methods of birth control. Malthus of course could not leave it at that and in his *Essay on the Principle of Population* (1798) he argued that population grows faster than food supply and that vice and misery must therefore remain in place as necessary checks. But Godwin counter-attacked with his doctrine of moral restraint or prudence, questioned the validity of Malthus's evidence, and rightly suggested that people would have fewer children as their living standards improved.

Education

The principal means of reform for Godwin is through education and his original reflections on the subject make him one of the great pioneers of libertarian and progressive thought. Godwin, perhaps more than any other thinker, recognizes that freedom is the basis of education and education is the basis of freedom. The ultimate aim of education, he maintains, is to develop individual understanding and to prepare children to create and enjoy a free society.

In keeping with his view of human nature, he believed that education has far greater power than government in shaping our characters. Children are thus a 'sort a raw material put into our hands, a ductile and yielding substance'.[61] Just as nature never made a dunce, so genius is not innate but acquired. It follows that the so-called vices of youth derive not from nature but from the defects of education. Children are born innocent: confidence, kindness and benevolence constitute their entire temper. They have a deep and natural love of liberty at a time when they are never free from the 'grating interference' of adults. Liberty is the 'school of understanding' and the 'parent of strength'; indeed children probably learn and develop more in their hours of leisure than at school.[62]

For Godwin all education involves some form of despotism. Modern education not only corrupts the hearts of children, but undermines their reason by its unintelligible jargon. It makes little effort to accommodate their true capacities. National or State education, the great salvation of many progressive reformers, can only make matters worse. Like all public establishments, it involves the idea of permanence and actively fixes the mind in 'exploded errors': as a result, the knowledge taught in universities and colleges is way behind that which exists in unshackled members of the community.[63]

In addition, a system of national education cannot fail to become the mirror and tool of government; they form an alliance more formidable than that of Church and State, teaching a veneration of the constitution rather than of truth. In these circumstances, it is not surprising that the teacher becomes a slave who is constantly obliged to rehandle the foundations of knowledge; and a tyrant, forever imposing his will and checking the pleasures and sallies of youth.

Godwin admits that education in a group is preferable to solitary tuition in developing talents and encouraging a sense of personal identity. In existing society, he therefore suggests that a small and independent school is best. But Godwin goes further to question the very foundations of traditional schooling.

The aim of education, he maintains, must be to generate happiness. Now virtue is essential to happiness, and to make a person virtuous he or she must become wise. Education should develop a mind which is well-regulated, active and prepared to learn. This is best achieved not by inculcating in young children any particular knowledge but by encouraging their latent talents, awakening their minds, and forming clear habits of thinking.

In our treatment of children, we should therefore be egalitarian, sympathetic, sincere, truthful, and straightforward. We should not become harsh monitors and killjoys; the extravagances of youth are often early indications of genius and energy. We should encourage a taste for reading but not censure their choice of literature. Above all, we should excite their desire for knowledge by showing its intrinsic excellence.

Godwin, however, goes on to suggest that if a pupil learns only because he or she desires it the whole formidable apparatus of education might be swept away. No figures such as teacher or pupil would then be left; each would be glad in cases of difficulty to consult someone better informed, but they would not be expected to learn anything unless they desired it. Everyone would be prepared to offer guidance and encouragement. In this way, a mind would develop according to its natural tendencies and children would be able to develop fully their potential.

Free Society

While Godwin does not offer a blueprint of his free society – to do so would be opposed to his whole scheme of progress and his notion of truth – he does outline some of the general directions it might take. In the first place, he is careful to show that freedom does not mean licence, that is to say, to act as one pleases without being accountable to the principles of reason. He distinguishes between two sorts of independence: natural independence, 'a freedom from all constraint, except that of reasons and inducements presented to the understanding', which is of the utmost importance; and moral independence, which is always injurious.[64] It is essential that we should be free to cultivate our individuality, and to follow the dictates of our own understanding, but we should be ready to judge and influence the actions of each other. External freedom is of little value without moral growth. Indeed, it is possible for a person to be physically enslaved and yet retain his sense of independence, while an unconstrained person can voluntarily enslave himself through passive obedience. For Godwin civil liberty is thus not an end in itself, but a means to personal growth in wisdom and virtue.

Godwin did not call himself an anarchist and used the word 'anarchy' like his contemporaries in a negative sense to denote the violent and extreme disorder which might follow the immediate dissolution of government without the prior acceptance of the principles of political justice. In such a situation, he feared that some enraged elements might threaten personal security and free enquiry. The example of the French revolutionaries had shown him that the people's 'ungoverned passions will often not stop at equality, but incite them to grasp at power'.[65] And yet Godwin saw the mischiefs of anarchy in this sense as preferable to those of despotism. A State despotism is permanent, while anarchy is transitory. Anarchy diffuses energy and enterprise through the community and disengages people from prejudice and implicit faith. Above all, it has a 'distorted and tremendous likeness, of truth and liberty' and can lead to the best form of human society.[66] It was always Godwin's contention that society for the greater part carries on its own peaceful and productive organization.

In place of modern Nation-States with their complex apparatus of government, Godwin proposes a decentralized and simplified society of face-to-face communities. The ideas of 'a great empire, and legislative unity' are plainly the 'barbarous remains of the days of military heroism'.[67] It is preferable to decentralize power since neighbours are best informed of each other's concerns, and sobriety and equity are characteristic of a limited circle. People should therefore form a voluntary federation of districts (a 'confederacy of lesser republics') in order to co-ordinate production and secure social benefits.

In such a pluralistic commonwealth, Godwin suggests that the basic social unit might be a small territory like the traditional English 'parish' – the self-managing commune of later anarchists. Democracy would be direct and participatory so that the voice of reason could be heard and spoken by all citizens. Such a decentralized society need not however be 'parochial' in the pejorative sense since with the dissolution of Nation-States and their rivalries the whole human species would constitute 'one great republic'.[68]

Godwin recognizes that in a transitional period a temporary co-ordinating body might be necessary in order to solve disputes between districts or to repel a foreign invader. He therefore suggests that districts might send delegates to a general assembly or congress of the federation, but only in exceptional emergencies. The assembly would form no permanent or common centre of authority and any officials would be unpaid and supported voluntarily.

At the local level, popular juries could be set up to deal with controversies and injustices amongst individuals within the community. Cases would be judged according to their particular circumstances in the light of the general good. In the long run, however, both assemblies and juries would lose any authority and it would suffice to invite districts to co-operate for the common advantage or to ask offenders to forsake their errors.

If the social system were simplified, Godwin is confident that the voice of reason would be heard, consensus achieved, and the natural harmony of interests prevail. As people became accustomed to governing themselves, all coercive bodies would become increasingly superfluous and obsolete. Government would give way to the spontaneously ordered society of anarchy. People would live simple but cultivated lives in open families in harmony with nature. Marriage would disappear and be replaced by free unions; any offspring would be cared for and educated by the community.

In such a free and equal society, there would be the opportunity for everyone to develop their intellectual and moral potential. With the abolition of the complicated machinery of government, the end of excessive luxuries, and the sharing of work by all, the labour required to produce the necessaries of life would be drastically reduced – possibly, Godwin calculates, to half an hour a day.

Far from ignoring the Industrial Revolution, Godwin further looks to technology – 'various sorts of mills, of weaving engines, steam engines', and even one day to an automatic plough – to reduce and alleviate unpleasant toil.[69] Unlike Tolstoy, he sees no dignity in unnecessary manual labour. Appropriate technology would not only lessen the enforced co-operation imposed by the present division of labour, but increase the incomparable wealth of leisure in which people might cultivate their minds. Science, moreover, might one day make mind omnipotent over matter, prolong life, and, Godwin suggests in a rare flight of wild conjecture, even discover the secret of immortality!

Although Godwin's decentralized society finds undoubtedly some inspiration in the organic communities of pre-industrial England, it is by no means a purely agrarian vision. His confidence in the potentially liberating effects of modern technology and science shows that he was not looking backwards but forward to the future. Indeed, while the nineteenth and twentieth centuries have seen increased centralization of production, the new technology may well as Godwin hoped lead to a dissolution of monolithic industries and a break-up of great cities. In this he anticipates Kropotkin's vision in *Fields, Factories and Workshops*.

While he does not enter into details, Godwin implies that production would be organized voluntarily, with workers pursuing their own interests or talents. A certain division of labour might still exist, since people with particular skills might prefer to spend their time in specialized work. There would be a voluntary sharing of material goods. Producers would give their surplus to those who most needed them, and would receive what was necessary to satisfy their own wants from the surplus of their neighbours. In this way goods would pass spontaneously to where whey were needed. Economic relationships however would always be based on free distribution and not on barter or exchange.

Godwin was anxious to define carefully the subtle connection between the individual and the group in such a free and equal society. His position has been seriously misunderstood, for he has been equally accused of 'extreme individualism' and of wanting to submerge the individual in 'communal solidarity'.[70] In fact, he did neither.

It is true that Godwin wrote 'everything that is usually understood by the term co-operation is, in some degree, an evil.'[71] But the co-operation he condemned is the uniform activity enforced by the division of labour, by a restrictive association, or by those in power. He could not understand why we must always be obliged to consult the convenience of others or be reduced to a 'clockwork uniformity'. For this reason, he saw no need for common labour, meals or stores in an equal society; they are 'mistaken instruments for restraining the conduct without making conquest of the judgement'.[72]

It is also true that society for Godwin forms no organic whole and is nothing more than the sum of its individuals. He pictured the enlightened person making individual calculations of pleasure and pain and carefully weighing up the consequences of his or her actions. He stressed the value of autonomy for intellectual and moral development; we all require a sphere of discretion, a mental space for creative thought. He could see no value in losing oneself in the existence of another:

> Every man ought to rest upon his own centre, and consult his own understanding. Every man ought to feel his independence, that he can assert the principles of justice and truth without being obliged

treacherously to adapt them to the peculiarities of his situation and the errors of others.[73]

This recognition of the need for individual autonomy should be borne in mind when considering one of the major criticisms levelled at Godwin, namely that in his anarchist society the tyranny of public opinion could be more dangerous than that of law. Godwin certainly argues that we all have a duty to amend the errors and promote the welfare of our neighbours; that we must practise perfect sincerity at all times. Indeed, he goes so far as to suggest that the 'general inspection' which would replace public authority would provide a force 'no less irresistible than whips and chains' to reform conduct.[74]

Now while this might sound distinctly illiberal, Godwin made clear that he was totally opposed to any collective vigilance which might tyrannize the individual or impose certain ideas and values. In the first place, the kind of sincerity he recommends is not intended to turn neighbours into priggish busybodies but to release them from their unnecessary repressions so that they might be 'truly friends with each other'. Secondly, any censure we might offer to our neighbours should be an appeal to their reason and be offered in a mild and affectionate way. Thirdly, Godwin assumes that people will be rational and independent individuals who recognize each other's autonomy: 'My neighbour may censure me freely and without reserve, but he should remember that I am to act by my deliberation and not his.'[75]

While Godwin certainly values personal autonomy, he repeatedly stresses that we are social beings, that we are made for society, and that society brings out our best qualities. Indeed, he sees no tension between autonomy and collectivity since 'the love of liberty obviously leads to a sentiment of union, and a disposition to sympathize in the concern of others'.[76] Godwin's novels show only too vividly the psychological and moral dangers of excessive solitude and isolation. His whole ethical system of universal benevolence is inspired by a love for others.

In fact, Godwin believes that people in a free and equal society would be at once more social and more individual: 'each man would be united to his neighbour, in love and mutual kindness, a thousand times more than now: but each man would think and judge for himself.' Ultimately, the individual and society are not opposed for each person would become more individually developed and more socially conscious: the 'narrow principle of selfishness' would vanish and 'each would lose his individual existence, in the thought of the general good'.[77] One of Godwin's greatest strengths is the way he reconciles the claims of personal autonomy and the demands of social life. As such, Godwin's anarchism is closer to the communism of Kropotkin than the egoism of Stirner or the competition of Proudhon.

Means of Reform

Having witnessed the French Revolution turn into the Terror, Godwin did not give his wholehearted support to revolution in the sense of a sudden and violent transformation of society. Revolution might be inspired by a horror of tyranny, but it can also be tyrannical in turn, especially if those who seize power try to coerce others through the threat of punishment.

Godwin was not an absolute pacifist, but non-violence was his strategy of liberation. He did not think human reason sufficiently developed to persuade an assailant to drop his sword. Armed struggle might also be necessary to resist the 'domestic spoiler' or to repulse an invading despot.[78] Nevertheless, he accepted the minimal use of physical force only when all persuasion and argument had failed. It follows that the duty of the enlightened person is to try to postpone violent revolution.

Godwin thus looked to a revolution in opinions, not on the barricades. The proper means of bringing about change is through the diffusion of knowledge: 'Persuasion and not force, is the legitimate instrument of influencing the human mind.' True equalization of society is not to reduce by force all to a 'naked and savage equality', but to elevate every person to wisdom. The reform Godwin recommends (that 'genial and benignant power!') is however so gradual that it can hardly be called action.[79] Since government is founded in opinion, as people become wiser and realize that it is an unnecessary evil, they will gradually withdraw their support. Government will simply wither away. It is a process which clearly cannot be realized by political parties or associations.

Godwin looks to thoughtful and benevolent guides who will speak the truth and practise sincerity and thereby act as catalysts of change. The kind of organization he recommends is the small and independent circle, the prototype of the modern anarchist 'affinity group'. In the anarchist tradition, Godwin thus stands as the first to advocate 'propaganda by the word'. By stressing the need for moral regeneration before political reform, he also anticipates the idea that the 'political is the personal'.

While Godwin's gradualism shows that he was no naive visionary, it does give a conservative turn to his practical politics. He criticized the kind of isolated acts of protest that Shelley engaged in. He felt it was right to support from a distance any movement which seemed to be going in the right direction. In his own historical circumstances, he declared: 'I am in principle a Republican, but in practice a Whig. But I am a philosopher: that is a person desirous to become wise, and I aim at this object by reading, by writing, and a little conversation.'[80] He thought at one time during the 1790s that he might be in Parliament, but quickly dismissed the idea since it would infringe his independence and would grate against his character which was more fitted for contemplation than action.

Godwin failed to develop an adequate praxis. His cautious gradualism meant that he was obliged to abandon generations to the disastrous effects of that political authority and economic inequality which he had so eloquently described. While he demonstrated vividly how opinions are shaped by circumstances, he sought only to change opinions rather than to try and change circumstances. He was left with the apparent dilemma of believing that human beings cannot become wholly rational as long as government exists, and yet government must continue to exist while they remain irrational. His problem was that he failed to tackle reform on the level of institutions as well as ideas.

As a social philosopher, Godwin is undoubtedly on a par with Hobbes, Locke, Rousseau and Mill. He was the most consistent and profound exponent of philosophical anarchism. With closely reasoned arguments, he carefully drew his libertarian conclusions from a plausible view of human nature. He believed that politics is inseparable from ethics, and offered a persuasive view of justice. His criticisms of fundamental assumptions about law, government and democracy are full of insight. From a sound view of truth, he developed one of the most trenchant defences of the freedom of thought and expression.

In place of existing tyrannies, Godwin proposed a decentralized and simplified society consisting of voluntary associations of free and equal individuals. In his educational theory, he showed the benefits of learning through desire. In his economics, he demonstrated the disastrous effects of inequality and outlined a system of free communism. If Godwin's practical politics were inadequate, it is because he was primarily a philosopher concerned with universal principles rather than their particular application. By the intrepid deduction from first principles, he went beyond the radicalism of his age to become the first great anarchist thinker.

Max Stirner

The Conscious Egoist

MAX STIRNER STANDS FOR the most extreme form of individualist anarchism. He denies not only the existence of benevolence but also all abstract entities such as the State, Society, Humanity and God. He rebels against the whole rational tradition of Western philosophy, and in place of philosophical abstraction, he proposes the urgings of immediate personal experience. His work stands as a frontal assault on the fundamental principles of the Enlightenment, with its unbounded confidence in the ultimate triumph of Reason, Progress and Order.

Stirner's place in the history of philosophy is as controversial as his status as an anarchist. It has been argued that he is more of a nihilist than an anarchist since he destroys all propositions except those which fulfil a purely aesthetic function in the egoist's 'overriding purpose of self-enjoyment and self-display'.[1] Camus saw Stirner's metaphysical revolt against God leading to the absolute affirmation of the individual and a kind of nihilism which 'laughs in the impasse'.[2] Others place Stirner in the existential tradition, stressing his concern with the ontological priority of the individual; Herbert Read called him 'one of the most existentialist of philosophers'.[3]

Certainly Stirner offered a root-and-branch attack on existing values and institutions. Like Kierkegaard, he celebrated the unique truth of the individual and sought to liberate him from the great barrel organ of Hegelian metaphysics. In his attack on Christian morality and his call for the self-exaltation of the whole individual, he anticipated Nietzsche and atheistic existentialism. But while there are nihilistic and existentialist elements to his work, Stirner is not merely a nihilist, for he does not set out to destroy all moral and social values. Neither is he, strictly speaking, a proto-existentialist, for he rejects any attempt to create a higher or better individual. He belongs to the anarchist tradition as one of its most original and creative thinkers. While many may find his views shocking and distasteful, every libertarian is obliged to come to terms with his bold reasoning.

Marx and Engels took Stirner seriously enough to devote a large part of their *German Ideology* to a refutation of the infuriating thinker whom they dubbed 'Saint Max', 'Sancho' and the 'Unique'.[4] In fact, Stirner shares many points with Marx: his dialectical method, his criticism of abstractions and the 'human essence', his analysis of labour, his rejection of static materialism, and his stress on human volition in social change. Engels even admitted to Marx that after reading Stirner's book he was converted to egoism, and although it was only temporary, he still maintained that 'it is equally from egoism that we are communists'.[5]

In his principal work *Der Einzige und sein Eigenthum* (1845), usually translated as *The Ego and His Own*, Stirner offers the most consistent case in defence of the individual against authority. He presents a searching criticism of the State and social institutions, and proposes in their place a 'union of egoists' who would form contractual relationships and compete peacefully with each other. Stirner's defence of personal autonomy not only influenced Benjamin Tucker and the American individualists, but also the social anarchists Emma Goldman and Herbert Read in our own century. Kropotkin had little time for his anti-social thrust and what he called his 'superficial negation of morality', but the early Mussolini in his socialist days wanted to make his celebration of the 'elemental forces of the individual' fashionable again.[6] Stirner continues to inspire and exasperate libertarians of both the Left and the Right.[7]

Max Stirner's life was as timid as his thought was bold. Born in 1806 at Bayreuth in Bavaria, his real name was Johann Kaspar Schmidt. His parents were poor. After the death of his father, his mother remarried and followed her husband around north Germany before they settled once again at Bayreuth. She eventually became insane. Her son attended the University of Berlin from 1826 to 1828 where he studied philosophy and listened to the lectures of Hegel. But his academic career was far from distinguished.

After a brief spell at two other universities, Stirner returned to Berlin in 1832 and just managed to gain a teaching certificate. He then spent eighteen months as an unsalaried trainee teacher, but the Prussian government declined to appoint him to a full-time post. In 1837, he married his landlady's daughter but she died in childbirth a few months later. It is difficult not to put down his misanthropy and egoism to a lonely childhood, unsuccessful career and bad luck. His fortunes only began to turn a little when he landed a post at Madame Gropius's academy for young girls in Berlin. During the next five years Johann Kaspar had a steady job and began to mix with some of the most fiery young intellectuals of the day. They called themselves *Die Freien* – the Free Ones – and met in the early 1840s at Hippel's Weinstube on Friedrichstrasse. Bruno Bauer and Edgar Bauer were the leading lights of the group but Marx and Engels occasionally attended. Engels has left a sketch of the Young Hegelians during a visit by Arnold Ruge which depicts Johann Kaspar as an isolated figure, looking on at the noisy debate.

It was during this period that he wrote 'The False Principle of Our Education', which was published in Marx's journal, *Rheinische Zeitung*, in 1842. The essay shows the libertarian direction Stirner was already taking. Distinguishing between the 'educated man' and the 'freeman', he argued that, in the former case, knowledge is used to shape character so that the educated become possessed by the Church, State or Humanity, while in the latter it is used to facilitate choice:

> If one awakens in men the idea of freedom then the freemen will incessantly go on to free themselves; if, on the contrary, one only educates them, then they will at all times accommodate themselves to circumstances in the most highly educated and elegant manner and degenerate into subservient cringing souls.[8]

The Free Ones came to be known as the Left Hegelians because they met to discuss and eventually oppose the philosophy of the great German metaphysician. It was in reaction to Hegel and the habitués of the Free Ones that Johann Kaspar wrote his only claim to fame, *The Ego and His Own*. The work is quite unique in the history of philosophy. Its uneven style is passionate, convoluted and repetitive; its meaning is often opaque and contradictory. Like a musical score it introduces themes, drops them, only to develop them at a later stage; the whole adds up to a triumphant celebration of the joy of being fully oneself and in control of one's life – something Stirner himself never achieved.

Stirner has an almost Wittgensteinian awareness of the way language influences our perception of reality and limits our world. 'Language', he writes, 'or "the word" tyrannizes hardest over us, because it brings up against us a whole army of *fixed ideas*'. He stresses that the 'thrall of *language*' is entirely a human construct but it is all-embracing. Truth does not correspond to reality outside language: 'Truths are phrases, ways of speaking . . . men's thoughts, set down in words and therefore just as extant as other things.'[9] Since truths are entirely human creations expressed in language they can be consumed: 'The truth is dead, a letter, a word, a material that I can use up.'[10] But since this is the case, Stirner recognizes the possibility of being enslaved by language and its fixed meanings. It also implies that it is extremely difficult to express something new. Ultimately, Stirner is reduced to verbal impotence in face of the ineffable, of what cannot be said or described. He calls the 'I' 'unthinkable' and 'unspeakable': 'Against me, the unnameable, the realm of thoughts, thinking, and mind is shattered.'[11]

The author of *The Ego and His Own* adopted the *nom de plume* Max

Stirner so as not to alarm Madame Gropius, the owner of the highly respectable academy for young girls where he taught. The German word 'Stirne' means 'brow', and the would-be philosopher felt that it was appropriate not only because he had a prominent forehead but because it matched his self-image as a 'highbrow'. His denunciation of all religious and philosophical beliefs which stood in the way of the unique individual earned him instant notoriety and inspired among others Ludwig Feuerbach, Moses Hess, and Marx and Engels to refute him.

Whilst writing his *magnum opus*, Stirner married Marie Dähnhardt, an intelligent and pretty member of the Free Ones. It proved the happiest period of his life. Madame Gropius was apparently unaware of the writings of the subversive and inflammatory thinker she was harbouring in her genteel establishment. But that still did not prevent her from firing her timid employee. He was then obliged to do hack work to earn a living, translating several volumes of the work of the English economists J. B. Say and Adam Smith. After the failure of a dairy scheme his wife left him, only to recall years later that he was very egoistical and sly. He spent the rest of his life in poverty, twice landing in prison for debt. He attended occasionally the salon of Baroness von der Goltz, where his radical philosophical opinions caused considerable surprise, especially as he appeared outwardly calm. The only work to emerge from this period was a *History of Reaction* (1852) (*Geschichte der Reaction*), as dull and ordinary as the author's own end in 1856. Stirner was the author of one great work: it proved to have been a desperate but unsuccessful attempt to escape from the stifling circumstances of his life and times.

Philosophy

Stirner's philosophy can only be understood in the context of the Left-Hegelian critique of religion that developed in Germany in the 1840s. Opposing the philosophical idealism of Hegel, which saw history as the realization and unfurling of Spirit, the Left Hegelians argued that religion is a form of alienation in which the believer projects certain of his own desirable qualities onto a transcendent deity. Man is not created in God's image, but God is created in man's ideal image. To overcome this alienation, they argued that it is necessary to 'reappropriate' the human essence and to realize that the ideal qualities attributed to God are human qualities, partially realized at present but capable of being fully realized in a transformed society. The critique of religion thus became a radical call for reform.

Stirner developed the Hegelian manner, including its dialectical progression of thesis, antithesis and synthesis, and adopted his theme of alienation and reconciliation. He saw his philosophy of egoism as the culmination of world history. Indeed, Stirner has been called the last and most logical of the Hegelians. Instead of attempting to replace Hegel's 'concrete universal' by any general notions such as 'humanity' or 'classless society', he only believed in the reality of the concrete individual.[12]

But Stirner went even further than the Left-Hegelians in his critique. Where Feuerbach argued that instead of worshipping God, we should try and realize the human 'essence', Stirner declared that this kind of humanism was merely religion in disguise: 'the Christian yearning and hungering for the other world'.[13] Since the concept of human essence is merely abstract thought, it cannot be an independent standard by which we measure our actions. It remains, like the fixed ideas of God, the State, and Justice, nothing more than 'wheels in the head' which have no more reality than a 'spook'.[14]

Although Stirner celebrates the primacy of the unique individual, he is not in metaphysical terms a solipsist. He recognizes the independent existence of the external world and of other people: 'I can make very little of myself; but this little is everything, and is better than what I allow to be made out of me by the might of others.'[15] The ego does not therefore create all, but looks upon all as means towards its own ends: 'it is not that the ego *is* all, but that the ego *destroys* all.'[16] Again, Stirner talks sometimes as if others are the property and creation of the ego, but he usually means that they should only be considered so: 'For me you are nothing but – my food, even as I too am fed upon and turned to use by you. We have only one relation to each other, that of *usableness*, of utility, of use.'[17] While the ego is not the only reality or all of reality, it is therefore the highest level of reality. It uses all beings and things for its own purposes.

The exact nature of the ego is not entirely clear in Stirner's work. The ego is prior to all supposition, neither a thing nor an idea, without enduring form or substance. As such, the ego is a 'creative nothing', not one self but a series of selves: 'I am not nothing in the sense of emptiness, but I am the creative nothing, the nothing out of which I myself as creator create everything.'[18] The ego is therefore a process, existing through a series of selves. Unfortunately Stirner is not entirely explicit or consistent here. He does not explain how an enduring ego can become a series of selves. Nor does he tally his conception of the self-creating ego with his assertion that people are born intelligent or stupid, poets or dolts.

As well as being creative, the ego is also *einzig* – unique. Each individual is entirely single and incomparable: 'My flesh is not their flesh, my mind is not their mind.'[19] Stirner thus has a completely atomistic conception of the self. But he does not suggest like Rousseau that man was originally independent: 'Not isolation or being alone, but society is man's original state . ... Society is our *state of nature*.'[20] But society is something which the individual should emancipate himself from to become truly himself. It is for this reason that Marx and Engels ironically dubbed 'Saint Max' as 'the Unique'.

As an atheist and materialist, Stirner considers the ego as finite and transitory and often seems to identify it with the body. To the question 'What am I?', Stirner replies: 'An abyss of lawless and unregulated impulses, desires, wishes, passions, chaos without light or guiding star'.[21] In addition, as the ego is corporeal, the products of the intellect or ideas can have no independent existence.

This leads Stirner to a nominalist position, rejecting universals or species since reality only consists of particular things. Abstractions or general ideas like 'man' are therefore only concepts in the mind, whatever Feuerbach or Marx might say. At times, Stirner seems to recognize that objective truth does exist, but it has no value apart from its uses for the ego. Stirner is principally concerned with the type of existential truth which is lived, not merely known. He does not say like Kierkegaard that truth is subjective, but holds subjectivity to be more important than truth.[22]

Unlike Godwin, Stirner is no perfectibilist. Indeed, the ego is completely perfect in its present state in every moment: 'We are perfect altogether, and on the whole earth there is not one man who is a sinner!'[23] What is possible is only what is. If this might seem paradoxical given his stress on development, it becomes less so if we interpret it to mean that the perfect ego can develop in the sense of becoming more aware of itself and other things as its property. It can thus develop its 'ownness' (*eigenheit*), its sense of self-possession. The problem still remains that if we are 'perfect', why do we need more knowledge and awareness? Although he does not, as Marx suggested, make a new God out of it, Stirner becomes almost mystical in his negative description of the ego. It is not only unspeakable but unthinkable, comprehensible through non-rational experience alone.

In his psychology, Stirner divides the self into desires, will and intellect. But it is the will which is the ruling faculty for to follow the intellect or desires would fragment the ego. The self is a unity acting from a self-seeking will: '*I* am everything to myself and I do everything *on my account*.'[24] But rather than achieving a balance between desire and intellect, the will seeks power over things, persons and oneself. Stirner thus anticipates Freud in his stress on the force of the desires to influence the intellect, and Adler in his description of the will as the highest faculty of the ego.

Stirner develops the psychological egoism of the eighteenth-century moralists to its most extreme form. It is in the nature of every ego to follow its own interest. Altruism is a complete illusion. The apparent altruist is really an unconscious, involuntary egoist. Even love is a type of egoism: I love 'because love makes me happy, I love because loving is natural to me, because it pleases me'.[25] The same applies to creativity, religion, and friendship. The argument however remains a tautology, and as such is no proof. Apart from mere assertion, Stirner offers no evidence to support his belief that universal self-interest is a true description of human conduct.

The corollary of psychological egoism for Stirner is ethical egoism. He tries to show that conscious egoism is better than egoism disguised as altruism since it allows the development of the will which gives one the dignity of a free man.

Ethics

In his ethics, Stirner argues that the ego is the sole creator of moral order. There are no eternal moral truths and no values to be discovered in nature: 'Owner and creator of my right, I recognize no other source of right than – me, neither God nor the State nor nature nor even man himself.'[26] One has no duty even to oneself since it would imply a division of the ego into a higher and a lower self. Since this is the case, the conscious egoist must choose what pleases him as the sole good: the enjoyment of life is the ultimate aim. The question is not therefore how a person is to prolong life or even to create the true self in himself, but how he is 'to dissolve himself, to live himself out'.[27] He has no moral calling any more than has a flower. If he acts, it is because he wants to. If he speaks, it is not for others or even for the truth's sake but out of pure enjoyment:

> I sing as the bird sings
> That on the bough alights;
> The song that from me springs
> Is pay that well requites.[28]

In the public realm, moral right is just another ghostly wheel in the head. There are no natural rights, no social rights, no historical rights. Right is merely might: 'What you have the *power* to be you have the *right* to.' It is completely subjective: 'I decide whether it is the *right thing* in me; there is no right *outside* me.'[29] The dominant morality will therefore be furnished with the values of the most powerful. The individual has no obligation to law or morality; his only interest is the free satisfaction of his desires. The conscious egoist is thus beyond good and evil, as conventionally defined:

> Away, then, with every concern that is not altogether my concern! You think at least the 'good cause' must be my concern? What's good, what's bad? Why, I myself am my concern, and I am neither good nor bad. Neither has meaning for me.

The divine is God's concern; the human, man's. My concern is neither the divine nor the human, not the true, good, just, free, etc., solely what is *mine*, and it is not a general one, but is – unique, as I am unique.

Nothing is more to me than myself![30]

Indeed, Stirner goes so far as to place one's 'ownness' above the value of freedom. He recognized that his freedom is inevitably limited by society and the State and anyone else who is stronger, but he will not let 'ownness' being taken from him:

one becomes free from much, not from everything . . . 'Freedom lives only in the realm of dreams!' Ownness, on the contrary, is my whole being and existence, it is I myself. I am free from what I am *rid* of, owner of what I have in my *power* or what I *control. My own* I am at all times and under all circumstances, if I know how to have myself and do not throw myself away on others.[31]

With this stress on the primacy of the ego, Stirner goes on to develop a view of freedom which involves the free and conscious choice of the uncircumscribed individual: 'I am my *own* only when I am master of myself.'[32] Stirner's analysis of freedom is penetrating and profound. In the first place, to make freedom itself the goal would be to make it sacred and to fall back into idealism. Secondly, the negative freedom from physical constraint could not guarantee that one would be mentally free from prejudice and custom and tradition. Thirdly, the kind of positive freedom advocated by Hegel – serving a higher cause – would be no different from slavishly performing one's duty. As Stirner points out, the problem with all these theories is that they are based on 'the desire for a *particular* freedom', whereas it is only possible to be free if one acts with self-awareness, self-determination and free will.[33] But whatever stress Stirner places on individual freedom it is always subordinate to the ego, a means of achieving one's selfish ends. He therefore places ownness (*eigenheit*) above freedom. It follows for Stirner that 'all freedom is essentially – self-liberation – that I can have only so much freedom as I procure for myself by my ownness.'[34]

What is owned by the ego is property. This central concept in Stirner's thought is equated with actual possession, but the ego can also look on everything as a candidate for ownership. The only limit to property is the possessor's power: 'I think it belongs to him who knows how to take it, or who does not let it be taken from him.'[35] The egoist can, however, never forfeit what is most important – the ego. He can treat everything else 'smilingly' and 'with humour', whether he succeeds or fails in the battle to acquire property.[36] Thus, while Stirner usually urges the maximum exploitation of others and the world, at times he implies an almost Stoic acceptance of the limitations of one's power.

Politics

While most anarchists make a sharp distinction between the State and society, and reject the former in order to allow the peaceful and productive development of the latter, Stirner rejects both the State and society in their existing form. The State, he argues, has become a 'fixed idea' demanding my allegiance and worship. In practice, it is utterly opposed to my individuality and interest. Its sole purpose is always 'to limit, tame, subordinate the individual – to make him subject to some *generality* or other'.[37] As such it is a 'stalking thistle-eater' and stands as 'an enemy and murderer of *ownness*'.[38]

Stirner finds no justification for the State in the theory of sovereignty and the Social Contract so dear to Rousseau. To claim that the State has a legitimate right to rule and make law because it expresses the will of the sovereign overlooks the irreducible fact that only the individual ego has a claim to sovereignty. Even if it could be shown that every individual had expressed the same will, any law enforced by the State would freeze the will and make the past govern the future. As for democracy based on majority rule, it leaves the dissenting minority in the same position as in an absolute monarchy. Since sovereignty inevitably involves domination and submission, Stirner concludes that there can be no such thing as a 'free State'. This criticism of the social contract theory is undoubtedly as trenchant as Godwin's.

In reality, the State is controlled by the bourgeoisie who developed it in the struggle against the privileged classes. The class of labourers therefore remains a 'power hostile to this State, this State of possessors, this "citizen kingship"'. The State also claims a monopoly of legitimate force: 'The State practises "violence", the individual must not do so. The State's behaviour is violence, and it calls its violence "law"; that of the individual, "crime".'[39] But the State is not merely a legal superstructure imposed on society, issuing orders as laws; it penetrates into the most intimate relationships of its subjects and creates a false bonding; it is 'a tissue and plexus of dependence and adherence; it is a *belonging together*, a holding together . . .'[40]

Stirner makes it crystal-clear that 'I am free in *no* State', and declares that no one has any business 'to command *my* actions, to say what course I shall pursue and set up a code to govern it.'[41] But rather than turning to society as a healthy and beneficial alternative to the State, Stirner sees existing society as a coercive association, demanding that each member think of the well-being of the whole. Given the ontological priority of the

individual, there is no organic society which can preserve individual freedom. The only way forward is therefore to transform both existing society
and the State which by their very natures oppose and oppress the individual.

Given his account of human nature, Stirner, no less than Hobbes, sees
society as a war of all against all. As each individual tries to satisfy his
desires he inevitably comes into conflict with others: 'Take hold, and take
what you require! With this, the war of all against all is declared. I alone
decide what I will have.'[42] But while Stirner's view of human nature as
selfish, passionate and power-seeking is close to that of Hobbes, they come
to opposite conclusions. Where Hobbes called for an all-powerful State
resting on the sword to enforce its laws and to curb the unruly passions of
humanity, Stirner believed that it is possible and desirable to form a new
association of sovereign individuals:

> There we two, the State and I, are enemies. I, the egoist, have not at
> heart the welfare of this 'human society', I sacrifice nothing to it, I
> only utilize it; but to be able to utilize it completely I transform it
> rather into my property and my creature; that is, I annihilate it, and
> form in its place the *Union of Egoists*.[43]

Unlike society which acts as a fused group, crystallized, fixed and dead, the
union of egoists is a spontaneous and voluntary association drawn together
out of mutual interest. Only in such a union will the individual be able to
assert himself as unique because it will not possess him; 'you possess it or
make use of it.'[44] Although it will expand personal freedom, its principal
object is not liberty but ownness, to increase the personal ownership of
property. By voluntary agreement, it will enable the individual to increase
his or her power, and by combined force, it will accomplish more than he
or she could on their own. From an extreme individualist position, Stirner
therefore destroys existing society only to reinvent it in a new form. Conscious egoists combine in a union because they realize that 'they care best
for their welfare if they *unite* with others'.[45] As in Adam Smith's market
model of society, individuals co-operate only so far as it enables them to
satisfy their own desires.

Although Stirner shares many of the assumptions of classical liberalism
in his view of the self-interested, calculating individual, he did not in fact
embrace its political theory. Political liberalism, he declared, abolished
social inequalities; social liberalism (socialism) made people propertyless;
and humanist liberalism, made people godless. While these goals were
progressive to a degree all three creeds allowed the master to rise again in
the form of the State.

Stirner does not endorse capitalism or the Protestant ethic behind it.
The ascetic and striving capitalist is not for Stirner: 'Restless acquisition

does not let us take breath, take a calm *enjoyment*: we do not get the comfort of our possessions.' He is extremely critical of the factory system which alienates workers from themselves and their labour: 'when every one is to cultivate himself into man, condemning a man to *machine-like labour* amounts to the same thing as slavery.' He accepts that only labour creates value. But when one performs mechanically a routine task a person's labour 'is nothing by itself, has no object *in itself*, is nothing complete in itself; he labours only into another's hands, and is *used* (exploited) by this other.'[46] And to complete his remarkable analysis of alienation and exploitation, Stirner argues that just as work should be fulfilling and useful to oneself, so one should enjoy the fruits of one's labour.

At the same time, Stirner rejects the 'sacred' right of private property. He points out that Proudhon is illogical in calling property 'theft'; the concept 'theft' is only possible if one allows validity to the concept 'property' in the first place. He does not therefore call like Proudhon for possession as opposed to property but believes that they coincide since property is merely the expression for *'unlimited dominion* over somewhat (thing, beast, man)' which I can dispose of as I see fit. It is not right but only might which legitimizes property and I am therefore entitled 'to every property to which I – *empower* myself'.[47]

But surely if everyone tried to seize whatever they desired for themselves, an unequal society would result? Not so, says Stirner. In his proposed union of egoists, all would be able to secure enough property for themselves so that poverty would disappear. Stirner even urges workers to band together and strike to achieve better pay and conditions, and be prepared to use force to change their situation if need be. This did not make him a proto-communist, for he contemptuously dismissed the 'ragamuffin communism' of Weitling which would only lead to society as a whole controlling its individual members.[48]

While rejecting the social contract of liberal theory, Stirner reintroduces the notion of contract as the basis of social relations between egoists. Stirner's 'contract', however, is a voluntary agreement which is not binding. Egoists meet as rational calculators of their own interests, making agreements between each other. While Stirner claims that this would not involve any sacrifice of personal freedom, it would only be the case if all contracting parties had the same bargaining power, which they clearly do not. The idea of a relationship based on the gift is beyond Stirner's comprehension.

Since it is the law which defines a crime and the State which punishes the criminal, in a Stateless society comprising unions of egoists there would be no punishment for wrongdoers. Stirner rejects all idea of punishment; it only has meaning when it brings about expiation for injuring something sacred and there is nothing sacred in Stirner's scheme of things. Nor will he accept the idea of using curative means to deal with wrongdoers since this is only the reverse side of punishment. Where the latter sees in an action a sin against right, the former takes it as a sin of the wrongdoer against himself. This insight is overlooked by most anarchists who prefer 'rehabilitation' to punishment. Rejecting the notion of 'crime' and 'disease', Stirner insists that no actions are sinful; they either suit me or do not suit me.

In place of punishment, Stirner suggests that individuals take the law into their own hands and demand 'satisfaction' for an injury.[49] But while this suggests an authoritarian trend in Stirner's thought, he maintains that conscious egoists would eventually see the advantage of making peaceful agreements through contract rather than resorting to violence. The aim after all is to enjoy life.

The reason why the State and even formal institutions of society can be done away with and replaced by a union of egoists is because we are more or less equal in power and ability. It is enough for people to become fully and consciously egoist to end the unequal distribution of power which produces a hierarchical society with servants and masters. A long period of preparation and enlightenment is not therefore necessary, as Godwin argues, before establishing a free society. People simply have to recognize what they are: 'Your nature is, once for all, a human one; you are human natures, human beings. But just because you already are so, you do not still need to become so.'[50]

In the 'war of each against all', force might be necessary to change society and redistribute wealth. It might also be used to free oneself from the State. The State calls the individual's violence 'crime' and 'only by crime does he overcome the State's violence when he thinks that the State is not above him, but he is above the State.' But this is not the only way; we can withdraw our labour and the State will collapse of itself: 'The State rests on the – *slavery of labour*. If *labour* becomes *free*, the State is lost.'[51]

In the final analysis Stirner goes beyond any violent revolution which seeks to make new institutions in his famous celebration of individual self-assertion and rebellion. He calls on individuals to refuse to be arranged and governed by others:

> Now, as my object is not the overthrow of an established order but my elevation above it, my purpose and deed are not a political and social, but (as directed myself and my ownness alone) an *egoistic* purpose and deed.
>
> The revolution commands one to make *arrangements*; the insurrection demands that he *rise or exalt himself*.[52]

Stirner does not celebrate the will to power over others but rather over oneself. If all withdrew into their own uniqueness, social conflict would be diminished and not exacerbated. Human beings might be fundamentally selfish but it is possible to appeal to their selfishness to make contractual agreements among themselves to avoid violence and conflict and to pursue their own selfish interests.

The problem with Stirner is that, given his view of human beings as self-seeking egoists, it is difficult to imagine that in a free society they would not grasp for power and resort to violence to settle disputes. Without the sanction of moral obligation, there is no reason to expect that agreements would be enacted. If such agreements were only kept out of prudence, then it would seem pointless making them in the first place. Again, to say that because human beings have a substantial equality, a truce would emerge in the struggle for power seems unlikely. Finally, an extreme egoist might well find it in his interest to seize State power or manipulate altruists to serve his ends rather than form voluntary unions of free individuals.

Like Hobbes', Stirner's model of human nature would seem to reflect the alienated subjectivity of his own society. He applied the assumptions of capitalist economics to every aspect of human existence and reproduced in everyday life what is most vicious in capitalist institutions. As such his view differs little from that of Adam Smith, whose *Wealth of Nations* he translated into German, and he stands in the tradition of possessive individualism.[53]

In the final analysis Stirner is not consistent in his doctrine of amoral egoism. The consistent egoist would presumably keep quiet and pursue his own interest with complete disregard for others. Yet by recommending that everyone should become an egoist, Stirner implies a moral ground. A complete egoist might encourage others to act altruistically towards him, but Stirner asks others, 'Why will you not take courage now to really make *yourselves* the central point and the main thing altogether?'[54] Again, Stirner may reject all objective values, but he celebrates some values, even if they are only egoistic ones. He cannot therefore be called a nihilist for he takes some things seriously, especially the ego.

Although Stirner's egoist encounters another 'as an *I against* a You altogether different from me and in opposition to me', it implies nothing 'divisive or hostile'.[55] Again, love is selfish exchange, and should be based not on mercy, pity or kindness but 'demands *reciprocity* (as thou to me, so I to thee), does nothing "gratis", and may be won and – *bought*'.[56] Yet this cynical view did not prevent Stirner from feeling love and dedicating *The Ego and His Own* 'To my sweetheart Marie Dähnhardt'. In his later writing, Stirner even underplays the artificial and calculating nature of his proposed union of egoists, likening it to the companionship of children at play, or the relationship between friends or lovers in which pleasure is the principal motive.[57]

Stirner's corrosive egoism makes him reject society as an organic being, but his celebration of the individual does not lead him to deny the existence of others. Sartre may have found that 'Hell is other people', but for Stirner they are individuals who enable one to fulfil oneself by uniting with them. As Emma Goldman pointed out, Stirner is not merely the apostle of the theory '"each for himself, the devil take the hind one"'.[58]

Marx's and Engels' rightly accused Stirner of being still sufficiently Hegelian to have an idealist approach to history, believing that 'concepts should regulate life'.[59] Looking for the 'sacred' everywhere to overcome, he overlooked the material base of society. This led him to believe that it was only necessary to change ideas about the individual's relationship to the State for it to wither away. He was also guilty of doing precisely what he reproached Feuerbach for in his attack on the 'holy', implying that it is only a matter of destroying mental illusions to liberate humanity. Again, while rejecting abstractions, Stirner's concept of the 'ego' is itself an abstraction and he fails to recognize that the individual is a set of relationships. Finally, Stirner does not go far enough in urging the workers merely to strike and claim the product of their labour. But while all this may be true, it is not enough to dismiss Stirner as a 'petit-bourgeois utopian' as Marxists have done, or to suggest that he was a harbinger of fascism.

Stirner is an awkward and uncomfortable presence. By stating things in the most extreme way, and taking his arguments to their ultimate conclusions, he jolts his readers out of their philosophical composure and moral smugness. His value lies in his ability to penetrate the mystification and reification of the State and authoritarian society. His criticism of the way communism can crush the individual is apt, and he correctly points out that a workers' State is unlikely to be any freer than the liberal State. Beyond this, he demonstrates brilliantly the hold 'wheels in the head' have upon us: how abstractions and fixed ideas influence the very way we think, and see ourselves, how hierarchy finds its roots in the '*dominion of thoughts, dominion of mind*'.[60] He lifts the social veil, undermines the worship of abstractions, and shows how the world is populated with 'spooks' of our own making. He offers a powerful defence of individuality in an alienated world, and places subjectivity at the centre of any revolutionary project. While his call for self-assertion could lead to violence and the oppression of the weak, and his conscious egoism is ultimately too limited to embrace the whole of human experience, he reminds us splendidly that a free society must exist in the interest of all individuals and it should aim at complete self-fulfilment and enjoyment. The timid and nondescript teacher at a girls' academy turned out to be one of the most enduringly unsettling thinkers in the Western tradition.

Pierre-Joseph Proudhon
The Philosopher of Poverty

PIERRE-JOSEPH PROUDHON WAS the first self-styled anarchist, deliberately adopting the label in order to provoke his opponents, who saw anarchy as synonymous with disorder. In *What is Property?* (1840), his first work to bring him notoriety, he presented his paradoxical position in the eloquent and classical French prose which earned him the admiration of Sainte-Beuve and Flaubert:

> 'You are a republican.' Republican, yes, but this word has no precise meaning. *Res publica*, that is, the public good. Now whoever desires the public good, under whatever form of government, can call himself a republican. Kings too are republicans. 'Well, then you are a democrat?' No. 'What, you cannot be a monarchist!' No. 'A Constitutionalist?' Heaven forbid! 'Then you must be for the aristocracy.' Not at all. 'Do you want a mixed government?' Even less. 'What are you then?' I am an anarchist.
>
> 'I understand, you are being satirical at the expense of government.' Not in the least. I have just given you my considered and serious profession of faith. Although I am a strong supporter of order, I am in the fullest sense of the term, an anarchist.[1]

As his famous maxims 'Property is Theft', 'Anarchy is Order', and 'God is Evil' imply, Proudhon gloried in paradox. He is one of the most contradictory thinkers in the history of political thought, and his work has given rise to a wide range of conflicting interpretations. He is also one of the most diffuse writers: he published over forty works and left fourteen volumes of correspondence, eleven volumes of notebooks and a large number of unpublished manuscripts.

To have a clear understanding of Proudhon is no easy task. He did not always digest his learning and he made no attempt to be systematic or consistent in the presentation of his arguments. He could appreciate both sides of any question but was often uncertain which side to adopt: truth for him tended to be the movement between two opposites. The exact meaning of his work is further obscured by the fact that he changed his mind several times throughout his career.

His style did not help matters either. At its best, it can be clear and eloquent, but it too often becomes diffuse and turbid. He was given to polemical exaggeration, and did not know when to stop. Much to the bemusement of his opponents and the confusion of his critics, he was a self-conscious ironist.

Like many social thinkers in the mid-nineteenth century, Proudhon combined social theory with philosophical speculation. He dived boldly into almost every sphere of human knowledge: philosophy, economics, politics, ethics and art were all grist to his mill. He held outrageous views on government, property, sexuality, race, and war. Yet behind his voluminous and varied output there was an overriding drive for justice and freedom.

He shared his century's confidence that reason and science would bring about social progress and expand human freedom. He saw nature and society governed by laws of development and believed that if human beings lived in harmony with them they could become free. Freedom thus becomes a recognition of necessity: only if man knows his natural and social limits can he become free to realize his full potential. From this perspective Proudhon considered himself to be a 'scientific' thinker and wanted to turn politics into a science. But although he liked to think that his 'whole philosophy is one of perpetual reconciliation', the dialectical method he adopted often failed to reach a satisfactory resolution of its contradictory ideas.[2]

Proudhon would often present himself as an isolated and eccentric iconoclast. In 1848, he wrote: 'My body is physically among the people, but my mind is elsewhere. My thinking has led me to the point where I have almost nothing in common with my contemporaries by way of ideas.' He liked to think of himself as the 'excommunicated of the epoch' and was proud of the fact that he did not belong to any sect or party.[3] In fact, this was more a pose than a correct assessment.

After the publication of *What is Property?* in 1840, Proudhon soon began to wield considerable influence. Marx hailed it as a 'penetrating work' and called it 'the first decisive, vigorous and scientific examination of property'.[4] Proudhon began to haunt the imagination of the French bourgeoisie as *l'homme de la terreur* who embodied all the dangers of proletarian revolution.

As the French labour movement began to develop, his influence grew considerably. His ideas dominated those sections of the French working class who helped form the First International and the largest single group in the Paris Commune of 1871 were Proudhonians. After Bakunin's rupture with Marx, which marked the parting of the ways of the libertarian and statist socialists, the organ of the first militant anarchist group based in Switzerland asserted: 'Anarchy is not an invention of Bakunin . . . Proudhon is the real father of anarchy'.[5] And Bakunin himself was the first to admit that 'Proudhon is the master of us all'.[6]

Proudhon's stress on economic before political struggle and his call for the working class to emancipate themselves by their own hands also made him the father of anarcho-syndicalism. Proudhon's disciples not only founded the Confédération Générale du Travail, the French trade union movement, but Fernand Pelloutier in his Fédération des Bourses du Travail tried to educate the working class along mutualist lines as laid out by Proudhon.

Proudhon's influence was not only restricted to France. During the 1870s, his ideas inspired Pi y Margall and the federalists in Spain, and the *narodniks* in Russia. The great Russian socialist Alexander Herzen became a close friend. Tolstoy was struck by his ideas on property and government, sought him out, and borrowed the title of Proudhon's *War and Peace* (1861) for his great novel. In Germany, he had an enormous influence on the early socialist movement; in the 1840s, Lassalle was regarded as the greatest hope of Proudhonism in the country. In America, his views were given wide publicity, especially by Charles Dana of the Fourierist Brook Farm, and William B. Greene. Benjamin R. Tucker – 'always a Proudhonian without knowing it' – took Proudhon's *bon mot* 'Liberty is not the Daughter but the Mother of Order' as the masthead of his journal *Liberty*. In Britain, his ideas pervaded the syndicalist movement before the First World War, and even G. D. H. Cole's version of guild socialism closely resembled his proposals.[7]

This century Proudhon has remained as controversial as ever. His attempt to discover the laws which govern society has earned him the reputation as a founding father of sociology. His ideas have been adopted by socialist writers as applicable to developing countries in the Third World.[8] He has also been taken up by the nationalists on the Right for his defence of small-property owners and French interests. He has not only been hailed as one of the 'masters of the counter-revolution of the nineteenth century', but as a 'harbinger of fascism'.[9] He continues to be most remembered, however, as the father of the historic anarchist movement.

Proudhon was born the son a tavern-keeper and cooper in Besançon in the department of Franche-Comté near the Swiss border. His family had been rugged and independent peasants in the mountainous region for generations and he boasted that he was 'moulded with the pure limestone of the Jura'.[10] He looked back to his early childhood as a lost golden age. From five to ten, he spent much of his time on his family's farm in the country, a life which gave a realistic base to his thinking. It probably encouraged his fiery individuality which led him later to declare: 'Whoever lays his hands on me to govern me is a usurper and a tyrant: and I declare him my enemy.'[11] It may also have fostered the puritanical and patriarchal attitudes which made him insist on chastity and see women primarily as subservient handmaids. What is certain is that the experience of growing up in the country left him with lifelong roots in the land and a powerful mystique of the earth. It fostered an ecological sensibility which led him to lament later the loss of 'the deep feeling of nature' that only country life can give:

> Men no longer love the soil. Landowners sell it, lease it, divide it into shares, prostitute it, bargain with it and treat it as an object of specu-lation. Farmers torture it, violate it, exhaust it and sacrifice it to their impatient desire for gain. They never become one with it.[12]

At the age of twelve, the young Pierre-Joseph started work as a cellar-boy in his father's business in Besançon. He managed however to get a scholarship to the Collège de Besançon, the best school in town with a fine academic reputation. Unfortunately, his father, better at brewing beer than doing business, was declared bankrupt when Pierre-Joseph was eighteen. He had to drop out of school and earn a living; in 1827 he decided to become a printer's apprentice. Proudhon's subsequent life as a craftsman gave him an independent view of society, while the personal control he exercised over his work only highlighted by contrast the alienation of the new factory system. It also gave him time and space to continue his studies. By 1838 he had not only developed a new typographical process but pub-lished an essay on general grammar.

Proudhon's workshop printed the publications for the local diocese and they inspired his own religious speculation. Not content to proof-read and set the writings of others, he started composing his own. He contributed to an edition of Bible notes in Hebrew (learning the language in the process) and later wrote for a Catholic encyclopaedia. The Bible became his principal authority for his socialist ideas. At the same time, his extensive knowledge of Christian doctrine did not deepen his faith but had the reverse effect and made him staunchly anti-clerical. He went on to reject God's providen-tial rule and to conclude that 'God is tyranny and poverty; God is evil.'[13]

More important to his subsequent development, Proudhon came into contact with local socialists, including his fellow townsman Charles Fourier who rejected existing civilization with its repressive moral codes. He even supervised the printing of Fourier's greatest work *Le Nouveau monde industriel et sociétaire* (1829) which gave the clearest account of his economic views. It also advocated a society of ideal communities or 'phalansteries' destined 'to conduct the human race to opulence, sensual pleasures and global unity'.[14] Fourier maintained that if human beings attuned to the 'Universal Harmony', they would be free to satisfy their passions, regain their mental health, and live without crime. Proudhon acknowledged that he was a captive of this 'bizarre genius' for six whole weeks and was impressed by his belief in immanent justice, although he found his phalansteries too utopian and his celebration of free love distasteful.

Determined to strike out on his own, Proudhon left Besançon and spent several years as a journeyman wandering throughout France from town to town, finding work wherever he could. His travels took him to Lyon, where he came into contact with workers advocating co-operative workshops, and to Paris, which he detested. His *tour de France* demonstrated only too well Alexis de Tocqueville's observation that authority in France at that time consisted of 'a single central power controlling the administration throughout the country' by means of rigid rules covering every administrative detail.[15]

Proudhon eventually returned to Besançon where he became a partner in a small printing firm. But he was not content to live the obscure life of a provincial printer; he could not make up his mind whether to become a scholar or to serve the working class. In 1838 he applied for a scholarship from the Besançon Academy to continue his studies, declaring himself to be 'born and raised in the working-class, and belonging to it in heart and mind, in manners and in community of interests and aspirations'.[16] Echoing the last testament of Henri de Saint-Simon, he asserted that he wanted to improve 'the physical, moral and intellectual condition of the most numerous and poorest class'.[17] He won the scholarship as well as the prize in a competition for an essay on *Sunday Observance*. The hero of the essay is Moses, founder of the Sabbath; he is depicted as a great social scientist for having laid the foundations of society based on 'natural' law and for discovering, not inventing, a code of laws. It was an achievement which Proudhon wanted to develop in drawing up the moral rules for people to live in equality and justice.

Proudhon dedicated his next work *What is Property? First Memoir* (1840) to the respectful scholars and burghers of the Besançon Academy. They were deeply shocked when they read the contents for the book questioned the twin pillars of their privilege: property and government. Not surprisingly, they insisted that the dedication be removed. As the obscure author later recalled, after a long, detailed and above all impartial analysis he had arrived at the astonishing conclusion that 'property is, from whatever angle you look at it, and whatever principle you refer it to – a contradictory notion! Since denying property means denying authority, I immediately deduced from my definition the no less paradoxical corollary that the true form of government is *anarchy*.'[18]

Proudhon replied to his own question 'What is Property?' with the bold paradox: 'Property is Theft'. It became his most famous slogan and its implications have reverberated ever since. But although Proudhon claimed that the principle came to him as a revelation and was his most precious thought, Morelly had expressed a similar idea in the previous century and Brissot had been the first to declare it during the French Revolution.

In fact, Proudhon had a very specific view of property and his slogan was not as revolutionary as it might appear. Stirner was quick to point out that the concept of 'theft' can only be possible if one allows the prior validity of the concept of property.[19] Proudhon did not attack private property as such; indeed, in the same work he called those communists who wanted to collectivize it as enemies of freedom. He was principally opposed to large property-owners who appropriated the labour of others in the form of revenue, who claimed the *droit d'aubaine*. At this stage, he was in favour of property as long as it meant 'possession', with the privileges of ownership restricted to the usufruct or benefits accruing from it.

In *What is Property?*, Proudhon not only threw down a gauntlet at the capitalists but also at his contemporary socialists. He attacked bitterly communism as oppression and servitude. Man, he believed, likes to choose his own work, whereas the communist system 'starts from the principle that the individual is entirely subordinate to the collectivity'.[20] It therefore violates both the principles of equality and the autonomy of the conscience which are so close to Proudhon's heart.

Is there a way through the Scylla of accumulated property and Charybdis of communism? Can society exist without capital and government or a communist State? Proudhon thought he had discovered the answer. He was convinced that the authority man has over man is in inverse ratio to his intellectual development. In his own society, he believed that force and cunning were being limited by the influence of justice and would finally disappear in the future with the triumph of equality. He concluded:

> Property and royalty have been decaying since the world began. Just as man seeks justice in equality, society seeks order in anarchy.
>
> *Anarchy*, that is the absence of a ruler or a sovereign. This is the form of government we are moving closer to every day.[21]

Proudhon, as he acknowledged in a footnote, was fully aware that the meaning usually given to the word 'anarchy' is 'absence of principles, absence of laws', and that it had become synonymous with 'disorder'.[22] He deliberately went out of his way to affirm the apparent paradox that 'anarchy is order' by showing that authoritarian government and the unequal distribution of wealth are the principal causes of disorder and chaos in society. By doing so, he became the father of the historic anarchist movement.

What is Property? was under threat of being proscribed, but the Ministry of Justice eventually decided that it was too scholarly to be dangerous. Undeterred, Proudhon followed up his strident squib by a new memoir entitled *Warning to the Property Owners* (1842). He called for economic equality and insisted that the man of talent and genius should accept it gracefully. This time Proudhon was prosecuted but was acquitted by a jury who again thought the work was too complicated for ordinary people to understand.

In his desire to discover the underlying laws of society, Proudhon turned to philosophy and his next major work was *On the Creation of Order in Humanity* (1843). His starting-point is similar to Lao Tzu's and Hegel's. While we cannot penetrate to the essence of the universe, we can observe that it is in a state of flux. This constant movement in nature and society takes the form of a 'dialectical series', that is it operates through the reconciliation of opposing forces. Nevertheless, Proudhon is at pains to stress that he is not offering an idealist interpretation of the world in which creatures are just ideas. According to what he calls his 'ideo-realist theory', the 'reality of being' increases progressively from the mineral world through the vegetable and animal kingdoms to man. It reaches its highest peak in human society, which is 'the freest organization and least tolerant of the arbitrariness of those who govern it'. While stressing that 'Man is destined to live without religion', Proudhon argues that the moral law still remains eternal and absolute once its outer religious shell has been removed.[23]

Proudhon also began developing his view of history. He argued that a scientific study of history should be based on the influence of labour on society. But while recognizing that all events depend on general laws inherent in nature and man, Proudhon asserts that there is no inevitability in particular events which may 'vary infinitely according to the individual wills that cause them to happen'. The main facts are therefore arranged in a causal sequence, but history has little predictive value. Thus while progress in the long term is inevitable, there is room for human volition, deliberation and ingenuity: 'it is upon ourselves that we must work if we wish to influence the destiny of the world'.[24]

In the winter of 1844–5 Proudhon went to Paris to write his next mammoth onslaught against government and property. In the Latin Quarter, he met many political exiles, including Marx, Herzen and Bakunin, who all sought the acquaintance of the notorious author of *What is Property?* In their garrets and cafés, they discussed passionately Hegelian philosophy and revolutionary tactics. Bakunin and Herzen became permanent friends of Proudhon. Bakunin developed his ideas and spread them amongst the growing international anarchist movement, while Herzen took them to sow in the soil of Russian populism.

With Marx, relations were more problematic. At first Marx welcomed *What is Property?*, and he and Proudhon were friendly for a while in Paris. Indeed, Marx later claimed that he had introduced Proudhon to Hegel. Engels also wrote that Proudhon's writings had left him with the 'greatest respect' for the author.[25] Marx tried to get Proudhon to join their international communist group, but Proudhon became quickly disenchanted both with Marx's doctrinaire and dominating personality and his authoritarian communism. Their desultory correspondence ended when Proudhon agreed to collaborate on seeking the laws of society but insisted:

> for God's sake, when we have demolished all *a priori* dogmas, do not let us think of indoctrinating the people in our turn . . . I wholeheartedly applaud your idea of bringing all shades of opinion to light. Let us have a good and honest polemic. Let us set the world an example of wise and farsighted tolerance, but simply because we are leaders of a movement let us not instigate a new intolerance. Let us not set ourselves up as the apostles of a new religion, even if it be the religion of logic or reason.[26]

No doubt angered by Proudhon's implied accusation of intolerance, Marx chose not to answer the letter. Instead, when Proudhon's next work *System of Economic Contradictions, or The Philosophy of Poverty* appeared in 1846, Marx took the opportunity to attack the author at length. He wrote soon after reading the book that it was a 'formless and pretentious work', singling out its 'feeble Hegelianism' and false hypothesis of 'universal reason'.[27] In his more deliberate reply written in French, *The Poverty of Philosophy*, Marx continued to portray Proudhon as a petty-bourgeois idealist who failed to recognize that human nature is not an unchanging essence but a product of history. His principal argument was that Proudhon's individualistic economic model made him see humanity or society as a static 'final subject'.[28] Henceforth, Marx invariably referred to Proudhon in his writings as a 'bourgeois socialist' or as a socialist 'of the small peasant and mastercraftsman'.[29] It would seem that Marx either simply failed to understand Proudhon's book, or deliberately misrepresented it.

Proudhon was furious. He considered writing a reply for a time but contented himself with a note in his diary (23 September 1847) to the effect that 'Marx is the tapeworm of socialism!' Their parting of the ways marked the beginning of the split between the libertarian and authoritarian socialists which came to a head in the dispute between Marx and Bakunin within the First International. Marx continued to attack Proudhon for advocating class collaboration and proscribing trade-union and parliamentary activity, and he could never forgive him the fact that the French working class adopted his ideas rather than his own.

The two great volumes of Proudhon's *System of Economic Contradictions, or The Philosophy of Poverty* were published in 1846. As Marx observed, it was full of sub-Hegelian dialectics and Proudhon freely admitted later that at this stage in his life he was 'intoxicated with the dialectic'.[30] In *On the Creation of Order in Humanity* (1843), he had already adopted Fourier's notion of a 'serial law' of development in both nature and society which he called the 'Serial Dialectic'. Now in the *Economic Contradictions*, he adopted the Kantian term of 'antinomies' to express Hegel's dialectic: the 'theory of antinomies', he wrote, 'is both the representation and the base of all movement in customs and institutions.'[31] By assuming that laws of development applied both to the material world and human society, Proudhon hoped that the discovery of these laws would turn politics and economics into a science. In practice, however, his use of the dialectic was invariably wooden and mechanical and Marx rightly observed that his antinomies were presented as mutually exclusive entities. It was all very well for Proudhon to assert that 'My whole philosophy is one of perpetual reconciliation', but in the *Economic Contradictions* he failed to reach a satisfactory synthesis, arguing for instance that property is 'liberty' as well as 'theft'.[32]

It was in this work that Proudhon declared that 'God is Evil' and that 'for as long as men bow before altars, mankind will remain damned, the slave of kings and priests'.[33] He also returned to his twin onslaught on government and property. He was critical of all forms of political democracy. While better than autocracy, constitutional government tends to be unstable and can become an instrument of bourgeois domination or degenerate into dictatorship. Even direct democracy is unacceptable since it often prevents subjects executing their own decisions; on occasion, it can be worse than autocracy since it claims legitimacy in oppressing its citizens. As for communism, Proudhon was particularly dismissive:

> The communists in general are under a strange illusion: fanatics of State power, they claim that they can use the State authority to ensure, by measures of restitution, the well-being of the workers who created the collective wealth. As if the individual came into existence after society, and not society after the individual.[34]

Not surprisingly, *Economic Contradictions* brought Proudhon further notoriety and hostility from the Right and the Left.

On the positive side, Proudhon elaborated in the work his economic system of mutualism. It was intended to be a 'synthesis of the notions of private property and collective ownership' and to avoid the abuses of both.[35] In place of *laissez-faire* and State control, he put forward a 'natural' economy based on work and equality, a kind of socialism based on exchange and credit. Accepting the labour theory of value, he argued that workers should form associations to exchange the products of their work, the value of which would be calculated by the amount of necessary labour time involved.

He later described his system of mutualism as the 'ancient law of retaliation, *an eye for an eye, a tooth for a tooth, a life for a life*' applied to the tasks of labour and fraternity. The workers themselves would control their own means of production. They would form small as well as large associations, especially in the manufacturing and extractive industries. As mutualism developed economic organization would replace the political one and the State would eventually wither away. In this system 'the labourer is no longer a serf of the State, swamped by the ocean of the community. He is a free man, truly his own master, who acts on his own initiative and is personally responsible.'[36] As people began to reach one common level, social harmony would prevail.

It would not however be a state of complete equality, for the industrious would be rewarded more than the lazy. Proudhon had a strong Puritan streak which made him see idleness as a vice and work as a virtue in itself: 'It is not good for man to live in ease', he declared. He also praised poverty for being clean and healthy: 'the glorification of poverty in the Gospel is the greatest truth that Christ ever preached to men'.[37] The positive aspect of Proudhon's frugality is the contention that if men limited their needs and lived a simple life, nature would provide enough for all. He did not moreover condemn luxury outright. He did not think that abundance would ever exist in the sense of there being more goods and services than were consumed, but he was ready to admit affluence into his mutualist scheme if it were spread fairly around.

It was not long before Proudhon had a chance to put his ideas into practice. He had moved to live in Paris in 1847, and a year later revolution broke out and the monarchy of Louis Philippe was overthrown. Concerned that it was a revolution 'made without ideas', Proudhon threw himself into the struggle. He spoke at many of the popular clubs and in February 1848 brought out *Le Représentant du Peuple*. Its circulation soared to forty thousand. Closed by the public censor, it was resurrected three times under a different name.

In his *Journal du Peuple*, he issued in November 1848 a mutualist manifesto which anticipated aspects of modern industrial 'self-management'. While defending property and the family, he called for 'the free disposition of the fruits of labour, property without usury'. Above all, he insisted: 'We want the unlimited liberty of man and of the citizen, except for the respect of the liberty of others: liberty of association, liberty of assembly, liberty of religion, liberty of the press, liberty of thought and speech, liberty of work, commerce and industry, liberty of education, in a word, absolute liberty'.[38]

Proudhon also made a brief foray into parliamentary politics at the time. He was elected to the National Assembly for the Seine *département* in June 1848, and in the autumn presidential elections supported the leftist candidate Raspail. In keeping with his principles, he voted against the new constitution of the Second Republic simply because it was a constitution which would prevent further progress. He tried to pose the social question before political issues, calling for a partial moratorium on debts and rents. It was all part of his scheme for reducing property to possession without revenue. The proposal however caused an uproar in the assembly. He not only told the deputies that 'in case of refusal we ourselves shall proceed to the liquidation without you', but when asked what he meant by 'we' he declared: 'When I say we, I identify myself with the proletariat, and when I say you, I identify you with the bourgeois class.'[39] 'It is the social war!' cried the horrified deputies and voted out his motion 691 to 2.

His parliamentary experience was not a happy one and it only confirmed his belief that economic reform was more important than political change. 'Universal Suffrage', he came to realize, 'is the Counter-Revolution.' Elected only a fortnight before the June insurrection, he completely failed to anticipate it. As he wrote of this time:

> As soon as I set foot in the parliamentary Sinai, I ceased to be in touch with the masses; because I was absorbed by my legislative work, I entirely lost sight of the current of events . . . One must have lived in that isolator which is called the National Assembly to realize how the men who are most completely ignorant of the state of the country are almost always those who represent it . . . fear of the people is the sickness of all those who belong to authority; the people, for those in power, are the enemy.[40]

Having realized the impossibility of bringing about fundamental change through parliament, Proudhon tried to set up a People's Bank with free credit to show the way for a mutualist transformation of the economy. Its business was to be limited to the exchange of commodities for an equivalent sum of money and to the issue of interest-free loans. The values of commodities would be based on the sum of labour and the expense involved in their production. It was clearly a consensual strategy for change, for it would have most benefited the small businessmen and workers who shared the same interests. Moreover it did not effect the driving force of capitalism for Proudhon continued to believe that competition is 'the spice of exchange, the salt of work. To suppress competition is to suppress liberty itself.'[41] In the outcome, the effectiveness of the People's Bank was never put to the test for although it managed to enlist twenty-seven thousand members, it collapsed within a year.

It was hardly a time to make bold experiments. Severe repression followed the successful *coup d'état* of Louis Napoleon in December 1848. Proudhon himself was arrested in January for attacking the usurper and sentenced to three years in prison. At first he fled to Belgium, but returned to Paris in June 1849 and gave himself up. Fortunately, the prison regime was light: he was allowed the books, visitors and food he liked, and could go out on parole one day each week.

He could even see his new wife and begat a child, the first of three daughters who became the joy of his life. The marriage had followed a singular proposal. While worrying about the failure of his bank and the collapse of his revolutionary hopes, the forty-one year old bachelor happened to notice a simple young woman in the streets. He at once made enquiries about her and then asked her to marry him, explaining that he wanted a 'working girl, simple, full of grace, naive, devoted to her work and her duties'. It was entirely a cerebral affair, and as he wrote to his brother 'I am taking a wife for the commodity of my poor existence . . .'⁴²

Proudhon did not remain idle in prison. He wrote about the 1848 revolution, about free credit and compiled his *Confessions of a Revolutionary* (1849). The latter was a colourful and lively account of his life and views. He took the opportunity to reiterate his belief that 'We do not admit the government of man by man any more than the exploitation of man by man.' He also reasserted his prickly sense of independence: 'Whoever lays his hands on me to govern me is a usurper and a tyrant.'⁴³

He wrote a Machiavellian pamphlet called *The Social Revolution Vindicated by the Coup d'État of December Second* (1852) in which he defended collaboration with Napoleon in the hope that he would bring about economic reform. The great scourge of property, government and hierarchy now declared: 'The Second of December is the signal for a forward march on the revolutionary road, and . . . Louis Napoleon is its general'.⁴⁴ It was a grave misreading of Napoleon's character and Proudhon lived to regret this temporary aberration which was at odds with his previous thought and action.

Proudhon drew the lessons of the 1848 Revolution in one of his most important works, *General Idea of the Revolution in the Nineteenth Century* (1851). It made a spirited defence of revolution as a permanent and continual process regulated by the 'natural laws' of society. 'My whole faith', Proudhon wrote, 'is contained in the following definition: "Revolution is, in the order of moral facts, an act of sovereign justice proceeding from the necessities of things. Consequently it is self-justifying, and it is a crime for any statesman to oppose it." '⁴⁵

Proudhon once again returned to his condemnation of State power, governmental prejudice, and man-made law. Few anarchist thinkers have offered such a telling analysis. The State is entirely a fictitious being, entirely without morality. It has become reified into a monster, possessing nothing but debts and bayonets.

Tracing the origins of the State, Proudhon finds it in embryo in the patriarchal family. It derives from the hierarchical form in which the first men conceived order, that is, 'in principle, authority, in action, government'.[46] He follows Rousseau in arguing that a self-interested minority originally deceived the majority into thinking that it contributed to the general good. It then penetrated deep into human consciousness so that even the boldest thinkers came to see it as a necessary evil.

There is no way to mitigate its defects. Democratic government is a contradiction, for the people can never be truly consulted or represented. It cannot express the will of constituents who vote for it and remain powerless between elections. As Proudhon wrote in a notebook, representative government is 'a perpetual abuse of power for the profit of the reigning caste and the interests of the representatives, against the interests of the represented'.[47] Universal suffrage is thus a real lottery, ensuring the triumph of mediocrity and the tyranny of the majority. 'To be governed', Proudhon concludes in one of his most famous tirades,

> is to be watched over, inspected, spied on, directed, legislated, regimented, closed in, indoctrinated, preached at, controlled, assessed, evaluated, censored, commanded; all by creatures that have neither the right, nor wisdom, nor virtue ... To be governed means that at every move, operation, or transaction one is noted, registered, entered in a census, taxed, stamped, priced, assessed, patented, licensed, authorized, recommended, admonished, prevented, reformed, set right, corrected. Government means to be subjected to tribute, trained, ransomed, exploited, monopolized, extorted, pressured, mystified, robbed; all in the name of public utility and the general good. Then, at the first sign of resistance or word of complaint, one is repressed, fined, despised, vexed, pursued, hustled, beaten up, garroted, imprisoned, shot, machine-gunned, judged, sentenced, deported, sacrificed, sold, betrayed, and to cap it all, ridiculed, mocked, outraged, and dishonoured. *That is* government, *that* is its justice and its morality! ... O human personality! How can it be that you have cowered in such subjection for sixty centuries?[48]

As for law, Proudhon starts like Rousseau by arguing that no one should obey a law unless they have consented to it themselves. If this is the case laws in a parliamentary democracy can have no legitimacy since individuals are not directly involved in their making: 'Law has been made without my participation, despite my absolute disapproval, despite the harm it makes me suffer.'[49] Unlike Rousseau, however, Proudhon rejects the definition of freedom as the capacity to obey self-imposed laws. If there must be legislation, Proudhon argues cogently, I should be my own legislator; and if I am, there is no need to make laws for myself.

All law for Proudhon is inevitably coercive and restricts the choice and action of the individual; it puts 'external authority . . . in the place of citizens' immanent, inalienable, untransferable authority'.[50] Indeed, he went so far in private as to assert that 'Organization of any kind is equivalent to the suppression of liberty, so far as free persons are concerned.'[51] Furthermore he rejected the common argument that law and virtue are interconnected and that the just person is the law-abiding person. He makes a clear distinction between man-made laws and general moral rules, and while he accepts the latter if voluntarily accepted, he condemns the former. As he wrote in his *Confessions* at this time, 'the true judge for every man is his own conscience, a fact that implies replacement of the systems of courts and laws with a system of personal obligations and contracts, in other words, repression of legal institutions'.[52]

Proudhon concludes that government is not necessary to maintain order, despite the popular equation between 'law and order'. In the first place, there is no logical connection for '*Order* is a genus, *government* a species'.[53] Secondly, there is no causal link between the two for political rule regularly fails to control social conflict. It follows that government and law are unnecessary evils and should be eliminated. Proudhon therefore declares in a passage which could stand as a summary of his anarchist beliefs:

> The sovereignty of reason having been substituted for that of revelation; the notion of contract succeeding to that of compulsion; economic critique revealing that political institutions must now be absorbed into the industrial organism: we fearlessly conclude that the revolutionary formula can no longer be direct government or any kind of government, but must be: no more government.[54]

Proudhon makes clear that instead of law he would have free contract or voluntary agreement which he considers to be the negation of authority. Such a contract would be based not on distributive justice, or distribution according to need, but on commutative justice, that is, on mutual exchange. It would take the form of contracts in which the parties would undertake mutual obligations and reciprocal guarantees for exchanging goods of equal value. It would be subject to no outside authority and impose no obligations on the contracting parties except those resulting 'from their personal promise of reciprocal service'.[55] This was to become the basis of his mature anarchism.

Proudhon was freed from prison in 1852, but the atmosphere of repression under Napoleon III made it almost impossible for socialists to publish their ideas. In 1854, the prolific and irrepressible author reluctantly confessed to an old friend 'The literary career is now more or less closed to me. No printer, no bookseller in Paris would dare publish or sell anything of mine . . . it seems that Society, really convinced that I am its greatest enemy, has excommunicated me. *Terra et qua interdictus sum!*'[56]

But he was far from finished. Four years later, he was inspired by a Catholic pamphleteer to write his greatest work on ethics, *Justice in the Revolution and the Church* (1858). In it, he laid out the ethical principles which were implicit in all his earlier works and clarified his view of human nature.

Human Nature

Although like Godwin, Proudhon believed that human beings are potentially rational, progressive and just, he starts from a very different position. To begin with, he believed that human nature is constant and unchangeable. The first characteristic of our nature is that we are individuals; society comes after the individual. But it is only in the abstract that the individual may be regarded in a state of isolation; he is 'an integral part of collective existence'.[57] Society is as real a thing as the individuals who compose it. The collectivity or group thus is the fundamental condition of all existence and society like the individual has a 'force, will and consciousness of its own'.[58] Proudhon thus went beyond the atomistic approach of Godwin and Stirner, and argued that individuals in a group create a 'collective force' and a 'collective reason' which are over and above the sum of individual forces and intelligences which compose the group. He also saw the family as the most important socializing agency in society, the source of our moral sentiments and social capacities.

Our social being does not however prevent us from being aggressive. It is our pugnacity which gives rise to conflict and war. According to Proudhon, man is naturally free and selfish. He is capable of self-sacrifice for love and friendship but as a rule selfishly pursues his own interest and pleasure.[59] The result is that left to himself he will inevitably try to gain power over others.

To avoid conflict Proudhon suggests that primitive men sought a leader and created a social hierarchy. This led to the exploitation of the weak by the strong. To constrain social conflict religion was first used but when it proved insufficient it was supported by the coercive force of government. But the drastic remedy of government for conflict eventually became an additional cause for its existence: 'Government was progressive when it defended a society against savages. There are no more savages: there are only workers whom the government treats like savages.'[60]

Thanks to our potential rationality, there is however a way out of this apparent impasse. As Proudhon wrote in his *Confessions*, 'in society as well as in the individual, reason and reflection always triumph over instinct and spontaneity. This is the characteristic feature of our species and it accounts for the fact that we progress. It follows that Nature in us seems to retreat while Reason comes to the fore.'[61] As man develops his reasoning powers and matures morally, he is therefore able to rebel against religious and political authority and reaches a stage where the artificial restrictions of government and law can be done away with. Liberation is within reach.

Ethics

In his ethics, Proudhon rejected the sanction of both Church and State. He had of course long thrown off his childhood Catholicism and had concluded that 'God is evil'. Although the statement assumes the existence of God and his moral nature, Proudhon in fact had become a convinced atheist. Man cannot therefore rely on some providence to ensure progress; indeed, 'Each step in our progress represents one more victory in which we annihilate the Deity.'[62] But Proudhon did not conclude like Stirner that only human beings create moral values. He still held firm to the idea that justice is immanent in the world and innate in human consciousness. We can therefore count on a sure guide and ultimate standard in our attempts to create a better world.

It is our social being which makes us capable of morality:

> Man is an integral part of collective existence and as such he is aware both of his own dignity and that of others. Thus he carries within himself the principles of a moral code that goes beyond the individual ... They constitute his essence and the essence of society itself.[63]

Like Kant, Proudhon based his case for intrinsic goodness in the world and man on *a priori* intuition: 'There are things that I judge good and praiseworthy *a priori*, even though I do not yet have a clear idea of them.'[64] The propositions that the universe is founded on the laws of justice and that justice is organized in accordance with the laws of the universe are therefore present 'in the human soul not only as ideas or concepts but as emotions or feelings'.[65] In addition, Proudhon believed intrinsic values are not means to an end, but ends in themselves.

Like Godwin, he argued that each individual is the judge of right and wrong and is 'empowered to act as an authority over himself and all others'. But while each person has a right to private judgement, there is only one single inherent good: Justice. Proudhon devotes long, rapturous passages to this capitalized principle; indeed, having boldly overthrown the Christian God, he reintroduces him in the different guise of Justice: 'Justice is the supreme God,' we are told, 'it is the living God'.[66]

This *idée princesse*, as Proudhon calls justice, is never clearly defined. It is often associated with equality, but would seem closer to respect. Proudhon tries to define it as: 'the respect, spontaneously felt and reciprocally guaranteed, of human dignity, in whatsoever person and in whatsoever circumstance it may be compromised, and to whatsoever risk its defence may expose us'.[67] Yet even his definition is not entirely clear. In practice, Proudhon would appear to mean that we should respect others as we would wish to be respected if we were in their place – a principle which is not very different from the Christian golden rule. In the social and economic field, it means that all men should receive according to their worth.

Justice for Proudhon further entails the duty to respect others simply as moral beings and to defend their dignity and freedom. It flows not from a spontaneous sense of benevolence but from a rational calculation of desert: altruism is 'an instinctive feeling, which it is useful and laudable to cultivate, but which, far from engendering respect and dignity, is strictly incompatible with them'.[68] But this position left Proudhon with a basic ethical problem.

On the one hand, it would seem that I am to be the sole judge of my actions and others should respect my right to choose and act as I see fit. On the other hand, others have a duty to ensure that I behave morally. Society has its 'own functions, foreign to our individuality, its ideas which it communicates to us, its judgements which resemble ours not at all, its will, in diametrical opposition to our instincts'.[69] It follows that there will be an inevitable conflict between our personal morality and the moral conventions of society. Proudhon fails to resolve this central ambivalence in his ethics. Sometimes he celebrates tolerance, yet he can also write: 'Conformity is just and deviance is reprehensible'.[70] This moral and cultural relativism leads him to defend practices like slavery in a society where it was generally accepted.

Proudhon's theoretical confusion comes to a head at the end of *Justice in the Revolution and the Church* where he introduces social pressure or public opinion as the means to bring about the triumph of virtue: 'society' should 'use the powerful stimuli of collective conscience to develop the moral sense of all its members'. He tries to mitigate its disrespectful tendency by arguing that unlike the decrees of God, rulers or scientists who impose pressure from without, social pressure can only operate if internalized in the individual like 'a sort of secret commandment from himself to himself'.[71] But this recourse has no logical connection with the rest of

Proudhon's theory. It is also false since all social pressure by its very nature must be disrespectful to the individual.

To make matters worse, in an unpublished *Treatise on Political Economy* (1849–55) Proudhon even contemplated a secret band of vigilantes to enforce public opinion. This puritanical elite would ensure that the individual conscience would be taught to identify with the social conscience for the sake of social survival. The vigilantes would be involved in the private execution of the wicked as well as punishing treason and adultery. Proudhon here reached his lowest ebb. In his published work on justice, he finally rejected vigilante justice but chiefly on practical rather than on moral grounds. It would simply be too difficult to find men pure enough to perform their task and their rule could easily degenerate into a reign of terror or pious moralizing. The result is that Proudhon never managed to resolve successfully in his ethics the tension between private judgement and public opinion and between moral autonomy and convention.

The outspoken attack on Church and State in *Justice in the Revolution and Church* led once again to its author's prosecution. Proudhon was sentenced to three years' imprisonment, but this time discretion was the better part of valour. He went into exile in Belgium where he remained until he was pardoned in an amnesty in 1860. He returned to France only two years later when the hostility of the local population obliged him to leave after he had written a critical article on nationalism.

Whilst living in Belgium, Proudhon wrote *War and Peace* which was to have such a profound influence on Tolstoy. The work bears witness to the paradoxical nature of Proudhon's mind. At first sight, he glorifies war to such an extent that he appears as an apologist for the right of force. This was partly due to his bellicose temperament which led him to celebrate struggle: 'To act is to fight', he declared.[72] But Proudhon also believed war was rooted in our being: 'War is divine, that is to say it is primordial, essential to life and to the production of men and society. It is deeply seated in human consciousness and its idea embraces all human relationships.'[73] War is nothing less than 'the basis of our history, our life and our whole being'; without it, mankind would be in a state of 'permanent siesta'.[74] Indeed, Proudhon goes so far as to represent war as a revelation of ideal justice since it is a great leveller and eliminates the weak. War will endure as long as humanity endures.

Sometimes Proudhon offers a psychological explanation of human conflict and suggests that 'our irascible appetite pushes us towards war'.[75] On other occasions, he gives an economic explanation and argues that its primary cause is poverty. But he also depicts war in logical terms as 'the abstract formulation of the dialectic'.[76] In the final analysis, Proudhon is no economic determinist like Marx for he argues that poverty is essentially a psychological fact and sees aggression as an innate part of unchanging human nature.

It does not follow however that we are forever condemned to a Hobbesian nightmare of the war of all against all. There comes a time in human development according to Proudhon when war can give way to peace. Again reason provides the key out of the impasse. In the course of history repressive institutions gradually perform the task of educating conscience and reason so that belligerent impulses can be transformed into creative ones. Proudhon felt that this stage had been reached in the middle of the nineteenth century and that no one could begin an aggressive war without being subject to 'foul suspicion'. But even this admission went against the grain: 'God forbid that I should preach the gentle virtues and joys of peace to my fellow man!', Proudhon exclaimed.[77] Like Milton's Satan, Proudhon seems to reserve his best rhetoric for war not peace.

In his final years, Proudhon was active as ever in his writing. Inspired by his friend Gustave Courbet, he wrote a work *On the Principle of Art* (1861) in which he saw its social task as 'to improve us, help us and save us'. He also developed a realist theory of art, calling on the artist to work from true observation. In a phrase which recalls Godwin's definition of truth and the original title of his novel *Caleb Williams*, Proudhon declares that not only must we begin by 'seeing things as they really are' but the task of the artist is to portray us 'as we really are'.[78] Ironically, this doctrine became the basis for the Soviet notion of socialist realism in art, while anarchism made a much stronger impact on avant-garde artists in the Dadaist and Surrealist movements of the early twentieth century.

Politics

Keen to clarify his ideas on social organization, Proudhon next wrote *The Federal Principle* (1863). He reiterates that 'the Government based on liberty is the government of each man by himself, that is *anarchy* or *self-government.*' This is to be achieved through the principles of federalism and decentralism. His treatment of federalism represents one of his most important contributions to anarchist theory, and has become particularly relevant today as empires break up and nations forge new alliances. In order to resist the tendency of power to accumulate more power, he proposed that society be broken up into a federation of autonomous regions. A contract between them in the form of an explicit agreement could then be discussed, adopted and amended at the contracting parties' will. Indeed, tracing the word to its Latin root, Proudhon calls federation a 'political contract'.[79]

The fundamental unit of society would remain the commune in which mutualist associations of property-owning and independent workers exchanged the products of their labour and organized their relationships through free contracts which are bilateral and based on equal exchange. Agricultural production would be based on the family, although Proudhon recognized the possibility of large industrial associations working as well as small ones.

Society however would still be arranged from the bottom up. The largest units within the federation would be assigned the fewest powers and the smallest ones the most. The higher levels would also be subordinated to the lower ones. Each unit of society would be sovereign and have the right to secede from the federation. Delegates would be sent to the federal assembly, while officers of the federal authority would be recallable and the authority itself would withdraw as soon as it had accomplished its specific task.

Proudhon argued that such a federal system is the very reverse of hierarchy or centralized administration and government. Nevertheless, it becomes clear that in order to resolve disputes, parties would have to submit to the authority of an independent arbiter. For the political contract to be binding, the citizen must abandon a degree of liberty in order to attain the special object for which the contract is made, namely to ensure that they keep to their contracts. While Proudhon denies that such an authority amounts to a government, and is merely the agent of the contracting parties, it is difficult to believe that it would not develop into one. Moreover, Proudhon drastically qualifies the right of secession from the federation by asserting that, in disputes over the interpretation and application of the terms of the federal contract, the majority has the right to compel minority compliance. Authority yet again raises its ugly head in his scheme and seriously infringes each member's autonomy. By arguing that authority and liberty presuppose each other, Proudhon crosses the boundary from anarchism to liberalism with its belief in a minimal State to ensure contracts are kept. The threat of sanctions by the federal authority would also probably undermine the self-assured ties of obligation between citizens.

As Proudhon grew older, he showed signs of an increasing conservatism, especially regarding property and government. He still wanted to see a just distribution of property in which the worker received the value of his labour. In a work on the *Theory of Property* written between 1863 and 1864, he clarified his earlier position by saying that he was not against the private ownership of wealth itself, but only against the sum of abuses which might spring from it.[80] He now identified property with the family, the most sacred of institutions, and with it defended the right of inheritance. He even preferred private property in its absolute and inalienable sense rather than as 'possession' since he considered it the only power that could act as a counterweight to the State. After waging war against the abuses of property for most of his life, Proudhon concluded that it had qualities inherent in its nature of the greatest value. Above all, it was 'liberal, federalist, decentralizing, republican, egalitarian, progressive, just'.[81] In the supreme irony of his complex life, the man who had once boldly declared that 'Property is Theft' came to see private property as the greatest bastion against State tyranny.

Proudhon also had second thoughts about authority and government. He had long considered them incompatible with man's dignity and freedom. In 1853, he reiterated his political faith of 1840: '*I am an anarchist*, declaring by this word the negation – or better – the insufficiency, of the principle of authority'.[82] But ten years later he began to talk about the 'government' of anarchy rather than the 'union of order and anarchy' as the highest form of society:

> I have already mentioned ANARCHY, or the government of each man by himself – or as the English say, *self-government* – as being one example of the liberal regime. Since the expression 'anarchical government' is a contradiction in terms, the system itself seems to be impossible and the idea absurd. However, it is only language that needs to be criticized.[83]

There was not merely a linguistic question at stake but also a conceptual one. Proudhon now maintained that far from being incompatible with authority, liberty 'assumes an Authority that bargains with it, restrains it, tolerates it'.[84] It follows that in any society, even the most liberal, a place is reserved for authority. Since the two contrary principles of authority and liberty which underlie all forms of organized society cannot be resolved or eliminated, the problem is to find a compromise between the two. The new formula was '*the balancing of authority by liberty*, and vice and versa' – no longer the destruction of the former in order to realize the latter.[85]

In fact, Proudhon in the end accepts the need for some form of minimal government. Central government in his federal and mutualist society is not merely a neutral arbiter and enforcer but an initiator. While leaving the execution of policies to the local authorities, he insists that 'In a free society the role of the State or Government is essentially one of legislating, initiating, creating, inaugurating and setting up'. Far from withering away, the functions of the State 'as prime mover and overall director never come to an end'.[86]

Yet although Proudhon now accepted the need for government and authority in a transitional period in his published work, he still looked forward in private to a time when centralized political authority would disappear, to be replaced by federal institutions and a pattern of life based on the commune. When individual and collective interests become identical and all constraint disappears, we will eventually reach 'a state of total liberty or anarchy' in which 'Society's laws will operate by themselves through universal spontaneity, and they will not have to be ordered or controlled.'[87]

Proudhon saw in the principle of federalism a way of overcoming national boundaries and hoped Europe would eventually become a confederation of federations. But his own nationalism became increasingly narrow and xenophobic. He liked to claim that his patriotism was not exclusive: he would never put devotion to his country before the rights of man. If he had to choose, he would be prepared to sacrifice his country to justice. Nevertheless, he argued that a federal republic should always give its citizens preference over foreigners in all transactions.

Proudhon moreover began to express an almost Messianic belief in the destiny of his own country, systematically opposing anything that was hostile or foreign to the 'sacred land of Gaul'. He wanted to see France return to its 'original nature', liberated once and for all from foreign beliefs and alien institutions: 'Our race for too long has been subject to the influence of Greeks, Romans, Barbarians, Jews and Englishmen.'[88] For Proudhon, France became the ultimate expression of the Revolutionary Idea and he judged foreign affairs chiefly from the perspective of its interests.

As a result, he opposed nationalist movements in Poland and Hungary. In his *Federation and Unity in Italy* (1862), he was also critical of the attempt by the 'Jacobin Mazzini' to create a centralized nation since he feared that a strongly united Italy would threaten France's role as a major Catholic power. It further led him to defend Napoleon's support of the Pope against Garibaldi and the King of Sardinia. It is easy to see why French nationalist writers earlier this century should turn to Proudhon for inspiration.

These views were not a temporary aberration on Proudhon's part. There were aspects of his thought which were reactionary from the beginning. This is most evident in his doctrine of equality.

Proudhon's definition of justice was so closely linked with the principle of equality that in his vocabulary they almost seem interchangeable terms. He insisted that equality is a law of nature: men are born equal and society itself is moving towards an equality of talents and knowledge. Existing inequalities are therefore simply the result of social custom and education. He believed that hierarchy is one of the most powerful instruments of oppression and he resumed Rousseau's battle against deference being made towards those who had wealth, power and prestige. Hierarchy not only results in exploitation, but deference engenders 'special perquisites, privileges, exemptions, favours, exceptions, all the violations of justice'.[89] It followed for Proudhon that equality is a necessary condition for liberty.

Proudhon believed that the 1789 Revolution had declared the principles of Equality and Liberty in the political arena; in the middle of the following century, the time had come to extend it to the economic sphere. His strong adherence to the principle of equality made him base his scheme of mutualism on the equivalent exchange of equal goods and services on commutative, not distributive, justice. Indeed, he opposed the socialist principle espoused by Louis Blanc and Etienne Cabet of distributive justice according to need since it preserves a degree of inequality.

But for all these noble sentiments, there was from the beginning a glaring hole in Proudhon's doctrine of equality. Like the lawyers of the French Revolution with their rights, Proudhon only applied it to European males. As might be guessed from his attitude to his wife, Proudhon considered women innately inferior to men in both intelligence and virtue. Few men have been so categorical in their male supremacy: 'The complete being ... is the male. The female is a diminutive of man.'[90] He went on to declare that woman is a mean term between man and the rest of the animal realm. He idealized man as the maker, woman as the user; where the former has a thinking mind, the later only has a feeling heart. Proudhon even calculated woman's total inferiority to man as a ratio of 27:8.

Woman's proper place is therefore in the home and her proper role is as an instrument of reproduction. She has no right to contraception; 'reliance must be exclusively on *abstinence*' within marriage in the matter of population control.[91] Marriage itself should be undissolvable: it is a union of male 'power' and female 'grace' with man remaining superior in 'labour, knowledge and rights'.[92] While recognizing that authority is born with the family, and the family is the embryo of the State, Proudhon is adamant about the need to preserve the 'natural' institution of patriarchy within the family. Authority in his scheme of things is to be banished from all parts of society except the home where man is to remain the undisputed master and his wife his submissive handmaiden. Proudhon even wrote just before he died a third of a work called *Pornocracy, or Women of Modern Times* (1875) in which he cruelly attacked the Saint-Simonian feminists who demanded intellectual and sexual freedom. To his eternal shame, the so-called father of anarchism sided with the most crude reactionaries by counting himself proudly amongst those men who think 'a woman knows enough if she knows enough to mend our shirts and cook us a steak'.[93]

It comes as no surprise to learn that Proudhon thought that women simply do not count in public life: 'society does no injustice to woman by refusing her equality before the law. It treats her according to her aptitudes and privileges. Woman really has no place in the world of politics and economics.' If she were to be on an equal footing with man in public life, it would mean 'the death of love and the ruin of the human race'.[94]

Proudhon was no less prejudiced and dogmatic when it came to race. For all his eloquent celebration of male equality, he maintained that there are 'badly born and bastard races' whose inferiority will be underlined by any attempt to educate them. In the forward march of progress they will be wiped out: in capital letters Proudhon declares that the 'law of revolution' is 'L'EGALITE OU LA MORT!'[95] He was profoundly anti-Semitic and wanted all Jews except those married to Frenchwomen to be expelled from France: 'The Jew is the enemy of the human race. This race must be sent back to Asia, or exterminated.'[96]

He further anticipated the German Nazis in his stress on the link between blood and soil. He insists that *'Land belongs to the race of people born on it*, since no other is able to develop it according to its needs. The Caucasian has never been able to take root in Egypt.' As to the mixing of the races, while it can give vigour to the native race, 'blood can be mixed but that it does not become *fused*. One of the two races always ends by reverting to type and absorbing the other.'[97] In his position on race and women nothing so clearly revealed Proudhon's roots in the puritanical, narrow-minded, and reactionary peasants of Franche-Comté.

The conservative tendency in his thinking which is so transparent in his views on women and race came to the fore in his old age in other fields. He replaced the bold Hegelian dialectic of his youth, for instance, and came closer to the liberal John Stuart Mill by arguing that opposites should not realize a higher synthesis or fusion but rather an equilibrium. It is from this perspective that he came to recommended property as a counterweight the power of the State, and wanted authority to balance liberty.

His growing caution is also apparent in his view of progress. In his *Economic Contradictions*, he had written that humanity in its development obeys an 'inflexible necessity'.[98] In a work on the *Philosophy of Progress* (1853), he continued to define progress as 'an affirmation of universal movement' and claimed that what had dominated his studies and constituted his originality as a thinker was that 'in all things and everywhere, I proclaim *Progress*, and that no less resolutely, in all things and everywhere, I denounce the *Absolute*'. By the time he came to write *Justice in the Revolution and Church* (1858), however, he stressed that 'We are not moving toward an ideal perfection or final state'. Moreover since humanity like the creation is ceaselessly changing and developing 'the ideal of Justice and beauty we must attain is changing all the time.'[99]

Despite his declining health and growing conservatism, Proudhon still took a strong interest in the emancipation of the working class. In the presidential elections of 1863, he urged abstention or the 'silent vote' against those who argued that it was necessary to gain political power through the ballot box. Impressed by the 'Manifesto of the Sixty' issued by a working class committee in support of their candidate Henri Tolain in a by-election in Paris in 1864, he recognized in an open letter the sharpening class conflict which was dividing 'society in two classes, one of employed workers, the other of property-owners, capitalists, entrepreneurs'.[100] Just before he died, he was working on a book entitled *On the Political Capacity of the Working Classes* (1865) in which he singled out the proletariat as the torch-bearers of revolution and recommended a new tactics for them to achieve freedom and justice.

Proudhon had never been an able tactician and had adopted widely differing strategies throughout his life. At first he had relied on Godwin's method of rational education: 'Stimulate, warn, inform, instruct but do not inculcate.'[101] He had no time for the alternatives put forward by his socialist contemporaries. Workers' control of industry, he argued, would only reduce enterprise and productivity while a progressive income tax would legitimize privilege rather than bring about equality. At the outbreak of the 1848 Revolution in France, he further condemned the proposals of Louis Blanc since his welfare State would need dictatorial authority and his plan to nationalize industry would only change the managers and stockholders. As for Auguste Blanqui's revolutionary dictatorship, it was nothing but a glorification of force: 'It is the theory of all governments turned against the governing classes; the problem of tyrannical majorities resolved in favour of the workers, as it is today in favour of the bourgeoisie.'[102]

After his disastrous experience of the 'parliamentary Sinai', Proudhon turned to economic remedies in an attempt to bring about a mutualist society. But even if his People's Bank had succeeded it would only have checked the power of the big bourgeoisie and primarily benefited the commercial middle class. Despairing at the course of events, Proudhon even considered, after his brief and ignominious flirtation with Napoleon III, a scheme for the 'dictatorship of the people of Paris'.[103] He quickly realized however that it would be both disrespectful and impotent, and he retreated into gradualism. Emphasizing moral renovation before political economy, it was now a question of '*attente révolutionnaire*'.

In his last work *On the Political Capacity of the Working Classes* (1865), Proudhon suddenly offered a new and incisive strategy. He had come to see social change primarily in terms of a class struggle. As the commercial middle class was being smothered, there was a growing polarization between the big bourgeoisie and proletariat. It was the proletariat who were in the ascendancy, growing in political capacity and class consciousness. The revolutionary task had thus fallen to them to rally under their leadership the peasants and the rump of the middle class.

Combined with this Marxian analysis was a renewed stress on the education of the working class. Proudhon had always celebrated work as one of the greatest human activities and looked forward to a time when 'Labour would become divine, it would become the religion.'[104] He hated the division of labour under the factory system, which required overspecialization, and reduced workers to mere instruments. He therefore wanted a young worker to be apprenticed to many trades. He also recommended the simultaneous education of mind and body, combining the study of arts and sciences with work in fields and factories. In this way, he hoped to form the all-round worker.

Proudhon continued to criticize both the political left and right. He maintained that the *laissez-faire* of the free-market economists is as oppressive as government since it assured 'the victory of the strong over the weak, of those who own property over those who own nothing'.[105] At the same time, he returned to the attack against 'State socialism', especially Louis Blanc's communist version. With prophetic clarity, Proudhon at the end of his life observed that

> the doctrinaire, authoritarian, dictatorial, governmental, communist system is based on the principle that the individual is essentially subordinate to the collective; that from it alone he has his right and life; that the citizen belongs to the State like a child to the family; that he is in its power and possession, *in manu*, and that he owes it submission and obedience in all things.[106]

As for the dictatorship of the proletariat advocated by Marx, Proudhon argued prophetically that it would ensure universal servitude, all-encompassing centralization, the systematic destruction of individual thought, an inquisitorial police, with 'universal suffrage organized to serve a perpetual sanction to this anonymous tyranny'.[107] In place of *laissez-faire* capitalism and State socialism, Proudhon finally proposed once again his system of mutualism as the only way to create a free society: 'In this system the labourer is no longer a serf of the State, swamped by the ocean of the community. He is a free man, truly his own master, who acts on his own initiative and is personally responsible.'[108]

When it came to practical tactics, Proudhon rejected the remedy of the trade unions and the parliamentary road to power. In their place, he recommended the tactic of complete withdrawal from organized politics in order to convert the whole of France to mutualism and federalism: 'Since the old world rejects us' the way forward is to 'separate ourselves from it radically'.[109] He was confident that the most important factor in popular movements is their spontaneity and that a revolution could spontaneously transform the whole of society.

Proudhon died in 1865. He had lived long enough to learn that many in the French working class were taking his advice and that the First International had been established largely by his followers. The crowning irony of his life was that the man who felt excommunicated from his contemporaries was accompanied to his grave in the cemetery in Passy by a crowd of several thousand mourners. Proudhonians went on to form the largest group in the Commune of Paris six years later. Proudhon's reputation became so high that one communard simply carried around an uncut copy of *On the Political Capacity of the Working Classes* to demonstrate the strength of his revolutionary commitment.

Proudhon was undoubtedly one of the most paradoxical and inconsistent social thinkers of the nineteenth century. His combative view of human nature is undoubtedly one-sided and his version of history highly speculative. He presents man as a self-governing individual and recognizes the 'collective force' of social groups, but fails to arrange these insights into a coherent whole. He sees man torn by destructive passions and yet capable of rational control. He does not properly define the relationship between the egoistic and benevolent impulses. Above all, as Marx pointed out, he fails to see that human nature is not an unchanging essence but a product of history which changes in the course of development.

In his ethics, Proudhon does not properly define the meaning of justice. While his concept of respect involves a duty to forbear as well as to intervene in the affairs of others, he fails to delineate the boundaries between personal autonomy and social intervention. Again, he does satisfactorily solve the dilemma between the individual conscience and the moral conventions of society. Autonomy requires that we should follow our own consciences, not what society prescribes, yet Proudhon is ready to utilize social pressure to make the individual conform to the norms of society.

His ethical intuitions by their very nature cannot be affirmed or denied, and as such are beyond discussion. He offers no evidence to prove that the laws of justice are either inherent in nature or in humanity. His claims for social science are also untestable, and he makes the classic error of making moral judgements about so-called 'facts'.

In his economics, Proudhon presents bargaining as the primary pattern of social relations. After rejecting the State and any form of central planning he looks to the market to achieve equivalent exchange. His mutualist society would be made up of rational individuals who calculate their own interests, yet this would seem to overlook the 'collective force' of social groups and organizations. It is a weakness shared by all forms of market socialism. Aware of the corrosive nature of such bargaining, Proudhon does not extend it to the patriarchal family where love replaces calculation and respect enjoins 'complete sacrifice of the person'.[109] It is a clear sign of the weakness of his position that he feels compelled to fall back on the family in order to compensate public self-interest with private altruism. Ironically, the family provides the moral foundation for his contractual scheme; without it there would be no moral sense.

In his mutualist society, Proudhon looks to contracts to replace laws and government. But his version of contracts as mutually acceptable agreements imposes no obligation on the contracting parties except that which flows from their personal promises. Given his pugnacious view of human nature, it is difficult to see why they should not degenerate into endless wrangles or dictated settlements. Even if, as he suggests, the contracts are made public, formal and explicit, and public opinion reinforces the purely moral obligation of promises, there is no final certainty that people will keep their agreements. His resort to a federal authority to solve disputes, and his call for an express oath of fidelity to the rules of contracting show that he was aware of the difficulty, but their introduction would doubtless lead to the reconstitution of the State.

Since Proudhon believes that human beings are naturally aggressive, selfish, and domineering, it would seem inevitable that they would grasp for power in a society without government. Proudhon tries to mitigate the danger by equalizing the power of organizations and by encouraging their diversity: 'the greatest independence of individuals and groups' must go with 'the greatest variety of combinations'.[110] But the principle of social diversity is not fully developed. Again, although Proudhon adopts a version of commutative justice as a rule for all bargains to bring about equality, under his mutualist scheme hard workers would receive more and a new labour hierarchy would bound to re-emerge in the long run. As Kropotkin later pointed out, the criterion of need is more just than productivity as a principle of distribution.

But if Proudhon remains theoretically confused, he at least draws attention to the central problems of government and property which oppress humanity. For all his lamentable racism, chauvinism and patriotism, it is unreasonable to see him as forerunner of fascism; if anything he was a liberal in proletarian clothing. He may have grown more conservative in his views of government and property as he grew older, and less certain about the course of progress, but bitter experience had taught him the difficulties of achieving his ideals. His recognition of the political capacity of the working class was a considerable improvement on his earlier tactical positions.

Despite the authoritarian dimension to his work, freedom was Proudhon's ultimate goal and the key to his thought. For him, freedom denotes complete liberation from every possible hindrance: the free man is 'liberated from all restraint, internal and external'. Freedom in this absolute sense not only rejects all social pressure, public opinion, and physical force from outside, but also the voice of conscience or the drive of passion from within. It allows the individual to think and act as he pleases, to become completely autonomous. It recognizes 'no law, no motive, no principle, no cause, no limit, no end, except itself'.[111] It is not surprising that any attempt to realize such boundless freedom would encounter overwhelming obstacles. But even if it is an impossible goal, Proudhon's flawed attempt to achieve it makes him one of the greatest of all libertarians. It is not without good reason that Bakunin recognized him as the father of the historic anarchist movement.

18

Michael Bakunin

The Fanatic of Freedom

BAKUNIN IS A PARADOXICAL THINKER, overwhelmed by the contradictory nature of the world around him. His life too was full of contradictions. He was a 'scientific' anarchist, who adopted Marx's economic materialism and Feuerbach's atheism only to attack the rule of science and to celebrate the wisdom of the instincts. He looked to reason as the key to human progress and yet developed a cult of spontaneity and glorified the will. He had a desire to dominate as well as to liberate and recognized that 'the urge to destroy is also a creative urge'. He called for absolute liberty, attacking all forms of institutionalized authority and hierarchy only to create his own secret vanguard societies and to call for an 'invisible' dictatorship.

Not surprisingly, Bakunin in his own lifetime inspired great controversy, and it continues until this day. On the one hand, he has been called one of 'the completest embodiments in history of the spirit of liberty'.[1] On the other, he has been described as 'the intellectual apologist for despotism', guilty of 'rigid authoritarianism'.[2] Camus maintained that he 'wanted total freedom; but he hoped to realize it through total destruction'.[3] It is usual to present him as a man 'with an impetuous and impassioned urge for action', or as an example of anarchist 'fervour in action'.[4] Yet it has also been argued that he was primarily an abstract thinker who elaborated a philosophy of action.[5] Far from being the intellectual flyweight dismissed by Marx as a 'man devoid of all theoretical knowledge', he increasingly appears to be a profound and original thinker.[6]

What is indisputable is that Bakunin had great charisma and personal magnetism. Richard Wagner wrote: 'With Bakunin everything was colossal, and of a primitive negative power ... From every word he uttered one could feel the depth of his innermost convictions ... I saw that this all destroyer was the love-worthiest, tender-hearted man one could possibly imagine'.[7] His magnanimity and enthusiasm coupled with his passionate denunciation of privilege and injustice made him extremely attractive to anti-authoritarians. In the inevitable comparisons with Marx, he appears the more generous and spontaneous. But his character remains as enigmatic as his theory is ambivalent. He attacked authority and called for absolute freedom, but admired those who were born to command with iron wills. He rejected arbitrary violence, but celebrated the 'poetry of destruction' and felt unable to condemn terrorists. He had a strong moral sense and yet doted on fanatics who believed that the revolution sanctifies all.

The contradictory nature of his life and thought has been put down to his 'innate urge to dominate' alongside a desire to rebel.[8] Others have hinted more darkly that Bakunin's eccentricity tottered on the verge of madness, that he was a 'little cracked' and showed 'hints of derangement'.[9]

It has even been argued that his violence and authoritarianism were rooted in Oedipal and narcissistic disorders and that his concern with freedom was born of 'weakness, fear and flight'.[10] From this perspective, his most genuine voice is that of a frightened youth.

Certainly Bakunin was brought up in a very special situation, and his relationships with his parents and siblings played a major part in shaping his personality. But he also suffered from being a superfluous aristocrat and intellectual who had no positive role to play under the despotic rule of Nicholas II. Herzen correctly observed that Bakunin had within him 'the latent power of a colossal activity for which there was no demand'.[11] His early longing to feel part of the whole, fired by his passionate involvement with German idealism, also left an indelible mark which led him to seek salvation in the cataclysmic upheaval of revolution.

Despite recent interest in him as a case study of utopian or apocalyptic psychology, Bakunin made an outstanding contribution to anarchist thought and strategy. He undoubtedly broke new ground. His critique of science is profound and persuasive. He reveals eloquently the oppressive nature of modern States, the dangers of revolutionary government, and, by his own lamentable example, the moral confusion of using authoritarian means to achieve libertarian ends, of using secret societies and invisible dictators to bring about a free society. He developed anarchist economics in a collectivist direction. He widened Marx's class analysis by recognizing the revolutionary potential of the peasantry and the lumpenproletariat.

In his historic break with Marx and his followers in the First International Working Men's Association, he set the tone of the bitter subsequent disputes between Marxists and anarchists. By rejecting the political struggle and arguing that the emancipation of the workers must be achieved by the workers themselves, he paved the way for revolutionary syndicalism. In his own life, he turned anarchism into a theory of political action, and helped develop the anarchist movement, especially in France, French-speaking Switzerland and Belgium, Italy, Spain and Latin America. He has not only be called the 'Activist-Founder of World Anarchism' but hailed as the 'true father of modern anarchism'.[12] Indeed, he became the most influential thinker during the resurgence of anarchism in the sixties and seventies.[13]

It is extremely difficult to assess Bakunin as a thinker. He was more of a popularizer than a systematic or consistent thinker. He was the first to admit that: 'I am not a scholar or a philosopher, not even a professional writer. I have not done much writing in my life and have never written except, so to speak, in self-defence, and only when a passionate conviction forced me to overcome my instinctive dislike for any public exhibition of myself.'[14] His writings were nearly always part of his activity as a revolutionary and as a result he left a confused account of his views written for different audiences. As in his life, there is a bewildering rush in his writing; just as he is beginning to develop an argument well, he drops it to pick up another. He not only appeals to abstract concepts like justice and freedom without properly defining them, but he often relies on clichés: the bourgeoisie are inevitably 'corrupt', the State always means 'domination', and freedom must be 'absolute'. His mental universe is Manichean, with binary opposites of good and evil, life and science, State and society, bourgeoisie and workers.

He wrote when he could during a lifetime of hectic travelling and agitation, but when begun his works sprawled in all directions. He rarely managed to finish a complete manuscript, and of his main works only *Statisn and Anarchy* was published in his lifetime and *God and the State* soon after his death. The bulk of his writings therefore remain unedited drafts. As a result, he often repeats himself and appears inconsistent and contradictory. He talks for instance of the need for the 'total abolition of politics' and yet argues that the International Working Men's Association offers the 'true politics of the workers'.[15] He uses the term 'anarchy' both in its negative and popular sense of violent chaos as well as to describe a free society without the State.[16] This can partly be explained by the inadequacy of existing political language for someone trying to go beyond the traditional categories of political thought, but it also resulted from a failure to correct his drafts or order his thoughts. Yet for all the fragmentation, repetition, and contradiction, there emerges a recognizable leitmotif.

Bakunin was born on 30 May 1814 in the province of Tver, north-west of Moscow. He was the son of a retired diplomat, a member of a long-established Russian family of the nobility who had become landed gentry. His mother, née Muraviev, came from a family ennobled by Catherine the Great. He was the third of ten children, but the eldest son, with two elder and two younger sisters, followed by five brothers. He therefore by sex and age enjoyed a dominant position in the family, and by tradition would have inherited the family's property. This did not prevent him from doting on his sisters with whom he shared his most intimate feelings and ambitions. He later became extremely jealous of their suitors.

His father had liberal sympathies, while one of his cousins on his mother's side had been involved in the Decembrist uprising in 1825 against Tsar Nicholas I by a group of aristocrats and poets under the influence of Western ideas. Bakunin was eleven at the time and like Herzen and Turgenev belonged to the unfortunate generation which reached adulthood under the despotism of Nicholas I.

Bakunin grew up in a fine eighteenth-century house on a hill above a broad and slow river. He spent a comfortable childhood playing with his sisters on the family estate which had five hundred serfs. Nettlau suggested that Bakunin's family circle was the most ideal group to which he ever belonged, the 'model for all his organizations and his conception of a free and happy life for humanity in general'.[17] In fact, it would appear far from ideal. His father was forty when he married his young mother and she always sided with the old man. Bakunin in later years attributed 'his passion for destruction to the influence of his mother, whose despotic character inspired him with an insensate hatred of every restriction on liberty'.[18]

He certainly seems to have been a timid, gentle and withdrawn boy, although it goes too far to assert that his mature anarchism reflected an 'elemental, permanent dread of society' and that he created secret organizations in order to submerge and lose himself in them.[19] Although he later married, he allowed the children to be fathered by a close friend. His intimate relationship with his sisters, especially Tatiana, may also have accounted for his sexual impotence owing to an incest taboo. Certainly his later fantasies of fire and blood would appear to offer an outlet for his sexual frustration, or at least a partial sublimation of his repressed libido. His apocalyptical visions undoubtedly fulfilled some profound psychological need.

Bakunin received a good education from private tutors, but when he reached fifteen, it was decided to send him to the Artillery School in St Petersburg. Here he experienced the pleasures of high society, and had his first love affair, although it seems to have been largely Platonic. In contrast to his 'pure and virginal' aspirations, he hated the 'dark, filthy and vile' side of barrack life.[20] He graduated and was gazetted as an ensign early in 1833, being posted to an artillery brigade in Poland.

The sensitive and thoughtful young aristocrat quickly found garrison life boring and empty. Everything in him demanded activity and movement, but as he wrote to his parents 'my strong spiritual urges, in their vain fight against the cold and insuperable obstacles of the physical world, sometimes reduce me to exhaustion, induce a state of melancholy . . .'[21] Taking his future into his own hands, Bakunin resigned from the army and decided to go to Moscow in 1836 to teach and to study philosophy.

He did much more of the latter. He found in German Idealism a meaning and purpose lacking in the lifeless chaos of the world around him. The new philosophy, he wrote to a friend is 'like a Holy Annunciation, promises a better, a fuller, more harmonious life'.[22] In August 1836, he wrote enthusiastically to his sisters that, strengthened by their love, he had overcome his fear of the external world: 'My inner life is strong because it is not founded on vulgar expectation or on worldly hopes of outward good fortune; no, it is founded on the eternal purpose of man and his divine nature. Nor is my inner life afraid, for it is contained in your life, and our love is eternal as our purpose.' While he recommends the 'religion of divine reason and divine love' to be the basis of their life, he had already decided to devote his life to expanding the freedom of all beings:

> Everything that lives, that exists, that grows, that is simply on the earth, should be free, and should attain self-consciousness, raising itself up to the divine centre which inspires all that exists. Absolute freedom and absolute love – that is our aim; the freeing of humanity and the whole world – that is our purpose.[23]

Whilst in Moscow, Bakunin came under the spell of Fichte, who believed that freedom is the highest expression of the moral law and saw the unlimited Ego as striving towards consciousness of its own freedom. He translated in 1836 Fichte's *Lectures on the Vocation of the Scholar*, his first publication. He was also intoxicated by Hegel who argued that the real is the rational and presented history as the unfolding and realization of Spirit in a dialectical reconciliation of opposites. He translated in 1838 Hegel's *Gymnasial Lectures* with an introduction: this was the first of Hegel's works to appear in Russian. Overwhelmed by their visions of wholeness, Bakunin began to swing from self-assertion and self-surrender: 'One must live and breathe only for the Absolute, through the Absolute . . .', he wrote to his sister Varvara.[24]

Like many of his generation, it was natural for Bakunin to search for enlightenment in Europe. After five years in Moscow, he decided in 1840 to go to Berlin to study Hegelianism at first hand. He made friends there with the radical poet Georg Herwegh and the publicist Arnold Ruge. Young intellectuals like Feuerbach, Bauer and Stirner were also involved in developing a left-wing critique of Hegel, rejecting his idealism and religion in favour of materialism and atheism. Bakunin was particularly impressed by Feuerbach's anthropological naturalism, and adopted his materialist and progressive view of history in which the human species gradually grows in consciousness and freedom. For many years thereafter, he apparently planned to write a book on Feuerbach, whom he called the 'disciple and demolisher of Hegel'.[25] The Left-Hegelians also found the existing State a principle which had to be negated in order to realize the higher synthesis of a free society. Bakunin, like Marx, was deeply influenced, and a reading of *Politics for the Use of the People* (1837) by the French religious socialist Lamennais further directed his energies towards the improvement of the human condition.

But it was not all study in Berlin. Bakunin moved in Russian *émigré* circles, and met Turgenev who later modelled the hero of his novel *Rudin* (1856) on the young Bakunin; and Belinsky, who believed in universal revolution and saw the young Bakunin as a bizarre mixture of comic poseur and vampire.

Bakunin also began to formulate his own ideas. In 1842, he went to Dresden in Saxony and published in April in Arnold Ruge's *Deutsche Jahrbücher* an article on 'The Reaction in Germany'. It advocated the negation of the abstract dialectic and rejected any reconciliation between opposing forces. It also called for revolutionary practice, ending with the famous lines:

> Let us therefore trust the eternal Spirit which destroys and annihilates only because it is the unfathomable and eternal source of all life. The passion for destruction is a creative passion, too![26]

The article launched Bakunin on his revolutionary career. From now on he began to preach revolution to the people rather than universal love to his sisters. He experienced the period of 1841–2 as a watershed in his life: 'I finally rejected transcendental knowledge', he later wrote, 'and threw myself headlong into life.'[27] He saw it as marking an irreversible transition from abstract theory to practice: 'To know truth', he wrote to his family at the time, 'is not only to think but to live; and life is more than a process of thought: life is a miraculous realization of thought.'[28]

Bakunin in fact did not abandon philosophy for mere action, but rather began to develop a new philosophy of action. And far from recovering from the disease of German metaphysics, he retained much of its influence, particularly its dialectical movement and search for wholeness. The longing to become one with the Absolute was transformed into a desire to merge with the people. His yearning to be a complete human being and save himself now combined with a drive to help others. At the end of 1842, he characteristically had a discussion with Ruge about 'how we must liberate ourselves and begin a new life, in order to liberate others and pour new life into them'.[29] The need for movement and excitement was the same, only the object changed. As he wrote later in his *Confessions*:

There was always a basic defect in my nature: a love for the fantastic, for unusual, unheard-of adventures, for undertakings that open up a boundless horizon and whose end no one can foresee. I would feel suffocated and nauseated in ordinary peaceful surroundings . . . my need for movement and activity remained unsatisfied. This need, subsequently, combined with democratic exaltation, was almost my only motive force.[30]

Bakunin left Saxony in 1843 and went to Zürich in Switzerland, where he met and was deeply impressed by Wilhelm Weitling. A self-educated German communist, Weitling preached a form of primitive Christianity which predicted the coming of the Kingdom of God on earth. He had written in 1838 the first communist programme for a secret German organization called the 'League of the Just'. Bakunin wrote to Ruge about his 'really remarkable book' *Guarantees of Harmony and Freedom*, quoting the passage: 'The perfect society has no government, but only an administration, no laws but only obligations, no punishments, but means of correction.'[31] Coupled with a reading of the 'immortal Rousseau', Weitling helped Bakunin stride towards anarchism.

In an unfinished article on *Communism*, written in 1843, Bakunin was already laying the foundations of his future political philosophy with its faith in the people: 'Communism derives not from theory, but from practical instinct, from popular instinct, and the latter is never mistaken.' By the people, he understood 'the majority, the broadest masses, of the poor and oppressed'.[32] But he was not entirely under Weitling's sway for he criticized his ideal society as 'not a free society, a really live union of free people, but a herd of animals, intolerably coerced and united by force, following only material ends utterly ignorant of the spiritual side of life'.[33]

The relation between the ardent aristocrat and tailor was cut short when Weitling was imprisoned. Hearing of their connection, the Tsarist government called Bakunin back to Russia. He refused to comply, and after a short stay in Brussels, made his way to Paris early in 1844.

It proved a crucial period in his development. He met Proudhon, still basking in the notoriety of *What is Property?* (1840) and putting the finishing touches to his *Economic Contradictions, or Philosophy of Poverty* (1844). He exclaimed to an Italian friend while reading Proudhon: 'This is the right thing!'[34] They engaged in passionate discussions, talking all night about Hegel's dialectic. Bakunin was impressed by his critique of government and property, and Proudhon no doubt also stressed the authoritarian dangers of communism and the need for anarchy. But it was Proudhon's celebration of freedom which most fired Bakunin's overheated imagination. By May 1845, Bakunin was writing home: 'My . . . unconditional faith in the proud greatness of man, in his holy purpose, in freedom as the sole source and sole aim of his life, has remained unshaken, has not only not diminished but grown, strengthened . . .'[35]

An equally important meeting for the subsequent history of socialism was with Marx in March 1844. Although Marx was four years younger, Bakunin was impressed by his intellect, his grasp of political economy and his revolutionary energy. By comparison, he admitted his own socialism was 'purely instinctive'. But he also recognized that from the beginning they were temperamentally incompatible: Marx accused him of being a 'sentimental idealist', while Bakunin found him vain, morose, and devious.[36]

Between Proudhon and Marx, it was the libertarian Frenchman that Bakunin preferred. He thought that Proudhon had understood and felt freedom much better than Marx: 'It is possible that Marx can rise theoretically to a system of liberty more rational than Proudhon, but he lacks Proudhon's instinct. As a German and as a Jew, he is from head to foot an authoritarian.'[37] Bakunin's enduring anti-Semitism and his anti-German feeling were among his most repellent characteristics for he wrongly believed that Jews and Germans were both by nature opposed to freedom. In the last years of his life, Bakunin described his own thought to his Spanish followers as a development of Proudhon's anarchism, but without his idealism, for which he had substituted a materialist view of history and economic processes.[38] Indeed, Bakunin's philosophy consists largely of Proudhonian politics and Marxian economics.

The cause which first appealed to Bakunin's burning desire to serve the people was the liberation of the Slavs. Hegel believed that each people had a historic mission; Bakunin now thought it was time for the Slavs to destroy the old world. Moreover with all their freshness and spontaneity, the Slavs appeared to Bakunin the very opposite of German pedantry and coldness. He anticipated a grand cataclysm in Europe. In September 1847, he wrote to the poet Georg Herwegh and his wife in mystical and sexual terms: 'I await my . . . fiancée, revolution. We will be really happy – that is, we will become ourselves, only when the whole world is engulfed in fire.'[39] Bakunin's visions of an apocalyptic holocaust is the underside of his eloquent and familiar defence of freedom, harmony, peace and brotherhood. After delivering a speech towards the end of 1847 which called for the independence of Poland from Russia, he was expelled from Paris as a result of Russian diplomatic pressure on the French government. But it did not cool his enthusiasm : the Slavo-Polish cause remained a ruling passion for many years.

Bakunin at first went to Brussels, but when the Revolution broke out in France several months later in February 1848, he returned immediately to Paris. He saw it as an opportunity to create at last a new society, and hoped that the revolution would end only when Europe, together with Russia, formed a federated democratic republic. It was his first real contact with the working class, and he was ecstatic about their innate nobility. On the barricades he preached communism, permanent revolution and war until the defeat of the last enemy. Bakunin was in his element – his dream of revolution was being realized, and he was able to divert his colossal energy into the orchestration of the downfall of the bourgeois State. At last, it was no longer a case of drawing-room chatter, but bloody action on the streets. Serving in the barracks with the Workers' National Guard, his inspiring example drew from the Prefect of Police the famous verdict: 'What a man! The first day of the revolution he is a perfect treasure; but on the next day he ought to be shot.'[40] The Prefect was no doubt aware that his own position would eventually be in jeopardy if the social revolution à la Bakunin triumphed!

The revolution spread to Germany in a few weeks, but Bakunin looked towards central Europe, hoping to start a Russian Revolution in Poland. He was intoxicated by the revolutionary turmoil in Europe and exulted in the destruction of the old world it seemed to presage. He wrote to Herwegh: 'Evil passions will bring about a peasant war, and that delights me because I do not fear anarchy, but desire it with all my heart.'[41] At this stage, Bakunin was still not an anarchist, and used the term 'anarchy' in its negative sense of disorder and tumult; his urge to destroy was still stronger than his creative urge. The days of parliaments and constitutions were over, he wrote to Herwegh: 'We need something different: passion and life and a new world, lawless and thereby free.'[42]

Hoping to incite a Panslavic revolution, Bakunin attended the Slav Congress in Prague in June 1848. In his fiery *Appeal to the Slavs* written in the autumn, he not only celebrated the 'admirable instinct of the masses' but called for a federation of all Slav peoples headed by a council which would settle internal disputes and decide on foreign policy. Bakunin was still primarily interested in encouraging nationalist independence movements, but already he had espoused the cult of popular spontaneity. In addition, by calling for the first time for the destruction of the Austrian Empire his *Appeal to the Slavs* is a landmark in European history.

At the same time, he developed during the Prague Congress and during the following year a project for a revolutionary dictatorship based on a secret society. It was the first of several such organizations which Bakunin tried to establish, a move which sits ill with his publicly avowed libertarian beliefs and opposition to revolutionary government. The aim of the society was to direct the revolution, extend it to all Europe and Russia, and overthrow the Austrian Empire. As he wrote later in his *Confessions* to Nicholas I, it would consist of three separate groups for the youth, peasantry and townspeople entirely unknown to each other. These groups would be organized 'on strict hierarchical lines, and under absolute discipline', enforced by a central committee of three or four members who could draw on the support of a battalion of three to five hundred men.[43] The secret society as a whole would act on the masses as an 'invisible force', and if successful would set up a government after the revolution with unlimited powers to wipe out 'all clubs and journals, all manifestations of garrulous anarchy'. Bakunin intended to be its 'secret director' and if his plan had been carried out 'all the main threads of the movement would have been concentrated in my hands' and the projected revolution in Bohemia would not have strayed from the course he had laid down for it.[44]

It has been suggested that we should not take all this too literally.[45] But there can be few fantasies for exercising absolute dictatorial power as lamentable as this in the history of political thought. It would seem that Bakunin was almost schizoid, celebrating absolute freedom and condemning dictatorship in his public writings only to fantasize about an invisible dictatorship which he would lead in private. It reveals an unsavoury authoritarian streak to his personality, undermines his criticism of Marx, and shows a profound flaw in his tactics. Yet this undoubted lacuna does not change the validity of his public statements on freedom nor does it alter his importance in the history of anarchism. It merely shows his failure to achieve an adequate praxis.

Bakunin was unable to realize his secret society at this stage, but he manned the barricades again during the brief Prague rising in 1848. After its failure, he wandered around Germany only to take part in another insurrection in Dresden in May 1849. The workers, according to Engels, found Bakunin 'a capable and cool-headed leader', although he has been accused of causing many casualties by persuading them to rise against impossible odds.[46]

Bakunin had little interest in supporting the pro-constitutional forces who sought German unification against the King of Saxony, and he did not think the rebellion would succeed, but he could not stand idly by. In the streets of Dresden, he came across Richard Wagner, the conductor of the Dresden Opera, and they went together to the City Hall to see what was happening. The new Provisional Government had just been announced. Bakunin immediately advised the leaders to fortify the city against the approaching Prussian troops who arrived that night. Only one of the provisional triumvirate held firm, and Bakunin backed him to the hilt, doing the rounds on the barricades to keep morale up. The soldiers however fought their way through. Bakunin urged the rebels to blow themselves up in the City Hall but they fell back to Freiburg and then to Chemnitz instead. The exhausted revolutionaries were arrested in their beds.

Bakunin was so tired he made no attempt to escape – his energy had at last run out. This time he was sentenced to death. He was woken up one night and led out as if to be beheaded only to learn that his sentence had been commuted to life imprisonment. He was then handed over to the Austrians who again sentenced him to death for high treason but he was eventually deported to Russia. He spent the next eight years in solitary confinement in the notorious Peter-and-Paul and the Schlüsselburg fortresses. It not only ruined his health – he developed scurvy and his teeth fell out – but it produced his remarkable *Confessions*.

Addressed to Tsar Nicholas I, it contained a bizarre blend of political prophecy, self-accusation and dramatization, as well as genuine personal insight. He calls himself the 'repentant sinner' and declares: 'I am a great criminal and do not deserve forgiveness.' At the same time, he suggests that he suffered from the 'philosophical disease' of German metaphysics and that his follies sprang in large part from false concepts, 'but even more from a powerful and never satisfied need for knowledge, life, action'.[47] This highly ambivalent document appears to be both a cunning ruse as well as an outright betrayal of his beliefs.

Bakunin's voluntarism comes clearly through when he relates how, after failing to foment an uprising in Bohemia, he reasoned that since the revolution is essential, it is possible. At this stage, revolutionary will was more important for Bakunin than objective conditions: 'faith alone', he declares, ' is already half of success, half the victory. Coupled with a strong will, it gives rise to circumstances, it gives rise to people, it gathers, unites, and merges the masses into one soul and one power.'[48] After outlining his scheme for an invisible dictatorship, and appealing to the despotic Tsar to bring about reforms, he maintains that he was not capable of being a dictator:

> To look for my happiness in the happiness of others, my personal dignity in the dignity of all those who surrounded me, to be free in the liberty of others, that is my credo, the aspiration of my whole life. I considered it as the most sacred of duties to revolt against all oppression, whoever was the author or the victim.[49]

Whatever his intentions in his *Confessions*, the man of action in Bakunin undoubtedly felt despair in prison at being cut off from the world. When his beloved sister came to see him and failed to gain admittance, he slipped out the note:

> You will never understand what it means to feel yourself buried alive, to say to yourself every moment of the day and night: I am a slave, I am annihilated, reduced to impotence for life; to hear even in your

cell the echoes of the great battle which has had to come, which will decide the most important questions of humanity – and to be forced to remain idle and silent. To be rich in ideas, some of which at least could be useful, and to be unable to realize even one of them ... capable of any sacrifice, even of heroism in the name of a cause that is a thousand times holy, and to see all these impulses shattered against four bare walls, my only witnesses, my only confidants! That is my life![50]

In keeping with his new philosophy of action, he regretted the time he had wasted with the 'Chinese shadows' of metaphysics, and urged his brothers to concentrate on improving their estates.[51]

It was only after the accession of Alexander II in 1855 that Bakunin's family managed to change his sentence from imprisonment to banishment. He left for Siberia where he married in 1857 an eighteen-year-old Polish girl called Antonia Kiriatkowska. She later bore two children by a family friend Carlo Gambuzzi but seemed quite happy to follow her itinerant revolutionary husband across the face of the earth. The Governor of Eastern Siberia, General Nikolai Muravev, turned out to be a second cousin on the Decembrist side of the family. Bakunin became deeply impressed by his colonizing methods: he told Herzen that he was the 'best man in Russia' who seemed 'born to command'; he was a true statesman 'who will not tolerate chatter, whose word has been his deed all his life, with a will of iron'.[52] It would seem that Bakunin saw in Muravev a potential leader of one of his secret societies. The Governor moreover hoped that one day it would be possible to free the peasants by giving them the land they culti-vated, and to establish 'self-government, the abolition of the bureaucracy and, as far as possible, the decentralization of the Russian empire, without constitution or parliament'. In the process, it would be necessary to establish an 'iron dictatorship' which would liberate all the Slavs, and declare war on Austria and Turkey.[53] Kropotkin later met Muravev in Siberia after he had annexed the Amúr region to Russia, but he was not taken in as Bakunin had been; 'like all men of action of the governmental school', Kropotkin wrote of Muravev, 'he was a despot at the bottom of his heart'.[54]

Bakunin spent four years in Siberia, from 1857 to 1861. He broke his word to Muravev's successor while acting as an agent for a trading company. On an expedition to the river Amúr, he took an American ship to Japan and then to San Francisco. He crossed the United States, and mingled with the leading lights of the progressive and abolitionist circles in Boston. He liked the country and was impressed by its federalist system, but he left no discernible impact on the embryonic labour movement. Only later did Benjamin Tucker publicize his ideas.[55] Bakunin stayed little more than a month in America, and eventually reached England at the end of 1861. In London, he met his old socialist friend Alexander Herzen and his cousin Nikolai Ogarev. His first statement for thirteen years 'To my Russian, to my Polish and all my Slav friends' appeared in their journal *The Bell* in February 1862. Quoting the journal's motto 'Land and Liberty', he reaffirmed his faith in the instincts of the people and called for a revolution which would bring about the self-government of the Slavs in a fraternal union organized from the bottom up and based on the peasant commune. While this clearly echoed Proudhon's federalism, Bakunin went beyond his economic mutualism to insist on the communal possession of land.

Herzen left a vivid picture of Bakunin at this time: 'His activity, his idleness, his appetite, and all his other characteristics, such as his gigantic height and his continual sweat, were of superhuman dimensions, as he was himself – a giant with a leonine head and a tousled mane.' He saw in him more of an 'abstract theorist' than a man of action, and told him candidly:

> Cut off from life, thrown from early youth into German Idealism . . . you have lived to the age of fifty in a world of illusions, of student expansiveness, of great aspirations and petty failings . . . unscrupulous in money matters, with a streak of discreet but stubborn epicureanism and with an itch for revolutionary activity that lacks a revolution.[56]

It was stunningly accurate, but Bakunin had little choice but to ignore it. He tried to go to Poland after the insurrection in January 1863, but the expedition he joined collapsed and he ended up in Sweden. He then made his way to Italy where he began to put his Panslavist hopes behind him and moved closer to fully fledged anarchism. His search for a revolution was as strong as ever. But as he wrote to a Russian acquaintance in 1864 he felt that he was living in a transitional period, an unhappy age for unhappy people:

> Civilization is rotting, barbarism has not yet developed into a force and we find ourselves *entre deux chaises*. It is very hard – if only one could live at least until the great day of Nemesis, the last judgement, which this despicable European society is not destined to escape. Let my friends build – I thirst only for destruction, because I am convinced that to build on carrion with rotten materials is a lost cause, and that new living materials and with them, new organisms, can arise only from immense destruction . . . For a long time ahead I see no poetry other than the grim poetry of destruction, and we will be fortunate if we get the chance to see even destruction.[57]

In Italy, Bakunin lived first in Florence and then moved to Naples in October 1865. After the failure of the Polish insurrection, he no longer believed in a national liberation movement as a revolutionary force and began to advocate a social revolution on an international scale. Although he had met the Italian revolutionary Mazzini in London and had respected him as person, he now found his religious idealism and nationalism irksome. Bakunin also took leave at this time of his early philosophical idealism and developed a materialist and atheistic view of the world. He was helped in this direction by the positivist Comte but more especially by Marx. He praised Marx for having been the first to understand 'that all the intellectual and political developments of society are nothing other than the ideal expression of its material and economic developments'.[58]

On Marx's request, Bakunin met him as he was passing through London in November 1864. Bakunin was still smarting about a report which had appeared in Marx's journal *Neue Rheinische Zeitung* that he was a Russian spy, but Marx assured him that he had no part in it nor in the defamatory articles on Bakunin in the English press. Marx was charmed by the encounter and wrote to Engels that Bakunin was one of the few men who had developed instead of retrogressing during the previous sixteen years.[59] At the same time, Bakunin was impressed by the International Working Men's Association Marx had just help set up, and apparently agreed to work on its behalf in Italy. It turned out to be their last meeting.

It was during his stay in Italy that Bakunin's anarchist ideas took final shape. The way had been prepared by his conversations with Proudhon and the reading of his works, but he now met Giuseppe Fanelli, a friend of the anarchist leader Carlo Pisacane. Pisacane defined property and government as the principal sources of slavery, poverty and corruption, and called for a new Italy organized from the bottom up on the principle of free association. This was to become the central plank of Bakunin's programme.

Yet despite his conversion, Bakunin was still unable to abandon his love of conspiracy and penchant for secret societies. In the absence of a well-organized workers' movement, he still relied on a vanguard to ensure the triumph of the social revolution. In Florence in 1864, he created a secret society, although it consisted of only a few men and women. When he moved to Naples, he set up a secret revolutionary Brotherhood and in 1866 wrote down *Principles and Organization of the International Brotherhood*. He wrote to Herzen and Ogarev at this time telling them how he had spent the last three years engaged in the 'foundation and organization of a secret international revolutionary society' and sent them a statement of its principles.[60]

The document not only offers the most detailed glimpse of Bakunin's version of a free society but also sketches the prototype of all his subsequent secret societies. The Brotherhood was to be organized into two 'families', national and international, with the latter controlling the former. Its aim was to overthrow the existing States and to rebuild Europe and then the world on the principles of liberty, justice and work.

But while the Brotherhood would be hierarchical and centralized, Bakunin in the main document entitled 'Revolutionary Catechism' elaborated his fundamental anarchist principles. In the first place, he insists that '*individual and collective freedom*' is the only source of order in society and morality. Next, he identifies, like Proudhon, justice with equality, and argues that liberty is inextricably linked with equality: 'The *freedom* of each is therefore realizable only in the equality of all. The realization of freedom through equality, in principle and in fact is *justice*.'[61] But unlike the patriarchal Proudhon, Bakunin maintains that women and men have equal rights and obligations. They would be able to unite and separate in '*free* marriage' as they please, and have their children subsidized by society. Children belong neither to their parents nor to society but 'to themselves and to their own future liberty'.[62] Finally, true freedom can only be realized with the complete destruction of the State, with the '*Absolute rejection of every authority including that which sacrifices freedom for the convenience of the State*'. The Brotherhood would therefore strive to destroy the '*all-pervasive, regimented, centralized State*, the alter ego of the Church, and as such, the permanent cause of the impoverishment, brutalization, and enslavement of the multitude'.[63]

Although Bakunin's secret societies never functioned as influential organizations, they reveal a central strand in his thought. He hopes they will act as 'invisible pilots in the thick of the popular tempest'. Their task is first 'to assist the birth of the revolution by sowing seeds corresponding to the instincts of the masses, then to channel the revolutionary energy of the people'. But the tension between Bakunin's libertarian sympathies and his authoritarian strategy of manipulating others through secret societies comes across only too clearly. One of the 'cardinal functions' of the leaders is to 'inculcate' in their followers the need to prevent 'all consolidation of authority' through the foundation of free associations.[64] In Bakunin's overheated imagination, there are still leaders and led, sage pilots and ignorant crews.

At this stage, Bakunin does not call for a direct and immediate expropriation of private industry. Instead, he relies on the abolition of the right of inheritance and formation of co-operative workers associations to ensure the gradual disappearance of private ownership and economic inequality. All property belonging to the State and to reactionaries would be confiscated. Economic and political equality would not however lead to the uniform levelling of individual differences, for diversity in capacities constitutes the 'abundance of humanity'.[65]

In place of existing nation states, society should be organized '*from the base to the summit-from the circumference to the centre – according to the principles* of free association and federation'. The basic unit of society would be the autonomous commune which would always have the right to secede from the federation. Decisions would be made by majority vote based on universal suffrage of both sexes. The commune would elect all functionaries, law-makers and judges and create its own constitution. There would be the *'absolute freedom of individuals'*, while society would meet their basic needs.[66]

This document, which has been called the 'spiritual foundation of the anarchist movement', nonetheless appears profoundly contradictory and authoritarian at times.[67] Bakunin writes that the only legitimate restraint would be the 'natural salutary power of public opinion'. Yet he also declares that society can deprive all 'antisocial' adults of political rights and those who steal or break their agreements and violate the freedom of individuals will be 'penalized according to the laws of society'.[68] Corruption and exploi-tation are allowed, but not of minors. Children would be educated only by the commune and not by their parents so as to inculcate 'human values' in them and to train them as specialized workers. Every able-bodied person is expected to work or else be considered a 'parasite' or a 'thief', since work is the sole source of wealth and the foundation of human dignity and morality. Each adult is expected to fulfil three obligations: 'that he remain *free*, that he *live by his own labour*, and that he *respect the freedom of others*'.[69] And as to the means to bring about the social revolution, Bakunin recognizes that it will involve war. It will very likely be 'bloody and vindictive' although he felt that it would not last long or degenerate into 'cold, systematic terrorism'. It would be war, not against particular men, but primarily against 'antisocial institutions'.[70]

But while there are undoubtedly some authoritarian elements in the document, Bakunin only wishes to retain political government in its most extenuated form. Certainly he still uses the word 'government' to describe the elected parliament at the provincial level which defines the rights and obligations of the communes and the elected tribunal which deals with disputes between communes. But by parliament he means here little more than a 'coordinating association'.[71] Again, Bakunin's use of the word 'State' at the end of the document might suggest that he is not yet fully an anarchist. But when he writes that the revolution seeks 'the absolute agglomerations of communes into provinces and conquered countries into the State', he is not referring to the compulsory legal order of existing states; instead, he is using it to describe the federal organ which forms the 'central unity of the country'.[72] While there would be a national parliament co-ordinating production and solving disputes, the nation would remain a voluntary feder-ation of autonomous units, with 'absolute liberty and autonomy of regions, provinces, communes, associations, and individuals'. There would be no standing armies and defence would be organized by people's militias. In the long run, Bakunin hoped that existing nations states would give way in the future to a 'Universal Federation of Peoples' with free commerce, exchange and communication.[73]

After leaving Italy, Bakunin went to Geneva in 1867 to attend the inaugural Congress of the League for Peace and Freedom, a liberal body which was supported by Garibaldi, Victor Hugo, Herzen, and John Stuart Mill among others. Bakunin thought it could provide a forum for his ideas and he quickly made a considerable stir. Baron Wrangel wrote later:

> I no longer remember what Bakunin said, and it would in any case scarcely be possible to reproduce it. His speech had neither logical sequence nor richness in ideas, but consisted of thrilling phrases and rousing appeals. It was something elemental and incandescent – a raging storm with lightning flashes and thunderclaps, and a roaring of lions. The man was a born speaker made for the revolution. The revolution was his natural being. His speech made a tremendous impression. If he had asked his hearers to cut each other's throats, they would have cheerfully obeyed him.[74]

In fact, in his first speech Bakunin made a clear denunciation of nationalism. He recognized that 'Every nationality has the indubitable right to be itself, to live according to its own nature' but he argued that aggressive nationalism always comes from centralized States.[75] He further expounded his anarchist views on human nature, society, and the State, although he acknowledged that the full realization of socialism 'will no doubt be the work of centuries'.[76]

In his unfinished address, later known as *Federalism, Socialism, Anti-Theologism*, he emphasized during a critique of Rousseau that man is not only the most individualistic being on earth but also the most social: '*Society* is the natural mode of existence of the human collectivity, independent of any contract. It governs itself through the customs or the traditional habits, but never by laws.'[77] Every human has a sense of justice deep in their conscience which translates itself into 'simple *equality*'. Human beings are born morally and intellectually equal, regardless of sex and colour, and instances of criminality and stupidity are '*not due to their nature; it is solely the result of the social environment in which they were born or brought up*'.[78] Like Godwin, Bakunin therefore believes that human beings are born with the same intelligence and moral sense but are otherwise entirely products of their environment. They are naturally social and are capable of governing themselves without man-made laws.

On the other hand, it is the State which is the principal cause of social evils; 'it is *the most flagrant, the most cynical, and the most complete negation of humanity*'. Bakunin expatiates in rhetoric worthy of Proudhon that

> the entire history of ancient and modern states is merely a series of revolting crimes ... There is no horror, no cruelty, sacrilege, or perjury, no imposture, no infamous transaction, no cynical robbery, no bold plunder or shabby betrayal that has not been or is not daily being perpetrated by the representatives of the states, under no other pretext than those elastic words, so convenient and so terrible: '*for reasons of state*'.[79]

Bakunin made the first clear and public statement of his anarchism in a speech in September 1868 at the Second Congress in Berne of the League for Peace and Freedom. He declared in no uncertain terms that all States are founded on 'force, oppression, exploitation, injustice, elevated into a system and made the cornerstone of the very existence of society'. They offer a double negation of humanity, internally by maintaining order by force and exploiting the people, and externally, by waging aggressive war. By their very nature they represent the 'diametrical opposite of human justice, freedom and morality'.[80] He concluded that freedom and peace could only be achieved through the dissolution of all States and the creation of a universal federation of free associations with society reorganized from the bottom up. It was to become a central theme in his anarchist philosophy.

In the summer of 1868 Bakunin joined the Geneva branch of the International, and in the following year acted as its delegate to the Fourth Congress of the International Working Men's Association in Basel. It marked a turning-point in his career and in the history of the anarchist movement for he came into direct contact for the first time with organized industrial workers. He soon found support amongst the watchmakers of the French-speaking Jura who provided him with a base, and he went on to win over workers especially in France and Italy. His Italian comrade Giuseppe Fanelli went to Spain and soon converted the Spanish Federation, the largest organization within the International, to Bakunin's collectivist and federalist programme. It was from the libertarian sections of the International that revolutionary syndicalism or 'anarcho-syndicalism' eventually sprung.

Bakunin's immediate suggestion of an affiliation with the League for Peace and Freedom however was rejected by the General Council of the International and by Marx who dominated it. When the Congress of the League also rejected the proposal for the 'economic and social equalization of classes and individuals', Bakunin left with fourteen others, including James Guillaume, a young schoolmaster from the Jura, to form the International Alliance of Social Democracy with a central bureau in Geneva.

In the following year, after again being refused affiliation with the International, Bakunin formally dissolved the Alliance early in 1869, but he privately maintained his connections with its members, and through them set up groups in Switzerland, Belgium, Italy and Spain. The exact status of the Alliance, and its relationship with the International, was ambiguous and has remained shrouded in controversy. Marx claimed that Bakunin never disbanded his Alliance and intended to turn it into 'a second *International within the International*'.[81] Guillaume said it was disbanded in January 1869 although the 'free contact of men united for collective action in an informal revolutionary fraternity' was continued.[82] Bakunin himself saw the Alliance as a necessary complement to the International, and although they had the same ultimate aims they performed different functions. While the International endeavoured to unify the workers, Bakunin wanted the Alliance to give them a really revolutionary direction. As such Bakunin asserted in Hegelian style that the programme of the Alliance 'represents the fullest unfolding of the International'.[83]

Bakunin threw himself into propaganda on behalf of the International. In a series of articles for *L'Egalité*, the journal of the French-speaking Swiss Federation of the International, he insisted that every new member must pledge 'to subordinate your personal and family interests as well as your political and religious beliefs to the supreme interests of our association: to the struggle of labour against capital, i.e., the economic struggle of the workers against the bourgeoisie'. This sounds distinctly authoritarian, and would horrify Godwin, who thought the right to private judgement paramount: one should not join a political association which insists on loyalty and obedience contrary to one's own conscience.

Bakunin defined the principal task of the International as providing the great mass of workers, who are 'socialistic *without knowing it*', with socialist thought, so that each worker could become 'fully conscious of what he wants, to awaken in him an intelligence which will correspond to his inner yearnings'. But this is not to be achieved only by propaganda and education, since the best way for workers to learn theory is through practice: '*emancipation through practical action*'. The fundamental principle of the International is therefore entirely correct: 'The emancipation of the workers is the task of the workers themselves.'[84]

Although it had little substance in reality, Bakunin continued to draw up programmes for the 'International Brotherhood'. In a draft of 1869, he clarified his ideas about revolutionary strategy, calling for the confiscation of private, Church, and State property and its transformation into collective property under a free federation of agricultural and industrial associations. He now gave a positive meaning to anarchy. 'We do not fear anarchy', he declared,

we invoke it. For we are convinced that anarchy, meaning the unrestricted manifestation of the liberated life of the people, must spring from
liberty, equality, the new social order, and the force of the revolution
itself against the reaction. There is no doubt that this new life – the
popular revolution – will in good time organize itself, but it will create
its revolutionary organization from the bottom up, from the circumference to the centre, in accordance with the principle of liberty.[85]

At the same time, while rejecting dictatorship and centralization, Bakunin
still writes about a 'new revolutionary State' and the need for the '*secret and
universal association of the International Brothers*' to be the organ to give life
and energy to the revolution. This anarchist vanguard movement would
consist of 'a sort of revolutionary general staff, composed of dedicated,
energetic, intelligent individuals, sincere friends of the people above all,
men neither vain nor ambitious, but capable of serving as intermediaries
between the revolutionary idea and the instincts of the people'.[86]

The rumbling dispute between Marx and his followers and Bakunin
and his supporters came to a head in at the Basel Congress of the International in September 1869. Bakunin could only count on twelve of the
seventy-five delegates but the force of his oratory and the charisma of his
presence almost made the Congress approve his proposal for the abolition
of the right of inheritance as one of the indispensable conditions for the
emancipation of labour. The supporters of Marx argued that since the
inheritance of property is merely a product of the property system, it would
be better to attack the system itself. In the outcome, both the proposals of
Bakunin and Marx were voted down but the issue led the partisans of
collective property to split into two opposing factions. According to Guillaume, those who followed Marx in advocating the ownership of collective
property by the State began to be called 'state' or 'authoritarian communists', while those like Bakunin who advocated ownership directly by the
workers' associations were called 'anti-authoritarian communists', 'communist federalists' or 'communist anarchists'.[87] The terms 'collectivist' and
'communist' were still used loosely; Bakunin preferred to call himself a
'collectivist' by which he meant that since collective labour creates wealth,
collective wealth should be collectively owned. He believed that distribution
should take place according to work done, not according to need.

The orthodox Marxist view is that Bakunin tried to seize control of the
International and was motivated by personal ambition.[88] A Russian emigré
called Utin in Switzerland fuelled the controversy and rumours were circulated from Marx's camp that Bakunin was a Russian spy and unscrupulous
in money matters. Yet Bakunin still admired Marx as a thinker and even
took an advance from a publisher to do a Russian translation of the first

volume of *Capital*. The real dispute was not between an ambitious individual (Bakunin) and an authoritarian one (Marx), or even between conspiracy and organization, but about different revolutionary strategies.

Bakunin now devoted all his energies to inciting a European revolution which he hoped would eventually embrace the entire world. In a series of hastily written speeches, pamphlets and voluminous unfinished manuscripts, he tried to set out his views. In the process, he began to transform anarchism into a revolutionary movement.

It was in Russia that he thought the world revolution could begin. Early in 1870, he criticized the attempt of his old friend Herzen to appeal to the Tsar and the Russian aristocracy to bring about reform. In particular, he asked him to reject the State, precisely because he was socialist: 'you practise State socialism and you are capable of reconciling yourself with this most dangerous and vile lie engendered by our century – official democracy and red bureaucracy.'[89] According to Bakunin, the only way to transform Russia was through popular insurrection.

In his search for likely catalysts, Bakunin became involved at this time with a young revolutionary called Sergei Nechaev. It proved a disastrous relationship and did immense harm to the anarchist movement. Nechaev, who later inspired the character Peter Verkhovensky in Dostoevsky's *The Possessed*, was an extraordinary character: despotic, power-hungry, egoistic, rude and yet strangely seductive. He exemplifies the unscrupulous terrorist who will stop at nothing to realize his aim.

Nechaev managed to convince both Bakunin and Herzen's colleague Ogarev that he had a secret organization with a mass following in Russia. At first, he seemed to Bakunin the ideal type of the new breed of Russian revolutionaries, a perfect conspirator with a piercing mind and the *diable au corps*. 'They are charming these young fanatics', Bakunin wrote to Guillaume, 'believers without a god, and heroes without flowering rhetoric'.[90] Bakunin could not stop himself from being seduced by someone who seemed to have his own extreme energy and dedication, and that despite his tender years. He appeared to be a reincarnation of the legendary Russian bandits Stenka Razin and Pugachev.

Whilst in Geneva with Bakunin, Nechaev wrote between April and August 1869 a *Catechism of a Revolutionary* which proved to be one of the most repulsive documents in the history of terrorism. The guiding principle of this work is that 'everything is moral that contributes to the triumph of the revolution; everything that hinders it is immoral and criminal.' It calls upon the would-be revolutionary to break all ties with past society, to feel a 'single cold passion' for the revolutionary cause and to adopt the single aim of 'pitiless destruction' in order to eradicate the State and its institutions and classes. The second part of the pamphlet opens:

> The revolutionary is a doomed man. He has no personal interests, no affairs, no sentiments, attachments, property, not even a name of his own. Everything in him is absorbed by one exclusive interest, one thought, one passion – the revolution.

The pamphlet not only recommends drawing up lists of persons to be exterminated but also declares that the central committee of any secret society should regard all other members as expendable 'revolutionary capital'.[91] Another unsigned pamphlet called *Principles of Revolution* written at the time, which has the stamp of Nechaev, declares in a similar vein:

> We recognize no other activity but the work of extermination, but we admit that the forms in which this activity will show itself will be extremely varied – poison, the knife the knife, the rope etc. In this struggle, revolution sanctifies everything alike.[92]

Both works have been assigned jointly to Bakunin and Nechaev, and their alleged authorship has provoked bitter controversy.

Certainly Bakunin was impressed by the spontaneous energy of Russian brigands, and wrote to Nechaev 'these primitive men, brutal to the point of cruelty, have a nature which is fresh, strong and untouched.' He also came close to Nechaev's moral relativism when he declared that 'Where there is war there are politics, and there against one's will one is obliged to use force, cunning and deception.' The *Catechism of a Revolutionary* was written during a period of close co-operation between the two men, but though Bakunin may have helped with the writing, the work most likely came in the main from Nechaev's hand. In the final analysis, Bakunin categorically repudiates Nechaev's 'Jesuitical system' and his unprincipled use of violence and deception. 'In your Catechism', he wrote unambiguously to Nechaev, 'you ... wish to make your own self-sacrificing cruelty, your own truly extreme fanaticism, a rule of life for the community.' He roundly condemns his 'total negation of man's individual and social nature'.[93]

Unlike Lenin who admired the *Catechism of a Revolutionary*, Bakunin would have no truck with Nechaev's nihilism. He came to doubt the existence of Nechaev's secret organization in Russia, and was repelled – while refusing to condemn – his political murder of a student called Ivanov. Bakunin finally broke with Nechaev after learning that his young protégé had threatened with dire punishment the publisher's agent who had given an advance for a translation of *Capital* if he caused any difficulties. But the damage had been done. Their association earned Bakunin an unfounded reputation for terrorism, and the works were used selectively to justify the acts of later anarchist terrorists as well as to denigrate anarchist ideals. Bakunin went on to recommend the selective killing of individuals as a preliminary to social revolution and saw in Russian banditry the spearhead of the popular revolution, but he was undoubtedly repelled by Nechaev's total amoralism.[94]

When the Franco-Prussian war broke out in July 1870, Bakunin's revolutionary hopes were aroused again for the first time since the Polish insurrection of 1863. Marx at first supported Prussia in its attempt to defeat a Bonapartist France he regarded as an obstacle to the working class. He wrote: 'If the Prussians are victorious, the centralization of the State power will be useful to the centralization of the German working class . . . On a world scale the ascendancy of the German proletariat over the French proletariat will at the same time constitute the ascendancy of our theory over Proudhon's.'[95] Bakunin on the other hand thought Prussian militarism even more dangerous than Bonapartism. He hoped that the defeat of the regime of Napoleon III would lead to a popular uprising of peasants and workers against the Prussian invaders and the French government, thereby destroying the State and bringing about a free federation of communes. To inspire such a revolutionary movement he wrote some draft *Letters to a Frenchman on the Present Crisis* which made a unique contribution to the theory and practice of revolution.

Bakunin advocates the turning of the war between the two States into a civil war for the social revolution: a guerrilla war of the armed people to repulse a foreign army and domestic opponents in 'a war of destruction, a merciless war to the death'.[96] Once again, Bakunin expresses his love of destruction. His anarchy is not merely the peaceful and productive life of the community, the 'spontaneous self-organization of popular life' which will revert to the communes. It is also violent turmoil – nothing less than 'civil war'.[97] He argues that the only feasible alternative is to awaken 'the primitive ferocious energy' of the French people and to 'Let loose this mass anarchy in the countryside as well as in the cities, aggravate it until it swells like a furious avalanche destroying and devouring everything in its path.'[98]

On the more positive side, Bakunin emphasizes the revolutionary capacity of the peasantry while depicting them as noble savages: 'Unspoiled by overindulgence and indolence, and only slightly affected by the pernicious influence of bourgeois society'. He stresses the need for an alliance between peasants and workers but sees the city proletarians taking the revolutionary initiative. Although recognizing the key influence of economic conditions in bringing about social change, the voluntarist in Bakunin underlines the importance of the consciousness and will of the people in the process : 'the revolutionary temper of the working masses does not depend solely on the extent of their misery and discontent, but also on their faith in the justice and the triumph of their cause.'⁹⁹

After the fall of the Second Empire and the establishment of the Third Republic, Bakunin went to Lyon in September 1870 with a few members of his clandestine Alliance to try to trigger off an uprising which he hoped would lead to a revolutionary federation of communes. It marked the beginning of the revolutionary movement which was to culminate in the Paris Commune the following spring. With the help of General Cluseret, Bakunin took over the Town Hall in Lyon and immediately declared the abolition of the State. On 25 September 1870, wall posters went up around town announcing:

ARTICLE 1: The administrative and governmental machinery of the state, having become impotent, is abolished.

ARTICLE 2: All criminal and civil courts are hereby suspended and replaced by the People's justice.

ARTICLE 3: Payment of taxes and mortgages is suspended. Taxes are to be replaced by contributions that the federated communes will have collected by levies upon the wealthy classes, according to what is needed for the salvation of France.

ARTICLE 4: Since the state has been abolished, it can no longer intervene to secure the payment of private debts.

ARTICLE 5: All existing municipal administrative bodies are hereby abolished. They will be replaced in each commune by committees for the salvation of France. All governmental powers will be exercised by these committees under the direct supervision of the People.

ARTICLE 6: The committee in the principal town of each of the nation's departments will send two delegates to a revolutionary convention for the salvation of France.

ARTICLE 7: This convention will meet immediately at the town hall of Lyon, since it is the second city of France and the best able to deal energetically with the country's defence. Since it will be supported by the People this convention will save France.

TO ARMS!!!

In the event, the Lyon uprising was quickly crushed. But while it earned Marx's contempt, it was in keeping with Bakunin's strategy. As he explained in a letter to his fellow insurrectionist Albert Richard, Bakunin rejected those political revolutionaries who wanted to reconstitute the State and who gave Paris a primary role in the revolution. On the contrary:

There must be anarchy, there must be – if the revolution is to become and remain alive, real, and powerful – the greatest possible awakening of all the local passions and aspirations; a tremendous awakening of spontaneous life everywhere . . . We must bring forth anarchy, and in the midst of the popular tempest, we must be the invisible pilots guiding the Revolution, not by any kind of overt power but by the collective dictatorship of all our allies, a dictatorship without tricks, without official titles, without official rights, and therefore all the more powerful, as it does not carry the trappings of power.[100]

In a fragment on 'The Programme of the Alliance' written at this time, Bakunin further elaborated on the correct relationship between his Alliance as a conscious revolutionary vanguard and the workers' movement in and outside the International. In the first place, he rejects class collaboration and parliamentary politics. Next, he attacks union bureaucracy in which the elected leaders often become 'absolute masters' of the rank-and-file, and replace popular assemblies by committees. Finally, he insists that his recommended libertarian organization is quite distinct from State structures since it involves the diffusion of power. Whereas the 'State is the organized authority, domination, and power of the possessing classes over the masses . . . the International wants only their complete freedom, and calls for their revolt'. For Bakunin, the fundamental idea underlying the International is 'the founding of a new social order resting on emancipated labour, one which will spontaneously erect upon the ruins of the Old World the free federations of workers' associations'.[101] This rejection of parliamentary politics and insistence that the workers' organizations should reflect the structure of future society helped lay the foundations of the revolutionary syndicalist movement.

It is difficult not to conclude that Bakunin's invisible dictatorship would be even more tyrannical than a Blanquist or Marxist one, for its policies could not be openly known or discussed. It would be a secret party; it would operate like conspirators and thieves in the night. With no check to their power, what would prevent the invisible dictators from grasping for absolute power? It is impossible to imagine that Bakunin's goal of an open and democratic society could ever be achieved by distorting the truth and manipulating the people in the way he suggests.

It is not enough to excuse Bakunin's predilection for tightly organized, authoritarian, hierarchical secret organizations by appealing to his 'romantic temperament' or the oppression of existing States.[102] His invisible dictatorship is a central part of his political theory and practice, and shows that for all his professed love of liberty and openness there is a profound authoritarian and dissimulating streak in his life and work. His habit of simultaneously preaching absolute liberty in his polemics with the Marxists while defending a form of absolute dictatorship in his private correspondence with members of his clandestine Alliance would certainly seem to point to 'acute schizophrenia' on Bakunin's part.[103] His love of destruction and struggle also prevented him from realizing that it is impossible to employ violence and force as means to achieve libertarian and peaceful ends.

After the collapse of the Lyon uprising, Bakunin retreated to Locarno, deeply depressed. The Paris Commune in the spring of 1871, the greatest urban uprising in the nineteenth century, temporarily raised his hopes. It seemed to confirm his belief that a war could trigger off a social revolution. Harking back to the revolutions of 1793 and 1848, it also rejected centralized authority and experimented with women's rights and workers' control. Bakunin immediately recognized its decentralist and federalist tendencies; it was not Marx's proletarian dictatorship that it exemplified, but 'the bold and outspoken negation of the state', bringing about 'a new era of the final emancipation of the people and their solidarity'. In his essay *The Paris Commune and the Idea of the State*, Bakunin further wrote:

> society in the future ought only to be organized from the bottom upwards, by the free association and federation of workers, in associations first, then in communes, regions, nations, and finally in a great international and universal federation. It is only then that the true and vital order of liberty and general happiness will be realized.[104]

The Lyon uprising and the Paris Commune inspired some of Bakunin's greatest writing. From the end of 1870 to 1872, he composed his first and last book, the sprawling *The Knouto-Germanic Empire and the Social Revolution*. The strange title of the work was meant to suggest that there was an alliance between the Tsar of Russia on the one hand and Wilhelm I and Bismarck of the new German Empire on the other to use the Russian whip (*knout*) to prevent the social revolution. But the work went far beyond international politics and Bakunin developed his views on a whole range of subjects in an attempt to give a philosophical foundation to his anarchism. One section was published in 1882 as a pamphlet entitled *God and the State* and became Bakunin's most famous work. For a long time, it was the only sizeable part of his writing translated into English.

Philosophy

Although Bakunin was a philosophical idealist as a young man with a spiritual yearning to become part of the whole, he had since the early 1840s been a materialist and a determinist. But while he had become a militant atheist, he was not uncompromising; he did not want atheism to become a fundamental principle of the International for fear of alienating many superstitious peasants. Nothing, he felt, is more natural than that the people, especially in the country, should believe in God as the creator, regulator, judge, master and benefactor of the world. People would continue to believe in a Superior Being until a social revolution provided the means to realize their aspirations on earth and overcome their instinctive fear of the world around them. Religious beliefs are therefore not so much 'an aberration of mind as a deep discontent at heart. They are the instinctive and passionate protest of the human being against the narrowness, the platitudes, the sorrows, and the shame of a wretched existence.'[105]

Nevertheless, while recognizing religious belief as an inevitable consequence of the oppressive and miserable life here on earth, Bakunin goes out of his way to deny its metaphysical truth. He develops the Left-Hegelian critique of religion, to argue like Feuerbach that the religious heaven is nothing but a mirage in which man discovers his own image divinized. Christianity is for Bakunin the religion *par excellence* which exhibits the essence of every religious system, which is *'the impoverishment, enslavement, and annihilation of humanity for the benefit of divinity'*.[106]

The idea of God implies *'the abdication of human reason and justice; it is the most decisive negation of human liberty, and necessarily ends in the enslavement of mankind, both in theory and practice'*. But since man is born free, slavery is not natural. As all Gods, according to Bakunin, desire to enslave man they too must be unnatural. Hence they cannot exist. Bakunin puts his ontological refutation of God in the form a syllogism: 'If God is, man is a slave; now, man can and must be free; then, God does not exist. I defy anyone whomsoever to avoid this circle.' Bakunin's sentiments might be admirable but his logic is faulty: he not only assumes paradoxically that God exists as an idea in order to disprove his existence, but his syllogism is only valid if we accept his initial premiss that the essence of God is always to enslave man. Be that as it may, Bakunin considers God to be such a threat to human liberty and virtue that he reverses the phrase of Voltaire to say *'if God really existed, it would be necessary to abolish him'*.[107]

Although dogmatically denying the existence of God, Bakunin is sceptical in his epistemology. There are inevitable limits to man's understanding of the world, and we must content ourselves with only 'a tiny bit of knowledge about our solar system'.[108] Nevertheless, Bakunin accepts the reality of a Newtonian universe governed by natural laws. The laws are not known by nature itself, and are only of a relative character, but they are discovered by human reason as constant and recurrent patterns.

Yet Bakunin is not a mechanical materialist like Feuerbach. He adopts an evolutionary perspective and argues that the gradual development of the material world is a 'wholly natural movement' from the simple to the complex, from the lower to the higher, from the inferior to the superior, the inorganic to the organic.[109] But like Marx, he sees change occurring through the clash of opposite forces both in nature and society: 'the harmony of the forces of nature appears only as the result of a continual struggle, which is the real condition of life and of movement. In nature, as in society, order without struggle is death.'[110] There is thus a mutual interaction in nature which produces a 'natural authority' which dominates all life.

Human Nature

When it comes to humanity's place in nature, Bakunin rejects all dualism which tries to separate the two. Indeed, far from being separate, 'Man forms with Nature a single entity and is the material product of an indefinite number of exclusively material causes.'[111] The human species is only one species amongst others, with two basic drives of sex and hunger. Nevertheless, Bakunin claims that the human world is the highest manifestation of animality. Our first ancestors, if not gorillas, were 'omnivorous, intelligent and ferocious beasts'.[112] But they were endowed to a higher degree than the animals of any other species with two faculties – the power to think and the desire to rebel. In addition, while denying free will in an absolute sense of some contra-causal autonomous power, Bakunin argues that man is alone among all the animals on earth in possessing a relatively free will in the sense of 'conscious self-determination'.[113] Due to his intelligence man can develop his will to modify his instinctive drives and regulate his own needs. It follows that moral responsibility exists but it is only relative.

It is the ability to think and to act deliberately which enables human beings to negate the animal element in themselves and to develop their consciousness and freedom. It is man's rational will which enables him to free himself gradually from the hostility of the external world. Whereas Jehovah wanted man to remain an 'eternal beast', ignorant and obedient, Satan urged him to disobey and eat of the tree of knowledge. As such, Satan is 'the eternal rebel, the first freethinker and the emancipator of worlds'.[114] Indeed, Bakunin believed that in general the vitality and dignity of an animal can be measured by the intensity of its instinct to revolt. The 'goddess of revolt', he declared in one of his resounding phrases, is the 'mother of all liberty'.[115]

As the human species revolts and rises from other animal species, they not only become more complete and free, but also more individual: 'man, the last and most perfect animal on earth, presents the most complete and remarkable individuality.'[116] Like Hegel, Bakunin saw the complete emancipation of the individual as the supreme aim of history which can only be achieved by growth in consciousness.

But while born with an innate ability to think and to rebel, Bakunin believed that human beings are almost entirely shaped by their environment, products of history and society. Every individual inherits at birth in different degrees the capacity to feel, to think, to speak and to will, but these rudimentary faculties are without content. It is society which provides the ideas and impressions which form the common consciousness of a people. It is the same with moral dispositions. We are born with a capacity to be egoistic or sociable, but not innate moral characteristics. Our moral behaviour will result from our social tradition and education.

Man is therefore largely a product of his environment, but it does not follow that he is its eternal victim. In the final stage of his development, man, unlike other animal species, managed to transform the greater part of the earth, and to make it habitable for human civilization. Although an inseparable part of nature, man in the past came to conquer nature, turning 'this enemy, the first terrible despot, into a useful servant'. For all his evolutionary perspective and stress on the animal origins of man, Bakunin is no ecologist and believes that we must continually struggle against external nature: 'Man ... can and should conquer and master this external world. He, on his part, must subdue it and wrest from it his freedom and humanity.'[117]

Although Bakunin refers to the human species in the habit of the day by the abstraction 'Man', he did not believe that he was merely an atomized creature. Indeed, 'Man is not only the most individual being on earth – he is also the most social being.' Bakunin totally rejects Rousseau's portrayal of primitive man as a self-sufficient individual living in isolation. Society is the basis of human existence: 'Man is born into society, just as an ant is born into an ant-hill or a bee into its hive.'[118] It is necessarily anterior to our thought, speech and will and we can only become humanized and emancipated in society. Outside society, not only would a human being not be free, he would not even become genuinely human, 'a being conscious of himself, the only being who thinks and speaks'.[119]

Society is also essential to our development. In the first place, the basis of morality can only be found in society, and the moral law to observe justice is a social fact, a creation of society. Secondly, human beings can only free themselves from the yoke of external nature through collective labour. Thirdly, a person can only realize his individual freedom and his personality through the individuals who surround him. Fourthly, solidarity is a fundamental law of human nature: 'All social life is nothing but the incessant mutual interdependence of individuals and of masses. All individuals, even the strongest and most intelligent, are at every moment of their lives both the producers and the products of the will and action of the masses.'[120]

Liberty and Authority

Bakunin called himself 'a fanatical lover of Liberty; considering it as the only medium in which can develop intelligence, dignity, and the happiness of man'.[121] He invariably called for 'absolute liberty'. By liberty in this sense he did not mean the 'liberty' regulated by the State, nor the 'individual liberty' of the liberals who see the rights of individuals protected by the rights of the State. Nevertheless, Bakunin acknowledges that liberty has a natural and social context and is inevitably limited by certain boundaries. Without recognizing these limits, liberty remains an empty and abstract concept. Thus the only liberty which Bakunin believes worthy of the name is

> the liberty which consists in the full development of all the material, intellectual and moral powers which are to be found as faculties latent in everybody, the liberty which recognizes no other restrictions that those which are traced for us by the laws of our own nature; so that properly speaking there are no restrictions, since these laws are not imposed on us by some legislator, beside us or above us; they are immanent in us, inherent, constituting the very basis of our being, material as well as intellectual and moral; instead, therefore, of finding them a limit, we must consider them as the real conditions and effective reason for our liberty.[122]

Liberty for Bakunin is therefore a condition of being free from all external restraints imposed by man, but in keeping with natural laws. It cannot escape the Tao of things. Liberty thus becomes an inevitable consequence of natural and social necessity.

At the same time, liberty does not begin and end with the individual, as with Stirner, where the individual is a self-moving atom. Bakunin makes clear that 'absolutely self-sufficient freedom is to condemn oneself to non-existence'; indeed such absolute independence is a 'wild absurdity' and the 'brainchild of idealists and metaphysicians'.[123]

Instead, Bakunin recognizes the social context of liberty; society is 'the root, the tree of freedom, and liberty is its fruit'.[124] He also acknowledges that the liberty of one must involve the liberty of all: I am truly free only when all human beings, men and women, are equally free, 'only in society and by the strictest equality'.[125] For Bakunin, liberty without equality means the slavery of the majority; equality without liberty means the despotism of the State and the unjust rule of a privileged class. Equality and liberty are therefore inextricably connected and confirm each other. It follows that the liberty of the individual 'far from halting as at a boundary before the liberty of others, finds there its confirmation and its extension to infinity; the illimitable liberty of each through the liberty of all, liberty by solidarity, liberty in equality . . .'[126] Bakunin correctly sees that liberty is meaningless unless people treat each other equally and have similar economic conditions in which to realize their potential.

Intimately connected with his notion of liberty is authority. Indeed, Bakunin defines liberty as an *'absolute rejection of any principle of authority'*.[127] Authority is the principal evil in the world: 'If there is a devil in human history, the devil is the principle of command. It alone, sustained by the ignorance and stupidity of the masses, without which it could not exist, is the source of all the catastrophes, all the crimes, and all the infamies of history.'[128] Since authority is the 'negation of freedom', Bakunin called for the revolt of the individual against all divine, collective and individual authority and repudiated both God and Master, the Church and the State.

But Bakunin was not so naive as to deny all power and authority at a stroke. All men possess a 'natural instinct for power' in the struggle for survival which is a basic law of life. This lust for power is however the most negative force in history and the best men amongst the oppressed necessarily become despots. Bakunin opposed power and authority precisely because they corrupt those who exercise them as much as those who are compelled to submit to them. No one therefore should be entrusted with power, inasmuch as 'anyone invested with authority must, through the force of an immutable social law, become an oppressor and exploiter of society'.[129]

Again, Bakunin may have rejected all imposed authority and usurped power in the form of the State and its laws, but he acknowledged that there was such a thing as the 'authority of society'. Indeed, the authority of society is 'incomparably more powerful than that of the State'. Where the State and the Church are transitory and artificial institutions, society will always exist. As a result, the action of social tyranny is 'gentler, more insidious, more imperceptible, but no less powerful and pervasive than is the authority of the State'. But while it is easier to rebel against the State than society around us, Bakunin is convinced that it is possible to go against the 'stream of conformity' and revolt against all divine, collective and individual authority in society.[130]

While this may be true of society, it is not of nature. Bakunin's political philosophy might well be an argument against 'the social institutionalization of authority', but he accepted 'natural' authority as legitimate and efficacious. As a determinist, he accepts the natural laws governing phenomena in the physical and social worlds. It is impossible to revolt against the authority of these laws, for 'Without them we would be nothing, *we simply would not exist.*'[131] Bakunin is not against all authority *per se*, but only against imposed external authority. Thus it makes sense to talk about a man being free if 'he obeys natural laws because he has *himself* recognized them as such, and not because they have been externally imposed upon him by an extrinsic will whatever, divine or human, collective or individual'.[132]

When it comes to the authority of knowledge, Bakunin is more circumspect. For special matters, he will consult the appropriate expert: 'In the matter of boots, I refer to the authority of the bootmaker; concerning houses, canals, or railroads, I consult that of the architect or engineer.'[133] But he will consult several and compare their opinions and choose what he thinks is most likely to achieve his desired end. Bakunin recognizes no infallible authority and will not allow anyone to impose their will upon him. Like Godwin, Bakunin believed that the right of private judgement is paramount, 'my human right which consists of refusing to obey any other man, and to determine my own acts in conformity with my convictions'.[134] Bakunin is thus ready to accept in general the 'absolute authority of science' because it is rational and in keeping with human liberty. But outside this legitimate authority, he declares all other authorities to be 'false, arbitrary and fatal'.[135]

But even in the special case of science Bakunin had his reservations. At a time when confidence in science to interpret the world and bring about progress was at its height, whether in the form of Comte's positivism or Marx's scientific socialism, Bakunin raised doubts about its universality. Science, he argued, cannot go outside the sphere of abstractions, and cannot grasp individuality or the concrete. For this reason, science is inferior to art which is 'the return of abstraction to life'. On the contrary, it is 'the perpetual immolation of life, fugitive, temporary, but real, on the altar of eternal abstractions'. Bakunin therefore preached the '*revolt of life against science*, or rather against the *government of science*'. Bakunin set out not to destroy science but rather to reform it and keep it within legitimate boundaries. It would be better for the people to dispense with science altogether than be governed by *savants*, for 'Life, not science, creates life; the spontaneous action of the people themselves alone can create liberty.'[136]

Bakunin is not simplistically anti-reason or anti-science, but is principally concerned with the authoritarian dangers of a scientific elite. Instead of science remaining the prerogative of a privileged few, he would like to see it spread amongst the masses so that it would represent the 'collective consciousness' of society.[137] Yet even when science is in the reach of all, men of genius should be allowed to devote themselves exclusively to the cultivation of the sciences.

Bakunin thus called for freedom both in its negative sense as freedom from imposed authority and in its positive sense as freedom to realize one's nature. The latter is most important in his philosophy and Bakunin remained enough of a Hegelian to see freedom primarily in terms of a state of wholeness in which all duality between the individual and society, between humanity and nature, is dialectically overcome. But it is as misleading to claim that he had a yearning to identify with 'a universal, omnipotent force' as it is to assert that individualism is 'the essence of Bakunin's social and political system and his opposition to Marx'.[138] In the final analysis, Bakunin recognized man as an individual as well as a social being, and asserted that the freedom of one can only be realized with the freedom of all. Collective liberty and prosperity, he asserts, exist only in so far as they represent 'the sum of individual liberties and prosperities'.[139] At the same time, he stressed the need for human solidarity and international associations. More than any other classic anarchist thinker Bakunin perceived that personal and social freedom are intertwined and that they can only be grounded in a form of communal individuality.

Bakunin was never a consistent or systematic thinker, but he was a powerful thinker nonetheless. After his conversion from German idealism to historical materialism he tried to give his abstract definition of liberty a social and natural dimension. He saw the intimate connection between liberty and authority and recognized natural and social boundaries to liberty. His notion of freedom is a form of collective self-discipline within the inescapable boundaries of nature and society. It was not so much a case of exerting 'maximum authority' over the conditions of one's life, but rather of accepting the context of freedom.[140] Far from offering a theory of liberty based on a 'hotchpotch of empty rhetoric' or 'glib Hegelian claptrap', Bakunin's position is both realistic and plausible.[141]

The State

The supreme case of illegitimate and imposed authority for Bakunin is the State. It is an artificial growth which negates individual liberties. All States are by their very nature oppressive since they crush the spontaneous life of the people: 'The State is like a vast slaughterhouse or an enormous cemetery, where all the real aspirations, all the living forces of a country enter generously and happily, in the shadow of that abstraction, to let themselves be slain and buried.'[142] With it comes economic centralization and the concentration of political power which inevitably destroy the spontaneous action of the people.

All Bakunin's mature writings are devoted to showing how the State is hostile to a free existence. He never tires of asserting that the State means domination: 'If there is a State, there must be domination of one class by another and, as result, slavery; the State without slavery is unthinkable – and this is why we are enemies of the State.'[143]

Bakunin further develops his critique by arguing that the modern State is by its very nature a military State and 'every military State must of necessity become a conquering, invasive State; to survive it must conquer or be conquered, for the simple reason that accumulated military power will suffocate if it does not find an outlet.'[144] Bakunin concludes that

> The State denotes violence, oppression, exploitation, and injustice raised into a system and made into the cornerstone of the existence of any society. The State never had and never will have any morality. Its morality and only justice is the supreme interest of self-preservation and almighty power – an interest before which all humanity has to kneel in worship. The State is the complete negation of humanity, a double negation: the opposite of human freedom and justice, and the violent breach of the universal solidarity of the human race.[145]

Bakunin traces the origin of the State to a mutual understanding between exploiters who then used religion to help them in the 'systematic organization of the masses called the State'. It is only in this sense that 'The State is the younger brother of the Church'. Like Marx, he sees class struggle as inevitable in society between the privileged classes and the working classes, and the former will always control 'the power of the State' in order to maintain and enjoy their privileges.[146] Political power and wealth are therefore inseparable. But unlike Marx, he sees nothing but harm resulting from the conquest of political power by the workers.

The liberal defence of the State which portrays it as the guarantor and protector of political rights holds little water for Bakunin since he is convinced that the State will always be controlled by an exploitative and oppressive elite. He makes clear that 'right' in the language of politics is 'nothing but the consecration of fact created by force'. To call for 'equality of rights' therefore implies a flagrant contradiction for where all equally enjoy human rights, all political rights are automatically dissolved. The same is true of a so-called 'democratic State'. The State and political law denote 'power, authority, domination: they presuppose inequality in fact'.[147] Even in the most radical political democracy, as in Switzerland in his own day, the bourgeoisie still governs.

Although many workers believed at the time that once universal suffrage was established, political liberty would be assured, it inevitably leads, according to Bakunin, to the collapse or demoralization of the radical party. The whole system of representative government is an immense fraud since it rests on the fiction that executive and legislative bodies elected by universal suffrage represent the will of the people. Irrespective of their democratic sentiments, all rulers are corrupted by their participation in government and begin to look down upon society as sovereigns regarding their subjects: 'Political power means domination. And where there is domination, there must be a substantial part of the population who remain subjected to the domination of their rulers.' Even if a government composed exclusively of workers were elected by universal suffrage, they would become tomorrow 'the most determined aristocrats, open or secret worshippers of the principle of authority, exploiters and oppressors'. They would rapidly lose their revolutionary will. It follows that representative government is 'a system of hypocrisy and perpetual falsehood. Its success rests on the stupidity of the people and the corruption of the public mind.'[148]

Bakunin was opposed to universal suffrage because he felt that it would not fundamentally change the distribution of power and wealth. Whereas Marx believed that universal suffrage could eventually lead to communism, Bakunin quoted Proudhon approvingly to the effect that '*Universal suffrage is the counter-revolution*'.[149] Nevertheless, Bakunin was never dogmatic about general principles, and while he was in theory a determined abstentionist from politics, in the particular circumstances of Italy and Spain at the time of the Paris Commune, he advised members of his Alliance to become deputies or help the socialist parties. He held that the most imperfect republic would always be preferable to the most enlightened monarchy.

Bakunin not only distinguished between different kinds of States, but also between the State and government. Every revolutionary government represents the principle of the minority rule over the majority in the name of the alleged 'stupidity' of the latter. But it is impossible for such a dictatorship of the minority to bring about the freedom of the people since it only perpetuates itself and enslaves the people. In one of his resounding aphorisms, Bakunin declares: 'Freedom can be created only by freedom, by a total rebellion of the people, and by a voluntary organization of the people from the bottom up.'[150] A People's State even in a transitional period is therefore an absurd contradiction in terms: 'If their State is effectively a popular State, why should they dissolve it? If on the other hand its suppression is necessary for the real emancipation of the people, why then call it a popular State?'[151]

The issue of revolutionary government in the form of the dictatorship of the proletariat was the principal source of conflict between the 'revolutionary socialists' or anarchists in Bakunin's Alliance and the 'authoritarian communists' who followed Marx. As Bakunin acknowledged, their ultimate aim was similar – to create a new social order based on the collective organization of labour and the collective ownership of the means of production. But where the communists looked to the development of the political power of the working classes, especially the urban proletariat in alliance with bourgeois radicals, the anarchists believed that they could succeed only through 'the development and organization of the non-political or antipolitical social power of the working classes in city and country, including all men of goodwill from the upper classes'.[152]

This led to a fundamental divergence in tactics. The communists wanted to organize the workers in order to seize the political power of the State, while the anarchists wished to liquidate the State. The former advocated the principle and practice of authority; the latter put their faith in liberty. Both equally favoured science, but the communists wanted to impose it by force, while the anarchists sought to propagate it so that groups could organize themselves spontaneously and in keeping with their own interests. Above all the anarchists believed that 'mankind has far too long submitted to being governed; that the cause of its troubles does not lie in any particular form of government but in the fundamental principles and the very existence of government, whatever form it may take'.[153] Bakunin concludes that the people were therefore left with a simple choice: 'the State, on one hand, and social revolution, on the other hand, are the two opposite poles, the antagonism which constitutes the very essence of the genuine social life of the whole continent of Europe'. And in one of his famous maxims, Bakunin insists that *'freedom without Socialism is privilege and injustice, and Socialism without freedom is slavery and brutality'*.[154]

Free Society

Bakunin did not provide any detailed sketch of a free society and only elaborated its most general principles of voluntary association and free federation. Indeed, he singled out for criticism 'all those modern Procrusteans who, in one way or another, have created an ideal of social organization, a narrow mould into which they would force future generations'. He insisted however that there is no middle path between rigorously consistent federalism and bureaucratic government. The future social organization should be carried out 'from the bottom up, by the free associations, then going on to the communes, the regions, the nations, and, finally, culminating in a great international and universal federation'.[155] Land would be appropriated by agricultural associations and capital and the means of production by industrial associations.

Such communes would have little in common with existing rural communes. Bakunin was particularly critical of the Russian *mir* or peasant commune. Although the Russian peasants felt that the land belonged to the community and were hostile to the State, they were weakened by paternalism, which made the family patriarch a slave and a despot; by confidence in the Tsar, which followed from the patriarchal tradition; and by the absorption of the individual into the community.

By contrast, the new commune in an emancipated society would consist of a voluntary association of free and equal individuals of both sexes. Unlike Proudhon, who extended his anarchist principles to only half the human species, Bakunin insists on the complete emancipation of women and their social equality with men. Perfect freedom can only exist with complete economic and social equality: 'I am free only when all human beings surrounding me – men and women – are equally free. The freedom of others, far from limiting or negating my liberty, is on the contrary its necessary condition and confirmation.' Every person would be personally free in that he or she would not surrender his or her thought or will to any authority but that of reason. They would be 'free collectively', that is by living among free people. Thus freedom involves the development of solidarity. Such a society would be a moral society, for socialism is justice and the basic principle of socialism is *that every human being should have the material and moral means to develop his humanity*.[156]

Human relations would be transformed. With the abolition of the patriarchal family, marriage law and the right of inheritance, men and women would live in free unions more closely united to each other than before. The upbringing and education of children would be entrusted to the mother but remain mainly the concern of society. Indeed, an integral 'equal education for all' is an indispensable condition for the emancipation of humanity. Such a system of education would not only eradicate existing differences, but prepare every child of either sex for a life of thought and work, imbibe him or her with 'socialist morality', and encourage respect for the freedom of others which is the 'highest duty'. Children cannot, however, choose not to be educated or to remain idle.

Bakunin lays down the law here: '*Everyone shall work, and everyone shall be educated*', whether they like it or not. No one will be able to exploit the labour of others. Every one will have to work in order to live, for 'social and political rights will have only one basis – the labour contributed by everyone'. Without the use of positive law, the pressure of public opinion should make 'parasites' impossible, but exceptional cases of idleness would be regarded 'as special maladies to be subjected to clinical treatment'.[157] Such authoritarian statements open up a potential world of tyranny and oppression in Bakunin's so-called free society.

Revolutionary Strategy

Bakunin is not only prepared to establish an invisible dictatorship but also to employ widespread revolutionary violence. Bakunin is quite frank about the issue: 'Revolution, the overthrow of the State means war, and that implies the destruction of men and things.' Although he regrets it, he insists that 'Philosophers have not understood that against political forces there can be no guarantees but complete destruction.' At the same time, he argues that terrorism is alien to a genuine social revolution; it should not be directed against individuals who are merely the inevitable products of society and history. Once the 'hurricane' has passed, true socialists should oppose 'butchery in cold blood'.[158]

Bakunin further recommended certain forms of economic struggle, such as organizing strikes which train workers for the ultimate struggle. While not opposed to workers' co-operatives, he pointed out that they cannot fundamentally change society, cannot compete with big capital, and, if they are successful, they must result in a drop in wages as well as prices. As to the agents of change, Bakunin consistently called for an alliance between peasants and industrial workers. Although the city workers might take the initiative in the revolutionary movement, they should not underestimate the revolutionary potential of the peasantry and should try to win their support.

Even while elaborating his mature political philosophy, Bakunin was never one to rest in theory. He constantly searched for opportunities to put his ideas into practice, or at least have them confirmed by experience. The failure of the Lyon rising of 1870 in which he had participated left him with little confidence in the triumph of the social revolution, but the great social upheaval of the Paris Commune which followed shortly after from March to May in 1871 raised his hopes once again. Although the majority were Jacobins calling for a revolutionary government and centralized State, many of the communards were Proudhonians, and the most active members of the committee of the twentieth *arrondissement* and the central committee of the National Guard were followers of Bakunin. Not surprisingly, Bakunin welcomed the Paris Commune as a striking and practical demonstration of his beliefs and called it 'a bold, clearly formulated negation of the State'. On its defeat, he wrote: 'Paris, drenched in the blood of her noblest children – this is humanity itself, crucified by the united international reaction of Europe'.[159]

When Mazzini attacked the International for being anti-nationalist, decried the Commune for being atheistic, and declared that the State is ordained by God, Bakunin immediately took up his pen and wrote hundreds of pages against Mazzini. He defended his own version of atheism and materialism in a pamphlet entitled *The Response of an Internationalist*, which was followed up with a second pamphlet called *The Political Theology of Mazzini*. Bakunin respected Mazzini as 'incontestably one the noblest and purest personalities' of the century and preferred him to Marx, but criticized him as 'the last high priest of an obsolescent religious, metaphysical and political idealism'.[160] The pamphlets helped to extend the International in

Italy and ensured that anarchism took firm root amongst the Italian working class.

Marx himself saw in the federalist programme of the communards a 'self-government of producers' and described it as 'the political form at last discovered under which the economic emancipation of work could be realized'.[161] Engels went on to call it the first demonstration of the 'Dictatorship of the Proletariat'. It is an irony of history that both Marx, Engels and Lenin all should hail the Paris Commune as a model of the proletarian revolution, while its attempt to abolish the machinery of the State at a stroke was clearly more in accord with the anarchist and federalist ideas of Proudhon and Bakunin.

Their common praise for the Commune did not prevent a new row breaking out between Marx and Bakunin in the International soon after. The defeat of the Paris Commune prevented the congress from taking place in Paris in 1871, and at the conference which was held in London the supporters of Bakunin from the Jurassian Federation were not invited. The two previous congresses had avoided any philosophical and political principles and merely asserted that 'the economic emancipation of the workers in the great aim to which must be subordinated every political movement'. Without the Bakuninist opposition, Marx now was able to get accepted the conquest of political power as an integral part of the obligatory programme of the International.

In addition, according to Bakunin, he managed to establish 'the dictatorship of the General Council, that is, the personal dictatorship of Marx, and consequently the transformation of the International into an immense and monstrous State with himself as chief'. What Marx proposed with his scientific socialism, Bakunin wrote, was 'the organization and the rule of the new society by socialist *savants*... the worst of all despotic governments!'[162]

For his part, Marx wrote in November 1871 that Bakunin was ' a man devoid of all theoretical knowledge' and wanted to make his 'children's primer' of a programme the propaganda of his 'second *International within the International*'. His doctrine moreover was a secondary matter – 'merely means to his own personal self-assertion'.[163] Engels also wrote that Bakunin's 'peculiar theory' was a medley of Proudhonism and communism. He saw the State as the main evil to be abolished, maintaining that it is the State which has created capital; hence his strategy of complete abstention from politics and his wish to replace the State with the organization of the International. For Marx and Engels, however, Bakunin had got it the wrong way round. To abolish the State without a previous social revolution is nonsense since 'the abolition of capital *is* precisely the social revolution'.[164]

The final battle took place at the Congress of the International held at the Hague in September 1872. Marx attended in person for the first time.

He alleged with Engels in a note on Bakunin's secret Alliance to the General Council that 'these intransigent defenders of openness and publicity have, in contempt of our statutes, organized in the bosom of the International a real secret society with the aim of placing its sections, without their knowledge, under the direction of the high priest Bakunin.'[165] They accused him of founding with Nechaev a secret society in Russia and produced the latter's threatening letter to the publisher's agent who had commissioned the translation of *Capital*. They also claimed that he had tried to control his Alliance groups in France, Spain and Italy. Paul Lafargue, Marx's Cuban son-in-law, was the principal source of their information.

At the Congress, Bakunin and his closest collaborator James Guillaume were expelled from the International. The headquarters were then moved to New York to save it from the control of the non-Marxist majority but it soon collapsed. Engels went on to write in an essay 'On Authority' that it is impossible to have any organization without authority since modern technology imposes upon men 'a veritable despotism independent of all social organisation'. It is absurd to want to abolish political authority in the form of the State at a stroke for a 'revolution is certainly the most authoritarian thing there is; it is the act whereby one part of the population imposes its will upon the other.'[166]

The anarchists set up in 1872 a new International at St Imier in Switzerland (with delegates from the Jura, Italy and Spain) as a loose association of fully autonomous national groups devoted to the economic struggle only. Its programme as outlined by Bakunin formed the basis of revolutionary syndicalism: '*the organization of solidarity in the economic struggle of labour against capitalism*'.[167]

While the tactics of character assassination employed by the Marxist camp, reviving claims that Bakunin was a Russian spy and unscrupulous with money, were contemptible, it is difficult to refute the main thrust of their accusation. At the height of his campaign against Marx's centralism and authoritarianism, Bakunin undoubtedly tried to establish a secret, centralized and hierarchical organization with the intention of directing the International. In a letter to his Spanish followers, he described the Alliance as 'a secret society which has been formed in the very bosom of the International in order to give the latter a revolutionary organization, to turn it ... into a force sufficiently organized to exterminate all the political-clerical-bourgeois reaction and destroy all the economic, legal, religious and political institutions of the state'.[168] The Alliance, as Guillaume asserted, might have been principally an 'informal revolutionary fraternity', held together by affinity rather than a rule-book, but they undoubtedly formed a secret network of cells within the International.[169] The anarchist historian Max Nettlau admitted that the Alliance was a 'secret society so to speak'.[170] Arthur Lehning, former editor of the Bakunin Archives, on the other hand insisted that the secret Alliance did not exist within the International, although he recognized that it may have been 'reconstructed in one form or another' after 1869.[171] But even if Bakunin's secret societies remained vague and unreal (in the sense that they did not have a coherent existence) they were still central to his notion of anarchist strategy.

Bakunin tried to justify his position and vented his anger against Marx and his followers in a letter to the Brussels paper *La Liberté* which was never sent. He reiterated his belief that the revolutionary policy of the proletariat should be the destruction of the State for its immediate and only goal. The Marxists on the other hand remained devoted Statists: 'As befits good Germans, they are worshippers of the power of the State, and are necessarily also the prophets of political and social discipline, champions of the social order built from the top down.'[172]

He also qualified Marx's economic determinism. He had long argued that facts come before ideas. He followed Proudhon, by claiming that the ideal is a flower whose root lies in the material conditions of existence, and Marx, by asserting that 'the whole history of humanity, intellectual and moral, political and social, is but a reflection of its economic history.'[173] Now he argued that while the economic base determines the political superstructure, the superstructure can in turn influence the base. According to Bakunin, Marx says: '" Poverty produces political slavery, the State." But he does not allow this expression to be turned around, to say: "Political slavery, the State, reproduces in its turn and maintains poverty as a necessary condition for its own existence; so that to destroy poverty, it is necessary to destroy the State!" '[174] And while recognizing the inevitable linking of economic and political facts in history, Bakunin refused to accept as Marx did that all events in the past were necessarily progressive, particularly if they revealed themselves to be in contradiction to the 'supreme end' of history which is nothing less than '*the triumph of humanity, the most complete conquest and establishment of personal freedom and development – material, intellectual, and moral – for every individual, through the absolutely unrestricted and spontaneous organization of economic and social solidarity*'.[175]

Bakunin further qualified Marx's version of historical materialism by stressing the importance in history of the particular character of each race, people, and nation. He claimed, for instance, that the spirit of revolt is an instinct found in more intense form in the Latin and Slav peoples than in the German. He also felt that patriotism, love of the fatherland, is a natural passion – a passion of social solidarity. It involves an instinctive attachment to a traditional pattern of life, and hostility towards any other kind of life. It is thus 'collective egoism on one hand, and war on the other'. Its roots are in man's 'bestiality' and it exists in inverse ratio to the development of civilization. Again nationality, like individuality, is a natural and social fact, but it should be imbued with universal values. In the final analysis, we should place 'human, universal justice above national interests'. Bakunin therefore recommends a form of 'proletarian patriotism' which takes into account local attachments but which is internationalist in scope.[176]

Finally, Bakunin rejected Marx's designation of the urban proletariat as the most progressive and revolutionary class since it implied the rule of the factory workers over the 'rural proletariat'. To consider the city proletariat as the vanguard class is a form of 'aristocracy of labour' which is the least social and the most individualist in character. On the contrary, Bakunin considers the *'flower of the proletariat'* to be the most oppressed, poorest and alienated whom Marx contemptuously dismissed as the *'lumpenproletariat'*. 'I have in mind', he wrote, 'the "riffraff", that "rabble" almost unpolluted by bourgeois civilization, which carries in its inner being and in its aspirations, in all the necessities and miseries of its collective life, all the seeds of the socialism of the future . . .'[177] Just as Marx idealized the proletariat, so Bakunin romanticized the lumpenproletariat.

In the last years of life, Bakunin grew increasingly pessimistic about the triumph of the social revolution. The Franco-Prussian war had not led to revolution in Europe and his attempts to foment rebellion in Russia achieved little. By 1872, his hopes for the political consciousness and spirit of revolt of the masses were at a nadir:

> Alas! It must be acknowledged that the masses have allowed themselves to become deeply demoralized, apathetic, not to say castrated, by the pernicious influence of our corrupt, centralized, statist civilization. Bewildered, debased, they have contracted the fatal habit of obedience, of sheepish resignation. They have been turned into an immense herd, artificially segregated and divided into cages for the greater convenience of their various exploiters.[178]

By now Bakunin was prematurely old, his health ruined by his years in Russian prisons and by a precarious life of incessant movement. In a letter dated 26 September 1873, he announced his retirement as a professional revolutionary:

> I feel I no longer possess either the necessary strength or perhaps the necessary faith to continue rolling the stone of Sisyphus against the forces of reaction which are triumphing everywhere. I am therefore retiring from the lists, and ask if my dear contemporaries only one thing – oblivion.[179]

With the help of his Italian comrade Carlo Cafiero a house was bought for him and his family near Locarno but peace still eluded him. The house proved too expensive and Bakunin was obliged to move on and spend the last two years of his life in Lugano. The sap of the old revolutionary could still rise however: he came out of retirement to join a final abortive insurrection in the province of Bologna in May 1874. It left him even more disillusioned, and in February 1875 he wrote to the anarchist geographer Elisée Reclus of his 'intense despair' since there was 'absolutely no revolutionary thought, hope, or passion left among the masses'. The only hope remaining was world war. 'These gigantic military states must sooner or later destroy each other. But what a prospect!'[180] The crumbling colossus, who had exhausted himself in the sisyphean task of inspiring a world revolution, eventually died in Berne on 1 July 1876, just before his sixty-second birthday. He was buried in the city.

But Bakunin's life and work were not in vain. While Marx may have won the initial dispute within the International subsequent events have tended to prove the validity of Bakunin's warnings about centralism, State socialism, and the dictatorship of the proletariat. He had prophetic insight into the nature of Communist States which have all become to varying degrees centralized, bureaucratic and militaristic, ruled by a largely self-appointed and self-reproducing elite. The string of Marxist regimes in Eastern Europe were overthrown in the 1980s by a mass display of the Popular Will, and progressive forces in the former Soviet Union are calling for a loose federation of independent republics. Bakunin, not Marx, has been vindicated by the verdict of history.

Soviet scholars liked to compare Bakunin's notion of invisible dictators with Lenin's concept of a disciplined elite of committed revolutionaries and saw it as a 'great step forward' in theoretical terms.[181] He certainly called like Lenin for violent revolution and shared a faith in a secret vanguard controlled by himself. But it is Bakunin's critique of Marxism which has been most remembered in the West. While the historical controversy between anarchists and Marxists has tended to exaggerate the differences between Bakunin and Marx, in fact they both adopted a form of historical materialism, accepted class struggle as the motor of social change, and saw the goal of history as a free and equal society. They both wanted the collective ownership of the means of production.

Their principal difference lay in strategy. Bakunin rejected parliamentary politics, called for the immediate destruction of the State, and insisted that the workers and peasants should emancipate themselves. Marx on the other hand dismissed as 'nonsense' his belief in the 'free organization of the working class from below upwards'.[182] Where Marx despised the peasantry as rural idiots and the lumpenproletariat as riffraff, Bakunin recognized their revolutionary potential. To Marx's call for the conquest of political power, Bakunin opposed economic emancipation first and foremost. Bakunin further tempered Marx's determinism by stressing the role of the people's spontaneous will in bringing about revolution.

Beyond their theoretical differences, Bakunin and Marx became symbols of different world-views. Bakunin is usually presented as the more attractive personality – generous and spontaneous, the embodiment of a 'free spirit'.[183] Bakunin was the more impetuous and Marx doubtlessly envied him for his ability to charm and influence others. Bakunin possessed what he admired most in others: 'that troublesome and savage energy characteristic of the grandest geniuses, ever called to destroy old tottering worlds and lay the foundations of new.'[184] Yet for all his turbulent eccentricities and contradictions, he was invariably kind, considerate and gentle with his friends.

Among the most disconcerting of the contradictions which characterized Bakunin as man and writer was that while he called for the equality of all humanity, he remained sufficiently nationalist and racist to see Germans and Jews as authoritarian, and Slavs as spontaneous and freedom-loving. His call for absolute liberty is counterbalanced by his authoritarian desire to lead and control other people in his secret societies. His eloquent advocacy of social harmony and peace was matched by his ferocious celebration of 'evil passions', 'blood and fire', 'complete annihilation', 'storm of destruction', the 'furious avalanche, devouring, destroying everything' and so on.[185] It comes as no surprise to learn that he advised Wagner to repeat in his music the same text in various melodies: 'Struggle and Destruction'.[186] It is difficult not to conclude that Bakunin's apocalyptic fantasies owed something to his sexual impotence.

Although he did not have a belief in the virtue of violence for its own sake, and 'a confidence in the technique of terrorism', there is something profoundly sinister in his celebration of the 'poetry of destruction'.[187] Bakunin stands at the fountainhead of a minor tradition of destructive and violent anarchism which prefers the gun to reason, coercion to persuasion. He confirms the popular view of anarchy as tumult and violent disorder in his indiscriminate use of the term 'anarchy' to describe both the violent and chaotic process of revolt and the goal of an ordered society without government. Indeed, by identifying anarchy with civil war and destruction, Bakunin is the shadow behind the later bomb-throwers and assassins who shook bourgeois society towards the end of the nineteenth century.

Bakunin's call for an invisible dictatorship and his belief in the importance of secret societies and small vanguard groups of militants are inescapably fraught with authoritarian and oppressive dangers. There is a fundamental contradiction between his awareness that 'Freedom can be created only by freedom' and his readiness to use a dictatorship in order to achieve 'absolute liberty'.[188] He dismally failed to realize that only libertarian means can be used to achieve libertarian ends. That the 'passionate seeker after Truth' and the 'fanatical lover of Liberty' should resort to dissimulation and fraud rather than reasoned argument and free choice in open association inevitably undermines his personal authenticity and moral example.[189] He was so thoroughly corrupted by the love of power that he singularly failed to see that the dangers he described in Marx's revolutionary dictatorship were equally applicable in his own.[190] Although his aim was to transform the instincts of people into conscious demands, there is no reason to think that his vanguard would wither away any more than Marx's.

Although not a great political philosopher, Bakunin nevertheless made a major contribution to anarchist and socialist theory. Far from being 'intellectually shallow and built on clichés', Bakunin's anarchism broke new ground and pointed the way for others to follow.[191] He was the first Russian to preach social revolution in international terms. In his analysis of the State, he anticipated Max Weber who saw bureaucracy as an inevitable consequence of the modern division of labour, and Robert Michels, whose 'iron law of oligarchy' asserts that an elite of technical experts will emerge from any political organization. In his concept of class, his stress on the revolutionary potential of the peasantry has been confirmed by all the major revolutions this century in Russia, Spain, China, and Cuba. His faith in the revolutionary potential of the 'lumpenproletariat' has become an essential part of the ideological baggage of the New Left. His critique of the authoritarian dangers of science and of scientific elites has been further developed by the Frankfurt School, notably Herbert Marcuse. During the 1968 rebellion in Paris, Bakuninist slogans reappeared on city walls: 'The urge to destroy is a creative urge.' It is Bakunin, not Marx, who was the true prophet of modern revolution.[192]

In the long run, the best image of Bakunin is not that of the revolutionary on the barricades calling for the bloody overthrow of Church and State, but the penetrating thinker who elaborated reasoned arguments for a free society based on voluntary federation of autonomous communes. His message, the message of the First International, was that the emancipation of the workers must be the task of the workers themselves. His historical importance was to have helped spread the ideas of anarchism amongst the working-class movement in the latter part of the nineteenth century. His influence, especially in France, Italy, Spain and Latin America, ensured that anarchism became a significant, if not dominating, influence amongst their labour movements well into the following century. The ideological roots of the Spanish Revolution reach deeply in Bakuninian soil, both in the libertarian aspirations of the anarchists as well as in the readiness of some to resort to aggressive vanguard organizations.

Since the Second World War, there has been a renewed interest in

Bakunin, not only from the students' movements in the sixties but from intellectuals like Noam Chomsky. Bakunin's cult of spontaneity, his celebration of revolutionary will and instinctive rebellion, his advocacy of workers' control, his faith in the creative energies of the people, his critique of science – all have appealed to the rebellious young in modern technological States. Even Che Guevara was hailed as the 'new Bakunin'. Bakunin's search for wholeness in a divided society is not merely the product of a diseased form of romanticism or an unbalanced psyche, but rather a bold and inspiring attempt to reclaim one's humanity in an alienated world.

19

Peter Kropotkin

The Revolutionary Evolutionist

KROPOTKIN IS BEST KNOWN as a geographer, the author of *Mutual Aid*, and one of the leading Russian revolutionaries. He is the most systematic and profound anarchist thinker of the nineteenth century. He attempted to ground anarchism in science and argued that it was in keeping with existing tendencies within nature and society. Above all, he developed anarchist theory in a communist direction and gave it a philosophical respectability at a time when it was increasingly being associated in the popular press with mindless terrorism.

Peter Kropotkin was born in 1842 into a family in the highest rank of Russian aristocracy under the autocratic tsarship of Nicholas I. His father was an officer in the imperial army, and the owner of a large house in Moscow and an estate with twelve hundred serfs in the province of Kaluga some one hundred and sixty miles away. Peter had little time for his father who ordered his serfs to be flogged, married them against their will, and sent them away into the army as a punishment; he even questioned whether the serfs were really 'people'.[1] According to his closest brother Alexander, their father was 'nasty, revengeful, obstinate and mean', and a cheat to boot.[2] They greatly preferred their mother whose romantic tastes they imbibed. She may well have encouraged Peter's optimistic frame of mind which at times could be almost fatalistic in its confidence in progress. She might also have been responsible for his later exaggerated reverence for women. Unfortunately, she died young, and her son never got on well with his 'cursed stepmother'.[3]

Peter found solace in the countryside which fired his ambition to become a geographer. He was fortunate enough to have a good tutor who encouraged his enquiring mind. Attending a Muscovite ball Nicholas I noticed the young Kropotkin and had him enrolled at the Corps of Pages, the most select military academy in Russia. He read widely in his spare time in literature and philosophy, including Voltaire and Kant, and his interest in science, especially astronomy, led him to find inspiration not in God but in nature:

> The never-ceasing life of the universe, which I conceived as *life* and evolution, became for me an inexhaustible source of higher poetical thought, and gradually the sense of Man's oneness with Nature, both animate and inanimate – the poetry of nature – became the philosophy of my life.[4]

At this time he also visited different factories in Moscow and appreciated the 'poetry of the machine' and the pleasure a person may derive from their use.

Kropotkin did so well at the military academy that he was nominated sergeant of the Corps of Pages, and became the personal *page de chambre* of the new Tsar Alexander II. At first, Kropotkin was deeply impressed by the Emperor and regarded him as a sort of hero for liberating the serfs in 1861, but the growing brutality of his regime, especially his crushing of the Polish rebellion of 1863, eventually made him distrust court politics and governments in general. At the same, he had also been impressed by Alexander Herzen's magazine *The Pole Star*, whose cover represented the heads of the five 'Decembrists' whom Nicholas I had hanged after the rebellion of 14 December 1825, and whose contents brought Kropotkin into contact with the powerful radical tradition in Russia. Soon after he began editing for his classmates his first revolutionary paper which advocated a liberal constitution for Russia.

On leaving the military academy, Kropotkin spent the next five years in a Cossack regiment as a military administrator in eastern Siberia. The post allowed him to explore the region which he did with great alacrity. It taught him how little a person really needs as soon as he leaves the circle of conventional civilization. His researches formed the foundation of his later reputation as a geographer and enabled him eventually to elaborate his major contribution to the subject: that the structural lines of Asia run diagonally. His close observations of the behaviour of animals led him to revise Darwin's theory and insist that co-operation is the most important factor in evolution. Above all, his contact with the peasants and their communities gave him a lasting faith in the solidarity and the creative spontaneity of the people. He enjoyed the feeling of simplicity and natural relations of equality, as well as of 'hearty goodwill' amongst the peasants.[5]

The years in Siberia were crucial for Kropotkin in other ways. They taught him the impossibility of doing anything really useful for the mass of the people by means of the 'administrative machine'. He came to share Tolstoy's view about leaders and masses and began to appreciate the difference between acting on the principle of command and discipline and that of common understanding. Living with the peasants and seeing at work the complex forms of their social organization stored up 'floods of light' illuminated by his subsequent reading. In short, as he wrote later in his memoirs, 'I lost in Siberia whatever faith in State discipline I had cherished before. I was prepared to become an anarchist.'6

Kropotkin returned to the capital St Petersburg in 1867 to study mathematics whilst acting as a secretary to the Geographical Society. He continued his scientific researches, but in 1871, he received news of the Paris Commune. For all its defects, its example inspired his hopes for European revolution, and he later called the Commune the 'precursor of a great social revolution – the starting-point for future revolutions'.7 But while Paris was in flames, Kropotkin set off again to explore the glacial deposits in Sweden and Finland. He concluded correctly that the ice cap had once covered the whole of Northern Europe and that Eurasia had undergone a long process of desertification.

In the following year, he visited Western Europe for the first time. In Switzerland, he met amongst the watchmakers of the Jura members of the libertarian wing of the First International (called federalists at the time). He became particularly friendly with James Guillaume, Bakunin's friend, the uncompromising editor of the *Bulletin of the Jurassian Federation*. Guillaume saw in the Paris Commune a 'federalist revolution', opening the way to 'a true state of anarchy, in the proper sense of the word'.8

The Jurassian federation was inspired by Bakunin who was felt not so much as an intellectual authority but as a moral personality. Kropotkin later recognized that Bakunin had established the leading principles of modern anarchism by proclaiming the abolition of the State and despite his collectivist statements was 'at heart a communist'.9

Bakunin and the libertarian delegates were deeply involved in a dispute with the general council controlled by Marx. The council was not content to be merely a correspondence bureau but wanted to direct the movement and participate in parliamentary elections. Kropotkin later claimed that the dispute fired the 'first spark of anarchism' since it set people thinking about the evils of government, however democratic in origin.10 He recalled later: 'when I came away from the mountains, after a week's stay with the watchmakers, my views upon socialism were settled. I was an anarchist.'11

On his return to St Petersburg, Kropotkin became involved in radical politics which had been stimulated by the nihilists and the *narodniks*. The nihilists had influenced the whole life of the educated classes of Russia. They had attacked the conventions of civilization and tried to transform the customs of everyday life. They refused to bend to any authority and analysed all existing institutions in the sole light of their reason. Kropotkin had been impressed by them and felt that nihilism 'with its affirmation of the rights of the individual and its negation of all hypocrisy' was the first step toward a higher type of man and woman.[12]

The *narodniks* in the early sixties had developed out of the nihilist movement and went to live with and educate the people (*narod*). Adopting a mixture of revolutionary populism and philosophical materialism, they called for a new society based on a voluntary association of producers on the lines of the traditional Russian *mir* or village commune.

Kropotkin soon began to move in the Chaikovsky Circle, the most revolutionary populist organization of the day. He stayed with them for two years. He later recalled that he was 'in a family of men and women so closely united in their common object, so broadly and delicately humane in their mutual relations', that there was not a single moment of even temporary friction marring the life of the circle.[13] Although they certainly formed a close-knit affinity group, Kropotkin may have exaggerated their unity. His friend Sergei Kravchinksy, for instance, felt at the time that Kropotkin was 'too exclusive and rigid in his theoretical convictions', admitting no departure from his 'ultra-anarchical program'.[14]

The majority of the circle were for non-militant agitation, but Kropotkin advocated peasant uprisings and the seizure of land and property. He contributed in November 1873 a lengthy manifesto entitled *Must We Occupy Ourselves with an Examination of the Ideal of a Future System?* It was his first major political statement and shows that many of his fundamental ideas were already formed. Like Proudhon and Bakunin, he calls for the ownership of the land and factories by the producers themselves in village communities. All should work and education should be universal, combining mental and manual skills. All these arguments, Kropotkin claims, lead to 'the idea of the harmfulness of any central authority and consequently, to anarchy'.[15] He therefore urges that a society be organized without government. This can only be achieved by a complete social revolution conducted by workers and peasants themselves. In the mean time populist agitators should spread their ideas, form a common organization, and go to the people. The only difference with his later communist position is that Kropotkin still retains like Proudhon a scheme of labour cheques in place of money.

Kropotkin's subversive activities were suddenly brought to a halt by his arrest in March 1874. He was condemned, whilst a trial was being prepared, to solitary confinement in the dreaded Peter and Paul fortress, without sunlight in his cell and only half an hour's exercise a day. He was allowed books however and continued his scientific enquiries. Despite his natural cheerfulness and careful exercising, he eventually caught scurvy and grew increasingly depressed. The experience left him a permanent hatred of prisons and confirmed his belief that punishment is never a suitable means of reforming conduct.

After three years of imprisonment, Kropotkin made a daring and dramatic escape from a prison hospital with the help of his friends in 1876. He left for Scotland and then England, determined to throw in his lot with the workers and to help develop the ideals and principles underlying the coming revolution, 'not as an order coming from their leaders, but as a result of their own reason; and so to awaken their initiative'.[16] In the following year, he returned to Switzerland to join the anarchist watchmakers of the Jurassian Federation with whom he felt so much at home.

Kropotkin spent all his energy during the next five years in the anarchist cause, helping to set up the journal *Le Révolté* in 1879 in which many of his most incisive articles first appeared, and encouraging both collective and individual acts of revolt which might trigger off a revolution. At this stage, he also saw the value of strikes, which might conceivably be transformed into an insurrection. Proscribed by the government for its anti-military propaganda, *Le Révolté* reappeared under the name *La Révolte*. Kropotkin and his comrades helped keep alive the anarchist idea during the difficult years following the defeat of the Paris Commune and the collapse of the First International to the early 1880s when the French movement started to grow again.[17] The defeat of the Paris Commune, which ended in the slaughter of twenty-five thousand communards, and saw fourteen thousand more incarcerated, five thousand deported and thousands more driven into exile, meant that a decade would pass before the devastated anarchist movement could pick up momentum again.

The great French geographer and anarchist Elisée Reclus edited many of Kropotkin's articles of this period, including the collection *Paroles d'un révolté* which was published in Paris in 1885 (and translated into Italian by the socialist Mussolini in 1905). In the same year, the Marxist H. M. Hyndman translated into English his *Appeal to the Young*, a work which he considered 'a masterpiece, alike in conception and execution. Nothing ever written so completely combined the scientific with the popular, the revolutionary with the ethical.'[18] Inspired by Kropotkin's *narodnik* impulse, it was a plea to young men and women of the professional classes and of the working class to join the revolutionary movement and to experience a more meaningful life of comradeship. It had the widest influence of all his pamphlets.

The Conquest of Bread was also first published in Paris in 1892. In it, Kropotkin argued the case for a communist form of anarchism, and offered his most constructive account of a future anarchist society. It was strongly influenced by the experience of the Paris Commune of 1871 which had declared the absolute autonomy of the commune throughout France. Kropotkin considered it to be the first time that the people had tried to implement the anarchist ideal of a decentralized and federal society.

Kropotkin was expelled from Switzerland for his activities. After returning to Lyon in 1882, he was arrested by the French authorities. He was condemned this time to five years in prison. Conditions however were much better at Clairvaux than in Russia, and he could see his new wife Sophie regularly. Owing to the international outcry of liberal thinkers, including Victor Hugo and Swinburne, he was eventually released in 1886.

In the following months, he wrote *In Russian and French Prisons* (1887), giving an objective account of his experiences and demonstrating the uselessness of imprisonment as a means of reforming conduct. Prisons are simply universities of crime. Since they cannot be meaningfully improved, the only solution would be to abolish them altogether and to treat wrongdoers humanely. Kropotkin later wrote in his *Memoirs of a Revolutionist* (1899):

> Incarceration in a prison of necessity entirely destroys the energy of a man and annihilates his will. In prison life there is no room for exercising one's will; to possess one's own will in prison means surely to get into trouble. The will of the prisoner *must* be killed, and it is killed. Still less room is there for exercising one's natural sympathies, everything being done to prevent free contact with those, outside and within, with whom the prisoner may have feelings of sympathy.[19]

Rather than reform the character of a prisoner, prison life merely encourages a deeper dislike of regular work, contempt for current rules of morality, and, worse of all, a morbid development of prisoner's sensuality.

In his article *Law and Authority*, Kropotkin further criticizes the legal and penal system. Originally people regulated themselves by unwritten customs. But law was introduced when primitive superstitions were exploited by a few in order to ensure their rule, and was later enforced by the decrees of conquerors: 'Law made its appearance under the sanction of the priest, and the warrior's club was placed at its service.' In recent times, laws have primarily been aimed at protecting private property and the machinery of government, with political authority making and applying them. Kropotkin however contends that they are not only unnecessary, but positively harmful:

> consider what corruption, what depravity of mind is kept up among men by the idea of obedience, the very essence of law; of chastisement; of authority having the right to punish, to judge irrespective our conscience and the esteem of our friends; of the necessity for executioners, jailers, and informers – in a word, by all the attributes of law and authority.[20]

Crimes, Kropotkin argues, are supported mainly by idleness, law and authority. In a society without government and property, there would be little incentive to crime, and the crimes of passion which might still exist are not likely to increase because of lack of punishment. Those who remained mentally disturbed or consistently anti-social would be given fraternal treatment and moral support within the community. In place of law, he therefore proposes to return to the traditional network of custom and free agreement which has united and regulated human relationships for centuries.

After his release from prison, Kropotkin this time decided to settle in England and came to London in 1886. He was still active in politics, and in 1886 helped set up the Freedom Press Group which has been publishing libertarian literature ever since. It was not a particularly happy time in exile in England: 'How did I survive this after France and Switzerland!' he wrote in 1904. He described British anarchism as '*anarchie de salon* – epicurean, a little Nietzschean, very *snobbish*'.[21] Nevertheless for several years, he wrote dozens of articles and gave many lectures each year in an effort to expand British anarchism. He was considered the most famous living anarchist in the world, and was on good terms with prominent figures on the Left in Britain, notably Edward Carpenter, William Morris, H. M. Hyndman, Keir Hardie, and Bernard Shaw. He earned his living by journalism, especially for the scientific press, and enjoyed a growing reputation as a scientist.

Amongst many intellectuals, he was known primarily as a scientist who happened to have extreme views on anarchy and communism. His refusal for instance to stand and toast the King's health at a banquet given for him by the Royal Geographical Society was dismissed as an eccentric oddity. He was allegedly offered the chair as Professor of Geography at Cambridge University in 1896, but refused since he thought it would compromise his political activity. Instead, he chose to live a quiet life with his caring wife, his beloved daughter, neat garden, and curious library in the suburbs of London and then in Brighton. Although he occasionally had unusual visitors, none of his neighbours would have believed the claim in a report by the French secret police that he was helping to run the internationalist anarchist movement from London.

From 1890, Kropotkin grew less involved in the active anarchist movement, arguing that a free society would best be achieved by the gradual ripening of public opinion. The spate of terrorist outrages in the 1890s earned anarchism a destructive reputation, and Kropotkin was keen to show that it was grounded not in mindless and desperate actions, but in a clear scientific and philosophical base. Moreover from 1893, British anarchism began to decline into a sect as State socialism began to dominate the labour movement. Kropotkin responded by showing how anarchist principles could be applied in everyday life and felt that it was important to encourage any tendency which checked government power and promoted solidarity and co-operation.

It was not a question of Kropotkin taking a pacifist stance like Tolstoy. Although he admired his compatriot greatly, he wrote that 'I am not in sympathy with Tolstoy's asceticism, nor with his doctrine of non-resistance to evil, nor with his New Testament literalism.'[22] Kropotkin thought aggressiveness a virtue; he was not merely a philosophical anarchist. Indeed, under the influence of Bakunin, Kropotkin had actively advocated revolution in the 1870s in the pages of *Le Révolté* and *La Révolte*. He saw the spirit of revolt spreading, and since the existing framework of society was incapable of fundamental reform, he felt that revolution would be most likely. Indeed, his optimism was so strong at this time that he often talked as if the anarchist revolution was imminent and inevitable. In 1880 he wrote: 'One courageous act has sufficed to upset in a few days the entire governmental machinery, to make the colossus tremble. The government resists; it is savage in its repressions. But . . . in rapid succession these acts spread, become general, develop.'[23] At the 1883 Lyon trial of anarchists, Kropotkin forecast that social revolution would burst out within a decade and felt that an insurrectional period might then last for five years. While the Italian Federation of the International advocated 'propaganda by the deed', Kropotkin stood more in the Russian *narodnik* tradition, seeking to work amongst and educate the people. He thought that small revolutionary groups should submerge themselves in workers' organizations, and act as catalysts to bring about the social revolution which would take on the nature of a mass uprising. He also recommended working through militant trade unions and was sympathetic to revolutionary syndicalism.

Although he has been associated with the doctrine of 'propaganda by the deed', Kropotkin was opposed to indiscriminate violence, and tried to distance himself from the doctrine. Individual acts of violence were only legitimate if part of a revolutionary struggle with anarchist goals directed at a specific form of oppression. He understood the despair which led to acts of terrorism, and refused to condemn anarchist terrorists outright, recognizing that the State itself engaged in terrorism of the people. He put great stress on the context and the motives of terrorists: 'Individuals are not to blame;' he wrote to his friend Georg Brandes, 'they are driven mad by horrible conditions.'[24] He personally found violence abhorrent but recognized that in certain situations it could not be avoided. But it should primarily be directed against economic targets, not against individuals, whatever their social class or position in the State. Economic 'terrorism' in the sense of industrial sabotage was therefore all right, but not throwing dynamite and bombs into bourgeois cafés.

Kropotkin saw 'revolution' and 'evolution' as inevitable processes in social change. He recognized that revolutions, that is 'periods of accelerated rapid evolution and rapid changes', are as much in the nature of human society as slow evolution which incessantly goes on in civilized societies. The question was not so much how to avoid revolution, as 'how to attain the greatest results with the most limited amount of civil war, the smallest number of victims', and a minimum of mutual embitterment.[25]

As he grew older he did not believe less in revolution. In the first edition of *Freedom* in 1886, he wrote that the social revolution was imminent and inevitable and that it would be proletarian and international: 'we are as unable to prevent the storm as to accelerate its arrival.'[26] Twelve years later, he stated optimistically at the end of *Memoirs of a Revolutionist* (1899) that at the age of fifty-seven he was more deeply convinced than ever that a revolution could occur by chance in Europe 'in the sense of a profound and rapid social reconstruction' although it would not assume the 'violent character' which revolutions in the past had assumed.[27] While he quoted Proudhon 'in demolishing we shall build' in the first edition of *The Conquest of Bread*, he stressed in a footnote to the last Russian edition how difficult it is to build 'without extremely careful consideration beforehand' and preferred the inversion 'in building we shall demolish'.[28] Nevertheless, he remained convinced that the gains in the past had always been made by 'the force of the popular revolution' and not 'an evolution created by an elite'.[29]

Philosophy

It was during the thirty years that Kropotkin lived in England that he elaborated his mature thought. Like Godwin he based his anarchist hopes on a particular view of nature and human nature. Indeed, his view of nature as governed by necessary laws, his stress on man as a social being, and his recognition that change will often be gradual recall Godwin's teaching. What was new was his confidence in the creativity and virtue of people living in simple societies, his desire to give a scientific grounding to his anarchist conclusions, and his overall evolutionary perspective.

Kropotkin's approach to nature and man (as he called the human species in the habit of his day) is rigorously scientific. He came to realize soon after settling in England that

> anarchism represents more than a mere mode of action and a mere conception of a free society; that it is part of a philosophy, natural and social, which must be developed in a quite different way from the metaphysical or dialectical methods which have been employed in

sciences dealing with men. I saw it must be treated by the same methods as natural sciences . . . on the solid basis of induction applied to human institutions.[30]

In *Modern Science and Anarchism*, first published in Russian in 1901, he recognized that anarchism like socialism in general was born among the people, but he maintains:

Anarchism is a world-concept based upon a mechanical explanation of all phenomena, embracing the whole of nature – that is, including in it the life of human societies and their economic, political and moral problems. Its method of investigation is that of the exact natural sciences, and, if it pretends to be scientific, every conclusion must be verified by the method by which every scientific conclusion must be verified. Its aim is to construct a synthetic philosophy comprehending in one generalization all the phenomena of nature – and therefore also the life of societies.[31]

He goes on to argue that the movement of both natural and social science was in the direction of the anarchist ideal.

A man of his time, Kropotkin shared Spencer's and Comte's positivistic faith in science to bring about progress, but he also wanted to extend scientific methods of thinking into the educational, moral and political spheres. In a letter to a friend in 1899, he wrote:

So long as three-quarters of the education of this country is in the hands of men who have no suspicion of there being such as a thing as *scientific* (inductive and deductive) thinking, and so long as science herself will do everything in her power to preach most absurd and unethical conclusions, such as *woe to the weak*, then all will remain as it is.[32]

Kropotkin was referring here to those thinkers who were trying to use Darwin's theory of evolution to justify existing inequalities. The Social Darwinists, as they came to been known, attempted to give pseudo-scientific support to capitalism, racism and imperialism: as there was struggle for survival in society as well in nature, it was right and inevitable that the fittest should survive and rule, whether it be a group of individuals, a race or a nation. T. H. Huxley, Darwin's bulldog, presented the animal world as a perpetual 'gladiator's show' and the life of primitive man as a 'continuous free fight'.[33] Kropotkin threw himself into the controversy and offered an alternative interpretation of the evolutionary process.

Kropotkin's views were first inspired by a lecture delivered in 1880 'On the Law of Mutual Aid' by the Russian zoologist and Dean of St Petersburg University Karl Kessler, who argued that mutual aid is as much a law of nature as mutual struggle, but the former was far more important in the progressive evolution of the species. Kropotkin went on to argue that there is far more evidence in nature of co-operation within a species than of competition. In his most famous work *Mutual Aid* (1902), he suggests with a rich array of data that in the struggle for life mutual aid appears to be a rule among the most successful species and argues that it is the most important factor in evolution:

> we maintain that under *any* circumstances sociability is the greatest advantage in the struggle for life. Those species which willingly or unwillingly abandon it are doomed to decay; while those animals which know best how to combine have the greatest chances of survival and of further evolution.[34]

Kropotkin makes clear that the struggle of existence which takes place is a struggle against adverse circumstances rather than between individuals of the same species. Where the other Social Darwinists argued that the struggle between individuals leads to the survival of the fittest, Kropotkin asserted that the unit of competition is the species as a whole and that the species which has the greatest degree of co-operation and support between its members is most likely to flourish. He concludes:

> The animal species, in which individual struggle has been reduced to its narrowest limits, and the practice of mutual aid has attained the greatest development, are invariably the most numerous, the most prosperous, and the most open to further progress. The mutual protection which is obtained in this case, the possibility of attaining old age and of accumulating experience, the higher intellectual development, and the further growth of sociable habits, secure the maintenance of the species, its extension, and its further progressive evolution.[35]

Mutual aid within the species thus represents the principal factor, the principal active agency in evolution. Progress, biological and social, is best fostered not by force or cunning, but by the practice of mutual support and co-operation.

Kropotkin did not hesitate to apply these observations of the animal world to the human species. He maintains that society is a natural phenomenon existing anterior to the appearance of man, and man is naturally adapted to live in society without artificial regulations. Man is and always has been a social species. Kropotkin draws on the findings of anthropology to argue that in traditional societies human beings have always lived in clans and tribes in which customs and taboos ensure co-operation and mutual aid. Unbridled individualism is therefore a modern growth. He maintains from his historical studies that mutual aid reached its apogee in the communal life of the medieval cities. Even the appearance of coercive institutions and the modern State from the sixteenth century has not eradicated voluntary co-operation:

> The State, based upon loose aggregations of individuals, and undertaking to be their only bond of union, did not answer its purpose. The mutual-aid tendency finally broke down its iron rules; it reappeared and reasserted itself in an infinity of associations which now tend to embrace all aspects of life, and to take possession of all that is required by man for life.[36]

Evolutionary theory, if properly understood, will not justify the inevitability of capitalist competition or the need for a strong State but rather point to the possibility of anarchy. Indeed, it forms the cornerstone of Kropotkin's philosophy.[37]

It follows that anarchism is not against but in keeping with evolving human nature. Indeed, Kropotkin insisted that the anarchist thinker studies society and tries to discover its tendencies and in his ideal merely points out the direction of evolution: 'The ideal of the Anarchist is thus a mere summing-up of what he considers to be the next phase of evolution. It is no longer a matter of faith; it is a matter of scientific discussion.'[38]

Ethics

Kropotkin not only argues that this is an accurate and true description of nature and the human species, but sees it as providing the ground for morality. By studying human society from the biological point of view, he believes that it is possible and desirable 'to deduce the laws of moral science from the social needs and habits of mankind'.[39] 'Nature', he writes in his incomplete *Ethics*,

> has thus to be recognized as the *first ethical teacher of man*. The social instinct, innate in men as well as in all the social animals, – this is the origin of all ethical conceptions and all the subsequent development of morality.[40]

Human beings are therefore by nature moral. Moreover, by living in society they develop their natural collective sense of justice which grows to become a habit. They are therefore morally progressive and their primitive instinct of solidarity will became more refined and comprehensive as civilization develops. Indeed, Kropotkin inferred from his study of nature and human history 'the permanent presence of a *double tendency* – towards a greater development on the one side, of *sociality*, and, on the other side, of a consequent increase of the intensity of life, which results in an increase of happiness for the *individuals*, and in progress – physical, intellectual, and moral.'[41]

Kropotkin never completed his work on ethics, and what exists is principally an account of the evolutionary origins of the moral sense and a history of ethics from the Greeks to the end of the nineteenth century. In an earlier work on *Anarchist Morality* (1890) he sketched the outline of a system of ethics devoid of the metaphysical and the supernatural. He distinguishes between our innate moral sense and the rigid moral codes imposed by authority. Where the former gives rise to sympathy and solidarity, the latter find their origin in primitive superstitions taken over by priests and conquerors to support their rule.

The moral sense is expressed in mutual aid, without which society cannot exist. Kropotkin attempts to derive an objective system of ethics from observations of nature. He defines good as what is useful to the preservation of the species and evil as what is harmful to it. Morality is therefore a 'natural' need of animal species. And the morality which emerges from observations of the whole of the animal world may be summed up as: '*Do* to others what you would have them do to you in the same circumstances.'[42]

But this definition of justice as equal treatment to be discovered in nature is not enough to hold society together. Altruism must also exist, a readiness to give more than is asked or required, and it is this moral quality which has inspired those who have most contributed to human progress. Like J. M. Guyau who sketched a scheme of morality independent of obligation or sanction, Kropotkin argues that this altruism comes from a feeling of the superabundance of life. It leads the individual to overflow with emotional and intellectual energy. Kropotkin therefore suggests as the summary of moral teaching: 'spread your intelligence, your love, your energy of actions broadcast among others!'[43] The goal to be aimed for is the plenitude of existence and the free development of every individual's faculties.

Kropotkin was highly critical of the egoistical kind of individualism advocated by Stirner and Nietzsche. In his view, it led to a destructive and selfish form of hedonism. Instead, he sought the individuality which attains 'the greatest individual development possible through practising the highest communist sociability.'[44] He did not however suggest like Kant that doing one's duty is inevitably unpleasant. He believed like Godwin that the greatest pleasure comes from benevolence, that 'personal gratification will come from the gratification of others'. In the final analysis, Kropotkin rejected both religious and utilitarian ethics in favour of a third system of morality which sees in moral actions 'a mere necessity of the individual to enjoy the joys of his brethren, to suffer when some of his brethren are suffering;

a habit and a second nature, slowly elaborated and perfected by life in society'.[45]

Human Nature

Kropotkin was the first to recognize that man is an 'extremely complicated animal'.[46] He believed our unconscious life to be very much wider than our conscious one, indeed that it comprises three-quarters of our relations with others. We are also rooted in nature. But man is part of society just as society is part of nature: 'Man did not create society; society existed before Man.'[47] And the leading characteristic of all animals living in society is the feeling of solidarity. The most important factor in human development has been mutual aid, and it our innate moral sense which makes us capable of altruism.

Unlike Proudhon, Kropotkin does not therefore think us naturally aggressive: 'Man has always preferred peace and quiet. Quarrelsome rather than fierce, he prefers his cattle, land, and his hut to soldiering.'[48] Progress has resulted from the resolution of conflict, not, as in Marx's view, through a dialectical synthesis of opposing forces, but through the triumph of co-operation. But is has not always been easy. He recognizes that history has been 'nothing but the struggle between the rulers and the ruled' and in the process both groups have been corrupted by authority.[49] Only through higher education and the equality of conditions will human beings be able to free themselves from their slavish instincts.

But Kropotkin's stress on the similarities between the human species and other species does not mean that he rejects the gains of civilization and culture. Indeed, he celebrates the intellectual faculty as being eminently social. Human beings like other animals need their basic needs satisfied but they are also creative and imaginative. In *The Conquest of Bread* (1892) his principal criticism of the present unequal distribution of property is that it does allow the leisure to develop the full human personality:

> Man is not a being whose exclusive purpose in life is eating, drinking, and providing a shelter for himself. As soon as his material wants are satisfied, other needs, which, generally speaking, may be described as of an artistic nature, will thrust themselves forward. These needs are of the greatest variety; they vary with each and every individual; and the more society is civilized, the more will individuality be developed, and the more will desires be varied.[50]

In the development of civilization, social human beings will not only evolve the full range of their artistic and intellectual abilities but become more truly individual. Man is therefore both social and individual, with physical and mental needs. For Kropotkin 'the strength of Anarchy lies precisely in that it understands *all* human faculties and *all* passions, and ignores none.'[51] Although he felt Emma Goldman and her companions were wasting too much space in their journals discussing the 'sex question', when the thirty year-old feminist reminded the fifty-seven year-old thinker how important it was for the young, he replied with a twinkle in his eye, 'Perhaps you are right after all.'[52]

Kropotkin's anarchism is thus, like Godwin's, firmly based on a particular view of human nature. Mutual aid is a principal factor in natural and human evolution. There is a moral principle in nature which ensures that human beings have a sense of justice. We are naturally social, co-operative and moral. But while society is a natural phenomenon, the State and its coercive institutions are an artificial and malignant growth.

The State

Kropotkin of course is left with the problem of explaining how social inequalities and oppressive institutions came to be if human beings are naturally co-operative. In his essay *The State: Its Historic Role* (1897), he examined the origin and nature of the State, the entity he considered the greatest obstacle to the birth of a free and equal society. He distinguishes like all anarchists between the State and society and sees the State as only one form of political organization adopted by society in the course of history. He also argues that the idea of the State is quite different from that of government, despite the tendency of some anarchists to confuse the two. The idea of the State

> not only includes the existence of a power situated above society, but also of a *territorial concentration* as well as the *concentration of many functions of the life of societies in the hands of a few*. It carries with it some new relationships between members of society which did not exist before the establishment of the State. A whole mechanism of legislation and of policing has to be developed in order to subject some classes to the domination of others.[53]

In tracing the origins of the State, Kropotkin still maintains that human societies originally were based on mutual aid. Man lived in clans or tribes before the founding of the patriarchal family, and did not accumulate private property. Tribal morality was kept alive by usage, custom and tradition only, not imposed by authority. During the course of migrations, the early tribes settled down and formed federated village communities of individual families but with the communal ownership of land. In Europe, from the twelfth century on, associations called guilds formed for mutual support.

From the village community and the guilds emerged the commune or free city of the Middle Ages, which struggled for federative principles and the liberty of the individual citizen. This for Kropotkin, in his idealized version of history, amounts to the high point of European history thus far.

The village communities and the urban communes flourished up until the late Middle Ages and the Renaissance when the corrosive principle of authority in the form of the State began to establish itself. Kropotkin presents the rise of the centralized European State after the sixteenth century as an aberration from the mainstream of Western social organization. Believing that the natural human tendency is towards mutual aid and community, Kropotkin is left with the problem of explaining how the State came to predominate.

Dominant minorities in the traditional village communities, Kropotkin suggests, managed to combine the military power of professional warriors hired for defence with the judicial power of those who had a specialized knowledge of customary law. A single man assumed these two functions, and won the support of the priest. It was not long before serfdom, capitalism and finally the State came into existence. Men then 'fell in love with authority' and called for a 'municipal Caesar' to solve disputes. And the State by its very nature cannot recognize a freely formed union operating within itself; it only recognizes subjects: 'The State and its sister the Church arrogate to themselves alone the right to serve as the link between men.'[54]

In the history of human societies, the State is thus an institution developed 'to prevent the direct association among men, to shackle the development of local and individual initiative, to crush existing liberties, to prevent their new blossoming – all this in order to subject the masses to the will of the minorities'.[55]

Kropotkin recognized as much as Marx the influence of economic conditions on political institutions: 'The *political* regime to which human societies are submitted is always the expression of the economic regime which exists within that society.'[56] He also maintained that throughout history a new form of political organization has 'corresponded to each new form of economic organisation'.[57] But the relationship between the two is not one in which an economic base determines the political superstructure as in Marx, but rather one of symbiosis. They influence each other to different degrees depending on the circumstances.

Nevertheless, in his account of the origin of the State Kropotkin implies political power was initially more important than economic power. It would seem that he had to posit in human nature a will to power which leads to the domination and exploitation of one's fellows. But the will to altruism is stronger. Although Malatesta accused Kropotkin of being a victim of 'mechanistic fatalism', this would imply that human volition can change the present course of events.[58] At the end of his essay on the State, he suggests that we are faced with the clear choice of death or renewal:

> *Either* the State for ever, crushing individual and local life, taking over in all fields of human activity, bringing with it its wars and its domestic struggles for power, its palace revolutions which only replace one tyrant by another, and inevitably at the end of this development there is ... death!
>
> *Or* the destruction of States, and new life starting again in thousands of centres on the principle of the lively initiative of the individual and groups and that of free agreement.
>
> The choice lies with you![59]

Kropotkin was thus confident that the dispossessed majority would resist, destroy the new coercive institutions of the State and re-establish mutual aid. If political authority was removed with all other unnatural restrictions, human beings would act socially, that is in accordance with their natures.

While Kropotkin distinguished between the State and government, he felt that they were equally oppressive and should be abolished. In his analysis of representative government, he argues that the workers' call for universal suffrage can accomplish nothing since political systems will always be manipulated by those who control the economy. Representative government corresponds to 'Capital-rule'. Only direct action can persuade legislators to make concessions.

The inherent tendency of representative government is always to centralize and unify its functions. It cannot attend to the innumerable affairs of the community. As for elections, they do not magically unearth men who can genuinely represent the nation, and who can manage, other than in a party spirit, the affairs they are compelled to legislate on. The legislator is expected to be a veritable Proteus and is compelled to make laws about things he knows nothing for thirty or forty million inhabitants. Parliamentary rule is 'pre-eminently a middle class rule' and majority rule is always a 'mediocrity rule'.[60]

Kropotkin is no less dismissive of the kind of revolutionary government advocated by State socialists in the transitional stage to a free society. Since a revolution is a growing and spontaneous movement, any centralized political authority will check and crystallize its progress and in turn will become a counter-revolutionary force by resisting any development beyond itself. The immense and profound complexity of reorganizing society and elaborating new social forms moreover can only be achieved by the collective suppleness of mind of the whole people, not by an elected or dictatorial minority in government. As for the *Volkstaat* or 'Popular State' advocated by some socialists, it is 'as great a danger for liberty as any form of autocracy'.[61]

Revolutionary groups should not therefore assume power, but restrict their activity to awaken the consciousness of the people and to remind them of fundamental goals. On the morrow of the revolution, it will be necessary however to satisfy grievances and needs immediately so that the people can recognize that the situation has been transformed to their advantage and is not merely a change of persons and formulae. This can only be achieved by the satisfaction of the basic needs of the people through the full expropriation of social goods and the means of production and the introduction of communism.

Free Society

Like all anarchists, Kropotkin does not give a blueprint of what a free society would be like but he does suggest certain directions it might take. Such a society would be composed of a network of voluntary associations of equal individuals who are consumers and producers. They would represent 'an interwoven network, composed of an infinite variety of groups and federations of all sizes and degrees, local, regional, national and international – temporary or more or less permanent – for all possible purposes'.[62] The 'commune', linked by local interests and sympathies, will become the basic social unit and the centre of life in town and country. For Kropotkin the commune is not just a territorial agglomeration, but

a generic name, a synonym for the grouping of equals, knowing neither frontiers nor walls. The social commune will soon cease to be a clearly defined whole. Each group of the commune will necessarily be drawn towards other similar groups in other communes; it will be grouped and federated with them by links as solid as those which attach it to its fellow citizens, and will constitute a commune of interests whose members are scattered in a thousand towns and villages.[63]

In place of law, people will regulate their relationships by a combination of custom and free agreements. Such voluntary contracts will be kept without the intervention of authority to enforce them; they are 'entered by free consent, as a free choice between different courses equally open to each of the agreeing parties'.[64] The only incentive to keep them would be common interest. With the eradication of private property and poverty the incentives to crime will be few – three-quarters of crimes are due to the unequal distribution of property, not the perversity of human nature. The few disputes which might arise would easily be settled by arbitrators. And those who do commit anti-social acts will not be punished or rendered worse in prison but treated with kindness and understanding.

When it came to organizing the economy, Kropotkin went beyond Proudhon's mutualism, and Bakunin's collectivism, to advocate a form of anarchist communism. It meant politically a society without government, that is anarchy, and economically, the complete negation of the wage system and the ownership of the means of production in common: 'everybody, contributing for the common well-being to the full extent of his capacities, shall enjoy from the common stock of society to the fullest possible extent of his needs.'[65] Moreover, Kropotkin believed 'Anarchy leads to Communism, and Communism to Anarchy.'[66] He felt that anarchist communism was the union of the two fundamental tendencies of his society, a tendency towards economic equality and a tendency towards political liberty.[67]

As he points out in the *The Conquest of Bread*, Kropotkin felt that economic communism is the only fair solution since wealth results from collective effort and the means of production are the collective work of humanity:

> Individual appropriation is neither just nor serviceable. All belongs to all. All things are for all men, since all men have need of them, since all men have worked in the measure of their strength to produce them, and since it is not possible to evaluate everyone's part in the production of the world's wealth.[68]

The means of production would be owned not by the State but by associations or communes of producers. They would be organized on a voluntary basis and connected federally. Each person would do whatever work he could and receive from the common stock according to his needs without money, exchange or labour notes. Kropotkin makes no distinction between qualified or professional work and simple work like Marx. Without an obligatory division of labour, people would be able to choose their work and use both their mental and manual skills.

Kropotkin further advocates industrial decentralization, regional self-sufficiency, integration of town and country, and more intensive methods of food production. Unlike the Marxist and liberal economists, he argues that the troubles of capitalist economy are not the result of over-production but under-consumption. At the same time, well-being for all is quite possible. He is convinced that five hours a day for 150 days a year would suffice to satisfy the basic needs of food, shelter and clothing, and another 150 days to provide secondary necessities. The aim would be to produce 'the greatest amount of goods necessary to the well-being of all, with the least possible waste of human energy'.[69]

Kropotkin is no Stoic and sees a need for luxury and the satisfaction of sensual pleasure and artistic feeling. 'After bread has been secured, leisure is the supreme aim.' Leisure would enable people to develop their whole personality, to cultivate the arts and sciences, and satisfy their varied tastes. In this way 'Luxury, ceasing to be a foolish and ostentatious display of the bourgeois class, would become an artistic pleasure.'[70]

All adults would be expected to do some manual labour, and no doubt writers and artists would benefit from the variety of work. While he does not share Tolstoy's celebration of the dignity of labour, Kropotkin sees no reason why manual labour should not be attractive if it is voluntarily undertaken and performed without strain. Like William Morris, he felt 'the most important economy, the only reasonable one, is to make life pleasant for all, because the man who is satisfied with his life produces infinitely more than the man who curses his surroundings.'[71] But he criticized Morris for his antipathy to machinery, and, like Godwin, welcomed the impending arrival of technology which would reduce drudgery and toil, and allow time for more fulfilling occupations.

The division of labour, which has led to the split between manual and mental workers, and specialization in a narrow field, is one of the most destructive features of capitalism:

> The division of labour means labelling and stamping men for life –
> some to splice ropes in factories, some to be foremen in a business,
> others to shove huge coal baskets in a particular part of a mine; but
> none of them to have any idea of machinery as a whole, nor of business,
> nor of mines. And thereby they destroy the love of work and the
> capacity for invention.[72]

Kropotkin would like people to be free to choose their own work and vary it as they wish. He looked to new mechanical devices and communal domestic services to liberate women from household drudgery; if not, 'half humanity subjected to the slavery of the hearth would still have to rebel against the other half.' He was delighted to hear of the invention of the washing machine, for example. Nevertheless, he implies a certain sexual division of labour for he assumes women would be mainly involved in the education and rearing of children, and fails to call on men to share domestic tasks or child care. Equally, a certain racial prejudice would seem to enter the reckoning when he suggests, for example, that the workers of a given French market gardener 'work like blacks'.[73]

As for living arrangements, Kropotkin is no advocate of Fourier's communal phalansteries and suggests that it is up to the people to choose whether they want communal living-quarters or not. Unlike many communists, he recognizes that privacy is essential for many, and 'isolation, alternating with time spent in society, is the normal desire of human nature.'[74] And while every able-bodied adult might find pleasure in performing some manual and mental work each day, after a certain age – say forty or more

– they might be released from the moral obligation of manual labour to devote themselves to whatever activity they choose.

Kropotkin is well aware of the stock objections to his free society and endeavours in *The Conquest of Bread* to answer them. His form of free communism recognizes 'the absolute liberty of the individual, that does not admit of any authority, and makes use of no compulsion to drive men to work'.[75] It is a society based on voluntary work, on moral rather than material incentives. But if subsistence is guaranteed and there is no need to earn wages, why should anyone work? Kropotkin points out that compulsion – whether in the form of slavery, serfdom or wagedom – has never made anyone work well; on the contrary, it is 'Well-being – that is to say, the satisfaction of physical, artistic and moral needs, [which] has always been the most powerful stimulant to work'.[76]

Voluntary work has always been more productive than work stimulated by wages. The incentive to work would not be the threat of want or the rod but the conscious satisfaction of the work itself and a sense of contributing to the general happiness. If work is made agreeable and meaningful, fulfilling human nature and not degrading it, there is no reason why it should be avoided like the plague or appear the curse of fate. Manual work is despised now simply because of the bad conditions and low status it has. There is no intrinsic reason why it should not be enjoyable; sports, after all, could be seen as a disguised form of manual labour. Kropoktin thus sought to humanize work and to make it 'the free exercise of *all* the faculties of man'.[77]

While rejecting all forms of economic or physical coercion, Kropotkin suggests that social disapproval and ostracism could be used to influence the loafer or sluggard. He might be looked upon as 'a ghost of bourgeois society' and even asked to leave the federation and look elsewhere in the wide world. If people did not keep their engagements they would earn the disapproval of the community. Like Godwin, Kropotkin recommends the use of public opinion to change the conduct of 'anti-social' individuals, but it is difficult not to see in this a potentially oppressive form of moral coercion. He also insists that all 'will have to work with their hands' as 'their duty towards society' whether they like it or not.[78] And on the morrow of the revolution if monopolizers cannot be checked by the boycott or other forms of social pressure, then Kropotkin countenances the use of violence against them.

Kropotkin is on firmer ground however when he suggests most idleness is due to lack of proper training or some form of mental or physical sickness and would be very rare in a free society. As he says elsewhere, work is a habit and a physiological necessity while idleness is 'an artificial growth'.[79] Only overwork is repulsive to human nature.

In order to make work attractive and satisfy the needs of all, Kropotkin advocated a fundamental reorganization of production. To end economic imperialism, he argued that each country should become as self-sufficient as possible. No country would then be dependent on another, and in a revolutionary situation starved into submission. In place of the concentration of large factories in cities, he called for economic as well as political decentralization, believing that 'diversity is the surest pledge of the complete development of production by mutual cooperation.'[80] He therefore favoured the scattering of industry throughout the country and the integration of industry and agriculture at the local level so that there would be industrial villages and small industries. Energy in the form of electricity made this increasingly possible. His ideal is:

> A society where each individual is a producer of both manual and intellectual work; where each able-bodied human being is a worker, and where each worker works both in the field and in the industrial workshop; where every aggregation of individuals, large enough to dispose of a certain variety of natural resources – it may be a nation, or rather a region – produces and itself consumes most of its agricultural and manufactured produce.[81]

Agriculture moreover could be made much more intensive and productive by the aid of science and technical inventions, and it would be quite possible for a family of five to be required to do less than a fortnight's work each year in order to grow its annual staple food. It would be quite possible for Britain, for example, to become self-sufficient in food production, and regional self-sufficiency is entirely desirable for providing fresh produce. By decentralizing industry, and combining industrial with agricultural work, it would not only give people more choice in their work but give them greater control of production and distribution. There is also a sense of unity and solidarity which comes from working the land in common. Where necessary, federal bodies would be able to co-ordinate economic life. In his *Fields, Factories, and Workshops* (1899), he gathered a wealth of data to show how this could be possible and concluded:

> Have the factory and the workshop at the gates of your fields and your gardens, and work in them. Not those large establishments, of course, in which huge masses of metals have to be dealt with and which are better placed at certain spots indicated by Nature, but the countless variety of workshops and factories which are required to satisfy the infinite diversity of tastes among civilized men ... factories and workshops into which men, women and children will not be driven by hunger, but will be attracted by the desire of finding an activity suited

to their tastes, and where, aided by the motor and the machine, they will choose the branch of activity which best suits their inclinations.[82]

Above all, such an arrangement would encourage integrated education, combining mental and manual work. The aim would be to produce 'the *complete* human being, trained to use his brain and his hands', especially as an initiator and an inventor in both science and technics. The principle should be 'Through the eyes *and* the hand to the brain.'[83] Learning would be best achieved by doing, since children prefer real work to abstract theory. The chief aim of education is not to make a specialist from a beginner, but

> to teach him the elements of knowledge and the good methods of work, and, above all, to give him that general inspiration which will induce him, later on, to put in whatever he does a sincere longing for truth, to like what is beautiful, both as to form and contents, to feel the necessity of being a useful unit amidst other human units, and thus to feel his heart at unison with the rest of humanity.[84]

Like Ruskin and Morris, he argues that art, in order to develop, must be bound up with industry by a thousand intermediate degrees.

Kropotkin sees overpopulation as no threat to his free society. His reply to Malthus is to argue that the stock of potential energy in nature is 'little short of infinite' in comparison with the present population of the globe. He also infers from the laws of evolution that the available means of subsistence grow at a rate 'which increases itself in proportion as population becomes denser – unless it be artificially (and temporarily) checked by some defects of social organisation'.[85] Improved methods of cultivation can increase food supply so that we have no need to fear overpopulation in the future. This century would seem to have confirmed Kropotkin's analysis. It is precisely in the most densely populated areas that agriculture has increased productivity, and population has eased most in those countries where a high standard of living prevails.

War and Revolution

While elaborating his anarchist philosophy in England, Kropotkin did not change any of his fundamental ideas about anarchy or communism. He did however shift his ground on two traditional anarchist principles – internationalism and anti-militarism. He had espoused both as a young man, and both had played a key part in the European anarchist movement. In the 1890s however he began to emphasize the importance of national character, and argued that the Marxist Social Democrats and the political regime in Germany expressed the country's militaristic and authoritarian nature. At the same time, he showed a marked preference for France, with its revolutionary tradition, and Britain, with its liberal culture which tolerated political refugees. He always considered France and Britain to be the two nations most likely to have a social revolution, while he put down Germany's defeat of France in 1871 as the chief cause of the failure of revolution in Europe. He wrote to a friend that 'Since 1871 Germany has become a standing menace to European progress . . . the chief support and protection of reaction.'[86]

After 1905 Kropotkin began to call for further military conscription in preparation for war against Germany. When the war broke out in 1914, he gave immediate support for the allies. He wrote to Jean Grave, editor of *Les Temps Nouveaux*: 'Arm yourself! Make a superhuman effort – this is the only way France will reconquer the right and strength to inspire the people of Europe with her civilization and her ideas of liberty, communism and fraternity.'[87] As a result, he isolated himself from the mainstream of the anarchist movement which wanted nothing to do with this 'ruling class' conflict. His old friends at *Freedom* in London tried to remind anarchists of their principles of anti-militarism, arguing that supporting the allied governments in the war was tantamount to supporting Statism, patriotism and nationalism. As late as 1916, Malatesta accused Kropotkin, along with Grave and others, of being 'Pro-government Anarchists' in their wish to see the complete defeat of Germany.[88] Trotsky noted drily that 'the superannuated anarchist Kropotkin, who had a weakness ever since youth for the populists, made use of the war to disavow everything he had been teaching for almost half a century.'[89]

Unrepentant, the ailing geographer turned increasingly towards his homeland for inspiration. He had not returned to Russia since his escape from prison in 1876, but had kept up his contacts. His works, especially *The Conquest of Bread*, had been widely distributed there.

To most of his contemporaries, Kropotkin appeared mainly as a European, but during his two visits to North America, he appeared very much a representative of Russian culture. After the first trip in 1897, when he travelled as a delegate of the British Association for the Advancement of Science to a convention in Toronto, he helped the persecuted Dukhobors find a home in Canada. During his second visit in 1901, he gave a series of lectures which were later published as *Ideals and Realities in Russian Literature* (1905). He was enthusiastically received in North America and lent considerable impetus to the burgeoning anarchist movement there; his *Appeal to the Young* was particularly influential. During both tours, he took every opportunity to make his views known to the Press, who seemed more interested in his aristocratic roots than his philosophy. To reporters in Jersey City in 1897, he insisted:

I am an anarchist and am trying to work out the ideal society, which I believe will be communistic in economics, but will leave full and free scope for the development of the individual. As to its organization, I believe in the formation of federated groups for production and distribution. The social democrats are endeavouring to attain the same end, but the difference is that they start from the centre – the State – and work toward the circumference, while we endeavour to work out the ideal society from the simple elements to the complex.[90]

On hearing of the outbreak of the Revolution in 1905, Kropotkin was ready to return to Russia immediately to support the revolutionary cause, and even practised his marksmanship at the age of sixty-three. He wrote a long article 'The Revolution in Russia' for the prestigious *Nineteenth-Century* journal describing the situation in his homeland and hoping that it would spark off a social revolution which would lead to anarchism. After the crushing of the revolt, he worked with the Parliamentary Russian Committee in London to help the victims of the reaction and produced a booklet called *The Terror in Russia* (1909).

By this stage, he was working mainly with the Social Revolutionary Party, a member of which married his daughter. The events inspired him to finish *The Great French Revolution 1789–1793* (1909) which he had been working on and thinking about for twenty years. In its final form, it focused on popular action during the period and spelled out the dangers of the Jacobin dictatorship.

When the revolution broke out again in 1917, there was nothing to hold him back. He returned to his homeland after more than forty years of exile. He contacted the liberals in the Provisional Government and was even offered a cabinet post as Minister of Education by the moderate socialist Alexander Kerensky, although he was still enough of an anarchist to reject the offer. At the all-party State Conference in Moscow in August 1917, he called for a federal republic in Russia and a renewed offensive against Germany. But when the Bolsheviks seized power in November, he commented prophetically: 'This buries the revolution.'

The growing dictatorial powers of the new regime led Kropotkin to renew contact with the Russian anarchist movement. He wrote to the Danish critic Georg Brandes in April 1919 that the Bolsheviks were acting like the Jacobins by socializing the land, industry and commerce by dictatorial methods: 'Unfortunately, the method by which they seek to establish communism like Babeuf's in a strongly centralized state makes success absolutely impossible and paralyzes the constructive work of the people.'[91]

In order to check the worst excesses, Kropotkin met Lenin in the spring of 1919. In their conversation, Kropotkin complained of the persecution of the co-operatives and of the bureaucratized local authorities which had been established, commenting 'Anywhere you look around, a basis for non-authority flares up.' Lenin for his part declared that the anarcho-syndicalist movement was harmful and made clear that the only kind of struggle that can be crowned with success is in the masses, 'only through the masses and with the masses, from underground work to massive red terror if it is called for, to civil war, to a war on all fronts, to a war of all against all . . .'[92]

Lenin agreed to receive letters from the old anarchist describing any injustices. Kropotkin took up the opportunity in March 1920, arguing that the dictatorship of the Communist Party was harmful to the creation of a new socialist system. Without the participation of local forces, without an organization 'from below' of the peasants and workers themselves, it seemed impossible to build a new life. Russia had become a Soviet Republic only in name, Kropotkin warned prophetically: 'at present it is not the soviets which rule in Russia but the party committees'; and if the situation were to continue 'the very word "socialism" will become a curse, as happened in France with the idea of equality for forty years after the rule of the Jacobins'.[93] Again in December of the same year, Kropotkin complained to Lenin that the practice of taking hostages by the Red Army in the civil war represented a return to the worst period of the Middle Ages and was tantamount to a restoration of torture.[94] But his pleas fell on deaf ears. Lenin soon became tired of the letters and told one of his associates: 'I am sick of this old fogy. He doesn't understand a thing about politics and intrudes with his advice, most of which is very stupid.'[95]

In the following year, Kropotkin wrote a *Letter to the Workers of the West*, in which he argued against foreign intervention in Russia which would only strengthen the 'dictatorial tendencies' of the Bolshevik rulers.[96] In *What to Do?*, he further argued, like Emma Goldman and Alexander Berkman, that the Bolsheviks were 'perpetuating horrors' and ruining the whole country. He had returned to the full-blown anarchism of his maturity.[97]

Kropotkin moved in 1920 from Moscow to Dmitrov, a small village forty miles from the metropolis. It symbolized his isolation from the Revolution. In his despair, he returned to his work on ethics. He also grew increasingly fatalistic and maintained that the revolution Russia had gone through was not 'the sum total of the efforts of separate individuals, but a natural phenomenon, independent of human will'.[98] The only thing one could do was to try and lessen the force of the approaching reaction.

When Kropotkin died in February 1921, the Bolshevik government offered a State funeral, but his family refused. As it happened, his funeral proved to be the last great anarchist demonstration in Russia, for later that year the movement was crushed. Although the house where he was born became the Kropotkin Museum, it was closed down in 1938. His anarchist writings were not available in Russia, but his memory lived on in the name of a metro station, of a town in Caucasia, and of the mountain range in Siberia which he was the first to cross in 1866. More recently, however, in the post-*glasnost* era in the Soviet Union, his insights and recommendations have been increasingly appreciated. It may well be that in a future federation of independent republics Kropotkin, and not Lenin, will have the last word.

Influence

Kropotkin undoubtedly appears as one of the most attractive of anarchist thinkers and his influence has been acknowledged by people as diverse as Kōtoku in Japan, Pa Chin in China, Gandhi in India, and Lewis Mumford and Paul Goodman in the United States. He was a major inspiration of anarchist movements in Russia and Britain, and helped shape those in France, Belgium and Switzerland. He remains the greatest exponent of a decentralized society based on a harmonious balance between agriculture and industry. His call for 'integrated education' of mental and manual skills still demands attention. His pragmatic and inventive approach is appreciated by those who wish to develop alternative institutions within the shell of the existing State and encourage the further development of libertarian tendencies within society. His keen awareness that society is as much a part of nature as the individual is part of society makes him a forerunner of modern social ecology.

Although Kropotkin could be tediously repetitive at times, his clear and simple style makes him eminently readable and easily understood. While dealing with complex philosophical arguments or difficult scientific data, he always addressed the common person. He illustrated his arguments by lively examples, whether it was the Lifeboat Association to show how successful voluntary organizations can be, international railways to demonstrate how complex agreements to provide a service can be negotiated without a central authority, or the British Museum Library to explain how distribution could be organized according to need in a communist society.

Oscar Wilde described Kropotkin as 'a man with a soul of that beautiful white Christ which seems coming out of Russia' and thought that his was one of the two most perfect lives he had come across (the other being Verlaine's).[99] Such a romantic and extravagant view was clearly unfounded. But by all accounts, Kropotkin was generous and considerate, and possessed great intelligence, sincerity and warmth. He was always ready to go out of his way to help those in need, whether they were his friends or strangers. Although he was born into Russia's highest aristocracy, he gave up the privileges of his rank and wealth to throw in his lot with the poor and oppressed. It led not only to spells in prison but exile for most of his life. Yet despite personal difficulties, he continued to work and write for what he considered to be the cause of freedom until the very end of his life.

To many Kropotkin appeared good without knowing it and he is often portrayed as a kind of gentle angel, or, as Paul Avrich calls him, 'a saint without God'.[100] But this picture is misleading. Kropotkin was never a strict pacifist. He longed for the coming revolution to end oppression and injustice, but recognized that it would inevitably be violent. He always believed that idealism had to be translated into action, and welcomed serious acts of revolt which might trigger off an insurrection, and, of course, he recognized the revolutionary potential of syndicalism and the labour movement.[101] He may have been disturbed by terrorism and the taking of individual life, but he refused to condemn the terrorists, explaining their behaviour in terms of a desperate reaction to inhuman conditions. His growing nationalist sentiments led him to take sides during the First Word War, a position which was tantamount to accepting militarism, nationalism and Statism.

At the same time, Kropotkin rejected the kind of deceit and manipulation practised by Bakunin, preferring open and sincere propaganda. In his personal and revolutionary morality, he did not accept the idea that the end justified the means; on the contrary, the means inevitably shaped the ends. It was this awareness that led him into a head-on collision with Lenin over the direction of the Russian Revolution.

Kropotkin's great value as a thinker lies in his endeavour to demonstrate that anarchism represents existing tendencies in society towards political liberty and economic equality. He further tried to adopt the methodology of the exact sciences in order to show that all the conclusions of anarchism could be scientifically verified. As a result, he attempted to prove that it is a philosophy which finds confirmation in evolutionary theory, sociology, anthropology and history.

His greatest contribution to science, apart from his geographical discoveries, was his stress on mutual aid amongst sociable species as a factor in evolution. His thesis has been confirmed by many recent findings.[102] Despite the clamourings of modern socio-biologists, with their talk of 'territorial imperatives' and 'selfish genes', Kropotkin's arguments retain all the force they possessed in his opposition to the Social Darwinists of his day who were usually trying to find justification for capitalism and imperialism in the biological roots of human behaviour. Kropotkin correctly saw that human beings are co-operative, social animals, and when least interfered with by coercive authority tend most to practise solidarity and mutual aid. All societies rest on the principles of harmony and co-operation, even if their customs can be coercive and public opinion tyrannical.

But while Kropotkin's scientific method undoubtedly had its rewards, it tended to be more deductive than inductive and tried to explain everything in terms of one principle. While he aspired to be scientific, he often used science to justify his social yearnings, refusing to consider evidence which did not fit in with his scheme; indeed, there is something rigid and inflexible about his approach. As Malatesta pointed out, he was a victim of 'mechanistic fatalism' in adopting a materialist philosophy which saw anarchy as a social organization in keeping with natural laws.[103] He was right to see that anarchy is natural order and that harmony is a law of nature, but he erred by talking of nature as if it were a kind of providence. By insisting that anarchy is a tendency within a mechanical universe which must inevitably triumph, he underestimated the role of the creative will.

His view of history is too deterministic in stressing the inevitability of the coming revolution. After the Russian Revolution, he became increasingly fatalistic and felt that the individual played little part in the historic process. But he was not always consistent. He recognized like Marx the importance of economic organization in influencing the political regime, but he also stressed the importance of consciousness in shaping history and what he called 'the spirit of revolt'. Indeed, at times he gave too much influence to the State as a reified force in society. And he was quite wrong, as the twentieth century has shown, in predicting that the transient aberration of the State would rapidly diminish in strength and density.

Kropotkin's attempt to deduce an objective ethics from a philosophy of nature is also problematic. By drawing moral conclusions from observations of natural phenomena, he committed the 'naturalistic fallacy', that is to say, he unjustifiably inferred an 'ought' from an 'is', a statement of how things should be from a statement of how things are. Human values are human creations, and even if nature operates in a particular way it does not necessarily follow that we should follow suit. Indeed, despite his scientific trappings, it would seem that Kropotkin was primarily a moralist. His anarchism ultimately rests on a moral base on which his scientific, historical and economic theories are built.

In his sociology, Kropotkin fails to see the necessity of any difference of approach when studying nature and society: 'there is no cause', he writes, 'for suddenly changing our method of investigation when we pass from the flower to man, or from a settlement of beavers to a human town.'[104] There is however an important distinction to be made between the laws governing nature and the laws governing society. Whereas natural laws can be disproved in experiments with repeatable conditions, since society has history and its conditions are constantly changing it is impossible to repeat any experiment to verify any laws. At best, we can talk about social trends, not laws of society.

On the other hand, Kropotkin's account of the origin of man-made laws from customs is excellent, and he brings out well the failure of prisons to reform wrongdoers and the immorality of punishment. His attempt to replace law with public opinion makes him open to the same criticism as Godwin that it can lead to moral coercion. Indeed, Kropotkin thinks that it is right for public opinion to oblige all people to do manual work and he believes it is justifiable to use force against inveterate monopolizers. There are authoritarian elements here which cannot be dismissed.

In his evolutionary perspective and in his emphasis on the close link between nature and society, Kropotkin appears as a forerunner of modern social ecology. He recognized the possibility of economic abundance with the appropriate use of technology and the careful husbandry of resources.[105] But while he felt that mutual aid was more advantageous than mutual struggle in bringing about industrial progress, Kropotkin still felt it involved the 'conquest over nature'.[106] It was a contemporary view which went against the logic of his own evolutionary arguments and his deep appreciation of the overall harmony of nature.

With Kropotkin anarchism develops into its most developed form in the nineteenth century. Even those who are generally hostile to anarchism single out Kropotkin as worth reading. He not only tried to base his anarchist philosophy on the findings of science, but to demonstrate its validity by appealing to existing trends within society. Although he countenanced violence and supported war in certain circumstances, he sought to create a society where they would no longer exist. He brought out the importance of mutual aid in evolution, and solidarity in society, but he was never prepared to sacrifice individuality. Indeed, perhaps his most important insight was that only a genuine community can allow the full development of the free individual.

20

Elisée Reclus

The Geographer of Liberty

ELISÉE RECLUS WAS THE most competent French exponent of anarchism at the end of the nineteenth century. He was a firm friend of Kropotkin and they not only shared a professional interest in geography but tried to give a scientific basis to their anarchist beliefs. They popularized in France a version of anarchist communism, and at the time Reclus's stature was second only to that of Kropotkin in anarchist circles.

Although Reclus became one of the foremost geographers of his age, it was always clear where his heart lay; he told the Dutch anarchist Ferdinand Domela Nieuwenhuis: 'Yes, I am a geographer, but above all I am an anarchist.'[1] He not only supported *Le Révolté* and *La Révolte* with money and contributions but his purely anarchist pamphlets like *A mon frère, le paysan* (1893) and *Evolution et révolution* (1880) had a wide circulation. For the anarchist historian Max Nettlau, Reclus represented 'a true realization of anarchy'.[2]

Despite his Calvinist upbringing and education, Reclus developed like Godwin a strong optimistic and idealistic outlook on rejecting his childhood religion. As early as twenty-one, he had laid the foundation of his mature thinking in an essay entitled 'Development of Liberty in the World' (1851) in which he argued that 'For each particular man liberty is an end, but it is only a means to attain love, to attain universal brotherhood.' He also reflected the influence of Proudhon at this stage when he declared: 'Our destiny is to arrive at that state of ideal perfection where nations no longer have any need to be under the tutelage of a government or any other nation. It is the absence of government; it is anarchy, the highest expression of order.'[3]

As a young man, Reclus visited the United States which only confirmed his hatred of slavery. He returned to France to marry Clarisse, the daughter of a French sea captain and a Senegalese woman. They lived with his brother Elie and his companion. After flirting with freemasonry and the freethinking movement, Elisée and his brother became involved and may have joined Bakunin's secret International Alliance of Social Democracy in the mid-sixties. They were both involved with Bakunin in the League for Peace and Freedom and tried to push it in a radical direction.

It was the experience of the Paris Commune however which finally turned Elisée into a militant anarchist. He stood as a Republican candidate but was arrested and imprisoned after the defeat of the Commune. In 1872, he went into exile for ten years in Switzerland, and from 1894 to 1904 he lived in Belgium. To the end of his days, he would say: 'How good it would be with no god and no master to live like brothers.' But while Elisée's anarchist faith never wavered, his brother Elie turned to anthropology, publishing *Les Primitifs* (1903). Thereafter he took an increasing interest in myths and religions.[4]

It was of course as a geographer that Elisée Reclus was principally known in academic circles during his lifetime. He was author of the nineteen-volume *La Nouvelle géographie universelle* (1878–94) as well as popular works such as local histories of a stream and a mountain. In his posthumous six-volume *L'Homme et la terre* (1905–8), he made a synthesis of his geographical and social views. These works earned him a world-wide reputation as a pioneer of human and social geography.

For Reclus, geography is a study of people's changing relationships with each other and with their environment. By looking at the spatial dimension of human life, he concluded that there are natural settings for peoples which are ignored by the artificial boundaries of States. People naturally co-operate when they share similar living conditions. Reclus refused to acknowledge the national status of European States, since they represented the coerced and distorted legal unity of disparate peoples in different environments.

Central to Reclus's social philosophy is the idea of progress. He believed that evolution and revolution both take place in history, but was confident in the eventual success of the revolutionary cause. Biologically and socially, people tend to progress from the simple to the complex, and mutual aid is an essential factor in the process: 'whether it is a question of small or large groups of the human species, it is always through solidarity, through the association of spontaneous, co-ordinated forces that all progress is made.'[5] In addition, Reclus maintained that there are three main laws determining human progress: the class struggle; the search for equilibrium; and the 'sovereign decision of the individual'.[6] While the initiative of the individual is the most important factor in progress, there is a constant oscillation between struggle and equilibrium in society. Reclus spent a long life of scholarly research and militant agitation to bring about the equilibrium of the natural order of anarchy.

At the same time, Reclus rejected the role of race in historical development. He insisted that all races are fundamentally equal, and that their outer differences are determined entirely by their different environments. He further championed the fusion of different races and cultures. While he welcomed the 'Europeanization' of other countries to create an interrelated world, this was not a disguised form of imperialism but a recognition of the technological advances and social freedoms of Europe at the time.

Reclus not only opposed racism but he also championed the emancipation of women and the equality of the sexes. In *L'Homme et la terre*, he argued that patriarchy, based on the brutal sexual force of man, had emerged when man claimed woman as private property. On the other hand, matriarchy, based on the natural attachment of the child to the mother, led to a refinement of mores and a higher stage of social evolution. European civilization was still patriarchal and only when private property was eradicated would women become truly liberated. In the mean time, Reclus called for complete co-education. He believed that men and women should form free unions and create a family solely based upon affection. Although his first marriage was traditional, he 'married' his second two companions without official or religious recognition. Brought up as rational and free beings, his two daughters followed suit when they chose their partners.

Like Kropotkin, Reclus insisted that human beings are social animals. They are not isolated atoms, but parts of a living whole. The individual is related to society like the cell to the body; both have independent existences but both are entirely dependent on each other. Reclus further claimed that the study of sociology established two laws: that a person is interdependent with every other person, and that social progress is achieved through individual initiative. To be true to their nature, people must conform to both laws and by doing so they will be able to liberate themselves. Reclus's conception of anarchy is therefore based on existing tendencies in society and observed regularities in nature. The social order of anarchy reflects the organic unity to be found in the natural world.

After the defeat of the Paris Commune Reclus rejected parliamentary politics and fought for the destruction of the State in a war until the end. '*Voter, c'est abdiquer!*' he declared on 10 October 1885 in *La Révolte* and never changed his mind. Like Descartes in philosophy, he sought in society to make a *tabula rasa* 'of kings and institutions which weigh on human societies'. He was convinced that if the individual was allowed to make all key decisions which affect him, he would move naturally towards anarchism, like a child grows into an adult. He was also certain that 'the solidarity of interests and the infinite advantages of a life at once free and communal will suffice to maintain the social organism'.[7] On 3 March 1877, in an address on 'Anarchy and the State' to the Congress of the Jurassian

Federation at St Imier, he defended the use of the term 'anarchy' on etymological and logical grounds to describe a free society.

Reclus was also one of the first to adopt the theory of anarchist communism propagated by the Italian section of the International (notably by
Malatesta, Cafiero and Costa) in 1876. But where Cafiero stressed the
slogan 'From each according to his abilities, to each according to his needs',
Reclus preferred to say that distribution should be regulated according to
solidarity.[8] The concept of need, he argued, is still an egoistic principle,
while solidarity, or the consideration of one's needs within the context of
the needs of others, represents a higher level of humanity.

According to Reclus, the State should be superseded by a 'free association of the forces of humanity' and law should give way to 'free contract'.[9]
But Reclus declined to describe a free society in detail for he considered
anarchy to be an ideal for the distant future. It would be impossible to
describe the institutions since they would never be permanent and would
adapt to meet changing needs. Nevertheless, he was prepared to outline the
anarchist ideal as the 'complete liberty of the individual and the spontaneous functioning of society by the suppression of privilege and of
governmental caprice, by the destruction of the monopoly of property, by
the mutual respect and reasoned observation of natural laws'.[10] It was at
Reclus's instigation that the Congress of the Jura Federation at La Chaux-
de-Fonds adopted in 1880 the 'natural commune' as opposed to the existing
administrative commune as the basic unit of a free society. In *A mon frère,
le paysan* (1893), he further called on the peasants to take over their land and
work it in common.

Reclus looked to advanced technology to increase production and to
provide the means of life for all. Despite a revival of neo-Malthusianism
amongst anarchist circles in France at the end of the century, his geographical studies convinced Reclus that the earth was rich enough to enable all
humanity to live in ease. Moreover, this could be achieved without the
destructive conquest of nature. As a forerunner of social ecology, Reclus
was repelled by the destruction which a 'pack of engineers' could wreak in
a beautiful valley.[11] He was more advanced than many contemporary social
ecologists (including Murray Bookchin) in his opposition to the slaughter
of animals for meat. He felt that we could learn a great deal from other
species: 'the customs of animals will help us penetrate deeper into the
science of life, will enlarge both our knowledge of the world and our love.'[12]
Reclus presented humanity evolving to a higher stage of civilization, but the
study of earlier human societies and the behaviour of animals could help us
understand our own potential.

Despite his ecological sensibility and vegetarianism, Reclus did not balk
at the use of violence in the human realm. His passionate opposition to the

State was so strong that he advocated in the 1880s propaganda by the deed as well as by the word. He had a preference for reasoned argument, but was ready to countenance individual acts of terrorism if they exposed the vulnerability of the State. In 1882, he declared that there were only two principles at work in society: 'on the one side, that of government, on the other, that of anarchy, authority and liberty . . . All revolutionary acts are, by their very nature, essentially anarchical, whatever the power which seeks to profit from them.'[13] Every revolt against oppression is therefore good to a degree. Means in themselves are neutral; Reclus disapproved of the use of dynamite not so much because of its explosive nature, but because it was inefficient.

In *Ouvrier, prends la machine! Prends la terre, paysan!* (1880), he made it quite clear that the real enemies were the owners and defenders of private property. Since private property is the unjust appropriation of collective property by a few, he considered *la reprise individuelle*, the individual recovery of the fruits of labour, justifiable theft. His only proviso was that the theft should be committed in the name of the happiness of the human race. What is important in an act is the intention behind it, not the act itself or its consequences. Although he did not approve of it, Reclus considered vengeance as an inevitable response to injustice. The bomber Ravachol may have been primitive, but at least he was a rebel.

The lifelong vegetarian once called himself 'a fighting cock'. Far from being a Tolstoyan, Reclus declared that he would defend the weak with force: 'I see a cat that is tortured, a child that is beaten, a woman who is mistreated, and if I am strong enough to prevent it, I prevent it.'[14] To make use of force can therefore be an expression of love. In the final analysis, it was not so much that violence is desirable, but that it is inevitable: 'a law of Nature, a consequence of the physical shock and counter-shock'.[15] Reclus's position on the necessity of violence is a far cry from Kropotkin's principle of anarchist morality: '*Do* to others what you would have them do to you in the same circumstances.'[16]

Although Reclus had in the 1860s been involved in the co-operative movement, after the Paris Commune he came to see co-operatives and communities as not enough since they benefit only a few and leave the existing order intact. He looked to a complete transformation of society which could only be achieved by the combined actions of the workers and the peasants. Later in life, he distanced himself from anarcho-syndicalism and opposed the Second International since he refused to collaborate with socialists who maintained a belief in government and laws.

With the failure of the anarchist campaign of terror in the early 1890s and the subsequent governmental repression of the revolutionary movement, Reclus like Kropotkin came to stress the gradual and evolutionary side of social change. At the turn of the century, he argued that 'evolution and revolution are two successive acts of the same phenomenon, evolution preceding revolution, and the latter preceding a new evolution, mother of future revolutions.'[17] Evolution is the natural and habitual course of events and revolution occurs only when the old structures become too limited and insufficient for an organism. Life then moves suddenly to realize a new form.

Reclus rejected Marx's and Bakunin's form of historical materialism, insisting that it is not economic factors which primarily shape the growth of consciousness, but consciousness that transforms society: 'it is blood which makes man; it is ideas which make society.'[18] In the preface to the first French edition of Kropotkin's *La Conquête du pain* (1892), Reclus declared: 'The first of the laws of history is that society models itself upon its ideal.'[19] Towards the end of his life, he chose to work almost entirely on the level of consciousness in order to eradicate human prejudice and domination.

In his ethics, Reclus felt the individual should draw on his own experience as well as listen to the interior voice of his conscience. He recommended to his comrades the maxim of 'our great ancestor Rabelais: "Do what you please!" ' At the same time, this did not imply some egoistic self-assertion which paid no heed to the wishes of others. The only resemblance Reclus found between individualist anarchists and anarchist communists was the name: he felt that every individual should act by always considering the welfare of all. He therefore defined liberty as the individual's 'right to act according to his liking, to "do as he pleases", at the same time associating naturally his will to those of other men in all the collective tasks'.[20] This concern for others should not be considered a constraint since like Godwin he believed that a person experiences the highest gratification in working for the general good.

Reclus's anarchism is persuasive. He made a compelling case for a form of voluntary communism which respects individuality while being based on solidarity. As a geographer, he had a profound ecological sensibility; as a moralist, he considered the suffering of animals as well as humans. Despite his early defence of revolutionary violence, he came to stress the need for gradual change through the spread of knowledge. For all his scientific interests, he was concerned with spiritual as well as material well-being, insisting that anarchists had a triple ideal to realize: bread for the body (food), bread for the mind (education), and bread for the spirit (brotherhood). Reclus stands not only as one of the most attractive of nineteenth-century anarchist thinkers but as a forerunner of modern liberation and social ecology.

21

Errico Malatesta

The Electrician of Revolution

THE MOST PROMINENT ANARCHIST thinker to emerge in Italy at the end of the nineteenth century was undoubtedly Errico Malatesta. If his thought does not appear as a coherent whole, it is because he was primarily a propagandist and agitator. He was at the centre of the international anarchist movement for nearly sixty years and his ideas were invariably developed in the social struggle. He never wrote a complete work and despite many requests failed to commit his memoirs to paper. But he edited, and wrote prolifically, for many journals and his collected articles show a penetrating mind and warm sensibility at work. He was no philosopher, but he had the knack of making complex ideas easily understood and wrote in a lively and incisive style. He not only interpreted anarchist thought for a wider audience but made a valuable contribution of his own.

Despite his weak constitution, Malatesta's life was one of continual movement. He spent most of his time either seeking out revolutionary situations or being obliged to move from one country to another to escape the wrath of the authorities. Nearly half his life was passed in exile, mostly in London, and although he never lost his love for Italy, he considered his country to be the whole world. States not only hindered his passage across their borders but they also denied him his freedom; he spent more than ten years in different prisons, mostly awaiting trial. Even there he did not waste his time; he considered most policemen 'poor devils' and did his best to convert them to the banner of freedom. Resolute and brave, he once described himself at a trial as 'a man with a cause' (*un uomo di fede*). Although he was reluctant to take unnecessary risks, the anarchist cause was more important to him than his own liberty and comfort.

Malatesta was born in 1853, the son of a small liberal landowner in Caserta Province in South Italy. He was sent to a Jesuit school but by the time he was fourteen years old, his republican sympathies inspired by Mazzini and Garibaldi led to his arrest after he had written a letter to King Victor Emmanuel II complaining about a local injustice. His father warned that if he continued on this path he would end up on the gallows. Undeterred, Malatesta became a medical student at Naples University but was expelled after taking part in a republican demonstration. It was not long after that he discovered the writings of Bakunin, and he joined the Italian section of the International in 1871.

Full of idealism, Malatesta and his young friends believed at the time that it was only necessary to criticize the bourgeoisie for the people to rebel. They quickly came to realize that extreme hunger often prevents rather than encourages revolution, and their propaganda proved most effective in the least depressed regions and amongst the more affluent workers. Malatesta did not lose his idealism, but he recognized the need to organize and to employ propaganda with realistic and practical goals in mind.

Handing over his inherited property to his tenants, he learned the electrician's and mechanic's trade in order to support himself independently and to live among the working people. After leaving university, he travelled widely in the 1870s around the Mediterranean, from Spain to the Ottoman Empire. In 1872, he met Bakunin for the first time, in Switzerland. He later acknowledged him as 'our spiritual father', especially in his criticism of the principle of authority and of the State, but he found his views on political economy and history too Marxist.[1]

In order to rival the feats of the followers of Garibaldi and Mazzini, the Italian anarchists organized strikes and demonstrations, but also resorted to the well-tried tactic of the Italian revolutionary tradition – the insurrection. In 1874, Malatesta, Andrea Costa, and members of a group within the International, who called themselves the Italian Committee for the Social Revolution, planned an uprising in Bologna in order to trigger off similar actions and eventually the 'social liquidation' throughout Italy. Bakunin was waiting to join them, but the *carabinieri* had been informed and foiled the insurgents as they were marching on Bologna.

The message of direct action was not lost on the international anarchist movement. At the Berne Conference of the International in 1876, Malatesta explained the background to the Bologna uprising and argued: 'the revolution consists more in deeds than words ... each time a spontaneous movement of the people erupts ... it is the duty of every revolutionary socialist to declare his solidarity with the movement in the making.' The movement should seek to destroy existing institutions by force; a 'river of blood separated them from the future'.[2] Three months later Malatesta and Carlo Cafiero gave a clearer definition of their strategy in the *Bulletin of the Jura Federation*: 'The Italian federation believes that the insurrectional fact, destined to affirm socialist principles by deeds, is the most efficacious means of propaganda.'[3] The view of the Italians came to dominate European anarchist activities during the 1880s, especially in France and Spain.

Despite the persecution of the authorities a national congress was held in a wood outside Florence in 1876, where Malatesta and Cafiero persuaded the delegates to move from a form of Bakuninite collectivism to communism. Those present accepted the proposition: 'Each must do for society all that his abilities will allow him to do, and he has the right to demand from society the satisfaction of all his needs, in the measure conceded by the state of production and social capacities.'[4] The congress also confirmed the insurrectional position of the Italian anarchist movement.

Malatesta, Cafiero and Costa lost no time in putting their preaching into practice. In the following year, they entered two villages near Benevento in Campania with an armed band, burning the tax registers and declaring the end of the reign of King Victor Emmanuel. The peasants, including their priests, welcomed them at first but feared to join them; as a result, Italian troops soon arrived and captured the insurgents.

This second abortive rising provoked another round of persecution. The Italian sections of the outlawed International called for a general insurrection on a national scale but when it failed to materialize individuals turned to their own acts of terror. In 1878, the new King Umberto was stabbed by a republican cook from Naples and on the following day a bomb was thrown in a monarchist parade. Even greater repression followed. The International was broken up and Malatesta went into exile.

Whilst staying with members of the Jurassian Federation of the International in Switzerland, Malatesta became friends with Elisée Reclus and Kropotkin, the leading anarchist communists of the day. He still continued to travel afar. In 1879 he went to Rumania. He attended the congress of the International in London in 1881 and in the following year went to Egypt hoping to foment rebellion in the days of Arabi Pasha.

He returned to Italy in 1883 where he tried to help reorganize the Italian sections and edited the journal *La Questione Sociale*.

It was at this time that he wrote his most widely read pamphlet *Fra contadini* (Between Peasants; 1884), an exposition of anarchist communist ideas for those who had little knowledge of social questions. Malatesta defined anarchy as 'without government . . . the government only serves to defend the bourgeois, and when it is a question of our interests, the best is to manage them ourselves'. On the grounds of human solidarity, he advocated a form of communism which involved the common ownership of property and the socialization of production. It was therefore necessary 'to establish a perfect solidarity between men of the entire world' based on the principle of 'from each according to his abilities, to each according to his needs'. After the revolution, he recommended that society be divided into communes in which different trades will form associations. Only anarchist communism could liberate humanity and bring about 'the destruction of political power, that is to say of the government, and the conquest of the soil and of all existing riches'.[5]

Soon after writing this pamphlet Malatesta was arrested and sentenced in 1884 to three years' imprisonment. After helping out in a cholera epidemic in Naples, he jumped bail and sailed to Buenos Aires in 1885. He spent the next four years in Argentina, leaving an indelible anarchist stamp on the labour movement there. When he returned to Europe, he visited France, England, Switzerland and Spain before settling again in Italy in 1897.

During his second stay in London in 1889, he began what was to become a lifelong friendship with his biographer Max Nettlau. He also met William Morris at the Socialist League, and got to know Joseph Lane and Frank Kitz well. He was deeply impressed by the London Dock Strike of 1889–90, although he did not think it would lead to a general insurrection. At the 1890 Conference of the Socialist League, he advocated the seizure of property in general; in its journal *The Commonweal* on 6 August 1890, he is quoted as saying 'Let us urge the people to seize the property and go and dwell in the mansions of the rich; do not let us paralyse our efforts by discussion as to the future.' As for those workers who were calling for a general strike in England, he urged: 'The General Strike would be good if we were ready to make use of it at once by immediate military action whether by barricades or otherwise.' These oft-quoted sentiments were however out of keeping with Malatesta's condemnation of terrorism and his call for a new syndicalism in the following decade.

In 1891 Malatesta issued one of his most influential pamphlets *Anarchy*, reprinted in English by Freedom Press in 1892. Malatesta considered it the best pamphlet he ever wrote, and it certainly expressed his ideas in a lively and polemical style.

The influence of Bakunin is immediately clear in the pamphlet; Malatesta quotes him on 'the natural and social law of human solidarity' and the need to recognize that 'My freedom is the freedom of all.'[6] But the impact of Malatesta's old schoolfriend F. S. Merlino, a lawyer and social historian, is also apparent. They both came to criticize the economic determinism of Marx, arguing that the revolution is not inevitable and that the State can have an influence on the economic structure of society.

Malatesta's starting-point in the pamphlet is that there is a fundamental law of solidarity which ensures that the development of human well-being is achieved through mutual aid or co-operation. But the resulting harmony of interests is very different from Kropotkin's vision, for Malatesta describes mutual aid as '*association for the struggle* against all natural factors antagonistic to the existence, the development and well-being of the associates'. The view that human progress is achieved in a struggle *against* nature leads

Malatesta to trace man's preference for domination to the 'fierce and anti-social instincts inherited from his animal ancestry'.[7] According to Malatesta, man is instinctively driven to defend his individual existence as well as his offspring. We therefore need society to redirect our natural desires, our 'animal' desires, into co-operative behaviour since co-operation is the only means towards progress and security. It is a view similar to Bakunin's but which also finds echoes in Kropotkin.

For Malatesta anarchy means a society without government. While recognizing the various meanings given to the word 'State', he prefers in his drive to destroy all political authority to collate the State and government and to call simply for the abolition of government. Government, however much it provides public services, is by its very nature plundering and oppressive. Since it is also 'the property owners' *gendarme*', its abolition would also involve the abolition of private property. It is essential to convince people that government is both harmful and useless and that with anarchy (in the sense of the absence of government) will come 'natural order, unity of human needs and the interests of all, complete freedom within complete solidarity'.[8] By stressing solidarity and the equality of conditions, Malatesta defines an anarchism closer to socialism than liberalism.

In place of government, he calls for the spontaneous groupings of individuals united by sympathies and interests in voluntary associations. Life would be managed on the basis of free initiative, free compact and voluntary co-operation. The real being, Malatesta insists, is the individual, and society or the collectivity is only made up of individuals. He sees little likelihood of conflict in a free and equal society as long as personal freedom is based on voluntary solidarity and an awareness of the community of interests. He proclaims the maxim 'DO AS YOU WISH' since 'in a harmonious society, in a society without government and property, each one will WANT WHAT HE MUST DO.'[9] It would appear that at this stage in his life Malatesta therefore held the optimistic view that in an anarchist society there would be no clash between desire and duty. As for the means to realize such a society, the only way is 'to crush those who own social wealth by revolutionary action'.[10]

In the early 1890s, Malatesta travelled widely in Europe. He was in Spain in 1891 at the time of the Jerez uprising and tried to ease the conflict between collectivists and communists by calling for an 'anarchism without adjectives'. With Charles Malato in Belgium, he witnessed in 1892–3 the general strike for universal suffrage and recognized its limitations. In the mean time, he found himself in Italy intermittently, maintaining his contacts and advocating a new unionism. Then in 1896, Malatesta helped organize the London Congress of the Second International where the anarchists were finally expelled from the international socialist movement.

His thoughts turned once again to Italy. With bad harvests and rising prices triggering off many peasant revolts, the country seemed ripe for revolution. In 1897 Malatesta therefore returned secretly to the port of Ancona and started editing *L'Agitazione* from a room; in it he called for the formation of a broad front of anarchists, syndicalists and socialists. It was probably the most important of the many publications edited by him, and his articles in it show signs of a maturing intellect informed by experience.

He reiterates that anarchy is a '*society organised without authority*, meaning by authority the power to *impose* one's own will'.[11] Such a society would not be disorganized or chaotic as the apologists of government maintain. Where Engels had argued that organization is impossible without authority, Malatesta maintains that organization, far from creating authority, is the only cure for it. Alone one is powerless; it is 'by co-operation with his fellows that man finds the means to express his activity and his power of initiative'. He also countered Engels' argument that once classes disappear the State as such has no *raison d'être* and transforms itself from a government over men into an administration of things: 'Whoever has power over things has power over men; who governs production also governs the producers; who determines consumption is the master of the consumer.'[12] The crucial question is for things to be administered on the basis of free agreement among the interested parties, not according to laws made by administrators. To achieve this end, he proposed the formation of an anarchist 'party' working outside parliament. Its task would be not to emancipate the people, but to help the people to emancipate themselves.

Malatesta's activities were soon curtailed for he was arrested again early in 1898 during a public demonstration in Ancona and was charged with 'criminal association'. Anarchists in the past had denied the charge on the grounds that they were opposed to organization, but Malatesta and his comrades declared that they were organized and demanded the right to organize a 'party' in the sense of an association with a common purpose. Although Malatesta and his comrades managed to turn the trial into a campaign for civil liberties, he was still sent to the penal island of Lampedusa for five years. In a daring escapade, he managed to flee to the United States. He stayed in New Jersey, where he was shot in the leg during an overheated discussion at a meeting of anarchists.[13] After visiting Cuba, where he was allowed to stay for ten days and address several meetings as long as he did not use the word 'anarchy', he returned to London in 1900.

Whilst living in London for the next thirteen years, Malatesta wrote articles and pamphlets mainly for the Italian anarchist press and did not involve himself directly with the British anarchist movement centred on Kropotkin and *Freedom*. This was partly because he felt that English comrades should write for an English paper, but also because he did not want to engage in public polemic with Kropotkin and undermine his prestige. Although he quietly went about earning his living as a mechanic and electrician, the police tried to implicate him in the Sidney Street affair in 1910 (as an electrician, he had supplied a bottle of gas to one of the gang) but without success. In 1909 he was imprisoned, with Rudolf Rocker, for three months on a charge of criminal libel brought by his fellow Italian Belleli, who had been called an Italian police spy. Malatesta was also recommended for deportation, but the threat was lifted after a vigorous campaign by workers' organizations and by the radical press which led to a mass demonstration in Trafalgar Square, organized by Guy Aldred and attended by several MPs. The *Daily Herald*, in particular, took up the cause, publishing one letter which referred to Malatesta as an 'international Tom Mann'. The growing influence of the movement at this time led the alarmed *Daily Telegraph* to report on 12 March 1912:

> The authorities have now, we understand, received evidence establishing the fact that sections of the Communists, the Syndicalists, and the Anarchists share common aims and are working together for one common object, and, in fact, it may be said that present labour unrest is almost entirely due to a great conspiracy on the part of those agitators to promote dissatisfaction and resentment amongst the working classes.

But while he tried to keep a fairly low profile in Britain, Malatesta was concerned with developing the international anarchist movement. He was a member of the British Industrial League and with the growth of anarcho-syndicalism, especially in Italy and France, he emphasized at the International Anarchist Congress held at Amsterdam in 1907 the link between revolutionary syndicalism and anarchist communism. Although he was considered one of the last representatives of insurrectional anarchism, Malatesta had always seen the need for some form of organization in small groups united by mutual solidarity; he had called for a new broad-front unionism throughout the 1890s. He was worried however that the new syndicalist movement might divide rather than unite the working class. In addition, he thought that syndicalism should not be limited to one class, even if they were the most oppressed, and argued that anarchist revolution has as its aims the complete liberation of the whole of humanity.

As for syndicalist methods, Malatesta felt that 'the general strike is pure utopia'. Far from being the great weapon of the non-violent revolution, it is fraught with difficulties. If everyone stopped work, there simply would not be enough food and essential goods in the storehouses to meet people's immediate needs. Rather than starving the bourgeoisie, the first to starve during a general strike would be the workers themselves. The answer is not therefore to lay down tools but to occupy and expropriate the factories and land and to increase production as quickly as possible. Above all, the general strike could be no substitute for the insurrection. As soon as the workers try to gain possession of the 'fruits of production by open force', they will be opposed by 'soldiers, policemen, perhaps the bourgeoisie themselves, and then the question will have to be resolved by bullets and bombs. It will be insurrection, and victory will go to the strongest.' In a homely image typical of his polemical style, Malatesta declared: 'To adopt the policy of neither cannons nor corn is to make all revolutionists the enemies of the people. We must face the cannons if we want the corn.'[14]

Before the First World War, the Italian anarchist movement was undergoing one of its periodic revivals. Malatesta decided to leave London in 1913 and return home again. He settled in Ancona and immediately threw himself into the struggle. A Captain of the local *carabinieri* described with reluctant admiration how

> His qualities as an intelligent, combative speaker who seeks to persuade with calm, and never violent, language, are used to the full to revive the already spent forces of the party and to win converts and sympathizers, never losing sight of his principal goal which is to draw together the forces of the party and undermine the bases of the State, by hindering its workings, paralysing its services and doing antimilitary propaganda, until the favourable occasion arises to overturn the existing State.[15]

Unlike Bakunin with his fascination with secret societies, Malatesta considered it essential for anarchists to give their activities a maximum of publicity to reach as many people as possible. He edited with Luigi Fabbri the journal *La Volontà* from Ancona and lectured in the principal cities in Italy. In 1914, he was involved in a general strike which spread rapidly after the killing in Ancona of unarmed anti-militarist demonstrators by police. During the 'Red Week' which followed, the monarchy seemed about to topple. The revolutionary Unione Sindacale set the pace and workers began to reorganize social life on a new basis. Then the moderate General Confederation of Labour, which controlled the majority of trade-unions, ordered their members back to work. The strike faltered and then collapsed. Once again, Malatesta was obliged to go into exile.

He spent the rest of the First World War in London. Despite his reluctance to engage in any public polemic which might split the anarchist movement, he openly attacked Kropotkin's support for the Allies – he considered his old friend to be a 'truly pathological case' – and tried to remind the minority of anarchists who wavered of their anti-militarist principles. He was no pacifist; indeed, he was prepared to fight for the 'triumph of peace and of fraternity amongst all human beings' and considered attack to be often the best means of defending oneself. But while he believed that wars of liberation and revolution are necessary, he could see no element of emancipation in the First World War.[16] In a letter to *Freedom* in December 1914, he reminded Kropotkin that 'anti-militarism is the doctrine which affirms that military service is an abominable and murderous trade, and that a man ought never to consent to take up arms at the command of the masters, and never fight except for the Social Revolution.' Attacking 'Pro-government Anarchists' like Kropotkin, Jean Grave, Elisée Reclus and Charles Malato who supported the Allies in the war, he further declared that there was only one remedy:

> More than ever we must avoid compromise; deepen the chasm between capitalists and wage-slaves, between rulers and ruled; preach expropriation of private property and the destruction of States. Such is the only means of guaranteeing fraternity between the peoples and Justice and Liberty for all; and we must prepare to accomplish these things.[17]

When he returned to Italy in 1919 he started up the first anarchist daily *Umanità Nova* in Milan. It survived for two years and reached a circulation of fifty thousand copies. Malatesta addressed meetings throughout the country. Some workers hailed him as the 'Lenin of Italy', a view he quickly rejected. Many of the Italian anarchists had welcomed enthusiastically the Russian Soviets and as late as June 1919 Camillo Berneri hailed the Bolshevik regime as 'the most practical experiment in integral democracy on the largest scale yet attempted ... the antithesis of centralizing state socialism'.[18] Malatesta however warned that the new government had been set up in Russia 'above the Revolution in order to bridle it and subject it to the purposes of a particular party ... or rather the leaders of a party'.[19] After the death of Lenin, he further wrote that 'even with the best intentions, he was a tyrant who strangled the Russian revolution – and we who could not admire him while alive, cannot mourn him now he is dead. Lenin is dead. Long live Liberty!'[20]

True to his anarchist beliefs, Malatesta continued to reject all parliamentary action and was deeply critical of any trade-union movement which set up a central committee with permanent officials. He synthesized his ideas in the draft text of an Anarchist Programme which was accepted by the Unione Anarchica Italiana at its Congress in Bologna in 1920. The articles of the Programme included the abolition of private property and government and the organization of social life by means of federations of free associations of producers and consumers. It insisted that the means of life should be guaranteed to all those who cannot provide for themselves.

It also declared war on 'patriotic prejudices' and on 'religions and all lies, even if they shelter under the cloak of science'. The family was to be reconstructed and would emerge 'from the practice of love, freed from every legal tie'.[21]

As for the means, Malatesta argued that the oppressed should be persuaded of the truth and beauty of the anarchist ideal based on equal liberty of all. While recognizing the importance of the economic struggle to improve workers' conditions, he insisted that one must pass to the political struggle, that is the struggle against government. All struggles for partial freedom are worth supporting, but in the last analysis the struggle must involve physical force since the only limit to the oppression of government is the power with which people oppose it. A successful insurrection is the most powerful factor in the emancipation of the people; it is therefore the task of anarchists to 'push' the people to expropriate the bosses, to put all goods in common and to organize their lives themselves. Only by the complete destruction of the domination and exploitation of man by man will there be well-being for all.

At the same time, Malatesta tried to bring together all the libertarian forces on the Left in a united front against fascism, with the proviso that if any party took power and became the government, it would be opposed as an enemy. Malatesta was always flexible and open to new alliances. He did not hanker for the old insurrectionary days, nor did his subtle thought crystallize into dogma. 'We do not boast that we possess absolute truth', he wrote in *Umanità Nova*; 'on the contrary, we believe that *social truth* is not a fixed quantity, good for all times, universally applicable or determinable in advance ... Our solutions always leave the door open to different and, one hopes, better solutions.'[22] Moreover, he wanted to show that anarchy is something possible and attainable in a relatively short time. Hence his concern with practical means to achieve the anarchist ideals.

He reiterated his view that anarchists are opposed to violence and seek a society without the intervention of the *gendarme*, but that violence is justifiable to defend oneself and others from violence. Even though violence is in itself an evil, he felt that revolution must necessarily be violent because the privileged classes would be unwilling to renounce their status voluntarily. He was prepared to use force against government, since it is by force that government keeps the people in subjection. Violence is therefore an unpleasant necessity which must cease as soon as the moment of liberation is achieved. He had refused to condemn the assassinations of King Umberto and President McKinley and he still held it possible for assassins to be 'saints' and 'heroes'. But he had gone beyond his youthful enthusiasm for fiery insurrection, as inspired by Bakunin. At this stage in his life, he steered a middle path between the 'propaganda by the deed' of the revolutionaries on the one hand, and the 'passive anarchy' of the Tolstoyans on the other.[23]

In his articles for *Umanità Nova*, Malatesta also clarified his view of freedom. It is fine to strive for maximum freedom but one's self-love should be tempered by a love of others: 'That aspiration towards unlimited freedom, if not tempered by a love for mankind and by the desire that all should enjoy equal freedom, may well create rebels who, if they are strong enough, soon become exploiters and tyrants, but never anarchists.' He now argued that men are not naturally harmonious and absolute freedom is impossible since social life involves sacrificing desires which are irreconcilable with those of others. While advocating freedom as the power to do as one wishes, he pointed out that it presupposes social freedom, the 'equal freedom for all, an equality of conditions such as to allow everybody to do as they wish, with the only limitation, imposed by inevitable natural necessities and the equal freedom of others'.[24] He did not therefore recognize the right of the majority to impose laws on the minority, and was even more opposed to the domination of the majority by a minority. Differences should be solved by mutual agreement and compromise. It is not necessary to 'educate' people for freedom; only liberty fits one for liberty.

It was Malatesta's contention that communism is the only possible system, 'based on natural solidarity, which links all mankind; and only a desired solidarity linking them in brotherhood, can reconcile the interests of all and serve as the basis for a society in which everyone is guaranteed the greatest possible well-being and freedom'. He was not so naive as to believe that all crime, in the strict sense of action which tends to increase human suffering and violate the right to equal freedom, will cease once government and private property are abolished, but it will undoubtedly diminish when its social causes are removed. It will be up to the people in a free society to defend themselves directly against criminals and delinquents, treating them 'as brothers who have strayed, as sick people needing loving treatment'.[25] Even the transitory violence of the people is always preferable to the legalized State violence of the judiciary and the police.

The period from 1919–22 saw a great revival of anarchist fortunes in Italy and it proved one of the most active and fulfilling times of Malatesta's long life. The revolutionary Unione Sindacale had renewed its vigour and had about 400,000 members. Malatesta urged anarchists to work within the unions as anarchists, trying to strengthen the revolutionary consciousness of the workers. In March 1920, he was calling in *Umanità Nova* for the workers not only to strike but to take over the factories. After widespread agitation the metal-workers occupied their places of work in Milan and Turin in 1920. They armed themselves for defence and began to organize production on their own. Other workers and peasants occupied factories and the land. The revolution seemed imminent. But the pattern of the 'Red Week' of 1914 was repeated.

The Socialist Party and the Confederazione Generale del Lavoro (General Confederation of Labour) were determined to prevent revolutionary action by arguing that there was a lack of raw materials in Italy. They went on to concoct with the government a token form of workers' control and the workers obeyed their order to return to work. The experience convinced Malatesta that the internationalization of natural wealth is not the precondition for socialism, as Rudolf Rocker had argued, but the result. It also confirmed his view that a general strike which did not lead to insurrection was bound to be defeated.

For their part in the strike, Malatesta, Armando Borghi (Secretary of the syndicalist union), and eighty other anarchists were arrested in October and held in prison awaiting trial until the following July when they were freed by a jury. Malatesta then directed all his energy towards uniting the libertarian forces against fascism through a 'Workers' Alliance'.

He recognized the working-class movement as at that time the most powerful force for social transformation. While co-operatives and trade-unions in capitalist society tend to be reformist because they serve sectional interests and develop an *esprit de corps*, they can be valuable in a revolutionary situation. In Malatesta's view, the syndicalists were mistaken however in seeing the workers' organizations as the only framework for future society. The general strike which they advocated could be a powerful weapon in raising their consciousness but too much faith in it could do harm to the revolutionary cause. In a revolution, it would be best for the workers' organizations to disappear and be absorbed in new popular groupings. Malatesta therefore recommended anarchists to work as anarchists within the unions, advocating and practising as far as possible direct action, decentralization and individual initiative.

This did not mean abandoning anarchist organization which must allow for complete autonomy and independence to individuals who co-operate for common aims. The decisions of congresses moreover should not be binding but simply suggestions based on free agreement. Having accepted a programme however, Malatesta considered it the moral duty of an anarchist to fulfil his or her pledges. At the same time, a libertarian organization should only hold together as long as it maintains a 'spiritual affinity' amongst its members and adapts its constitution to continually changing circumstances.[26]

After the collapse of the factory occupations and the general strike, things went from bad to worse. In 1921, some anarchists undertook a series of bombings in Milan which not only alienated many workers but provided the Fascists with an excuse to use counter-violence against the Left. The paralysed Socialist Party split into three different factions. Mussolini's 'march' on Rome in 1922 heralded the defeat of the working-class movement in Italy. Nevertheless, despite constant police harassment and government censorship, Malatesta managed with great difficulty from 1924 to 1926 to bring out *Pensiero e Volontà* which contained some of his most thoughtful and penetrating articles.

After a lifetime of study and agitation, he concluded that anarchism is not linked to any philosophical system and is born of a 'moral revolt against social injustice'. The common factor amongst anarchists divided into different schools is the 'searching for a more secure guarantee of freedom'. It was Malatesta's view that freely accepted communism is the best guarantee for individual freedom, for only in association can human beings overcome the 'hostile forces of Nature'.

Whereas he had earlier argued like Bakunin that there is a natural law of solidarity which predominates in nature as in society, he came to stress that in nature brute force alone rules and that all human life is 'a struggle against outside nature, every step forward is adaptation, is the overcoming of a natural law'.[27] Far from being based on natural harmony, anarchy is 'a human aspiration, which is not founded on any real or imagined natural necessity, but which can be achieved through the exercise of the human will. It takes advantage of the means that science offers to Man in his struggle against nature and between contrasting wills.'[28] Malatesta is the first major anarchist thinker to reject the notion of a prior natural order, a notion which had formed the bedrock of previous anarchist philosophy, and which had been habitually counterpoised to the artificial disorder of government. It marks a major shift in anarchist thought and adapts the creed to a metaphysical belief in chaos.

Malatesta was as insistent as ever about the need for a social revolution preceded by an insurrection to overthrow the government. He believed that only violent revolution could solve the social question and that it was an act of will and not the inevitable outcome of economic and political forces. Revolution for Malatesta was not merely speeded up social change; it was a fundamental transformation of society:

> The Revolution is the creation of new living institutions, new group-ings, new social relationships; it is the destruction of privileges and monopolies; it is the new spirit of justice, of brotherhood, of freedom which must renew the whole of social life, raise the moral level and material conditions of the masses by calling on them to provide, through their direct and conscious action, for their own futures.[29]

At the same time, he stressed that anarchist revolution should not destroy all institutions but only those based on authority such as the army, police, judiciary and prison. Other existing institutions should be taken over and used by the people to manage their own affairs. The first task on the morrow of the revolution is therefore to destroy all political power and for the workers and peasants to take over the factories and land and work them in common. The landowners, the industrialists and the financiers must be expropriated, the banks abolished, title deeds destroyed, and the people armed. Intellectuals and members of the bourgeoisie would have to work like everybody else if they wanted to enjoy the same benefits. Those workers and peasants who do not want to join in the collectives would be given tools to provide for themselves. Anarchists, Malatesta adds, ought to be tolerant of all social concepts as long as they do not threaten the equal freedom of others.

As realistic as ever, he recognizes that anarchists would probably play a minority role in any foreseeable revolution so it would be their special mission to be 'vigilant custodians of freedom'.[30] If any group tried to reconstitute the State they should rebel against its demands and refuse to support it in any shape or form. Malatesta had come to believe that in the long run, the complete triumph of anarchy would come gradually by evolution rather than by violent revolution once the initial period of insurrection was over.

An anarchist attempt on Mussolini's life in 1926 was used as an excuse to ban not only the libertarian but the whole of the independent press. All opposition was silenced. Malatesta spent the remaining five years of his life with his companion and daughter under house arrest, guarded night and day by Mussolini's police. Whoever went to see him was arrested and questioned.

It did not prevent him from writing articles, including his recollections and criticisms of his 'old friend' Kropotkin whom he believed erred in his theory of scientific determinism and in his excessive optimism. He was a 'victim of mechanistic fatalism' who underestimated the importance of the will in human affairs. By believing communist-anarchism would triumph inevitably as if by a law of nature, he had failed to see the difficulties ahead:

> At bottom Kropotkin conceived Nature as a kind of Providence, thanks to which there had to be harmony in all things, including human societies.
>
> And this has led many anarchists to repeat that *'Anarchy is Order'*, a phrase with an exquisite Kropotkinian flavour.
>
> If it is true that the law of Nature is harmony, I suggest one would be entitled to ask why Nature has waited for anarchists to be born, and goes on waiting for them to triumph, in order to rid us of the

terrible destructive conflicts from which mankind has always suffered.
Would one not be closer to the truth in saying that anarchy is the
struggle, in human society, against the disharmonies of Nature?[31]

At the end of his life, anarchy for Malatesta was not so much a form of
natural order as a human creation. The idea of natural harmony, he now
felt in his old age, is an invention of human laziness.

Malatesta had long espoused anarchism not because it is a scientific
truth and a natural law but because it corresponded 'better than any other
way of social life, to my desire for the good of all, to my aspiration towards
a society which reconciles the liberty of everyone with co-operation and
love among men'. It was enough for him that it did not contradict any known
law of nature. Indeed, he argued that 'Science stops where inevitability ends
and freedom begins . . . it is in this ability to exercise will-power that one
must seek for the sources of morality and the rules of behaviour.'[32] Science
leads to fatalism, the denial of free will and of freedom, and a mechanical
and deterministic interpretation of phenomena (like Kropotkin's) leaves no
room for moral responsibility. Anarchy on the other hand is a human
aspiration achieved through the exercise of the human will which can
achieve new effects. It would be misleading however to suggest that Malatesta was an extreme voluntarist opposed to science. He was flattered to be
alleged to possess a 'scientific mind' and criticized Kropotkin precisely
because he felt he was a 'poet of science' who was 'too passionate to be an
accurate observer'.[33]

Malatesta's view that it is necessary to struggle *against* nature in order
to achieve abundance reflects the prevailing nineteenth-century notions
about economic scarcity. He agreed with Marx's view that overproduction
is inherent in capitalism, arguing that it places obstacles in the way of producing useful commodities. Since the *raison d'être* of capitalism is profit
there needs to be an artificial scarcity of goods. But he was convinced that
modern technology made abundance a real possibility. Unfortunately, his
emphasis on struggle against nature in order to achieve well-being for all is
too harsh. As modern social ecologists have pointed out, it is necessary to
co-operate with and not conquer the forces of nature.

Malatesta was right however to insist that anarchism is not linked to
any particular philosophical system. In his case, he took a consistently
sceptical and anti-metaphysical stance, but it did not turn him into a mechanical atheist. Not only did he oppose his own doctrine of the creative
power of the will to Kropotkin's deterministic and mechanistic system, but
more tellingly he assumed that people *can* do what they *will*. Although he
called for war on religions, he constantly emphasized the importance of
moral and spiritual values: the moral basis of anarchism is love for all

humanity. However dark the prison he found himself in, Malatesta never lost sight of his own shining ideal of freedom and love.

Although Malatesta reluctantly accepted the need for revolutionary violence, he insisted that the end does not justify the means. Indeed, 'every end needs its means'; since morality must be sought in the aims, the means is determined.[34] It follows that while the capitalist who appropriates the labour of others is a thief, if an anarchist steals the property of another, he is no less a thief. Unlike Reclus, Malatesta was no apologist for '*la reprise individuelle*', the individual 'rip-off'.

Malatesta also argued that one must not and cannot defend the revolution with means which contradict the ends. He was totally opposed to revolutionary terror; 'if in order to win it [the revolution] it were necessary to erect the gallows in the public square', he wrote, 'then I would prefer to lose.'[35] The great advocate of insurrection and revolution, pointed to the horror of indiscriminate violence the day before he died. He wrote in his notebook: 'He who throws a bomb and kills a pedestrian, declares that as a victim of society he has rebelled against society. But could not the poor victim object: "Am I society?"'[36] Only the kind of violence which was not motivated by hatred and which aimed at the liberation of all was justifiable in Malatesta's eyes. He did not want to impose anarchy by force in order to defend its gains against violent opponents.

Malatesta sounds more authoritarian when he argued that the task of the anarchist propagandist is to 'push' the people to seize all the freedom they can and to 'push' the revolution as far as it will go.[37] Yet he made clear that such 'pushing' is a question of 'education for freedom' in which people are stimulated to think and act for themselves. Finally, Malatesta still felt as late as 1920 that it was necessary for groups and parties who are 'joined by free agreement, under oath of secrecy' to provide a network of speedy communications to inform each other of all incidents likely to provoke a widespread popular movement. Such oaths and secrecy, which hark back to Bakunin's conspiracies, would appear an unreasonable restriction on the free exercise of individual judgement. In general, however, Malatesta insisted that anarchists should work in the open as much as possible in 'the full light of day'.[38] What shines through all of Malatesta's writings is his openness, his sincerity, and his honesty.

Malatesta died in 1932, aged seventy-nine, still faithful to his vision of a society 'without bosses and without *gendarmes*'.[39] The indomitable international revolutionary, renowned for his warmth, humanity, and unflagging optimism, remained a symbol of the fragmented Italian anarchist movement which was forced into exile and only regrouped after the Second World War. He was not only one of the great anarchist thinkers, but a key link in the movement from the late nineteenth to the early twentieth centuries. Uniting his theory and action with rare consistency, he combined idealism with common sense, philosophical rigour with practical experience. Rejecting the role of prophet or leader, he stands as an outstanding example of the modest, independent individual which the anarchist movement has so often produced.

Leo Tolstoy
The Count of Peace

ALTHOUGH TOLSTOY DID NOT like to call himself an anarchist, because of its popular association with violence, he may be considered one of the greatest anarchist thinkers for his eloquent and reasoned defence of freedom. He was a Russian aristocrat like Bakunin, but he utterly repudiated his call for violent revolution. Tolstoy's politics were inextricably connected with his moral views which in turn were based on a highly unorthodox version of Christianity. He was one of the most powerful critics of the fraud of government, the immorality of patriotism, and the danger of militarism. He not only tried to live according to his principles – however unsuccessfully – but his religious anarchism gave rise to many communities of Tolstoyans. He was a major influence in shaping Gandhi's philosophy of non-violence and continues to inspire many libertarian pacifists.

Leo Tolstoy at first sight seems an unlikely candidate to become one of the most uncompromising of anarchists. He was born in 1828 on the family estate of Yasnaya Polyana in Tula province, the third of five children. His father Count Nikolai was a veteran of the 1812 campaign against Napoleon. He was orphaned at an early age: his mother died when he was not quite two, and his father died when he was nine. He was brought up by a pious and elderly aunt who was concerned with the spiritual welfare of the poor. This did not prevent him from having a happy childhood. His father never used corporal punishment and taught the young Leo to be polite to the servants.

The enlightened atmosphere of the home encouraged the utopian dreams of the children. The game which Tolstoy most enjoyed was invented by his elder brother Nikolai who claimed to have discovered a remarkable secret written on a green stick in a nearby forest. When known it would make all men happy; there would be no more disease, no misery, no anger and all would love one another. They would become like 'the brotherhood of ants', referring it seems not to a hierarchical colony of insects, but to the religious sect of Moravians whose name in Russian sounds like the word for ants!¹ The existence of such a secret truth haunted all Tolstoy's later spiritual expeditions.

Tolstoy was educated at home; at one stage there were eleven tutors living in the house. In 1844, he went to Kazan University were he intended to study oriental languages, but lost interest and did not graduate. Whilst at university he began his lifelong habit of keeping a diary of his thoughts and plans. He tried to write down some 'Rules of Life' but he did not get very far: the constant struggle in his life between his strong moral conscience and his strong sensual desires had begun. He later described the period of his youth and early manhood as one of 'coarse dissoluteness, employed in the service of ambition, vanity, and, above all, lust', but he was not much different from other young Russian aristocrats of his time.² His later anarchist morality called for the repression, not the liberation, of his strong and unruly sensual desires.

At this time Tolstoy still wanted to follow a rigorous course of self-study but he played the gentleman-farmer for a while on his estate. He then enjoyed the pleasures of Moscow for several years, before turning his back on polite, frivolous society in 1851 to accompany his brother Nikolai to the North Caucasus, where he joined an artillery regiment. He was stationed in a Cossack village, and went on expeditions to subdue the mountain tribes, on one occasion nearly being killed by a grenade, and, on another, narrowly escaping capture. He could not stop himself gambling and womanizing, and he loved the wild nature all around.

The example of the peasant communities, regulating their affairs through custom and voluntary agreement, also impressed him deeply. He later wrote that he witnessed, in the communes of the Cossacks, who did not acknowledge private ownership of land, 'such well-being and order that did not exist in society where landed property is defended by the organized violence of government'.³ But he did not yet reach anarchistic conclusions. After reading Plato and Rousseau, he wrote in his diary, on 3 August 1852: 'I will devote the rest of my life to drawing up a plan for an aristocratic, selective union with a monarchical administration on the basis of existing elections. Here I have an aim for a virtuous life. I thank thee, O Lord. Grant me strength.'

It was in the Caucasus that Tolstoy began his literary career, producing several autobiographical stories and his first novel *Childhood*. As he later acknowledged: 'I didn't become a general in the army, but I did in literature.'

Commissioned at the outbreak of the Crimean war in 1854, he was given the command of a battery during the defence of Sevastopol. It was to have a traumatic effect. He described the horrors of the war in *Tales from Army Life* and *Sketches of Sevastopol* (1856) and then left the army in 1856.

He went on to see in conscription one of the worst expressions of governmental violence and later urged the young to refuse to serve in the army. In the Crimea, Tolstoy also recovered his earlier aim in life – the ideal of virtue – which had been long forgotten because of the temptations of military society. He now decided at the age of twenty-seven that it would be his purpose in life to found a new religion corresponding to the development of mankind: 'the religion of Christ, but purged of beliefs and mysticism, a practical religion, not promising future bliss but giving bliss on earth'.[4]

After returning to the capital, Tolstoy circulated in the literary *demimonde* of St Petersburg. In 1857 he left for Western Europe, spending six months in France, Switzerland and Germany. In Paris he witnessed the public guillotining of a murderer which was to prove a key event in his life and the beginning of his gradual conversion to anarchism. He was filled with horror at the State's 'insolent, arrogant desire to carry out justice and the law of God'. In a letter to a friend, he wrote of this nonsensical law contrived by man:

> The truth is that the state is a conspiracy designed not only to exploit, but above all to corrupt its citizens . . . I understand moral laws, and the laws of morality and religion, which are not binding, but which lead people forward and promise a harmonious future; and I sense the laws of art which always bring happiness; but the laws of politics are such terrible lies for me that I can't see in them a better or a worse . . . as from today I will certainly never go and see such a thing again, and I will never serve *any* government anywhere.[5]

As he later wrote in *A Confession* (1882), the sight of the execution revealed to him the instability of his belief in inevitable progress.[6]

Tolstoy still was not confident that socialism could transform existing States, but he was now prepared to contemplate their abolition. He was deeply impressed by Proudhon's belief, as expressed in *What is Property?* (1844), that the government of man by man is oppression, and that the union of order and anarchy is the highest form of society. In his notebook, he was critical of Proudhon's one-sided materialist philosophy, yet added 'it is better to see this one side in past thinkers and workers, especially when they complement each other. From this comes love, uniting all these views into one, and this is the simple infallible law of humanity.'[7]

Tolstoy was not only groping towards his mature conception of universal love. His notebooks show that he was struggling already with many of his future concerns. He was convinced that 'Nationality is the one single bar to the growth of freedom.' He was ready to accept that 'the absence of laws is possible, but there must be security against violence'.[8] It was this preoccupation with violence, which he saw in himself as well as on a grand scale in the Crimean War, which prevented him from supporting the cause of revolutionary socialism. He could see no justification for shedding blood for any political gain, however beneficial. But he was willing (and remained so for the rest of his life) to accept Proudhon's proposition: 'All governments are in equal measure good and evil. The best ideal is anarchy.'[9]

After his travels abroad, Tolstoy returned home to Yasnaya Polyana and threw himself into improving the condition of his estate and its serfs. He founded a school for peasant children in 1859 which occupied him for the next three or four years. He was not certain exactly what to teach them – his moral and religious views had not yet hardened – so he let them learn what they liked. He said to himself: 'In some of its developments progress has proceeded wrongly, and with primitive peasant children one must deal in a spirit of perfect freedom, letting them choose what path of progress they please.'[10] He based his method on individual freedom and became convinced that the principal part in educating people is played not by schools but by life.

Tolstoy developed his own theory of spontaneous learning. He wanted to eliminate all compulsory methods and allow the students to regulate themselves. Above the school entrance he placed the inscription: 'Enter and Leave Freely.' The school practised non-interference, with the students allowed to learn what they wanted to learn: 'When they submit only to natural laws, such as arise from their natures, they do not feel provoked and do not murmur; but when they submit to predetermined interference, they do not believe in the legality of your bells, programmes, and regulations.'[11]

From his experience, Tolstoy felt a certain amount of disorder was useful, and the need for order should come from the students themselves. He was convinced that natural relations between teacher and student could only be achieved in the absence of coercion and compulsion; force, in his view, is always used through haste or insufficient respect for human nature. The students were therefore left to settle their own disputes as far as possible. There were no examinations and no clear system of rewards and punishments. The essential task of education was to teach children 'as little as possible' and to encourage an awareness of the fact that 'all people are brothers and equal to one another'.[12]

Tolstoy made a sharp distinction between culture and education. Culture is free, but education, he argued, is 'the tendency of one man to make another just like himself'; it is 'culture under restraint'.[13] On these grounds, Tolstoy consistently opposed State education which tends to shape the young according to its needs: 'The strength of the government rests on the ignorance of the people, and it knows this, and therefore will always fight against education.'[14] For Tolstoy, the most important task was to develop the students' moral sensibility and ability to think for themselves.

To propagate his views, Tolstoy founded a monthly review called *Yasnaya Polyana* in January 1862 which went through twelve issues. In the first, he boldly declared the principle: 'In order to determine what is good and what is not, he who is being taught must have full powers to express his dissatisfaction or, at least, to avoid lessons that do not satisfy him. Let it be established that there is only one criterion in teaching: freedom!'[15]

In keeping with his principle that a school must be adapted to the particular needs of its students, Tolstoy was ready to admit that his school might be the worst possible example for others. Most contemporary experts condemned him as a 'pedagogical nihilist', but his libertarian approach based on children's needs not only developed Godwin's insights, but has had widespread influence on the growth of 'free schools' in the twentieth century.

Tolstoy's interest in educational theory led him to visit Western Europe again in 1860. In England, he heard Dickens read a lecture on education and met several times the Russian exile Alexander Herzen, who was editing *The Pole Star*. In Brussels, he met Proudhon who had just completed his work on armed conflict between nations – *War and Peace*. Tolstoy was impressed by the anarchist thinker who had the 'courage of his convictions', while Proudhon found the young Russian a 'highly educated man' and was thrilled by his news of the emancipation of the serfs in 1861.[16]

On his return to Yasnaya Polyana, Tolstoy was appointed an Arbiter of the Peace to solve disputes between the liberated serfs and their former masters. The experience left him with a permanent distaste for litigation and he later recommended that no one should take any grievance to the lawcourts. A police raid on his school which was intended to unearth subversive literature and revolutionaries further alienated him from the government. He wrote an indignant letter to Alexander II in which he denied that he was a conspirator and proudly described his chosen profession as 'the founding of schools for the people'.[17]

Tolstoy continued to have casual relations with prostitutes and a married serf on his estate bore him a son. He also had affairs with women of his own class, but in 1862 after a brief courtship he married Sophie Andreyevna Behrs. She bore him thirteen children, four of whom died. Although she became her husband's diligent and jealous amanuensis, she confirmed Tolstoy's view of woman (shared lamentably by Proudhon), namely that their principal role in life is motherhood. 'Every woman,' Tolstoy wrote, 'however she may dress herself and however she may call herself and however refined she may be, who refrains from childbirth without refraining from sexual relations is a whore. And however fallen a woman may be, if she intentionally devotes herself to bearing children, she performs the best and highest service in life – fulfils the will of God – and no one ranks above her.'[18] He later saw women as dangerous temptresses, diverting man from his spiritual life.

Despite, or perhaps because of, his strong sexual drive, Tolstoy eventually believed that it was best to remain single and celibate. In his story *Kreutzer Sonata* (1890), he made it clear that if desire drove one to marry, one should still try and remain as chaste as possible. No doubt reflecting on his own conjugal difficulties, Tolstoy is reported to have said: 'Man survives earthquakes, epidemics, terrible illnesses, and every kind of physical suffering, but always the most poignant tragedy was, is, and ever will be the tragedy of the bedroom.'[19] He eventually came to see sex as the greatest evil and recommended complete chastity – an ideal, despite supreme efforts, he was unable to fulfil even as an old man.

Nevertheless, although he thought woman's nature most fulfilled in motherhood and sex without procreation untenable, he did not, as Proudhon did, regard women as inferior to men. He advocated the same education for both men and women. He brought up his daughters in the same way as his sons, and they were his most ardent supporters. While he rejected free love, thought monogamy a natural law of humanity, and defended marriage as the only moral outlet for sex, he wrote in his diary: 'I am of course against all legal restrictions, and for complete liberty: only the ideal is chastity and not pleasure.'[20] In this, Tolstoy was following the teaching of St Paul who argued that it is better to marry than to burn, but best of all is to abstain completely from sexual passion. For Tolstoy the spiritual life involves the ceaseless effort to free oneself from the desires of the flesh. This does not excuse, nonetheless, his outrageous misogyny, which was eventually to broaden out into misanthropy.

After his marriage, Tolstoy settled on his Volga estate and combined its progressive management with writing *War and Peace* (1863–9), arguably the world's greatest novel. He originally planned to make the hero one of the Decembrist rebels who had been exiled to Siberia in 1825 but finally placed the novel in the period before Napoleon's invasion of 1812. The political considerations were gradually superseded by the characterization. In a draft introduction to the novel he declares: 'I shall write a history of people more freely than of statesmen.' In the event, he presents the fortunes of two families – the Rostovs and the Bolkonskis – against the background of Russia's struggle against Napoleon. The proud Prince Andrew and the hedonistic but searching Pierre mirror two aspects of Tolstoy's own personality.

But the work goes beyond psychological interest. The title was borrowed from Proudhon's *War and Peace*, and Tolstoy was keen to demonstrate that history is not made by exceptional individuals but is comprised of a myriad of circumstances. Military victories, for example, are not won as in a game of chess but are produced by unpredictable and chance events which make up the fortunes of war. His position comes close to Marx's but he does not share his confidence in inevitability.

In an article 'Some Words About *War and Peace*' (1868), Tolstoy clarified his philosophy of history. While man psychologically wishes to believe that he acts according to his own free will, and some actions do indeed depend on the will, the more he involves himself with the actions of others, the less free he is. Therefore, there is a law of predetermination guiding history, although it is difficult for men to predict or control it. This approach led Isaiah Berlin to describe Tolstoy as a fox, who knows many things, though Tolstoy himself believed he was a hedgehog, who knows only one big thing: 'Tolstoy perceived reality in its multiplicity, as a collection of separate entities round and into which he saw with clarity and penetration scarcely ever equalled, but he believed only in one vast, unitary whole.'[21]

Although he was principally committed to literature during this period, Tolstoy defended a private before a military court who had been charged with striking an officer. The soldier however was found guilty and executed. The event undoubtedly hardened Tolstoy's growing opposition to the judicial and military institutions of the State. He later wrote a moving indictment of capital punishment in *I Cannot Be Silent* (1908).

He continued to be interested in education and wrote stories and *A Primer* for peasant children. His next great work *Anna Karenina* (1874–82) depicted the dilemma between the creative artist and the committed moralist which Tolstoy himself experienced. The work took a great deal out of him. Like Anna, he felt torn between two contradictory forces – between a sense of vitality which grasps at life (Anna was 'too eager to live'), and a sense of life's pointlessness and tragedy. Tolstoy records how at this time he would travel through the muddy farms on his estate and say to himself 'very well – you will be more famous than Gogol or Pushkin or Shakespeare or Molière – and what of it?'[22]

Tolstoy was soon undergoing a deep spiritual crisis which took him to the verge of suicide. But while he felt that human life was a remorseless stream carrying all towards nothingness, he became convinced that there was a bank of God to hold it back. He became increasingly interested in religious matters, and visited several monasteries. As he described so movingly in *A Confession* (1882), he thought of his past with horror: 'Lying, robbery, adultery of all kinds, drunkenness, violence, murder – there was no crime I did not commit . . .'[23]

After a desperate search to find a meaning to his life in philosophy and religion, and then amongst the people, Tolstoy eventually was converted to a religion of love based on the literal interpretation of the Gospels, especially the Sermon on the Mount. This new Christianity confirmed the libertarian leanings of his youth and helped him develop a fully-fledged philosophy of pacifist anarchism. It was never fully consistent, however, and his desultory attempt to live out his philosophy – however sincere and earnest – has opened him up to accusations of hypocrisy.

Philosophy

In a series of books, pamphlets and commentaries issued in the 1880s and 1890s, Tolstoy elaborated a highly unorthodox version of Christianity. He came to believe that Christ is not the divine son of God but rather a great moral teacher. There is no afterlife, although we are all part of the infinite. At the same time, an inner light reveals itself in human reason, which comes from a source outside ourself and will endure after our death. Unlike the analytical reason of the *philosophes*, it leads us not away from but towards God, for the activity of reason is truth, and God is divine truth. God is far from being a personal being who judges us; 'God is that whole of which we acknowledge ourselves to be a part: to a materialist – matter; to an individualist – a magnified, non-natural man; to an idealist – his ideal, Love.' There is no Romantic separation or contradiction between love and reason, for 'reason should be loving' and 'love should be reasonable'.[24] This is at the centre of Tolstoy's philosophy.

Tolstoy became convinced that the teaching of Jesus in the Gospels provided the key of how a good life should be lived on earth. From his careful reading of the Gospels, he inferred the following five commandments:

(1) Do not be angry, but live at peace with all men. (2) Do not indulge yourself in sexual gratification. (3) Do not promise anything on oath to anyone. (4) Do not resist evil, do not judge and do not go to law. (5) Make no distinction of nationality, but love foreigners as your own people.

All these commandments are contained in one: all that you wish men to do to you, do you to them.[25]

Tolstoy thought that these principles formed the central message of Christianity and they became the basis of his moral teaching. The first commandment confirmed his anarchism since all governments are based on organized violence. The fourth commandment – 'Do not resist evil' – led him to develop his doctrine of non-resistance, that is to say, the refusal to resist evil by violence. It does not mean that one should not resist evil at all; on the contrary, it is right to resist evil by persuasion and to influence public opinion on which evil institutions rest. The fifth commandment was based on Tolstoy's interpretation of the maxim 'Love thy enemy' to mean one's national enemy; it involved rejecting every kind of patriotism, even the patriotism of the oppressed.

With these beliefs, it was a simple logical step for Tolstoy to argue that all governments, laws, police forces, armies and all protection of life or property are immoral. The law of God is always superior to the law of man. He therefore inferred: 'I cannot take part in any Governmental activity that has for its aim the defence of people and their property by violence; I cannot be a judge or take part in trials; nor can I help others to take part in lawcourts and Government offices.'[26] It also follows that no one has a right to keep anything that anyone else wishes to take.

Although Tolstoy condemned the passions of greed, anger and lust as vigorously as any tub-thumping Puritan, he was no other-worldly moralist. He recommended the happiness which is to be found in a life close to nature, voluntary work, family, friendship, and a painless death. He considered moreover that life is a blessing for the individual who identifies with Christ and tries to realize the kingdom of God on earth. According to Tolstoy, Christ demonstrated in his own life that if people live without resisting others by violence and without owning property they will find contentment.

Tolstoy's new moral and religious beliefs at first made him much more active in denouncing injustice. In 1881, he wrote to the new Tsar, asking him to pardon the assassins of Alexander II: 'Return good for evil, resist not evil, forgive everyone.'[27] Not surprisingly, the Tsar did not like being reminded that God's law is above all other laws; the call for forgiveness fell on deaf ears. Alexander III could not imprison the wayward Count, but he did his best to ban his works..'This ignominious L. Tolstoy', the Tsar later wrote, 'must be stopped. He is nothing but a nihilist and a non-believer.'

In 1882, Tolstoy took part in a census in Moscow and visited the slums for the first time. The horrifying experience only strengthened his concern for the poor. In an attempt to live out his beliefs, he refused to do jury service. He renounced blood sports and became a vegetarian since he felt it is immoral to take animal life for entertainment or appetite, especially when it is possible to be healthy without eating meat. In 1886, he made new contact with the Russian people during a 130-mile walk from Moscow to Yasnaya Polyana. During the serious famine which affected much of European Russia during 1891–2, he also threw himself – with the help of his family – into the campaign to alleviate the suffering of its victims.

In *The Kingdom of God is Within You* (1894), he summed up years of reading and meditating. He depicted the exploitation and oppression which are incompatible with true Christianity but which are often carried out in its name. With great energy, he also portrayed the hypocrisy of the wealthy and respectful, including himself:

> We are all brothers, yet every morning a brother or sister carries out my chamber-pot. We are all brothers, yet every morning I need a cigar, some sugar, a mirror and other objects produced by my equals, my own brothers and sisters, at the cost of their own health; I make use of these objects and even demand them ... We are all brothers, yet I only give my educational, medical and literary works to the poor in exchange for money.[28]

Tolstoy used the money from his next novel *Resurrection* (1899), which was about the moral regeneration of a young nobleman, to help the persecuted sect of Dukhobors to emigrate to Canada. The novel reflected his new aesthetic view already expressed in *What is Art?* (1897–8); art is an extension of morality, which in the Christian era should reflect a religious view of man's place in the world. It should also be simple enough for everyone to understand.

Many literary historians and biographers have suggested that the moralist got the better of the artist in the later part of Tolstoy's life. A. N. Wilson, for instance, has argued that 'the wilful absence of common sense in Tolstoy was ultimately the death of his artistic imagination.'[29] Yet this is far too simplistic a view. There was always a strong moral theme to Tolstoy's great early novels, and much of his later fiction, such as the short stories *The Death of Ivan Ilyich* (1886), *The Master and Man* (1895) and the short novel *Hadzhi Murad* (1911), show that his imaginative powers remained to the end. His decision to write simply and clearly so that the most uneducated peasant could understand often lends a powerful starkness to his best stories. Moreover, his ability to express himself with simple verve give his later moral and political works a peculiar strength of their own.

As a moral thinker and religious reformer, Tolstoy continued to develop a form of Christianity based on the Sermon on the Mount which rejected all earthly authority and which urged non-violent resistance to evil. He sought to purge Christianity of its mysticism and transform it into a moral code which could appeal to a rational person. But he went so far that the Holy Synod of the Russian Orthodox Church excommunicated him in 1901. His response was a simple declaration of faith:

> I believe in God, whom I understand as Spirit, as love, as the Source of all. I believe that He is in me and I in Him. I believe that the will of God is most clearly and intelligibly expressed in the teaching of the man Jesus, whom to consider as God and pray to, I consider the greatest blasphemy. I believe that man's true welfare lies in fulfilling God's will, and His will is that men should love one another and

should consequently do to others as they wish others to do to them –
of which it is said in the Gospels that in this is the law and the prophets.
I believe therefore that the meaning of the life of every man is to be
found only in increasing the love that is in him . . . that this increase
of love leads man . . . towards the establishment of the kingdom of
God on earth: that is, to the establishment of an order of life in which
the discord, deception and violence that now rule will be replaced by
free accord, by truth, and by the brotherly love of one for another.[30]

Rather than harming his reputation, Tolstoy's excommunication made him
even more popular amongst the Russian people.

Non-resistance became the key to Tolstoy's new political creed and it
was with considerable joy that he came across Thoreau's essay on civil
disobedience. In *The Kingdom of God is Within You*, he rigorously applied
the principle of non-resistant love to government, the Church, patriotism
and war. He was particularly critical of the evil caused by those who arrogate
to themselves the right to prevent evil by force which may occur but has
not yet occurred. This is equally true of holy inquisitions, the gaoling of
political prisoners, government executions, and the bombs of revolutionaries. True Christianity is revolutionary, but it looks to a moral reform in
the individual not a violent social revolution. It can only be accepted if it
involves a fundamental change in the life of the individual.

What makes Tolstoy's Christianity anarchistic is his claim that human
beings, in their spiritual journey from darkness to light, outgrow the governmental stage in history. A true Christian is free from every human authority
since the divine law of love implanted in every individual – made conscious
for us by Christ – is the sufficient and sole guide of life.

Tolstoy is as confident as Godwin that the State will wither away and
like him places his confidence in growing public opinion to bring about its
demise. There will come a time 'when all institutions based on violence will
disappear because it has become obvious to everyone that they are useless,
and even wrong'.[31] Human beings will become so reasonable that they will
no longer want to rob and murder each other. 'A time will come', Tolstoy
further prophesizes, 'and is already coming, when the Christian principles
of equality (the brotherhood of man, the community of property, and non-
resistance to evil by violence) will appear just as natural and simple as the
principles of family, social or national life do now.'[32] The sole meaning of
life therefore lies in serving the world by promoting the establishment of
the Kingdom of God by each individual's simple avowal of the truth. And
in this government and the State have no place.

Government

Although Tolstoy bases his case against government on spiritual grounds, few anarchists have portrayed so incisively the link between government and violence. He insists that governments by their very nature are based on violence. They compel their citizens to act contrary to their wishes and conscience whenever they introduce taxation or conscription. State power moreover cannot be the remedy for private violence since it always introduces fresh forms of violence. The stronger the State becomes, the greater the violence it perpetrates.

Tolstoy goes to the heart of the matter when he makes clear that it is physical force which makes men obey established laws. In a memorable definition, he asserts: 'Laws are rules made by people who govern by means of organized violence, for non-compliance with which the non-complier is subjected to blows, a loss of liberty, or even to being murdered.'[33] They are made not by the will of all but by those in power and always and everywhere they are made in the interests of those who have power.

Tolstoy was ready to admit that there may have been a time when government was necessary, or as he put it, the 'evil' of supporting a government was less than being left defenceless against the organized force of hostile neighbours. But he was convinced that humanity no longer needed it. Under the pretext of protecting its subjects, government only exercises a harmful influence. By claiming a moral right to inflict punishment, it merely attempted by immoral means to make a bad action appear good.[34]

Tolstoy's principal criticism of government is that it is inextricably linked with war. All governments are based on violence in the form of police, army, courts and prisons. As military organizations, their chief purpose is to wage war. They constantly increase their armies not only against external enemies but also against their oppressed subjects. It follows that a government entrusted with military power is the most dangerous organization possible.

At the same time, Tolstoy did not place the responsibility of war merely on government ministers: 'In reality war is an inevitable result of the existence of armies; and armies are only needed by governments in order to dominate their own working-classes.'[35] In addition, he recognized that war is caused by the unequal distribution of property and the false teaching which inspires feelings of patriotism.

On no account did Tolstoy accept the patriotism which supports governments. Patriotism, the spontaneous love for one's own nation above other nations, is always rude, harmful and immoral. In *Christianity and Patriotism* (1894) he illustrated forcibly how governments whip up national patriotism to support war. He went on to argue that patriotism is nothing less than a form of slavery:

> Patriotism in its simplest, clearest and most indubitable signification is nothing else but a means of obtaining for the rulers their ambitions and covetous desires, and for the ruled the abdication of human dignity, reason, and conscience, and a slavish enthralment to those in power.[36]

Tolstoy even rejected the patriotism of enslaved nations who are fighting for their independence. Preference for one's own nation can never be good or useful since it overrides the perception of human equality and respect for human dignity. The aim therefore should not be to support nationalist struggles for independence but for conquered nations to liberate themselves by refusing to participate in the violent measures of any governments.

In *Patriotism and Government* (1900), Tolstoy exposed the hypocritical profession of great powers calling for peace while preparing for war. Rejecting the deterrence argument (since made popular by apologists for nuclear weapons) that the invention of terrible instruments of destruction will put an end to war, he insisted that the only lasting remedy is to do away with governments which are the ultimate instruments of violence: 'To deliver men from the terrible and ever-increasing evils of armaments and wars, we want ... the destruction of those instruments of violence which are called Governments, and from which humanity's greatest evils flow.'[37] Unless there was universal disarmament, Tolstoy prophesized that more terrible wars were to come. If only people could recognize that they are not the sons of a fatherland or the slaves of a government, but the sons of God, 'those insane unnecessary, worn-out, pernicious organizations called Governments, and all the sufferings, violations, humiliations, and crimes they occasion, would cease'.[38] War, military conscription and all other coercive governmental actions will end only with the gradual dissolution of the State.

Tolstoy is an anarchist – and a vigorous one at that – because he specifically called for a society without government and the State. He argued as follows: 'Slavery results from laws, laws are made by Governments, and, therefore, people can only be freed from slavery by the abolition of Governments.' Even if the State were once necessary, Tolstoy concluded that 'it is now absolutely unnecessary, and is therefore harmful and dangerous'. He rejects the charge that without governments there will be chaos or a foreign invasion. His experience of Cossack communes in the Urals had shown him that order and well-being are possible without the organized violence of government. Rational beings can arrange their social life through agreement. It is therefore quite possible to create a society based on voluntary and 'reasonable agreement confirmed by custom'.[39] The only moral principle necessary would be to act towards others as one would like them to act towards oneself.

Tolstoy wrote: 'The anarchists are right in everything; in the negation of the existing order, and in the assertion that, without authority, there could not be worse violence than that of authority under existing conditions. They are mistaken only in thinking that anarchy can be instituted by a revolution.'[40] Tolstoy was well aware of the arguments of previous anarchist thinkers, recognizing that they wished to abolish power not by force but by a change in people's consciousness. He quoted Godwin on the possibility of organizing a society without government and law. He met Proudhon, borrowed his book title, and was impressed by his advocacy of ordered anarchy. Initially, he admired Bakunin, before learning about his celebration of violence. He referred to Kropotkin's *The Conquest of Bread* and *Fields, Factories and Workshops* to demonstrate the possibility of food for all.[41]

Nevertheless, he found the philosophy of Godwin and Proudhon lacking because of their utilitarian emphasis on general welfare and justice, and rejected the violent revolutionary means advocated by Bakunin and Kropotkin. He did not care for the appeal of Stirner and Tucker to personal interest. Above all, he felt that in their materialistic conception of life, atheistic anarchist thinkers lacked the spiritual weapon which has always destroyed power – 'a devout understanding of life, according to which man regards his earthly existence as only a fragmentary manifestation of the complete life'. What previous anarchists had failed to understand was that the highest welfare lies not in human happiness or the general good but in the fulfilment of the laws of this 'infinite life' which are far more binding than any human laws.[42]

Despite his metaphysical disagreement with most of the major nineteenth-century anarchist theorists, Tolstoy shared their ultimate goal of a society without government. To his critics who asked what he would put in the place of government, he simply replied that there was no need to replace it with anything: an organization, which being unnecessary had become harmful, would simply be abolished and society would continue on its own beneficial course as before. Indeed, 'even if the absence of Government really meant Anarchy in the negative, disorderly sense of that word – which is far from being the case – even then no anarchical disorder could be worse than the position to which Governments have already led their peoples, and to which they are leading them.'[43] Tolstoy sees no risk of chaos in abolishing the government and the State since he firmly believed that 'God has implanted His law in our minds and our hearts, that there may be order, not disorder, and that nothing but good can arise from our following the unquestionable law of God, which has been so plainly manifested to us.'[44]

Tolstoy based his case for anarchism on a love of freedom and a hatred of coercion. He did not for instance condemn Negro slavery merely because it was cruel, but because it was a particular case of universal coercion. His position, like that of the American abolitionist William Lloyd Garrison, was founded on the principle that 'under no pretext has any man the right to dominate, *i.e.*, to use coercion over his fellows.'[45] According to Tolstoy, true liberty consists in 'every man being able to live and act according to his own judgement' which is incompatible with the power of some men over others.[46]

It was Tolstoy's love of freedom which led him to condemn the factory system and to call for a return to the land. The misery of the factory hand and town worker consists not so much in his long hours and low pay, as in the fact that he is deprived of freedom and the 'natural conditions of life in touch with nature' and compelled to perform compulsory and monotonous labour at another man's will.[47]

Although Tolstoy sees a major cause of social evil in government, he does not overlook the question of property. In his address *To the Working People*, he emphasized the link between government and property, since the laws of government are intended to protect private property. The resulting exploitation is the root of all evils; it not only causes suffering to those who possess property and to those who are deprived of it, but gives rise to conflict between the two. War, executions, imprisonment, murder, and vice are all a direct result of the private ownership of property. If it were not eliminated, Tolstoy prophesized thirty-one years before the Russian Revolution: 'A worker's revolution with horrors of destruction and murder threaten us . . . The hatred and contempt of oppressed masses are growing and the physical and moral forces of the wealthy classes are weakening; the deception, on which everything depends, is wearing out.'[48]

Tolstoy not only called for the communal ownership of land but wished to overcome the division of labour, especially between manual and mental work. He made an impassioned plea for all to share in the manual labour of the world. Like Proudhon, he extolled the virtue and dignity of labour and called for a more simple life close to nature. He was confident that there would be enough land for all if it was fairly distributed.

Since it was a lack of land and the burden of taxes that drove men to work in the towns, Tolstoy recommended Henry George's Single Tax System to free land from its present owners and to allow the peasants to cultivate as much acreage as their needs would require. In the long run, he looked to a complete abolition of taxes and landed property. His ultimate ideal however was not some mythic Arcadia in the past. He recognized that under existing conditions nearly all agricultural labourers as well as factory workers were slaves. Nor was he opposed to technology as such and looked, like Kropotkin, to technical improvements which would give us 'control over nature' without destroying human life.[49]

Means of Reform

In order to bring about a free and just society, Tolstoy completely repudiated the use of physical force. He clearly understood that it is impossible to use violent means to bring about peaceful ends, to wield power to abolish power: 'All revolutionary attempts only furnish new justification for the violence of Governments, and increase their power.'[50] Even if a change in the existing order were to be brought about by violent means, nothing could guarantee that the enemies of the new order would not try and overthrow it by use of the same violence. The new order would therefore have to maintain itself by violence and very quickly be corrupted like the old order.[51] Again, Tolstoy rightly pointed out that political assassinations only strengthen the State and provide an excuse for its further repression of the people. To murder people is hardly a proper way of improving the condition of the people, and the killing of kings and presidents is as useful as cutting one of the Hydra's heads.[52] In a notebook, Tolstoy asked: 'Is there not a difference between the killing that a revolutionist does and that which a policeman does?' He replied bluntly: 'There is as much difference as between cat-shit and dog-shit. But I don't like the smell of either one or the other.'[53] Only by the ending of force, and the slavery which results from force, can an enlightened society be created.

In this, Tolstoy was one of the most consistent and far-sighted of anarchists. He saw public opinion not violence as the most valuable and effective instrument to eradicate government, although he overlooked its tyrannical potential to make people conform. In his writings, he continually appealed to the rational and the moral person. For him reason and love are not separate but two aspects of the same moral activity: 'Righteousness will be produced by reasonable love, verified by truth; and truth only by loving reason, having as its aim righteousness.'[54]

Tolstoy insisted that government is founded on opinion, so that 'Public opinion produces the power, and the power produces the public opinion.'[55] The solution is therefore to change public opinion through discussion and persuasion, by pointing out that all governments are harmful and obsolete. The essential thing for people to see is that strength lies not in force but in truth. Indeed, all the terrible organization of brute force is as nothing compared 'to the consciousness of truth, which surges in the soul of one man who knows the power of truth, which is communicated from him to a second and a third, as one candle lights an innumerable quantity of others'.[55] Like Godwin before him, and Gandhi after him, Tolstoy had an unswerving confidence in the omnipotence of truth.

For Tolstoy there can be only 'one permanent revolution – a moral one: the regeneration of the inner man'.[56] Since only a person living in accordance with his conscience can have a good influence on others, he urged that one try and achieve inner self-perfection. To the working people, he recommended what he called the law of reciprocity: 'for your true welfare you should live only according to the law of God, a brotherly life, doing unto others that which you wish others to do unto you.'[57]

But while Tolstoy was against resisting evil by physical force, he was no quietist. Impressed by Thoreau's example of refusing to pay a tax as a protest against slavery, he recommended civil disobedience to help dismantle evil institutions and practices. In order to abolish governments, he encouraged people to refuse to participate in them, to fight on their behalf, to pay taxes, to appeal to governmental violence for protection of their property or persons. Since to take part in elections, courts of law, or in the administration of government is the same thing as participation in the violence of government, he urged that they should be eschewed at all times.

Again, to get rid of landed property, Tolstoy suggested that the workers should simply abstain from participation in landed property: 'You should not support the iniquity of landed property, either by violence enacted by the troops, or by working on the lands of the landlords, or renting them.'[58] As for the upper classes, they can alleviate the suffering of the workers by not making people work for them, by doing themselves as far as possible all work that is tedious and unpleasant, and by inventing technological processes to diminish disagreeable work. He also encouraged co-operative activity and experiments: 'the founding of co-operatives and participation in them,' he wrote, 'is the only social activity which a moral, self-respecting person who doesn't wish to be a party to violence can take part in our time.'[59]

Convinced of the power of truth, Tolstoy wrote a long letter to the Tsar on the evils of autocracy and coercion and urged him to abolish the private ownership of land. In a letter to the Prime Minister he further advocated Henry George's single tax system on land and the abolition of private property. Not surprisingly, they declined the advice. Given his brilliant analysis of the corruption of power and the violence of government, Tolstoy should not have expected anything else.

At the time, the Tsar and the court were deeply disturbed by the unrest his works were causing throughout Russia. The spiritual censor K. P. Pobedonostsev, the Procurator of the Holy Synod, added to a report about a Tolstoyan to the Tsar:

It is impossible to conceal from oneself that in the last few years the intellectual stimulation under the influence of the works of Count Tolstoy has greatly strengthened and threatens to spread strange, perverted notions about faith, the Church, government, and society. The direction is entirely negative, alien, not only to the Church, but to the national spirit. A kind of insanity has taken possession of people's minds.[60]

Before Alexander III died in 1894, one of the last acts of his government was to ban Russian journalists from saying anything about Tolstoy's life and works in the foreign press.

In his old age, Tolstoy increasingly stressed the religious basis of his moral and political convictions. He liked to claim that he was not for the government nor for the revolutionaries, but for the people. He did not tire from reiterating that the only radical method capable of eliminating violence and oppressions is a revival of the religious consciousness of the people. While he wrote in a notebook in September 1905 'Socialism is unconscious Christianity', he later wrote in his diary: 'Socialists will never destroy poverty and the injustice of the inequality of capacities. The strongest and more intelligent will always make use of the weaker and more stupid. Justice and equality in the good things of life will never be achieved by anything less than Christianity, i.e., by negating oneself and recognizing the meaning of one's life in service to others.'

He had a prophetic awareness of the implications of the Marxist road to power: 'Even if that should happen which Marx predicted, then the only thing that will happen is that despotism will be passed on. Now the capitalists are ruling, but then the directors of the working class will rule.' Marxists go wrong, Tolstoy claimed, in seeing economics at the root of all things, whereas humanity develops through growth in consciousness. Tolstoy argued that Marx was therefore mistaken 'in the supposition that capital will pass from the hands of private people into the hands of the government, and from the government, representing the people, into the hands of the workers'.[61]

The failure of the 1905 Revolution in Russia only confirmed Tolstoy's views. He wrote to a correspondent: 'I rejoice for the revolution, but grieve for those who, imagining that they are making it, are destroying it. The violence of the old regime will only be destroyed by non-participation in violence, and not at all by the new and foolish acts of violence which are now being committed.' He considered what was being done by all the 'comic parties and committees' to be neither important nor good: 'unless the people, the real people, the hundred million peasants who work on the land, by their passive non-participation in violence make all this frivolous, noisy, irritable and touchy crowd harmless and unnecessary, we shall certainly arrive at a military dictatorship.'[62] In an article *On the Social Movement in Russia* (1905), he further rejected the liberal idea that a good society could be brought about by substituting constitutional government for autocracy, and went out of his way to demonstrate the lack of freedom in parliamentary regimes in the West.

In his more considered response in *The Significance of the Russian Revolution* (1906), Tolstoy repeated his view that the Russian people should stay on the land, and avoid the industrial civilization of the West. The only effective way to bring an end to coercive government is the practice of non-resistant love. The ideal cannot be realized by any organized movement but by each individual's moral self-improvement. Not surprisingly, Lenin, while praising his criticism of capitalist exploitation and governmental violence, saw in Tolstoy's advocacy of religion 'one of the most corrupt things existing in the world'. The Tolstoyan non-resistance to evil, he declared, was 'the most serious cause of the defeat of the first revolutionary movement'.[63]

Another admirer, Bernard Shaw, also had his doubts about certain aspects of Tolstoy's social and moral philosophy. He included him in a list of five men who are building up 'the intellectual consciousness of the race', but wrote that even if we embrace Tolstoyism, we cannot live for ever afterwards on one another's charity: 'We may simplify our lives and become vegetarians; but even the minimum of material life will involve the industrial problems of its production and its distribution, and will defy Anarchism ... Anarchism in industry, as far as it is practicable, produces exactly the civilization that we have today, and ... the first thing a Tolstoyan community would have to do would be to get rid of it.'[64] As a Fabian socialist, reneging on the anarchist sympathies of his youth, Shaw equated 'anarchism in industry' with the *laissez-faire* economics advocated by Benjamin Tucker (whose journal *Liberty* Shaw contributed to) rather than with the communism of Kropotkin which sought to abolish the wage-system.

In his old age, Tolstoy had increasing troubles at home with his wife and family, who found his righteousness irritating and his preaching insufferable. In public, he was as vigorous as ever in the cause of justice and peace. After reading in 1908 of the execution of twenty peasants for an attack on a landowner's home, he wrote his famous article *I Cannot Be Silent* against capital punishment. He accepted that revolutionary crimes are terrible, but they do not compare with the criminality and stupidity of the government's legalized violence. Since the government claimed that the executions were done for the general welfare of the Russian people, he felt as one of the people he was an unconscious participant in the crime. To free himself from this intolerable position, he wrote:

either these inhuman deeds may be stopped, or that my connection with them may be snapped and I put in prison, where I may be clearly conscious that these horrors are not committed on my behalf; or still better (so good that I dare not dream of such happiness) that they may put on me, as on those twelve or twenty peasants, a shroud and a cap and may push me also off a bench, so that by my own weight I may tighten the well-soaped noose around my old throat.[65]

Towards the end of his life, Tolstoy's Christian and pacifist version of anarchism won many followers and Yasnaya Polyana became a place of pilgrimage. He lent his support to many causes, including the emigration to Canada of the oppressed Dukhobors who shared his belief that one must not obey man rather than God. He was always ready to offer his advice to social reformers. Just before he died, Tolstoy wrote to Gandhi, who had been overwhelmed by a reading of *The Kingdom of God is Within You*, that 'love, i.e. the striving of human souls towards unity and the activity resulting from such striving, is the highest law and only law of human life.' Since it is incompatible with violence, he concluded that 'all our taxes collected by force, our judicial and police institutions and above all our armies must be abolished'.[66]

Whatever his failings, Tolstoy made a supreme effort to practise what he preached. His grand ideal of chastity was repeatedly defeated in his own bed; the wildness of his passions held sway over the calmness of his reason. But in the fields he did his share of manual labour like a pious *muzhik*. He dressed simply, refused to be served by servants, and took up boot repairing, living like a peasant on his own estate and adopting a vegetarian diet. He made his fortune over to his wife, and gave away the copyright on his last books. But while his conduct enhanced his international reputation, it only increased his problems with his family, who could not understand his new direction; only his youngest daughter sympathized.

Things got so bad that Tolstoy finally decided to go and live in a monastery. He left Yasnaya Polyana in the winter of 1910 at the age of eighty-two, accompanied by his doctor and youngest daughter. During the long train journey, he was suddenly taken ill and died in a small railway junction at Astapovo. In keeping with his wishes, he was buried in the forest on his former estate where as boys he and his brother believed a green stick was to be found which would cure the evils of the world.

After his death, Tolstoyan communities were set up throughout Europe. His later works struck a chord with those who were concerned with the survival of the individual in a world which was becoming more authoritarian and materialist. In America, his beliefs found an echo in the Christian anarchism of Dorothy Day and Ammon Hennacy and those associated with *The Catholic Worker*.

After the Bolshevik seizure of power, he was celebrated in his own country primarily as a literary artist; the authorities either ignored his social philosophy or tried to explain it away. Ironically enough, the property that the great anarchist abandoned at Yasnaya Polyana became a State museum, visited by as many as five thousand people a day. His subversive views on militarism, patriotism and government can be culled from the almost definitive edition of his writings which was published in ninety volumes in the Soviet Union in 1958.

Tolstoy's greatest indirect influence as a moral and social thinker has probably been in India. Gandhi developed Tolstoy's doctrine of non-resistance into a highly effective weapon in the campaign to oust the British imperial presence. But Gandhi went beyond Tolstoy to develop collective action and organize campaigns of mass disobedience. While he declared that 'the ideally non-violent state will be ordered anarchy', he accepted the need for a limited government and a form of indirect democracy as a step towards the ideal.[67] The Gandhian *Sarvodaya* movement, which developed in India after independence under the guidance of Vinoba Bhave, moved closer to Tolstoyan principles. Bhave emphasized the need for positive *satyagraha*, that is, non-violent assistance to others.[68]

In the West, Tolstoy's message, especially mediated by Gandhi who gave it a more practical application, found fertile ground in the peace movement after the Second World War when the superpowers used the threat of nuclear annihilation as an excuse to maintain their rule and control their peoples. Tolstoy proved an influential figure in the *rapprochement* at the time between the pacifist and anarchist traditions; his tactics of non-violent direct action and civil disobedience seemed for a while in the sixties capable of bringing about a peaceful revolution. An increasing number of libertarians have since come to acknowledge Tolstoy's central insight that violence cannot be used to abolish the violence of government, and that it is impossible to seize power in order to dissolve it.

It is still possible for a biographer like A. N. Wilson to call Tolstoy's religious anarchism the 'least Russian' and the 'silliest of his teachings'.[69] Nothing could be farther from the truth. It is hardly a coincidence that the Russian aristocracy should have produced three of the greatest anarchist thinkers in the nineteenth century in Bakunin, Kropotkin and Tolstoy. They were all able to witness at close quarters the tyranny of the Tsarist regime, and, conversely, the inspiring example of peasant communities living in an orderly and peaceful fashion without a trace of government.

Tolstoy's religious anarchism represents the fulfilment of a lifetime's erratic and desperate search for meaning. By stressing the light of reason and the kingdom of God within, he not only echoes the mystical anarchists of the Middle Ages but anticipates the best of modern radical theology.

Because Tolstoy interpreted the teaching of the Gospels in a pacifist and anarchist manner, and had the temerity to practise (if not always with success) what he preached, he will always irritate those who live in comforting churches, cushioned by bureaucracies and cynicism. He will always inspire those who seek a peaceful end to oppression and exploitation and who look forward to a world of creative fellowship.

23

American Individualists and Communists

THE UNITED STATES, WITH its traditional hostility to central government, has produced many original anarchists. Like their European counterparts, the individualists amongst them drew inspiration from Adam Smith's confidence in the market's capacity to bring about economic and social order, and they assumed that a modified form of capitalism would lead to anarchy. But while later in the century they were influenced by Proudhon, their anarchism was largely a home-grown affair.[1] It developed out of the American sense of independence and individuality which had been forged by the self-reliant settlers of the seventeenth and eighteenth centuries.

Josiah Warren

The first real American anarchist was the musician and inventor Josiah Warren.[2] He was first a member of Robert Owen's utopian colony New Harmony, but left in 1827 because of its communal property arrangements and system of collective authority which he felt prevented initiative and responsibility and suppressed individuality. Warren thought that it had failed to reconcile the need for personal autonomy and the demand for communal conformity; the 'united interests' of the members were directly at war with their individual personalities and the circumstances.

The experience did not lead Warren however to reject the principle of co-operative living, but rather made him aware that society should adapt to the needs of the individual and not *vice versa*. He henceforth adopted the principle that:

SOCIETY MUST BE SO CONSTRUCTED AS TO PRESERVE THE *SOVEREIGNTY OF EVERY INDIVIDUAL* INVIOLATE. That it must avoid all combinations and connexions of persons and interests, and all other arrangements, which will not leave every individual at all times at LIBERTY to dispose of his or her person, and time, and property, in any manner in which his or her feelings or judgement may

dictate, WITHOUT INVOLVING THE PERSONS OR INTER-
ESTS OF OTHERS.[3]

In his *Equitable Commerce* (1846), Warren further argued that each person
should be the final judge of right and wrong. He advocated a society in
which every agent is independent from his fellows and unable to suffer the
consequences of actions he does not commit. The only way to avoid discord
is to avoid all necessity for artificial organizations. 'The Individual', Warren
insisted ' "is by nature a law unto himself" or herself, and if we ever attain
our objects, this is not to be overlooked or disregarded.'[4] It is worthy of
note that Warren adds 'or herself'; unlike most of his contemporaries, he
was concerned with the individuality of women as much as men. His radical
individualism moreover did not prevent him from trying to establish libertarian communities in which people defined their own wants and received
according to their work done.

Although he worked out his principles independently, Warren has been
called the 'American Proudhon'.[5] Like Proudhon, he focused on property
as the key to human freedom. Each individual has the right to the product
of his or her labour, but no one could be entirely self-sufficient. Existing
forms of production made a division of labour inevitable. To overcome this
contradiction, Warren proposed like Robert Owen an exchange of notes
based on labour time, with the additional proviso that the intensity of labour
be taken into account in evaluating an individual's work. He wanted to
establish an 'equitable commerce' in which all goods are exchanged for
their cost of production. He therefore proposed 'labour notes' to replace
conventional money, assuming that each seller would accurately calculate
his or her labour time. In this way profit and interest would be eradicated
and a highly egalitarian order would emerge.

On leaving New Harmony, Warren tried out his system in a Time Store
which he set up in Cincinatti. It lasted three years and demonstrated the
practicality of his ideas. Goods were sold at cost price and customers gave
the storekeeper labour notes representing an equivalent time of their own
work to recompense his labour. Keen to spread the new gospel, Warren
managed to earn enough money from his patents (which included the first
design for a rotary press) to bring out a journal called *The Peaceful Revolutionist* in 1833, the first anarchist periodical to appear in America. He also set
up a model village based on the equitable exchange of labour which he
hoped would be the first of many such communities. In the long run, he
thought that two hours' labour a day would suffice to provide all necessaries.

The next experiment Warren undertook was called the Village of Equity
in Ohio. Half a dozen families bought a strip of land, built their own houses,
and set up a co-operative sawmill. With relationships based on voluntary

agreements, it proved to be the first anarchist community in any country since the Diggers tried to set up theirs on George's Hill during the English Revolution. Unfortunately, it collapsed through illness. Warren was not dismayed and immediately founded in 1846 another community called Utopia, mainly with former members of Fourierist communities. Based on stone quarries and sawmills, it attracted about a hundred members and lasted into the 1860s. At the beginning, it was entirely libertarian and voluntary in character. 'Throughout our operations on the ground', Warren observed in 1848,

> everything has been conducted so nearly upon the Individualist basis that no one meeting for legislation has taken place. No Organization, no indefinite delegated power, no 'Constitution', no 'laws' or 'Bye-laws', 'rules' or 'Regulations' but such as each individual makes for himself and his own business. No officers, no priests nor prophets have been resorted to – nothing of either kind in demand.[6]

Warren moved on in 1850 to establish a third community called the City of Modern Times on Long Island which survived for more than a decade. True to its individualist principles, the only way of dealing with a recalcitrant member was the boycott: 'When we wish to rid ourselves of unpleasant persons, we simply let them alone', a friend of Warren's recalled. 'We buy nothing of them, sell them nothing, exchange no words with them – in short, by establishing a complete system of non-interference with them, we show them unmistakably that they are not wanted here, and they usually go away on their own accord.'[7] The settlers showed remarkable mutual tolerance, and remained faithful to 'the great sacred right of Freedom even to do silly things'.[8]

Warren's form of individualism did not exclude co-operation for mutual advantage. He argued, for instance, that something like a communal kitchen would be cheap and efficient and would 'relieve the female of the family from the full, mill-horse drudgery to which they otherwise are irretrievably doomed'.[9] He also suggested that individuals could choose to live together, and that there could be 'hotels for children', organized according to the peculiarities of their wants and pursuits. Like Utopia, Modern Times did not collapse but rather evolved into a more traditional village with mutualist leanings.

In his theory, Warren remained consistent to the end, calling for complete religious freedom – 'every man his own church' – and asserting the absolute sovereignty of the individual – 'every man his own nation'.[10] He looked to a classless society of equal opportunity, with all coercive institutions abolished and replaced by a regime of voluntary contract. To enforce contracts and to sanction infractions against the 'law of equal liberty',

Warren advocated the deployment of rotating, voluntary juries who could shape general rules which would deal with individual cases. He even countenanced the use of public censure, imprisonment and death as possible sanctions, although he recognized that 'punishment is in itself an objectionable thing, productive of evil even when it prevents greater evil, and therefore it is not wise to resort to it for the redress of trivial wrongs.'[11]

The practical success of Warren's theories made them particularly attractive, and he went on to inspire individual anarchists like Lysander Spooner and Stephen Pearl Andrews. When William B. Greene introduced Proudhon's mutualism into America, its reception had already been prepared by Warren.

Even John Stuart Mill praised Warren as a 'remarkable American'. While noting abundant differences in detail, he accepted his general conception of liberalism and admitted that he had borrowed the phrase 'the sovereignty of the individual' from the Warrenites. Mill also correctly observed that while Warren's Village Community had a superficial resemblance to some aspects of socialism, it was opposed to them in principle since 'it recognizes no authority in Society over the individual, except to enforce equal freedom of development for all individualities'.[12]

The lawyer and linguist Stephen Pearl Andrews adopted Warren's notion of the sovereignty of the individual and his principle that cost should be the equitable limit of price. Throughout the universe, Andrews asserted, 'Individuality is the essential law of order'.[13] At the same time, he argued that the cost principle underlies individuality, or the 'disconnection of interests', since it ensures that I take as much of your labour for my benefit, as you take from me for your benefit.

But Andrews was not content to accept these principles merely in theory. He consistently opposed slavery and tried to free the state of Texas by raising money to buy off all of its slaves but the war with Mexico intervened. He also argued that sexual behaviour and family life should be matters of personal responsibility beyond the control of Church and State. Above all, he applied Warren's principle of the 'sovereignty of the individual' to both sexes, advocating the 'complete emancipation and self-ownership' of women as well as men.

Lysander Spooner

Another American individualist, Lysander Spooner, turned Lockean arguments to anarchist conclusions. In *Natural Law; or the Science of Justice* (1882), he asserted that justice requires each individual to respect the inviolability of person and property. Since in the state of nature men are at war when they forget justice, in civil society 'it is evidently desirable that men should associate, so far as they freely and voluntarily can do, for the maintenance of justice among themselves, and for mutual protection against wrong-doers.'[14] Such a voluntary association to maintain justice is nothing like a minimal State, but resembles more an insurance policy against fire or commercial loss. It is wholly a matter of contract.

As a lawyer, Spooner at first accepted the American Constitution. In his early writings, especially in a treatise on slavery, he recognized that it could not be reconciled with the right of private judgement. He also came to believe that trial by jury is more likely to bring about justice than government statutes. The Civil War finally convinced him that it is wrong for a people to be compelled to submit to, and support, a government they do not want. In his series of *No Treason* pamphlets, he argued 'if a man has never consented or agreed to support a government, he breaks no faith in refusing to support it. And if he makes war upon it, he does so as an open enemy, and not as a traitor.'[15] Consent must be unanimous, requiring the separate consent of every individual who is required to contribute, either by taxation or personal service, to the government.

Spooner was consistent, if nothing else: with irrefutable logic he demolished the contractual theory of the State in general, and the US Constitution in particular, on the grounds that it is impossible to say that every citizen has made a contract with government. People can contract for nobody but themselves; it is absurd to say that they can make political contracts binding on subsequent generations as the founding fathers tried to do. Any government that claims authority on the basis of an invalid social contract is clearly illegitimate. Indeed, all the great governments of the world, Spooner insists, have been

> mere bands of robbers, who have associated for purposes of plunder, conquest, and the enslavement of their fellow men. And their laws, as they have called them, have been only such agreements as they found it necessary to enter into, in order to maintain their organizations, and act together in plundering and enslaving others, and in securing to each his agreed share of the spoils.[16]

Unfortunately the 'tyrant-thief' of government dupes its subjects by convincing them that they are free simply because some of them can vote for a new master every few years. Voting is nothing more than an act of self-defence made in the vain hope that one will remain free while others are enslaved.

In his pamphlet *Poverty: Its Illegal Causes and Legal Cure* (1846), Spooner traced crime to poverty and fear of poverty which in turn is itself a sign of pernicious inequality and the unjust distribution of wealth. The remedy for crime is therefore to turn the present 'wheel of fortune' into 'an extended surface, varied somewhat by inequalities, but still exhibiting a general level, affording a safe position for all, and creating no necessity, for either force or fraud, on the part of any one, to enable him to secure his standing'.[17] To this end he recommends that every man should be his own employer, and he depicts an ideal society of independent farmers and entrepreneurs who have access to easy credit. If every person received the fruits of his own labour, the just and equal distribution of wealth would result.

Although he did not call himself an anarchist, Spooner invariably traced the ills of American society to its government and argued that civil society should be organized as a voluntary association. Contemporary right-wing libertarians in the United States like Murray Rothbard and Robert Nozick have been impressed by Spooner's arguments, but his concern with equality as well as liberty makes him a left-wing individualist anarchist. Indeed, while his starting-point is the individual, Spooner goes beyond classical liberalism in his search for a form of rough equality and a community of interests.

Benjamin R. Tucker

Benjamin Tucker was the first American thinker to call himself an anarchist with pride. He was influenced by Warren (whom he called his 'old friend and master'), but he further developed American individualist anarchism by drawing on Proudhon, Bakunin and Stirner. He was, a friend declared, 'an all-round man – Atheist, Anarchist, Egoist, Free Lover – not, like so many reformers, radical in one direction and reactionary in another'.[18] Although he was not an original thinker, Tucker was the most influential in spreading anarchism in America, arguing that it was not a system of philosophy but 'the fundamental principle in the science of political and social life'.[19] In 1878 he founded the *Radical Review* and, three years later, *Liberty*, which adapted from Proudhon the rubric: 'Not the Daughter but the Mother of Liberty'. It became the best anarchist periodical in English, celebrated for its aggressive and controversial tone. Tucker not only made pioneering translations of Proudhon and Bakunin into English, but published a whole series of books on anarchism and related topics over thirty years. Bernard Shaw admired him as a controversialist, and himself contributed to *Liberty*. Walt Whitman, who subscribed to *Liberty*, also said of its editor: 'I love him: he is plucky to the bone.'[20] Despite his hostility to Tucker's individualism, Kropotkin still applauded his criticism of the State as 'very searching' and his defence of the individual as 'very powerful'.[21]

Tucker came from a family of wealthy liberals and radical Protestants in New Bedford, inheriting from his parents their Painite individualism and formality of dress and manner. His experience of the best qualities of Quakerism made him confident that people could govern themselves without elected leaders, each following his or her light of reason in a community of fellowship. He went on to develop *laissez-faire* liberalism to its extreme and to express the aspirations of the small entrepreneur. 'The most perfect Socialism', he insisted, 'is possible only on the condition of the most perfect individualism.'[22] When he published his own translation of Bakunin's *God and the State*, Tucker advertised it as 'Paine's "Age of Reason" and "Rights of Man" Consolidated and Improved', a novel way of grafting Left Hegelianism onto the American individual tradition of natural rights.

Although personally timid and a man of thought rather than of action, Tucker was no less iconoclastic than Bakunin. His greatest fear was of inconsistency, and a friend described him as 'a glittering icicle of logic'.[23] He called for the destruction of every monopoly, including that worst of all monopolies and the mainstay of all privilege – the State. He rejected government as an invasion of the individual's private sphere, and the State as a monopoly of government in a particular area. All government, he recognized, is based on aggression and therefore tyrannical. By contrast, anarchism is 'the doctrine that all the affairs of men shall be managed by individuals or voluntary associations, and that the State should be abolished'. Anarchists are simply 'unterrified Jeffersonian Democrats' who believe that 'the best government is that which governs least, and that which governs least is no government at all.'[24] Even the police function of protecting persons and property could be done by voluntary associations and co-operatives for self-defence. Tucker was confident that the powers of every individual would be limited by the exercise of the equal rights of all others and equal liberty would eventually prevail. The fundamental law of social expediency for anarchism, he claimed, is 'the greatest amount of liberty compatible with equality of liberty'.[25]

No code of morals should be imposed on the individual. In Tucker's view, the only moral law is ' "Mind your own business" and the only crime is interference with another's business'.[26] Not surprisingly, Tucker asserted that anarchists should not only be utilitarians pursuing their own self-interest but egoists in the fullest sense. Yet he did not deny that individuals should influence their neighbours through the influence of reason, persuasion, example, public opinion, social ostracism and the influence of unhampered economic forces.

Although Tucker recognized that property is a social convention and labour is the only basis of the right of ownership, he believed strongly in competition and called anarchism 'consistent Manchesterism'.[27] He followed Warren in wanting prices to be fixed by costs of production and measured in labour time. But where Warren looked to 'equitable' individuals to work out the cost, Tucker relied on their self-interested conduct in a free market (that is, one which has abolished money, tariffs and patents). He also believed that absolute equality is not desirable: people should enjoy the results of their superiority of muscle or brain. But while retaining private property and admiring certain aspects of *laissez-faire* capitalism, he was critical of the 'system of violence, robbery, and fraud that the plutocrats call "law and order"'.[28] Although Emma Goldman complained that his attitude to the communist anarchists was 'charged with insulting rancor', he remained a left- rather than a right-wing libertarian.[29]

Like Godwin, Tucker looked to the gradual spread of enlightenment to bring about change. He made a plea for non-resistance to become a universal rule. But he distinguished between domination and defence, and accepted that resistance to encroachment from others is acceptable. Like Warren, he considered the use of violence as justified in enforcing contracts, and argued that individuals and groups have the right to any violence, including the use of capital punishment, in order to defend themselves. As Kropotkin observed, such a position opened the way to re-introduce in the name of 'defence' all the traditional functions of the State.[30]

Tucker saw like Proudhon the need for alternative institutions like schools, co-operative banks and trade unions, and hoped that, ultimately, massive civil disobedience and general strikes would bring about the collapse of the State. But he would refuse to be drawn on the exact nature of a free society beyond saying that natural patterns of organization would emerge. It was absurd, he argued, to predict 'A Complete Representation of Universal Progress for the Balance of Eternity'.[31]

Tucker was undoubtedly more effective in his critique of the State than in his alternative proposals. Indeed, he once confessed that it was easier to demonstrate why he was not anything else than to say why he was an anarchist: 'Archy once denied, only Anarchism can be affirmed. It is a matter of logic.'[32] While he kept individualist anarchism alive whilst anarcho-communism and anarcho-syndicalism were growing in strength, he became increasingly disillusioned. He spent the last thirty years of his life in silence in France, where his family lived an anarchistic life. His only daughter described him as a 'born nonteacher' who always considered himself right.[33] He endorsed, with Kropotkin, the cause of the Allies in the First World War, being anti-German from the outset. Still uncertain whether humanity had yet discovered the path to the goal of anarchy, he died in 1939 aged eighty-five.

Adin Ballou and John Humphrey Noyes

Although individualism dominated American indigenous anarchism, there was a communitarian tradition which was largely of Christian inspiration. Adin Ballou, for instance, had sought freedom with community in the

1830s. Admired later by Tolstoy, he insisted that the absolute authority of God must guide the life of humanity: 'The *will of man* (human government) whether in one, a thousand, or many millions, has no intrinsic authority – no moral supremacy – and no rightful claim to the allegiance of man. It has no original, inherent authority whatsoever over the conscience . . .'[34] While divine government is nurtured by persuasion and love, human government depends on cunning and physical force, expressed in its corruption, jails and wars. The Christian should therefore behave as though the millennium had already come, and refuse to support the secular authority by voting, legislating or fighting. In place of human government, Ballou proposed a 'neighbourhood society by voluntary association' like town meetings, in which public opinion would be enough to reform the disorderly individual. He tried to realize these ideals in the model community of Hopedale.

In the following decade, another Christian radical, John Humphrey Noyes, founded a community at Oneida, New York, believing like the Ranters that true Christians have thrown off the chains of Satan and become as innocent as Adam and Eve. Being in God's grace, they cannot sin. Under his system of 'Perfectionism', churches and governments are considered harmful impositions. The Bible, he insists, has depicted the coming of the kingdom of heaven on earth and in heaven 'God reigns over body, soul and estate, without interference from human governments.'[35]

Unlike the more repressive millenarian sects like the Shakers, Noyes' disciples at Oneida pooled their property and practised free love, believing in the physical and spiritual union of all. Solidarity was achieved and disputes solved through the practice of 'mutual criticism' by rotating committees. It proved remarkably successful in Oneida. Ironically the very success of Oneida's communism proved its undoing for the growing prosperity encouraged materialist and consumer values which eventually undermined its radical aims.

Towards the end of the century, European immigrants brought in a new kind of militant anarchist communism which rapidly overtook the indigenous variety. Nevertheless, middle-class society in New England could still produce fiery and rebellious youth. One such was Voltairine de Cleyre.

Voltairine de Cleyre

As a child de Cleyre attended a convent and wanted to become a nun. The Haymarket Massacre, a lecture on Paine, and a reading of Benjamin Tucker's journal *Liberty* eventually convinced her that 'Liberty is not the

Daughter but the Mother of Order.' She lost her religious vocation and began to give lectures on free-thinking, and worked as a language teacher amongst working-class Jewish immigrants. Her religious upbringing however led her to see anarchism as 'a sort of Protestantism, whose adherents are a unit in the great essential belief that all forms of external authority must disappear to be replaced by self-control only'.[36]

To begin with, De Cleyre was both a pacifist and non-resister, believing like Tolstoy that it was easier to conquer war by peace rather than force. Although she came to accept direct action as a form of public protest, she refused to advise anyone to do anything which involved a risk to herself. She thought that it was only from a peaceful strategy that a real solution to inequality and oppression would eventually emerge.

De Cleyre was fully aware that anarchists in the States at the time were divided in their conception of a future society between the individualists and the communists. Initially she favoured individual solutions to social problems, but increasingly stressed the importance of community. In her maturity, she envisaged a time when the great manufacturing plants of America would be broken up and society would consist of 'thousands of small communities stretching along the lines of transportation, each producing largely for its owns needs, able to rely upon itself, and therefore independent'.[37] She came to label herself simply 'Anarchist', and called like Malatesta for an 'anarchism without adjectives', since in the absence of government many different experiments would probably be tried in various localities in order to determine the most appropriate form.

Alexander Berkman

After the Haymarket Massacre in Chicago in 1886 and the subsequent repression, anarchism remained principally a movement of immigrants among the Italian and Jewish populations, and the Russian refugees in the larger cities. From the latter community emerged the most influential anarcho-communists in America in the early part of this century: Alexander Berkman and Emma Goldman. They were not only tireless campaigners but also produced the best journals, especially *Mother Earth* which ran from 1906 to 1917.

Berkman was born into a respectable Jewish family in Vilnius, Lithuania in 1870. Moving to St Petersburg he found the revolutionary movement inspirational, especially in the person of his uncle Mark Natanson, a revolutionary leader and founder of the Chaikovsky circle. After his parents' deaths, Berkman left Russia at the age of sixteen, arriving in America in 1882. On becoming the companion of Emma Goldman, and inspired by the martyrdom of the Haymarket anarchists, he tried to put his revolutionary beliefs into action by attempting unsuccessfully to shoot in 1892 the financier Henry Clay Frick, an employee of Andrew Carnegie who had ordered gunmen to kill strikers at a steel strike in Homestead. The action earned Berkman a twenty-two year sentence in prison, but it did not dampen his spirit. Unrepentant, he wrote in the *Prison Memoirs of an Anarchist* that 'Human life is indeed sacred and inviolate. But the killing of a tyrant, an enemy of the People, is in no way to be considered the taking of a life.' Despite the effect of prison on his nerves, Berkman wrote to Goldman after ten years inside: 'My youthful ideal of a free humanity in the vague future has become clarified and crystallized into the living truth of anarchy, as the sustaining elemental force of my every-day existence.'[38]

After serving fourteen years, he was released and immediately took up the revolutionary struggle once again. He helped organize the free Ferrer school in New York and edited with Goldman *Mother Earth*. They became the leading figures in the American anarchist movement, and both threw themselves into the anti-militarist campaign. Berkman went on to edit his own journal *Blast* which from 1915 to 1917 called stridently for direct action.

After being arrested and imprisoned for two years for opposing conscription on the US entry into the War, in 1919 Berkman was deported, with Emma Goldman, to Russia. At first, he worked with Bolsheviks and was even asked to translate Lenin's *'Left-Wing' Communism, An Infantile Disorder* (1920). But Berkman rapidly became disillusioned and witnessed at first hand the Bolsheviks' betrayal of the revolution and their persecution of the anarchists. The crushing of the Kronstadt rebellion was the final blow. In July 1921, he wrote in his diary: 'Grey are the passing days. One by one the embers of hope have died out. Terror and despotism have crushed the life born in October. The slogans of the Revolution are forsworn, its ideals stifled in the blood of the people ... Dictatorship is trampling the masses underfoot ... The Revolution is dead; its spirit cries in the wilderness.'[39] The disillusioned Berkman decided to leave Russia once and for all. He lived at first in Germany for a couple of years, then settled in Paris, and finally ended up in the south of France.

In his last years, Berkman remained faithful to the anarchist cause, which he still considered the 'very first thing humanity has ever thought of'.[40] But he became less certain about the efficacy of violence and wrote to Goldman in November 1928: 'I am in general now not in favour of terroristic tactics, except in very exceptional circumstances.' Whilst working on his pamphlet *What is Communism?* in the following year, he even wrote to his lifelong companion: 'There are moments when I feel that the revolution cannot work on anarchist principles. But once the old methods are followed, they never lead to anarchism.'[41] Rather than die slowly after an operation, he shot himself in 1936, only a few weeks before the Spanish anarchists decided to take up arms against Franco.

Berkman's *What is Communism?* was first published in 1929 in New York as *Now and After: the ABC of Anarchism*. The pamphlet proved one of the best introductions to anarcho-communism and has become an anarchist classic. Its value lies not so much in the originality of its ideas (mainly culled from Kropotkin) but in its plain and clear style and readiness to answer the traditional objections to anarchism.

Berkman defines anarchism as the ideal of 'a society without force and compulsion, where all men shall be equals; and live in freedom, peace and harmony'. It does not mean, as its enemies would allege, bombs or chaos, but that 'you should be free; that no one should enslave you, boss you, rob you, or impose upon you'. For Berkman anarchist communism implies 'voluntary communism, communism from free choice'.[42]

His most interesting arguments are in the chapter 'Will Communist Anarchism Work?' where he insists that laziness implies the 'right man in the wrong place' and asserts that freedom in practice implies diversification. As far as means are concerned, he points out that anarchists do not have a monopoly on violence any more than other social activists. Individual acts of violence are more an expression of temperament than theory and are the 'method of ignorance, the weapon of the weak'.[43] Indeed, in his chapter on the 'Defence of the Revolution', Berkman specifically condemns the suppression and terrorization of counter-revolutionaries and argues that the practice of liberty and equality is the best possible defence.

Emma Goldman

The Most Dangerous Woman

EMMA GOLDMAN WAS MORE of an activist than a thinker. Nevertheless, she made a lasting contribution to anarchist theory by giving it a feminist dimension which had only been hinted at in the work of Godwin and Bakunin. She not only stressed the psychological aspects of women's subordination but made a creative synthesis of personal individualism and economic communism. As a lecturer on anarchism, agitator for free speech, pioneer of birth control, critic of Bolshevism, and defender of the Spanish Revolution, she was considered to be one of the most dangerous women of her time. Ever since her death her star has been rising in the firmament of reputation.

Goldman was born in 1869 in a Jewish ghetto in Russia, the unwanted child of her father's second marriage. She grew up in the remote village of Popelan, where her parents had a small inn. She later recalled that she had always felt a rebel. As a girl, she was instinctively repelled by the knouting of a servant and shocked that love between a Jew and Gentile should be regarded a sin. When she was thirteen, the family moved in 1882 to the Jewish quarter in St Petersburg. Coming just after the assassination of Alexander II, it was a time of intense political repression and the Jewish community in Russia suffered a wave of pogroms. It was also a time of severe economic hardship. Due to her family's poverty Goldman was obliged to leave school in St Petersburg only after six months and find work in a factory.

Mixing with radical students, she was introduced to Turgenev's *Fathers and Sons* (1862) and was impressed by the definition of a nihilist as 'a man who does not bow down before any authority, who does not take any principle on faith, whatever reverence that principle may be enshrined in'. More important to her subsequent development, she secured a copy of Nikolai Chernyshevsky's *What is to be Done?* (1863) in which the heroine Vera is converted to nihilism and lives in a world of easy friendship between the sexes and enjoys free enquiry and co-operative work. The book not only offered an embryonic sketch of her later anarchism, but strengthened her determination to live her life in her own way.[1]

Unfortunately her father would have none of it. The archetypal patriarch, he became the 'nightmare' of her childhood.[2] He not only whipped her in an attempt to break her spirit, but tried to marry her off at fifteen. When she refused and begged to continue her studies, he replied: 'Girls do not have to learn much! All a Jewish daughter needs to know is how to prepare *gefüllte* fish, cut noodles fine, and give the man plenty of children.'[3] It was eventually agreed in the family that such an impossible child should go to America with a half-sister to join her other half-sister who had already settled in Rochester.

As a Russian Jew without connections, Emma quickly realized that the paradise of America was, for the poor at least, hell on earth. She gained her real education in the slums and sweatshops, earning her living as a seamstress. The difficulties of her early years undoubtedly strengthened her sense of injustice and inspired her impassioned love of freedom.

What drew Goldman initially to anarchism in America was the outcry which followed the Haymarket Square tragedy in 1886 in Chicago. After a bomb had been thrown in a crowd of police during a workers' rally for an eight-hour day, four anarchists were eventually hanged. Convicted on the flimsiest evidence, the judge at the trial had openly declared: 'Not because you have caused the Haymarket bomb, but because you are Anarchists, you are on trial.'[4] These events not only shaped the radical conscience of a generation but made Goldman undergo a profound conversion. On the day of the hanging, she decided to become a revolutionary and to find out what exactly had inspired the ideals of the martyrs.

At the age of twenty, she divorced the Russian immigrant she had married out of loneliness and decided to go to New York. Here she met Johann Most, the fiery editor of the German-language anarchist paper *Freiheit* and adopted his violent brand of communism as her own. She was soon giving lectures on anarchism herself. Increasingly repelled by Most's destructive ire, she became interested in the rival German anarchist journal *Die Autonomie*. It introduced her to the writings of Kropotkin whom she immediately recognized as anarchism's clearest thinker.

Goldman was never one to rest in theory. In keeping with her views on free love, she became the lover of the anarchist Alexander Berkman, the 'Sasha' of her autobiography. It was the beginning of a lifetime's relationship. They lived in a *ménage à trois* with an artist comrade Modest Stein called Fedya, rejecting jealousy as an outmoded form of honour and possession.

Keen to carry out some spectacular deed to advance the workers' cause, she planned with Berkman the assassination of Henry Clay Frick during a steel-strike at Homestead in 1892. Goldman even tried unsuccessfully to work as a prostitute on Fourteenth Street to raise money for the gun but eventually borrowed the money from her sister.

Berkman managed to enter Frick's office and shot him, but the manager was only wounded. Although Berkman was sentenced to twenty-two years' imprisonment, Goldman openly tried to explain and justify the attempted assassination. The trial not only confirmed the growing reputation of anarchism for violence but made Goldman a marked woman. Thereafter her lectures were regularly disrupted by the authorities. They were certainly lively affairs: when on one occasion, Most condemned Berkman's act, Goldman was so enraged that she took out a horsewhip and tried to give him a fierce lashing.

In 1893, Goldman was arrested for allegedly urging the unemployed to take bread 'by force' and given a year in prison on Blackwell's Island. At the trial the Assistant District Attorney questioned her about her beliefs:

> Do you believe in the Supreme Being, Miss Goldman?
>
> No, sir, I do not.
>
> Is there any government on earth whose laws you approve?
>
> No, sir, for they are all against the people.
>
> Why don't you leave this country if you don't like its laws?
>
> Where shall I go? Everywhere on earth the laws are against the poor, and they tell me I cannot go to heaven, nor do I want to go there.[5]

Her replies were hardly intended to endear her to the respectable jury. After her release, Goldman found herself a celebrity, the notorious 'Red Emma', renowned and feared for her espousal of free love, atheism and revolution. She did little to dissuade her critics. When asked by the editor of the *Labor Leader* in 1897 for an account of a free society, she simply replied: 'I am really too much of an anarchist to work out a programme for the members of that society; in fact, I do not bother about such trifling details, all I want is freedom, perfect, unrestricted liberty for myself and others.'[6]

When the young Polish immigrant Czolgosz assassinated President McKinley in 1901, it was said that Goldman had incited him to commit the act. Although she denied any connection, her sympathy for the defenceless assassin only made her more dangerous in the public mind. The repression of anarchists which followed meant that she could not return to public life until 1906.

It was then that she began publishing with Berkman the monthly *Mother Earth*. Originally called the 'Open Road' after a poem by Walt Whitman, the title was particularly appropriate, invoking the goddess of fertility and the beauty of freedom. Its pages not only discussed anarchist ideas but became a platform for literature and art, introducing writers like Ibsen, Strindberg, Hauptmann, Thoreau, Nietzsche and Wilde to the American public.

Goldman's writing and editorial activities did not prevent her from organizing her lecture tours. She became one of the most magnetic and volatile orators in American history, despite the attempts of the police and vigilante groups to silence her. In 1910, when her most theoretical work *Anarchism and Other Essays* came out, she undertook a tour during which she spoke 120 times in 37 cities to 25,000 listeners. Her drama lectures were published in 1914 as *The Social Significance of the Modern Drama*. She not only saw drama as a powerful disseminator of radical thought and championed the work of Hauptmann and Ibsen, but was consistently concerned with the aesthetic dimension to the struggle for freedom.

Not surprisingly, the little revolutionary with the pince-nez repeatedly fell foul of the authorities for her outspoken attack on the scourge of law, government and property. She was imprisoned a second time for distributing birth control literature, but her longest sentence resulted from her involvement in setting up No-Conscription Leagues and organizing rallies against the First World War. She and Berkman were then arrested in 1917 for conspiracy to obstruct the draft and given two years. Afterwards, they were stripped of their American citizenship and deported with other undesirable 'Reds' to Russia in 1919. J. Edgar Hoover, who directed her deportation hearing, called her 'one of the most dangerous women in America'.

In the circumstances, Goldman was not too disappointed to return to her homeland and to witness at first hand the Russian Revolution which she had extolled in America as 'the promise and hope of the world'.[7] For the sake of the revolution, she was at first willing to repress her distaste of Marxist centralism and Statism and to work with the Bolsheviks. She was immediately disappointed by the gagging of free speech and by the special privileges enjoyed by Communist Party members. She and Berkman travelled throughout the country to collect documents for the revolutionary archives and were horrified at the growing bureaucracy, political persecution and forced labour they found.

Their breaking-point was reached when the Kronstadt rebellion broke out. A series of strikes took place in March 1921 in Petrograd, supported by the sailors of Kronstadt. Among their demands, the workers and sailors called for an equalization of rations, freedom of speech for Left groups, and elections to the Soviets. When they were brutally crushed by Trotsky and the Red Army, Goldman and Berkman felt unable to stay in Russia, convinced that the triumph of the Bolshevik State had meant the defeat of the Revolution. In December 1921 they were issued passports and they left for Europe.

Goldman set down her two years in Russia in a book entitled *My Disillusionment in Russia* (1923), followed up by *My Further Disillusionment in Russia* (1924), which were published together as a single volume in Britain the following year. In her moving account, she describes how she had tried to raise the question of the New Economic Policy in an interview with Lenin but quickly came to realize that the 'centralized political State was Lenin's deity, to which everything else was sacrificed'. Although the libertarian principle had been strong in the early days of the Revolution, she put down its failure to the 'fanatical governmentalism' of Marxism and to its concept of the 'dictatorship of the proletariat'.[8] Goldman later argued that Bolshevism in practice was not a form of voluntary communism but rather 'compulsory State Communism'.[9] With its nationalized economy, its rigid central planning, its wage system, its class divisions and privileges, its vast bureaucracy, its dominant and exclusive Communist Party, it was little different from State capitalism. Indeed, she even claimed that Stalin's dictatorship was more absolute than any tsar's had been.

After leaving Russia, Goldman and Berkman were not allowed to return to America. Berkman settled in France and she in England. Here she was championed by Rebecca West, who wrote an introduction to *My Disillusionment in Russia*, but she was unable to capture the public attention with her unwelcome message. She was almost alone amongst radicals in condemning the Bolsheviks. Bertrand Russell recalled that although she had been welcomed enthusiastically by Rebecca West and others to give a speech in 1924, she sat down in dead silence after severely criticizing the Bolsheviks. Increasingly her public lectures were poorly attended. She was even unable to find a publisher for a perceptive manuscript on the Russian dramatists. On hearing that she might be deported in 1925, James Colton, an old self-taught Welsh miner, offered to marry her in order to give her British nationality and she accepted his expression of 'sweet solidarity'. With a British passport, she was then able to travel to France and Canada. In 1934, she was even allowed to give a lecture tour in the States.

The greatest experience of her old age was the Spanish Revolution. Depressed by Berkman's suicide in 1936 and the rise of fascism, she was greatly cheered to hear of the republican stand against Franco in Spain. At the age of sixty-seven, she went to Barcelona in September 1936 to join in the struggle. At last anarchism seemed about to triumph. She told a rally of Libertarian Youth: 'Your revolution will destroy forever [the notion] that anarchism stands for chaos.'[10] She worked with the anarchist CNT-FAI (Confederación Nacional del Trabajo and the Federación Anarquista Ibérica); on one occasion, ten thousand of their members turned out to hear her call them 'a shining example to the rest of the world'.[11] She edited the

English language edition of the Bulletin of the CNT-AIT-FAI and was given the task of publicizing their cause in Britain.

But once again her high hopes for revolution were to be dashed. She disagreed with the participation of the anarchists of the CNT-FAI in the coalition government of 1937 and the concessions they made to the increasingly powerful communists for the sake of the war effort. She correctly foresaw that it would do irreparable harm to the anarchist cause; the social revolution ought to have gone ahead simultaneously with the fight against Franco. However, Goldman felt unable to condemn her anarchist comrades for their understandable compromises by joining in the government and accepting militarization since she felt the alternative at the time was communist dictatorship.

At the International Working Men's Association Congress held in Paris late in 1937, she declared that in the 'burning house' of Spain, it seemed a breach of solidarity to pour the 'acid' of criticism on their 'burned flesh'.[12] She wrote a year later to Vernon Richards:

> though I disagreed with much that our Spanish comrades had done I stood by them because they were fighting so heroically with their backs to the wall against the whole world, misunderstood by some of their own comrades and betrayed by the workers as well as by every Marxist organisation. Whatever verdict future historians will give the struggle of the CNT-FAI they will be forced to acknowledge two great actions of our people, their refusal to establish dictatorship when they had power, and having been the first to rise against Fascism.[13]

Despite her profound disappointment at the triumph of Franco in Spain and the spread of fascism throughout Europe, she refused to compromise her anarchist principles. She wrote just before her death in 1940: 'I am against dictatorship and Fascism as I am opposed to parliamentary regimes and so-called political democracy.'[14] She continued to consider anarchism the 'most beautiful and practical philosophy' and was confident that one day it would be vindicated.[15]

She died in 1940 three months after a stroke, in Toronto. Her body was finally allowed to return to America and was buried in a Chicago cemetery, not far from the Haymarket martyrs whose fate had changed the course of her life over fifty years before.

Philosophy

Although primarily an activist, Goldman developed an original and persuasive view of anarchism. In her metaphysics, she was a thoroughgoing atheist, and felt that the Church was as oppressive an institution as the State. She believed like Bakunin that religion originated in our mental inability to solve natural phenomena and that the Church had always been 'a stumbling block to progress'. As for Christianity, with Christ's exaltation of the meek and determination to fulfil the law of the prophets, it is 'most admirably adapted to the training of slaves, to the perpetuation of slave society'. In terms reminiscent of Nietzsche, she concluded that 'Atheism in its negation of gods is at the same time the strongest affirmation of man, and through man, the eternal yea to life, purpose, and beauty.'[16]

Goldman defined anarchism as 'The philosophy of a new social order based on liberty unrestricted by man-made law; the theory that all the forms of government rest on violence, and are therefore wrong and harmful, as well as unnecessary'. She repudiated entirely the objections that it is an impractical ideal and that it stands for destruction and violence. On the contrary, anarchism, she believed, is 'the only philosophy which brings to man the consciousness of himself; which maintains that God, the State, and society are non-existent'. As such, it is a great liberator from the 'phantoms' of religion and property. Government which makes and enforces law moreover is unnecessary since 'crime is naught but misdirected energy' and prison is a social crime and failure which only creates anti-social beings.[17]

While none of this is particularly original, her most striking contribution was her defence of individuality. She counted Stirner and Nietzsche as allies in her struggle for freedom and became convinced that 'if society is ever to become free, it will be so through liberated individuals'. As a woman, she had directly experienced the intolerance and prejudice of the average American, and consequently repudiated the 'mass as a creative factor'.[18] She was also only too well aware of the readiness of the majority of people to become dependent on leaders and bow before authority:

> the mass itself is responsible for this horrible state of affairs. It clings to its masters, loves the whip, and is the first to cry Crucify! the moment a protesting voice is raised against the sacredness of the capitalistic authority or any other decayed institution ... Yes, authority, coercion, dependence rest upon the mass, but never freedom or the free unfoldment of the individual, never the birth of a free society.[19]

It would be misleading however to call Goldman an elitist. Despite her realistic assessment of the revolutionary potential of her contemporaries she was still convinced that all human beings are ultimately capable of throwing off their chains and of reaching their full stature. There was nothing in human nature to prevent it and 'the love of freedom is a universal trait'.[20]

Again, while inspired by Stirner, Goldman is not an egoist. Anarchism may be the philosophy of 'the sovereignty of the individual' but it is also the theory of 'social harmony'.[21] She tried to achieve the central anarchist ideal of communal individuality. In her most widely read essay 'What I Believe' (1908), she insisted that anarchism is a theory of 'organic development'. Rejecting property as 'dominion over things', she argues moreover that liberated work is possible only 'in a society based on voluntary co-operation of productive groups, communities and societies loosely federated together, eventually developing into free communism, actuated by a solidarity of interests'.[22]

Having met leading French syndicalists, she saw syndicalism at the time, with its wish to overthrow the wage system and to replace the centralized State by the 'free, federated grouping of the workers', as the 'economic expression of Anarchism'.[23] She also praised the educational work of the French Labour Chambers and approved of their methods of direct action, industrial sabotage, and the general strike.

She returned to the question of 'The Place of the Individual in Society' (1940) in her last published essay. She reasserted her belief that 'The Individual is the true reality in life' and criticized government precisely because it not only seeks to widen and perpetuate power but has an inherent distrust of the individual and fear of individuality. Fully aware of the crippling influence of public opinion, she further suggested that 'even more than constituted authority, it is social uniformity and sameness that harass the individual most.' Like Oscar Wilde, whom she admired, she maintained that true civilization is to be measured by a person's 'individuality and the extent to which it is free to have its being, to grow and expand unhindered by invasive and coercive authority'. At the same time, she followed Kropotkin by asserting that mutual aid and voluntary co-operation have worked for the evolution of the species and can only create the basis of a 'free individual and associational life'.[24] Goldman's individualism was not therefore a rugged individualism which operates at the expense of others.

Goldman was scathing about the American Left as well as the Right. She considered the radical movement before the First World War to be in a state of 'sad chaos . . . a sort of intellectual hash, which has neither taste nor character'. She swiped at those 'intellectual proletarians' who preferred comfort to the ideal, and external success to the vital issues of life.[25] Though she frequently worked with individual socialists on particular issues, she attacked the American Socialist Party for treating every 'spook prejudice' with kid gloves and for following the 'crooked path' of politics as a means of capturing the State: 'if once economic dictatorship were added to the already supreme political power of the State, its iron heel would cut deeper into the flesh of labor than that of capitalism today.'[26]

As for Marxists in general, she felt keenly the split in the First International between Marx and Bakunin. She criticized moreover Marx's historical materialism for overlooking the 'human element' and for failing to recognize that the rejuvenation of humanity needs 'the inspiration and energising force of an ideal'. Class consciousness can never be expressed in the political arena but only through the 'solidarity of interests' forged in the determined effort to overthrow the present system.[27]

While she offered a telling critique of her own society and culture and rejected the programmes of other socialists, Goldman refused to impose 'an iron-clad programme or method on the future ... Anarchism, as I understand it, leaves posterity free to develop its own particular systems, in harmony with its needs.'[28] While some have seen this as a theoretical weakness, it is in fact in keeping with her view that the past or the present should not determine the future, and it is impossible to imagine how people in a free society would want to arrange their affairs.

When it came to the means of bringing about a free society and transformed humanity, Goldman was somewhat ambivalent. To begin with she accepted the need for individual acts of political violence and she not only supported Berkman in his assassination attempt but commiserated with Czolgosz after he was condemned to death for killing McKinley. The men who make violent protests are not cruel and heartless monsters, she argued, but rather it is their 'supersensitiveness to the wrong and injustice surrounding them' which compels them to pay 'the toll of our social crimes'.[29] Compared with the wholesale violence of capital and government, political acts of violence are but a drop in the ocean. Indeed, it is the 'terrible inequality and great political injustice that prompts such acts'.[30] But towards the middle of he life, she came to see Berkman and Czolgosz as victims who had committed deeds of misplaced protest. While she refused to condone them, neither did she condemn them.

The State, according to Goldman, is the greatest source of violence in our society, particularly by being the focal point for the twin evils of patriotism and militarism. Patriotism is a menace to liberty, fuels militarism, and should be replaced by universal brotherhood and sisterhood. She was totally opposed to militarism and like Tolstoy saw the soldier merely as a professional man-killer – 'a cold-blooded, mechanical, obedient tool of his military superiors'.[31] Whereas class war and war against false values and evil institutions are legitimate, to prepare for war between States is 'The Road to Universal Slaughter'.[32] As she said at her trial in July 1917 for conspiracy to avoid the draft: 'It is organized violence at the top which creates individual violence at the bottom.'[33]

Whilst living in America, Goldman thus advocated the use of collective violence to overthrow the State and capitalism and endorsed class war, direct action and industrial sabotage. But after her experience in Russia in 1920 and 1921, she had second thoughts. It is one thing to employ violence in combat as a means of defence, but to institutionalize terrorism as the Bolsheviks had done is altogether different: 'Such terrorism begets counter-revolution and in turn becomes counter-revolutionary.' In Russia, the all-dominating slogan of the Communist Party had become: 'THE END JUSTIFIES THE MEANS.'[34] Indeed, after her stay in Russia, she began to insist that methods and means cannot be separated from the ultimate aim.

In practice, this meant that all violent means to realize libertarian ends are suspect. Social revolution should not only recognize the sanctity of human life but aim at a fundamental transvaluation of values; it involves internal change in our moral values as well external social relations. As she wrote to a friend in 1923: 'The one thing I am convinced of as I have never been in my life is that the gun decides nothing at all.'[35] Five year later, she wrote to Berkman that it was time to reject revolution as a 'violent eruption destroying everything' and that the only choice was to accept terrorism and become Bolsheviks or to become Tolstoyans.[36] But she never relinquished her belief in revolution. When the Spanish Revolution broke out she not only refused to condemn those anarchists who collaborated in the republican government with socialists and communists but even condoned the military training of soldiers in the exceptional circumstances of the civil war.

In general, Goldman thought the most important way of reconstructing society was through example and education. She defined example as 'the actual living of a truth once recognized, not the mere theorizing of its life element'.[37] It was to this end that she wrote the two volumes of her frank and intimate autobiography *Living My Life* (1931).

In the area of education, she involved herself in the Modern School Movement, helping to establish one in an anarchist community in Stelton, New Jersey and another in Manhattan. They were inspired by the schools of the Frenchman Sébastien Faure and those of the Spaniard Francisco Ferrer, whose execution in 1909 had caused an international outcry in liberal circles. Goldman saw existing schools as drilling the young into absolute uniformity by compulsory mental feeding. The social purpose of the libertarian Modern School on the other hand was 'to develop the individual through knowledge and the free play of characteristic traits, so that he may become a social being'.[38]

To bring this about, there should be no rules and regulation. The educators should encourage the free expression of the child and to bring about his or her understanding and sympathy. Since 'man is much more of a sex creature than a moral creature', sex education should be given to recognize the central and beautiful part it plays in life.[39] But while Goldman insisted on the 'free growth' of the innate tendencies of a child, she did not foresee a time like Godwin and Ferrer when education would become an entirely spontaneous affair. She continued to believe in the creative power of the good teacher: 'The child is to the teacher what clay is to the sculptor.'[40]

Sexual Politics

Goldman's arguments on government, revolution and education were invariably clear and perceptive, but her most important contribution to anarchist theory was in giving it a feminist dimension. She was particularly incensed about the status and conditions of women in her day and her outspoken views caused much of her notoriety. She detested the double standard which prevailed in the relations between the sexes. She attacked the 'The Hypocrisy of Puritanism' which demeans natural impulses and depresses culture. She railed against the existing system which treated women as sex objects, breeders and cheap labour. Prostitution was the prime example of the exploitation of woman, but all women in different ways were obliged to sell their bodies. By stressing the personal as the political in this way, Goldman was isolated from feminists in her own day but it made her particularly appealing to the American feminists of the 1970s and 1980s.

Unlike the suffragettes, who saw the vote as the principal means of female emancipation and who wanted to bring men under the same restrictions as women, Goldman rejected completely the 'modern fetish' of universal suffrage. She criticized the existing suffrage movement in America for being 'altogether a parlor affair', detached from the economic needs of the people.[41] While the true aim of emancipation should make it possible for woman to be human in the fullest sense, 'The Tragedy of Woman's Emancipation' in America had been to turn her into an isolated and artificial being. Paradoxically, Goldman thought it necessary to emancipate her American sisters from 'emancipation' as it was then understood. The so-called 'free American citizen' had by the right of universal suffrage merely 'forged chains about his limbs'; she saw no reason why woman should not have the equal right to vote with man but felt it an absurd notion to believe that 'woman will accomplish that wherein man has failed'.[42]

No political solution is possible for the unequal and repressive relations between the sexes. Goldman therefore called for a Nietzschean 'transvaluation of all accepted values' coupled with the abolition of economic slavery. She invited her contemporaries to go 'Beyond Good and Evil' and assert 'the right to oneself, to one's personality'.[43] True emancipation begins neither at the polls nor in the courts; it begins in a 'woman's soul'. Above all, woman's emancipation must come from and through herself:

First, by asserting herself as a personality, and not as a sex commodity. Second, by refusing the right to anyone over her body; by refusing to bear children, unless she wants them; by refusing to be a servant to God, the State, society, the husband, the family etc., by making her life simpler, but deeper and richer. That is, by trying to learn the meaning and substance of life in all its complexities, by freeing herself from the fear of public opinion and public condemnation. Only that, and not the ballot, will set woman free, will make her a force hitherto unknown in the world, a force for real love, for peace, for harmony; a force of divine fire, of life-giving; a creator of free men and women.[44]

Goldman felt no compunction in tackling head on the most tabooed subjects and called for a frank and open discussion of sex, love and marriage. Far from being synonymous, Goldman believed that marriage and love are often mutually antagonistic. Whereas love has been the most powerful factor in breaking the bars of convention, marriage furnishes the State and Church with an opportunity to pry into our most intimate affairs. It is often purely an economic arrangement, furnishing the woman with an insurance policy and the man with a pretty toy and a means of perpetuating his kind. As such it 'prepares the woman for a life of a parasite, a dependent helpless servant, while it furnishes the man the right to a chattel mortgage over a human life'.[45] A woman therefore emancipates herself when she admires a man only for the qualities of his heart and mind, asserts the right to follow that love without hindrance, and declares the absolute right to free motherhood. No anarchist thinker other than Godwin has compiled such a trenchant critique of the 'market place of marriage'.

Goldman not only advocated free love but practised it. She had at least one affair with another woman. In her twenties, she lived with Berkman and the artist Fedya as a *ménage à trois*. In 1908 when she was thirty-eight she took a lover called Ben Reitman who was nine years her junior. He was known as the 'Hobo King' for his work as a doctor in Chicago among vagrants. For all her declarations of independence, she became obsessed by the 'handsome brute'. He aroused in her a 'torrent of elemental passion' she had never dreamed a man could evoke and she admitted 'I responded shamelessly to its primitive call, its naked beauty, its ecstatic joy.'[46]

Reitman continued to have frequent sex with other women during their ten-year relationship and, as their correspondence shows, Goldman could not help feeling jealous and anxious when he was with someone else. Her lamentations might be interpreted as at least a contradiction and perhaps a failure of her philosophy. She recognized the danger herself and wrote to Reitman 'I have no right to speak of Freedom when I myself have become an abject slave in my love.'[47] But her personal experience as a spurned and neglected lover does not contradict, but rather gives more weight to, her considered thoughts and public statements.

In an essay on 'Jealousy' probably written around 1912, she insisted that the anguish over lost love which inspired many Romantic poets has nothing to do with jealousy, which only makes people angry, petty and envious. Goldman traces its source to the idea of an exclusive sex monopoly endorsed by Church and State and sees it embodied in an outmoded code of honour based on possession and vengeance. It also involves the conceit of the male and the envy of the female. The cure is firstly to recognize that no one is the owner of the sex functions of another, and secondly, to accept only love or affection which is voluntarily given: 'All lovers do well to leave the doors of their love wide open.'[48] In a lecture called 'False Fundamentals of Free Love', Goldman further distinguished carefully between promiscuity and the free choice of committed love. As she wrote to Reitman at the same time 'My love is sex, but it is devotion, care, anxiety, patience, friendship, it is all . . .'[49] Goldman always had a romantic view of love, celebrating its 'savagery' as well as its ideal beauty, and was fully aware that it was a double-edged sword.

It could be argued that it was easy for Goldman to practise free love because she was infertile through endometriosis. But she could have had an operation to enable her to conceive; she chose not to. As such, her choice amounted to a voluntary form of birth control. Moreover, she was not without maternal feelings and wrote to Reitman: 'I have a great deep mother instinct for you, baby-mine; that instinct has been the redeeming feature in our relation.'[50] This did not prevent her from attacking at times the myth of motherhood and asserting the right of every woman to make a free choice of becoming a parent. In addition, she fought the laws against birth control until she was jailed in 1916. As the contemporary feminist Margaret Anderson observed, Goldman was sent to prison for advocating that 'women need not always keep their mouths shut and their wombs open'.[51]

Goldman called for a new society where individuals could read, write and say what they liked, and have equal opportunities regardless of their sex to realize their full potential. She wanted women to have control over their bodies and to be able to practise birth control. She hoped men and women would become truly individual whilst living in voluntary associations. She looked to a revolution to bring about both an internal and external change, economic communism as well as a complete transformation of values.

Although at the end of her life, Goldman acknowledged that she was hopelessly out of tune with her contemporaries, she has reached a new and broader audience since her death. She is now widely read and admired for her trenchant attack on repressive institutions and for her call for the complete fulfilment of the individual. One of the most dangerous women in America, once pilloried and then spurned, she has become the heroine of modern feminists and a founding mother of anarcho-feminism. She allegedly said at an anarchist ball: 'if I can't dance, it's not my revolution.' If the next revolution is libertarian and feminist, it will certainly be playing many of her favourite tunes.

German Communists

DESPITE THE OVERWHELMING INFLUENCE of Marxism in Germany at the end of the nineteenth century, a number of bold and original thinkers gravitated towards anarchism. Gustav Landauer was amongst those who struggled in the unfavourable political climate and were killed for their activities and views. Others like Johann Most and Rudolf Rocker were forced to move abroad to exert their influence.

Gustav Landauer

Gustav Landauer was the most important anarchist thinker in Germany after Max Stirner. He was born in 1870 of a middle-class Jewish family in Karlsruhe in southern Germany. As a student he joined the German Social Democratic Party (SPD). Due to his political activities, which led to a spell in prison, he was refused entrance to the School of Medicine at Freiburg University. Because of his extreme views, he was also one of a small group who were expelled from the SPD in 1891. Two years later, he became an anarchist, although he preferred to call himself an 'anarchist-socialist' to dissociate himself from the Stirnerite egoism which was fashionable in some anarchist circles at the time. As he wrote to his friend Martin Buber, 'anarchism is the negative side of that which, positively, is called socialism.'[1] He went on to edit, from 1892, the Berlin anarchist paper *Der Sozialist*, but changed its subtitle to *Organ für Anarchismus-Sozialismus* to stress the socialist nature of his anarchism and the libertarian nature of his socialism. In *Der Sozialist*, he wrote on 15 July 1911: 'Anarchy is the expression of the liberation of man from the idols of the state, the church and capital; socialism is the expression of the true and genuine community among men, genuine because it grows out of the individual spirit.'[2]

Landauer was always prepared to collaborate with socialists. In 1893 he was excluded, with Rosa Luxemburg and others, from the Zürich Congress of the Second International. Undismayed, he attended with Malatesta the Second International Congress held in London in 1896, and tried to put the anarchist case:

What we fight is *State* socialism, levelling from above, bureaucracy; what we advocate is free association and union, the absence of authority, mind freed from all fetters, independence and well-being of all. Before all others it is we who preach *tolerance* for all – whether we think their opinions right or wrong – we do not wish to crush them by force or otherwise.[3]

Despite his plea for tolerance, the anarchists were expelled. It was the last time anarchists tried to attend meetings of the Socialist International.

Such setbacks did not deter Landauer. He was primarily a thinker and a man of letters, elaborating a form of mystical anarchism which stood in the German idealist tradition stretching as far back as Meister Eckhart. His originality lies in the way he developed the romantic concern with the *Volk* in a libertarian rather than an authoritarian direction. The word *Volk* had come to mean something like the 'common people', but it was also used to described the German language, culture, and customs as distinct from the State. Landauer wanted to realize the potential unity of the *Volk*, to develop 'a connexion between people which is actually there; only it has not yet become bond and binding, it is not yet a higher organism'.[4] Landauer was thus an eloquent prophet of real community.

Drawing on the work of the German sociologist Ferdinand Toennies, Landauer developed the distinction between community (*Gemeinschaft*), which is an organic, long-standing living together, and atomized, mechanical, and transitory society (*Gesellschaft*). He wanted to see the reborn community develop out of the artificial shell of existing society and the State. His most penetrating and oft-quoted insight is the recognition that the State is not merely something standing above society but a force which permeates everyday life:

> The state is a condition, a certain relationship among human beings, a mode of behaviour between them; we destroy it by contracting other relationships, by behaving differently toward one another ... We are the state, and we shall continue to be the state until we have created the institutions that form a real community and society of men.[5]

The setting up of the community outside and alongside the State is therefore essentially a discovery of something actually present, something which has grown out of the past: 'This likeness, this equality in inequality, this peculiar quality that binds people together, this common spirit, is an actual fact.'[6]

While rejecting the artificial State and the atomistic society of capitalism, Landauer saw the nation as a peaceful community of communities: 'Every nation is anarchistic, that is, without force; the conceptions of nation and force are completely irreconcilable.' He also saw the nation as a stepping stone, not an obstacle, to internationalism. 'The goal of humanity', he wrote to Julius Bab in 1913, 'is the outer structure for which we strive; the way toward this goal, however, does not lead merely from our own humanity, but above all through our differentiated nationality.'[7] The nation is a circle within the ever-widening circles from the individual to the whole of humanity. This is Landauer's most important idea, and lays the ground for a nationalism which is not exclusive and xenophobic. He demonstrates that the nation can exist without the State; indeed, one of his principal objections to the State is that it destroys the organic unity of the nation. Each nation can contribute something unique and valuable to our common humanity.

Community for Landauer not is merely the liberal's view of society as a sum of individuals; it is an organic whole which has its own interests. According to Landauer, Stirner's absolute and independent individual is a myth, a phantom in the brain. Each individual is united not only to his own local community but also to the rest of humanity, both in a physical and spiritual sense: 'As the individual organism is only a part of a great, real physical community, so the individual soul is part of a great, real spiritual community.' Landauer did not reject genuine individualism but rather the atomistic, uprooted individualism of capitalism. In each individual there is a unique individuality which offers a different picture of humanity. The individual personality is therefore a 'vital part of a larger organic whole'.[8]

Landauer was not opposed to revolution. 'Revolution', he wrote, 'concerns every aspect of human life—not just the State, the class-structure, industry and commerce, arts and letters, education and learning, but a combination of all these social factors which is at a given moment in state of relative stability.' He did not consider revolution merely as a period of time or even a borderline between two social conditions, but 'a principle stepping over vast distances of time'.[9] He insisted on the identity of means and ends and the necessity of moral action in the present. He was totally opposed to violent revolution and individual acts of terrorism. The great error of revolutionary anarchists, he wrote, is 'the idea of being able to reach the ideal of powerlessness through power . . . every act of force is dictatorship'. For Landauer, anarchy should not involve more war and murder but a spiritual rebirth: 'The way to a new, higher form of human society leads from the dark, fateful gate of our instincts and *terra abscondita* of our soul, which is our world. Only from within to without can the world be formed . . .'[10]

Landauer recognized that in revolution, there rises up 'the image and feeling of positive union through the binding quality, through love' but it is impossible to solve social problems by political and violent means.[11] This can only be done by each individual's decision to refuse to co-operate with the existing State and its institutions in order to create positive alternatives:

there comes a time in the history of a social structure, which is a structure only as long as individuals nourish it with their vitality, when those living shy away from it as a strange ghost from the past, and create new groupings instead. Thus I have withdrawn my love, reason, obedience, and my will from that which I call the 'state'. That I am able to do so depends on my will.[12]

It is a process which is never complete, but constantly renews itself: 'No final security of measures should be taken to establish the millennium or eternity, but only a great balancing of forces, and the resolve periodically to renew the balance . . .'[13]

He therefore called for the development of self-managing communities and co-operatives which can bring people together and release them from their crippling dependence on authority. As he grew older, he talked less of class struggle and saw 'direct action' as the building of co-operatives coupled with Tolstoyan passive resistance to authority. The 'general strike' – the panacea of the anarcho-syndicalists – should not be a downing of tools but rather the reorganization of work under workers' control. In the end, he came to see revolution not as a violent cataclysmic upheaval but as the peaceful rejection of coercive society and the gradual creation of alternative institutions. Rejecting industrial urbanism, he further urged the renewal of the traditional rural community by a return of the workers to the land.

Although Landauer wrote a preface to a pamphlet by Max Nettlau on Bakunin, his mature anarchism drew on the writings of both Proudhon and Kropotkin (whose works he also translated). He considered Proudhon the greatest of all socialists and freely adopted his schemes for mutual credit and exchange. He tried to reconcile individual possession of property and mutualist co-operation by suggesting that there should be a profusion of different forms of possession – individual, communal and co-operative – in a free society. It would be for the members of each community to decide periodically on the right balance between the different forms of possession.

Landauer translated Kropotkin's *Mutual Aid* and was impressed by his *Fields, Factories and Workshops*. Like Kropotkin, he promoted the economic independence of local and regional communities which combined agriculture and industry on a small scale. For Germany, he advocated a confederation of local communities in order to release the creative and organic spirit which lay imprisoned within the State. But while sharing Kropotkin's vision of the integration of industry and agriculture, he called more insistently for a return to the land. Landauer even went so far as to argue that 'the struggle for socialism is a struggle for the land; the social question is an agrarian question'.[14] By identifying the genuine community with the land, Landauer turned his back on urban-based syndicalism.

The philosophical idealist in Landauer ultimately diverged from the scientifically-minded Kropotkin. He shared his stress on mutual aid and co-operation, but he insisted, like Malatesta, that they were the result of human will, not of natural laws at work in human society. In order to create a free society, he looked to spiritual awareness, not to the development of reason or science. A degree of high culture is reached only when a unifying spirit pervades social structures, 'a spirit dwelling in the individuals themselves and pointing beyond earthly and material interests'. Socialism, he wrote in 1915, is 'the attempt to lead man's common life to a bond of common spirit in freedom, that is, to religion'.[15]

Landauer was not very optimistic about the possibility of change in his own day. He felt that his German contemporaries were the most obedient of subjects, demonstrating only too well la Boétie's notion of voluntary servitude. The authoritarian State existed as a result more of human passivity than of externally imposed tyranny. He had little faith in the German working class and felt that only a few would be able to develop anarchism in exemplary co-operative settlements on the land.

Landauer remained an impressive figure in German literary circles, tall and gaunt with his long, dark beard and hair. 'One felt when he spoke', Rudolf Rocker recalled, 'that every word came from his soul, bore the stamp of absolute integrity.'[16] But he became increasingly isolated within the socialist movement before and during the First World War, earning the hatred of many compatriots for his principled opposition to it: 'War is an act of power, of murder, of robbery', he wrote in 1912. 'It is the sharpest and clearest expression of the state.'[17]

Nevertheless, Landauer participated as a minor leader in the Bavarian Revolution of 1918–19. In November 1918, he was invited to Munich by his friend Kurt Eisner, the new socialist President of the Bavarian republic. He threw himself into the struggle as a member of the Revolutionary Workers' Council and the Central Workers' Council, trying to create his ideal of a federalist and decentralized society of self-managing communities. After the assassination of Eisner, Landauer became minister of education in the 'cabinet' of the short-lived Munich Council Republic proclaimed in April 1919. It was an attempt by anarchists and intellectuals to establish a free and independent Bavaria. Landauer worked with the poet Erich Mühsam, Ernst Toller (the author of a play about the Luddites), and Ret Marut (later to become the author B. Traven) but their efforts were tragically cut short. Landauer's programme to provide libertarian education for people of all ages was never realized. In little more than a week, the anarchists were ousted by communists who rejected their 'pseudo-republic'. The revolution was eventually crushed by an army of 100,000 troops sent from Berlin by the Minister of Defence Gustav Noske.

In the aftermath, Landauer was beaten and murdered in Munich.

According to a worker who witnessed the event, 'an officer struck him in the face. The men shouted, "Dirty Bolshi! Let's finish him off!" and a rain of blows from rifle-butts drove him out in the yard . . . they trampled on him till he was dead; then stripped the body and threw it into the wash-house.' 'Kill me then!', he is reported as saying, 'To think that you are human beings!'[18] The unassuming pacifist had just turned forty-nine years old.

But he was not forgotten. The Anarchist Syndicalist Union of Munich, with workers' contributions, raised a monument to him, using his own words as his epitaph: 'Now is the time to bring forth a martyr of a different kind, not heroic, but a quiet, unpretentious martyr who will provide an example for the proper life.'[19] It was torn down by the Nazis after Hitler's rise to power.

Since his death, Landauer has exerted a strong influence on those who see the State as a set of relationships pervading society rather than as some mechanical superstructure. Through his friend Martin Buber (who edited his writings), Landauer influenced the Israeli communitarian movement. In the sixties and seventies, his call to drop out and to create alternative institutions found a resounding echo in the counter-culture.

The Jewish poet Erich Mühsam was also deeply influenced by Landauer and worked with him in Munich Council Republic. He was sentenced to fifteen years' hard labour in the aftermath. He was a brilliant journalist as well as lyric poet, combining the insights of Kropotkin and Nietzsche to develop his own eccentric anarchism. After the defeat of the Munich Council, Mühsam served more than four years of a long sentence before being released in 1924 in a general amnesty. He did not turn his back on politics: he became active in the Red Aid organization which assisted political prisoners, and edited a monthly anarchist review *Fanal*. He remained an outspoken critic of German militarism and warned of the growing dangers of Nazism. He not only continued to write poetry but also composed a volume of 'Unpolitical Memoirs'. One of his last works was called *The Liberation of Society from the State*. Mühsam was eventually arrested by the Nazis in 1933 and murdered in Oranienburg concentration camp the following year.

Johann Most

While Landauer expresses the most constructive side of anarchism, his compatriot Most probably contributed more than any other German to anarchism's reputation as a violent and destructive creed. Most was born at Augsburg in Bavaria, the son of a governess and a clerk. He left school at fourteen and became apprenticed to a bookbinder. As a member of the

German Social Democratic Party (SPD), he was elected a deputy to the Reichstag from 1874 to 1878. After writing against the Kaiser and clergy, he was forced into exile and arrived in London as a political refugee in 1878. His activities provided Henry James with a theme for his novel *The Princess Casamassima* (1886).

From 1879 Most began publishing the journal *Freiheit*. It was exported and mainly exerted an influence in Germany and Austria where its gospel of revolutionary violence and illegality appealed more to conspiratorial groups than to the socialist movement at large. As a result of writing an editorial celebrating the assassination of Tsar Alexander II, the British courts sentenced him to sixteen months' imprisonment.

On his release, Most set sail for the United States. When he arrived in New York in 1882, he rapidly became a fully-fledged anarchist. He began publishing *Freiheit* again and continued to do so until his death in 1906. He fervently promoted propaganda by the deed as well as by the word, undertaking lecture tours which preached violent revolution. Most became notorious for recognizing 'a "wild" anarchist in every criminal'.[20] In order to obtain specialised information on how to make bombs, he worked in an explosive factory. He then wrote the pamphlet *Revolutionäre Kriegswissenschaft* (Science of Revolutionary Warfare), a do-it-yourself 'manual of instruction in the use and preparation of Nitroglycerine, Dynamite, Gun-cotton, Fulminating Mercury, Bombs, Fuses, Poisons, etc.' Much of this was just bluster: Most did not employ such means himself, but his enthusiastic advocacy inspired disaffected rebels with more foolhardiness than himself. Nevertheless, like Nechaev, he believed for a while that the revolutionary end justifies any means, including the murder of individuals. 'Assassination', he wrote, 'is a concomitant of revolution, if you choose to call the forcible removal of insufferable oppression, assassination.'[21] Not surprisingly, Most rapidly became known as one of the most dangerous men in America, although after the Haymarket Massacre in 1886 he had second thoughts about violent revolution. He gloried in his reputation and always embraced class warfare with enthusiasm: 'Tyrants and the bourgeoisie hate me. I hate tyrants and the bourgeoisie. Our mutual hatred is my pride and joy.'[22]

Most was no original thinker; indeed, Max Nettlau correctly observed that he advanced 'in steps' in his own political development.[23] It is difficult to find in Most's writings many nuanced ideas. He was above all a propagandist, and felt obliged to express views which he thought his subscribers wanted to hear. As a social revolutionary, in 1882 he adopted for himself four 'rules' which sum up his positive teaching:

I follow four commandments. Thou shalt deny God and love truth; therefore I am an atheist. Thou shalt oppose tyranny and seek liberty; therefore I am a republican. Thou shall repudiate property and champion equality; therefore I am a communist. Thou shall hate oppression and foment revolution; therefore I am a revolutionary. Long live the Social Revolution![24]

For Most, it was as if revolution had replaced God, and he worshipped the new deity in every possible way. The ultimate goal was anarchism which, as a good lapsed socialist, he defined as 'socialism perfected'.[25]

Rudolf Rocker

Like Most, Rocker was a German by birth and reflected in his life the transnational and cosmopolitan nature of modern anarchism. He was born in 1873 in the ancient Rhine city of Mainz, South Germany, the scion of old burgher families. As a Rhinelander, he was exposed to the region's anti-Prussian and federalist traditions. His father was a printer but it was his uncle who introduced him to socialism. He joined a dissident Marxist group in Mainz known as 'Die Jungen' (Landauer was also a temporary member), a largely libertarian grouping within the SPD. The German socialist movement was dominated at the time by Marx and Lassalle and the young Rocker was soon repelled by its dogmatic narrow-mindedness. He became convinced that socialism was not only a question of a full belly but also a question of culture which 'would have to enlist the sense of personality and the free initiative of the individual'.[26] Looking for an alternative, he began to read the classic anarchist thinkers from Godwin to Kropotkin.

After leaving school, Rocker became a bookbinder and travelled through several European countries, contacting members of the international anarchist movement. Because of his political activities he went into exile in 1892, first in Paris and then, at the beginning of 1895, in London.

For the next twenty years, Rocker devoted the best years of his life to the Jewish anarchist movement in the East End of London. He quickly learned Yiddish and from 1898 edited the Yiddish paper *Arbeter Fraint* (The Worker's Friend) and from 1900 the literary monthly *Germinal*. The paper was responsible for one of the first criticisms of the Marxist conception of history to appear in Yiddish. Rocker argued that materialism and idealism are both different views of life; however much we try, we can never find absolute truth. It is therefore impossible to believe that there is a final goal as Marx suggested: 'Freedom will lead us to continually wider and expanding understanding and to new social forms of life. To think that we have reached the end of our progress is to enchain ourselves in dogmas, and that always leads to tyranny.'[27]

The experience of the poverty and suffering in what Rocker called 'Darkest London' rapidly disproved for him the idea, held by some revolutionaries about the condition of the poor, that 'The worse, the better'. He believed, to the contrary, that if people suffer terribly, they become demoralized and are unlikely to have the strength or inclination to fight for social emancipation. It was this concern and sympathy which enabled him to become accepted by the Jewish community. But he also helped galvanize them into action. When he turned *Arbeter Fraint* into a daily paper during the successful strike of sweatshop workers in 1912, he won the respect of thousands. He later recorded his experiences amongst the Jewish community in his lively autobiography *The London Years* (1956): 'I gave them all I had to give, and I gave it to them gladly, for there is no greater joy than to see the seed one has planted sprout. They were devoted to me because they saw that I was honestly devoted to them, that I was working with them, at their side, as one of them.'[28]

It was during his years amongst the Jewish Anarchist Group in Whitechapel that Rocker met his lifelong companion Milly Witcop. True to their anarchist beliefs, in 1898 they preferred to be turned back by the US Immigration Authority rather than go through the ceremony of a marriage imposed by the State. When they did eventually marry, it was on their own terms.

During the First World War, Rocker was interned in Britain as an 'enemy alien'. He was deported in 1918 and went back to Germany. He became a leading figure in the syndicalist International Working Men's Association which was set up in 1922 and which had its International Bureau in Berlin for the next decade.

Rocker was a competent and profuse writer. He defended the anarchists in the Spanish Revolution in the pamphlets *The Truth about Spain* (1936) and *The Tragedy of Spain* (1937) and produced an incisive account of *Anarcho-Syndicalism* (1938). His most important work was undoubtedly the monumental *Nationalism and Culture* (1937), completed shortly before the Nazi's seizure of power. Forced into exile again, he finally settled in the United States. His opposition to fascism led him to support the allies in the war against Hitler and the Nazi dictatorship. He also wrote *Pioneers of American Freedom* (1949), to remind his new compatriots of the depth and breadth of their own libertarian tradition. He died in 1958, aged eighty-five.

In his *Nationalism and Culture*, Rocker tried to present an outline of the causes of the general decline of our civilization, the most important of which being power politics. He offered a searching analysis of human culture and institutions throughout known history. It is the most important anarchist treatment of the subject; Rocker's standard of value is always the utmost possible freedom. The work was widely hailed as one of the great books of its time; Bertrand Russell, for instance, considered it an important contribution to political philosophy on account of its analysis of political thinkers as well as its 'brilliant criticism of state-worship'.

Rocker insists that the nation is not the cause, but the result of the State: *'It is the state which creates the nation, not the nation the state.'* At first sight this might seem strange since there are many 'nations' which are colonized and seek to create an independent State for themselves. But Rocker's position becomes clearer when he distinguishes between a 'people' and a 'nation'. A people is the 'natural result of social union, a mutual association of men brought about by a certain similarity of external conditions of living, a common language, and special characteristics due to climate and geographic environment'. On the other hand, the nation is 'the artificial result of the struggle for political power, just as nationalism has never been anything but the political religion of the modern state'. A people is always a 'community with rather narrow boundaries', whereas a nation generally encompasses a whole array of different peoples and groups of peoples who have 'by more or less violent means been pressed into the frame of a common state'. Nation-States are therefore *'political church organizations'.*[29]

Rocker rejects the idea that a nation is founded on communality of language as an arbitrary assumption since peoples change their language, and nations exist with different language districts. He also repudiated race as a delusive concept since it is merely an artificial classification of biological science and only humanity as a whole constitutes a biological unit, a species. Not surprisingly, Rocker felt that all nationalism is reactionary since it enforces artificial separations within the 'organic unity' of the great human family.[30]

Cultural nationalism according to Rocker appears in its purest form when people are subjected to a foreign rule, and cannot for this reason pursue their own plans for political power. For Rocker 'home sentiment' is natural and acceptable for it is not the same as patriotism or love of the State. Only when it is mixed with 'national consciousness' does it become 'one of the most grotesque phenomena of our time'.[31]

Rocker's principal thesis is that States create no culture. In this he placed himself within the important if minor German libertarian tradition. He admired Nietzsche for his views of the State, the decline of German culture, and the Apollonian and Dionysian spirit in art. He also appreciated Humboldt's ideas regarding the limitation of State action and his view that freedom is the basis of human progress and culture. Developing their ideas, Rocker argued that political power and culture are irreconcilable opposites;

the former always strives for uniformity, while the latter looks for new forms and organizations. It follows that 'Where states are dying or where their power is still limited to a minimum, there culture flourishes best.'[32] Culture gives man consciousness of his humanity and creative strength; but power deepens in him the sense of dependence and bondage. Indeed, Rocker compares the contest between power and culture, State and society, to the motion of a pendulum which proceeds from one of its poles – authority – towards its opposite – freedom.

Rocker however is no social ecologist. He defines culture as 'the conscious resistance of man against the course of nature, to which resistance alone he owes the preservation of the species'. The process of culture is therefore 'only a gradual mastery of nature by man'.[33]

The Nation-State has destroyed the old community and has turned gradually all social activity into an instrument to serve the special ends of organizations for political power. Rocker makes the characteristic anarchist point:

> *It is not the form of the state, it is the state itself which creates evil and continually nourishes and fosters it.* The more government crowds out the social element in human life or forces it under its rule, the more rapidly society dissolves into its separate parts.[34]

The great problem set for our age is not the government of men, but the administration of things: 'It is not so much *how* we are governed, but *that* we are governed at all.' Whether in the form of State socialism or State capitalism, Rocker argued that there is no tyranny more unendurable than that of an all-powerful bureaucracy.

In place of government and the State, Rocker proposes federalism as 'the organic collaboration of all social forces towards a common goal on the basis of covenants freely arrived at':[35] While rejecting 'positive' law made by governments, he accepts 'natural' law which existed before the growth of States and which is the 'result of mutual agreements between men confronting one another as free and equal, motivated by the same interests and enjoying equal dignity as human beings'.[36]

In an epilogue to *Nationalism and Culture* written at the end of the war in 1946, Rocker called for a real federation of European peoples as the first condition for a future world federation. Despite the rise of fascism and the defeat of the anarcho-syndicalists in Spain, Rocker was confident that 'just as there was once a time when might and right were one, so we are now apparently moving towards a time when every form of rulership shall vanish, law yield place to justice, liberties to freedom'.[37]

Rocker's social philosophy took off from the teachings of Kropotkin. He argued that modern anarchism is a confluence of the currents of socialism and liberalism and may be regarded as 'a kind of voluntary Socialism'.[38] It is not a patent solution for all human problems but believes in 'an unlimited perfectibility of social patterns and human living conditions'. It strives for the 'free unhindered unfolding of all the individual and social forces in life'.[39] Freedom is valuable not because it is an absolute goal but because it enables this process to take place.

Rocker defined anarchism as an intellectual current 'whose adherents advocate the abolition of economic monopolies and of all political and social coercive institutions in society'. In place of the capitalistic economic order, anarchists would have 'a free association of all productive forces based on co-operative labour'.[40] The State on the other hand is 'the defender of mass exploitation and social privileges, the creator of privileged classes and castes and of new monopolies'. He concludes that the liberation of humanity from economic exploitation and political oppression, which is only possible through the 'world-philosophy' of anarchism, is the first prerequisite for the evolution of a higher social culture and a new humanity.[41]

Rocker saw anarcho-syndicalism as the most relevant form of anarchism for the twentieth century. He rejected political struggle since all the political rights and liberties enjoyed by people are not due to the goodwill of their governments but to their own strength. Anarcho-syndicalists are not against political struggle – they fight political suppression as much as economic exploitation – but they see that the struggle lies not in the legislative bodies but in direct action, particularly in the form of the strike. Although opposed to militarism, Rocker was not a pacifist, and accepted the need for a determined people to fight for their freedom. The workers, he argued, 'can regain their rights only by incessant warfare against the dominant powers'.[42] He defended the anarchists in the Spanish Revolution and the fight against Franco and his troops. He also supported the allies in the war against Nazi Germany. Towards the end of his life, he took a more reformist stand, but he never lost the vision of a free society which he found in the writings of the great anarchist thinkers as a boy.

26

Mohandas Gandhi
The Gentle Revolutionary

THE MOST IMPORTANT AND outstanding libertarian thinker to emerge in India this century was undoubtedly Mohandas Gandhi. On several occasions he called himself a kind of anarchist and always opposed the centralized State and the violence it engendered. In a famous speech in 1916, referring to India's violent revolutionaries, he declared that he too was an anarchist, 'but of another type [than the terrorist kind]'.[1]

Gandhi's particular form of libertarian philosophy was strongly influenced by several Western thinkers. A reading of Tolstoy's *Kingdom of God is Within You* in 1893 inspired him to practise non-resistance to violence, but he went on to develop his own highly successful technique of non-violent direct action. In a South African prison in 1907, he found further confirmation of his approach in Thoreau's essay on *Civil Disobedience*. From Ruskin, he learned that the good of the individual is contained in the good of all and the life of labour is the life worth living. He was particularly influenced by Ruskin's *Unto This Last* and translated the title as *Sarvodaya*, welfare for all. Finally, it was from Kropotkin that he elaborated his vision of a decentralized society of autonomous village communes.

But despite the Western influences, Gandhi's anarchism is deeply embedded in Indian philosophy. He attempted to reconstruct an ancient tradition of Indian religious thought which depicts man as a divine being capable of perfection and of self-discipline by internalising moral norms. His appeal to all classes and groups was based on a metaphysical belief in the cosmic unity of all beings. Central to his world-view were also the principles of *satya* (truth), *karmayoga* (self-realization through disinterested action), *varnasramdharma* (the Hindu law of right conduct), and above all *ahimsa* (non-injury or non-violence). But the most revolutionary aspect of Gandhi's teaching was undoubtedly his social and political interpretation of *ahimsa* in which he turned the principle of individual self-realization into a principle of social ethics. He also drew on the traditional Indian values of village life and the joint family and the practice of making decisions by consensus.[2]

One looks in vain for a clear exposition of Gandhi's social philosophy in his writings. He was prepared to change his theory according to his experience and aptly called his autobiography *My Experiments with Truth*. In his voluminous writings, he left behind no clear system of moral or political philosophy but rather 'an existential pattern of thought and deed'.[3] Since he was mainly concerned with persuading people, his writings chiefly consist of the monotonous repetition of a few basic themes.

The primary motive of Gandhi's pacifism was religious but in South Africa he developed a specific method of resistance (against the registration laws for Indians) which he called *Satyagraha*. The term in Gujarati means 'firmness in the truth' but in Gandhi's hands it became a kind of non-violent struggle. Tolstoy had urged that the way to undermine the State is to refuse to co-operate with it but Gandhi shifted the emphasis from passive to active non-violent resistance. He regarded 'passive resistance' as the weapon of the weak, but he was also wary of the kind of 'civil disobedience' which implies angry defiance. His strategy was therefore a form of non-violent resistance which sought to fight with the power of truth rather than with the force of the body. Based on the precept 'Hate the sin but not the sinner', it aimed at defeating the enemy without harming him or arousing hatred. In practice, it involved the classical syndicalist tactic of the strike, but it also entailed refusing to hit back at charging police and lying on railway lines.

For all his commitment to non-violence, Gandhi was not in fact an absolute pacifist. He became a stretcher bearer on the British side in the Boer War, even acting as a kind of recruiting sergeant for the British Army. He was prepared to be a stretcher bearer in the First World War. He always thought it better to fight than to be a coward: 'where there is only a choice between cowardice and violence, I would advise violence', he declared.[4]

One of Gandhi's most important contributions to libertarian theory was his clarification of the relationship between means and ends. He insisted that the two cannot be separated; means are ends. Means are never merely instrumental, but create their own ends; they are ends-in-the-making.[5] If we concentrate on the right means then the desirable ends will follow automatically. Again, by acting here and now as if we are free agents capable of self-rule, we actually bring about the free society rather than seeing it as some distant goal. His non-violent revolution therefore does not involve the seizure of power but the transformation of everyday life and relationships.

Although his method was gradualist and piecemeal, Gandhi was a revolutionary who sought not only to end British rule in India but to transform traditional Indian society and eventually world society. His long-term goal was to realize a realm of peace and justice throughout the world, to bring about *Ram Raj*, the kingdom of God on earth. To this end, he deepened his campaign in the 1930s to uproot the worse aspects of the caste system by concentrating on the lot of the untouchables. He deliberately called them *Harijans* (Children of God) and set an example by doing their traditional work like cleaning out his own toilet. The campaign showed his profound wish to bring about a more equal and co-operative society. He was concerned to provide service to 'backward tribes' as well as to bring about the 'uplift of women'. Women he felt were equal in status, but different in function. He demanded the abolition of *purdah* and hoped that women would be able to practise sexual restraint once freed from male domination.

Gandhi's 'Constructive Programme', as it came to be known, not only included the end of untouchability and communal reconciliation, but also the renewal of village life. He told his co-workers in 1944:

> Through it you can make the villagers feel self-reliant, self-sufficient and free so that they can stand up for their rights. If you can make a real success of the constructive programme, you will win *Swaraj* (self-government) for India without civil disobedience.[6]

In Gandhi's view, it was essential to create a new society on the sound base of a decentralized economy, in which villages grew their own food and developed industries based on local materials. Suspicious of the nomadic hunter as much as the city slicker, he felt that the ideal society would combine good husbandry with a high level of craftsmanship. Artisans should be their own masters and the land should belong to those who cultivate it. Children ought to practise handicrafts before reading and writing in order to learn how to use their hands; like everyone else, they should do 'bread-labour' in field or workshop to help meet their basic needs. All should enjoy the benefits of a simple and self-reliant life.

Despite his emphasis on crafts, Gandhi was no Luddite opposed to technological progress. He was not against electricity although he thought each village should have its own power station to maintain its autonomy. The few remaining centralized factories would be run by workers with their former owners acting as trustees.

Gandhi's libertarian sensibility not only comes through in his description of his ideal society but also in his criticism of the State and parliamentary democracy. Like Tolstoy, he fully realized that the State represents violence in a concentrated and organized form. He feared the power of the State, even when it tries to minimize exploitation and provide welfare, since it destroys individuality which lies at the root of all progress. Instead, he advocated *swaraj* or self-government, by which he meant the 'continuous effort to be free of government control, whether it is foreign or whether it is national'.[7] It would be the first step towards his ultimate ideal, a form of enlightened anarchy in which social life is self-regulated and 'there is no political power because there is no state'.[8]

While Gandhi does not reject the notion of a State in a transitional period, it is clear in his writings that he does not mean anything more by it than a co-ordinating body in a decentralized society of autonomous villages. Although a person's concern would be first directed towards his neighbours, it would not end there:

> Life will not be a pyramid with the apex sustained by the bottom. But it will be an oceanic circle whose centre will be the individual always ready to perish for the village, the latter ready to perish for the circle of villages, till at last the whole becomes one life composed of individuals . . . The outermost circumference will not wield power to crush the inner circle but will give strength to all within and derive its strength from it.[9]

In place of parliamentary democracy, he proposed a form of indirect democracy in which each village would be ruled by its own traditional five-man council and would elect a representative to the district council. Each district would elect a representative to the regional council which in turn would choose members of the national council. The latter would have little to do other than co-ordinate communications, energy, minerals and other resources. There would be no need for an army: if the land were invaded, peace brigades would meet the invader and oppose them non-violently. The police might still have to use restraint on wrongdoers but they would not be punished and prisons would be turned into education centres. Disputes would be solved by arbitration amongst neighbours rather than by lawcourts.

It is easy to overestimate Gandhi's anarchist tendencies. Although he declared that 'The ideally non-violent state will be an ordered anarchy', he did not call for the immediate abolition of State and government.[10] Although he resigned from the Indian National Congress and had a diminishing influence on its policies, he initiated the 1942 Quit India movement. After independence, he made no frontal criticism of the Indian government.

While Gandhi wanted to end political coercion, many of his opponents felt morally coerced by him. It is almost as if he felt it necessary to internalize the laws of the State in the individual so that he or she would be capable of self-restraint. He constantly stressed the need for duty, and called for the willing submission of the individual to the well-being of society.

There was also a strong puritanical and repressive streak in his personality and teaching which led him to prohibit tobacco and alcohol. He recommended strict sexual continence, and for those incapable of it, he would only countenance sex for procreation and not pleasure. His society might be tolerant of different religions, but it would expect a rigid moral code. He ruled like a patriarch in his communes or *ashrams* in South Africa and India and did not always reject the role of the venerable *guru*. Like Godwin he believed that close friendship and loyalty can override the demands of impartial justice but his own imperfect practice of universal benevolence led to claims that he was inconsiderate to his own wife and children.

Gandhi also deliberately cultivated a power of his own which did not always have democratic tendencies. 'Non-violence', he declared, 'does not seize power. It does not even seek power. Power accrues to it.'[11] After the First World Gandhi helped organize, mainly through the Indian National Congress, collective acts of non-violent resistance, including the Salt March. After 1932 however he increasingly acted as a charismatic leader exerting moral and spiritual power over his opponents. As an outstanding *satyagrahi*, he grew more isolated, and by exercising so much power himself he prevented others from developing their own initiative. Indeed, for all his undoubted sincerity and humility, his form of persuasion could at times become a kind of moral coercion. *Satyagraha*, or the force of truth, could in practice degenerate into *duragraha*, the force of stubbornness.[12] Gandhi's chosen tactic was to oppose moral power against political power, but in the end the anarchist goal is to decentralize and dissolve power altogether. Just as Gandhi the patriarch prevented his *ashrams* from becoming wayward self-governing communities, so the example of India's most famous *satyagrahi* hindered the development of a mass libertarian movement of equals.

Nevertheless, Gandhi remained until the end deeply suspicious of political power. When asked what would happen to India if the British abdicated their responsibility, he replied: 'Leave India to God. If that is too much to believe, then leave her to anarchy.' After Indian independence, he suggested that his fellow constructive workers should not enter politics; their task was to mould the politics of the country without taking power for themselves. Just before he died, he also urged the leaders of Congress, his party, to avoid the 'ungainly skirmish for power' and to turn their organization into a 'body of servants of the nation engaged in constructive work, mostly in the villages, to achieve social, moral and economic freedom'.[13] Needless to say, his advice fell on deaf ears, and his 'political heir' Pandit Nehru proceeded to militarize and centralize the Indian State amidst mounting communal violence between Hindus and Muslims.

Through his spectacular feats of fasting, Gandhi tried to bring political and religious factions together. Despite his enormous prestige, he failed to unite the warring factions. Winston Churchill's 'half-naked fakir' had helped bring an empire to its knees but he was unable to hold back the violent passions checked by colonial rule. After being shot by a fellow Hindu in January 1948, the funeral of the penniless anarchist and pacifist became a huge State affair, organized by the military authorities, with a British general in charge. It was the final irony of a complex life.

Gandhi once defined himself as a politician trying to be a saint. He was certainly a practical politician, ready to make compromises and forge temporary alliances in his overriding drive to make India independent of colonial rule. Even so, as George Orwell observed, he managed to shake empires by sheer spiritual power and 'compared with the other leading political figures of our time, how clean a smell he has managed to leave behind!'.[14] Gandhi accepted the title of Mahatma, the teacher, but he once declared: 'There is no such thing as 'Gandhism' and I do not want to leave any sect after me.'[15] It was enough for him that he was his own follower. But while there are not many 'Gandhians', even in India, his experiments with truth and his technique of non-violence have had a wide influence. He demonstrated that non-violence is not only an effective means of resistance but that it can be used to transform society peacefully. He also showed that the individual, and a group of individuals, can by their example wield enormous moral power which can shake political authority to its roots.

In the West, Gandhi has primarily been seen as a national leader whose principal aim was to achieve independence for India.[16] But he was also influential in bringing pacifism and anarchism together. It has been argued that, after 1930, Gandhi came to accept the modern State, but apart from some ambiguous statements there is little evidence to support this view.[17] On the contrary, Gandhi remained an anarchist to the end, albeit of a distinctly Indian stamp, since he believed that the State is incompatible with the moral and spiritual nature of humanity. His ideal was always 'enlightened anarchy' even though he recognized that the State was likely to continue to exist for a long time. Above all, he insisted that any State is not simply a structure built to legitimize organized violence, but that it consists of a network of internal relations with its own citizens. It would never be adequate merely to 'overthrow' it; it will only disappear with the liberation of our own selves. This is Gandhi's central and most enduring insight.

In his lifetime, Gandhi's ideas were popularized in the West by books such as Richard Gregg's *The Power of Non-Violence* (1935). The Dutch anarchist Bart de Ligt in his *The Conquest of Violence* (1937) warned his fellow anarchists that 'The more violence, the less revolution' and linked Gandhi's moral non-violence with the non-violent direct action of the syndicalists, notably in their use of the general strike. In the 1950s and 1960s, anarcho-pacifism came to the forefront in the New Left and the campaigns for nuclear disarmament, and it looked for a time that a non-violent revolution might be possible towards the end of the sixties before the transatlantic reaction set in.

PART FIVE

Anarchism in Action

Anarchy is order: government is civil war.
ANSELME BELLEGARRIQUE

There is no such thing as revolutionary power, for all power
is reactionary by nature.
CONFEDERACIÓN NACIONAL DEL TRABAJO (SPAIN)

The greater the violence, the weaker the revolution.
BART DE LIGT

Life will not be a pyramid with the apex sustained by the
bottom, but an oceanic circle whose centre will be the
individual.
MOHANDAS GANDHI

France

FRANCE IN MANY WAYS was the cradle of the historic anarchist movement. Its seeds were scattered by the *enragés* during the French Revolution and began to grow amongst the workers in the 1840s. France produced in Pierre-Joseph Proudhon the 'father' of the organized anarchist movement. Proudhon not only inspired the varieties of anarchism which developed in the second half of the nineteenth century but the mutualist workers with whom he was associated helped set up the First International Working Men's Association. Towards the end of the century, France witnessed the worst examples of terrorist 'propaganda by the deed' as well as the great imaginative flowering of anarchism amongst the writers and artists of Symbolism and Post-Impressionism. It also gave rise to one of anarchism's most constructive forms – anarcho-syndicalism.

The libertarian spirit had been strong in France ever since the irreverent Rabelais coined his motto 'Do what you will', and la Boétie offered his insights about voluntary servitude. The anti-authoritarian utopias of Foigny and Fénelon had been followed by the searing criticisms of the *philosophes*, Morelly, Meslier, Diderot and Rousseau. They all fired the mood of discontent which was eventually to culminate, of course, in the French Revolution.

The French Revolution set the context of many of the disputes and struggles on the Left which were to follow in the nineteenth century. From the beginning there was a struggle between the libertarians and the federalists and the authoritarians and centrists. Condorcet, who believed in the perfectibility of man and the possibility of a free and classless society even while awaiting his execution at the hands of the authoritarian Jacobins, proposed a remarkable scheme of *mutualité*, that is a vast mutual aid association among all workers. The moderate Girondins also advocated a form of federalism as a means of saving France from a Jacobin Paris.

A more revolutionary and spontaneous form of federalism developed in the 'districts' or 'sections' into which Paris had been organized administratively for elections. Out of these emerged the Commune of Paris. Many popular societies and revolutionary committees also arose which soon replaced the Jacobin-dominated sections. But while it was argued that the Commune must legislate and administer itself, it remained a kind of federalist direct democracy. Mutualism and federalism not only became later the twin pillars of Proudhon's system but Kropotkin was convinced that the principles of anarchism found their origin in the deeds of the French Revolution.[1]

The term anarchist was still used as a term of abuse at the time. It was applied indiscriminately to libertarians and authoritarians alike by their opponents. In England, the utilitarian philosopher Jeremy Bentham in his anti-revolutionary *Anarchical Fallacies* (1791) attacked the French Declaration of Rights, arguing that it would replace the old tyranny of a single master by the new tyranny of collective anarchy. The Jacobins called the *sans culottes* anarchists and were called anarchist in turn by the Directory which replaced them. The *sans-culottes*, the revolutionary mob who took to the streets in the spring and summer of 1793, were not strictly speaking anarchists for they helped overthrow the Girondins and bring about the Jacobin dictatorship.

Once in power Robespierre employed the epithet to attack those on the Left whom he had used for his own ends. But it was also adopted as a term of pride: in September 1793, the *Sans-Culottes of Beaucaire* informed the Convention: 'We are poor and virtuous *sans-culottes*; we have formed an association of artisans and peasants . . . we know whom our friends are: those who have delivered us from the clergy and nobility, from the feudal system . . . those whom the aristocrats called anarchists, factious elements, Maratists.'[2] It was Marat of course who had called for revolution in 1789 and declared that 'the people have broken the yoke of nobility; in the same way they will break that of wealth'. He was however in practice an extreme authoritarian.

When the Directory came to call the authoritarian Jacobins whom they had replaced in 1795 as 'anarchists' the term began to develop its elasticity of meaning which makes it so misleading, especially since:

> By 'anarchists' the Directory means these men covered with crimes, stained with blood, and fattened by rapine, enemies of laws they do not make and of all governments in which they do not govern, who preach liberty and practice despotism, speak of fraternity and slaughter their brothers . . .[3]

Nevertheless, not only in practice but also in theory, there were popular leaders reaching characteristically anarchist conclusions, particularly amongst the *enragés*, a loose movement of revolutionaries who rejected parliamentary politics, practised direct action, and looked to economic reform. One of their leaders was named Anacharsis Clootz. When the Girondin Brissot called for the suppression of the *enragés* in 1793, he declared:

Laws that are not carried into effect, authorities without force and despised, crime unpunished, property attacked, the safety of the individual violated, the morality of the people corrupted, no constitution, no government, no justice, these are the features of anarchy.[4]

Apart from the references to the safety of the individual and the morality of the people, at least there was some element of truth in this definition.

Chief among the *enragés* was Jacques Roux, a country clergyman who became a member of the General Council of the Commune. He has been remembered for escorting the king to the guillotine and for urging the mob to direct action, such as the seizure of goods in shops. He was also one of the first to link political freedom with economic equality: 'Freedom is but an empty phantom if one class of men can starve another with impunity. Freedom is but an empty phantom when the rich man can through his monopoly exercise the right of life and death over his fellow men.'[5] The Jacobins accused him of telling the people that 'every kind of government must be proscribed'; he was arrested and condemned to death by them, but he committed suicide before they could enjoy their triumph. But for all his libertarian profession, Roux like Marat remained an extreme authoritarian.

It was Jean Varlet however who came closest to being an anarchist during the French Revolution. He asserted the absolute sovereignty of the Section. He was imprisoned during the Terror but survived to mount a blistering attack on the Jacobin dictatorship in a work entitled *L'Explosion*:

What a social monstrosity, what a masterpiece of Machiavellism is this revolutionary government. For any rational being, government and revolution are incompatible – unless the people is willing to set up its delegates in a permanent state of insurrection against themselves – which is absurd.[6]

The work may be considered the earliest anarchist manifesto in continental Europe.

Gracchius Babeuf with the support of the *enragés* tried in his *Conspiration des Égaux* to overturn the Directory in 1796. He called for perfect equality, attacked private property as the principal source of ills in society, and believed everything should be shared in common. Kropotkin saw a direct filiation from Babeuf's conspiracy to the International Working Men's Association set up in 1866.[7] But Babeuf was never an anarchist like Varlet for he looked to the State, run by a revolutionary dictatorship, to bring about his 'Republic of Equals'.

It was the French thinker Pierre-Joseph Proudhon who was the first to call himself deliberately and provocatively an anarchist. To the rhetorical question 'What are you then?', Proudhon replied unequivocally in *What is Property?* in 1840:

> I am an anarchist.
>   'I understand, you are being satirical at the expense of government.'
> Not in the least. I have just given you my considered and serious profession of faith. Although I am a strong supporter of order, I am in the fullest sense of the term, an anarchist.[8]

Aware of the derivation of the word anarchy from the Greek, Proudhon rejected the government of man by man as oppression, and insisted that society finds its highest perfection in the union of order and anarchy: 'Just as man seeks justice in equality, society seeks order in anarchy.'[9] This apparent paradox had a profound meaning: only society without artificial government could restore the natural order and social harmony.

Proudhon generally spelt the word 'an-archy' to emphasize its etymological meaning. He not only defined anarchy as a 'state of total liberty' but referred to 'absolute liberty, which is synonymous with order'.[10] He added to the potential confusion by occasionally using the word anarchy in its negative sense, associating it with property and exploitation, the complete *laissez faire* of 'Industrial Empire', and referring to the 'anarchy of commercial capitalism' and 'anarchical capitalism'.[11] Towards the end of his life, he grew more cautious and preferred to call himself a 'federalist' rather than an anarchist. His followers did not call themselves anarchists either but mutualists, after the principle of the mutual exchange of the products of labour. Bakunin however described anarchism as 'Proudhonism broadly developed and pushed to its extreme consequences'.[12]

Proudhon may have been the most influential anarchist thinker in France but he was not the only one. At the time of the 1848 Revolution an obscure revolutionary called Anselme Bellegarrique launched the slogan 'Anarchy is order: government is civil war' quite independently of Proudhon. Before disappearing into Central America, he went on to publish in 1850 two issues of *L'Anarchie, Journal de l'Ordre* which combined a form of Stirnerite egoism with a vision of a free society based on the commune, without government and armies. The physician Ernest Coeurderoy and the upholsterer Joseph Déjacque also participated in the 1848 Revolution and the bitterness of failure and exile led them to apocalyptic celebration of violence and barbarism. 'Anarchist revolutionaries', Coeurderoy declared, 'we can take hope only in the human deluge, we can take hope only in chaos, we have no recourse but a general war.'[13]

Déjacque edited the anarchist paper *Le Libertaire, Journal du Mouvement Social* in New York from 1858 to 1861. He advocated 'war on civilization by criminal means' and secret societies in *La Question Révolutionnaire* (1854). He let his utopian imagination run riot in *L'Humanisphère* in which man holds in his hand 'the sceptre of science' which had once been attributed to the gods. Each is his own representative in a 'parliament of anarchy'.[14] Déjacque's 'humanispheres' resemble Fourier's 'phalansteries' and while based on the principle of complete freedom reflect a similarly rigid planning.

Anarchism as a movement only started gathering momentum in the 1860s in France, mainly inspired by Proudhon's mutualism and his ideas expressed in *De la Capacité politique des classes ouvrières* (1865). Workers' associations and mutual credit schemes were considered the principal way forward. Towards the end of the 1860s men like Eugène Varlin and Benôit Malon helped shift the emphasis from mutualism to Bakuninite collectivism in the French sections of the First International. The Paris Commune of 1871, which declared 'the absolute autonomy of the Commune extended to all the localities of France', advocated in theory a form of Proudhonian federalism. In practice little could be done except to keep public services going and defend its existence. In the bloody aftermath, amongst the anarchists Varlin was shot, Louise Michel was transported to a penal settlement, and Elisée Reclus was imprisoned.[15]

The anti-authoritarians within in the International saw the Commune as the spontaneous expression of federalist, anti-statist ideas and it strengthened their argument for the Communal reconstruction of post-revolutionary society. The Federal Committee of the Jura Federation in 1872 saw the principle issue at stake in the socialist movement was the choice between the *Commune libre* or the *Volkstaat*. By 1875, the Commune was gradually becoming a myth. As *Le Révolté* declared on 1 November 1879, 'the people, who in modern times have first formulated in practice the anarchist programme of the proletariat by constituting the free Commune of Paris, cannot be for authoritarianism.'

For a decade after the Commune all anarchist and socialist activity was declared illegal in France. The Jura in Switzerland became the new centre of opposition to the General Council of the International, and the nucleus of the incipient European anarchist movement. Its principal leader James Guillaume argued that federalism in the sense given to it by the Paris Commune and Proudhon meant above all the negation of the nation and the State. In a federal revolution:

There is no more State, no more central power superior to groups and imposing its authority on them; there is only collective force resulting from the federation of groups . . . The national and central State no longer existing, and the Communes enjoying the fullness of their independence, there is truly *an-archy*.[16]

In 1873 Paul Brousse, a graduate of the medical school of Montpellier University, joined the Jura Federation and tried to give anarchism a scientific basis and make it more militant. He had been with the Republican opposition at the end of the Second Empire, but on joining the International he soon became an opponent of Marx and the General Council, and played a major role in the anti-authoritarian wing. He was expelled from the Montpellier section of the International in 1872. After a short period of exile in Spain where he became more influenced by Bakuninite ideas and was involved in an uprising in Barcelona in 1873, he moved to Switzerland.

Kropotkin became acquainted with him there and described him as 'a young doctor full of mental activity, uproarious, sharp, lively, ready to develop any idea with a geometrical logic to its utmost consequences'. At the Berne Congress of the International in 1874, Brousse had heard Malatesta and Cafiero insisting that revolution consists more in deeds than in words. Matching the violence of the Russian and Italian anarchists, Brousse became a leading exponent of 'propaganda by the deed', which led to conflict with the moderate James Guillaume.[17] He was sufficiently eminent to give a speech, along with Guillaume and Reclus, at Bakunin's funeral in Bern in 1876.

In the same year Brousse edited *Die Arbeiter-Zeitung*, and later launched from La Chaux-de-Fonds *L'Avant-Garde*. Under the rubric 'Collectivism, Anarchy, Free Federation', the latter organ called for the replacement of the State by a society based on contract and the free federation of groups formed around each need and interest. The strategy advocated by the journal was extremely violent, calling for the creation of the Commune by insurrection: 'It is necessary to desert the ballot boxes and man the barricades, and for that, it is necessary to get organized.'[18] Its motto was 'Rise, people, in your might!/ Worker, take the machine!/ Take the land, peasant!'

After being one of the most active anarchist organizers and militants, on his return to France in 1880 Brousse went over to the socialists and developed the reformist doctrine of 'possibilism' which sought improvements through factory legislation and municipal politics. 'The ideal', he wrote in 1883, 'divided into several practical stages; our aims should, as it were, be immediatized so as to render the *possible*.'[19] He formed the Possibilist Party which became the most powerful socialist organization in France in the 1880s.

A general awareness of the anarchist movement as a distinct strand within socialism did not appear until the beginning of the decade. Even as late as 1876 James Guillaume in the Jurassian Federation complained that the terms 'anarchist' and 'anarchy' expressed only a negative idea and led to 'distressing ambiguities'.[20] Elisée Reclus however soon argued that the notoriety of the term would aid their cause by attracting attention.[21]

At the same time, the Federation moved from collectivism to communism. The first mention of anarcho-communism was made by a French exile living in Geneva François Dumartheray who, in 1876 in *Aux Travailleurs manuels partisans de l'action politique*, announced the publication of a pamphlet on the subject which in the event has never been traced.

In October 1876 anarcho-communism was adopted by the Italian Federation at its Florence congress, and Malatesta and Cafiero travelled to Switzerland and told their Swiss comrades about it. In 1876 Guillaume in his pamphlet *Idées sur l'organisation sociale* also argued that after the revolution there would be a general sharing out of wealth and consumption need not be related strictly according to work. Kropotkin claimed that he was ignorant of the doctrine as late as 1889, but in the following year it was officially adopted on his insistence by the Congress of the Jurassian Federation at La Chaux-de-Fonds.

With the lifting of restrictions on political activity in France in 1881, anarchism became recognizable for the first time as an identifiable movement.[22] A remarkable group of activists emerged. The shoemaker Jean Grave, who edited *La Révolte* and *Les Temps Nouveaux*, was an able and indefatigable propagandist. Emile Pouget edited the scurrilous *Le Père Peinard* and went on to become a leading exponent of anarcho-syndicalism. The ex-Jesuit seminarist Sébastien Faure popularized anarchist theory in a series of pamphlets and founded the *Le Libertaire* in 1899 which continued into the 1950s. Kropotkin's presence in France at the time greatly inspired the movement and he wrote for the leading anarchist journals, especially *Le Révolté* and its successor *La Révolte*. Many of his works first appeared in French.

Elisée Reclus, the geographer, felt no compunction about using his knowledge to support the anarchist cause. His brother Elie also wrote about *Les Primitifs* (1903), employing the findings of anthropology to demonstrate the possibility of a free society, but he took an increasingly pessimistic interest in past myths and religions. Elisée Reclus remained an optimist and became the most competent French exponent of anarchism at the end of the nineteenth century. He not only supported *La Révolte* and *Le Révolté* with money and contributions but his purely anarchist pamphlets like *A mon frère, le paysan* (1893) and *Evolution et révolution* (1880) had a wide circulation.

But while these thinkers were elaborating a profound critique of the French State, and developing a persuasive anarcho-communist alternative, a series of spectacular and bloody acts of propaganda by the deed won anarchism its notorious reputation in the popular mind which it has never been able to shake off. In the desperate social unrest in the 1880s many anarchists thought that the only way to bring down the State was through a campaign of terror. Jean Grave for one concluded at the time that 'all the money spent to propose deputies would be more judiciously used to buy dynamite'.[23]

Charles Gallo agreed and threw a bottle of vitriol from the gallery of the Paris Stock Exchange and then starting firing his revolver at random. The legendary François-Claudius Ravachol placed bombs in the houses of two French judges (whom he held responsible for imposing severe sentences on two workers after a May Day demonstration). His name became immortalized in the verb – *ravacholiser* (to blow up). Théodule Meunier bombed a barracks and the restaurant where Ravachol had been betrayed to the police (killing the proprietor and a customer). Auguste Vaillant hurled a bomb into the Chamber of Deputies (killing no one).

The most notorious terrorist at this time was the young intellectual Emile Henry, who threw a bomb in the Café Terminus in the Gare St Lazare in Paris to show the vulnerable side of the bourgeoisie. He killed one customer and injured twenty others. At his trial, Henry declared:

> I wanted to show the bourgeoisie that henceforth their pleasures would not be untouched, that their insolent triumphs would be disturbed, that their golden calf would rock violently on its pedestal until the final shock that would cast it down among filth and blood.

He made clear that he saw himself as part of an international anarchist movement which no government could crush:

> You have hanged in Chicago, decapitated in Germany, garrotted in Jerez, shot in Barcelona, guillotined in Montbrison and Paris, but what you will never destroy is anarchy. Its roots are too deep. It is born in the heart of a society that is rotting and falling part. It is a violent reaction against the established order. It represents all the egalitarian and libertarian aspirations that strike out against authority. It is everywhere, which makes it impossible to contain. It will end by killing you![24]

On the scaffold, Henry exclaimed: 'Long live Anarchy! My death will be avenged.' It certainly was. In 1894, an Italian anarchist Santo Jeronimo Caserio stabbed to death President Sadi Carnot of France. Kropotkin and others tried to excuse such acts as desperate responses to an impossible situation, but no such tortuous arguments could assuage the public revulsion. As the writer Octave Mirbeau drily observed: 'A mortal enemy of anarchism could not have done better than Emile Henry when he hurled his inexplicable bomb in the midst of peaceful anonymous people who had come to a café to drink a beer before going to bed.'[25]

While anarchism showed its ugliest and most destructive side in the terrorists acts at the end of the nineteenth century in France, it also inspired many artists and writers in its most creative form. Gustave Courbet of course had been a friend of Proudhon who had argued that art must have a moral and social purpose, and that it should be 'an idealist representation of nature and ourselves with the aim of perfecting our species physically and morally'.[26] The view was shared by Courbet who depicted the life of the poor, and it eventually contributed to the theory of social realism. Courbet in his famous *Burial at Ornans* tried to negate the ideal of Romanticism and arrive at the emancipation of the individual. He became a member of the Commune and responsible for artistic policy; as a result he was involved in the decision to demolish the Vendôme Column in Paris, a symbol of Napoleon's military dictatorship.

Many of the Post-Impressionist painters found in anarchism a confirmation of their call for artistic freedom, their revolt against bourgeois society, and their sympathy for the poor and oppressed. Camille Pissarro and his son Lucien contributed regularly to *Le Père Peinard* and to Jean Grave's *Les Temps Nouveaux*. Pissarro like Courbet was exiled after the Commune and in 1894 had to move to Belgium to escape the persecution of the anarchists following the assassination of President Carnot. Paul Signac, who eventually ended up in the Communist Party, declared in 1902: 'The anarchist painter is not one who will show anarchist paintings, but one who without regard for lucre, without desire for reward, will struggle with all his individuality, with a personal effort, against bourgeois and official conventions . . .'[27] Steinlen and later Vlaminck and other Fauvist artists also contributed to *Les Temps Nouveaux*.

A young French philosopher who greatly impressed Kropotkin was J. M. Guyau who offered in his *Esquisse d'une morale sans obligation ni sanction* (1884) a view of morality free from all external duty and coercion. Guyau rejected the utilitarian calculus as well as metaphysical sanctions, arguing that we create our own morality through rational choice. Unlike Stirner and Nietzsche, however, he did not draw egoistic conclusions: we have a superabundance of energy which leads us to go beyond the instinct of self-preservation to feel compassion for others. Altruism is therefore based on a natural need to live a full, intense and productive life. Guyau was unable to develop these insights for he died when he was thirty-four, but Kropotkin felt that he was an anarchist without being conscious of it.

Amongst other writers, the novelist and playwright Octave Mirbeau, whom Degas called the 'pyromaniac fireman', came to anarchism in his maturity after reading Kropotkin, Tolstoy and Elisée Reclus. His ornate novels often show a fascination with the very vices he condemns, and his heroes are listless rebels. In *Sébastien Roch*, a study of a young man traumatized by his Jesuit education, Mirbeau raises the question whether youth will ever rebel against the suffocating system run by priests and police. *Le Jardin des supplices*, inspired by the Dreyfus affair, offers an Oriental allegory of Western corruption and legalized torture, while *Le Journal d'une femme de chambre*, made recently into a successful film, shows the bourgeoisie held together principally by its vices. Amongst his explicitly anarchist writings, Mirbeau wrote the immensely successful pamphlet *La Grève des électeurs* which sold in tens of thousands.[28] He was a lifelong anti-militarist, and his comment on the political violence of the 1880s proved the most astute of all his contemporaries: 'The biggest danger of the bomb is the explosion of stupidity that it provokes.' However, it did not stop him from describing Ravachol as 'the peal of thunder to which succeeds the joy of sunlight and of peaceful skies'.[29]

Anarchism at the turn of the century undoubtedly attracted many bohemian individualists, and for a while it became a broad cultural movement, giving expression to a wide range of social disenchantment and artistic rebellion.[30] Jean Grave, amongst others, was suspicious of their importance, and certainly many were more interested in attacking bourgcois convention than in exploring social theory. The writer Laurent Tailhade declared 'Qu'importe les vagues humanités, pourvu que le geste soit beau?' (Of what importance are the vague expressions of humanity, as long as the gesture is fine?) – although he might have changed his mind after a bomb exploded in a restaurant where he was eating and he lost an eye.

Maurice Barrès, influenced by Nietzsche, wrote a series of novels called *Le Culte du moi* which expressed an anti-social individualism. In *L'Ennemi des lois*, he depicted the protagonists who became anarchists after studying Saint-Simon, Fourier and Marx but they withdraw to the country to cultivate their refined sensuality and practice universal benevolence. Jean Grave declared that it was an anarchism only appropriate for millionaires who could free themselves from existing laws.

In Switzerland during the First World War a group of artists, pacifists and radicals, including Hugo Ball and Richard Huelsenbeck, met in Zürich and launched the Dada movement, a unique blend of art and anarchy. It claimed to be a total negation of everything that had existed before, but was very much in the tradition of the medieval Heresy of the Free Spirit. The Romanian-born French poet Tristan Tzara explained in his *Notes pour la bourgeoisie* that the *soirées* at the Cabaret Voltaire and Galerie Dada 'provided the possibility for the spectators to link for themselves suitable associations with the characteristic elements of their own personality'.[31] Dada aimed at destroying through art the entire social order and to achieve through art total freedom. Marcel Duchamp was among the leading exponents of Dada in France before leaving for the United States. Many Dadaists became involved in the Berlin rising of 1918, calling for a Dadaist Revolutionary

Central Council on the basis of radical communism and progressive unemployment. Although Tzara became a Stalinist, the Dadaists influenced the Surrealist movement in France which developed in the 1920s, as seen in the characteristic declaration of 1925 'Open the Prisons! Disband the Army!' which asserted 'Social coercion has had its day. Nothing . . . can force man to give up freedom.'[32]

The antics of the artists and writers were a far cry from the struggles of the revolutionary syndicalists who were forging the Conféderation Généralale du Travail in France at the turn of the century. Syndicalism not only redirected the impulses of the advocates of 'propaganda by the deed' but also took over many of the most positive ideas of anarchism.[33]

The origins of French syndicalism went as far back as the First International which had adopted the principle that 'The emancipation of the workers shall be the task of the workers themselves.' At the fourth congress of the International in Basel in 1869, it had further been argued by the French, Spanish, Swiss, Jurassian and Belgian delegates that the economic associations of the workers should be considered the social nucleus of the coming society. The advocates of this policy were strongly influenced by Bakunin who had asserted:

> The organization of the trade sections, their federation in the International, and their representation by the Labour Chambers, not only create a great academy, in which the workers of the International, combining theory and practice, can and must study economic science, they also bear in themselves the living germs of the *new social order*, which is to replace the bourgeois world.[34]

The organization of the new revolutionary syndicates therefore tried to reflect the organization of the new society; they were based on the principles of federalism and autonomy, recognizing the right of self-determination of each syndicate. Organized from the bottom up, the various committees in the federations acted merely as co-ordinating organs without any executive or bureaucratic power.

What distinguished the French anarcho-syndicalists from other trade unionists was their insistence that the movement should be completely independent of political parties and their refusal to participate in conventional politics. As the anarchist Emile Pouget succinctly put it, 'The aim of the syndicates is to make war on the bosses and not to bother with the politics.'[35] They insisted that the reconstruction of society must be carried out by the economic organization of the workers themselves. Their strategy was one of 'direct action' in the form of the boycott, labelling (buying goods from approved employers), sabotage, anti-militarist propaganda, and the strike in all its gradations. The strike was considered to be the most important tactic, especially the general strike which took on mythic proportions.

As early as 1874 the Jura anarchist Adhémar Schwitzguébel had argued that the general strike would 'certainly be a revolutionary act capable of bringing about the liquidation of the existing social order'.[36] Enthusiasm for the general strike rapidly spread amongst anarchists involved in the labour movement and it was soon considered as the best means of bringing about the collapse of the State and ushering in the new society.

Georges Sorel, inspired by Proudhon and the syndicalists, maintained in his *Reflections on Violence* (1908) that class war invigorates society. He opposed 'bourgeois force' with 'proletarian violence', arguing that the latter has a purifying effect and enables the people to take possession of themselves. The general strike moreover is of value as a 'social myth', an article of faith which inspires the workers in their struggle. For Sorel, social myths are important since they are 'not descriptions of things, but expression of a determination to act'. Although he later influenced Lenin, Mussolini and Action Française, he did not object to acknowledging himself an anarchist since 'Parliamentary Socialism professes a contempt for morality' and the new ethic of the producers.[37]

In the long run Sorel's celebration of revolutionary will and proletarian violence had more influence on the Right than the Left. The syndicalist movement certainly did not think that the general strike was a myth, and Sorel had only a slight influence on syndicalist theoreticians. Although he earned a bloodthirsty reputation, he was in fact opposed to industrial sabotage and argued that syndicalist revolution should not be defiled by abominations such as terror which had sullied bourgeois revolutions.

The most constructive phase of anarcho-syndicalism was at the turn of the century when the French trade union movement separated into revolutionary and reformist sections. It found fertile soil in France because of its long revolutionary tradition and because the political leaders had so clearly betrayed the workers in the revolutions of 1789, 1830, and 1848. The general strike became an economic alternative to the barricades.[38]

Many anarchists such as Fernand Pelloutier and Emile Pouget joined the Confédération Générale du Travail (CGT) and helped develop it in an anarcho-syndicalist direction. In 1895, the CGT declared itself independent of all political parties, and in 1902, it was joined by the Fédération des Bourses du Travail. Pelloutier became the secretary of the later, while Pouget edited the official organ of the CGT, *La Voix du Peuple*. The revolutionary Pouget was sufficiently impatient to maintain that there was a difference between *le droit syndical* and *le droit démocratique*, and that conscious minorities need not wait for majority approval of their action if it be intended to promote the interests of their fellow workers.[39]

After 1902, the CGT was organized into two federations of the Bourses du Travail (Labour Chambers) and of the Syndicats (syndicates or unions). The federation of Labour Chambers co-ordinated the activities of local syndicates. They had originally been set up to find jobs for workers, but soon became centres of education and discussion for all aspects of working-class life.

The syndicates had been formed in factories and, in some cases, in different branches of industry. Any syndicate, however small, had the right to be represented in the federation by a delegate chosen by itself. The confederal committee of the CGT which consisted of delegates from the labour chambers and the syndicates acted as a co-ordinating body and had no authority. Officers were kept to a minimum to avoid bureaucracy, and were instantly dismissible by the rank and file.[40] Each section of the CGT was autonomous but each syndicate was obliged to belong to a local labour chamber or equivalent organization.

The revolutionary influence in the CGT grew to such an extent that its Charter of Amiens in 1906 pledged the organization to class struggle, political neutrality, and the revolutionary general strike. While trying to achieve the immediate improvement in the workers' conditions, it was committed to

> preparing the way for the entire emancipation that can be realized only by the expropriation of the capitalist class. It commends the general strike as a means to this end and holds that the trade union, which is at present a resistance group, will be in the future the group responsible for production and distribution, the foundation of the social organization.[41]

The adversaries of the CGT called it anarchist, but the militant Pierre Monatte claimed that it had no official doctrine and was independent of all political tendencies. Nevertheless, he was ready to admit that syndicalism had recalled anarchism to an awareness of its working-class origins. It was moreover 'a school of will, of energy, and of fertile thinking'.[42]

But while the CGT engaged in a series of dramatic strikes, culminating in the campaign for an eight-hour day in 1906, it never attracted more than half of the total number of unionized workers in France and failed to provoke a revolutionary general strike. In the outcome, it tended to be pragmatic, appealing to a diverse work-force and trying to make the existing world more habitable.[43] After 1914, the CGT became largely a reformist trade union movement and abandoned its anarcho-syndicalist principles.

The French CGT however left the broad outline of anarcho-syndicalist organization which was copied in most other countries. Workers organized themselves into syndicates according to trade or industry in a given locality.

The syndicates then federated horizontally with other syndicates in the same area (town or rural district) to establish a local federation; and vertically, with other syndicates in the same industry or craft. These federations then united into a confederation to co-ordinate the movement. Taking the CGT as his model, Rudolf Rocker argued that in a revolutionary situation, it would be the task of the Federation of Labour Chambers to take over and administer existing social capital and arrange distribution in each community, while the Federation of Industrial Alliances would organize the total production of the country.[44] In practice, anarcho-syndicalism was to flourish most in Latin countries where there was little alternative for the labour movement other than revolutionary struggle.

The broader anarchist movement in France had an uneasy relationship with anarcho-syndicalism. The individualists and bohemians naturally wanted little to do with the unions. Amongst the anarchist communists, Jean Grave and *Les Temps Nouveaux* gave their qualified approval. The purist Sébastien Faure in *Le Libertaire* was at first hostile although he too came to tolerate it. The tension between the anarchists and the syndicalists came to the fore at the International Anarchist Congress held in Amsterdam in 1907. Pierre Monatte criticized the 'revolutionarism' of the pure anarchists which had 'taken superb retreat in the ivory tower of philosophic speculation'.[45] Emma Goldman replied that the syndicalists' principle of majority rule cramped the initiative of the individual: 'I will only accept anarchist organization on one condition. It is that it should be based on absolute respect for *all* individual initiatives and should not hamper their free play and development.'[46] For his part, Malatesta voiced the concern of many anarchist communists that syndicalism had too simple a conception of class struggle and placed too much confidence in the general strike – a 'pure utopia' which could degenerate into a 'general famine'.[47] Syndicalism should be considered only as *a* means to anarchy, not *the* sole one.

The French anarchist movement, both its communist and syndicalist wings, reached its peak before the outbreak of the First World War. Faure and the individualist E. Armand remained true to their anti-militarist principles, but most anarchists either joined the army or declared their support for the allies. After the war, the apparent success of the Russian Revolution ensured that communists gained ground in the CGT. Anarcho-syndicalists and communists formed a revolutionary group which split away in 1921 to form the CGT Unitaire, but the communists gained the upper hand in the following year and aligned themselves with Moscow. The anarchists left to form the Comité de Defence Syndicaliste Révolutionnaire which claimed to represent 100,000 workers at the syndicalist IWMA founded in Berlin 1923. It lingered on until 1939 but was never able to make much headway amongst the working class. Outside the syndicalist movement, a small band of ageing militants kept the anarchist message alive in a few papers with declining readership. Their international connections were maintained by the increasing number of anarchist refugees from the Soviet Union, Italy, Germany and Spain to seek asylum in France.

After the experience of the German occupation and the resistance, anarchism in France had something of a revival in the fifties and early sixties around magazines like *Le Libertaire* of the Anarchist Federation and the new *Noir et Rouge*. Alain Sergent and Claude Harmel (the latter a French Nazi during the occupation) produced an incomplete *Histoire de l'anarchie* in 1949 and Jean Maitron brought out his *Histoire du mouvement anarchiste en France* in 1951. The libertarian atmosphere affected Albert Camus who associated with French and Spanish anarchists and syndicalists, and studied anarchist history and philosophy. Although he was critical of Stirner and Bakunin in his *L'Homme révolté* (1951), he was even more critical of authoritarian communism. The work shows that he was moving towards a form of anarcho-syndicalism.

It was in the sixties that libertarian ideas really began to take hold on a new generation. Inspired by Dada and Surrealism, a small band of artists and intellectuals founded the Internationale Situationniste in 1957 which soon rediscovered anarchist history and developed a libertarian critique of consumer society and culture. In 1964 a French group, Jeunesse Libertaire, gave new impetus to Proudhon's slogan 'Anarchy is Order' by creating the circled A, a symbol which quickly proliferated throughout the world. Daniel Guérin, a former Marxist, developed a libertarian form of socialism and called in 1965 for *L'Anarchisme: de la doctrine à l'action*. Three years later the greatest outburst of libertarian energy since the Second World War occurred in the student rebellion of May 1968. During the general strike which followed, de Gaulle's regime tottered but did not fall. While the students lost the revolution, they won the argument, and authoritarian socialists and communists in France have been on the retreat ever since. A revived syndicalist organization – the Confédération Nationale du Travail – has since made headway, especially in south-west France and in the Paris region.

Amongst intellectuals, Michel Foucault developed a highly imaginative, and equally contentious, critique of power, while Cornelius Castoriadis as Paul Cardan posed the choice of libertarian *Socialisme ou Barbarie* as we reach the crossroads in the labyrinth of contemporary society and culture. French post-modernist thinkers like Jacques Derrida, Gilles Deleuze, Félix Guattari and Jean-François Lyotard have made a major contribution to renewing anarchist theory. In the new century, French anarchists have been at the forefront of the anti-capitalist and anti-globalization movements.

Italy

IN ITALY THE EARLY anarchists emerged from the republican and nation-alist movement led by Mazzini and Garibaldi. The methods of the clan-destine *Carbonari* with their loose organization and acts of insurrection left a mark on the developing anarchist strategy. The ideas of Proudhon were also nudging republican thought in a federal direction long before the arrival of Bakunin in 1864. But while he is often seen as the first inspiration of the Italian anarchist movement, he was with other Russian revolutionaries more of a catalyst than an originator.[1]

Carlo Pisacane, the Duke of San Giovanni, was a transitional figure between the old nationalists and the anarchist movement, acting as chief of staff in Mazzini's army and spreading Proudhon's and Fourier's ideas. He called for the creation of an independent nation through the social revol-ution. The only just and secure form of government, he asserted, was 'the anarchy of Proudhon', but he went beyond Proudhon by arguing that industrial factories should become collective property and the land be col-lectivized in communes. Above all, Pisacane was one of the earliest advo-cates of *propaganda dei fatti* (propaganda by the deed):

> The propaganda of the idea is a chimera. Ideas result from deeds, not the latter from the former, and the people will not be free when they are educated, but will be educated when they are free. The only work a citizen can do for the good of the country is that of co-operating with the material revolution.[2]

There were several old comrades of Pisacane amongst the Brotherhood founded by Bakunin in Florence in 1864 as well as in his International Brotherhood set up later in Naples. It was in Florence that Bakunin aban-doned his Panslavism, so it could be argued that the birth of anarchism in Italy coincided with the birth of the international anarchist movement.[3] Amongst the members of the Italian section of the International Brother-hood were Giuseppe Fanelli, a deputy at the Italian parliament, who went on a pioneering mission to Spain to spread the anarchist gospel, and Carlo Gambuzzi, who became for a long time one of the principal leaders of the Italian anarchist movement.

In 1869 the branches of Bakunin's Brotherhood were dissolved in

Italy and the they became sections of the International Working Men's Association (IWMA). It was from this time that the Italian anarchist movement really began to grow. When Bakunin replied to Mazzini's twin-pronged attack – on the Paris Commune for its atheism and on the International for denying genuine nationalism – the International in Italy went from strength to strength.[4] Disenchanted Mazzinian republicans and Garibaldian volunteers radicalized by the Paris Commune recruited some thirty thousand members to the International, mainly from central Italy and Naples. But it was not yet a workers' organization. It had been introduced by the bourgeoisie, and by 1872 its militants were still mainly young people from affluent families.[5]

Early in the 1870s a new group of militants emerged, led by young Carlo Cafiero, Errico Malatesta and Andrea Costa. Cafiero was a product of the Apulian nobility who had given up his family fortune and his career as a diplomat. As a member of the International Marx had hoped to use him to convert Italy and Spain to Marxism; he wrote a compendium of *Capital* and met Marx in 1871 in London. In the event, he was converted by Bakunin and Malatesta to the anarchist cause. Malatesta was the son of a liberally minded small-scale landowner, and was raised in the province of Caserta. He too cast in his lot, when a medical student, with the people. Andrea Costa came from Romagnole petty bourgeois stock, and studied law at Bologna University. All three young men were convinced positivists. Inspired by the sociology of Comte and Spencer, they saw society as a living organism whose natural growth was hindered by the institutions of private property and the State.

In order to rival the feats of the followers of Garibaldi and Mazzini, the anarchists organized strikes and demonstrations, but also resorted to the well-tried tactic of the Italian revolutionary tradition – the insurrection. In the 1860s there had been civil war in the south and the Italian State was particularly weak. It was therefore not unreasonable to hope that an uprising could spark off a general insurrection which would bring down the tottering State. In 1874, Andrea Costa, Malatesta, and members of a group within the International who called themselves the Italian Committee for the Social Revolution planned an uprising in Bologna in order to trigger off similar actions in other towns and cities throughout Italy. Bakunin was waiting to join them, but the *carabinieri* had been informed and foiled the insurgents as they were marching on Bologna.

The Italian message of direct action was not lost on the international anarchist movement. At the Berne Conference of the IWMA in 1876, Malatesta explained the background to the Bologna uprising and argued that 'the revolution consists more in deeds than words ... each time a spontaneous movement of the people erupts ... it is the duty of every revolutionary socialist to declare his solidarity with the movement in the making.'[6]

Three months later Cafiero and Malatesta gave a clear definition of propaganda by the deed in the *Bulletin of the Jura Federation*: 'The Italian federation believes that the insurrectional fact, destined to affirm socialist principles by deeds, is the most efficacious means of propaganda.'[7] The view of the Italians came to dominate European anarchist activities during the 1880s, especially in France and Spain.

Despite the persecution of the authorities a national congress was held in a wood outside Florence in 1876, where Cafiero and Malatesta persuaded the delegates to move from a form of Bakuninite collectivism to communism. Those present accepted the proposition:

> Each must do for society all that his abilities will allow him to do, and he has the right to demand from society the satisfaction of all his needs, in the measure conceded by the state of production and social capacities.[8]

The congress also confirmed the insurrectional position of the Italian anarchist movement.

Malatesta, Cafiero and Costa lost no time in putting their preaching into practice. In the following year, they entered two villages near Benevento in Campania with an armed band, burning the tax registers and declaring the end of the reign of King Victor Emmanuel. The peasants, including their priests, welcomed them at first but feared joining them; as a result, Italian troops soon arrived and captured the insurgents.

This second abortive rising provoked another round of persecution. The Italian sections of the outlawed International called for a general insurrection on a national scale but when it failed to materialize individuals turned to their own acts of terror. In 1878, the new King Umberto was stabbed and on the following day a bomb was thrown in a monarchist parade. Even greater repression followed. The International was broken up and Cafiero and Malatesta went into exile.

Costa soon turned his back on insurrectionary anarchism. He considered that 'insurrectionism, if practised, leads to nothing if not the triumph of reaction and, if not practised, it leads to the disesteem of him who preaches it and it remains merely verbal'.[9] He became a deputy, and played an important part in forming the Italian Socialist Party. Like Paul Brousse, whom he met in the spring of 1880, he developed a form of communalism with the tactic of formulating minimum and maximum programmes for local socialist parties. While collectivism was the means, he still saw anarchy as the end. Cafiero on the other hand suddenly went over to the parliamentary socialists; he eventually became insane, obsessed by the idea that he was enjoying more than his fair share of the sun.

The defection of Costa and Cafiero reflected a general shift to social democracy in the Italian labour movement. It was not long before anarchism in Italy became the preserve of constantly changing, largely autonomous groups in the small towns. Towards the end of the century, individual Italians were responsible for some of the most notorious assassinations, killing the French President Sadi Carnot in 1894, the Spanish Prime Minister Antonio Canovas in 1897, the Empress Elizabeth of Austria in 1898, and finally King Umberto after two attempts in 1900.

Some anarchists during this period went abroad to realize their ideals in utopian communities, such as the Cecilia Colony in Brazil which lasted four years in the early 1890s. In the twentieth century, many Italians emigrated and continued to propagate anarchist ideas, especially in Latin America and North America.

The most prominent anarchist thinker to emerge in Italy was undoubtedly Errico Malatesta who remained active in the international anarchist movement for nearly sixty years and the principal figure in the Italian anarchist movement during its most important years. In the late 1880s and early 1890s he tried to form a new nationalist anarchist 'party' but it failed to get off the ground. Nevertheless, his tolerant 'anarchism without adjectives' was widely influential.

Malatesta worked closely at this time with F. S. Merlino, a lawyer who showed in his studies of the Italian State that bureaucracy and State institutions can exert their influence on the economic base of society. Although Merlino went on to become a socialist, he helped lay the foundations of Italian syndicalism and weaned Malatesta off his early Marxian taste for economic determinism. Other anarchist intellectuals who collaborated with Malatesta at this time included Pietro Gori, a lawyer who composed some of the most popular inspirational songs of the era, and Luigi Fabbri, who popularized anarchist ideas about education, birth control, and militarism.

National congresses of the anarchist movement were held in 1891, 1907 and 1915 but there was no continuous national organization. Anarchists in the 1890s remained a minority group in the labour movement, seeing their role as being to foster revolutionary consciousness and to prod socialists to insurrection. They worked in their local Chambers of Labour (*camere de lavoro*), which remained largely autonomous. As a result, while anarchism remained weaker as a movement than socialism from the turn of the century to the First World War, its values, symbols and language dominated Italian working-class popular culture.[10] Localism, anti-Statism, *operaismo* (workerism), and anti-clerical and anti-militarist sentiments prevailed.

The anarchists too were the first to see syndicalism as a serious alternative to socialism for the workers. Modelled on the French CGT, the Confederazione Generale del Lavoro (CGL) was founded in 1906 and tried to centralize and control the local Chambers of Labour. The anarchist-inspired Unione Sindacale Italiana (USI) broke away in 1912 from the increasingly socialist and reformist CGL. The new organization grew rapidly and by 1919 claimed a membership of half a million, mainly in Central Italy and along the Ligurian coast. Although the railway workers were led by anarchists they did not join the USI, and except in Apulia, the Unione won a minority following amongst the landless peasants.

Despite his reservations about syndicalism voiced at the Amsterdam Anarchist Congress, Malatesta called in 1914 for a general strike after the shooting of some anti-militarist demonstrators in his base in Ancona. The call was taken up in different parts of Italy. In the 'Red Week' (*settimana rosa*) which followed the railway system virtually ground to a halt and fighting broke out in many areas. Small towns in the Marches declared themselves self-governing republics. The movement, led by the anarchists and the Unione Sindacale Italiana, seemed poised to overthrow the monarchy, but the CGL ordered its members back to work. The experience left many syndicalist leaders disillusioned with direct action. The syndicalists too became split during the crisis over Italy's intervention in the war in 1915.

News of the Russian Revolution greatly inspired the Italian syndicalist movement. By 1920, the USI had nearly recruited half a million members, although the CGL had two million. The Italian Federation of Metal Workers won an agreement in 1919 allowing them to elect 'internal commissions' in the factories; in a series of spectacular strikes and occupations, they then tried to turn them into factory councils. When in August 1920, the employers locked them out, the metal workers of Milan and Turin decided to take over the factories and run them themselves by workers' committees. As a culmination of the *biennio rosso*, the call for a general strike was endorsed by the Unione Sindacale Italiana, led by the journalist Armando Borghi.

Malatesta in the first Italian anarchist daily newspaper *Umanità Nova* founded at the time in Milan warned that the failure of the strike would lead to retribution. The reformist leadership of the moderate CGL again persuaded the workers to abandon their occupations in exchange for some minor reforms which never materialized. Within a few weeks, there were mass arrests of strike leaders and anarchist activists, including Malatesta and Borghi.

It was the last great experiment in workers' control in Italy before the rise of fascism. But the strike was of considerable importance for it had gone some way in realizing the aspirations of the group of libertarians and left-socialists associated with the weekly *L'Ordine Nuovo*. Edited by Antonio Gramsci, the journal called for factory councils to replace the reformist trade unions in order to prepare the workers for self-management. In line with anarcho-syndicalist teaching, the councils were also considered as embryos of the new socialist society.

Antonio Gramsci at this stage was developing a form of Marxism which was to prove hugely influential in revisionist Eurocommunist circles later in the twentieth century. He was opposed to the bureaucratic State as well as to the reformist trade union movement. His call for a party as a co-ordinating body for factory councils and soviets was not very different from Malatesta's earlier conception of an anarchist party.[11] Like many Italian anarchists at this time, he considered the Bolshevik regime to be genuinely democratic, and thought it possible to reconcile Bolshevism with the withering away of the State. The young anarchist intellectual Camillo Berneri, who was to die during the Spanish Revolution, also saw the Soviet system at this stage as one of *autogoverno* (self-management).

As early as 1919, however, Luigi Fabbri and Malatesta had warned that a new class was emerging in Russia. Malatesta wrote to Fabbri on 30 July 1919:

> In reality one is dealing with a dictatorship of a party; and a very real dictatorship with its decrees, penal sanctions, executions and above all its armed force that today helps defend the revolution from external enemies, but tomorrow will help impose the dictators' will on the workers, stop the revolution, consolidate and defend new interests of a new privileged class against the masses.[12]

At their congress at Ancona in November 1921, the recently formed Unione Anarchica Italiana denounced the Bolshevik government as the main enemy of the Russian Revolution.

Although anarchists were instrumental in the establishment of an anti-fascist front in 1921-2, Gramsci and his friends went on to set up the Italian Communist Party which soon affiliated to the Communist International. In an obituary on Lenin, Malatesta suggested in 1924 that his death should be celebrated as a holiday rather than an occasion for mourning, thereby further alienating the Communists. After Mussolini's March on Rome in 1922, anarchism as a movement began to disintegrate, but it went down fighting. Anarchists were imprisoned, sent to penal islands, put under house arrest (as in the case of Malatesta) or driven into exile.

The anarchists had been unable to pose a serious alternative to the fascists because of their uneven national distribution, their local disagreements, and their loose organization. During the war, anarchists fought in the resistance, especially in the north of the country. After the war, there was a slight revival of anarchism amongst disenchanted workers. The Italian Anarchist Federation was regrouped in Carrara, the traditional stronghold of the rebellious marble-cutters. *Umanità Nova* was revived and Cesare Zaccaria helped found *Volontà*, which is still published today. But when the New Left emerged in Italy in the 1960s it was strictly Marxist; the terrorist Red Brigades were especially authoritarian.

An international anarchist congress held in Carrara in 1968 helped revive libertarian spirits despite the failure of the students' insurrection earlier in the year. In the seventies, with the rise of the peace, Green and feminist movements, anarchism started to make a comeback, albeit mainly amongst students and the middle class. The Unione Sindacale Italiana was relaunched in 1983 and now has groups in every province. In the following year, the city of Venice welcomed three thousand people to an international congress which revived dormant contacts, and confirmed that the ideas of anarchism thrive once again. Anarchism may no longer shape Italian working-class life, but it still challenges the Italian State, and is a considerable thorn in its side.

Spain

TO DATE, SPAIN IS the only country in the modern era where anarchism can credibly be said to have developed into a major social movement and to have seriously threatened the State. There are some good local reasons why this should be the case. The anarchist principles of autonomy, association and federation are peculiarly suited to the independent cast of the Spanish social temperament. There was also a long tradition of independent communes which stretched back to the Middle Ages; these communes had had their own public charters and made their own *fueros* or local laws. The free commune was considered a self-governing organism capable of federating with others.

Very firmly in this tradition was the Catalan Pi y Margall, who, in the middle of the nineteenth century, became the leader of the Federalist Party. Referring to the brotherhoods formed by the municipalities chiefly in Castilla and León in the last third of the Middle Ages, he wrote:

> The citizens not content with their *fuero* or own law codes, attempted all the time to extract further privileges to buttress them. If for any reason they united with their neighbours, it was to defend local freedoms, even against the king himself, whom they always looked at with cautious and suspicious eyes.[1]

Pi y Margall was inspired by Hegel's principle of 'unity in diversity' and translated Proudhon into Spanish. He advocated a federal society based on self-governing communes. In *Reacción y Revolución* (1854), he declared that 'I shall divide and subdivide power; I shall make it changeable and go on destroying it'. The book was to have a profound influence on Spanish radicalism. When Pi became President for a short period during the 1873 revolution, he only managed to introduce a few liberal reforms.[2] But he was long considered the moving spirit of Spanish anarchism.

The European message of anarchism first arrived in Spain in 1868. On hearing of the military revolution which had driven Queen Isabella into exile, Bakunin sent several of his envoys to win supporters for his newly formed International Alliance of Socialist Democracy, a secret society within the First International. Despite his inability to speak Spanish, the Italian Giuseppe Fanelli managed to set up in Madrid a nucleus of twenty-one converts who formed the Federación Regional Española, the Spanish section of the First International. He also won over some students and workers to Bakunin's anti-authoritarian collectivism in Barcelona. The Spanish section of the First International was to remain firmly Bakuninist and immediately developed in an anarcho-syndicalist direction.[3]

Anarchism in Spain quickly took root amongst the rural poor. Itinerant apostles like the austere printer Anselmo Lorenzo (who had been inspired by Fanelli and Proudhon) carried the anarchist message from village to village, awakening revolutionary aspirations which would occasionally burst out in local insurrections. In the villages *obreros conscientes* (clear-thinking workers) would keep the anarchist flames alight. The peasants dreamed of the day of *el reparto*, the redistribution of land, when authority in the form of the landowner, priest and police would come to an end.[4]

But it was not only amongst the dispossessed in the south and east – the landless peasants and poor farmers of Andalucía and the Levante – that anarchism found fertile soil. It made headway in the mining districts of Catalunya and Oviedo. It appealed to the most advanced workers in Barcelona, Valencia and Madrid. Young intellectuals, like Francisco Ferrer who founded the Modern School Movement, were attracted by its militant atheism and rebellious spirit as well as to its confidence in human goodness and progress. Even the young Pablo Picasso came under its sway at the turn of the century.

Anarchism tended to take on a more violent form in Spain than elsewhere because political violence had come to seem unexceptional since the Napoleonic Wars. But while Spanish anarchism had a prophetic, and to some degree a millenarian ring, it is misleading to see it, as many historians have, as fundamentally religious in character. It was usually based on a clear understanding and analysis of the causes of social oppression and offered a realistic solution to agricultural impoverishment and industrial alienation.[5] It was rooted in popular culture and expressed in a new form ancient aspirations for land and liberty, bread and justice, education and freedom.

At the same time, Spanish anarchism placed a great stress on culture and lifestyle and sought to free everyday life from the traditional bonds of Church and State. Maturing in a period of economic scarcity, it developed on occasion a somewhat puritanical strain. But while the strong moral sense of many Spanish anarchists led them to reject usury and waste, they also celebrated free love and free enquiry. In their desire to live in harmony with nature, some even adopted simple dress, a vegetarian diet, and nudism. They were well organized and efficient and yet valued spontaneity and initiative. In their *grupos de afinidad* (affinity groups), they developed forms of organization which were based not only on ideological ties but more importantly on friendship and conviviality.[6]

As in France, there was an upsurge in the early 1890s of anarchist bombings and assassinations in Spain, which was met by brutal government repression. But the anarchists soon recognized the inability of terrorism to overthrow the State and turned to propaganda amongst the workers and peasants. A new wave of industrial unrest broke out at the turn of the century. Inspired by the successes of the French CGT, the libertarian unions of Catalunya formed a syndicalist organization called Solidaridad Obrera (Workers' Unity) in 1907.

It held its first congress the following year. When the government called for conscription in Catalunya in 1909 for its war with the Riffs in Morocco, Solidaridad Obrera called a general strike. Street battles broke out in Barcelona, and during the subsequent *Semana Trágica* (tragic week) some two hundred workers were killed, thousands injured, and many churches burnt down. In the merciless reprisals which followed Ferrer lost his life although he had not even been present during the fighting in Barcelona. In the aftermath the unions recognized the need to create a stronger organization and in 1911 the Confederación Nacional del Trabajo (CNT) was formed at a congress in Sevilla. It saw itself as the successor to the First International which had existed in Spain in one form or another since 1868.

The CNT was unable to operate legally until 1914. Five years later, its membership had soared to one million. Its main period of activity was between 1917 and 1923 when it organized all over Spain revolutionary strikes which almost provoked a civil war. Gunmen or *pistoleros* of the Left and Right shot it out in the streets, especially in Barcelona, and perpetrated revenge killings. But the CNT faced the same dilemma as the CGT had in France, since it was dedicated to improving the conditions of its members in the short term as well as aiming ultimately at the revolutionary transformation of society. At the CNT congress in 1919 it adopted the principles of *comunismo libertario* as its basic ideology, as proposed by the regional congress of the Catalan unions the previous year. It also committed itself to 'struggle in the purely economic field, that is by direct action, untrammelled by any political or religious prejudice'.[7]

A split developed between a moderate wing led by Salvador Seguí and Angel Pestaña, who were willing to compromise with employers and even the State, and extremists like Buenaventura Durruti who were ready to use virtually any means to bring about the revolution. But what united both wings in the CNT was their common opposition to authoritarian socialism. A delegate returned from a Congress of the Third International in Moscow in 1920 with the news that under the pretext of revolutionary power a new dictatorship, that of a single (if nominally socialist) party, was emerging in

Russia. In 1922 at its Zaragoza Congress, the CNT declared itself to be a 'firm defender of the principles of the First International maintained by Bakunin', and broke away from the Communist Third International because of its link with the Soviet Union. The constitution of the CNT adopted the principle 'The emancipation of the workers must be the work of the workers themselves'. They took it so far to begin with that only waged workers with a permanent employer were allowed to join.

At every opportunity the militant literature of the CNT attacked the State as the source of all evil and denounced political power with such well-known aphorisms as:

> there is no such thing as revolutionary power, for all power is reaction-
> ary by nature; power corrupts both those who exercise it and those
> over whom it is exercised; those who think they can conquer the State
> in order to destroy it are unaware that the State overcomes all its
> conquerors; there are no good and bad politicians, only bad ones and
> worse; the best government is no government at all; the Nation is not
> the People, nor is the State the same as Society; instead of the govern-
> ment of men, let us have the administration of things; peace to men,
> and war on institutions; dictatorship of the proletariat is dictatorship
> without the proletariat and against them; to vote for politicians is to
> renounce your own personality; your union is yourself.[8]

Unlike the French CGT with its dual structure of local *bourses du travail* and a national federation of trade unions, the CNT was at first based on the local *sindicatos únicos*. These syndicates brought together all workers in one factory or town and were loosely federated at a regional and national level. It had no permanent officials and the minimum of administrative arrangements: officers were unpaid and rotated annually to prevent them from becoming bureaucrats. All decisions were taken at a meeting of the branch, preferably by acclamation but if not, by majority vote. The consti-tution of the CNT, which was printed in every membership card, unequivo-cally stated: 'We recognize the sovereignty of the individual, but we accept and agree to carry out the collective mandate taken by majority decision. Without this there is no organization.'

Complete autonomy was the basis of the federation and the only ties were the general agreements reached at the national congresses. In carrying a resolution, it was usual to operate by majority vote, but proportional representation was also used to stop the small unions from the villages being crushed by the large unions from the cities. The delegates at conferences had the mandate to discuss fundamental themes but they had to submit the propositions agreed to referendum of individual unions. At all times the members had control over the delegates and could dismiss them.

As a union organization, the CNT was one of the most democratic. But there were some limitations to its libertarian structure. Interpreting strictly its principle that the emancipation of workers must be the work of the workers themselves, initially it only allowed workers who had a wage and an employer to join. This of course excluded self-employed workers, members of co-operatives, certain technicians and intellectuals. Its revolutionary impetus also had an anti-intellectual edge – in its constitution printed on membership cards, it declared: 'To lose time in talking in meetings by holding philosophical discussions, is anti-revolutionary. The adversary does not discuss, he acts.'⁹ With its emphasis on the slogan 'Unity is Strength', it overruled private judgement and free enquiry by insisting that each member be obliged to comply with majority decisions, even when they contravene his or her own principles. The union also insisted that there should be no public criticism of the organization.

The highly decentralized structure of the CNT however made it extremely resilient. When it went underground during the dictatorship of Primo de Rivera from 1923 to 1930, it re-emerged largely intact.

At the 1931 Madrid Congress, the moderate tendency within CNT carried a proposal to form, like the French CGT, national federations in each industry, in addition to the local *sindicatos únicos* which grouped workers from every factory into a town federation. At the same time, the extreme Federación Anarquista Ibérica (FAI), which had been formed in exile in 1927, began through its loose *grupos de afinidad* (affinity groups) to dominate the important committees and bureaux of the CNT. Its intention was to counter the reformist wing. While all the anarchists of the FAI were members of the CNT, not all the members of the CNT were anarchists. Those in the CNT who rejected the idea of revolution and a movement led by an audacious minority like the FAI began to be expelled.

The result was that from 1932 at least half of the Spanish trade-union movement was being guided by a dedicated anarchist nucleus – Bakunin's dream of a secret vanguard come true. The FAI succeeded in ousting the moderate leaders of the CNT, including Angel Pestaña and Juan Peiro. They were known as the *Treintistas* as thirty of them had signed a manifesto opposing the tactic of unprepared insurrection, violence for the sake of violence, and the 'myth of revolution'. When the moderates broke away, criticizing the *dictadura de la FAI*, they formed their own *sindicatos de oposición*, but they probably never gained more than sixty thousand members.

The FAI was also split into various tendencies, which ranged from the supporters of Diego Abad de Santillan who proposed a planned economy run by the industrial unions, to those who advocated like Federica Montseny a free federation of communes. The FAI did not come out into the open until the beginning of the Civil War in 1936. Despite its considerable influence, it never achieved more than thirty thousand members.

Amongst its ranks numbered not only a criminal element but also a group of puritanical idealists who were the first to advocate the burning of churches and the summary execution of priests and male prostitutes during the Civil War. Although it would be misleading to call these atheist militants fundamentally religious, they undoubtedly shared some of the hatred for organized religion felt by the puritanical sects of the Reformation.

Opponents accused the FAI of trying to seize power in the CNT, but in reality there was no central power to seize and on most issues the two organizations agreed.[10] In their tactic of using their affinity groups to spearhead the revolution and direct the CNT, the FAI has also been accused of adopting a theory of 'anarcho-Bolshevism'.[11] Murray Bookchin also acknowledges that the Peninsular Committee of the FAI walked 'a very thin line between a Bolshevik-type Central Committee and a mere administrative body'.[12] It certainly remained a secret organization, with its members carefully selected right up until the Civil War, although it could have acquired legal status after the founding of the republic. The *faistas* were also responsible for many of the revenge killings.

But while the affinity groups of the FAI undoubtedly had vanguardist tendencies, they were free associations held together voluntarily by mutual sympathy as well as ideology. They can hardly be compared to Communist Party cells or cadres with their strict discipline and hierarchy. With their ties of intimacy, they had something in common with an extended family. They often acted on their own initiative, which earned them the nickname of *los incontrolados* amongst the authoritarian Left. In addition, the FAI like the CNT was organized along confederal lines, with the delegated Peninsular Committee executing any general agreements rather than making policy. Trotsky, aware of their differences with Bolshevism but misjudging their true nature, called the FAI and CNT a 'fifth wheel on the cart of bourgeois democracy'.[13]

In the early thirties, there were many anarchist attempts to set up insurrectional communes, particularly in the Levante, Andalucía and Catalunya by militants like Buenaventura Durruti. The most famous was in a small village near Jerez called Casas Viejas, where a small group of local anarchists inspired by a veteran nicknamed *seisdedos* (six fingers) locked up the civil guards, unfurled the red and black flag, and announced *el reparto*. After fierce fighting with the Guardia Civil, the rebels were all killed, burnt alive in a shepherd's hut.[14]

Social unrest grew more bitter and widespread. In 1932 a general strike was attempted in Sevilla and in 1933 there were riots in Barcelona. As a result of an abstention campaign led by the CNT, the Republican-Socialist coalition was defeated at the 1933 elections. The alternative was more strikes and insurrections, especially in Aragón and the Rioja district. The CNT and the socialist Unión General de Trabajadores (UGT) supported a rising of seventy thousand miners in Asturias in October 1934 which was brutally put down with the help of Moroccan troops. Hundreds were killed and nine thousand sent up for trial. In the *bienno negro* (black two years) which followed, the country seemed to be drifting towards civil war.

The CNT in the mean time had consistently rejected voting in elections with the slogan: '*Frente a las urnas, la Revolución Social*' (Social Revolution instead of ballot boxes). Its abstention in the 1933 elections undoubtedly led to the formation of a right-wing government. But not all its members were happy with the policy and many voted early in 1936 in elections which brought the Popular Front coalition to power. At the national congress at Zaragoza in May 1936, representing some half million workers, the CNT also welcomed back moderate dissidents of the *sindicatos de oposición* and agreed to try and seek out an alliance with the socialist UGT.

The CNT at the Congress also reaffirmed its revolutionary anarchist beliefs: 'Once the violent aspect of the revolution is finished, the following are declared abolished: private property, the state, the principles of authority, and as a consequence, the classes which divide men into exploiters and exploited, oppressed and oppressors.' The revolution, it was made clear, was not only a sudden act of violence but would involve a profound psychological transformation.

The resolutions made at the ten-day congress add up to one of the most eloquent and incisive statements of libertarian communism. It was agreed that the new society would consist of communes, based on the freely associated syndicates, who would produce and exchange the necessities of life through regional and national federations. Elected committees in the communes, without any executive or bureaucratic character, would make decisions regarding agriculture, hygiene, culture, discipline, production, and statistics. There would be no social hierarchy: the producers would meet at the end of the day to discuss questions of detail which did not require the approval of the communal assemblies.

The individual was seen as the cell and cornerstone of all social, economic and moral creation, but the congress adopted the principle of economic communism. Everyone who freely gave assistance to the collective according to their strength and ability would receive from the commune the satisfaction of their needs. With ecological insight, it was further resolved that eventually the new society should assure each commune of all the agricultural and industrial elements necessary for its autonomy, 'in accordance with the biological principle which affirms that the man, and in this case, the commune, is most free, who has least need of others'.

Tolerance of diversity was one of the keynotes of the Congress. Every attempt was made to incorporate the many shades of anarchist opinion, from the collectivist to the individualist. It was recognized that the communes would take on many different forms, and opponents of industrial technology and advocates of nudism would be free to create their own. As for personal relations, it was affirmed that the revolution would not act violently against the family since at its best it encouraged solidarity in society. But it was recognized that *comunismo libertario* proclaims 'free love, with no more regulation than the free will of the men and women concerned, guaranteeing the children with the security of the community'.

There was to be no distinction between intellectuals and manual workers, but education would be developed to end illiteracy and help people to think for themselves. Courts and prisons would no longer be needed: '*Comunismo libertario* has nothing in common with coercion: a fact which implies the disappearance of the existing system of correctional justice and furthermore of the instruments of punishment.' It was clear to those gathered at the Congress that 'man is not bad by nature, and that delinquency is the logical result of the state of injustice in which we live'. As for anti-social people, it would be the task of the popular assemblies in a spirit of conciliation to seek the just solution to each individual case. They were confident that when a person's needs are satisfied and he or she receives a rational and humane education the principal causes of social injustice will disappear.

These remarkable resolutions of a congress which sought to define the 'Confederal Conception of Libertarian Communism' were not presented as a specific programme or a blueprint for a future society. They were offered as the broad outlines of an initial plan, as 'the point of departure for Humanity towards its integral liberation'.[15] But while these were all revolutionary demands, and revolution was in the air, the Congress made no concrete arrangements to prepare for one. A proposal that militias should be trained was defeated by one favouring the idea of guerrilla warfare. The revolutionary general strike was to be the answer to military rebellions. The vagueness about the means for realizing *comunismo libertario* did not however diminish its popularity. At the time of the Congress, the CNT had half a million members; by the end of the year, it had swelled to more than one and a half million.

When Franco rebelled against the republic on 19 July 1936, his forces were rapidly disarmed by popular militias. By the end of July, he was left in control of only half the country. The CNT responded by declaring the revolutionary general strike and by calling for the collectivization of the land and factories. For the following ten months the CNT and the FAI were amongst the dominant associations in republican Spain. The anarcho-syndicalists immediately took over the running of Barcelona. As George Orwell observed, most of the active revolutionaries were 'Anarchists with a mistrust of all parliaments'.[16]

Catalunya became virtually an independent republic. A Committee of Anti-Fascist Militias was set up to represent the workers' organizations and various political parties and groupings. But when confronted with the issue of dissolving the Generalitat, the provisional government of Catalunya, the leaders of the CNT-FAI made the crucial decision to leave it intact and support its President Lluis Companys. García Oliver lamely commented: 'The CNT and the FAI decided on collaboration and democracy, renouncing revolutionary totalitarianism which would lead to the strangulation of the revolution by the anarchist and Confederal dictatorship.'[17] Oliver spelt out the dilemma more clearly as a choice 'between Libertarian Communism, which meant anarchist dictatorship, and democracy which meant collaboration'.[18]

The decision to collaborate with the Catalan government however put a break on the further development of the social revolution. Within two months the Committee of the Anti-Fascist Militias was abolished. On 27 September 1936 the anarchist leaders of the CNT-FAI entered the government of the Generalitat, vainly trying to justify their action by referring to it as a Regional Defence Council. They had started down the slippery slide to parliamentary participation. Forgetting their function as delegates, they tried to direct the popular movement. They became mesmerized by the slogan: '*Sacrificamos a todo menos a la victoria!*' (We sacrifice all except victory!) In the long run, the social revolution itself was to be sacrificed for the war against Franco.

But while the CNT leadership rejected an 'anarchist dictatorship' and opted for collaboration with other republican political parties and unions, it still supported the collectivization process. With the co-operation of a large part of the socialist UGT, members of the CNT rapidly collectivized the land and took over factories in the areas under the control of the republican forces. Although short-lived, the successful outcome of the experiment demonstrated triumphantly that workers and peasants can manage their own affairs and that *comunismo libertario* is firmly in the realm of the possible.

The anarchists, like the other factions, formed themselves into militia groups, electing their own officers, and discussing orders before carrying them out. The militia columns may have been somewhat chaotic at first but as the professional soldier Colonel Jimenez de la Beraza observed: 'From a military point of view it is chaos, but it is chaos which works. Don't disturb it!'[19] The lack of military discipline was more than compensated by the initiative and courage of the columns. Orwell asserted that the anarchist militias were 'notoriously the best fighters amongst the purely Spanish forces'.[20]

As he went with papers from the Independent Labour Party, Orwell was drafted into the dissident Communist group POUM (Partido Obrero de Unificación Marxista), and he preferred it to the International Brigades. But he confessed that if he had understood the situation better he would have probably joined the anarchists.[21] Orwell moreover went out of his way to correct the misrepresentations of the anarchists and syndicalists in England and to stress the remarkable achievements of Spanish anarchism at the beginning of the war, especially in Catalunya.[22] Another Englishman, Walter Gregory, was deeply impressed by the anarchists, despite his communist affiliation: 'Their obvious sincerity, dedication and enthusiasm were wonderful to see. No amount of hardship seemed to lessen their deeply held conviction in the natural justice of their cause or the inevitably of its fulfilment.'[23] Yet despite the enthusiasm and bravery of the anarchist militias, after the initial drive of Durruti's column into Aragón, the principal anarchist front became one of the most static of the whole war.

In the country behind the war fronts, the peasants drawing on their own communal traditions collectivized their land in Andalucía, Catalunya, the Levante, Aragón and parts of Castilla immediately after Franco's rebellion in July 1936. By 1937 some three million people were living in rural collectives. In Aragón about three-quarters of the land was managed through the collectives which ranged from a hundred to several thousand members. In Andalucía, before it was overrun by Franco's troops early in the war, many village communes were set up, abolishing money, collectivizing the land, and attempting the direct exchange of goods. They set up plans to eradicate illiteracy and to provide elementary medical services. Free and equal poverty became the ideal. Having experienced centuries of poverty and oppression, they were notable for their austere moral fervour and revolutionary idealism.[24]

In general, the CNT syndicates were turned into popular assemblies of the entire population, often including women and children. The assemblies would elect an administrative committee which would be entirely accountable to the assemblies. Decision making was thus shared between the village or town assemblies and the CNT committees which were concerned with the day-to-day running. They operated through what might be called a system of 'voluntary authority'; no one was forced to join or remain a member of the collective, but was subject to the authority of the general assembly, and in most cases, to the local committees. Regional federations were set up to co-ordinate the collectives.[25]

In most areas, 'individualist' peasants were allowed to cultivate their own plots of land if they preferred and in some areas had consumer tickets printed especially for them. The members of the collectives wanted to persuade people to join them by example and not by force, although the powerful influence of public opinion played a role. Most of the collectives moved towards the communist goal of distribution according to need. New methods of cultivation were tried and overall production of agricultural production increased, despite the loss of labour to the war effort.[26]

In the cities, the CNT continued production with remarkable efficiency, considering the difficulties with supplies and in many cases the loss of the entire management structure and many technicians.[27] In some cases, owners remained but were directed by the elected committees. In Catalunya, which had seventy per cent of Spain's total industry, entire branches of industry (such as textiles and glass) were reorganized into larger units. A war industry, with its chemical plants to back it up, had to be created. In Barcelona, which was the centre of urban collectivization, the public services and industries were taken over and run with great success in such a large and complex city. From July until October 1936, virtually all production and distribution were under workers' control.

Even as late as the summer of 1937, Fenner Brockway, Secretary of the British Independent Labour Party, reported after a visit that it was evident that the CNT was the largest and most vital of the working-class organizations in Spain. He was

> immensely impressed by the constructive revolutionary work which is being done by the CNT. Their achievement of workers' control in industry is an inspiration . . . The Anarchists of Spain, through the CNT, are doing one of the biggest constructive jobs ever done by the working class. At the front they are fighting Fascism. Behind the front they are actually constructing the new Workers' Society. They see that the war against Fascism and the carrying through of the Social Revolution are inseparable.

Brockway also observed that 'the great solidarity that existed among the Anarchists was due to each individual relying on his own strength and not depending on leadership'.[28] In the long run, the anarchists might have lost the war, but their successful collectivization of the land and industry remained their most enduring and constructive achievement.

There were of course difficulties which sympathetic visitors did not always see. Relations between different enterprises were often casual, and some collectives continued to compete as if they were still privately owned. Wages fluctuated in different factories even within the same industry. With the Madrid government refusing to release funds from the gold reserve (the second largest in the world), there was a shortage of capital and materials.

The revolutionary process was halted on 24 October 1936 when the

provisional government of Catalunya, the Generalitat, issued a Collectivization Decree which recognized the collectives, but tried to bring them under
government and not workers' control. It not only checked their further
development but restricted collectivization of industry to those enterprises
employing more than a hundred workers. In privately owned factories a
Workers' Control Committee was established to increase production and
ensure strict discipline. A planning and co-ordinating body called the Economic Council (with powers of compulsion as the ultimate industrial authority) and a Council of Enterprises (with workers' representatives joined by
a 'controller' from the Generalitat) were set up. They both reflected the
drift towards central government control.

Yet for all the restrictions of a wartime economy, Orwell for one was
deeply impressed in Barcelona by the spectacle of a vibrant city where 'the
working class was in the saddle'.[29] Everyday relations were transformed.
Men called each other by the familiar *Tú*.

Women participated on a mass scale in the revolution. In the early part
of the war, they fought alongside men as a matter of course, and took part
in the communal decision-making in the village assemblies. Many wanted
to replace legal marriage with 'free unions' based on mutual trust and
shared responsibility. The more active feminists formed a libertarian group
called Mujeres Libres which worked towards freeing women from their
passivity, ignorance and exploitation and sought a co-operative understanding between men and women. By the end of September 1936 they had
seven labour sections and brigades.[30] The liberation of women however
was only partial: they were often paid a lower rate than men in the collectives; they continued to perform 'women's work'; they saw the struggle
primarily in terms of class and not sex. But in a traditionally Catholic and
patriarchal society, there were undoubtedly new possibilities for women
and they appeared unaccompanied in public for the first time with a new
self-assurance.

The experiment however was short-lived. The CNT-run factories were
unable to provide the militias with the necessary equipment because of the
shortage of raw supplies. They failed to win the support of the majority of
the working class, and their attempt to develop the social revolution was
checked by the war with Franco's army and the struggle with other Republican factions, notably the Communists. In September 1936 the Madrid
paper of the CNT was still insisting that 'the libertarian transformation of
society can only take place as a result of the abolition of the state and the
control of the economy by the working class'.[31] Yet towards the end of
October, as Franco's troops were closing in on Madrid, the CNT in Barcelona agreed with the UGT to accept the need for a unified command,
military discipline, and conscription. It also halted the expropriation of small

proprietors and businesses. The CNT-FAI in Barcelona not only had a Propaganda Bureau in which members were expected to toe the line, but also set up a School for Militants which smacked of vanguard elitism.

The anarchist leaders further checked the social revolution by their collaboration with government. Some joined in November 1936 the Generalitat of Catalunya, with the feeble excuse that it was a regional defence council. Four leaders of the CNT then became ministers in the socialist government of Largo Caballero (known as the 'Spanish Lenin') in December, breaking at a stroke the honoured tradition of abstention from all forms of parliamentary politics. Juan López and Juan Peiró were made Ministers of Commerce and Industry respectively. The FAI militant García Oliver accepted the post of Minister of Justice; he introduced some liberal reforms, but was reduced to defending work camps for political prisoners.

After much agonizing the anarchist intellectual Federica Montseny became Minister of Health even though she had always believed that 'the state could achieve absolutely nothing, that the words Government and Authority meant the negation of any possibility of liberty for individuals and peoples'.[32] The strength of the CNT had always lain in its rejection of the State and political intrigue. It was independent of political parties and committed to the revolution through direct action. In an unparalleled bout of dissimulation, the CNT daily paper *Solidaridad Obrera* declared that, at the very moment its leaders joined Caballero, the government 'as a regulating instrument of the organisms of the State, has ceased to be an oppressive force against the working class, just as the State no longer represents the organism which divides society into classes'.[33]

The leaders of the CNT felt that it had to compromise to obtain foreign aid and to win the war against Franco. But inevitably they were obliged to reinforce the very institutions which they had so vehemently denounced in the past. They checked the collectivization process. They oversaw the transformation of the popular militias into an army. Minister of Justice García Oliver went so far as to tell the students of the new Military School early in 1937: 'Officers of the Popular Army, you must observe an iron discipline and impose it on your men who, once they are under your command, must cease to be your comrades and be simply cogs in the military machine of our army.'[34] The subsequent regimentation and militarization demoralized many of the anarchist militias and workers.

The anarchist participation in government has been described by Vernon Richards as the unavoidable outcome of the FAI's original collaboration with the CNT.[35] Others like Emma Goldman tried to excuse it on grounds of expediency in order to unite the republican forces and to defeat fascism. It certainly demonstrated the constant danger which awaited anarcho-syndicalism if it became involved in parliamentary politics. By the middle of 1937 the greatest anarchist experiment in history was virtually over; it had lasted barely a year.

The Communists increased their influence because the Soviet Union was the sole foreign supplier of arms to the Republican cause, and together with the socialists they began to replace the anarchist committees with municipal government. The militia columns were converted into orthodox brigades with a centralized command structure. On 16 December, 1936, *Pravda* declared: 'As for Catalunya, the purging of the Trotskyists and Anarcho-syndicalists has begun; it will be conducted with the same energy with which it was conducted in the USSR.' A Communist-controlled secret police, based on the Cheka model, began a reign of terror. By the end of April 1937 open hostilities were taking place between the members of the Partido Socialista Unificat de Catalunya (PSUC – the combined Socialist and Communist Parties of Catalunya) and the supporters of the CNT who were joined by the dissident Marxist group POUM.

Fighting broke out in Barcelona in early May, when the Communist-controlled police attacked the Telephone Building of Barcelona which was in the hands of the CNT. The street battles which followed left four hundred people dead, including the Italian anarchist intellectual Camillo Berneri. A group calling themselves the Friends of Durruti (who had been shot in the back in mysterious circumstances) criticized the capitulation of the CNT leadership and called for a fresh revolution led by an elected Revolutionary Junta to manage the war and to supervise revolutionary order, propaganda, and international affairs while the unions dealt with the economic affairs with an Economic Council. They argued that 'the revolution needs organisms to oversee it, and repress, in an organised sense, hostile sectors'.[36]

By this stage however they were a voice in the revolutionary wilderness, and the Federación Ibérica de Juventudes Libertarias (FIJL – Iberian Federation of Libertarian Youth) and the Regional Committee of the CNT rejected the call. The government however with the support of the PSUC put down the anarchist resistance. Strict censorship was imposed. It marked the end of anarchist ascendancy in Catalunya. The conflict between the anarchists and Communists was to prove one of the principal causes of the defeat of the republican forces.

Largo Caballero's government fell directly after the 'May Days'. It was replaced by Juan Negrin's government which was even more strongly influenced by the Stalinists; one of its first acts was to declare POUM illegal. It was argued that the war demanded the concentration of the authority of the State. This attitude came to the foremost in the Extended National Economic Plenum of January 1938, the first full gathering of the CNT since the Zaragoza Conference in 1936. It accepted the need for work inspectors, work norms, and workers' cards. Censorship of the CNT press was approved to prevent public disagreements. It was even agreed to form an Executive Committee of the CNT, FAI and FIJL.

Soon after the meeting the CNT formed a pact with the UGT, over which the Socialist leader Luis Araquistina said 'Bakunin and Marx would embrace'. It was however never implemented and at least the Barcelona anarchist weekly *Tierra y Libertad* had the clarity of thought to point out:

> There is 'embrace' for a common revolutionary upheaval. But authority and freedom, the State and Anarchism, dictatorship and the free federation of peoples, remain irreconcilably antagonistic until such a time as we all will understand that no real union is possible except by the free choice of the people.[37]

At a national congress held in October 1938 attended by delegates from the CNT, the FAI and the FIJL, the secretary-general of the CNT argued that it was the refusal of his comrades to accept militarism from the start which was responsible for the mess they were in. The movement reaffirmed its belief in decentralization and workers' control but Franco's victory soon made their realization impossible. Half a million Spaniards went into exile. The anarchist groups formed a Movimiento Libertario Español (Spanish Libertarian Movement) which mulled over what had gone wrong in exile.

The defeat of the anarchist movement in Spain did not result from a failure of anarchist theory and tactics but rather a failure to carry through the social revolution. If the latter had not been sacrificed for the war effort, and the Communists had not seized power, the outcome may well have been very different.

After Franco's death, the CNT re-emerged in Spain in 1976 as a vigorous force in the trade-union movement, but it is the socialist UGT who now makes the running.[38] The new CNT is still a loose association of *sindicatos* administered by committees, unpaid officers, and dedicated workers. The programme of the 1936 Zaragoza Congress with its commitment to *comunismo libertario* remains its goal. Their numbers are small but their idealism is intact, as old veterans pass on their experience to new generations of workers and students.

For a time, the CNT seemed poised to become a considerable force in the labour movement once again. Unfortunately the movement split, after the Sixth National Congress in 1983, into two factions – the CNT-AIT (Asociación Internacional de Trabajadores) and the CGT (Confederación General de Trabajadores) – one broadly revolutionary, the other more reformist. These wings have been locked in a dispute over who owns the historical assets of the confederation which had been seized by Franco's State. The CGT has taken on board social ecology, and now calls itself an anarcho-syndicalist trade union that struggles for a libertarian society, and 'a future in which neither the person nor the planet is exploited'.

Spanish anarchists were cheered by the appearance of anarchist ideas and tactics briefly during the Portuguese Revolution in the early 1970s.[39] But few believe that revolution is possible in post-Franco Spain, increasingly entrenched as it is in the European Community. As elsewhere in Europe, anarchism finds its chief expression in the campaign for workers' control and self-management, in the counter-culture, in the peace and green movements and in the anti-capitalist and anti-globalization campaigns.

Russia
and the Ukraine

ALTHOUGH RUSSIA PRODUCED THREE of the greatest anarchist thinkers in Bakunin, Kropotkin and Tolstoy, they had remarkably little influence in their own country. The anarchist movement started in Russia late and remained small. Only in the mid 1890s did it really get under way and not until the Russian Revolution did anarchists play a significant part. At the same time, early Russian socialism was remarkably libertarian.

The State in Russia hardly reached many parts of the empire, and was mainly recognizable outside the towns in the form of the soldier, policeman and taxman. It was generally considered an unnecessary and unwelcome burden. Russian peasants moreover had lived for centuries in autonomous communities (*obshchina*), working their land in common and managing their affairs through village councils, *mir*. Disputes were solved through arbiters and juries. They had no need for laws; they arranged their transactions through custom and followed their own consciences.

The Russian revolutionary tradition tended to take an anti-Statist form from the beginning. The great peasant revolts led by Stenka Razin and Pugachev in the seventeenth and eighteenth centuries were directed against the interference of central authority and sought a decentralized and egalitarian society. In the 1830s Konstantin Aksakov and his fellow Slavophiles were hostile not only to the St Petersburg State but to Statism in general, even though they looked for an ideal autocracy to replace it.

Amongst Russian intellectuals, Alexander Herzen in the 1840s began to spread Proudhon's ideas in radical circles in Moscow, rejecting both utopian and Jacobin socialism. He looked to the *mir* as the fundamental organism of a transformed Russia. Bakunin's influence was indirect and desultory in the Russian revolutionary movement, and like Herzen his message reached his homeland chiefly through Russian *emigrés*.

The first Russian anarchist organization was formed in Switzerland as a section of Bakunin's International Brotherhood in the late sixties. It managed to print in 1873 a number of pamphlets in Russian, as well as Bakunin's *Statism and Anarchy*. Bakunin also collaborated at the time with Nicholas Zhukovsky on the journal *Narodnoe Delo* (People's Cause), calling for a collectivist and anarchist revolution in order to bring about a voluntary federation of workers' *artels* and peasant *mirs*. But the journal was soon taken over by the anti-Bakuninist Russian section of the International.

In the 1870s the publications of the Revolutionary Community of Russian Anarchists, set up in Geneva by Zhukovsky and friends in 1873, were the only ones to be widely circulated in Russia. In 1878 they brought out *Obschina* (Community) which rejected constitutional government and insisted that the peasants and workers must emancipate themselves. But their influence remained infinitesimal.

The move towards terrorism in the Russian revolutionary movement reached its apogee in the assassination of Tsar Alexander II in 1881 by the Narodnaya Volya (People's Will). In the repression which followed, the Russian Social Revolutionary Party emerged to gain considerable support amongst the peasants. It was not until the 1890s that the first openly anarchist groups in Russia appeared and the works of Bakunin and Kropotkin began to be circulated. From his exile, Kropotkin contributed to the anarchist journal *Khleb i Volya*. But at the time of the 1905 Revolution the anarchists groups still remained tiny, completely overshadowed by the Social Revolutionary Party in the country and by the Social Democratic Party in the cities.

The outbreak of the October 1905 Revolution surprised many revolutionaries. It seemed to confirm anarchist tactics of the general strike and their faith in spontaneous revolution. When the revolution failed the Social Democrats were discredited, but the anarchists gained support. During the subsequent years of repression, new groups formed in the larger towns, especially in the Urals and the Ukraine. Anarcho-syndicalism too began to make rapid headway. For the first time in Russian history the anarchists were a force to be reckoned with. Lenin, Trotsky and their supporters were sufficiently concerned to make sure that the Second International in 1907 voted for the exclusion of the followers of Bakunin and Kropotkin.

When the Revolution broke out in February 1917, the anarchists still only formed a small minority on the Left, compared to the Social Revolutionaries and the Social Democrats. The anarchists were divided amongst themselves into syndicalists, anarcho-communists, Tolstoyans and individualists. But when the Revolution broke out, workers and peasants started spontaneously to form soviets, and they seized their chance. Throughout Russia people were calling for the traditional libertarian demands of Russian populism: land and liberty, bread and justice for all, with production organized through industrial and agricultural collectives.

Few anarchist organizations existed in Russia at the time, but in Moscow at least there was a small federation of anarchist groups. The writer V. M. Eikhenbaum, better-known as Volin, returned from America and joined the Union for Anarcho-Syndicalist Propaganda in St Petersburg and helped edit its daily paper *Golos Truda* (The Voice of Labour), which

became the most influential of its type. His *nom de guerre* Volin was formed
from the Russian *volia* meaning 'freedom'.[1] He was involved in setting up
one of the first soviets. Trotsky later wrote without irony: 'The activity of
the soviet represented the organization of anarchy. Its existence and its
subsequent development the consolidation of anarchy.'[2] Towards the end
of 1918 a Confederation of Anarchist Organizations called *Nabat* (Alarm)
was formed in Kharkov, also with the help of Volin; it offered a social model
of 'communist anarchism' different from those of both the Whites and the
Reds. Needless to say, both tried to ban it.

A few anarchists from the beginning opposed the slogan 'All Power to
the Soviets!' because they were against the concept of power as such. Most
of them however threw themselves behind the call since they hoped to
transform the soviets into genuine organs of direct democracy for the
workers and peasants, and to develop them in a libertarian direction. A
whole 'unknown revolution' did in fact get underway with the decentralization of authority, the creation of autonomous communes and councils, and
the development of self-management in factory and farm.[3] Apart from the
worker and peasant movements throughout Russia, anarchist women played
an important role on the barricades as well as in creating free schools,
day-care centres, and a libertarian atmosphere in the family.

The initial euphoria soon evaporated. Volin wrote prophetically at the
end of 1917 in *Golos Truda*:

> Once their power has been consolidated and legalized, the Bolsheviks,
> as state socialists, that is as men who believe in centralized and authori-
> tarian leadership – will start running the life of the country and the
> people from the top. Your soviets ... will gradually become simple
> tools of central government ... You will soon see the inauguration of
> an authoritarian political and state apparatus that will crush all oppo-
> sition with an iron fist ... 'All power to the Soviets' will become 'All
> power to the leaders of the party'.[4]

Leninist ideology, with its concept of a vanguard party leading the masses
and its commitment to the dictatorship of the proletariat, was directly
opposed to the syndicalist principle established by the inaugural declaration
of the IWMA that 'The emancipation of the workers must be brought about
by the workers themselves'. The Bolsheviks moreover had no appreciation
of the anarchist idea that socialism must be free or it will not be at all.
Lenin however was sufficiently astute to realize that in order to achieve
power, he would have to rely at first on the masses and to develop their
aspirations. On the eve of the October Revolution, he therefore wrote the
libertarian-sounding *State and Revolution*, and advocated workers' management. He even praised the anarchists for criticizing parliamentarism and

for describing the opportunist character of most socialist parties in their attitude to the State. At this stage, he sought to forge an alliance with the anarchists by arguing that Marx and Proudhon both stood 'for the "smashing" of the present state machine' and that the opportunists were unwilling to accept the similarity between Marxism and anarchism (of both Proudhon and Bakunin). He even went so far as to castigate Plekhanov for his clumsy depiction of anarchists as 'bandits'.[5] As a result, the Marxists and anarchists between March and October 1917 were able to struggle side by side in their call for the distribution of the land to the peasants and the occupation of factories by the workers.

The Bolsheviks seemed at first prepared to subordinate their Marxist theory to anarchist practice by calling for the redistribution of land and dismantling of the bourgeois State. Although their organizations numbered only twelve thousand active members, the anarchists wielded considerable influence from 1917 to 1918 through their press and their work in the soviets. There were two weeklies in Petrograd and a daily in Moscow, each appearing in twenty-five thousand copies. According to one visitor, they represented the 'most active party, the most combative, and probably the most popular of the opposition groups'.[6]

Many anarchists took an active part in the October Revolution and four anarchists actually sat on the Military-Revolutionary Committee. Some like Anatolii Zhelezniakov remained anarchists to the end; others like Victor Serge became converted to the Bolshevik cause. At the beginning of 1918, Lenin told the Third Congress of Soviets that 'Anarchist ideas have now taken on living form'. At the Trade Union Congress in the spring of 1918, he even borrowed anarchist terminology to describe the factories as the 'self-governing communes of producers and consumers'.

But the delicate alliance between the Bolsheviks and the anarchists was only temporary. It soon became clear that Lenin and the Bolsheviks wanted to centralize power for themselves and to gain control over the people. They were happy to use libertarian language only if it suited their own ends. Despite its libertarian tone, Lenin had made clear in *State and Revolution* that it was necessary in a transitional period to establish the 'dictatorship of the proletariat' in a 'proletarian' State in order to crush the resistance of the bourgeoisie. By March, the Bolshevik Party had become the sole party in Russia. It used the Civil War and the threat of foreign invasion as its excuse for the clamp-down; it started to confiscate grain from the peasants and to suppress its opponents. Lenin did not balk at using mass terror to consolidate his power.

In the following month, a detachment of the Red Guards and of the Cheka, the newly formed political police force, raided anarchist circles in Moscow, arresting several hundred people. They were denounced as common criminals and bandits, 'the armed detachments of counter-revolutionary burglars and robbers which had taken refuge under the black flag of anarchy'.[7] It marked the turning-point: from the spring of 1918 the anarchists stopped being reluctant allies of the Bolsheviks and became their bitter enemies. Within three years, the Bolsheviks had succeeded in wiping out by military means the anarchist movement completely. Emma Goldman and Alexander Berkman, who had returned in 1920 after being deported from America and had swallowed their initial reservations for the cause of the social revolution, left in 1921 deeply disillusioned by their experience.

Only in the Ukraine, under the inspiration of Nestor Makhno, did the anarchist cause make any further head way. After the October Revolution, he took the initiative in organizing an area of some four hundred square miles with a rough population of seven million into an autonomous region. The factories were occupied and the collectives had to co-ordinate their production; Makhno even managed to negotiate a direct exchange of grain for textiles produced by anarchist workers in Moscow. For more than a year, anarchists were in charge of a large territory, one of the few examples of anarchy in action on a large scale in modern history.

The great libertarian experiment was under threat from the beginning. Makhno was obliged to fight Reds and Whites, Ukrainian nationalists, and the Germans and Austrians who had been given control of the Ukraine under the Treaty of Brest-Litovsk with Germany in March 1918 by the Bolshevik government.

When he visited Moscow in June 1918, Lenin received him at the Kremlin. The Bolshevik leader complained of the 'empty fanaticism' of most anarchists, and he declared to Makhno 'if only one-third of the anarchists-communists were like you, we Communists would be ready, under certain conditions, to join with them in working towards a free organization of producers.'[8] After denying that the anarchists were utopian dreamers, Makhno returned to the Ukraine.

By September his partisan army had captured the regional capital Gulyai-Polye from the Austrians. Even under war conditions, the social revolution was continued. In the areas under Makhno's sway, 'communes' or 'free-work soviets' were set up. When they passed through a district, his partisans would put up posters announcing:

> The freedom of the workers and the peasants is their own, and not subject to any restriction. It is up to the workers and peasants themselves to act, to organize themselves, to agree among themselves in all aspects of their lives, as they themselves see fit and desire ... The Makhnovists can do no more than give aid and counsel ... In no circumstances can they, nor do they wish to, govern.[9]

The land was tilled in common and affairs managed by temporary delegates elected by the commune. Each commune had as much land as it could cultivate without hired labour. The commune was merely the executive of the decisions of the peasants in a locality. Groups of producers were federated into districts, and districts into regions. Free assembly, free speech and a free press were declared. It was planned to develop a form of libertarian education and in place of traditional courts it was proposed that 'Law and order must be upheld by the living force of the local community and must not be left to police specialists.'[10]

From November 1918 to June 1919 Makhno and his supporters thus helped set up a society based on communes which went far in achieving the anarchist vision of a free society in the region east of the Dnieper.[11] In January, February and April of 1919, they held a series of Regional Congresses of Peasants, Workers and Insurgents to discuss economic and military matters, and elected a Regional Military Revolutionary Council. In practice, they formed the beginning of a loose-knit government, and authority emanated from Makhno and his staff, accountable though they were in theory.

However sincere his anarchist beliefs, Makhno was no theorist and his movement lacked intellectuals, even though it was joined by Peter Arshinov (who had been Makhno's anarchist mentor in jail) and Volin. Makhno himself was primarily a military leader, and the *bat'ko*, as his comrades called him, sometimes succumbed to the dictatorial antics of a warrior chief. But he was more than a primitive rebel, or libertarian Robin Hood, for while the roots of his anarchism lay in the rough-and-ready democracy of the Cossack peasants, he consciously tried to put anarchist theory into practice.

At first, the army was organized on a libertarian and voluntary basis, with the rules of discipline drawn up by elected commissions and then voted on by general assemblies of the partisans. In the end, however, Makhno resorted to a voluntary mobilization which amounted to conscription to swell his Revolutionary Insurrectionary Army to some fifteen thousand troops.

Alarmed by the growing influence of the Makhnovist movement, the Bolshevik government tried to reach an agreement with Makhno in 1920. He insisted that in the area in which the Makhnovist army was operating 'the worker and peasant populations shall create its own free institutions for economic and self-administration; these institutions shall be autonomous and linked federally by agreements with the governing organs of the Soviet Republics'. In April 1919, the Third Regional Council met despite being banned by the Soviet authorities, and invited delegates from the Red Army. This was clearly too much for the Bolshevik government. After

Makhno's army had defeated the White Army under General Wrangel in October 1920, the Bolsheviks finally ordered his units to be absorbed into the Red Army under the supreme command of Trotsky. Makhno resisted. The officers of the Crimean Makhnovist army were then arrested while attending a joint military council and shot in November 1920. Makhno managed to fight on for another nine months against hopeless odds until August 1921. He went into exile – slandered as a bandit and a pogromist by the Bolsheviks – and died of poverty and drink in Paris.

Although the anarchist experiment in the Ukraine was unable to last in the exceptional conditions of civil war and repression, it proved to be the first major historical example of constructive anarchy in action. Wherever they went, Makhno's partisans carried the black flag of anarchy at their head, embroidered with 'Liberty or Death' and 'The Land to the Peasants, the Factories to the Workers'.

As for the workers' and peasants' soviets in the rest of Russia, they were taken over, centralized and organized from the top down by the Bolsheviks. In December 1917 a Supreme Economic Council was set up to direct industry and in the following May industry as a whole was collectivized and nationalized by decree. At the Congress of Factory Councils in June 1918, Lenin declared; 'You must become basic cells of the State'. The councils rapidly became subject to the directives of the government and the Bolshevik party, and the unions were turned mainly into tame organs for disciplining the work-force. The German anarcho-syndicalist Augustin Souchy observed after his visit in 1920 that the soviets were already being elected on a partisan basis, and that in the villages the administrative delegates were behaving like the former landowners.[12] The All-Russian Congress of Anarchists which was planned to take place at he end of 1920 never materialized; the Cheka rounded up members of the Nabat Confederation, including Volin, in Kharkov.

Even the communist Alexandra Kollantai complained of the loss of initiative which followed the economic centralization and the dismantling of the collectives. She was a member of the group within the Bolshevik Party called the 'Workers' Opposition' which called for a return to the democracy of the original soviets. At the Tenth Party Congress in November 1920, Lenin accused the 'Workers' Opposition' of 'petty-bourgeois and anarchist deviations' and declared that their 'syndicalism' and 'semi-anarchism' were a direct danger to the Revolution. Henceforth there was to be 'unquestioning obedience to the orders of individual representatives of the Soviet government during work time', as well as 'iron discipline while at work, with unquestioning obedience to the will of a single person, the Soviet leader'.[13] As Lenin told Alexander Berkman in no uncertain words: 'Liberty is a luxury not to be permitted at the present stage of development.'[14] There was to be no opposition to his one-party State and centralized economy.

In his *Message to the Workers of the West*, Kropotkin pointed out in 1920 that Russia had shown the way in which Socialism cannot be realized:

> so long as the country is dominated by the dictatorship of a party, the workers' and peasants' councils naturally lose their significance. They are thereby degraded to the same passive role which the representatives of the estates used to play at the time of the absolute monarchies.

He concluded that the attempt 'to build a communist republic on the basis of a strongly centralized state, under the iron law of the dictatorship of one party, has ended in a terrible fiasco. Russia teaches us how not to impose communism.[15]

Just before he died Kropoktin also wrote that the Russian Revolution

> is perpetrating horrors. It is ruining the whole country. In its mad fury it is annihilating human lives. That is why it is a revolution and not a peaceful progress, because it is destroying without regarding what it destroys and wither it goes. And we are powerless for the present to direct it into another channel, until such a time as it will have played itself out. It must wear itself out.[16]

When Kropotkin died in February 1921, it was the last time that the anarchists' black flag was carried amongst the red ones through the streets of Moscow in an immense funeral convoy of a hundred thousand people.

The last glimmer of hope for the anarcho-syndicalists and anarchists in Russia was in the uprising of the Petrograd sailors and workers in March 1921 at the Kronstadt fortress two weeks after Kropotkin's death. The sailors had played a heroic role in October 1917 – Trotsky had called them the 'pride and glory of the Russian Revolution' – and although their ranks had been swelled by peasants they were still considered the revolutionary vanguard of the Navy. The mutiny was primarily an attempt to renew the revolution and restore the original Soviet idea in face of the Bolshevik dictatorship and the centralization of 'War Communism'.

Sixteen thousand sailors, workers and soldiers attended a meeting held on 1 March 1921. The rebels condemned the usurpation of power by the Bolshevik government. They called for new elections for the Soviets by secret ballot, liberty for the trade unions, and the release of political prisoners. Their programme also included the call for 'Freedom of speech and press to workers and peasants, to anarchists and left socialist parties' (though not for Mensheviks).[17] Some anarchists called the Kronstadt rebellion the 'Third Revolution'.

Although the Kronstadt rebels insisted that they wanted to work within the framework of the Revolution, the Bolshevik government refused to negotiate. Following the great Leningrad strikes of January and February, they were in no mood for compromise. At the Tenth Congress of the Bolshevik Party in March 1921 the New Economic Policy was adopted which met most of the rebels' economic demands, but the Party refused to make terms with the Workers' Opposition. Soon afterwards an ultimatum to the rebels in Kronstadt appeared on billboards over the signature of Lenin and Trotsky: 'Surrender or Be Shot Like Rabbits!' The mutiny was labelled an anarchist conspiracy, and the sailors treated as White Guards. The rebels were ruthlessly suppressed by the Red Army and the Chekà under Trotsky's orders. Trotsky boasted soon after: 'At last the Soviet government, with an iron broom, has rid Russia of anarchism.'[18]

By the end of 1921, Goldman and Berkman had decided to leave Russia. The latter wrote in his diary: 'The revolution is dead; its spirit cries in the wilderness'.[19] It became clear to anarchists inside and outside Russia that the Bolsheviks had become the chief adversary of the social revolution in the country. Gaston Leval who went with the Spanish delegation to the Third Congress of the Communist International held in Moscow in the summer of 1921 returned to France to argue that the 'dictatorship of the proletariat' had become a dictatorship *over* the proletariat.[20] The result, anticipated so forcefully by Bakunin, was that the Bolshevik revolution made in the name of Marxism had degenerated into a form of State capitalism which operated in the interests of a new bureaucratic and managerial class. Rocker later observed that the dictatorship of the proletariat had become a new Russian 'commissar-ocracy'.[21]

After 1925 no anarchist activity was allowed in the Soviet Union. Russian exiles in Paris launched the controversial 'Organizational Platform' which called for a general union of anarchists with a central executive committee to co-ordinate policy and action, but although it was supported by Arshinov and Makhno, Volin and others argued that its central committee was not in keeping with the anarchist stress on local initiative. It failed to get off the ground. As for Kropotkin, his revolutionary and scientific reputation was stressed in his homeland but his political works were banned; in 1938 the Kropotkin Museum was symbolically closed. Anarchists were dismissed in official publications as bandits or irresponsible hotheads. The only good anarchist was one who had been saved miraculously by the Communist Party. During Stalin's purges, Solzhenitsyn came across several young anarchists in the Gulag Archipelago. In the forties and fifties a few

Tolstoyans were known to be in the camps, and Khrushchev had to deal with some Ukrainian Makhnovists.[22]

In the late seventies, clandestine groups distributed *samizdat* texts by Bakunin, Kropotkin, Tolstoy and Cohn-Bendit. Since the rise to power of Gorbachev and the era of *glasnost*, there has been a sudden revival of libertarian ideas and goals. On the Left, the cry for 'All Power to the Soviets!' has gone up.

In 1987 the anarcho-syndicalist monthly *Obshchina* began to appear in Moscow, and in 1989 the Confederation of Anarcho-Syndicalists (KAS) was founded, chiefly by young students and teachers. In 1990 it claimed some five hundred members and three thousand supporters. Those members see anarchy as the maximum realization of human freedom, and place themselves in the non-violent tradition pioneered by Tolstoy and Gandhi. Its membership mainly centres on Russia and the Ukraine, and, to a lesser extent, Siberia. As yet, it has not attracted much support in the smaller republics whose immediate goal is national autonomy. A much smaller anarchist-communist revolutionary union – AKRU – has also emerged, calling for the violent overthrow of the State.

The issues of the dominant part played by the State in steering the economy and the leading role of the Communist Party in society are clearly on the political agenda once again. Anarchist plans for decentralization and federalism are now proposed as a dam to stem the rising nationalism in the peripheral republics. Following the revolutions of 1989–90 in what was the Eastern bloc of the Soviet empire, communist imperialism is collapsing; the centre cannot hold. The Soviet Union itself has now followed suit.

The main call has been for social democracy in a multi-party State, but for some the centralized State is the principal obstacle to progress. The Soviet Union may well end up as a loose federation of autonomous republics, a model of organization for that region once imagined by Bakunin over a century ago. During the May Day Parade in Moscow in 1990, a large group – with placards declaring 'Let the Communist Party Live at Chernobyl' and 'Down with the Empire and Red Fascism' – eventually forced the leadership to leave the platform. After the failed coup of August 1991, the Communist Party itself committed hara-kiri. Anarchism, apparently destroyed by the Bolsheviks in the early twenties, is now re-emerging from the ashes of the Stalinist system.

Northern Europe

Germany

DESPITE THE MYTH THAT the German character is intrinsically authoritarian and given to State worship, Germany has produced some remarkable libertarian thinkers and its own lively anarchist movement. The forerunners of the movement may be traced to Wilhelm von Humboldt who drew narrowly at the time of the French Revolution the *Limits of State Action* (1792). In the 1840s Max Stirner opposed the prevailing barrel organ of Hegelianism and attacked all absolute abstractions, including the society and the State, in the name of the unique individual. Nietzsche too in the second half of the century mounted a devastating philosophical assault against the German State and culture and celebrated the creativity of the fully developed individual.

Although Stirner had virtually no influence on the labour movement other social thinkers in the 1840s were moving towards a libertarian form of socialism. The first anarchist journal published in German, *Berliner Monatsschrift*, appeared in Mannheim in 1844, with Stirner and Edgar Bauer among the contributors.

Wilhelm Weitling, influenced by Fourier and Saint-Simon, advocated in *Guarantees of Harmony and Freedom* (1842) a 'harmonious' communist society without property and the wage system, although like Fourier's utopia it remained somewhat regimented. When Weitling left for the United States in 1849, he moved closer to Proudhon's mutualism and became primarily concerned with setting up a Bank of Exchange. Weitling had an important influence on Bakunin; the latter quoted to Arnold Ruge his declaration that 'the perfect society has no government, but only an administration, no laws but only obligations, no punishments, but means of correction'.[1] Arnold Ruge himself was a Left-Hegelian who favoured federalism in Germany.

Another German Proudhonist was Karl Grün, who kept the French thinker informed of developments in Germany. He wrote the first work *The Social Movement in France and Belgium* (1844) which spread Proudhon's ideas in Germany. He translated Proudhon's *Philosophy of Poverty*, although he went beyond his mentor to denounce the wage system and to argue that production and distribution should result from the free choice of the individual. Not surprisingly, Marx dismissed Grün as a 'literary hack'.

Moses Hess called Proudhon's system 'anarchy' in *The Philosophy of the Deed* and in *Socialism and Communism* (both 1843). Like Proudhon and Bakunin (whom he knew), Hess rejected organized religion and the State. Yet while stressing the importance of individual inclinations, he called in an unanarchist way for national workshops and universal suffrage.

Wagner joined Bakunin on the barricades in the Dresden uprising in April 1849. He shared Bakunin's apocalyptic vision and in *Volksblatter* declared that 'the old world is in ruins from which a new world will arise'. He considered revolution to be 'ever-rejuvenating ever-creating life' which will destroy 'the domination of one over many ... the power of the Almighty, of law, of property'.[2] He called for an ideal community made up of natural alliances or associations brought about for the sole purpose of satisfying common need. At this stage, Wagner seemed explicitly anarchist and Johann Most later quoted approvingly his view that:

> Freedom means not to suffer authority that is against our purpose and desire ... Only were we to consider ourselves ignorant and without will could we believe useful an authority that showed us the right thought and purpose. To tolerate an authority that we realize does not know and do right is slavery.[3]

After the failure of the 1848–9 revolutions in several German States, there followed the dissolution of the German Confederation and the unification of the German State under Bismarck. During this period anarchism in its Stirnerite or Proudhonian form had virtually no impact. The German delegates during the early years of the First International supported Lassalle and Marx, not the anti-authoritarian groups inspired by Proudhon and Bakunin. In 1876–7 the journal *Die Arbeiter-Zeitung*, which numbered Kropotkin among its editors, was published in Bern and had some influence, especially in southern Germany. In the 1880s anarchism began to make further ground in the German socialist movement, especially within the German Social Democratic Party.

Johann Most played a significant role. A former member of the Reichstag, Most became a social revolutionary and was eventually forced into political exile. He began publishing *Freiheit* from London in 1879, but moved to New York, taking the journal with him, in 1882. Most soon became an anarchist and exported his message back to his homeland.

Anarchism at this time failed to inspire a mass movement in Germany and won over only a few small groups in Berlin and Hamburg. There was however one abortive attempt to blow up the Kaiser and his princes when they opened the National Monument at Rudesheim on the Rhine in 1883. A young compositor called August Reinsdorf was condemned to death for the attempt; on going to his execution, he declared: 'Down with barbarism! Long live Anarchy!'[4] Shortly before he was executed, a police officer called Rumpff was murdered and a young German anarchist, Julius Lieske, arrested and decapitated. Lieske was one of a team of three who had prepared the assassination, although the Bohemian anarchist August Peschmann committed the deed itself.

At the time, anarchism was making a much greater impact in Austria, Bohemia and Hungary: the radical wing of the Austro-Hungarian labour movement were deeply imbued with anarchist ideas. Joseph Peukert with his paper *Die Zukunft* also exerted an influence alongside Most's *Freiheit*. The violent confrontations between anarchist and socialist workers and the police reached a climax in January 1884 when a state of siege was declared in Vienna. In the repression which followed, anarchist activists engaged in criminal activities were executed and Peukert left the country. Nevertheless, a few scattered anarchist groups survived in the Austrian Empire. The writers Jaroslav Hašek and Franz Kafka were both exposed to anarchist ideas in the bohemian circles of Prague before the First World War. Kropotkin's memoirs became one of Kafka's favourite books.

After 1884, it has been argued that anarchist ideas in Germany virtually vanished.[5] But this is too severe a judgement. A group called Die Jungen (The Young Ones) developed about 1889 inside the Social Democratic Party; members included Rudolf Rocker, Bernhard Kampffmeyer (the future founder of the German Garden City movement), and Max Baginski, who eventually became editor of the *Chicagoer Arbeiter-Zeitung* and one of Emma Goldman's lovers. Their paper *Der Sozialist* turned expressly anarchist after Gustav Landauer became one of its editors.

Syndicalism also gained a foothold when a group calling themselves Localists formed a parallel grouping around 1892 within the Social Democratic trade unions and formed their own federation in 1897 called the Frei Vereinigung Deutscher Gewerkschaften. Before the First World War, they cut their ties with the German Social Democratic Party and rejected parliamentary politics like their French counterparts in the CGT. The federation was renamed the Frei Arbeiter Union at a congress in Dusseldorf in 1919 and became more distinctly anarcho-syndicalist. In the early revolutionary twenties, it grew fast and claimed a membership of 120,000 at the International Syndicalist Congress held in Berlin in 1923; the journal *Der Syndikalist* had for some time between 150,000 and 180,000 subscribers.[6] The syndicalist movement began to weaken with the rise to power of the Nazis, and in 1933 it suffered the same fate as other left-wing organizations in Germany.

Apart from the influence of anarchism on the labour movement, Stirner's and Nietzsche's ideas became fashionable in literary and artistic circles in the 1890s. Germany also produced in Gustav Landauer at the turn of the century the most important anarchist thinker in the country after Stirner. After joining the Berlin *Der Sozialist* as one of its editors, he attacked State socialism and called for a renewal of the organic community. He wanted to create, not to destroy – to develop alternative communities alongside or outside the State so that it would become obsolete. In general, he was opposed to indiscriminate violence – 'every act of force is dictatorship' – but not to revolution. His revolution was not merely directed to changing social structures but to transforming everyday life itself.

Landauer's form of anarchism was not very influential at the time, partly because of the 'literary' nature of his language. But he was directly involved in one of the most notable episodes in theh history of German anarchism during the Weimar Republic. In the Bavarian Revolution of 1918–1919, he became a 'minister of education' in the week-long Munich Council Republic which wanted to create a free and independent Bavaria. With the help of the anarchist poet Erich Mühsam, he also tried to organize 'Revolutionary Workers' Councils'. But it was crushed by troops sent from Berlin, and in the aftermath Landauer was murdered. Mühsam was sentenced to fifteen years' hard labour; though he was released in 1924, he was murdered in a Nazi concentration camp ten years later.

With the rise of Nazism the German anarchist movement was destroyed. The cause however was kept alive by Rudolf Rocker, a bookbinder born in Mainz in South Germany, who went into exile in 1892. At the beginning of 1895, he left for England, where he chose to live amongst the Jewish community in the East End of London and edited the anarchist journal in Yiddish *Arbeter Fraint*. After being interned during the First World War as an enemy alien, he was deported in 1918 back to Germany where he became a leading figure in the German syndicalist movement, and initiated the founding of the syndicalist International (IWMA), which was set up in Berlin in 1922. He expounded the principles of anarcho-syndicalism, took up the cause of the Spanish anarchists during the Spanish Revolution, and in his most important book explored the link between *Nationalism and Culture* (1937). By his principled stand against Nazism, Rocker provided the link between the old anarchist movement in Germany and the new.

After the Second World War, there was a small but ideologically influential anarchist movement. East Germany groaned under a communist dictatorship which allowed no libertarian dissent, but in West Germany, in the early sixties, the New Left took on a libertarian aura. By the late sixties, the West German student movement had entirely rejected the old Marxist myths of class struggle and in Rudi Dutschke found an eloquent exponent of anti-authoritarian struggle against bureaucracy and the State. In France, the German-born Daniel Cohn-Bendit became a student leader during the 1968 rebellion and took a distinctly anarchistic stand.

Like many German libertarians, Cohn-Bendit later joined the Green movement. Despite the parliamentary success of the German Green Party, there is a deepening rift between the libertarian 'fundos' who reject much of parliamentary politics and call for fundamental change and the 'realists' who seek political compromise. It is a split which resembles that of the German Social Democratic Party towards the end of the nineteenth century.

While the anarchist movement remains heterogeneous and fragmented, the ideas of anarchism are kept alive in a few journals, including the umbrella *Schwarzer Faden*, the anarcho-syndicalistic *Direkte Aktion* of the Frei Arbeiter Union (FAU), and the pacifist *Graswurzelrevolution*. The FAU was partly reinvigorated by Spanish 'guest-workers', but because the German State bars its members from holding jobs in the public sector, its work has mainly been in education and propaganda. The collapse of the Iron Curtain in 1989 and the subsequent reunification of Germany released a surge of libertarian hopes, but they may well be channelled to capitalist rather than anarchist ends. In the early 1990s, nationalism and authoritarianism were more visible revenants than the inheritors of the German anarchist legacy, although the latter are showing renewed vigour in the new century.

Sweden and Norway

Elsewhere in Northern Europe, anarchism never found fertile ground like it did in the south except in Sweden and Holland. In Sweden, anarchists joined the Social Democratic Party in the 1880s as in Germany but were expelled in 1891. They then worked in the growing labour movement. By 1909, the Swedish anarcho-syndicalists were numerous enough to break away to form their own federation Sveriges Arbetares Central (SAC) on the French CGT pattern. By 1922 it had 32,000 members while its counterpart in Norway – Norsk Syndikalistik Federasjon – had 20,000. But while the Norwegian federation fell away, the SAC has continued with its daily paper as a significant force within the Swedish labour movement and has helped maintain the syndicalist International Working Men's Association. Although they have accepted a form of collective bargaining, the Swedish syndicalists still keep clear of political activity and defend the local syndicates as the centres of union power.

Holland

Holland has developed one of the most original anarchist movements in Europe. In the first International the Dutch delegates supported Bakunin and the anti-authoritarians against Marx and the General Council and went on to affiliate to the Saint-Imier International. In the 1880s a growing Dutch anarchist tendency was felt in the socialist movement led by the ex-pastor Ferdinand Domela Nieuwenhuis. Nieuwenhuis helped found the Social Democratic League in 1881 which devoted itself to organizing the trade union movement and to anti-war campaigns. Although Nieuwenhuis was elected to parliament as a socialist in 1888, he rapidly became disillusioned. Before French syndicalism had got underway, he started to call for direct action and the general strike as a means to oppose war and bring about the social revolution. He played an important role in international congresses, and tried to hold together the anarchist and socialist wings of the labour movement.

Nevertheless, Nieuwenhuis openly opposed the reformists at the Zürich Congress in 1893 by arguing that war between the nations should be turned into an international revolutionary struggle between classes with the general strike as the principal weapon. After the congress, he wrote *Socialism in Danger* (1894), categorically rejecting the conquest of political power and stressing that liberty is 'the faculty of allowing each to express his opinion freely and to live according to that opinion'.[7] Nieuwenhuis followed Bakunin in arguing that 'libertarian socialism' came from France while 'authoritarian socialism' was born in Germany. In 1898 he founded the anarchist paper *De Vrije Socialist* (The Free Socialist) which continues to be published as *De Vrije*.

In 1893 a split occurred in the Social Democratic League, with the minority leaving the anarchist majority to form the Social Democratic Party. In the same year the syndicalist Nationaal Arbeids Secretariaat (NAS) was founded. Nieuwenhuis was never an active supporter, but Christaan Cornelissen played a major part in the international syndicalist movement until he supported with Kropotkin the allies at the outbreak of the First World War. At first the NAS led the running in the Dutch labour movement, although it lost most of its membership to the reformist trade unions after the failure of a general strike in 1903. After the First World War it began to expand again, and in 1922 it could boast 22,500 members at the Syndicalist Convention in Berlin which founded the syndicalist International Working Men's Association. But it was in the process of being taking over by communist sympathizers. When the anarcho-syndicalists split away in the following year to form the Nederlandsch Syndicalistisch Vakverbond they were unable to maintian their momentum, despite the efforts of Albert de Jong and Bakunin-specialist Arthur Lehning who edited *De Syndicalist*.

While anarcho-syndicalism in Holland faltered after the 1903 strike, Dutch anarchist thinkers have been particularly influential this century. After the First World War, Nieuwenhuis' anti-war propaganda appeared to have influenced a new generation of anarchists, mostly former Christian pacifists. The central figures were Albert de Jong and the ex-pastor Bart de Ligt, who published the monthly *Bevrijding* (Liberation) in the 1920s and 1930s. Other prominent activists were Clara Wichmann, a lawyer who sought to reform the criminal law and abolish prisons, and Kees Boeke, a Christian anarchist who in the late twenties started a free school called De Werkplaats (The Working Place), which still survives and boasts Queen Beatrix as a former pupil.

De Ligt's essay on war and revolution *The Conquest of Violence* (1937) was widely influential, especially in the English-speaking world. His slogan 'the greater the violence, the weaker the revolution' became a rallying-cry for pacifists. He advocated passive resistance, non-cooperation and civil disobedience (including the general strike) against regimes preparing for war and foreign invaders. Modern warfare, de Ligt argued, is total warfare, so that the 'in every country the political and military directors are absolutely the enemies of the entire population'. In his view barricades are usually raised by those who wish to rule; do away with governments and 'govern ourselves in reasonable fashion, and all barricades will be superfluous'.[8]

It was this message which reached a new generation of anarchists in the fifties and sixties. Peter Heintz in *Anarchismus und Gegenwart* (1951) noticed the death of the traditional anarchist movement in Holland, but saw a 'quiet anarchist revolution' taking place in society and culture. In the early sixties the monthly *Buiten de Perken* (Beyond the Limits) with an anarcho-syndicalist background began to appear. Nieuwenhuis and de Ligt were rediscovered. Then the Campaign for Nuclear Disarmament, Dada, and the 'happenings' of Robert Jaspar Grootveld against consumerism helped trigger off the 'Provo' movement.

The Provos set out to provoke the staid burghers of Amsterdam and upholders of the Dutch State. In their journal *Provo*, they announced a series of White Plans to deal with city problems. These included the White Bicycle Plan, which set up a number of white bikes around the city to be used communally; unfortunately, and perhaps predictably, many were stolen. They also mooted the White Chicken Plan (*kip*, or chicken, is slang for policeman); this would have seen policemen dressed in white uniforms and had them distributing contraceptives. *Provo* (which as a monthly reached a circulation of ten thousand) regarded anarchism as the 'inspirational source of resistance' and wanted to revive anarchism and to teach it to the young.[9] The happenings and demonstrations of the Provos reached its climax in a violent confrontation with the police during a royal wedding on 10 March 1966.

While the Provos engaged in local elections in 1966 and won one seat on the municipal council of Amsterdam, the 'death of Provo' was declared on May 1967. In the light of the growing institutional tendencies in the Provo movement, its funeral was very libertarian. Nevertheless, Provo had proved a catalyst in the quiet revolution. Roel van Duyn, the principal Provo theorist, who took over the seat in Amsterdam municipal council in 1969, and who had written enthusiastically about Kropotkin, then helped launch Kabouter (elf).

Like the anarcho-syndicalists who wanted to create the new society in the shell of the old, the Kabouters in their proclamation of the Orange Free State on 5 February 1970 declared:

> Out of the subculture of the existing order an alternative society is growing. The underground society grows out of the ground now and it begins – independent of the still ruling authorities – to live its own life and to rule itself. This revolution takes place now. It is the end of the underground, of protest, of demonstrations; from this moment we spend our energy on the construction of an anti-authoritarian society.[10]

They wanted to change things in the present and build alternative institutions, not wait for a cataclysmic revolution. They participated in the 1970 municipal elections, and were very successful in Amsterdam and other cities, but, since there was no planned follow-up in the 1984 elections, they expired silently.

If the Provos pitched the imagination against power, the Kabouters showed what the imagination could create. They stood in the constructive anarchist tradition which stemmed from Proudhon and Landauer, not the apocalyptic one associated with Bakunin. The Provos and the Kabouters in fact have proved to be one of the most creative phases in the anarchist tradition, concerning themselves with the environment as well as society. Their legacy of play, spontaneity, fun and idealism has not been lost.

The Kabouters eventually went the same way as the Provos but its veterans went on to develop the Green movement in Holland. Roel van Duyn founded Groen (Green) Amsterdam, which became part of the libertarian De Groenen (The Greens) in 1987, competing with the reformist Groen Links (Green Left). The more strictly anarchist tradition has been kept alive by *De As*, founded by Hans Ramaer in 1972 with the veteran free-thinking journalist Anton Constandse and Albert de Jong's son Rudolf. It maintains the essentially ethical character of Dutch anarchism.

Britain

Britain's libertarian tradition may be traced back to the Peasants' Revolt of 1381, which began as a mass protest against a new poll tax. But behind the reasonable demands of Wat Tyler to end the worse burdens of feudalism was a millenarian vision expressed most vividly by the medieval Heresy of the Free Spirit, which looked for the advent of Christ to establish on Earth the Kingdom of the Saints, without priest or sacrament, law or oath, king or government.

This underground heretical movement emerged again during the English Revolution in the seventeenth century, especially amongst the Diggers and the Ranters. The Ranters were isolated preachers who believed like the Brethren of the Free Spirit that the moral law no longer applied to them. God's elect therefore could do no wrong. The Ranters were the most libertarian in their uncompromising call for freedom from all restraint, but the Diggers were a more organized force and may be considered the first recognizably anarchistic movement. Their spokesman Gerrard Winstanley not only anticipated Tolstoy in declaring Reason as the 'Kingdom of God within man', but equated Christ with 'universal liberty'. In his early work, he rejected not only authority and property, but called like Kropotkin for the whole earth to become a 'common treasury'.

Nevertheless, the Diggers and the Ranters were only called 'anarchist' in a pejorative sense. By the sixteenth century the word 'anarchy' in English (derived from the medieval Latin *anarchia*) had come to mean primarily disorder, whether in the political, moral or intellectual sphere, which results from the absence or non-recognition of authority. Thus Milton, an ardent lover of freedom, could write in *Paradise Lost* of 'the waste /Wide anarchy of Chaos'.[11] By 1678, an anarchist in Britain was seen as one who admits of no ruling power, and by implication, one who upsets settled order.[12]

In the following century, for all his conservative politics, the Tory Dean Swift in Book IV of his *Gulliver's Travels* (1726) depicted in his society of rational horses a fully-fledged anarchist utopia. Burke too in his early *Vindication of Natural Society* (1756) made a case of a society without law and government which was taken seriously by later anarchists. Paine at the end of the century came to the conclusion in the second part of his *Rights of Man* that the great part of that order which reigns among mankind is not the effect of government and that 'the more perfect civilization is, the less occasion it has for government'.[13]

It was William Godwin at the time of the French Revolution who gave the first clear statement of anarchist principles. In his *Enquiry concerning Political Justice* (1793), he forcibly exposed the evils of government and concluded:

With what delight must every well informed friend of mankind look forward to the auspicious period, the dissolution of political government, of that brute engine which has been the only perennial cause of the vices of mankind, and which . . . has mischiefs of various sorts incorporated with its substance, and no otherwise removable than by its utter annihilation![14]

Godwin's son-in-law Shelley put his philosophy of political justice to resounding verse. William Blake's radiant vision of transformed humanity living in harmony without the constraints of Church or State makes him one of the seminal figures in the history of British anarchism. But, it must be said, neither poet ever called himself an anarchist. Even Godwin, the father of anarchism, understood 'anarchy' at the time in the sense of tumult and violent disorder, albeit preferable to despotism, and despite its 'distorted and tremendous likeness, of true liberty'.[15] As in France, anarchist was still a label of abuse: the followers of 'Modern Philosophy, and the Godwynian System' were called anarchists, at least by Zachary Macaulay who ended his poetic satire :

> Ah! grieve not, Anarchists, if heav'n assign
> A transient hour to visions so divine,
> If Nature reassume her ravish'd right,
> And Godwyn's goddess vanish into night.

The future British Prime Minister George Canning also attacked Godwin (along with Paine and John Thelwall) in an ode to 'The Anarchists' in the *Anti-Jacobin Review* in 1798, mocking his

> New scenes of joy at distance hail;
> When tyrant kings shall be no more,
> When human wants and wars shall fail,
> And sleep and death shall quit the hallow'd shore.[16]

Although Britain produced many great libertarian thinkers in the nineteenth century, as a social movement anarchism remained marginal. This is surprising since Robert Owen, who acknowledged Godwin as one of his principal literary companions, had an enormous influence on the growing labour movement. His Grand National Consolidated Trades Union developed a form of economic syndicalism, and his ideal was of a society of decentralized self-governing communities. William Benbow also anticipated anarcho-syndicalism in his concept of a millennial strike which would usher in a new world. Yet with the Chartists the labour movement became overwhelmingly reformist and concerned itself with exerting pressure on parliament rather than manning the barricades.

In fact anarchism proper was largely an import of foreign workers and political refugees who came to London from the 1840s. There were a few isolated revolutionaries with anarchist leanings, but until the 1880s there were no organized groups.[17] It was then that individuals came together in clubs like the Rose Street Club and the Autonomie Club in Soho, and the International Club in Whitechapel.

At the end of 1878 the fiery German Johann Most turned up in London as a refugee from Hamburg and started printing *Freiheit* a week later – it was mainly intended for distribution in Germany and Austria. Most was imprisoned for approving of the assassination of the Tsar Alexander II in 1881. When his friends lauded the assassination of Lord Cavendish in Phoenix Park by Irish nationalists the journal was closed down. On his release, Most made his way to the States.

English revolutionaries began to move towards anarchism after the International Social Revolutionary Congress of 1881. Frank Kitz and Joseph Lane formed the Labour Emancipation League from a faction of the Stratford Dialectical and Radical Club. The object of the League was 'the establishment of a Free Social Condition of Society based on the principles of Political Equality with Equal Social Advantages for All'. They soon gained support amongst East End workers for their opposition to parliamentary politics and State socialism. They were prepared however to work with other socialists and joined the Social Democratic Federation (SDF). Lane in tandem with a small group called the Social Democratic Association issued in 1883 a *Manifesto to the Working Men of the World*, which asserted that 'Governments, no matter of what party, are but the instruments of [ruling] classes and under different disguises of judges and police, priests or hangmen, use their strength and energies to support the monopolies and privileges of the exploiters . . .'[18]

But when the Marxist leader H. M. Hyndman tried to impose his will on the SDF, they broke away with William Morris, Eleanor Marx Aveling and Belfort Bax to form a new organization called the Socialist League. Its manifesto specifically rejected 'State Socialism' and called for 'equality and brotherhood for all the world'. Morris began editing their journal *Commonweal*. He approved of the majority decision to adopt an anti-parliamentarian stance in 1887 but left when the faction which denied all authority and advocated violent revolution took over the executive council. Lane issued in 1887, his own *Anti-Statist Communist Manifesto*, calling for 'the abolition of the State in every form and variety'. The *Commonweal* eventually folded in October 1894 after its editor H. B. Samuels had welcomed acts of 'daring and lawlessness' like 'smashing windows, robbing misers, coining counterfeit or smuggling' to weaken the machinery of government.[19] The explosion of a bomb in Greenwich Park in the same year killing a French anarchist confirmed the popular view of anarchism and inspired the sinister depiction of the anarchist terrorist in G. K. Chesterton's *The Man Who Was Thursday* and in Joseph Conrad's *The Secret Agent*.

The Socialist League at this time adopted a revolutionary position. But other anarchist tendencies were emerging. The individualist Henry Seymour first published *The Anarchist* in 1885 which expressed the view of Proudhon and Tucker on private ownership as a bastion of personal freedom. Seymour went on to publish several other journals from an individualist point of view. The main tendency in the growing anarchist movement however was towards communism as on the continent. The eccentric Dan Chatterton published his *Chatterton's Commune – the Atheistic Communistic Scorcher* from 1884 until his death in 1895.

In 1886 a group including the exiled Kropotkin who had collaborated with Seymour founded *Freedom* which proved to be the longest running anarchist journal and is still published today.[20] While Kropotkin collaborated with fellow revolutionaries like Nicholas Chaikovsky, English anarchists were also involved. The Cambridge-educated Charlotte Wilson became the editor in 1886 until 1895. Kropotkin remained the main intellectual inspiration of the group until he broke with them over his support for the allies in the First World War.

During the zenith of the anarchist movement in Britain in the 1880s and 1890s, the Jewish community formed the largest anarchist group in the country.[21] In 1885 the Yiddish journal *Arbeter Fraint* appeared which by 1891 had moved from expressing broad socialist to anarchist views. Rudolf Rocker, who had come to London in 1893 as a political refugee, learnt Yiddish and became its editor in 1898. He remained so until his internment at the beginning of the First World War.[22] *Arbeter Fraint* became a daily during the successful strike of the sweatshop workers in 1912. The Jewish anarchists not only published literary translations but set up the Jubilee Street Institute as a centre for workers' education and the Workers' Circle as a welfare and educational group.

In the eighties and nineties, there was a great libertarian interest amongst intellectuals and artists in Britain. George Bernard Shaw contributed to Seymour's *The Anarchist* before writing for the Fabian Society about the impossibilities of anarchism because of its attitude to authority. William Morris was closely involved in the Socialist League and wrote the romance *News from Nowhere* which proved to be the most attractive anarchist utopia ever written. Edward Carpenter criticized existing repressive civilization and called for a 'non-governmental society'. Oscar Wilde defended with his habitual eloquence and wit the importance of individuality and presented a marvellous picture of *The Soul of Man Under Socialism*. Henry Salt advocated animal rights, reprinted Godwin on property and promoted Shelley's revolutionary vision.

The most directly anarchist amongst London literary circles were the teenage daughters of the Pre-Raphaelite William Michael Rossetti. The two sisters Olivia and Helen and their brother Arthur published from their house *The Torch: A Revolutionary Journal of Anarchist Communism*, managing to attract a couple of drawings from Pissarro as well as including articles by Louise Michel, Sébastien Faure, Malatesta, Zola, Octave Mirbeau and the young Ford Madox Hueffer (later Ford) before it fizzled out. Many other *fin de siècle* writers and artists were attracted by the anarchist ideal of absolute freedom, but repelled by the terrorism practised by the exponents of propaganda by the deed.

On the other hand, anarchism made little inroads in the British labour movement. Despite the anti-political example of Owen's Grand National Consolidated Trades Union, syndicalism developed late in Britain and failed to win over the reformist trade union movement. In *The Industrial Syndicalist* (1911), Guy Bowman, Tom Mann and his comrades tried to encourage the formation of unions on the model of the American Industrial Workers of the World (IWW) and argued for workers' control as opposed to the State nationalisation of industry. Tom Mann advocated class war and a revolutionary workers' movement 'because it will refuse to enter into any long agreements with masters, whether with legal or State backing, or merely voluntarily; and because it will seize every chance of fighting for the general betterment – gaining ground and never losing any'.[23] These ideas influenced the Irish labour militant James Larkin at the time.

The strongly libertarian pamphlet *The Miners' Next Step* (1912) published anonymously in South Wales by Noah Ablett and others, rejected the notion of leadership – 'all leaders become corrupt despite their own good intentions' – and called for the unions to become cells of the new society with branches having supreme control and the executive being a purely administrative body.[24] Another group associated with the *The Syndicalist* (1912) was more directly anarcho-syndicalist in inspiration and stressed the need for greater decentralization. Its chief spokesman was Guy Bowman who was influenced by the French CGT. But British syndicalism remained a minority movement and waned after the First World War.[25]

The anarchist movement proper lost its way at the turn of the century, although some anarchists involved themselves in communities like Clousden Hill near Newcastle and Whiteway in the Cotswolds. The First World led to a split between the minority who like Kropotkin supported the allies and those who opposed the war. Despite Guy Aldred's brave efforts in journals entitled *The Herald of Revolt* and *Spur*, he had little effect on the working class. By 1924 the anarchist movement in Britain was in disarray. *Freedom* was discontinued in 1927. Only some pockets of working-class anarchists remained, mainly in London,- Sheffield, South Wales and Glasgow.

It was not until the Spanish Civil War that the anarchist movement began to revive again. *Spain and the World*, edited by Vernon Richards, came out in 1936 and helped revitalize the Freedom Press. Marie-Louise Berneri, the daughter of Camillo, soon collaborated on the journal. It was succeeded by *Revolt!* in 1939. During the war the Freedom Press group brought out *War Commentary*, resulting in the arrest in 1944 and imprisonment in 1945 of the editors John Hewetson, Vernon Richards and Philip Sansom for spreading disaffection in the army.[26] A new generation of intellectuals became involved in anarchism, including John Cowper Powys, Ethel Mannin, Herbert Read, Augustus John, and George Woodcock. Woodcock was associated with Freedom Press during and after the war. He edited the literary journal *Now*, wrote about syndicalism and posed the alternative *Anarchy or Chaos* (1944). He subsequently went to Canada where he became a respected man of letters, continuing to write anarchist biography and history. During and after the war Alex Comfort also wrote articles for Freedom Press.

There was a gradual revival of anarchism in the fifties in Britain before the rise of the New Left. Anarchists became influential in the Campaign for Nuclear Disarmament, especially in the Committee of One Hundred. But the nature of the anarchist movement had changed. In 1944 the Freedom Group withdrew from the Anarchist Federation of Great Britain when it was taken over by syndicalists, who in 1954 renamed it the Syndicalist Workers' Federation. Despite the publication of *Direct Action*, they made few inroads amongst their chosen constituency. In a 1960 survey by *Freedom* the majority of readers were professionals and only fifteen per cent were workers.[27]

In the sixties Colin Ward edited the remarkable journal *Anarchy* which attracted contributions from a wide range of libertarian writers including Alan Sillitoe, Adrian Mitchell and George Melly. With much insight, Ward has been concerned with *Anarchy in Action* (1973) in fields as diverse as town planning, housing, education and allotments. Like Landauer, he wishes to create new relationships and institutions in the shell of the old society. Nicolas Walter has written persuasively *About Anarchism* (1969), edited many anarchist classics and been deeply involved in anti-militarist and humanist activities. For many decades the thoughtful centre of anarchism in Britain has remained the Freedom Press, formed over a century ago by Kropotkin and his friends, which continues anarchist education through its journals and publications.

In academic circles, Michael Taylor has recently developed an anarchist critique of the liberal State, using arguments drawn from modern logic and political theory. In *Anarchy and Co-operation* (1976), he argued cogently that social order exists in inverse proportion to the development of the State, and went on in *Community, Anarchy, and Liberty* (1982) to maintain that anarchy as a stateless social order can only exist in a stable community with a rough equality of material conditions.

The minor revolutionary trend in British anarchism has been kept alive by anarchists like Stuart Christie and Albert Meltzer who have been associated with the paper *Black Flag* and have adopted a class-war form of anarchism which calls for *The Floodgates of Anarchy* (1970) to be opened. In the early seventies, the Angry Brigade revived old terrorist images of anarchism, although none of its members were identified as anarchists.

Anarchy in Britain not only permeated youth culture towards the end of the sixties, a time of student sit-ins and squatting, but spilled into the seventies in the alternative movement of communes and co-operatives. Anarchists played a vital role in the 'counter-culture', seeing anarchism not merely as a system of beliefs but a way of living. They adapted their dress and manner to their politics, and sought to create new free institutions. A whole alternative network developed amongst so-called 'hippies' and 'travellers' who wanted to be left alone to live their own lives. A recognizable culture of resistance to the State emerged from the world of free festivals, city gigs, fanzines, squats, and food co-ops, and around ancient sites like Glastonbury and Stonehenge. Conflict with the authorities and owners of private property reached a head in the battle of Stonehenge in 1985 when police prevented the 'Peace Convoy' from celebrating the summer solstice. The ecological tendency of the movement is expressed in the *Green Anarchist* which sees industrialization destroying the planet and urbanization encouraging crime and despair. In their place, it calls for the creation of autonomous self-sufficient villages where all can have a roof over their heads and work the land.

Towards the end of the seventies, there was an explosion of anarchistic attitudes and symbols amongst the urban youth in the form of punk. When the Sex Pistols' anthem *Anarchy in the UK* stormed the charts in 1977, anarchy and punk were indissolubly connected: 'I am an anarchist/I am Antichrist' shrieked Johnny Rotten. 'No Future' they proclaimed. God and State, work and sex, home and family – all the lynchpins of bourgeois living they demolished, one by one; all condemned as bad jokes in the still better joke of the music. Johnny Rotten styled himself an anarchist, and their first four singles consciously or unconsciously echoed – some say turned into music – the rebellion. Yet it was not entirely a new phenomenon. The band's graphic artist Jamie Reid and their manager Malcolm McLaren were certainly aware of the theories and stunts of the Situationists whose influence had been felt in British art colleges in the late sixties and in the popular music scene in the seventies. Rotten himself became the medium for an ancient libertarian instinct of which he was only dimly aware.[28]

Anarchy gave punk its shock tactics and do-it-yourself thrust, as a distinctive culture developed around the provocative music, dress and lifestyle. 'We're pretty vacant', the new anti-elite disclaimed, 'And we don't care.' Vivienne Westwood made ageing feminists like Germaine Greer look coy by suggesting that sex gives the establishment the horrors and by urging the young to live out their 'wildest fantasies to the hilt'. With the revolutionary pacifist band Crass, anarcho-punk became more serious in 1979; their commune in the Epping Forest linked such experiments of the sixties with the eighties. The Clash further evoked modern British alienation in 'Lost in the Supermarket' in denouncing the special offer of 'guaranteed personality'. The Mekons, The Slits, X-ray Spex and Subway Sect continued the musical subversion.

The 'acid house' scene of the late eighties and early nineties, in which youth take over temporarily empty buildings for a rave, is less overtly political but still confounds the elders, those who man the State institutions, who have consistently proved psychologically unable to allow youngsters a freedom to let themselves ago, to relinquish their given authority over them. Inspired by the Situationists and anarchist theory, another post-punk anti-authoritarian tendency emerged in the late 1980s around the 'Free University' collective in Scotland, and from journals like *Smile*, *Here and Now* and the more scholarly *Edinburgh Review*. Much of the new libertarian writing is in the Ranter and Dadaist tradition of poetic declamation. It fuses fact and fiction, history and myth, and opposes the primitive to the civilized. Rather than resorting to agit-prop, it tries to politicize culture and transform everyday life.

The most popular anarchist tendency in the eighties has been the Class War Federation. While it shares some of the shock tactics and 'fuck-off' graphics of punk, the similarity stops there. While making a broad assault on culture, Class War still seeks the 'destruction of the ruling class by the working class'. Its principal line, developed by Ian Bone and other middle-class organizers, has been to urge its followers indiscriminately to have a go at bashing the rich and taking on authority.[29] Class War members (and fellow travellers) were prominent in the 'Stop the City' of London campaign in 1984, and in the Poll Tax riots in Trafalgar Square of March 1990. Both inspired the British press to raise again the spectre of the 'anarchist menace'. Being the most populist and violent of the recent anarchist groupings, they have attracted fascistic elements who are more interested in a brawl than the creation of free institutions.

Other strands within British anarchism have been kept alive by the syndicalist Direct Action Movement which re-formed in 1979 and seeks independent organization in the workplace and 'a system where workers alone control industry and its community'. Some claim that the tiny Socialist Party of Great Britain was anarchist in inspiration. The Anarchist Communist Federation, who were also prominent in what they call the 'Battle of Trafalgar Square' during the Poll Tax riots, demand the 'abolition of all hierarchy, and work for the creation of a worldwide classless society'. Like Class War, they have little to do with industrial union politics, but they are aware of the subtleties of the anarchist tradition. *Solidarity* and *Peace News* call for libertarian socialism and non-violent revolt respectively. Some anarchists are active in the growing animal liberation movement, arguing that freedom should not be restricted merely to the human species.

The most recent development in Britain, as in other advanced industrial societies, has been to recognize the anarchist possibilities inherent in capitalism's reliance on computers. This not only involves computer hacking (breaking into computers to steal or alter data), but in creating alternative information networks. As the black flag of anarchy flies from London's fashionable West End to the ancient hills of Stonehenge, the new black chip moles away in the most automated offices of the city.

The new century sees anarchism alive and kicking in Britain and back in the news. Anarchists have been prominent in the anti-war and anti-globalization movements, sections of which organize themselves on anarchist lines and engage in direct action.

United States

THERE HAS OF COURSE been a long libertarian tradition in the United States. The early settlers came to escape religious persecution, and from the beginning were hostile to any form of government and were fiercely jealous of their personal independence. As early as 1636 Roger Williams was arguing that forced belief was 'soul-rape' and that each person must have the liberty to 'try all things'.[1] At the same time Anne Hutchinson asserted that the godly were no longer sanctified by obligations to law but were purified by the covenant of grace, 'the indwelling of the spirit'.

Both Williams and Hutchinson were banished, but after the English Revolution the Quakers arrived with their contempt for man-made law, their refusal to make political oaths, their rejection of war, taxes, and military duty, and their unconventional behaviour. In 1682, William Penn might have solemnly prayed that the government of his colony be respected as 'a part of religion itself, a thing sacred in its institution and its end', but even he felt that earthly laws were superficial compared with the 'fundamental laws' revealed by conscience.[2] The Protestant right of private judgement or conscience became an ineradicable part of American political culture, and formed the basis of the defence of freedom of thought and speech. It also accounts for the deeply ingrained sense of individualism in American society.

Whatever civic leaders might think or want, life in the New World was largely self-reliant and self-governing, based on mutual aid in difficult and often hostile circumstances. Vast areas were beyond the reach of government. The later expansion to the West was notoriously 'lawless', albeit distinguished by greed and injustice, especially from the indigenous peoples' viewpoint. After the American War of Independence, the founding fathers of the new republic were convinced like Locke for the need for government to protect private property and the individual rights to life, liberty and the pursuit of happiness. Yet they were still keen to keep governmental interference to a minimum and adopted the principle of federation to spread political authority throughout the regions. Immediately after the American Revolution, the Articles of Confederation established a minimal government which was both libertarian and decentralized, although it powers were inexorably strengthened in the following decades.

The self-reliant settlers were well aware without reading Thomas Paine's common-sense strictures on government that 'Society in every state is a blessing, but government even in its best state is but a necessary evil; in its worst state an intolerable one.'[3] Indeed, life in the commonwealth passed off so quietly, and the people spent their time in such peaceful and productive activities that Benjamin Franklin apparently warned the delegates of the Pennsylvania Constitutional Convention not to stall in drawing up a new government: 'Gentleman, you see that in the anarchy in which we live society manages much as before. Take care, if our disputes last too long, that the people do not come to think that they can very easily do without us.'[4] Although Franklin's ideal was a free and educated people helping themselves and exchanging ideas and goods, he did not go beyond laissez-faire liberalism and question minimal government.

It was Thomas Jefferson who came closest to formulating an anarchist position at this time. He warned against the 'wolfish' instincts of the State and suggested that society without government 'as among our Indians' might be the happiest condition of humanity.[5] The maxim attributed to him 'That government is best which governs least' did not appear in his writings, but it has been a rallying cry to libertarians down the centuries. In fact, Jefferson was principally interested in increasing popular participation in government through universal suffrage, not in abolishing political authority all together. 'The influence over government must be shared among the people,' he wrote. 'If every individual which composes the mass participates in the ultimate authority, the government will be safe; because the corrupting of the whole mass will exceed any private resources of wealth.'[6] In addition, as a member of the slave-owning landed gentry, he did not wish to rock the principal pillar of government: private property. But like Proudhon later, he felt that private property could ensure personal autonomy: he acquired the Louisiana Purchase in order to divide it into small farms as a mainstay of freedom.

In the nineteenth century, the indigenous anarchist tradition in the United States took a mainly individualist direction.[7] Inspired by the libertarian ideals of Jefferson and Paine and Protestant Dissent, they rejected the State and wanted to turn American society into an association of voluntary agencies. But they did not question the market economy and saw like Proudhon that private property was a guarantee of personal independence. As such most American individualist anarchists might be called 'right-libertarians' since they felt capitalism would encourage anarchy.[8]

In the middle of the century, it was the Transcendentalists Emerson and Thoreau, and their kindred spirit Walt Whitman who expressed most keenly the libertarian ideal. Their independent stance directly inspired later anarchists and their combination of 'transcendental individualism' with a search for a simple and creative life close to nature finds echoes this century. The first self-conscious American anarchist however was the musician and inventor Josiah Warren. He became a member of Robert Owen's utopian colony New Harmony, but left in 1827 convinced that it had failed. Dubbed the 'American Proudhon', he tried to realize a system of 'equitable commerce' in which goods are exchanged for the costs of production first in a Time Store and then in the Village of Equity in Ohio and Modern Times on Long Island. He influenced the individualists Stephen Pearl Andrews and Lysander Spooner. William B. Greene then engrafted Proudhon's mutualism onto the native individualist tradition although the Proudhonians never made many converts.

The most outstanding American individualist anarchist was undoubtedly Benjamin R. Tucker whose journal *Liberty* lasted from 1881 to 1907. He combined Warren's and Proudhon's teachings but gave them his own personal stamp and made them applicable to capitalist America. Tucker translated Proudhon and Bakunin into English and supported Kropotkin during his trial at Lyon in 1883, while disagreeing with the declaration of the accused. He called anarchists 'unterrified Jeffersonians' and defined anarchism as complete laissez-faire or 'consistent Manchesterism'. The subtitle of his journal however made sure that Proudhon's maxim that 'Order is the daughter of Liberty' reached a wide audience.

While the indigenous American anarchist tradition was primarily individualist, there was a minority communitarian trend developed by Christian radicals like Adin Ballou and John Humphrey Noyes. They believed that respect for the authority of God meant rejecting the authority of human governments. Ballou advocated a voluntary 'neighbourhood society' while Noyes practised a form of communism in the Oneida community which he helped found.

Although Spooner and Greene were both members of the First International, there was no organized anarchist movement in the United States as in Europe until the arrival of anarchist immigrants at the end of the seventies. After the International Social Revolutionary Congress in 1881, two American federations formed. One was a group of Chicago-based Socialist Revolutionaries, made up mainly of immigrants from Germany and the Austro-Hungarian Empire. They formed the International Working People's Association (known as the Black International) which was committed to revolutionary action. Another group of Americans in San Francisco founded in the mean time a secret society called the International Workmen's Association (known as the Red International) which was affiliated to the London International.

The new Europeans immigrants in the 1880s brought in a new wave of communitarian anarchism. Unlike the native American individualists, who despised the State because it hindered the liberty of the individual and his property, the new left-libertarians attacked the State because it was the mainstay of property and privilege. Rather than stressing the liberty of the individual, they talked of the advantages of solidarity and community.

When Johann Most arrived in New York in 1882, and set up again his journal *Freiheit*, he attempted to channel and organize the energies of the brightly hopeful but desperate workers – with considerable success.[9] He wished to unite revolutionaries in their opposition to State and capital. The centre of the anarchist movement remained in Chicago however, especially among the city's German and Czech immigrants. They sent more delegates than any other city to the second congress of the International held in Pittsburgh in 1883, and made up half of the total American membership of six thousand. Three anarchist papers were published in Chicago alone and enjoyed a wide readership amongst the working class. Initially opposed to the call for an eight-hour day, from 1886 they supported it for tactical reasons, and matched police violence with worker violence.

The agitation reached its peak in Chicago in 1886. On 3 May the police fired on a crowd outside the McCormick Reaper Works which had locked out its men, killing several people. At a protest rally held the next day in Haymarket Square, a bomb was thrown from a side alley when two hundred police marched into the square as crowds were dispersing in the rain. In the shoot-out which followed seven policemen were killed and possibly three times as many demonstrators, along with sixty others wounded. There was a huge public outcry. Seven anarchists were accused, including Albert Parsons, editor of *Alarm*, and August Spies, one of the editors of *Chicagoer Arbeiter-Zeitung*, despite the absence of evidence to link them to the bombing. One got fifteen years, the others the death penalty, although in the event two had their sentence commuted to life imprisonment. They were released a few years later when an inquiry ordered by Governor Altgeld concluded that the trial had been judicial murder. Of the five condemned to death, one committed suicide the night before the execution. The incident inspired Frank Harris's novel *The Bomb*, and has been regarded as the greatest inquisition in America since the Salem witch trials.[10]

The general public really became aware of anarchism in 1886 when news of the Haymarket tragedy hit the headlines. The Chicago anarchists became martyrs for the labour movement, but demons for those in power. The new image of anarchism as a terrorist movement rather than the absurd creed of a few individualist cranks was confirmed when the Russian immigrant Alexander Berkman tried to assassinate in 1892 the financier Henry Clay Frick in revenge for the killing of workers during the Homestead steel strike. The assassination of President McKinley by a young Polish immigrant Leon Czolgosz in 1901 was the last straw. Theodore

Roosevelt, the new President, denounced anarchism in his message to Congress in December 1901 as 'a crime against the whole human race,' and urged that 'all mankind should band against anarchists'. Two years later a law was passed banning alien anarchists and any person 'who disbelieves in or is opposed to all organized governments'. The new wave of terror led Most to change his tack, since he realized that the masses were as alienated as the rulers by the violence.

The anarchist movement went into decline because of its violent reputation. Most died in 1906, and his *Freiheit* survived him by only four years. With the demise of Tucker's journal *Liberty* in 1907, American home-grown individualist anarchism lost its principal voice. Primarily amongst the Jewish and Italian groups in the large cities did anarchism stay alive. *Mother Earth*, edited by Emma Goldman and Alexander Berkman among others, spread the anarchist message from 1906 to 1917. Berkman moved to San Francisco and brought out *Blast* during 1916 and 1917. During the First World War, they helped form the No Conscription League which was crushed in 1917. After the Russian Revolution, they went back with thousands of others to their country of origin, only to become rootless political refugees with the rise of Leninism. In 1919, 247 anarchists and socialists (including Goldman and Berkman) were deported, chiefly to Italy and Eastern Europe.

At the turn of the century, syndicalism began to take off in the American labour movement. Most had been advocating syndicalism and communism throughout the previous decade. In 1905 the Industrial Workers of the World (IWW) was founded. At first the majority of its delegates were anarchists, but they soon became outnumbered by socialists. The anarchists helped form the syndicalist wing led by 'Big Bill' Haywood which broke away from the reformist group led by the Marxist Daniel de Leon. The IWW, or Wobblies as they came to be called, attracted migrant workers in the mines and lumber camps of the West as well as in the factories of the East and Midwest which depended on cheap immigrant labour. They abolished the office of president and insisted that the 'rank and file must conduct the affairs of the organization directly through an executive based on a central committee'.[11]

They departed however from the anarcho-syndicalist principle of federalism and tried to organize workers into a dozen or so national unions (although there was some provision for local industrial councils). Berkman lamented in October 1913 in *Mother Earth* that the Wobblies had lost sight of the fact that 'no organization of independent and self-reliant workers is thinkable without complete local autonomy'.[12] The issue between local autonomy and central control remained unresolved. As a result, it has been argued on the one hand that syndicalism in America was 'at most a parallel movement to anarchism', and on the other, that it substituted 'romantic anarcho-utopianism for hard analysis of social and economic realities'.[13] In fact, the IWW ended up as a curious blend of Marxism, syndicalism and anarchism.

Despite its impact during a wave of dramatic strikes in 1912 and 1913, it failed to develop in a revolutionary direction and was overtaken by the reformist American Federation of Labor. After the execution of the poet Joe Hill in 1915, it failed to maintain its momentum for long. The initial success of the Russian Revolution won over many of the more militant workers to communism.

While the anarchist movement lost ground after the First World War, a few isolated but vigorous groups, mainly to be found amongst Jewish, Italian and Spanish immigrants, continued to carry forth the message. The Jewish *Fraye Arbeter Shtime* and the Italian *Il Martello* and *L'Adunata dei Refrattari* (which published the writings of Luigi Galleani among others) kept anarchist ideas alive.

Before the depression, anarchism hit the headlines not so much because of its influence, but because of the tragic case of Nicola Sacco and Bartolomeo Vanzetti, a shoemaker and a fishmonger. In 1921 they were condemned to death ostensibly for an armed robbery which took place at a shoe factory in South Braintree, Massachusetts, but insidiously for their foreign birth and anarchist beliefs. Despite international protests, they were electrocuted in the State of Massachusetts six years later. Anarchism was certainly their strongest passion and they believed in revolutionary violence.[14] While Sacco may have been guilty of the robbery, Vanzetti's innocence is almost certain. Their case became a *cause célèbre*, joining up anarchists and communists in their defence and radicalizing a whole generation of liberals. 'Give flowers to the rebels failed', translated Vanzetti from an anarchist poem whilst awaiting execution; at least he and his comrade have had their fair share of garlands, if not an official pardon.

Most historians pronounce the death of the anarchist movement in the United States with the passing of Sacco and Vanzetti, but its ideas were still kept alive. The Catholic Ammon Hennacy was converted to anarchist pacifism in prison during the First World War for opposing the 'blood tax'. Inspired by Tolstoy, he went on with Dorothy Day to develop the Catholic Worker movement. He called for a 'One-Man Revolution', advocating rural simplicity and voluntary poverty. Dorothy Day who set up *The Catholic Worker* in 1933 went on to find the social answer to *The Long Loneliness* (1952) in community.

Peter Maurin, who was involved in the Catholic Worker movement in New York City, called for 'personalism and communitarianism'. Like the IWW, he wanted to build the new society in the shell of the old, believing that the best way to find God is through brotherly love. He advocated houses of hospitality based on mutual aid to replace State welfare: 'he who is a pensioner of the State is the slave of the State'.[15] In the long-term, he called for a 'Green Revolution' which would bring about workers' control in decentralized factories and a shift from the city to the land. In the place of the State, he advocated a community of families, combining private and communal property.

With the growing prosperity of the United States and its workers seemingly won over to the American dream, anarchism as an organized movement virtually disappeared after the depression. Before the Second World War, Emma Goldman returned to the United States, agitated on behalf of her Spanish comrades, but was taken up more as a relic of a bygone era than as an exponent of a dangerous creed. Her earlier support for Francisco Ferrer's method of rational education after his execution had helped sparked off the influential Modern School Movement in the United States. It insisted on the child being the centre of gravity in the educational process. In practice, the movement tended to be hostile to academic learning, but it prepared a whole generation of libertarians.[16]

During the Second World War, anarchist ideas were revived by a new generation of young intellectuals who recognized the unseemly health of the State. On the east coast, David Wieck, Paul Goodman and others in New York asked *Why*, and moved on to *Resistance*, while Dwight Macdonald brought out the anarchist-pacifist journal *Politics*. On the west coast, Kenneth Rexroth helped set up the San Francisco Anarchist Circle, attracting old Italian and Jewish anarchists and young poets like Kenneth Patchen, who was eventually to achieve some fame as a Beat.

After the war, anarchists involved themselves in the Civil Rights Movement and the Students for a Democratic Society. Paul Goodman called for revitalized self-governing communities to replace the increasingly centralized and militarized American State. The New Left in the sixties, with its emphasis on decentralization, participation and direct action, reflected many of the fundamental beliefs of anarchism. The emerging counter-culture also concerned itself with the transformation of everyday life. A massive non-conformist youth culture developed across the land, especially in California, New York and New England, although its libertarian rhetoric was often a disguise for a self-indulgence which never really threatened the Establishment. It petered out into street-fighting amongst the Yippies inspired by Abbie Hoffman and Jerry Rubin, and the spluttering pyrotechnics of the Weathermen.

The seventies and eighties in the United States saw a resurgence of right-libertarianism, with 'anarcho-capitalists' like Murray Rothbard drawing inspiration from Spooner and Tucker. The Libertarian Party became in the eighties the third largest party in the country. Philosophers like

Robert Paul Wolff have argued in *Defence of Anarchism* (1970), rejecting all political authority on grounds of the individual's moral autonomy. Paul Feyerabend attempted an anarchist theory of knowledge in his work *Against Method* (1975), maintaining that historical explanations are the only feasible accounts of scientific success and that 'anything goes' in science. The ex-Marxist Fredy Perlman journeyed via Situationism to become an anarchist visionary in his neo-primitivist *Against His-story, Against Leviathan!* (1983).

The rump of the Industrial Workers of the World still exists, and the Libertarian Workers Group formed in New York in the late 1970s became a section of the International Workers Association in 1984. At the same time, the communitarian tradition in North American anarchism has come through in the social ecology of Murray Bookchin and cultural and philosophical writings of John Clark. Journals like *Anarchy: Journal of Desire Armed* in Columbia, Missouri, *Social Anarchism* in Baltimore, *Kick It Over* in Toronto, *Black Rose* in Boston, *Fifth Estate* in Detroit, and *Our Generation* in Montréal are breaking new ground in libertarian theory. American anarchists are *Reinventing Anarchy* in the peace, feminist and Green movements.[17] Anarchist thinking and practice pervade much contemporary radical debate and alternative culture and have been a major influence on the anti-capitalist and anti-globalization movements.

Latin America

THE VAST UNDERDEVELOPED CONTINENT of Latin America has proved a fertile ground for anarchism. Despite the continent's rich potential, its perennial problems of poverty, military rule and imperialism made the uncompromising stance and extreme demands of anarchism particularly attractive. The fraud, corruption and violence of political life made the coercive nature of the State only too transparent.

The original Indian empires of the Aztecs and Incas had of course been highly hierarchical and authoritarian. But the Spanish destroyed the indigenous civilizations and reduced most of the Indians to landless peasants. In the mid nineteenth century, the *latifundia* system developed in which lands were seized from the Indians and vast estates were concentrated in the hands of a few families. A *patrón – peón* relationship, based on patriarchy and subservience, became part of the rural culture.

Throughout the nineteenth century, the ex-colonies were still closely linked to Spain and Portugal and anarchist ideas were brought in by waves of European immigrants to the towns. It was primarily in the industrial centres in the Eastern countries of Latin America that the strongest labour movements developed and anarchism took root.

Foreign capital and a large influx of immigrant labour, especially from Italy and Spain, were the two principle causes of industrialization in the second half of the nineteenth century. The factory owners, many of whom were foreigners, were attracted by the chance of easy profits, and industrial relations tended to be violent and rough. As a result, anarchism, especially in its syndicalist form, dominated the working class movement in Latin America until at least 1930.[1] In several countries, the struggles between the anarchists and the State from 1900–20 virtually reached the proportion of an undeclared civil war. Even after the success of Russian Revolution encouraged many workers to turn to communism in the 1930s, anarchism left a permanent mark on the continent and continues to make its presence felt today.

Argentina

Argentina best illustrates the general principle that the degree of anarchist activity in a Latin American country depended on the extent of its industrialization and the number of its Italian and Spanish immigrants. As the most industrialized and urbanized country in the region, Argentina developed the most powerful anarchist movement. While some contacts were made with the peasants, it remained a predominantly a workers' movement based in the cities.

Argentinian sections supporting Bakunin were affiliated to the First International in 1872 and delegates attended the Saint-Imier Conference in 1877.[2] Malatesta stayed in the country from 1885 to 1889 and his *Questione Sociale* had a widespread influence on the Italian workers who were at the centre of the growing anarchist movement. The celebrated anarchist paper *La Protesta* was founded in 1897 and has continued on and off ever since.

Due to the sudden growth of trade-unionism, the Federación Obrera Regional Argentina (FORA) was set up in 1901, largely inspired by the Italian Pietro Gori. Its unions were called *sociedades de resistencia* and were considered the principal weapons to propagate the anarchist ideal amongst the proletariat and to undertake strikes, direct action and 'revolutionary gymnastics'.

At the fifth Congress of FORA in 1905 the anarchists emerged victorious in the struggle against the social democrats. The Congress passed a resolution declaring that 'it advises and recommends the widest possible study and propaganda to all its adherents with the object of teaching the worker the economic and philosophical principles of anarchist communism'. FORA was opposed to any other form of trade-unionism, including revolutionary syndicalism since the latter wanted to maintain the class structure beyond the social revolution: 'We must not forget that a union is merely an economic by-product of the capitalist system, born from the needs of this epoch. To preserve it after the revolution would imply preserving the system which gave rise to it.'[3]

FORA then launched a series of spectacular strikes; in one year alone, twelve local ones became general. In the first decade of the century, the government declared a state of emergency five times. The violence culminated on May Day 1909 in Buenos Aires when an anarchist procession was suddenly fired on by the police. In revenge, a young anarchist called Simon Radowitsky shot the Chief of Police. The familiar pattern of strikes, bombings and arrests continued, with all civil liberties being revoked. Despite the repression, *La Protesta* continued to be circulated. In 1919, the membership of FORA had reached twenty thousand once again, and the country came near to revolution during the *Semana Trágica* (Tragic Week) following a general strike organized by FORA. Over a thousand people were killed, and fifty-five thousand imprisoned.

Although the Bolshevik success weakened FORA in the twenties, it remained the largest working-class organization in Argentina. It declined in the following decade until FORA was finally merged with the socialist Unión General de Trabajadores into the Confederación General de Trabajadores in 1929. In the mean time, more purist anarchist groups were revitalized by militant immigrants like the Italian Severino di Giovanni.[4]

From 1931 the era of military governments began. Yet anarcho-syndicalism still left its impact in the country's political culture and even contributed to the rise of Peronism after the Second World War.[5] In 1951, the populist President Peron declared paradoxically that 'We are moving towards the Syndicalist State' and organized one million people into 'self-governing collectives'. During his rule, which ironically allowed greater participation of the people, the whole anarchist movement went underground.

In 1955 the Argentine Anarcho-Communist Federation (founded 1935) changed its name to the Argentine Liberation Front (FLA). In the sixties the FLA came out strongly against Castro's communism.[6] But while rejecting doctrinaire Marxism it believed that capitalism could transform itself into a more libertarian structure. The events in Paris in May 1968 radicalized a new generation while a popular rebellion in Rosario and Córdoba in the following year renewed revolutionary hopes. Since then the brutal military dictatorships, the Malvinas war, and the rise of social democracy have kept Argentinian anarchism on the political margins. Nevertheless, the economic crisis of 2001–2 gave rise to factory occupations and neighbourhood assemblies run on anarchistic lines.

Uruguay

In Uruguay, the anarchist movement developed in a similar way as had happened in Argentina. But since the country was less industrialized and Italian and Spanish immigrants were fewer, it did not prove such a threat to the State. As early as 1875 the Regional Federation of the Eastern Republic of Uruguay affiliated with the Bakuninist anti-authoritarian International which emerged from the split at the Hague Conference. From this time anarchism in Uruguay held sway in the workers' movement and revolutionary circles until the end of the 1920s.

The anarcho-syndicalist Uruguayan Workers' Regional Federation (FORU) was formed in 1905 and most of the important trade unions affiliated. It adopted the same line as the Argentinian FORA:

> Our organization is purely economic and is unlike and opposed to all bourgeois and worker political parties in that they are organized to take over political power while our aim is to reduce the existing legal

and political state forms to purely economic functions and to replace them with a free federation of free associations of free producers.[7]

It became the only workers' organization in the country and concerned itself with social questions like alcoholism as well as rationalist schools and workers' libraries. Anarchist intellectuals gravitated to the Centro Internacional de Estudios Sociales which issued many publications. There was a continuing and unresolved debate between the 'finalists' pushing for the social revolution, and those who pursued immediate aims. Direct action, in the form of the boycott, sabotage and the general strike, was seen as the chief means of struggle.

The Mexican Revolution was supported warmly by the Uruguayan anarchists and contact was made with the Partido Liberal Mexicano (PLM) of the brothers Flores Magón. FORU reached a high-point in 1918 with a membership of twenty-five thousand. But the success of the Russian Revolution won the support of most of the revolutionary workers and finally led to a split in FORU in the early twenties. The introduction of a Welfare State and a more democratic constitution further led to its decline.

In 1956 however the Uruguayan Anarchist Federation (FAU) was formed. After a split in the early 1960s it became a semi-clandestine organization based on workers' groups with influence over several important unions within the Convención Nacional de Trabajadores (CNT). The CNT was founded in 1964, bringing together almost all the workers' movements. It specified that member-unions should be independent of the State, political parties, and unions (although there was some provision for local industrial councils). Unlike the Argentinian anarchists, the FAU also defended the Cuban Revolution in the 1960s. The other major anarchist grouping in Uruguay has been the *Comunidad del Sur* which sees the commune as the basis of the new society and tries to prepare the way for a change in human relationships.

Brazil

Like Argentina and Uruguay, anarchism in Brazil became the dominant radical ideology by the turn of the century. The movement was developed mainly by immigrants or immigrant families who arrived between the 1880s and the First World War from Portugal, Spain, and Germany, but above all from Italy.

The anarchist movement first began as early as the 1870s when the ideas of Proudhon and Bakunin reached the New World. It was further galvanized by news of the Haymarket Massacre in 1887 in the United

States. Kropotkin's version of anarchist communism grew stronger in the 1880s, and in 1890 Dr Giovanni Rossi, an Italian agronomist, founded in the famous Cecilia colony in Paraná one of the first anarchist communities in Latin America.[8]

As in Portugal and Spain, anarchism in Brazil tended to be highly ascetic and intense, embracing anti-clericalism and vegetarianism and rejecting the use of tobacco and alcohol. The self-educated anarchist workers not only engaged in strikes and rallies, but founded libertarian schools and organized concerts, plays and lectures for themselves and families.[9] The movement included such colourful characters as the Italian Oreste Ristori who founded the weekly *La Battaglia* in São Paulo and who was deported twice; the Spaniard Everardo Dias who edited the free-thinking *O Livre Pensador*; and the Portuguese intellectual Neno Vasco who edited *Aurora* (Dawn) and *A Terra Livre* (Free Earth). More controversial was the Brazilian poet and philosopher José Oiticica who threw in his lot with the anarchist cause, calling for the 'aristocratization of democrats'.[10]

By the beginning of the First World War the anarchists controlled the Brazilian Confederation of Labour (founded in 1906) and mounted a series of strikes from 1917 to 1919 which seriously disrupted the industrial centres. At first, they welcomed the Bolshevik insurrection and even condoned the 'dictatorship of the proletariat', until news began reaching them in 1920 of the repression of their anarchist comrades, the rout of the Kronstadt rebellion, and the growing tyranny of the Soviet government.

The labour movement continued to be predominantly anarcho-syndicalist well into the 1920s. Although the Brazilian Communist Party, inspired by the apparent success of the Russian Revolution, came to dominate the trade unions, it remained comparatively libertarian until the Stalinist thirties. Internal disputes between anarchist communists and syndicalists, government repression, and the growth of the Communist Party all contributed to anarchism's decline. Small anarchist groups survived beyond the Second World War in the main centre São Paulo and to a lesser extent in Rio de Janeiro. Although the military dictatorship which took power in 1964 all but quenched their fire, the flag of anarchy still flies.

Peru, Chile, Bolivia, Venezuela, Nicaragua

Elsewhere in South America, anarchism has never found such a strong foothold as in Argentina, Brazil and Uruguay.

Peru followed the familiar pattern. Anarcho-syndicalism took root along industrialized centres on the coast and the period after the First World

War saw the greatest agitation. In 1918 the anarchist-led struggle for an eight-hour day led to many strikes and the formation of the Regional Federation of Labour which intended to 'do away with capitalism and substitute for it a society of free producers'. Manuel Prada, founder of the National Union and Director of the National Library, fought for the abolition of all State and private property. One of his associates Victor Haya founded in 1921 the popular University for Workers and Indians. The anarchist movement in the country was suppressed soon after, although it left a remarkable collection of popular poetry.

In Chile, apart from a few journals, there was little anarchist activity until 1919 when the Industrial Workers of the World (IWW) was formed as 'a revolutionary organization fighting capital, the government and the church'. It was represented at the Syndicalist Congress in Berlin in 1923, claiming a membership of twenty thousand. Because of its late appearance, it had always to vie with the other communist trade unions. After 1931, it exerted little influence.

In Bolivia, the Labour Federation of La Paz affiliated with the IWMA and anarchist ideas reached the tin-workers. In Venezuela, a Regional Labour Federation was set up in Caracas by the CNT after the Spanish Civil War. But elsewhere on the Latin American continent anarchism made little inroads.

In the Central American Republics, the US 'back-yard', periodic visits by American marines ensured that their man remained in the Presidential Palace. In Nicaragua in the 1920s, the anarcho-syndicalist Augustino Sandino led a popular revolt, but although the revolutionaries in the eighties called themselves 'Sandinistas', they had all but forgotten his form of libertarian socialism. Only in Mexico and Cuba have anarchists participated in making successful revolutions.

Mexico

Mexico differed markedly from the anarchist movements in Argentina and Uruguay. From the beginning there were two trends, one in the urban labour movement and the other amongst the peasantry. The first anarchist group established in Mexico seems to have been organized by Plotino Rhodakanaty in Mexico City as early as 1863. He was to have a profound influence for the next thirty years.

Rhodakanaty was a Greek immigrant who had been influenced by Fourier and Proudhon (whom he had once met), and a professor of philosophy. He moved in 1865 with Francisco Zalacosta to Chalco in the extreme south of Mexico where he opened an Escuela Moderna y Libre for peasants. They then founded a group called La Social in 1871 which soon spawned more than sixty similar anarchist groups; they even sent a delegate to the

Saint-Imier conference of the International in 1877. In their journal *La Internacional*, the editor Zalacosta defined its programme as 'social anarchy, the abolition of all government, and a social revolution'.[11]

Towards the end of the century, Spanish immigrants started to spread anarcho-syndicalism in the towns and cities. The urban-based labour movement soon became predominantly anarcho-syndicalist.

In the mean time, anarchist ideas reached the 'bandits' who were waging a constant guerrilla war against the landlords of the vast semi-feudal estates known as *haciendas*. Traditionally, in many parts of Mexico the land around each village, the *ejidos*, was held and worked communally. There were no deeds of ownership since they had not been considered necessary. Under the military dictatorship of Porfirio Díaz from 1884 to 1911 these lands were seized by large landowners with private armies. The peasants, as well as a growing number of Indians, looked to the 'bandits' in the hope of getting their land returned and of winning a degree of local autonomy.

In 1869 Chavas López, a former pupil of Rhodakanaty's free school, started in Chalco an insurrection which soon spread to several neighbouring towns before he was captured and killed. Rhodakanaty and Zalacosta issued a *Manifiesto a todos los oprimidos y pobres de México y del Universo* in which they called for a 'Universal Republic of Harmony' which would give freedom to the people 'to unite under the form they estimate to be the most convenient' and 'to sow in the place that suits them without having to pay tribute'.[12] Zalacosta went on to engage in a running battle with government troops until his death in 1880 when the movement collapsed.

At the turn of the century a *mestizo* called Ricardo Flores Magón emerged as an eloquent and impassioned propagandist against Díaz's dictatorship. As a boy in Oaxaca State, Ricardo was able to see at first hand a primitive form of anarchist communism in which the peasant community worked the land in common and shared its fruits equally. A reading of Kropotkin, Bakunin, Jean Grave and Malatesta added a theoretical framework to this experience. From 1900, Ricardo with his brothers Jesús and Enrique began publishing their anarchist journal *Regeneración* in Mexico City, which reached a circulation of nearly thirty thousand. In 1904 they were forced into exile but they continued to edit the journal from across the border in the United States. Ricardo was never to return to his native land, and spent more than half of the rest of his life in prison.

In 1905, the brothers helped form the Junta Organizadora del Partido Liberal Mexicano (PLM). It was not so much a 'party' in the traditional sense but more of an association of like-minded people. For Ricardo, the choice of the name of the 'party' was a question of tactics. He wrote from an American jail soon afterwards: 'we will continue to call ourselves liberals during the course of the revolution, and will in reality continue propagating anarchy and executing anarchistic acts.'[13] Amongst its demands (many of which were met in the 1917 Mexican Constitution), the PLM called for the return of communal and uncultivated lands to the villages, the protection of indigenous Indians, and the transformation of prisons into reform colonies. The PLM became the most serious threat to the Díaz regime. The attempts of the Magón brothers and the PLM to incite rebellion in 1906 and in 1908 not only helped prepare the way for the Revolution of 1910, but pushed it in an egalitarian and libertarian direction.[14] In the following year, they issued a manifesto calling for the expropriation and socialization of all wealth and began to form an alliance with Emiliano Zapata.

Under the banner of *Tierra y Libertad* (Land and Liberty), they directly inspired a revolt in Baja California which established short-lived communes at Mexicali and Tijuana. After the capture of Mexicali, Jack London sent Flores Magón the following message: 'We socialists, anarchists, hoboes, chicken-thieves, outlaws and undesirable citizens of the United States are with you heart and soul in your effort to overthrow slavery and autocracy in Mexico.'[15]

Long before the 1910 Revolution, Emiliano Zapata had been active in his home state of Morelos, a small, densely-populated sugar-growing area in the South. Many villages had been destroyed and the land of the peasants seized to make way for great plantations or *haciendas*. Zapata had been involved in the struggle of one such village to reclaim a well, and was condemned to forced labour. When the Revolution broke out in 1910, the peasants in Morelos began taking back their stolen lands and occupied the main towns. Zapata soon emerged as a leader of the movement, rather like Makhno had done in the Ukraine, but he continued for a while to listen to the politicians and to believe in legal means. He was denounced by the press as a bandit, a 'modern Attila' no less. When a government force was sent to crush the rising in Morelos it was defeated instead by Zapata's forces.

They became known as the 'Agrarians' as well as the 'Liberating Army of the South'. They swept down from the mountains and eventually reached the gates of Mexico City, killing government officials and dividing up the *haciendas* on the way. In the liberated regions, the peasants were free to work the land together with the landlords and government off their backs. Zapata's forces would help turn the plough and gather in the harvest. Although primarily an egalitarian movement which sought the redistribution of the land and the right to be left alone, they resembled the peasant anarchists of Andalucía during the Spanish Civil War in their moral purity and contempt for politics. They had a deep-grained suspicion of all authority, and distrusted in particular the clergy and politicians.

In the mean time, another uprising had ousted President Díaz in the capital after fraudulent presidential elections. The free-thinking liberal Francisco Madero formed a government which tried to end corruption. Madero had managed to persuade many supporters of the PLM to join forces with his party. Ricardo Flores Magón however insisted that the *Maderistas* merely wanted political reform whereas the PLM was fighting for economic as well as political freedom by handing over the land to the people, without distinction according to sex. In *Regeneración* on 25 February 1911, Ricardo attacked bitterly Madero as 'a traitor to the cause of liberty' and reasserted his own anarchist principles:

> I am firmly convinced that there is not, and cannot be, a good govern-ment. They are all bad, whether they call themselves absolute mon-archies or constitutional republics. Government is tyranny, because it curtails the individual's free initiative, and the sole purpose it serves is to uphold a social system which is unsuitable for the true develop-ment of the human being. Governments are the guardians of the interests of the rich and the educated classes, and the destroyers of the sacred rights of the proletariat. I have no wish, therefore, to be a tyrant. I am a revolutionist, and a revolutionist I shall remain until I draw my last breath.[16]

Undeterred, Madero signed a peace treaty with Díaz and began to suppress the PLM. But his government was unable to assert its authority over the regions where land expropriation continued on an increasing scale. In Sep-tember 1911, Ricardo wrote a new manifesto for the Junta of the PLM, declaring war against 'Capital, Authority and the Church' and calling on the people of Mexico to fight under the red flag with the cry of 'Land and Liberty'.[17] The manifesto most fully expressed his anarchist-communist ideas. It not only called for the expropriation of the land and the means of production by those who worked them, but for armed struggle against those in power in order to bring about equality.

When Madero became president in October 1911, Zapata rose against him after issuing his *Plan de Ayala*. It was based to a large extent on Ricardo Flores Magón's September manifesto. The peasant leader had finally lost all faith in politicians. In his *Plan de Ayala*, he criticized bitterly the 'deceitful and traitorous men who make promises as liberators but who, on achieving power, forget their promises and become tyrants'. He called for: 'The land free, free for all, without overseers and masters. Seek justice from tyrannical governments, not with a hat in your hand but with a rifle in your fists.'[18] Although Zapata was not strictly speaking an anarchist, he did much to disseminate Flores Magón's ideas.

In February 1913, right-wing rebels tried to overthrow Madero who managed to put them down during ten bloody and tragic days (*Década Trágica*). A week later Madero was assassinated on the orders of the commander of his own forces, General Victoriana Huerta. The revolution then flared up again between the federal army and the various revolutionary forces. When Huerta was forced to resign in 1914, Zapata's forces, in alliance with armies led by Pancho Villa, and Venustiano Carranza from the North, entered Mexico City. Where Zapata had strong libertarian sympathies, Villa was more motivated by revenge without any clear ideology, and Carranza, as commander of the Constitutional Army, was in a mould similar to Madero.

When two conventions failed to reach an agreement between the three leaders, fighting broke out between their forces. Carranza seized power in Mexico City and got the US government to recognize him and send him arms. With uprisings on his hands from the Left and Right, Carranza in 1916 further managed to enlist the support of the industrial workers organized in the anarcho-syndicalist Casa del Obrero Mundial (House of the World Worker). They agreed to join Carranza's army and formed 'Red Battalions' to fight against the peasant armies of Villa and Zapata. Tricked by their leaders, the workers destroyed what remained of the social revolution. Carranza then repaid them by threatening strikers with the death penalty and by closing down the Casa del Obrero Mundial.

Zapata and his army were beaten back to Morelos. Although the province was laid waste, they fought on for four more years from a mountain stronghold. 'Men of the South', he told his comrades, 'it is better to die on your feet than to live on your knees!' But despite his defiance, he was eventually betrayed in an ambush and killed in 1919. With him expired any hope that the Mexican Revolution would create a genuinely free and equal society. He died as he lived, an honest and courageous peasant, fighting for land and liberty for his people.

Ricardo Flores Magón, meanwhile, criticized the Mexican anarcho-syndicalist workers for betraying the natural class interests they shared with the peasants. He was arrested in the United States again after issuing a manifesto in March 1918 addressed from the PLM to 'the anarchists of the world and the workers in general'. It announced the approaching death of the old society and called for the social revolution. It also insisted that

> we, who do not believe in Government, that we, who are convinced
> that Government in all its forms and whoever is at its head is a tyranny
> . . . must use every circumstance to spread, without fear, our sacred
> anarchist ideal, the only human, the only just and the only true.[19]

At his trial, Ricardo Flores Magón was sentenced to twenty years for allegedly violating the US Espionage Laws. Four years later, he was found murdered in Leavenworth Penitentiary, Kansas. Like Kropotkin's funeral in Russia two years before, Flores Magón's in 1923 became a public demonstration. As the banners declared he 'died for Anarchy', but ironically the Mexican State presently came to honour its most rebellious citizen. The foremost Mexican anarchist of the twentieth century now lies entombed in the Rotunda of Illustrious Men in Mexico City, and he is remembered throughout Mexico as 'a great precursor of the Mexican Revolution'.[20]

Despite the failure of the Mexican Revolution, the labour movement remained predominantly anarcho-syndicalist. It had its first national congress in Mexico in 1921 and in 1922 the Mexican CGT was represented at the 1923 Syndicalist Congress in Berlin, claiming a membership of thirty thousand. As elsewhere in Latin America, it then steadily became more reformist.

The Mexican Revolution was the first major revolution in the twentieth century and had widespread repercussions. Although it degenerated into a squabble amongst politicians for power and privilege, its call for 'Land and Liberty' echoed across the Latin American continent. It has been taken up by the Zapatistas who rebelled in 1994 in Chiapas province and established a democratic form of self-government.

Cuba

Like Argentina and Uruguay, the anarchists in Cuba exerted the greatest influence on the labour movement at the turn of the century. Cuba was not only the largest island in the Caribbean, but also one of the richest. Despite two long wars of independence, slavery had not been abolished until 1886, and Cuba did not become nominally independent until after the Spanish-American War of 1898. Anarchists however played an important role in the independence struggle and when the labour movement developed it rapidly moved in an anarcho-syndicalist direction.

The earliest anarchist groups appeared in Cuba in the 1860s, largely organized by Spanish immigrants. They quickly influenced the tobacco workers who were the most militant and politically conscious in the country. From 1865, they published the libertarian journal *La Aurora* (Dawn) and a year later formed the first trade union in Cuba, the Association of Tobacco Workers of Havana. Other trades followed suit but the first Workers' Congress of Havana was not held until 1885. Inspired by the militant organizers Enrique Roig de San Martín, Enrique Messonier, and Enrique Cresci, Cuban workers, especially those in the tobacco industry, backed the openly anarchist organization La Alianza Obrera founded in 1887.

The paper *El Productor*, edited by Roig, called the members of the alliance 'revolutionary socialists', but they were known as anarchists for their rejection of political parties and for their militancy. While Cuba was still fighting for its independence from Spain, *El Productor* argued that there was a basic contradiction between nationalism and socialism. In an article on 'The Fatherland and the Workers', it asked pointedly: 'Is it that an independent fatherland consists in having its own government, in not depending on another nation ... although its citizens are in the most degrading slavery?'[21] Its own message was that only a society without government could be free and that the true fatherland of the workers should be the world.

Anarcho-syndicalist ideas spread rapidly. At the Workers' Congress held in Havana in 1892, the resolutions drafted by the anarchists Enrique Cresci, Enrique Suárez, and Eduardo González were passed, including the principle that 'The working class will not be emancipated until it embraces revolutionary socialism, which cannot be an obstacle for the triumph of the independence of our country.'[22] Indeed, the anarchists were so influential at this time that they had from the mid 1880s persuaded the Cuban tobacco workers in Florida and New York to bypass the political movement for national independence in favour of the social revolution.[23]

Even José Martí was affected by this libertarian tendency. He wrote in his journal *Patria*:

> The republic ... will not be the unjust dominance of one class of Cubans over the rest, but a sincere and open balance of all the nation's real forces, and the ideas and the free wishes of all Cubans. We do not want to redeem ourselves of one tyranny in order to enter into another. We do not want to free ourselves of one hypocrisy in order to fall into another. We will die for real freedom; not for a freedom that serves as a pretext to maintain some men in excessive wealth, and others in unnecessary pain.[24]

Known today as the 'intellectual author' of the Cuban Revolution, Martí knew that 'To change the master is not to be free'. But while he published the writings of Elisée Reclus in *Patria*, he cannot be called an anarchist. He appealed to the emerging Cuban working class but also cultivated conservative Cuban groups in exile by stressing the need for class co-operation and by trying to defuse the anarchist influence on the workers.

This did not prevent the anarchists from controlling the Cuban labour movement organized in the Confederación de Trabajadores Cubanos (CTC) from the 1890s. Many anarchists were also at the forefront of the struggle for independence, including Armando André, a commander in the rebel army. When Malatesta was invited to visit the island by the anarchist group publishing *El Mundo Ideal* in 1900, he was not allowed by the authorities to use the word 'anarchy', but he was able to trace the strong libertarian tradition of the Cuban independence movement:

> I assume that the libertarians fighting against the existing government will not put another government in its place; but each one will understand that as in the war of independence this spirit of hostility to all governments incarnated in every libertarian will now make it impossible to impose upon the Cuban people the same Spanish laws which martyrs like Martí, Cresci, Maceo and thousands of other Cubans died to abolish.[25]

In the first two decades of this century, the anarchists, with papers like *Tierra!* and *El Rebelde*, spread the ideas of Bakunin, Kropotkin and Reclus. They led the 1902 strike of the apprentices, the first major one of the new Republic. They helped form agrarian co-operatives and built up peasant organizations. They continued to be especially strong amongst the tobacco and construction workers.

The success of the Russian Revolution led to the CTC being eventually taken over by the communists in the 1920s. The anarchists formed the rival Confederación Nacional Obrera Cubana (CNOC) with the typographer Alfredo López as its general secretary. During the underground struggle against the Machado dictatorship, it led the call for the general strike, despite opposition from the communists, which eventually succeeded in ousting Machado in 1933. The communists however soon took over the CNOC and collaborated with Batista's dictatorship during the thirties and forties.

A minor revival of anarchism occurred during the Second World War, when the Asociación Libertaria de Cuba was formed. It held its first congress in 1944 which was attended by delegates from all over the island. Its rapid growth was strong enough for Batista to declare: 'The anarcho-syndicalist influence is as dangerous as communist intrusion!'[26] But where Batista went on to court the communists, even appointing some as ministers, he did his best to suppress the anarchists.

While Fidel Castro and Che Guevara and their small band of guerrillas were fighting in the Sierra Maestra mountains, the anarchists played an important role in the urban underground. Their paper *El Libertario* had a wide circulation, and they put out clandestine radio broadcasts. The organized food workers, an important group in the tourist paradise of Havana, were mainly anarchist and published the journal *Solidaridad Gastronómica*.

After the fall of Batista early in 1959, the anarchists continued to exert an influence on the course of the revolution. They were ready to go along with Castro when he promised, on the guerrillas' triumphant entry into Havana, 'humanistic democracy on the basis of liberty with bread for all peoples'. Slogans went up all over the city: 'Freedom with bread, bread without terror'; 'Neither dictatorship from the right nor dictatorship from the left.' The Agrarian Reform which distributed land to the peasants was widely popular. The old communists, who had collaborated with Batista, were kept out in the cold.

For many Western observers, including Jean-Paul Sartre, the Cuban Revolution seemed an example of direct democracy, if not anarchy, in the making. But when Castro tightened his hold over the revolutionary process and declared himself in December 1961 to be a Marxist-Leninist until the day he died, the anarchists became increasingly alarmed. Soon after the Bay of Pigs fiasco, Castro laid down the narrow limits for permissible dissent: 'Nothing against the Revolution, everything within the Revolution'.

As the Cuban State, controlled by Castro and a small group of former guerrillas, grew more bureaucratic, centralized and militarized, the 'Revolution' became virtually synonymous with the 'State'. What the State did not like was by definition against the Revolution. The Asociación Libertaria was disbanded and late in 1961 the anarchist papers *El Libertario* and *Solidaridad Gastronómica* ceased publication. Many anarchist militants decided exile was preferable to a Cuban jail. Declaring the Cuban Revolution to be counter-revolutionary, they have continued their agitation from abroad, especially from Miami.[27]

In the seventies, Castro moved closer to the Soviet Union. He consolidated his form of State socialism by adopting their centralized form of economic planning and by introducing a Constitution in 1976 based on the Eastern-bloc model. The new Cuban Communist Party, formed in 1965 from a purged coalition of revolutionary groups, did not hold its first congress until 1975. It then adopted a set of statutes in which it described itself as 'the organized vanguard of the working class' and declared its 'fidelity to Marxism-Leninism as its vanguard theory and guide for action'.[28] Not surprisingly, the ideologues of the Cuban Communist Party adopt Lenin's attitude to the 'infantile disorder' of left-wing communism; any political troublemakers are dismissed as *anarcholocos*, mad anarchists.

Nevertheless, there continues amongst the Cuban people a strong libertarian underswell which reveals itself in their traditional suspicion of authority, their individualism, and their profound dislike of regimentation. Moreover, the thought and action of Che Guevara keeps alive a libertarian strand within Cuban communism.

Che Guevara has been hailed as the 'new Bakunin'. He certainly shared the anarchist confidence in the revolutionary potential of the peasantry and sought to create a co-operative society of workers and peasants in which work is transformed into 'meaningful play'. He was very critical of any bureaucracy which checked individual initiative. He wanted to abolish money and to see people motivated by moral and not material incentives; to work for the good of the whole, not just for themselves. Above all, he wanted to transform human relations so that all, regardless of sex or race, could realize their full potential. 'We socialists are freer', he declared, 'because we are more complete; we are more complete because we are freer.'[29] Although Guevara was unable to overcome his admiration for strong leaders, the early years of the Cuban Revolution, when his influence was at its height, proved the most creative and original phase. Since his death in 1967, his legacy has not been forgotten and libertarian socialists still exist in Cuba who call for direct democracy and self-management.

The early success of the Cuban Revolution in standing up to the United States gave it enormous prestige amongst left-wing movements in Latin America, but its later connection with the Soviet Union and its continued suppression of the freedoms of thought, speech, and movement have tarnished its image amongst the libertarian left in Latin America.

Since Latin America remains a largely under-developed continent, still suffering from poverty, political corruption and authoritarian rule, anarchism is likely to have its voice heard in the foreseeable future. In its syndicalist form it continues to appeal to the most progressive urban workers while anarchist communism echoes the ancient aspiration of the poorest peasants to work the land in common without interference from boss or priest. New libertarian tendencies have emerged in the 'Pedagogy of the Oppressed' of the Brazilian educationist Paulo Freire and in Ivan Illich's search for institutional alternatives to the centralized, technocratic State.[30] The Liberation Theology developing in Latin America, which combines Marxism and Christianity, and juxtaposes images of Che and Jesus to potent effect in the shanty-towns, has a strong libertarian impulse which may well leave its historical roots behind.[31] It is still not impossible that one day genuine anarchy will rise out of the chaos of military dictatorships in Latin America. In the meantime, it has been a driving force in the anti-capitalist and anti-globalization movements which have swept across the Americas.

34

Asia

China

MODERN ANARCHISM CAME TO China at the beginning of the twentieth
century and became the central radical stream until after the First World
War and the rise of Marxism-Leninism. It was introduced by two groups
of young intellectuals who had studied abroad in Japan and France.
Although they were attracted to anarchism because it appeared the most
scientific and progressive of Western political ideologies, there was of course
a long-standing indigenous libertarian tradition in China.

For most of its history, China has been made up of self-governing
communities to whom the State appeared distant and impersonal. The
oldest debate in Chinese political thought was between the Taoists, who
advocated a simple life in harmony with nature, and the Legalists and
Confucians, who stressed the need for a strong centralized State and
bureaucracy.[1] Modern anarchism not only advocated the Taoist rural
idyll, but also echoed the peasant longing embedded in Chinese culture
for a frugal and egalitarian millennium which has expressed itself in
peasant rebellions throughout Chinese history. It further struck a chord
with two traditional concepts, *Ta-t'ung*, a legendary golden age of social
equality and harmony, and *Ching-t'ien*, a system of communal land tenure
which was probably practised locally at different periods during the first
millennium.[2]

At the turn of the century, China was almost completely dependent on
Japan for its knowledge of the West. It is not therefore surprising that the
formative stage of Chinese radicalism was closely linked to Japan's. A
Chinese group of students in Tokyo came under the influence of the Japanese anarchist thinker Kōtoku Shūsui. Amongst them was Chang Chi who
translated Malatesta's *Anarchy* into Chinese. The group published in 1907
the anarchist journal *Tien-i-pao*. The classical scholar Liey Shih-p'ei argued
that the realization of anarchism in China should not be too difficult because of the influence of Taoist principles of 'indifference' and 'non-
interference'.[3]

A more influential group of Chinese students came under the sway of anarchism while studying in Paris. They included the aristocratic Li Shih-tseng, Chang Ching-chiang and Wu Chih-hui. They established the journal *Hsin Shih-chi* (The New Century) in June 1907 which championed for three years the cause of revolutionary anarchism. The Paris group, as they came to be known, nonetheless rejected the attempt to link Lao Tzu with modern anarchism or the ancient co-operative well-field system with communism.[4] They were chiefly influenced by the evolutionary theory of Darwin, and the anarchism of Bakunin and Kropotkin. They were drawn to the anarchist-communism of the geographers Kropotkin and Elisée Reclus because of their emphasis on science. The greatest single influence was Kropotkin's *Mutual Aid*, which virtually became the bible of the Chinese anarchist movement. It was translated into Chinese and Japanese many times in the 1920s and 1930s.

The message of *Hsin Shih-chi* was uncompromisingly anarcho-communist. The Chinese anarchists who contributed to it were opposed to religion, tradition, the family, government, militarism and nationalism. They advocated science, freedom, humanism, communism, and universalism. They placed great emphasis on anarchist morality without religious sanctions, and were strongly anti-libertine; many rejected meat, alcohol and tobacco, and visiting prostitutes.

At the same time, they did not balk at violent revolution; like Bakunin, they saw that it was necessary to destroy in order to create. They were the first in Chinese political thought to call for a peasant – worker mass uprising, but since it was not forthcoming in China at the time, they turned to the pistol and the bomb. They advocated assassination of government officials, strikes against capitalism, and love towards society. Some even urged taking over the existing Chinese secret societies.

They defined anarchism like Kropotkin as meaning 'no authority'.[5] Like the European anarchists they saw all States and governments as the enemies of freedom and equality. But while they advocated economic communism, they still saw the individual as the basic unit in society: 'Together with others, he forms a village, and with other villages, a country is formed. Society in turn is formed through the process of bringing all countries together.' While the State is the destroyer of society, and governments are organized by the few in their own interest, the 'proper society is that which permits free exchange between and among individuals, mutual aid, the common happiness and enjoyment of all, and the freedom from force by the control of the few.'[6] True communism is not that of the ancient well-field system, but rather is based on common property held by a free federation of small, natural groups.

They totally rejected militarism – brute force exerted to uphold the State – and clashed with the nationalists in wanting to liberate all humanity and establish universal harmony. They argued that States and armies did not prevent a country from external attack.

The anarchists of the Paris group saw their role as modernizing China and overcoming its deadening tradition as well as its burdensome government. They were impressed by Western civilization, and believed that progress in China had to occur through the spreading of science and direct democracy. Both the Japanese and the French groups of Chinese anarchists were united in their detestation of the Manchu regime. On the eve of the Nationalist Revolution of 1911, the anarchists seemed in a strong position. Large sections of the revolutionary movement were adopting their goals and tactics.

Li and Chang of the Paris group returned to China after the 1911 Revolution and founded in 1912 the 'Society to Advance Morality'. If any member broke one of its complicated rules, then the others were supposed merely to 'raise their hats' in silent disapproval. The major spokesmen of the Paris group when they returned to China affiliated themselves increasingly with the nationalist movement of the Kuomintang, which itself had been founded in 1912. The nationalist leader Sun Yat-sen however was sympathetic to them, especially as he had been influenced during his stay in England in the 1890s by Henry George and his single-tax system. He used the word 'communism' in the sense of Kropotkin's anarcho-communism until his death in 1925.

One of the first to propagate actively the anarcho-communist ideas of *Hsin Shih-chi* in China was the charismatic ex-assassin Liu Szu-fu, better known as Shih fu. In Canton in 1912, he founded the 'The Society of Cocks Crowing in the Dark'; its conditions of membership included no eating meat, no riding in sedan chairs and rickshaws as well as no joining of political parties. In his anarchist journal, *Hui-ming-lu* (The Voice of the People), Shih fu declared that 'Our principles are communism, anti-militarism, syndicalism, anti-religion, anti-family, vegetarianism, an international language, and universal harmony. We also support all the new scientific discoveries which advance man's livelihood.'[7] All the anarchist groups were influenced by the Taoist and Buddhist ideal of the pure man who refuses to take office and who helps others by teaching and example.

The anarchists also initiated the famous work-study movement in China which was to have important repercussions for the future. Wu, Wang, Li and others founded 'The Society for Frugal Study in France' in 1912 and in 1915 'The Association for Diligent Work and Frugal Study' to promote simple living and scientific education. Mao Tse-tung was in the Peking class of the latter but did not go to France. He later admitted however that he had been strongly influenced by anarchism as a student.[8]

Ironically, anarchism in China paved the way for Marxism-Leninism.

The students sent to France by the predominantly anarchist association unintentionally became influenced by Marxist-Leninist dogma. They went on to help establish the Chinese Communist Party which had its first congress in 1921. But it was not long before a leading spokesman for the Communists, Ch'en Tu-hsiu, argued, against the anarchists, the case for an organized central power, an 'enlightened despotism' no less. He railed against the 'lazy, wanton, illegal sort of free thought that forms a part of our people's character', which he put down to 'Chinese-style anarchism', derived from Lao Tzu and Chuang Tzu, which was very different from Western anarchism.[9]

The impact of Western anarchism on China was short-lived but profound. It came with a rush of new political currents at the beginning of the century, arriving more or less simultaneously with liberalism and socialism. The decade following the 1911 Revolution was a period of intellectual and political turmoil. Between 1916 and 1920 anarchist thought probably had its greatest influence on young intellectuals, particularly in South China.

The famous Chinese novelist and translator Pa Chin (Le Fei Kan) also became an anarchist in 1919 after reading an article by Emma Goldman; on several occasions, he called her his 'spiritual mother'.[10] His *nom de plume* Pa Chin was a contraction of Bakunin and Kropotkin. The anarchists also had considerable influence in the federalist movement in China from 1920 to 1923. The General Association of Hunan Workers was led by anarchists and supported the movement. Students in Fukien in their journal *Tzu-chih* (Autonomy) argued that 'to govern oneself and to be governed are two contradictory things'.[11]

But the anarchists were soon eclipsed by the Marxist-Leninists in the mid 1920s. Anarchism paved the way for them by its opposition to tradition, the family and religion, by its stress on progress through science, by its call for a mass movement, even by its puritanical leanings. Apart from the successes of the Bolshevik Revolution, the Leninist theory of tutelage attracted many radical Chinese intellectuals who did not trust the allegedly stubborn and ignorant masses. Unlike anarchism, Leninism also embraced nationalism which helped it draw on a wider base of support.

Anarchism on the other hand is in many ways naturally Chinese, standing in a long tradition going back to Taoism. It is the opposite side of the coin to the Legalist and Confucian tradition, with their emphasis on a centralized State and mandarin rule. Even this century, China has remained relatively decentralized with the State playing only a small controlling part until 1949. Since then Communist China has largely comprised a vast number of relatively self-sufficient communities bound together primarily by a common identity rather than by a uniform administration.[12]

In the fifties and sixties, Mao's vision of a decentralized society was reminiscent of Kropotkin's. During the Great Leap Forward of 1958 and the Cultural Revolution of 1966–7, the Chinese communists tried to realize in some measure the anarchist ideal of a society of federated self-governing communes, but did so in such an inflexible and ruthless way that, generally speaking, they ushered in decades of misery, violence and injustice for the great mass of the people. Since then the ancient push and pull between the Taoist tendency to sponsor local autonomy and the Legalists' fondness for centralization has continued, with the central government periodically attempting to reassert control and enforce standardization on wayward regions by enforcing adherence to its national plans.

The anarchist opposition never died in China during the period of communist rule, with libertarians like Shen-wu-lieu keeping its message alive.[13] In recent years, the students have been leading the call for more freedom and democracy; there have even been those among them who do not merely want to get rid of the 'Government of Old Men' but central government itself. In May 1989, in a great upsurge of libertarian energy, millions of students, workers and civil servants occupied the major cities in a display of non-violent direct action. For weeks, the government lost control over the peaceful demonstrations, which saw workers calling for self-management and students for freedom of speech and assembly. The demonstrations grew into a peaceful popular revolution, with students using the hunger strike to bring Gandhian moral pressure to bear on the tottering government. At one stage, it looked as if the People's Army would throw in its lot with the pro-democracy movement.

But the octogenarian rulers prevailed. The general secretary of the Communist Party Zhao Ziyan delivered a stern warning: 'the government could not tolerate a state of anarchy in Beijing'.[14] Loyal troops were called up from the provinces. The tanks rolled into Tiananmen Square on 4 June 1989. Thousands were killed. The eighty-four year-old anarchist novelist Pa Chin, having survived half a century of 'struggle sessions', was arrested for expressing sympathy for the demonstrators. The Communist government may have won this time, but the Chinese people are used to long struggles.

Japan

Despite the popular Western image of Japan as a conformist, rigidly hierarchical and authoritarian nation, anarchism is not entirely an alien flower. Kōtuku Shūsui, the first to introduce Western anarchism to Japan during the Shōwa era, asserted that an anarchistic spirit of negation in Japanese life can be traced back to the influence of Buddhism (especially Zen) and Taoism.[15] An important forerunner of anarchism in seventeenth-century

Japan was also Audō Shōeki who advocated a form of agrarian communism.

The organized anarchist movement did not however get off the ground until 1906 at the time of the authoritarian rule of Emperor Meiji. Kōtoku was of lower Samurai origins but became the most brilliant radical of his generation. He wrote a biography of Rousseau and translated his works. He read Kropotkin whilst in prison during the Russo-Japanese War and habitually called him *sensei* ('teacher'). He became a philosophical material-ist and did not shrink from violence. During a stay in California in 1906–7 he even made contact with the Industrial Workers of the World.

On his return, Kōtuku led the anarchist faction within the short-lived Socialist Party of Japan; they caused a split in 1907 and the Party collapsed soon after. With his anarchist comrades, he then began to nudge the embry-onic labour movement in an anarcho-syndicalist direction. As editor of the anti-war paper *Heimin* (Common People), he also helped establish the anti-militarist tradition of Japanese anarchism. But he was involved in a plot against the Emperor Meiji and in the rigged High Treason trial of 1910–11, twelve anarchists including himself were executed.[16]

In prison at the time was another anarchist Ōsugi Sakae who became the next most important thinker to develop anarchism in Japan. He came from a family of eminent soldiers. When he joined Kōtoku's anti-militarist campaign, he deliberately called himself 'the son of a murderer'. Of a philosophical and literary turn of mind, he developed his own peculiar form of anarchism under the influence of Stirner, Nietzsche, Bergson and Sorel. He argued that the future growth of society would depend on 'an unknown factor' in man's reasoning to be developed by 'a minority who would strive for the expansion of each one's self'.[17] Like Sorel, he saw the labour movement as an attempt by the working man to regain himself.

Although the Japanese anarchists and socialists made little impact dur-ing the First World War, the success of the Russian Revolution and the fast growth of Japanese industry thereafter encouraged the development of the labour movement. It took place in difficult circumstances: unions were technically illegal and the Public Peace Police Law of 1900 legitimized the habitual intimidation of the workers. Ōsugi was interested in the Comintern but soon broke with those who established the Communist Party in Japan in 1922. He managed to win over a sizeable part of the labour movement to anarcho-syndicalism before being murdered by the military police in 1923. Anarchists then lost ground to the communists and the social demo-crats in the labour movement. Some anarchists turned to individual acts of terrorism, especially the members of the secret Guillotine Society. Others made a study of European anarchist thinkers, especially William Godwin and Kropotkin.[18]

During the period of Taishō Democracy, which saw the passing of the Universal Suffrage Act of 1925, the anarchists formed the Black Youth League to oppose the participation of the workers in parliamentary democracy. A school of 'pure anarchism' emerged which argued that socialist parties and reformist trade unions only assist the progress of capitalism. They believed that only an anarchist minority could achieve a social revolution by freeing the people from economic exploitation and political power. Not surprisingly, they clashed with the more reformist anarcho-syndicalists.

A leading exponent of 'pure anarchism' was Hatta Shūzō. An ex-Christian clergyman who drank himself to death in 1934, he translated the works of Bakunin and Kropotkin into Japanese and kept a picture of Nestor Makhno in his room. But he was not merely an interpreter; he developed Kropotkin's anarcho-communism in an original way and became its greatest Japanese exponent.[19] He saw the central evil of capitalism as the division of labour which prevented workers having an interest or sense of responsibility for what goes on outside their narrow sphere of work. On similar grounds, he criticized the class struggle of the syndicalists and their call for workers' councils or soviets since in a post-revolutionary situation such organs would continue the division of labour and require a co-ordinating machinery which would result in a new State. Although he believed in a Bakuninite vanguard of conscious activists, he called on the 'revolutionary masses' as a whole to create without a transitional period a decentralized society based on the free commune. Similar to the traditional Japanese village, the commune would be largely self-sufficient, but its members would be allowed to choose their own work and not become narrow specialists.

At the same time, Ishikawa Sanshiro, another anarchist in prison when Kōtoku was murdered, helped form a syndicalist federation in 1926 called *Zenkoku Jiren* (All-Japan Libertarian Federation of Labour Unions). Ishikawa had not only been deeply influenced by Edward Carpenter's *Towards Democracy* but had spent eight years in exile in Europe, mainly with the Reclus family in Brussels. At first *Zenkoku Jiren* consisted of more than eight thousand workers from twenty-five separate unions. Some of Hatta Shūzō's most important writings appeared in its *Libertarian Federation Newspaper*. The federation soon developed in a 'pure anarchist' direction which led to a syndicalist breakaway in 1929 and the forming of the rival *Nihon Jikyō* (Japanese Libertarian United Conference of Labour Unions).

Zenkoku Jiren grew to achieve a membership of over sixteen thousand members in 1931, compared to *Nihon Jikyō*'s three thousand. The syndicalist unions, formed mainly of workers in small firms, fought a series of strikes during the depression, but the Japanese invasion of Manchuria in 1931 – opposed vehemently by the anarchists – led to their suppression as well as that of the Left as a whole. A united front against fascism which the anarchists joined was finally crushed with *Zenkoku Jiren* in 1935. Some went on however to fight in the CNT militias during the Spanish Civil War.

After the Second World War the elderly Ishikawa wrote his celebrated anarchist vision of utopia *Japan Fifty Years Later*. He imagined Japanese society organized on a co-operative basis (with Proudhonist mutual exchange banks) to enable each individual to live a life of artistic creation. His celebration of nudity reflected Carpenter's influence, but the idea of retaining the Japanese Emperor as the symbol of communal affection was his very own.

In 1946 the Japanese Anarchist Federation was reformed with some syndicalist support. It favoured a revolutionary popular front but became increasingly opposed to the Communists. The Federation collapsed in 1950 along with the Japanese Left, partly due to the repressive policies orchestrated by MacArthur, the Supreme Commander of the Allied Powers, the atmosphere of the Cold War, and the revival of the Japanese economy.

In 1956, the Anarchist Federation reformed with *Kurohata* (Black Flag) as their journal. At its 1958 annual conference, the delegates argued that peaceful co-existence would only serve the rulers of the two superpowers and that the choice was between atomic death and the social revolution. They decided to support the militant students and workers 'from behind' and advocated direct action against the danger of a nuclear war. They remained a negligible force within the workers' movement, but increased support amongst the federation of students unions, the Zengakuren. The latter developed a militant tradition and called for local communes and the taking over of university power. In 1960, the anarchists joined the mainstream of the Zengakuren by calling for fighting rather than demonstration against the military alliance, known as the Security Treaty, with the United States.

A new anarchist theorist Osawa Masamichi emerged at this time. In the journal *Jiyu-Rengo* (Libertarian Federation) which had replaced *Kurohata*, he argued that dehumanization and alienation represented a new type of poverty in mass society and that the social revolution would best be achieved through the gradual structural change of various social groups towards free associations and communes. The revolution would be cultural and social rather than political.

The Vietnam War further mobilized the student movement. The anarchists however saw the danger that the struggle for national independence in underdeveloped countries could lead to national capitalism with a socialist mask at home and promote a world war between the superpowers. A series of direct actions against the war in Vietnam culminated in 1967 in a pitch battle between students and riot police near Haneda airport.

Translations of Marcuse, Guevara and Cohn-Bendit and news of the 'May Revolution' in Paris further radicalized the students. The Japanese Anarchist Federation declared a new era of direct action.

The high point of the struggle was the student occupation of Tokyo University which lasted for several months in 1968. One of the leaders of the 'Council of United Struggle' at the university declared that they were 'aristocratic anarchists' and that their struggle was not on behalf of the maltreated but rather 'the revolt of the young aristocrats who felt that they had to deny their own aristocratic attributes in order to make themselves truly noble'.[20] They happily accepted that epithet thrown by Leninists that their position was an 'infantile disorder' since they were involved in a struggle between the generations.

While the anarchist propagandist Osawa welcomed the 'revolutionary violence' of the students, he warned that it would become oppressive if it remained separated from the 'revolutionary masses'. In the event, the students singularly failed to turn their struggle for greater autonomy into a popular movement. The workers in Japan had become too wedded to the material gains of a thriving economy and too blinded by the ties of loyalty to their companies.

Anarchism in Japan has remained primarily the preserve of small groups of students and isolated intellectuals. In the late 1970s, however, a new anarcho-syndicalist organization called the Rodosha Rentai Undo (Workers' Solidarity Movement) was formed in the Tokyo area and is making headway in other regions. Parliamentary democracy in Japan still remains a delicate plant in stony soil, and the corruption and misrule of a series of conservative governments have sharpened the relevance of the anarchist critique. Direct action also remains part of Japanese political culture. While a social revolution in Japan seems remote, anarchism with its Buddhist and Taoist roots retains its moral force and its legacy will not be erased.

Korea

As in China and Japan, Korea has an old libertarian tradition, especially through Taoist influence. The roots of Korean anarchism have been traced back to Jeong Dasan (1760–1833) and Su-un (1824–64).[21] Dasan advocated a 'village-land system', an early form of anarcho-communism in which people possess jointly the land and cultivate it in common. Everyone is expected to work but can choose and receive according to need. Differences between rich and poor villages would be overcome through free transfers between them. Su-un was more of a philosopher than Dasan. As a humanist, he argued that 'Man is Heaven' and inferred that all human beings are of equal worth. He was executed for trying to upset the feudal order.

These ideas found expression in the Farmers' Revolution in Honan Province in 1894 during which the district which supplied half the rice production of Korea was taken over until it was crushed by the invading Japanese.

During the Japanese occupation from 1910 to 1945 the anarchist movement developed in Korea as part of the national resistance. In the Shimmin region, anarchists formed an independent administration from 1929 to 1931. One 'anarchist' Yu-Rim even took part in the 'Provisional Government'. Korean anarchists are therefore considered patriots today and have a section devoted to them in the Independence Hall in Seoul.

The devastating civil war of the 1950s split the country, with the north developing a Stalinist form of communism under Kim Il Sung which has remained as authoritarian and monolithic as ever. The rulers in the south chose to develop a form of State-directed capitalism. Free trade unions are still not allowed so anarcho-syndicalism has hardly got off the ground. A Federation of Anarchists of Korea however exists and its secretary Ha Ki-Rak, veteran of the Kwangju uprising against the Japanese in 1929, has translated many classic anarchist texts into Korean. The Korean anarchist movement still remains somewhat nationalist and reformist, with the centre of libertarian opposition to the regime remaining with the students and the young who are obliged to do three years' military service.

India

As in China and Japan, the Buddhist tradition of non-interference and indifference to political power made anarchism attractive to a few Indian intellectuals and spiritual teachers. The Buddha told of the first men who lived in perfect harmony but they are said to have had no corporeal bodies. Jaina too tells of a heaven on earth in which no person is discontent and all wants are satisfied by trees. Nevertheless, the mainstream Hindu tradition, with its rigid caste system, is static and hierarchical. Although there was no ideal of a stateless society in ancient Indian political thought, it is doubtful that there was ever a clear idea of the State as a living entity in pre-Muslim times.[22] The idea of the State is discouraged by the concept of *dharma* which is seen as a cosmic law which regulates the universe and sustains society. Indian mysticism moreover has always recognized the need for the individual to work out his or her liberation.

Modern anarchism has popularly been associated in India with violence and naturally has not appealed to those committed to non-violence. Whereas most Western anarchists have been 'anti-statist', Indian anarchism tends to be more 'non-statist', preferring to build an alternative society and to make the State redundant rather than trying to destroy it at one stroke. It is mainly for this reason that Tolstoy has been the most influential Western anarchist in India.

Before the Second World War no real anarchist movement on Western lines developed in India although isolated militants like the Bombay worker M. P. T. Acharya who moved in London anarchist circles in the thirties did their best to introduce anarcho-communism.[23] A Bombay publishing house also reprinted many Western anarchist classics, but they did not find fertile ground beyond a few student and intellectual circles. It was left to the heirs of revolutionary Gandhism to develop an authentically Indian anarchist movement.

While Gandhi has been the outstanding libertarian in India earlier this century, he was not the only one to draw on the country's spiritual traditions in order to reach anarchist conclusions. The central belief of Hindu philosophy is a belief in the divine nature of the unique individual. God is usually interpreted as a moral principle, not a person, synonymous with truth.

Vivekananda early this century reinterpreted the *Bhagavadgita* in a libertarian direction by arguing that every individual has a right to self-realization. 'Liberty is the first condition of growth', he argued, since it leads to individual self-awareness and to the realization of human solidarity and social harmony. The process of self-realization does not cut the individual off from others; on the contrary: 'You are part of the Infinite. This is your nature. Hence you are your brother's keeper.' Nevertheless, while insisting that all control should be voluntary, Vivekananda defined the freedom to which each soul aims in terms of 'freedom from the slavery of matter and thought, mastery of external and internal nature'.[24]

Aurobindo Ghose, who was educated in England, took up Vivekananda's teaching, and became an outstanding spokesman of the national liberation struggle. While advocating non-violent direct action, he sympathized with those prepared to fight against the British. In his philosophy, he tried to reconcile individual freedom with social unity and called for 'preservation by reconstruction'. The individual may exist outside society but once he has attained the personal realization he seeks he should return to the community in order to help others find their own truth and fullness of being. Although Aurobindo saw the Nation-State as a progressive stage in human history after the collapse of empires, in his study *The Ideal of Human Unity* (1918) he described that entity as a mechanical, constricting and uniform structure which should give way to the ideal of anarchy: 'the unity of the human to be entirely sound and in consonance with the deepest laws of life must be founded on free groupings and the groupings again must be the natural association of free individuals.'[25] Like modern social ecologists, he felt that unity is best achieved in diversity, that anarchy is in keeping with the ultimate aims of nature, and that freedom means self-fulfilment in harmony with the environment.

The Indian guru Osho, better known in the West as Bhagwan Shree Rajneesh, often celebrated anarchism as the ultimate goal of human evolution, but he had none of the philosophical rigour or clarity of style of Aurobindo. For him, revolutionary practice meant meditation, freeing the mind from restraint so that it might achieve the true realization of self. He was well aware of the work of Bakunin, Kropotkin, and Tolstoy, and argued that 'there is no need for any laws, any constitutions', but felt that the anarchist ideal could not be achieved without a spiritual transformation. Freedom for him meant being responsible for oneself: 'That you have to be left alone, that the government need not interfere with you, that the police need not interfere with you, that the law need not interfere with you, that the law has nothing to say to you – you are simply alone.'[26]

He once told a French journalist from *Le Figaro*: 'Whichever regime is closer to anarchism is better – the closest to anarchism is best – whatever is furthest from anarchism is worst.'[27] Osho proposes the simple life of economic communism coupled with spiritual growth which should flower into anarchism. Such aims are revolutionary enough, but his demands for a reborn spirituality offer little substantial guidance. The guru found hundreds of Western followers amongst disenchanted middle-class youth; many aped his ideas, and practised his teachings, but no organization was spawned comparable to that sponsored by Gandhi's spiritual tutelage. His fondness for acquiring many a Rolls-Royce car, a triumphantly capitalist icon, did little to bolster his credibility; as did reports of far-from-anarchistic financial corruption amongst his aides.

Gandhi of course was the most influential social thinker this century in India. He was deeply affected by the writings of Tolstoy, but developed his notion of non-resistant love into non-violent direct action and helped organize mass campaigns of civil disobedience to oust the British rulers. He not only saw the State as representing violence in a concentrated and organized form, but contemplated an increase in the power of the State 'with the greatest fear' since it destroys the kind of individuality which lies at the root of all progress. He came closest to anarchism when he declared that the ideal society would be one of 'enlightened anarchy' where 'everyone is his own ruler, and . . . there is not political power because there is no State.'[28] In practice, however, Gandhi was prepared to work with the National Congress and felt that some form of State was necessary in a transitional period before the ideal of anarchy could be realized. The *Sarvodaya* (welfare of all) movement however which Gandhi inspired went beyond his cautious position to a more overtly anarchist one.

The Sarvodaya Movement

After Gandhi's death, a few thousand constructive workers in the *Sarvodaya* movement followed their teacher's suggestion that they should not partici- pate in politics and formed in 1948 a loosely affiliated fellowship. In the following year, it united several Gandhian associations, notably the Spinners Association and the Village Industries Association, under an umbrella organization called Akhil Bharat Sarva Seva Sangh, the All India Associ- ation for the Service of All. They followed Gandhi in promoting a non- violent revolution in order to transform India into a society of self-governing village republics.

Vinoba Bhave soon emerged as the leader of the *Sarvodaya* movement which tried to bring about a land revolution. He launched the campaign for *Bhoodan*, in which landowners were persuaded to donate voluntarily a part of their land to the landless. From this policy developed in the mid 1950s the more ambitious *Gramdan* campaign which tried to bring about communal villages. It was seen as the immediate programme of a total revolution which would lead to the complete moral and social transformation not only of Indian society but of the entire world.[29]

Under the guidance of Vinoba Bhave who stressed the need to 'forget Gandhi' and made his own experiments with truth, the *Sarvodaya* movement took an increasingly anarchist direction.[30] It not only stressed the social implications of *ahimsa* but radically interpreted Gandhi's notion of 'trustee- ship' to support the policy of the common ownership of land. Like Godwin, Gandhi maintained that any property one has, including one's talents, should be used to the benefit of the whole. As in the family, so in society: property should be held in common, each giving according to his ability and each taking according to his needs. In the long run, this would lead to to social equality, as would the call for integrated labour and the recognition that all work is of equal value. The *Sarvodaya* movement was as committed as Gandhi to a decentralized economy of combined fields and workshops although it placed more stress on the value of appropriate technology. Despite the claims of their critics, they have no desire to turn back the clock but merely wish to avoid the disastrous consequences of unchecked industrial growth and to promote local autonomy.

Like Gandhi, the movement was also deeply suspicious of centralized political authority. By stressing the right of private judgement and the impor- tance of the individual conscience, Vinoba rejected the legitimacy of the State's claim to obedience. 'If I am under some other person's command, where is my self-government?', he asked.

> Self-government means ruling your own self. It is one mark of *swaraj* not to allow any outside power in the world to exercise control over

oneself. And the second mark of *swaraj* is not to exercise power over any other. These two things together make *swaraj* – no submission and no exploitation.[31]

Vinoba also believed that the State and government can provide no useful service, however benevolent they may appear: 'My voice is raised in opposition to good government . . . What seems to me to be wrong is that we should allow ourselves to be governed at all, even by good government.' And to dispense with the impression that these are just isolated statements, Vinoba insisted that his main idea is that all humanity should be set free from the burden of government: 'If there is a disease from which the entire world suffers, it is this disease called government.'[32]

This led naturally to a criticism of parliamentary democracy. In the first place, the Sarvodayites like their Western anarchist counterparts assert that those who seek political power are inevitably corrupted. Secondly, they believe that the principle of majority rule cannot express public opinion and bring about the welfare for all. Thirdly, they maintain that political parties are by their nature divisive and corrupting. Recognizing that revolutions are never achieved by power or party politics, the *Sarvodaya* movement therefore sought at this stage to develop a new form of politics based on the direct action of the people themselves. Through Vinoba's inspiration, the Sarva Seva Sangh (Association for the Service of All) adopted the basic rule that all decisions should be taken either unanimously (all members positively agreeing) or by consensus (no member actively disagreeing).

There are of course important differences from the mainstream of Western anarchism. Like Tolstoy's anarchism, the *Sarvodaya* movement is fundamentally religious, and while it sees all creeds as different paths to the same end and even tolerates atheism, it assumes the existence of God and the reality of spirit. Its appeal to all classes is ultimately based on a metaphysical belief in the unity of humankind and in the harmony of interests. Its confidence in an objective moral order means that its central principle of non-violence can take on the force of a categorical imperative. The Sarvodayites have also inherited Gandhi's ascetic, puritanical and repressive character. They rightly want to simplify life, but in pursuing non-attachment they wish to eliminate all sensual pleasure.

In addition, the Sarvodayites are gradualists and flexible in their application of theory. They believe that truth, the obverse of which is non-violence, exists in an absolute sense. But they acknowledge that human beings, however enlightened, are capable of expressing only relative truths. The world might be evolving towards non-violence, but violence is preferable to non-violence adopted out of cowardice. In the Sino-Indian border war of 1962, for instance, many Sarvodayites accepted military resistance as justifiable (while not resisting themselves) since the Indian people were not strong enough for *ahimsa*.

Their gradualism is also reflected in Vinoba's three-fold programme of political development which moves from national independence, via a decentralized self-governing State, to pure anarchy or freedom from all government. He saw himself working in his lifetime to develop the second stage; the last stage will only be reached when all the people, both rich and poor, powerful and weak, become self-reliant and self-governing. The State will eventually wither away, but only if people build an alternative society. And this will be possible only through the slow and thorough transformation of ideas and values.

Vinoba's two most important contributions to anarchism however were his views of non-violent direct action and popular politics. The first involves *satyagraha*. He preferred to work positively through non-violent *assistance* in right thinking rather than through Gandhi's non-violent *resistance* to evil. He wanted get rid of all coercion, moral as well as physical, confident that it is enough to reveal the truth for it to be immediately understood and acted upon. Secondly, Vinoba advocated the 'politics of the people', which involves the positive non-violence of truth and love instead of the 'politics of the State' which excites a craving for power. Even the Welfare State is wrong since it encourages dependence. He fully recognized that the 'only way to bring peace is to renounce power' since 'If you want to cut down a tree, it is no use to climb into its branches.'[33] To this end he called for a new politics of partyless democracy based on the consensus of all classes and groups.

At the peak of its campaign for land revolution in 1969, the *Sarvodaya* movement managed to get 140,000 villages to declare themselves in favour of modified version of *Gramdan* (in which landowners possessed ninety-five per cent of their land donated). Although the movement distributed over one million acres of *Bhoodan* land to half a million landless peasants, it failed to redeem the vast majority of pledges in favour of *Gramdan*, with the result that few villages became even partially communitarian. Many peasants were alienated by the volunteer workers, who on occasion appeared somewhat proud, if not arrogant, in their moral superiority. The movement also became identified to a degree with the National Congress since the government had actually endorsed *Gramdan* programme as a way of promoting its own more modest land reforms.

As the movement began to founder in the early 1970s, Jayaprakash Narayan (JP), an ex-socialist Party leader who had joined *Sarvodaya* in 1954, began to exert a dominant influence. On joining, he had argued that the way forward was 'to create and develop socialist living through the voluntary endeavour of the people rather than seek to establish socialism by use of the power of the State'.[34] He now began calling however for the 'politicalization' of the movement and the use of Gandhi's more aggressive form of non-violent struggle which involved active resistance to the State. Ninety per cent of the activists supported JP's revised strategy but Vinoba himself declined to endorse any departure from his 'non-political' and 'gentle to gentler to gentlest' approach.

In the ensuing crisis, JP and his supporters went on the offensive and tried to turn a students' rebellion in the northern State of Bihar into a 'people's movement' for 'Total Revolution'. No doubt recalling the Marxism of his youth, JP declared that it had become 'glaringly apparent' that the 'state system was subservient to a variety of forces and interests in keeping it a closed shop'.[35] Mass demonstrations opposed 'student power' and 'people's power' to 'State power' and through 'struggle committees' a parallel system of self-government was attempted. Indira Gandhi however responded by imposing in 1975 her State of Emergency for nearly two years, imprisoning the main opposition leaders.

Vinoba, Mahatma Gandhi's 'spiritual heir', had reacted to JP's campaign by a year's vow of silence as a mark of disapproval. Asked for his opinion of the Emergency, he vouchsafed the written comment without breaking his silence: 'an era of discipline'. It was immediately interpreted as support for Indira Gandhi's government and the State of Emergency. The old libertarian who had done so much to guide the *Sarvodaya* movement into a genuinely anarchist direction, was even hailed as the 'Saint of the Government'.[36] He later clarified his position by saying that he was referring to the discipline laid down by the *acharyas* (traditional teachers) to guide their pupils, but the harm had been done.

For his part, JP abandoned all anarchist pretensions. Throwing himself into the political struggle in Bihar, he reminded the students that he would not be a leader in name only and that while he would take the advice of all they would have to accept his decision. During the State of Emergency he then helped organize the coalition of non-Communist parties which formed the Janata (People) Party which defeated unexpectedly Indira Gandhi in 1977. He still held true to his vision of a community in which every individual is dedicated to serving the weak, in which individuals are valued for their humanity and in which every citizen participates in its affairs, but he now saw that a vote for the Janata Party was the way to realize it.[37] Composed of the same social forces and interests as its Congress predecessors, it singularly failed to change anything in India. Since Indira Gandhi's return in 1980 and the subsequent rule of her son and his successors, India has drifted further into authoritarian rule.

JP died in 1979 and Vinoba three years later. Although JP made his strategy of revolution more confrontational, Vinoba remained the purer anarchist of the two. JP like Gandhi had the dubious honour of a State funeral, but not Vinoba. As for the *Sarvodaya* movement itself, its disastrous engagement in conventional politics has left it weakened and uncertain. The failure of its political compromises has encouraged the landless and poor peasants who have not benefited from India's 'Green Revolution' in agriculture to look more to the Communist parties and to those who adopt the violent methods of the Naxalite movement.

From its political baptism of fire, the *Sarvodaya* movement emerged no longer as gentle and anarchistic as it had once appeared. Since 1978, the *Sangh* has modified the unanimity principle to accept majority decisions of eighty per cent. With the loss of its two principal leaders, it has developed more collective ways of forging policy. The main thrust of this policy is now directed towards building from below 'a non-party alternative' to the existing system, combining elements of both Vinoba's and JP's ideas. But the *Sangh* also promotes the idea of fielding non-party 'people's candidates' in elections.

Whatever the future, the *Sarvodaya* movement which developed from revolutionary Gandhism remains distinctly libertarian, and represents the fruitful union of Western economic and social thought with traditional Indian philosophy. It is still active in India and Sri Lanka in the new century.

PART SIX

Modern Anarchism

Neither Victims nor Executioners.
ALBERT CAMUS

Power is war, continued by other means.
MICHEL FOUCAULT

I am an anarchist/I am Antichrist.
'ANARCHY IN THE UK', SEX PISTOLS

Never Work.
Under the Paving Stones, the Beach.
I Take My Desires for Reality, Because I Believe in the
Reality of My Desires.
PARIS, 1968

35

The New Left and the Counter-culture

THE LAST GREAT ANARCHIST experiment on a large scale took place in the Spain of the 1930s, and the anarchists' defeat by Franco's forces destroyed libertarian activity in that country for a generation. The rise of fascism in Germany and Italy destroyed the movements there, while in Britain and France the small remaining bands of anarchists played only a minor role in the struggle against fascism during the Second World War. During the post-war period of reconstruction in Europe, capitalism not only failed to collapse as a result of its own inherent contradictions, as predicted by Marxists, but seemed to many workers to be delivering the goods. It appeared for a while that the 'end of ideology' had come. The European anarchist movement had become so fragmented by the late fifties and early sixties that historians of anarchism were sounding its death knell, burying it in valedictory tomes. Only the idea of anarchism seemed to remain as an unrealizable ideal, perpetually receding on the horizon.

The resurgence of anarchism in the sixties therefore came as a great surprise. With hindsight, however, it is possible to trace a gradual disillusionment on the Left with authoritarian socialism, especially in its Soviet form, after the invasion of Hungary in 1956. As the Cold War began to bite, the promises of Western social democracy – that it would liberate the peoples of Europe from fear and want – came to ring increasingly hollow. Towards the end of the decade, the campaign against the stationing of nuclear weapons in Europe, a campaign which proved especially vigorous in Britain, radicalized a large number of young people.

In the United States, the Civil Rights Movement and the Students for a Democratic Society made a new generation wary of the coercive power of the State. Although the demand was initially for 'one man, one vote', the protesters took to the street and practised non-violent direct action. The police replied with force. For many young people vaguely discontent with their lot, the direct confrontation with authority proved traumatic: 'The policeman's riot club functions like a magic wand', wrote Carl Oglesby in extravagant, existentialist tones, 'under whose hard caress the banal soul grows vivid and the nameless recover their authenticity – a bestower, this wand, of the lost charisma of the modern self: I bleed, therefore I am.'[1]

Tired of the grey monotony of bourgeois life, groups of the young began to 'drop out' and form their own subculture. They wanted to establish a free social space for their imaginative experiments. The cult of the anti-hero and the outsider suggested that all was not well in suburbia. Albert Camus' existentialist stress on rebellion in thought and action against the absurdity of life was widely appreciated. Although the young rebels had not yet found a cause, they wanted to leave their comfortable homes and take to the open road.

The New Left

It was in this context that the New Left emerged in the late fifties in the United States and Western Europe, rediscovering and developing a form of libertarian socialism which sought a third path between the organized lovelessness of capitalist States and the bureaucratic centralism of Communist States. In the West, social democratic parties seemed to be merely tampering with capitalism in order to make it more efficient, while Marxist-Leninist parties with their tired dogmas born of nineteenth-century circumstances had little relevance to workers in the affluent societies of the late twentieth century who had little to lose but their mortgages. The Communist Parties of Western Europe, following the parliamentary road to socialism, were desperately trying to make themselves respectable to a disinterested electorate. Marxism's apologists resorted to notions of 'alienation' and 'false consciousness' in order to try and explain away the lack of interest of the 'proletariat' in class struggle.

At the cultural level, many new ideas were fermenting on the Left. The American sociologist C. Wright Mills called on academics and intellectuals to resist the System. He had revised Marxism by opposing the notion of a power elite to the class model and by stressing the role of the military-industrial complex in American society. His 'Letter to the New Left' in 1961 was strongly libertarian in spirit, reflecting a utopian yearning for social justice and spontaneity. The work of the maverick psychoanalyst and Marxist Wilhelm Reich was rediscovered. His argument that the authoritarian personality is the *sine qua non* of authoritarian regimes and that a sexual revolution must accompany the next political revolution was taken to heart. He wished to create a worker democracy of self-governing individuals free of cruelty and dependency. A. S. Neill, the British educationist and founder of Summerhill, was strongly influenced by Reich: he advocated free schools in which each individual child governs herself and had a wide influence in educational circles.

The German-American philosopher Herbert Marcuse offered a highly libertarian analysis of the failings of Soviet Marxism. Recognizing with Freud that 'civilization has progressed as organised domination', he called in *Eros and Civilisation* (1955) for the release of the forces of repression and the eroticizing of culture. He went on to portray vividly the alienation of the *One-Dimensional Man* (1964) of Western society whose creativity and ability to dissent had been undermined. He concluded that only a non-repressive civilization would be able to give natural expression to unfettered human nature although he did not go so far as to reject the need for government. At the same time, social critics like Lewis Mumford were denouncing the 'megamachine' of the new military-industrial complex in the United States, while Paul Goodman was reminding people of the advantages of decentralized communities.

During the early part of the 1960s the ideology of the New Left remained ambiguous. The reigning orthodoxies of Liberalism and Marxism seemed exhausted and irrelevant, but there was no clear alternative. The old class analysis did not seem to fit post-scarcity society and the notion of vanguard parties had been sullied by the Soviet experience. It was not long however before the New Left began espousing the traditional anarchist principles of mutual aid, participatory democracy, and decentralization. Its activists challenged the pyramid of power in university, factory and State. They criticized the oppressive nature of contemporary culture, especially in the realm of the family and sexuality. They called for an end to hierarchy and domination. They opposed the living community to the centralized and bureaucratic State. They wanted to control their lives and forge their own destiny. Like Bakunin, they saw the 'lumpenproletariat' despised by Marx – blacks, students, women and the unemployed – as possessing truly revolutionary potential. Where they did turn to the Marxist tradition for inspiration, it was to its more libertarian and syndicalist strands.[2]

In the process, Marxism itself underwent a sea change. It was possible to talk of the 'anarcho-Marxism' of Herbert Marcuse, or for the student militant Daniel Cohn-Bendit to describe himself as a Marxist 'in the way Bakunin was'. The new 'libertarian Marxism' which emerged was closer to anarchism than the official Marxist movements, stressing the role of free will in history, the importance of consciousness in shaping social life, and the need for community-based organization. It was opposed to bureaucracy and militarism and called for the disassembly of the State.[3] In Britain, for instance, E. P. Thompson, Raymond Williams, and Stuart Hall called in their May Day Manifesto of 1967 for a new kind of socialist movement based on particular needs and issues; they urged us to withdraw our allegiance from the 'political machines' and to 'resume our own initiatives' in extra-parliamentary activity.[4]

The New Left movement has been called 'anarchist in its deepest impulses'.[5] Not all on the New Left however could be described as entirely libertarian, let alone anarchist; many like Wright Mills merely looked for reforms within a more enlightened form of capitalism. Its leaders rarely challenged the fundamental premisses of late capitalist society. Towards the end of the sixties, many New Left activists turned their backs on traditional radical theory and looked instead to Third World revolutions, especially those in Cuba and China, as model social insurrections. Yet these revolutions themselves were far from being thoroughly libertarian: Che Guevara may have been called the 'new Bakunin' but he emphasized the need for a vanguard party and strong leadership. Again, back in the United States, the Black Panthers reprinted Bakunin and Nechaev, yet their dominant ideology was the Third World Marxism of Mao and Frantz Fanon.

Even so, while these reformist and authoritarian strands existed, the mainstream of the New Left undoubtedly espoused many classic anarchist ideas such as workers' control, decentralization, and direct action. They recognized like Bakunin the revolutionary potential of the marginal and *déclassé* elements in society and argued that the organization of the movement itself inevitably foreshadows the structure of the new society. Above all, they saw the need to create counter-institutions and to build the new society from the bottom up in the womb of the old.[6] The anarchism of the New Left was different from its pre-war antecedents in that it was predominantly pacifist and largely existed outside strictly anarchist organizations. Crucially, it also saw feminism as a central issue. Where the main support for the old anarchist movement came from peasants and artisans, the new anarchists were principally disaffected middle-class intellectuals, especially teachers, social workers and students. As a result, there was a new emphasis on the importance of environment, culture and lifestyle.

The Counter-culture

While the New Left's confrontation with the State deepened over the Vietnam War, a remarkable shift in consciousness occurred which came to be known as the 'counter-culture'. Following the pioneering example of the Beats (notably Allen Ginsberg, Lawrence Ferlinghetti, Tuli Kupferberg and Gary Snyder), young people in the US began to challenge the lifestyle of their parents and the values of the nuclear family. Taking the advice of Timothy Leary, many dropped out and turned on to mind-expanding drugs. They began creating 'counter-institutions' such as communes, collectives, co-operatives, rock festivals, love-ins and sit-ins. They challenged authority whatsoever form it took and insisted on the right to think and act for themselves. They tried to create a real community in the heart of 'the lonely crowd'.

Although they practised different strategies, those who dwelled in the counter-culture were opposed to the modern technological, militarized, and centralized State which seemed to offer only instant death by nuclear war or gradual, lingering death by tedium in factory or office. Capitalism promised freedom and affluence, but all it seemed to deliver was bland conformity, the packaging of time and space, and boredom. Many of the young decided 'to do their own thing'. They celebrated tolerance and diversity and sought the free satisfaction of desire. The social nature of the movement found expression in slogans like 'Make Love, not War' – a principle with profound social and psychological implications since it recognized the link between sexual repression and organized violence.

While not a conscious anarchist, Jerry Rubin was infected by the libertarian tendency of the counter-culture in America when he declared:

[After the revolution] there will be no more jails, no courts, or police.

The White House will become a crash pad for anybody without a place to stay in Washington.

The world will be one big commune with free food and housing, everything shared.

All watches and clocks will be destroyed.

Barbers will go to rehabilitation camps where they will grow their hair long.

The Pentagon will be replaced by an LSD experimental farm.

There will be no more schools or churches because the entire world will become one church and school.

People will farm in the morning, make music in the afternoon and fuck whenever they want to.[7]

The counter-culture which erupted in America in the late 1960s has been described, not implausibly, as 'the new anarchism'.[8] Theodore Roszak, in his classic study *The Making of a Counter-Culture* (1970), specifically listed among its major sources and ingredients anarchist social theory. In his rhapsodic *Where the Wasteland Ends* (1972), he further recommended anarchism as a politics uniquely swayed by 'organic sensibility . . . born of a concern for the health of cellular structure in society and a confidence in spontaneous self-regulation'. His 'visionary commonwealth' on the far side of the urban-industrial wasteland is a decentralized society based on the commune and neighbourhood, combining Proudhon's economic mutualism with Kropotkin's harmonious blend of fields and workshops.[9]

The counter-culture was a product of the first American youth movement in history. The pioneers were the hippies, street people and flower children. They rejected the cultural templates of the dominant culture and tried to create their own alternative scene. Partly as a result of their 'mind-expanding' drug experiences – as encouraged by Aldous Huxley, Ken Kesey and Timothy Leary – they wanted to change people's consciousness and cleanse 'the doors of perception'. But it was also a question of change for change's sake, or as Yippie leader Abbie Hoffman put it, *Revolution for the Hell of It*.

Like the overtly political New Left movement, the counter-culture was fundamentally anarchist without being conscious of it, especially in its rejection of majority rule and its stress on the moral responsibility of the individual. The military draft became terminally emblematic of the authoritarian State in the United States, for on signing one not only pledged service to a State which was killing mindlessly and pointlessly in Vietnam, but also signed oneself over to the System in all its poisonous finery.

The counter-culture was also anarchist in its critique of the centralized and technological State and in its widespread desire to see a return to a simpler life closer to nature.[10] Faced with the prospect of collusion with suburbia and the military-industrial complex, American youth set up communes and collectives in the city centres or in the country. In the midst of affluence and consumerism, they chose voluntary poverty, like Thoreau in *Walden*, like the monastics of old, preferring to go without, borrow, improvise or steal rather than work.

The counter-culture was tolerant of diversity and eclecticism. Unlike the classic anarchist thinkers, who as heirs of the Enlightenment looked to reason and science to bring about progress, the gurus of the counter-culture rejected the 'rationality' and 'objectivity' which had been so debased by the dominant culture in its attempts to justify war, poverty and injustice. The pendulum swung in the other direction, towards a reinvigorated spirituality, towards subjectivity, feelings, sensations, play, mysticism, and magic. Critical thought was often a casualty, spurned in favour of blissing out, of abdicating entirely from careful thinking.

Unlike their more politicized counterparts in the New Left, the inhabitants of the counter-culture were not, strictly speaking, revolutionary. They did not seek to overthrow the government or State but rather tried to live out their dreams on its boundaries or in its interstices.[11]

The counter-culture was full of contradictions. A desire to eat organic foods often coexisted with chemical experimentation with drugs. The influence of women's liberation led to a convergence of sexual styles which encouraged androgyny (long hair, beads etc.), but in some communes traditional 'male' and 'female' roles were voluntarily adopted and accentuated. The communes also offered the apparent freedom to break with parental values and 'to do what you will', but there were also strong moral pressures to conform to certain 'alternative' norms and values. Letting it 'all hang out' was not always entirely inspiring or beautiful. The ideal was the 'together' person, who was 'cool', 'laid back', and in control of his or her life. In practice, much of what passed for 'freedom' was little more than self-indulgence. The experimentation with drugs did not always put people in touch with a 'higher reality', more usually rendering them less energetic, duller, in the long run. Excepting a small, dogged minority, the disaffected children of the affluent soon left the underground when the money and the kicks ran out.

The counter-culture never offered a real threat to the *status quo*; many of its fashions were taken up by the market, and many of its members eventually co-opted by the dominant society and culture. The political movement of the New Left, however, did have a real, if not a lasting, effect. In the United States, student unrest burst out on the Berkeley campus of the University of California in 1964 after the authorities tried to arrest a student activist. In the ensuing struggle with the police on campus, which left many injured, the Free Speech movement was born. In the following year, students combined with local youth to occupy a vacant lot, and tried to create a 'People's Park' but the police eventually ensured that the bulldozers prevailed. It marked a symbolic turning-point for those whose concern with democracy and nature led them into direct confrontation with the forces of the State.

For a while, it seemed possible that a social revolution might be achieved by non-violent direct action. Mao's power, which grew out of the barrel of a gun, was abandoned by the hippies and their fellow travellers for 'Flower Power'. The Beatles sang *All You Need Is Love* and the youth echoed the sentiment on both sides of the Atlantic. But the pacifist phase of the New Left was comparatively short-lived. The student unrest in Europe and America in 1967 and 1968 led to a violent confrontation with the State. The oppressive response of the authorities showed that the ruling elites would never peacefully acquiesce in change. The spontaneous uprising in France in the spring of 1968, initially triggered off by students and followed by a general strike and the occupation of factories, seemed to augur a revolution along classic anarchist lines.

In other European States, student movements, inspired by their comrades in America and France, called for educational reforms and deepened their analysis of the capitalist State. Small anarchist associations, along with dissident Trotskyist and Maoist groups, suddenly found their literature to be in demand. The prevailing mood of the movement was profoundly anti-authoritarian.

In Germany, Rudi Dutschke made this libertarian undertow amongst the students more explicit, despite his Marxist background. 'The present-day nationalization of the whole society', he insisted, 'creates the basis for an understanding of the anti-state and anti-institution struggle of the radical extra-parliamentary opposition.' The opposition was no longer directed against mistakes in the System but was aimed 'at the whole way of life of the authoritarian state as it has existed up to now'.[12] Since the aggression of the United States in Vietnam had prompted the symbolic entry into the Western capitals of the Third World and all its concerns, every radical opposition to the System must necessarily assume a global dimension. Dutschke therefore called for a student-worker alliance to overthrow capitalism and the State. His voice however was soon silenced: inspired by the assassin of Martin Luther King, Jr., in 1968 a young German right-winger put several bullets in Dutschke's head and body and nearly killed him.

In practice, the student movements in Germany and Britain did not go far beyond the occupation of academic institutions, the call for greater academic democracy, and street demonstrations against US aggression in Vietnam. There was no question of them directly challenging the State as in France. Although they were profoundly libertarian in tone, self-conscious anarchists did not play a major role in the student unrest.

France 1968

The greatest European uprising of the 1960s occurred in France during May 1968, when the student rebellion triggered off the occupation of the factories and one of the greatest general strikes in history. It had been long taken for granted on the European Left that a classic revolution was no longer possible in Western countries. As the British historian Eric Hobsbawm observed at the time, the events in France were 'totally unexpected and totally unprecedented'.[13] President de Gaulle ordered the French army in Germany to the frontier and moved troops up towards Paris. It seemed for a brief moment that the social revolution was about to happen.

But while the workers occupied the factories, they did not work in them and failed to turn their strike committees into administrative organs of self-management. In the event, a ten per cent pay rise accepted by the reformist Confédération Générale du Travail and the offer of new elections by de Gaulle led to the collapse of the strike, and the students left for their holidays and their comfortable family homes. They had failed to uncover the beach under the paving stones of Paris. Nevertheless, the May – June events proved the most important uprising in France since the Paris Commune of 1871.

The rebellion was distinctly libertarian in character. The French anarchist historian Jean Maitron described the events which shook France for six weeks in the spring of 1968 as a definite form of anarchism.[14] Daniel Guérin, whose book on anarchism became a best-seller at the time, wrote in a postscript afterwards that the revolution was 'profoundly libertarian in spirit' and that 'all authority was repudiated or denied'.[15] He was particularly impressed by the call for self-management which echoed in university and factory. In Britain Tom Nairn in his analysis of the events declared boldly soon afterwards: 'The anarchism of 1871 looked backwards to a pre-capitalist past, doomed to defeat; the anarchism of 1968 looks forward to the future society almost within our grasp, certain of success.'[16]

In retrospect, it would seem that many of the ideas and tactics at the time were profoundly anarchist in character, although those professing them would probably not have called themselves anarchists. The events marked a great resurgence of anarchist theory but they did not lead to an organized social movement. It was as if a sudden libertarian tidal wave had come from nowhere and threatened to wash away the State, only to subside as quickly as it had come. It was left for historians to pick over the confused flotsam which it discarded in its wake.

The slogans of the movement undoubtedly seemed directly inspired by the anarchist tradition. Graffiti on the walls in Paris declared: NEITHER GODS NOR MASTERS; THE MORE YOU CONSUME THE LESS YOU LIVE; ALL POWER TO THE IMAGINATION; IT IS FOR-BIDDEN TO FORBID; BE REALISTIC: DEMAND THE IMPOSS-IBLE. All this revealed a profoundly anarchist sensibility at work. But unlike previous revolutions which were primarily concerned with overcoming econ-omic scarcity, the French revolutionaries in a society of abundance were preoccupied with the transformation of every day life. They looked to self-liberation as the basis for social liberation. And while the revolt was started by the students, it developed into a mass movement, cutting across tra-ditional class divisions. The uprising rapidly passed from resistance to the State to a direct and permanent *contestation* with it.[17]

The first rumblings were heard at Strasbourg University in 1966 when the government-sponsored student union was taken over by those who wanted to destroy it. It inspired André Bertrand's comic strip account *The Return of the Durutti Column* – a direct reference to the legendary activities of Buenaventura Durruti during the Spanish Civil War. The Situationist Mustapha Khayati also issued his widely influential tract *The Poverty of Student Life*, in which he calls for a revolutionary alliance between workers and students, victims both of the spectacle of consumer society. The most revealing document to emerge, however, from the student movement was the Appeal issued from the open assembly of the occupied Sorbonne of 13–14 June 1968. Although some of the theses contradicted each other, they stated that there are 'no student problems' for students are workers themselves – the 'lumpenproletariat of the consumer society'. The global dimension of their struggle was recognized in the thesis that the 'solidarity of the bourgeoisie and the proletariat is set against the lumpenproletariat of the Third World'. Above all, they stressed that they chose the means of their ends, that is, 'the power from which every form of violence and repression can be excluded as the foundation of its existence and the means of its survival'.[18] The students reaffirmed personal liberty, the innocence of desire, and the joy of creativity, play and happiness. In the Sorbonne amphitheatre a slogan declared: I TAKE MY DESIRES FOR REALITY, BECAUSE I BELIEVE IN THE REALITY OF MY DESIRES. Outside in the Place de la Sorbonne one could read: FREEDOM IS THE CON-SCIOUSNESS OF OUR DESIRES.[19]

Anarchists in France at the time formed only small groups centred around magazines like *Socialisme ou Barbarie* and *Noir et Rouge*. Critical of its dogmatism, many had left the French Anarchist Federation and developed an eclectic critique of contemporary society. There was therefore no organized anarchist movement to speak of in France at the time. But individual anarchists undoubtedly influenced the anti-authoritarian groups called the 22 March Movement and the Situationist International who played an important role in the events. In addition, the anonymous crowds of *enragés* (fanatics) who belonged to no organization expressed profound anarchist sentiments without apparently being aware of their origin.

The libertarian impetus of the 22 March Movement, formed at the cradle of the revolt – Nanterre University – came through in its celebration of spontaneity, improvisation and self-expression. Its participants felt they were involved in a permanent festival, at home everywhere. In its assemblies they arrived at decisions by the 'sense of the assembly' and sought not the seizure of power but its dissolution.[20] They criticized both superpowers as being merely varieties of the same State capitalism. They challenged all forms of repression in existing society. Their tactics, slogans and propaganda were invented as they went along. They saw their actions as 'exemplary' in the struggle against the capitalist State. As de Gaulle correctly observed, they were 'in revolt against modern society, against consumer society, against technological society, whether communist in the East or capitalist in the West'.

Although the movement had no leaders, the media took up Daniel Cohn-Bendit, better known as 'Danny Le Rouge', as its spokesman. He was a twenty-three year-old Nanterre sociology student at the time. Typical of the eclecticism of the movement, he called himself both an anarchist and a 'libertarian Marxist': while Bakunin was the greatest influence on him, he also acknowledged that Trotsky, Mao and Marcuse had played an important part in his intellectual education. His anarchism was evident in his opposition to capitalism and the State, his condemnation of Soviet communism, and his advocacy of workers' control and self-management.

In his book written soon after the events with his brother Gabriel, *Le Gauchisme, remède à la maladie sénile du communisme* (1968; translated into English as *Obsolete Communism: The Left Wing Alternative*), he drew out the libertarian implications of the 22 March Movement. A great part of the book was a sustained polemic against Bolshevism, both Leninist and Stalinist, focusing in particular on the repression of the anarchist opposition during and after the Russian Revolution. At the same time, it recorded how the students recognized that all revolutionary activity is collective and involves a degree of organization, but they challenged the need for a revolutionary leadership as well as the need for a party, since the latter inevitably reduces the freedom of the people to 'freedom to agree with the party'.[21] New forms of organization were developed in the students' local action committees which were seen as evolving the means of coping with specific situations. They welcomed the vast chain of workers' committees which emerged to bypass the calcified structure of the trade unions.

The anarchist nature of their recommendations is clear in their insistence that in the future the movement must resolve to respect and guarantee 'the plurality and diversity of political currents within the revolutionary mainstream', to struggle against the formation of any kind of hierarchy, and to ensure that all factories and businesses are run by those who work in them.[22] Above all, they argued that the revolution was not made in the name of some abstract ideal or on behalf of a party: '*C'est pour toi que tu fais la révolution*' (You make the revolution for yourself). Daniel Cohn-Bendit has since thrown himself into the activities of the Green Party in Germany, but he has not entirely forgotten his libertarian youth and he continues to seek greater social autonomy within the confines of the State.

The Situationists

The other important libertarian group which came to prominence during the May – June events in France in 1968 were the Situationists. They originated in a small band of avant-garde artists and intellectuals influenced by Dada, Surrealism and Lettrism. The post-war Lettrist International, which sought to fuse poetry and music and transform the urban landscape, was a direct forerunner of the group who founded the magazine *Situationniste Internationale* in 1957. At first, they were principally concerned with the 'supersession of art', that is to say, they wished like the Dadaists and the Surrealists before them to supersede the categorization of art and culture as separate activities and to transform them into part of everyday life.[23] Like the Lettrists, they were against work and for complete *divertissement*.

Under capitalism, the creativity of most people had become diverted and stifled, and society had been divided into actors and spectators, producers and consumers. The Situationists therefore wanted a different kind of revolution: they wanted the imagination, not a group of men, to seize power, and poetry and art to be made by all. Enough! they declared. To hell with work, to hell with boredom! Create and construct an eternal festival.

At first the movement was mainly made up of artists, of whom Asger Jorn was the most prominent. From 1962 the Situationists increasingly applied their critique not only to culture but to all aspects of capitalist society. Guy Debord emerged as the most important figure: he had been involved in the Lettrist International, and had made several films, including *Hurlements en faveur de Sade* (1952). Inspired by the libertarian journal *Socialisme ou Barbarie*, the Situationists rediscovered the history of the anarchist movement, particularly during the period of the First International, and drew inspiration from Spain, Kronstadt, and the Makhnovists. They described the USSR as a capitalist bureaucracy, and advocated workers' councils. But they were not entirely anarchist in orientation and retained elements of Marxism, especially through Henri Lefebvre's critique of the alienation of everyday life. They believed that the revolutionary movement in advanced capitalist countries should be led by an 'enlarged proletariat' which would include the majority of waged labourers. In addition, although they claimed to want neither disciples nor a leadership, they remained an elitist vanguard group who dealt with differences by expelling the dissenting minority. They looked to a world-wide proletarian revolution to bring about the maximum pleasure.

At the end of 1967, Guy Debord in *The Society of the Spectacle* and Raoul Vaneigem in *The Revolution of Everyday Life* presented the most elaborate expositions of Situationist theory which had a widespread influence in France during the 1968 student rebellion. Many of the most famous slogans which were scribbled on the walls of Paris were taken from their theses, such as FREE THE PASSIONS, NEVER WORK, LIVE WITHOUT DEAD TIME. Members of the Situationist International (SI) co-operated with the *enragés* from Nanterre University in the Occupations Committee of the Sorbonne, an assembly held in permanent session. On 17 May the Committee sent the following telegram to the Communist Party of the USSR:

SHAKE IN YOUR SHOES BUREAUCRATS STOP THE INTERNATIONAL POWER OF THE WORKERS' COUNCILS WILL SOON WIPE YOU OUT STOP HUMANITY WILL NOT BE HAPPY UNTIL THE LAST BUREAU-CRAT IS HUNG WITH THE GUTS OF THE LAST CAPITALIST STOP LONG LIVE THE STRUGGLE OF THE KRONSTADT SAILORS AND OF

THE MAKHNOVSCHINA AGAINST TROTSKY AND LENIN STOP LONG
LIVE THE 1956 COUNCILIST INSURRECTION OF BUDAPEST STOP
DOWN WITH THE STATE STOP

Groups of *enragés* in Strasbourg, Nantes and Bordeaux were also inspired
by the Situationists and attempted to 'organize chaos' on the campuses.
The active thinkers however never numbered much more than a dozen.

In their analysis, the Situationists argued that capitalism had turned all
relationships transactional, and that life had been reduced to a 'spectacle'.
The spectacle is the key concept of their theory. In many ways, they merely
reworked Marx's view of alienation, as developed in his early writings. The
worker is alienated from his product and from his fellow workers and finds
himself living in an alien world:

> The worker does not produce himself; he produces an independent
> power. The *success* of this production, its abundance, returns to the
> producer as an *abundance of dispossession*. All the time and space of his
> world become *foreign* to him with the accumulation of his alienated
> products . . .[24]

The increasing division of labour and specialization have transformed work
into meaningless drudgery. 'It is useless', Vaneigem observes, 'to expect
even a caricature of creativity from a conveyor belt.'[25] What they added to
Marx was the recognition that in order to ensure continued economic
growth, capitalism has created 'pseudo-needs' to increase consumption.
Instead of saying that consciousness was determined at the point of production, they said it occurred at the point of consumption. Modern capitalist
society is a consumer society, a society of 'spectacular' commodity consumption. Having long been treated with the utmost contempt as a producer, the
worker is now lavishly courted and seduced as a consumer.

At the same time, while modern technology has ended natural alienation
(the struggle for survival against nature), social alienation in the form of a
hierarchy of masters and slaves has continued. People are treated like passive objects, not active subjects. After degrading being into having, the
society of the spectacle has further transformed having into merely appearing. The result is an appalling contrast between cultural poverty and economic wealth, between what is and what could be. 'Who wants a world in
which the guarantee that we shall not die of starvation', Vaneigem asks,
'entails the risk of dying of boredom?'[26]

The way out for the Situationists was not to wait for a distant revolution
but to reinvent everyday life here and now. To transform the perception of
the world and to change the structure of society is the same thing. By
liberating oneself, one changed power relations and therefore transformed
society. They therefore tried to construct situations which disrupt the ordi-

nary and normal in order to jolt people out of their customary ways of thinking and acting. In place of petrified life, they sought the *dérive* (with its flow of acts and encounters) and *détournement* (rerouting events and images). They supported vandalism, wildcat strikes and sabotage as a way of destroying the manufactured spectacle and commodity economy. Such gestures of refusal were considered signs of creativity. The role of the SI was to make clear to the masses what they were already implicitly doing. In this way, they wished to act as catalysts within the revolutionary process. Once the revolution was underway, the SI would disappear as a group.

In place of the society of the spectacle, the Situationists proposed a communistic society bereft of money, commodity production, wage labour, classes, private property and the State. Pseudo-needs would be replaced by real desires, and the economy of profit become one of pleasure. The division of labour and the antagonism between work and play would be overcome. It would be a society founded on the love of free play, characterized by the refusal to be led, to make sacrifices, and to perform roles. Above all, they insisted that every individual should actively and consciously participate in the reconstruction of every moment of life. They called themselves Situationists precisely because they believed that all individuals should construct the situations of their lives and release their own potential and obtain their own pleasure.

As for the basic unit of the future society, they recommended workers' councils by which they meant 'sovereign rank-and-file assemblies, in the enterprises and the neighbourhoods'.[27] As with the communes of the anarcho-communists, the councils would practise a form of direct democracy and make and execute all the key decisions affecting everyday life. Delegates would be mandated and recallable. The councils would then federate locally, nationally and internationally.

In their call for the 'concrete transcendence of the State and of every kind of alienating collectivity' and in their vision of communist society the Situationists come closest to the anarchists.[28] They not only referred to Bakunin for their attack on authoritarian structures and bureaucracy, but Debord argued that 'anarchism had led in 1936 [in Spain] to a social revolution and to a rough sketch, the most advanced ever, of proletarian power'.[29] The Situationists differ however from traditional anarchism in their elitism as an exclusive group and in their overriding concern with coherence of theory and practice. In their narrow insistence on the proletariat as the sole revolutionary class, they overlooked the revolutionary potential of other social groups, especially the students. They also denied that they were 'spontaneists' like the 22 March Movement and rejected the 'ideology' of anarchism in so far as it was allegedly another restrictive ideology imposed on the workers.

Despite the acuteness of their critique of modern capitalism, the Situationists mistakenly took a temporary economic boom in post-war France for a permanent trend in capitalist societies. Their belief in economic abundance now seems wildly optimistic; not only underproduction but also underconsumption continue in advanced industrial societies. In many parts of the globe, especially in the southern hemisphere, so-called 'natural alienation', let alone social alienation, has yet to be overcome. Nevertheless, for all their weaknesses, the Situationists have undoubtedly enriched anarchist theory by their critique of modern culture, their celebration of creativity, and their stress on the immediate transformation of everyday life. Although the SI group disbanded in 1972 after bitter wrangling over tactics, their ideas have continued to have widespread influence in anarchist and feminist circles and inspired, at times almost subconsciously it seemed, much of the style and content of punk rock.

Provos and Kabouters

The only place in Europe where a profoundly libertarian movement got underway outside France was in Holland where the 'Provo' movement which emerged in the mid sixties had been inspired by anarchist militants. The movement began when the philosophy student Roel van Duyn, who had participated in anarchist artist Robert Jaspar Grootveld's staged 'happenings', set up the monthly magazine *Provo*. The 'Provos' – short for provocateurs – brought social issues to public attention by means of well-orchestrated protests and demonstrations.

The approach of the Provos was non-violent, playful, and utopian; they were determined to release the *homo ludens* buried in each of their staid compatriots. They used games, satire and mimicry in order to make authority reveal the coercive nature hidden under its tolerant mask. One of their more memorable plans was to leave white bicycles all over Amsterdam for anyone to use to counteract the effect of the private motor car on the environment. The campaign grew until the police began to confiscate the bicycles, not on the grounds that they might affect the car industry but because they might be stolen!

Given the highly industrialized and densely populated nature of their society, the Provos were particularly concerned with environmental issues. They did not look to the proletariat like the Situationists in France but to the 'provotariat' – hippies, drop-outs, students and the disaffected young – as the agents of change. The were self-consciously anarchist. The journal *Provo*, which reached a circulation of 10,000, included in its declaration of principles: 'PROVO regards anarchism as the inspirational source of resistance' and 'PROVO wants to revive anarchism and teach it to the young'.[30]

Roel van Duyn, the principal theoretical spirit, specifically identified himself with the anarchist tradition. A former art and philosophy student, van Duyn had emerged from an anarchist group inspired by the Dutch anarcho-pacifist Ferdinand Domela Nieuwenhuis. He was also profoundly influenced by Kropotkin's arguments for co-operation as the key factor in evolution, his call for a total revolution of society, and his vision of a balance between town and country.[31]

The Provos participated in the 1966 municipal elections in Amsterdam, and won one seat, but their provocative nature inevitably led to clashes with the police. The movement reached a climax in 1966 when it disrupted Princess Beatrix's wedding with smoke bombs – a riot followed. It began to flounder soon afterwards and wound itself up in 1967. On 13 May 1967 a Provo happening took place, proclaiming the 'death of Provo'.

Concerned about the violent and destructive direction the Provos had taken, van Duyn concluded that it was not enough to protest against consumer society and centralized power; like the anarcho-syndicalists before him, he decided that it was essential to try and build a new society in the shell of the old. He now felt that the Provos should have put more emphasis on love than on creativity. In order to remind people of their close bond with nature, he chose as a symbol of a revitalized libertarian movement the figure of the 'kabouter', an elf or gnome.

It was the role of the modern kabouter, van Duyn argued, to become a 'playful technologist'. In his *Message of a Wise Kabouter* (1969), he further tried to link cybernetics with anarchism since it teaches that a healthy organism controls itself. At the same time, he was less optimistic than Kropotkin in his estimate of the reasonableness of human beings; there is a 'screwed up little dictator in each of us' who has to be overcome.[32] He also went beyond Kropotkin's positivism to develop a formal dialectics based on the marriage of love and aggression. Whereas Kropotkin's symbol was said to be the industrious and co-operative ant, van Duyn chose the peacock butterfly. Its normal mode of existence is based on love and co-operation, but it can also frighten its predator by spreading its wings and revealing menacing eyes.

In February 1970 the Kabouters announced the formation of an alternative community called the 'Orange Free State' (the royal house of Holland is the House of Orange). They set up twelve departments paralleling existing government ministries. In their playful proclamation, they declared that the new society would emerge out of the old society like a toadstool from a rotting trunk; from the subculture of the existing order will grow an alternative community. It will create a new culture with a new human being – the 'culture elf' – who will bring to an end the tension between nature and the old culture. The tension between riches and poverty will also be overcome by collectivizing property.

The 'Free State' will be a society without government in which everybody is responsible for his or her own destiny. Its form will be anti-authoritarian and decentralized, based on a council democracy which will never resort to force. In order to build their new autonomous society in the midst of the old order, the Kabouters recommended non-violent direct action, sabotage and 'erotics'. In short, their social philosophy is not 'the socialism any more of the clenched fist, but of the interlaced fingers, of the erect penis, of the flying butterfly, of the moved glance, of the Holy Cat. It is anarchism.'[33] An orange tree was planted as a symbol for the new society and the citizens of Amsterdam were invited to dance around it, singing the new national anthem, 'The Cuckoo Song'.

The Kabouters never formed a party and remained a broad libertarian movement, but, six months after the formation of the Free State, they caused a sensation by winning seats in six municipalities in Holland with eleven per cent of the vote and gaining five seats in the forty-five-member council of Amsterdam. Groups on similar lines were formed in other parts of Europe. Although such parliamentary action was clearly a retreat from pure anarchism and a 'Free State' is a contradiction in terms, van Duyn saw it as a peaceful way of creating a free society on libertarian lines. When the Kabouters began to falter in 1971, he formed a new group called the 'Panic Sowers', after expressing his views in personal form in a *Panic Diary* (1971). While his comrades evoked the Greek God Pan in their attempt to defend nature against its enemies, they singularly failed to create panic in the authorities. The movement collapsed silently in Holland in the early seventies, but the electoral strategy and the concern with the environment of the Kabouters made them forerunners of the European Greens.

Social Ecology

One of the most influential expressions of anarchism has come in the growing Green movement, which has attracted not only libertarian socialists like Cohn-Bendit in Germany but avowed anarchist thinkers like Murray Bookchin in the United States. The new 'social ecology', which finds the roots of the ecological crisis in society and calls for an end to hierarchy and domination, has proved to be one of the most fruitful developments in contemporary anarchism.

Whereas nineteenth-century anarchists like Kropotkin still saw the need for the 'conquest of nature' and industrial progress in order to eradicate poverty, social ecologists argue that in our post-industrial and post-scarcity society the principal concern must be to overcome the drive to conquer and master nature. As Murray Bookchin has argued, the very idea of dominating nature probably first evolved from man's prior domination of woman. In their search for power and desire to dominate, human beings have gone on not only to oppress each other, but also to devastate the planet which sustains them. The traditional anarchist demand to eradicate authority and domination in *society* must therefore be widened to include *nature* as a whole.

In fact, modern ecology confirms many of the central themes of classic anarchism. It offers a model of nature which embraces unity in diversity, equality with difference, equilibrium with change, all within a non-hierarchical framework. It presents the planet as a self-regulating and evolving organism, which reflects the self-regulating and evolving capacity of human beings. As the ecological crisis deepens, social ecology has been a major influence in the new century.

Anarcha-Feminism

Feminism too has developed the libertarian message of traditional anarchism. Taking their cue from women like Louise Michel, Charlotte Wilson, Voltairine de Cleyre and Emma Goldman, feminists have been drawn to the subtle analysis of power and hierarchy put forward by anarchists. They have also been impressed by their insistence that moral regeneration come before political reform.

In a study of anarchist women in America earlier in the century, Margaret Marsh observed that anarcha-feminists considered themselves exempt from the notions of womanhood that restricted their less liberated sisters and advocated sexual experimentation. They focused primarily on the family, seeing the roots of sexual inequality embedded in the nuclear family. They did not therefore think that reform of laws alone could bring about equality; it was necessary to struggle for personal autonomy and economic independence. They also went further than their socialist sisters by insisting that roles should always be based on preference, not gender, whether it be in sexual relationships, child rearing, or work.[34] Indeed, Emma Goldman's most important contribution to anarcha-feminism was her recognition that the revolutionary process must take place within the individual mind as well as in society at large.[35]

These points were taken up by the second wave of anarcha-feminists in the late sixties who maintained that 'anarchism is the logically consistent expression of feminism' since it does not separate political activities from personal dreams of liberation.[36] They argued that as women generally live on the boundaries of capitalism and yet are its most unfortunate victims, they have a remarkably clear insight into its nature. Their position makes them particularly aware of patriarchy in the family as well as in the State. To anarcha-feminists, the State and patriarchy are twin aberrations; they are both part of the fundamental social and psychological model of hierarchy and domination. It is therefore necessary to destroy 'all vestiges of the male-dominated power structure, the State itself'.[37]

Stressing the principle 'the personal is political', the anarcha-feminists have developed a radical critique of everyday life. With relationships being split between subject and object, women have become either commodities to be used by men or passive spectators of the male world. Rejecting the polarities between male and female, adult and child, work and play, sanity and madness, they seek to create a society in which individuals whatever their gender or age can choose their own way of life.[38] They do not want to transfer power from one set of boys to another as has always happened previously in 'his-story'. Their principal aim is to erode power and authority; in personal terms, they seek individual control over their own bodies and lives – 'Power to no one, and to every one: to each power over his/her own life, and no others.'[39]

In the women's movement as a whole, there are undoubtedly many 'natural' anarchist tendencies. Penny Kornegger contends that 'feminists have been unconscious anarchists in both theory and practice for years'.[40] From this perspective, it has been suggested that feminism practises what anarchism preaches. Indeed, it has even been argued that feminists are the only existing protest group that can honestly be called practising anarchists.[41]

The feminist movement which began in the late sixties developed its own organizational form and practice at the heart of which lay the small 'consciousness-raising' group. Spontaneous and non-competitive, without leaders and followers, they resemble the 'affinity groups' which played such an important part in the Spanish Civil War. As an international movement, the women's movement has also adopted the central anarchist principles of decentralization and federalism.

Anarcha-feminists have noted this tendency and have tried to develop it as fully as possible. They wish to avoid the oppression of patriarchy on the one hand and the 'tyranny of structurelessness' on the other. They steer clear of reformist campaigns and left-wing parties, preferring to undertake independent direct action over specific issues. Unlike their sisters earlier in the century who worked alongside men in the anarchist movement, many anarcha-feminists prefer to work mainly within the radical women's movement.[42] They have shown by their example what can be done in a decentralized mass movement based on federally-linked affinity groups.

A New Era: Reinventing Anarchy

Anarchism was pronounced moribund in the early sixties and then made a remarkable and unexpected revival towards the end of the decade. But in America and Europe the New Left underwent a crisis after 1968. The riot following the Democratic Party Convention in Chicago in 1968 proved the high-point of mass opposition to the State in America, as did the uprising and general strike in France the same year. By the early 1970s, the New Left had disintegrated as a coherent movement. In desperation, splinter groups like the Weathermen in the US, the Baader-Meinhof Gang in Germany, the Red Brigades in Italy, and the Angry Brigade in Britain, all of whose libertarian credentials were doubtful to say the least, resorted to bombings and kidnappings in order to speed up the collapse of the capitalist State. Their actions only made it all the more vigilant and repressive.

In the meantime, the world-wide economic recession of 1973–4 checked post-scarcity utopianism; the vast majority of rebellious youth put away their beads and tried to make it once again in straight society. They reverted to type. Only a few persevered with the commune movement. Nevertheless, the libertarian legacy of the sixties remained powerful, and the seventies saw widespread experimentation with alternative ways of living, especially in urban and rural communes and co-operatives. Anarchy was no longer a forgotten dream.

Proudhon's maxim 'Anarchy is Order', commonly reduced to the symbol Ⓐ, has become one of the most common graffiti on the urban landscape. The feminist, pacifist, municipal and Green movements which emerged in the seventies and eighties were distinctly libertarian in their organization and goals.[43] They have gone from strength to strength. Punk rock, whose themes echoed those of the Situationists, helped a new generation to see the limitless possibilities in rebellion. Anarchism today is no longer dismissed as the creed of bomb-throwers, but is increasingly recognized as that of thoughtful individuals who are asking awkward questions and proposing new ways of seeing and doing. Anarchy has been reinvented and the new anti-capitalist, anti-war and anti-globalization movements reflect its decentralized and non-hierarchical ways of organizing and its libertarian goals.

36

The New Right and Anarcho-capitalism

ANARCHO-CAPITALISM HAS RECENTLY had a considerable vogue in the West where it has helped put the role of the State back on the political agenda. It has become a major ideological challenge to the dominant liberalism which sees a role for government in the protection of property. The anarcho-capitalists would like to dismantle government and to allow complete *laissez-faire* in the economy. Its adherents propose that all public services be turned over to private entrepreneurs, even public spaces like town halls, streets and parks. Free market capitalism, they insist, is hindered not enhanced by the State.

Anarcho-capitalists share Adam Smith's confidence that somehow private interest will translate itself into public good rather than public squalor. They are convinced that the 'natural laws' of economics can do without the support of positive man-made law. The 'invisible hand' of the market will be enough to bring social order.

Anarcho-capitalism has recently had the greatest impact in the United States, where the Libertarian Party has been influenced by it, and where Republicans like Ronald Reagan wanted to be remembered for cutting taxation and for getting 'the government off people's backs'. In the United Kingdom, neo-Conservatives argue that 'there is no such thing as society' and wish to 'roll back the frontiers of the State' – a view adopted evangelically, in theory if not always in practice, by Margaret Thatcher, Prime Minister from 1979 to 1990. State socialism is attacked not so much because it is egalitarian but because it seeks to accrue more powers for the State to exercise centrally.

The phenomenon of anarcho-capitalism is not however new. With the demise of Benjamin Tucker's journal *Liberty* in 1907, American individualist anarchism lost its principal voice; but its strain of libertarianism continued to re-emerge occasionally in the offerings of isolated thinkers. The young essayist Randolph Bourne, writing outside the anarchist movement, distinguished between society and the State, invented the famous slogan

'War is the Health of the State', and drew out the authoritarian and conformist dangers of the 'herd'.[1]

Franz Oppenheimer's view of the State as 'the organization of the political means' and as the 'systematization of the predatory process over a given territory' influenced libertarians and conservatives alike in the twenties.[2] The Jeffersonian liberal Albert Jay Nock reached anarchist conclusions in *Our Enemy the State* (1935) at the time of the New Deal. A conservative of the *laissez-faire* school, he foresaw 'a steady progress in collectivism running into a military despotism of a severe type'.[3] It would involve steadily-increasing centralization, bureaucracy, and political control of the market. The resulting State-managed economy would be so inefficient and corrupt that it would need forced labour to keep it going.

Nock's warning did not go unheeded. Friedrich A. Hayek spelt out in *The Road to Serfdom* (1944) the dangers of collectivism. In his restatement of classic liberalism in *The Constitution of Liberty* (1960), he rejected the notion of social justice and argued that the market creates spontaneous social order. But while he wished to reduce coercion to a minimum, he accepted the need for the coercion of a minimal State to prohibit coercive acts by private parties through law enforcement. He also accepted taxation and compulsory military service. While a harsh critic of egalitarianism and of government intervention in the economy, he was ready to countenance a degree of welfare provision which cannot be adequately provided by the market. His views have had an important influence on neo-Conservatives, especially those on the right wing of the Conservative Party in Britain.

Anarcho-capitalists like David Friedman and Murray Rothbard go much further. In some ways, their position appears to be a revival of the principles of the Old Right against the New Deal which sought government interference in the economy, but they are not only motivated by a nostalgia for a thoroughly free market but are aggressively anti-authoritarian. Where Tucker called anarchism 'consistent Manchesterism', that is taking the nineteenth-century *laissez-faire* school of economists to their logical conclusion, anarcho-capitalists might be called consistent Lockeans.

Following Locke, classic liberals argue that the principal task of government is to protect the natural rights to life, liberty and property because in a 'state of nature' where there is no common law the enjoyment of such rights would be uncertain and inconvenient. The anarcho-capitalists also ask, like Locke in his *Second Treatise*, 'If Man in the state of Nature be so free as has been said, if he be absolute lord of his own person and possessions, equal to the greatest and subject to nobody, why will he part with his freedom?'[4] Unlike Locke, however, the anarcho-capitalists do not find such a state of nature without a common judge inconvenient or uncertain. They maintain that even the minimal State is unnecessary since the defence of person and property can be carried out by private protection agencies.

David Friedman sees such agencies as both brokers of mini-social contracts and producers of 'laws' which conform to the market demand for rules to regulate commerce. Each person would be free to subscribe to a protective association of his choice, since 'Protection from coercion is an economic good'.[5] Apart from adumbrating *The Machinery of Freedom* (1971), Friedman sees capitalism as the best antidote to the serfdom of collectivism and the State.

The writings of Ayn Rand, a refugee from the Soviet Union, best represent the intellectual background to the new right-wing libertarianism in the United States. In her *The Virtue of Selfishness: A New Concept of Egoism* (1964), she attempted a philosophical defence of egoism while in her novels she portrayed a superior individual fighting the forces of collectivism, particularly in the form of the State. Her superior individual, driven by a Nietzschean will to power, appears in the guise of a capitalist entrepreneur who is presented as the source of all wealth and the creator of all progress. Rand claimed that she had a direct knowledge of objective reality, and her 'Objectivist' movement had a considerable vogue in the sixties. She was convinced of the objective truth of her own views, which to others appear mere dogma. She remained a minimal statist and explicitly rejected anarchism.

Amongst anarcho-capitalist apologists, the economist Murray Rothbard is probably most aware of the anarchist tradition. He was originally regarded as an extreme right-wing Republican, but went on to edit la Boétie's libertarian classic *Of Voluntary Servitude* and now calls himself an anarchist. 'If you wish to know how the libertarians regard the State and any of its acts,' he wrote in *For a New Liberty: The Libertarian Manifesto* (1973), 'simply think of the State as a criminal band, and all the libertarian attitudes will logically fall into place.' He reduces the libertarian creed to one central axiom, 'that no man or group of men may aggress against the person or property of anyone else'.[6] Neither the State nor any private party therefore can initiate or threaten the use of force against any person for any purpose. Free individuals should regulate their affairs and dispose of their property only by voluntary agreement based on contractual obligation.

Rejecting the State as a 'protection racket' with an illegitimate claim on the monopoly of force, Rothbard would like to see it dissolved, as would Friedman, into social and market arrangements. He proposes that disputes over violations of persons and property may be settled voluntarily by arbitration firms whose decisions are enforceable by private protection agencies.

Rothbard describes an anarchist society where 'there is no legal possibility for coercive aggression against the person or the property of any individual'. But where Tucker recognized no inherent right to property,

Rothbard insists on the need for a 'basic libertarian code of the inviolate right of person and property'.[7] In addition, for all his commitment to a Stateless society, Rothbard is willing to engage in conventional politics. He helped found the Libertarian Party in the USA which wants to abolish the entire federal regulatory apparatus as well as social security, welfare, public education, and taxation. Accepting Bourne's view that war is the health of the State, the Party wants the United States to withdraw from the United Nations, end its foreign commitments, and reduce its military forces to those required for minimal defence.

Rothbard argued at the 1977 Libertarian Party Convention that to become a true libertarian it was necessary to be 'born again', not once but twice, in a baptism of reason as well as of will. Since in his view libertarianism is the only creed compatible with the nature of man and the world, he is convinced that it will win because it is true. Whatever the workers and bureaucrats might think or want, Statism will collapse of its own contradictions and the free market will prevail throughout the world.

However libertarian in appearance, there are some real difficulties in the anarcho-capitalists' position. If laws and courts are replaced by arbitration firms, why should an individual accept their verdict? And since he 'buys' justice, what assurances are there that the verdicts would be fair and impartial? If the verdicts are enforced by private protection agencies, it would seem likely, as Robert Nozick has pointed out, that a dominant protective agency (the one offering the most powerful and comprehensive protection) would eventually emerge through free competition.[8] A *de facto* territorial monopoly would thus result from the competition among protective agencies which would then constitute a proto-State. The only difference between the 'ultraminimal' State of a dominant protection agency and a minimal State would be that its services would be available only to those who buy them.

Nozick's work *State, Anarchy and Utopia* (1974) is widely regarded as one of the most important works in contemporary political philosophy. Inspired in part by individualist anarchist arguments, especially those of Spooner and Tucker, and replying to the libertarian views of Rothbard and Rand, he calls for a minimal State to oversee private protection agencies to ensure contracts are kept by property-owning individuals. He insists however that a man ruled by others against his will, whose life and property are under their control, is no less a slave because he has the vote and periodically may 'choose' his masters.

Nozick has helped to make libertarian and anarchist theory acceptable in academic circles. But in the end he opts for a nightwatchman State in order to protect the individual's rights to life, liberty and property. In his 'framework for utopia', he proposes a society of independent city-States organized according to their inhabitants' preferences. He defends capitalism under the theory of just entitlement, arguing that just acquisitions and just transfers made in the absence of force or fraud legitimize the distribution of wealth resulting from capitalist exchange. However poorly a person may fare in the exchange, he argues, his rights remain inviolate. Since the outcome is the exercise of human liberty, there is no moral reason to correct market forces by redistributing wealth. The acceptable maxim of capitalism for Nozick is therefore: 'From each as they choose, to each as they are chosen'.[9]

Nozick joins a group of American philosophers like John Hospers and Eric Mack who adopt 'minarchy' rather than anarchy. They call for a minimal State, restricting the scope of the modern state to Locke's 'common judge with authority' to make laws (for the protection of property), to punish thieves and malefactors, and to defend the nation against foreign aggression.[10] They are right-wing libertarians rather than anarchists in the tradition of Jefferson, insisting 'that government is best which governs least'.

An ambivalent 'defense of anarchism' has been put forward by Robert Paul Wolff. He rejects the political legitimacy of the State on a neo-Kantian principle of moral autonomy. He assumes that in so far as people are rational and are to act they must be autonomous. The autonomous man who determines his own acts refuses to be ruled and denies all claims to political authority: 'For the autonomous man, there is no such thing, strictly speaking, as a command.'[11] Wolff does not however see any immediate implications for his philosophical anarchism and ethical individualism. In his 'Utopian Glimpses of a World Without States' in *In Defense of Anarchism* (1970), he maintains that a high order of social co-ordination in a society in which no one claims legitimate authority would only be possible after its members had achieved a high level of moral and intellectual development. Indeed, rather than offering a defence of anarchism as a political theory, he seems more concerned with elaborating a form of moral and political scepticism.[12]

Wolff's practical proposals are also problematic. He recommends a form of 'instant direct democracy' based on a system of 'voting machines' in every home linked to a computer in Washington. Each Bill would then be voted on by all the people after it had been discussed by their representatives in a national assembly. But such a system could easily lead to representatives manipulating their voters as they do in existing parliamentary democracies. There is also a big difference, recognized in part by Wolff, between the passive role of listener and the active role of participant in a debate. The kind of direct democracy practised in ancient Athens, which actively involved all the citizens, would appear to be preferable to television viewers being merely able to register their response to decisions made by an elected elite. Wolff's proposal would turn citizenship into little more than a spectator-sport. He allows no meaningful debate or collective discussion of ends.

Although he recommends extreme economic decentralization, Wolff aligns himself with the anarcho-capitalists and right-libertarians by wanting to retain private property and the market to co-ordinate human behaviour. Again, he suggests that the army could be run on the basis of voluntary commitment and submission to orders but this would seem little different from existing forms of conscription.

In the utopias of the anarcho-capitalists, there is little reason to believe that the rich and powerful will not continue to exploit and oppress the powerless and poor as they do at present. It is difficult to imagine that protective services could impose their ideas of fair procedure without resorting to coercion. With the free market encouraging selfishness, there is no assurance that 'public goods' like sanitation and clean water would be provided for all. Indeed, the anarcho-capitalists deny the very existence of collective interests and responsibilities. They reject the rich communitarian tradition of the ancient Greek *polis* in favour of the most limited form of possessive individualism. In their drive for self-interest, they have no conception of the general good or public interest. In his relationship with society, the anarcho-capitalist stands alone, an egoistic and calculating consumer; society is considered to be nothing more than a loose collection of separate individuals.

The anarcho-capitalist definition of freedom is entirely negative. It calls for the absence of coercion but cannot guarantee the positive freedom of individual autonomy and independence. Nor does it recognize the equal right of all to the means of subsistence. Hayek speaks on behalf of the anarcho-capitalist when he warns: 'Above all we must recognize that we may be free and yet miserable.'[13] Others go even further to insist that liberty and bread are not synonymous and that we have 'the liberty to die of hunger'.[14] In the name of freedom, the anarcho-capitalists would like to turn public spaces into private property, but freedom does not flourish behind high fences protected by private companies but expands in the open air when it is enjoyed by all.

Anarcho-capitalists are against the State simply because they are capitalists first and foremost. Their critique of the State ultimately rests on a liberal interpretation of liberty as the inviolable rights to and of private property. They are not concerned with the social consequences of capitalism for the weak, powerless and ignorant. Their claim that all would benefit from a free exchange in the market is by no means certain; any unfettered market system would most likely sponsor a reversion to an unequal society with defence associations perpetuating exploitation and privilege. If anything, anarcho-capitalism is merely a free-for-all in which only the rich and cunning would benefit. It is tailor-made for 'rugged individualists' who do not care about the damage to others or to the environment which they leave in their wake. The forces of the market cannot provide genuine conditions for freedom any more than the powers of the State. The victims of both are equally enslaved, alienated and oppressed.

As such, anarcho-capitalism overlooks the egalitarian implications of traditional individualist anarchists like Spooner and Tucker. In fact, few anarchists would accept the 'anarcho-capitalists' into the anarchist camp since they do not share a concern for economic equality and social justice. Their self-interested, calculating market men would be incapable of practising voluntary co-operation and mutual aid. Anarcho-capitalists, even if they do reject the State, might therefore best be called right-wing libertarians rather than anarchists.[15]

Modern Libertarians

IN THIS CENTURY, THERE have been few outstanding libertarian thinkers but libertarian thought has been remarkably profound and varied. It has been enriched by intellectuals as diverse as the British philosopher Bertrand Russell and the novelist Aldous Huxley, the Jewish existentialist philosopher Martin Buber, the American cultural critic Lewis Mumford and the linguist theoretician Noam Chomsky, and the French writer Albert Camus and the social thinker Michel Foucault. They have taken socialism or liberalism to the borders of anarchism, and occasionally stepped over. As States east and west have grown more centralized, militarized, and bureaucratic they have held up the vision of a free society as the ultimate ideal.

Bertrand Russell

Bertrand Russell was attracted to anarchism and remained a lifelong libertarian despite his espousal of the idea of a World State to end war between nations. At the age of twenty-three, the young aristocrat was described by Beatrice Webb in 1895 as 'anarchic', and he later confessed to a temperamental leaning towards anarchism.[1] In 1938, the Spanish secretary of the IWMA included all his works in a bibliography to an encyclopaedia article on anarchism because, as Gerald Brenan's wife put it, 'they have the "tendency" as old Anarchists say.'[2]

Russell knew what anarchism stood for. In his *Roads to Freedom: Socialism, Anarchism, and Syndicalism* (1918), written just before he was imprisoned for denouncing the validity of the First World War, he included on the title page the sentiments of Lao-Tzu:

Production without possession
action without self-assertion
development without domination.

In an informed and thoughtful discussion, he defines anarchism as the theory which is opposed to 'every kind of forcible government'. Liberty is the supreme good of the anarchist creed, and liberty is sought by 'the direct road of abolishing all forcible control over the individual by the community'.[3] Russell endorsed such a view and argued that anarchism should be 'the ultimate ideal, to which society should continually approximate'.[4] He felt that anarchism is particularly strong in matters of science and art, human relations and the joy of life.

However, he still felt that for the time being it was impossible to realize such an ideal. In an earlier work on *Principles of Social Reconstruction* (1916), he had acknowledged that the State and private property are the two most powerful institutions of the modern world. But while he wished to show how harmful and unnecessary many of the powers of the State were, he still held it useful for bringing about the substitution of law for force in human relations: 'The primitive anarchy which precedes law is worse than law.'[5] The State also had a positive role in ensuring compulsory education and sanitary measures and in diminishing economic justice.

Despite close consideration of Bakunin's and Kropotkin's arguments against government and the State, Russell still concluded in *Roads to Freedom* that some coercion by the community is unavoidable in the form of law and that the State is a necessary institution for certain limited purposes. Without government, the strong would only oppress the weak. Of all the ideologies treated, he came down in favour of guild socialism. But it remained his belief that 'the free growth of the individual must be the supreme end of a political system which is to refashion the world'.[6] In a review, the anarchist journal *Freedom* (founded by Kropotkin and others) quoted at length from *Roads to Freedom*, recommended it as a 'very readable book', and observed that Russell's work showed 'very strong leanings to anarchism in its constructive proposals'.[7]

Russell visited Russia in the summer of 1920 where he met several prominent anarchists, including Emma Goldman and Alexander Berkman who showed him around Moscow, as well as Bolshevik leaders. His book *The Practice and Theory of Bolshevism* (1920) which resulted from the visit was a critical account of his experiences at a time when, on the Left, it was considered a kind of treachery for a socialist to criticize the Bolshevik dictatorship.

When Goldman sought political refuge in Britain two years later, Russell took up her case with the Home Office, informing them that she would not engage 'in the more violent forms of Anarchism'.[8] At a dinner in Oxford to welcome her, the only person to applaud her vehement attack on the Soviet government was Russell. *Freedom* reported that his was by far the best speech (along with William C. Owen's): 'Mr Russell, who has the most acute philosophical mind in England, made the most complete avowal of anarchist convictions of the evening.'[9]

Russell, however, still kept his distance from the anarchists. He refused to help Goldman in her efforts to form a committee to aid Russian political prisoners since he was not prepared to advocate an alternative government in Russia which might be even more cruel. He wrote to Goldman: 'I do not regard the abolition of all government as a thing which has any chance of being brought about in our life times or during the twentieth century.'[10] He was clearly worried about his utilitarian position nonetheless, and went on to condemn the Bolsheviks' appalling treatment of their political opponents. When Sacco and Vanzetti were executed, he was forced to conclude that they had been condemned unjustly on account of their political opinions.

Russell's libertarian stance and his reluctance to follow it to anarchist conclusions were rooted in his view of humanity and the universe. He was well aware of the logical error known as the 'naturalistic fallacy', committed by Kropotkin and many other anarchists, of drawing arguments from the laws of nature as to what we ought to do, for to imitate nature may merely be slavish. Nevertheless, he acknowledged that 'if Nature is to be our model it seems that the anarchists have the best of the argument. The physical universe is orderly, not because there is a central government but because every body minds its own business.'[11]

As an atheist and atomist, Russell had a dark vision of humanity despite his hopes for a better world. He considered man to be the outcome of an 'accidental collocation of atoms' destined to meet extinction in the vast death of the solar system. Only on the 'firm foundation of unyielding despair, can the soul's habitation henceforth be safely built'.[12] But although man has a strangely accidental and ephemeral position in the universe, it does not mean that he cannot struggle to improve his lot.

As a humanist, Russell was interested in expanding human freedom and happiness. The task however is not easy. While man had evolved to be the most rational and creative of animals, prepared even to engage in unpleasant activities as means to desirable ends, he was still prey to destructive and aggressive desires. These natural impulses cannot be eradicated, thought Russell, only channelled into less injurious outlets. The theme runs throughout Russell's work as a disruptive undertow in the bright stream of rational thought. In his work on *Power* (1938), written as the Nazis were preparing for war, Russell suggests, like Hobbes before him, that among the infinite desires of man the chief are those for power and glory. Morality is therefore needed to restrain 'anarchic self-assertion'.[13]

Russell was never a complete pacifist and supported the war against Nazi Germany, but the experience only made him more pessimistic about human possibilities. After the war, he even called on the United States to threaten the Soviet Union in order to enforce international agreement about atomic weapons. In the Preface to the 1948 edition of *Roads to Freedom*, he said that if he were to write it again, he would be much less sympathetic towards anarchism. In a world of scarcity, 'only stringent regulations can prevent disastrous destitution'. Moreover, the totalitarian systems in Germany and Russia had led him to take a 'blacker view' of what men are likely to become without 'forcible control over their tyrannical impulses'.[14]

In his Reith Lectures, published in 1949 as *Authority and the Individual*, Russell argued that human nature had not changed much over the centuries and that we instinctively divide mankind into friends and foes, co-operating with the one and competing with the other. He therefore sees the need for government, whose primary aim should be 'security, justice and conservation'. In this Russell remains a liberal, calling for the protection of life and property since law is 'an indispensable condition for the existence of any tolerable social order'.[15] Taking up an idea he launched as early as 1916, Russell further advocated the creation of a World State to bring about unity between nations and to prevent war.

In the late fifties and early sixties, Russell became involved once again with anarchists in the Committee of 100 of the Campaign for Nuclear Disarmament. Since lawful persuasion had proved ineffectual, the veteran dissident now called again for non-violent direct action and large-scale civil disobedience. But he remained estranged from the anarchist movement, for he considered that British unilateral disarmament and subsequent multilateral disarmament could be achieved by strong national governments and eventually by a world government. As anarchists pointed out, the venerable philosopher thereby tried to place the responsibility for disarmament in the very hands of the people and institutions who were responsible for armament in the first place.[16]

The passionate sceptic became even more cynical in his old age. Meditating on the progressive school he had helped set up with his wife Dora, he wrote in his autobiography: 'To let the children go free was to establish a reign of terror, in which the strong kept the weak trembling and miserable. A school is like the world: only government can prevent brutal violence.'[17]

Nevertheless, despite the parting of the ways from the anarchists over the unruly nature of man, Russell's writings were profoundly libertarian. He remained throughout his life a staunch defender of freedom of thought:

> Thought is subversive and revolutionary, destructive and terrible. Thought is merciless to privilege, established institutions and comfortable habits. Thought is anarchic and lawless, indifferent to authority, careless of the well-tried wisdom of the ages.[18]

His free thinking was not only apparent in works like *Sceptical Essays* (1928) and *Why I am Not a Christian* (1957) but also in *Marriage and Morals* (1929) where he called for the liberation of Woman and promoted the value of a healthy sex-life. He wrote widely on education. His *The Conquest of Happiness* (1930) recalls the title and some of the contents of Kropotkin's *Conquest of Bread*. In his marvellous essay 'In Praise of Happiness' (1932), he roundly rejected the Protestant Ethic (urging the Young Man's Christian Association to start a campaign to induce the young to do nothing) and argued that the road to happiness lies in 'the organized diminution of work'.[19] Equally his celebration of 'useless' knowledge echoes the thoughts of many an anarchist since Godwin on the value of leisure and free enquiry.

Russell's writings achieved an enormous circulation in many languages. They acted as a great liberating influence on generations of readers in their call for greater personal and social freedom and the joyful flowering of human personality. Even in the political field, he insisted that the necessary evil of government should be kept to a minimum, and that individuality, personal initiative and voluntary organization should be allowed to flourish. As a public figure, he was ready to stand up for the beliefs he held, even if it meant going to prison in their defence. One of his last campaigns was to end *War Crimes in Vietnam* (1967). His own varied life, which straddled the twentieth century, exemplified his maxim that the best life is 'that which is most built on creative impulses, and the worse that which is most inspired by love of possession'.[20]

Aldous Huxley

Amongst earlier British libertarians this century, the novelist Aldous Huxley stands out boldly. He was born in 1894, the grandson of T. H. Huxley, and, after being educated at Oxford, he settled in California in 1937. Huxley called himself a decentralist but his analysis of power and authority, his hatred of war, and his vision of a free society are undoubtedly anarchist in spirit. In his anti-utopian novel *Brave New World* (1932), he depicted the direction in which Western science and society seemed to be developing, with human embryos conditioned to collectivism and passivity. Order is achieved by creating a society of robots for whom happiness is synonymous with subordination. A 'savage' who has educated himself by reading Shakespeare and believes in free moral choice is unable to cope with the new world and eventually commits suicide.

In *Ends and Means* (1937), Huxley expressed his own philosophy more directly: the ultimate 'end' is the free person who is non-attached – non-attached to desires, possessions, exclusive love, wealth, fame, and status, even to science, art, speculation and philanthropy. Such an ethic assumes the existence of a spiritual reality underlying the phenomenal world. To realize this libertarian ideal, Huxley insists, like Tolstoy, that good ends can only be achieved by good means.

The tendency of modern States is towards authoritarian and centralized rule which happens to be the principal obstacle to social and individual progress. Huxley proposes a move in the opposite direction to what he calls 'responsible self-government'.[21] Indeed, he insists, like all anarchists, that the State should be abolished;

> in so far as it serves as the instrument by means of which the ruling class preserves its privileges, in so far as it is a device for enabling paranoiacs to satisfy their lust for power and carry out their crazy dreams of glory, the state is obviously worthy of abolition.[22]

At the same time, Huxley argues that in a complex society there must be some organization responsible for co-ordinating the activities of the various constituent groups. There must also be a body to which is delegated the power of acting in the name of the society as a whole. Huxley goes on: 'If the word "state" is too unpleasantly associated with ideas of domestic oppression and foreign war, with irresponsible domination and no less irresponsible submission, then by all means let us call the necessary social machinery by some other name.'[23] Since there is no general agreement as to what that name should be, Huxley decided to go on using 'the bad old word' until some better one be invented. In describing the functions of this form of 'self-government', he clearly has in mind a pattern of responsible, communal living in which the government of men has been replaced by the administration of things. As an alternative to State socialism and capitalism, he advocated a form of small-scale, decentralized industrial democracy in which greater economic equality would encourage co-operation amongst its people.

After the Second World War, Huxley showed, in his *Science, Liberty and Peace* (1947), how applied science and technology had helped concentrate power in the hands of a small ruling minority and equipped 'the political bosses who control the various national states with unprecedentedly efficient instruments of coercion'.[24] In place of the all-embracing modern State, with its large-scale production, he urged the progressive decentralization of the population, greater accessibility to land, and the common ownership of the means of production. Science should be used to help form self-governing, co-operative groups working for subsistence and the local market. While international trade should be kept to a minimum in order to lessen nationalist passions, technology should be used to increase self-sufficiency within individual nations.

Despite his readiness to resort to 'appropriate legislation' to bring about these reforms, Huxley clearly reveals the influence of Gandhi and Tolstoy in his call for a peaceful return to the land. He reiterates moreover that 'any government enjoying a monopoly of political and economic power is exposed to almost irresistible temptations to tyranny'.[25] He therefore recommends an increase in personal autonomy, the expansion of voluntary co-operation, and of all 'de-institutionalized activity'.[26]

Yet in his eagerness to avoid wars perpetrated by nationalism, Huxley is still willing, as was Bertrand Russell, to contemplate some form of world government. In keeping with his pacifism, he spelled out in the pamphlet *What Are We Going To Do About It* (1936) that the only way to resist belligerent and authoritarian governments is via Gandhian non-violent resistance and direct action. Like Godwin and Tolstoy, Huxley believed that not only is government founded on opinion, but it is possible to change people's opinions peaceably.

As he grew older, Huxley became increasingly interested in mysticism. In his anthology, *The Perennial Philosophy* (1945), he argues that each person is in their innermost being part of the Ultimate Reality of God and the final purpose is to lose one's earthly personality and be absorbed in the whole. In the heart of things, there is a divine serenity and goodwill. Huxley now insists that while society is good to the extent that it encourages contemplation, the ultimate goal is a free mind. Huxley experimented with mescaline to achieve mystical insight and encouraged others in *The Doors of Perception* (1954) to use drugs in order to achieve a higher order of consciousness. The work became a key text of the counter-culture.

Throughout Huxley's mystical writings and fiction, there is a constant undertow of anti-authoritarianism. Huxley is principally concerned with liberation – economic, social, mental and finally spiritual. When he came to sketch his ideal society in his novel *Island* (1962), it transpired that his vision of utopia comprises a decentralized and co-operative community based on ecological principles. On Pala, his imaginary island of freedom and happiness in South-East Asia, the only religion is Buddhism; the crippling creeds of Christianity, Freudianism and Leninism are absent. Where Lenin claimed electricity plus socialism equals communism, the equation of Palanese civilization is quite different: 'Electricity minus heavy industry plus birth control equals democracy and plenty.'[27] Applied science is only used to solve agricultural problems. The horrors of the nuclear family have been replaced by a Mutual Adoption Club (MAC) which enables each child to feel secure in the company of twenty or more adults without being possessed by them.

In theory, the island of Pala is a constitutional monarchy with an elected parliament, but there is neither an established church nor omnipotent politicians nor bureaucrats. In practice, it is a 'federation of self-governing units, geographical units, professional units, economic units – so there's plenty of scope for small-scale initiative and democratic leaders, but no place for any kind of dictator at the head of a centralized government'.[28]

Since they do not fight wars or prepare for them, there is no conscription, military hierarchy, or unified command. Its economy is neither capitalist nor State communist, but rather co-operative socialist. Thanks to preventive medicine and education, few crimes are committed; criminals are dealt with by their own MAC and undergo group therapy.

Bringing his interests in Eastern wisdom and Western science together, Huxley observes that 'Elementary ecology leads straight to elementary Buddhism.' Palanese education is therefore founded on a 'conservation-morality' in which the children learn that 'we shall be permitted to live on this planet only for as long as we treat all nature with compassion and intelligence'.[29] The only interference with nature is in the Palanese use of Artificial Insemination and Deep Freeze to improve the race and to control the population. They believe that 'begetting is merely postponed assassination'.[30]

The drive to power and domination is sublimated in rock-climbing and other dangerous sports. Not torn between body and spirit, the Palanese experience the joy of sex. They overcome the essential horror of physical disease and death and the sorrow inherent in the human condition by taking *moshka*, the 'truth and beauty' drug which brings them into direct contact with God. Clearly such a society would find it difficult to survive in the existing world. The presence of oil on the island brings a 'liberating invasion' from a neighbouring military dictator.

Huxley's vision of a decentralized society in harmony with nature is similar in many respects to Murray Bookchin's version of social ecology. But Huxley's ideal society has a uniform religion and morality. Every one is expected to conform on Pala; they are not free to question the underlying values and beliefs of their society. Oscar Wilde, for one, would not feel at home there, unable to develop his individuality and pursue his own artistic quest. *Island* is Huxley's personal utopia, and like all utopias it has a stationary air about it. Nevertheless, Huxley took it as an act of faith that 'man is here for the purpose of realizing as much as possible of his desirable potentialities within a stable and yet elastic society'.[31] He remained a libertarian in spirit until his dying day.

Martin Buber

The Jewish existentialist philosopher Martin Buber comes from a very different intellectual background. He was a close friend of Gustav Landauer and devoted an enthusiastic chapter to him (as well as to Proudhon and Kropotkin) in his influential *Paths in Utopia* (1949). Buber was mainly responsible for bringing Landauer's work to international attention. They both shared a concern with developing the organic community within the shell of the existing State and wanted to base social regeneration on a moral and spiritual change. Buber also admired Proudhon's rejection of systems and readiness to steep himself in contradiction. But while praising his view of the group as an organic association of individuals, Buber felt that Proudhon had overlooked the nature of the federative combination which constitutes the 'nation'. Again, Buber approved of Kropotkin's stress on the need for pre-revolutionary structure-making so that the revolution is not so much a creative as a delivering force. But he considered Kropotkin's stark antithesis between society and the State to be too simple.

Buber made a clear distinction between society and the State, and argued that there is an inverse relationship between the 'social principle' and the 'political principle' in any society. He also recognized that the State develops a 'political surplus' of power to maintain order in any latent crisis. While believing that all social structures have a certain measure of power and authority, Buber wanted to see the decentralization of political power and hoped that the social principle, with its free unfolding of energy and spontaneity, would gradually replace the rigid political principle of the State: 'Government should, as much as possible, turn into Administration.'[32]

But while this analysis follows Landauer closely and confirms the traditional anarchist view of the State, Buber ultimately parted company with the anarchists by arguing that the State can in certain circumstances have a legitimate role. In the present condition of humanity, he considered the State necessary to maintain external security and solve internal conflicts between different groups. It should not however act as a machine but as the *communitas communitatum*, as 'the great nourishing mother who carefully folds her children, the communities, to her bosom'.[33]

Despite his admiration for the anarchist principles of decentralization and federalism, Buber remained a communitarian socialist rather than an anarchist by accepting the legitimate role of the State as a framework in which to consolidate self-managing communities and associations. He saw the need to rebuild the State as a community of communities, since only 'a community of communities merits the title of Commonwealth'. He even proposed the formation of a new kind of Supreme Court which would act like Plato's 'custodians' and draw up the boundaries between the degree of centralization of representative government and the degree of local autonomy of the communities.[34]

Buber's most positive plea was for the renewal and deepening of the co-operative movement, taking the village commune as a model in which communal living is based on the amalgamation of production and consumption, and agriculture is united organically with industry. He attempted to relate the early collective settlements in Palestine to the anarchist tradition of Proudhon, Kropotkin and Landauer. He did not want a Jewish State and sought co-operation with the Arabs and as a result his idea of binationalism made him ostracized by orthodox Zionists as an 'enemy of the people'.[35] The subsequent history of Israel has shown the danger of Buber's view of the State as the 'mother' of communities. He should have heeded more carefully Proudhon's insight that order is the daughter and not the mother of liberty.

Lewis Mumford

Lewis Mumford's concern with the relationship between society and technology led him to adopt a strongly libertarian position. From his first work *The Story of Utopia* in 1922, he tried to set out the conditions for the rational use of technology for human liberation. His fundamental thesis is that from late neolithic times in the Near East two technologies have recurrently existed side by side: 'one authoritarian, the other democratic, the first system-centred, immensely powerful but inherently unstable, the other man-centred, relatively weak, but resourceful and durable'.[36] The former has become so dominant that Mumford believes we are rapidly approaching a time when our surviving democratic technics will be completely suppressed or supplanted unless we radically alter course and begin to reassert control over our runaway technology.

The problem lies not so much in the nature of the technology itself but in the question of who is to control it. In *The Myth of the Machine: Technics and Human Development* (1967), Mumford found in the contemporary alliance between scientists and the higher agents of government a parallel with the coalition between royal military authority and supernatural authority in ancient Egypt which formed a 'megamachine'. He warned in *The Pentagon of Power* (1970) that if technology continues to be controlled by the 'military-industrial-scientific' elite, the consequences will be devastating.

Technology will be truly beneficial, Mumford insists in all his writings, only when it is used for our ends rather than for the purposes of the 'megamachine' and of those who direct it. To prevent authoritarian technics from dominating us, we must redeem it by the democratic process and bring it under the control of ordinary individuals. Only then will the machine be used to release humanity from drudgery and provide enough leisure time for work which is dependent on special skill, knowledge and aesthetic sense.

In *Technics and Civilization* (1934), written at the height of the depression, Mumford used the language of archaeology to distinguish three succeeding phases in industrialization which he defined in terms of their motive power and characteristic materials: the *eotechnic*, the age of water and wood; the *paleotechnic*, the age of coal and iron; and the *neotechnic*, the age of electricity and alloys. All three overlap and interpenetrate. We have further entered the age of nuclear energy and the silicon chip. However, Mumford was not just concerned with the nature of different technologies, but with the people who use them and their long-term effects. He saw the machine arising out of the denial of the organic and the living and found its apogee in the 'cult of death'. The threat of nuclear war is simply the 'supreme drama of a completely mechanized society'.[37]

The answer according to Mumford does not lie in the destruction of the machine and a return to a more primitive way of life. It involves on the contrary, the 'rebuilding of the individual personality and the collective group, and the re-orientation of all forms of thought and social activity toward life'.[38] It involves the radical transformation of our society and environment.

In *Technics and Civilization*, Mumford proposes a form of 'basic communism' in which production and consumption are 'normalized' to meet basic needs. There should be complete equality of basic income. Beyond that, individual wants can be satisfied by direct effort. Mumford suggests that this form of communism implies obligation to share in the work of the community, but there will be no coercion. To the objection that some would not want to work without being forced to, he replies that since we give a minimum of food and shelter and medical attention to criminals, why then should we deny it to the lazy and stubborn. He also recognizes that the quality of work is all important in order to make it attractive and he calls for work for the amateur and not the automaton. 'As social life becomes mature,' he insists, 'the social unemployment of machines will become as marked as the present technological unemployment.'[39] At the same time, he acknowledges the potential emancipatory effect of technology in alleviating drudgery and increasing personal autonomy. Finally, he proclaims the slogan 'Socialize creation!' – creativity should not be the prerogative of a small caste, but the practice of all.

Such changes cannot occur without a major shift in consciousness, without a move from a mechanical to an organic ideology. We must think in terms of the organic whole, of life in its fullest manifestation rather than in terms of abstractions and fragments. By calling for a 'dynamic equilibrium' and not indefinite progress in society, Mumford is a pioneer of social ecology. He looks to a new equilibrium in the environment, with the restoration of the balance between humanity and nature. It would also involve a harmonious balance between industry and agriculture, the decentralization of population, and economic regionalism.

Mumford was never a complete anarchist and sometimes used 'anarchy' in the negative sense of chaos. He considered, for instance, the existence of complicated weapons as a mark of 'international anarchy'. Again, while he calls for workers' control and the creation of consumers' groups in his new social order, he sees industries still operating within the political framework of co-operating States. Nevertheless, while he suggests that the State can take over all banking functions, his vision of regenerated society, of decentralized communities designed to the human scale, is distinctly libertarian.

In his widely influential book *The Culture of Cities* (1938), Mumford went on to offer an iconoclastic study of urban civilization, and to advocate a decentralist, regionalist approach to town and country planning. In the *The Myth of the Machine* (1967) in which he traced back technology to pre-history, he further asserted that man is more than a tool-using animal; he is 'pre-eminently a mind-making, self-mastering, and self-designing animal; and the primary locus of all his activities lies first in his own organism, and in the social organization through which it finds fuller expression'. Mumford was not just concerned with the hard facts of technology but the mental processes which underlie them.[40]

Mumford was a great synthesizer. In his positive proposals, he drew on the insights of biologist Patrick Geddes and garden-city pioneer Ebenezer Howard. He was particularly impressed by Kropotkin's vision of a decentralized society in which people govern themselves and fulfil themselves in work. He felt that Kropotkin's *Fields, Factories and Workshops* was more important in the 1960s than when it was first written at the end of the nineteenth century. Kropotkin had not only seen how electricity and intensive farming had laid the foundations for a more decentralized urban development, but that they provided 'the opportunity for a more responsible and responsive local life, with greater scope for the human agents who were neglected and frustrated by mass organizations'.[41]

The libertarian and democratic aspects of Mumford's thought comes through especially in his later work. Autonomy, which is an essential attribute for any organism to develop, was his central concern. It is his contention that it can only be sustained if technology is made democratic in a democratic society. Final authority should therefore be given to the whole, which involves 'communal self-government, free communication as between equals, unimpeded access to the common store of knowledge, protection against arbitrary external controls, and a sense of individual moral responsibility for behavior which affects the whole community'.[42]

For Mumford, like most anarchists, the best life possible is one that calls for an ever greater degree of 'self-direction, self-expression, and self-realization. In this sense, personality, once the exclusive attribute of kings, belongs on democratic theory to every man. Life itself in its fullness and wholeness cannot be delegated.'[43] Murray Bookchin, whose own work betrays the influence of Mumford, has complained that he has denatured the term libertarian into 'the more socially respectable and amorphous term democratic'.[44] Indeed, Mumford liked to style himself a 'radical conservative'. Be that as it may, his view of technics and his version of democracy remain profoundly libertarian.

Noam Chomsky

The American linguist – philosopher Noam Chomsky has created a revolution in his own field, but he has also become one of the most lively social critics of the United States' government and its policies. As a linguist, he is principally known for his thesis that all human beings have an innate 'universal grammar' which enables them to learn their different languages. At the same time, he shares Bertrand Russell's 'humanistic conception' which regards the young as a gardener regards a young tree, an organism with the potential to be nurtured and encouraged.[45] And like Russell, he sees the supreme end in society to be the free growth of the individual.

Chomsky however goes beyond Russell's radical humanism to draw inspiration directly from the anarchist tradition. He has been deeply impressed by Wilhelm von Humboldt's attempt to draw *The Limits of State Action* (1801) and by his emphasis on the importance of the free choice of the individual.[46] But he freely admits that he has been most influenced by Rudolf Rocker, the 'last serious thinker', in the direction of anarcho-syndicalism. Ultimately, he bases his libertarian socialism on a belief that all human beings have 'intrinsic needs for liberty and for being able to exercise *control over themselves*'.[47]

Chomsky does not see a necessary connection between his social and political views and his linguistic theory. As a Cartesian rationalist, he has argued however that the 'libertarian left should have a vested interest in innateness'.[48] While most socialists and anarchists have argued that character is largely a product of the environment, Chomsky has tried to formulate a biological concept of 'human nature' with its own innate intellectual and cognitive aspects.[49] In his view, only humans have an ability to use language creatively. He claims that there is no inconsistency in believing that the 'essential attributes of human nature give man the opportunity to create social conditions and social forms to maximize the possibilities for freedom and diversity, and individual self-realization'.[50]

To support this view, Chomsky has quoted Bakunin's view of liberty as the full development of all the powers that are latent in each person, a form of liberty that recognizes 'no restrictions other than those determined by the laws of our own individual nature, which cannot be regarded as restrictions since these laws are not imposed by any outside legislator or above us'.[51] Such natural laws do not limit humans but are the real and immediate conditions of their freedom.

But while Chomsky compares Bakunin's remarks with his own approach to creative thought, he is reluctant to press the link between his linguistic and social views. He readily admits that one cannot simply deduce social or political consequences from any insights into language. While one may hope to be able to show that 'structures of authority and control limit and distort intrinsic human capacities and needs, and to lay a theoretical basis for a social theory that eventuates in practical ideas as to how to overcome them', there are nevertheless 'huge gaps' in any such argument.[52]

In fact, rather than trying to develop a philosophical foundation for his social beliefs, Chomsky has chosen to express his libertarian sympathies in a persistent critique of American culture and politics. He has been particularly critical of the servility of the American intellectual establishment and the American media who hide their real interests behind a mask of 'liberal objectivity'.[53] Such intellectuals have come to form a secular priesthood who try to justify the inhuman policies of the State by disguising them in morally acceptable terms. Chomsky has also been one of the most trenchant critics of American administrations, especially in their execution of an aggressive foreign policy from Vietnam to the Gulf War. The key problem lies in what he calls 'military Keynesianism', that is, the need for the military-industrial complex in America to find an enemy in order to maintain a high level of military spending.[54]

Chomsky's libertarian sympathies are clearest in his unswerving critique of power and in his view that all States of whatever complexion are controlled by privileged elites who rule in their own interests. He has been called a 'left-wing Marxist' as well as an anarchist but he tends to call himself a libertarian socialist or socialist anarchist.[55] He sees anarchism as the libertarian wing of socialism. He rejects the American individualist tradition of Tucker and stands in the collectivist and syndicalist one inspired by Bakunin. But he sees anarchism not as a doctrine but as a historical tendency of thought and action which has many ways of developing and which will remain a permanent strand of history. 'What attracts me about anarchism personally', he openly admits, 'are the tendencies in it that try to come to grips with the problem of dealing with complex organized industrial societies within a framework of free institutions and structures.'[56] In all his social and political writings, he has tried to do precisely that.

Albert Camus and Existentialism

Existentialism undoubtedly influenced many anarchists after the Second World War. Not only have the libertarians Stirner and Nietzsche been called precursors of existentialism, but there is a close link between the existentialists' stress on the individual, free choice, and moral responsibility and the main tenets of anarchism. Herbert Read for one found many parallels between the two, and considered both superior to Marxism.[57]

The most influential exponent of atheistic existentialism was Jean-Paul Sartre, who devoted the whole of his intellectual life to expanding human freedom. In his essay on *Existentialism and Humanism* (1946), he stressed the ineradicable nature of freedom. Since God does not exist, everything is permitted and all moral values are human creations. Again, as there is no fixed human nature ('existence precedes essence'), man is free to fashion himself: 'there is no determinism – man is free, man *is* freedom.' But while offering the heady prospect of humanity transforming itself and making its own future, Sartre suggested that the experience of freedom is not one of joy but of anguish: man is 'condemned to be free'.[58] Moreover, as he made clear in his plays, there is no natural solidarity between human beings: 'Hell is others.'

After the war, Sartre was prepared to collaborate with the Stalinist French Communist Party; and he became a Marxist in 1960. While he developed a libertarian form of Marxism, insisting that we can say no to our conditioning, and called for a form of direct democracy, he aligned himself with the Maoists rather than the anarchists during the 1968 rebellion in France. He found Che Guevara to be the most complete man of his age, not Cohn-Bendit. Towards the end of his life, Sartre acknowledged his affinity with anarchism, but it was with classical anarchism rather than its modern offspring: 'by way of philosophy', he said in 1975, 'I discovered the anarchist in me. But when I discovered it I did not call it that, because today's anarchy no longer has anything to do with the anarchy of 1890.'[59] His road to freedom nonetheless remained within the Marxist tradition, albeit alleviated by an existentialist concern with individual freedom.

With Albert Camus, the links with anarchism and the anarchist movement are much closer. Camus was born in Algeria, a *pieds-noirs*, the son of poor-white settlers in the French colony. Despite his childhood poverty, the open-air life in the sun left him with a permanent love of the Mediterranean and its clarity. Having learned his ethics on the football pitch, he left university to become a journalist. In 1934, he became a member of the Communist Party, conducting propaganda amongst the Algerians. He left soon after to develop his own brand of libertarian humanism.

In his short novel *The Outsider* (1939), Camus depicted a young man who simply refuses to play the game and to lie about his feelings, whether to his girlfriend or to the judge who condemns him to death for the killing of an Arab. Camus described his deadpan hero as dying for the sake of truth

– 'the only Christ we deserved', no less. But for all its lyrical celebration of a young working-class demi-god of the beaches, the novel has little overt political message, except perhaps in its implication that, in bourgeois society, the man who seeks truth is bound to be an outsider.

In the more philosophical essay *The Myth of Sisyphus* (1942), Camus developed his doctrine of the absurd. The work opens with the statement: 'There is one truly serious philosophical problem and that is suicide.'[60] To the question whether life is worth living, Camus argues that the human condition is fundamentally absurd. There is an ineradicable discrepancy between human desire and reality: man is born to die, and yet he seeks eternity; he longs for certain knowledge, and yet he is surrounded by a sea of doubt. The absurd therefore lies in 'the confrontation of the irrational and the wild longing for clarity'.[61]

Yet the answer does not lie in killing oneself. Camus insists that we should rebel against absurdity by continuing to live. The authentic man is 'He who, without negating it, does nothing for the eternal . . . Assured of his temporally limited freedom, of his revolt devoid of future and of his mortal consciousness, he lives out his adventure within the span of his lifetime.' Like Sisyphus he rolls his stone uphill in the firm knowledge that it will roll down again, sharing 'his scorn for the gods, his hatred of death and his passion for life'.[62] He knows that his task is ultimately futile but he completes it all the same, with a certain satisfaction in work well done. Within the confines of his condition, he is master of his days, and in this sense, the absurdity of the world can be seen as an invitation to happiness.

While denying any transcendental reality, Camus felt that it was possible to work on earth for the improvement of humanity. In this, he remained a resolute humanist. As he wrote during the war in *Letter to a German Friend*, 'I have chosen justice to remain faithful to the earth. I still think that the world has no final meaning, but I know that something in it has meaning, and that is man, because he is the only being to demand that he should have one.'[63]

When the Second World War broke out, Camus moved to France and worked in the Resistance, collaborating with Sartre on the journal *Combat* from 1943 to 1946. Although he liked to think of himself first and foremost as an artist, a pagan apostle of the absurd, he threw himself into the political turmoil of the period. Despite his Communist youth, he became increasingly suspicious of the abstract political ideals which had led to Nazism and Stalinism. Rather than revolution, he began calling for rebellion. Where the former often ends in the sacrifice of the individual, the latter involves an instinctive refusal to obey authority and an affirmation of personal identity. As his play *Caligula* demonstrates, one cannot destroy everything without destroying oneself.

But Camus' evolution was gradual. Although he had left the Communist Party before the war, in 1944 he was still defending in *Combat* the foreign policy of the Soviet Union: 'we must never forget that Russia adopted the nationalistic policy which she now pursues only after she had in vain proposed a system of collective security. Neither must we forget that, alone among all other states, she offered general disarmament.'[64] In the same year, he also called for a popular, working-class democracy to be established in France.

After the war when resistance did not lead to the expected revolution in France, Camus argued that all revolutions lead to new tyrannies. He was convinced that none of the evils which totalitarianism claimed to be fighting against were worse than totalitarianism itself. In opposition to Communism, he began preaching the politics of tolerance and moderation; he told his critics that he did not learn about freedom from Marx, but from poverty. He now preferred piecemeal change and addressed specific ills. In 1946 he took up the theme of some earlier *Reflections on the Guillotine*, which had dwelt on the horrors of legalized murder, to write, in *Neither Victims nor Executioners* (1946), a brilliant denunciation of the death penalty as the vengeance of an unjust society.

Camus at the time came in contact with Spanish anarcho-syndicalists in France, supporting the Spanish Federation of Political Prisoners and associating with the editor of the CNT's paper *Solidaridad Obrera*. He also became friendly with the editors of the French syndicalist and anarchist magazine *Témoins*, *Le Libertaire* and *Le Monde Libertaire*. They helped him appreciate the libertarian tradition and showed that it was quite possible to be an anti-communist on the Left.

The most substantial expression of his new position appeared in his widely influential study *The Rebel* (1951). In his Preface to the 1953 English translation of the work, Herbert Read welcomed it enthusiastically: 'With the publication of this book, a cloud which has oppressed the European mind for more than a century begins to lift. Once again it becomes possible to hope – to have confidence again in man and in the future.' The work is a sustained onslaught on those abstract ideals which too readily degenerate into nihilism and terrorism. It explores the perversion of rebellion in which rebels, rather than electing to live in a godless world, erect new tyrannical divinities to worship.

In detailed studies, Camus explores literary and philosophical examples of revolt which show that he had studied, albeit in a partisan spirit, anarchist and libertarian thought. He argues, for instance, that de Sade demanded absolute liberty for himself in order to satisfy his desires regardless of others, and despite his generous nature entertained fantasies of absolute dictatorship. Again, Nietzsche's denial of God and all values became easily distorted and were used to justify National Socialism. By destroying all abstractions, Stirner made of himself an abstraction; his 'individual-king' ends up on the ruins of the world, ready to commit any form of destruction. Bakunin and Nechaev both called for total liberty, but the result was that one contributed to the Leninist notion of dictatorship, while the other fostered the cult of murder for political ends. Camus saves his greatest ire for Hegel who maintained there were no values but those produced by history, and his follower Marx whose utopian Messianism found final expression in the Soviet police State.

Camus' distinction between revolution and rebellion directly echoes Stirner's between revolution and insurrection. Revolution changes little since it merely substitutes one set of masters for another, whereas rebellion may change human nature by creating a new metaphysics and morals. Rebellion protests against absurdity, suffering and injustice and creates a moral value based on the idea of moderation. It implies recognition of the integrity of the individual and seeks relative aims in politics. According to Camus, rebellion is the refusal to be treated as an object and to be reduced to simple historical terms.

Nevertheless, rebellion is not a lonely and solitary act. It does not destroy human solidarity but rather affirms the common nature of all humans which thereby eludes the world of power. In the experience of the absurd, suffering is individual, but when it moves to rebellion, it is aware of being collective, 'the adventure of all'. The first step of the estranged spirit is to recognize that he or she shares such estrangement with all human beings. Rebellion therefore takes the individual out of solitude: 'I rebel, therefore we are.'[65]

At the end of his long study, Camus celebrates the libertarian and rebellious spirit in history and comes out in favour of anarcho-syndicalism as the only alternative to bourgeois nihilism and authoritarian socialism: 'Syndicalism, like the commune, is the negation, to the benefit of reality, of abstract and bureaucratic centralism.'[66] It alone expresses the message of the libertarian tradition which has been submerged by prevailing authoritarian thought.

Camus' new approach led to a public dispute with Sartre in 1952 over the French Communist Party. Camus refused to have anything to do with Stalinism, while Sartre like most left-wing intellectuals at the time argued that it had to be taken into account since it had the support of a large part of the working class. The uprising in Hungary in 1956 led to a further clash. Although both condemned its suppression, Sartre argued that Stalinism had been a necessary evil and that Russian Communism could still become more democratic. Camus, on the other hand, insisted in the *Franc-Tireur* in February 1957 that there is no possible evolution in a totalitarian society:

'Terror does not evolve except towards a worse terror, the scaffold grows no more liberal, the gallows are not tolerant. Nowhere in the world has there been a party or a man with absolute power that did not use it absolutely.'[67]

But rather than developing his anarcho-syndicalist sympathies, Camus soon veered in the opposite direction. In the 1955 elections, he supported the campaign of Mendès-France and called for a French Labour Party. In a speech ironically published in 1957 in the revolutionary syndicalist journal *La Révolution Prolétarienne*, he argued that the liberty of each is bounded by the liberty of his fellows, and that this liberty is defined by a body of law whose supremacy the State must recognize. He had reached the classic liberal defence of parliamentary democracy.

Camus was ready to admit that Gandhi was the 'greatest man of our time' and that nuclear weapons had fundamentally changed the nature of international relations. But over the question of Algeria, his birthplace, he refused to budge. Where Sartre wholeheartedly advocated Algerian independence, Camus merely called for moderation on all sides during the war of independence and equal rights for Algerians and French under the colonial system. He was unable to go beyond the myth of a French Algeria and tried to organize a truce. When accepting the Nobel prize in 1957 (refused by Sartre), Camus' speech was interrupted by an Algerian student who asked him why he did not condemn the use of torture in Algeria. Camus replied that he loved justice, but if he had to choose between justice and his mother, he would choose his mother. It was the very opposite of Godwin's stance: Godwin had asked what magic there is in the word 'my' to overturn the dictates of everlasting justice. By choosing his mother before justice, Camus by extension chose his tribe, his nation and his race. As a result, he remained faithful to his roots, a left-wing colonialist, an outsider on the African shore and in metropolitan France, a man who was prepared to accept injustice for a place to live in the sun with his kind.

Unfortunately, Camus was unable to extricate himself from his dilemma. Two years later, in January 1960, he was killed in a car crash; a return railway ticket was in his pocket. Once again, the absurd had triumphed.

Michel Foucault

The French social theorist Michel Foucault has been called a modern anarchist, although like Sartre he did not use the term and even denied that he was one.[68] There can be no doubt that a profound libertarian spirit pervades his work, and he has made a brilliant analysis of how knowledge is used as an instrument of power and domination, an analysis which has influenced many anarchists. Foucault attempted in *The Order of Things*

(1966) nothing less than an archaeology of the human sciences by revealing the fundamental codes ('epistemes') underlying our culture. Far from celebrating the Enlightenment as bringing about progress through reason and science, he saw it as an intensification of human suffering and social control.

In *Madness and Civilization* (1961), he located towards the end of the eighteenth century the shift in the perception of madness from it being accepted as meaningful unreason (the 'wisdom of folly') to it being considered a disease. He went on in *Discipline and Punish* (1975) to trace eloquently, if at times inaccurately, the ideological foundations of modern punitive society in the Enlightenment. Foucault's central insight turns on the recognition that the power to punish is not essentially different from the power to cure or to educate. 'Is it surprising', he asks, 'that prisons resemble factories, schools, barracks, hospitals, which all resemble prisons?'[69] This tendency is best symbolized by the 'model' prison called the Panopticon designed by the utilitarian philosopher Jeremy Bentham which allowed complete surveillance of the inmates.[70]

Foucault's study of prisons led him to an analysis of social power in general. What characterizes modern culture for Foucault is coercion. He follows Nietzsche, not Marx, in seeing power in non-economic terms: 'Power is war, a war continued by other means', that is to say 'unspoken warfare'.[71] Even repression is a subordinate effect of power. Although power is an ineradicable part of the human condition, bourgeois society invented a new type of power – disciplinary power. Unlike sovereign power which was exercised chiefly over the earth and its products, disciplinary power is concentrated on 'human bodies and their operations' in the form of surveillance.[72] Thus in the dialectic of knowledge as the will to power, reason becomes a technology of power, and science an instrument of domination.

In his unfinished multi-volume *History of Sexuality* (1978–84), Foucault further showed how the self had become prey to power from within. He traced the change in sexuality from the *ars erotica* of the ancients to the confessional control of the Christian era. As a 'confessing animal', Western man became subject to socio-sexual control.[73] In the early nineteenth century, the individual had become self-aware as a subject of sexuality, at roughly the same time as the psychiatrization of insanity and the spread of the penitentiary occurred. The bourgeoisie built a code of sex for its own self-assertion by erecting the monogamous heterosexual couple as exemplar and fount of morality, and pillar of society. Sex was thus reconstructed as the preoccupation of self-searching and confessing individuals, rather than being, as it had been to the ancients, a sophisticated and impersonal source of pleasure.

Foucault pitted Nietzschean psychological understanding of power against Marxist economic analysis. Yet he rejected Wilhelm Reich's view that repression is a product of authoritarian societies. For Foucault the will to power, particularly in the form of sexual domination, will always be present in humanity although its form may change in the course of history. This led him to a marked anti-utopianism in his attitude to revolution. He offered no alternative to existing capitalist society. In a televised debate with Chomsky in Amsterdam in 1971, he refused to draw a model of society and argued that the task of the revolutionary is to conquer power, not to try and bring about justice which is merely an abstraction mirroring the dominant class interests of society.[74]

There is clearly much in Foucault which makes him of interest to anarchists. His critique of power and his depiction of modern culture as a form of domination are illuminating and persuasive. He rejected politics in its conventional form since he believed that all revolutions, if they retain the State, tend to deteriorate into Stalinism.[75] Instead, he favoured decentralized and spontaneous revolutionary movements.

This led him to support the student rebellion in Paris in 1968. At the time, he argued that it was the duty of prisoners to try to escape. Because of his distrust of institutions he rejected revolutionary tribunals as well as courts of justice. And while not rejecting traditional class struggle, he called for specific struggles against 'particularized power' by women, prisoners, conscripted soldiers, hospital patients and homosexuals.[76]

Foucault, like many contemporary anarchists, rejected the rational, liberal culture of the West which he saw as a disastrous and coercive offshoot of the Enlightenment. His intellectual fire harks back to the early pyrotechnical tradition in anarchism which prefers explosive outburst to cool analysis. He once confessed: 'I would like my books to be . . . Molotov cocktails or minefields; I would like them to self-destruct after use, like fireworks.'[77] Nevertheless, it is too great an exaggeration to say that he was with Marcuse 'the high priest who presided over the wedding of anarchism and the counter-culture'.[78] Foucault offers no concrete way to conquer power, and argues that it can never be entirely dissolved. Ultimately, Foucault's maverick form of structuralism is inspired more by Nietzschean individualism than by anarchism. He might inspire anarchists in his analysis of power and his criticism of modern culture, but he himself vigorously denied that he was an anarchist.

38

Modern Anarchists

THIS CENTURY HAS PRODUCED few great original thinkers of an
anarchist stamp. Most anarchists have merely adopted the ideas of the
classic nineteenth-century thinkers or tried to put them into action. Only
Emma Goldman and Murray Bookchin have helped develop new anarchist
currents, notably feminism and social ecology. Several others like Noam
Chomsky have been drawn to anarchism but have made their main contribution in fields other than anarchist political theory; they have smudged the
narrow line between anarchism and libertarianism but have not completely
erased it. Three outstanding exceptions to this trend have been Herbert
Read and Alex Comfort in Britain and Paul Goodman in the United States.

Herbert Read

Herbert Read was directly involved in the anarchist movement before and
after the Second World War, wrote several impressive works on anarchist
philosophy and helped make surrealism respectable in Britain. But he was
primarily a man of letters, a social commentator and art critic, rather than
a man of action. Born on a remote Yorkshire farm in 1893, he acknowledged, as Proudhon had done, that by birth and tradition he was a peasant.
On his father's death in 1903, he left the North York Moors to go to an
orphan's school in Halifax, thereby leaving a 'world of innocent wonder'
which he tried to recapture throughout his adult life. After leaving school,
he went to work in the Savings Bank in Leeds, before moving to London,
and becoming a civil servant in the Ministry of Labour and the Treasury,
where he acquired an enduring dislike of bureaucrats. He eventually
became an assistant keeper at the Victoria and Albert Museum, a post
which provided a base for his subsequent career as an art critic, poet and
educationist.

As a young man in Leeds, Read was at first a fanatical Tory. He traced
his conversion to anarchism through a reading of Edward Carpenter's *Non-
Governmental Society* before the First World War. It opened up a whole new
range of thought. He went on to read eagerly the works of Proudhon,
Bakunin and Kropotkin. He was also influenced by Nietzsche, Sorel, Ibsen

and Tolstoy who supported anarchist philosophy and Marx and Shaw who attacked it.

As Read makes clear in his autobiography *Annals of Innocence and Experience* (1940), his experience of the First World War as an officer only confirmed his libertarian opposition to militarism and the State. As early as April 1918, he wrote to a friend that his political sentiment was 'a revolt of the individual against the association which involves him in activities which do not interest him; a jumping to the ultimate anarchy which I have always seen as the ideal of all who value beauty and intensity of life. "A beautiful anarchy" – that is my cry.'[1] He became an anarchist and pacifist although he did not publicly profess his anarchism until 1937.

Read wanted to change the world and tried to show through his works on art and education how people could liberate themselves from authoritarian ways of seeing and being. But he was not ready to engage in mere propaganda aimed at the working class: 'Intellectuals writing for proletarians will not do', he wrote. 'It is merely another form of *la trahison des clercs*.'[2] Nevertheless, he was closely associated from 1938 to 1953 with the Freedom Press (which had been set up by Kropotkin at the end of the nineteenth century).

Read's anarchist development was gradual but irreversible. At first he was ready to give the Russian Revolution the benefit of the doubt because of Lenin's commitment to the withering away of the State and his maxim that 'While the State exists there is no freedom. When there is freedom, there will be no State.'[3] But the suicide of the poet Vladimir Mayakovsky in 1930 triggered off Read's doubts and henceforth he lost few opportunities to denounce the central control of the Communist State. His hopes were greatly aroused by the Spanish Revolution, and he supported enthusiastically the anarcho-syndicalism of the CNT. He was particularly impressed by the religious intensity of the Spanish anarchists; in a poem he wrote for them, he declared:

> The golden lemon is not made
> but grows on a green tree:
> A strong man and his crystal eyes
> is a man born free.[4]

Read, like Wilde, saw his anarchist philosophy flower directly from his aesthetic concerns. A life without art, he believed, would be a 'graceless and brutish existence'.[5] Taking up Eric Gill's cry 'To hell with culture', he criticized the elitist culture of his day as 'dope, a worse dope than religion'.[6] In its place, he wanted to develop a democratic culture which could best be achieved through the expansion of personal and social freedom. Read believed human beings to be naturally creative: 'If we follow this Natural Order in all the ways of our life, we shall not need to talk about culture. We shall have it without being conscious of it.'[7] At the same time, the artist can only realize his full creative potential if he is free and art autonomous. There is therefore a vital and organic link between freedom and culture.

Read looked to education as the principal means of encouraging the growth of the creative and autonomous person; indeed, his greatest contribution to anarchist theory was probably in the area of education. He saw an inextricable link between the disordered state of modern civilization and the traditional systems of schooling. The cause of our ills can be traced to the suppression of the creative spontaneity of the individual which is the result of coercive discipline, authoritarian morality, and mechanical toil. Existing schools, he felt, were nothing more than 'abattoirs of sensibility'.[8]

In his *Education through Art* (1943), Read advocated a libertarian form of education which George Woodcock has called 'a method of creating anarchists by stealth'.[9] It was consciously intended to be 'deeply anarchist in its orientation'.[10] In Read's view, the aim of education should be the 'individuation of the self', which involved both the concurrent development of the 'uniqueness' and the 'social consciousness' of the individual.[11] Education must be not only a process of personal development but also of social integration and reciprocity.

It was Read's contention that the social virtues necessary for a free life are more likely to be encouraged by developing an aesthetic sensibility in the young rather than by inculcating knowledge and science. He therefore advocates a system of education which makes the innate sensibility of the child the basis of mental development. Children are natural artists, and by practising creative art, they can develop a balanced personality and become lively members of the group or community to which they belong. The child however can only enter the world of co-operation if he or she is liberated from fear by adult sympathy and understanding.

But how is this then to be achieved? By no apparent method at all, Read suggests. The necessary self-discipline arises out of the activity itself:

> The good teacher is not a dictator, but rather a pupil more advanced in technique than the others, more conscious of the aim to be achieved and the means that must be adopted, who works with the children, sympathizes with them and encourages them, gives them that priceless possession which is self-confidence.[12]

He will try and establish a relationship of reciprocity and trust which will encourage mutual aid amongst his pupils. Discipline will not then be imposed but discovered. It was the same message as that preached by

Godwin two centuries before, but was considered entirely modern and progressive when reiterated by Read.

Apart from his writings on education and art, Read wrote two libertarian classics *Poetry and Anarchism* (1938) and *The Philosophy of Anarchism* (1940). He felt anarchism to be the only political philosophy which advocates the kind of freedom necessary for creativity, the only approach consistent with a love of justice. Like Bakunin, he recognized that 'in order to create it is necessary to destroy', that is, to break existing forms in order to change the nature of our civilization.[13] It seemed just as important to him to destroy the established bourgeois ideals in literature, painting and architecture as it was to destroy the established bourgeois ideals in economics. In Read's view, the English in particular have no taste merely because of their lack of social freedom.

It was Read's Wildean concern with the development of true individuality which most preoccupied him. In his *Philosophy of Anarchism*, he asserted that the measure of progress is the 'degree of differentiation in a society' and the richness and intensity of experience. The farther a society progresses, the more clearly the individual stands out of the group. The future unit of society is 'the individual, a world in himself, self-contained and self-creative, freely giving and freely receiving, but essentially a free spirit.'[14] But Read recognized that the kind of complete personal freedom advocated by Stirner means 'inevitable decadence'; the individual must find his place within the organic community of a co-operative commonwealth.[15] The whole case for anarchism rests on the assumption that the right kind of society is an 'organic being' for the organic life of the group is self-regulative, like the life of all such entities.[16]

Read also accepted that liberty is always relative to man's control over natural forces. In his opinion, the ideal of anarchy can best be realized through the practical organization of anarcho-syndicalism. As an anarcho-communist, he further argued that we should surrender all our material rights and put our property into a common fund. Only this way could a classless society be realized – 'society without a bureaucracy, without an army, without any closed grade or profession, without functionless components'.[17] This can only be achieved by federal devolution, by decentralizing the economy.

There might be the need, Read admits, for a kind 'parliament of industry' to adjust relations between the various collectives and to decide on general questions of policy, but it would in no sense form an administrative, legislative or executive body. Work in general should be subordinated to the enjoyment of life and be considered no more than a necessary interval in the day's leisure. Anarchism thus implies a 'universal decentralization of authority, and a universal simplification of life'.[18]

Read sketched his social ideal in more detail in *The Politics of the Unpolitical* (1943), in which he argued that society must begin with the family and then with the guild. Among the essential features of what he calls 'natural society' are:

I. The liberty of the person. II. The integrity of the family. III. The reward of qualifications. IV. The self-government of the guilds. V. The abolition of parliament and centralized government. VI. The institution of arbitrament. VII. The delegation of authority. VIII. The humanization of industry.

Clearly not all these principles, especially the seventh, are strictly anarchist, and Read is prepared to allow an independent judiciary to exist merely as 'the arbiter, to decide, in the interests of the whole, the conflicts which emerge in the parts'.[19]

Read is not a complete egalitarian in calling for equal shares and work. He believes that a hierarchy of talent and the division of labour would always exist in a free society. Although no special powers would be enjoyed by an elite, there would probably be an aristocracy of the intellect. Since there is no uniformity of desires, society would not be reduced to the dull mediocrity of a common level. An anarchist society however would give everyone the full opportunity to develop their minds and imaginations. For Read lust for power and fear of death are the original sins and his final aim is neither to suffer nor renounce but 'to accept, to enjoy, to realize the anarchy of life in the midst of the order of living'.[20]

Read's interest in psychology and philosophy led him to draw on the insights of many thinkers to support his anarchist philosophy. Within a Freudian context, he defined the anarchist as 'the man who, in his manhood, dares to resist the authority of the father'.[21] At the same time, he rejected the psychological need for leadership, particularly denouncing the leader of the group. The only alternative to leadership is the principle of co-operation and mutual aid; not the father – son relationship, but the relationship of brotherhood. Read also drew on Jung's description of the individuation process to support his view of the gradual emancipation of the individual from the group.

Read valued freedom above all else, and his treatment of the concept, a concept often lazily abused by other anarchists, is suggestive. He recognized that freedom implies freedom from some kind of control, but in its positive condition it means the freedom to create, 'freedom to become what one *is*'. It is not therefore a state of rest, but 'a state of action, of projection, of self-realization'. It is a positive self-regulating form of responsibility. He also contrasted perceptively the use of the words 'freedom' and 'liberty' in English: 'A man *is* free: he is given his liberty'.[22] The latter is abstract and essential; the former concrete and existential. Liberty is a political ideal and is expressed in social organization. Freedom is the condition in which the 'spirit of man' achieves spontaneity and creativity.[23]

From the anarchist point of view, Read thought that it is not good enough merely to control ourselves and external nature, a view subscribed to by most doctrinaire Marxists who see freedom as the knowledge of necessity. On the contrary, we must allow for 'spontaneous developments'. Whereas Marxism is based on economics, Read argued that anarchism is based on biology, in the sense that it insists on 'the consciousness of an overriding human solidarity'. Unlike the ideologies of Marxism and existentialism, anarchism, for Read, is the only political philosophy that combines 'an essentially revolutionary and contingent attitude with a philosophy of freedom. It is the only militant libertarian doctrine left in the world, and on its diffusion depends the progressive evolution of human consciousness and of humanity itself.'[24]

Read was no original thinker and the philosophical foundations of his anarchism are eclectic. Like Kropotkin he discerns a natural order which predates the birth of society, and he celebrates mutual aid and human solidarity. Like Godwin, he believes in universal truth – 'a universal order of thought, which is the order of the real world'. Like Proudhon, he argues that we should discover the true laws of nature and live in accordance with them, especially 'the principles of equality and fairness inherent in the natural order of the universe'.[25] And like Tolstoy, he maintains that when we follow reason, we listen to the voice of God: 'we discover God's order, which is the Kingdom of Heaven'.[26]

All this sounds extremely rational, yet for all his stress on reason, Read believed that a new religion is a necessary element in a free and organic society; he admired the Spanish anarchists during the Civil War precisely because they had a 'religious intensity'.[27]

As for the means to realize a free society, Read argued that anarchism naturally implies pacifism. It should not entail, as it does with Huxley, a fight against one's instincts, but should work through reason and persuasion. He accepted Wilhelm Reich's view that all forms of aggressive behaviour may be explained in terms of 'prior frustrations'.[28] Even if the will to power is a biological factor, it is offset by the drive to mutual aid. Moreover, any 'aggressive instinct' as the basis of the will to power can be turned into creative instead of destructive channels.[29] There is therefore no insurmountable biological or psychological obstacle to peace. It is nationalism and collectivism which encourage war, and war increases in intensity as society develops a central organization. War will exist as long as States exist, whereas 'Peace is anarchy'.[30]

But this does not mean that Read remained quiescent. He developed

Stirner's distinction between revolution and insurrection and Camus's between revolution and rebellion to argue that we should aim to get rid of political institutions by rebellion or insurrection. Guided by instinct rather than reason, insurrection and rebellion act like shock therapy on the body of society and may change human nature, 'in the sense of creating a new morality, or new metaphysical values'.[31] On a practical level, he also advocated a General Strike of the entire community against the State to bring about a spontaneous and universal insurrection. Until this happens, we can try and persuade each other by reason and set an example to emulate within a 'cell of good living'. But whatever means the anarchist employs, Read insisted that revolutionary realism in an age of atoms bombs is necessarily pacific: 'the bomb is now the symbol, not of anarchy, but of totalitarian power'.[32]

Read once remarked that 'it is perfectly possible, even normal, to live a life of contradictions'.[33] He certainly exemplified the sentiment in his own life. A virulent anti-Catholic, he left his first wife and married a Catholic convert who brought up their children in the faith he had profoundly despised. Although a professed pacifist, he fought in the First World War, and was decorated with the DSO and MC for bravery. Later in life he left the Committee of 100 of the Campaign for Nuclear Disarmament (CND) because its policy of non-violence he found 'too provocative'. Despite his attack on the prevailing political and artistic culture and his description of the House of Commons as descending 'below mediocrity to some absolute zero of vulgarity and ineptitude', he was honoured by the Establishment with a knighthood in 1952.[34] Read wrote perceptively about the paradox of anarchism, but he is remembered by many anarchists as that great paradox, an anarchist knight. For all his revolutionary views of culture and his call for social rebellion, he remained deeply conservative in many respects. Towards the end of his life, he lost his faith in the goodness of humanity and felt that the only possible protest was to establish one's individuality.[35]

Yet despite his paradoxical position, Read remained all his life on the side of organic growth in freedom, culture and community against the artificial organization of liberty, civilization and the State. While he did not advance anarchist philosophy to any great extent, he gave fresh and vital expression to the traditional themes of anarchism. He was the most prominent British anarchist intellectual of his day, and he reached a wide audience. With his peasant roots, his careful dress, his country retreat and his anarchist ideals, Read was part of that romantic movement which seeks 'the application of a total "metaphysical sensibility", exploring without fear the confines of man's fate and destiny'.[36] Many were dismayed by his apparent arrogance and opportunism, but he undoubtedly affirmed the irreducible freedom of humanity.

Alex Comfort

Amongst British anarchist writers, Alex Comfort has been one of the most prolific as poet, novelist and biologist. Like Read, he has remained on the margins of the organized anarchist movement, but like Kropotkin, he has used modern science to back up his arguments for anarchism. He has approached gerontology and sexology from a libertarian point of view, emphasizing the dignity of the old and the need for personal responsibility in sex.

In the forties and early fifties Comfort was particularly active as an anarchist and wrote pamphlets for the Freedom Press. In *Barbarism and Sexual Freedom* (1948), originally a series of lectures on the sociology of sex from the standpoint of anarchism, he insisted that a free society consists of 'politically, a form of society without central or other governmental power, and without extra-personal forms of coercion, and sociologically, one based on mutually-accepted obligations maintained solely by the existence of a social group ethic'.[37] As a pacifist, he also wrote at the time pamphlets for *Peace News* calling for *Peace and Disobedience* (1946) and *Social Responsibility in Science and Art* (1952).

In *Authority and Delinquency in the Modern State* (1950), Comfort's most important book from an anarchist point of view, he argued that the modern State is a haven for delinquents since power attracts the maladjusted – a neat reversal of the familiar claim that left-wing politics, and especially anarchism, is an infantile disorder. The scope of crime, Comfort points out, depends directly on legislation, but delinquency in the sense of 'action and attitude prejudicial to the welfare of others' is a psychiatric condition.[38]

According to this definition, he maintains that centralized societies with established governments have put delinquents in power, notably in the law enforcement agencies of police, army and prison. Their main preoccupation is a desire for authority, for powers of control and direction over others. Party politics also attracts aggressive personalities in search of power as an end in itself, 'psychopathic persons or groups who will exhibit delinquent behaviour'.[39]

In a lecture on delinquency given at the anarchist summer school organized by the Freedom Press in 1950, Comfort went even further to declare:

As anarchists the desire to dominate is the 'crime' which worries us most. We recognize that at the moment the delinquent activities of governments, and of individual psychopaths in them, are a greater threat to social advance than even the most serious examples of punishable crimes.[40]

In his analysis of the sociology of power, Comfort draws on the insights of social anthropology and psychoanalysis. He makes the interesting observation that organized government first appears in history at the same time as anti-social patterns of behaviour: 'at the point in any culture when it ceases to be capable of absorbing its own abnormal members, the demand for coercion appears hand in hand with the emergence of individuals who desire to coerce.'[41] He suggests that 'power-centred' cultures are found in 'patriform' societies, those based upon jealousy of the father, which emphasize command, prohibition and coercion. 'Life-centred' cultures on the other hand develop in 'matriform' societies, where co-operation, production and creation are more important. Among the components for the desire for power he suggests is self-identification with the coercive father and power as a sexual substitute, or as a form of compensation for failure to secure status and affection. As social animals, humans desire the approval and affection of others, and prohibition may well be a substitute for participation and recognition.

For all its Freudian overtones, Comfort's argument is very suggestive. It offers a wider anthropological and psychological dimension to the traditional anarchist analysis of the State. Comfort however is less convincing on aggression and domination. He suggests that dominance patterns are 'apparently inseparable' from all types of relationship among men and animals. And while he suggests that interpersonal aggression is at root a desire to recognize and to be recognized, he asserts 'Humanity maintains itself by an aggressive attitude towards its environment'.[42] It is a view which most modern anarchists, especially those influenced by social ecology, would reject. Dominance and hierarchy are not inevitable elements of the human condition, and a genuinely free society would encourage the practice of 'matriform' values not only amongst its individual members, but also in relation to other species and nature as a whole.

Comfort returned to the issue of aggression in his *Nature and Human Nature* (1966), where he discusses from an evolutionary perspective the origins of humanity, the development of their sexual and social behaviour, their emotional needs, and their place in the world. He sees aggression more common in 'Man' [sic] than in other social species and higher primates, suggesting that self-destructive behaviour is 'one of the most characteristically "human" features'. While an eighteenth-century optimist like Godwin would have seen human beings as social animals liable to outbursts of irrational aggression, Man appears to Comfort 'more like an irrationally aggressive animal capable of outbursts of sociality'.[43] At the same time, Comfort suggests like Kropotkin that our capacity for love and sociality, even our 'moral sense', is in direct continuity with the mutual aid of lower animals. A large part of our aggression is therefore part of our alienation from our animal mode. As a result, Man has become his own worse enemy. Even freedom forced upon us makes us anxious. Aggression is thus presented as a stress disorder, internalized in suicide and externalized in war.

The cause of this state of affairs, according to Comfort, is the absence in our centralized and technological culture of the orgiastic and socializing experience for which we seem to be programmed by evolution. In the past, religion and art helped organize human feelings and wishes. Comfort now calls for 'A Technology of the Emotions' to release the socializing forces within us through fulfilling work.

In his discussion of paternalism or what he calls 'baboonery', Comfort strikes a particularly anarchist note when he suggests that since the development of institutional authority, human societies have used 'government' to express two incompatible social activities, 'namely organization or communication and individual or group dominance behaviour – whether the eldest, the strongest, the entrenched or the magic-possessor'.[44] A sign that baboonery is on its way out will come when we stop considering government as a matter of power and begin to regard it as a matter of communication. To do this, Comfort recommends a kind of democracy as direct as that of the old Greek city or the small club, in which everyone can be consulted by voting through computers against any policy undertaken by administrators. The government of men would then be replaced by the administration of things.

As a medical biologist concerned with physical and mental well-being, Comfort advocates the complete fulfilment of sexuality. In *Barbarism and Sexual Freedom*, he argued that coercion or institutions sponsored by the State and other such bodies, civil or religious, have no place in sexuality. Like Reich he maintained that a revolution in the moral and personal sexuality of the individual entails an equally radical revolution in the social order. But while rejecting sexual repression, he condemns untrammelled licentiousness in a social vacuum. The bases of sexual freedom, he insists, are: 'responsibility of the individual for his own acts and their consequences, absence of interference of coercive institutions, economic freedom and security, and social order orientated towards life rather than death'.[45]

Comfort went on to write widely about *Sexual Behaviour and Society* (1950) and his books on the subject helped shape the 'permissive society' of the sixties. But it was in his best-selling *The Joy of Sex* (1972; 2nd edn., 1991) that he developed his hedonistic and libertarian message in its most popular form. Drawing on different cultural traditions, the work offers 'A Gourmet Guide to Lovemaking'. It is Comfort's contention that every individual should be free to explore the full range of their sexuality. But again with freedom comes responsibility. The only basic rule is that one should not injure or exploit anyone: 'you don't take a novice climbing and abandon them halfway up when things get difficult . . . A cad can be of either sex.'[46] Comfort also wisely suggests that no one should feel obliged to do anything that they do not want to do, and adults should never involve children in their sexual activities. While it is one of the least inhibited books on sex ever written, its dominant note is one of tenderness and joy.

Paul Goodman

Amongst anarcho-communists in the United States, Paul Goodman has undoubtedly had the widest influence since the Second World War. Born in New York in 1911, he became a teacher, essayist, poet, novelist, playwright, psychotherapist, and critic. His main concern was to avoid war and to apply anarchist principles to the problems of urban America. He was not primarily an anarchist thinker, but like Colin Ward in Britain was keen to show in concrete ways the practical applicability of anarchist ideas. He helped develop and gave expression to the wave of libertarianism and pacifism in the fifties and sixties which formed part of the New Left in America. His advocacy of anti-militarism, radical decentralization, participatory democracy, and organic community also deeply influenced the counter-culture at the time.

Goodman first proposed his alternative to the size, sprawl and bureaucracy of contemporary America in *Communitas: Means of Livelihood and Ways of Life* (1947), a work he wrote with his architect brother Percival. It offers a libertarian perspective on urban organization, calling for a restoration of the community as a face-to-face voluntary association of individuals united by common needs and interests. They wanted to eliminate the difference between production and consumption and stop 'quarantining' work from homes and vice versa. Like William Morris, they recognized that people like to work and be useful, 'for work has a rhythm and springs from spontaneous feelings just like play, and to be useful makes people feel right'.[47] But with its emphasis on discipline, the modern factory system had destroyed the instinctive pleasures of work.

To overcome this state of affairs, the Goodmans recommended workers' participation and control, and relatively small units with relative self-sufficiency. This would enable each community to enter into a larger whole with solidarity while retaining an independent outlook. They further advocated like Kropotkin the integration of factory and farm, town and country as well as decentralization and regional autonomy. The economy should be based on the production of useful things rather than of profit.

Goodman saw himself as a creative artist preserving and developing the anarchist tradition. He did not think that there could be a history of anarchism in the sense of establishing a permanent state of things called anarchist. What anarchists must do is to decide where 'to draw the line' against the authoritarian and oppressive forces at work in society.[48]

For Goodman anarchism is grounded in the proposition that

> valuable behaviour occurs only by the free and direct response of
> individuals or voluntary groups to the conditions presented by the
> historical environment. It claims that in most human affairs, whether
> political, economic, military, religious, moral, pedagogic or cultural,
> more harm than good results from coercion, top-down direction, cen-
> tral authority, bureaucracy, jails, conscription, states, pre-ordained
> standardisation, excessive planning, etc. Anarchists want to increase
> intrinsic functioning and diminish extrinsic power. This is a social-
> psychological hypothesis with obvious political implications.[49]

Goodman described himself as a 'community anarchist who believes
that coercive sovereign power is always a poor expedient'. He always considered freedom and health to be absolute goods and was convinced that
'organism-self-regulation' works out best. His anarchism went beyond liberalism since he felt the negative definition of freedom as mere freedom
from interference is both trivial and in fact indefensible. Instead, he advocated freedom in the positive sense as '*the condition of initiating activity*'.[50]
Without this ability, people might be formally free, but in practice powerless
and enslaved.

At the same time, Goodman was pragmatic and argued that the 'relativ-
ity of the anarchist principle to the actual situation is of the essence of
anarchism'. He therefore affirmed the Jeffersonian Bill of Rights (as
opposed to the Constitution) as a great historical achievement, fundamental
to further progress. In their day, Congregational churches and the free
medieval cities were anarchist in spirit. Even the civil rights movement in
the United States was 'almost classically decentralist and anarchist'. Far
from being directed only to a glorious future, anarchism for him involved
perpetual vigilance to make sure that past freedoms are not lost and do not
turn into their opposite; it is 'always a continual coping with the next
situation'.[51]

Goodman thought utopian thinking necessary in our era in order to
combat the emptiness of the technological life and to think up new social
forms. On the other hand, he liked to call himself a 'Neolithic Conservative'.
He recognized that in the modern world the anarchist should be a conservator of libertarian traditions as well as pressing for gradual change by
fostering beneficial tendencies in society. Like Landauer, he wrote: 'A free
society cannot be the substitution of a "new order" for the old order; it is
the extension of spheres of free action until they make up most of the social
life.'[52]

Goodman was ready to accept voting for candidates in national elections
who were unambiguously opposed to the Cold War and believed that an

electoral campaign could be a powerful means of educating the public. Nevertheless, he was totally opposed to traditional politics as 'a matter of "getting into power", and then "deciding", directing, controlling, coercing, the activities of society'.[53] In the normal functioning of a free community of interests, there is no need for abstract power except in the case of emergencies. Abstract power, in the form of discipline, bureaucracy and management, universally debases the persons involved and thwarts normal and healthy activities.

In tracing the evolution of government, Goodman describes how in the past conquerors and pirates intervened in traditional, peaceful, 'community-anarchy'. Piracy then became government, 'the process of getting people to perform by extrinsic motivations, of penalty and blackmail, and later bribery and training'. A continual state of emergency was created. The result today is that some individuals aspire to be top managers and obtain power for its own sake, while most people experience utter powerlessness. In modern centralized States, 'we mostly see the abortions of lively social functioning saddled, exploited, prevented, perverted, drained dry, paternalized by an imposed system of power and management'.[54]

Goodman, like Bourne, argues that the principal lesson of modern history is that 'War is the health of the State'. Sovereign national States have grown by preparing for war and waging war. Even education has become regimented to 'apprentice-training for war'. The only pacifist conclusion is therefore the anarchist one – to decentralize regionally and localize wherever possible for such a process promotes peace, encourages initiative, and creates a more 'vivid and intimate life'.[55]

Goodman's pacifism is necessarily revolutionary. It does not look to traditional politics but tries to dispel the mesmerism of abstract power. It practises civil disobedience and direct action. Above all, it tries to live communally and without authority, to do useful work and feel friendly, and so positively '*to replace an area of power with peaceful functioning*'.[56]

Given his psychoanalytic background, Goodman was not opposed to all forms of violence. He felt that face-to-face violence, like a fist-fight, is natural; if anything, it does damage to try and repress it. Again he felt it was inevitable that oppressed people, like blacks in the US or the French during the Nazi occupation would fight back. He refused to make a moral judgement about this kind of violence because it was like a force of nature. But when violence becomes organized as in modern warfare, and some abstract policy rather than personal anger leads people to kill, then he was completely opposed to it: 'all war is entirely unacceptable because it mechanises human beings and inevitably leads to more harm than good. Therefore I am a pacifist.'[57] While Goodman recognized guerrilla fighting to be a classic anarchist technique and refused to condemn it, he felt that especially in modern conditions, '*any* violent means tends to reinforce centralism and authoritarianism'.[58] In *A Message to the Military Industrial Complex* (1965) of the United States, he declared in characteristic style:

> You are ... the most dangerous body at present in the world, for you not only implement our disastrous policies but are an overwhelming lobby for them, and you expand rigidly the wrong use of brains, resources, and labour so that change becomes difficult.[59]

In order to change people and society, Goodman primarily looked to education. Probably his single most important contribution was to libertarian education. His starting-point was that there is no right education except 'growing up into a worthwhile world'. Beyond this, education should foster independent thought and expression, rather than conformity. Since compulsory education had become a universal trap, Goodman boldly suggested like Godwin that very many of the young might be better off if they had no formal schooling at all: 'it by no means follows that the complicated artifact of a school system has much to do with education, and certainly not with good education'.[60] There is good evidence that normal children will make up the first seven years' school-work with four to seven months of good teaching. At least students should be able to leave and return to education periodically. Where school does exist it must be voluntary for there is no growth to freedom without intrinsic motivation.

Goodman's educational alternatives included using the city itself as a school, involving adults from the community, making class attendance voluntary, and decentralizing urban schools and enabling children to live temporarily on marginal farms. In *Art and Social Nature* (1946), Goodman stressed like Read the importance of the aesthetic sensibility, but he came to believe that contemporary education must also be heavily weighted towards the sciences so that people can feel at home in the modern technological environment and understand the morality of a scientific way of life.

In *The Community of Scholars* (1962), Goodman dealt with higher education and showed how inadequate it was to meet the real educational needs of the young. With the huge growth of administrators and the relationships between teachers and pupils increasingly distant and official, he called for a return to the traditional university which was a small, face-to-face community of scholars, autonomous and self-governing – in short, 'anarchically self-regulating'.[61] Since teaching and learning always involve a personal relation, the teacher should be not an institutional hybrid but a veteran with experience of life.

Goodman thought that contemporary problems are not just the result of bad formal education in school and university. The whole of 'normal' child-rearing is to blame. In his best-selling book *Growing Up Absurd* (1960), he showed how irrational are the traditional ways of bringing up children through coercion and discipline. But he did not despair. He was impressed by the young in America, who were dismissed by their elders as beatniks and delinquents, for their simpler fraternity and sexuality. They offered a direct contrast to the mores of the ' "organized system", its role playing, its competitiveness, its canned culture, its public relations, its avoidance of risk and self-exposure'.[62]

To remedy the alienation and division felt by members of modern society, Goodman worked as a psychotherapist, and in his remarkable contribution to *Gestalt Therapy* (1951) he searched for a new harmony between the individual and his social and physical environment. In 1968, at a time of social upheaval in the West, he declared simply:

> The important crisis at present has to do with authority and militarism. That's the real danger, and if we could get rid of militarism and if we could get rid of the principle of authority by which people don't run their own lives, then society could become decent, and that's all you want of society. It's not up to governments or states to make anybody happy. They can't do it.[63]

On a broader front, Goodman called just before he died in 1972 for a *New Reformation* which would radically transform industrialized civilization. Thousands of people influenced by Goodman in the counter-culture in the sixties and seventies tried to do just that by creating alternative ways of living and seeing in communes and collectives. The 'Flower Power' generation, whom Goodman inspired and admired, attempted to put into practice the kind of pacifist anarchism to which he devoted his life.

Murray Bookchin
and the Ecology of Freedom

ONE OF THE MOST influential thinkers to have renewed anarchist thought and action since the Second World War is undoubtedly Murray Bookchin. His main achievement is to have combined traditional anarchist insights with modern ecological thinking to form what he calls 'social ecology'. In this way, he has helped develop the powerful libertarian tendency in the contemporary Green movement. Just as Kropotkin renewed anarchism at the end of the nineteenth century by giving it an evolutionary dimension, so Bookchin has gone further to give it a much needed ecological perspective.

Bookchin has recently reached a wider audience, but he has been involved in Left politics for most of his life. Born in 1921 the son of poor Russian immigrants in the United States, he spent his early years as a worker in industry. As a young man he steeped himself in Marxism; first he was a Communist and then a Trotskyist. A reading of Herbert Read and George Woodcock helped wean him from Marx and Engels, and in the sixties he emerged as a powerful and controversial anarchist thinker. The first book to bring him to prominence was *Post-Scarcity Anarchism* (1971), a collection of essays inspired by the revolutionary optimism of the sixties which argued that for the first time in history the prospect of material abundance created by modern technology made possible a free society for all. The vitriolic essay 'Listen, Marxist!' reflected the controversial and sometimes abusive nature of his style.

In the meantime, Bookchin continued to develop his interest in environmental issues. His first published work was about the problems of chemicals in food published in German as *Lebensgefährliche Lebensmittel* (1952) which looked at the social origins of environmental pollution. It was followed by *Our Synthetic Environment* (1962), issued under the pseudonym of Lewis Herber, which reflected his interest in the way technology mediated our relationship with nature. A concern about the quality of city life led him to write his critical study of urbanism *Crisis in our Cities* (1965). In *The Limits of the City* (1973; many essays therein dated from the

1950s), he attacked the modern megalopolis and centralized planning and tried to bring a human and democratic dimension which he saw in the Greek *polis* back to modern city life. City air should make people free, not cough. This interest is further reflected in *The Rise of Urbanization and the Decline of Citizenship* (1987). It became a central theme in Bookchin's writing that municipalism, with its emphasis on the human scale, local control, and decentralization, must be a fundamental anarchist goal. The citizens' assembly should foster autonomous selfhood as well as civic virtue.

It was in his essay 'Ecology and Revolutionary Thought' (1964) which appeared in *Post-Scarcity Anarchism* that Bookchin first clearly argued that a free society should be an ecological one. He took up the theme in *Toward an Ecological Society* (1980) where he developed his central thesis that the notion of the domination of nature by man stems from the very real domination of man and woman by man. In his wide-ranging work *The Ecology of Freedom* (1982) he draws on history and anthropology to demonstrate the emergence of hierarchy and to argue for its dissolution. It was called at the time by John Clark 'the most important book to appear so far in the history of anarchist thought' and by Theodore Roszak to be 'the most important contribution to ecological thought in our generation'.[1]

Unfortunately, it is not an easy book to read for those not well versed in philosophy and critical social theory, and the style can sometimes be obscure, repetitive and tangential. Bookchin has tried to remedy the drawback by writing *Remaking Society* (1989) as a 'primer' on his ideas in a more accessible and readable form. In all these later works, he developed a form of cultural politics grounded in an organic and ecological world-view. Taken together, they form an original contribution to political theory.

Like the great nineteenth-century social thinkers, Bookchin proposes a grand synthesis of philosophy, science, anthropology, and history. If he does not always weave ideas culled from different and often incompatible traditions into a coherent whole, he cannot at least be accused of not being ambitious. Bookchin's intellectual background is remarkably wide-ranging but it is firmly placed in the Western tradition of critical theory and the Enlightenment.

His Marxist apprenticeship has left a Leninist cast to his thought: he claims to think dialectically and recognizes the central importance of history in understanding culture. Among the German Romantic thinkers, he shares Schiller's emphasis on the imagination and art, and Fichte's view of human consciousness as nature rendered self-conscious. He is influenced by the Frankfurt school of social theorists, especially Adorno and Horkheimer, in their critique of instrumental reason and modern civilization although he rejects their pessimistic view that man must dominate nature in order to create economic abundance. Yet despite the wide variety of his influences and sources, he has tried to digest them into a remarkable synthesis of his own. Coherence, he admits, is his favourite word – although he does not always achieve it.

Bookchin's anarchism draws inspiration from Bakunin in its revolutionary fervour and from Kropotkin in its proposals. His study of the Spanish Revolution, which resulted in *The Spanish Anarchists* (1976), reflects his awareness of a living anarchist tradition. Towards the end of his life, he looked back to the American Revolution and to ancient Greece for libertarian and democratic precedents.

At the same time, Bookchin unabashedly places himself in the utopian tradition. For him utopia is not a dreamy vision, but rather a matter of foresight. The power of utopian thinking lies precisely in 'a vision of society that questions *all* the presuppositions of present day society'.[2] It stirs the imagination to consider new alternatives to everyday life while having a passion for concrete proposals. He is particularly inspired by Rabelais, Charles Fourier and William Morris who offer a vision of society in which work is transformed into play, and who stress the importance of sensuousness and creativity. Bookchin thus adds his voice to the call of the Parisian students of 1968 for 'Imagination to seize Power' and shares with the Situationists a desire to change our habits and perceptions in everyday life.

But while Bookchin readily admits his utopian inspiration, he is keen to stress that anarchism is extremely realistic and more relevant than ever. In the past, the anarchist was often regarded 'as a forlorn visionary, a social outcast, filled with nostalgia for the peasant village or the medieval commune', but today the anarchist concepts of a balanced community, a face-to-face democracy, a humanistic technology and decentralized society are not only 'eminently practical' but preconditions to human survival.[3] Bookchin's utopian thinking is therefore firmly based on the realities of human experience.

One of Bookchin's most important achievements is to have helped develop a new approach to analyse economic exploitation and social oppression. He goes beyond the rather simplistic denunciation of the State and capitalism found in the classic anarchist thinkers and prefers to talk in terms of 'hierarchy' rather than class, 'domination' rather than exploitation. He eschews tired abstractions like the 'masses' or the 'proletariat'. Exploitation and class rule are particular concepts within more generalized concepts of domination and hierarchy. And by hierarchy, he means not only a social condition but a state of consciousness; it involves 'the cultural, traditional and psychological systems of obedience and command' as well as the economic and political systems of class and State.[4]

The State moreover is according to Bookchin not merely a constellation of bureaucratic and coercive institutions but also a state of mind, 'an instilled mentality for ordering reality'. The State as an instrument of organized violence did not suddenly evolve in society as Proudhon and Kropotkin suggest. It emerged with the gradual politicization of certain social functions and it has become meshed with society to such an extent that it is difficult to distinguish the two: 'It not only *manages* the economy but *politicizes* it; it not only *colonizes* social life but *absorbs* it.'[5]

It follows for Bookchin that any future revolution should not only aim to dissolve the State but to reconstruct society along new communal lines. It should develop new libertarian institutions and be concerned with nothing less than the liberation of daily life. It is this personal dimension which is most important in Bookchin's work. Indeed, he argues that the slogan 'power to the people' is meaningless since the people can never have power until they disappear as a 'people'.[6] The value of direct action for Bookchin lies precisely in the fact that it makes people aware of themselves as individuals who can affect their own destiny. Revolution is not therefore some abstract inevitable upheaval but a concrete form of self-activity.

Philosophy of Nature

Bookchin tried to develop a comprehensive philosophy of nature in which to ground his ethics and politics. It stands in a tradition of organismic and holistic thinking and may best be described – to use Bookchin's own phrase – as a kind of dialectical naturalism. Rejecting both the mechanical materialism which sees nature as a dead body of resources to exploit, and the 'spiritual mechanism' in which all is dissolved in cosmic oneness, he develops the Hellenic concept of a world *nous* which finds meaning and purpose in nature.[7] Nature is not just a 'lump of minerals' but a 'complex web of life' which is charged with ethical meaning. It has its own order and abhors 'the incoherence of disorganization, the lack of meaning that comes with disorder'.[8] The whole is greater than the sum of its parts.

In Bookchin's view, nature is potentially rational and conscious and even wilful. Reason in nature appears as the 'self-organizing attributes of substance; it is the latent subjectivity in the inorganic and organic levels of reality that reveal an inherent striving towards consciousness'.[9] There seems, Bookchin argues, to be 'a kind of intentionality latent in nature, a graded development of self-organization that yields subjectivity and, finally, self-reflexivity in its highly developed human form'.[10] Indeed, he follows Aristotle and Fichte in seeing human consciousness as one of the necessary manifestations of nature and echoes Elisée Reclus by describing it as 'nature rendered self-conscious'.[11] But while Bookchin discerns a purpose within nature, this does not mean that it is deterministic. It simply implies the development of each being must be understood in terms of its interaction with other beings. Like a plant or a child, nature has a potential which it tries to unfold with a dim sense of 'will' and 'choice' but its realization depends on its relationships with other beings and things in its total environment.

Like Kropotkin, Bookchin believes that nature can offer the basis for objective ethics. Since '*nature is writing its own nature philosophy and ethics*', it is possible to draw moral lessons from the ways of nature.[12] And the most important lesson is that nature is not blind, mute or stingy, but provides the grounds for human freedom.[13] Rejecting the market-place image of nature, he adopts an ecological image which sees it as essentially creative, directive, mutualistic and fecund.

Bookchin develops Hegel's argument that substance is subjectivity but tries to release it from its idealist implications. He maintains that nature organizes itself into more complex and conscious forms, ever greater 'complexity, subjectivity and mind'.[14] Bookchin further gives an account of evolution which confirms Kropotkin's stress on co-operation as the key factor in the survival of the species but adds that it takes place through an immanent striving rather than as the chance product of external forces. He sees the earth as a self-regulating organism but refuses to see it anthropomorphically as a personified deity.

In his discussion of human nature, Bookchin pays particular attention to the self and human consciousness and is not afraid to use such words as the 'psyche' or the 'human spirit'.[15] But he is not a philosophical idealist and he places the human species firmly within nature. Human society constitutes a 'second nature', a cultural artifact, out of 'first nature', or primeval, non-human nature. Where 'first nature' is in large part the product of biological evolution, the 'second nature' of society is a product of social evolution, of a mind that can act purposefully and creatively.[16] Nature thus has within it latent consciousness and subjectivity; human consciousness is nature made self-conscious. But while human beings evolve from nature they are unique in that they are creative, conscious and purposeful beings able to shape societies and make their own history.

This evolutionary view of human consciousness does not prevent Bookchin from asserting that there is such a thing as human nature. He defines it as 'proclivities and potentialities that become increasingly defined by the installation of social needs'.[17] Although he moved later in a more rationalist direction, in his early work he talks in terms of releasing the 'Eros-derived impulses' and affirming the 'life-impulses' in human nature – 'the urgings of desire, sensuousness, and the lure of the marvelous'. He is convinced that a 'basic sense of decency, sympathy and mutual aid lies at the core of human behavior'.[18]

At the same time, while stressing the importance of the concrete individual, Bookchin is no rugged individualist. He repeatedly condemns the type of modern individualism which presents the individual wandering through life as a free-floating and egoistical monad. He sees 'selfhood' not merely as a personal dimension but also a social one: 'The self that finds expression in the assembly and community is, literally, the assembly and community that has found self-expression – a complete congruence of form and content.'[19] We are above all social beings, and have a need to associate, and to care for our own kind.

History and Society

Like Kropotkin, Bookchin finds evidence for his arguments for a free society in the findings of anthropology and history. Like Hegel, he adopts a historical approach in understanding society and culture, recognizing that their nature can only be appreciated in terms of their origins and development. In *The Ecology of Freedom*, he offers an 'anthropology of hierarchy and domination' out of which he tries to rescue the 'legacy of freedom'.[20]

In the past, the domination of woman by man, man by man, and nature by man led to the emergence of social hierarchies justified by 'epistemologies of rule' which encourage competitive and hierarchical thinking. Nevertheless, there are historical precedents for a free society. Bookchin endorses the outlook of pre-literate 'organic' society which allegedly had no hierarchical thinking, established an equality of unequals (recognizing individual differences), and practised the principles of usufruct (the use of resources based on desire rather than exclusive right), complementarity (based on interdependence and mutual aid), spontaneity, and the guarantee of the 'irreducible minimum' (every one's basic material and social needs being met regardless of their contribution to society).

Drawing on the work of anthropologists Paul Radin and Dorothy Lee among others, Bookchin argues that organic society emphasized the uniqueness of each person as well as co-operation between them. Where leadership exists it is functional and does not involve hierarchical institutions. Such societies saw nature as a harmonious whole and their tribal communities as an inseparable part of it. Their view of nature was primarily decided by the nature of their social structures. They developed a system of needs which was possible to satisfy without a struggle *against* nature. What they lacked was a developed sense of self-consciousness.

According to Bookchin, a sense of community and co-operation became more important in agricultural society. But in other hunter-gatherer societies a division of labour between hunting and defence contributed to the emergence of domination and hierarchy. Elderly men searched for power and won the support of the warriors. But a true class system did not evolve until the formation of cities: with them came the State, authoritarian technology and organized markets. Needs multiplied and the ruling class appropriated the growing economic surplus. In the meantime, as man increasingly dominated woman and man, the attitude to nature changed from one of co-operation to one of domination. In order to create wealth it was now considered necessary to conquer nature. What is original about all this is that Bookchin shows the origins of hierarchy to be the result of a complex combination of economic, political and cultural factors, of changes in the way people think and feel as well as in their social organization.

Bookchin is not however a primitivist who calls for a return to Stone-Age living. He sees the development of Greek civilization as a great step forward for humanity, and particularly chastises those who would turn to Oriental philosophy for enlightenment.[21] He praises the Greeks for having a teleological view of nature in which nature is seen as having a purpose and meaning. The Greeks also placed technology (*techne*) in an ethical context. Above all, they did not separate ethics and politics in their search for the 'good life' and 'living well'.

According to Bookchin, the Hellenic notion of *autarkia*, commonly seen as self-sufficiency, sought to find a balance between mind and body, needs and resources, and the individual and society. Indeed, their concept of individuality integrated the 'constellations' of the individual and the social. And in the Athenian *polis*, Bookchin finds a radiant example of direct, face-to-face democracy, especially in the *ecclesia* of the Periclean period where all the citizens met as a whole to make policy and chose administrators by lot and disputes were solved by popular juries. The human scale of the *polis*, which according to Aristotle should be 'taken in at a single view', has important lessons for urban planners.[22]

While subsequent history in the West led to a legacy of domination, especially with the foundation of the Nation-State and the development of capitalism, Bookchin traces an alternative underground libertarian tradition. In this 'legacy of freedom', Bookchin singles out the millenarian Christian sects of the Middle Ages, the Diggers' colony in the English Revolution, the town meetings in New England after the American Revolution, the Parisian sections during the French Revolution, the Paris Commune, and the anarchist communes and councils of the Spanish Revolution as providing models for the forms of freedom for the future. Only in the latter did a system of working-class self-management succeed, since the Spanish anarcho-syndicalists consciously sought to limit centralization.

Social Ecology

However interesting we might find his anthropological and historical studies, Bookchin's principal achievement lies in his impressive synthesis of anarchist and ecological thought. He became a leading exponent of 'social ecology' which traces the roots of the environmental crisis to society and which argues that only the creation of a free society will solve the present threat of ecological disaster confronting humanity.

Bookchin's starting-point is that modern technology (or technics, as he calls it) has created a new stage in history by enabling humanity to pass from a realm of material scarcity to one of abundance. In the past material scarcity not only provided the rationale for the patriarchal family, private property, class domination and the State but fostered a repressive morality of denial and guilt. The immediate prospect of material abundance however has outdated earlier socialist theories, including Marxism, which saw the primary goal as overcoming scarcity. In *Post-Scarcity Anarchism*, Bookchin argued that for the first time in history the 'technology of abundance' has created the necessary preconditions for a free society, a society without class rule, exploitation, toil or material want. There is no longer any obligation to pass through a transitional period of austerity and sacrifice as Marx and Engels argued in order to move from the realm of necessity to the realm of freedom. It follows that the age-old ambition to satisfy basic needs can now be replaced by the fulfilment of desire. Utopia is no longer a dream but an actual possibility.

Bookchin has stressed that post-scarcity does not mean mindless affluence, but a 'sufficiency of technical development that leaves individuals free to select their needs autonomously and to obtain the means to satisfy them'.[23] He is eager to demystify the notion of a 'stingy nature' which has led some ecologists to call for 'limits to growth', 'voluntary poverty' and a 'life-boat' ethic. At the same time, he identifies freedom more with personal autonomy than material abundance, with greater choice rather than more goods.

But while the conditions of post-scarcity provide a real possibility, the recent thrust to increase production in both capitalist societies and communist States has led to a new crisis, the threat of ecological disaster. Bookchin argues however that the roots of the present ecological crisis do not lie in technology, overpopulation, or industrial growth alone but rather in the practice of domination and hierarchy. In the past, to transcend scarcity, it was thought necessary to dominate and conquer nature. But the very concept of dominating nature first emerged from man's domination of woman in patriarchal society and man's domination of man in hierarchical society. Both human beings and nature have therefore become common victims of domination to such a degree that they are now faced with ecological extinction.

There is however a 'redemptive dialectic' to this process. We have the power to create as well as the power to destroy. The technology which now helps to enslave us and destroy our environment can also provide the preconditions of freedom. But this can only be done if we radically transform our society. Where Marx posed the choice between socialism or barbarism, Bookchin suggests that we are confronted with the more drastic alternatives of 'anarchism or annihilation'.[24] It is only by creating a free and ecological society that humanity will have a future.

It is Bookchin's principal contention that we must turn to ecology for the essential guidelines of how a free society should be organized. Ecology deals with the dynamic balance of nature, with the interdependence of living and non-living things. In its critical dimension, it shows not only how man has produced imbalances in nature but also the absurdity of his pretension to achieve mastery over the planet.

The most important principle in ecology is that overall harmony in an ecosystem is best realized in diversity. Mankind on the other hand is undoing the work of organic evolution, by replacing a highly complex, organic environment with a simplified, inorganic one. The critical message of ecology is that if we diminish variety in the natural world, we debase its unity and wholeness. Its constructive message is that if we wish to advance the unity and stability of the natural world, we must preserve and promote variety. Ecological wholeness is thus a dynamic unity of diversity in which balance and harmony are achieved by an ever-changing differentiation. Slipping from the natural order to the social realm, Bookchin asserts: 'From an ecological viewpoint, balance and harmony in nature, in society and, by inference, in behavior, are achieved not by mechanical standardization but by its opposite, organic differentiation.'[25]

Anarchism is the only social philosophy which offers the possibility of achieving unity in social diversity. And just as anarchism can help realize ecological principles, so ecology can enrich anarchism. Bookchin stresses that his definition of the term 'libertarian' is guided by his description of the ecosystem: 'the image of unity in diversity, spontaneity, and complementary relationships, free of all hierarchy and domination'.[26]

Bookchin's transition 'by inference' from the scientific principles of ecology to social and moral theory of anarchism runs the logical risk of the 'naturalistic fallacy', that is, it tries to develop a moral imperative from an empirical observation, an 'ought' from an 'is'. But Bookchin makes no apology for drawing ethical imperatives from an ecological interpretation of nature. Nature itself is not an ethics, he claims, but it is the 'matrix' for an ethics, and ecology can be a 'source of values and ideals'.[27] It offers the two basic moral principles of participation and differentiation in a non-hierarchical framework.

Bookchin supports his case for an objective ecological ethics in several ways. Firstly, he asserts that in so far as man is part of nature, an expanding natural environment enlarges the basis for social development. Secondly, he maintains that both the ecologist and anarchist place a common stress on the importance of spontaneity in releasing potentialities and that anarchism best approximates the ecological ideal. Thirdly, he claims that both view differentiation as measure of progress, so that '*An expanding whole is created by growing diversification and enrichment of its parts*'.[28] Anarchism is thus scientifically vindicated and presented as the only possible alternative to the threatening ecological extinction.

Bookchin calls his revolutionary version of ecology and anarchism 'social ecology'. It was a term used by E. A. Gutkind in his *Community and Environment* (1954) but for Bookchin the root conceptions of a radical social ecology are hierarchy and domination. Inspired by the ecological principles of unity in diversity, spontaneity and complementarity, it sees the balance and the integrity of the biosphere as an end in itself. It aims to create a movement to change the relations of humans to each other and of humanity to nature, to transform how we see nature and our place within it.

As such, Bookchin distinguishes social ecology from environmentalism which merely reflects an instrumental sensibility, views nature as a passive habitat composed of objects, and is principally concerned with conservation and pollution control. Environmentalism does not question the most basic premisses of our society based on domination and hierarchy. Bookchin also stresses its difference from so-called 'deep ecology' as expounded by Arne Naess, David Foreman, George Sessions and Bill Devall. Deep ecology in his view is not only a 'black hole' of half-baked ideas but also dismally fails to understand that ecological problems have their ultimate roots in society.[29] Above all, deep ecologists do not show satisfactorily how consciousness and society have emerged from nature.

Ecotopia

Bookchin refuses to draw up a blueprint of his ecological and anarchist society which he calls 'ecotopia'. He does however offer some basic considerations. In the first place, cultural as well as social revolution will have to take place; this will involve nothing less than the 'remaking of the psyche'.[30] In place of all hierarchical and domineering modes of thought, a new 'ecological sensibility' must develop which has a holistic outlook and celebrates 'play, fantasy and imagination'. Such a sensibility should be accompanied by a 'new animism' which leads to a 'respiritization' of the natural world by seeing in human consciousness 'a natural world rendered self-conscious and self-active'.[31] An 'animistic imagination' moreover would not separate the 'how' of things from the 'why'.

Secondly, in a free society it will be necessary to develop a libertarian approach to reason. Like Horkheimer and Adorno, Bookchin believes in 'objective' reason which makes the universe a rational and meaningful order. He is also critical of the kind of instrumental reason which turns ends into means. But he wishes to go beyond both of them 'to integrate rationality with subjectivity in order to bring nature within the compass of *sensibility*'. In order to achieve this, 'We must recover the continuum between our "first nature" and our "second nature", our natural world and our social world, our biological being and our rationality.'[32] A genuinely libertarian reason for Bookchin will be infused with sensibility, work in an ethical context, and recognize unity in diversity. In his later work, he called for a 're-enchantment' of humanity by a 'fluid, organismic and dialectical rationality'.[33]

A libertarian ethics according to Bookchin should be based on rational analysis. It sees freedom as unhindered volition and self-consciousness. A libertarian ethics therefore should be concerned more with freedom than justice, more with pleasure than happiness. The principle of justice developed by the Greeks asserts the rule of equivalence – equal and exact exchange. Inspired by the example of organic societies, freedom for Bookchin presupposes an equality based on a recognition of the inequality of capacities, needs and responsibilities. It abandons the notion of right as it provides an 'irreducible minimum' to survive. Freedom thus involves the equality of unequals.

Whereas organic societies lived in a condition of limited needs, advanced industrial societies are now in a position to choose freely their needs. We are faced with the broadest freedom known thus far: '*the autonomous individual's freedom to shape material life in a form that is . . . ecological, rational, and artistic*'.[34] Because of this freedom we are able to go beyond need to desire, happiness to pleasure: where happiness is the mere satisfaction of physical needs, pleasure by contrast is the satisfaction of sensuous and intellectual desires. It is a spiritual as well as a physical condition, since the essence of ecology for Bookchin is 'a return to earthy naturalism'.[35]

Bookchin maintains that human intervention in nature is inevitable since human nature is part of nature: our second social nature has evolved from our first biological nature. Ecological ethics definitely involves 'human stewardship' of the planet. Man can play his part in the management of the ecological situation by fostering diversity and spontaneity and in organic evolution by helping to realize its potential life forms. But he agrees with the ecologist Charles Elton that such intervention should not be like a game of chess but more like steering a boat.[36] Knowledge of ecology is not a question of power but of insight. In an ecological society, the 'second nature' of human society would help actualize the potentiality of 'first nature' to achieve 'mind and truth'. Ultimately, it would transcend both first and second nature into a new domain of 'free nature' which is both ethical and rational. Bookchin argues that we should therefore talk not in terms of natural evolution but of 'participatory evolution'.[37]

In practical terms, Bookchin suggests that his 'ecotopia' would be made up of a confederation of self-governing communes. Each commune would govern itself through a form of direct democracy. Like the Greek *polis*, it would be a face-to-face democracy without representation or delegated authority. Administrative tasks might be rotated but fundamental policies would be made in popular assemblies open to all. Society would become a 'body politic' in the sense that the citizens would be in direct control of the social process. Such a direct democracy would offer the most advanced form of direct action and the emphasis in 'self-management' would be on the 'self'.

In the economic sphere, Bookchin's 'ecotopia' would practise 'anarcho-communism' which presupposes the abolition of private property, the distribution of goods according to individual needs, the dissolution of commodity relationships, the rotation of work, and a reduction in the time devoted to labour.[37] Old ideas of justice, based on exchange value and the rule of equivalence, would be replaced by the ideal of freedom which recognizes the equality of unequals. Need, the agony of the masses, would give way to desire, the pleasure of individuals. And needs would no longer be dictated by scarcity or custom, but become the object of conscious choice.

Distribution would thus be based on usufruct, complementarity and the irreducible minimum. According to Bookchin, it would be an advance on nineteenth-century anarchism since usufruct is a more generous principle than the communist maxim 'to each according to his needs'. It would also go beyond Proudhon's appeal to contract to regulate relationships without the law. However freely entered, contract is inevitably based on the notion of equivalence, 'a system of "equity" that reaches its apogee in bourgeois conceptions of right'.[18] Every contract reflects a latent antagonism, and lacks an understanding of care and complementarity. No contracts would therefore be made in Bookchin's free society; all would receive the basic minimum to live and give freely without considerations of return. The market economy would be transformed into a 'moral economy' in which people would change the way they relate to each other.[39] Care, responsibility and obligation would be the new watchwords, not interest, cost or profitability.

Bookchin calls the basic units of his federated society of communes 'ecocommunities'. Tailored to the local ecosystem, they would approximate local or regional autarky, with a balanced mix of small-scale agriculture and industry. Small for Bookchin is not only beautiful but also ecological, humanistic and above all emancipatory. They would try and restore 'natural arts' to 'artificial crafts'.[40] Above all, they would form confederations in harmony with their ecosystems, bioregions and biomes. Bookchin envisages them artistically tailored to their natural surroundings:

> We can envision that their squares will be interlaced by streams, their places of assembly surrounded by groves, their physical contours respected and tastefully landscaped, their soils nurtured caringly to foster plant variety for ourselves, our domestic animals, and wherever possible the wildlife they may support on their fringes.[41]

The communities would develop 'ecotechnologies', using flexible and versatile machines which not only make use of local materials and energy sources with the minimum of pollution but favour diversity in the ecosystem and consciously promote the integrity of the biosphere. Bookchin not only stresses the cultural and social context of technology but maintains that technology is not morally neutral, like a knife which can either cut bread or murder. It is not merely a means to an end but a system which embodies specific meanings and values. He distinguishes between technics as a system of objective social forces and technical rationality, which is a system of organization and a way of knowing. There can be authoritarian and libertarian technics, exemplified in a factory as opposed to a craft workshop.

Bookchin advocates an emancipatory technology which acknowledges its ethical dimension as in the Greek notion of *techne* and sees each form as part of an organic whole. It involves developing a technological imagination which considers matter as an 'active substance' developing 'meaningful patterns' and not a dead collection of atoms.[42] An emancipatory technology would also be decentralized, subject to democratic control and compatible with ecological values. It would be small and appropriate, linked to the human scale, but above all would be rooted in the new culture and develop new meanings as well as designs.

Bookchin believes that an ecological community would overcome the existing contradictions between town and country, work and play, mind and body, individual and society, humanity and nature. It would realize the Greek ideal of the rounded and complete person and social life would fall into 'a well balanced, harmonious whole'.[43]

Such a society would take up the legacy of freedom from the past, especially the commitment of traditional societies to usufruct, complementarity, the equality of unequals, and the irreducible minimum. It would go beyond the claims of existing class society to private property, the sanctity of contract, and its adherence to the rules of equivalence. It would also develop the Renaissance sense of universal humanity and the modern emphasis on individual autonomy, without the loss of strong communal ties enjoyed by earlier organic societies. Above all, it would replace domination and hierarchy by interdependence and mutual aid.

Remaking Society

In order to achieve a free and ecological society, Bookchin refuses to separate the revolutionary process from the revolutionary goal; only libertarian means can achieve libertarian ends. The revolution must therefore not aim at the seizure of power but its dissolution. While he defends the anarchist terrorist at the end of the nineteenth century who practised 'propaganda by the deed' as imbued with 'ethical and visionary concepts', he believes in our own time that a long period of enlightenment will be necessary before the revolutionary project of an ecological society can be realized.

A continual theme in Bookchin's writings is a critique of authoritarian and proletarian forms of socialism, especially in their Marxist form. While recognizing Marx's stature as a social thinker, Bookchin argues that Marxism has ceased to be applicable to our time. It was born of an era of scarcity: Marx and Engels saw the need for a State in a transitional period precisely to increase the total of productive forces as rapidly as possible. Modern technology however has created a new industrial revolution which offers the possibility of material abundance, thereby enabling humanity to pass from the realm of necessity to the realm of freedom. Marxism should therefore be transcended just as Marx transcended Hegelian philosophy. Indeed, Bookchin argues that Marxism is the ideology of capitalism *par excellence* because it focuses on capitalist production without challenging the underlying 'cultural sensibilities' that sustain it. Marxism is therefore not only the culmination of the 'bourgeois Enlightenment' but also a form of bourgeois sociology.[44]

Bookchin is particularly critical of 'scientific' socialism because its stress on economic factors in determining human affairs leads it to reject ethical goals. Overlooking the early Marx's concern with self-realization and his critical theory of needs, Bookchin argues that Marx's later reduction of ethics to natural laws opens the doors to domination as the 'hidden incubus of the Marxian project'. The theme of domination is latent in Marx's interpretation of communism, he argues, since the conquest of nature is given as a necessary precondition for freedom. Nature for Marx is 'simply an object for mankind, purely a matter of utility'.[45]

Bookchin singles out the Marxist 'myth' of class for special criticism. In the first place, domination and hierarchy in the form of patriarchy, gerontocracy and even bureaucracy antedate the formation of classes and cannot be subsumed by class rule and economic exploitation. Secondly, Marx's class analysis which sees the proletariat as the principal agent of revolution is outmoded and incomplete. The industrial working class is no longer the majority of the population and is not becoming increasingly impoverished as Marx prophesied. On the contrary, there is a tendency for classes to decompose into entirely new subcultures which are not strictly economic groups anymore. In these new circumstances, the worker becomes revolutionary not by becoming class-conscious but by undoing his 'workerness'.[46] Indeed, Bookchin considers the workers' movement to be dead and the most advanced elements are now the drop-out youth, blacks, students, intellectuals and artists – those very *declassé* elements which Marx condemned as the lumpenproletariat.

Bookchin also assails the Marxist 'myth' of the Communist Party which struggles for power by means of hierarchy and centralization. Such a project is permeated with hierarchy, sexism and renunciation which do not disappear with the foundation of a 'worker's State' or a planned economy. Even the neo-Marxism of Herbert Marcuse is 'an exotic flower with a prickly stem' because it argues that delegated authority and representation are necessary in modern society.[47]

Bookchin is critical of the syndicalist interpretation of self-management which adopts a narrow economic interpretation of industrial democracy or workers' control. It is not enough for workers merely to take over the running of a factory; Bakunin, Bookchin reminds us, agreed with Engels that the traditional factory is inherently authoritarian. It is necessary to recognize the ethical context of technology and to transform the factory so that self-management is recast in the 'industrial management of self' and work becomes 'meaningful self-expression'.[48]

The way forward is not therefore to seize power as the authoritarian socialists propose. Power not only corrupts but it destroys. The only act of power excusable in a popular revolution is to dissolve power as far as possible. This would involve the 're-empowerment' of the individual to shape his or her life. Above all, it is essential that the revolutionary process is not separated from the revolutionary goal: '*A society based on self-administration must be achieved by self-administration.*'[49] The revolutionary process must aim at the formation of popular assemblies and communities which will involve all members of the community and enable them to act as individuals.

Bookchin proposes the 'affinity group' as a cell of the new society. Translated from the Spanish *grupo de afinidad*, a term used earlier this century by the Spanish anarchists for their form of organization, Bookchin defines it as 'a collective of intimate friends who are no less concerned with their human relationships than with their social goals'. Indeed, it is a 'new type of extended family in which kinship ties are replaced by deeply empathetic relationships'.[50] Such a group overcomes the split between the psyche and the social world, and is based on voluntarism and self-discipline, not coercion or command. It should affirm not only the rational, but also the joyous, the sensuous, and the aesthetic side of the revolution.

Affinity groups should only act as catalysts and not take a vanguard or leadership role. While remaining autonomous and local, they can federate by means of local, regional and national assemblies. Bookchin does not deny the need for co-ordination and planning, but insists that they should be achieved voluntarily through assemblies and conferences of the organs of self-management. Anarchist praxis thus emphasizes direct action, in which people become aware of themselves as individuals who can affect their own destiny, have control over their everyday life, and make each day as joyous and marvellous as possible. It also leaves room for spontaneity which releases 'the inner forces of development to find their authentic order and stability'.[51]

Spontaneity has a special meaning in Bookchin's writings and does not preclude organization and structure. It might be free of external constraint, but it is not mere impulse: 'It is self-controlled, *internally* controlled, behaviour, feeling and *thought*, not an uncontrolled effluvium of passion and action.' Bookchin stresses that self-control is an active form of selfhood in which the self is formed by 'the light of spirit, reason, and solidarity'.[52] As such, it creates its own liberated forms of organization.

Revolution for Bookchin is important not only because it tries to overthrow the established order but also because it subverts the kind of mentality it breeds. It is a 'magic moment' which should become a festival in the streets. In its purest form, the 'dialectic' of revolution is 'a gentle transcendence that finds its most human expression in art and play'.[53]

Changing the World

Despite its profound libertarian sensibility and utopian vision, there are still some authoritarian elements in Bookchin's vision of social ecology. For all his celebration of a harmonious relationship with nature, he is silent about other species. Indeed, the conditions for the kind of material abundance he contemplates would seem to presuppose the continued exploitation and enslavement of other species. Every attempt, he says, will be made to 'use' animals 'rationally and humanistically' in the best anthropocentric way. Animals with distinct and complex patterns of behaviour are neutralised into 'livestock'. Again, Bookchin's eco-farms are synthetic environments; he waxes lyrically about the 'augermatic feeding of livestock . . . in feed pens', without recognizing that such pens are very similar to prisons and deny the claim of every being to free movement.[54] It comes as no surprise to learn that Bookchin should find a place for hunting as well as 'stock-raising' and 'aquaculture' in his 'ecotopia'. Bookchin laments our alienation from nature, by which we lose part of ourselves as feeling beings, but he would still appear to be a victim of the process.

Bookchin rightly points out that the very concept of rights is becoming suspect as the expression of a patronizing elite. But while he might be sound about eradicating human privileges, he has nothing to say about animal rights. Indeed, he ridicules the reasonable contention of the ecologists Devall and Sessions that 'we have no right to destroy other living beings without sufficient reason'. Bookchin would like to see an end to domination of man by man and nature by man, but is ready to accept the continued domination of animals by man. Unaware of the complex family life of pigs and the danger of imposing human values on animal behaviour, he can still write belligerently: 'The very troughs that turned men into swine, however, contain the nutrients for armoring men against swinishness.'[55]

Again, Bookchin's interventionist ethics in nature would seem to go too far. He rails against the 'biocentric' ethics of the 'deep ecologists' who argue that all creatures have intrinsic worth by calling them anti-humanist. Bookchin is certainly a humanist, and on occasion an arrogant one. He calls for active human stewardship of the rest of the creation and is still sufficiently Marxist to insist that 'Our re-entry into natural evolution is no less a humanization of nature than a naturalization of humanity.'[56] The intervention in nature he recommends would involve 'consciously abetting the thrust of natural evolution toward a more diversified, varied, and fecund biosphere'.[57] Indeed, his humanist arrogance leads him to think that it is possible to create a '*free* nature', a synthesis of first and second nature in which an emancipated humanity will become 'the voice, indeed the expression, of a natural evolution rendered self-conscious, caring, sympathetic to the pain, suffering, and incoherent aspects of an evolution left to its own, often wayward, unfolding'.[58] Like Marx and other humanists before him, Bookchin insists that humanity must be an *active* agent in the world, ordering nature into a more coherent form.

In Bookchin's teleological world, it is not clear who decides what exactly the 'thrust' of evolution is and how it is to be encouraged. Is it up to the ecological 'experts' to decide or will it be decided by popular vote? In the end, Bookchin's humanism is still somewhat anthropocentric and anthropo-morphic, words he does not like but which he cannot avoid. He sees the rest of nature as serving man's ends and imposes human ideas of freedom, will, choice, consciousness and subjectivity on natural processes. Ultimately, Bookchin's view of nature, like any metaphysical presupposition, cannot be confirmed or denied. Moreover his 'ecological image' of nature is simply that – an image which works as a metaphor.

In his approach to technology, Bookchin argues that new technics can be used in an ecological manner to promote balance in nature, the full development of natural regions, and the creation of organic communities. Technology in his view is also a precondition of a free society by potentially eliminating toil, material insecurity and centralized economic control. In long passages, he describes laboriously the hardware of technology with all the enthusiasm of a technician. 'The modern tractor', we are told, 'is a work of superb mechanical ingenuity' but he makes no mention of the fact that the introduction of tractors in the Third World has in many places completely destroyed self-sustaining agriculture and its ecosystems.[59] He foresees a time when an organized economy could automatically manufac-ture small 'packaged' factories without human labour. He even recommends the use of 'controlled thermonuclear reactions'.[60]

The long-term aim of a future revolution should be according to Bookchin 'to produce a surfeit of goods with a minimum of toil'.[61] While he nods in favour of crafts (supported of course by technology), he overlooks Tolstoy's awareness of the dignity and satisfaction of physical labour. He fails to realize that some technology is intrinsically life-denying. He betrays at times the very instrumental mentality in his discussions of technology which he allegedly rejects. Not surprisingly, he denies Jacques Ellul's argument that modern technology not only affects the ways we think and feel but is inevitably debasing.[62]

It would seem most likely that the material abundance Bookchin recommends would lead to hedonism. But while he celebrates pleasure rather than happiness, there is still a puritanical streak in his ethics. He argues for instance that an anarchist society must be simple: 'clothing, diet, furnishing and homes would become more artistic, more personalized and more Spartan.'[63] Again, there are echoes of moral rearmament when Book-chin praises the ethical 'character building' which direct democracy would bring about.[64] His ecological society appears as a highly sensible utopia in which there is little room for extravagance, ostentation, or creative awkwardness.

Bookchin maintained that we are on the 'threshold' of a post-scarcity society. He also argues that the United States is at the centre of the social revolution that can overthrow 'hierarchical society as a world-historical system' because of its technological potential.[65] Yet even in the United States, the material well-being of the privileged is achieved as a result of the impoverishment of the rest of the world, for it consumes forty per cent of the world's resources to support only five per cent of its population.

Abundance for all would seem a long way off. It is not enough to assert that hunger is not born of a natural shortage of food or of population growth but is merely the result of social and cultural dislocations.[66] Many parts of the Third World, especially in Africa and the Indian subcontinent, are under constant threat of malnutrition, if not actual famine. Population growth, encouraged by poor living conditions, can be a serious threat to overall well-being. There are also definite limits to certain non-renewable resources. Bookchin's optimistic arguments for abundance would seem to apply only to very advanced industrialized societies.

In his ethics, Bookchin makes the same logical error (known as the naturalistic fallacy) as Kropotkin when arguing that because nature works in a particular way, society should follow suit. There is no logical connection to make us move from fact to value, from what is to what ought to be. Bookchin rejects this criticism by arguing in a Hegelian way that the ethical 'ought' is the 'actualization of the potential "is" ', in the same way that an oak tree 'objectively inheres in an acorn'. His form of objective ethics is therefore rooted in 'the objectivity of the potential'.[67] But values are not like trees. While there are pristine values like free activity, growth and life in nature, it depends on us how we value them. One of the alleged 'laws' of ecology is that there is no 'free lunch' in nature, yet we might well choose to have 'free lunches' in society. If the ways of nature are considered inhumane, there is no reason why we should follow them.

Bookchin himself recognizes that our relationships with nature are always mediated by our technology and knowledge. There is no one given 'true' interpretation of nature and the ecological description of how nature works may be a temporary model to be superseded by another more accurate one, in the same way that Newton's mechanical model has been superseded by Einstein's relative one. Human beings not only decide what is valuable, but so-called 'laws of nature' are merely observed regularities in nature.

For all his emphasis on biological and social evolution, in his description of an ecological society, Bookchin often uses words like harmony, equilibrium, and stability. The same words are used by functionalist sociologists and systems theorists as well as ecologists. Yet the historical anarchist movement has always been opposed to stasis; indeed its principal criticism of government is that it tries to check social change and development. Most anarchists are opposed to authority and authoritarian institutions precisely because they do not recognize the constant flow of nature and the flux of society.

Again, like Hegel and Marx, Bookchin talks of his ecological society as though it is the final end of history, the culmination of man's struggle for survival, the ultimate actualization of human and natural potential in which nature itself becomes 'free, rational, and ethical'. But while he criticizes the overreaching teleology of Aristotle's and Hegel's use of the dialectic which tends to subordinate 'the element of contingency, spontaneity, and creativity', he would seem to be to a degree guilty of the same thing.[68]

Much of Bookchin's early work now reads as wildly optimistic. He was writing on the great swell of the counter-culture of the sixties, with its celebration of a natural diet, extended family, tribalism, sexual freedom, community and mutual aid. To drop out at the time was considered a mode of 'dropping in' to a more genuine community. The new agents of change were no longer Marx's proletariat but the *déclassé* elements he despised such as the blacks, hippies and students. What unified the essays of Bookchin's *Post-Scarcity Anarchism* was the belief that 'man's most visionary dreams of liberation have now become compelling necessities . . . hierarchical society, after many bloody millennia, has finally reached the culmination of its development'. The last essay in the book, written in New York in 1967, ended with the words: 'Our Science is Utopia. Our Reality is Eros. Our Desire is Revolution.'[69]

By the end of the sixties, the student movement had collapsed and the counter-culture began to lose its way, breaking up into isolated pockets. The 'revolutionary project' of the 1960s in America was replaced in the 1980s by the right-wing libertarianism of Reaganism. Many radical hippies and students went into big business and the legal profession, while black leaders ended up as mayors and politicians. By 1980, Bookchin was obliged to admit that the workers' movement was dead and that hardly any authentic revolutionary opposition existed in North America and Europe. Nevertheless, he continued to argue that the creation of utopia is possible and that 'In our own time, in the era of the final, generalized revolution, the general interest of society can be tangibly and *immediately* consolidated by a post-scarcity technology into material abundance for *all*.'[70] In this respect, he remained unconvinced by ecological arguments about the limits of growth, the dangers of overpopulation, the dwindling of finite resources and the threat of global warming.

Writing in 1987, Bookchin asserted that social ecology in the political sphere is radically green:

> It takes its stand with the left-wing tendencies in the German Greens and extra-parliamentary street movements of European cities, with the

American radical eco-feminist movement that is currently emerging, with the demands for a new politics based on citizens' initiatives, neighborhood assemblies, New England's tradition of town meetings, with unaligned anti-imperialist movements at home and abroad, with the struggle by people of color for complete freedom from the domination of privileged whites and from the superpowers of both sides of the Iron Curtain.[71]

The new social movements of the 1980s and 1990s, centred around environmentalism, feminism, municipalism, and pacifism, all developed the libertarian impetus of the sixties against growing centralized States. It was still Bookchin's fundamental thesis – a thesis shared with the younger Marx – that the 'harmonization of nature cannot be achieved without the harmonization of human with human'.[72] If the modern crisis is to be resolved, he insisted, the colour of radicalism must turn from red to green.[73] The black and red flag of anarchy seems to have been furled up and put away.

Bookchin with his strong sense of history and tradition has always taken a long-term view of things. Whatever the outcome of the libertarian and ecological struggles underway, he is probably right in seeing a major shift in human consciousness taking place at the end of the second millennium. We may well be living in a period of a new Enlightenment, as Bookchin suggests, which closely resembles the revolutionary Enlightenment of the eighteenth century, except that it not only challenges the authority of established institutions and values, but the principle of authority itself.[74] No-one, Bookchin included, was able to forecast the sudden collapse of the rusty Iron Curtain in 1989–90, or the popular explosion of libertarian energy which led to the overthrow of State communism in Eastern Europe and the Soviet Union.

For all the shortcomings of his Hegelian teleology, his naturalistic ethics, his faith in modern technology and his confidence in the prospect of economic abundance, Bookchin stands as an outstanding social thinker. His style may be difficult at times and his tone unduly virulent, but his thought is fresh and stimulating. His greatest contribution was undoubtedly to have renewed anarchist theory and practice by combining libertarian and utopian ideas with ecological principles in the creative synthesis of social ecology. It is unfortunate that towards the end of his life – he died in 2006 – he should have become increasingly sectarian and vituperative and finally returned to the Marxism of his youth.

PART SEVEN

The Legacy of Anarchism

A map of the world that does not include Utopia is not worth
even glancing at, for it leaves out the one country at which
Humanity is always landing. And when Humanity lands there,
it looks out, and, seeing a better country, sets sail. Progress
is the realization of Utopias.

OSCAR WILDE

Either the State for ever, crushing individual and local life,
taking over in all fields of human activity, bringing with it its
wars and its domestic struggles for power, its palace revolutions which only replace one tyrant by another, and inevitably
at the end of this development there is . . . death!

Or the destruction of States, and new life starting again
in thousands of centres on the principle of the lively initiative
of the individual and groups and that of free agreement.
The choice lies with you!

PETER KROPOTKIN

If I can't dance, it's not my revolution.

EMMA GOLDMAN

Be Realistic: Demand the Impossible!

PARIS, 1968

Ends and Means

'ANARCHISTS ARE SIMPLY UNTERRIFIED Jeffersonian Democrats', as Benjamin Tucker put it.[1] They believe that the best government is that which governs least, but better still is no kind of government at all. But what kind of society would they like to see in place of existing governments and States?

Anarchists reject authoritarian organization but not organization itself. They believe that for most of their history people have been able to organize themselves and create their own self-managed institutions in order to satisfy their needs. But they vary considerably in the kind of libertarian institutions they would like to see in the place of the State and government. It is against the nature of anarchism to offer a blueprint for a free society, for free people must decide themselves how they want to live. Nevertheless, anarchists do offer some rough outlines and glimpses of how the economy in a free society might be organized based on the principles of self-management, association, and federation.

In anarchist society, no centralized body would exist to impose its will on the people. No political authority would be recognized as legitimate and there would be no coercive apparatus to enforce laws. With the dismantling of the State, society would organize itself into a decentralized federation of autonomous districts. The fundamental unit of society varies according to the anarchist thinkers – for Godwin it is the parish; for Proudhon, the association; for Bakunin and Kropotkin, the commune – but they all propose a model of society in which decisions are made in the local assemblies of the sovereign people.

Godwin started from an individualist position and argued that all co-operation to a degree is an evil since it interferes with personal autonomy. He also maintained that the producer has a permanent right to the produce of his labour but argued that he has a duty to distribute any surplus beyond his subsistence needs to the worthiest recipients. But just as a person has a duty to help others, they also in turn have a claim to assistance. We should therefore consider the good things of the world as a trust to be used in the most beneficial way. In the long run, Godwin believed that this form of voluntary distribution would lead to communism.

Proudhon at first sight appears inconsistent in his economic views, but this is because he often used language in an idiosyncratic way and developed his thought as he adapted to changing circumstances in his life. At the time of the 1848 revolution in France, he proposed that the workers should begin to manage their own industries – an idea far more revolutionary than the prevailing rallying-call, universal suffrage. While his followers, the mutualists, tried to retain private ownership for agriculture (because of the individualism of the French peasantry), they accepted collective ownership for transport and proposed a form of industrial self-management. Proudhon himself thought that in the future, large-scale industry must be the fruit of association, that is to say, the means of production and exchange must be managed by associations of workers themselves. Making a distinction between possession and ownership, he proposed that the workers should possess their means of production, but not be their exclusive owners. They would exchange goods whose value would be measured by the amount of labour necessary to produce them. Workers would receive wages in 'work vouchers' according to the amount of work done. A People's Bank would accept such vouchers and offer free credit.

Adopting the assumptions of capitalism, Proudhon argued that competition and association are interdependent and should be allowed to find their equilibrium. Competition provides an irreplaceable stimulus since it is the 'motive force' of society, as long as it does not lead to monopoly and operates on the basis of fair exchange and in the spirit of solidarity.[2] Proudhon wanted to replace political centralization with economic centralization through his People's Bank. Affairs would be managed through 'contracts of mutuality', which he thought would combine the principles of authority and freedom. The producers' associations would finally associate in a great industrial and agricultural federation. Indeed, Proudhon envisaged a vast economic federation covering the entire world which would act as a co-ordinating body, provide information, balance supply and demand, and distribute products of agriculture and industry.

Josiah Warren came to similarly mutualist conclusions independently of Proudhon. He set up successfully a Time Store where people changed goods directly on the basis of the labour time required to produce them. He insisted on the principle that the price of any good should be the same as its cost, thereby eliminating profit. The individualist Tucker, who was much influenced by Warren, called anarchism 'consistent Manchesterism'. He considered labour to be the only just basis of the right of ownership, but defined that right as 'that control of a thing by a person which will receive either social sanction, or else unanimous individual sanction, when the laws of social expediency shall have been fully discovered'.[3] If allowed to be universal and unrestricted, he believed that competition would result in the most perfect peace and the truest co-operation.

Bakunin recognized that it would be difficult for Proudhon's self-managed associations to compete with capitalist enterprises and that the associated workers could eventually themselves become exploiters of other workers. He therefore called for all private property (except that retained for personal use) to be pooled as the collective property of workers' associations (for both agricultural and industrial production) which are freely organized and federated among themselves. He looked to trade unions – 'the natural organizations of the masses' – to become the embryo of the administration of the future, and urged workers to think more in terms of co-operatives than of strikes. Federations of unions should also act as planning agencies. Such ideas later became the intellectual basis for anarcho-syndicalism, according to which the syndicate or union was seen as the embryo of the future society.

While Bakunin felt that workers should still be paid according to the amount of work done, anarchist communists like Kropotkin and Malatesta thought that it was more just to distribute according to need. Most wealth, they argued, comes from the accumulated labour of the past and it is difficult to judge the value of labour only according to hours done. Service to the community cannot be measured. Proudhon's competition, even amongst associations, undermines solidarity, while Bakunin's wage system continues the morality of debit, credit and self-interest.

The anarchist communists were also confident that labour in a new society would produce more than enough for all. From Kropotkin to Bookchin, they have been confident that the common ownership of production and the appropriate use of technology will enable humanity to pass from the realm of scarcity to relative abundance. As Kropotkin concluded after investigating different agricultural and industrial methods: 'Well-being for all is not a dream.'[4] The geographer Elisée Reclus was also convinced that Malthus's threat of overpopulation was unfounded and that 'the earth is vast enough to support all of us on its breast; it is rich enough to enable us to live in ease.'[5]

While different anarchists propose different economic arrangements for a free society, many communists like Malatesta would accept that a form of collectivism may well exist in a transitional period. Mutualism, collectivism and communism moreover need not be incompatible; they can be different means to the same end. It would be up to each locality to decide freely what kind of system it would like to adopt and this of course will depend on their degree of economic development and social consciousness.

Although anarchists have carefully outlined their economic proposals, it is not always clear how they think society should organize itself outside the economic sphere. For Godwin the fundamental unit would be the self-governing parish or district although he suggested that a national assembly with delegates from the parishes might be called in emergencies at the national level. Proudhon thought a 'natural group' would emerge at the local level asserting 'itself in unity, independence, and autonomy'.[6] It would associate with neighbouring groups and form a higher group for mutual security. The fundamental unit would remain the autonomous association which should be entirely sovereign with the right to administer itself, to impose taxes, to dispose of its revenue and to provide education.

But what of the relationship between the workers' associations and the communes? Bakunin argued that the former would link up within the communes and the communes federate freely amongst themselves. He saw the task of the commune as being to expropriate the means of production. It should be administered by a council of elected delegates who would be always accountable to the electorate and subject to immediate recall. The elected councils should be working bodies with executive functions; they would also be able to elect from amongst themselves executive committees for each area of the administration of the commune.

Yet Proudhon and Bakunin still continued to see society as a pyramid, even though they spoke of organizing it from the bottom up. As Kropotkin observed of the Paris Commune of 1871, to retain a system of representation is to continue the evils of parliamentarianism and to crush popular initiative. He therefore looked to a form of direct democracy in which all the members of the commune would meet in a general assembly. Only this would be worthy of the name of self-government, of government of oneself by oneself. Unlike the medieval commune, which remained in many respects an isolated State, the commune of the future would not be a territorial agglomeration but rather a 'generic name, a synonym for a grouping of equals, not knowing frontiers, nor walls'.[7] The natural sentiment of sociability would then be able to develop itself freely.

The social form proposed by anarchists is therefore of a simplified and decentralized society in which people manage and govern themselves. It would involve overlapping economic and administrative organizations: a federation of self-managing workers' associations within the communes which would federate amongst themselves. The communes could form federations at the regional and national level, with mandated delegates, to resolve disputes, deal with foreign threats, and co-ordinate economic life. Proudhon called for a binding contract between the various communes of a federation in a large territory to ensure unity, but Bakunin insisted that real unity can only derive 'from the freest development of all individuals and groups, and from a federal and absolutely voluntary alliance . . . of the workers' associations in the communes and, beyond the communes, in the regions, beyond the regions, the nations'.[8] The communes would remain absolutely autonomous.

Since Bakunin most anarchists have envisaged the whole social organization as a network of local groups which associate freely: the commune or council as a territorial nucleus, and the syndicate or workers' council as the economic organization. These would federate together not so much like a pyramid but like a net, with the knots forming the communes. They would be based on the principles of autonomy, self-management, decentralization and federalism. In this way, a living unity could emerge which respected and encouraged local and regional differences. Freed from the strait-jacket of the State, society would be able to develop more spontaneously and individuals become more fully themselves. Anarchists are confident that the natural solidarity of interests and the advantages of a free and communal life will be enough to maintain social order, and with the principal causes of strife – imposed authority and unequal property – eradicated, social harmony will prevail.

Means

The anarchists do not agree on the means to achieve their common goal of a stateless society, although most believe that it is wrong to separate the means from the end. Anarchists have often be accused of relying in a voluntaristic way on 'the instincts of the masses' to mount a social revolution which would somehow turn violence into its opposite.[9] Anarchism moreover is often linked in the popular imagination with terrorism. Despite the evidence to the contrary, the anarchist continues to be seen more as a savage terrorist than as a gentle dreamer or quiet philosopher. The image of the anarchist as a bomb-throwing desperado in a black cloak has stuck. It is an image immortalized in literature, by Henry James in *The Princess Casamassima* (1886) and by Joseph Conrad in *The Secret Agent* (1907). It was an image forged in the desperate 1880s and 1890s when there were a series of political assassinations and bombings in Europe linked to the anarchist movement.

In fact, anarchists have contributed far less to the sum of human violence than nationalists, monarchists, republicans, socialists, fascists and conservatives, not to mention the Mafia, organized crime, and banditry. They have never organized the indiscriminate slaughter that is war or practised genocide as governments have. They have never coolly contemplated the complete nuclear annihilation of the earth as nuclear scientists, generals and presidents have. They have never adopted a deliberate policy of terror in power as Robespierre, Stalin, or Pol Pot did. While most anarchists would accept some violent action which might involve damage to a person or property as part of an insurrection, very few indeed have advocated terror in the form of premeditated acts of violence. At its most violent their action has typically not gone much beyond throwing up barricades or entering a village armed with rudimentary weapons. And yet the terrorist reputation sticks, and the very word 'anarchist' continues to evoke a shiver of anxiety among the respectable and well-off. Of the leftist political groups, the police still believe that 'the anarchists are usually the most violent of all'.[10]

It is easy to see why those who control the State should fear the anarchists for they have most to lose from their success. The myth that anarchists are the most violent of all no doubt stems from the fact that they question the need for the State with its coercive apparatus. They not only believe that rulers, standing armies and professional police forces are harmful, but argue that they would no longer be necessary in a free society. Few people feel sympathy towards those who would like to see them abolished.

But even a superficial acquaintance with the classic anarchist texts demonstrates that anarchists are remarkable not for their violence but for the varied tactics they recommend to realize the goal of a free society.

There is little justification for violent action amongst the early thinkers. Godwin wrote as a philosopher concerned with universal principles rather than their practical application. He sought to bring about gradual change through reasoned discussion, not physical action; his was a revolution in opinion, not on the barricades. Since government is founded on opinion, all that is necessary is to change people's opinions through education and enlightenment. But while Godwin opposed violent revolution, and called for gradual change, he was not an absolute pacifist for he believed that reason was not yet sufficiently developed to persuade an assailant to drop his sword.

Proudhon used the motto *Destruam ut Aedificabo* ('I destroy in order to build up') in his *System of Economic Contradictions* (1846) but that was to emphasize the need to create new libertarian institutions to replace existing ones. He not only sought to bring about reform through instruction (hence his journalism and books) but also through co-operative experiments like the People's Bank and worker associations. During his life, he employed a whole range of different tactics. At first he employed reasoned argument alone. Then he tried the parliamentary road by entering parliament as a deputy during the 1848 revolution. After the failure of the revolution, he even appealed to Louis Napoleon to become the 'general' of the social revolution. In the end, he advocated abstention from parliamentary politics and urged the working class to emancipate itself through the labour movement by building its own economic institutions.

With Bakunin however the emphasis was more on destruction than innovation. Bakunin more than any other anarchist thinker is responsible for the violent and menacing shadow of anarchism. Intoxicated with the 'poetry of destruction', he not only sided with Satan ('the eternal rebel, the first freethinker and the emancipator of worlds') in his rebellion against God, but declared that the 'The passion for destruction is a creative passion, too!'[11] To further the cause of freedom, he was willing to resort to secret societies, manipulation and deceit and called for an invisible dictatorship once the revolutionary storm broke out. Under his influence the Jurassian Federation in Switzerland adopted the principle of class dictatorship in 1874, although they specified: 'The dictatorship that we want is one which the insurgent masses exercise directly, without intermediary of any committee or government.'[12] Although Bakunin was against systematic terror and suggested that 'there will be no need to destroy men' he welcomed civil war as a prelude to social revolution.[13] He undoubtedly contributed to the sinister side of anarchism which has attracted disturbed and criminal elements, individuals who delight more in illegality and conspiracy than in building and creating.

Bakunin further enhanced his reputation as a destructive revolutionary by his association in the 1870s with the young Russian student Sergei Nechaev who partly inspired the character of Stavrogin in Dostoevsky's *The Possessed* (1871–2). Nechaev was not only involved in the political murder of a student but wrote a series of pamphlets arguing that the revolution justifies any means, however destructive. In his *Catechism of a Revolutionary*, he declared of the revolutionary: 'Day and night he must have one thought, one aim – merciless destruction.' In his *Principles of Revolution*, he went even further:

> We recognise no other activity but the work of extermination, we admit that the form in which this activity will show itself will be extremely varied – the poison, the knife, the rope, etc. In this struggle, revolution sanctifies everything alike.[14]

But while Nechaev was no anarchist, and it is now known that Bakunin was not the author of the pamphlet, the stance came to be seen as characteristically anarchist. Marx and Engels tried to associate Bakunin with Nechaev's amoral position, and describe his anarchism as synonymous with terrorism: 'There [in Russia] anarchy means universal, pan destruction; the revolution, a series of assassinations, first individual and then *en masse*; the sole rule of action, the Jesuit morality intensified; the revolutionary type, the brigand.'[15] The victim could plead innocence but the accusation stuck.

After the bloody suppression of the Paris Commune of 1871, and the repressive measures of governments throughout Europe against radicals, it is true that some anarchists grew impatient with gradual reform through education and participation in the labour movement and began to adopt a strategy of 'propaganda by the deed' to speed up the advent of the revolution. The doctrine had been advocated earlier by the Italian Republican Carlo Pisacane, a follower of Garibaldi and Proudhon. In his political testament, he wrote:

> The propaganda of the idea is a chimera. Ideas result from deeds, not the latter from the former, and the people will not be free when they are educated, but educated when they are free. The only work a citizen can do for the good of the country is that of co-operating with the material revolution.[16]

Another Italian, Carlo Cafiero, who had once been Marx's and Engels' trusted agent, came under the spell of Bakunin and developed the doctrine in a more destructive direction. After the failure of the Bologna rising in 1874, Cafiero and Errico Malatesta decided to resort to symbolic actions like taking over a village to encourage the Italian peasantry to revolt. They also led the move in the international anarchist movement towards more violent forms of action. After attending, in October 1876, the Bern Congress of the International, they urged that 'the *insurrectionary deed* designed to affirm socialist principles by actions, is the most effective means of propaganda'.[17] In *Le Révolté* in Switzerland in 1880, Cafiero went even further by arguing like Nechaev that the revolutionary end justifies any means:

> Our action must be permanent rebellion, by word, by writing, by dagger, by gun, by dynamite, sometimes even by ballot ... We are consistent, and we shall use every weapon which can be used for rebellion. Everything is right for us which is not legal.[18]

During the desperate social unrest of the 1880s many anarchists felt that the only way to speed up the collapse of the capitalist State and bring about the revolution was to go on the attack. They felt justified in opposing the 'State terrorism' of the masses with acts of individual terrorism against the agents of the State or the owners and managers of industry, arguing that the force which maintained the existing order had to be overthrown by force. Others decided that they wanted to defend the workers against the State, to demoralize the ruling class, and to create a revolutionary consciousness amongst the workers. They did not expect the acts themselves to overthrow capitalism or the State: assassinating a despot would not get rid of despotism. But as Alexander Berkman observed 'terrorism was considered a means of avenging a popular wrong, inspiring fear in the enemy, and also calling attention to the evil against which the act of terror was directed.'[19]

The anarchist practice of 'propaganda by the deed' reached its apogee in the 1880s and 1890s when kings, presidents and ministers were attacked throughout Europe. The perpetrators were often motivated by a sense of retribution.

These acts of terrorism not only sparked off repressive measures against anarchists in general but gave the anarchist cause a reputation for violence which it has never been able to live down. It has consequently done enormous harm to the movement. It even became the fashion for criminals to claim a link with anarchism after being caught for a sensational crime.

In the midst of the terrorist outrages and growing class war at the end of the nineteenth century, Kropotkin appeared to many of his contemporaries to rise above the anarchist movement as a kind of gentle saint. Oscar Wilde pronounced Kropotkin's life one of the two most perfect lives he had come across: 'a man with a soul of that beautiful white Christ which seems coming out of Russia'.[20] But Kropotkin's attitude to revolutionary violence was ambivalent at best, and there is an uncomfortable mixture of quietist and aggressive elements in his thinking which is typical of many an anarchist. He certainly rejected Bakunin's tendency to resort to deceit and manipulation, and went beyond Godwin's reliance on an intellectual elite; he stressed the need to propagandize amongst the people. He had a great confidence in the capacity of even illiterate peasants and workers for clear thinking. In his early days, he offered a limited defence of terror and felt that illegal protest and violent struggle are acceptable if the people involved have a clear idea of what they are doing and aiming at.[21] Indeed, like Sorel, he even suggested that violent revolution can have a beneficial effect on the oppressed: 'revolutionary whirlwind ... revive[s] sluggish hearts'.[22]

Towards the end of his life, Kropotkin was repelled by the spate of terrorist acts and the disastrous effect they were having on the anarchist movement. And yet he still tried to explain them as the inevitable outcome of repressive social conditions. 'Personally', he wrote to a friend, 'I hate these explosions, but I cannot stand as a judge to condemn those who are driven to despair.'[23] In a speech commemorating the Paris Commune in London, Kropotkin further rejected the slur that anarchism was *the* party of violence, arguing that all parties resort to violence when they lose confidence in other means. On the contrary, he maintained:

> Of all parties I now see only one party – the Anarchist – which respects human life, and loudly insists upon the abolition of capital punishment, prison torture and punishment of man by man altogether. All other parties teach every day their utter disrespect of human life.[24]

Eventually, by the 1890s, he came to disapprove of acts of violence except those undertaken in self-defence during the revolution. He now argued that conditions favoured peaceful evolution rather than violent revolution.

As his friend Elisée Reclus wrote: 'Evolution and revolution are two success-ive acts of the same phenomenon, evolution preceding revolution, and the latter preceding a new evolution born of a future revolution.'[25] Kropotkin therefore increasingly sought to encourage existing libertarian and voluntary tendencies in society.

Of all the great anarchist thinkers, Tolstoy was of course the most uncompromising in his pacifist rejection of violence. His position was based on a strict interpretation of the Christian commandment: 'Thou shalt not kill'; he even interpreted the principle to mean that you should not kill a criminal who seems about to murder a child. It is precisely because govern-ment is ultimately based on violence – the soldier's gun – that Tolstoy wanted to see it abolished; it is nothing less than 'an organization for the commission of violence and for its justification'.[26] The means he adopted was to refuse to co-operate with the violence of government through civil disobedience and non-resistance.

Gandhi, who called himself a kind of anarchist and looked to an ideal of 'enlightened anarchy', developed Tolstoy's method of non-violent action into an effective means of mass struggle, and managed to break the British hold on India. His declared that 'The ideally non-violent state will be an ordered anarchy.'[27] By being prepared to break the law and to be punished accordingly, Gandhi's followers wielded enormous moral power which proved greater than the force of the bayonet. Such a course of action of course relies on widespread public sympathy and at least a minimal moral sensibility on the part of the oppressing authorities. The Sarvodaya move-ment has continued his strategy of non-violent direct action.

Although she collaborated as a young woman with Alexander Berkman in his attempt on an industrialist's life, Emma Goldman became an anarchist precisely because she felt human beings are capable of leading peaceful, ordered, and productive lives when unrestricted by the violence of man-made law. Indeed, she defined anarchism as 'the theory that all forms of government rest on violence, and are therefore wrong and harmful, as well as unnecessary'.[28] Towards the end of her life, she increasingly felt that the Tolstoyans who renounced all violence were right.

Although by the turn of the century, propaganda by the deed in the form of isolated acts of terror was largely abandoned in favour of education and industrial action, it had done great harm to the anarchist movement. It not only meant that governments introduced severe measures against anarchists, but the fear of anarchism continued long after, as the trial of Sacco and Vanzetti in the 1920s in America demonstrated.

While the terrorist strand within the anarchist tradition has been sig-nificant, it has always been a minority trend. The advocates of terrorism are more than balanced by a pacifist wing. Godwin was not the only anarchist to recognize that war is 'the inseparable ally of political institutions'.[29] Claiming to be the supreme authority within a territory, the State is ready to use its monopoly of force in the form of its police and armed services against its dissenting citizens as well as foreign peoples. Since a State compels its people to fight the people of another State, the war of one State against another State invariably becomes a war of the State and its military apparatus against its own people. It was on these grounds that Tolstoy opposed the State and government. To deliver men from the terrible evils of armaments and wars, Tolstoy called for 'the destruction of those instruments of violence which are called Governments, and from which humanity's greatest evils flow'.[30]

The carnage of the First World War led Randolph Bourne to conclude that 'War is the health of the State.' The experience of war has disastrous psychological consequences:

> The State is the organization of the herd to act offensively or defensively against another herd similarly organised. War sends the current of purpose and activity flowing down to the lowest level of the herd, and to its most remote branches . . . The slack is taken up, the crosscurrents fade out, and the nation moves lumberingly and slowly, but with ever accelerated speed and integration, towards the great end, towards that *peacefulness of being at war*.[31]

Bourne further noted how in wartime the State achieves a uniformity of feeling and hierarchy of values which it finds difficult to realize in peacetime. The herd instinct drives people into conformity and obedience to the State and encourages a kind of filial mysticism.

Other pacifist anarchists began to stress that violence is the most authoritarian and coercive way of influencing others, and authoritarian means cannot be used to achieve libertarian ends. The use of violence encourages authoritarian and hierarchical organization, as standing armies show only too vividly. A violent person moreover is unlikely to develop a libertarian character. As the Dutch anarchist Bart de Ligt wrote:

> the violence and warfare which are characteristic conditions of the imperialist world do not go with the liberation of the individual and society, which is the historic mission of the exploited classes. The greater the violence, the weaker the revolution, even where violence has deliberately been put at the service of the revolution.[32]

Violence always produces the results of violence. The result in the victim is either resentful hostility, leading ultimately to counter-violence, or abject subjection. In the perpetrator, it encourages a habit of brutality and a readiness to resort to further violence. A violent revolution is therefore unlikely to bring about any fundamental change in human relations.

There has therefore been a highly ambivalent attitude to violence and revolution in the anarchist tradition. All anarchists have recognized the State as perpetrating 'organized violence', and most have taken part in anti-militarist agitation and opposed wars between States. But there has been a terrorist wing of anarchism, as well as a pacifist wing, and the defenders of minimum use of violence have probably predominated.[33] Bakunin and Kropotkin both accepted the violence of a popular uprising, believing that it differed from the violence of the State since it benefited the poor and powerless and would lead to a free society. In addition, they would have been unable to carry out the widespread expropriation they advocated without recourse to some violence against property and persons. They defended their position by a kind of 'just war' theory which accepts the discriminate use of violence as a regrettable necessity for a just end.

When the opportunity to put his theory into action occurred during the Spanish Civil War, the anarchist Buenaventura Durruti did not shrink from executing landowners. Like Proudhon and Bakunin, he felt it was necessary to destroy the old world in order to create anew:

> We are not in the least afraid of ruins. We are going to inherit the earth. There is not the slightest doubt about that. The bourgeoisie may blast and ruin their own world before they leave the stage of history. But we carry a new world in our hearts.[34]

All anarchists look forward to a peaceful and non-violent society, even those who see it as necessary to use violence to end the violence of the State with its coercive apparatus of police, army and prisons. They are not naive. They see like Hobbes that the force of the State rests on the sword and observe that in time of war and social conflict the State comes into its own and reveals its violent nature. They see the State claiming a monopoly of violence in society, with its wars as mass murder, its soldiers as assassins, its conscription as slavery, and its taxation as physical aggression. They are repelled by the inhumanity of the State's mass executions and deportations and the cruel absurdity of war which it unleashes upon the world.

Anarchists also recognize that violence is not only physical force but constitutes the foundation of institutionalized forms of domination. As Alexander Berkman pointed out the lawful world is itself violent: 'our entire life is built on violence or fear of it. From earliest childhood you are subjected to the violence of parents or elders. At home, in school, in the office, factory, field, or shops, it is always someone's *authority* which keeps you obedient and compels you to do his will.'[35] People are so invaded and violated that they subconsciously revenge themselves by invading and violating others over whom they have authority. Indeed, the word violence comes from the

Latin *violare* and etymologically means violation. Strictly speaking, to act violently means to treat others without respect. All forms of domination are inherently disrespectful and violent – economical exploitation, political authoritarianism, as well as sexual and racial discrimination.

Given the anarchists' respect for the sovereignty of the individual, in the long run it is non-violence and not violence which is implied by anarchist values. As April Carter has written: 'The utopianism of anarchism logically entails also the utopianism of pacifism, in the sense of rejecting all forms of organized violence.'[36] Unfortunately, the association of anarchism with violence, both in a brief period of its history, and in the popular imagination, has left a dilemma for its adherents. On the one hand, its reputation for illegality has undoubtedly attracted certain individuals who are interested in mindless violence for its own sake. On the other, its philosophical rigour and idealism appeal to those who are most repelled by indiscriminate acts of violence.

The nineteenth-century anarchists were part of the tradition of revolutionary violence forged by the success of the American and French Revolutions. In this they were at one with the Jacobins, the followers of Mazzini and Garibaldi, the Russian populists and the Marxists who saw non-violence as either ineffectual or as objectively supporting the existing order. Engels spoke on behalf of most socialist revolutionaries when he wrote:

> a revolution is certainly the most authoritarian thing there is; it is the act whereby one part of the population imposes its will upon the other part by means of rifles, bayonets and cannon – authoritarian means, if such there be at all; and if the victorious party does not want to have fought in vain, it must maintain this rule by means of the terror which its arms inspire in the reactionaries.[37]

The Russian and Spanish Revolutions saw the last great outbursts of anarchist violence on a large scale. Since the Second World War, the modern anarchist movement, inspired by Tolstoy, Gandhi and de Ligt, has tended to be non-violent and constructive. Most anarchists recognize that not only do the means influence the ends, but means are ends-in-the-making. In a nuclear era of total war, anarchists have tried to undermine the State by refusing to obey or co-operate with its immoral demands. They seek to create free zones and libertarian institutions rather than to overthrow the State in a cataclysmic revolution. To raise consciousness and challenge authorities, they have adopted a whole range of tactics from passive to active non-violent resistance, including demonstrations, boycotts, strikes, sit-ins, occupations, and refusing to pay taxes.[38] They hope to change the public opinion on which the legitimacy of the State rests so that people will come to realize that it is not only harmful but also unnecessary. They see like

Godwin that government is founded on opinion as well as the sword: if enough people stop believing that it is right for the State to use violence, the moral authority of the State will disintegrate, and the sword will become useless.

While their long-term goal is to replace the State by a federation of self-managing communes, contemporary anarchists are not content to dream of a mythic future. They try and change their lives here and now. As such, the strategy of most anarchists of 'dropping out' to create an alternative lifestyle is closer to Stirner's view of insurrection rather than Bakunin's view of revolution:

> The Revolution aimed at new *arrangements*; insurrection leads us no longer to *let* ourselves be arranged, but to arrange ourselves, and sets no glittering hopes on 'institutions'. It is not a fight against the established, since, if it prospers, the established collapses of itself; it is only the working forth of men out of the established.[39]

This does not mean that some anarchists are not prepared to take to the streets and even raise barricades, as in May 1968 in France. Anarchists also joined in the riot against the Poll Tax in London in March 1990. But the vast majority of modern anarchists prefer, like the Provos in Holland, to provoke rather than to destroy; they choose to work in the Green, peace and women's movements, not underground. After their somewhat apocalyptic past, they have come to realize the ultimate folly of trying to realize peaceful ends through violent means. Violence is undoubtedly the method of the ignorant and the weak, and the more enlightened people become, the less they will resort to compulsion and coercion.

The Relevance of Anarchism

THE RIVER OF ANARCHY which has flowed continuously since ancient times – sometimes fitfully, sometimes at flood level – has carried a wide variety of theories and movements to the far corners of the earth. As a political philosophy, anarchism not only questions many of the fundamental ideas and values by which most people have lived their lives, but also offers a trenchant, empirical critique of existing practices. It seeks to create a society without government or State, a non-coercive, non-hierarchical world in which fully realized individuals associate freely with one another.

As a movement, anarchism has only partially realized its aims on a large scale for brief periods at times of social upheaval, but it has gone a long way in creating alternative institutions and transforming the everyday life of many individuals. It has a whole range of strategies to expand human freedom right here and now. As a result, it has an immediate and considerable relevance to contemporary problems as well as to future well-being. It provides a third and largely untried path to personal and social freedom beyond the domain of the tired social models of State-orchestrated capitalism or socialism.

The Nature of Anarchism

Although anarchism offers an interpretation of both history and society, it cannot be called a 'political' theory in the accepted sense since it does not concern itself with the State. It calls for non-participation in politics as conventionally understood, that is the struggle for political power. It places the moral and economic before the political, stressing that the 'political' is the 'personal'. If anything, it wishes to go beyond politics in the traditional sense of the art or science of government.

Political theorists usually classify anarchism as an ideology of the extreme Left. In fact, it combines ideas and values from both liberalism and socialism and may be considered a creative synthesis of the two great currents of thought. With liberalism, it is wary of the State and shares a concern for the liberty of the individual. Like liberals, anarchists stress the liberty of choice, the liberty to do what one likes. They advocate the freedom of enquiry, of thought, of expression, and of association. They call for tolerance and forbearance in relations with others and are opposed to force and dogma. They assume that if people are left to pursue their natural desires and interests, the general well-being will result.

At the same time, anarchism like liberalism is suspicious of centralized bureaucracy and concentrated political authority. It recognizes that power corrupts and absolute power corrupts absolutely. It is fearful of the triumph of mediocrity and the tyranny of the majority. It calls for social pluralism and cultural diversity. It echoes Alexis de Tocqueville's ideal of liberty and community and J. S. Mill's celebration of individuality. In many of these values, anarchism links up with the libertarian Right.

Unlike liberalism, however, anarchism extends the principle of freedom to the political as well as the economic sphere, confident that a natural harmony of interests will prevail if people are left to themselves. It is opposed to the State, believing that freedom cannot be achieved *through* the State, but only *from* the State.[1] It rejects the need for a constitution or social contract to set up government. It goes beyond the liberal justification of law to establish rights, to protect freedom and to solve disputes. Where liberals rely on the rule of law established through parliament and political parties, the anarchists argue that such institutions are not the bulwark but the grave of genuine freedom. They see no need for the government to defend society against external threat or internal dissension. They do not want to limit the powers of the State, but to dissolve them altogether. Where the principle attributed to Jefferson 'That government is best which governs least' is liberal, the anarchists join Thoreau in saying 'That government is best which governs not at all.'

At the same time, mainstream anarchism contains many elements of socialism. As Malatesta wrote liberalism is 'a kind of anarchy without socialism' whereas true anarchy is based on a socialist concern with the equality of conditions.[2] Since the 1840s anarchism has usually been seen as part of a wider socialist movement. It embraces the socialist critique of capital, property and hierarchy, and stresses the need for solidarity and mutual aid. It is closer to Marxism than democratic socialism in so far as it recognizes that sudden change may be necessary and that the State should ultimately wither away. Both look forward to a free and equal society. Anarchism differs from Marxism however in its scrupulousness about the means required to reach such a society – it rejects political parties and the parliamentary road to socialism as well as the establishment of any form of workers' State. It stresses that means cannot be separated from ends, and that it is impossible to use an authoritarian strategy to achieve a libertarian goal.

Depending on whether they are individualists stressing the liberty of the individual, or collectivists emphasizing social solidarity, anarchists align themselves with liberalism or socialism. In general, anarchism is closer to socialism than liberalism. Kropotkin called anarchy 'the No-Government system of Socialism', Johann Most declared that anarchism is 'socialism perfected', and Rudolf Rocker regarded it as 'a kind of voluntary socialism'.[3] More recently, Daniel Guérin has argued that anarchism is only one of the streams of socialist thought and is really a synonym for socialism.[4] But while this approach might help to rehabilitate anarchism amongst other socialists, it would inevitably exclude individualist anarchists like Max Stirner and Benjamin Tucker and modern anarcho-capitalists like Murray Rothbard. Anarchism finds itself largely in the socialist camp, but it also has outriders in liberalism. It cannot be reduced to socialism, and is best seen as a separate and distinctive doctrine.

The word 'libertarian' has long been associated with anarchism, and has been used repeatedly throughout this work. The term originally denoted a person who upheld the doctrine of the freedom of the will; in this sense, Godwin was not a 'libertarian' but a 'necessitarian'. It came however to be applied to anyone who approved of liberty in general. In anarchist circles, it was first used by Joseph Déjacque as the title of his anarchist journal *Le Libertaire, Journal du Mouvement Social* published in New York in 1858. At the end of the last century, the anarchist Sébastien Faure took up the word, to stress the difference between anarchists and authoritarian socialists.[5]

For a long time, libertarian was interchangeable in France with anarchist but in recent years, its meaning has become more ambivalent. Some anarchists like Daniel Guérin will call themselves 'libertarian socialists', partly to avoid the negative overtones still associated with anarchism, and partly to stress the place of anarchism within the socialist tradition. Even Marxists of the New Left like E. P. Thompson call themselves 'libertarian' to distinguish themselves from those authoritarian socialists and communists who believe in revolutionary dictatorship and vanguard parties. Left libertarianism can therefore range from the decentralist who wishes to limit and devolve State power, to the syndicalist who wants to abolish it altogether. It can even encompass the Fabians and the social democrats who wish to socialize the economy but who still see a limited role for the State.

The problem with the term 'libertarian' is that it is now also used by the Right. Extreme liberals inspired by J. S. Mill who are concerned with civil liberties like to call themselves libertarians. They tend to be individualists who trust in a society formed on the basis of voluntary agencies. They reject a strong centralized State and believe that social order, in the sense of the security of persons and property, can best be achieved through private firms competing freely in the market-place. In its moderate form, right libertarianism embraces *laissez-faire* liberals like Robert Nozick who call for a minimal State, and in its extreme form, anarcho-capitalists like Murray Rothbard and David Friedman who entirely repudiate the role of the State and look to the market as a means of ensuring social order.

While undoubtedly related to liberalism and socialism, true anarchism goes beyond both political tendencies. It maintains that liberty without equality means the liberty of the rich and powerful to exploit (as in capitalist States), and equality without liberty means that all are slaves together (as in communist States). Anarchism leaves Left and Right libertarianism behind since it finds no role for the State and government, however minimal. Its roots may entwine and its concerns overlap, but ultimately anarchism forms a separate ideology and doctrine, with its own recognizable tradition.

Human Nature

The most common criticism of anarchism is that it is based on a simplistic view of human nature. Certainly anarchists all insist that humanity has a largely untried libertarian potential. Human beings, they believe, are capable of living without imposed authority and coercion. A system of punishments and rewards is not essential to shape their behaviour and rulers and leaders are unnecessary to organize society. Human beings, anarchists point out, have regulated themselves for most of history and are capable of leading productive and peaceful lives together. While a few individualist anarchists appeal to self-interest to bring about the natural order of anarchy, most anarchists emphasize the potential for solidarity and believe that in a non-coercive society the values of mutual aid, co-operation, and community would flourish.

The main weakness of the argument that anarchism is somehow against 'human nature' is the fact that anarchists do not share a common view of human nature. Amongst the classic thinkers, we find Godwin's rational benevolence, Stirner's conscious egoism, Bakunin's destructive energy, and Kropotkin's calm altruism. Some like Godwin and Stirner stress the importance of enlightenment and education, others like Bakunin and Kropotkin have great faith in the creative energies of the masses. Emma Goldman had little time for existing majorities, but still thought that all human beings are ultimately capable of becoming free and governing themselves.

The majority of anarchists believe that human beings are products of their environment, but also capable of changing it. Some of the more existentially minded among them insist that 'human nature' does not exist as a fixed essence. We may be born into a particular situation, but we are largely what we make of ourselves.[6] The aim is not therefore to liberate some 'essential self' by throwing off the burden of government and the

State, but to develop the self in creative and voluntary relations with others.

Another traditional criticism of anarchism is that it assumes the natural goodness of man. It is true that from Godwin onwards the classic anarchist thinkers have depicted human beings as corrupted and deformed by the burden of the State, and they have argued that people will not be able to realize their full potential until it is abolished. But it is not simply a question of pitching some mythical 'natural man' in a state of innocence against corrupt 'political man'. Few anarchists believe in natural goodness. Godwin argued that human beings are born neither good nor bad, but made so by their circumstances. Bakunin felt that man is born a 'ferocious beast' but his reason enables him to develop into a social being. Stirner felt that we are irredeemably egoistical; all we can do is to become conscious of the fact. Kropotkin came closest to a notion of 'natural goodness', but felt not that it is intrinsic as Rousseau had argued, but rather that it has evolved in the form of a moral sense in the co-operative behaviour of human beings in their struggle for survival.

It was George Bernard Shaw's view that we are simply not good enough for anarchism. In his Fabian tract *The Impossibilities of Anarchism* (1893), he rejected Kropotkin's claim that man is naturally social and gregarious. It would have been impossible, Shaw argues, for the institution of property to come into existence unless nearly every man had been eager 'to quarter himself idly on the labour of his fellows, and to domineer over them whenever the law enabled him to do so'.[7] But such a Hobbesian view of man, as countless anarchists have pointed out, is profoundly unhistorical; there have been societies where people do not desire to exploit and dominate each other. Even within existing Western society, there are many people who do not do what Shaw considers 'natural'. If this is the case, then the ability to live without domination and exploitation is part of the legacy and potentiality of human beings. Since such an ability has existed and continues to exist, there is no reason to suppose that it cannot exist on a wider scale in the future.

If anything, it could be argued that the anarchists have not only a realistic, but even a pessimistic view of human nature. This is not merely because some anarchists like Emma Goldman have little faith in the masses. More importantly, it is the profound awareness of anarchists of the corruption inherent in the exercise of power that leads them to criticize political authority. The rise to prominence of Hitler and Stalin this century does not make the anarchist argument weaker but stronger. Precisely because the concentration of power in the hands of a few rulers has led to such enormous oppression, it is prudent to decentralize political authority and to spread power over as wide an area as possible. Power should be dispersed not because people are good, but because when a few wield it exclusively they tend to cause immense injury.

The State

The central issue which distinguishes anarchists from liberals and authoritarian socialists and communists is of course the role of the State in society. The anarchist critique of the Marxist-Leninist State has been only too painfully vindicated. The great Communist revolutions this century in Russia, China, Vietnam and Cuba have all underlined the danger of the 'dictatorship of the proletariat' swiftly becoming the dictatorship of a party, if not the dictatorship of a party leader. They have vividly demonstrated the implausibility of the State ever 'withering away' once political control has been centralized and its apparatus colonized by a bureaucratic elite. Wherever vanguard parties have existed, the people have been left behind. It is the Marxist-Leninists, and not the anarchists, who have been naive in thinking that, after a society had suffered the centralization of authority and the concentration of power, the resultant State could then gradually be dismantled. As George Orwell observed, the totalitarian State governs its subjects not only by naked force but by trying to define reality, even to the extent of manipulating their thoughts through the control of permissible language.

The anarchists have been equally vociferous in condemning the liberal State as an unnecessary and harmful check to social development. Far from creating social order, they see it as the principal cause of social disorder. They point out that at the root of the modern democratic State there is a fundamental paradox: its rhetoric celebrates the participation of the people in the political process and yet asks them to sign away their liberty periodically in elections and prevents them from participating directly in the decisions which most affect their lives. Rather than defending the 'national interest' or promoting the 'general good', governments still tend to further the interests of those with power, privilege and wealth. At best they perpetrate the tyranny of the majority; at worst, the tyranny of a minority.

In his spirited defence of social democracy, Shaw maintained that anarchist fears about the tyranny of the majority in a parliamentary democracy are unfounded since under such a system it usually proves too costly to suppress even a minority of one. There is moreover a 'fine impartiality about the policeman and the soldier, who are the cutting edge of State power'.[8] He was convinced that once the workers had ousted the 'gentlemen' in the House of Commons, they would use the State against the upper classes and landlords in order to buy land for the people. At the end of the nineteenth century Shaw's argument may have seemed plausible, but, unfortunately, where the workers have been able to send their representatives to parliaments those representatives have tended to join the ruling class and be corrupted by political power. The political establishment has proved far more subtle in co-opting its enemies than Shaw foresaw or imagined.

The central liberal contention that the State is necessary to fight the enemies of liberty from within and without has more weight. As L. T. Hobhouse wrote: 'The function of State coercion is to override individual coercion, and, of course, coercion exercised by any association within the State.'[9] From this point of view, every liberty rests on a corresponding act of control. Clearly a liberal State which respects basic human rights is preferable to a despotic State which does not, and the use of soldiers to prevent the lynching of innocent minorities is preferable to their use in shooting dissidents and so-called 'counter-revolutionaries'.

Bertrand Russell, who considered pure anarchism 'the ultimate ideal, to which society should continually approximate', made a similar defence of the minimal State.[10] He agreed with the anarchists that a good community springs from the unfettered development of individuals, that the positive functions of the economy should be in the hands of voluntary organizations, and that anarcho-syndicalism was more nearly right than socialism in its hostility to the State and private property. But he still felt a limited State to be necessary: to exercise ultimate control in the economic sphere; to establish a just system of distribution; to maintain peace between rival interests; and to settle disputes whether within or outside its borders.

But this liberal and social democratic defence offered by apologists for the State can be pressed too far. The coercive nature of the State, exemplified by its army, police, and prisons, is invariably greater than its protective nature. Equally, it is presumptuous to consider the State essential to the protection of the people of a country from internal disruption or external threat. A nation which consists of a network of decentralized communities would be more difficult to conquer than a centralized State, and a foreign invasion can be foiled by well-organized civil disobedience. A people-in-arms is preferable to a professional standing army, but the best form of defence is non-violent direct action which seeks to dissuade the enemy rather than to kill him. In the absence of a professional police force, communities are quite capable of maintaining public security for themselves and have done so for centuries.

Another substantive liberal argument for the State is that it can provide for the welfare of its disadvantaged citizens. Clearly, some anarchists have committed the 'genetic fallacy' in thinking that because the State originated in conquest and fraud, it must always remain conquering and fraudulent. The struggles of reformers and working people over the centuries have ensured that the liberal-democratic State does provide some basic social services and welfare for its citizens. But these positive provisions can be better supplied by voluntary associations than State agencies. Released from top-heavy bureaucracies, such organizations will encourage personal initiative and mutual aid. They will be able to satisfy more directly the needs of the people and involve them in their management. To be effective, medicine and education do not require State sponsorship any more than industry and agriculture do. What they need is to be managed by the producers and consumers in democratic committees and councils.

A powerful argument in favour of the State is its role as 'the guardian of national identity'.[11] There is no doubt a deep-seated desire among people to feel part of a larger whole, particularly in modern societies which are often composed of lonely crowds of individuals who float around like nounless adjectives. Many people feel more secure by identifying with a nation with a common tradition, culture and language. But a State is not a prerequisite for the integrity of a nation, nor does it always guard its identity. Many nations are either arbitrarily sliced up by different State boundaries or forcibly yoked together within one State.

With their principles of federalism and decentralization, anarchists would encourage a more organic and voluntary grouping of peoples, based on cultural, geographical and ecological lines. They accept the validity of 'bioregions', living areas shaped by natural boundaries like watersheds rather than by the bureaucrat's ruler on a map. Cosmopolitan and inter-nationalist, they would like to go beyond the narrow ties of tribe, class, race and nation. They see no beauty in xenophobic nationalism and the exclusive love of one's country. But they are not all opposed to the nation as a community of communities, and see it as part of a widening circle of humanity.

Authority and Power

Anarchism of course seeks to create a society without political authority. It is on the question of authority that socialists have departed from the anarchists. For many, brought up in an authoritarian society, they believe that without some central authority the centre will not be able to hold and chaos will be loosed on the world. People are so conditioned to thinking that leaders are necessary that they are at a loss when not told what to do. Those who fear this imminent collapse feel the need for some reference point, whether it be God, King, President, or General, to hold everything together with bands of law and the threat of the sword. With their ancient theory of spontaneous order, confirmed by recent scientific hypotheses about the self-regulation of nature, anarchists do not fear the spontaneous order of apparent 'chaos'.

The principal argument of the anarchists is that authority, especially in its political form, prevents the free development of the individual. They believe that political authority is not the remedy for social disorder but rather its main cause. Society flourishes best when least interfered with, and people work most creatively and efficiently when not compelled to work. To authoritarians, the anarchist critique of authority and power may seem naive, but in fact the disastrous example of authoritarian leaders and governments this century only confirms the relevance of their analysis.

Their position on authority is not however entirely clear-cut. Bakunin for instance was ready to accept the 'authority' of competence, although he stressed that the individual should always be the final arbiter in accepting the advice of an expert. More recently, it has been argued by some anarchists that it is acceptable for a person to be '*in* authority' so long as such leadership is not coercive and is exercised in an egalitarian framework.[12] For some, delegated authority is acceptable if it does not entail power over persons; others insist that the 'rule of authority' by competent individuals is permissible if based on consent and accountability.[13] From this perspective, anarchists are said to reject authoritarianism, not authority itself.

Most anarchists, however, still do not believe that because someone knows more than another he or she should have more authority and influence, for this simply amounts to the tyranny of 'merit'. For Godwin the authority of competence which involves reliance on experts is the worst form of authority since it undermines individual judgement and prevents intellectual and moral development. You can be *an* authority in a certain field, in the sense of having special knowledge, and you may for some *have* authority, in the sense of special wisdom, but no one has a monopoly of knowledge or wisdom which entitles them to a special place in some chain of command. When journalists described Daniel Cohn-Bendit as a leader of the 1968 Revolution in Paris, he insisted in true anarchist spirit that the student movement did not need any chiefs: 'I am neither a leader nor a professional revolutionary. I am simply a mouthpiece, a megaphone.'[14]

A certain ambivalence has also crept into anarchist discussions of power. In general, anarchism has recognized that power is one of the principal causes of oppression; that as much as wealth, it is at the root of all evil. Influenced by loose slogans such as 'power to the people', some anarchists and feminists have called for the 'empowerment' of the weak. But while their concern shows a fine wish to redistribute power, the long-term aim of all true anarchists is to decentralize power and where possible to dissolve it altogether. Indeed, one of the most important themes of anarchism is that all relations based on power are imperfect. They have not only been traditionally opposed to power over persons, but increasingly they are opposed to power over other species and nature itself.

Law

The rule of law – made, interpreted and enforced by the State – is considered essential by liberals to maintain order and to prevent anti-social behaviour in society. Undoubtedly what Russell calls 'primitive anarchy' based on the force of the strongest is worse than the law which follows known procedures and treats everyone equally.[15] But as Kropotkin's research and countless anthropological studies have shown, not all pre-industrial societies without written laws are in a Hobbesian condition of universal and permanent war. They generally manage their affairs through custom and solve disputes through agreed convention.

The constant refrain of the anarchist song is that the system of government and law in modern States is often the cause of, rather than the remedy for, disorder. Most laws in Western democracies protect private property and economic inequality rather than civil rights. An authoritarian society with a repressive morality encourages the psychological disorders which lead to rape, murder and assault. And punishment by its very nature tends to alienate and embitter rather than reform or deter.

In a freer and more equal society, anarchists argue, there would be less occasion for crimes against property since all would have their basic needs satisfied and, where possible, share luxuries. But while crime born of injustice and repression might be diminished, if not eradicated, in an anarchist society, it may still not be possible to eliminate entirely *crimes passionnels* and apparently random crime. What about those individuals who simply do not want to fit in with a reasonable, just and decent society, who might prefer to stick out their tongue – just for the hell of it – at a well-ordered community without political authority? How would an anarchist society deal with the kind of self-assertion which involves injury to others and to the perpetrator? Why should an individual be virtuous, and act according to the dictates of reason or in the interest of self and society? Indeed, as Dostoevsky's Underground Man declares, it may be possible and beneficial to act in a manner directly contrary to one's best interest: 'One's own free and unfettered volition, one's own caprice, however wild, one's own fancy, inflamed sometimes to the point of madness – that is the one best and greatest good.'[16] If a person suddenly wants to push another in front of a train, why shouldn't he?

It is a question that all libertarian visionaries must take into account. The conventional anarchist response would be first to point out that since a free society would not impose any social or moral blueprint, there would be no prompt to non-conformity, nothing to rebel against. Its vitality would be measured by the degree of individuality and the diversity of lifestyles it could accommodate without falling apart. It would constantly try and adjust the fine balance between individual and social freedom to maximize both. Secondly, where our repressive society encourages destructive and arbitrary acts, those growing up in a freer one would probably feel it unnecessary to assert themselves by inflicting injury on their own person or on others. Even if there remained people intent on injuring themselves, they should be allowed to do so (as John Stuart Mill argued); if it involved others, then that too would be acceptable as long as mutual consent obtained. But clearly, any such society, however free, would have to restrain child abusers, serial killers or drugged maniacs, if they existed, and deal with the residue of arbitrary and random evil. The inescapable freedom of one is the freedom of all.

The anarchist answer would not however include the demand to punish such wrongdoers since punishment neither deters nor reforms. Nor would offenders be ostracized from society in prisons to be further criminalized. Restraint would be kept to the absolute minimum necessary; the best remedy for anti-social behaviour is to be found in common human sympathy. Every attempt would be made to rehabilitate wrongdoers in the community, not by brainwashing or re-education but by friendly and dignified treatment which respects their humanity, individuality and will. Foucault is not the only analyst to have pointed out the similarities between old-fashioned penal culture and modern techniques of 'curing' which perceive 'madness' as a disease and try to turn individuals into docile citizens, uniformly obedient. To solve disputes, regularly rotated juries drawn from the local community would be able to consider each case in the light of its particular circumstances. The aim would be not to apportion blame or to punish the guilty but to restore social harmony and to compensate the victim. Public opinion and social pressure could also act as deterrents as they do now, while traditional techniques of influencing the anti-social through boycott and ostracism could operate as powerful sanctions. But even the latter should be applied carefully and only in extreme cases since they contain the seeds of intolerance and unfair psychological pressure. Non-cooperation is perhaps the most effective sanction: a person who regularly fails to keep their contracts and agreements will eventually find it difficult to enter into agreement with anyone.

In a free society, based on trust and friendship, a new social morality would undoubtedly develop which would make disputes increasingly unlikely. Political and moral coercion would give way to freely adopted customs and norms. Such a society would be based on a tolerance of different lifestyles and beliefs, treating individuals, including children, as ends-in-themselves. It would encourage the values of autonomy, self-determination, mutual aid, creativity, and respect for all living forms.

Public Opinion

There is of course a real danger that the tyranny of public opinion could replace the oppression of law in a society without government. Godwin suggested that public opinion can provide a force 'not less irresistible than whips or chains' to reform conduct.[17] There can be no doubt that in traditional and close-knit communities, public opinion can be a powerful sanction to make people conform. It can be intolerant, repressive and dogmatic. In their efforts to shape public opinion through 'propaganda by the word', some anarchists have undoubtedly been guilty of trying to inculcate anarchist principles instead of letting them be critically discussed and freely adopted. The very word 'propaganda' conjures up the over-zealous proselytizer, not the careful and sensitive thinker. The different schools of anarchism have also engaged in sectarian disputes, the most sustained being that between the individualists and the communists. Social anarchists, who wish to abolish the State and Capital, have nothing but contempt for the right-wing libertarians who wish to get rid of the State in order to achieve unfettered *laissez-faire* in the economy.

Orwell observed that there is often an authoritarian strain in the pacifist anarchists who take the high moral ground. Tolstoy, for instance, may have completely abjured violence, but 'it is not easy to believe that he abjured the principle of coercion, or at least the *desire* to coerce others'.[18] Again, Gandhi by his fasts exerted a moral force on people which had coercive overtones. His followers have sometimes been guilty of exerting undue pressure on people to think and act like themselves, a pressure which at times verges on moral coercion. If you are convinced that you are in the right, it is easy to bully others into thinking likewise, but to make someone think like you simply because you are certain does not encourage free enquiry or real conviction.

There is undoubtedly a totalitarian danger in the anarchist vision of society where the only arbiter of behaviour is public opinion and everyone is constantly exhorted and advised to act by meddling busybodies. Orwell rightly pointed out that, because of the tremendous urge to conformity in human beings, public opinion can be less tolerant than any system of law: 'When human beings are governed by "thou shall not", the individual can practise a certain amount of eccentricity: when they are supposedly governed by "love" or "reason", he is under continuous pressure to make him behave and think in exactly the same way as everyone else.'[19] In addition, in a society in which public opinion replaces law there is also the additional danger of that kind of collective vigilance and moral watchfulness developing which has made many religious sects and socialist States so oppressive.

Most anarchists however are keenly aware of these dangers, especially because of their concern with the sovereignty of the individual. The fundamental moral law, according to Benjamin Tucker, is 'Mind your own business.' This is not only true of individualists. The social anarchists have tried hard to reconcile the freedom of the individual with the freedom of others; to allow the maximum degree of individuality of all; and to achieve the apparent paradox of communal individuality. The measure of a free society would be the degree of eccentricity and deviance it could tolerate. Anarchists are committed to a pluralist society. They encourage variety and experimentation in lifestyles and social forms; to let not just a thousand but as many flowers as possible blossom. In addition, all anarchists have insisted on the individual's right of private judgement and opposed rigid censorship.

The foundation of anarchist educational theory has been to encourage people to think and act for themselves, not to rely on the opinion of others simply because they happen to be in authority. Their aim is to form critical judgement and deploy the creative imagination, not pander to intellectual orthodoxy and social conformity. As Godwin observed, a person may advise others but he should not dictate: 'He may censure me freely and without reserve; but he should remember that I am to act by my deliberation and not his.'[20] Public opinion would undoubtedly play an important part in an anarchist society in encouraging social cohesion and in dissuading 'wrongdoers', but its use would be much more deliberate and circumspect.

Like most critics of anarchism, Shaw, Russell and Orwell see no alternative to the rule of law. What such critics underestimate is not so much the goodness of man without the pressure of coercive institutions but the importance of social morality. Without legal and political coercion, new social customs and norms would emerge to hold society together. Anarchists assume that people can act morally and govern themselves, without compulsion, as they did before the creation of States, and that there is enough solidarity, love, reason, and good will in human beings to enable them to get on with each other in a fairly harmonious way when not interfered with.

History of course shows that human beings are equally capable of aggression as of peaceful living. Anarchists believe that without States and governments, which are primarily the cause of war and conflict, the more co-operative and gentler aspects of humanity will have an opportunity to flourish. And the social anarchists would add, without private property and capital, a social morality which satisfies real desires and encourages respect for the freedom of others would grow with the experience of communal work and play.

Social and Economic Arrangements

It has been argued that anarchist thinking is based on a 'romantic backward-looking vision of an idealized past society of artisans and peasants, and on a total rejection of the realities of twentieth-century social and economic organization'.[21] It is true that in the nineteenth century, many skilled artisans were undoubtedly attracted to Proudhon's mutualism which seemed to provide an alternative to the factory system of modern industry. Anarchism also attracted the independent clockmakers of the Swiss Jura who developed it in a communist direction. In the Mexican and Spanish Revolutions, it was the most backward peasants who embraced anarchism with the greatest fervour.

But it is quite misleading to see anarchism merely as a peasant or artisan ideology. In the form of anarcho-syndicalism, it attracted the most advanced workers in France and Spain. In the last century, anarchism appealed to sons of aristocrats like Bakunin, Kropotkin and Tolstoy, of peasants like Proudhon, and of landowners like Malatesta. In this century, anarchism has found in advanced industrial countries its greatest support among 'white collar' workers, especially students, teachers, doctors, architects, artists and other intellectuals. The new anarchism is not merely a revolt of the underprivileged but of the affluent who do not find fulfilment as passive consumers and spectators.

While anarchism has no specific class base like Marxism, it has traditionally found its chief support amongst workers and peasants. Bakunin established an important anarchist tradition by stressing the revolutionary potential of the peasantry, whom Marx dismissed as reactionary 'rural idiots', and of the lumpenproletariat, whom Marx considered to be anti-social elements. The great revolutions of the twentieth century have all confirmed Bakunin's rather than Marx's prognosis; they have not occurred in advanced industrial societies, but in predominantly agricultural ones. Moreover, in advanced industrial societies, it is the lumpenproletariat – students, the unemployed, ethnic minorities, and women on the margins of capitalism – who have proved the most rebellious.

The accusation that anarchism is opposed to the dominant economic trend of the twentieth century has more substance. It is certainly hostile to the centralized large-scale industry and agriculture found in modern capitalist and socialist States. It is not committed to a policy of economic growth and mass production and consumption.

But while it was possible a quarter of a century ago to suggest that anarchism was out of step with existing economic trends, it would now seem that State communism and international capitalism are failing to achieve their stated aims. The New Left and the growing Green movement have all taken up the classic anarchist demands of a decentralized economy with small-scale units and a harmonious balance between field and factory. Anarchism extolled the virtues of 'Small is Beautiful' before it became a popular slogan, and has long stressed the benefits of self-reliance and self-sufficiency. It has always put human beings before things, and seen no value in economic growth for its own sake. As the twenty-first century approaches, anarchists are no longer idealists swimming against the economic current. Indeed, their recommendations may well prove prerequisites to survival.

There are of course two main strains in anarchist economic thinking. Individualists and their contemporary counterparts, the anarcho-capitalists, rely entirely on the free market to supply public goods, and they retain the profit motive and the wage system. Social anarchists, including the collectivists, syndicalists and communists, seek to organize production for use through co-operatives, collectives, syndicates and communes.

Undoubtedly real difficulties exist with the economic position of the individualists. If occupiers became owners overnight as Benjamin Tucker recommended, it would mean in practice that those with good land or houses would merely become better off than those with bad. Tucker's advocacy of 'competition everywhere and always' among occupying owners, subject to the only moral law of minding your own business might well encourage individual greed rather than fair play all round. His argument for labour as the sole measure of price further conflicts with the market model in which values are dependent on supply and demand.

The economic proposals of modern anarcho-capitalists suffer from similar shortcomings, only in a more extreme form. In their system of complete *laissez-faire*, those who have wealth and power would only increase their privileges, while the weak and poor would go to the wall. The economy might be 'free' in the sense of unrestrained, but most people would not be free from want and fear. Private protection agencies would merely serve the interests of their paymasters. Right-wing libertarians merely want freedom for themselves to protect their privileges and to exploit others. They talk about freedom but remain silent about equality.

On the other hand, social anarchists all try to realize a society which is both equal and free. They recognize that every person has an equal right to basic liberties and material goods. They would assure a basic minimum for every member of society. There are however differences of degree between collectivists and communists. The collectivists would retain the wage system, rewarding individuals according to the amount of work done. The communists would rely on each contributing according to his or her ability and receiving according to need. In both cases production and distribution would be arranged through the basic economic unit of society, whether it be the syndicate, collective, council or commune.

In general, anarchists look to a decentralized economy which is managed at the local level by the producers and consumers themselves. Production and distribution would be organized through co-ordinating bodies at local, regional and national levels which would also seek to balance regional differences. And if this may appear utopian to some, anarchists point to the way in which highly complex agreements between international airlines and railways can be reached through negotiation without a central authority imposing its will.

In practice, anarchists have adopted different methods, sometimes at the same time, to achieve their ultimate goal of a free and equal society. During the Spanish Revolution, for instance, most theorists had talked about the benefits of co-operatives and syndicates, but collectives emerged in the early days of the civil war which rapidly proceeded to a form of communism by pooling the land and establishing common storehouses. The collective, based on universal solidarity and mutual aid, encompassed all those who wished to join, whether producers or not. Money was abolished in some cases and any surplus produce exchanged directly with neighbouring collectives. Small private farmers who did not wish to join were allowed to continue alongside the collectives. At the same time, in highly industrialized Catalunya, the factories were run by workers' committees who retained the wage system and in some cases even the managers as advisers. The whole resulted in a surprisingly diversified form of economic federalism.

What these collectives in Spain demonstrate is that farms and factories can be successfully organized through self-management and workers' control. They also show that there is no inevitable tension between liberty and efficiency. Many impartial observers in Catalunya noted how production in the factories increased and public services improved. This was not a result of better material incentives, for in many instances the value of real wages actually dropped. Even if collective decision-making took longer than issuing orders, in the long run the decisions were better implemented since they were properly understood and those affected felt involved and committed.

The example of Spain further exposes the myth that anarchists are somehow against organization. They are certainly against hierarchical and centralized organization, but not the kind of organization which is reached through negotiation and agreement. A few individualists might wish to remain aloof from all organization, and it is their prerogative if they so wish, but the great majority of anarchists find that they work best within voluntary associations which are small and functional.

In the economic sphere, the traditional arguments against anarchism have therefore proved increasingly hollow, even within capitalist societies. Innumerable practical examples of industrial self-management and workers' control have made a mockery of Engels' nineteenth-century contention that it is impossible to organize a factory without authority. Orwell's end-of-the-war comment that a planned, centralized society is necessary in order to make an aeroplane has been scotched by the success of private aerospace companies. In the post-scarcity world of advanced industrial societies, it can no longer be said that anarchism implies a low standard of living. 'Unless there is some unpredictable change in human nature', a deflated Orwell observed, 'liberty and efficiency must pull in opposite directions.'[22] It is not an unpredictable change which has occurred but merely a growing awareness that people are more efficient when they undertake their work voluntarily and participate freely in the process of decision-making.

Work

Human beings of course cannot survive without work. Once compulsion has been abolished, anarchist critics ask, who will then do the dirty work? Indeed, why should one bother to work at all? There is of course no intrinsic good in work, and aristocrats for centuries have enjoyed without complaint their unemployment and leisure. Unlike Marxists and Protestants, most anarchists (with the notable exception of Tolstoy) do not have a strong work ethic and find more happiness in comfortable idleness than in hard labour. They would agree with Russell that work has largely been of two kinds: moving matter around on the earth's crust and telling people to do so.[23] In a free society, the latter type of work would of course no longer exist, but who would carry on the former which is necessary to our existence?

Shaw argued forcibly that it is unlikely for men trained under the present economic system to be trusted to pay for their food in a scheme of voluntary communism if they could take it with impunity. Only the dire threat of want forces people to labour and the strong hand of the law can make them pay for what they consume. Even the pressure of social disapproval could not prevent them from taking advantage of voluntary communism for 'a man could snap his fingers at public opinion without starving for it'.[24]

It is not only 'authoritarian' socialists who have made this point. Some anarchists have insisted on compulsory work for all; others that those who refuse to work should be asked to leave the community since by refusing they are coercing others. Camillo Berneri proposed the compromise: 'no compulsion to work, but no duty towards those who do not want to work'.[25]

Clearly material incentives are not the only way to get people to work. The threat of want or the promise of material gain do not exhaust human motivation. Social anarchists stress that in a free society without compulsion, a morality based on mutual aid and solidarity would develop which would foster satisfaction in working for the good of the whole. In addition, there would be the moral incentive of social approval for those who work for others, and the sanction of disapproval for those who work only for themselves or not at all. Work which might usually be considered unpleasant can be enjoyable if it is felt to be socially useful and worthwhile. And where work cannot be made more agreeable and attractive, and machines cannot perform unpleasant tasks, there would doubtless be enough public-spirited people to share the work willingly.

But it is not only a question of moral versus material incentives. The nature of work itself would be changed in a free society. Anarchists promote useful work, not useless toil. They wish to end the division of labour so that people can make use of their mental and physical abilities. There would be much greater variety which would make life and work more interesting and exciting. If some people find labour-intensive work agreeable, then there is no reason why they should not engage in it.

When people are able to choose the nature of their work and control its process they do not wish to avoid it like the plague. The most important principle is that every one should be free to decide when, where and how they work. Work can only be fulfilling if it is undertaken voluntarily. The worker can hate his work in the factory, and be mentally and physically exhausted at the end of the day, but a couple of hours in his allotment in the evening can completely restore him.

As for the 'work-shy', it is generally the case, as Berkman pointed out, that laziness implies the right person in the wrong place. Many find little pleasure in their work simply because they do not know how to work well. In an anarchist society, there would no longer be any physical compulsion to work, and material incentives in the form of money and goods would not operate. Nevertheless, every member of the community would have the opportunity to realize his or her mental and physical potential while mixing their labour with nature. Without a rigid division and hierarchy of labour, without the tyranny of the clock and the wage system, people would be able to undertake freely the work which suits them best and remain in control of their labour and their product. As a result, it would be extremely unlikely if there were not enough able-bodied people to satisfy the basic needs and elementary comforts of the entire community.

In our post-scarcity society in the West, the need to work is far less than it was in the nineteenth century. With the development of modern technology we have now reached an era of potential abundance for all. It is no longer necessary for everyone to work, and certainly not in stultifying and degrading labour. As with the body, so with society: the health of a free community might well be measured by the number of 'parasites' it could support as an organism without going under. So-called loafers, idlers, wastrels and good-for-nothings should all have their place in the sun. Apart from excluding the young, the elderly and the infirm, it is a mean principle which says that a person who does not work cannot eat. In an anarchist society based on voluntary and integrated labour, there would room for *homo ludens* as well as *homo faber*. Work would finally lose its coercive character and be transformed into meaningful play; it would no longer involve suffering but become a joyful and graceful affirmation of life.

Reform or Revolution?

A major criticism of anarchism is that by refusing to participate in traditional politics, its adherents are inevitably left out in the cold. In general, it is undoubtedly anti-political in the traditional sense, in that it does not offer a specific programme of political change but a platform for personal and social liberation. As a result of their rejection of parliamentary and representative government, anarchists have tended to remain on the fringe of organized politics. In their refusal to compromise they may have maintained their theoretical purity, but they have also been practically ineffective, condemned to wallow in the political doldrums. Whether it be in one-party States or pluralist democracies, political parties have now become an almost universal demand. But what for many democrats is seen as a practical weakness can also be a theoretical strength. The anarchists remain the conscience of the Left, offering a profound critique of authority and power and holding up the combined ideals of equality and freedom. They are the most persistent critics of the Left and Right, and offer a third, largely untried path, to freedom.

Not all anarchists however are uncompromising. Even though they do not see a solution in parliamentary politics in the long run, some anarchists are prepared to support democratic movements if they think they are going in a libertarian direction. Godwin was in theory a republican, but in practice a Whig. Proudhon became a deputy in the National Assembly during the 1848 Revolution. Bakunin urged the boycott of elections not as a principle but as a strategy. And in Spain, many anarchists voted in the 1936 elections for the Popular Front and some of their leaders were prepared to become ministers in the Republican government in order to fight Franco's rebels. Since then, Paul Goodman has argued that a general election can be an educational experience and approved of voting for candidates committed to particular policies. Many anarchists are prepared to engage in local rather than national politics, since to do so is in keeping with their views on decentralization and autonomy.

Whether to use violence or not to achieve their aims has also divided anarchists. Some in the past have advocated terrorism as a last resort while others have been absolute pacifists. In its purest form, anarchism stands for peace and freedom while governments and States perpetrate violence and disorder. However, most anarchists have made a distinction between the violence of the oppressor and the violence of the oppressed, and have justified the use of revolutionary violence as a legitimate weapon with which to resist and eventually overthrow the organized violence of the State. A revolution is by its very nature one of the most violent processes in history, even if it remains relatively bloodless.

In the nineteenth century, anarchist thinkers vacillated on the question of violence. Godwin hoped to bring about gradual and peaceful change through education and enlightenment, but he felt that man was not yet sufficiently rational to be able to persuade an assailant to drop his sword through the mere use of reason. While Proudhon countenanced revolution and participated in the 1848 Revolution, he directed most of his energies to building up alternative institutions. Bakunin more than any other anarchist thinker celebrated the 'poetry of destruction', but he was opposed to arbitrary violence and isolated acts of terrorism. Kropotkin always preferred reason to the sword, and eventually favoured evolution rather than revolution to bring about social change, yet still he refused to condemn terrorists. Only Tolstoy and Gandhi were strict pacifists, although the latter felt that it was better to fight than to refuse to bear arms out of cowardice.

Following the Civil War of the Spanish Revolution, the carnage of the Second World War, and the continued threat of nuclear annihilation, an increasing number of anarchists have adopted a reformist and gradual approach to change. They are still prepared to take direct action, but in a non-violent way. They have recognized with Tolstoy and Gandhi that means cannot be separated from ends; they are ends-in-the-making. As activists in the 1968 Paris rebellion observed: 'The revolutionary organization has to learn that it cannot combat alienation through alienated forms.'[26] It is as impossible to create a free society by using coercive means as it is to use violence in order to bring about lasting peace.

Rather than attempting a violent confrontation with the State, which only leads to more repression, many modern anarchists seek like Gustav Landauer to make it obsolete by forming new relationships and institutions. By changing themselves, they change the character of social relationships. Since government is founded on opinion, as Godwin and Tolstoy observed, it will only wither away when enough people believe that it is unnecessary and withdraw their support. Such a process will inevitably be long and gradual, especially as many authoritarian values have been internalized and people are brought up to be dependent on bosses and rulers. But an anarchist society will only be achieved when society consists of anarchists; liberation will occur only when individuals have liberated themselves.

Despite the dominant authoritarian trend in existing society, most contemporary anarchists therefore try and extend spheres of free action in the hope that they will one day become the mainstream of social life. In difficult times, they are, like Paul Goodman, revolutionary conservatives, maintaining older traditions of mutual aid and free enquiry when under threat. In more auspicious moments, they move out from free zones until by their example and wisdom they begin to convert the majority of people to their libertarian vision. Aware that the political is the personal, they work from their particular situation, but they do not rest there. Part of the whole, they reach out to embrace humanity, transcending State boundaries and cultural barriers alike.

Anarchists now recognize that there are many rooms in the communal house of change and that there is no clear-cut distinction between reform and revolution: revolution after all is merely accelerated evolution. They therefore support all movements which seem to be headed in a libertarian direction. They seek to dismantle power pyramids and develop networks of co-operation. They build alternative institutions: free schools, which encourage learning by desire and respond to individual needs; factories based on the principles of self-management and workers' control; housing associations and communes which pool resources and share skills and conviviality. They try and develop a counter-culture which overcomes the split between science and art, reason and imagination, mind and body. They are concerned with the here and now, not merely with a mythical future; they are unwilling to postpone pleasure indefinitely.

With the collapse of anarcho-syndicalism as a major movement in the 1930s, it seemed for a time that anarchism would remain more of a personal philosophy than a social force. All that was changed with the resurgence of anarchism in the fifties and sixties. In India, the *Sarvodaya* movement attempted to develop Gandhi's vision of a decentralized society of self-sufficient, self-governing village republics. The popular revolution in Hungary in 1956 threw up workers' councils on the anarchist pattern. Many of the chief preoccupations of the New Left – such as participatory democracy, decentralization, workers' control and self-management – were central anarchist themes. The uprising in France in 1968, which was largely anarchist in character, provided an unprecedented example of a large-scale revolutionary struggle in late capitalist, late twentieth-century Europe. It was this event, coupled with the widespread resurgence of anarchism among the young throughout the world, which obliged historians of anarchism to add postscripts to their books admitting that they had been too hasty in announcing the demise of the movement.

Anarchism today is still very much a living and vibrant tradition. In the West anarchist individualism has inspired much of the thinking on the libertarian Right. On the Left, socialism has had to develop in a libertarian direction, to concern itself with personal freedom as well as social equality in order to retain its appeal.

In Eastern Europe, the Marxist-Leninist States have collapsed from their own internal contradictions and failure to win popular support. The old centralized bureaucracies have been dismantled and there has been a renewed call for fundamental freedoms. The success of the massive demonstrations for freedom and democracy in East Germany, Czechoslovakia, and Poland in the 1980s demonstrated the efficacy of the anarchist tactic of non-direct action and the general strike. Even in the republics of the former Soviet Union the role of the State is being discussed critically once again, with the leading role of the Communist Party roundly rejected. The student-inspired democracy movement which flourished all too briefly in China in 1989, with its call for autonomous unions and freedom of speech and assembly, was strongly libertarian. Before the tanks finally rolled into the centre of Peking, it provided a remarkable example of spontaneous popular organization without leaders. While the main thrust of the recent social movements in former Communist States has undoubtedly been towards greater democracy, not all wish to imitate the capitalist West. Many seek to reconstruct a form of libertarian socialism with a human face in the crumbling ruins of Marxist-Leninist centralism.

Anarchism might reject many of the realities of twentieth-century social and economic organization, but the signs are that it will help form and be in tune with those of the twenty-first century. It is totally opposed to the highly industrialized, centralized and militarized modern States. It is not committed to economic growth and consumerism. It does not want to exploit people and other species and destroy and pollute the environment. On the contrary, it poses personal autonomy against remote bureaucracies, the organic community against mass society, the balanced integration of town and country against rural deprivation and urban anomie, human relations inspired by trust and solidarity against those based on fear and self-interest. It wishes to end psychological dependence and social injustice so that all can develop the full harmony of their being.

Bourgeois Sport, Infantile Disorder or Utopian Dream?

Ever since the furious dispute between Marx and Bakunin which led to the schism in the international labour movement and the demise of the First International, Marxists have lost no opportunity to criticize anarchism as a puerile and extravagant dream. Most Marxists have taken their cue from

George Plekhanov who asserted at the end of the last century that anarchism is a kind of 'bourgeois sport' and argued that 'in the name of revolution, the Anarchists serve the cause of reaction; in the name of morality they approve the most immoral acts; in the name of individual liberty they trample under foot all the rights of their fellows'.[27]

Lenin at least derided Plekhanov's 'Philistine' and 'clumsy' dissertation on the theme that an anarchist cannot be distinguished from a bandit. He also criticized him for completely ignoring the 'most urgent, burning, and politically most essential issue' in the struggle against anarchism, namely the relation between the Revolution and the State.[28] Yet although Lenin agreed with the anarchists that it was necessary 'to smash the bourgeois State', he still called for the dictatorship of the proletariat in a centralized State and dismissed anarchism along with other forms of left-wing communism as an 'infantile disorder'.[29] In similar vein, the historian Alexander Gray damned anarchists when he declared magisterially: 'Anarchists are a race of highly intelligent and imaginative children, who nevertheless can scarcely be trusted to look after themselves outside the nursery pen.'[30]

Such criticism, which merely asserts that anarchists are 'immature' and treats most human beings as naughty children is so obviously vacuous it does not deserve any serious refutation. A more pertinent criticism of anarchism is that it is utopian. From Marx and Engels, who attacked all forms of unscientific socialism as 'utopian', onwards, anarchism has been dismissed as chimerical and fanciful – at best a romantic dream, at worst a dangerous fantasy. It is true that anarchism shares with utopian thought a longing for perfection and holds up the ideal of absolute liberty. There is also a continuous messianic and millenarian strand in the anarchist tradition. Like the Brethren of the Free Spirit and the Anabaptists of the Middle Ages, many anarchists have hoped to create heaven on earth in a society of perfect freedom and complete equality. The fight against rulers and the State has often been pitched as a struggle of cosmic proportions between good and evil. During the great social upheavals, some anarchists have tried to realize their ideals with religious fervour, especially in the peasant communities in Spain and Mexico during their revolutions. With Bakunin and his followers, there also creeps in an apocalyptic vision of revolution in which all is suddenly transformed in an orgy of violent destruction.

The failure of anarchism to establish thus far a free society for any great length of time further supports the utopian claim. Anarchism undoubtedly presents a non-coercive and decentralist vision of society which is entirely different from existing centralized and hierarchical States. Its ideal of complete freedom has also never been realized and strictly speaking can only be imagined. And despite the many attempts to realize the anarchist ideal, to put anarchism into practice, notably in the Russian Revolution and the Spanish Revolution, the embryonic experiments were crushed by more powerful forces.

Nevertheless, it says little to dismiss anarchism merely as a historical failure and a utopian dream. Wary of the utopian accusation, the towering anarchist thinkers of the nineteenth century, Bakunin and Kropotkin, were keen to stress that their social philosophy was 'scientific', in keeping with human psychology and the laws of nature. Despite his dispute with Marx over strategy and the role of the State, Bakunin adopted a tempered version of historical materialism. Kropotkin also constantly emphasized the scientific character of his anarchist beliefs, arguing that the existing tendencies in nature and society supported the anarchist ideal and were moving in its direction. Since Malatesta, who was critical of such a mechanical and determinist approach, anarchists have tended to lay greater stress on the role of human consciousness and volition in social change. Unlike other 'utopian' thinkers, they have consistently refused to offer a detailed blueprint of a free society.

At the same time, anarchists do share some positive aspects of the utopian tradition. The hard-headed 'realist' who rejects utopianism is often trying to discredit any alternative to the *status quo* in a most unrealistic way. As Oscar Wilde observed:

> A map of the world that does not include Utopia is not worth even glancing at, for it leaves out the one country at which Humanity is always landing. And when Humanity lands there, it looks out, and, seeing a better country, sets sail. Progress is the realization of Utopias.[31]

Utopian thought is valuable precisely because it has the imagination to visualize a society which is different from our own. By doing so, it questions the implicit assumptions of existing society and presents alternatives in a concrete way. It offers an ideal to strive for and a goal to approximate constantly. Moreover what was long considered utopian in the sense of fanciful or impossible has in our century become a reality. To dismiss anarchism as a 'romantic luxury at best' or as 'a cry of pain for the future' is an expression of prejudice entirely bereft of philosophical rigour.[32]

While the epithet utopian need not be an insult or a condemnation, in many ways anarchism is far from utopian. It offers a clear-sighted critique of existing society and a coherent range of strategies to realize its ideal both in the present and the future. It bases itself on a sound understanding of human potential. It looks to existing libertarian tendencies within society and believes that they can be more fully developed in the future. It draws on the experiences of the past, especially of earlier Stateless societies, and sees no reason why their best qualities cannot be transformed in a more libertarian direction in the future. It combines age-old patterns of co-operation with a modern concern with individuality. Far from sacrificing generations to some unknown future or individuals to some great cause, it argues that everyday relations can be changed here and now. It offers a platform for social change as well as an ideal of personal liberation and self-determination. For the time being, an anarchist society might seem unlikely, since it still remains a minority interest, but it cannot be said that it is implausible or impossible.

While the authoritarian trend remains dominant in most parts of the world, Colin Ward has correctly observed that 'an anarchist society, which organizes itself without authority, is always in existence, like a seed beneath the snow'.[33] It can be seen in all groups and associations which are organized like networks rather than pyramids, and which are voluntary, temporary and small. It emerges in groups which are based on affinity between members rather than on the rigours of the rule-book; which are in flux rather than in aspic. It begins to take shape in self-help, mutual aid and direct action organizations, in co-operatives, learning networks, and community action. It emerges spontaneously when people organize themselves outside the State during emergencies, disasters, strikes, and revolutions.

If not accused of being utopian, anarchism is often dismissed as being a shallow creed without great theoretical substance. It is presented as more of a mood than a doctrine, as a form of therapy rather than a serious social philosophy. This is a view usually levelled by historians rather than philosophers against anarchism. The historian James Joll, for instance, has talked of the 'somewhat incoherent nature of anarchist philosophy' and argued that if there is a living anarchist tradition, it should be sought in 'psychological and temperamental attitudes in society'.[34]

Again the historian Eric Hobsbawm, who at least recognized the historical importance of anarchism as a social movement, has argued that 'with the exception of Kropotkin, it is not easy to think of an anarchist theorist who could be read with real interest by non-anarchists'.[35] In his view, there is 'no real intellectual room for anarchist theory' and its only useful contribution to socialism has been its critical element. In his study of 'primitive' anarchism in Andalucía, Hobsbawm further emphasized its religious dimension and suggested that it was the dying ideology of historically condemned craftsmen and peasants.

Anarchism has certainly attracted a certain type of temperament. Like all extreme ideologies, it has its share of unbalanced individuals who seek a solution to their personal problems in apocalyptic revolution and who revel in illegality and criminality for their own sake. But these are exceptions. The great majority of anarchists are inspired by a vision of universal freedom, love and peace. For this ideal, they have often been prepared to give up their privileges and comforts, living on the margins of society in a state of permanent protest and open rebellion. They have sometimes gone so far as to cut from the trunk the branch on which they sit.

The anarchist ideal has appealed to a wide variety of people. It has inspired intellectuals who like to take their principles to their logical conclusions and who are prepared to adopt an uncompromising moral stance. The anarchist stress on creativity and spontaneity has attracted many artists among the Post-Impressionists, Dadaists and Surrealists who have called for artistic freedom and tried to create new forms to express their aspirations and feelings. Anarchism appeals to the young in heart who wish to think for themselves and question authority, who wish to throw off the oppressive burden of history and create the world anew.

At the same time, anarchists have certainly not engaged in the tortuous and scholastic debates of many would-be Marxist thinkers. The classic anarchist thinkers, except for Stirner, are notable for the clear and simple exposition of their fundamental principles. Apart from the philosophical anarchists, they have preferred to address the thoughtful worker or peasant rather than the closeted intellectual. But it would be wrong to imply that anarchists are less interested in theory than other socialists or liberals. On the contrary, since there have been relatively few occasions when they have been able to put their principles fully into practice, much of their energy has been devoted to the realm of thought. If some contemporary anarchists are short on theory and long on rhetoric, it is not because of the poverty of anarchist philosophy, but because anarchism attracts a wide range of support outside the world of intellectuals.

Far from being the puerile, naive, utopian fantasy imagined by superficial observers, anarchist thought, as the present study should hopefully have demonstrated, is profound, complex and subtle. It is more than a doctrine of personal living. It questions and has answers for many of the fundamental concerns of moral and political philosophy. It addresses itself to many of the burning issues of the day. As a result, it remains one of the most important and stimulating intellectual currents in the modern era.

Anarchists are unashamedly optimistic. Many base their optimism on the existence of self-regulation in nature, on the spontaneous harmony of interests in society, and on the potential goodwill of humanity. These beliefs may be under attack in our age of crisis and anxiety but they are still worthy of being taken seriously. They can map our future even if they may never be fully vindicated. Anarchism has been with us as a recognizable philosophy for two and a half millennia; the signs are that it will grow as a social movement and develop even more vigorously as a way of thinking and being in the coming millennium.

Anarchism remains not only an ultimate ideal, but increasingly a practical possibility. If we are to survive nuclear annihilation and ecological disaster, if we can steer between the Scylla of roaring capitalism and the Charybdis of authoritarian socialism, then we may reach the land where a free society of relative abundance exists in harmony with nature, where the claims of the free individual are reconciled with general solidarity. Even if we cannot reach it in our lifetimes, we can at least enjoy the exhilaration of the journey, sailing our ship together towards the beckoning horizon without fettering slaves in the hold or shooting the albatross on the way.

EPILOGUE

The Phoenix Rising

You must have chaos within you to give birth to a
dancing star.
FRIEDRICH NIETZSCHE

Demanding the Impossible was partly inspired by the enthusiasm and experience of the sixties through which I lived. It was a moment when the authoritarian and centralized State was challenged by mass social movements, especially in Europe and North America. It was a time when after the dreary post-war period of reconstruction it seemed that the imagination could at last seize power. In many countries in the West the State was in retreat in face of the civil rights movement, anti-Vietnam demonstrations, campaigns for Nuclear Disarmament and the rising feminist and green movements. There were widespread calls for workers' control, participatory democracy and the decentralization of power. The concepts of hierarchy and authority became central to discussions on the Left. Many alternative communities were set up, based on libertarian principles and promoting justice, creativity and concern for the environment.

In the seventies, the Left in Europe and America largely abandoned the hope of revolution. Instead, they attempted the 'long march of the institutions', that is, they tried to subvert and reform the State from within. The attempt failed but the eighties and nineties saw the emergence of non-violent revolutions within the Soviet camp, and the eventual overthrow of Marxism-Leninism as a State ideology. Unfortunately, the newly liberated countries followed the *laissez-faire* model of Western capitalism, often with fewer safeguards for workers and the environment. In the meantime in the West, the organized working-class movement more or less abandoned its militancy. Only a few small groups of Leftists continued to promote class war and violent revolution.

With the collapse of authoritarian communism, it became fashionable to talk of the end of history, in the sense that the titanic clash between the two opposing ideologies during the Cold War was over. With the triumph of neo-liberalism, the ruling elites claimed that representative democracy was the only universally applicable and desirable form of government. There was moreover no alternative to market economics. Yet despite the ideology of rolling back the frontiers of the State to 'free up' the economy, corporate power and State authority grew stronger and became more entrenched.

The millennium dawned not with a new age of personal and social transformation but with the West's military involvement in the Middle East, especially in Iraq and Afghanistan. After 9/11, the fear of terrorism was whipped up and used to expand and strengthen the coercive forces of the State. Hard-won civil rights were gleefully abandoned in the name of homeland security. The Society of the Spectacle was joined by the Surveillance Society: never before in history have the lives of citizens been so intimately surveyed. With the erosion of public welfare and older traditions of civil liberty, the fear of unemployment and poverty has meant that most people live in constant anxiety, exhausted by an endless round of gruelling work with little leisure to alleviate it.

Many have adopted a form of voluntary servitude in the hope of survival. Things are in the saddle. There is a collective hallucination that consumer goods will bring fulfilment and happiness. People are alienated from themselves, each other and the natural world. The Megamachine, not the human spirit, has triumphed. We seem to be entering a new Dark Age where global heating threatens, smog hangs over cities obscuring the sun, and the minds of the young are clouded with despair and melancholy. Naked military force and invisible economic power rule over the fate of billions.

The interests of transnational corporations and States have been integrated into an increasingly powerful system. A common culture of hedonism and consumerism, enflamed by the media and advertising in order to maximize profit and power, has spread across the world, from China to the US, from India to South Africa. Fundamentalist Christianity and Islam are the only mass movements making gains.

Yet to a growing number of the earth's population capitalism and its by-products – imperialism, war, racism, poverty and the destruction of environment – are no longer acceptable. The globalization of corporate power, encouraged and defended by the most developed industrial States, has spawned a dynamic and inventive grassroots movement of opposition and resistance throughout the world. Ever since the 'Battle of Seattle' at the World Trade Organization summit in 1999, international gatherings of the most powerful governments and corporations have been made uncomfortable by the anti-globalization movement and their leaders have been reminded of the plight of the poor nations of the world and the wretched of the earth. After the invasion of Iraq, eleven million people around the world protested in demonstrations in February 2003. A strong dissident culture, particularly among the young, has emerged – and much of it is very anarchistic, both in its methods and orientation.[1]

There are also other important libertarian developments around the world. South America has seen the growth of libertarian Left movements and the alternative 'solidarity economy'. In Asia grassroots campaigns of 'people's power' have threatened and even toppled dictatorships and the *Sarvodaya* movement in India and Sri Lanka is maintaining its momentum. And in China, a swelling libertarian underground current offers a powerful challenge to the Chinese State.

The Phoenix in the desert continues to rise, stretching its wings, multi-coloured, far-seeing and wise.

Wave upon Wave

In a 1975 postscript to his classic history of *Anarchism* (1962), George Woodcock observed that there had been 'an autonomous revival of the anarchist idea' on almost a world-wide scale.[2] But in the twenty-first century anarchism is not only an inspiring idea but part of a broader historical movement. The continuing protests against capitalism, globalization and war have reawakened an interest in the subject, partly because anarchists have been deeply involved in the struggles and partly because the movement itself shares the non-hierarchical, decentralized, participatory and co-operative forms of organization associated with anarchism. As a result, at the beginning of the third millennium anarchism is as vibrant and more relevant than ever.

The end of the Spanish Civil War saw the defeat of classical anarchism, but as George Woodcock recognized in the sixties and seventies, a new surge of anarchism took place associated with the New Left, the counter-culture, the communes movement, feminism, and the peace and green movements. In the eighties and nineties a 'second wave' of anarchism rose up, even more diverse and diffuse than before.

It was responding to the decline of the organized working class in Western countries, to the globalization of capital, to the propaganda of consumption of the mass media, and the stultifying emptiness and alien-ation of much of the prevailing culture. This recent wave of anarchism is concerned not only with the abolition of Capital and the State but all rela-tions of domination and hierarchy. It wants to diffuse relations of power as much as it can, and if possible, dissolve them entirely. It is fundamentally anti-dogmatic and protean and ready to break with the past. It wishes to create areas of freedom and equality, here and now, not in some mythical future. It does not look to a receding horizon but to the present and the immediate.

Partly inspired by the Situationists, many anarchists today look for the beach below the' paving stones and call for the imagination, not the pro-letariat, to seize power. They attack the deathly forces of the Pentagons of the world with poetic terrorism and oppose the cold rationality of the Panopticon of the surveillance society with the magical and the marvellous.

They liven up the bland monochrome of contemporary culture with sense-less acts of beauty and joy. They advocate a radical individualism and autonomy without rejecting the ethos of co-operation and communality.

Contemporary anarchists further explore imaginatively the tactics of protest and resistance, issues of identity and sexuality, mental and physical well-being, the degradation of the environment, the effects of technology and the possibility of living in a sustainable world.[3] They find the affinity group, based on friendship, mutual aid and respect, a basis for a new commonwealth. They create new forms of self-organization which run parallel to existing ones. They create zones of freedom and joy in the shell of the old society of deference and despair; they confront the forces of the State in mass demonstrations; they defend woodlands and fight new road schemes; they form communes and co-operatives; they reject technology and wish to return to a simpler life close to nature. And as States become more global in reach and corporations more transnational, they celebrate the small, the local, the regional, the wild and the free.

Some iconoclasts of the new wave of anarchy like to claim that classical anarchism is outmoded and the struggles of the past are no longer relevant. Yet a broader sense of history shows that they have not made a completely radical break; they not only reveal an ancient anarchist sensibility but are developing existing currents and eddies in the long and deep flow of the river of anarchy.

Given the fashion for describing what is allegedly new as 'post', it is not surprising that recent thinkers have come up with the term 'post anarchism'. The term embraces the new forms of anarchist thinking and strategy which have emerged at the turn of the twenty-first century. Having an extremely protean and open nature, it rejects the idea that it should form a coherent set of beliefs and actions. There are also lively streams of 'post-structuralist anarchism', 'post-modern anarchism', and even 'post-left anarchy'. Social ecology, which forged a creative union between anarchism and ecology, has been joined and enriched by 'anarcho-primitivism', 'green anarchy' and 'liberation ecology'. There are thinkers, like Noam Chomsky and Colin Ward, still working creatively in the older tradition of post-war anarchism and offering telling analyses of the present malaise. And anarcha-feminism too is into its second wave and contributing to the boys' own theory and practice and in many cases showing them the way.

Anarcha-feminism

The women's groups of first-wave feminists aimed at raising awareness of their oppression undoubtedly revealed an unconscious libertarian consciousness, both in their non-hierarchical structure and attempts to reach consensus among themselves.[4] But as L. Susan Brown has pointed out, not all feminists were or are anarchists. For her part, she has developed a form of 'existential individualism' which values autonomy of the self, voluntary co-operation and the process of becoming.[5] Some activists involve themselves with the working class and unions, while others have been promoting social ecology. Starhawk (Miriam Simos) calls herself a modern witch and anarchist and has reported regularly about the actions of the anti-globalization and anti-capitalist movements.

Most contemporary anarcha-feminists follow Voltairine de Cleyre and Emma Goldman, who saw no contradiction between the emancipation of the individual and social solidarity. The Anarcha-feminist International, for instance, demands that the 'traditional patriarchal nuclear family should be replaced by free associations between men and women based on equal right to decide for both parts and with respect for the individual person's autonomy and integrity'.[6] Feminists, no longer content to cook and carry for their radical *compañeros*, are very much part of the modern anarchist movement. They have engaged in turbulent demonstrations as well as direct actions. Their *Quiet Rumours* (2003) are becoming much more vocal.[7]

Manufacturing Dissent

Like the anarcha-feminists, Noam Chomsky, schooled in classical anarchism, was impressed by the social experiments during the Spanish Civil War. He has been the most influential critic of capitalism in the US from a libertarian point of view. In a long series of books on the media and American foreign policy, he has resoundingly demonstrated how Western elites have supported genocide, wars and repression throughout the world in the name of liberal democracy and Western civilization. He has shown how both 'liberal' and 'conservative' opinion in the US is committed to a State capitalist ideology which seeks to establish a global system in which US-based corporations can operate freely. The 'fifth freedom' of the US constitution, he says, is the freedom to exploit and dominate other peoples.

Chomsky has vividly demonstrated how corporations have joined governments to manipulate the media in order to promote their own interests, thereby perpetuating injustice and inequality and blocking any attempts to create a more direct and participatory democracy. He has repeatedly stressed the double standards of the US government, which rhetorically promotes freedom and democracy abroad yet supports some of the most tyrannical regimes in the world if they further its interests. In *Hegemony or Survival: America's Quest for Global Dominance* (2003), he presented a scathing overview of American foreign policy and its imperial ambitions since the Second World War.

Chomsky has never claimed to be an original anarchist thinker, prefer-ring to call himself a 'derivative fellow traveller'. Even so, he has long aligned himself with the anarchist tradition, and has been particularly influ-enced by Bakunin, Kropotkin, Rudolf Rocker and Daniel Guérin's anthol-ogy of anarchist writings *No Gods, No Masters*. By the age of twelve or thirteen, he admits identifying more fully with the anarchist cause. While he often calls himself a libertarian socialist, he is particularly critical of right-wing libertarians who would inevitably create 'private tyrannies' and an all-encompassing form of command economics. Indeed, if the ideals of the US Libertarian Party were realized they would create 'the worst totalitarian monster that the world has ever seen'.[8]

Chomsky of course has earned a major reputation for his work in lin-guistics and for his notion of 'universal grammar' innate in human beings. His belief in a human essence places him within the tradition of the Enlightenment. But he does not try to use science to justify his view that 'normal human emotions are sympathy and solidarity, not just for people but for stranded dolphins'.[9]

Chomsky still recognizes the reality of a class struggle in existing society, since there is a huge difference between giving orders and taking them. On the other hand, he sees little difference between wage slavery and slavery itself. Like his father, a Jewish émigré from the Ukraine, he has long been a member of the syndicalist Wobblies (IWW) and still stresses the relevance of anarcho-syndicalism and council communism to advanced capitalist societies like the US. He would like to see 'centralized power eliminated, whether it's the state or the economy, and have it diffused and ultimately under the direct control of the participants'.[10] Political power is always illegitimate and the essence of anarchism is the conviction that 'the burden of proof has to be placed on authority, and that it should be dismantled if that burden cannot be met'.[11]

Nevertheless, Chomsky is not an uncompromising anarchist. In his view, a degree of State intervention will be necessary during the transition from capitalist rule to direct democracy. While his long-term goal is to abolish the State, he is prepared to defend and even strengthen elements of existing State authority in order to protect the human rights, welfare, social security and limited democracy that have been won through past popular struggles.

Chomsky is also a pragmatist by refusing to sketch out the nature of a future anarchist society, except to say that by general agreement 'whatever social structures and arrangements are developed, they ought to maximize the possibilities for people to pursue their own creative potential'.[12] He imagines such an anarchist society would be under the direct control of its participants. This would mean workers' councils in industry, popular democracy in the communities, and 'interaction between free associations in larger groups, up to organization of international society'.[13] And while general agreement would be preferable, he is willing to countenance a form of democracy based on majority rule as long as any individual through conscious choice is able to refuse to go along with it.

Chomsky has remained a scourge of the media. His analysis of how the mass media are *Manufacturing Consent* (1988) has been followed up by *How it Keeps the Rabble in Line* (1994). He is particularly persuasive in showing how governments and corporations attempt to use the language of the media to distort systematically the fundamental meaning of words and thereby cloud an understanding of social reality. In this way, 'democracy' means the rule of an elite rather than the direct participation of the people in running their own affairs; the 'war on terrorism' really signifies the use of State violence against dissidents; and the 'war on drugs' targets potentially subversive groups and criminalizes certain substances as means of social control. Many people are so brainwashed by State propaganda, the media and public relations that they are not even aware that they are oppressed themselves. They become passive consumers and voluntary slaves. Chomsky often celebrates the value of the consciousness-raising of the women's movement in making women realize how oppressed they are.

Chomsky opposes censorship and believes in the free exchange of ideas – to the extent that he refuses to take legal action against those who may libel him under the present laws. He still argues that the majority of Western intellectuals – the 'new mandarins' – work behind a veneer of objective scholarship for the State and corporate power and interests. Moreover, while he is personally committed to the pursuit of truth and knowledge, he does not believe that it is the special preserve of intellectuals and experts but can be discovered by anyone with an open mind and a degree of common sense. Where many contemporary anarchists adopt a poetic, ranting and declamatory style, Chomsky is remarkable for his careful reasoning, clear analysis, telling evidence and transparent style.

Not all anarchists are happy with Chomsky's approach. He has been criticized for an overly narrow class analysis and for espousing anarcho-syndicalism. Primitivists are particularly dismissive: the Unabomber Theodore Kaczynski had him on his hit-list while the anarcho-primitivist John Zerzan, who was in touch with the bomber, dismisses him as irrelevant because of his emphasis on the workplace. It is clear why Chomsky should not endear himself to them. In his view, 'technology is a pretty neutral instrument' and while it can turn factory workers into robots there are 'virtual communities which are very real'. Indeed, he cannot believe that the anarcho-primitivists who want to abandon cities are serious. Because of the way urban society is now organized, they are calling for 'the worst mass genocide in human history'.[14]

Like his philosophical mentors Bertrand Russell and John Dewey, Chomsky is a child of the eighteenth-century Enlightenment and shares its faith in reason, science and technology to improve the human condition. The MIT professor is certainly not green: as a Cartesian rationalist and radical humanist, he lacks an ecological perspective in his writings. Nevertheless, as a persistent and doughty gadfly, he has remained the most influential anarchist critic of American corporations and the US government and their ruthless policy of world domination.

Seeds beneath the Snow

In Britain, Colin Ward is another anarchist working in the older tradition. He was part of the movement which developed after the Second World War, contributing to the paper *Freedom* and editing the remarkable journal *Anarchy*. With his background in town planning and architecture, his works primarily explored the relations between people and their built environment, looking at life from an anarchist perspective in fields as diverse as squatting, housing, planning, education, transport and water.[15]

In his widely influential book *Anarchy in Action* (1973), he revealed the influences of Gustav Landauer's view that the State is a set of relationships, Martin Buber's distinction between the 'social principle' and the 'political principle', and Paul Goodman's belief that a free society is not a new order but an expansion of existing spheres of free action. For Ward, anarchism is a description of human organization which is rooted in the experience of everyday life. In an often-quoted passage, he declared that

> A society which organizes itself without authority, is always in existence, like a seed beneath the snow, buried under the weight of the state and its bureaucracy, capitalism and its waste, privilege and its injustices, nationalism and suicidal loyalties, religious differences with their superstitious separatism.[16]

Anticipating post-left anarchy, Ward maintained that rather than speculating about the distant future, or waiting for the revolution to occur, anarchist alternatives are already present in the interstices of the existing State. Moreover, it is an everyday choice whether we wish to encourage libertarian or authoritarian tendencies within society and the structures of political power. His do-it-yourself approach is very much in tune with the practical anarchy of 'second wave' anarchy. And he ends his lively short introduction to *Anarchism* (2004) with the view that the best future prospects of anarchism lie with the ecological movement. Indeed, anarchism is the 'the only political ideology capable of addressing the challenges posed by our new green consciousness to the accepted range of political ideas. Anarchism becomes more and more relevant for the new century.'[17]

A more analytical approach to an anarchist theory of history and of the State has been developed by the British political philosopher Alan Carter. After undertaking a radical critique of *Marx* (1987) which was distinctly libertarian, he explored *The Philosophical Foundations of Property Rights* (1989). In keeping with his non-violent and anarchist sympathies, in *A Radical Green Political Theory* (1999), he elaborated what he called a 'State-Primacy Theory' against Marx's economic one and called for a form of anarcho-communism which would lead to an egalitarian, decentralist and pacifist society. Arguing that there is 'more mileage' in anarchist political theory than might be at first assumed, he has from his professorial seat in Glasgow tried to rescue anarchist political thought and the 'often profound insights it contains from an otherwise premature burial' by both liberal and Marxist academics.[18]

Past the Post

The term 'post anarchism' was first used by intellectuals influenced by the French post-modernist thinkers, especially in their opposition to 'totalizing systems' and their analysis of power. They employ the deconstructive techniques of post-structuralism and post-modernism and criticize the legacy of the Enlightenment and its epistemology. The processes of surveillance and control in Western society, for example, are seen as a logical unfolding of the Enlightenment. They also question the universal application of ethical systems, arguing that humans create values and the principles of morality are specific to particular cultures and times. And they challenge the idea of the individual as an essential self and of human nature as innate and universal.

Post-modernist thinkers, however, tend to be libertarians rather than anarchists. Michel Foucault for one maintains that power in the sense of 'a mode of action upon the action of others' is everywhere and cannot be escaped, whether in the arena of society or in the realm of knowledge.[19] While the relations of domination can be changed, the relations of power will always remain. Where anarchists seek to dissolve the structures of power, for Foucault it is senseless to try to create a world outside power: 'there are no margins for those who break with the system to gambol in'.[20] Indeed, in his view power does not emanate from the State but the State from power: the State is thus a congealed assemblage of power relations.

The American Todd May has tried to elaborate a form of 'post-structuralist anarchism'. Unlike a formal or strategic philosophy like Marxism, which locates power emanating from a single place (the economic substructure), May calls anarchism a tactical political philosophy since it avoids an overarching explanation of politics and sees power existing at multiple sites and different levels (such as the State, Church, capitalism and patriarchy). Nevertheless, he misunderstands the richness and diversity of anarchist thought by arguing that classical anarchism relies on 'naturalism' and presents the individual as a benign essence oppressed by the State. Anarchists have had very different views of human nature, and not all are essentialist.[21] Moreover, Todd goes against the general trend of post-structuralist thought in his ethics as well as anarchism by arguing that binding principles of conduct are 'universal in scope'. He is even ready to accept for himself 'the rules of law, the techniques of management, and also the ethics, the ethos, the practice of self, which would allow these games of power to be played with a minimum of domination'.[22]

For his part, the Australian Saul Newman has attempted to make the case for 'post anarchism' in his book *From Bakunin to Lacan* (2001). Comparing classical anarchist thought with post-structuralist thought, he finds in them a common thread of anti-authoritarianism. He also acknowledges that the most pressing political problem today is the proliferation and intensification of power and points out the dangers of radical political theories and movements which reaffirm power in their very attempt to overcome it. Taking up Stirner's idea that the individual has no essence but 'nothingness' and Jacques Lacan's notion of 'lack', Newman argues that this 'empty space' not only enables the subject to shape his or her own subjectivity but provides a ground for resistance against social power.[23] By focusing on the isolated individual, however, Newman overlooks the fact that human beings are sets of relations and that society comes before the individual surges up into the world.

Like Nietzsche, Foucault and May, Newman is convinced that one can never be completely free from relations of power: the more one tries to repress power, the more obstinately it rears its head. In his version of 'post anarchism', he wishes to affirm power like Nietzsche rather than deny it. He calls for a new 'heroic' philosophy which is based on the will to power as long as it is over oneself rather than others. In his view it would lead to a community which sought to overcome itself 'continually transforming itself and revelling in the knowledge of its power to do so'.[24]

The American Lewis Call describes his version as 'postmodern anarchism' and draws on post-modernist thinkers as well as cyberpunk science-fiction writers to support his case. He calls them anarchist since their critiques allegedly 'constitute, in part, a massive theoretical challenge to the very existence of capital and the state'.[25] Following Deleuze, he proposes an anarchism grounded in desire, desire which he believes is inherently revolutionary. Although he denies free will and intentionality, he says the goal of 'postmodern anarchism' is to 'reprogram and redesign ourselves' – as if we were computers. This, he tells us, would involve killing 'our inner fascist'.[26] Call's most significant contribution however is in his notion of the gift which he takes up from Jean Baudrillard: 'the symbolic violence of the gift without return is the only violence which has any chance against the omnipresent semiotic codes of political economy'.[27] As a cyberpunk enthusiast, he naturally celebrates the Internet as opening up a space where such non-capitalistic exchanges can take place.

In their analysis of power, these 'post anarchists' remain libertarian rather than anarchist. Instead of recognizing that all relationships of power are unacceptable, they distinguish between repressive and productive relationships of power. As Bakunin recognized, it is precisely because human beings can have a deep craving for power that they should not be trusted with it. Power corrupts and absolute power corrupts absolutely. It may well be that some residue of power will remain in an anarchist society, but it will be denied rather than affirmed. Power in its political form is inevitably dehumanizing, exploitative and oppressive. Power in the loose sense of the ability to influence others through persuasion would be acceptable, as long as it remains uncoercive, that is, without the use of emotional, mental or physical force. We all have 'powers' as capacities and abilities which can be creative and productive but for anarchists asserting power over others against their will is unacceptable. While they have traditionally called for the 'decentralization of power', they would also like to see power as a coercive force dissolved completely.

Post-left Anarchy

Another refreshing wave of original and imaginative thinking among contemporary anarchists is 'post-left anarchy'. It distances itself from the traditional Left with its involvement in trade unions and the working-class movement, stress on class struggle and goal of social revolution. It is wary of the traditional militant who knows the text and arguments but silences all questioning or opposition. Post-leftists have been influenced by postmodernist thinkers such as Foucault, Derrida, Lacan, Deleuze, Guattari, Jean-François Lyotard and Judith Butler who are not explicitly anarchist but whose analysis of power is profoundly anti-authoritarian. They share their criticism of the denaturalization of the body and their deconstruction of gender roles and reject the analytical rationality of the Enlightenment, and the binary opposites of Western thought.

A few, following the Italian Alfredo M. Bonanno, author of *Armed Joy*

(1977), advocate insurrection – Bonanno himself ended up in gaol for armed robbery. The vast majority though are interested in creating areas of freedom here and now and encouraging existing libertarian tendencies rather than struggling for some imaginary future. In their view, the satisfaction of desire need not be postponed; joy is available for the taking; the imagination can be immediately powerful. And they are not afraid of celebrating 'anarchy' in the popular sense of chaos rather than in the traditional anarchist sense of an ordered society without government. They tend to work within loosely affiliated 'affinity groups'.

Associated with 'post-left anarchy' in the US, where the movement first emerged, are the journals *Crimethinc, Anarchy: A Journal of Desire Armed*, and *Green Anarchy*. Bob Black has written a diatribe against Murray Bookchin called *Anarchy after Leftism* (1997). Many primitivists are post-leftists, although one of their most influential thinkers, John Zerzan, likes to call himself 'anti-Leftist'.

Crimethinc, a loose association of post-leftists in the North America calling themselves an Ex-Workers Collective, takes its name from George Orwell's concept of 'Thought Crime' in his anti-utopian novel *Nineteen Eighty-Four*. Their members are influenced by Situationism, anarcho-punk and green anarchy. Their influential pamphlet *Fighting for Our Lives* not only rails against the State and Capital but calls for a transformation of everyday life which involves a 'straight edge' lifestyle, refusal to work and the suppression of gender roles. In the pamphlet *Anarchy in the Age of Dinosaurs*, the authors describe as dinosaurs capitalism, the State, hierarchy and the 'countless other guises worn by Authority'. Crimethinc activists reject ideology and adopt the DIY approach of so-called 'folk' anarchy. They call for *Days of War, Nights of Love* (2000).

Temporary Autonomous Zones

The most delightfully exasperating post-left anarchist is undoubtedly Hakim Bey. 'Who is Hakim Bey? I love him,' said Timothy Leary, the Harvard psychologist who recommended his students in the sixties to drop out and turn on. Hakim Bey (Bey being Turkish for 'Prince') is in fact the *nom de plume* of Peter Lamborn Wilson, scholar, historian, poet and visionary. Murray Bookchin considered Bey as one of 'the most unsavoury examples' of so-called 'lifestyle-anarchism', attacking him for his dangerous Orientalism, extravagant rhetoric and cyber enthusiasm.[28] He could have added his interest in tantra, Hermeticism and paganism. Not surprisingly, for Bey lived for a decade in the East and acknowledges the Ranters, Dadaists and Situationists as influences and has written about Hindu tantrists, heretical Sufis, Muslim pirates, American spiritual anarchists,

French utopians and Avant Gardeners. Cultivating the 'art of chaos', he employs 'metarational' thinking in order to transform everyday life and to attain unmediated experiences. A large number of his essays and communiqués, now collected in books, first appeared in the anarcho-punk underground and on-line.

As Peter Lamborn Wilson, he has investigated the *Orgies of Hemp Eaters* (2005) and searched in *Ploughing the Clouds* (1999) for the psychedelic Irish Soma plant. For him *Angels* (1994) are the *Messengers of the Gods*. Faced with the tyranny of mechanical and analytical reason and the all-pervasive surveillance of the modern State, he believes that one of the best ways to subvert them is in the realm of the 'magical' and the 'marvellous' in which images can be manipulated to influence actions and events.

In *Pirate Utopias* (2003), he imagines the adventures of Muslim corsairs and pirates from the Barbary coast who set up an independent republic. His essays on the margins of Islam in *Sacred Drifts* (1993) show him to be a radical Muslim in the tradition of Sufi mysticism. Rejecting the authoritarianism and sexual repression of contemporary Islam, he explores the esoteric spirituality of its misfits and outlaws. He believes that religions can provide a form of 'subversive orthodoxy': 'Capital triumphs over the Social as against all spiritualities, spirituality itself finds itself re-aligned with revolution.'[29] In an essay on 'Crazy Nietzsche', he argues that the wounded madman was a prophet of a religion 'without authority'.

Hakim Bey's most influential book to date however has been *T.A.Z.: The Temporary Autonomous Zone* (1985). Its subtitle is 'Ontological Anarchy, Poetic Terrorism': the former reflects the 'Chaos of Being' while the latter is a tactic to overthrow the Society of the Spectacle. In the book, he celebrates ecstasy, joy and the marvellous, calling for gratuitous generosity rather than violence. He advocates a 'syncretism of anarchy and tantra' and an '*amour fou*' to subvert the relations of power.

As for his notion of a 'Temporary Autonomous Zone' (TAZ), which has struck a resounding chord among the young, he refrains from defining it precisely. It is clear however that he considers them as 'free enclaves' which can be created here and now, within the shell of the 'megacorporate information State, the empire of the Spectacle and Simulation'. As such, the TAZ is like 'an uprising which does not engage directly with the State, a guerrilla operation which liberates an area (of land, of time, of imagination) and then dissolves itself to re-form elsewhere/elsewhen, *before* the State can crush it'.[30] It thereby offers a microcosm of the 'anarchist dream' of a free culture. They have existed in the past – during the Paris Commune, in the Ukraine during the Russian Revolution and in Catalunya in the Spanish Civil War – but in the present era when the State is all powerful they offer a tactic for creating free space and time in its cracks and vacancies. It is 'an encampment of guerrilla ontologists' and aims at the 'structures of control, essentially at ideas'.[31] Although they risk violence, the best tactic in most cases is not to be engaged in it but to strike and run away. TAZs need not be isolated experiments; they can link up with others across the globe, both in the physical world and in cyberspace. Constantly changing and ephemeral, they take on the shape of a temporary uprising or insurrection rather than a permanent revolution. Above all, they manifest the pleasure and openness of a carnival, a festival, a rave or even a convivial dinner party.

In his collection of essays *Immediatism* (1994), Bey reveals the influence of Nietzsche and post-modernist theorists by asserting that the meaning of life and the true nature of things cannot be predicted with any certainty. At the same time, a dance with 'Chaos' can lead to the affirmation of life. Not only can the imagination free us from mental slavery imposed by authority but events and situations can be created to subvert mainstream culture and envisage an alternative reality. In this way, he believes that a new society based on the economy of reciprocity and the gift can be created in the shell of the old. 'Immediatism' is meant in both senses of the word – to seek experiences without mediation and to act here and now.

Although highly critical of modern means of surveillance, Bey is by no means a Luddite or neo-primitivist. Indeed, he has argued that cybernetic technology, freed from all political control, could make possible a world of autonomous zones. Rather than abandoning computers, we can use them to expand zones of freedom by creating a non-hierarchical, shadowy network which he calls the 'Counter-Net' or 'Web' within the mainstream Internet. Indeed, he recognizes that most people could not do without cars, computers and even cell phones. 'Culture is our Nature,' he provocatively declares.[32]

Faced with global capital and an all-pervasive State, Bey has argued in *Millennium* (1996) that there is no alternative except to enter the system or oppose it. As multinational corporations undermine its sovereignty, the nation state is becoming increasingly irrelevant as a focus of opposition. Nationalism however can be a force against Capital and the State if it is coupled with regionalism, devolution and organic democracy. The only long-term solution is 'enlightened anarchy' in which 'custom and right' replace the laws of the State. It is clear that Bey here not only draws on Gandhi but is also inspired by Proudhon's mutualism. More recently, since revolution now seems tactically impossible, Bey/Wilson recommends dropping out to form small utopian communities: 'Success or failure remains unforeseeable – but adventure is something that can be willed.'[33]

Some anarchists have dismissed Bey's work as a form of poetic hedonism of little use to anyone seriously concerned with remaking society on a large scale. On the other hand, with its subversive call to embrace Chaos, its exotic recipes for poetic terror and black anarchist magic and its joyful advocacy of a 'congress of weird religions', TAZ has become something of a cult underground classic. The idea also has had considerable influence among anti-globalization campaigners, environmental activists and those who have tried to reclaim the streets, occupy disused buildings, organize rave parties, free festivals and carnivals – in short, all those including myself who wish to create enclaves of light, freedom and play in the shadow of the Leviathan.

Many anarchists like Hakim Bey have enthusiastically embraced the Internet and espied its libertarian potential, especially with its borderless and ownerless structure. They plan in cyberspace, creating horizontal and decentralized networks of communication throughout the world. They are involved in alternative organizations like Indymedia, a global, non-hierarchical network of independent journalists and media. They reject censorship and notions of intellectual property and copyright. They practise the gift relationship rather than capitalist exchange, sharing software, music and text. Their credo is that information is free and should be freely available for all. A few engage in criminal activity, hacking into major corporations and government departments in order to hinder their work and reveal their exploitative and coercive nature. But most are active in the free software and open-source movement. Moreover, the anti-capital and anti-globalization movements which they help co-ordinate mirror the organic and decentralized pathways of the Internet.

The Wild and the Free

At the same time, one of the major new strands of 'second wave' anarchism, particularly in the most advanced industrial societies, has been the rise of primitivism. Where Jean-Jacques Rousseau in his personal moral reform abandoned the trappings of civilization – in his case the wig, the sword and the watch – the new primitivists turn their back on modern technology and try to adopt a 'primitive' lifestyle close to nature. They claim that it is not the use or the kind of technology which is the problem today, but the technology itself. It is not neutral, as Chomsky has argued, but affects our whole way of being. They have mounted a penetrating critique of modern technology and would like to smash television and surveillance screens to escape the Society of the Spectacle, Surveillance and Simulation. They stand in the revolutionary tradition of the Luddites ('No King but King Ludd') at the beginning of the Industrial Revolution in Britain who resisted the kind of technology – in their case the new textile machines – which they felt harmful to their community.

For the anarcho-primitivists, it is not the centralized and militarized State which is the principal cause of social, political and ecological crisis, as most anarchists maintain, but Civilization itself. In their view, human society has gone wrong since it abandoned the nomadic way of life around 7,000 BC and settled down to domesticate animals and to grow crops. This was the true fall of humanity from authenticity. By contrast, in the Palaeolithic period, according to David Watson, the world was 'affluent because its needs are few, all its desires are easily met. Its tool kit is elegant and light . . . It is anarchic . . . a dancing society, a singing society, a celebrating society, a dreaming society.'[34]

Like Rousseau, anarcho-primitivists call for a return to nature; like Thoreau, they believe that the salvation of the world lies in wildness; and like Edward Carpenter, they would like to live lightly on the land. With the deep ecologists, they wish to have an unmediated experience of nature, and with Edward Abbey and the members of Earth First! they are prepared to engage in 'monkey-wrenching' and eco-sabotage to defend ecosystems and non-human species.

Many of those primitivists critical of civilization in the US, such as Fredy Perlman, John Zerzan and Derrick Jensen, advocate, even if they do not live it, a revival of the way of life of hunter-gatherers of the Palaeolithic era and of indigenous peoples who still live close to the land and sea. They would like to see the dismantling of urban civilization. They wish to go 'feral', that is, return to a condition of 'wildness'.[35] As well as 'born to be free', their slogan might be 'born to be wild'.

If they cannot flee to the woods, deserts and mountains, they prefer to live in the interstices of urban life, reclaiming abandoned buildings and sites, growing their own vegetables and building their own low-impact dwellings. Rejecting the bourgeois life of a steady job, pension and mortgage, they try to become active agents rather than passive subjects and consumers.

Long before primitivism became fashionable among young urban sophisticates, Fredy Perlman, associated with the Detroit-based journal *Fifth Estate*, wrote a fiery roll against Western civilization and its deep-rooted patriarchy in *Against His-story, Against Leviathan!* (1983). This passionate rant traced the emergence of the first State in Mesopotamia during the Bronze Age when a king began to enslave neighbouring tribes. The resulting Leviathan of a State, Perlman argued, developed a 'hive mind' which tried to absorb or destroy any egalitarian peoples and cultures it came across. It became deeply authoritarian and repressive: whereas Nature springs from our inner voice and says 'Thou Canst and Thou Shalt Be', the Leviathan has 'closed gates' and with its laws declares 'Thou Shall Not'.[36] Wherever the Leviathan emerged – whether in ancient Mesopotamia, India or China – it saw the beginning of the rule of kings and emperors, the origins of hierarchy and domination and the foundation of State and Empire.

Perlman's alternative was to create and live in 'nomadic communes' in the belly of the Beast in the hope that one day it would be overthrown. This will not be easy, as Perlman more than most was aware of *The Continuing Appeal of Nationalism* (1985). This neo-primitivist prophet died in his early fifties after a life, in the words of his wife, of 'having little and being much'. While the historical evidence for his thesis is somewhat sketchy, his trenchant critique of the origins of modern civilization has been widely influential.

The Forest beneath the Streets

It is however John Zerzan who has been the most controversial of the anarcho-primitivists, one who is not afraid of quarrelling with his fellow anarchists. Calling himself an 'anti-leftist', he has attacked Chomsky for being too conservative and for saying little about women and nature.[37] He is no less dismissive of Murray Bookchin's social ecology and libertarian municipalism, which in his view are part of the old Left which anarchists should leave behind.

Zerzan makes no bones about it; he is quite simply *Against Civilization* (1999) and all that it stands for: its wars, hierarchy, division of labour, symbolic thought, machines, environmental destruction and mass psychology of misery. As the best form of human society so far, he looks back to the hunter-gatherers who lived lightly on the land and shared goods without a central authority and hierarchy. The 'wrong turn' for humanity was therefore the Agricultural Revolution, which was much more fundamental than the Industrial Revolution. Drawing on archaeology and anthropology, he further argues for the superior health and well-being of the hunter-gatherers: 'life before domestication/agriculture was in fact largely one of leisure, intimacy with nature, sensual wisdom, sexual equality, and health.'[38] The Great Settlement led to social hierarchy, the oppression of the many by the few, the subjugation of women and the exploitation and destruction of the planet. Ever since human beings abandoned their nomadic ways, they have become domesticated, complacent, obedient, violent and alienated. We have been going downhill ever since, except for a few indigenous cultures which have managed to survive on the margins or in the interstices of modern civilization.

Zerzan combines a traditional anarchist analysis with radical ecological thought. As a neo-Luddite, he has long been questioning technology.[39] But like all anarcho-primitivists, he argues that it is not the type of technology which is the problem but modern technology itself, with its inevitable division of labour and overspecialization and alienating effects. This goes against the flow of many classical anarchists and syndicalists who saw technology as liberating people from drudgery and reducing the working day so that workers could have more leisure to develop their full potential. Zerzan even finds intermediate and alternative technology unacceptable, although some hand-held tools might be tolerated in his brave new world.

Zerzan now sees Western civilization as *Running on Emptiness* (2002). On a cultural level, the 'catastrophe' of post-modernism, with its eclecticism, relativism, nihilism and lack of historical imagination, is only one symptom of its vacuity. The increasing trend to use symbolic representation, especially through language, not only cuts us off from each other but prevents a direct experience of the natural world. As a result, we are 'estranged from our own experiences, dislodged from a natural mode of being'.[40] And the experience of time as a linear process rather than as a constant process further prevents us from living in the here and now.

There is no point trying to tinker with modern civilization for it cannot be reformed. As Zerzan makes clear in *Elements of Refusal* (1999), there are ways of resisting its worst aspects, from taking up voluntary unemployment to running feral, but the only long-term remedy is a thoroughgoing dismantling of modern civilization and a return to a simpler way of life. We must transcend the last 8,000 years of civilization and empire and move forward to a *Future Primitive* (1994) in which we live in a world close to nature without technology beyond hand-held tools.

Zerzan's onslaught on modern civilization is penetrating and his analysis of its ills, made with wit and passion, is persuasive. But he romanticizes and simplifies the life of the hunter-gatherers. He cites the ! Kung San (Bushmen) and Mbuti (pygmies) as examples of people living a non-alienating and non-oppressive life. Having spent time with the nomadic Baka pygmies in the rainforests of Cameroon and travelled widely in Africa, I recognize that they are healthier and have more leisure than town people, but I find it difficult to imagine that they offer the ultimate ideal of human society.[41] While one can appreciate the wisdom of tribal and aboriginal peoples and their close kinship with the natural world, one should not overlook in many of them the lack of sexual equality, personal autonomy, freedom of thought and tolerance of eccentricity.

Zerzan's harmonious 'state of nature' pre-existing civilization might be different from Hobbes' war of all against all, Locke's free but uncertain condition or Rousseau's life of solitary individuals, but he makes a similar error in imagining a hypothetical state in order to justify the kind of society he would like to see. Indeed, his way of glorifying hunter-gatherers may not be very different from those colonialists who projected their desires and fears on to tribal societies in the nineteenth and twentieth centuries although they did it for different ends.

Neolithic Anarchy

Contrary to Zerzan, I would argue that in Europe at least the initial stage of settled agriculture – the first 3,000 years or so before the Bronze Age – was not a decline but an actual improvement in the well-being of human beings. It was a creative period during which society was co-operative, egalitarian, creative and comparatively free. Graves, for instance, were communal, dwellings similar, and magnificent astronomically aligned buildings were raised in collective surges of energy. It was also a peaceful society: the megalithic monuments were undefended and no signs of battles have been found near them.[42] It was only when warriors with metal weapons arrived in Europe from the East in the Bronze Age that hierarchy, domination, chiefs, private property and war began to appear, and have been with us ever since. In my view, it is this period of Neolithic anarchy rather than the earlier period of hunter-gatherers which can offer an inspiring vision for the future. It cannot be a question of going back, even if it were possible, but we can draw on the insights of our ancient ancestors and distant forebears to create our own values and actions in the here and now. As Rousseau himself observed, the golden age is not behind us but within us, waiting to be renewed.

It is a common phenomenon for the over-sophisticated to celebrate the primitive. It is impossible to escape the inventions of civilization and return to some pristine wilderness. Even Zerzan makes use of the conveniences of modern civilization: he may live in a co-operative in Oregon, but he still uses the phone, borrows a neighbour's computer and allows trees to be cut down to produce his books. Ironically, anarcho-primitivists are well-organized on the web.[43]

In evolutionary terms, human civilization is a very recent development and nature is only temporarily held at bay: grass and trees are forever ready to burst through the paving stones of the streets. But given the present human population, it would be impossible for all of us to abandon cities and re-create the lifestyle of hunter-gatherers. If many tried to return to the little fragile wilderness that remains, there would very rapidly be no more wilderness at all. The only real wilderness left is not on the land – which only makes up about thirty per cent of the Earth's surface – but at sea or within ourselves. We were born to be wild and free; the great question for the new millennium is how to expand our freedom and preserve the remaining wilderness, faced as we are with the inexorable increase in human population and consumption of the world's resources.

Zerzan unduly dismisses other anarchists who seek urban and work-based solutions to the exploitation and oppression of Capital and the State. He might inspire some to leave their jobs and try and dwell in the woods, mountains and deserts, to live in a continuous flow of communion with nature rather than counting the hours and minutes at work, but it cannot be a solution for all. Nevertheless, his searching critique of industrialism, capitalism and the megamachine is both trenchant and compelling. He is right to question the alleged benefits of civilization, the notion of linear progress and the limitations of symbolic thought. Zerzan's vision is utopian and offers no clear programme for social change, apart from personal resistance, wildcat strikes and public demonstrations, but it powerfully illuminates the disasters of Western civilization and shows the human potential for another, more ancient way of being connected with the Earth. To have encouraged people to recognize themselves as members of the wider community of beings is no mean achievement in itself.

Another polemical American primitivist is Derrick Jensen, who admires Zerzan's work. In his view civilization is inherently violent and unsustainable and can only be remedied by an end to industrialism and return to a more harmonious way of life. He draws inspiration from indigenous peoples who do not treat the natural world as a metaphor or as a resource to exploit. Jensen has not only explored in *Welcome to the Machine* (2004) the science, surveillance and culture of control, but in the two volumes of *Endgame* (2006) has looked at the problem of civilization and the ways it can be resisted, whether by blowing up dams or paralysing the capitalist system by sabotaging the commercial infrastructure and means of communication. Nevertheless, like Zerzan he offers us no clear way forward.

Green Shoots

Many green anarchists, like the primitivists, are radically 'anti-civilization'. For them it is civilization and not capitalism which is the prime cause of authority and domination. They too trace the downfall of humans to the era when they moved from the carefree nomadic life of the hunter-gatherers who worked a few hours a day to the sedentary and busy ways of the horticulturalists, agriculturalists and pastoralists.

Green anarchists believe in direct action; they are involved in protest and resistance movements against the State and contemporary civilization, including anti-capitalist, anti-colonial and ecological struggles. One of their banners is 'Destruction of Civilization and Reconnection with Nature'. They wish to replace the present 'civilized' lifestyle with more primitive living and to experience nature as far as possible unmediated by symbolic thought and cultural representation.

But not all green anarchists want to return to a deep Palaeolithic era, even if that were possible. Some try to return to the 'wilderness' of woods and fields, developing earth and survival skills, practising self-sufficiency and using applied technology. Some live in small communities coexisting with other beings without dominating them. Some develop the art of doing nothing yet leave nothing undone. Some try to simplify their lives while they continue to live in the cities, resisting the authoritarian and alienating elements of modern culture and the destruction of the wider environment. Others go in for 'Rewilding', attempting to reclaim our 'lost knowledge of living with the earth'.[44] What unites green anarchists is the belief that the present form of industrial civilization, spreading across the world with global capital and political imperialism, will lead to a social and ecological catastrophe unless there is a major shift in values and a new relationship with the Earth.

Green anarchists particularly stress the importance of local identity, rehabilitation of the land and bioregionalism while keeping a wider perspective. They say that we should act locally and think globally: the principle fits in well with the ecological principle of unity-in-diversity. They recognize that humans are inevitably part of the natural ecosystems in which they live and work. A region, they point out, is not defined by artificial boundaries like a State, but is a product of the imagination as well as of nature. It draws on older historical, cultural and linguistic traditions.

Shoots of green anarchy, like rhizomes of irises, have sprung up in different places. Syndicalists such as Graham Purchase and the Wobbly organizer Judi Bari have tried to develop a form of green syndicalism, in which unions committed to direct action and workers' self-management take up ecological concerns.[45] Anarchists have been involved in the Animal Liberation and Animal Rights movement, extending their concern for freedom from the human to the animal sphere. Many contemporary anarchists, following in the footsteps of Elisée Reclus, are vegetarian or vegan in order to minimize the human exploitation of animals. Wild Greens and members of Earth First! and the Earth Liberation Front defend the planet, and its species threatened by humans, with a wide variety of tactics carried out by autonomous groups and individuals, from tree-squatting and road-blocking to monkey-wrenching. One movement to emerge from green anarchy is Freeganism (coined from free-veganism), which advocates voluntary joblessness and tries to escape the economic system based on exploitation. They live off abandoned products of modern industrial society, such as the food thrown away by supermarkets.

Many green anarchists have been inspired by the poet and essayist Gary Snyder, who finds 'Buddhist anarchism' to have 'nation-shaking' implications.[46] Inspired by the closeness of Native Americans to the earth and their sense of belonging, he has called for a return in 'Turtle Island' (the North American continent) to a tribal way of life based on bioregions defined by natural and cultural boundaries. His concern for the *Earth House Hold* (1969) was followed up by calling for *The Practice of the Wild* (1990), a defence of bioregionalism, of truly dwelling in and caring for the land where we live. He reminds us that the most immediate and ordinary can often be the most sacred and wondrous and that wildness is not just wilderness in nature but the wild culture of free peoples and the wild mind and imagination of creators. For Snyder, nature is not a place to visit but home.

Aragorn!, one of the editors of *Anarchy*, who is immersed in the American Indian tradition, has called for a 'Non-European Anarchism' which combines 'decentralization, mutual aid, power, cultural bias, single solutions to political questions, and rejection of authority'. To resolve questions regarding organization and social change, he suggests people should look to their own cultural heritage and traditions and make decisions among themselves through consensus.[47]

The science-fiction writer Ursula K. Le Guin has continued to have a great influence and introduced many people to anarchism and Taoism, particularly through her utopian novel *The Dispossessed* (1974). On the moon Annares, she depicts a society without government and coercive institutions. Even its language, Pravic, reflects its anarchist foundations, with no word for 'my'. The novel also shows the dangers of centralization and bureaucracy developing if they are not constantly challenged. As the hero Shevek makes clear: 'You cannot take what you have not given, and you must give yourself. You cannot buy the Revolution. You cannot make the Revolution. You can only be the Revolution. It is in your spirit, or it is nowhere.'[48] In her great work of utopian fiction *Always Coming Home* (1985) she tells the story of the gentle, joyful, creative and co-operative Kesh, a peaceful valley culture, and the ruthless, aggressive Condor people who live in the mountains. They present vividly aspects of how the world is and how it could be. Le Guin in her other writings has shown that the wild is all around us, even in the most domesticated landscapes. If we can only see it the possibility of utopia is already in our midst.

At the same time, there has been a growing interest in pagan anarchism which finds reverence for the Earth leading inevitably to anarchist solutions. Starhawk, for example, shows that an appreciation of the Great Goddess does not necessarily involve hierarchy. Her book *The Spiral Dance* (1979), a classic work on Wicca and eco-feminism, argued that the Goddess is not a transcendental deity like the Christian God but an immanent life force to be nurtured and celebrated.

Pagan anarchists wish to protect the Earth, celebrate the cycle of the seasons and honour the Earth Goddess and the Green Man. They combine earth-based spirituality with libertarian activism, performing rituals to transform the relationships of humans with each other and with nature. Many accept the Wiccan Rede ('Counsel'), which is said to summarize the Wicca religion: 'An [if] it Harm None; Do as thou wilt.' The principle recalls St Augustine's saying: 'Love, and do what you will.' Such a position implies ethical reciprocity; that is to say, while satisfying one's own desires one should actively avoid doing harm to others.

Social Ecology

On the face of it, anarcho-primitivism and green anarchy would seem to have much in common with social ecology for they all combine a deep concern with the environment with a telling critique of modern culture. But Murray Bookchin, one of the key figures in social ecology, has since the 1990s alienated potential recruits to his cause by attacking vituperatively those who do not agree with him. In the name of reason, progress and civilization, he mounted a wildly irrational onslaught on deep ecologists and primitivists as counter-revolutionary mystics.[49] He dismissed anarcho-syndicalism, espoused by Chomsky and others, as having too narrow a class base and declared that the workers' movement was essentially dead. As for Hakim Bey's post-left anarchy, he saw it as the whimsy of retarded adolescents obsessed with themselves.

The dispute between 'second wave' anarchists and Bookchin came to a head in his acrimonious essay *Social Anarchism or Life-Style Anarchism: An Unbridgeable Chasm* (1995). Rather than forming bridges, like Malatesta, Emma Goldman and Colin Ward, he tried to create a chasm between what in many ways had been a fruitful exchange between different strands of the anarchist and ecological movements. Like the worst Leninist sectarian, Bookchin mounted a rancorous tirade against what he called 'alternative café' radicals, deep ecologists and, 'Thousands of self-styled anarchists [who] have slowly surrendered the social core of anarchist ideas to the all-pervasive Yuppie and New Age personalism that marks this decadent, bourgeosified era.'[50] He lumped together in one distasteful bag such diverse people as primitivists, mystics, lumpenproletarians, post-modernists, New Agers, Stirnerites, irrationalists, liberals and fascists. He accused them of abandoning class-consciousness and revolutionary fervour, replacing an egoistic, undisciplined, do-your-own-thing mentality for solidarity and revolutionary commitment. In his drive to 'demystify the primitive', he further launched a sustained attack on 'primitivity', which he saw as a projection of irrational nostalgia by misguided romantics on allegedly pristine primitive society. Still believing, as he had written in *Post-Scarcity Anarchism* (1971), that maximum consumption with minimum effort could be attained through modern technology, he derided the primitivists as retreating 'into the shadowy world of brutishness, when thought was dim and intellectuation was only an evolutionary promise'.[51] At this stage, Bookchin still hoped for a social anarchism which is committed to rationality, while opposing the rationalization of experience; to technology, while opposing the 'megamachine'; to social institutions, while opposing class rule and hierarchy; to a genuine politics based on the confederal co-ordination of municipalities or communes by the people in direct face-to-face democracy, while opposing parliamentarism and the State.[52]

Ensconced in his Institute of Social Ecology in Vermont, Bookchin however was simply out of tune with the direction of the new wave of anarchism. Instead, he advocated what he called 'libertarian municipalism', that is a libertarian, participatory and confederal politics based on municipal assemblies, which in his view offered nothing less than a 'kind of human destiny'. He called the municipality the 'living cell' which forms the basic unit of political life.[53] To this end, he recommended anarchists to engage in local elections and accept the principle of majority rule. Partly inspired by the Greek *polis* and New England town meetings, he believed that this model could lead eventually to a decentralized society consisting of a 'Commune of communes' replacing the centralized State.

Rooted in the old politics of the working-class movement and committed to the rationalist humanism of the Enlightenment, he eventually returned to the socialist sectarianism of his youth. He preferred the word 'communalism' to describe his position, by which he meant a libertarian ideology that includes 'the best of the anarchist tradition as well as the best in Marx'.[54] In 2004, he was even prepared to countenance government and laws in an ecological society: 'There can be no society without institutions, systems of governance and laws. The only issue is whether these structures and guidelines are authoritarian or libertarian, for they constitute the very forms of social existence.'[55] Before he died in 2006, Bookchin declared that he was no longer an anarchist. The man who had so effectively revitalized the anarchist tradition by linking it with ecology finally rejected anarchism as no longer relevant to creating a 'rational' society.

Social ecology did not die with Bookchin and still has its supporters. The British anthropologist Brian Morris, who is particularly inspired by Kropotkin's politics of community, sees 'Socialist Anarchism' as the 'only viable political tradition that complements ecology, and offers a genuine response to the social and ecological crisis that we now face'.[56] Many anarchists however have found Bookchin's opposition between 'life-style' anarchism and social anarchism both false and misleading. In his carefully argued *Beyond Bookchin* (1996), David Watson (aka George Bradford, who has been long associated with the journal *Fifth Estate*) sees the rational and technological version of social ecology espoused by Bookchin at an impasse. Although critical of some aspects of deep ecology, he accepts that primitivism offers a 'legitimate response to real conditions of life under civilization'.[57] While social ecology, liberated from Bookchin, can, like the anarchist ideal, serve as a general orientation, he believes we may also learn from our 'primordial kinship' with the phenomenal world and the wisdom of archaic civilizations. He has further made his views clear on empire and its enemies in *Against the Megamachine* (1998). In his book *Anarchy after Leftism* (1997) Bob Black dissected the philosophy of 'Dean Bookchin' only to conclude that he was not a true anarchist but part of the Old Left which needed to be left behind.

On a more philosophical level, John Clark continues to develop the libertarian potential of social ecology. In the eighties, he worked closely with Bookchin but the two eventually fell out. Having written studies of Godwin and Stirner, he was already arguing in his collected essays in *The Anarchist Moment* (1984) that anarchism offered 'both a strategy for human liberation and a plan for avoiding global ecological disaster'.[58] This already reflected the growing influence of the organic philosophy of Taoism and Buddhism as well as a deep concern for individual autonomy. For him 'personal growth' was not just a New Age fad; it takes place 'only through dialectical interaction within the self and others . . . the self can be as much a complex unity-in-diversity as are the community and nature'.[59]

As an academic philosopher, Clark began developing a form of social ecology which had room for Eastern as well as Western thought within the broader context of the anarchist tradition of social and political engagement. He found the thought of Elisée Reclus particularly inspiring.[60] When Bookchin learned that he took an interest in the insights and practices of deep ecology, it seemed an ominous involvement in the mystical. Clark broke away from Bookchin, refusing to be Engels to his Marx, and came to see him as an incoherent thinker who had lost touch with the anarchist tradition.[61] To his version of libertarian municipalism, Clark counterposed a form of 'ecocommunitarian' politics inspired by 'a vision of human communities achieving their fulfillment as an integral part of the larger, self-realizing earth community'.[62]

But while Clark came to see the inadequacy of Bookchin's Aristotelian way of thinking, he still continues to work within the tradition of social ecology in order to reinvigorate it and develop it in a more dialectical, spiritual and communal direction. He is also keen to promote a political movement based on small primary communities, including affinity groups, intentional communities and co-operatives, which he sees as playing a potentially significant liberatory role in society. Clearly social ecology is not the special reserve of Bookchin but a fertile land with open borders.

While educated in the Enlightenment and the Western humanist tradition, Clark's interest in Taoism, Zen, Surrealism and Situationism has led him to explore the realm of the magical and the imaginary. Delighting in paradox and verbal wit, he has written under the pseudonym of Max Cafard a *Surre(gion)alist Manifesto* (2003), which advocates local identity, rehabilitation of the land and bioregionalism while retaining a global outlook. Clark is deeply rooted in Louisiana and has been directly involved in the renovation work in New Orleans following hurricane Katrina, which wreaked so much devastation but has resulted in so many positive examples of anarchy in action.

Liberation Ecology

I myself, in an earlier edition of this book, gave a positive portrayal of Bookchin's attempt to bring together the insights of the anarchist tradition and ecology but have since become increasingly exasperated by his vituperative tone and his rejection of any other strand of anarchism which did not fit in with his increasingly narrow version of social ecology. His claim that there was an unbridgeable chasm between so-called 'life-style' anarchism and social anarchism seems both muddled and absurd.

I believe that the philosophical anarchism of William Godwin and the visionary anarchism of William Blake are not incompatible. To appreciate the imagination, the unconscious and the magical does not mean abandoning reason but accepting its inadequacy in certain areas of human experience and creativity. I have written about the imaginary and the magical as well as exploring the libertarian potential in Taoism and Buddhism. And I have investigated alternative ways of seeing the world and transforming oneself in the Hermetic tradition. And I have found inspiration for a peaceful and egalitarian society among the Neolithic megalith builders in Europe.

Having explored ecological thinking in *Nature's Web* (1992) from a libertarian perspective, I developed in *Riding the Wind* (1998) a new philosophy for the new millennium which I call 'liberation ecology'. It has been called a holistic adventure in love. Based on ancient wisdom and modern insights, it is holistic, deep, social and libertarian and seeks to free all beings from their burdens so that they can realize their full potential. It offers an environmental ethics based on reverence for the Being of beings and anarchistic solutions to work, education, economics and social arrangements. In my view, the golden age is neither behind nor ahead of us but within us and can be renewed at any time. We can transform ourselves and society here and now as well as work towards a more harmonious relationship with nature and a more egalitarian, free and sustainable future.

Anarchy in Action

There has not only been a new wave of anarchist thinking but a vibrant renewal of the anarchist movement. Indeed, the most creative energy for radical politics is now coming from anarchism with its libertarian spirit, tactic of direct action, decentralized and horizontal methods of organization and traditions of mutual aid and solidarity.[63]

As we have seen, most contemporary anarchists have given up the hope of large-scale revolution and armed insurrection and think in terms of protest and resistance. They are interested in creating practical experiments of anarchy in action in the present. Only a few still advocate 'class war' and 'bashing the rich': the Class War Federation in Britain, for instance, has gone into decline after a split in 1997. Alfredo Bonanno might call for armed insurrection and John Zerzan refuse to condemn the 'counter-terror' of the Unabomber, but they are distinctly minority voices.[64] As an Australian anarchist pamphlet puts it, *You Can't Blow Up a Social Relationship*.

Propaganda by the deed, guerrilla warfare and insurrection may still be contemplated by those living under dictatorships but seem hardly appropriate in representative democracies. Nevertheless, anarchists reject political representation in favour of direct and participatory democracy and have generally boycotted parliamentary elections. 'Don't Vote. It Only Encourages Them!' they say. 'What is the point of voting when the same old politicians always get in?' Bookchin however encouraged people to engage in municipal elections and John Clark has argued that in certain circumstances tactical voting may be beneficial if candidates are trying to educate rather than gain power, especially at local elections.

Propaganda by the word – raising awareness through education and persuasion – continues apace. Following in the tradition of Paul Goodman and Colin Ward, it advocates that anarchy is an existing tendency in society and the task of anarchists is to develop its potential in a web of free associations for the realization of human desires. They do not simply dream and do nothing but work in the realm of everyday life to expand freedom, equality and solidarity.

Contemporary anarchists also are involved in different forms of resistance and protest against globalization, capitalism and war. As the demonstrations at recent international meetings of governments and economic corporations have shown, tactics range from non-violent civil disobedience to direct action, such as squatting, sabotage, monkey-wrenching, urban climbing, defacing ads, reclaiming the streets, parties and the destruction of business property. Symbolic actions are intended to raise awareness and confidence, often taking the form of bearing witness (such as a vigil) or obstruction (as in marches or sit-downs). 'Critical mass' actions by small groups attempt to trigger off a sustained chain reaction among the wider populace. Carnival, festival, theatre and pranks are used to deconstruct the coercive forces of the State. A magical process of *détournement* overturns conventional ideas and misappropriates the images and symbols of the Society of the Spectacle. It helps to release individuals from their 'mind-forged manacles' (Blake) and the 'spooks' in their head (Stirner) in order to become more truly themselves.

These forms of protest and resistance not only challenge the authority of the State and the power of transnational corporations but reveal the empty charade of consumer society. By their very nature, they show a different way of doing things which is decentralized, democratic, egalitarian and fun. They are intended to demonstrate that the more you consume and gawp, the less you live, while the more you act and create, the more fulfilled and alive you become.

My own view is that any means employed inevitably influence the ends; indeed, means are ends-in-the-making. You cannot use violence against individuals as the principal means to bring about a peaceful society. You cannot use a secret elite to overthrow an elite without the danger of creating another one. You cannot use coercion to bring about a free society. You cannot force others to be free. Non-violent resistance, civil disobedience and direct action may be necessary sometimes against an oppressive tyranny, but the best way to bring about change is to persuade people openly of the benefits of a decentralized society without government through creative thought, imagination, action and example. When there are enough people who want to be free, then we shall have a free society. To try and impose by force an anarchist solution on society is against the whole tenor of anarchism, which seeks to end coercion and expand freedom. And confronted with the mad rationality of the Panopticon and Pentagon society, love is truly subversive.

Just as the notion of 'self-organization', partly inspired by new cybernetics, became popular in the seventies, so the more organic image of the 'rhizome', used by the French philosophers Gilles Deleuze and Felix Guattari, has caught on to delineate anarchist organization. In typically convoluted prose, they describe the concept as containing the principles of connection, heterogeneity and multiplicity: 'an acentred, non-hierarchical, non-signifying system without a General and without an organizing memory or central automation, defined solely by a circulation of states'.[65] In botany, the rhizome is a thick, horizontal underground stem of plants, the buds of which develop like irises or mint into new plants. The metaphor is particularly appropriate to describe the kind of libertarian grassroots, non-hierarchical, leaderless networks of groups and movements which have emerged in the international campaigns against globalization, capitalism and war. They are like nature's web itself, interconnected, diverse and fecund.

By working within the mainstream society, it is also possible to create a 'transfer culture', gradually building libertarian relationships of trust, support and co-operation in ever-widening and overlapping circles.[66] These networks are often made up of 'affinity groups', convivial gatherings of like-minded individuals, which are autonomous, fluid, flexible and responsive. They come and go according to need and desire. They can form loose clusters and confederations, and where necessary send delegates or 'spokes' to larger assemblies or 'spoke councils' to co-ordinate their thinking and action through a process of consensus decision-making. To facilitate this, highly effective procedures have been developed to accommodate minority views and to resolve conflicts of opinion.

No longer ready to work or wait for a post-revolutionary utopia in an imaginary future, many contemporary anarchists have taken up the anarcho-syndicalist idea of creating 'the new world in the shell of the old' by adopting a DIY approach. Better to do it yourself, they say, than be told what to do or do nothing. Such practical anarchy ranges from experiments in communal living, alternative economic systems and the development of libertarian institutions. These vary from LETS (Local Exchange and Trade Systems), co-ops, community centres to temporary autonomous zones and liminal spaces of transformation and passage. Groups like Critical Mass (originating in California) and Reclaim the Streets (first appearing in London) further try to reinhabit the over-regulated and constantly surveyed public spaces across Europe, Australasia and the Americas.

The Movement of Movements

Anarchism has emerged as one of the most influential and dynamic currents in the anti-globalization movement, not so much as capital-'A' anarchist groups as a network of small-'a' anarchist activists. Indeed, in many ways the soul of the movement is anarchist.[67] The term 'anti-globalization' describes a variety of groups which are all united in opposing the political and economic power of the multinational corporations and the free-trade agreements brokered by the leading industrial States which undermine local democracy, worsen labour conditions and harm the environment. Some however prefer to give it the more positive definition of Global

Justice Movement; others call it a movement of movements. Whatever the name, those involved wish to expose the mechanisms and machinations of corporate and State power and expand autonomous spaces within and outside their reaches.

The activists are anti-capital, anti-neoliberalism and anti-war; they are for human rights, biological and cultural diversity and the free movement of ideas and peoples across borders. They have no parties, no leaders and no centralized bureaucracy. Using the latest information technology, they organize and co-ordinate campaigns of direct action and civil disobedience across the globe. There can be no doubt that as a decentralized, leaderless network of self-organizing and autonomous groups, the international Global Justice Movement is very anarchistic. As Naomi Klein has observed, there is a general consensus that 'building community-based decision-making power – whether through unions, neighbourhoods, farms, villages, anarchist collectives or aboriginal self-government – is essential to countering the might of the multinational corporations'.[68]

Anarchists have been involved in the World Social Forums, first held in Porto Alegre in Brazil in 2001, with the slogan 'Another World is Possible', and in the first European Social Forum in Florence in 2002, which defined itself as 'Against the War, Against Racism, Against Neoliberalism'. They have been active in the international People's Global Action, founded in Geneva in 1998, which is an instrument for co-ordination, based on the principles of autonomy and decentralization, for those struggling against economic liberalization and corporate rule. A Direct Action Network of anarchist and anti-authoritarian affinity groups, autonomous and regional, was also set up to co-ordinate actions.

Not only does the organization of the Global Justice Movement reflect anarchist principles but anarchists have been prominently involved in a series of demonstrations at international summits of the most powerful and wealthy States and corporations. These have taken place in Seattle in 1999 (which shut down the meeting of the World Trade Organization), the IMF summit in Prague in 2000, the Genoa meeting of the G8 in 2001 (which led to the death of the Genoese anarchist Carlo Giuliani), the World Trade Forum in New York in 2002, the Anti-War demonstration in Washington DC in 2003, and the G8 summit in Rostock and Heiligendamm in 2007. The movement is generally committed to non-violent civil disobedience and direct action and attempts a carnivalesque disruption of order at the international gatherings.

Active in the movement is the organization Food not Bombs, started in Cambridge, Massachusetts, in the eighties and now with some 200 chapters all over the world. They are against war and poverty and for immigration and self-managing communities. The Love and Rage Anarchist Federation in North America firmly adopted in the nineties a 'Platformist' approach, inspired by the Russian Dielo Truda's *Organizational Platform of the General Union of Anarchists (Draft)* (1917), which emphasized the need for anarchists to organize themselves and adopt a common approach. They also took up the tactic of forming 'Black Blocs' at demonstrations which were first seen in the protests against the Gulf War in 1991.

Since Seattle, the Black Blocs have been joined by other anarchists, autonomists and anti-capitalist groups who are prepared to engage in vandalism and property destruction without wishing to harm human beings. The Black Bloc tactic developed out of the Autonomism movement in Germany, Holland, Italy and France in the eighties (influenced by the thinkers Antonio Negri and Cornelius Castoriadis), whose members wore black clothes and urged the working class to force changes outside the trade unions and the State. Despite their commitment to liberty and equality, their confrontational tactics have attracted media interest, *agents provocateurs* and police repression as well as resurrecting the popular but mistaken image of anarchism as violent and dangerous.

Other anarchists adopt a more playful form of cultural subversion. Ya Basta! (Enough Already) groups in the US and the Wombles (White Overalls Movement Building Libertarian Effective Struggles) in Britain have dressed up in white overalls for symbolic actions, taking their cue from the Tute Bianche (White Overalls) group in Italy and the Provos in Holland. Reclaim the Streets groups, which first appeared in Britain, arrange direct actions from mass cycling to street parties in order to re-inhabit public spaces. Acts of senseless beauty and absurd theatre, pink fairies and Michelin men have delighted and subverted the media and helped to raise awareness about the plight of those who most suffer from the effects of globalization, Capital and the State.

Anarchy around the World

Given the confines of space, this brief survey of recent developments in anarchism is somewhat Atlantic-centric, but it should not be forgotten that anarchism is a vibrant, world-wide movement. In Russia, a hard-hitting anarchist punk rock scene emerged in the eighties and nineties, more concerned with personal rebelliousness than class struggle. The New Revolutionary Alternative appeared however in 1991, carrying out a number of direct actions in protest against the Second Chechen War, attacking government buildings and military and police centres. The increasingly authoritarian government in Russia gives little room for opposition but anarchist-inspired groups include Autonomous Action, New Light and the Siberian Confederation of Labour. In the old Soviet Union, there is also a lively anarchist scene, more engaged in cultural subversion than class struggle, especially in the Czech Republic and Hungary.

On the eastern fringe of Europe, in Greece, there has been a strong interest in social ecology. A new wave of young anarchists emerged in the nineties, especially among school and university students, whose actions culminated in the violent police invasion of the Polytechnic of Athens in 1995. They were involved again in clashes with police in 2007 while protesting against government plans to privatize higher education. Some insurrectionists, known as 'Thieves in Black', have engaged in bank robberies, while in 2006 a group called 'Anti-Justice' let off a few symbolic bombs. In neighbouring Turkey, anarchists have published the magazine *Ates Hirsizi*, and offered a federal solution for Kurdistan. A translation of *Demanding the Impossible* has also appeared.

Travelling further east, the *Sarvodaya* movement, inspired by Gandhi, who called for an 'enlightened anarchy', is still active. In India, where it is often translated as 'Welfare for All', it has been working for the voluntary donation and redistribution of land and the development of a decentralized, self-managing society. In Sri Lanka, the Buddhist-inspired movement is known as 'Awakening for All' and has been involved in grassroots development and peace projects.

On the other hand, many countries in Asia have had severe restrictions on free speech and assembly although their authoritarian governments and dictatorships allow multinational corporations a free hand. Having experienced decades of brutal communist dictatorships and Marxist propaganda, the rallying cry of class war does not go down very well. Nevertheless, anarchist groups are active in Cambodia, the Philippines and in Indonesia (where the Jarkata Anarchist Resistance operates and where *Demanding the Impossible* is being translated).

Anarchism has played a very significant part in Korean history, a tradition kept alive today by the Korean Anarchist Network in the South. The week-long uprising in the South Korean town of Kwangju in 1980, during which neighbourhood assemblies were established, inspired other revolts against dictatorships in East Asia. Libertarian 'people-power revolutions' have helped overthrow dictatorships in the Philippines and in Indonesia. Despite the highly conformist and hierarchical structure of Japanese society, groups like Anarchy in Nippon are challenging the *status quo*. There is also a lively and creative anarchist movement in Australia, and to a lesser extent in New Zealand.

Libertarian impulses in China were given temporary and joyous expression in Tiananmen Square in 1989, especially by the Autonomous Beijing Group. After the tanks rolled in, the implacable censorship and brutal repression of the Chinese Communist Party have prevented an anarchist movement from surfacing, although a strong anarchist current is flowing in the underground labour and anti-dictatorship movements. The Falun Gong movement, based on the principles of truthfulness, compassion and forbearance, also offers a powerful challenge to the Chinese Communist State.

In Africa, most people have managed their lives communally outside or despite their corrupt and dictatorial governments. Indeed, many aspects of the traditional village are quite anarchistic, especially the reliance on consensus decision-making. The decentralized and participatory democracy of many ethnic groups – so-called tribes without rulers – are moreover an inspiration to the wider movement. At the same time, a self-conscious anarchist movement has developed in South Africa, Swaziland and Lesotho, where the Zabalaza Anarchist Communist Federation is active. Uganda has anarchist voices. Nigeria, the largest African nation, has a dynamic anarchist movement called the 'Awareness League'. Two of its members, Sam Mbah and I. E. Igariwey, have produced the first history of *African Anarchism* (1997). Even Nobel-prize winning writer Wole Soyinka has been linked to the cause.

In Central and South America, the Cuban government has so far failed to widen civil liberties, despite the efforts of the Cuban Libertarian Movement, which mainly works in exile. The Commission of Anarchist Relations in Venezuela has been struggling on two fronts, against the Hugo Chávez government as well as the US-backed opposition. On the other hand, the anarcha-feminists of the Mujeres Creando Collective have made a colourful impact in Bolivia, challenging traditional gender roles and poverty through imaginative direct and symbolic actions.

In South America, *Especifismo*, a concept developed by the Uruguayan Anarchist Federations (FAU), has been taken up by other federations in Brazil and Argentina. Partly inspired by Dielo Truda's 'Platformism', it calls for a specifically anarchist organization with clear objectives to serve as a guide to popular social movements. The Landless Workers' Movement in Brazil has had some success. The economic crisis in Argentina in the winter of 2001–2 saw anarchy in action when millions of citizens took to the streets for days, setting up neighbourhood assemblies and developing local alternative economic systems. Workers occupied their factories and many are still under their control. The popular slogan *Que se vayan todos* ('All of them should go') reflected not only frustration with corrupt politicians but with the principle of government itself.

Walking and Questioning

It is however the theory and tactics of the Zapatista movement in southern Mexico which have most caught the attention of anarchists. Named after the revolutionary Emiliano Zapata and partly inspired by the anarchist Ricardo Flores Magón, the Zapatista Army of National Liberation rose up in 1994 in the poor Chiapas province and demanded the right of the indigenous people in southern Mexico to be different and self-governing. While holding off the armed forces of the Mexican State, they have organized their lives in autonomous municipalities. These are made up of delegates who express the decisions of local assemblies open to all and with no hierarchy. They make 'laws', though those who break them are not imprisoned but are obliged to help their communities in some way. Ready to learn from their mistakes, they practise what they call *caminar preguntando* ('to walk while questioning'). Although they do not call themselves anarchists, they are democratic in many ways. The Zapatista movement has no fixed leadership, no executive body and no headquarters. Their charismatic spokesman known as Subcomandante Insurgente Marcos – probably the missing professor of philosophy Rafael Sebastián Guillén Vicente – playfully expresses Left-libertarian views. He likes to criticize himself and says he wears his mask as a 'vaccine against *caudillismo*', against the danger of becoming a boss.[69] Nevertheless, his self-promotion and courtship of the media seem close to creating a personality cult.

The example of the Zapatistas has inspired anti-globalization activists. At the International Encounter for Humanity and against Neoliberalism held in Chiapas in 1996, the participants issued the anarchistic declaration, read by Marcos, that it was 'not an organizing structure; it has no central head or decision maker; it has no central command or hierarchies. We are the network, all of us who resist.'[70] It is a far cry from the approach of the 'Supreme Chief' Castro or President Chávez. Ya Basta! groups supporting the Zapatistas have emerged around the world and been involved in setting up the People's Global Action. The Zapatista struggle for self-determination and resistance against economic dictatorship has been an inspiration throughout the world.

Dancing in the New Millennium

The anarchist sensibility, as I have argued, is much older than biblical or classical times and has existed ever since humans first evolved in Africa and spread across the world. Anarchy has flourished wherever they have rejected authority, hierarchy and domination. Left to themselves, humans have always managed their own affairs creatively and well. Indeed, for most of human evolution and history people have lived peaceful, co-operative lives without rulers, leaders, politicians, soldiers, policemen and taxmen.

Anarchism today is not only with us in remote areas of the globe outside the reach of the tentacles of the State but also in the free spaces within society which escape its heavy hand. Even in the harshest State environment, a free society exists in embryo ready to break through the shell of the old. Anarchist and libertarian ideas are no longer dormant seeds in the desert, dreaming for life-giving rain. The period of hibernation is over. New shoots are growing up everywhere, all over the world, not only in the crevices and cracks of centralized States, but in expanding enclaves of freedom. Appearing and disappearing like the sun behind clouds, anarchism reveals itself in the most common aspects of everyday life. Just as the world is turning green, so people, especially the young, are acting in an anarchistic way, often without being aware of it.

In most countries, it is now accepted that the onus is on authoritarians to justify their assertions of authority, rather than on libertarians to defend the principle of freedom. It is increasingly recognized that freedom is the mother and not the daughter of order. It is not the honest advocate of freedom who would turn the world upside down, but the brazen juggler of imposed authority and naked power. Freedom is like water: it cannot be contained and wears away the hardest rock.

In these circumstances, anarchism is even more relevant today than in the early nineties when *Demanding the Impossible* was first published. It is still realistic to demand the impossible; indeed, it is more urgent than ever if we are to survive the ecological crisis and reverse the growing injustice and inequality in the world. We need to imagine and realize an alternative future and social reality, one based on autonomy, individuality, community, solidarity and a deep concern for the natural world.

When it comes to choosing between different currents of anarchism, it need not be a question of either/or. They are not mutually exclusive and all flow in the great river of freedom. Like Malatesta, Reclus and Voltairine de Cleyre more than a century ago, I advocate 'anarchism without adjectives', anarchism which embraces rather than spurns, which encourages mutual tolerance between different strands and schools. It does not try to impose a common economic system: mutualism can evolve into collectivism, which in turn can develop into voluntary communism. As in republican Spain during the Civil War, land can be held in common while at the same time allowing some to work their own plots. Individualism and community, no more than liberty and equality, are not necessarily opposed. Individualism can be supported by community just as every person should have the equal claim to be free. Indeed, the ideal would be a form of communal individuality in which the maximum degree of individuality is encouraged compatible with social solidarity. The health of an anarchist society might then be judged by the number of so-called 'parasites' it could support and the degree of diversity, individuality and eccentricity it could tolerate.

You can be an individualist on your own or join up with other individualists, forming what Stirner called 'a union of conscious egoists'. You can be a social anarchist who values both her autonomy and individuality. So-called 'life-style' anarchism is not necessarily opposed to anarcho-syndicalism, self-management or libertarian municipalism. You can adopt an anarchist life style, challenge authority and domination in the workplace, participate in unions striving for better and freer conditions, and at the same time defend the wilderness and other species and enjoy the sensuality and adventure of the natural world.

You can run free in the woods (where they still exist), dive into the sea (where it is not polluted) as well as link up with neighbours and friends in affinity groups where you live and love. You can be rooted in your own bioregion, promoting its diversity and well-being. You can create horizontal webs of co-operation to replace pyramids of power. You can become involved in alternative networks of communication which have no central control. You can undermine and dissolve coercive power, whether it be in yourself, at home, in the streets, in the workplace, or in the institutions of the State. You can challenge the mechanical reason which leads to the Panopticon and the Pentagon and celebrate the imagination, intuition, the playful, the magical, the marvellous, the wild and the free. You can transform yourself and the world around you. No one path is paramount: there are many different ways up a mountain.

The threats to human freedom and equality are local and global; the response cannot fail to be interconnected. The organized warfare of modern States, the ruthless exploitation of transnational corporations and the blind hatred of religious fundamentalists can be subverted by an ethos of universal love, justice and reverence for all life. There is no need to despair or feel powerless, for as the 'velvet revolutions' in the former Soviet bloc, the self-managing citizens of Argentina and the Zapatista peasants of Chiapas in Mexico have shown, if enough people do not accept those in power they cannot stay there for long.

In the meantime, we can challenge and dissolve relations of power and domination. We can form convivial affinity groups, develop libertarian communities and co-operatives, create permanent as well as temporary autonomous zones within the fissures of authoritarian society. We can develop grassroots, participatory institutions. Depending on how it is used, the Internet can also create networks of like-minded people all over the world sharing their experiences and knowledge and organizing protest and resistance.

This history of anarchist thought and action demonstrates that anarchism constantly reinvents itself in new guises according to changing conditions and has flourished at different times at a local and national level. Many experiments were short-lived and often in times of social dislocation, but the fact they took place at all shows that they are part of the creative experience of humanity. If it has happened on a small scale in the past, it can take place on a larger scale in the future. If the free citizens of Athens could set up a form of direct and participatory democracy two and a half thousand years ago, then with all our subsequent experience the creation of a free and ecological society is well within the realm of possibility. It is realistic to demand what others find impossible.

In one sense, anarchism is utopian in that it imagines the world as it could be. But it is also realistic in that it conserves and develops ancient traditions of self-help and mutual aid and profound libertarian tendencies within society. Above all, anarchism addresses itself to *homo ludens* (playful humanity) along with *homo faber* or *homo sapiens* (working or thinking humanity). Emma Goldman allegedly once said: 'If I can't dance, it's not my revolution.' I would add, if there be no joy, imagination, spontaneity, conviviality and fun, it isn't my free society.

REFERENCE NOTES

Place of publication is London, unless otherwise specified; n.d. indicates that no date of publication was given on the copyright page of the book referred to.

Introduction

1 See *Roget's Thesaurus* (Harmondsworth: Penguin, 1965), p.165
2 Quoted in James D. Forman, *Anarchism: Political Innocence or Social Violence* (New York: Watts, 1975), p. 4
3 William Butler Yeats, 'The Second Coming', *Collected Poems of W. B. Yeats* (Macmillan, 1950), p. 211
4 John Locke, 'An Essay concerning the True Original, Extent and End of Civil Government' (1690), *Of Civil Government, Two Treatises* (Dent, 1936), pp. 118, 126 (Bk. II, para. 4, 19)
5 George Woodcock, *Anarchism: A History of Libertarian Ideas and Movements* (1962) (Harmondsworth: Penguin, 1983), p. 450
6 James Joll, *The Anarchists* (1964), (2nd edn.: Methuen, 1979), p. ix; Irving L. Horowitz, ed., *The Anarchists* (New York: Dell, 1964), p. 588
7 See Daniel Guérin, 'Postscript: May 1968', *Anarchism: From Theory to Practice* (1965) (New York: Monthly Review Press, 1970), p. 156
8 Joll, *The Anarchists*, op. cit., p. 262; see also his 'Anarchism – a Living Tradition', *Anarchism Today*, eds. David E. Apter & James Joll (Macmillan, 1971), pp. 212–25
9 Woodcock, *The Anarchist Reader* (Fontana, 1977), p. 55; see also his Preface to the Second Edition of *Anarchism*, op. cit., pp. 7–8

10 See David Miller, *Anarchism* (Dent, 1984)
11 Peter Kropotkin, 'Anarchism', *Encyclopaedia Britannica* (1910), reprinted in *Anarchism and Anarchist Communism*, ed. Nicolas Walter (Freedom Press, 1987), p. 10.
12 See Murray Bookchin, *The Ecology of Freedom: The Emergence and Dissolution of Hierarchy* (Palo Alto: Cheshire Books, 1982), ch. vii
13 For other anarchists writers, see Michael Scrivener, 'The Anarchist Aesthetic', *Black Rose*, I, 1 (1979), 7–21
14 See V. I. Lenin, *'Left-Wing' Communism, An Infantile Disorder* (1920)

Chapter One

1 Peter Kropotkin, *The State: Its Historic Role* (1897) trans. Vernon Richards (Freedom Press, 1969), p. 55
2 *The Anarchist Writings of William Godwin*, ed. with introd. Peter Marshall (Freedom Press, 1986), p. 92
3 *Selected Writings of Pierre-Joseph Proudhon*, ed. Stewart Edwards (Macmillan, 1970), p. 89
4 Michael Bakunin, *Oeuvres*, ed. J. Guillaume (Paris: P.V. Stock, 1910), IV, 252
5 Bart de Ligt, *The Conquest of Violence:*

An Essay on War and Revolution, trans. Honor Tracey, introd. Aldous Huxley (Routledge, 1937), p. 75

6 Rudolf Rocker, *Anarcho-syndicalism* (Secker & Warburg, 1938), p. 89

Chapter Two

1 See Ernest Barker, *Principles of Social and Political Theory* (Oxford University Press, 1967), p. 3

2 Thomas Paine, *Common Sense*, ed. Isaac Kramnick (Harmondsworth: Penguin, 1976), p. 65

3 Guérin, *Anarchism*, op. cit., p. 13

4 Godwin, *Anarchist Writings*, op. cit., pp. 89, 50

5 See Taylor, *Community, Anarchy and Liberty*, op. cit., pp. 6–10; Ward, 'Harmony through Complexity', *Anarchy in Action*, op. cit., pp. 44–52; John Pilgrim, 'Anarchism and stateless societies', *Anarchy*, 58 (December 1965), 353–68; 'Primitive Societies and Social Myths', *A Decade of Anarchy 1961–70*, ed. Colin Ward (Freedom Press, 1987), pp. 59–71; Harold Barclay, *People Without Government: An Anthropology of Anarchism* (Kahn & Averill, 1982); and John Middleton & David Tait, eds., *Tribes without Rulers* (Routledge & Kegan Paul, 1958)

6 Proudhon, quoted in Rocker, *Nationalism and Culture* (Freedom Press, c.1947), p. 231

7 Sébastien Faure, *La Douleur universelle, la philosophie libertaire* (Paris: Savine, 1895), p. 217

8 *Chuang Tzu*, trans. Herbert A. Giles (1889) (Allen & Unwin, 1980), pp. 98–9

9 *Anarchist Reader*, op. cit., p. 16

10 See Arthur O. Lovejoy, *The Great Chain of Being* (1936) (Cambridge, Mass.: Harvard University Press, 1971), pp. 196–7

11 Proudhon, *Selected Writings*, op. cit., p. 249

12 *Bakunin on Anarchy*, op. cit., p. 271

13 *Errico Malatesta; His Life and ideas*, ed. Vernon Richards (Freedom Press,

1977) pp. 267, 277

14 See my article, 'The Natural Order of Anarchy', *The New Internationalist* (February 1979), pp. 20–1; and Ward, 'The Theory of Spontaneous Order', *Anarchy in Action*, op. cit., pp. 28–38

15 See April Carter, *The Political Theory of Anarchism* (Routledge & Kegan Paul, 1971), pp. 78–9

16 Kropotkin, *The State*, op. cit., p. 31

17 Godwin, *Anarchist Writings*, op. cit., p. 89; Kropotkin, *Anarchism and Anarchist Communism*, op. cit., p. 9

18 Benjamin R. Tucker, *Instead of a Book* (New York: B. R. Rucker, 1899), pp. 21–3

19 Godwin, *Anarchist Writings*, op. cit., p. 90

20 Max Stirner, *The Ego & Its Own*, trans. Steven T. Byington (1907), in *Anarchist Reader*, op. cit., p. 240

21 Proudhon, *Selected Writings*, op. cit., pp. 89, 110

22 Proudhon, *General Idea of the Revolution in the Nineteenth Century* (1851), quoted in Guérin, *Anarchism*, op. cit., pp. 15–16

23 Bakunin, ibid., p. 61

24 Malatesta, *Anarchy* (Freedom Press, 1974), pp. 13–14

25 *Kropotkin's Revolutionary Pamphlets*, ed. Roger N. Baldwin (1927), reprinted (New York: Benjamin Blom, 1968), pp. 46, 284

26 Kropotkin, *The State*, op. cit., pp. 10, 52

27 Gustav Landauer, quoted in Martin Buber, *Paths in Utopia* (Boston: Beacon Press, 1958), p. 46

28 Bookchin, *Ecology of Freedom*, op. cit., pp. 94, 124

29 L. T. Hobhouse, *Liberalism* (Williams & Norgate, n.d.), pp. 146–7

30 Kropotkin, *Paroles d'un révolté* (Paris: Marponet Flammarion, 1885), p. 34

31 Godwin, *Anarchist Writings*, op. cit., p. 114

32 Lysander Spooner, *No Treason* (1870), quoted in Miller, *Anarchism*, op. cit., pp. 37–8

33 Proudhon, quoted in *Anarchist Reader*, op. cit., p. 111

34 Bakunin, ibid., p. 109
35 Nicolas Walter, *About Anarchism* (Freedom Press, 1969), p. 10
36 Woodcock, 'Tradition and Revolution', *The Raven*, II, 2 (1988), p. 104
37 Engels, 'The Origin of the Family, Private Property and the State', Marx & Engels, *Selected Works* (Lawrence & Wishart, 1968), p. 589
38 Marx & Engels, *The Communist Manifesto*, ed. A. J. P. Taylor (Harmondsworth: Penguin, 1967), p. 105
39 Quoted by Lenin, *The State and Revolution* (1917) (Peking, 1965), p. 19
40 Engels, 'On the Occasion of Karl Marx's Death', *Anarchism and Anarcho-syndicalism: Selected Writings by Marx, Engels*, ed. N. Y. Kolpinsky (New York: International Publishers, 1972), pp. 171–3
41 Lenin, *The Tasks of the Proletariat in our Revolution*, quoted in Alexander Gray, *The Socialist Tradition*, op. cit., p. 469
42 Robert Conquest, *Lenin* (Fontana, 1972), p. 85
43 Lenin, *The State and Revolution*, op. cit., p. 124
44 Marx, 'Instructions', *The First International and After*, ed. David Fernbach (Harmondsworth: Penguin, 1974), p. 89
45 Marx to Paul Lafargue, 19 April 1870, Marx, Engels & Lenin *Anarchism and Anarcho-syndicalism*, op. cit., p. 46
46 Marx, 'Conspectus of Bakunin's *Statism and Anarchy*' in *The First International and After*, op. cit., p. 334
47 Paul Thomas, *Karl Marx and the Anarchists*, (Routledge & Kegan Paul, 1980) p. 351
48 Lenin, *The State and Revolution*, op. cit., pp. 63, 71
49 See Conquest, *Lenin*, op. cit., p. 86
50 Lenin, *'Left-Wing' Communism, An Infantile Disorder* (1920) (Peking, 1965), pp. 16–17, 94
51 Lenin, *The State* (1929) (Peking, 1965), pp. 24–5

52 See Barker, *Principles of Social and Political Theory*, op. cit., p. 227
53 Tolstoy, 'The Slavery of our Times', *Anarchist Reader*, op. cit., p. 118
54 Tolstoy, 'Patriotism and Government', *The Works of Leo Tolstoy*, trans. Aylmer Maude (Henry Frowde, 1904), XLVI, 1, p. 250
55 Jean Grave, *L'Anarchie, son but, ses moyens* (Paris: Stock, 1899), p. 3. For a discussion, see Thom Holterman & Henevan Maarsween, *Law and Anarchism* (Montréal: Black Rose, 1984)
56 Godwin, *Anarchist Writings*, op. cit., pp. 94, 98
57 Ibid., pp. 79, 95
58 Kropotkin, 'Law and Authority', *Revolutionary Pamphlets*, op. cit., p. 205
59 Kropotkin, *In Russian and French Prisons* (1887), in *Anarchist Reader*, op. cit., p. 363
60 Ibid., p. 124
61 Kropotkin, 'Law and Authority', in *Anarchist Reader*, op. cit., p. 116. See also C. Cahm, 'Kropotkin and Law', *Anarchism and Law*, op. cit., pp. 119–40
62 Stirner, *The Ego and Its Own*, op. cit., p. 91
63 See Geoffrey Ostergaard, 'Resisting the Nation-State: the Pacifist and Anarchist Traditions', *The Nation-State: The Formation of Modern Politics*, ed. Leonard Tivey (Oxford: Martin Robertson, 1981), pp. 171–95
64 Godwin, *Anarchist Writings*, op. cit., pp. 107, 164
65 Tolstoy, 'Patriotism and Government', op cit., p. 252
66 Proudhon, quoted in Guérin, *Anarchism*, op. cit., p. 68
67 Bakunin, ibid.
68 Bakunin, quoted in *Socialism and Nationalism*, eds. E. Cahm & V. C. Fisera (Nottingham: Spokesman, 1978), p. 42
69 *The Political Philosophy of Bakunin: Scientific Anarchism*, ed. G. P.

Maximoff (New York: Free Press, 1953), Part Two, chs. x – xi

70 Bakunin, quoted in Guérin, *Anarchism*, op. cit., pp. 6–7

71 Rudolf Rocker, *Nationalism and Culture*, op. cit., pp. 200–1

72 Gustav Landauer, quoted in Ward, *Anarchy in Action*, op. cit., p. 11

73 Landauer, quoted by Buber, *Paths in Utopia*, op. cit., p. 49

Chapter Three

1 Sébastien Faure, 'Anarchie', *Encylopédie anarchiste* (Paris, n.d.). Cf. Anthony Arblaster, 'The Relevance of Anarchism', *The Socialist Register* (1971), p. 198

2 Herbert Read, 'Chains of Freedom', *Anarchy & Order*, op. cit., p. 164

3 Quoted in Kenneth Rexroth, *Communalism: From its Origins to the Twentieth Century* (New York: Seabury Press, 1974), p. 236

4 For the distinction between negative and positive freedom, see Isaiah Berlin, *Two Concepts of Liberty* (Oxford: Clarendon Press, 1958). Paul Thomas errs in thinking that anarchists are chiefly concerned with the negative view of liberty. See his *Karl Marx and the Anarchists*, op. cit., p. 8.

5 See Gerald C. MacCalham, Jr., 'Negative and Positive Freedom', *Contemporary Political Theory*, ed. Anthony de Crespigny & Alan Wertheimer (Nelson, 1971), pp. 107–26

6 Bakunin, 'Revolutionary Catechism' (1866), *Bakunin on Anarchy*, ed. Sam Dolgoff (Allen & Unwin, 1973), pp. 76, 261

7 Read, *Anarchy & Order*, op. cit., p. 23

8 Sébastien Faure, *Autorité et liberté* (Paris: Aux Bureaux de la Révolte, 1891), no folios.

9 Elisée Reclus, *L'Evolution, la révolution, et l'idéal anarchiste* (Paris: Stock, 1896), p. 143

10 Godwin, *Anarchist Writings*, op. cit., p. 158

11 *Bakunin on Anarchy*, op. cit., p. 257

12 Fyodor Dostoevsky, *Notes from Underground*, trans. Jessie Coulson (Harmondsworth: Penguin, 1977), pp. 33–4

13 Malatesta, *Life and Ideas*, op. cit., p. 24

14 Ibid., p. 53

15 Benjamin R. Tucker, *Instead of a Book. By a Man Too Busy to Write One. A Fragmentary Exposition of Philosophical Anarchism culled from the Writings of Benjamin R. Tucker, editor of Liberty*, 2nd edn. (New York: Benj. R. Tucker, 1897), p. 15

16 Ibid., p. 13

17 Jean-Jacques Rousseau, *The Social Contract and Discourses*, ed. G. D. H. Cole (Dent, 1973), p. 177

18 See Emma Goldman, *Anarchism and Other Essays*, op. cit., p. 194; *Red Emma Speaks*, ed. Alix Kates Shulman (Wildwood House, 1979), p. 354

19 Godwin, *Anarchist Writings*, op. cit., p. 65

20 Bakunin, *Marxism, Freedom and the State*, ed. K.J. Kenafick (Freedom Press, 1984), p. 17

21 Malatesta, *Life and Ideas*, op. cit., p. 23

22 Franz Kafka, *The Castle* (1926) trans. Willa & Edwin Muir (Harmondsworth: Penguin, 1966), p. 105

23 Malatesta, *Life and Ideas*, op. cit., p. 48

24 Godwin, *Anarchist Writings*, op. cit., p. 159.

25 Alan Ritter, *Anarchism: A Theoretical Analysis* (Cambridge University Press, 1980), pp. 3, 24, 38

26 Godwin, *Anarchist Writings*, op. cit., pp. 77, 171

27 Quoted in Ritter, *Anarchism*, op. cit., p. 27

28 Malatesta, *Life and Ideas*, op. cit., pp. 25, 87

29 Randolph Bourne, 'The State' (1919), quoted in *Anarchist Reader*, op. cit., p. 101

30 Eric Fromm, *The Fear of Freedom* (Routledge & Kegan Paul, 1960), p. 28

31 Wilhelm Reich, *The Function of the*

Orgasm (New York: Noonday Press, 1942), Introduction

32 Malatesta, *Life and Ideas*, op. cit., p. 47

33 Murray Bookchin, 'Thinking Ecologically: A Dialectical Approach', *Our Generation*, 18, 2 (March 1987), p. 36

34 Woodcock, *Anarchism* (1st edn.), op. cit., p. 7. Cf. Gerald Runkle, *Anarchism Old and New* (New York: Delta, 1972), p. 3

35 *Bakunin on Anarchy*, op. cit., p. 77; Kropotkin, 'Anarchism: Its Philosophy and Ideal', *Revolutionary Pamphlets*, op. cit., p. 137

36 Malatesta, *Life and Ideas*, op. cit., p. 20

37 Ward, *Anarchy in Action*, op. cit., p. 11

38 See Michael Taylor, *Community, Anarchy and Liberty* (Cambridge University Press, 1982), p. 24

39 Robert Paul Wolff, *In Defense of Anarchism* (New York: Harper Colophon Books, 1976), p. 18

40 Max Weber, *Economy and Society*, eds. G. Roth & C. Wittick (New York: Bedminster Press, 1968), I, 215

41 Faure, *Autorité et liberté*, op. cit., no folios; see also Jean Grave, *La Société mourante et l'anarchie* (Paris: Stock, 1893), p. 8

42 William McKercher, *Libertarian Thought in the Nineteenth Century* (Garland Press, 1987), pp. vi – vii

43 Richard De George, 'Anarchism and Authority', *Anarchism* (reprint of *Nomos*, XIX) (New York University Press, 1978), p. 101

44 Godwin, *An Enquiry concerning Political Justice* (G. G. Robinson, 1793), II, 565

45 Bakunin, *Oeuvres*, op. cit., III, 69n

46 Giovanni Baldelli, *Social Anarchism* (Harmondsworth: Penguin, 1971), p. 93

47 David Wieck, 'The Negativity of Anarchism', *Reinventing Anarchy*, op. cit., p. 140

48 Ritter, 'The Anarchist Justification of Authority', *Nomos*, XIX, op. cit., p. 138

49 Miller, *Anarchism*, op. cit., p. 57

50 Godwin, *Political Justice* (1793 edn.), op. cit., II, 708

51 Taylor, *Community, Anarchy, and Liberty*, op. cit., p. 23

52 Ritter, 'The Anarchist Justification of Authority', op. cit., p. 138

53 Bertrand Russell, *Power: A New Social Analysis* (Basic Books, 1940), p. 35

54 Alex Comfort, *Authority and Delinquency in the Modern State* (Routledge & Kegan Paul, 1950), p. 75

55 See Bookchin, 'The Power to Create, The Power to Destroy', *Toward an Ecological Society* (Montréal & Buffalo: Black Rose Books, 1980), ch. 1

56 Tucker, *Instead of a Book*, op. cit., p. 59

57 See Paul Goodman, *People or Personnel: Decentralizing and the Mixed System* (New York: Random House, 1965), pp. 175–89

58 Alfred Adler, *Understanding Human Nature*, quoted in Russell, *Power*, op. cit., p. 17

59 Kropotkin, *Mutual Aid: A Factor of Evolution* (Harmondsworth: Penguin, 1939), p. 233

60 Malatesta, *Life and Ideas*, op. cit., pp. 35, 267

61 See Bookchin, *The Ecology of Freedom*, op. cit.

62 John Clark, *The Anarchist Moment* (Montréal: Black Rose Books, 1984), p. 15

63 See Taylor, *Liberty, Anarchy and Community*, op. cit., pp. 80–1

64 Quoted in George Woodcock, *Pierre-Joseph Proudhon: A Biographical Study* (Routledge & Kegan Paul, 1956), p. 34

65 Tucker, *Instead of a Book*, op. cit., p. 347

66 Bakunin, 'Revolutionary Catechism', *Bakunin on Anarchy*, op. cit., p. 76

67 Malatesta, *Life and Ideas*, op. cit., p. 49

68 John Rawls, 'Justice as Fairness', *Contemporary Political Theory*, op. cit., p. 193

69 Tucker, *Instead of a Book*, op. cit., p. 132

Chapter Four

1 See John Clark, 'Master Lao and the Anarchist Prince', *The Anarchist Moment*, op. cit., p. 165. Reprinted from the symposium on Taoism and anarchism in *Journal of Chinese Philosophy* 10 (1983). The consensus of all the contributors is that Taoism offers a workable form of anarchism.

2 Lao Tzu, *Tao te ching*, trans. Gia-Fu Feng & Jane English (New York: Vintage, 1972), ch. 1 (*hereafter the chapters are referred to in brackets after each quotation in the text*)

3 Joseph Needham, *Science and Civilization in China* (Cambridge University Press, 1956), II, 35

4 Ibid., II, 37

5 Roger T. Ames, 'Is Political Taoism Anarchism?', *Journal of Chinese Philosophy*, op. cit., p. 34

6 Cf. Needham, *Science and Civilization in China*, op. cit., II, 70

7 Ames, 'Is Political Taoism Anarchism?', op. cit., p. 35

8 Bookchin, 'Thinking Ecologically', op. cit., pp. 8–9

9 Cf. Clark, 'Master Lao and the Anarchist Prince', op. cit., p. 186; Brian Morris, 'Lao Tzu and Anarchism', *Freedom Anarchist Review*, 42, 17 (22 August 1981), p. 14

10 *Chuang Tzu*, trans. H. A. Giles (Unwin, 1980), pp. 98–9

11 Ibid., p. 87

12 Ibid., p. 106

13 Quoted in Ames, 'Is Political Taoism Anarchism', op. cit., p. 36

14 *Chuang Tzu*, op. cit., pp. 255–6

15 Gary Snyder, 'Buddhist Anarchism', first printed in the *Journal for the Protection of All Beings*, ed. Lawrence Ferlinghetti. In a revised version of the essay called 'Buddhism and the Coming Revolution', reprinted in *Earth House Hold* (New York: New Directions, 1969), Snyder drops the reference to anarchism.

16 Christmas Humphreys, *Buddhism* (Harmondsworth: Penguin, 1971), p. 75

17 Snyder, 'Passage to More than India', *Earth House Hold*, op. cit., p. 105

18 John Clark, correspondence with the author

19 Humphreys, *Buddhism*, op. cit., p. 179

20 D.T. Suzuki, *Essays in Zen Buddhism*, First Series (1949), p. 111

21 *Zen Buddhism: Selected Writings of D. T. Suzuki*, ed. William Barrett (New York: Anchor, 1956), p. 9

22 Humphreys, *Buddhism*, op. cit., p. 76

23 *Zen Flesh, Zen Bones*, compiled by Paul Reps (Harmondsworth: Penguin, 1986), p. 39

24 *The Sutra of Wei Lang* (Hui-neng), quoted in Humphreys, *Buddhism*, op. cit., p. 183

25 Ibid., p. 186

26 *Zen Flesh, Zen Bones*, op. cit., pp. 75, 54

27 See ibid., pp. 40–1

28 Quoted in Suzuki, *Zen Buddhism*, op. cit., p. 118

29 *A Source Book in Chinese Philosophy* (Princeton, NJ: Princeton University Press, 1963) p. 447

30 *Zen Flesh, Zen Bones*, op. cit., p. 128

31 Ibid., p. 63

32 Suzuki, *Zen Buddhism*, op. cit., p. 258

Chapter Five

1 Sophocles, *Antigone* (*c.*441 BC), in *Seven Famous Greek Plays*, eds. W. J. Oates & E. O'Neil, Jr. (New York: Modern Library, 1950), p. 202. For Antigone as an anarchist heroine, see Henry Nevinson, 'An Anarchist Play', *Essays in Freedom* (Duckworth, 1911), pp. 209–14

2 *Heraclitus: The Cosmic Fragments*, ed. G. S. Kirk (Cambridge University Press, 1970), p. 105.

3 Ibid., p. 307

4 Quoted in Bertrand Russell, *History of Western Philosophy* (George Allen & Unwin, 1962), p. 60

5 Quoted in J. B. Bury, *A History of Freedom of Thought* (Williams & Norgate, 1920), p. 34

6 See D. Ferraro, 'Anarchism in Greek

Philosophy', *Anarchy*, 45 (November 1964), pp. 322–3

7 Quoted in Russell, op. cit., p. 241

8 See D. Novak, 'The Place of Anarchism in the History of Political Thought', *The Review of Politics*, 20, 3 (July 1958), 308; Alexander Gray, *The Socialist Tradition* (Longmans, 1963), pp. 28–9

9 Kropotkin, *Anarchism*, op. cit., p. 10

10 Diogenes Laertius, *Lives of Eminent Philosophers*, trans. R. D. Hicks (Loeb Classical Library, 1925), II, 195

11 Ibid., II, 225–9

12 Ibid.

13 Thucydides, *History of the Peloponnesian War*, trans. Rex Warner (Harmondsworth: Penguin, 1954), pp. 117–19

14 A. H. M. Jones, *Athenian Democracy* (Oxford: Blackwell, 1957), p. 132

15 See Bookchin, *Ecology of Freedom*, op. cit., p. 132

16 Thucydides, *History of the Peloponnesian War*, op. cit.; quoted in Bookchin, ibid., p. 130

17 See Martin Small, 'Athenian Democracy', *Anarchy*, 45 (November 1964), p. 343

Chapter Six

1 See Bookchin, *Ecology of Freedom*, op. cit., p. 195

2 Jacques Ellul, 'Anarchism and Christianity', *Katallagete*, 7, 3 (1980), 14–24

3 See Kenneth Rexroth, *Communalism: From its Origins to the Twentieth Century*, op. cit., p. 25

4 Gray, *The Socialist Tradition*, op. cit., pp. 35–8

5 St Ambrose, *The Duties of the Clergy*, Book 1, ch. 28

6 See Franz Neumann, *The Democratic and Authoritarian State* (New York: The Free Press of Glencoe, 1957), p. 6

7 *St Francis of Assisi. His Life and Writings as Recorded by His Contemporaries*, trans.

L. Sherley-Price (A. R. Mowbray, 1959), p. 145

8 William Blake *Complete Writings*, ed. Geoffrey Keynes (Oxford University Press, 1974). pp. 689. 402, 400, 600, 158, 151, 393, 401; see also my *William Blake: Visionary Anarchist* (Freedom Press, 1988), pp. 34–42

9 Blake, *Complete Writings*, op. cit., pp. 615, 158, 395, 879, 413

10 Godwin, *Sketches of History*, in *Six Sermons* (T. Cadell, 1784), pp. 5, 20

11 See my *William Godwin* (New Haven & London: Yale University Press, 1984), pp. 26–8

12 Proudhon, *Selected Writings*, op. cit., pp. 156, 223, 221

13 Stirner, *The Ego and Its Own*, op. cit., p. 239

14 Bakunin, *God and the State* in *The Essential Works of Anarchism*, ed. Marshall S. Shatz (New York: Bantam, 1971), pp. 135

15 Ibid., pp. 136, 138

16 Bakunin, *Oeuvres* (1910), IV, quoted in *Anarchist Reader*, op. cit., p. 88

17 Adin Ballou, *Non Resistance and Government* (1839), in *Patterns of Anarchy*, eds. Leonard I. Krimerman & Lewis Perry (New York: Anchor, 1966), pp. 141, 143, 148–9

18 Tolstoy, *A Confession. The Gospel in Brief, and What I Believe*, trans. Aylmer Maude (Oxford University Press, 1974), pp. 531–2

19 Tolstoy, *Patriotism and Government*, *Works*, op. cit., XLVI, 1, 261

20 Ammon Hennacy, *Autobiography of a Catholic Anarchist* (New York: Catholic Worker Books, 1954), p. 128

21 Dorothy Day, *The Long Loneliness* (New York: Harper & Row, 1952), p. 286

22 Hennacy, *Autobiography of a Catholic Anarchist*, op. cit., p. 130

23 Ibid., pp. 365, 368

24 Ibid., preface

25 Nicholas Berdyaev, *Slavery and Freedom*, trans. E. M. French (Geoffrey Bles, 1943), in *Patterns*

of Anarchy, op. cit., pp. 155, 159, 153

26 Berdyaev, quoted in Ellul, 'Anarchism and Christianity', op. cit., p. 22

27 Berdyaev, *Slavery and Freedom*, in *Patterns of Anarchy*, op. cit., p. 152

28 Ibid., p. 160

29 Ciaron O'Reilly, 'The Anarchist Implication of Christian Discipleship', *Social Alternatives*, II, 3 (1982), 11

Chapter Seven

1 See Ahmad Amin, *The Dawn of Islam* (Beirut, 1969). Translated for me by Bargas Hatem.

2 See Norman Cohn, *The Pursuit of the Millennium: Revolutionary Millenarians and Mystical Anarchists of the Middle Ages* (Paladin, 1984), p. 148

3 Ibid., p. 177

4 Ibid., p. 178

5 Ibid., p. 179

6 Ibid., p. 183

7 Ibid., pp. 184, 185

8 See George H. Williams, *The Radical Reformation* (Weidenfeld & Nicolson, 1962), p. 61

9 Quoted in *A Radical Reader: The struggle for Change in England, 1381–1914*, ed, Christopher Hampton (Penguin, 1984), p. 51

10 Ibid., p. 62

11 Quoted in Rexroth, *Communalism*, op. cit., p. 69

12 Quoted in Cohn, *The Pursuit of the Millennium*, op. cit., p. 215

13 See Rexroth, *Communalism*, op. cit., p. 86

14 Ibid., p. 91

15 Quoted in Cohn, *The Pursuit of the Millennium*, op. cit., p. 215

16 Peter Chelčický, *The Net of Faith*, trans. into German by Carl Vogl (Munich, 1925), p. 145, quoted in Rudolf Rocker, *Nationalism and Culture*, op. cit., p. 109

17 Rocker, ibid.; Kropotkin, *Anarchism*, op. cit., p. 11

18 Williams, *The Radical Reformation*, op. cit., p. 846

19 Quoted in Rexroth, *Communalism*, op. cit., pp. 104–5.

20 Quoted in Cohn, *The Pursuit of the Millennium*, op. cit., p. 255

21 Quoted in Rexroth, *Communalism*, op. cit., p. 125

Chapter Eight

1 See Christopher Hill, *The World Turned Upside Down: Radical Ideas During the Revolution* (Harmondsworth: Penguin, 1978), p. 123; A.L. Morton, *The World of the Ranters: Religious Radicalism in the English Revolution* (Lawrence & Wishart, 1979), pp. 70–1

2 *The Works of Gerrard Winstanley*, ed. G. H. Sabine (Ithaca, NY: Cornell University Press, 1941) (*hereafter referred to as Works*), p. 199

3 Gerrard Winstanley, *The True Levellers' Standard Advanced* (1649), quoted by Cohn, *The Pursuit of the Millennium*, op. cit., p. 288

4 Hill, *The World Turned Upside Down*, op. cit., p. 154

5 Ibid, p. 48

6 See D. W. Petegorsky, *Left-wing Democracy in the English Civil War: A Study of the Social Philosophy of Gerrard Winstanley* (Victor Gollancz, 1940), p. 161

7 Winstanley, *The Law of Freedom and Other Writings*, ed. Christopher Hill (Cambridge University Press, 1983), p. 128 (*hereafter known as Writings*)

8 See Hill, 'Introduction', Winstanley, *Writings*, op. cit., p. 30. Cf. Leslie S. A. Jones, *The Digger Movement 1649* (Hyde Park Pamphlet, n.d.), pp. 7–8

9 Winstanley, *A Declaration from the Poor Oppressed People of England* (June, 1649), *Writings*, op. cit., p. 108

10 Winstanley, *A Watch-Word to the City of London* (August 1649), *Writings*, op. cit., p. 128

11 Winstanley, *The Saint's Paradise or the Fathers Teaching the only Satisfaction to Waiting Souls* (?1648), p. 78

12 Winstanley, *True Levellers' Standard*, *Writings*, op. cit., p. 77

13 Ibid., 78

14 Cf. Hill, 'Introduction', Winstanley, *Writings*, op. cit., p. 41; *The World Turned Upside Down*, op. cit., p. 135

15 Winstanley, *The New Law of Righteousness* (1649), p. 6

16 Ibid., p. 5

17 Winstanley, *Works*, op. cit., p. 159

18 Ibid., p. 283

19 Quoted in Woodcock, *Anarchism*, op. cit., p. 44

20 Hill, *The World Turned Upside Down*, op. cit., p. 134

21 See Edmund Dell, 'Gerrard Winstanley and the Diggers', *The Modern Quarterly*, IV, 138–9 and Hill, *The World Turned Upside Down*, op. cit., pp. 134–5

22 Winstanley, *The Law of Freedom*, *Writings*, op. cit., p. 295

23 Ibid., p. 302

24 Winstanley, *A New-year's Gift for the Parliament and Armie* (1650), *Writings*, op. cit., p. 170

25 Winstanley, *The Law of Freedom*, *Writings*, op. cit., p. 305

26 Ibid., pp. 374, 357

27 Ibid., p. 276

28 Hill, *The World Turned Upside Down*, op. cit., p. 134

29 Lawrence Clarkson, *A Single Eye All Light No Darkness; or Light and Darkness One* (1650), quoted in Morton, *The World of the Ranters*, op. cit., p. 134

30 Godwin, *History of the Commonwealth of England* (H. Colburn, 1824–8), III, 82

31 Woodcock, *Anarchism*, op. cit., p. 41

32 Thomas Collier, *A Looking-Glasse for the Quakers* (1657), p. 73

33 Joseph Salmon, *Heights in Depths* (1651), p. 15, quoted in Morton, *The World of the Ranters*, op. cit., pp. 94–5

34 Winstanley, *Works*, op. cit., p. 539

35 Quoted in Cohn, *The Pursuit of the Millennium*, op. cit., p. 289

36 William Penn, Preface to Fox's *Journal*, I, xlix; quoted in Hill, *The World Turned Upside Down*, op. cit., p. 253

37 Quoted in Cohn, *The Pursuit of the Millennium*, op. cit., p. 291

38 Clarkson, *A Single Eye All Light*, op. cit., quoted in Morton, *The World of the Ranters*, op. cit., p. 134

39 Clarkson, *A Single Eye All Light*, op. cit., quoted in Cohn, *The Pursuit of the Millennium*, op. cit., p. 311

40 Ibid., p. 313

41 Ibid., p. 312

42 Ibid., p. 183

43 Ibid., p. 302

44 Abiezer Coppe, *A Second Fiery Flying Roule* (1649), p. 12

45 George Fox, *Gospel-Truth* (1656), p. 81

46 Winstanley, *The Law of Freedom*, *Writings*, op. cit., p. 388

47 Coppe, *A Second Fiery Flying Roule*, op. cit., p. 13

48 *The Routing of the Ranters* (1650), quoted in Cohn, *The Pursuit of the Millennium*, op. cit., p. 297

49 Coppe, *A Second Fiery Flying Roule*, op. cit., p. 3–4

50 *A Fiery Flying Roll* (1649), p. 2

51 Ibid., p. 5

52 *A Second Fiery Flying Roule*, op. cit., p. 15

53 *A Fiery Flying Roll*, op. cit., p. 4

54 Ibid., p. 7

55 *A Second Fiery Flying Roule*, op. cit., p. 8

56 Preface, *A Fiery Flying Roll*, op. cit., p.3

57 Cohn, *The Pursuit of the Millennium*, op. cit., p. 317

58 See 'Introduction', Coppe, *Selected Writings*, ed. Andrew Hopton (Aporia Press, 1987), p. 7

59 *Copps Return to the wayes of Truth* (1651), p. 14

60 J. C. Davis, *Fear, Myth and History* (Cambridge University Press, 1986), p. 91

61 Morton, *The World of the Ranters*, op. cit., p. 112

Chapter Nine

1 François Rabelais, *Gargantua and Pantagruel*, Bk 1 (1534). My translation. See Marie Louise Berneri,

Journey through Utopia (London: Freedom Press, 1982), p. 141

2 Etienne de la Boétie, *Discours de la servitude volontaire*, ed. Maurice Rat (Paris: Librairie Armand Colin, 1963), p. 55. My translation.

3 Ibid., p. 55

4 Ibid., p. 57

5 Ibid., p. 63

6 Ibid., p. 72

7 Ibid., p. 87

8 Ibid., p. 92

9 See Nicolas Walter, 'Introduction' to *Discourse of Voluntary Servitude*, *Anarchy* 63 (May 1966), p. 135

10 Max Nettlau, *Bibliographie de l'anarchie* (Paris: Stock, 1897), p. 2; see also E. V. Zenker, *Anarchism* (Methuen, 1898), pp. 15–16

11 See Murray N. Rothbard, 'Introduction', *The Politics of Obedience: The Discourse of Voluntary Servitude* (New York: Free Life, 1975)

12 Gabriel de Foigny, *A New Discovery of Terra Incognita Australis* (1693), quoted in Berneri, *Journey through Utopia*, op. cit., p. 193

13 Ibid., p. 196

14 Ibid., pp. 198–200

15 Ibid., p. 201

16 Ibid.

17 François de Salignac de La Mothe Fénelon, *Télémaque* (1699), quoted in Gray, *The Socialist Tradition*, op. cit., p. 72

18 Claude Harmel, *Histoire de l'anarchie* (Paris: Editions Champ Libre, 1984), p. 26

19 *Le Testament de Jean Meslier*, ed. Rudolf Charles (Amsterdam: R. C. Meijer, 1864), I, p. 4

20 Ibid., pp. 6–7

21 Quoted by Joll, *The Anarchists*, op. cit., p. 14

22 Morelly, *Code de la nature, ou le véritable esprit de ses lois* (1755), ed. Edouard Dolléans (Paris, 1910), Preface

23 Ibid., p. 71

24 Ibid., p. 30

25 Quoted in Joll, *The Anarchists*, op. cit., p. 13

26 Denis Diderot, 'Passions', *Encyclopedia*,

quoted in Charles Vereker, *Eighteenth-Century Optimism* (Liverpool University Press, 1967), p. 168

27 Diderot, 'Législation', ibid., p. 191

28 Diderot, *Rameau's Nephew, D'Alembert's Dream*, trans. Leonard Tancock (Harmondsworth: Penguin, 1966), p. 65

29 Diderot, 'Le Code de Denis', quoted in Berneri, *Journey through Utopia*, op. cit., p. 201. My translation.

30 Diderot, 'Les Eleuthéromanes ou abdication d'un roi de la fève', Ibid., p. 202

31 Diderot, 'Entretiens d'un père avec ses enfants', *Contes morales et nouvelles idylles* (Paris, 1773)

32 Diderot, 'Supplément au voyage de Bougainville', *Diderot: Selected Philosophical Writings*, ed. John Lough (Cambridge University Press, 1953), p. 190

33 Ibid., pp. 168, 169

34 Ibid., p. 197

35 Ibid., p. 203

36 Jean-Jacques Rousseau, 'A Discourse on the Arts and Sciences' (1750), *The Social Contract and Discourses*, trans. and introd. G. D. H. Cole, eds. J. H. Brumfitt & John C. Hall (J. M. Dent, 1973), p. 26

37 Rousseau, 'A Discourse on the Origin of Inequality' (1754), *The Social Contract and Discourses*, op. cit., pp. 39, 45, 74

38 Ibid., p. 68

39 Ibid., pp. 55, 74

40 Ibid., p. 68

41 Ibid., p. 76

42 Ibid., pp. 83, 86, 89

43 Ibid., pp. 94, 95

44 Ibid., p. 93

45 Ibid., p. 96

46 Rousseau, *Confessions* (1781–8), *Oeuvres complètes*, eds. B. Gagnebin & M. Raymond (Paris, 1959–70), I, 404

47 'A Discourse on the Origin of Inequality', op. cit., p. 104

48 Ibid., p. 82

49 Godwin, *Political Justice* (1798), ed. Isaac Kramnick (Harmondsworth: Penguin, 1976), pp. 496–7n

50 See Ronald Grimsley, *The Philosophy of*

Rousseau (Oxford University Press, 1973), pp. 91, 115; Peter Gay, *The Enlightenment: An Interpretation* (Wildwood House, 1973), II, 534

51 Rousseau, *Emile ou de l'éducation* (1762) (Paris: Garnier-Flammarion, 1966), p. 35

52 Ibid., pp. 628, 629

53 Rousseau, *The Social Contract*, op. cit., p. 174

54 Ibid., p. 240

55 Ibid., pp. 208–9, 210, 228

56 Gay, *The Enlightenment*, op. cit., II, 549

57 Rousseau, *The Social Contract*, op. cit., pp. 165, 170, 177

58 Godwin, *Political Justice*, op. cit., p. 497n

59 Bakunin, quoted in Rocker, *Nationalism and Culture*, op. cit., pp. 162–3. See also J. L. Talmon, *The Origins of Totalitarian Democracy* (1952) (Sphere, 1970), pp. 38–49

60 See Judith N. Shklar, 'Rousseau's Images of Authority', *Hobbes and Rousseau: A Collection of Critical Essays*, eds. Maurice Cranston & R. S. Peters (New York: Anchor, 1972), p. 341

61 See John Plamenatz, 'On le forcera d'être libre', ibid., pp. 323–4

62 Rousseau, *The Social Contract*, op. cit., p. 178

63 Rousseau, 'Discourse on the Origin of Inequality', op. cit., p. 70

64 Rousseau, *Emile*, op. cit., p. 466

Chapter Ten

1 Locke, *Two Treatises of Civil Government*, op. cit., p. 118

2 See C. B. Macpherson, *The Theory of Possessive Individualism* (Oxford University Press, 1962)

3 See Irvin Ehrenpreis, 'Swift on Liberty (1952)', *Swift*, ed. A. Norman Jeffares (Nashville/London: Aurora, 1970), pp. 59–60

4 Jonathan Swift, *Gulliver's Travels and Other Writings*, ed. Ricardo Quintana (New York: The Modern Library, 1958), p. 101

5 J. Middleton Murray, *Swift* (Longmans, Green & Co., 1966), p. 5

6 Godwin, *Political Justice* (G. G. & J. Robinson, 1798 edn.), II, 209n

7 Swift, *Gulliver's Travels*, op. cit., p. 202

8 Ibid., p. 229

9 Ibid., .p. 226

10 George Orwell, 'Politics *vs.* Literature: an examination of *Gulliver's Travels*' (1950), *Swift*, ed. A. Norman Jeffares, op. cit., p. 2

11 Ibid., pp. 202. Orwell adds that both Tolstoy and Swift have 'the same anarchistic outlook covering an authoritarian cast of mind'. Ibid., p. 203

12 Quoted in my *William Godwin*, op. cit., p. 49. For Swift's influence on Godwin, see also James A. Preu, *The Dean and the Anarchist* (Tallahassee: Florida State University Press, 1959)

13 Edmund Burke, *A Vindication of Natural Society* (M. Cooper, 1756), pp. 3–4

14 Ibid., pp. 5, 8

15 Ibid., p. 13

16 Ibid., p. 90

17 Ibid., pp. 67, 104

18 Godwin, *Political Justice* (1798 edn.), op. cit., I, 13n

19 Burke, *The Inherent Evils of all State Governments Demonstrated* (Holyoake & Co., 1858), Preface, p. iii; Appendix, pp. 59–60

20 Thomas Paine, *Rights of Man*, ed. Henry Collins (Harmondsworth: Penguin, 1971), p. 241

21 Ibid., p. 250

22 Ibid., p. 181

23 Thomas Paine, 'An Occasional Letter to the Female Sex' (1775), *The Writings of Thomas Paine*, ed. M. D. Conway & C. Putnam (New York, 1906), II, 60

24 Paine, *Common Sense*, op. cit., p. 100

25 Ibid., p. 65

26 Paine, *Rights of Man*, op. cit., p. 168

27 Burke, *Reflections on the Revolution in France* (1790), ed. Conor Cruise O'Brien (Harmondsworth: Penguin, 1969), p. 173

28 Paine, *Rights of Man*, op. cit., p. 64
29 See Olivia Smith, *The Politics of Language 1791–1819* (Oxford: Clarendon Press, 1984), p. 139
30 Paine, *Rights of Man*, p. 90
31 Ibid., pp. 211, 220, 232
32 Ibid., p. 109
33 Ibid., p. 168
34 Ibid., p. 185
35 Ibid., pp. 230, 186
36 Ibid., pp. 187–8
37 Ibid., p. 187
38 Ibid., pp. 220, 209
39 Ibid., p. 206

Chapter Eleven

1 Quoted in Geoffrey Gorer, ed., *The Life and Ideas of the Marquis de Sade* (Panther, 1965), pp. 15–16
2 Ibid., p. 32
3 Ibid., p. 51
4 Ibid., p. 182
5 Ibid., p. 177
6 Ibid., p. 97
7 Ibid., p. 105
8 Ibid., p. 101
9 Ibid., p. 109
10 Ibid., p. 105
11 Ibid., pp. 123–4
12 Ibid., pp. 124–5
13 Ibid., p. 126
14 Ibid., p. 131
15 Ibid., p. 134
16 Ibid., p. 135
17 Ibid., p. 136
18 Ibid., pp. 135–6
19 Ibid., p. 146
20 Ibid., p. 156
21 See *Guardian Weekly*, 13 March, 1988, p. 15. In the interview with Michel Contat, Robbe-Grillet asserts that he is 'an anarchist all the way'.
22 Gorer, *The Life and Ideas of the Marquis de Sade*, op. cit., p. 142
23 Pierre Klossowski, *Sade mon prochain* (Paris: Editions du Seuil, 1947), p. 34
24 Cf. Berneri, *Journey through Utopia*, op. cit., p. 178
25 Kropotkin, *Anarchist Communism*, op. cit., p. 31

26 Bookchin, *The Ecology of Freedom*, op. cit., p. 328. See also Edward Mason, 'Fourier and Anarchism', *The Quarterly Journal of Economics*, XLII, 2 (February 1928), 228–62
27 *The Utopian Vision of Charles Fourier*, ed. Jonathan Beecher & Richard Bienvenu (Boston: Beacon Press, 1971), p. 1
28 Ibid., p. 161
29 Ibid., pp. 196, 177, 321
30 Ibid., p. 23
31 Ibid., p. 353. See also Frank Manuel, 'Charles Fourier: The Burgeoning of Instinct', *The Prophets of Paris* (Cambridge, Mass.: Harvard University Press, 1962)
32 *The Utopian Vision of Charles Fourier*, op. cit., p. 43
33 Ibid., p. 169
34 Ibid., p. 317
35 Ibid., p. 69

Chapter Twelve

1 See John W. Burrow, 'Introduction', Wilhelm von Humboldt, *The Limits of State Action* (Cambridge University Press, 1969), p. xvii
2 Max Nettlau, *Bibliographie de l'anarchie* (Paris, 1897; New York: Burk Franklin, 1968), p. 31
3 See Noam Chomsky, *Problems of Knowledge and Freedom* (Fontana, 1972), pp. 48–9; and his Introduction to Guérin, *Anarchism*, op. cit., p. xi
4 See Burrow, 'Introduction', *The Limits of State Action*, op. cit., p. xviii
5 Ibid., p. 16
6 Ibid., p. 20
7 Ibid., pp. 131, 40
8 Ibid., p. 28
9 Ibid., pp. 10, 11
10 Ibid., p. 63
11 Ibid., p. 91
12 Ibid., p. 130
13 Ibid., p. 131
14 See Peter Kropotkin to Max Nettlau, 5 March 1902, in P. Kropotkin, *Selected Writings on Anarchism and Revolution*,

ed. Martin A. Miller (Cambridge, Mass.: MIT Press, 1970), p. 305

15 Emma Goldman, *Anarchism and Other Essays*, ed. Richard Drinnon (New York: Dover, 1969), p. 44

16 Rudolf Rocker, *Nationalism and Culture*, op. cit., p. 83

17 Herbert Read, 'The Philosophy of Anarchism' (1940), *Anarchy & Order*, op. cit., pp. 39–40

18 Nietzsche, *Twilight of the Idols and the Anti-Christ*, trans. R. J. Hollingdale (Harmondsworth: Penguin, 1969), p. 86

19 Nietzsche, 'Maxims and Reflections', *A Nietzsche Reader*, ed. R. J. Hollingdale (Harmondsworth: Penguin, 1977), p. 279

20 Nietzsche, *The Gay Science* (1882), quoted in Walter Kaufmann, *Nietzsche: Philosopher, Psychologist, Antichrist* (Princeton, N.J.: Princeton University Press, 1974), p. 375

21 Nietzsche, *The Case of Wagner* (1888), quoted in Kaufmann, ibid., p. 731

22 See R. J. Hollingdale, *Nietzsche* (Routledge & Kegan Paul, 1973), p. 194

23 Nietzsche, *Thus Spoke Zarathustra*, trans. R. J. Hollingdale (Harmondsworth: Penguin, 1964), p. 116

24 Ibid., pp. 83, 91, 93

25 See Kropotkin to Max Nettlau, 5 March 1902, Kropotkin, *Selected Writings*, op. cit., p. 297

26 See Hollingdale's comments, Nietzsche, *Twilight of the Idols*, op. cit., p. 108

27 *Thus Spoke Zarathustra*, op. cit., p. 86

28 Nietzsche, *Beyond Good and Evil* (1886), quoted in Hollingdale, *Nietzsche*, op. cit., pp. 145–6

29 Kaufmann, *Nietzsche*, op. cit., p. 360.

30 Nietzsche, *The Gay Science* (1882), quoted in Hollingdale, *Nietzsche*, op. cit., p. 96

31 *Twilight of the Idols*, op. cit., p. 110

32 Ibid., p. 92

33 Ibid., pp. 96, 101

34 *Thus Spoke Zarathustra*, op. cit., p. 88

35 Ibid., p. 77

36 Ibid., pp. 75–6

37 Ibid., pp. 75–6, 154

38 *Twilight of the Idols*, op. cit., p. 92

39 Ibid., pp. 60, 63

40 *Thus Spoke Zarathustra*, op. cit., p. 227

41 Emma Goldman, *Anarchism and Other Essays*, op. cit., p. 44

42 Goldman, *Living My Life* (New York: Alfred Knopf, 1931), I, 194

Chapter Thirteen

1. John Stuart Mill *On Liberty* (1859) in *Utilitarianism, On Liberty, Essay on Bentham*, ed. Mary Warnock (Fontana, 1970), p. 186

2 Mill, *Autobiography* (1873) (New York: Signet, 1964), pp. 182–3

3 See Alan Ryan, *J. S. Mill* (Routledge & Kegan Paul, 1974), p. 183

4 Mill, *Autobiography*, op. cit., p. 168. Max Nettlau quotes the sentence approvingly in his *Bibliographie de l'anarchie*, op. cit., p. 225

5 *On Liberty*, op. cit., p. 171. Cf. p. 180

6 Ibid., p. 138

7 Ibid., p. 227

8 Ibid., p. 185

9 Ibid., p. 135

10 Ibid., p. 250

11 Ibid., p. 136

12 Ryan, *J. S. Mill*, op. cit., p. 127. Cf. p. 130

13 See Kropotkin, *Anarchism and Anarchist Communism*, op. cit., pp. 21, 30–1; *Ethics*, op. cit., pp. 288–322; Emma Goldman, 'What I Believe', *Red Emma Speaks*, ed. Alix Kates Shulman (Wildwood House, 1979), p. 35. See also Max Nettlau, *Bibliographie de l'anarchie*, op. cit., p. 225

14 See Donald Macrae, Introduction to Herbert Spencer, *The Man versus The State* (1884) (Harmondsworth: Pelican, 1969), p. 35

15 Spencer, 'The Sins of Legislators', ibid., p. 112

16 Ibid., p. 183

17 'The Great Political Superstition', *Essays, Scientific, Political and Speculative* (London & New York, 1892), III, 42, quoted in Kropotkin, *Anarchist Communism*, op. cit., p. 30

18 See Spencer, 'Representative Government – What is it Good For?' (1857), *The Man versus the State*, op. cit., p. 271

19 'The Great Political Superstition', ibid., p. 151

20 'The Coming Slavery', *ibid.*, pp. 100, 107

21 See 'Postscript', *The Man versus the State*, op. cit., p. 184; and 'From Freedom to Bondage' (1891), ibid., p. 334

22 See T. H. Huxley's 'Administrative Nihilism', *Fortnightly Review* (1871), pp. 525–43

23 See Spencer, 'Specialized Administration' (1871) in *The Man versus The State*, op. cit., p. 306

24 Kropotkin, *Anarchist Communism*, op. cit., p. 30n

25 Spencer, *The Proper Sphere of Government* (1842)

26 'Specialized Administration', op. cit., p. 288

27 Spencer, *Social Statics* (Williams & Norgate, 1868), p. 306

28 See J. D. Y. Peel, *Herbert Spencer: The Evolution of a Sociologist* (1971)

29 Spencer, *Principles of Ethics* (1893 edn.), para 391. Spencer associates anarchism with 'the doctrine of Ravachol' – see Kropotkin, *Ethics*, op. cit., p. 320

30 See David Wiltshire, *The Social and Political Thought of Herbert Spencer* (Oxford University Press, 1978), p. 13

31 Henry W. Nevinson, 'Edward Carpenter', *Great Democrats*, ed. A. Barratt Brown (Nicholson & Watson, 1934), p. 111. Nettlau in his *Bibliographie de l'anarchie* (op. cit., p. 220) also refers to Carpenter's 'socialisme libertaire'.

32 Edward Carpenter, *Civilization: Its Causes and Cure* (1889) (Swann Sonnenschein, 1897 edn.), p. 5

33 Ibid., p. 31. Cf. Edward Carpenter,

Edward Carpenter 1844–1929 (Dr Williams's Trust, 1970), p. 20

34 Ibid., p. 42

35 Carpenter, *Non-Governmental Society* (A. C. Fifield, 1911), p. 214

36 See Carpenter, *Prisons, Police and Punishment: An Inquiry into the Causes of Crime and Criminals* (A. C. Fifield, 1905)

37 Carpenter, *Towards Democracy* (1883) (Allen & Unwin, 1931), p. 111

38 Ibid., p. 62

39 See Thomas H. Bell, *Edward Carpenter: The English Tolstoi* (Los Angeles: The Libertarian Group, 1932)

40 Quoted by E. P. Thompson, *William Morris: Romantic to Revolutionary*, 2nd edn. (Merlin Press, 1977), p. 244

41 Ibid., p. 802

42 Ibid., p. 772

43 William Morris, 'The Society of the Future' (1887), *Political Writings of William Morris*, ed. A. L. Morton (Lawrence & Wishart, 1973), p. 192

44 Ibid., p. 201

45 Morris, *News from Nowhere, or An Epoch of Rest* (1890) (Longmans, Green & Co., 1907), p. 121

46 Ibid., p. 83

47 Ibid., pp. 84, 83, 87

48 Ibid., p. 102

49 Ibid., p. 64

50 See Paul Meier, *William Morris: The Marxist Dreamer*, trans. Frank Gubb, 2 vols. (Hassocks: Harvester, 1978)

51 Morris, 'Communism' (1893), *Political Writings*, op. cit., p. 234

52 'How I Became a Socialist' (1894), ibid., p. 242

53 See Thompson, *William Morris*, op. cit., p. 770

54 Morris, 'How I Became a Socialist', *Political Writings*, op. cit., p. 242

55 Morris to James Tochatti, 21 December 1893, quoted in Thompson, *William Morris*, op. cit., p. 596

56 Morris, 'Socialism and Anarchism' (1889), *Political Writings*, op. cit., pp. 212–13

57 Ibid., p. 213

58 Ibid., p. 214

59 May Morris, *William Morris: Artist,*

Writer, Socialist, 2 vols. (Blackwell, 1936), quoted by Edmund Penning-Rowsell, *TLS*, 11 August 1978

60 Oscar Wilde, 'The Soul of Man under Socialism', *De Profundis and Other Writings*, ed. Hesketh Pearson (Harmondsworth: Penguin, 1973), p. 34

61 Richard Ellmann, *Oscar Wilde* (Hamish Hamilton, 1987), p. 9

62 Ibid., p. 41

63 Ibid., p. 116

64 'The Soul of Man under Socialism', op. cit., p. 23

65 Ibid., p. 22

66 Quoted in George Woodcock, *The Paradox of Oscar Wilde* (T.V. Bondman, 1949), p. 147

67 Ibid.

68 Quoted in Ellmann, *Oscar Wilde*, op. cit., p. 273n

69 Wilde, 'De Profundis' (1905), *De Profundis and Other Writings*, op. cit., p. 180

70 'The Soul of Man under Socialism', op. cit., p. 46

71 Ibid., p. 21

72 Ibid., pp. 30–1

73 Ibid., pp. 30, 46

74 Ibid., p. 40

75 Ibid., p. 22

76 Ibid., p. 20

77 Ibid., p. 32

78 Ibid., p. 36

79 Ibid., p. 47

80 Ibid., p. 53

81 Ibid., p. 49

82 Wilde to Cunninghame Graham, quoted in Ellmann, *Oscar Wilde*, op. cit., p. 526

83 'The Ballad of Reading Gaol' (1896), *The Works of Oscar Wilde* (Collins, c.1933), p. 197

Chapter Fourteen

1 Ralph Waldo Emerson, 'Politics' (1844), *The Complete Essays and Other Writings of Ralph Waldo Emerson*, ed. Brooks Atkinson (New York: Modern Library, 1940), p. 430; *Journals of Ralph Waldo Emerson*, ed. E. W. Emerson & W. E. Forbes (Boston: Houghton, Mifflin, 1909–14), III, 200

2 *Journals*, op. cit., V, 302–3

3 *The Letters of Ralph Waldo Emerson*, ed. Ralph L. Rusk (New York: Columbia University Press, 1939), I, pp. 412–13

4 Emerson to Walt Whitman, 21 July 1855, quoted by Justin Kaplan, 'Introduction', Walt Whitman, *Leaves of Grass* (1892) (New York: Bantam, 1983), p. xix

5 Whitman, 'A Backward Glance o'er Travel'd Roads', ibid., p. 451

6 'Thought', ibid., p. 223

7 'A Backward Glance', ibid., pp. 452–3

8 'To the States', ibid., p. 224

9 'To the States', ibid., p. 7

10 Quoted by W. Harding, *A Thoreau Handbook* (New York University Press, 1959), p. 201

11 Henry David Thoreau, 'Civil Disobedience' *The Portable Thoreau*, ed. Carl Bode (Harmondsworth: Penguin, 1979), p. 122

12 Ibid., p. 111

13 Ibid.

14 Ibid., p. 109

15 Ibid., pp. 127, 130

16 'Walking' (1861), *The Portable Thoreau*, op. cit., p. 592

17 Quoted by Harold Beaver, 'The Transcendental Savage', *TLS* (6 October 1978)

18 'Life without Principle' (1861), *The Portable Thoreau*, op. cit., p. 650

19 Quoted in Albert Keiser, *The Indian in American Literature* (New York: Oxford University Press, 1933), p. 227

20 See Thoreau, *Walden; or, Life in the Woods* (1854) (New York: Signet, 1960), p. 74

21 Ibid., p. 143

22 'Civil Disobedience', op. cit., p. 130

23 *Walden*, op. cit., p. 78. Cf. Richard Drinnon, 'Thoreau's Politics of the Upright Man', *Anarchy*, 3, 26 (1963), pp. 122–3

24 *Walden*, op. cit., pp. 636, 653

25 'Civil Disobedience', op. cit., p. 115

26 Ibid., p. 120

27 Ibid., pp. 111, 131

28 Ibid., p. 133

Chapter Fifteen

1 William Hazlitt, *The Spirit of the Age; or, Contemporary Portraits* (1825) (Oxford University Press, 1954), pp. 19–20

2 For Godwin's influence, see my *William Godwin* (New Haven & London: Yale University Press, 1984), ch. viii

3 Thomas de Quincey, *Collected Writings*, ed. David Masson (1897), III, 25

4 Percy Bysshe Shelley to William Godwin, 3 January 1812, *The Letters of Percy Bysshe Shelley*, ed. Frederick L. Jones (Oxford University Press, 1964), I, 220

5 William Godwin, *Sketches of History, In Six Sermons* (T. Cadell, 1784), pp. 5, 20; Godwin, *An Enquiry concerning Political Justice*, 3rd edn. (G. G. & J. Robinson, 1798), I, 323

6 *The Anarchist Writings of William Godwin*, ed. Peter Marshall (Freedom Press, 1986), p. 140. Most of this chapter first appeared in the introduction to this work.

7 Godwin, *History of the Internal Affairs of the United Provinces* (1787), p. 332

8 Quoted in my *William Godwin*, op. cit., p. 77

9 Godwin to Sheridan, ibid., p. 81

10 Mary Shelley, C. Kegan Paul, *William Godwin: His Friends and Contemporaries* (Kegan Paul, 1876), I, 76

11 Godwin, *Political Justice*, op. cit., I, x

12 Godwin, *Things as They Are; or The Adventures of Caleb Williams* (1794), ed. Maurice Hindle (Harmondsworth: Penguin, 1987), p. 3

13 *Political Justice*, op. cit., I, xii

14 Godwin, *Considerations on Lord Grenville's and Mr Pitt's Bills* (J. Johnson, 1795), p. 21

15 See De Quincey, *Collected Writings*, op. cit., XI, 328; Kropotkin, *Anarchism*, op. cit., p. 12

16 T. J. Mathias, quoted in my *William Godwin*, op. cit., p. 215

17 Government spy report, ibid., p. 290

18 *Shelley's Prose: or, The Trumpet of Prophecy*, ed. D. L. Clark (Albuquerque, 1954), pp. 237, 252, 240. For Godwin's central influence on Shelley's political philosophy, see Michael H. Scrivener, *Radical Shelley. The Philosophical Anarchism and Utopian Thought of Percy Bysshe Shelley* (Princeton, NJ: Princeton University Press, 1982), p. 8

19 Godwin, *History of the Commonwealth of England* (1824–8), I, 90; II, 333

20 Godwin, *Thoughts on Man, his Nature, Productions and Discoveries* (Effingham Wilson, 1831), pp. 112–13

21 Ibid., p. 471

22 *Political Justice* (1st edn., 1793), I, 11

23 Godwin, *Essays. Never Before Published*, ed. C. Kegan Paul (H. S. King, 1873), p. 87

24 *Anarchist Writings*, op. cit., p. 61

25 *Political Justice* (1798 edn.), I, 81; I, xxvi

26 *Anarchist Writings*, op. cit., p. 64. Mark Philp (*Godwin's Political Justice*, Duckworth, 1986, p. 83) has recently argued that Godwin's moral philosophy is a 'form of perfectionism', but John P. Clark, *The Philosophical Anarchism of William Godwin* (Princeton, NJ: Princeton University Press, 1977), p. 110; and Don Locke, *A Fantasy of Reason* (Routledge & Kegan Paul, 1980), pp. 172–3, support my interpretation.

27 *Anarchist Writings*, op. cit., p. 95

28 Ibid., p. 65

29 Ibid., p. 49

30 *Political Justice* (1793 edn.), I, 121, 88

31 *Anarchist Writings*, op. cit., p. 69

32 Quoted in my *William Godwin*, op. cit., p. 204

33 *Anarchist Writings*, op. cit., p. 75

34 Ibid., p. 77

35 Ibid., p. 79

36 *Political Justice* (1793 edn.), I, 163

37 Ibid., II, 850

38 Ibid., I, 237

39 *Anarchist Writings*, op. cit., pp. 50, 89

40 Ibid., p. 92

41 Ibid., p. 93

42 Ibid., pp. 91–2

43 Ibid., p. 94

44 Ibid., p. 98
45 *Caleb Williams*, op. cit., pp. 218–9
46 *Anarchist Writings*, op. cit., pp. 99–100
47 Ibid., p. 101
48 Ibid., p. 107
49 Ibid., p. 108
50 Ibid., p. 114
51 Ibid., p. 115
52 Ibid., p. 89, 125
53 Ibid., p. 127
54 Ibid., pp. 127, 126
55 Ibid., p. 129
56 Ibid., p. 130
57 Ibid., pp. 132, 134
58 Ibid., p. 135
59 See Marx to Engels, 17 March 1845, quoted by Max Nettlau, *Der Vorfrühling der Anarchie* (Berlin: Fritz Kater, 1925), p. 73. Rudolf Rocker rightly observed that Godwin was 'really the founder of later communist Anarchism', *Anarcho-syndicalism*, op. cit., p. 14.
60 *Anarchist Writings*, op. cit., p. 136
61 Ibid., p. 141
62 Ibid., p. p. 144
63 Ibid., p. 146
64 Ibid., p. 158
65 Ibid., p. 161
66 Ibid., p. 162
67 Ibid., p. 164
68 Ibid., pp. 163–4
69 Ibid., p. 172
70 See Clark, *The Philosophical Anarchism of William Godwin*, op. cit., p. 312; Isaac Kramnick, Introduction, *Political Justice* (Harmondsworth: Penguin, 1976), p. 52
71 *Anarchist Writings*, op. cit., p. 171
72 Ibid., pp. 171, 172
73 Ibid., pp. 60–1
74 *Political Justice* (1793 edn.), II, 565
75 Ibid., I, 335, 168
76 *Anarchist Writings*, op. cit., pp. 172–3
77 Ibid., p. 173
78 Ibid., p. 77
79 Ibid., pp. 123, 121
80 Quoted in my *William Godwin*, op. cit., p. 343

Chapter Sixteen

1 R. W. K. Paterson, *The Nihilistic Egoist: Max Stirner* (Oxford University Press, 1971), pp. 292–3. See also pp. 102, 127
2 Albert Camus, *L'Homme révolté* (Paris: Gallimard, 1951), p. 83
3 Herbert Read, *Anarchy and Order*, op. cit., p. 165
4 See C. J. Arthur, 'Introduction', Marx & Engels, *The German Ideology* (Lawrence & Wishart, 1970), p. 23
5 Quoted by Paterson, *The Nihilistic Egoist*, op, cit., p. 117
6 Kropotkin, *Ethics*, op. cit., p. 338; Mussolini, quoted in Joll, *The Anarchists*, op. cit., p. 155
7 See John P. Clark, *Max Stirner's Egoism* (Freedom Press, 1976), pp. 87–90; James J. Martin, *Men against the State: The Expositors of Individualist Anarchism in America, 1827–1908* (Colorado Springs: Ralph Myles, 1970), p. 250
8 Max Stirner, *The False Principle of Our Education* (Colorado Springs: Ralph Myles, 1967), p. 23
9 Stirner, *The Ego & Its Own*, trans. Steven Byington (Rebel Press, 1982), pp. 346–7. This edition is a reprint of the English translation by Byington entitled *The Ego and His Own* and published by the Libertarian Book Club in 1963.
10 Ibid., p. 354
11 Ibid., p. 143
12 David McLellan, *The Young Hegelians and Karl Marx* (New York: Praeger, 1969), p. 119
13 Stirner, *The Ego & Its Own*, op. cit., p. 32
14 Ibid., pp. 43, 39
15 Ibid., p. 182
16 Ibid., p. 182
17 Ibid., pp. 296–7
18 Ibid., p. 5
19 Ibid., p. 138
20 Ibid., pp. 305–6
21 Ibid., p. 161
22 See Clark, *Max Stirner's Egoism*, op. cit., p. 30

23 Stirner, *The Ego & Its Own*, op. cit.,
   p. 359
24 Ibid., p. 162
25 Ibid., p. 291
26 Ibid., p. 205
27 Ibid., p. 320
28 Ibid., p. 296
29 Ibid., p. 189
30 Ibid., p. 5
31 Ibid., p. 157
32 Ibid., p. 169
33 Ibid., p. 159
34 Ibid., p. 167
35 Ibid., p. 191
36 Ibid., p. 358
37 Ibid., p. 227
38 Ibid., pp. 224, 308
39 Ibid., p. 115–16, 197
40 Ibid., p. 223
41 Ibid., pp. 195, 226
42 Ibid., p. 257
43 Ibid., p. 179
44 Ibid., p. 312
45 Ibid., p. 309
46 Ibid., pp. 119–20
47 Ibid., p. 256
48 Ibid., p. 118
49 Ibid., p. 241
50 Ibid., p. 332
51 Ibid., pp. 197, 116
52 Ibid., p. 316
53 Cf. Clark, *Max Stirner's Egoism*, op. cit.,
   pp. 57–8
54 Stirner, *The Ego & Its Own*, op. cit.,
   p. 161
55 Ibid., pp. 179, 209
56 Ibid., p. 310
57 See Stirner, *Kleinere Schriften und seine
   Entgegnungen auf die Kritik seines
   Werkes: Der Eiznige und sein Eigentum*
   (Berlin: Schuster und Loeffler, 1898),
   p. 164
58 Goldman, *Anarchism and Other Essays*,
   op. cit., p. 44
59 Marx & Engels, *The German Ideology*,
   op. cit., p. 26. Cf. *The Ego & Its Own*,
   op. cit., p. 96
60 Ibid., p. 74

Chapter Seventeen

1 *Selected Writings of Pierre-Joseph
   Proudhon*, ed. Stewart Edwards, trans.
   Elizabeth Fraser (Macmillan, 1969),
   p. 88 (*hereafter referred to as SW*)
2 Proudhon, *System of Economic
   Contradictions or the Philosophy of
   Poverty* (1846), SW, p. 231
3 Proudhon to Maurice, 25 February
   1848, SW, p. 155; *Correspondence* (Paris,
   1874–5), VI, 313
4 Marx, *The Holy Family*, quoted by
   Edward Hyams, *Pierre-Joseph
   Proudhon: His Revolutionary Life, Mind
   and Works* (John Murray, 1979), p. 40
5 *Bulletin de la Fédération Jurassienne*, 39
   (24 September 1884); quoted by Jean
   Maitron, *Histoire du mouvement
   anarchiste en France (1880–1914)*
   (Paris: Société Universitaire, 1955),
   p. 32
6 Quoted by George Woodcock, 'On
   Proudhon's "What is Property?"',
   Anarchy 106 (December 1969), p. 353
7 See Alan Ritter, *The Political Thought of
   Pierre-Joseph Proudhon* (Princeton, NJ:
   Princeton University Press, 1969), pp.
   198–9; Paul Avrich, 'Proudhon and
   America', *Anarchist Portraits*
   (Princeton, NJ: Princeton University
   Press 1988), pp.14–17
8 See, for instance, René Dumont, *False
   Start in Africa* (1966)
9 See Louis Dimier, *Les Maîtres de la
   contre-révolution au XIXème siècle*
   (Paris, 1907); J. Salwyn Schapiro,
   'Pierre-Joseph Proudhon, Harbinger of
   Fascism', *American Historical Review*, L
   (1945), 714–37; Henri Bachelin, *P.-J.
   Proudhon, socialiste national* (Paris,
   1941); and Ritter, *Proudhon*, op. cit.,
   pp. 7–8
10 Proudhon to Pierre Leroux, 7
   December, 1849, SW, p. 197
11 *Confessions of a Revolutionary* (1849)
   (1851 edn.), p. 31
12 *Justice in the Revolution and the Church*
   (1858), SW, p. 261
13 *Economic Contradictions*, op. cit., SW,
   p. 223
14 *The Utopian Vision of Charles Fourier*, ed.

Jonathan Beecher & Richard
Bienvenu (Boston: Beacon, 1972), p. 1

15 Alexis de Tocqueville, *The Old Regime
and the French Revolution* (New York:
Anchor, 1955), p. 57

16 Quoted in Hyams, *Proudhon*, op. cit.,
p. 29

17 Proudhon, *What is Property?* (1840)
(1841 edn.), p. v

18 *Confessions* (1849), op. cit., SW, p. 241

19 See Stirner, *The Ego & Its Own*, op. cit.,
p. 251

20 Quoted in Guérin, *Anarchism*, op. cit.,
p. 21

21 Proudhon, *What is Property?*, op. cit.,
SW, p. 89

22 Ibid., p. 89n

23 *On the Creation of Order in Humanity*
(1843), SW, pp. 226, 227n, 224

24 *Confessions*, op. cit., SW, pp. 237, 71

25 Marx, *The Holy Family*, quoted in
Hyams, *Proudhon*, op. cit., p. 40

26 Proudhon to Marx, 17 May 1846,
Confessions, op. cit., SW, pp. 150–1

27 Marx to P. V. Annenkov in Paris, 23
December 1846, Marx and Engels,
Selected Works (Lawrence & Wishart,
1968), p. 669

28 See Shlomo Avineri, *Karl Marx: Social
and Political Thought* (Cambridge
University Press, 1971), p. 71

29 Marx and Engels, *Selected Works*,
op. cit., pp. 59, 260. See also Paul
Thomas, *Karl Marx and the Anarchists*
op. cit., for a very one-sided account
of the relationship.

30 Proudhon, *Confessions* (1851 edn.),
op. cit., p. 147

31 *Economic Contradictions*, op. cit., quoted
in Guérin, *Ni Dieu ni Maître: anthologie
de l'anarchisme* (Paris: Maspero, 1972),
I, 57

32 *Economic Contradictions*, op. cit., SW,
p. 231; Guérin, *Ni Dieu ni Maître*,
op. cit., I, 55

33 *Economic Contradictions*, op. cit., SW,
p. 223

34 Quoted in Hyams, *Proudhon*, op. cit.,
pp. 85–6

35 *Economic Contradictions*, op. cit., SW,
p. 58

36 *Political Contradictions: Theory of the*

*Constitutional Movement in the 19th
Century* (1863–4), SW, p. 60

37 *War and Peace* (1861), SW, p. 260

38 *Journal du Peuple* (8–15 November
1848), Guérin, *Ni Dieu ni Maître*,
op. cit., pp. 84, 83

39 Ibid., p. 62

40 Quoted in *Anarchist Reader*, op. cit., p.
111

41 *General Idea of the Revolution in the 19th
Century* (1851) (1923 edn.), p. 132

42 Hyams, *Proudhon*, op. cit., pp. 93, 173

43 Proudhon, *The Social Revolution
Vindicated by the Coup d'Etat of
December Second* (1852) (1936 edn.), p.
177

44 *Confessions* (1851 edn.), op. cit., pp. 12,
31

45 *General Idea of the Revolution*, quoted in
Hyams, *Proudhon*, op. cit., p. 182

46 *General Idea of the Revolution*, quoted in
Guérin, *Ni Dieu ni Maître*, op. cit.,
p. 86

47 *Carnets* (1843–1864), X, 52

48 *General Idea of the Revolution*, quoted in
Guérin, *Anarchism*, op. cit., pp. 15–16

49 Ibid., in Guérin, *Ni Dieu ni Maître*, op
cit., pp. 96–7

50 *General Idea of the Revolution* (1923
edn.), pp. 374, 378

51 *Correspondance* (Paris, 1875), IV, 149

52 *Confessions* (1929 edn.), p. 236

53 *General Idea of the Revolution* (1923
edn.), p. 116

54 Ibid., quoted in Guérin, *Ni Dieu ni
Maître*, op. cit., p. 91

55 *General Idea of the Revolution*, op. cit.,
SW, p. 97

56 Proudhon to Bergmann, March 1854,
quoted in Hyams, *Proudhon*, op. cit.,
p. 210

57 *Justice*, op. cit., SW, p. 249

58 Ibid., p. 233

59 *Justice* (1930–5 edn.), I, 306

60 *Carnets*, op. cit., VII, 219

61 *Confessions*, op. cit., SW, p. 243

62 *Economic Contradictions*, op. cit., SW,
p. 221

63 *Justice*, op. cit., SW, p. 249

64 *Justice* (1858 edn.), III, 340

65 Ibid., IV, 433

66 *Justice* (1868 edn.), I, 326, 43

67 Ibid., I, 225. Ritter, *Proudhon*, op. cit., p. 68, defines justice as respect; Gray, *The Socialist Tradition*, op. cit., p. 235, and Woodcock, *Pierre-Joseph Proudhon* (Routledge & Kegan Paul, 1956), p. 208, equate it with equality.

68 *Justice* (1858 edn.), I, 416

69 *Philosophy of Progress* (1853) (1946 edn.), pp. 66–7

70 Quoted in Ritter, *Proudhon*, op. cit., pp. 63–4

71 *Justice* (1858 edn.), IV, 368; I, 325. For an interesting discussion of this contradiction, see Ritter, *Proudhon*, op. cit., p. 83

72 *War and Peace* (1861), SW, p. 204

73 Ibid., p. 23

74 Ibid., p. 207

75 *War and Peace* (1927 edn.), p. 121

76 Ibid., p. 347

77 *War and Peace*, op. cit., SW, p. 210

78 *On the Principle of Art* (1861), SW, pp. 215–16

79 *The Federal Principle* (1863), SW, pp. 103, 106

80 See *Theory of Property* (1863–4), p. 17

81 Ibid., p. 208

82 *Philosophy of Progress* (1853), SW, p. 90

83 *Federation*, op. cit., SW, p. 91

84 Ibid. (1959 edn.), pp. 271–2

85 Ibid., SW, p. 102. Cf. p. 104

86 Ibid., pp. 108, 110

87 Letter, 20 August 1864, SW, p. 92

88 Proudhon to Pierre Leroux, 7 December 1849, ibid., p. 196

89 *Justice* (1930–5 edn.), III, 174

90 *Justice* (1868 edn), IV, 134

91 Proudhon to Joseph Garnier, February 1844, quoted by Hyams, *Proudhon*, op. cit., p. 64

92 *Justice*, op. cit., SW, p. 254

93 Quoted by Hyams, *Proudhon*, op. cit., p. 274

94 *Justice*, op. cit., SW, pp. 255, 256

95 *Justice* (1868 edn.) I, 304–5

96 *Carnets*, op. cit., SW, p. 228n

97 *Justice*, op. cit., SW p. 260

98 *Economic Contradictions* (1923 edn.), I, 385

99 *Philosophy of Progress*, op. cit., SW, p. 246; *Justice*, op. cit., SW, p. 245

100 Quoted in Guérin, *Ni Dieu ni Maître*, op. cit., p. 122

101 *Carnets*, op. cit., VI, 269

102 Ibid., IX, 2

103 Quoted in Ritter, *Proudhon*, op. cit., p. 172

104 *Justice*, op. cit., SW, p. 83

105 *On the Political Capacity of the Working Classes* (1865) (1924 edn.), p. 141

106 Quoted in Guérin, *Ni Dieu ni Maître*, op. cit., p. 135

107 Ibid., p. 138

108 *Political Capacity*, op. cit., SW, p. 60

109 *Political Capacity* (1924 edn), p. 236

110 *Justice* (1930–5 edn.), III, 429

111 Ibid., III, 409, 424

Chapter Eighteen

1 E. H. Carr, *Michael Bakunin* (Macmillan, 1937), p. 440

2 Aileen Kelly, *Mikhail Bakunin: A Study in the Psychology and Politics of Utopianism* (Oxford: Clarendon Press, 1982), p. 293; Arthur P. Mendel, *Michael Bakunin: Roots of Apocalypse* (New York: Praeger, 198), p. 1. See also Max Nomad's chapter, entitled 'Bakunin: The Apostle of Pan-Destruction', *The Apostles of Revolution* (Secker & Warburg, 1961) – an epithet which Eugene Pyziur asserted that he 'richly deserved', *The Doctrine of Anarchism of Michael A. Bakunin* (Chicago: Henry Regnery, 1965), p. 33

3 Albert Camus, *L'Homme révolté* (1951) (Paris: Gallimard, 1974), p. 194

4 Rudolf Rocker, 'Introduction', *The Political Philosophy of Bakunin: Scientific Anarchism*, ed. G. P. Maximoff (New York: The Free Press, 1953), p. 17 (*hereafter referred to as Max*); Joll, *The Anarchists*, op. cit., p. 7

5 See Kelly, *Bakunin*, op. cit., p. 97 (*hereafter referred to as Kelly*)

6 Marx to F. Bolte, 23 November 1871, Marx & Engels, *Selected Works*, op. cit., p. 682; Richard B. Saltman, *The Social and Political Thought of Michael*

Bakunin (Westport, Connecticut: Greenwood Press, 1983), p. 170; Arthur Lehning, 'Introduction', *Michael Bakunin: Selected Writings* (New York: Grove Press, 1973), p. 10. Paul Thomas in his *Marx and the Anarchists*, op. cit., follows Marx in arguing that Bakunin was opposed to theory.

7 Quoted in Guy A. Aldred, *Bakunin* (Glasgow: Bakunin Press, 1940), p. 31

8 Carr, *Bakunin*, op. cit., 2nd edn. (New York, 1975), p. 229

9 Paul Avrich, *The Russian Anarchists* (Princeton, NJ: Princeton University Press, 1967), pp. 20–1; Edmund Wilson, *To the Finland Station: A Study in the Writing and Acting of History* (1940) (Fontana, 1970), p. 283 (*hereafter referred to as Wilson*)

10 Mendel, *Bakunin*, op. cit., pp. 419, 1

11 Wilson, p. 269

12 *Bakunin on Anarchy: Selected Works of the Activist-Founder of World Anarchism*, ed. Sam Dolgoff (Allen & Unwin, 1973); Saltman, *The Social and Political Thought of Michael Bakunin*, op. cit., p. 170

13 See Anthony Masters, *Bakunin: The Father of Anarchism* (Sidgwick & Jackson, 1974), pp. xix–xx

14 *Bakunin on Anarchy*, op. cit., p. 261. After Bakunin's death, his friend James Guillaume edited five out of six volumes of his *Oeuvres* (Paris: P. V. Stock, 1895–1913). Max Nettlau edited the first. The Russian historian M. Steklov intended to publish fourteen volumes of Bakunin's work, but after four (M. A. Bakunin, *Sobranie sochinenii i pisem 1828–76*, ed. Yu. M. Steklov, 4 vols. (Moscow, 1934–5) (*hereafter referred to as Bakunin*), the project was dropped; even these four volumes were later withdrawn from circulation in the Soviet Union. Arthur Lehning began to edit an edition of fifteen volumes of Bakunin's Archives held at the International Institute of Social History in Amsterdam. So far seven volumes of *Archives Bakounine* have appeared (Leiden: E. J. Brill, 1961 –).

Lehning also edited *Michael Bakunin: Selected Writings* (New York: Grove Press, 1974) (*hereafter referred to as Lehning*). Other collections referred to are *The Political Philosophy of Bakunin*, ed. G. P. Maximoff, with an Introduction by Rudolf Rocker (New York: The Free Press, 1953) (*hereafter referred to as Max.*), which arranges selections thematically; and *Bakunin on Anarchy*, op. cit. (*hereafter referred to as Dol.*), which arranges them chronologically.

15 Max., pp. 314, 313

16 Dol., p. 139

17 Max., p. 30

18 Wilson, p. 270

19 Mendel, p. 419

20 Ibid., p. 29

21 Bakunin to his parents, 19 December 1834, *Bakunin*, I, 154

22 Bakunin to A. P. Efremov, 29 July 1835, ibid., I, 174–5

23 Bakunin to his sisters, 10 August 1836, Lehning, pp. 31–2, 34–5

24 Bakunin to Varvara, 22 December 1836, *Bakunin*, I, 376

25 Bakunin, *God and the State*, ed. Benjamin Tucker (1893) (New York: Dover, 1970), p. 72

26 Dol., p. 57. The usual translation of the last sentence is: 'The urge to destroy is also a creative urge.' See Lehning, p. 58

27 Bakunin to I. Skorzewski, January 1849, *Bakunin*, III, 370

28 Bakunin to his family, May 1843, ibid., III, 216

29 Bakunin to Pavel and Turgenev, 20 November 1842, ibid., III, 164

30 *Materialy dlya biografii M. Bakunina*, ed. V. Polonsky, 3 vols. (Moscow, Petrograd, 1923), I, 175 (*hereafter referred to as Materialy*). See also *The Confessions of Mikhail Bakunin*, trans. Robert C. Howes, ed. Lawrence D. Orton (Ithaca: Cornell University Press, 1977), p. 92

31 Bakunin to Arnold Ruge, 19 January 1843, *Bakunin*, III, 176–7

32 Ibid., III, 222–31; Kelly p. 115

33 Lehning, pp. 123–4

34 Max., p. 37

35 Bakunin to his brothers and sisters, 1
    May 1845, *Bakunin*, III, 249–50
36 *Materialy*, III, 301
37 H.-E. Kaminski, *Bakounine: la vie d'un
    révolutionnaire* (1938) (Paris:
    Bélibaste, 1971), p. 77 (*hereafter referred
    to as* Kaminski)
38 *Materialy*, III, 367. Cf. Bakunin's letter
    to *La Démocratie*, ibid., III, 145,
    acknowledging Proudhon's influence
    on his anarchism.
39 Bakunin to Georg and Emma
    Herwegh, 6 September 1847,
    Bakunin, III, 265
40 Wilson, p. 271
41 Bakunin to Georg Herwegh, 8
    December 1848, *Bakunin*, III, 368
42 Bakunin to Herwegh, August 1848,
    ibid., III, 318
43 Dol., p. 70
44 *Confessions*, op. cit., pp. 112, 119
45 See Franco Venturi, *Roots of Revolution*
    (New York: Grosset & Dunlap, 1966)
    p. 58; Dol., p. 62
46 Quoted in Lehning, p. 144
47 *Confessions*, op. cit., pp, 149–50, 34
48 Ibid., p. 79
49 Quoted in Kaminski, p. 167
50 Bakunin to Tatyana, February 1854,
    Bakunin, IV, 244–5
51 Bakunin to his family, *Materialy*, I, 269
52 Bakunin to Herzen, 7 November 1860;
    8 December 1860, Kelly, p. 147
53 Quoted in Kaminski, p. 179
54 Peter Kropotkin, *Memoirs of a
    Revolutionist*, ed. J. A. Rogers
    (Cresset, 1988), p. 133
55 See Avrich, 'Bakunin and the United
    States', *Anarchist Portraits*, op. cit.,
    pp. 16–31
56 A. I. Herzen, *Sobranie sochinenii
    v tridtsati tomakh* (Moscow, 1954–65),
    XI, 360; Herzen to Bakunin, 20 August
    1863
57 *Bakunin*, II, 273–4
58 'Réflexions philosophiques sur le
    fantôme divin, le monde réel, et
    l'homme', *Oeuvres*, op. cit., III, 397
59 See Marx to Engels, 4 November 1864,
    Wilson, p. 283
60 Bakunin to Herzen and Ogarev, 19 July
    1866, Lehning, p. 59

61 Dol., p. 76. Guérin reproduces in his
    anthology *Ni Dieu ni Maître* the two
    related texts 'The Programme of the
    Brotherhood' and the 'Revolutionary
    Catechism' from Nettlau's handwritten
    biography of Bakunin in their original
    French and argues that they are the
    'least known and perhaps the most
    important of Bakunin's anarchist
    writings' (Guérin, *Ni Dieu ni Maître*,
    op. cit., p. 169). A shortened version of
    the manuscript is also reprinted in
    Lehning, pp. 64–93
62 Ibid., pp. 93, 94
63 Dol., pp. 76, 78
64 Lehning, p. 20
65 Dol., p. 88
66 Ibid., pp. 77, 78
67 Kaminski, p. 214
68 Dol., pp. 79, 80–81
69 Ibid., pp. 89, 99, 95
70 Ibid., p. 100
71 Ibid., pp. 83, 82
72 Ibid., p. 96; Guérin, *Ni Dieu ni Maître*,
    op. cit., I, 170
73 Dol., pp. 98, 85
74 Wilson, p. 277
75 Kelly, p. 179
76 Dol., p. 103
77 Ibid., p. 129
78 Ibid., pp. 125, 147
79 Ibid., pp. 133, 134
80 Kelly, p. 179
81 Marx to F. Bolte, 23 November 1871,
    Marx and Engels, *Selected Works*,
    op. cit., p. 682
82 James Guillaume, 'Michael Bakunin: A
    Biographical Sketch', Dol., p. 38
83 Dol., p. 157
84 Ibid., pp. 162, 166, 167
85 Ibid., p. 152
86 Ibid., pp. 154–5
87 Ibid., p. 158
88 See Marx to F. Bolte, 23 November
    1871, Marx and Engels, *Selected
    Works*, op. cit., pp. 682–3; Nikolai
    Ivanov, *Karl Marx: A Short Biography*
    (Moscow: Novosti Press, 1982),
    p. 176
89 Kaminski, p. 222
90 Bakunin to Guillaume, 13 April 1869,
    Kelly, p. 270

91 Kelly, p. 266. For a French translation, see M. Confino, *Violence dans la violence. Le débat Bakounine – Nečaev* (Paris, 1973), pp. 100–5
92 Carr, p. 379
93 Bakunin to Sergei Nechaev, 2 June 1870, *Archives*, IV, 114, 125, 106–7. Carr (p. 386) argues from internal evidence that both the *Principles of Revolution* and *Catechism of a Revolutionary* were written by Bakunin. On the other hand, Kelly follows Steklov (*Bakunin*, III, 463–5) by asserting that Bakunin wrote the *Principles* and that, because of the similarities in style and content, he probably helped edit Nechaev's *Catechism* (Kelly, pp. 271, 269). At the same time, P. Pomper (*Sergei Nechaev* (New Brunswick, NJ: 1979), pp. 79–83) assigns authorship of *The Principles* to Nechaev, as does Paul Avrich, 'Bakunin and Nechaev', *Anarchist Portraits*, op. cit., p. 40
94 See *Letter to a Frenchman*, Kelly, p. 212; and *Statism and Anarchy*, *Archives*, III, 174
95 Marx, quoted in Lehning, p. 284
96 Dol., p. 184
97 Ibid., pp, 207, 206
98 Ibid., p. 200
99 Ibid., pp. 189, 209
100 Quoted in Eugene Schulkind (ed.), *The Paris Commune of 1871: The View from the Left* (Cape, 1972), p. 39; Bakunin to Albert Richard, 1871, pp. 180–1
101 Ibid., pp. 245, 256, 249
102 Ibid., p. 182
103 Kelly, p. 193
104 *The Paris Commune and the Idea of the State*, ed. Nicolas Walter (Cira, 1971)
105 *The Essential Works of Anarchism*, ed. Marshall S. Shatz (New York: Bantam, 1971), p. 134 (*hereafter referred to as Shatz*)
106 Shatz, p. 135
107 Ibid., pp. 136, 138
108 Max., p. 58
109 Shatz, 130–1
110 Dol., p. 271
111 Max., p. 83

112 Shatz, p. 126
113 Max., p. 95
114 Shatz, p. 127
115 Dol., p. 308
116 Shatz, 147
117 Max., pp. 88, 90
118 Ibid., pp, 136, 157
119 Dol., p. 271
120 Ibid., p. 257
121 *Michael Bakunin: Marxism, Freedom and the State*, ed. K. J. Kenafick (Freedom Press, 1984), p. 16 (*hereafter referred to as Ken.*)
122 Ken., p. 17
123 Dol., p. 257
124 Max., 165
125 Dol., pp. 237–8
126 Ken., p. 17
127 Lehning, p. 65
128 Dol., pp. 245, 238
129 Max., p. 249
130 Dol., pp. 240, 239, 241
131 Max., p. 239
132 Shatz, p. 141
133 Ibid., p. 143
134 Dol., p. 238
135 Shatz, pp. 144–5
136 Ibid., pp. 147, 149, 153
137 Ibid., p. 152
138 Kelly, p. 255; Carr, p. 435
139 Shatz, p. 147
140 Saltman, *Bakunin*, op. cit., p. 150
141 Kelly, p. 196; Isaiah Berlin, *A Remarkable Decade: Russian Thinkers* (1978), p. 107. Cf. Chomsky's Introduction to Guérin's *Anarchism*, op. cit., pp. x–xi
142 Dol., p. 269
143 Ibid., p. 330
144 Ibid., p. 337
145 Max., p. 224
146 Ibid., pp. 354, 346, 196
147 Ibid., pp. 241, 240
148 Dol., pp. 221, 224
149 Max., p. 214
150 Dol., pp. 329, 332
151 *Archives*, III, 149
152 Dol, pp. 262–3
153 Dol., p. 263
154 Max., pp. 373, 269
155 Dol., pp. 325, 270

156 Max., pp. 267, 341, 295
157 Ibid., pp. 328, 341, 328, 345
158 Ibid., pp. 372, 376, 413
159 Dol., p. 264
160 Lehning, p. 214
161 Marx, 'Civil War in France', Marx and Engels, *Selected Works*, op. cit., pp. 292, 294
162 Dol., pp. 292, 295
163 Marx to F. Bolte, 23 November 1871, Marx and Engels, *Selected Works*, op. cit., pp. 682–3
164 Engels to Theodor Cuno, 24 January 1872, *Marx and Engels, Basic Writings on Politics and Philosophy*, ed. L. S. Feuer (Fontana, 1979), p. 481
165 *Archives*, II, 276
166 Marx and Engels, *Basic Writings*, op. cit., pp. 521, 522
167 Dol., p. 303
168 *Materialy*, III, 263–4
169 Dol., p. 38
170 Max., p. 44
171 Lehning, Bakunin's Conceptions of Revolutionary Organizations and their Role: A Study of his Secret Societies', *Essays in Honour of E. H. Carr*, ed. C. Abramsky (1974), p. 74
172 Dol., p. 277
173 Shatz, p. 126
174 Dol., p. 282
175 Ibid., pp. 310–11
176 Max., pp. 227, 325, 235
177 Dol., pp. 280, 294
178 Ibid., p. 309.
179 *Bakunin*, IV, 316
180 Bakunin to Elisée Reclus, 15 February 1875, Dol., pp. 354–5
181 *Bakunin*, III, 119
182 See Marx's commentary to Bakunin's *Statism and Anarchy*, Marx, Engels & Lenin, *Anarchism and Anarcho-syndicalism*, op. cit., p. 152
183 Carr, pp. 439–40
184 Shatz, p. 142
185 Mendel, p. 425
186 Aldred, *Bakunin*, op. cit., p. 31
187 Joll, *The Anarchists*, op. cit., p. 67
188 Shatz, p. 164
189 Ken., p. 17
190 See Clark, 'Marx, Bakunin, and Social Revolution', *The Anarchist Moment*, op. cit., 73–4
191 Kelly, p. 186
192 See Avrich, 'The Legacy of Bakunin', in *Anarchist Portraits*, op. cit., pp. 5–15

Chapter Nineteen

1 See Martin A. Miller, *Kropotkin* (Chicago University Press, 1976), p. 12
2 Quoted by George Woodcock & Ivan Avakumović, *The Anarchist Prince: A Biographical Study of Peter Kropotkin* (T. V. Boardman, 1950), p. 15
3 Ibid., p. 23
4 Peter Kropotkin, *Memoirs of a Revolutionist*, ed. Allen Rogers (Cresset, 1988), p. 91
5 Ibid., p. 84
6 Ibid., pp. 147–8
7 *The Commune of Paris*, ed. Nicolas Walter (Freedom Press, 1971)
8 Kropotkin, quoted in Avrich, 'The Paris Commune', *Anarchist Portraits*, op. cit., p. 23
9 'Modern Science and Anarchism', *Kropotkin's Revolutionary Pamphlets*, ed.Roger Baldwin (New York: Vanguard Press, 1927), p. 166
10 *Memoirs*, op. cit., p. 185
11 Ibid., p. 188
12 Ibid., p. 195
13 Ibid., p. 210
14 Sergei Kravchinsky, *Underground Russia* (New York, 1885), p. 89
15 Kropotkin, *Selected Writings on Anarchism and Revolution*, ed. Martin A. Miller (Cambridge, Mass.: M. I. T. Press, 1970), p. 63
16 Kropotkin, *Memoirs*, op. cit., p. 260
17 For a detailed account of Kropotkin's involvement in the anarchist movement at the time see Caroline Cahm, *Kropotkin and the Rise of Revolutionary Violence, 1872–1886* (Cambridge University Press, 1988)
18 Woodcock & Avakumović, *Kropotkin*, op. cit., p. 218
19 Kropotkin, *Memoirs*, op. cit., p. 293.

See also the essay 'Prisons and their Moral Influence on Prisoners', *Revolutionary Pamphlets*, op. cit., pp. 220–35

20 'Law and Authority', ibid., pp. 205, 217
21 Miller, *Kropotkin*, op. cit., p. 169
22 Kropotkin, *Memoirs*, op. cit., p. 303
23 'The Spring Revolt', *Revolutionary Pamphlets*, op. cit., pp. 40–1
24 Kropotkin to Georg Brandes, *Freedom* (October 1898), pp. 68–9
25 *Memoirs*, op. cit., p. 191
26 'The Coming Revolution', *Act for Yourselves: Articles from Freedom 1886–1907*, eds. Nicolas Walter & Heiner Becker (Freedom Press, 1988), p. 22
27 *Memoirs*, op. cit., p. 301
28 *The Conquest of Bread* (1906) (Elephant Editions, 1985), p. 173n
29 Kropotkin to Max Nettlau (5 March 1902), *Selected Writings*, op. cit., p. 305
30 Quoted by Woodcock & Avakumović, *Kropotkin*, op. cit., p. 165
31 *Modern Science and Anarchism* (1901) (Simian, n.d.), p. 5
32 Quoted by Woodcock & Avakumović, *Kropotkin*, op. cit., p. 256
33 Kropotkin, *Mutual Aid* (1902) (Harmondsworth: Pelican, 1939), p. 23
34 Ibid., pp. 60–1
35 Ibid., p. 230
36 Ibid., p. 231
37 Cf. Avrich, 'Kropotkin's Ethical Anarchism', in *Anarchist Portraits*, op. cit., p. 59
38 *Anarchism and Anarchist Communism*, ed. Nicolas Walter (Freedom Press, 1987), p. 25
39 Ibid., p. 30
40 *Ethics: Origin and Development* (1922), ed. N. Lebedev (Dorchester: Prism Press, n.d.), p. 45
41 Ibid., pp. 19–20
42 'Anarchist Morality', *Revolutionary Pamphlets*, op. cit., p. 92
43 Ibid., p. 109. For Kropotkin's appreciation of Guyau, see *Ethics*, op. cit., pp. 322–31
44 Kropotkin to Nettlau (5 March 1902), *Selected Writings*, op. cit., p. 297

45 *Anarchist Communism*, op. cit., pp. 31, 58
46 Quoted by Woodcock & Avakumović, *Kropotkin*, op. cit., p. 199
47 *The State: Its Historic Role*, trans. Vernon Richards (Freedom Press, 1969), p. 12
48 Ibid., p. 21
49 *Act for Yourselves*, op. cit., p. 84
50 *Conquest of Bread*, op. cit., p. 108
51 Ibid., p. 110
52 Goldman, *Living My Life*, op. cit., I, 253
53 *The State*, op. cit., p. 10
54 Ibid., pp. 35, 39
55 Ibid., p. 52
56 Quoted by Woodcock & Avakumović, *Kropotkin*, op. cit., p. 307
57 *Act for Yourselves*, op. cit., p. 38
58 Malatesta, 'Peter Kropotkin – Recollections and Criticism of an Old Friend', *Malatesta: His Life & Ideas*, op. cit., p. 263
59 *The State*, op. cit., p. 56
60 *Conquest of Bread*, op. cit., p. 159; *Anarchist Communism*, op. cit., p. 28
61 *Revolutionary Pamphlets*, op. cit., p. 249; *Anarchist Communism*, op. cit., p. 27
62 *Anarchism*, op. cit. p. 7
63 Quoted by Woodcock & Avakumović, *Kropotkin*, op. cit., p. 312
64 *Anarchist Communism*, op. cit., p. 52
65 Ibid., p. 43
66 *Conquest of Bread*, op. cit., p. 45
67 See *Anarchism in Socialist Evolution* (Freedom Press, pamphlet no. 7, n.d.), p. 13; *Act for Yourselves*, op. cit., p. 102
68 *Conquest of Bread*, op. cit., p. 33
69 Ibid., p. 103
70 Ibid., pp. 108, 120
71 Quoted by Woodcock & Avakumović, *Kropotkin*, op. cit., p. 321
72 *Conquest of Bread*, op. cit., p. 183
73 Ibid., pp. 128, 204
74 Ibid., p. 124
75 Ibid., p. 143
76 Ibid., pp. 146–7
77 Ibid., p. 148
78 Ibid., pp. 154, 111, 117
79 *Anarchist Communism*, op. cit., p. 53
80 *Conquest of Bread*, op. cit., p. 189

81 *Fields, Factories and Workshops Tomorrow*, ed. Colin Ward (Allen & Unwin, 1974), p. 26

82 Ibid., p. 197

83 Ibid., pp. 194, 175

84 Ibid., p. 178

85 *Anarchist Communism*, op. cit., p. 33. Cf. *Fields, Factories and Workshops*, op. cit., pp. 77–9

86 Kropotkin to Gustav Steffens, *Selected Writings*, op. cit., pp. 310–11

87 Kropotkin to Jean Grave (November 1914), 'Epilogue', *Memoirs*, op. cit., p. 304

88 See Malatesta, 'Anarchists have Forgotten their Principles', *Freedom* (November 1914), and 'Pro-government Anarchists', ibid. (April 1916)

89 Leon Trotsky, *History of the Russian Revolution*, trans. Max Eastman (New York, 1932), I, 75

90 Avrich, 'Kropotkin in America', *Anarchist Portraits*, op. cit., p. 85

91 Kropotkin to Georg Brandes, April 1919, *Selected Writings*, op. cit., p. 320

92 'Conversation with Lenin', ibid., p. 330

93 Avrich, ed., *The Anarchists in the Russian Revolution* (Ithaca, NY: Cornell University Press, 1973), pp. 147–8

94 Kropotkin to Lenin, 4 March 1920, ibid., pp. 336–7; 21 December 1920, ibid., p. 338. See also David Shub, 'Kropotkin and Lenin', *Russian Review* XII (1953), 227–34

95 Quoted in 'Epilogue', *Memoirs*, op. cit., p. 313

96 'Letter to the Workers of the West', *Revolutionary Pamphlets*, op. cit., p. 253

97 'What to Do?', ibid., p. 258

98 'Epilogue', *Memoirs*, op. cit., p. 314

99 Wilde, *De Profundis and Other Writings*, op. cit., p. 80

100 Avrich, 'Kropotkin's Ethical Anarchism', *Anarchist Portraits*, op. cit., p. 78

101 See Cahm, *Kropotkin and the Rise of Revolutionary Violence, 1872–1886*, op. cit., pp. 279–80

102 See John Hewetson, 'Mutual Aid and Social Evolulution', *Anarchy*, 55 (September 1965), 257–70

103 Malatesta, *Life and Ideas*, op. cit., p. 263

104 'Modern Science and Anarchism', *Revolutionary Pamphlets*, op. cit., p. 152

105 See Ward's edition of *Fields, Factories and Workshops Tomorrow*, op. cit., where Kropotkin's arguments are supported by recent data.

106 *Mutual Aid*, op. cit., p. 233

Chapter Twenty

1 Quoted in Marie Fleming, *The Anarchist Way to Socialism: Elisée Reclus and Nineteenth-Century European Anarchism* (Croom Helm, 1979), p. 9

2 Max Nettlau, *Elisée Reclus: La vida de un sabio justo y rebelde* (Barcelona, 1929), quoted in Fleming, *The Anarchist Way to Socialism*, op. cit., pp. 10–11

3 Ibid., pp. 37, 39

4 See Joseph Ishill, *Elisée Reclus and Elie Reclus: In Memoriam* (Berkeley Heights, 1927)

5 Reclus, Preface to Leon Metchnikoff, *La Civilisation et les grands fleuves historiques* (Paris, 1889), p. xxvii. See also Fleming, 'Life, Liberty and the Pursuit of a Natural Order: The Anarchism of Elisée Reclus', *Social Anarchism*, II, l (1981), 19–35

6 Reclus, Preface, *L'Homme et la terre* (Paris, 1905), I, iv

7 Reclus, *L'Evolution légale et l'anarchie* (Paris: Bibliothèque des Temps Nouveaux, 1898), p. 14

8 *Le Révolté* (17 October 1880)

9 *Bulletin de la Fédération Jurassienne* (11 March 1877)

10 Reclus, *L'Idéal et la jeunesse* (Paris: Editions de la Société Nouvelle, 1894), p. 3

11 Reclus, 'On Vegetarianism', *The Humane Review* (January 1901)

12 Reclus, 'La Grande Famille', *Magazine International* (January 1897), trans. Edward Carpenter as *The Great Kinship* (1900)

13 *Le Révolté* (21 January 1882)

14 Quoted in Fleming, *The Anarchist Way to Socialism*, op. cit., pp. 180, 210

15 Reclus, *An Anarchist on Anarchy* (1894), p. 14

16 Kropotkin, 'Anarchist Morality', *Revolutionary Pamphlets* op. cit., p. 92

17 Reclus, *L'Evolution, la révolution, et l'idéal anarchique* (Paris: P. V. Stock, 1898), p. 15

18 Ibid., p. 186. See also Reclus, *Evolution et révolution* (Paris: Publications de la Révolte, 1891), p. 10

19 Reclus, Preface to Kropotkin's, *La Conquête du pain* (Paris, 1892). Reclus helped with the proofs and suggested the title of the work.

20 Reclus, *L'Evolution, la révolution, et l'idéal anarchique*, op. cit., p. 143

Chapter Twenty-One

1 *Malatesta: His Life and Ideas*, ed. Vernon Richards (1965) (Freedom Press, 1977), p. 208 (*hereafter referred to as Malatesta*)

2 *Compte rendu du VIIIème Congrès générale, Berne* (Berne, 1876), pp. 10, 97

3 Quoted in R. Hostetter, *The Italian Socialist Movement, 1. Origins (1860-1882)* (Princeton, NJ: Van Nostrand, 1958), p. 368

4 Quoted in Woodcock, *Anarchism*, op. cit., p. 320

5 Malatesta, *Entre Paysans* (Paris, 1887), pp. 61, 58, 67

6 Malatesta, *Anarchy*, trans. V. Richards (Freedom Press, 1974), pp. 50, 27

7 Ibid., pp. 24, 28

8 Ibid., pp. 19, 13

9 Ibid., p. 41

10 Ibid., p. 53

11 *Malatesta*, op. cit., p. 20

12 Ibid., pp. 87, 145

13 For an account of this incident, see Richards, ibid., Appendix III, pp. 252-6

14 *Compte rendu analytique des séances du Congrès anarchiste tenu à Amsterdam 24-31 août 1907* (Paris, 1908), p. 83

15 Quoted in Richards, 'Introduction' to Malatesta, *Anarchy*, op. cit., p. 5

16 Malatesta's 'Anarchists have forgotten their Principles', *Freedom* (November 1914), *Malatesta*, op. cit., p. 243

17 *Freedom* (April 1916), ibid., p. 251

18 Camillo Berneri, *Auto-Democracy* (1 June 1919)

19 Quoted in Guérin, *Anarchism*, op. cit., p. 112

20 Malatesta, *Scritti scelti*, ed. C. Zaccaria & G. Berneri (Naples, 1947), p. 326

21 *Malatesta*, op. cit., p. 184

22 Ibid., p. 21

23 Ibid., pp. 66, 60

24 Ibid., pp. 24, 49

25 Ibid., pp. 98, 107

26 Ibid., p. 88

27 Ibid., pp. 19, 31, 35, 47

28 Ibid., p. 42

29 Ibid., p. 153

30 Ibid., p. 161

31 Ibid., p. 267

32 Ibid., pp. 25, 40

33 Ibid., p. 261

34 Ibid., p. 68

35 Ibid., p. 173

36 Quoted by Richards, 'Introduction', Malatesta, *Anarchy*, op. cit., p. 8

37 *Malatesta*, op. cit., pp. 178, 170

38 Ibid., pp. 164, 180

39 Ibid., p. 177

Chapter Twenty-Two

1 See Henri Troyat, *Tolstoy*, trans. Nancy Amphoux (W. H. Allen, 1968), p. 16

2 Quoted in Ernest J. Simmons, *Tolstoy* (Routledge & Kegan Paul, 1973), p. 24

3 Tolstoy, 'The Slavery of our Times', *Social Evils and Their Remedy*, ed. Helen Chroushoff Matheson (Methuen, 1915), p. 102

4 Diary entry, 4 March 1855, *Tolstoy's Diaries*, ed. R. F. Christian (Athlone Press, 1985), p. 101

5 Tolstoy to V. P. Botkin, 24-5 March/5-6 April 1857, *Tolstoy's Letters*, ed. R. F. Christian (Athlone Press, 1978), I, 95-6

6 *A Confession, The Gospel in Brief, and What I Believe*, trans. Aylmer Maude (Oxford University Press, 1974), p. 12

7 Notebooks, 25 May 1857, quoted in Simmons, *Tolstoy*, op. cit., p. 54

8 Ibid., 13 April 1957

9 Ibid., 24 May 1857

10 *A Confession, The Gospel in Brief, and What I Believe*, op. cit., p. 13

11 'The School at Yásnaya Polyána', *Patterns of Anarchy*, op. cit., p. 476

12 Tolstoy to S. N. Tolstaya, 15 May 1902, *Letters*, op. cit., II, 618–19

13 'Education and Culture', in *Tolstoy on Education*, trans. Leo Wiener (Chicago: University of Chicago Press, 1967). See also Joel Spring, *A Primer of Libertarian Education* (New York: Free Life Editions, 1977), pp. 47–8

14 Tolstoy to A. M. Kalmykova, 31 August 1896, *Letters*, op. cit., II, 539

15 Quoted in Troyat, *Tolstoy*, op. cit., p. 220

16 Ibid., p. 205

17 Tolstoy to the Emperor Alexander II, 22 August 1862, *Letters*, op. cit., I, 164

18 'What Then Must We Do?' (1886), *The Works of Leo Tolstoy*, trans. Louise & Aylmer Maude (1929–1937), XIV, 384

19 Quoted in Simmons, *Tolstoy*, op. cit., p. 154

20 *Social Evils*, op. cit., pp. 235–6

21 Isaiah Berlin, *The Hedgehog and the Fox: an essay on Tolstoy's view of history* (New York, 1953), p. 39

22 *A Confession, The Gospel in Brief and What I Believe*, op. cit., p. 17

23 Ibid., p. 8

24 *Social Evils*, op. cit., p. 206; 'Introduction', *A Confession, The Gospel in Brief and What I Believe*, op. cit., p. xv

25 Ibid., p. 167

26 Ibid., pp. 531–2

27 Tolstoy to Alexander III, 8–15 March 1881, *Letters*, op. cit., II, 343

28 'The Kingdom of God is Within You', *The Lion and the Honeycomb: The Religious Writings of Tolstoy*, ed. A. N. Wilson (Collins, 1987), pp. 89–90

29 A. N. Wilson, *Tolstoy* (Hamish Hamilton, 1988)

30 Tolstoy, 'A Reply to the Synod's Edict of Excommunication' (1901), *On Life and Essays on Religion, Works*, op. cit., XII, 223

31 *The Kingdom of God and Peace Essays*, ibid., XX, 135

32 Ibid., p. 330

33 'The Slavery of our Time', *Social Evils*, op. cit., p. 97

34 'Patriotism and Government', *Works*, op. cit. XLVI, 1, 250

35 'Letter to a Non-Commissioned Officer', *Tolstoy on Civil Disobedience and Non-Violence*, (New York: Mentor, 1967), p. 121

36 'On Patriotism', *On Civil Disobedience*, op. cit., p. 79

37 Tolstoy, 'Patriotism and Government', *Works*, op. cit., XLVI, 1, 252

38 Ibid., p. 261

39 'Slavery of our Times', *Social Evils*, op. cit., p. 105

40 Tolstoy, 'On Anarchy', ibid., p. 185

41 See 'To the Working People', ibid., p. 24

42 'Government', ibid., p. 135

43 'Patriotism and Government', *Works*, op. cit., XLVI, 1, 259

44 A Letter addressed to *The Daily Chronicle* (1895), *Tolstoy on Civil Disobedience*, op. cit., p. 138

45 'On the Negro Question' (1904), ibid., p. 283

46 'Government', *Social Evils*, op. cit., p. 132

47 'The Slavery of Our Times', ibid., p. 68

48 'What Then Must We Do?', *Works*, op. cit., XIV, 357–8

49 'Slavery of our Times', *Social Evils*, op. cit., p. 79

50 'Government', ibid., p. 138

51 See Tolstoy to A. M. Kalmykova, 31 August 1896, *Letters*, op. cit., II, 540

52 See '"Thou Shalt Not Kill" – On the Death of King Humbert' (1900), *On Civil Disobedience*, op. cit., p. 155

53 Quoted in Simmons, *Tolstoy*, op. cit., p. 212

54 *Social Evils*, op. cit., p. 206

55 Ibid., p. 93
56 Ibid., p. 190
57 'To the Working People', ibid.,
    p. 47
58 Ibid., p. 45
59 Tolstoy to V. F. Totomiants, 23
    January 1910, *Letters*, op. cit., II, 696
60 Quoted in Simmons, *Tolstoy*, op. cit.,
    p. 204
61 Ibid., p. 212
62 Tolstoy to A. Y. Alipov, 20 September
    1906, *Letters*, op. cit., II, 659
63 *Lenin o Tolstom* (Moscow-Leningrad,
    1928), p. 24. Among Lenin's several
    articles devoted to Tolstoy, the most
    important is *Leo Tolstoy as a Mirror of
    the Russian Revolution*.
64 Shaw to R. Ellis Roberts, February
    1900, *Letters*, op. cit., II, 677
65 'I Cannot Be Silent', *Works*, op. cit.,
    XXI, 404–11
66 Tolstoy to Mohandas Gandhi, 7
    September 1910, *Letters*, op. cit., II,
    706
67 Gandhi, *Democracy, Real and Deceptive*
    (Ahmedabad, 1961), p. 28
68 For the Sarvodaya movement, see
    Geoffrey Ostergaard & M. Currell,
    The Gentle Anarchists (Oxford:
    Clarendon Press, 1971); and
    Ostergaard, *Nonviolent Revolution in
    India* (New Delhi: Gandhi Peace
    Foundation, 1985)
69 Wilson, 'Introduction', *Religious
    Writings*, op. cit., p. 16

Chapter Twenty-Three

1 See Martin, *Men Against the State: The
   Expositors of Individualist Anarchism in
   America, 1827–1908*, op. cit.
2 See William Bailie, *Josiah Warren: The
   First American Anarchist* (Boston:
   Small, Maynard & Co., 1906)
3 Josiah Warren, *Practical Details in
   Equitable Commerce* (New Harmony,
   Ind., 1852), I, 12
4 Warren, *Equitable Commerce* (New
   Harmony, Ind., 1846), p. 96
5 See Eunice M. Schuster, *Native
   American Anarchism: A Study of*

   Left-Wing Anarchist Individualism
   (1932) (New York: Da Capo Press,
   1970), pp. 92–106
6 Quoted in Woodcock, *Anarchism*,
   op. cit., p. 433
7 Quoted in David De Leon, *The
   American as Anarchist: Reflections on
   Indigenous Radicalism* (Baltimore and
   London: Johns Hopkins University
   Press, 1978), p. 79
8 Warren, *Practical Applications of the
   Elementary Principles of 'True
   Civilization'* (Princeton, NJ: The
   Author, 1873), p. 19
9 Warren, *Equitable Commerce* (New
   York: Fowler & Wells, 1852), p. 69
10 Warren, *Practical Details in Equitable
   Commerce* (Princeton, NJ: Cooperative
   Publishing Company, 1872), p. 73
11 *Liberty*, XI (8 February 1896), 5
12 *Autobiography of John Stuart Mill*
   (1873) (New York: Signet, 1964),
   pp. 182–3
13 Stephen Pearl Andrews, *The Science of
   Society* (New York: Fowler & Wells,
   1852). For Andrews, see also Schuster,
   Native American Anarchism, op. cit., pp.
   106–12
14 Lysander Spooner, *Natural Law: or The
   Science of Justice* (1882) in *Collected
   Works of Lysander Spooner*, ed. Charles
   Shively (Weston, Mass.: M & S Press,
   1971), I, 9
15 Spooner, *No Treason* (Boston: The
   Author, 1867)
16 *Natural Law*, op. cit., I, 18
17 *Poverty: Its Illegal Causes and Legal Cure*
   (1846), *Collected Works*, op. cit., V, 59
18 George Schumm, 'Benjamin R.
   Tucker – A Brief Sketch of his Life
   and Work', *Freethinker's Magazine*, 2
   (July 1893), 439
19 Benjamin R. Tucker, *Instead of a Book*
   (New York: Benj. R. Tucker, 1897),
   p. 80
20 Quoted in Horace Traubel, *With Walt
   Whitman in Camden* (Boston, 1906), I,
   350
21 Kropotkin, *Anarchism and Anarchist
   Communism*, op. cit., p. 18
22 *Liberty*, VIII (16 July 1892), 2
23 Quoted in Avrich, 'Benjamin Tucker

and His Daughter', *Anarchist Portraits*, op. cit., p. 146

24 Tucker, *Instead of a Book*, op. cit., pp. 9, 14

25 Ibid., p. 131

26 Ibid., p. 15

27 Ibid., p. 404

28 *Liberty*, X (28 August 1894), 1

29 Goldman, *Living My Life*, op. cit., I, 232

30 See Kropotkin, *Anarchism and Anarchist Communism*, op. cit., p. 18

31 *Liberty*, III (3 June 1885), 4

32 Tucker, 'Why I am an Anarchist', *Twentieth Century Magazine*, 4 (29 May 1890), 5–6

33 Quoted in Avrich, 'Benjamin Tucker and His Daughter', op. cit., p. 151

34 Adin Ballou, *Remarks* at the First Annual Meeting of the Non-Resistance Society (Massachusetts, 25 September 1839). See also his *Non-Resistance in Relation to Human Government* (Boston: Non-Resistance Society, 1839)

35 John Humphrey Noyes, *History of Socialisms* (Trübner, 1870), p. 624

36 Voltairine de Cleyre, 'The Making of an Anarchist', *Selected Writings of Voltairine de Cleyre*, ed. Alexander Berkman (New York: Mother Earth Publishing Association, 1914)

37 Ibid., p. 134. See also Avrich, *An American Anarchist: The Life of Voltairine de Cleyre* (Princeton, NJ: Princeton University Press, 1978), ch. vi

38 Alexander Berkman, *Prison Memoirs of an Anarchist* (New York: Mother Earth Publishing Association, 1912), pp. 7, 415

39 Berkman, *The Bolshevik Myth: Diary 1920–1922* (New York: Boni & Liveright, 1925), p. 319

40 Berkman to Ben Capes, 25 April 1927, quoted in Avrich, 'Alexander Berkman: A Sketch', *Anarchist Portraits*, op. cit., p. 200

41 Berkman, *ABC of Anarchism*, ed. Peter E. Newell (Freedom Press, 1973), pp. xii, xiii

42 Ibid., pp. 8, 2, 11

43 Ibid., pp. 20, 8

Chapter Twenty-Four

1 See Richard Drinnon, *Rebel in Paradise: A Biography of Emma Goldman* (Chicago: University of Chicago Press, 1982), pp. 9–10

2 Quoted in Alix Kates Shulman, 'Introduction', *Red Emma Speaks* (Wildwood House, 1979), p. 6

3 Ibid., p. 10

4 Quoted by Goldman, *Anarchism and Other Essays*, ed. Richard Drinnon (New York: Dover, 1969), p. 87

5 *Red Emma Speaks*, op. cit., p. 60

6 Ibid., p. 102

7 Ibid., p. 332

8 Ibid., pp. 242, 346

9 Ibid., p. 360.

10 Ibid., p. 333

11 Drinnon, *Rebel in Paradise*, op. cit., p. 302

12 Goldman, 'Address' (1937), *Red Emma Speaks*, op. cit., p. 385

13 Goldman to Vero Richards, 10 September 1938, *Anarchy* 114 (August 1970), p. 246

14 Goldman, 'The Individual, Society and the State' (1940), *Red Emma Speaks*, op. cit., p. 87

15 'Was My Life Worth Living?', ibid., p. 392

16 'What I Believe' (1908), ibid., p. 42; 'The Failure of Christianity', ibid., p. 187; 'The Philosophy of Atheism', ibid., p. 202

17 'Anarchism', *Anarchism*, op. cit., pp. 50, 52, 59

18 Preface, ibid., pp. 44, 45

19 'Minorities versus Majorities', ibid., pp. 77–8

20 'Was My life Worth Living?', *Red Emma Speaks*, op. cit., p. 393

21 'Anarchism', *Anarchism*, op. cit., p. 67

22 'What I Believe' (1908), *Red Emma Speaks*, pp. 35, 36

23 'Syndicalism: Theory and Practice' (1913), *Red Emma Speaks*, op. cit., p. 68

24 'The Place of the Individual in Society' (1940), ibid., pp. 90, 93, 97, 95

25 *Red Emma Speaks*, op. cit., pp. 65, 176

26 'Socialism: Caught in a Political Trap', ibid., 79

27 Ibid., pp. 100, 84

28 'Preface', *Anarchism*, op. cit., p. 43
29 'The Psychology of Political Violence', ibid., p. 80
30 'What I Believe', *Red Emma Speaks*, op. cit., p. 45
31 Ibid., p. 38
32 'Preparedness: The Road to Universal Slaughter' (1915), ibid., p. 301
33 'Address to the Jury', ibid., p. 318
34 *My Disillusionment in Russia*, ibid., pp. 207, 355
35 Quoted by Shulman, ibid., p. 207
36 Goldman to Berkman, 3 July 1928, Drinnon, *Rebel in Paradise*, op. cit., p. 267
37 *Red Emma Speaks*, op. cit., p. 46
38 'The Social Importance of the Modern School' (c. 1812), ibid., p. 121
39 Ibid., p. 125
40 'The Child and its Enemies', ibid., p. 115; 'Francisco Ferrer and The Modern School', *Anarchism*, op. cit., p. 148
41 Ibid., p. 207
42 'Woman Suffrage', ibid., p. 198
43 'The Traffic in Women', ibid., p. 194; 'Jealousy', *Red Emma Speaks*, op. cit., p. 169
44 'Woman Suffrage', *Anarchism*, op. cit., p. 211
45 'What I Believe', *Red Emma Speaks*, op. cit., p. 43
46 Candace Falk, *Love, Anarchy and Emma Goldman* (1985) (rev. edn., New Brunswick: Rutgers University Press, 1990), pp. 45, 50
47 Ibid. p. 75
48 'Jealousy: Causes and a Possible Cure', *Red Emma Speaks*, op. cit., p. 175
49 Falk, *Love, Anarchy and Emma Goldman*, op. cit., p. 75
50 Ibid., p. 54
51 Quoted in *Red Emma Speaks*, op. cit., p. 105

Chapter Twenty-Five

1 Gustav Landauer to Martin Buber, quoted in Charles B. Maurer, *Call to Revolution: The Mystical Anarchism of Gustav Landauer* (Detroit: Wayne State University Press, 1971), p. 101
2 *Der Sozialist* (15 July 1911)
3 Landauer, *Social Democracy in Germany* (Freedom Press, 1896), p. 8
4 Quoted in Martin Buber, 'Landauer', *Paths in Utopia*, op. cit., p. 46
5 Landauer, *Die Revolution* (Frankfurt, 1907), quoted in Eugene Lunn, *The Prophet of Community: The Romantic Socialism of Gustav Landauer* (Berkeley: University of California Press, 1973), p. 226
6 Quoted in Buber, *Paths in Utopia*, op. cit., p. 49
7 Quoted in Lunn, *The Prophet of Community*, op. cit., pp. 257–8
8 Ibid., pp. 107, 110
9 Landauer, *Die Revolution*, op. cit., quoted in Landauer, 'Thoughts on Revolution', *Anarchy* 54 (August 1965), pp. 252, 254
10 Quoted in Lunn, *The Prophet of Community*, op. cit., pp. 135, 136–7
11 Landauer, *Die Revolution*, op. cit., a work written at Buber's request and quoted extensively in his *Paths in Utopia*; ibid., p. 5
12 Gustav Landauer to Margarete Susmann, reprinted in *Gustav Landauer, sein Lebensgang in Briefen*, ed. Martin Buber (Frankfurt, 1929)
13 Buber, *Paths in Utopia*, op. cit., pp. 55–7
14 Ibid., p. 218
15 Ibid., pp. 53, 55
16 Rocker, *The London Years* (Robert Anscombe, 1956), p. 90
17 Quoted in Lunn, *The Prophet of Community*, op. cit., p. 242
18 Quoted by Colin Ward, 'Gustav Landauer', *Anarchy* 54 (August 1965), 250; and Avrich, 'The Martyrdom of Gustav Landauer', *Anarchist Portraits*, op. cit., pp. 247–54. See also Russell Berman & T. Luke, 'On Gustav Landauer', *The Radical Papers*, ed. Dimitrios Roussopolous (Montréal: Black Rose, 1987), 97–114
19 Lunn, *The Prophet of Community*, op. cit., p. 342
20 Rudolf Rocker, *Johann Most: Das Leben*

eines Rebellen (Berlin, 1924–5), p. 301

21 Quoted in Frederic Trautmann, *The Voice of Terror: A Biography of Johann Most* (Westport, Conn.: Greenwood Press, 1980), p. xxiii

22 Ibid., p. xxi

23 Nettlau, *Anarchisten und Sozialrevolutionäre* (Berlin, 1931), p. 96

24 Johann Most, *Freiheit* (15 July 1882), quoted in Trautmann, *The Voice of Terror*, op. cit., p. 96. For an account of Most's early views, see Heiner Becker, 'Johann Most in Europe', *The Raven*, 4 (March 1988), 291–321

25 Most, 'Der Anarchie', *Internationale Bibliothek* (1888), quoted in Trautmann, *The Voice of Terror*, op. cit., p. 103

26 Quoted in Translator's Preface to Rudolf Rocker, *Nationalism and Culture*, op. cit., p. xv

27 Rocker, *The London Years*, op. cit., p. 196

28 Ibid., Foreword

29 *Nationalism and Culture*, op. cit., pp. 200–21

30 Ibid., p. 213

31 Ibid., p. 214

32 Ibid., p. 81

33 Ibid., pp. 342, 343

34 Ibid., p. 529

35 Ibid., p. 535

36 Ibid., p. 86

37 Ibid., p. 88

38 *Anarchism and Anarcho-syndicalism* (Freedom Press, 1973), p. 11

39 Ibid., pp. 14–15

40 *Anarcho-syndicalism* (Secker & Warburg, 1938), p. 9

41 Ibid., pp. 29, 33

42 Ibid., p. 130

Chapter Twenty-Six

1 Speech at Benares Hindu University, 6 February 1916, reprinted in M. K. Gandhi, *The Collected Works* (Delhi: Government of India, 1964), XIII, 214

2 See Geoffrey Ostergaard, 'Indian Anarchism: The Sarvodaya Movement', *Anarchism Today*, op. cit., pp. 150–1

3 Woodcock, *Gandhi*, op. cit., p. 7

4 *Young India* (11 August 1920)

5 For this aspect of Gandhi's thought, see Joan V. Bondurant, *The Conquest of Violence: The Gandhian Philosophy of Conflict* (Princeton, NJ: Princeton University Press, 1959); Ostergaard, 'Indian Anarchism', op. cit., p. 156

6 See Gandhi, *The Constructive Programme* (Ahmedabad: Navajivan, 1945)

7 Woodcock, *Gandhi*, op. cit., p. 86

8 *Young India* (2 July 1931)

9 Gandhi, *Sarvodaya* (Ahmedabad: Navajivan, 1954), pp. 70–1

10 Quoted in Woodcock, *Gandhi*, op. cit., p. 86

11 Ibid., p. 90

12 For the distinction between the two, see Joan Bondurant, 'Satyagraha versus Duragraha', in G. Ramachandran and T. K. Mahadevan, eds., *Gandhi – His Relevance for our Times* (Bombay: Bharatiya Vidya Bhavan, 1964), and Epilogue to the new edition of her *Conquest of Violence* (Princeton, NJ: Princeton University Press, 1988)

13 Woodcock, *Gandhi*, op. cit., p. 95

14 George Orwell, 'Reflections on Gandhi', *The Collected Essays*, op. cit., pp. 459–60

15 Quoted by Ostergaard, 'Indian Anarchism', op. cit., p. 148

16 See Ostergaard, 'Resisting the Nation-State: The Pacifist and Anarchist Traditions', *The Nation-State: The Formation of Modern Politics*, ed. Leonard Tivey (Oxford: Martin Robertson, 1981), p. 191

17 See Bhikhu Parekh, *Gandhi's Political Philosophy* (Macmillan, 1989). For the view that Gandhi remained an anarchist, see Ostergaard's review of Parekh, *Bulletin of Anarchist Research* 19 (December 1989), 22–3

Chapter Twenty-Seven

1 See Kropotkin, *The Great French Revolution* (Heinemann, 1909)

2 Quoted by Albert Soboul, *Les Sans-Culottes parisiens en l'An II* (Paris, 1958), p. 411

3 Quoted in Woodcock, *Anarchism*, op. cit., pp. 8–9

4 Ibid.

5 Quoted by Soboul, *Les Sans-Culottes parisiens en l'An II*, op. cit., p. 459

6 Quoted by Alain Sergent and Claude Harmel, *Histoire de l'anarchie* (Paris, 1949), p. 59

7 Kropotkin, *The Great French Revolution*, op. cit., p. 580

8 *Selected Writings of Pierre-Joseph Proudhon* op. cit., p. 88

9 Ibid., p. 89

10 Ibid., pp. 92, 95

11 Ibid., p. 134, 166, 168, 182

12 Bakunin, *Oeuvres*, op cit., IV, 252

13 Quoted in Woodcock, *Anarchism*, op. cit., pp. 261–2

14 *L'Humanisphère* was first published in series in *Le Libertaire* and then reprinted by Sébastien Faure in 1899.

15 See Avrich, 'The Paris Commune and its Legacy', *Anarchist Portraits*, op. cit., pp. 229–39. For Michel, see Edith Thomas, *Louise Michel*, trans. Penelope Williams (Montréal: Black Rose Books, 1980)

16 Quoted in C. Rihs, *La Commune de Paris: sa structure et ses doctrines* (Geneva, 1955), pp. 260–1

17 Kropotkin, *Memoirs of a Revolutionist*, op. cit., p. 393. An article entitled 'La propagande par le fait' first appeared on 5 August 1877 in the *Bulletin de la Fédération Jurassienne* written by Brousse whilst he was a temporary editor in Guillaume's absence.

18 Quoted in David Stafford, *From Anarchism to Reformism: A Study of the Political Activities of Paul Brousse (1870–90)* (Weidenfeld and Nicolson, 1971), p. 108

19 Quoted in Avrich, 'Paul Brousse: The Possibilist Anarchist', *Anarchist Portraits*, op. cit., p. 245

20 *Bulletin de la Fédération Jurassienne* (30 April, 7 May 1876)

21 Elisée Reclus, 'A Propos de l'anarchie', *Le Travailleur* (February – March 1878)

22 See my 'The Principal Conceptions of the State held by the Leading Anarchist Communists in France, 1880–1896', MA thesis (University of Sussex, 1971)

23 Jean Grave: *Le Mouvement libertaire sous la troisième République* (Paris: Oeuvres Représentatives, 1930), p. 7

24 Emile Henry, 'A Terrorist's Defence', *Anarchist Reader*, op. cit., p. 193. See also M. Fleming, 'Propaganda by the Deed: Terrorism and Anarchist Theory in Late Ninteteenth Century Europe', *Terrorism in Europe*, eds. Y. Alexander and K. A. Myers (Croom Helm, 1982); Miller, *Anarchism*, op. cit., pp. 115–21

25 Octave Mirbeau, *Le Journal* (19 February 1894), quoted in Joll, *The Anarchists*, op. cit., p. 127

26 Proudhon, *Du Principe de l'art et sa destination sociale* (Paris, 1865), p. 43

27 Quoted in Joll, *The Anarchists*, op. cit., p. 150

28 See Reg Carr, *Anarchism in France: The Case of Octave Mirbeau* (Manchester University Press, 1977), Appendix

29 Quoted in Woodcock, *Anarchism*, op. cit., p. 290

30 See Richard Sonn, *Anarchism and Cultural Politics in Fin-de-siècle France* (University of Nebraska Press, 1989)

31 See Hans Richter, *Dada – Art and Anti-Art* (Thames and Hudson, 1965)

32 *La Révolution Surréaliste*, 2 (1925)

33 See G. D. H. Cole, 'Marxism and Anarchism', *A History of Socialist Thought* (1954) (Macmillan, 1974), II, 336

34 Quoted in Rocker, *Anarcho-syndicalism*, op. cit., pp. 77–8

35 Quoted in Maitron, *Histoire du mouvement anarchiste en France*, op. cit., p. 252

36 Ibid., p. 261

37 Georges Sorel, *Reflections on Violence* (1908), trans. T. E. Hulme and J.

Roth, intro. Edward A. Shils (Collier-Macmillan, 1969), pp. 50, 223

38 See F. F. Ridley, *Revolutionary Syndicalism in France: The Direct Action of its Time* (Cambridge University Press, 1970), p. 14

39 Emile Pouget, *Les Bases du syndicalisme* (Paris: Bibliothèque Syndicaliste, n.d.), pp. 20–4

40 See Maitron, *Histoire du mouvement anarchiste en France*, op. cit., p. 251

41 Charter of Amiens, quoted in G. D. H. Cole, *The Second International, A History of Socialist Thought*, op. cit., III, 371

42 *Congrès anarchiste tenu à Amsterdam*, op. cit., p. 19

43 See Barbara Mitchell, *The Practical Revolutionaries: A New Interpretation of the French Anarchosyndicalists* (New York: Greenwood Press, 1987), pp. 10–11

44 See Rocker, *Anarchism and Anarcho-Syndicalism*, op. cit., p. 34; see also his *Anarcho-Syndicalism*, op. cit., ch. iv

45 *Congrès anarchiste tenu à Amsterdam*, op. cit., quoted in *Anarchist Reader*, op. cit., pp. 214, 218

46 Ibid., p. 46

47 Ibid., pp. 223, 224

Chapter Twenty-Eight

1 See Carl Levy, 'Italian Anarchism, 1870–1926, For Anarchism: History, Theory and Practice*, ed. David Goodway (Routledge, 1989) p. 26

2 Quoted in Hostetter, *The Italian Socialist Movement*, op. cit, p. 23

3 See Woodcock, *Anarchism*, op. cit., p. 309

4 See Bakunin, *Mazzini's Political Theology and the International* (1871)

5 See Malatesta, Preface to Max Nettlau, *Bakunin e l'Internazionale in Italia del 1864 al 1872* (Geneva, 1928)

6 *Compte rendu du VIIIème Congrès générale, Berne* (Berne, 1876), pp. 10, 97

7 Quoted in Hostetter, *The Italian Socialist Movement*, op. cit., p. 368

8 Quoted in Woodcock, *Anarchism*, op. cit., p. 320

9 Quoted in Hostetter, *The Italian Socialist Movement*, op. cit., p. 410

10 See Levy, 'Italian Anarchism', op. cit., pp. 45, 75

11 Ibid., p. 61

12 Quoted in ibid., p. 73

Chapter Twenty-Nine

1 Pi y Margall, *Nationalities*, quoted in José Peirats, *What is the CNT?* (Simian, 1974), pp. 9–10

2 See Bookchin, *The Spanish Anarchists: The Heroic Years 1868–1936* (New York: Free Life Editions, 1977), pp. 21, 80–1

3 Ibid., p. 8

4 See J. Díaz del Moral's massive *Historia de las agitaciones campesinas andaluzas* (Madrid, 1929)

5 The religious interpretation of Spanish anarchism was first put forward by Juan Díaz del Moral in his *Historia de las agitaciones campesinas andaluzas*, op. cit., pp. 187–192. It was taken up by the British historians Gerald Brenan, *The Spanish Labyrinth* (New York: Macmillan, 1943), p. 157; E. J. Hobsbawm, *Primitive Rebels* (Manchester University Press, 1959), p. 84f.; Franz Borkenau, *The Spanish Cockpit* (Faber & Faber, 1937), p. 220. Brenan (p. 75) and Hobsbawm (p. 84) also suggest, on scanty evidence, that Spanish puritanism led to sexual abstinence during anarchist strikes. For a cogent and persuasive dismissal of the traditional view, see Temma Kaplan, *Anarchists of Andalucía (1869–1903)* (Princeton, NJ: Princeton University Press, 1977) and Jerome R. Mintz, *The Anarchists of Casas Viejas* (Chicago University Press, 1982).

6 See Bookchin, *The Spanish Anarchists*, op. cit., pp. 4–5

7 Peirats, *What is the CNT?*, op. cit., p. 2

8 Ibid., p. 12. See also Peirats' *La CNT*

en la Revolución Española (Toulouse, 1951); reprinted in *Anarchists in the Spanish Revolution* (Detroit: Black & Red, 1977)

9 Peirats, *What is the CNT?*, op. cit., pp. 19–20

10 See Juan Gomez Casas, *Anarchist Organization: The History of the FAI*, trans. A. Bluestein (Montréal: Black Rose Books, 1986), p. 16

11 Robert W. Kern, *Red Years/Black Years: A Political History of Spanish Anarchism (1911–1937)* (Philadelphia: ISHI, 1978), p. 3

12 Bookchin, *The Spanish Anarchists*, op. cit., p. 214

13 Quoted in Kern, *Red Years/Black Years*, op. cit., p. 3

14 See Mintz, *The Anarchists of Casas Viejas*, op. cit. Mintz agrees with Kaplan that Spanish anarchism was not fundamentally religious; he suggests that it makes more sense to see it as a 'revitalization' movement in the anthropological sense; ibid., pp. 3–4

15 Peirats, *La CNT en la Revolución Española*, op. cit., I, 109ff. See also Bookchin, *The Spanish Anarchists*, op. cit., pp. 290–5

16 George Orwell, *New English Weekly* (29 July & 2 September 1937), reprinted in *The Collected Essays, Journalism and Letters of George Orwell*, eds. Sonia Orwell & Ian Angus (Harmondsworth: Penguin, 1970), I, 307

17 Quoted in Vernon Richards, *Lessons of the Spanish Revolution* (1953) (Freedom Press, 1983), p. 34

18 Ibid., p. 35. As Richards points out, the concept of an 'anarchist dictatorship' is a contradiction in terms.

19 Quoted by Richards, *Lessons of the Spanish Revolution*, op. cit., pp. 59–60

20 See Orwell, *Homage to Catalonia* (1938) (Harmondsworth: Penguin, 1962), p. 61

21 Orwell to Jack Common, October 1937, *The Collected Essays*, op. cit., I, 323

22 See Orwell's review of Mairin Mitchell's *Spanish Rehearsal* in *Time and Tide* (11 December 1937) quoted in *The Collected Essays*, op. cit., I, 324

23 Walter Gregory, in Walter Gregory, David Morris & Anthony Peters, *The Shallow Grave* (Gollancz, 1986)

24 See Borkenau, *The Spanish Cockpit*, op. cit., p. 167

25 See Pierre Broué and Emile Témine, *The Revolution and the Civil War in Spain* (Cambridge, Mass.: MIT Press, 1970); Gaston Leval, *Collectives in the Spanish Revolution* (Freedom Press, 1975); Sam Dolgoff, ed., *The Anarchist Collectives: Workers' Self-Management in the Spanish Revolution 1936–1939* (Montréal: Black Rose, 1974)

26 See Hugh Thomas, 'Anarchist Agrarian Collectives in the Spanish Civil War', M. Gilbert, ed., *A Century of Conflict 1850–1950* (Hamish Hamilton, 1966), pp. 253–7

27 See Borkenau, *The Spanish Cockpit*, op. cit., pp. 90–1; Richards, *Lessons of the Spanish Revolution*, op. cit., pp. 110–11

28 Quoted in Rocker, *Anarcho-syndicalism*, op. cit., p. 101n

29 Orwell, *Homage to Catalonia*, op. cit., p. 8

30 See Liz Willis, *Women in the Spanish Revolution* (Solidarity Pamphlet, no. 48, 1975)

31 *CNT* (5 September 1936), quoted by Burnett Bolloten, *The Grand Camouflage: The Communist Conspiracy in the Spanish Civil War* (New York, 1968), p. 156

32 Quoted by Joll, *The Anarchists*, op. cit., p. 247

33 *Solidaridad Obrera* (4 November 1936)

34 Quoted in Richards, *Lessons of the Spanish Revolution*, op. cit., p. 159

35 Ibid., p. 200

36 The Friends of Durruti Group, *Towards a Fresh Revolution* (Barcelona, 1938) (Sanday, Orkney: Cienfuegos Press, 1978), p. 42. For Durruti, see Pai Ferrer, *Durruti* (Barcelona: Planeta, 1985)

37 Quoted in Richards, *Lessons of the Spanish Revolution*, op. cit., p. 176

38 See Gary Prevost, 'Contemporary Spanish Anarchism', *Social Anarchism*, II, 2 (1982), 22–32

39 See P. Mailer, *Portugal: The Impossible*

Revolution (Solidarity, 1977); Hugo
Gil Ferreira & Michael W. Marshall,
Portugal's Revolution: Ten Years On
(Cambridge University Press, 1986)

Chapter Thirty

1 See Avrich, 'V. M. Eikhenbaum
(Volin): the Man and His Book',
Anarchist Portraits, op. cit., p. 126

2 Quoted in Guérin, *Anarchism*, op. cit.,
p. 83

3 See also Volin [Vsevolod Mikhailovitch
Eikhenbaum], *The Unknown Revolution
(1917-1921)* (New York, 1955), the
most important anarchist history of the
Russian Revolution.

4 Quoted in Daniel & Gabriel
Cohn-Bendit, *Obsolete Communism: The
Left-Wing Alternative*, trans. Arnold
Pomerans (André Deutsch, 1968), pp.
218-19

5 Lenin, *The State and Revolution*, op. cit.,
pp. 62, 124

6 Jacques Sadoul, report dated 6 April
1918, *Notes sur la révolution bolchévique*
(Paris, 1919), pp. 286-7

7 Quoted in Joll, *The Anarchists*, op. cit.,
p. 172

8 Quoted in Avrich, 'Nestor Makhno:
The Man and the Myth', *Anarchist
Portraits*, op. cit., p. 112

9 Quoted in Guérin, *Anarchism*, op. cit.,
p. 99

10 Quoted in David Footman, *Civil War
in Russia* (Faber & Faber, 1961), p.
284. See also Peter Arshinov, *History of
the Makhnovist Movement (1918-1921)*
(Detroit: Black & Red, 1974)

11 See Nestor Makhno, *La Révolution russe
en Ukraine* (Paris, 1927). See also
Michael Palij, *The Anarchism of Nestor
Makhno, 1918-1921* (Seattle:
University of Washington Press, 1976);
Michael Malet, *Nestor Makhno and the
Russian Civil War* (Macmillan, 1982)

12 See A. Souchy, *Wie lebt der Arbeiter und
der Bauer in Russland und in der
Ukraine* (Berlin, n.d.), Preface

13 Quoted in Cohn-Bendit, *Obsolete
Communism*, op. cit., p. 226

14 Alexander Berkman, *The Bolshevik
Myth* (1925), pp. 90-1

15 Quoted in Rocker, *Anarcho-syndicalism*,
op. cit., pp. 96-7; Guérin, *Anarchism*,
op. cit., p. 106

16 Quoted in Woodcock & Avakumović,
The Anarchist Prince, op. cit.,
p. 430

17 See Paul Avrich, *Kronstadt 1921*
(Princeton, NJ: Princeton University
Press, 1970); see also Victor Serge's
testimony, *Kronstadt '21* (Solidarity
pamphlet, n.d.) and his *Memoirs of a
Revolutionary 1901-1941* (New York,
1967)

18 Quoted in Voline, *Nineteen-Seventeen:
The Russian Revolution Betrayed* (New
York: Libertarian Book Club, 1954), p.
154

19 Berkman, *The Bolshevik Myth*, op. cit.,
p. 319

20 See Gaston Leval, 'Choses de Russie',
Le Libertaire (11-18 November 1921)

21 Rocker, *Anarcho-syndicalism*, op. cit.,
p. 27

22 See *Notes sur l'anarchisme en URSS de
1921 à nos jours* (Paris: Les Cahiers
du Vent du Chemin, 1983)

Chapter Thirty-One

1 Bakunin to Arnold Ruge (19 January
1843), in Bakunin, *Oeuvres*, op. cit.,
III, 176-7

2 Richard Wagner, *Kurstwerk der Zukunft*
(1850), quoted in Andrew Carlson,
*Anarchism in Germany, I: The Early
Movement* (Metuchen, NJ: Scarecrow,
1972), pp. 16-17

3 Quoted by Johann Most, 'Der
Anarchie', *Internationale Bibliothek*
(1888)

4 Joll, *The Anarchists*, op. cit., p. 122

5 Carlson, *Anarchism in Germany*, op. cit.,
p. 191

6 Rocker, *Anarchism and
Anarcho-Syndicalism*, op. cit.,
p. 44

7 Ferdinand Domela Nieuwenhuis, *Le
Socialisme en danger* (Paris: Stock,
1897), p. 115

8 Bart de Ligt, *The Conquest of Violence*, op. cit., pp. 84, 109

9 Rudolf de Jong, 'Provos and Kabouters', *Anarchism Today*, op. cit., p. 173

10 Ibid., p. 177

11 John Milton, *Paradise Lost* (1667), X, 283–4, *Poetical Works*, ed. Douglas Bush (Oxford University Press, 1966), p. 405

12 See *The Shorter Oxford English Dictionary*

13 Paine, *Rights of Man*, op. cit., p. 187

14 Godwin, *Anarchist Writings*, op. cit., p. 169

15 Ibid., p. 162

16 Quoted in my *William Godwin*, op. cit., pp. 232, 215

17 See John Quail, *The Slow Burning Fuse: The Lost History of the British Anarchists* (Paladin, 1978), pp. 4–5

18 Ibid., pp. 22, 31

19 Ibid., pp. 37–8, 67, 145

20 See *Freedom: A Hundred Years, October 1886 to October 1986* (Freedom Press, 1986)

21 See William J. Fishman, *East End Jewish Radicals 1875–1914* (Duckworth, 1975) and Hermia Oliver, *The International Anarchist Movement in Late Victorian England* (Croom Helm, 1983)

22 See Rudolf Rocker, *The London Years*, op. cit., abridged from the Yiddish edition

23 Quail, *The Slow Burning Fuse*, op. cit., p. 263

24 *The Miners' Next Step* (Tonypandy, 1912)

25 See R. J. Holton, *British Syndicalism, 1900–1914* (Pluto Press, 1975)

26 See Albert Meltzer, *The Anarchists in London 1935–1955* (Sanday, Orkney: Cienfuegos Press, 1976)

27 See *Anarchy*, 12 (February 1962), 50–7

28 See Greil Marcus, *Lipstick Traces: A Secret History of the Twentieth Century* (Secker & Warburg, 1989), pp. 440–1

29 See Stewart Home, *The Assault on Culture: Utopian Currents from*

Lettrisme to Class War (Aphoria Press and Unpopular Books, 1988), pp. 95–101

Chapter Thirty-Two

1 Quoted in De Leon, *The American as Anarchist*, op. cit., p. 16

2 Ibid., pp. 19–20

3 Paine, *Common Sense*, op. cit., p. 65

4 Quoted in *Patterns of Anarchy*, op. cit., p. xv

5 De Leon, *The American as Anarchist*, op. cit., p. 53

6 Quoted in Woodcock, *Anarchism*, op. cit., p. 47

7 See James J. Martin, *Men against the State*, op. cit.; William O. Reichert, *Partisans of Freedom: A Study in American Anarchism* (Bowling Green, Ohio, 1976)

8 De Leon, *The American as Anarchist*, op. cit., pp. 9, 74–5. For an opposing view, see Schuster, *Native American Anarchism*, op. cit.

9 See Avrich, 'Jewish Anarchism', *Anarchist Portraits*, op. cit., p. 178

10 See Avrich, *The Haymarket Tragedy* (Princeton, NJ: Princeton University Press, 1984)

11 Quoted in P. F. Brissenden, *The IWW: A Study of American Syndicalism* (New York: Columbia University Press, 1920), p. 139

12 Ibid., p. 318

13 Woodcock, *Anarchism*, op. cit., p. 440; Melvyn Dubofsky, *We Shall Be All: A History of the Industrial Workers of the World* (Chicago: Quadrangle, 1969), p. 480

14 See Avrich, 'Sacco and Vanzetti: The Italian Anarchist Background', *Anarchist Portraits*, op. cit., pp. 163, 175

15 Quoted in *Patterns of Anarchy*, op. cit., pp. 375–6

16 See Avrich, *The Modern School Movement: Anarchism and Education in the United States* (Princeton, NJ: Princeton University Press, 1980)

17 See *Reinventing Anarchy*, eds. Howard J. Ehrlich, Carol Ehrlich, David De

Leon & Glenda Morris (Routledge & Kegan Paul, 1979)

Chapter Thirty-Three

1　See Alfredo Gomel, *Anarquismo y anarcosindicalismo en América Latina* (Paris: Rudeo Iberico, c.1980); Ian R. Mitchell, 'The Anarchist Tradition in Latin America', *Anarchy* 79 (September 1967), 262–3; and Fanny F. Simon, 'Anarchism and Anarcho-syndicalism in South America', *Hispanic American Historical Review*, XXVI (1946), 38–59

2　See Max Nettlau, *Contribución a la Bibliografía Anarquista en América Latina hasta 1914* (Buenos Aires: Ediciones La Protesta, n.d.)

3　Quoted in Eduardo Colombo, 'Anarchism in Argentina and Uruguay', *Anarchism Today*, op. cit., p. 185

4　See Osvaldo Bayer, *Anarchism and Violence; Severino di Giovanni in Argentina, 1923–1931*, trans. Paul Sharkey (Elephant Editions, 1986)

5　See Ronaldo Munck with Ricardo Falcon & Bernardo Galitelli, *Argentina: From Anarchism to Peronism: Workers, Unions and Politics, 1855–1985* (Zed, 1987)

6　See Acción Libertaria, 'Cuba: Revolution and Counter-Revolution', reprinted in *Anarchy* 79 (September 1967)

7　Colombo, 'Anarchism in Argentina and Uruquay', op. cit., p. 191

8　See Newton Stadler de Souza, *O anarquismo da Colônia Cecília* (Rio de Janeiro, 1970)

9　See Avrich, 'Brazilian Anarchists', *Anarchist Portraits*, op. cit., p. 256

10　Quoted in John W. Dulles, *Anarchists and Communists in Brazil, 1900–1935* (Austin, TX: University of Texas Press, 1973), p. 328

11　Quoted in *Land and Liberty. Anarchist Influences in the Mexican Revolution. Ricardo Flores Magón*, ed. David Poole (Sanday, Orkney Islands: Cienfuegos Press, 1977), p. 10

12　Ibid., p. 9

13　Ibid., p. 17

14　See John M. Hart, *Anarchism and the Mexican Working Class 1860–1931* (Austin: University of Texas Press, 1978)

15　*Regeneración* (11 February 1911)

16　*Land and Liberty*, op. cit., p. 21

17　Ibid., pp. 98, 100

18　See John Womack, *Zapata and the Mexican Revolution* (Thames & Hudson, 1972), pp. 393–404 for the complete *Plan de Ayala*

19　*Land and Liberty*, op. cit., pp. 104–5 Enrique Flores Magón insisted on the close links between Zapata's 'Agrarians' and the PLM in an article in *Freedom* (London, February 1917)

20　See Avrich, 'Ricardo Flores Magón in Prison', *Anarchist Portraits*, op. cit., p. 208

21　*El Productor* (26 July 1889). See also the Introduction to *Enrique Roig de San Martín: artículos publicados en el periódico 'El Productor'*, ed. Aleida Plasencia (Havana, 1967)

22　See my *Cuba Libre: Breaking the Chains?* (Victor Gollancz, 1987), p. 29

23　See Gerald Poyo, 'The Anarchist Challenge to the Cuban Independence Movement, 1885–1890', *Cuban Studies*, 15, 1 (1985), 29–42

24　José Martí, *Obras completas*, 28 vols. (Havana, 1963–73), II, 255

25　*Solidaridad Gastronómica* (Havana, 15 August 1955)

26　Quoted by Mitchell, 'The Anarchist Tradition in Latin America', *Anarchy*, op. cit., p. 269

27　See Sam Dolgoff, *The Cuban Revolution: A Critical Perspective* (Montréal: Black Rose, 1976) for the early anarchist campaign against Castro's regime

28　See my *Cuba Libre*, op. cit., pp. 79–80

29　Che Guevara, *Socialism and Man* (New York: Pathfinder Press, 1968), p. 22

30　See Paulo Freire, *Pedagogy of the Oppressed* (1970) (Harmondsworth: Penguin, 1972), and Ivan Illich's

Celebration of Awareness (1971)
(Harmondsworth: Penguin, 1973)
31 See Linda H. Damico, *The Anarchist
Dimension of Liberation Theology* (New
York: P. Lang, 1987)

Chapter Thirty-Four

1 See Jack Gray, *Modern China in Search
of a Political Form* (Oxford University
Press, 1969), p. 345
2 See Martin Bernal, 'The Triumph of
Anarchism over Marxism, 1906–1907',
*China in Revolution: The First Phase,
1906–1913*, ed. Mary C. Wright (New
Haven: Yale University Press, 1971),
pp. 67, 70; Gray, *Modern China*, op. cit.,
p. 67
3 See Robert A. Scalapino and George
T. Yu, *The Chinese Anarchist Movement*
(1961) (Bristol: Drowned Rat
Publications, 1985), p. 9
4 See Ch'u Min-i, 'Looking at the Past',
Hsin Shih-chi, 24 (30 November 1907),
25
5 'On Anarchism', ibid., 60 (15 August,
1908), 5
6 Answers to a letter by Li Shih-tseng,
ibid., 8 (10 August, 1907), 2–3
7 'Declaration', *Hui-ming-lu*, 1 (20
August, 1913), 1–2
8 Edgar Snow, *Red Star over China*
(Gollancz, 1937), p. 149
9 Ch'en Tu-hsiu, 'Chinese-style
Anarchism', *Hsin Ch'ing-nien* 9, 1
(1 May 1921), 5–6
10 Pa Chin, letter of 27 November 1962.
See also Olga Lang, *Pa Chin and his
Writings* (Cambridge, Mass.: Harvard
University Press, 1967)
11 Quoted by Jean Chesneaux, 'The
Federalist Movement in China,
1920–23', *Modern China*, op. cit.,
p. 129
12 See Gray, *Modern China*, op. cit., p. 345
13 See John F. Walsh, 'Shen-wu-lieu:
China's Anarchist Opposition', *Social
Anarchism*, II, 1 (1981), 3–15
14 *Guardian* (19 May 1989)
15 See Kōtoku Shūsui in *Hikari* (Light)
(15 December 1906)

16 See F. G. Notehelfer, *Kotoku Shusui:
Portrait of a Japanese Radical*
(Cambridge University Press, 1971).
See also Hyman Kublin's life of Sen
Katayama, *Asian Revolutionary*
(Princeton, NJ: Princeton University
Press, 1964)
17 Quoted in Chushichi Tsuzuki,
'Anarchism in Japan', *Anarchism Today*,
op. cit., p. 107. See also Thomas A.
Stanley, *Ōsugi Sakae: Anarchist in Taisho
Japan* (Cambridge, Mass.: Harvard Uni-
versity Press, 1982) and Tatsuo Arima,
The Failure of Freedom (Cambridge,
Mass.: Harvard University Press, 1969)
18 See Otsushi Shirai, 'The Impact on
Japan of William Godwin's Ideas',
*American Journal of Economics and
Sociology*, 29 (1970), 89–96
19 See John Crump, 'Communists vs.
Syndicalists in the Japanese Anarchist
Movement', *Bulletin of Anarchist
Research*, 17 (May 1989), 7. See also
his 'Anarchist Opposition to Japanese
Militarism, 1926–37', ibid. 24 (1991),
34–36
20 *Jokyo (Situation)* 8 (1969), 37
21 See Hai Ki-Rak, 'Speech to First
International Seminar for World Peace,
October 1988', *Freedom*, 50, 1 (January
1989), pp. 8–9. See also his *History of
the Korean Anarchist Movement* (Tuega,
Korea: Anarchist Publishing
Committee, 1986)
22 See Adi Doctor, *Anarchist Thought in
India* (Bombay: Asia Publishing
House, 1964), p. 15
23 See Albert Meltzer, *The Anarchists in
London 1935–1955* (Sanday, Orkney
Islands: Cienfuegos Press, n.d.), p. 30
24 Dalton Dennis, 'The Theory of
Anarchism in Modern India – an
analysis of the political thought of
Vivekananda, Aurobindo and Gandhi',
Tradition and Politics in South Asia, ed.
R. J. Moore (New Delhi: Vikas, 1979),
pp. 211, 209
25 Aurobindo Ghose, *The Ideal of Human
Unity* (Madras, 1919), p. 77. See also
Brian Morris, 'Politics of the Divine
Life: Notes on the Social Philosophy
of Aurobindo Ghose', *Bulletin of*

Anarchist Research, 22 (November 1990), 33–5

26 Osho, *Rebellion, Revolution and Religiousness* (Santa Monica: Falcon Press, 1989)

27 Quoted by Stuart Edwards, 'Spiritual Anarchism', *Bulletin of Anarchist Research* 21 (July 1990), p. 26

28 Gandhi, *Democracy: Real and Deceptive*, op. cit., pp. 28–9

29 For a sociological analysis of the *Sarvodaya* movment, see Geoffrey Ostergaard and M. Currell, *The Gentle Anarchists* (Oxford: Clarendon Press, 1971)

30 For the anarchistic elements of the the *Sarvodaya* movement, see Geoffrey Ostergaard, 'Indian Anarchism: The Sarvodaya Movement', *Anarchism Today*, op. cit., pp. 150–3

31 Vinoba Bhave, *Democratic Values* (Kashi: Sarva Seva Sangh Prakashan, 1962), pp. 13–14

32 Ibid, pp. 12–13, 64

33 *Bhoodan* (28 November 1956); Bhave, *Democratic Values*, op. cit., p. 226

34 Jayaprakash Narayan, *Socialism, Sarvodaya and Democracy*, ed. Bimal Prasad (Bombay: Asia Publishing House, 1964), p, 161

35 *Everyman's Weekly* (27 April 1975)

36 See Ostergaard, 'Indian Anarchism: The Curious Case of Vinoba Bhave – Anarchist Saint of Government' in *For Anarchism*, op. cit., pp. 201–15

37 See Ostergaard, *Nonviolent Revolution in India* (New Delhi: Gandhi Peace Foundation, 1985), p. 281

Chapter Thirty-Five

1 Carl Oglesby, 'The Idea of the New Left', *The New Left Reader* (New York: Grove Press, 1969), p. 15

2 See Nigel Young, *An Infantile Disorder: The Crisis and Decline of the New Left* (Routledge & Kegan Paul, 1977), pp. 132–3

3 Ibid., pp. 134, 142

4 *The New Left Reader*, op. cit., p. 142

5 Mitchell Goodman, ed., Introduction,

The Movement towards a New America: The Beginnings of a Long Revolution (New York: Knopf, 1970), p. vii

6 See Young, *An Infantile Disorder*, op. cit., p. 136. Apter also adds unreason, spontaneous violence, and irresponsibility but these are not characteristically anarchist tendencies. Apter, 'The Old Anarchism and the New', *Anarchism Today*, op. cit., p. 1

7 Jerry Rubin, *Do It!* Quoted in De Leon, *The American as Anarchist*, op. cit., p. 85

8 Oglesby, quoted in Goodman, Introduction, *The Movement towards a New America*, op. cit.

9 Theodore Roszak, *Where the Wasteland Ends* (Faber & Faber, 1973), pp. 424, 431–2

10 See Keith Melville, 'The Anarchist Response', *Communes in the Counter-Culture* (New York: Morrow, 1972), pp. 114–33; Judson Jerome, *Families of Eden: Communes and the New Anarchism* (New York: Seabury, 1974), pp. 231–51; and L. Veysey, *The Communal Experience: Anarchist and Mystical Counter-Cultures in America* (New York: Harper & Row, 1973)

11 See Michael Lerner, 'Anarchism and the American-Counter-Culture', *Anarchism Today*, op. cit., p. 52

12 Rudi Dutschke, 'On Anti-authoritarianism', *The New Left Reader*, op. cit., p. 246

13 Eric Hobsbawm, *The Black Dwarf* (1 June 1968)

14 See Jean Maitron, 'Anarchisme', *Le Mouvement Social*, 69 (October – December 1969)

15 Guérin, *Anarchism*, op. cit., p. 158. See also his interview in *Le Fait Public* (6 May 1969) where he describes the dominant ideology as a form of 'libertarian Marxism'.

16 Tom Nairn in Angelo Quattrochi and Tom Nairn, *The Beginning of the End* (Panther, 1968). See also David Caute, *Sixty Eight: The Year of the Barricades* (Hamish Hamilton, 1988)

17 See Richard Gombin, 'The Ideology and Practice of Contestation seen

through Recent Events in France', *Anarchism Today*, op. cit., p. 14

18 *Appeal*, issued by the assembly of the Sorbonne (13–14 June 1968). Theses 1, 7, 6, 24, quoted in Quattrochi and Nairn, *The Beginning of the End*, op. cit.

19 Ibid., pp. 36, 79

20 See Murray Bookchin, 'May – June Events in France: I', *Post-Scarcity Anarchism* (Wildwood House, 1974), p. 254

21 Daniel Cohn-Bendit and Gabriel Cohn-Bendit, *Obsolete Communism: The Left Wing Alternative*, trans. Arnold Pomerans (Deutsch, 1968), p. 250. The original French title *Le Gauchisme, remède à la maladie sénile du communisme* makes ironic play with Lenin's attack on anarchism in his *'Left-Wing' Communism, An Infantile Disorder* (1920)

22 Ibid., p. 254

23 See Mark Shipway, 'Situationism', *Non-Market Socialism in the Nineteenth and Twentieth Centuries*, ed. Maximilien Rubel and John Crump (Macmillan, 1987), p. 152. See also Peter Wollen, 'The Situationist International', *New Left Review*, 174 (March – April, 1989); Home, *The Assault on Culture*, op. cit., ch. v, vi; and Marcus, *Lipstick Traces*, op. cit.

24 Guy Debord, *The Society of the Spectacle* (Detroit: Black and Red, 1977), thesis 31

25 Raoul Vaneigem, *The Revolution of Everyday Life* (1967) (Rebel Press, 1983), p. 38

26 Ibid., p. 8. See also Vaneigem's *The Book of Pleasure* (Pending Press, 1983)

27 'The Beginning of an Era' (September 1969), in K. Knabb, *Situationist International Anthology* (Berkeley: Bureau of Public Secrets, 1981), p. 253

28 Vaneigem, *The Revolution of Everyday Life*, op. cit., p. 211

29 Debord, *The Society of the Spectacle*, op. cit.

30 *Provo*, 1 and 2, quoted by Rudolf de Jong, 'Provos and Kabouters', *Anarchism Today*, op. cit., p. 173

31 See Roel Van Duyn, 'Kropotkin: A Universal Specialist', *Message of a Wise Kabouter* (1969) (Duckworth, 1972), ch. i

32 Ibid., p. 48

33 'Proclamation of the Orange Free State', *The Essential Works of Anarchism*, op. cit., p. 574

34 See Marsh, *Anarchist Women*, op. cit., pp. 173–4

35 See Marsha Hewitt, 'Emma Goldman: The Case for Anarcho-Feminism', *The Anarchist Papers*, ed. Dimitrious I. Roussopoulus (Montréal: Black Rose, 1986), p. 170

36 'Blood of the Flower: An Anarchist-Feminist Statement' *Siren – A Journal of Anarcho-Feminism*, I, 1 (1971)

37 'Who We Are: An Anarcho-Feminist Manifesto', ibid.

38 See Penny Kornegger, 'Anarchism: the feminist connection', *Reinventing Anarchy*, op. cit., p. 240

39 Carol Ehrlich, 'Socialism, anarchism, feminism', *Reinventing Anarchy*, op. cit., p. 265

40 Kornegger, 'Anarchism: the feminist connection', ibid., p. 240

41 Lynne Farrow, 'Feminism as Anarchism', *Quiet Rumours: An Anarcha-Feminist Anthology* (Dark Star, n.d.), p. 11

42 See Marian Leighton, 'Anarcho-feminism', *Reinventing Anarchy*, op. cit., p. 258

43 See Murray Bookchin, 'New Social Movements: The Anarchic Dimension', *For Anarchism*, op. cit., pp. 259–74

Chapter Thirty-Six

1 Randolph Bourne, 'The State', *Untimely Papers* (New York: Huebsch, 1919)

2 Franz Oppenheimer, *The State* (New York: Vanguard Press, 1926), p. 27

3 Albert Jay Nock, *Our Enemy the State* (1935) (New York: Free Life Editions, 1977), p. 88

4 John Locke, *Of Civil Government, Second*

Treatise (1690), op. cit., sec. 123, p. 179

5 David Friedman. *The Machinery of Freedom* (New York: Harper & Row, 1971), p. 156

6 Murray Rothbard, *For a New Liberty: The Libertarian Manifesto*, rev. edn. (New York: Collier Books, 1978), pp. 46, 23–24

7 Rothbard, 'Society without a State', *Nomos*, op. cit., pp. 191, 206. See also his *Power and Market* (Kansas City: Sheed Andrews & McMeel, 1977)

8 Robert Nozick, *Anarchy, State and Utopia* (Oxford: Basil Blackwell, 1974), pp. 16–17

9 Ibid., p. 160

10 See Stephen L. Newman, *Liberalism at Wits' End: The Libertarian Revolt against the Modern State* (Ithaca: Cornell University Press, 1984), ch. vi

11 See Robert Paul Wolff, *In Defense of Anarchism* (New York: Harper Colophon, 1970). It also contains a reply to Jeffrey H. Reiman's criticism of his work *In Defense of Political Philosophy*.

12 See Graham Baugh, 'The Poverty of Autonomy: the Failure of Wolff's Defence of Anarchism, *The Anarchist Papers*, op. cit., p. 110

13 Friedrich Hayek, *The Constitution of Liberty*, (Chicago: Chicago University Press, 1960), p. 137

14 Pierre Limeux, *Du Libéralisme à l'anarcho-capitalisme* (Paris: Presses Universitaires de France, 1983), p. 32

15 See Henri Arvon, *Les Libertariens américains: de l'anarchisme à l'anarcho-capitalisme* (Paris: Presses Universitaires de France, 1983), p. 9

Chapter Thirty-Seven

1 Quoted in Vivian Harper, 'Bertrand Russell and the Anarchists', *Anarchy*, 109 (March 1970), pp. 68, 77

2 Mrs Gerald Brenan to Russell, November 1938, *The Autobiography of Bertrand Russell* (Allen & Unwin, 1968), II, 210

3 Russell, *Roads to Freedom: Socialism, Anarchism, and Syndicalism* (1918), 3rd edn. (Allen & Unwin, 1973), pp. 38–9

4 Ibid., p. 15

5 Russell, *Principles of Social Reconstruction* (1916) (Allen & Unwin, 1971), p. 34

6 *Roads to Freedom*, op. cit., p. 97

7 See Harper, 'Bertrand Russell and the Anarchists', *Anarchy*, op. cit., p. 71

8 Russell to Emma Goldman, 8 July 1922, *Autobiography*, op. cit., II, 123

9 *Freedom*, quoted in Harper, 'Bertrand Russell and the Anarchists', op. cit., p. 73

10 Russell to Goldman, ibid., p. 74

11 *Freedom*, ibid., p. 73

12 Russell, 'A Free Man's Worship' (1903), *Mysticism and Logic* (1918) (Harmondsworth Penguin, 1953), p. 51

13 Russell, *Power: A New Social Analysis* (1938) (Basis Books, 1940), p. 9

14 Preface to *Roads to Freedom*, op. cit., p. 14

15 Russell, *Authority and the Individual* (Allen & Unwin, 1949) pp. 89, 109

16 See Nicolas Walter, *Freedom* (21 April 1962)

17 Russell, *Autobiography*, op. cit., II, 154

18 Harper, 'Russell and the Anarchists', op. cit., p. 75

19 Russell, *In Praise of Idleness* (1932) (Allen & Unwin, 1963), p. 11

20 Preface to *Principles of Social Reconstruction*, op. cit.

21 Aldous Huxley, *Ends and Means* (Chatto & Windus, 1937), p. 63

22 Ibid., p. 70

23 Ibid.

24 Huxley, *Science, Liberty and Peace* (Chatto & Windus, 1947), p. 6

25 Ibid., p. 41

26 Ibid., p. 44

27 Huxley, *Island* (Frogmore, St Albans: Triad/Panther, 1976), p. 169

28 Ibid., p. 171

29 Ibid., p. 249

30 Ibid., p. 97

31 Quoted in Philip Thody, *Aldous Huxley*

(New York: Charles Scribner's Sons, 1973), p. 128

32 Martin Buber, 'Society and the State' (1950), reprinted in *Anarchy* 54 (August 1965), pp. 241–2

33 Martin Buber, *Paths in Utopia* (1949) (Boston: Beacon Press, 1958), p. 39

34 Ibid., pp. 137, 134

35 See John Ellerby, 'Martin Buber', *Anarchy*, 54 (August 1965), p. 230

36 Lewis Mumford, 'Authoritarian and Democratic Technics', *Questioning Technology*, eds. Alice Carnes & John Zerzan (Freedom Press, 1988), p. 14

37 Mumford, *The Future of Technics and Civilization* (Freedom Press, 1986), p. 58

38 Ibid., p. 182

39 Ibid., p. 175

40 See Theodore Roszak, 'Scholar, Poet, Prophet', *Manas*, Los Angeles, 31 January 1968)

41 See Mumford, *The City in History* (Secker & Warburg, 1961), quoted in Colin Ward, 'Introduction', *The Future of Technics and Civilization*, op. cit., p. 14

42 Mumford, 'Authoritarian and Democratic Technics', op. cit., p. 13

43 Ibid.

44 Bookchin, *The Ecology of Freedom*, op. cit., p. 241

45 Noam Chomsky, *Problems of Knowledge and Freedom: The Russell Lectures* (Fontana, 1972), p. 46

46 See 'Introduction', Guérin, *Anarchism*, op. cit., p. xi

47 Paul Barker, 'Noam Chomsky's Two Worlds', *New Society* (2 April 1981), p. 61

48 Ibid.

49 Chomsky, *Language and Responsibility* (New York: Pantheon Books, 1979), p. 77

50 Chomsky, *For Reasons of State* (New York: Pantheon Books, 1973), pp. 395–6

51 Introduction to Guérin, *Anarchism*, op. cit., p. x. In the original review article from which the introduction is taken, Chomsky compares in note 11

Bakunin's remarks on the laws of individual nature with his own approach to creative thought in his works *Cartesian Linguistics* (1966) and *Language and Mind* (1968) (*New York Review of Books*, 21 May 1970).

52 Interview with Graham Baugh, *Open Road* (Summer, 1984)

53 With reference to the treatment of the Spanish Civil War, see Chomsky's 'Objectivity and Liberal Scholarship', *American Power and the New Mandarins* (New York: Random House, 1969), 72–124

54 Interview in *The Guardian* (14 January 1989)

55 See George Woodcock, 'Chomsky's Anarchism', *Freedom* (16 November 1974) who argues that he is a 'left-wing Marxist'; and Carlos Otero, 'Introduction', Chomsky's *Radical Priorities* (Montréal: Black Rose, 1981) and Paul Marshall, 'Chomsky's Anarchism', *Bulletin of Anarchist Research*, 22 (November 1990), 22–6, who claim that he is an authentic anarchist.

56 Interview, *The Chomsky Reader*, ed. James Peck (Serpent's Tail, 1987), pp. 22–3

57 See Read, 'Existentialism, Marxism and Anarchism' (1949), *Anarchy and Order*, op. cit., pp. 141–60

58 Jean-Paul Sartre, *Existentialism & Humanism* (1946), trans. Philip Mairet (Eyre Methuen, 1975), p. 34

59 'Sartre at Seventy: An Interview', *New York Review of Books* (August, 1975)

60 Camus, *The Myth of Sisyphus* (1942), trans. Justin O'Brien (Harmondsworth: Penguin, 1977), p. 11

61 Ibid., p. 26

62 Ibid., pp. 64, 108

63 Quoted in Philip Thody, *Albert Camus, 1913–60* (Hamish Hamilton, 1961), p. 81

64 Ibid., p. 90

65 Camus, *L'Homme révolté* (1951) (Paris: Gallimard, 1972), pp. 35–6

66 Ibid, p. 356

67 Quoted in Thody, *Albert Camus*, op. cit., p. 203

68 See J. G. Merquior, *Foucault* (Fontana Press, 1985), p. 154
69 Michel Foucault, *Discipline and Punish: The Birth of the Prisons*, trans. Alan Sheridan, III, 1 (New York: Pantheon, 1977), p. 228
70 See Foucault's Preface 'The Eye of Power' to the French edition of Benthams's *Panopticon* (1977)
71 Foucault, *Power/Knowledge: Selected Inerviews and Other Writings 1972–1977*, eds. Colin Gordon, Leo Marshall, John Meplam and Kate Soper (Brighton: Harvester Press, 1980), pp. 87–90, 110
72 Ibid., p. 151. Cf. Ibid., pp. 104–5
73 Foucault, *The History of Sexuality*, trans. Robert Hurley (New York: Pantheon, 1978), I, p. 59
74 Merquior, *Foucault*, op. cit., p. 149
75 See Interview in *Le Nouvel Observateur* (12 March 1977)
76 Foucault, 'Réponse à une question', *Esprit*, 371 (May, 1968), 850–74
77 Interview with Jean-Lousiézine in *Nouvelles Littéraires*, 2477 (17–23 March 1977)
78 Merquior, *Foucault*, op. cit., p. 156

Chapter Thirty-Eight

1 Quoted in Woodcock, 'The Philosopher of Freedom', *Herbert Read: A Memorial Symposium*, ed. Robin Skelton (Methuen, 1970), p. 74; see also James King, *The Last Modern: A Life of Herbert Read* (Weidenfeld & Nicolson, 1990)
2 Quoted in Woodcock, *Herbert Read: The Stream and the Source* (Faber & Faber, 1972), p. 232
3 Lenin, *The State and Revolution*, quoted by Read, 'Poetry and Anarchism' (1938), in *Anarchy and Order: Essays in Politics* (Souvenir Press, 1974), p. 93
4 Quoted in *The Anarchist Reader*, op. cit., p. 256
5 Read, *To Hell with Culture: Democratic Values are New Values* (Kegan Paul, Trench, Trubner, 1941), p. 43
6 Ibid., p. 7
7 Ibid., p. 17
8 Read, 'Chains of Freedom', *Anarchy and Order*, op. cit., p. 186
9 Woodcock, *The Anarchist Reader*, op. cit., p. 379
10 Read, 'My Anarchism', *Anarchy and Order*, op. cit., p. 244
11 Read, *Education through Art* (Faber & Faber, 1943), p. 5
12 Read, *The Grass Roots of Art* (1955), quoted in *The Anarchist Reader*, op. cit., p. 283
13 'Poetry and Anarchism' (1938), *Anarchy and Order*, op. cit., p. 58
14 'Philosophy of Anarchism', *Anarchy and Order*, op. cit., pp. 37, 39
15 Ibid., pp. 81, 88
16 'Philosophy of Anarchism', op. cit., p. 50
17 'Poetry and Anarchism', op. cit., p. 87. For an outline of Read's anarchist society, see ibid., pp. 101–2; and 'Philosophy and Anarchism, op. cit, pp. 49–50
18 'The Paradox of Anarchism', *Anarchy and Order*, op. cit., p. 134
19 Read, *The Politics of the Unpolitical* (Routledge, 1943), pp. 11, 10
20 'Poetry and Anarchism', op. cit., p. 125
21 Ibid., p. 96
22 'Chains of Freedom', op. cit., pp. 162, 163
23 'Revolution and Reason', ibid., p. 23
24 'Existentialism, Marxism and Anarchism', *Anarchy and Order*, op. cit., pp. 157, 155, 158
25 'Poetry and Anarchism', op. cit., p. 107
26 Ibid., pp. 41–2
27 'Philosophy of Anarchism', op. cit., p. 48
28 'The Chains of Freedom', op. cit., p. 195
29 Ibid., p. 212
30 'The Prerequisite of Peace', *Anarchy and Order*, op. cit., p. 121
31 'Revolution and Reason', op. cit., p. 17
32 Ibid., p. 31
33 Woodcock, *Herbert Read*, op. cit., p. 13
34 'Chains of Freedom', op. cit., p. 175
35 Read, *The Contrary Experience* (Faber & Faber, 1963), p. 11
36 Read, *A Concise History of Modern*

Painting (Thames & Hudson, 1972), p. 14

37 Alex Comfort, *Barbarism and Sexual Freedom* (Freedom Press, 1948), p. 34

38 Comfort, *Authority and Delinquency in the Modern State: A Criminological Approach to the Problems of Power* (Routledge & Kegan Paul, 1950), p. ix

39 Ibid., p. 17

40 Comfort, *Delinquency* (Freedom Press, 1951), p. 9

41 *Authority and Delinquency*, op. cit., p. 78

42 Ibid., pp. 80–1

43 Comfort, *Nature and Human Nature* (Weidenfeld & Nicolson, 1966), p. 191

44 Ibid., p. 201

45 *Barbarism and Sexual Freedom*, op. cit., p. 42

46 Comfort, ed., *The Joy of Sex: A Gourmet Guide to Lovemaking*, (Quartet, 1986), p. 34

47 Paul and Percival Goodman, *Communitas: Means of Livelihood and Ways of Life* (1947) (New York: Vintage, 1960), p. 153

48 See Goodman's political essays, *Drawing the Line*, ed. Taylor Stoehr (1962) (New York: Free Life Editions, 1977)

49 Goodman, 'The Anarchist Principle', *A Decade of Anarchy*, op. cit., p. 38

50 Goodman, 'Reply' on Pornography and Censorship, *Commentary* 32, 2 (1961), 159–61

51 Goodman, 'The Anarchist Principle', *A Decade of Anarchy*, op. cit., p. 39

52 Cf. Woodcock, 'Paul Goodman: The Anarchist as Conservator', *The Anarchist Papers*, op. cit., pp. 66–72

53 Goodman, *People or Personnel*, op. cit., p. 179

54 Ibid., p. 181

55 Ibid., pp. 175, 176

56 Ibid., p. 189

57 Goodman to Richard Boston, 'Conversations about Anarchism', *A Decade of Anarchy*, op. cit., p. 16

58 Goodman, 'The Anarchist Principle', ibid., p. 38

59 Goodman, *A Message to the Military Industrial Complex* (1965) (Housmans, 1969), p. 3

60 Goodman, *Compulsory Miseducation* (1964) (Harmondsworth: Penguin, 1971), p. 20

61 Goodman, *The Community of Scholars* (New York: Random House, 1962)

62 Goodman, *Growing up Absurd* (1960) (Sphere, 1970), p. 193

63 Goodman to Boston, 'Conversations about Anarchism', *A Decade of Anarchy*, op. cit., p. 17

Chapter Thirty-Nine

1 John Clark, *The Anarchist Moment*, op. cit., p. 188n; Theodore Roszak, quoted on the back cover of Murray Bookchin's *Remaking Society* (Montréal & New York: Black Rose Books, 1989)

2 Bookchin, *Toward an Ecological Society*, op. cit., p. 280

3 Bookchin, *Post-Scarcity Anarchism*, op. cit., pp. 68–9

4 Bookchin, *The Ecology of Freedom*, op. cit., p. 4

5 Ibid., pp. 94, 127

6 *Post-Scarcity Anarchism*, op. cit., p. 21

7 Bookchin, 'Thinking Ecologically: A Dialectical Approach', *Our Generation*, 18, 2 (March 1987), 11–12

8 *Post-Scarcity Anarchism*, op. cit., p. 64; *Ecology of Freedom*, op cit., p. 237

9 Ibid., p. 11

10 Ibid., pp. 353–4

11 *Toward an Ecological Society*, op. cit., p. 109

12 *Ecology of Freedom*, op. cit., p. 355

13 See 'Thinking Ecologically', op. cit., pp. 6–7; Bookchin, 'Freedom and Necessity in Nature', *Alternatives*, 12, 4 (1986); *The Modern Crisis*, 2nd edn. (Montreal & New York: Black Rose, 1987), pp. 55, 71

14 Bookchin, 'Social Ecology versus "Deep Ecology"', *Green Perspectives*, 4–5 (Summer 1987), 20

15 *Post-Scarcity Anarchism*, op. cit., pp. 10, 69

16 'Social Ecology', op. cit., 9–10. See also

'Recovering Evolution: A Reply to Eckersley and Fox', *Our Generation*, 12 (1990), 253

17 *Ecology of Freedom*, op. cit., p. 114. For a criticism of Bookchin's view of human nature, see my article 'Anarchism and Human Nature', *For Anarchism*, op. cit., p. 148, n. 32

18 *Post-Scarcity Anarchism*, op. cit., pp. 39, 138

19 Ibid., p. 167n

20 *Ecology of Freedom*, op. cit., p. 318

21 See 'Thinking Ecologically', op. cit., pp. 3–4

22 *Toward an Ecological Society*, op. cit., p. 102. See also *Ecology of Freedom*, op. cit., pp. 130–3

23 Ibid., p. 251

24 *Post-Scarcity Anarchism*, op. cit., p. 40

25 Ibid., p. 70

26 *Ecology of Freedom*, op. cit., p. 352; cf. *Toward an Ecological Society*, op. cit., p. 60

27 *Ecology of Freedom*, op. cit., pp. 276, 278, 272. See also *The Modern Crisis*, op. cit., p. 25

28 *Post-Scarcity Anarchism*, op. cit., p. 78

29 See 'Social Ecology', op. cit., pp. 3–4; 'The Crisis in the Ecology Movement', *Green Perspectives*, 6 (May 1988), pp. 1–5

30 *Post-Scarcity Anarchism*, op. cit., p. 19

31 *Toward an Ecological Society*, op. cit., pp. 26, 93, 70

32 *Ecology of Freedom*, op. cit., pp. 276, 279

33 'Thinking Ecologically', op. cit., p. 20; see also 'The Crisis in the Ecology Movement', op. cit., pp. 5–6

34 *Ecology of Freedom*, op. cit., p. 218

35 'Social Ecology', op. cit., p. 10

36 See *Post-Scarcity Anarchism*, op. cit., p. 71n; *Toward an Ecological Society*, op. cit., p. 59

37 'Thinking Ecologically', op. cit., pp. 35–6; *Remaking Society*, op. cit., p. 201

38 *Ecology of Freedom*, op. cit., p. 320

39 See ibid., p. 218

40 Ibid., p. 312

41 Ibid., p. 344

42 Ibid., p. 266

43 *Post-Scarcity Anarchism*, op. cit., p. 81

44 *Toward an Ecological Society*, op. cit., pp. 29, 193

45 Ibid., pp. 201, 202. See also *Remaking Society*, op. cit., p. 136

46 *Post-Scarcity Anarchism*, op. cit., p. 188. See also *Toward an Ecological Society*, op. cit., p. 208, and *The Modern Crisis*, op. cit., p. 168

47 *Toward an Ecological Society*, op. cit., p. 222

48 Ibid., pp. 126, 118

49 *Post-Scarcity Anarchism*, op. cit., p. 167

50 Ibid., pp. 19–20, 221

51 Ibid., p. 21

52 *Toward an Ecological Society*, op. cit., pp. 259, 245

53 Ibid., pp. 264, 274

54 *Post-Scarcity Anarchism*, op. cit., pp. 119, 115

55 Bill Devall and George Sessions, *Deep Ecology* (Salt Lake City: Peregrine Smith Books, 1985), p. 75, quoted in 'Social Ecology', op. cit., p. 12; *The Modern Crisis*, op. cit., p. 119

56 *Ecology of Freedom*, op. cit., p. 315

57 Ibid., p. 342

58 'Thinking Ecologically', op. cit., p. 36; *Remaking Society*, op. cit., p. 203

59 *Post-Scarcity Anarchism*, op. cit., p. 116

60 Ibid., p. 119

61 Ibid., p. 130

62 See Jacques Ellul, *The Technological Society* (New York: Vintage, 1964). For a broader discussion of the issue, see Carnes & Zerzan, eds., *Questioning Technology*, op. cit.

63 *Post-Scarcity Anarchism*, op. cit., p. 134

64 *Ecology of Freedom*, op. cit., p. 339

65 *Post-Scarcity Anarchism*, op. cit., p. 23

66 See 'Social Ecology', op. cit., p. 17; 'The Population Myth, I – II', *Green Perspectives*, 8 (July 1988), pp. 1–6; 15 (April 1989), pp. 1–8

67 'Thinking Ecologically', op. cit., 31, 34n, 32

68 Ibid., pp. 36, 26

69 *Post-Scarcity Anarchism*, op. cit., p. 27

70 *Toward an Ecological Society*, op. cit., p. 256

71 'Social Ecology', op. cit., pp. 19–20. See also 'New Social Movements', *For*

Anarchism, op. cit., pp. 259–74;
'Radical Politics in an Era of
Advanced Capitalism', *Green
Perspectives*, 18 (November 1989), pp.
1–6

72 *Remaking Society*, op. cit., p. 171
73 See *The Modern Crisis*, op. cit., p. 45
74 See *Toward an Ecological Society*, op. cit.,
   p. 257

Chapter Forty

1 Tucker, *Instead of a Book*, op. cit., p. 14
2 Proudhon, quoted in Guérin,
   Anarchism, op. cit., p. 53
3 Tucker, *Instead of a Book*, op. cit., pp.
   404, 131
4 Kropotkin, *The Conquest of Bread*, op.
   cit., p. 35
5 Elisée Reclus, *L'Evolution, la révolution,
   et l'idéal anarchique*, op. cit., p. 135
6 Proudhon, quoted in Guérin,
   Anarchism, op. cit., p. 57
7 Kropotkin, *Les Paroles d'un révolté*, op.
   cit., p. 117
8 Bakunin, quoted in Guérin, *Anarchism*,
   op. cit., p. 65
9 See Thomas, *Karl Marx and the
   Anarchists*, op. cit., pp. 2, 9
10 Richard Clutterbuck, 'Lecture to the
   Silver Jubilee Meeting of International
   Police', *The Police Journal* (July, 1975),
   p. 204
11 'The Reaction in Germany', *Bakunin on
   Anarchy*, op. cit., p. 57
12 *Bulletin de la Fédération Jurassienne*, 38
   (12 July 1874)
13 *Michael Bakunin: Selected Writings*,
   op. cit., p. 168
14 Sergei Nechaev, *Catechism of a
   Revolutionary* (1869) and *Principles of
   Revolution*, quoted in Carr, *Michael
   Bakunin* (1937 edn.), op. cit., p. 380
15 Marx and Engels, 'The Alliance of the
   Socialist Democrats and the
   International Working Men's
   Association' in Marx, Engels & Lenin,
   Anarchism and Anarcho-Syndicalism, op.
   cit., p. 117
16 Quoted in Woodcock, *Anarchism*,
   op. cit., p. 308

17 *Bulletin de la Fédération Jurassienne* (3
   December, 1876)
18 Carlo Cafiero, *Action et communisme*
   (1880), quoted in Nicolas Walter, 'Carlo
   Cafiero on Action and Communism',
   The Raven, II, 2 (October 1988), 177
19 Berkman, *ABC of Anarchism* (1973
   edn.), op. cit., p. 6
20 Wilde, *The Soul of Man Under Socialism*,
   op. cit., p. 180
21 See Miller, *Kropotkin*, op. cit., pp. 146,
   174–5
22 *Kropotkin's Revolutionary Pamphlets*, op.
   cit., p. 36
23 Kropotkin to Mrs Dryhurst, 1893,
   quoted in Woodcock & Avakumović, *The
   Anarchist Prince*, op. cit., p. 248
24 Kropotkin, quoted in *The Anarchist
   Reader*, op. cit., p. 184
25 Elisée Reclus, *L'Evolution et la
   révolution, et l'idéal anarchique*, op. cit.,
   p. 15
26 Tolstoy, 'Patriotism and Government',
   Works, op. cit., XLVI, 1, 252
27 Quoted in Woodcock, *Gandhi*, op. cit.,
   p. 86
28 Goldman, *Anarchism and Other Essays*,
   op. cit., p. 51
29 Godwin, *Anarchist Writings*, op. cit.,
   p. 55
30 Tolstoy, 'Patriotism and Government',
   op. cit., 252
31 Bourne, 'The State', op. cit., quoted
   in Ward, *Anarchy in Action*, op. cit.,
   p. 22
32 Bart de Ligt, *The Conquest of Violence*,
   op. cit., p. 75
33 See April Carter, 'Anarchism and
   Violence', *Nomos XIX: Anarchism*,
   op. cit., p. 320. See also Ostergaard,
   'Resisting the Nation State', *The
   Nation-State*, op. cit., p. 188
34 Buenaventura Durruti, *Montreal Star*
   (30 October 1936), quoted in Hugh
   Thomas, *The Spanish Civil War* (Eyre
   & Spottiswoode, 1961), p. 289
35 Berkman, *ABC of Anarchism*, op. cit.,
   p. 8
36 See Carter, 'Anarchism and Violence',
   op. cit., p. 334. See also Ostergaard,
   'Resisting the Nation State', op. cit.,
   p. 188; Ronald Sampson, *The*

Anarchist Basis of Pacifism (Peace Pledge
Union, 1970)

37 Engels, 'On Authority', Marx, Engels
& Lenin, *Anarchism and Anarcho-
Syndicalism*, op. cit., p. 105

38 See April Carter, 'Direct Action, Law,
and Anarchism', *Anarchism and the Law*,
op. cit., 141–3

39 Stirner, *The Ego and Its Own*, op. cit.,
p. 316

40 Berkman, *ABC of Anarchism*, op. cit., p. 8

Chapter Forty-One

1 For this distinction, see Guido de
Ruggiero, *The History of European
Liberalism*, trans. R. G. Collingwood
(Boston: Beacon Press, 1959), p. 350

2 Malatesta, *Anarchy*, op. cit., p. 47

3 Kropotkin, *Anarchism and Anarchist
Communism*, op. cit., p. 23; Most, 'Die
Anarchie', *Internationale Bibliothek*
(1888); Rocker, *Anarchism and
Anarcho-Syndicalism*, op. cit., p. 11

4 Guérin, *Anarchism*, op. cit., p. 12

5 See Faure, *La Douleur universelle*,
op. cit., p. 357

6 See my essay, 'Anarchism and Human
Nature', in *For Anarchism*, ed. David
Goodway, op. cit., pp. 127–49

7 George Bernard Shaw, 'The
Impossibities of Anarchism' (1893), in
Patterns of Anarchy, op. cit., p. 508

8 Ibid., p. 514

9 Hobhouse, *Liberalism*, op. cit., p. 146

10 Russell, *Roads to Freedom*, op. cit., p. 15

11 Miller, *Anarchism*, op. cit., p. 178

12 See Howard J. Ehrlich, 'Anarchism
and formal organizations', *Reinventing
Anarchy*, op. cit., p. 108

13 See David Wieck, 'The Negativity
of Anarchism', *Reinventing Anarchy*,
op. cit., p. 140; Giovanni Baldelli,
Social Anarchism, op. cit., p. 95

14 Quoted in Ward, *Anarchy in Action*,
op. cit., p. 38

15 Russell, *Principles of Social
Reconstruction*, op. cit., p. 3

16 Dostoevsky, *Notes from Underground*,
op. cit., pp. 33–4

17 Godwin, *Political Justice* (1793 edn.),
op. cit., II, 565

18 Orwell, 'Lear, Tolstoy and the Fool'
(1947), *Collected Essays*, op. cit., p. 432.

19 Orwell, 'Politics vs. Literature' (1946),
ibid., p. 405. Cf. Shaw, 'The Impossibilities of Anarchism', op. cit., p. 508

20 Godwin, *Political Justice* (1798 edn.),
op. cit., I, 168

21 Joll, *The Anarchists*, op. cit., p. 259

22 Orwell, *Poetry Quarterly* (Autumn 1945)

23 See Russell, *In Praise of Idleness*, op. cit.,
p. 11

24 Shaw, 'The Impossibilities of
Anarchism', op. cit., p. 508

25 Camillo Berneri, 'The Problem of Work'
(1938), *Why Work? Arguments for the
Leisure Society*, ed. Vernon Richards
(Freedom Press, 1983), p. 74

26 *Adresse à tous les travailleurs* (30 May
1968) (Paris: Comité Enragés –
Internationale Situationniste, 1968)

27 G. Plechanoff, *Anarchism and Socialism*,
trans. Eleanor Marx Aveling (Chicago:
C. H. Kerr, 1912), pp. 141, 148

28 Lenin, *The State and Revolution*, op. cit.,
p. 124

29 See Lenin, '*Left-Wing' Communism, An
Infantile Disorder* (1920)

30 Gray, *The Socialist Tradition*, op. cit.,
p. 380

31 Wilde, 'The Soul of Man under
Socialism', op. cit., p. 34

32 Apter, 'The Old Anarchism and the
New – Some Comments', *Anarchism
Today*, op. cit., p. 1

33 Ward, *Anarchy in Action*, op. cit.,
p. 11

34 Joll, 'Anarchism – a Living Tradition',
Anarchism Today, op. cit., p. 225

35 Hobsbawm, 'Reflections on Anarchism'
(1969), *Revolutionaries: Contemporary
Essays* (Weidenfeld and Nicolson, 1973),
p. 83

Epilogue

1 See Richard Day, *Gramsci is Dead:
Anarchist Contributions to the Newest
Social Movements* (Pluto Press, 2005)

2 Woodcock, *Anarchism* (1975), op. cit., p. 454

3 See Jonathan Purkis & James Bowen, eds., *Twenty-first Century Anarchism: Unorthodox Ideas for a New Millennium* (Cassell, 1997), p. 3. See also their *Changing Anarchism: Anarchist Theory and Practice in a Global Age* (Manchester: Manchester University Press, 2004)

4 See Penny Kornegger, 'Anarchism: The Feminist Connection', H. J. Ehrlich, ed., *Reinventing Anarchy, Again* (Edinburgh: AK Press, 1996), p. 175

5 See L. Susan Brown, *The Politics of Individualism: Liberalism, Feminism and Anarchism* (Montréal: Black Rose, 2003)

6 Bulletin of the Anarcha-feminist International in Ruth Kinna, *Anarchism: A Beginner's Guide* (Oxford: Oneworld, 2005), p. 79

7 See Roxanne Dunbar-Ortiz, ed., *Quiet Rumours* (Edinburgh: AK Press, 2003)

8 Noam Chomsky, 'Anarchism, Intellectuals and the State'(1996), *Chomsky on Anarchism*, ed. Barry Pateman (Edinburgh: AK Press, 2005), p. 215

9 Chomsky, Interview with Barry Pateman (2004), ibid., p. 223

10 Chomsky, *Language and Politics*, ed. C. Otero (Montréal: Black Rose, 1988), p. 162

11 Chomsky, 'Anarchism, Marxism and Hope for the Future'(1995), *Chomsky on Anarchism*, op. cit., p. 178

12 Chomsky, Interview with Barry Pateman, op. cit., p. 222

13 Chomsky, Interview with Zida Vodnovik, op. cit., p. 238

14 Chomsky, Interview with Barry Pateman, op. cit., p. 226

15 See David Goodway, *Anarchist Seeds Beneath the Snow* (Liverpool: Liverpool University Press, 2006), pp. 309–25. See also Colin Ward and David Goodway, *Talking Anarchy* (Nottingham: Five Leaves, 2003)

16 Ward, *Anarchy in Action* (Allen & Unwin, 1973), p. 11

17 Ward, *Anarchism: A Very Short Introduction* (Oxford: Oxford University Press), p. 98

18 Alan Carter, 'Analytical Anarchism: Some Conceptual Foundations', *Political Theory*, 28, 2 (2000), p. 230

19 Michel Foucault, 'The Subject and Power', Hubert L. Dreyfus and Paul Rabinow, *Michel Foucault: Beyond Structuralism and Hermeneutics* (Brighton: Harvester Press, 1982), p. 221

20 Foucault, 'Power and Strategies', in *Power/Knowledge*, op. cit., p. 141

21 Todd May, *The Political Philosophy of Poststructuralist Anarchism* (Philadelphia: Pennsylvania University Press, 1994), p. 63. See my 'Human Nature and Anarchism', *For Anarchism: History, Theory and Practice*, ed. David Goodway (Routledge, 1989)

22 Ibid., p. 119, p. 123

23 Saul Newman, *From Bakunin to Lacan: Anti-Authoritarianism and the Dislocation of Power* (Lanham: Lexington Books, 2001), p. 153

24 See Newman, 'Anarchism and the Politics of *Ressentiment*', *Theory & Event*, 4, 3 (2000)

25 Lewis Call, 'Anarchy in the Matrix: Postmodern Anarchism in the Novels of William Gibson and Bruce Sterling', *Anarchist Studies*, 7, 2 (Cambridge, 1999), p. 100

26 Call, *Postmodern Anarchism* (Lanham: Lexington Books, 2002), pp. 52–3

27 Ibid., p. 97

28 See Murray Bookchin, *Social Anarchism or Life-Style Anarchism: An Unbridgeable Chasm* (Edinburgh: AK Press, 1995)

29 Peter Lamborn Wilson, 'Crazy Nietzsche', *I Am Not A Man, I Am Dynamite!: Friedrich Nietzsche and the Anarchist Tradition*, eds. John Moore with Spencer Sunshine (Brooklyn, NY: Autonomedia, 2004), p. 147

30 Hakim Bey, *T.A.Z: The Temporary Autonomous Zone: Ontological Anarchy, Poetic Terrorism* (1985) (Brooklyn, NY: Autonomedia, 1991), pp. 98–9

31 Ibid., p. 100

32 Bey, *Immediatism* (Brooklyn, NY: Autonomedia, 1994), p. 106

33 Wilson, 'Secular Antinomian Anabaptist Neo-Luddism', *Fifth Estate*, 372 (Spring, 2006), p. 39

34 George Bradford, 'Civilization in Bulk', *Fifth Estate* (Spring, 1991)

35 John Zerzan, *Future Primitive and Other Essays* (Brooklyn, NY: Autonomedia, 1994), p. 144

36 Fredy Perlman, *Against His-story, Against Leviathan!* (Detroit: Black & Red, 1983), p. 57

37 Zerzan, 'Who is Chomsky?', *Running on Emptiness: The Pathology of Civilization* (Los Angeles: Feral House, 2002), p. 34

38 Zerzan, *Future Primitive*, op. cit., p. 16

39 See Zerzan and Alice Carnes, eds., *Questioning Technology: A Critical Anthology* (Freedom Press, 1988)

40 Zerzan, *Running on Emptiness*, op. cit., p. 80

41 See my *Around Africa: From the Pillars of Hercules to the Strait of Gibraltar* (London and New York: Simon & Schuster, 1994), pp. 127–31

42 See my *Europe's Lost Civilization: Uncovering the Mysteries of the Megaliths* (Headline, 2004), pp. 8–10, 285–90

43 See www.primitivism.com

44 'Rewilding', *Back to Basics*, vol. 3, www.greenanarchy.org

45 See Graham Purchase, 'Social Ecology, Anarchism and Trades Unionism', *Deep Ecology and Anarchism* (Freedom Press, 1993)

46 Gary Snyder, 'Buddhist Anarchism', *Journal for the Protection of All Beings* (San Francisco: City Lights, 1961)

47 Agorn!, *Towards an Anarchist Theory of Race* (Detroit, n.d.)

48 Ursula K. Le Guin, *The Dispossessed* (New York: Harper & Row, 1974), p. 241

49 See Murray Bookchin, *Re-enchanting Humanity: A Defense of the Human Spirit against Anti-Humanism, Misanthropy, Mysticism and Primitivism* (Cassell, 1995)

50 Bookchin, *Social Anarchism or Life-Style Anarchism: An Unbridgeable Chasm* op. cit., p. 1

51 Ibid., p. 56

52 Ibid., p. 9

53 Bookchin, 'Libertarian Muncipalism: An Overview', *Society and Nature*, 1, 1 (1992), p. 94. See also Janet Biehl and Murray Bookchin, *The Politics of Social Ecology: Libertarian Municipalism* (Montréal: Black Rose, 1997)

54 Bookchin, Interview with David Vanek, *Harbinger: A Journal of Social Ecology*, 2, 1 (Spring, 2003), p. 2

55 Bookchin, Introduction, third edition, *Post-Scarcity Anarchism* (Edinburgh: AK Press, 2004)

56 Brian Morris, *Ecology and Anarchism: Essays and Reviews on Contemporary Thought* (Malvern Wells: Images, 1996), p. 5. See also his *Kropotkin: The Politics of Community* (New York: Humanity Books, 2004)

57 David Watson, *Beyond Bookchin: Preface for a Future Social Ecology* (Brooklyn, NY: Autonomedia, 1996), p. 240

58 John P. Clark, *The Anarchist Moment*, op. cit., p. 160

59 Clark, 'What is Social Ecology?', *Renewing the Earth*, op. cit., pp. 10–11

60 See John P. Clark and Camille Martin, eds., *Anarchy, Geography, Modernity: The Radical Thought of Elisée Reclus* (Lanham: Lexington Books, 2004)

61 Clark, 'Municipal Dreams: A Social Ecological Critique of Bookchin's Politics', *Social Ecology after Bookchin*, ed. Andrew Light (New York: Guilford Press, 1998)

62 See Clark, 'Bridging the Unbridgeable Chasm: On Bookchin's Critique of the Anarchist Tradition', forthcoming in *Perspectives on Anarchist Theory*

63 See David Graeber, 'The New Anarchists', *New Left Review*, 13 (January–February, 2002). See also his *Fragments of an Anarchist Anthropology* (Chicago: Prickly Paradigm Press, 2004)

64 See Benjamin Franks, *Rebel Alliances: The Means and Ends of Contemporary British Anarchisms* (Edinburgh: AK Press, 2006); Zerzan, *Running on Emptiness*, op. cit., p. 162

65 Gilles Deleuze and Felix Guattari, *A Thousand Plateaus: Capitalism and Schizophrenia*, trans. Brian Massumi (Continuum, 1999), p. 74

66 See Erlich, 'How to Get from Here to There: Building Revolutionary Transfer Culture', *Reinventing Anarchy, Again*, op. cit., p. 352

67 See Séan M. Sheehan, *Anarchism* (Reaktion, 2003), pp. 7–12, 150

68 Naomi Klein, 'Does Protest Need a Vision?', *New Statesman* (3 July 2000)

69 In Bill Weinberg, *Homage to Chiapas* (Verso, 2002), p. 198. See also Subcomandante Insurgente Marcos, *Ya Basta! Ten Years of the Zapatista Uprising*, ed. Ziga Vodovnik (Edinburgh: AK Press, 2004)

70 In Subcomandante Marcos, *Our Word Is Our Weapon*, ed. Juan Ponce de León (New York: Seven Stories Press, 2002)

SELECT BIBLIOGRAPHY

This select bibliography consists mainly of the works consulted, as a definitive bibliography of anarchism would run to several volumes. Specific details of articles referred to are given in the Reference Notes. As there, the place of publication of the titles listed below is London, unless otherwise stated. 'n.d.' indicates that no date of publication was printed in the volume consulted. The broad distinction between 'General' and 'Anarchist and Libertarian Works' is not hard and fast, but intended as a useful guide.

Anthologies

Berman, Paul, ed., *Quotations from the Anarchists* (New York: Praeger, 1972)

Ehrlich, Howard J. et al, eds., *Reinventing Anarchy* (Routledge & Kegan Paul, 1979); *Reinventing Anarchy, Again* (Edinburgh: AK Press, 1996)

Graham, Robert, ed., *Anarchism: A Documentary History of Libertarian Ideas*, vol. 1 (Montréal: Black Rose, 2005); vol. 2 (2009)

Guérin, Daniel, ed., *Ni Dieu ni Maître: anthologie de l'anarchisme*, 4 vols. (Paris: Maspero, 1972)

Horowitz, Irving L., ed., *The Anarchists* (New York: Dell, 1964)

Krimerman, Leonard I. & Lewis Perry, eds., *Patterns of Anarchy: A Collection of Writings on the Anarchist Tradition* (New York: Anchor, 1966)

Shatz, Marshall S., ed., *The Essential Works of Anarchism* (New York: Bantam, 1971)

Woodcock, George, ed., *The Anarchist Reader* (Fontana, 1977)

General

Alexander, Y. & K. A. Myers, eds., *Terrorism in Europe* (Croom Helm, 1982)

Antliff, Allan, *Anarchist Modernism: Arts, Politics and the First American Avant-garde* (Chicago: Chicago University Press, 2001)

Apter, David E. & James Joll, eds., *Anarchism Today* (Macmillan, 1971)

Arias de la Canal, Fredo, *La Revolución Mexicano fue anarquista: Flores Magón, poeta revolucionaria* (Mexico: G. de Anda, 1977)

Arvon, Henri, *L'Anarchisme* (Paris: Presses Universitaires de France, 1977)

Arvon, Henri, *L'Anarchisme au XXe siècle* (Paris: Presses Universitaires de France, 1979)

Arvon, Henri, *Les Libertariens américains: de l'anarchisme individualiste à l'anarcho-capitalisme* (Paris: Presses Universitaires de France, 1983)

Avineri, Shlomo, *Karl Marx: Social and Political Thought* (Cambridge: Cambridge University Press, 1971)

Avrich, Paul, *The Russian Anarchists* (Princeton, NJ: Princeton University Press, 1967)

Avrich, Paul, *Kronstadt 1921* (Princeton, NJ: Princeton University Press, 1970)

Avrich, Paul, ed., *The Anarchists in the Russian Revolution*, (Ithaca, NY: Cornell University Press, 1973)

Avrich, Paul, *Bakunin and Nechaev* (Freedom Press, 1973)

Avrich, Paul, *An American Anarchist: The Life of Voltairine de Cleyre* (Princeton, NJ: Princeton University Press, 1978)

Avrich, Paul, *The Modern School Movement: Anarchism and Education in the United States* (Princeton, NJ: Princeton University Press, 1980)

Avrich, Paul, *The Haymarket Tragedy* (Princeton, NJ: Princeton University Press, 1984)

Avrich, Paul, *Anarchist Portraits* (Princeton, NJ: Princeton University Press, 1988)

Bachelin, Henri, *P.-J. Proudhon, socialiste national* (Paris, 1941)

Bailie, William, *Josiah Warren: The First American Anarchist* (Boston: Small, Maynard, 1906)

Barber, Benjamin, *Superman and Common Men: Freedom, Anarchy and the Revolution* (Harmondsworth: Penguin, 1972)

Barclay, Harold, *People without Government* (Kahn & Averill and Cienfuegos Press, 1982)

Barker, Ernest, *Principles of Social and Political Theory* (1951) (Oxford: Oxford University Press 1967)

Barker, Jeffrey M., *Individualism and Community: The State in Marx and Early Anarchism* (New York: Greenwood Press, 1986)

Barrat, Jean, *What is Situationism?* (Unpopular Books, 1987)

Bayer, Osvaldo, *Anarchism and Violence: Severino di Giovanni in Argentina, 1923–31*, trans. Paul Sharkey (Elephant Editions, 1986)

Bell, Thomas, *Edward Carpenter: The English Tolstoi* (Los Angeles: Libertarian Group, 1932)

Benello, George & Dimitri Roussopoulos, eds., *The Case for Participatory Democracy* (New York: Grossman, 1971)

Bernal, Martin, *Chinese Socialism to 1907* (Ithaca, NY: Cornell University Press, 1976)

Bhattacharyya, Buddhadeva, *Evolution of the Political Philosophy of Gandhi* (Calcutta, 1969)

Bolloten, Burnett, *The Grand Camouflage: The Communist Conspiracy in the Spanish Civil War* (1961) (Pall Mall, 1968)

Bondurant, Joan V., *Conquest of Violence: The Gandhian Philosophy of Conflict* (Princeton, NJ: Princeton University Press, 1958)

Borkenau, Franz, *The Spanish Cockpit* (Faber & Faber, 1937)

Brailsford, H. N., *Shelley, Godwin and their Circle* (Oxford: Oxford University Press, 1945)

Brenan, Gerald, *The Spanish Labyrinth* (New York: Macmillan 1945)

Brissenden, P. F., *The I. W. W.: A Study of American Syndicalism* (New York: Columbia University Press, 1920)

Brogan, D. W., *Proudhon* (Hamish Hamilton, 1934)

Broué, Pierre & Emile Témine, *The Revolution and the Civil War in Spain* (Cambridge, Mass.: MIT Press, 1970)

Brown, Barratt A., ed., *Great Democrats* (Nicholson & Watson, 1934)

Brown, Bernard E., *Protest in Paris: Anatomy of a Revolt* (Morristown, NJ: General Learning, 1974)

Bury, J. B., *A History of Freedom of Thought* (1913) ed. H. J. Blackham (Oxford: Oxford University Press, 1952)

Cahm, Caroline, *Peter Kropotkin and the Rise of Revolutionary Anarchism, 1873–1886* (Cambridge: Cambridge University Press, 1989)

Cahm, E. & V. C. Fisera, eds., *Socialism and Nationalism* (Nottingham: Spokesman, 1978)

Carlson, Andrew, *Anarchism in Germany I: The Early Movement* (Metuchen, NJ: Scarecrow, 1972)

Carnes, Alice & John Zerzan, eds., *Questioning Technology* (Freedom Press, 1988)

Carr, E. H., *Michael Bakunin* (Macmillan, 1937) (2nd edn., New York, 1975)

Carr, E. H., *Studies in Revolution* (Macmillan, 1950)

Carr, E. H., *The Romantic Exiles* (Harmondsworth: Penguin, 1949)

Carr, Reg, *Anarchism in France; The Case of Octave Mirbeau* (Manchester: Manchester University Press, 1977)

Carroll, John, *Break-out from the Crystal Palace: The Anarcho-Psychological Critique: Stirner, Nietzsche, Dostoevsky* (Routledge & Kegan Paul, 1974)

Carter, April, *The Political Theory of Anarchism* (Routledge & Kegan Paul, 1971)

Casas, Juan Gómez, *Anarchist Organization: The History of the FAI* (Montréal: Black Rose, 1986)

Caute, David, *Sixty Eight: The Year of the Barricades* (Hamish Hamilton, 1988)

Cohn, Norman, *The Pursuit of the Millennium: Revolutionary Millenarians and Mystical Anarchists in the Middle Ages* (1957) (Paladin, 1984)

Cole, G. D. H., *A History of Socialist Thought*, Vol. I: *The Forerunners* (Macmillan, 1953), Vol. II: *Marxism and Anarchism* (Macmillan, 1954)

Compte rendu analytique des séances du congrès anarchiste tenu à Amsterdam, 24–31 août, 1907 (Paris, 1908)

Compte rendu du VIIIème congrès général, Berne (Berne, 1876)

Confino, M., *Violence dans la violence: le débat Bakounine – Necaev* (Paris, 1973)

Conquest, Robert, *Lenin* (Fontana, 1972)

Creagh, Ronald, *Histoire de l'anarchisme aux États-Unis*, 2 vols. (Paris: Didier Erudition, 1986)

Crowder, George, *Classical Anarchism: The Political Thought of Godwin, Proudhon, Bakunin, and Kropotkin* (New York: Oxford University Presss, 1992)

Crump, John, *Origins of Socialist Thought in Japan* (Croom Helm, 1983)

D'Agostino, Anthony, *Marxism and the Russian Anarchists* (San Francisco: Germinal Press, 1977)

Damico, Linda H., *The Anarchist Dimension of Liberation Theology* (New York: Lang, 1987)

Davis, J. C., *Fear, Myth and History* (Cambridge: Cambridge University Press, 1986)

Day, Richard, *Gramsci is Dead: Anarchist Contributions to the Newest Social Movements* (Pluto Press, 2005)

De Jasay, A., *Against Government: On Government, Anarchy and Politics* (New York: Routledge, 1997)

De Leon, David, *The American as Anarchist: Reflections on Indigenous Radicalism* (Baltimore: Johns Hopkins University Press, 1978)

De Souza, Newton Stadler, *O anarquismo da Colônia Cecília* (Rio de Janeiro, 1970)

Dirlik, Arif, *Anarchism in the Chinese Revolution* (New York: Oxford University Press, 1989)

Doctor, Adi Hormusji, *Anarchist Thought in India* (Bombay: Asia Publishing House, 1964)

Doctor, Adi Hormusji, *Sarvodaya: A Political and Economic Study* (Bombay: Asia Publishing House, n.d.)

Dolléans, Eduard, *Proudhon et la Révolution de 1848*, (Paris: Presses Universitaires de France, 1948)

Dostoevsky, Fyodor, *Notes from the Underground* (Harmondsworth: Penguin, 1977)

Dreyfus, Hubert L. & Paul Rabinow, *Michel Foucault: Beyond Structuralism and Hermeneutics* (Brighton: Harvester Press, 1982)

Drinnon, Richard, *Rebel in Paradise: A Biography of Emma Goldman* (Chicago: Chicago University Press, 1961; new edn. 1982)

Dubofsky, Melvyn, *A History of the Industrial Workers of the World* (Chicago: Quadrangle, 1969)

Dubois, Félix, *Le Péril anarchiste* (Paris, 1894)

Dulles, John W., *Anarchists and Communists in Brazil, 1900–1935* (Austin: University of Texas Press, 1973)

Ellmann, Richard, *Oscar Wilde* (Hamish Hamilton, 1987)

Eltzbacher, Paul, *Anarchism: Exponents of the Anarchist Philosophy* (1908), (New York: Libertarian Book Club, 1960)

Esenwein, George R., *Anarchist Ideology and the Working Class Movement in Spain, 1868–1898* (Berkeley: University of California Press, 1989)

Everett, Martyn, *War and Revolution: The Hungarian Anarchist Movement in World War I and the Budapest Commune* (1919) (Kate Sharpley, 2006)

Falk, Candace, *Love, Anarchy and Emma Goldman* (New York: Holt, Rinehart & Winston, 1985; rev. edn. New Brunswick: Rutgers University Press, 1990)

Fernbach, David, ed., *The First International and After* (Harmondsworth: Penguin, 1974)

Ferreira, Hugo Gil & Michael W. Marshall, *Portugal's Revolution: Ten Years On* (Cambridge: Cambridge University Press, 1976)

Ferrer, Pai, *Durruti* (Barcelona: Planeta, 1985)

Fishman, W. J., *East End Jewish Radicals 1875–1914* (Duckworth, 1975)

Fleming, Marie, *The Anarchist Way to Socialism: Elisée Reclus and 19th-Century European Anarchism* (Croom Helm, 1979)

Footman, David, *Civil War in Russia* (Faber & Faber, 1961)

Forman, James D., *Anarchism: Political Innocence or Social Violence* (New York: Watts, 1975)

Freedom: A Hundred Years, October 1886 to October 1986 (Freedom Press, 1986)

Franks, Benjamin, *Rebel Alliances: The Means and Ends of Contemporary British Anarchisms* (Edinburgh: AK Press, 2006)

Fromm, Erich, *The Fear of Freedom* (Routledge & Kegan Paul, 1960)

Gans, C., *Philosophical Anarchism and Political Disobedience* (New York: Cambridge University Press, 1992)

Garaud, R., *L'Anarchie et 'la répression* (Paris, 1895)

Gay, K. &. M., *Encyclopaedia of Political Anarchy* (Santa Barbara: ABC-CLIO, 1997)

Gibbs, Benjamin, *Freedom and Liberation* (Brighton: Sussex University Press, 1976)

Goehlert, Robert & Claire Herczeg, *Anarchism: A Bibliography* (Monticello, Illinois: Vance Bibliographies, 1982)

Gombin, Richard, *The Origins of Modern Leftism* (Harmondsworth: Penguin, 1975)

Gombin, Richard, *The Radical Tradition* (Methuen, 1978)

Gomel, Alfredo, *Anarquismo y anarcosindicalismo en América Latina* (Paris: Ruedo Ibérico, c. 1980)

Goodman, Mitchell, ed., *The Movement toward a New America: The Beginning of a Long Revolution* (New York: Knopf, 1970)

Goodway, David, ed., *For Anarchism: History, Theory and Practice* (Routledge, 1989)

Goodway, David, ed., *Herbert Read Reassessed* (Liverpool: Liverpool University Press, 1998)

Goodway, David, *Anarchist Seeds beneath the Snow: Left-Libertarian Thought from William Morris to Colin Ward* (Liverpool: Liverpool University Press, 2006)

Graeber, David, 'The New Anarchists', *New Left Review*, 13 (January–February, 2002)

Graeber, David, *Fragments of an Anarchist Anthropology* (Chicago: Prickly Paradigm Press, 2004)

Graham, Robert, ed., *Anarchism: A Documentary History of Libertarian Ideas*, vol. 1 (Montréal: Black Rose, 2005); vol. 2 (2009)

Gray, Alexander, *The Socialist Tradition* (1946) (Longmans, 1 63)

Gray, Christopher, ed., *Leaving the Twentieth Century: The Incomplete Work of the Situationist International* (Free Fall, 1974)

Gray, Jack, *Modern China in Search of a Political Form* (Oxford: Oxford University Press, 1969)

Gregg, Richard B., *The Power of Non-Violence* (George Routledge & Sons, 1938)

Gregory, Walter, David Morris & Anthony Peters, *The Shallow Grave* (Victor Gollancz, 1986)

Hall, David, *Eros and Irony: A Prelude to Philosophical Anarchism* (New York: State University of New York, 1982)

Hamon, A., *Psychologie de l'anarchiste-socialiste* (Paris, 1895)

Hampton, Christopher, ed., *A Radical Reader: The Struggle for Change in England 1381–1914* (Harmondsworth: Penguin, 1984)

Hardy, Dennis, *Alternative Communities in Nineteenth-Century England* (Longman, 1979)

Harmel, Claude, *Histoire de l'anarchie: des origines à 1880* (Paris: Editions Champ Libre, 1984)

Hart, John M., *Anarchism and The Mexican Working Class 1860–1931* (Austin: University of Texas Press, 1978)

Herbert, Eugenia, *The Artist and Social Reform: France and Belgium, 1885–1898* (New Haven: Yale University Press, 1961)

Heredia, Luis, *El Anarquismo en Chile (1897–1931)* (Mexico: Antorcha, 1981)

Herzen, Alexander, *My Past and Thoughts*, 4 vols. (Chatto & Windus, 1968)

Hill, Christopher, *The World Turned Upside Down: Radical Ideas during the English Revolution* (1972) (Harmondsworth: Penguin, 1975)

Hobhouse, L. T., *Liberalism* (Williams & Norgate, n.d.)

Hobsbawm, E. J., *Primitive Rebels: Studies in Archaic Forms of Social Movement in the 19th and 20th Centuries* (Manchester: Manchester University Press, 1959)

Hobsbawm, E. J., *Bandits* (Weidenfeld & Nicolson, 1969)

Hobsbawm, E. J., *Revolutionaries: Contemporary Essays* (Weidenfeld & Nicolson, 1973)

Hoffman, Robert L., *Revolutionary Justice: The Social and Political Theory of P.-J. Proudhon* (Urbana: University of Illinois Press, 1972)

Hollingdale, R. J., *Nietzsche* (Routledge & Kegan Paul, 1973)

Holterman, Thom & Henevan Maarsween, *Law and Anarchism* (Montréal: Black Rose, 1984)

Holton, R. J., *British Syndicalism, 1900–1914* (Pluto Press, 1973)

Holton, R. J., *British Syndicalism, 1900–1914* (Pluto Press, 1975)

Home, Stewart, *The Assault on Culture: Utopian Currents from Lettrisme to Class War* (Aporia Press & Unpopular Books, 1988)

Hostetter, R., *The Italian Socialist Movement, I: Origins 1860–1882* (Princeton, NJ: Van Nostrand, 1958)

Humphreys, Christmas, *Buddhism* (Harmondsworth: Penguin, 1971)

Hyams, Edward, *Pierre-Joseph Proudhon: His Revolutionary Life, Mind and Works* (John Murray, 1979)

Ishill, Joseph, *Elisée and Elie Reclus: In Memoriam* (Berkeley Heights, 1927)

Jenning, Jeremy R., *Georges Sorel: The Character and Development of his Thought* (Macmillan, 1985)

Jerome, Judson, *Families of Eden: Communes and the New Anarchism* (New York: Seabury, 1974)

Joll, James, *The Second International 1889–1914* (Weidenfeld & Nicolson, 1955)

Joll, James, *The Anarchists* (Eyre & Spottiswoode, 1964; 2nd edn. Methuen, 1979)

Jones, Leslie A., *The Digger Movement 1649* (Hyde Park Pamphlet, n.d.)

Kafka, Franz, *The Castle* (Harmondsworth: Penguin, 1966)

Kaminski, H. E., *Michel Bakounine: la vie d'un révolutionnaire* (1938) (Paris: Bélibaste, 1971)

Kaplan, Temma, *Anarchists of Andalusia (1868–1903)* (Princeton, NJ: Princeton University Press, 1977)

Kaufmann, Walter, *Nietzsche: Philosopher, Psychologist, Antichrist* (Princeton, NJ: Princeton University Press, 1974)

Kedward, Roderick, *The Anarchists* (Macdonald, 1971)

Kelly, Aileen, *Mikhail Bakunin: A Study in the Psychology and Politics of Utopianism*, (Oxford: Clarendon Press, 1982)

Kern, Robert W., *Red Years / Black Years: A Political History of Spanish Anarchism (1911–1937)* (Philadelphia: Institute for the Study of Human Issues, 1978)

King, James, *The Last Modern: A Life of Herbert Read* (Weidenfeld & Nicolson, 1990)

Ki-Rak, Ha, *A History of the Korean Anarchist Movement* (Tuegu, Korea: Anarchist Publishing Committee, 1986)

Kline, Gary W., *The Individualist Anarchists* (New York, 1987)

Klossowski, Pierre, *Sade mon prochain* (Paris: Seuil, 1947)

Knabb, K., ed., *Situationist International Anthology* (Berkeley: Bureau of Public Secrets, 1981)

Kravchinsky, Sergei, *Underground Russia* (New York, 1885)

Kublin, Hyman, *Asian Revolutionary* (Princeton, NJ: Princeton University Press, 1964)

Lang, Olga, *Pa Chin and his Writings* (Cambridge, Mass.: Harvard University Press, 1967)

Lehning, Arthur, *Anarchisme et marxisme dans la révolution russe* (Paris: Spartacus, 1971)

Leighton, Patricia, *Re-ordering the Universe: Picasso and Anarchism, 1897–1914* (Princeton, NJ: Princeton University Press, 1989)

Leval, Gaston, *Collectives in the Spanish Revolution*, trans. Vernon Richards (Freedom Press, 1975)

Lenin, V. I., *'Left-Wing' Communism, An Infantile Disorder* (Peking: Foreign Languages Press, 1965)

Lenin, V. I., *The State and Revolution* (Peking: Foreign Languages Press, 1965)

Lenin, V. I., *The State* (Peking: Foreign Languages Press, 1965)

Light, Andrew, ed., *Social Ecology after Bookchin* (New York: Guilford, 1998)

Limeux, Pierre, *Du Libéralisme à l'anarcho-capitalisme* (Paris: Presses Universitaires de France, 1983)

Locke, Don, *A Fantasy of Reason: The Life and Thought of William Godwin* (Routledge & Kegan Paul, 1980)

Locke, John, *Two Treatises of Civil Government* (Dent, 1936)

Longmore, C., *The IWA Today* (DAM – IWA, 1985)

Lubac, Henri de, *The Un-Marxian Socialist: A Study of Proudhon* (Sheed & Ward, 1948)

Lunn, Eugene, *The Prophet of Community; The Romantic Socialism of Gustav Landauer* (Berkeley, CA: University of California Press, 1973)

Mackay, J. H., *The Anarchists: a Picture of Civilization at the Close of the Nineteenth Century*, trans. George Schumm (Boston: Benj. R. Tucker, 1891)

Mackay, J. H., *Max Stirner, sein Leben und sein Werk* (Berlin, 1898)

Mailer, P., *Portugal: The Impossible Revolution* (Solidarity, 1977)

Maitron, Jean, *Histoire du mouvement anarchiste en France (1880–1914)* (Paris: Société Universitaire, 1951); 3rd edn., *Le Mouvement anarchiste en France*, 2 vols., (Paris: Maspero, 1975)

Malet, Michael, *Nestor Makhno and the Russian Civil War* (Macmillan, 1982)

Manuel, Frank, *The Prophets of Paris* (Cambridge, Mass.: Harvard University Press, 1962)

Marsh, Margaret, *Anarchist Women, 1870–1920* (Philadelphia: Temple University Press, 1987)

Marshall, Peter, *William Godwin* (London & New Haven: Yale University Press, 1984)

Marshall, Peter, ed., *The Anarchist Writings of William Godwin* (Freedom Press, 1987)

Marshall, Peter, ed., *Damon and Delia*, by William Godwin (Croesor: Zena, 1988)

Marshall, Peter, *William Blake: Visionary Anarchist* (Freedom Press, 1988)

Marshall, Peter, *Cuba Libre: Breaking the Chains?* (Victor Gollancz, 1987: Unwin Paperbacks, 1988; New York: Faber & Faber, 1988; rev. edn. Mexico City: Diana, 1991)

Martin, James J., *Men against the State: The Expositors of Individualist Anarchism in America, 1827–1918* (1953) (Colorado Springs: Ralph Myles, 1970)

Marx, Karl, *The Poverty of Philosophy* (New York: International Publishers, 1963)

Marx & Engels, *The Communist Manifesto*, ed. A. J. P. Taylor (Harmondsworth: Penguin, 1967)

Marx & Engels, *Selected Writings* (Lawrence & Wishart, 1968)

Marx & Engels, *The German Ideology*, ed. C. J. Arthur (Lawrence & Wishart, 1970)

Marx, Engels & Lenin, *Anarchism and Anarcho-syndicalism: Selected Writings*, ed. N. Y. Kolpinsky (New York: International Publishers, 1972)

Masters, Anthony, *Bakunin: The Father of Anarchism* (New York: Saturday Review Press, 1974)

Maurer, Charles B., *Call to Revolution: The Mystical Anarchism of Gustav Landauer* (Detroit: Wayne State University Press, 1971)

Mbah, Sam & I. E. Igariwey, *African Anarchism: The History of a Movement* (Tucson, AZ: Sharp Press, 1997)

McKay, George, *Senseless Acts of Beauty: Cultures of Resistance since the Sixties* (Verso, 1996)

McKercher, William, *Libertarian Thought in Nineteenth-Century England* (Garland Press, 1987)

McLellan, David, *The Young Hegelians and Karl Marx* (New York: Praeger, 1969)

Melville, Keith, *Communes in the Counter-Culture* (New York: Morrow Quill, 1979)

Mendel, Arthur P., *Michael Bakunin: Roots of Apocalypse* (New York: Praeger, 1981)

Merquior, J. G., *Foucault* (Fontana Press, 1985; 2nd edn., 1991)

Middleton, John & David Tait, eds., *Tribes Without Rulers* (Routledge & Kegan Paul, 1958)

Miller, David, *Anarchism* (Dent, 1984)

Miller, Martin A., *Kropotkin* (Chicago: Chicago University Press, 1976)

Miller, W., *Dorothy Day* (New York: Harper & Row, 1982)

Mintz, Jerome R., *The Anarchists of Casas Viejas* (Chicago: Chicago University Press, 1982)

Mitchell, Barbara, *The Practical Revolutionaries: A New Interpretation of the French Anarchosyndicalists* (New York: Greenwood Press, 1987)

Moore, John, ed., with Spencer Sunshine, *I Am Not A Man, I Am Dynamite! Friedrich Nietzsche and the Anarchist Tradition* (New York: Autonomedia, 2004)

Moral, J. Diaz del, *Historia de las agitaciones campesinas andaluzas*, (Madrid, 1929)

Morris, Brian, *Kropotkin: The Politics of Community* (New York: Humanity Books, 2004)

Morris, May, ed., *William Morris: Artist, Writer, Socialist*, 2 vols. (Blackwell, 1936)

Morton, A. L., *The English Utopia* (Lawrence & Wishart, 1952)

Morton, A. L., *The World of the Ranters: Religious Radicalism in the English Revolution* (Lawrence & Wishart, 1979)

Munck, Ronaldo with Ricardo Falcon & Bernardo Galitelli, *Argentina: From Anarchism to Peronism: Workers, Unions, Politics, 1855–1985* (Zed, 1987)

Narayan, Jayaprakash, *Socialism, Sarvodaya and Democracy*, ed. Bimal Prasad (Bombay: Asia Publishing House, 1964)

Nataf, André, *La Vie quotidienne des anarchistes en France, 1880–1910* (Paris: Hachette, 1986)

Needham, Joseph, *Science and Civilisation in China*, Vol. II, (Cambridge: Cambridge University Press, 1956)

Neocleous, Mark, 'Changing Anarchism: Anarchist Theory and Practice in a Global Age', *Radical Philosophy*, 130 (March, 2005)

Neumann, Franz, *The Democratic and Authoritarian State* (New York: The Free Press of Glencoe, 1957)

Newman, Saul, *From Bakunin to Lacan: Anti-Authoritarianism and the Dislocation of Power* (Lanham: Lexington Books, 2001)

Newman, Stephen L., *Liberalism at Wits' End: The Libertarian Revolt against the Modern State* (Ithaca, NY: Cornell University Press, 1984)

Nomad, Max, *Rebels and Renegades* (New York: Macmillan, 1932)

Nomad, Max, *Marx and Bakunin* (New York: Hound & Horn, 1933)

Nomad, Max, *Apostles of Revolution* (Secker & Warburg, 1939)

Nomad, Max, *Dreamers, Dynamiters and Demagogues: Reminiscences* (New York: Waldon Press, 1964)

Notehelfer, F. G., *Kotoku Shusui: Portrait of a Japanese Radical* (Cambridge: Cambridge University Press, 1971)

Notes sur l'anarchisme en URSS de 1921 à nos jours (Paris: Les Cahiers du Vent du Chemin, 1983)

Oglesby, Carl, ed., *The New Left Reader* (New York: Grove Press, 1969)

Oliver, Hermia, *The International Anarchist Movement in Late Victorian London* (Croom Helm, 1983)

Orwell, George, *Collected Essays* (Secker & Warburg, 1968)

Orwell, George, *Homage to Catalonia* (1938) (Harmondsworth: Penguin, 1962)

Orwell, George, *The Collected Essays, Journalism and Letters*, eds. Sonia Orwell & Ian August, 2 vols. (Harmondsworth: Penguin, 1970)

Ossar, Michael, *Anarchism in the Dramas of Ernst Toller: The Realm of Freedom* (Albany: State University of New York Press, c. 1980)

Osterfield, David, *Freedom, Society and the State: An Investigation into the Possibility of Society without Government* (New York: University Press of America, 1983)

Ostergaard, Geoffrey, *Nonviolent Revolution in India* (New Delhi: Gandhi Peace Foundation, 1985)

Ostergaard, Geoffrey, & M. Currell, *The Gentle Anarchists* (Oxford: Clarendon Press, 1971)

Paddison, Ronald, *The Fragmented State: The Political Geography of Power* (Basil Blackwell, 1983)

Palij, Michael, *The Anarchism of Nestor Makhno, 1918–1921: An Aspect of the Ukrainian Revolution* (Seattle: University of Washington Press, 1976)

Parekh, B., *Gandhi's Political Philosophy: A Critical Examination* (Macmillan, 1989)

Pateman, Carol, *Participation and Democratic Theory* (Cambridge: Cambridge University Press, 1973)

Paterson, R. W. K., *The Nihilistic Egoist: Max Stirner* (Oxford: Oxford University Press, 1971)

Paul, C. Kegan, *William Godwin: His Friends and Contemporaries*, 2 vols., (Henry S. King, 1876)

Paz, Abel, *Durruti: The People Armed*, trans. Nancy Macdonald (Montréal: Black Rose, 1976)

Pennock, J. Roland & John W. Chapman, eds., *Anarchism: Nomos XIX* (New York: New York University Press, 1978)

Perlin, Terry M., ed., *Contemporary Anarchism* (New Brunswick, NJ: Transaction Books, 1979)

Petegorsky, *Left-Wing Democracy in the English Civil War: A Study of the Social Philosophy of Gerrard Winstanley* (Victor Gollancz, 1940)

Philp, Mark, *Godwin's Political Justice* (Duckworth, 1986)

Piehl, Mel, *Breaking Bread: The Catholic Worker and the Origins of Catholic Radicalism in America* (Philadelphia: Temple University Press, 1982)

Plechanoff (Plekhanov), George, *Anarchism and Socialism*, trans. Eleanor Marx Aveling (Chicago: C. H. Kerr, 1912)

Pomper, Philip, *Sergei Nechaev* (New Brunswick, NJ: Rutgers University Press, 1979)

Poole, David, ed., *Land and Liberty: Anarchist Influences in the Mexican Revolution* (Sanday, Orkney: Cienfuegos Press, 1977)

Porton, R., *Film and the Anarchist Imagination* (Verso, 1999)

Le Procès des anarchistes devant la police correctionnelle à la Cour d'Appel à Lyons (Lyons: Imprimerie Nouvelle, 1883)

Purkis, Jonathan & James Bowen, *Twenty-first Century Anarchism: Unorthodox Ideas for a New Millennium* (Cassell, 1997)

Purkis, Jonathan & James Bowen, *Changing Anarchism: Anarchist Theory and Practice in a Global Age* (Manchester: Manchester University Press, 2004)

Pyziur, Eugene, *The Doctrine of Anarchism of Michael A. Bakunin* (1955) (Chicago: Henry Regnery, 1968)

Quail, John, *The Slow Burning Fuse: The Lost History of the British Anarchists* (Paladin, 1978)

Quattrocchi, Angelo & Tom Nairn, *The Beginning of the End: France, May 1968* (Panther, 1968)

Rama, Carlos M., *Fascismo y anarquismo en la España contemporanea* (Barcelona: Bruguera, 1979)

Ramachandran, G., & T. K. Mahadevan, eds., *Gandhi – His Relevance for Our Times* (Bombay: Bharatiya Vidya Bharan, 1964)

Ravindranathan, T. R., *Bakunin and the Italians* (Kingston, Ont.: McGill Queen's University Press, 1988)

Reichert, William O., *Partisans of Freedom: A Study in American Anarchism* (Bowling Green, Ohio: Bowling Green University Popular Press, 1976)

Reps, Paul, ed., *Zen Flesh, Zen Bones* (Harmondsworth: Penguin, 1986)

Rexroth, Kenneth, *Communalism: From its Origins to the Twentieth Century* (New York: Seabury Press, 1974)

Richter, Hans, *Dada, Art and Anti-Art* (Thames & Hudson, 1965)

Ridley, F. F., *Revolutionary Syndicalism in France: The Direct Action of its Time* (Cambridge: Cambridge University Press, 1970)

Rihs, C., *La Commune de Paris: sa structure et ses doctrines* (Geneva, 1955)

Ritter, Alan, *The Political Thought of Pierre-Joseph Proudhon* (Princeton, NJ: Princeton University Press, 1969)

Ritter, Alan, *Anarchism: A Theoretical Analysis* (Cambridge: Cambridge University Press, 1980)

Rubel, Maximilien & John Crump, eds., *Non-Market Socialism in the Nineteenth and Twentieth Century* (Macmillan, 1987)

Runkle, Gerald, *Anarchism: Old and New* (New York: Delta, 1972)

Ryan, Alan, *J. S. Mill* (Routledge & Kegan Paul, 1974)

Saltman, Richard R., *The Social and Political Thought of Michael Bakunin* (Westport, Conn.: Greenwood Press, 1983)

Scalapino, Robert A. & George T. Yu, *The Chinese Anarchist Movement*, (Berkeley: University of California Press, 1961; Bristol: Drowned Rat, 1985)

Schulkind, Eugene, ed., *The Paris Commune of 1871: The View from the Left* (Cape, 1972)

Schuster, Eunice M., *Native American Anarchism: A Study of Left-Wing Anarchist Individualism* (1932) (New York: Da Capo Press, 1970)

Scrivener, Michael Henry, *Radical Shelley: The Philosophical Anarchism and Utopian Thought of Percy Bysshe Shelley* (Princeton, NJ: Princeton University Press, 1982)

Sergent, Alain & Claude Harmel, *Histoire de l'anarchie* (Paris, 1949)

Shaw, George Bernard, *The Impossibilities of Anarchism*, Fabian Tract, no. 45 (Fabian Society, 1893)

Sheehan, Séan M., *Anarchism* (Reaktion, 2003)

Simmons, Ernest J., *Tolstoy* (Routledge & Kegan Paul, 1973)

Skelton, Robin, ed., *Herbert Read* (Methuen, 1970)

Smith, Michael P., *The Libertarians and Education* (Allen & Unwin, 1983)

Snow, Edgar, *Red Star Over China* (Gollancz, 1937)

Soboul, Albert, *Les Sans-culottes parisiens en l'An II*, (Paris, 1958)

Soboul, Jacques, *Notes sur la révolution bolchévique* (Paris, 1919)

Sonn, Richard D., *Anarchism and Cultural Politics in Fin de Siècle France* (Lincoln, NA: Nebraska University Press)

Spring, Joel, *A Primer of Libertarian Education* (New York: Free Life, 1975)

Stafford, David, *From Anarchism to Reformism: A Study of the Political Activities of Paul Brousse 1870–90* (Weidenfeld & Nicolson, 1971)

Stanley, Thomas A., *Osugi Sakae, Anarchist in Taisho Japan* (Cambridge, Mass.: Harvard University Press, 1982)

Suzuki, D. T., *Zen Buddhism: Selected Writings* ed. William Barrett (New York: Anchor, 1956)

Talmon, J. L., *The Origins of Totalitarian Democracy* (1952) (Sphere, 1970)

Tatsuo Arima, *The Future of Freedom* (Cambridge, Mass.: Harvard University Press, 1968)

Taylor, Michael, *Anarchy and Cooperation* (John Wiley, 1976)

Taylor, Michael, *Community, Anarchy and Liberty* (Cambridge: Cambridge University Press, 1980)

Taylor, Michael, *The Possibility of Cooperation* (Cambridge: Cambridge University Press, 1987)

Thody, Philip, *Albert Camus, 1913–1916* (Hamish Hamilton, 1961)

Thody, Philip, *Aldous Huxley* (New York: Charles Scribner's Sons, 1973)

Thomann, C., *Le Mouvement anarchiste dans les montagnes neuchâteloises et le Jura bernois* (La Chaux-de-Fonds, 1947)

Thomas, Edith, *Louise Michel*, trans. Penelope Williams (Montréal: Black Rose, 1980)

Thomas, Hugh, *The Spanish Civil War* (1961), 3rd edn., (Harmondsworth: Penguin, 1977)

Thomas, Paul, *Karl Marx and the Anarchists* (Routledge & Kegan Paul, 1980)

Thompson, E. P., *William Morris: Romantic to Revolutionary* (1955) (Merlin Press, 1977)

Tivey, Leonard, ed., *The Nation State* (Martin Robertson, 1981)

Torres, Manuel, ed., *Breve antología del pensamiento anarquista en el Perú* (La Molina, 1979)

Trautmann, Frederic, *The Voice of Terror: A Biography of Johann Most* (Westport, CN: Greenwood Press, 1980)

Troyat, Henri, *Tolstoy*, trans. Nancy Amphoux (W. H. Allen, 1968)

Tzuzuki, Chushishi, *Edward Carpenter, 1844–1929* (Cambridge: Cambridge University Press, 1980)

Venturi, Franco, *The Roots of Revolution: A History of the Populist Socialist Movements in Nineteenth-Century Russia* (Weidenfeld & Nicolson, 1960)

Vereker, Charles, *Eighteenth-Century Optimism* (Liverpool: Liverpool University Press, 1967)

Veysey, Laurence, *The Communal Experience: Anarchist and Mystical Counter-Cultures in America* (New York: Harper & Row, 1973)

Viénet, René, *Enragés et Situationnistes dans le mouvement des occupations* (Paris: Gallimard, 1968)

Vizetelly, Ernest Alfred, *The Anarchists: Their Faith and their Record, including sidelights on the royal and other personages who have been assassinated* (John Lane, 1911)

Wall, Derek, *Babylon and Beyond: The Economics of the Anti-capitalist, Anti-globalist and Radical Green Movements* (Pluto Press, 2005)

Weinberg, Bill, *Homage to Chiapas* (Verso, 2002)

Weir, David, *Anarchy and Culture: The Aesthetic Politics of Modernism* (Amherst: University of Massachusetts Press, 1957)

Wexler, Alice, *Emma Goldman: An Intimate Life* (Virago, 1984)

Wexler, Alice, *Emma Goldman in Exile: From the Russian Revolution to the Spanish Civil War* (Boston: Beacon Press, 1989)

Williams, George Hunston, *The Radical Reformation* (Weidenfeld & Nicolson, 1962)

Willis, Liz, *Women in the Spanish Revolution* (Solidarity Pamphlet, no. 48, 1975)

Wilson, A. N., *Tolstoy* (Hamish Hamilton, 1988)

Wilson, Edmund, *To the Finland Station* (Fontana, 1970)

Wiltshire, David, *The Social and Political Thought of Herbert Spencer* (Oxford: Oxford University Press, 1978)

Womack, John, *Zapata and the Mexican Revolution* (Thames & Hudson, 1972)

Woodcock, George, *Anarchy or Chaos* (Freedom Press, 1944)

Woodcock, George, *Anarchism and Morality* (Freedom Press, 1945)

Woodcock, George, *William Godwin* (Porcupine Press, 1946)

Woodcock, George, *The Paradox of Oscar Wilde* (T. V. Boardman, 1949)

Woodcock, George, *Pierre-Joseph Proudhon* (Routledge & Kegan Paul, 1956)

Woodcock, George, *Anarchism: A History of Libertarian Ideas and*

Movements (Harmondsworth: Penguin, 1963); with Postscript (1975); 2nd edn. (1986)

Woodcock, George, *The Crystal Spirit: A Study of George Orwell* (Cape, 1966)

Woodcock, George, *Dawn and the Darkest Hour: A Study of Aldous Huxley* (Faber & Faber, 1972)

Woodcock, George, *Herbert Read: The Stream and the Source* (Faber & Faber, 1972)

Woodcock, George, *Gandhi* (Fontana, 1972)

Woodcock, George, ed., *The Anarchist Reader* (Fontana, 1977)

A George Woodcock Reader, ed. Doug Fetherling (Ottawa: Deneau & Greenberg, 1980)

Woodcock, George & Ivan Avakumović, *The Anarchist Prince: The Biography of Prince Peter Kropotkin* (T. V. Boardman, 1950)

Wright, Mary C., *China in Revolution: The First Phase, 1900–1913* (New Haven: Yale University Press, 1971)

Young, Nigel, *An Infantile Disorder: The Crisis and Decline of the New Left* (Routledge & Kegan Paul, 1977)

Zarrow, Peter Gue, *Anarchism and Chinese Culture* (New York: Columbia University Press, 1990)

Zenker, Ernst Victor, *Anarchism: A Criticism and History of the Anarchist Theory* (Methuen, 1898)

Anarchist and Libertarian Works

Adresse à tous les travailleurs (30 May 1968) (Paris: Comité Enragés – Internationale Situationniste, 1968)

Aldred, Guy A., *Bakunin* (Glasgow: Bakunin Press, 1940)

Anderson, Benedict, *Under Three Flags: Anarchism and the Anti-colonial Imagination* (New York: Verso, 2005)

Andrews, Stephen Pearl, *The Science of Society* (New York: Fowler & Wells, 1852)

Arshinov, Peter, *History of the Makhnovist Movement (1918–1921)* (Detroit: Black & Red, 1974)

Aurobindo, Ghose, *The Ideal of Human Unity* (1918)

Aurobindo, Ghose, *The Essential Aurobindo*, ed. R. A. McDermott (New York, 1974)

Bakunin, Michael, *Oeuvres (1868–1872)*, 6 vols., eds. M. Nettlau (Vol. I) & J. Guillaume (Vols. II–VI) (Paris: Stock, 1895–1913)

Bakunin, Michael, *Correspondance de Michel Bakounine. Lettres à Herzen et à Ogareff 1860–74*, ed. M. Dragomanov (Paris, 1896)

Bakunin, Michael, *The Political Philosophy of Bakunin: Scientific*

Anarchism, ed. G. P. Maximoff (New York: Free Press, 1953)

Bakunin, Michael, *Archives Bakounine* (Leiden: E. J. Brill, 1961) *I: Bakounine et l'Italie, 1871–2* (1961–3); II: *Bakounine et les conflits dans l'Internationale, 1872* (1965); III: *Etatisme et anarchie 1873* (1967); IV: *Bakounine et ses rélations avec Sergej Nečaev 1840–1872*, (1971); V: *Bakounine et ses rélations slaves, 1870–1875* (1974); VI: *Bakounine sur la guerre franco-allemande et la révolution sociale en France, 1870–1871* (1977); VII: *L'empire knouto-germanique et la révolution sociale, 1870–1871* (1981)

Bakunin, Michael, *The Paris Commune and the Idea of the State*, ed. Nicolas Walter (Cira, 1971)

Bakunin, Michael, *Michael Bakunin: Selected Writings*, ed. Arthur Lehning (Cape, 1973)

Bakunin, Michael, *Bakunin on Anarchy*, ed. Sam Dolgoff (George Allen & Unwin, 1973)

Bakunin, Michael, *The Confessions of Mikhail Bakunin*, trans. Robert C. Howes, ed. Lawrence D. Orton (Ithaca, NY: Cornell University Press, 1977)

Bakunin, Michael, *Marxism, Freedom and the State*, ed. K. J. Kefanick (Freedom Press, 1984)

Bakunin, Michael, *From out of the Dustbin: Bakunin's Basic Writings, 1869–1871*, ed. Robert M. Cutler (Ann Arbor, MI: Ardis, 1985)

Bakunin, Michael, *Statism and Anarchy*, ed. Marshall S. Shatz (Cambridge: Cambridge University Press, 1990)

Baldelli, Giovanni, *Social Anarchism* (Harmondsworth: Penguin, 1971)

Ballou, Adin, *Non-resistance in Relation to Human Government* (Boston: Non-Resistance Society, 1839)

Ballou, Adin, *Practical Christian Socialism* (New York: Fowles & Wells, 1854)

Berdyaev, Nicholas, *The Bourgeois Mind & Other Essays* (Sheed & Ward, 1934)

Berdyaev, Nicholas, *Slavery and the Freedom* (1938) (Geoffrey Bles, 1943)

Berdyaev, Nicholas, *The Meaning of the Creative Act* (New York: Harper, 1955)

Berkman, Alexander, *Prison Memoirs of an Anarchist* (New York: Mother Earth, 1912)

Berkman, Alexander, *The Russian Tragedy* (Berlin: Der Syndikalist, 1922)

Berkman, Alexander, *The Bolshevik Myth (Diary 1920–21)* (New York: Boni & Liveright, 1925)

Berkman, Alexander, *The ABC of Anarchism* (1929) (Freedom Press, 1973)

Berneri, Camillo, *Peter Kropotkin: His Federalist Ideas* (Freedom Press, 1942)

Berneri, Marie Louise, *Journey through Utopia* (1950) (Freedom Press, 1982)

Berneri, Marie Louise, *Neither East Nor West: Selected Writings, 1939–1948* (Freedom Press, 1988)

Bey, Hakim, *T.A.Z.: The Temporary Autonomous Zone, Ontological Anarchy, Poetic Terrorism* (Brooklyn, NY: Autonomedia, 1985)

Bey, Hakim, *Immediatism* (Edinburgh: AK Press, 1994)

Bey, Hakim, *Millennium* (Brooklyn, NY: Autonomedia, 1996)

Bhave, Vinoba, *Democratic Values* (Kashi: Sarva Seva Sangh Prakashan, 1962)

Biehl, Janet, *Finding Our Way: Rethinking Ecofeminist Politics* (Montréal: Black Rose, 1990)

Biehl, Janet & Murray Bookchin, *The Politics of Social Ecology: Libertarian Municipalism* (Montréal: Black Rose, 1997)

Black, Bob, *Anarchy after Leftism* (Columbia: CAL Press, 1997)

Blake, William, *Complete Writings*, ed. Geoffrey Keynes (Oxford: Oxford University Press, 1974)

Bonanno, Alfred, *Armed Joy*, trans. Jean Weir (Elephant Editions, 1998)

Bookchin, Murray, *Post-Scarcity Anarchism* (1971) (Wildwood House, 1974); 3rd edn. (Edinburgh: AK Press 2004)

Bookchin, Murray, *The Spanish Anarchists: The Heroic Years, 1868–1936* (1976) (New York: Harper Colophon, 1978)

Bookchin, Murray, *Toward an Ecological Society* (1980) (Montréal and Buffalo: Black Rose, 1986)

Bookchin, Murray, *The Ecology of Freedom: The Emergence and Dissolution of Hierarchy* (Palo Alto, California: Cheshire Books, 1982)

Bookchin, Murray, *The Rise of Urbanization and the Decline of Citizenship* (San Francisco: Sierra Club, 1987)

Bookchin, Murray, *The Modern Crisis*, 2nd edn. (Montréal: Black Rose, 1987)

Bookchin, Murray, *Remaking Society* (Montréal: Black Rose, 1989)

Bookchin, Murray, *The Philosophy of Social Ecology: Essays on Dialectical Naturalism* (Montréal: Black Rose, 1990)

Bookchin, Murray, *Re-enchanting Humanity: A Defense of the Human Spirit against Anti-Humanism, Misanthropy, Mysticism and Primitivism* (Cassell, 1995)

Bookchin, Murray, *Social Anarchism and Life-Style Anarchism: An Unbridgeable Chasm* (Edinburgh: AK Press, 1995)

Bookchin, Murray, *Anarchism, Marxism and the Future of the Left* (Edinburgh: AK Press, 1999)

Bookchin, Murray, *Social Ecology and Communalism* (Edinburgh: AK Press, 2007)

Bourne, Randolph, *Untimely Papers* (New York: Huebsch, 1919)

Bourne, Randolph, *War and the Intellectuals: Collected Essays (1915–1919)* (New York, 1964)

Brown, L. Susan, *The Politics of Individualism: Liberalism, Feminism and Anarchism* (Montréal: Black Rose, 2003)

Buber, Martin, *Gustav Landauer, sein Lebensgang in Briefen* (Frankfurt, 1929)

Buber, Martin, *Paths in Utopia* (1949) (Boston: Beacon Press, 1958)

Burke, Edmund, *A Vindication of Natural Society* (M. Cooper, 1756); reprinted as *The Inherent Evils of All State Governments Demonstrated* (Holyoake, 1858)

Burke, Edmund, *Reflections on the Revolution in France* (1790), ed. Conor Cruise O'Brien (Harmondsworth: Penguin, 1969)

Cadogan, Peter, *Direct Democracy*, 2nd edn. (1975)

Cafard, Max (John Clark), *The Surre(gion)alist Manifesto and Other Writings* (Baton Rouge: Exquisite Corpse, 2003)

Cafard, Max (John Clark), 'Zen Anarchy', *Fifth Estate*, 368–9 (2005), pp. 69–73

Cafiero, Carlo, *Anarchie et communisme* (1880)

Camus, Albert, *The Myth of Sisyphus* (1942) (Harmondsworth: Penguin, 1977)

Camus, Albert, *L'Homme révolté* (1951) (Paris: Gallimard, 1972)

Carpenter, Edward, *Civilization: Its Cause and Cure* (1889) (Swann Sonnenschein, 1897)

Carpenter, Edward, *Non-Governmental Society* (A. C. Fifield, 1911)

Carpenter, Edward, *Prisons, Police and Punishment* (A. C. Fifield, 1905)

Carpenter, Edward, *Towards Democracy* (1883) (George Allen & Unwin, 1931)

Carter, Alan, *Marx: A Radical Critique* (Brighton: Wheatsheaf Books, 1988)

Carter, Alan, *The Philosophical Foundations of Property Rights* (Hemel Hempstead: Prentice Hall/ Harvester Wheatsheaf, 1989)

Carter, Alan, *A Radical Green Political Theory* (Routledge, 1999)

Carter, Alan, 'Analytical Anarchism: Some Conceptual Foundations', *Political Theory*, 28, 2 (2000), pp. 230–53

Chomsky, Noam, *American Power and the New Mandarins* (New York: Random House, 1969)

Chomsky, Noam, Introduction to Daniel Guérin, *Anarchism* (New York: Monthly Review Press, 1971)

Chomsky, Noam, *Problems of Knowledge and Freedom* (Fontana, 1972)

Chomsky, Noam, *For Reasons of State* (New York: Pantheon, 1973)

Chomsky, Noam, *Language and Responsibility* (New York: Pantheon, 1979)

Chomsky, Noam, *Radical Priorities*, ed. Carlos Otero (Montréal: Black Rose, 1981)

Chomsky, Noam, *The Chomsky Reader*, ed. James Peck (Serpent's Tail, 1987)

Chomsky, Noam, *Language and Politics*, ed. C. P. Otero (Montréal: Black Rose, 1988)

Chomsky, Noam, *Hegemony or Survival: America's Quest for Global Dominance* (Penguin, 2004)

Chomsky, Noam & Edward Herman, *Manufacturing Consent: The Political Economy of the Mass Media* (New York: Pantheon, 1988)

Christie, Stuart, *Granny Made Me an Anarchist* (Scribner, 2004)

Chuang Tzu: Taoist Philosopher and Chinese Mystic, trans. Herbert A. Giles (Unwin, 1980)

Clark, John P., *Max Stirner's Egoism* (Freedom Press, 1976)

Clark, John P., *The Philosophical Anarchism of William Godwin* (Princeton, NJ: Princeton University Press, 1977)

Clark, John P., *The Anarchist Moment: Reflections on Culture, Nature and Power* (Montréal: Black Rose, 1984)

Clark, John P., ed., *Renewing the Earth: The Promise of Social Ecology* (Green Print, 1990)

Clark, John P., 'A Social Ecology', *Capitalism, Nature, Socialism*, 31 (1997), pp. 3–33

Clark, John P., 'Municipal Dreams: A Social Ecological Critique of Bookchin's Politics', *Social Ecology after Bookchin*, ed. Andrew Light (New York: Guilford Publications, 1998), pp. 137–90

Clark, John P., 'Bridging the Unbridgeable Chasm: On Bookchin's Critique of the Anarchist Tradition', forthcoming in *Perspectives on Anarchist Theory*

Clark, John P. & Camille Martin, eds., *Anarchy, Geography, Modernity: The Radical Social Thought of Elisée Reclus* (Lanham, MD: Lexington Books, 2004)

Cleyre, Voltairine de, *Selected Writings*, ed. Alexander Berkman (New York: Mother Earth, 1914)

Cohn-Bendit, Daniel & Gabriel, *Obsolete Communism: The Left-Wing Alternative*, trans. A. Pomerans (André Deutsch, 1968)

Colson, Daniel, *Petit léxique philosophique de l'anarchisme: de Proudhon à Deleuze* (Paris: Le Livre de Poche, 2001)

Comfort, Alex, *Peace and Disobedience* (Peace News, 1946)

Comfort, Alex, *Barbarism and Sexual Freedom* (Freedom Press, 1948)

Comfort, Alex, *Sexual Behaviour in Society* (Duckworth, 1950)

Comfort, Alex, *Authority and Delinquency in the Modern State: A Criminological Approach to the Problems of Power* (Routledge & Kegan Paul, 1950)

Comfort, Alex, *Delinquency* (Freedom Press, 1951)

Comfort, Alex, *Social Responsibility in Science and Art* (Peace News, 1952)

Comfort, Alex, *Nature and Human Nature* (Weidenfeld & Nicolson, 1966)

Comfort, Alex, ed., *The Joy of Sex* (Quartet, 1974)

Comfort, Alex, *Writings Against Power & Death*, ed. David Goodway (Freedom Press, 1994)

Coppe, Abiezer, *A Fiery Flying Roll* (1649), bound and issued with *A Second Fiery Flying Roule* (1649)

Coppe, Abiezer, *Selected Writings*, ed. Andrew Hopton (Aporia Press, 1987)

Day, Dorothy, *The Long Loneliness* (New York: Harper & Row, 1952)

Debord, Guy, *The Society of the Spectacle* (1967) (Detroit: Black & Red, 1970)

Déjacque, Joseph, *L'Humanisphère* (Paris, 1899)

Déjacque, Joseph, *A bas les chefs!* (Paris: Champ Libre, 1971)

Deleuze, Gilles & Felix Guattari, *A Thousand Plateaus: Capitalism and Schizophrenia* (Continuum, 1999)

De Ligt, Bart, *The Conquest of Violence* (Routledge, 1937)

De Sade, Marquis, *The Life and Ideas of the Marquis de Sade*, compiled by Geoffrey Gorer (1934) (Panther, 1963)

Diderot, Denis, *Contes morales et nouvelles idylles* (Paris, 1773)

Diderot, Denis, *Diderot: Selected Philosophical Writings*, ed. John Lough (Cambridge: Cambridge University Press, 1953)

Diderot, Denis, *Rameau's Nephew. D'Alembert's Dream*, trans. Leonard Tancock (Harmondsworth: Penguin, 1966)

Dolgoff, Sam, ed., *The Anarchist Collectives: Workers' Self-Management in the Spanish Revolution, 1936–1939* (Montréal: Black Rose, 1974)

Dolgoff, Sam, *The Cuban Revolution: A Critical Perspective* (Montréal: Black Rose, 1976)

Emerson, Ralph Waldo, *Journals*, eds. E. W. Emerson & W. E. Forbes, (Boston: Houghton, Mifflin, 1909–14)

Emerson, Ralph Waldo, *The Letters of Ralph Waldo Emerson*, ed. Ralph L. Rusk, (New York: Columbia University Press, 1939)

Emerson, Ralph Waldo, *The Complete Essays and other Writings*, ed. Brooks Atkinson (New York: Modern Library, 1940)

Faure, Sébastien, *Autorité el liberté* (Paris: Aux Bureaux de la Révolte, 1891)

Faure, Sébastien, *La Douleur universelle, philosophie liberatire* (Paris: Savine, 1895)

Faure, Sébastien, *L'Encyclopédie anarchiste*, 4 vols. (Paris, n.d.)

Fernandez, Frank, *Cuban Anarchism: The History of a Movement*, trans. Chaz Bufe (Tucson, AZ: Sharp Press, 2001)

Ferrer, Francisco, *The Origins and Ideals of the Modern School* (New York: Putnam, 1913)

Feyerabend, Paul, *Against Method* (1975) (Verso, 1988)

Foigny, Gabriel de, *A New Discovery of Terra Incognita Australis* (1693)

Foucault, Michel, *Discipline and Punish: The Birth of Prisons*, trans. Alan Sheridan (New York: Pantheon, 1977)

Foucault, Michel, *The History of Sexuality*, trans. Robert Hurley (New York: Pantheon, 1978)

Foucault, Michel, *Power/Knowledge: Selected Interviews and Other Writings, 1972–1977*, eds. Colin Gordon, Les Marshall, John Meplam & Kate Soper (Brighton: Harvester Press, 1980)

Fourier, Charles, *The Utopian Vision of Charles Fourier*, eds. Jonathan Beecher & Richard Bienvenu (Boston: Beacon Press, 1971)

Fourier, Charles, *Harmonian Society: Selected Writings*, ed. Mark Poster (New York: Doubleday, 1971)

Freire, Paulo, *Pedagogy of Oppressed* (1970) (Harmondsworth: Penguin, 1972)

Friedman, David, *The Machinery of Freedom* (New York: Harper, 1971)

Friends of Durruti Group, *Towards a Fresh Revolution* (1938) (Sanday, Orkney: Cienfuegos Press, 1978)

Gandhi, Mohandas, *The Constructive Programme* (Ahmedabad: Navajivan, 1945)

Gandhi, Mohandas, *Sarvodaya* (Ahmedabad: Navajivan, 1954)

Gandhi, Mohandas, *Democracy: Real and Deceptive* (Ahmedabad: Navajivan, 1961)

Gandhi, Mohandas, *Collected Works* (Delhi: Government of India, 1964)

Godwin, William, *An Enquiry Concerning Political Justice*, 2 vols. (G. G. & J. Robinson, 1793); facsimile 3rd edn. 1798, ed. F. E. L. Priestley (Toronto: Toronto University Press, 1946); 3rd edn. 1798, ed. Isaac Kramnick (Harmondsworth: Penguin, 1976)

Godwin, William, *Caleb Williams* (1794), ed. Maurice Hindle (Harmondsworth; Penguin, 1987)

Godwin, William, *Cursory Strictures* (D. I. Eaton, 1794)

Godwin, William, *Considerations* (J. Johnson, 1794)

Godwin, William, *The Enquirer* (G. G. & J. Robinson, 1797)

Godwin, William, *Of Population* (Longman, Hurst, Rees, Orme & Brown, 1820)

Godwin, William, *History of the Commonwealth of England*, 4 vols. (H. Colburn, 1824–8)

Godwin, William, *Thoughts on Man, his Nature, Production and Discoveries* (Effingham Wilson, 1831)

Godwin, William, *Uncollected Writings (1785–1822)*, ed. J. W. Marken & B. R. Pollin (Gainesville, Florida: Scholars' Facsimiles, 1968)

Godwin, William, *The Anarchist Writings of William Godwin*, ed. with introd. Peter Marshall (Freedom Press, 1986)

Goldman, Emma, *Anarchism and Other Essays* (1911) (New York: Dover, 1969)

Goldman, Emma, *My Disillusionment in Russia* (Garden City: Doubleday, Page, 1923)

Goldman, Emma, *My Further Disillusionment in Russia* (Garden City: Doubleday, Page, 1924)

Goldman, Emma, *Living my Life*, 2 vols. (New York: Alfred Knopf, 1931) (New York: Dover, 1970)

Goldman, Emma, *Red Emma Speaks*, ed. Alix Kates Shulman (Wildwood House, 1979)

Goodman, Paul, *Growing up Absurd* (1960) (Sphere, 1970)

Goodman, Paul, *Drawing the Line* (1962) (New York: Free Life, 1977)

Goodman, Paul, *The Community of Scholars* (New York: Random House, 1962)

Goodman, Paul, ed., *Seeds of Liberation* (New York: Brazillier, 1965)

Goodman, Paul, *People or Personnel: Decentralizing and the Mixed System* (New York: Random House, 1965)

Goodman, Paul, *A Message to the Military-Industrial Complex* (1965) (Housmans, 1969)

Goodman, Paul, *Compulsory Miseducation* (1964) (Harmondsworth: Penguin, 1971)

Goodman, Paul & Percival, *Communitas: Means of Livelihood and Ways of Life* (1947) (New York: Vintage, 1960)

Grave, Jean, *La Société au lendemain de la Révolution* (Paris: Au Bureau de la Révolte, 1889)

Grave, Jean, *La Société mourante et l'anarchie* (Paris: Tresse et Stock, 1893)

Grave, Jean, *La Société future* (Paris: Stock, 1895)

Grave, Jean, *L'Individu et la société* (Paris: Stock, 1897)

Grave, Jean, *L'Anarchie, son but, ses moyens*, (Paris, 1899)

Grave, Jean, *Le Mouvement libertaire sous la troisième République* (Paris: Les Oeuvres Représentatives, 1930)

Grave, Jean, *Quarante ans de propagande anarchiste* (Paris: Flammarion, 1973)

Griffuelhes, V., *L'Action syndicaliste* (Paris, 1908)

Guérin, Daniel, *Anarchism: From Theory to Practice* (1965) (New York: Monthly Review Press, 1970)

Guevara, Che, *Socialism and Man* (New York: Pathfinder Press, 1968)

Guillaume, James, *Idées sur l'organisation sociale* (La Chaux-de-Fonds, 1876)

Guillaume, James, *L'Internationale. Documents et Souvenirs (1864–1878)*, 4 vols. (Paris, 1905–10)

Guyau, J. M., *A Sketch of Morality Independent of Obligation or Sanction* (Watts, 1898)

Harper, Clifford, *Anarchy: a Graphic Guide* (Camden Press, 1987)

Harrison, Frank, *The Modern State: An Anarchist Analysis* (Montréal: Black Rose, 1983)

Hayek, F. A., *The Constitution of Liberty* (Chicago: Chicago University Press, 1960)

Hennacy, Ammon, *The Autobiography of a Catholic Anarchist* (New York: Catholic Worker Books, 1954)

Heyd, Lewis, *The Gift: Imagination and the Erotic Life of Property* (New York: Vintage Books, 1983)

Humboldt, Wilhelm von, *The Limits of State Action*, ed. John W. Burrow (Cambridge: Cambridge University Press, 1969)

Huxley, Aldous, *Ends and Means* (Chatto & Windus, 1937)

Huxley, Aldous, *Science, Liberty and Peace* (Chatto & Windus, 1947)

Huxley, Aldous, *Island* (Frogmore, St Albans: Triad/Panther, 1976)

Illich, Ivan, *Celebration of Awareness* (Harmondsworth: Penguin, 1973)

Illich, Ivan, *Deschooling Society* (Harmondsworth: Penguin, 1973)

Jensen, Derrick, *Welcome to the Machine* (White River Jct., VT: Chelsea Green Publishing, 2004)

Jensen, Derrick, *Endgame*, 2 vols. (New York: Seven Stories Press, 2006)

Kropotkin, Peter, *Paroles d'un révolté* (Paris: Marpon et Flammarion, 1885)

Kropotkin, Peter, *The Place of Anarchism in Socialist Evolution* (Freedom Press, 1886)

Kropotkin, Peter, *In Russian and French Prisons* (1887), ed. Paul Avrich (New York: Schocken Books, 1971)

Kropotkin, Peter, *The Commune of Paris* (1895), ed. Nicolas Walter (Freedom Press, 1971)

Kropotkin, Peter, *L'Anarchie, sa philosophie, son idéal* (Paris: Stock, 1896)

Kropotkin, Peter, *The State: Its Historic Role* (1897) trans. Vernon Richards (Freedom Press, 1969, 1987)

Kropotkin, Peter, *Fields, Factories and Workshops* (Hutchinson, 1899);

Fields, Factories and Workshops Tomorrow, ed. Colin Ward (George Allen & Unwin, 1974)

Kropotkin, Peter, *Memoirs of a Revolutionist* (1899), ed. Allen Rogers (Cresset, 1980); ed. Nicolas Walter (Dover, 1980)

Kropotkin, Peter, *Mutual Aid: A Factor of Evolution* (1902) (Harmondsworth: Penguin, 1939)

Kropotkin, Peter, *The Conquest of Bread* (1906) (Elephant Editions, 1985)

Kropotkin, Peter, *The Great French Revolution* (1909) (New York: Schocken Books, 1971)

Kropotkin, Peter, *Modern Science and Anarchism* (1912) (Freedom Press, 1923)

Kropotkin, Peter, *Ethics: Origins and Development* (1924) (Dorchester: Prism Press, n.d.)

Kropotkin, Peter, *Kropotkin's Revolutionary Pamphlets*, ed. Roger N. Baldwin (New York: Vanguard Press, 1927; Benjamin Blom, 1968)

Kropotkin, Peter, *Selected Writings on Anarchism and Revolution*, ed. Martin Miller (Cambridge, Mass.: MIT Press, 1970)

Kropotkin, Peter, *Anarchism and Anarchist Communism*, ed. Nicolas Walter (Freedom Press, 1987)

Kropotkin, Peter, *Act for Yourselves: Articles from Freedom 1886–1907*, eds. Nicolas Walter & Heiner Becker (Freedom Press, 1988)

The Essential Kropotkin, eds. E. Capouya & K. Tompkins (New York: Live Right, 1975)

Labadie, Joseph Antoine, *Anarchism: What It Is and What It Is Not* (Detroit: International Anarchist Group of Detroit, 1896)

La Boétie, Etienne de, *Discours de la servitude volontaire*, ed. Maurice Rat (Paris: Armand Colin, 1963)

La Boétie, Etienne de, *The Politics of Obedience: The Discourse of Voluntary Servitude*, ed. Murray Rothbard (New York: Free Life, 1975)

Landauer, Gustav, *Social Democracy in Germany* (Freedom Press, 1896)

Landauer, Gustav, *Die Revolution* (Frankfurt, 1907)

Landauer, Gustav, *For Socialism*, trans. D. J. Parent (St Louis: Telos Press, 1978)

Lao Tzu, *Tao te Ching* (New York: Vintage, 1972)

Lefebvre, Henri François, *Introduction à la critique de la vie quotidienne* (Paris: Grasset, 1947)

Lefebvre, Henri François, *Everyday Life in the Modern World* (1968) (Allen Lane, 1971)

Le Guin, Ursula K., *Always Coming Home* (Berkeley: University of California Press, 2001)

Le Guin, Ursula K., *The Dispossessed* (New York: Harper & Row, 1974)

Makhno, Nestor, *La Révolution russe en Ukraine* (Paris, 1927)

Malatesta, Errico, *Entre Paysans* (Paris, 1887)

Malatesta, Errico, *Anarchy* (1892), trans. Vernon Richards (Freedom Press, 1974)

Malatesta, Errico, *Vote. What for?* (Freedom Press, 1945)

Malatesta, Errico, *Scritti scelti*, ed. Cesare Zaccaria & Giovanna Berneri (Naples, 1947)

Malatesta, Errico, *Errico Malatesta: His Life and Ideas*, ed. Vernon Richards (Freedom Press, 1965)

Malatesta, Errico, *Errico Malatesta: His Life and Ideas*, ed. Vernon Richards (Freedom Press, 1965)

Malato, Charles, *Philosophie de l'anarchie* (Paris, 1889)

Malato, Charles, *De la Commune à l'anarchie* (Paris, 1894)

Marcos, Subcomandante, *Our Word Is Our Weapon*, ed. Juan Ponce de León (New York: Seven Stories Press, 2002)

Marcos, Subcomandante, *Ya Basta! Ten Years of the Zapatista Uprising*, ed. Ziga Vodovnik (Edinburgh: AK Press, 2004)

Marshall, Peter, *Around Africa: From the Pillars of Hercules to the Strait of Gibraltar* (London & New York: Simon & Schuster, 1994)

Marshall, Peter, *Nature's Web: An Exploration of Ecological Thinking* (London & New York: Simon and Schuster, 1992)

Marshall, Peter, *Riding the Wind: A New Philosophy for a New Era* (Cassell, 1998)

Marshall, Peter, *Europe's Lost Civilization: Uncovering the Mysteries of the Megaliths* (Headline, 2004)

Maximoff, G. P., ed., *Constructive Anarchism* (Chicago: Maximoff Memorial Publications Committee, 1952)

Maximoff, G. P., ed., *The Political Philosophy of Bakunin: Scientific Anarchism* (New York: Free Press, 1953)

May, Todd, *The Political Philosophy of Poststructuralist Anarchism* (Philadelphia: Pennsylvania University Press, 1994)

Meltzer, Albert, *The Anarchists in London, 1935–1955* (Sanday, Orkney: Cienfuegos Press, 1976)

Meltzer, Albert, *Anarchism: Arguments For and Against* (Black Flag, 1986)

Meltzer, Albert & Stuart Christie, *The Floodgates of Anarchy* (Sphere, 1972)

Meslier, Jean, *Le Testament de Jean Meslier*, ed. Rudolf Charles (Amsterdam: R. C. Meijer, 1864)

Michel, Louise, *La Commune* (Paris, 1898)

Mill, John Stuart, *Utilitarianism, On Liberty, Essay on Bentham*, ed. Mary Warnock (Fontana, 1970)

Mill, John Stuart, *Autobiography* (1873) (New York: Signet, 1964)

The Miners' Next Step (Tonypandy, 1912)

Morelly, *Code de la Nature, ou le véritable esprit de ses lois*, (1755), ed.
Edouard Dolléans (Paris, 1910)

Morris, Brian, *Ecology & Anarchism: Essays and Reviews on Contemporary
Thought* (Malvern Wells: Images, 1996)

Morris, William, *News from Nowhere* (1891) (Longmans, Green, 1907)

Morris, William, *Political Writings of William Morris*, ed. A. L. Morton
(Lawrence & Wishart, 1973)

Morris, William, *William Morris' Socialist Diary*, ed. Florence Boos
(Journeyman Press, 1985)

Mumford, Lewis, *The City in History* (Secker & Warburg, 1961)

Mumford, Lewis, *The Myth of the Machine: Technics and Human
Development* (New York: Harcourt, Brace & World, 1967)

Mumford, Lewis, *The Future of Technics and Civilization*, ed. Colin Ward
(Freedom Press, 1986)

Nettlau, Max, *M. Bakunin, Eine Biographie*, 2 vols. (Lithograph,
1896–1900)

Nettlau, Max, *Bibliographie de l'anarchie* (Paris: Stock, 1897)

Nettlau, Max, *Bakunin und die Internationale in Spanien 1868–1873*
(Leipzig, 1913)

Nettlau, Max, *Errico Malatesta: Das Leben eines Anarchisten* (Berlin,
1922)

Nettlau, Max, *Der Vorfrühling der Anarchie* (Berlin, 1925; Glashutten,
1972)

Nettlau, Max, *Der Anarchismus von Proudhon zu Kropotkin* (Berlin, 1927;
Glashutten, 1972)

Nettlau, Max, *Elisée Reclus: Anarchisten und Gelehrter* (Berlin, 1927)

Nettlau, Max, *Bakunin e l'Internazionale in Italia del 1846 al 1872*
(Geneva, 1928)

Nettlau, Max, *Anarchisten und Sozialrevolutionäre* (Berlin, 1931;
Glashutten, 1972)

Nettlau, Max, *Contribución a la Bibliografía Anarquista en América Latina
hasta 1914* (Buenos Aires: Ediciones La Protesta, n.d.)

Nettlau, Max, *Die erste Blütezeit der Anarchie* (Vaduz, 1981)

Nettlau, Max, *Anarchisten und Syndikalisten*, I, (Vaduz, 1984)

Nettlau, Max, *A Short History of Anarchism*, ed. Heiner Becker, trans. Ida
Pilat Isca (Freedom Press, 1996)

Nietzsche, Friedrich, *Thus Spoke Zarathustra* (Harmondsworth: Penguin,
1964)

Nietzsche, Friedrich, *Twilight of the Idols, and the Anti-Christ*
(Harmondsworth: Penguin, 1968)

Nietzsche, Friedrich, *The Portable Nietzsche*, ed. Walter Kaufmann (New York: Viking, 1972)

Nietzsche, Friedrich, *A Nietzsche Reader*, ed. R. J. Hollingdale (Harmondsworth: Penguin, 1977)

Nieuwenhuis, Ferdinand Domela, *Le Socialisme en danger* (Paris: Stock, 1897)

Nock, Albert Jay, *Our Enemy the State* (1935) (New York: Free Life, 1977)

Noyes, John Humphreys, *History of Socialisms* (Trübner, 1870)

Nozick, Robert, *Anarchy, State, and Utopia* (Oxford: Blackwell, 1974)

Oppenheimer, Franz, *The State* (New York: Vanguard Press, 1920)

Osho, *Rebellion, Revolution and Religiousness* (Santa Monica, CA: Falcon Press, 1989)

Osho, *The Rebel* (Cologne: Rebel Publishing House, 1989)

Paine, Thomas, *Common Sense* (1776), ed. Isaac Kramnick (Harmondsworth: Penguin, 1976)

Paine, Thomas, *Rights of Man* (1791–2), ed. Henry Collins (Harmondsworth: Penguin, 1971)

Pataud, E. & E. Pouget, *Syndicalism and Co-operative Commonwealth* (Oxford: New Internationalist Publications, 1913)

Peirats, José, *What is the CNT?* (Simian, 1974)

Peirats, José, *Anarchists in the Spanish Revolution* (Detroit: Black & Red, 1977)

Pelloutier, F., *L'Organisation corporative et l'anarchie* (Paris, 1896)

Pelloutier, F., *Histoire des Bourses du Travail* (Paris, 1902)

Perlman, Fredy, *Against His-story, Against Leviathan!* (Detroit: Black & Red, 1983)

Perlman, Fredy, *The Continuing Appeal of Nationalism* (Detroit: Black & Red, 1985)

Pouget, Emile, *La Confédération du Travail* (Paris, 1908)

Proudhon, Pierre-Joseph, *Qu'est-ce que la propriété? ou recherche sur le principe du droit et du gouvernment* (Paris, 1840); *What is Property?* trans. Benjamin Tucker (1876) (New York: Humbold, 1890; Dover, 1970)

Proudhon, Pierre-Joseph, *De la Création de l'ordre dans l'humanité* (Besançon, 1843)

Proudhon, Pierre-Joseph, *Système des contradictions économiques, ou philosophie de la misère*, 2 vols. (Paris, 1846); *System of Economic Contradictions; or, The Philosophy of Misery*, Vol. 1, trans. Benjamin R. Tucker (Boston: Benj. R. Tucker, 1888)

Proudhon, Pierre-Joseph, *Solution du problème social* (Paris, 1848); *Proudhon's Solution of the Social Problem* (New York, 1927)

Proudhon, Pierre-Joseph, *Les Confessions d'un révolutionnaire* (Paris, 1849)

Proudhon, Pierre-Joseph, *Idée générale de la révolution au XIXème siècle* (Paris, 1851); *The General Idea of the Revolution in the Nineteenth Century*, trans. John Beverley Robinson (Freedom Press, 1923)

Proudhon, Pierre-Joseph, *La Révolution sociale démontrée par le coup d'état du deuxième décembre* (Paris, 1852)

Proudhon, Pierre-Joseph, *Philosophie du progrès, programme* (Brussels, 1853)

Proudhon, Pierre-Joseph, *De la Justice dans la révolution et dans l'église*, 3 vols. (Paris, 1858)

Proudhon, Pierre-Joseph, *La Guerre et la paix*, 2 vols. (Paris, 1861)

Proudhon, Pierre-Joseph, *Du Principe fédératif et de la nécessité de reconstituer le parti de la révolution* (Paris, 1863); *The Principle of Federation*, ed. Vernon Richards (Toronto: University of Toronto Press, 1979)

Proudhon, Pierre-Joseph, *Du Principe de l'art et de sa destination sociale* (Paris, 1865)

Proudhon, Pierre-Joseph, *De la Capacité politique des classes ouvrières* (Paris, 1865)

Proudhon, Pierre-Joseph, *Oeuvres complètes*, 26 vols. (Paris, 1867–70); *Oeuvres complètes*, 19 vols., eds. C. Bouglé & H. Moysset (Paris: Marcel Rivière, 1923–65)

Proudhon, Pierre-Joseph, *Correspondance*, 14 vols. (Paris, 1874–5)

Proudhon, Pierre-Joseph, *Les Carnets*, 11 vols. (Paris, 1843–64); 2 vols. (Paris, 1960)

Proudhon, Pierre-Joseph, *Selected Writings of Pierre-Joseph Proudhon*, ed. Stewart Edwards, trans. Elizabeth Fraser (Macmillan, 1969)

Quiet Rumours: An Anarcha-Feminist Anthology (Dark Star, n.d.)

Rabelais, François, *Gargantua and Pantagruel* (1534) (Harmondsworth: Penguin, 1955)

Rand, Ayn, *The Virtue of Selfishness: A New Concept of Egoism* (New York: Signet, 1964)

Read, Herbert, *To Hell with Culture: Democratic Values are New Values* (Kegan Paul, Trench, Trubner, 1941)

Read, Herbert, *The Politics of the Unpolitical* (Routledge, 1943)

Read, Herbert, *Education through Art* (Faber & Faber, 1943)

Read, Herbert, *The Education of Free Men* (Freedom Press, 1944)

Read, Herbert, *Anarchy and Order* (Faber & Faber, 1954); (Souvenir Press, 1974)

Read, Herbert, *The Contrary Experience* (Faber & Faber, 1963)

Read, Herbert, *A Concise History of Modern Painting* (Thames & Hudson, 1972)

Read, Herbert, *A One-Man Manifesto and Other Writings*, ed. David Goodway (Freedom Press, 1994)

Reclus, Elie, *Les Primitifs* (Paris, 1903)

Reclus, Elisée, *Ouvrier, prends la machine! Prends la terre, paysan!* (Genève: Imprimerie Jurassienne, 1880)

Reclus, Elisée, *L'Evolution et la révolution* (Paris: Publications de la Révolte, 1891)

Reclus, Elisée, *A mon frère, le paysan* (Genève: Imprimerie Jurassienne, 1893)

Reclus, Elisée, *An Anarchist on Anarchy* (Freedom Press, 1894)

Reclus, Elisée, *L'Idéal et la jeunesse* (Paris: Editions de la Société Nouvelle, 1894)

Reclus, Elisée, *L'Anarchie* (Paris: Publications des Temps Nouveaux, 1895)

Reclus, Elisée, *L'Evolution, la révolution et l'idéal anarchique* (Paris: Stock, 1896)

Reclus, Elisée, *L'Evolution légale et l'anarchie* (Paris: Bibliothèque des Temps Nouveaux, 1898)

Reclus, Elisée, *L'Homme et la terre*, 6 vols. (Paris, 1905–8)

Reclus, Elisée, *Correspondance, 1850–1905*, 3 vols. (Paris, 1911–25)

Reich, Wilhelm, *The Function of the Orgasm* (New York: Noonday Press, 1942)

Richards, Vernon, *Lessons of the Spanish Revolution* (1953) (Freedom Press, 1983)

Richards, Vernon, ed., *Errico Malatesta: His Life and Ideas* (1965) (Freedom Press, 1977)

Richards, Vernon, *The Impossibilities of Social Democracy* (Freedom Press, 1978)

Richards, Vernon, *Protest without Illusions* (Freedom Press, 1981)

Richards, Vernon, ed., *Why Work? Arguments for the Leisure Society* (Freedom Press, 1983)

Rocker, Rudolf, *Johann Most: das Leben eines Rebellen* (Berlin: Der Syndikalist, 1924)

Rocker, Rudolf, *Nationalism and Culture*, trans. Ray E. Chase (Los Angeles, 1937); (Freedom Press, *c.* 1947)

Rocker, Rudolf, *Anarcho-syndicalism* (Secker & Warburg, 1938)

Rocker, Rudolf, *Pioneers of American Freedom* (Los Angeles: Rocker Publications Committee, 1949)

Rocker, Rudolf, *The London Years* (Robert Anscombe, 1956)

Rocker, Rudolf, *Anarchism and Anarcho-Syndicalism* (Freedom Press, 1973)

Roszak, Theodore, *The Making of a Counter-Culture: Reflections on the*

Technocratic Society and its Youthful Opposition (Faber & Faber, 1970)

Roszak, Theodore, *Where The Wasteland Ends* (Faber & Faber, 1973)

Roszak, Theodore, *Person/Planet* (Garden City, New York: Doubleday, 1978)

Rothbard, Murray N., *Power and Market* (Kansas City: Sheed Andrews & McMeel, 1977)

Rothbard, Murray N., *For a New Liberty: The Libertarian Manifesto*, rev. edn. (New York: Collier, 1978)

Rousseau, Jean-Jacques, *Emile ou de l'éducation* (1762) (Paris: Garnier-Flammarion, 1966)

Rousseau, Jean-Jacques, *The Social Contract and Discourses*, trans. G. D. H. Cole, eds. J. H. Brumfitt & John C. Hall (Dent, 1973)

Roussopoulos, Dimitrios, ed., *The Anarchist Papers* (Montréal: Black Rose, 1986)

Roussopoulos, Dimitrios, ed., *The Radical Papers* (Montréal: Black Rose, 1987)

Rubin, Jerry, *Do It!* (Cape, 1970)

Russell, Bertrand, *Principles of Social Reconstruction* (1916) (Allen & Unwin, 1971)

Russell, Bertrand, *Roads to Freedom; Socialism, Anarchism, Syndicalism* (1918) (Allen & Unwin, 1973)

Russell, Bertrand, *In Praise of Idleness and Other Essays* (1935) (Allen & Unwin, 1963)

Russell, Bertrand, *Power: A New Social Analysis* (Basis Books, 1940)

Russell, Bertrand, *Authority and the Individual* (Allen & Unwin, 1949)

Russell, Bertrand, *History of Western Philosophy* (Allen & Unwin, 1962)

Russell, Bertrand, *The Autobiography of Bertrand Russell*, 2 vols. (Allen & Unwin, 1968)

Sampson, Ronald, *The Anarchist Basis of Pacifism* (Peace Pledge Union, 1970)

Sampson, Ronald, *Tolstoy on the Causes of War* (Peace Pledge Union, 1987)

Santillan, D. A., *Reconstrucción Social* (Buenos Aires, 1933)

Santillan, D. A., *El Organismo Económico de la Revolución* (Barcelona, 1936)

Santillan, D. A., *La Revolución y la Guerra en España* (Buenos Aires, 1937)

Serge, Victor, *Memoirs of a Revolutionary (1901–1941)* (New York, 1967)

Serge, Victor, *Kronstadt '21* (Solidary Pamphlet, n.d.)

Snyder, Gary, *Earth House Hold* (New York: New Directions, 1969)

Snyder, Gary, *The Practice of the Wild* (1990) (Emeryville, CA: Shoemaker & Hoard, 2003)

Sorel, Georges, *Reflections on Violence* (1908) (Collier-Macmillan, 1969)

Spencer, Herbert, *Social Statics* (Williams & Norgate, 1868)

Spencer, Herbert, *Essays, Scientific, Political and Speculative* (Library Edition, 1892)

Spencer, Herbert, *The Man versus the State*, ed. Donald Macrae (Harmondsworth: Penguin, 1969)

Spooner, Lysander, *No Treason* (Boston, MA: The Author, 1867)

Spooner, Lysander, *Natural Law; or, The Science of Justice* (Boston, MA: A. Williams, 1882)

Spooner, Lysander, *Collected Works*, ed. Charles Shively, 6 vols. (Weston, MA: M & S Press, 1971)

Starhawk, *The Spiral Dance: A Rebirth of the Ancient Religion of the Great Goddess* (1979)

Stirner, Max, *The Ego and Its Own*, trans. Steven T. Byington (1963) (Rebel Press, 1982)

Stirner, Max, *The False Principle of our Education*, trans. Robert Beebe (Colorado Springs: Ralph Myles, 1967)

Stirner, Max, *Die Geschichte der Reaktion* (Berlin, 1852)

Stirner, Max, *Kleinere Schriften und seine Entgegnungen auf die Kritik seines Werkes: Der Einzige und sein Engenthum* (Berlin: Schuster & Loeffler, 1898)

Swift, Jonathan, *Gulliver's Travels and Other Writings*, ed. Ricardo Quintana (New York: Modern Library, 1958)

Thoreau, Henry David, *Walden, or Life in the Woods* (1854) (New York: Signet, 1960)

Thoreau, Henry David, *A Thoreau Handbook*, ed. W. Harding (New York: New York University Press, 1959)

Thoreau, Henry David, *The Portable Thoreau*, ed. Carl Bode (Harmondsworth: Penguin, 1979)

Tolstoy, Leo, *Social Evils and their Remedy*, ed. Helen Choustchoff Matheson (Methuen, 1915)

Tolstoy, Leo, *Tolstoy Centenary Edition*, 21 vols., trans. Louise & Aylmer Maude, (Oxford: Oxford University Press, 1928–37)

Tolstoy, Leo, *Tolstoy on Education*, trans. Leo Weiner (Chicago: Chicago University Press, 1967)

Tolstoy, Leo, *Tolstoy on Civil Disobedience and Non-Violence* (New York: Mentor, 1968)

Tolstoy, Leo, *A Confession, The Gospel in Brief and What I Believe*, trans.

Aylmer Maude (Oxford: Oxford University Press, 1974)

Tolstoy, Leo, *Tolstoy's Letters*, ed. R. F. Christian, 2 vols. (Athlone, 1978)

Tolstoy, Leo, *Tolstoy's Diaries*, ed. R. F. Christian (Athlone, 1985)

Tolstoy, Leo, *The Lion and the Honeycomb: The Religious Writings of Tolstoy*, ed. A. N. Wilson (Collins, 1987)

Tucker, Benjamin R., *Instead of a Book* (New York: Benj. R. Tucker, 1897)

Tucker, Benjamin R., *Individual Liberty* (New York: Vanguard Press, 1926)

Van Duyn, Roel, *Message of a Wise Kabouter* (1969) (Duckworth, 1972)

Vaneigem, Raoul, *The Revolution of Everyday Life* (Rebel Press, 1983)

Vaneigem, Raoul, *The Book of Pleasures* (Pending Press, 1983)

Vaneigem, Raoul, *Le Mouvement du Libre Esprit* (Paris: Editions Ramsay, 1986)

Volin, E. M. V., *Nineteen-Seventeen: The Russian Revolution Betrayed* (New York: Libertarian Book Club, 1954)

Volin, E. M. V., *The Unknown Revolution (1917–1921)* (Freedom Press, 1955)

Walter, Nicolas, *About Anarchism* (Freedom Press, 1969; new edn. 1977)

Walter, Nicolas, *The Anarchist Past and Other Essays*, ed. David Goodway (Nottingham: Five Leaves, 2006)

Ward, Colin, *Anarchy in Action* (Allen & Unwin, 1973)

Ward, Colin, *Housing: An Anarchist Approach* (Freedom Press, 1976)

Ward, Colin, ed., *A Decade of Anarchy (1961–1970)* (Freedom Press, 1987)

Ward, Colin, *Anarchism: A Very Short Introduction* (Oxford: Oxford University Press, 2004)

Ward, Colin & David Goodway, *Talking Anarchy* (Nottingham: Five Leaves, 2003)

Warren, Josiah, *Equitable Commerce* (New Harmony, IN, 1846; New York: Fowler & Wells, 1852)

Warren, Josiah, *Practical Details in Equitable Commerce* (New Harmony, IN, 1852; Princeton, NJ: Cooperative Publishing Company, 1872)

Warren, Josiah, *True Civilization an Immediate Necessity and the Last Grain of Hope for Mankind* (Long Island, NY, 1861)

Warren, Josiah, *Modern Education* (Boston, 1863)

Warren, Josiah, *Practical Applications of the Elementary Principles of 'True Civilization'* (Princeton, NJ: Cooperative Publishing Company, 1873)

Watson, David, *Beyond Bookchin: Preface for a Future Social Ecology* (Brooklyn, NY: Autonomedia, 1996)

Watson, David, *Against the Megamachine: Essays on Empire and its Enemies* (Brooklyn, NY: Autonomedia, 1998).

Whitman, Walt, *Leaves of Grass* (1892) (New York: Bantam, 1983)

Wilde, Oscar, *Works* (Collins, *c.* 1933)

Wilde, Oscar, *De Profundis and Other Writings*, ed. Hesketh Pearson (Harmondsworth: Penguin, 1973)

Wilson, Peter Lamborn, *Sacred Drift: Essays on the Margins of Islam* (San Francisco: City Lights, 1993)

Wilson, Peter Lamborn, *Angels: Messengers of the Gods* (Thames & Hudson, 1994)

Wilson, Peter Lamborn, *Ploughing the Clouds: The Search for Irish Soma* (San Francisco: City Lights, 1999)

Wilson, Peter Lamborn, *Pirate Utopias* (Brooklyn, NY: Autonomedia, 2003)

Wilson, Peter Lamborn, ed., with Abel Zag, *Orgies of Hemp Eaters* (Brooklyn, NY: Autonomedia, 2003)

Winstanley, Gerrard, *Works*, ed. G. H. Sabine (Ithaca, NY: Cornell University Press, 1941)

Winstanley, Gerrard, *The Law of Freedom and other Writings*, ed. Christopher Hill (Cambridge: Cambridge University Press, 1983)

Wolff, Robert Paul, *In Defense of Anarchism* (New York: Harper Colophon Books, 1976)

Zerzan, John, *Future Primitive: And Other Essays* (Brooklyn, NY: Autonomedia, 1994)

Zerzan, John, ed., *Against Civilization: Readings and Reflections* (1999) (Los Angeles: Feral House, 2005)

Zerzan, John, *Elements of Refusal* (1999) (Columbia: CAL Press, 2006)

Zerzan, John, *Running on Emptiness: The Pathology of Civilization* (Los Angeles: Feral House, 2002)

Zerzan, John & Alice Carnes, *Questioning Technology: A Critical Anthology* (Freedom Press, 1988)

Some Anarchist and Allied Websites

A Infos
http://www.ainfos.ca/
Anarchist Black Cross
http://www.anarchistblackcross.org/
Anarchy Archives
http://dwardmac.pitzer.edu/Anarchist_archives/index.html
Anarchist Encyclopedia
http://recollectionbooks.com/bleed/gallery/galleryindex.htm

Anarchist Platformist Network
   www.anarkismo.net
Anarchist Studies Network
   www.sgsa.org.uk
Autonomedia
   http://www.autonomedia.org/
Crimethinc
   http://www.crimethinc.com/
Divergences
   http://divergences.be/
Earth First!
   http://www.earthfirstjournal.org/
Green Anarchy
   http://www.greenanarchy.org/
Information
   http://www.infoshop.org
Industrial Workers of the World (Wobblies)
   http://www.iww.org/
Indymedia
   http://www.indymedia.org.uk/
Insurgent Desire
   http://www.insurgentdesire.org.uk/
Institute for Anarchist Studies
   http://www.anarchiststudies.org/
Institute for Social Ecology
   www.social-ecology.org/
International Workers' Association (IWA)
   http://www.iwa-ait.org/
Kate Sharpley Library
   http://www.katesharpleylibrary.net/
Peace Pledge Union
   http://www.ppu.org.uk/
Peoples' Global Action
   http://www.agp.org/
Primitivism
   http://www.primitivism.com/
Research on Anarchism
   http://raforum.info/
Schnews
   http://www.schnews.org.uk/
Situationist International Text Library
   http://library.nothingness.org/

Social Anarchism
   http://www.socialanarchism.org/
Spunk Library
   http://www.spunk.org/

INDEX

WOBBLIES AND ZAPATISTAS

Conversations on Anarchism, Marxism and Radical History
Paperback | 5" x 8" | 300 pages | $20.00 | ISBN: 978-1-60486-041-2

"There's no doubt that we've lost much of our history. It's also very clear that those in power in this country like it that way. Here's a book that shows us why. It demonstrates not only that another world is possible, but that it already exists, has existed, and shows an endless potential to burst through the artificial walls and divisions that currently imprison us. An exquisite contribution to the literature of human freedom, and coming not a moment too soon."
—DAVID GRAEBER, author of *Fragments of an Anarchist Anthropology and Direct Action: An Ethnography*

Wobblies and Zapatistas offers the reader an encounter between two generations and two traditions. Andrej Grubacic is an anarchist from the Balkans. Staughton Lynd is a lifelong pacifist, influenced by Marxism. They meet in dialogue in an effort to bring together the anarchist and Marxist traditions, to discuss the writing of history by those who make it, and to remind us of the idea that "my country is the world." Encompassing a Left libertarian perspective and an emphatically activist standpoint, these conversations are meant to be read in the clubs and affinity groups of the new Movement.

The authors accompany us on a journey through modern revolutions, direct actions, anti-globalist counter summits, Freedom Schools, Zapatista cooperatives, Haymarket and Petrograd, Hanoi and Belgrade, 'intentional' communities, wildcat strikes, early Protestant communities, Native American democratic practices, the Workers' Solidarity Club of Youngstown, occupied factories, self-organized councils and soviets, the lives of forgotten revolutionaries, Quaker meetings, antiwar movements, and prison rebellions. Neglected and forgotten moments of interracial self-activity are brought to light. The book invites the attention of readers who believe that a better world, on the other side of capitalism and state bureaucracy, may indeed be possible.

"I have been in regular contact with Andrej Grubacic for many years, and have been most impressed by his searching intelligence, broad knowledge, lucid judgment, and penetrating commentary on contemporary affairs and their historical roots. He is an original thinker and dedicated activist, who brings deep understanding and outstanding personal qualities to everything he does."
—NOAM CHOMSKY

REVOLUTION AND OTHER WRITINGS: A POLITICAL READER

Gustav Landauer

Paperback | 6" x 9" | 528 pages | $32.95 | ISBN: 978-1-60486-054-2

"At once an individualist and a socialist, a Romantic and a mystic, a militant and
an advocate of passive resistance… He was also the most influential German
anarchist intellectual of the twentieth century."
—PAUL AVRICH, author of *Anarchist Voices*

"Landauer is the most important agitator of the radical
and revolutionary movement in the entire country." This
is how Gustav Landauer is described in a German police
file from 1893. Twenty-six years later, Landauer would
die at the hands of reactionary soldiers who overthrew the
Bavarian Council Republic, a three-week attempt to realize libertarian socialism amidst the turmoil of post-World
War I Germany. It was the last chapter in the life of an
activist, writer, and mystic who Paul Avrich calls "the
most influential German anarchist intellectual of the
twentieth century."

This is the first comprehensive collection of Landauer
writings in English. It includes one of his major works,
Revolution, thirty additional essays and articles, and a
selection of correspondence. The texts cover Landauer's entire political biography, from
his early anarchism of the 1890s to his philosophical reflections at the turn of the century, the subsequent establishment of the Socialist Bund, his tireless agitation against the
war, and the final days among the revolutionaries in Munich. Additional chapters collect
Landauer's articles on radical politics in the US and Mexico, and illustrate the scope of
his writing with texts on corporate capital, language, education, and Judaism. The book
includes an extensive introduction, commentary, and bibliographical information, compiled by the editor and translator Gabriel Kuhn.

"Gustav Landauer was, without doubt, one of the brightest intellectual lights within
the revolutionary circles of fin de siècle Europe. In this remarkable anthology, Gabriel
Kuhn brings together an extensive and splendidly chosen collection of Landauer's
most important writings, presenting them for the first time in English translation.
    With Landauer's ideas coming of age today perhaps more than ever before,
Kuhn's work is a valuable and timely piece of scholarship, and one which should
be required reading for anyone with an interest in radical social change."
—JAMES HORROX, author of *A Living Revolution: Anarchism in the Kibbutz Movement*

DRAWING THE LINE ONCE AGAIN
Paul Goodman's Anarchist Writings
Paperback | 6" x 9" | 128 pages | $14.95 | ISBN: 978-1-60486-057-3

> "Paul Goodman has been one of the few integrated and hence liberated
> people of our age… He may well have been the only truly
> seminal libertarian thinker in our generation."
> —GEORGE WOODCOCK, historian of anarchism

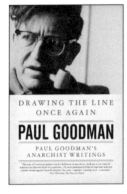

Five years after his death in 1972, Paul Goodman was characterized by anarchist historian George Woodcock as "the only truly seminal libertarian thinker in our generation." In this new PM Press initiative, Goodman's literary executor Taylor Stoehr has gathered together nine core texts from his anarchist legacy to future generations.

Here will be found the "utopian essays and practical proposals" that inspired the dissident youth of the Sixties, influencing movement theory and practice so profoundly that they have become underlying assumptions of today's radicalism. Goodman's analyses of citizenship and civil disobedience, decentralism and the organized system, show him Drawing the Line Once Again, mindful of the long anarchist tradition, and especially of the Jeffersonian democracy that resonated strongly in his own political thought. This is a deeply American book, a potent antidote to US global imperialism and domestic anomie.

> "Paul Goodman brought a new invigorating stream into American anarchism,
> simply through his insistence that in all the problems of daily life we are faced
> with the possibility of choice between authoritarian and libertarian solutions.
> Taylor Stoehr's sympathetic editing introduces Goodman's social criticism
> to a new generation."
> —COLIN WARD, community planner and public intellectual

> "When I get confused about what is happening and what to do about it,
> I miss Paul's eager and perceptive counsel… The important thing about Paul is
> that he raises the right questions. The fact that most of his answers are
> brilliant gives the reader an extra bonus."
> —DAVE DELLINGER, peace activist and founder of *Liberation* magazine

> "The core of Goodman's politics was his definition of anarchism…look not to
> the state for solutions but discover them for yourselves… He most passionately
> believed that man must not commit treason against himself,
> whatever the state—capitalist, socialist, et al—commands."
> —NAT HENTOFF, *The Village Voice*

FOR ALL THE PEOPLE

Uncovering the Hidden History of Cooperation, Cooperative Movements, and Communalism in America

Paperback | 6" x 9" | 506 pages | $28.95 | ISBN: 978-1-60486-072-6

> "It is indeed inspiring, in the face of all the misguided praise of 'the market', to be reminded by John Curl's new book of the noble history of cooperative work in the United States."
> —HOWARD ZINN, author of *A People's History of the United States*

The survival of indigenous communities and the first European settlers alike depended on a deeply cooperative style of living and working, based around common lands, shared food and labor. Cooperative movements proved integral to the grassroots organizations and struggles challenging the domination of unbridled capitalism in America's formative years. Holding aloft the vision for an alternative economic system based on cooperative industry, they have played a vital, and dynamic role in the struggle to create a better world.

Seeking to reclaim a history that has remained largely ignored by most historians, this dramatic and stirring account examines each of the definitive American cooperative movements for social change—farmer, union, consumer, and communalist—that have been all but erased from collective memory. Focusing far beyond one particular era, organization, leader, or form of cooperation, For All the People documents the multigenerational struggle of the American working people for social justice. With an expansive sweep and breathtaking detail, the chronicle follows the American worker from the colonial workshop to the modern mass-assembly line, ultimately painting a vivid panorama of those who built the United States and those who will shape its future.

John Curl, with over forty years of experience as both an active member and scholar of cooperatives, masterfully melds theory, practice, knowledge and analysis, to present the definitive history from below of cooperative America.

> "This new edition is greatly welcome, because we need a cooperative movement and spirit more than ever before. Curl surveys all, and explains much. New generations of readers will find this a fascinating account, and aging co-opers like myself will understand better what we did, what we tried to do, where we succeeded and where we failed. Get this book and read it, Curl will do you good."
> —PAUL BUHLE, co-editor of the *Encyclopedia of the American Left*, founding editor of *Radical America* (SDS)

FRIENDS OF PM PRESS

These are indisputably momentous times—the financial system is melting down globally and the Empire is stumbling. Now more than ever there is a vital need for radical ideas.

In the year since its founding—and on a mere shoestring—PM Press has risen to the formidable challenge of publishing and distributing knowledge and entertainment for the struggles ahead. We have published an impressive and stimulating array of literature, art, music, politics, and culture. Using every available medium, we've succeeded in connecting those hungry for ideas and information to those putting them into practice.

Friends of PM allows you to directly help impact, amplify, and revitalize the discourse and actions of radical writers, filmmakers, and artists. It provides us with a stable foundation from which we can build upon our early successes and provides a much-needed subsidy for the materials that can't necessarily pay their own way.

It's a bargain for you too. For a minimum of $25 a month, you'll get all the audio and video (over a dozen CDs and DVDs in our first year) or all of the print releases (also over a dozen in our first year). For $40 you'll get everything that is published in hard copy. Friends also have the ability to purchase any/all items from our webstore at a 50% discount. And what could be better than the thrill of receiving a monthly package of cutting edge political theory, art, literature, ideas and practice delivered to your door?

Your card will be billed once a month, until you tell us to stop. Or until our efforts succeed in bringing the revolution around. Or the financial meltdown of Capital makes plastic redundant. Whichever comes first.

For more information on the Friends of PM, and about sponsoring particular projects, please go to www.pmpress.org, or contact us at info@pmpress.org.

ABOUT PM PRESS

PM Press was founded at the end of 2007 by a small collection of folks with decades of publishing, media, and organizing experience. PM co-founder Ramsey Kanaan started AK Press as a young teenager in Scotland almost 30 years ago and, together with his fellow PM Press co-conspirators, has published and distributed hundreds of books, pamphlets, CDs, and DVDs. Members of PM have founded enduring book fairs, spear-headed victorious tenant organizing campaigns, and worked closely with bookstores, academic conferences, and even rock bands to deliver political and challenging ideas to all walks of life. We're old enough to know what we're doing and young enough to know what's at stake.

We seek to create radical and stimulating fiction and non-fiction books, pamphlets, t-shirts, visual and audio materials to entertain, educate and inspire you. We aim to distribute these through every available channel with every available technology—whether that means you are seeing anarchist classics at our bookfair stalls; reading our latest vegan cookbook at the café; downloading geeky fiction e-books; or digging new music and timely videos from our website.

PM Press is always on the lookout for talented and skilled volunteers, artists, activists and writers to work with. If you have a great idea for a project or can contribute in some way, please get in touch.

PM Press
PO Box 23912
Oakland, CA 94623
www.pmpress.org